The GALE
ENCYCLOPEDIA
of SCIENCE

The GALE ENCYCLOPEDIA of SCIENCE

VOLUME 2

Calibration – Embolism

Bridget Travers,
Editor

An ITP Information/Reference Group Company

Changing the Way the World Learns

NEW YORK • LONDON • BONN • BOSTON • DETROIT
MADRID • MELBOURNE • MEXICO CITY • PARIS
SINGAPORE • TOKYO • TORONTO • WASHINGTON
ALBANY NY • BELMONT CA • CINCINNATI OH

The GALE ENCYCLOPEDIA *of* SCIENCE

Bridget Travers, *Editor*

Sheila M. Dow, *Coordinating Editor (Advisors)*
James Edwards, *Coordinating Editor (Databases)*
Paul Lewon, *Coordinating Editor (Illustrations)*
Jacqueline Longe, *Coordinating Editor (Contributors)*
Donna Olendorf, *Coordinating Editor (Submissions, Indexing)*

Christine B. Jeryan, Kyung-Sun Lim, Kimberley A. McGrath, Robyn V. Young, *Contributing Editors*

Kristine M. Binkley, Zoran Minderovic, *Associate Editors*

Nicole Beatty, Pamela Proffett, Carley Wellman, *Assistant Editors*

Linda R. Andres, Shelly Andrews, Dawn R. Barry, Ned Burels, Melissa Doig, David Oblender, *Contributors*

Marlene S. Hurst, *Permissions Manager*
Margaret A. Chamberlain, *Permissions Specialist*
Susan Brohman, *Permissions Associate*

Victoria B. Cariappa, *Research Manager*
Maureen Richards, *Research Specialist*

Mary Beth Trimper, *Production Director*
Evi Seoud, *Assistant Production Manager*
Shanna Heilveil, *Production Assistant*

Cynthia Baldwin, *Product Design Manager*
Mary Krzewinski, *Art Director*
Barbara Yarrow, *Graphic Services Manager*
Randy Bassett, *Image Database Supervisor*
Robert Duncan, *Digital Imaging Specialist*
Pamela A. Hayes, *Photography Coordinator*

Benita L. Spight, Manager, *Data Entry Services*
Gwendolyn S. Tucker, *Data Entry Supervisor*
Beverly Jendrowski, *Senior Data Entry Associate*
Francis L. Monroe, *Data Entry Associate*

Jeffrey Muhr, Roger M. Valade, III, *Editorial Technical Services Associates*

Indexing provided by the Electronic Scriptorium

ISBN 0-8103-9841-9 (set)
0-8103-9836-2 (Vol. 1)
0-8103-9837-0 (Vol. 2)
0-8103-9838-9 (Vol. 3)
0-8103-9839-7 (Vol. 4)
0-8103-9840-0 (Vol. 5)
0-8103-9892-3 (Vol. 6)

I(T)P™ Gale Research, an International Thomson Company
The ITP logo is a trademark under license.

Printed in the United States of America
10 9 8 7 6 5 4 3 2

Gale encyclopedia of science / Bridget E. Travers, editor.
p.   cm.
Includes bibliographical references and index.
Summary: Contains 2,000 entries ranging from short definitions to major overviews of concepts in all areas of science.
ISBN 0–08103–9841–9 (alk. paper)
1. Science--Encyclopedias, Juvenile.   [1. Science--Encyclopedias.]   I. Travers, Bridget.
Q121.G35   1995
503--dc20   95-25402
CIP
AC

CONTENTS

ORGANIZATION OF THE ENCYCLOPEDIA

The Gale Encyclopedia of Science has been designed with ease of use and ready reference in mind.

- Entries are **alphabetically arranged** in a single sequence, rather than by scientific field.
- Length of entries varies from **short definitions** of one or two paragraphs to longer, more **detailed entries** on complex subjects.
- Longer entries are arranged so that an **overview** of the subject appears first, followed by a detailed discussion conveniently arranged under subheadings.
- A list of **key terms** are provided where appropriate to define unfamiliar terms or concepts.
- Longer entries conclude with a **further reading** section, which points readers to other helpful sources.
- The **contributor's name** appears at the end of longer entries. His or her affiliation can be found in the "Contributors" section at the front of each volume.
- **"See-also" references** appear at the end of entries to point readers to related entries.
- **Cross-references** placed throughout the encyclopedia direct readers to where information on subjects without their own entries can be found.
- A comprehensive **general index** guides readers to all topics and persons mentioned in the book.

ADVISORY BOARD

A number of experts in the library and scientific communities provided invaluable assistance in the formulation of this encyclopedia. Our advisory board performed a myriad of duties, from defining the scope of coverage to reviewing individual entries for accuracy and accessibility. We would therefore like to express our appreciation to them:

Academic Advisors

Bryan Bunch
Adjunct Instructor
Department of Mathematics
Pace University

David Campbell
Head
Department of Physics
University of Illinois at Urbana
Champaign

Neil Cumberlidge
Professor
Department of Biology
Northern Michigan University

Bill Freedman
Professor
Department of Biology and
School for Resource and Environmental Studies
Dalhousie University

Clayton Harris
Assistant Professor
Department of Geography and
Geology
Middle Tennessee State University

William S. Pretzer
Curator
Henry Ford Museum and Greenfield Village
Dearborn, Michigan

Theodore Snow
Fellow and Director
Center for Astrophysics and
Space Research
University of Colorado at Boulder

Robert Wolke
Professor emeritus
Department of Chemistry
University of Pittsburgh

Richard Addison Wood
Meteorlogical Consultant
Tucson, Arizona

Librarian Advisors

Donna Miller
Director
Craig-Moffet County Library
Craig, Colorado

Judy Williams
Media Center
Greenwich High School
Greenwich, Connecticut

Carol Wishmeyer
Science and Technology Department
Detroit Public Library
Detroit, Michigan

CONTRIBUTORS

Nasrine Adibe
Professor Emeritus
Department of Education
Long Island University
Westbury, New York

Mary D. Albanese
Department of English
University of Alaska
Juneau, Alaska

James L. Anderson
Soil Science Department
University of Minnesota
St. Paul, Minnesota

Susan Andrew
Teaching Assistant
University of Maryland
Washington, D.C.

John Appel
Director
Fundación Museo de Ciencia y
   Tecnología
Popayán, Colombia

David Ball
Assistant Professor
Department of Chemistry
Cleveland State University
Cleveland, Ohio

Dana M. Barry
Editor and Technical Writer

Center for Advanced Materials
   Processing
Clarkston University
Potsdam, New York

Puja Batra
Department of Zoology
Michigan State University
East Lansing, Michigan

Donald Beaty
Professor Emeritus
College of San Mateo
San Mateo, California

Eugene C. Beckham
Department of Mathematics and
   Science
Northwood Institute
Midland, Michigan

Martin Beech
Research Associate
Department of Astronomy
University of Western Ontario
London, Ontario

Massimo D. Bezoari
Associate Professor
Department of Chemistry
Huntingdon College
Montgomery, Alabama

John M. Bishop III
Translator
New York, New York

T. Parker Bishop
Professor
Middle Grades and Secondary
   Education
Georgia Southern University
Statesboro, Georgia

Carolyn Black
Professor
Incarnate Word College
San Antonio, Texas

Larry Blaser
Science Writer
Lebanon, Tennessee

Jean F. Blashfield
Science Writer
Walworth, Wisconsin

Richard L. Branham Jr.
Director
Centro Rigional de
   Investigaciones Científicas y
   Tecnológicas
Mendoza, Argentina

Patricia Braus
Editor
American Demographics
Rochester, New York

David L. Brock
Biology Instructor
St. Louis, Missouri

Leona B. Bronstein
Chemistry Teacher (retired)
East Lansing High School
Okemos, Michigan

Brandon R. Brown
Graduate Research Assistant
Oregon State University
Corvallis, Oregon

Lenonard C. Bruno
Senior Science Specialist
Library of Congress
Chevy Chase, Maryland

Scott Christian Cahall
Researcher
World Precision Instruments, Inc.
Bradenton, Florida

G. Lynn Carlson
Senior Lecturer
School of Science and
    Technology
University of Wisconsin—
    Parkside
Kenosha, Wisconsin

James J. Carroll
Center for Quantum Mechanics
The University of Texas at Dallas
Dallas, Texas

Steven B. Carroll
Assistant Professor
Division of Biology
Northeast Missouri State
    University
Kirksville, Missouri

Rosalyn Carson-DeWitt
Physician and Medical Writer
Durham, North Carolina

Yvonne Carts-Powell
Editor
Laser Focus World
Belmont, Massachustts

Chris Cavette
Technical Writer
Fremont, California

Kenneth B. Chiacchia
Medical Editor

University of Pittsburgh Medical
    Center
Pittsburgh, Pennsylvania

M. L. Cohen
Science Writer
Chicago, Illinois

Robert Cohen
Reporter
KPFA Radio News
Berkeley, California

Sally Cole-Misch
Assistant Director
International Joint Commission
Detroit, Michigan

George W. Collins II
Professor Emeritus
Case Western Reserve
Chesterland, Ohio

Jeffrey R. Corney
Science Writer
Thermopolis, Wyoming

Tom Crawford
Assistant Director
Division of Publication and
    Development
University of Pittsburgh Medical
    Center
Pittsburgh, Pennsylvania

Pamela Crowe
Medical and Science Writer
Oxon, England

Clinton Crowley
On-site Geologist
Selman and Associates
Fort Worth, Texas

Edward Cruetz
Physicist
Rancho Santa Fe, California

Frederick Culp
Chairman
Department of Physics
Tenneesse Technical
Cookeville, Tennessee

Neil Cumberlidge
Professor

Department of Biology
Northern Michigan University
Marquette, Michigan

Mary Ann Cunningham
Environmental Writer
St. Paul, Minnesota

Les C. Cwynar
Associate Professor
Department of Biology
University of New Brunswick
Fredericton, New Brunswick

Paul Cypher
Provisional Interpreter
Lake Erie Metropark
Trenton, Michigan

Stanley J. Czyzak
Professor Emeritus
Ohio State University
Columbus, Ohio

Rosi Dagit
Conservation Biologist
Topanga-Las Virgenes Resource
    Conservation District
Topanga, California

David Dalby
President
Bruce Tool Company, Inc.
Taylors, South Carolina

Lou D'Amore
Chemistry Teacher
Father Redmund High School
Toronto, Ontario

Douglas Darnowski
Postdoctoral Fellow
Department of Plant Biology
Cornell University
Ithaca, New York

Sreela Datta
Associate Writer
Aztec Publications
Northville, Michigan

Sarah K. Dean
Science Writer
Philadelphia, Pennsylvania

Sarah de Forest
Research Assistant
Theoretical Physical Chemistry
 Lab
University of Pittsburgh
Pittsburgh, Pennsylvania

Louise Dickerson
Medical and Science Writer
Greenbelt, Maryland

Marie Doorey
Editorial Assistant
Illinois Masonic Medical Center
Chicago, Illinois

Herndon G. Dowling
Professor Emeritus
Department of Biology
New York University
New York, New York

Marion Dresner
Natural Resources Educator
Berkeley, California

John Henry Dreyfuss
Science Writer
Brooklyn, New York

Roy Dubisch
Professor Emeritus
Department of Mathematics
New York University
New York, New York

Russel Dubisch
Department of Physics
Sienna College
Loudonville, New York

Carolyn Duckworth
Science Writer
Missoula, Montana

Peter A. Ensminger
Research Associate
Cornell University
Syracuse, New York

Bernice Essenfeld
Biology Writer
Warren, New Jersey

Mary Eubanks

Instructor of Biology
The North Carolina School of
 Science and Mathematics
Durham, North Carolina

Kathryn M. C. Evans
Science Writer
Madison, Wisconsin

William G. Fastie
Department of Astronomy and
 Physics
Bloomberg Center
Baltimore, Maryland

Barbara Finkelstein
Science Writer
Riverdale, New York

Mary Finley
Supervisor of Science Curriculum
 (retired)
Pittsburgh Secondary Schools
Clairton, Pennsylvania

Gaston Fischer
Institut de Géologie
Université de Neuchâtel
Peseux, Switzerland

Sara G. B. Fishman
Professor
Quinsigamond Community
 College
Worcester, Massachusetts

David Fontes
Senior Instructor
Lloyd Center for Environmental
 Studies
Westport, Maryland

Barry Wayne Fox
Extension Specialist,
 Marine/Aquatic Education
Virginia State University
Petersburg, Virginia

Ed Fox
Charlotte Latin School
Charlotte, North Carolina

Kenneth L. Frazier
Science Teacher (retired)
North Olmstead High School

North Olmstead, Ohio

Bill Freedman
Professor
Department of Biology and
 School For Resource and
 Environmental Studies
Dalhousie University
Halifax, Nova Scotia

T. A. Freeman
Consulting Archaeologist
Quail Valley, California

Elaine Friebele
Science Writer
Cheverly, Maryland

Randall Frost
Documentation Engineering
Pleasanton, California

Robert Gardner
Science Education Consultant
North Eastham, Massachusetts

Gretchen M. Gillis
Senior Geologist
Maxus Exploration
Dallas, Texas

Kathryn Glynn
Audiologist
Portland, Oregon

Natalie Goldstein
Educational Environmental
 Writing
Phoenicia, New York

David Gorish
TARDEC
U.S. Army
Warren, Michigan

Louis Gotlib
South Granville High School
Durham, North Carolina

Hans G. Graetzer
Professor
Department of Physics
South Dakota State University
Brookings, South Dakota

Jim Guinn
Assistant Professor
Department of Physics
Berea College
Berea, Kentucky

Steve Gutterman
Psychology Research Assistant
University of Michigan
Ann Arbor, Michigan

Johanna Haaxma-Jurek
Educator
Nataki Tabibah Schoolhouse of
  Detroit
Detroit, Michigan

Monica H. Halka
Research Associate
Department of Physics and
  Astronomy
University of Tennessee
Knoxville, Tennessee

Jeffrey C. Hall
Astronomer
Lowell Observatory
Flagstaff, Arizona

C. S. Hammen
Professor Emeritus
Department of Zoology
University of Rhode Island

Beth Hanson
Editor
The Amicus Journal
Brooklyn, New York

Clay Harris
Associate Professor
Department of Geography and
  Geology
Middle Tennessee State
  University
Murfreesboro, Tennessee

Catherine Hinga Haustein
Associate Professor
Department of Chemistry
Central College
Pella, Iowa

Dean Allen Haycock
Science Writer
Salem, New York

Paul A. Heckert
Professor
Department of Chemistry and
  Physics
Western Carolina University
Cullowhee, North Carolina

Darrel B. Hoff
Department of Physics
Luther College
Calmar, Iowa

Dennis Holley
Science Educator
Shelton, Nebraska

Leonard Darr Holmes
Department of Physical Science
Pembroke State University
Pembroke, North Carolina

Rita Hoots
Instructor of Biology, Anatomy,
  Chemistry
Yuba College
Woodland, California

Selma Hughes
Department of Psychology and
  Special Education
East Texas State University
Mesquite, Texas

Mara W. Cohen Ioannides
Science Writer
Springfield, Missouri

Zafer Iqbal
Allied Signal Inc.
Morristown, New Jersey

Sophie Jakowska
Pathobiologist, Environmental
  Educator
Santo Domingo, Dominican
  Republic

Richard A. Jeryan
Senior Technical Specialist
Ford Motor Company
Dearborn, Michigan

Stephen R. Johnson
Biology Writer
Richmond, Virginia

Kathleen A. Jones
School of Medicine
Southern Illinois University
Carbondale, Illinois

Harold M. Kaplan
Professor
School of Medicine
Southern Illinois University
Carbondale, Illinois

Anthony Kelly
Science Writer
Pittsburgh, Pennsylvania

Amy Kenyon-Campbell
Ecology, Evolution and
  Organismal Biology Program
University of Michigan
Ann Arbor, Michigan

Eileen M. Korenic
Institute of Optics
University of Rochester
Rochester, New York

Jennifer Kramer
Science Writer
Kearny, New Jersey

Pang-Jen Kung
Los Alamos National Laboratory
Los Alamos, New Mexico

Marc Kusinitz
Assistant Director Media
  Relations
John Hopkins Medical Instituition
Towsen, Maryland

Arthur M. Last
Head
Department of Chemistry
University College of the Fraser
  Valley
Abbotsford, British Columbia

Nathan Lavenda
Zoologist
Skokie, Illinios

Jennifer LeBlanc
Environmental Consultant
London, Ontario

Benedict A. Leerburger
Science Writer
Scarsdale, New York

Betsy A. Leonard
Education Facilitator
Reuben H. Fleet Space Theater
  and Science Center
San Diego, California

Scott Lewis
Science Writer
Chicago, Illinois

Frank Lewotsky
Aerospace Engineer (retired)
Nipomo, California

Karen Lewotsky
Cartographer
Portland, Oregon

Kristin Lewotsky
Editor
Laser Focus World
Nashua, New Hamphire

Stephen K. Lewotsky
Architect
Grants Pass, Oregon

Sarah Lee Lippincott
Professor Emeritus
Swarthmore College
Swarthmore, Pennsylvania

David Lunney
Research Scientist
Centre de Spectrométrie
  Nucléaire et de Spectrométrie de
  Masse
Orsay, France

Steven MacKenzie
Ecologist
Spring Lake, Michigan

J. R. Maddocks
Consulting Scientist
DeSoto, Texas

Gail B. C. Marsella
Technical Writer
Allentown, Pennsylvania

Karen Marshall
Research Associate
Council of State Governments
  and Centers for Environment
  and Safety
Lexington, Kentucky

Liz Marshall
Science Writer
Columbus, Ohio

James Marti
Research Scientist
Department of Mechanical
  Engineering
University of Minnesota
Minneapolis, Minnesota

Elaine L. Martin
Science Writer
Pensacola, Florida

Lilyan Mastrolla
Professor Emeritus
San Juan Unified School
Sacramento, California

Iain A. McIntyre
Manager
Electro-optic Department
Energy Compression Research
  Corporation
Vista, California

G. H. Miller
Director
Studies on Smoking
Edinboro, Pennsylvania

J. Gordon Miller
Botanist
Corvallis, Oregon

Christine Miner Minderovic
Nuclear Medicine Technologist
Franklin Medical Consulters
Ann Arbor, Michigan

David Mintzer
Professor Emeritus
Department of Mechanical

Engineering
Northwestern University
Evanston, Illinois

Christine Molinari
Science Editor
University of Chicago Press
Chicago, Illinois

Frank Mooney
Professor Emeritus
Fingerlake Community College
Canandaigua, New York

Partick Moore
Department of English
University of Arkansas at Little
  Rock
Little Rock, Arkansas

Robbin Moran
Department of Systematic Botany
Institute of Biological Sciences
University of Aarhus
Risskou, Denmark

J. Paul Moulton
Department of Mathematics
Episcopal Academy
Glenside, Pennsylvania

Otto H. Muller
Geology Department
Alfred University
Alfred, New York

Angie Mullig
Publication and Development
University of Pittsburgh Medical
  Center
Trafford, Pennsylvania

David R. Murray
Senior Associate
Sydney University
Sydney, New South Wales
Australia

Sutharchana Murugan
Scientist Three Boehringer
  Mannheim Corp.
Indianapolis, Indiana

Muthena Naseri
Moorpark College

Moorpark, California

David Newton
Science Writer and Educator
Ashland, Oregon

F. C. Nicholson
Science Writer
Lynn, Massachusetts

James O'Connell
Department of Physical Sciences
Frederick Community College
Gaithersburg, Maryland

Dónal P. O'Mathúna
Associate Professor
Mount Carmel College of
   Nursing
Columbus, Ohio

Marjorie Pannell
Managing Editor, Scientific
   Publications
Field Museum of Natural History
Chicago, Illinois

Gordon A. Parker
Lecturer
Department of Natural Sciences
University of Michigan—
   Dearborn
Dearborn, Michigan

David Petechuk
Science Writer
Ben Avon, Pennsylvania

John R. Phillips
Department of Chemistry
Purdue University, Calumet
Hammond, Indiana

Kay Marie Porterfield
Science Writer
Englewood, Colorado

Paul Poskozim
Chair
Department of Chemistry, Earth
   Science and Physics
Northeastern Illinois University
Chicago, Illinois

Andrew Poss
Senior Research Chemist
Allied Signal Inc.
Buffalo, New York

Satyam Priyadarshy
Department of Chemistry
University of Pittsburgh
Pittsburgh, Pennsylvania

Patricia V. Racenis
Science Writer
Livonia, Michigan

Cynthia Twohy Ragni
Atmospheric Scientist
National Center for Atmospheric
   Research
Westminster, Colorado

Jordan P. Richman
Science Writer
Phoenix, Arizona

Kitty Richman
Science Writer
Phoenix, Arizona

Vita Richman
Science Writer
Phoenix, Arizona

Michael G. Roepel
Researcher
Department of Chemistry
University of Pittsburgh
Pittsburgh, Pennsylvania

Perry Romanowski
Science Writer
Chicago, Illinois

Nancy Ross-Flanigan
Science Writer
Belleville, Michigan

Gordon Rutter
Royal Botanic Gardens
Edinburgh, Great Britain

Elena V. Ryzhov
Polytechnic Institute
Troy, New York

David Sahnow
   Associate Research Scientist

John Hopkins University
Baltimore, Maryland

Peter Salmansohn
Educational Consultant
New York State Parks
Cold Spring, New York

Peter K. Schoch
Instructor
Department of Physics and
   Computer Science
Sussex County Community
   College
Augusta, New Jersey

Patricia G. Schroeder
Instructor
Science, Healthcare, and Math
   Division
Johnson County Community
   College
Overland Park, Kansas

Randy Schueller
Science Writer
Chicago, Illinois

Kathleen Scogna
Science Writer
Baltimore, Maryland

William Shapbell Jr.
Launch and Flight Systems
   Manager
Kennedy Space Center, Florida

Anwar Yuna Shiekh
International Centre for
   Theoretical Physics
Trieste, Italy

Raul A. Simon
Chile Departmento de Física
Universidad de Tarapacá
Arica, Chile

Michael G. Slaughter
Science Specialist
Ingham ISD
East Lansing, Michigan

Billy W. Sloope
Professor Emeritus
Department of Physics

Virginia Commonwealth University
Richmond, Virginia

Douglas Smith
Science Writer
Milton, Massachusetts

Lesley L. Smith
Department of Physics and Astronomy
University of Kansas
Lawrence, Kansas

Kathryn D. Snavely
U.S. General Accounting Office
Policy Analyst, Air Quality Issues
Raleigh, North Carolina

Charles H. Southwick
Professor
Environmental, Population, and Organismic Biology
University of Colorado at Boulder
Boulder, Colorado

John Spizzirri
Science Writer
Chicago, Illinois

Frieda A. Stahl
Professor Emeritus
Department of Physics
California State University, Los Angeles
Los Angeles, California

Robert L. Stearns
Department of Physics
Vassar College
Poughkeepsie, New York

Ilana Steinhorn
Science Writer
Boalsburg, Pennsylvania

David Stone
Conservation Advisory Services
Gai Soleil
Chemin Des Clyettes
Le Muids, Switzerland

Eric R. Swanson
Associate Professor

Department of Earth and Physical Sciences
University of Texas
San Antonio, Texas

Cheryl Taylor
Science Educator
Kailua, Hawaii

Nicholas C. Thomas
Department of Physical Sciences
Auburn University at Montgomery
Montgomery, Alabama

W. A. Thomasson
Science and Medical Writer
Oak Park, Illinois

Marie L. Thompson
Science Writer
Ben Avon, Pennsylvania

Melvin Tracy
Science Educator
Appleton, Wisconsin

Karen Trentelman
Research Associate
Archaeometric Laboratory
University of Toronto
Toronto, Ontario

Robert K. Tyson
Senior Scientist
W. J. Schafer Assoc.
Jupiter, Florida

James Van Allen
Professor Emeritus
Department of Physics and Astronomy
University of Iowa
Iowa City, Iowa

Julia M. Van Denack
Biology Instructor
Silver Lake College
Manitowoc, Wisconsin

Kurt Vandervoort
Department of Chemistry and Physics
West Carolina University
Cullowhee, North Carolina

Chester Vander Zee
Naturalist, Science Educator
Volga, South Dakota

Jeanette Vass
Department of Chemistry
Cuyahoga Community College
Timberlake, Ohio

R. A. Virkar
Chair
Department of Biological Sciences
Kean College
Iselin, New Jersey

Kurt C. Wagner
Instructor
South Carolina Governor's School for Science and Technology
Hartsville, South Carolina

Cynthia Washam
Science Writer
Jensen Beach, Florida

Joseph D. Wassersug
Physician
Boca Raton, Florida

Tom Watson
Environmental Writer
Seattle, Washington

Jeffrey Weld
Instructor, Science Department Chair
Pella High School
Pella, Iowa

Frederick R. West
Astronomer
Hanover, Pennsylvania

Glenn Whiteside
Science Writer
Wichita, Kansas

John C. Whitmer
Professor
Department of Chemistry
Western Washington University
Bellingham, Washington

CONTRIBUTORS

Donald H. Williams
Department of Chemistry
Hope College
Holland, Michigan

Robert L. Wolke
Professor Emeritus
Department of Chemistry
University of Pittsburgh
Pittsburgh, Pennsylvania

Jim Zurasky
Optical Physicist
Nichols Research Corporation
Huntsville, Alabama

ACKNOWLEDGEMENTS

Photographs appearing in the *Gale Encyclopedia of Science* were received from the following sources:

© Account Phototake/Phototake: **Genetic disorders**; © James Allem, Stock Market: **Gazelles**; © A. W. Ambler, National Audubon Society Collection/Photo Researchers, Inc.: **Goats, Newts, Sedimentary rock**; © Toni Angermayer, National Audubon Society Collection/Photo Researchers, Inc.: **Hamsters**; © Mark Antman/Phototake: **Textiles**; AP/Wide World Photos: **Elements, formation of**; © Archiv, National Audubon Society Collection/Photo Researchers, Inc.: **Astrolabe**; © Bachman, National Audubon Society Collection/Photo Researchers, Inc.: **Wombats**; © Bill Bachman, National Audubon Society Collection/Photo Researchers, Inc.: **Grasslands**; Baiyer River Sanctuary, New Guinea © Tom McHugh, National Audubon Society Collection/Photo Researchers, Inc.; © M. Baret/RAPHU, National Audubon Society Collection/Photo Researchers, Inc.: **Biotechnology**; Jen and Des Bartlett, National Audubon Society Collection/Photo Researchers, Inc.: **Sea lions**; © Jen and Des Bartlett, National Aububon Society Collection/Photo Researchers, Inc.: **Cicadas, Langurs and leaf monkeys, Aardvark, Bandicoots, Grebes, Lorises, Monitor lizards, Opossums, Pipefish, Sea horses, Secretary bird, Spiny anteaters**; © Bat Conservation Int'l: **Bats**; © John Bavosi, National Audubon Society Collection/ Photo Researchers, Inc.: **Hernia**; Tom Bean: **Archaeology**; © Tom Bean, Stock Market: **Volcano**; © James Bell, National Audubon Society Collection/Photo Researchers, Inc.: **Buds and budding**; © Pierre Berger, National Audubon Society Collection/Photo Researchers, Inc.: **Beech family**; © J. Bernholc et al, North Carolina State University/Science Photo Library, National Audubon Society Collection/Photo Researchers, Inc.: **Buckminsterfullerene**; © The Bettmann Archive: **Chemical warfare, Photography**; © Art Bileten, National Audubon Society Collection/Photo Researchers, Inc.: **North America**; © Biophoto Associates, National Audubon Society Collection/Photo Researchers, Inc.: **Acne, Chromosome, Tropical diseases, Spina bifida**; © Wesley Bocxe, National Audubon Society Collection/Photo Researchers, Inc.: **Oil spills**; © Mark Boulton, National Audubon Society Collection/Photo Researchers, Inc.: **Bustards, Erosion**; © Malcolm Boulton, National Audubon Society Collection/Photo Researchers, Inc.: **Porcupines, Baboons**; © Mark N. Boulton, National Audubon Society Collection/Photo Researchers, Inc.: **Yak**; © Dr. Tony Brain/Science Photo Library, National Audubon Society Collection/Photo Researchers, Inc.: **Aerobic**; © Thomas H. Brakefield, Stock Market: **Cats**; © Tom Brakefield, Stock Market: **Wolverine**; © 1980 Ken Brate, National Audubon Society Collection/Photo Researchers, Inc.: **Citrus trees**; Andrea Brizzi, Stock Market: **Sewage treatment**; © S. Brookens, Stock Market: **Mynah birds**; © John R. Brownlie, National Audubon Society Collection/Photo Researchers, Inc.: **Lyrebirds**; © Dr. Jeremy Brugess/Science Photo Library, National Audubon Society Collection/ Photo Researchers, Inc.: **Leaf, Chloroplast, Aphids, Battery**; © John Buitenkant 1993, National Audubon Society Collection/Photo Researchers, Inc.: **Buttercup**; © 1994, Michele Burgess/Bikderberg, Stock Market: **Elephant**; © Michele Burgess, Stock Market: **Flightless birds**; © Jane Burton, National Audubon Society Collection/Photo Researchers, Inc.: **Pangolins**; © Diana Calder/Bikderberg, Stock Market: **Barometer**; © Scott Camazinr, National Audubon Society Collection/Photo Researchers, Inc.: **AIDS**; © Tardos Camesi/Bikderberg, Stock

Market: **Transformer**; © John Cancalosi: **Numbat**; © Robert Caputo, National Audubon Society Collection/Photo Researchers, Inc.: **Hyena**; © Alan D. Carey, National Audubon Society Collection/Photo Researchers, Inc.: **Captive breeding and reintroduction, Coffee plant**; © Carolina Biological Supply Company/Phototake: **Chemoreception, Microscopy, Plant, Cashew family, Yeast**; © Tom Carrill/Phototake: **Pollution control**; © Tom Carroll/Phototake: **Air pollution, Bridges, Freeway**; © CBC/CBC/Phototake: **Petrels and shearwaters**; © Jean-Loup Charmet, National Audubon Society Collection/Photo Researchers, Inc.: **Anesthesia, Rabies**; © Ann Chawatsky/Phototake: **Burn**; © Ron Church, National Audubon Society Collection/Photo Researchers, Inc.: **Barracuda**; © Geoffrey Clifford,Stock Market: **Fractal**; © CNRI/ Science Photo Library, Nationa Audubon Society Collection/Photo Researchers, Inc.: **Influenza**; © CNRI/Phototake: **Leprosy**; © CNRI/Science Photo Library, National Audubon Society Collection/ Photo Researchers, Inc.: **Enterobacteria**; © Pedro Coll, Stock Market: **Cave, Machine tools**; © Holt Confer/Phototake: **Cranes**; © Judd Cooney/Phototake: **Weasels**; © Tony Craddock, National Audubon Society Collection/Photo Researchers, Inc.: **Microwave communication**; © Allan D. Cruickshank, National Audubon Society Collection/Photo Researchers, Inc.: **Cuckoos, Gila monster**; © Russell D. Curtis, National Audubon Society Collection/ Photo Researchers, Inc.: **Sleep disorders**; © Tim Davis, National Audubon Society Collection/Photo Researchers, Inc.: **Colobus monkeys, Finches**; © John Deeks, National Audubon Society Collection/Photo Researchers, Inc.: **Clouds**; © E.R. Degginger, National Audubon Society Collection/Photo Researchers, Inc.: **Tundra**; © Nigel Dennis, National Audubon Society Collection/Photo Researchers, Inc.: **Flamingos**; © Jack Dermid, National Audubon Society Collection/Photo Researchers, Inc.: **Dune**; © Jack Dermid 1979, National Audubon Society Collection/Photo Researchers, Inc.: **Bromeliad family**; © Jack Dermid, National Audubon Society Collection/Photo Researchers, Inc.: **Puffer fish**; © 1992 Alan L. Detrick, National Audubon Society Collection/Photo Researchers, Inc.: **Amaranth family**; © Mike Devlin, National Audubon Society Collection/Photo Researchers, Inc.: **Prosthetics**; © Richard Dibon-Smith, National Audubon Society Collection/Photo Researchers, Inc.: **Sheep**; © Gregory G. Dimijian 1990, National Audubon Society Collection/Photo Researchers, Inc.: **Coca**; © Thomas Dimock, Stock Market: **Crabs**; © Martin Dohrn, National Audubon Society Collection/Photo Researchers, Inc.: **Interference, Skeletal system**; © Martin Dohrn/Science Photo Library, National Audubon Society Collection/Photo Researchers, Inc.: **Wave motion**; © Dopamine-CNRI, National Audubon Society Collection/Photo Researchers, Inc.: **Ulcers**; © A. B. Dowsett/Science Photo Library, National Audubon Society Collection/ Photo Researchers, Inc.: **Virus**; © John Dudak/Phototake: **Arrowroot, Composite family**; © Richard Duncan,National Audubon Society Collection/Photo Researchers, Inc.: **Geometry**; © Hermann Eisenbeiss, National Audubon Society Collection/Photo Researchers, Inc.: **Surface tension**; © Thomas Ernsting, Stock Market: **Metric system**; © Thomas Ernsting/Bikderberg, Stock Market: **Virtual reality**; © 1992 Robert Essel/Bikderberg, Stock Market: **Electricity**; © Robert Essel, Stock Market: **Moose**; © Kenneth Eward/BioGrafx, National Audubon Society Collection/Photo Researchers, Inc.: **Atom**; © Dr. Brian Eyden, National Audubon Society Collection/Photo Researchers, Inc.: **Cancer**; © Douglas Faulkner, National Audubon Society Collection/Photo Researchers, Inc.: **Manatee, Coral reef**; © Fawcett, National Audubon Society Collection/ Photo Researchers, Inc.: **Cell**; © Fawcett/Phillips, National Audubon Society Collection/Photo Researchers, Inc.: **Flagella**; © Kenneth W. Fink, National Audubon Society Collection/Photo Researchers, Inc.: **Turacos**; © Cecil Fox/Science Source, National Audubon Society Collection/Photo Researchers, Inc.: **Alzheimer's disease**; © Carl Frank, National Audubon Society Collection/Photo Researchers, Inc.: **Rivers**; © Stephen Frink, Stock Market: **Squirrel fish**; © Petit Fromat/Nestle, National Audubon Society Collection/Photo Researchers, Inc.: **Embryo and embryonic development**; © G.R. Gainer, Stock Market: **Spiral**; Gale Research Inc.: **Jet engine**; © Gordon Garrado/Science Photo Library, National Audubon Society Collection/Photo Researchers, Inc.: **Thunderstorm**; © Frederica Georgia, National Audubon Society Collection/Photo Researchers, Inc.: **Hydrothermal vents**; © Ormond Gigli, Stock Market: **Frigate birds**; © 1989 Ned Gillette, Stock Market: **Mass wasting**; © A. Glauberman, National Audubon Society Collection/Photo Researchers, Inc.: **Cigarette smoke**; © F. Gohier 1982, National Audubon Society Collection/Photo Researchers, Inc.: **Amaryllis family**; © Francois Gohier, National Audubon Society Collection/Photo Researchers, Inc.: **Stromatolites**; © Spencer Grant, National Audubon Society Collection/Photo Researchers, Inc.: **Robotics**; © Stephen Green-Armytage, Stock Market:

ACKNOWLEDGEMENTS

Boas; © Al Greene and Associates, National Audubon Society Collection/Photo Researchers, Inc.: **Coast and beach**; © Barry Griffiths, National Audubon Society Collection/Photo Researchers, Inc.; © Tommaso Guicciardini/Science Photo Library, National Audubon Society Collection/Photo Researchers, Inc.: **Gravity**; © Dan Guravich 1987, National Audubon Society Collection/Photo Researchers, Inc.: **Atmospheric optical phenomena**; © Dan Guravich, National Audubon Society Collection/Photo Researchers, Inc.: **Alluvial systems**; © A. Gurmankin 1987/Phototake: **Begonia**; © Clem Haagner, National Audubon Society Collection/Photo Researchers, Inc.: **Giraffes and okapi**; © Hugh M. Halliday, National Audubon Society Collection/Photo Researchers, Inc.: **Shrikes**; © David Halpern, National Audubon Society Collection/Photo Researchers, Inc.: **Oil drilling**; © Chris Hamilton, Stock Market: **Waterwheel**; © Craig Hammell/Bikderberg, Stock Market: **Caliper**; © Hammond Incorporated, Maplewood, New Jersey.: **Bar code**; © 1993 Brownie Harris, Stock Market : **Antenna**; © Brownie Harris, Stock Market: **Turbine**; © Adam Hart-Davis/Science Photo Library, National Audubon Society Collection/Photo Researchers, Inc.: **Electrostatic devices**; © Adam Hart-Davis, National Audubon Society Collection/Photo Researchers, Inc.: **Thermometer, Integrated circuit**; © Anne Heimann, Stock Market: **Horseshoe crabs**; © Robert C. Hermes,National Audubon Society Collection/Photo Researchers, Inc.: **Mayflies**; © John Heseltine, National Audubon Society Collection/Photo Researchers, Inc.: **Geodesic dome**; © Andrew Holbrooke, Stock Market: **Landfill, Prosthetics**; © Holt Studios International, National Audubon Society Collection/Photo Researchers, Inc.: **Cashew family**; © Eric Hosking, F.R.P.S., National Audubon Society Collection/Photo Researchers, Inc.: **Auks**; © Eric Hosking, National Audubon Society Collection/Photo Researchers, Inc.: **Kingfishers, Loons, Mice, Stilts and avocets**; © John Howard, National Audubon Society Collection/Photo Researchers, Inc.: **Electromagnetic Field**; Robert J. Huffman/Field Mark Publications.: **Anoles, Anteaters, Armadillos, Bison, Blackbirds, Butterflies, Cactus, Capybaras, Carnivorous plants, Carnivorous plants, Composting, Cormorants, Cranes, Crayfish, Crows and jays, Deer, Ducks, Eagles, Falcons, Fossil and fossilization, Frogs, Fungi, Geese, Goats, Gulls, Hawks, Herons (2 photos), Horsetails, Ibises, Iguanas, Juniper, Koalas, Mockingbirds and thrashers, Moths (2 photos), Nuclear fission, Nuthatches, Oaks, Owls (2 photos), Parrots, Peafowl, Peccaries, Pelican, Pheasants, Pigeons and doves, Prairie dog, Praying mantis, Quail, Recycling, Rhinoceros, Sandpipers, Seals, Sparrows and buntings, Squirrels, Starfish, Swallows and martins, Swans, Terns, Thistle, Thrushes, Turkeys, Turtles, Tyrant flycatchers, Warblers, Waste management, Wetlands, Wrens, Zebras**; IBM Almaden: **Compact disc**; © Institut Pastuer/Phototake: **Immune system**; © Bruce Iverson/Science Photo Library, National Audubon Society Collection/Photo Researchers, Inc.: **Electric motor**; © Jacana, National Audubon Society Collection/Photo Reasearchers, Inc.: **Tuna**; © Y. Lanceau Jacana, National Audubon Society Collection/Photo Researchers, Inc.: **Carp**; JLM Visuals: **Acid rain, Africa, Agricultural machines, Agronomy, Alternative energy sources, Animal breeding, Antarctica, Arachnids, Astroblemes, Australia, Barrier Islands, Bitterns, Blue revolution, Brick, Bridges, Buoyancy, Principle of, Camels, Carnivore, Chameleons, Coal, Cotton, Crop rotation, Cycads, Deposit, Desert, Dinosaur, Disturbance, ecological, Dogwood tree, Dust devil, Earthquake, Endangered species, Europe, Fault, Ferns, Ferrets, Flax, Flooding, Fold, Fossil and fossilization, Freshwater, Gerbils, Ginger, Ginkgo, Glaciers, Goatsuckers, Gourd family, Grasses, Grasshoppers, Groundwater, Heath family, Hornbills, Horse chestnut, Ice ages, Igneous rocks, Introduced species, Iris family, Irrigation, Karst topography, Lagomorphs, Lake, Land use, Legumes, Lice, Lichens, Liverwort, Lobsters, Mangrove tree, Marmots, Mass wasting, Milkweeds, Mint family, Mistletoe, Mulberry family, Muskoxen, Mutation, Myrtle family, Nightshade, Octopus, Olive family, Orchid family, Oviparous, Paleobotany, Palms, Pandas, Penguins, Peninsula, Petroleum, Pigs, Pike, Plate tectonics, Pollination, Poppies, Prairie chicken, Pythons, Radio astronomy, Rushes, Savanna, Saxifrage family, Scavenger, Scorpionfish, Sculpins, Sea anemones, Sea level, Sedges, Sediment and sedimentation, Segmented worms, Sequoia, Shrimp, Silk cotton family, Skinks, Snails, Species, Spiderwort family, Storks, Swamp cypress family, Symbiosis, Tea plant, Terracing, Territoriality, Thermal expansion, Tides (2 photos), Trains and railroads, Turbulence, Vireos, Volcano, Vultures, Walnut family, Waterlilies, Wheat, Woodpeckers**; © Mark A. Johnson, Stock Market: **Jellyfish**; © Verna Johnston 1972, National Audubon Society Collection/Photo Researchers, Inc.: **Amaryllis family**; © Verna R. Johnston, National Audubon Society Collection/Photo

Researchers, Inc.: **Gophers**; © Darrell Jones, Stock Market: **Marlins**; © Chris Jones Photo, Stock Market: **Mining**; © Chris Jones, Stock Market: **Mass Production**; © Joyce Photographics, National Audubon Society Collection /Photo Researchers, Inc.: **Soil, Eutrophication**; © Robert Jureit, Stock Market: **Desert**; © John Kaprielian, National Audubon Society Collection/Photo Researchers, Inc.: **Buckwheat**; © Ed Kashi/Phototake: **CAD/CAM/CIM**; © Ted Keane, National Audubon Society Collection/Photo Researchers, Inc.: **Arum family**; © Michael A. Keller 1989, Stock Market: **Nutrition**; © Tom Kelly/Phototake : **Submarine**; © Karl W. Kenyon, National Audubon Society Collection/Photo Researchers, Inc.: **Otters**; © Paolo Koch, National Audubon Society Collection/Photo Researchers, Inc.: **Ore**; © Carl Koford, National Audubon Society Collection/Photo Researchers, Inc.: **Condors**; © Stephen J. Krasemann, National Audubon Society Collection/Photo Researchers, Inc.: **Prescribed burn**; © Charles Krebs, Stock Market: **Dating techniques, Walruses**; © J. Kubec A. NR.m, Stock Market: **Glass**; © Dr. Dennis Kunkel/Phototake: **Membrane, Natural fibers**; © Dennis Kunkel/Phototake : **Blood**; Dennis Kunkel (2) /Phototake: **Mites**; © Maurice & Sally Landre, National Audubon Society Collection/Photo Researchers, Inc.: **Bromeliad family**; © Lawrence Livermore National Laboratory/Science Photo Library, National Audubon Society Collection/Photo Researchers, Inc.: **States of matter**; © Lawrence Berkeley Laboratory/Science Photo Library, National Audubon Society Collection/Photo Researchers, Inc.: **Cyclotron, Particle detectors**; © Francis Leroy, Biocosmos/Science Photo Library, National Audubon Society Collection/Photo Researchers, Inc.: **Hydrothermal vents**; © Tom & Pat Lesson, National Audubon Society Collection/Photo Researchers, Inc.: **Old-growth forests**; © Yoav Levy/Phototake: **Acupuncture, Motion, Machines, simple, Phases of matter, Superconductor, Viscosity, Water pollution**; © Dr. Andrejs Liepins, National Audubon Society Collection/Photo Researchers, Inc.: **Hodgkin's disease**; © Norman Lightfoot, National Audubon Society Collection/Photo Researchers, Inc.: **Albinism**; © Suen-O Linoblad,National Audubon Society Collection/Photo Researchers, Inc.: **Eland**; © R. Ian Lloyd, Stock Market: **Island**; © Paul Logsdon/Phototake: **Contour plowing**; Courtesy of Jacqueline Longe.: **Ultrasonics**; © Dr. Kari Lounatimaa/ Science Photo Library, National Audubon Society Collection/Photo Researchers, Inc.: **Asexual reproduction**; © Alexander Lowry, National Audubon Society Collection/Photo Researchers, Inc.: **Hazardous wastes**; © Renee Lynn, National Audubon Society Collection/Photo Researchers, Inc.: **Capuchins**; © John Madere, Stock Market: **Mass transportation**; © Dr. P. Marazzi, National Audubon Society Collection/Photo Researchers, Inc.: **Edema**; © Andrew J. Martinez, National Audubon Society Collection/Photo Researchers, Inc.: **Flatfish**; © Bob Masini/Phototake: **Radial keratotomy**; © Karl H. Maslowski, National Audubon Society Collection/Photo Researchers, Inc.: **Caribou, Weaver finches**; © Don Mason, Stock Market: **Bats**; © Cynthia Matthews, Stock Market: **Birth**; © C. G. Maxwell, National Audubon Society Collection/Photo Researchers, Inc.: **Cattails**; © Henry Mayer, National Audubon Society Collection/Photo Researchers, Inc.: **Beech family**; © Fred McConnaughey, National Audubon Society Collection/Photo Researchers, Inc.: **Boxfish, Cuttlefish, Mackerel**; © Tom McHugh/Science Source, National Audubon Society Collection/Photo Researchers, Inc.: **Fossil and fossilization**; © Tom McHugh, National Audubon Society Collection/Photo Researchers, Inc.: **Bowerbirds, Canines, Elapid snakes, Elephant shrew, Gibbons and siamangs, Gorillas, Mole-rats, Skates, Sturgeons, Vipers, Salamanders**; © Will and Deni McIntyre, National Audubon Society Collection/Photo Researchers, Inc.: **Canal, Dyslexia, Amniocentesis, Lock**; © Eamonn McNulty, National Audubon Society Collection/Photo Researchers, Inc.: **Pacemaker**; © Dilip Mehia/Contact Giza, Stock Market: **Pyramid**; © Anthony Mercieca Photo, National Audubon Society Collection/Photo Researchers, Inc.: **Bluebirds**; © Astrid & Hanns-Frieder Michler/Science Photo Library, National Audubon Society Collection/Photo Researchers, Inc.: **Precipitation**; © 1983 Lawrence Midgale, National Audubon Society Collection/Photo Researchers, Inc.: **Composite family**; Courtesy of J. Gordon Miller.: **Horses**; © Mobil Solar Energy Corporation/Phototake: **Photovoltaic cell**; © Viviane Moos, Stock Market: **Perpendicular, Smog**; © Moredun Animal Health LTD, National Audubon Society Collection/Photo Researchers, Inc.: **Thrombosis**; © Hank Morgan, National Audubon Society Collection/Photo Researchers, Inc.: **In vitro fertilization**; © Hank Morgan, National Audubon Society Collection/Photo Researchers, Inc.: **Radiation detectors**; © Roy Morsch, Stock Market: **Bioluminescence, Seeds, Toucans**; © Roy Morsch/Bikderberg, Stock Market: **Dams**; © John Moss, National Audubon Society Collection/Photo Researchers, Inc.: **Aqueduct**; © Prof. P. Motta/Dept. of Anatomy/University La Sapienza,

Rome/Science Photo Library, National Audubon Society Collection/Photo Researchers, Inc.: **Connective tissue, Skeletal system, Osteoporosis**; © Prof. P. Motta/G. Macchiarelli/University La Sapienza, Rome/Science Photo Library, National Audubon Society Collection/ Photo Researchers, Inc.: **Heart**; © Mug Shots, Stock Market: **Electrocardiogram**; © Joe Munroe, National Audubon Society Collection/Photo Researchers, Inc.: **Amaranth family, Starlings**; © Dr. Gopal Murti, National Audubon Society Collection/Photo Researchers, Inc.: **Sickle cell anemia**; © S. Nagendra, National Audubon Society Collection/Photo Researchers, Inc.: **Spider monkeys**; © NASA/Science Photo Library, National Audubon Society Collection/Photo Researchers, Inc.: **Radar**; © NASA, National Audubon Society Collection/Photo Researchers, Inc.: **Satellite**; NASA: **Aircraft (2 photos), Airship, Balloon, Black Hole, Comets, Constellation, Dark Matter, Earth, Jupiter (3 photos), Mars (3 photos), Mercury (2 photos), Meteors and meteorites, Moon (3 photos), Neptune (2 photos), Planetary nebulae, Pluto, Rockets and missiles, Saturn (2 photos), Saturn, Solar flare, Solar system, Space Shuttle, Spacecraft, manned, Sun (2 photos), Sunspots, Telephone, Tropical cyclone, Uranus (2 photos), Venus (2 photos)**; © National Aububon Society Collection/Photo Researchers, Inc.: **Monoculture, Aye-ayes, Bass, Chinchilla, Crocodiles, Fossa, Lemur, Plastics, Pneumonia**; © Tom Nebbia, Stock Market: **Drought**; © Nelson-Bohart & Associates/Phototake: **Metamorphosis**; © Ray Nelson/Phototake: **Amplifier**; © Joseph Nettis, National Audubon Society Collection/Photo Researchers, Inc.: **Computerized axial tomography**; © Mark Newman/Phototake: **Glaciers**; © Newman Laboratory of Nuclear Studies, Cornell University, National Audubon Society Collection/Photo Researchers, Inc.: **Subatomic particles**; © NIH, National Audubon Society Collection/Photo Researchers, Inc.: **Artificial heart and heart valve**; © Novosti Press Agency, National Audubon Society Collection/Photo Researchers, Inc.: **Nuclear fusion, Spacecraft, manned**; © Richard Nowitz/Phototake: **Engraving and etching**; © Gregory Ochocki, National Audubon Society Collection/Photo Researchers, Inc.: **Ocean sunfish**; © John Olson , Stock Market : **Brewing, Metal production**; © Omikron, National Audubon Society Collection/Photo Researchers, Inc.: **Lampreys and hagfishes, Squid**; © Omikron, National Audubon Society Collection/Photo Researchers, Inc.: **Tarsiers**; © Stan Osolinski 1993, Stock Market: **Predator**; © Stan Osolinski 1992, Stock Market: **Evolution**; © 1992 Gabe Palmer/Bikderberg, Stock Market: **Sextant**; © David Parker, ESA/National Audubon Society Collection/Photo Researchers, Inc.: **Rockets and missiles**; © David Parker/Science Photo Library, National Audubon Society Collection/Photo Researchers, Inc.: **Oscilloscope**; © David Parker, National Audubon Society Collection/Photo Researchers, Inc.: **Computer, digital**; © Claudia Parks, Stock Market: **Coast and beach**; © David Parler, National Audubon Society Collection/Photo Researchers Inc.: **Particle detector**; © Pekka Parviatnen, National Audubon Society Collection/Photo Researchers, Inc.: **Auroras**; © Alfred Pasieka/Science Photo Library, National Audubon Society Collection/Photo Researchers, Inc.: **Magnetism**; © Bryan F. Peterson, Stock Market: **Natural Gas**; © David M. Phillips/The Population Council/Science Source, National Audubon Society Collection/Photo Researchers, Inc.: **Fertilization**; © Mark D. Phillips, National Audubon Society Collection/Photo Researchers, Inc.: **Monkeys**; © Phototake: **Oryx**; Phototake (CN) /Phototake: **Abscess**; © Photri, Stock Market: **Explosives**; © 1973 Photri/Bikderberg, Stock Market: **Tornado**; © Roy Pinney, National Audubon Society Collection/Photo Researchers, Inc.: **Arum family**; © Philippe Plailly, National Audubon Society Collection/Photo Researchers, Inc.: **Hologram and holography, Microscopy, Gene therapy**; © Philippe Plailly/Eurelious/Science Photo Library, National Audubon Society Collection/Photo Researchers, Inc.: **Microscopy**; © Philippe Plailly/Eurelios, National Audubon Society Collection/Photo Researchers, Inc.: **Electrostatic devices**; © Rod Planck, National Audubon Society Collection/Photo Researchers, Inc.: **Mosquitoes**; © Planet Earth: **Coelacanth, Crocodiles, Orang-utan, Tapirs**; © 1986 David Pollack/Bikderberg, Stock Market: **Concrete**; © J. Polleross, Stock Market: **Emission**; © Marco Polo/Phototake: **Slash-and-burn agriculture**; © Cecilia Posada/Phototake: **Assembly line**; © Masud Quraishy, National Audubon Society Collection/Photo Researchers, Inc.: **Cats**; © E. Hanumantha Rao, National Audubon Society Collection/Photo Researchers, Inc.: **Bee-eaters**; © Rapho, National Audubon Society Collection/Photo Researchers, Inc.: **Dik-diks**; © G. Carleton Ray, National Audubon Society Collection/Photo Researchers, Inc.: **Sharks**; © Hans Reinhard/Okapia 1990, National Audubon Society Collection/Photo Researchers, Inc.: **Carrot family**; © H. Reinhard/Okapia, National Audubon Society Collection/Photo Researchers, Inc.: **Buzzards**; © Roger Ressmeyer/Starlight/for the W. M. Keck Observatory, cour-

ACKNOWLEDGEMENTS

tesy of California Associate for Research and Astronomy.: **Telescope**; © Chris Rogers/Bikderberg, Stock Market: **Laser**; © Otto Rogge, Stock Market: **Precious metals**; © Frank Rossotto, Stock Market: **Temperature regulation**; © Martin M. Rotker/Phototake: **Adrenals**, **Aneurism**; Neasaphus Rowalewkii: **Fossil and fossilization**; © Royal Greenwhich Observatory, National Audubon Society Collection/Photo Researchers, Inc.: **Atomic clocks**; © Royal Observatory, Edinburgh/AATB/Science Photo Library, National Audubon Society Collection/Photo Researchers, Inc.: **Star cluster**; © Royal Observatory, Edinburgh/National Audubon Society Collection/Photo Researchers, Inc.: **Telescope**; © Ronald Royer/Science Photo Library, National Audubon Society Collection/Photo Researchers, Inc.: **Star**; © Leonard Lee Rue III, National Audubon Society Collection/Photo Researchers, Inc.: **Groundhog**, **Kangaroos and wallabies**, **Mongooses**, **Muskrat**, **Coatis**, **Rats**, **Rusts and smuts**, **Seals**; © Leonard Lee Rue, National Audubon Society Collection/Photo Researchers, Inc.: **Camels**; © Leonard Lee Rue, National Audubon Society Collection/Photo Researchers, Inc.: **Shrews**; © Len Rue Jr., National Audubon Society Collection/Photo Researchers, Inc.: **Badgers**; © S.I.U.,National Audubon Society Collection/Photo Researchers, Inc.: **Lithotripsy**; © 1994 Ron Sanford, Stock Market: **Behavior**; © Nancy Sanford, Stock Market: **Mink**; © Ron Sanford, Stock Market: **Beavers**, **Raccoons**; © Science Photo Library, National Audubon Society Collection/Photo Researchers, Inc.: **Arthritis**, **Gangrene**, **Artificial fibers**; Science Photo Library: **Binary star, Galaxy, Halley's comet, Milky Way, Paleontology, Star formation**; Science Source: **Eclipses, Quasar**; © Secchi-Lecague/Roussel-UCLAF/CNRI/Science Photo Library, National Audubon Society Collection/Photo Researchers, Inc.: **Neuron**; © Nancy Sefton, National Audubon Society Collection/Photo Researchers, Inc.: **Sponges**; © Dr. Gary Settles/Science Source, National Audubon Society Collection/Photo Researchers, Inc.: **Aerodynamics**; James Lee Sikkema: **Elm , Gesnerias, Grapes, Holly family, Lilac, Lily family, Lily family, Maples, Mustard family, Nightshade, Pines, Rose family, Spruce, Spurge family, Swamp cypress family, Willow family**; © Lee D. Simon, National Audubon Society Collection/Photo Researchers, Inc.: **Bacteriophage**; © James R. Simon, National Audubon Society Collection/Photo Researchers, Inc.: **Sloths**; © Ben Simon, Stock Market: **Elephant;** © SIU, National Audubon Society Collection/Photo Researchers, Inc.: **Frostbite**; © SIU, National Audubon Society Collection/ Photo Researchers, Inc.: **Birth**; © Prof. D. Skobeltzn, National Audubon Society Collection/Photo Researchers, Inc.: **Cosmic rays**; © Howard Sochurek, Stock Market: **Gene**; © Dr. M.F. Soper, National Audubon Society Collection/Photo Researchers, Inc.: **Plovers**; Courtesy of Charles H. Southwick: **Macaques, Rhesus monkeys**; © James T. Spencer, National Audubon Society Collection/Photo Researchers, Inc.: **True eels**; © Hugh Spencer, National Audubon Society Collection/Photo Researchers, Inc.: **Spore**; © Spielman/CNRI/Phototake: **Lyme disease**; © St Bartholomew's Hospital, National Audubon Society Collection/Photo Researchers, Inc.: **Bubonic Plague**; © Alvin E. Staffan, National Audubon Society Collection/Photo Researchers, Inc.: **Walkingsticks**; © S. Stammers, National Audubon Society Collection/Photo Researchers, Inc.: **Interferons**; © Peter Steiner, Stock Market: **LED**; © Tom Stewart, Stock Market: **Icebergs**; © David Stoeklein, Stock Market: **Partridges**; © Streinhart Aquarium, National Audubon Society Collection/Photo Researchers, Inc.: **Geckos**; © Mary M. Thacher, National Audubon Society Collection/Photo Researchers, Inc.: **Genets**; © Mary M. Thatcher, National Audubon Society Collection/Photo Researchers, Inc.: **Carrot family**; © Asa C. Thoresen, National Audubon Society Collection/Photo Researchers, Inc.: **Slash-and-burn agriculture**; Geoff Tompkincon, National Audubon Society Collection/Photo Researchers, Inc.: **Surgery**; © Geoff Tompkinson, National Audubon Society Collection/Photo Researchers, Inc.: **Cryogenics**; © Tom Tracy, National Audubon Society Collection/Photo Researchers, Inc.: **Refrigeration**; © Alexander Tsiaras, National Audubon Society Collection/Photo Researchers, Inc.: **Cauterization, Transplant, surgical**; © George Turner, National Audubon Society Collection/Photo Researchers, Inc.: **Cattle family;** © U.S. Fish & Wildlife Service: **Canines, Kangaroo rats, Toads, Turtles**; © Akira Uchiyama, National Audubon Society Collection/Photo Researchers, Inc.: **Saiga antelope**; © Howard Earl Uible, National Audubon Society Collection/Photo Researchers, Inc.: **Marmosets and tamarins**; © Howard E. Uible, National Audubon Society Collection/Photo Researchers, Inc.: **Tenrecs**; © R. Van Nosstrand, National Audubon Society Collection/Photo Researchers, Inc.: **Gibbons and siamang**; © G. Van Heijst and J. Flor, National Audubon Society Collection/Photo Researchers, Inc.: **Chaos**; © Irene Vandermolen, National Audubon Society Collection/Photo Researchers, Inc.: **Banana**; © K. G. Vock/Okapia, National Audubon Society Collection/Photo

Researchers, Inc.: **Birch family**; © Ken Wagner/Phototake: **Herbicides, Agrochemicals**; © Susan Woog Wagner, National Audubon Society Collection/Photo Researchers, Inc.: **Down's syndrome**; © M. I. Walker/Science Photo Library, National Audubon Society Collection/Photo Researchers, Inc.: **Copepods**; © Kennan Ward, Stock Market: **Chimpanzees, Salmon**; Bill Wassman: **Dinosaur**; © C. James Webb/Phototake: **Smallpox**; C. James Webb/Phototake: **Elephantiasis**; © Ulrike Welsch, National Audubon Society Collection/Photo Researchers, Inc.: **Deforestation**; © Jerome Wexler 1981, National Audubon Society Collection/Photo Researchers, Inc.: **Carnivorous plants**; © Herbert Wexler, National Audubon Society Collection/Photo Researchers, Inc.: **Livestock;** © Jeanne White, National Audubon Society Collection/Photo Researchers, Inc.: **Hippopotamuses, Dragonflies**; © George Whiteley, National Audubon Society Collection/Photo Researchers, Inc.: **Horticulture**; © Mark Wilson, National Audubon Society Collection/Photo Researchers, Inc.: **Falcons**; © Charles D. Winters, National Audubon Society Collection/Photo Researchers, Inc.: **Centrifuge**; © Anthony Wolff/Phototake: **Boobies and Gannets**; Illustrations reprinted by permission of Robert L. Wolke.: **Air pollution (2 illustrations), Aluminum, Amino acid, Atom, Barbiturates, Calorimetry, Carbon (3 illustrations), Chemical bond (3 illustrations), Chemical compound (2 illustrations), Crystal, Deoxyribonucleic Acid (DNA), Earth's interior, Electrolysis, Electrolyte, Electromagnetic spectrum, Ester, Fatty acids, Gases, properties of (4 illustrations), Hydrocarbon (3 illustrations), Metric system, Metabolism, Molecule, Nuclear fission (2 illustrations), Plastics, Radiation, Soap, Solution, States of matter (2 illustrations), Water, X rays**; © David Woods, Stock Market: **Cockatoos**; © Norbert Wu, Stock Market: **Courtship, Rays**; © Zefa Germany, Stock Market: **Codfishes, Forests, Hummingbirds, Mole, Rain forest**; © 1994 Zefa Germany, Stock Market: **Bears, Mimicry, Pollination**.

Line art illustrations provided by Hans and Cassady of Westerville, Ohio.

Calibration

Calibration is the process of checking the performance of a measuring instrument or device against some commonly accepted standard. A watch, for example, has to be calibrated so that it keeps correct time, agreeing with the international standard. The dials on a radio must also be calibrated so that the correct frequency or station is actually being received. Calibration provides consistency in a variety of applications. Because rulers and calipers are calibrated, for instance, a 0.39 in (10 mm) nut made by one factory will fit a 0.39 in (10 mm) screw machined by another halfway around the world. Without calibration, such standardization and interchangeability would not be possible.

Laboratories exist that provide official calibration of various instruments. In addition to clocks, such instruments and tools as electrical meters, laser beam power analyzers, torque wrenches, thermometers, and surveyors' theodolites all need calibration to an accepted standard to be useful. Calibration is performed by comparing the results of the instrument or device being tested (the value you actually get) to the accepted standard (the value you should get), and adjusting the instrument/device being tested until the two agree.

Frequency of calibration varies according to the device being calibrated and the applications. A clock or a common ruler for home use, for example, will only be calibrated at the time it is manufactured. A torque wrench on a NASA project, on the other hand, may require calibration every year. Some sophisticated electronic instruments for such projects may require calibration every few months.

In the United States, calibration of instruments or devices for high precision applications is generally traceable to standards established by the National Institute of Standards and Technology (NIST). In other words, if a laboratory is calibrating a meter stick for distance measurement, they need to prove that the standard they are measuring against has also been calibrated against the NIST definition of the meter. NIST keeps standard definitions of mass, length, temperature, etc. Historically, standards have been based on a 'magic measure' such as the platinum–iridium bar initially used as the standard for the meter. The trend now is away from physical expressions of standards and toward standards based on some physical constant. One of the official definitions of the meter, for example, is based on the wavelength of light emitted by calcium atoms under certain specific conditions. Such a definition can be recreated at need and does not depend on the physical existence of a slab of metal. International standards have been agreed upon, simplifying international trade and science.

Traceability to NIST is not in and of itself a guarantee of accuracy, however. All measurements have some uncertainty associated with them. Common sense should thus be used when measurement accuracy requirements for an instrument or device are formulated. Accuracy is limited by calibration, and even calibration has its limits.

See also Caliper.

Californium see **Element, transuranium**

Caliper

A caliper is an instrument used for measuring linear dimensions that are not easily measured by devices such as meter sticks or rulers. Two examples of such measurements include the outer dimensions of a pipe or the internal diameter of a glass tube.

Although many kinds of calipers exist, they are all designed on a common principle: two legs are hinged at one end to allow movement of the free ends of the legs both towards and away from each other. A caliper looks like a common pair of tweezers. The distance between the free ends of the two legs is the linear dimension measured by the caliper.

The crescent–shaped legs of an outside caliper are curved inward toward each other. When the ends of the caliper are placed on the outside of some object, the distance between the ends of the legs can be read on a scale (usually incised on the pivot end of the caliper), giving the outside diameter of the object. The legs of an inside caliper, on the other hand, are curved away from each other, like an hourglass. To find an interior diameter, the caliper is placed inside an object and opened. Again, the distance between the ends of the caliper can be read on a scale.

The micrometer is one of the most common devices using the caliper principle. The micrometer consists of a metal handle around which a movable cylinder called the thimble is attached. As the thimble is rotated, a spindle connected to the handle moves toward or away from a fixed anvil. The dimensions of an object can be measured by placing the object between the anvil and the spindle and slowly rotating the thimble. When the object is in firm contact with the anvil on one side and the spindle on the other, its linear dimensions can be read on the scale located on the micrometer handle.

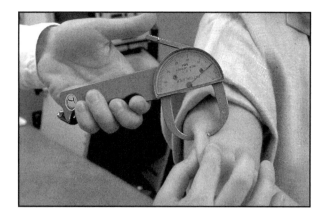

A fat caliper.

The micrometer caliper can provide precise measurements relatively easily. A turn of the thimble advances the spindle only a small distance. A single rotation of the thimble in most micrometers advances the spindle a distance of 0.025 in (0.064 cm). The thimble itself is divided into 25 segments, which enables the micrometer to measure distances as small as 0.001 in (0.0025 cm). The addition of a vernier scale to the micrometer can further improve the precision of a measurement by a factor of 10.

Calla see **Arum family**

Calomel see **Mercurous chloride**

Calorie

A calorie is the amount of energy required to raise the temperature of one gram of pure water by 1° C under standard conditions. These conditions include an atmospheric pressure of one atmosphere, and a temperature change from 15.5–16.5° C.

The calorie is also sometimes designated as a gram–calorie or small calorie (abbreviated: cal), to distinguish it from the Calorie of dieticians (abbreviated: Cal), also known as a large calorie, or kilocalorie (kcal), which is equal to 1000 (small) calories.

One calorie is equivalent to 3.968 British thermal units (btu), a non–metric measure of energy content. A calorie is also equivalent to 4.187 joules (also known as an International Table calorie), which is now the unit of energy that is most commonly used in science.

Scientists are often interested in the energy contents of organic materials. These data are usually obtained by completely oxidizing (burning) a known quantity of a substance by igniting it in an oxygen–rich atmosphere inside of a device known as a bomb-calorimeter. The quantity of energy released is determined by measuring the increase in temperature of a known quantity of water contained within the bomb.

Dieticians are interested in the calorie contents of foods of various sorts. The potential energy of food is utilized metabolically by animals to drive their physiological processes, and to achieve growth and reproduction. Foods vary tremendously in their energy contents, so careful planning of food intake requires an understanding of the balance of the nutrients, such as vitamins and amino acids.

On average, pure carbohydrates have a calorific content of about 4600 cal/g (or 4.6 Cal/g), while proteins contain about 4800 cal/g, and fats or lipids about 6000–9000 cal/g. Because fats are so energy–dense, they are commonly used by organisms as a compact material in which to store potential energy for future use. Of course, some of us store more of this potential energy of fat than others.

Engineers are often concerned with the energy contents of petroleum, coal, and natural gas, and of distillates or synthetic materials refined from any of these fossil fuels. Knowledge of the amounts of energy that are liberated through the complete oxidation of these materials is important in the design of engines, fossil–fueled generating stations, and other machines that we use to achieve mechanical work. In order to maximize the amount of useful work that is achieved per unit of fuel consumed, that is, the energy–conversion efficiency, engineers are constantly re–designing machines of these sorts, and tuning their operating parameters, such as fuel:oxygen ratios.

Ecologists are also interested in the energy contents of organic materials, and how these change over time. Although ecologists commonly measure biomass and productivity in terms of weight, these are often converted into energy units, in order to account for the greatly varying calorific contents of different sorts of biomass, as was described above for carbohydrates, proteins, and fats. In parallel with the interests of engineers, ecologists are concerned with the efficiency of ecosystems in converting solar energy into plant productivity, as well as the transfers of the energy of plants to herbivores and carnivores. These efficiencies are best determined through knowledge of the amounts and transfers of energy, as expressed in calorific units.

See also Energy.

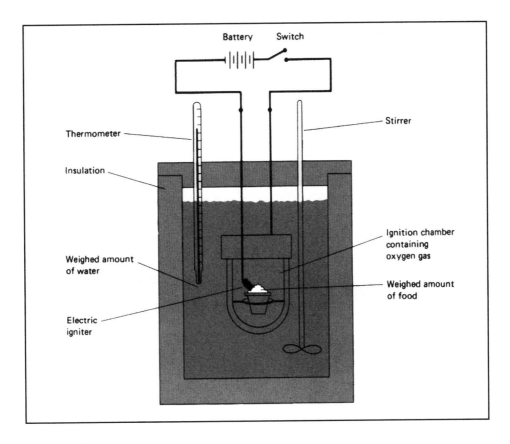

Battery   Switch

Thermometer

Insulation

Weighed amount
of water

Electric
igniter

Stirrer

Ignition chamber
containing
oxygen gas

Weighed amount
of food

A calorimeter.

Calorimetry

Calorimetry is the measurement of the amount of heat gained or lost during some particular physical or chemical change. Heats of fusion or vaporization, heats of solution, and heats of reaction are examples of the kinds of determination that can be made in calorimetry. The term itself derives from a very old word for heat, caloric, as is the name of the instrument used to make these determinations, the calorimeter.

History

Little productive work on the measurement of heat changes was accomplished prior to the mid–nineteenth century for two reasons. First, the exact nature of heat itself was not well understood. Until the work of the Scottish chemist Joseph Black in the late eighteenth century, the distinction between temperature and heat was not at all clear. It then took until about 1845 before the nature of heat as a form of energy and not of matter was made clear in the experiments of James Joule and others.

Secondly, given such uncertainties, it is hardly surprising that appropriate equipment for the measurement

of heat changes was not available until after the 1850s. Lavoisier and Laplace had made use of a primitive ice calorimeter to measure the heats of formations of compounds in 1780, but their work was largely ignored by their colleagues in chemistry.

In fact, credit for the development of modern techniques of calorimetry should probably be given to the French chemist Pierre Eugène Berthelot. In the 1860s, Berthelot became interested in the problems of heat measurement. He constructed what was probably the first modern calorimeter and invented the terms endothermic and exothermic to describe reactions in which heat is taken up or given off, respectively.

The calorimeter

In essence, a calorimeter is any device in which the temperature before and after some kind of change can be accurately measured. Probably the simplest of such devices is the coffee cup calorimeter so–called because it is made of a styrofoam cup such as the ones in which coffee is commonly served. A styrofoam cup is used because styrofoam is a relatively good insulating material. Heat given off within it as a result of some physical or chemical change will not be lost to the surrounding environment. To use the coffee cup calorimeter, one simply carries out the reaction to be studied inside the coffee cup, measures the temperature changes that take place, and then calculates the amount of heat lost or gained during the change.

The type of calorimeter more commonly used for precise work is called the bomb calorimeter. A bomb calorimeter designed to measure heats of combustion, as an example, consists of a strong–walled metal container set inside another container filled with water. The inner container is fitted with an opening through which oxygen can be introduced and with electrical leads to which a source of electricity can be connected.

The object to be studied is then placed in a combustion crucible within the bomb and ignited. The reaction occurs so quickly within the reaction chamber that it is similar to the explosion of a bomb. Hence the instrument's name. Surrounding the bomb in this arrangement is a jacket filled with (usually) water. Heat given off or absorbed within the bomb heats up the water in the jacket, a change that can readily be measured with a thermometer inserted into the water.

Many variations in the basic design described here are possible. For example, the use of liquids other than water in the insulating jacket can permit the study of heat changes at higher temperatures than the boiling point of water (100°C). Aneroid (without liquid) calorimeters are also used for special purposes, such as the measurement of heat changes over very large temperature ranges. Such calorimeters use metals with a high coefficient of thermal conductivity, like copper, to measure the gain or loss of heat in some type of change.

Calorimetry theory

Suppose that a cube of sugar is burned completely within the bomb of a calorimeter. How can an experimenter determine the heat released in that reaction?

To answer that question the assumption is made that all of the heat produced in the reaction is used to raise the temperature of the water in the surrounding jacket and the metal walls of the bomb itself. The heat absorbed by each is equal to its mass multiplied by its specific heat multiplied by the temperature change (ΔT). Using a word equation to express this fact: heat released in reaction = (mass of water $\times$ specific heat of water $\times$ ΔT) + (mass of bomb $\times$ specific heat of bomb $\times$ ΔT). The last part of this equation, (mass of bomb $\times$ specific heat of bomb $\times$ ΔT), is the same for any given calorimeter. Once measured, it is known as a constant value and, therefore, is given the name of calorimeter constant.

KEY TERMS

Heat—The form of energy that flows between two bodies because of a different in temperature.

Insulator—An object that does not conduct heat (or electricity) well.

Specific heat—The amount of heat required to raise the temperature of one gram of a substance one degree Celsius.

Temperature—A measure of the average kinetic energy of the particles of which a substance is made.

Furthermore, the specific heat of water is constant, 1.0 cal/g•°C, or 4.18 J/g•°C. In any given experiment, therefore, the only measurements that must be made are the mass of water used in the calorimeter and the change in temperature.

See also Heat; Temperature.

Further Reading:

Asimov, Isaac. *Asimov's Biographical Encyclopedia of Science & Technology.* 2nd revised edition. Garden City, NY: Doubleday & Company, Inc., 1982, pp. 443–444.

Masterson, William L., Emil J. Slowinski, and Conrad L. Stanitski. *Chemical Principles.* Philadelphia: Saunders, 1983, Chapter 5.

McCullough, John P., and Donald W. Scott, eds. *Experimental Thermodynamics.* New York: Plenum Press, 1968.

David E. Newton

Calvin cycle see **Photosynthesis**

Camels

Camels and their relatives, the llamas, are long-legged, hoofed mammals in the family Camelidae in order Artiodactyla, whose members have an even number of toes. All camels have a cleft in their upper lip, and all have the ability to withstand great heat and great cold.

Camels evolved in North America and spread into South America, Asia, and Africa. Camels in Asia and Africa today have been domesticated for up to 3,500 years. The two smaller South American species of camel have been bred to develop two purely domestic species, the llama and the alpaca.

A dromedary camel.

Like cattle, camels are cud–chewing animals, or ruminants. However, unlike other ruminants, which have four chambers to their stomachs, camels have only three. Both male and female camels have the same number of teeth for feeding, but the front incisor teeth of the males are large and sharp, making them useful for fighting. Camels have oval shaped red blood cells, whereas all other mammals have round red blood cells.

Both New World and Old World camels communicate in a variety of ways, including whistling, humming, and spitting. In zoos, camels have been known to spit the contents of their first stomach at annoying visitors.

Old world camels

The Bactrian, or two–humped, camel *(Camelus ferus)* is the largest species, native to the rocky deserts in Asia. These wild camels were the ancestors of the domestic Bactrian camel, *C. bactrianus*. These animals are named for the Baktria region of ancient Persia (now Iran), and can withstand severe cold as well as extreme heat (up to 122° F (50° C). Bactrian camels have a thick and shaggy coat, with very long hair growing downward from their necks. Domesticated bactrians have longer hair than the wild species.

The Bactrian camel stands about 6.5 ft (2 m) high at the shoulder and weighs up to 1,500 lbs (680 kg) and can run up to 40 mph (65 kph). Bactrian camels can carry loads of up to 1,000 lbs (454 kg), about twice as much as a dromedary can carry. Although Bactrian camels breed well in zoos, they are almost extinct in the wild, with probably only a few hundred left in the Gobi Desert of Asia.

The most common camel is the one–humped Arabian, or dromedary camel, which is known today only as a domesticated species, *C. dromedarius*. Although the name "dromedary" has now been given to all one–humped camels, it originated with a special breed developed for great speed in racing. Racing camels can also run over great distances – covering more than 100 mi (160 km) in a day.

Dromedary camels are taller but lighter than Bactrian camels, reaching 7 ft (2.1 m) at the shoulder, and an average weight of about 1,200 lbs (550 kg). The animals' hair can vary in color from dark brown to white, though most are the tan color referred to as "camel's hair." The Arabian camel has long been extinct in the wild, though feral populations (domestic animals living in the wild) occur in various parts of the world, including central Australia where the herds number up to 50,000.

Although one–humped and two–humped camels are given separate species names, they can interbreed fairly easily and are probably varieties of a single species. The product of interbreeding, called a tulu, usually has two humps. This is not surprising in view of the fact that the one–humped camel actually has another hump that lies unnoticeably in the shoulder region.

Both species are used primarily as pack animals in desert countries, where they travel at a leisurely pace of about 25 miles (40 km) a day, carrying both goods and people, mounted in saddles that fit over the single hump or between the two humps. A camel's hump contains 80 lbs (36 kgs) of fat, not water, which provides the animal with energy when no food is available. The hump shrinks and becomes flabby as the fat supply is used up, but it firms up again when the animal eats plants and drinks water. A camel can go for a week and even travel 100 mi (161 km) or more in a desert summer without drinking. Camels can withstand a great deal of dehydration and can lose more than 40 percent of their body weight without harm. In winter, camels can go for many weeks without drinking. When dehydrated camels do reach water, they make up for any previous lack by drinking as much as possible very quickly. They have been known to drink as much as 30–40 gal (114–150 l) in a single session to rehydrate.

Other adaptations of camels for dealing with desert conditions include a reduced number of sweat glands which only function in extreme heat or exertion. At heat stresses which would cause most animals to sweat to cool their bodies, and thus use up water, the camel's body temperature can temporarily rise several degrees, a strategy known as heat storage. The thick coat on the back of the camel prevents heat from the sun from being absorbed. The hoofed feet have broad, thick pads that provide a solid base on shifting sands. The thick, bushy eyebrows and double rows of eyelashes keep sand out of their eyes. Any sand that does enter the eye is dislodged by a transparent third eyelid that slides across the eye.

A domesticated llama in Peru.

Hair inside a camels ears prevents sand from easily blowing in the ear canal. In addition, camels can voluntarily squeeze shut both their slit–like nostrils and their mouth to prevent sand from entering. The camels mouth has a thick, leathery lining that prevents the thorny desert plants from damaging the mouth. The round, leathery kneepads of camels protect their knees when they kneel on the hot sand or on hard rocky ground.

Camels are central to the survival and culture of the nomadic peoples of the old world deserts. Camel hair, shed in large clumps, is woven into clothing and tents, while camel milk and meat provide nourishment, particularly on special occasions. Nomadic people often let their camels loose in the desert for several months at a time, which includes the mating season. Camels have a gestation period of about 14 months, after which the mother camel gives birth to a single 80 lb (36 kg) offspring, every other year. The long–legged calves, become independent at about four years, and domesticated camels can live up to about 50 years.

New world camels

New World camels are native to the Andes Mountains on the western side of South America. The wild New World camels are the vicuña *(Vicugna vicugna)* and the guanaco *(Lama guanicoe)* while the llama and alpaca are domestic animals.

Wild South American camels live primarily at high altitudes in both open grasslands and forests. Their family groups may include a male and half a dozen or so females, each with a single young. Young males are chased from the group when they are between a year and a year and a half old, then they join a bachelor herd until they can later form their own family groups. Young females join a new group and mate, producing young after a gestation period of about 11 to 12 months.

Vicuñas are extremely rare in the wild, and are small animals, often standing no more than 3 ft (90 cm) at the shoulder and weighing no more than about 110 lbs (50 kg). Vicuñas, are alone among the camels to have bottom incisor teeth that keep growing and enamel only on the outer surface. This characteristic has led taxonomists to assign them to a separate genus. Vicuñas are fast runners that can readily cover the dry, open grasslands where they live at altitudes between 11,500 and 18,700 ft (3,500–5,700 m). Male vicuñas defend both a grazing territory and a sleeping territory.

Vicuña fur can be woven into one of the softest textiles known and was for many centuries worn only by the Inca kings. After the Incan empire fell, Vicuñas were no longer protected, and were hunted for their meat and skins until they were close to extinction, with fewer than 10,000 animals left in 1967. Vicuñas are now protected in several Andean national parks, and their numbers are climbing once again.

The South American larger guanaco lives primarily in dry open country, from the coastal plains to the high mountains. Guanaco hair is cinnamon colored on their backs and white on their under parts. Unlike the smaller vicuñas, they have dark faces. Guanacos stand about 6 ft (less than 2 m) tall, and are the tallest South American camels, but are very light compared to camels, weighing only about 250 lbs (113 kg). Most guanacos now live in Patagonia, a temperate large grassland in southern Argentina and Chile, and are found from sea level to about 14,000 ft (4,200 m). Males guanacos will mark their territories with piles of dung. Female guanacos give birth every two years with their newborn being called a chulengo, which can run within minutes of being born. Young guanacos often make a playful prance in which they lift all four feet off the ground at once, and guanacos also like playing in the running water of streams.

Starting about 4,000 years ago, natives of the Andes Mountains bred the guanaco to develop two other domesticated camels, the sure–footed llama *(Lama glama),* bred for its strength, endurance, and its ability to carry great loads over steep mountains, and the long–haired alpaca *(Lama pacos).*

Llamas stand only about 4 ft (1.2 m) at the shoulder. Usually only male llamas are used for the long pack trains, while the females are kept for breeding. An average male llama weighs about 200 lbs (90 kg) but can carry a load weighing two–thirds that amount on its back, for about 15–20 mi (24–32 km) a day across mountain terrain. Llamas were used by the Incas to transport silver from their mountain mines.

The alpaca, the other domesticated breed, has long hair valued for warm blankets and clothing because it is soft, lightweight, and waterproof. Some breeds of alpaca have hair that almost reaches the ground before it is sheared. Llama hair is not used for weaving because it is too coarse. Llamas and alpacas are often crossed to get an animal that produces hair that is both sturdier and softer than either of the parents' hair.

Further Reading:

Arnold, Caroline. *Camel.* New York: Morrow Junior books, 1992.

Camels. Zoobooks series. San Diego, CA: Wildlife Education, 1984.

Green, Carl R. and Sanford, William R. *The Camel.* Wildlife Habits & Habitats series. New York: Crestwood House, 1988.

LaBonte, Gail. *The Llama.* Remarkable Animals series. Minneapolis: Dillon Press, 1989.

Lavine, Sigmund A. *Wonders of Camels.* New York: Dodd, Mead & Company, 1979.

Perry, Roger. *Wonders of Llamas.* New York: Dodd, Mead & Co., 1977.

Stidworthy, John. *Mammals: The Large Plant–Eaters.* Encyclopedia of the Animal World. New York: Facts on File, 1988.

Jean F. Blashfield

Canal

A canal is a man–made waterway or channel that is built for navigation, irrigation, drainage, or water supply. When the word is used today however, it is usually in the context of transport or navigation by boats. Canal transport should not be confused with navigating on a river, since a canal is entirely artificial (although often connected with a natural body of water). There are two major types of transport canals. One is best described as an inland waterway, or water route, that either follows the lay of the land or has locks; the other is a canal that is built to shorten a sea route. Examples of the latter are the well–known Suez Canal, which connects the Mediterranean and the Red Sea, and the Panama Canal, which shortens the voyage from Europe to America's west coast by 3,000 m (4800 km). From the earliest times, canals were built because they were the simplest and cheapest way of moving heavy goods. Despite the coming of railroads, automobile and truck transport, and airplanes, canals continue to play a vital and growing role in the world's economy.

History

The earliest canals were built by Middle Eastern civilizations primarily to provide water for drinking and for irrigating crops. In 510 B.C. Darius I, King of Persia, ordered the building of a canal that linked the Nile River to the Red Sea; this canal was a forerunner of the modern Suez Canal. The Chinese were perhaps the greatest canal builders of the ancient world, having linked their major rivers with a series of canals dating back to the third century B.C. Their most impressive project was the famous Grand Canal, the first section of which opened around 610 A.D. With a total length of 1,000 m (1600 km), it is the longest canal in the world. Canals were naturally employed by the highly practical Romans, but were neglected for the centuries after the fall of the Roman Empire. The commercial expansion of the 12th century spurred the revival of canals, and it is estimated that as much as 85% of the transport in medieval Europe was by canal.

Many early canals were called contour canals because they followed the lay of the land and simply went around anything in their way. Major changes in ground and water levels have always presented canal builders with their greatest engineering problem; at first, boats were simply towed or dragged over slipways to the next level. The invention of the modern lock in China solved this problem at once, causing the full development of canals. The modern two–gate lock evolved from the slow and unsafe Chinese "flash lock" that had only one gate; the "flash lock" eventually made its way to Renaissance Europe, where it was modified with a second gate. The development of the lock heralded a period of extensive canal construction across Europe, and it is not surprising that each nation responded in its own particular way. The Naviglio Grande Canale in Italy (1179–1209) and the Stecknitz Canal in Germany (1391–1398) are two that made

A Hanjin ship in the Panama canal.

important contributions to waterway technology. Also in China, a 700 m (1100 km) branch of the Grand Canal was finished in 1293. Over the next few centuries, France built the pioneering Briare Canal (completed in 1642) and the famous Canal du Midi (1681), which joined the Mediterranean and the Atlantic and would serve the world as an example of complex civil engineering at its best. This remarkable French canal stimulated the era of British canal construction that began with the completion of the Bridgewater Canal (1761). In Germany, the Friedrich Wilhelm Summit Canal was completed in 1669, and in other nations, extensive waterway systems were developed. With industrial production steadily growing in the 19th century, transport by canal became essential to the movement of raw materials and goods throughout Europe.

The United States has a shorter tradition of canal building; its first major canal was the Erie Canal, constructed during the beginning of the 19th century. Completed in 1824, the 364 m (586 km) canal provided a water route that brought grain from the Great Lakes region to New York and the markets of the East. With the coming of the railroads in the 1830s, the U.S. quickly abandoned its canals, believing that rail was now the best method for every transport task. The Europeans did not react the same way to the railroad, maintaining their canal systems as a complementary system not in competition with railroads. Today, inland waterways or canals play a major transportation role in the United States and the rest of the world, for it has been realized that canals are perfectly suited for carrying low–value, high–bulk cargoes over long distances.

Sea canals, the great canals that shorten sea routes, are glamorous, highly–visible engineering achievements. The three outstanding examples are the Kiel Canal connecting the North and Baltic Seas (1895), the Suez Canal linking the Mediterranean and Red Seas (1869), and the Panama Canal linking the Atlantic and Pacific Oceans (1914). However, sea–to–sea ship canals with and without locks all face the same problem of obsolescence—newer ships are too large for older canals. Both the Kiel and the Suez canals have been enlarged, but the Panama canal is not large enough to accommodate the world's monster transport ships.

Construction and Operation

Engineers who are designing a canal must take several things into consideration. Based on the number, frequency, and size of vessels that will use the canal, engineers must formulate the dimensions of the canal to accommodate predicted traffic. Natural obstacles in the path of the canal, such as rock formations, must also be taken into account; engineers must plan to modify, remove, or avoid the obstacle. There must be adequate vertical clearance above the canal; the clearance afforded by pre–existing bridges, for example, must be able to accommodate the vessels that will use the canal. Lastly, based on the canal design, engineers must decide the scale and location of associated structures, such as bridges, tunnels, and locks.

The paths of most canals are affected by variations in the levels of terrain. Engineers compensate for these variations with either locks or inclined planes. A lock is a segment of the waterway that is closed off by gates at either end. When a boat enters the lock, the front gate is already closed; the back gate is then closed behind the boat, and the water level within the lock is raised or lowered to the level of the water on the outside of the front gate. Valves on the gates control the level of the water. While locks are the most common means of compensating for elevation changes, the procedure is slow and uses great volumes of water. Inclined planes can be

---

KEY TERMS

Contour Canal—Usually early canals that followed the meandering natural contours of the earth.

Flash lock—A simple wooden gate that was placed across a moving body of water to hold it back until it had become deep; the sudden withdrawal of the gate would cause a "flash" of water that would carry a boat downstream and over the shallows below.

Inland waterway—An artificial waterway or channel that is cut through land to carry water and is used for transportation.

Lock—A compartment in a canal separated from the main stream by watertight gates at each end; as water fills or drains it, boats are raised or lowered from one water level to another.

Slipway—An inclined path or road leading into a body of water over which, in ancient times, boats were dragged or rolled from one body of water to another.

---

used to elevate and lower smaller vessels; they use no water and are often quicker. When boats reach certain stations along the waterway, they are pulled out of the water and moved on trucks up or down the plane.

Canal operators must monitor the canal's supply of water. If the natural supply of water at the upper end of the canal is deficient, it must be supplemented by water pumped into the reservoirs. If nature supplies the reservoir with excess amounts of water, some of the water must be diverted from the canal; otherwise, excess water may strengthen the current to the extent of disrupting canal operation.

Although canals are among the oldest works of civil engineering, they will continue to play a major role in commerce, as they are by far the cheapest form of inland transportation yet devised.

Further Reading:

Hadfield, Charles. *World Canals: Inland Navigation Past and Present*. New York: Facts On File, 1986.

Payne, P. S. Robert. *The Canal Builders: The Story of Canal Engineers Through the Ages*. New York: Macmillan Co., 1959.

Spangenburg, Ray and Diane K. Moser. *The Story of America's Canals*. New York: Facts On File, 1992.

Leonard C. Bruno

Canary see **Finches**

Cancel

Cancel refers to an operation used in mathematics to remove terms from an expression leaving it in a simpler form. For example, in the fraction 6/8, the factor 2 can be removed from both the numerator and the denominator leaving the irreducible fraction 3/4. In this instance the 2 is said to be canceled out of the expression. Canceling is particularly useful for solving algebraic equations. The solution to the equation $x - 7 = 4$ is obtained by adding 7 to each side of the equation resulting in $x = 11$. When we add 7 to the left side of the equation, we cancel the -7 and put the equation in a simpler form. Typically, canceling is performed by using inverse operations. These are operations such as multiplication and division or addition and subtraction which "undo" one another.

Further Reading:

Marcucci, Robert & Harold Schoen. *Beginning Algebra.* Boston: Houghton Mifflin Company, 1990.

Saxon, John. *Algebra I: An Incremental Development.* Norman: Grassdale Publishers Inc, 1981.

Cancer

Cancer is a disease of unregulated cell growth caused by carcinogen exposure, an inherited genetic defect, or viruses. The original cause of a particular cancer can be difficult to determine, but many cancerous cells maintain some trace of their original site. Cancerous cells can multiply and form a large multi–cellular mass (tumor) which disrupts the biological balance of the organ or tissue where it grows. Some tumors are found contained in one location and can be surgically removed. These encapsulated tumors may cause little harm and are called "benign". Other tumors may spread to several places in the body causing extensive damage. Those tumors which invade surrounding tissues or metastasize (literally "change position") are said to involve secondary sites. Such aggressive tumors are called "malignant". Those most likely to spread include bone, brain, and lung tumors. The study of cancer is called oncology.

History

Cancer is not just a modern phenomenon. Dinosaur fossils and Egyptian mummies have been discovered with evidence that cancer is no new adversary.

The ancient Greeks believed that good health resulted from the balance of the four elements: blood, phlegm, yellow bile, and black bile. They thought that cancer was due to an excess of black bile, because tumors were often darkened by vascularization, infiltration of blood vessels. In 500 B.C., the Greek physician Hippocrates wrote extensively about the tumors he found in patients. He gave cancer ("the crab") its name, because the tumors he saw appeared crab–shaped with a central mass and tumorous growth extending from the center like the appendages of a crab. Cancer is a word usually used to describe malignant, not benign, tumors.

Periods of discovery

Through the 1600s, cancer was often treated with bleeding, magical ointments, and surgery. Surgery of cancer patients allowed for a better understanding of tumorous tissues and dispelled the Greek notion of "black bile." Surgery shifted the classifications of tumors to specific body sites. Hence, cancers began to be termed using words to describe their tissue or organ of origin. For example, an epithelioma was a cancerous growth in epithelial tissue. Cancer had been viewed as an invisible assailant which always attacked the entire body. But surgery promoted the understanding that it often began in a single site.

Anthonie von Leeuwenhoek's development of the first high quality microscope around 1674 focused attention on the cellular and biochemical aspects of cancer. He made lenses capable of 300X magnification; this is equivalent to magnifications used in today's laboratories. Thereafter, cell biologists could actually see cellular differences between normal and cancerous cells in the microscope.

Oncology and an understanding of the causes and effects of cancer, however, are more recent advances. In 1775, cancer was linked to a substance by the English surgeon, Percivall Pott. Pott wrote a series of papers arguing his belief that the soot in chimneys was responsible for scrotal cancer in the young chimney sweeps who were hired to clean the filth out of these narrow spaces. Chimney soot was later found to contain hydrocarbons which are potent mutagens. Yet, many aspects of cancer remained a mystery.

As the 19th century was ending, the highly publicized cancer of General Ulysses S. Grant led the Ameri-

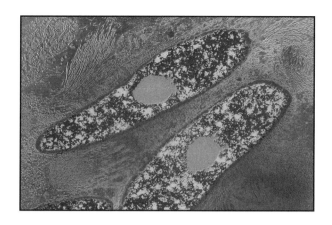

A transmission electron micrograph (TEM) of two spindle cell nuclei from a human sarcoma. Sarcomas are cancers of the connective tissue (bone, nerves, smooth muscle).

can public to openly discuss this powerful disease. Grant was a heavy tobacco user whom physicians diagnosed as having multiple tumors resulting from tobacco use. Grant lost his battle with cancer in 1885. No cancer case received so much public attention until the 1985's colo–rectal cancer of then–President Ronald Reagan.

The twentieth century

Into the 1900's, the battle against cancer was a quiet, terrifying battle fought with private prayers and desperate therapies. Cancer seemed to be an unyielding adversary which crept up on its victims and often went unnoticed until it was too late. Most cancer patients died. As the century progressed, cures for several other fatal diseases such as tuberculosis and polio were found. By contrast, the lack of advances in oncology reinforced the fear people had of cancer. In 1913, the American Cancer Society (ACS) was founded to inform the public about cancer. Today the ACS is one of the largest private funders of cancer research.

In 1937, the National Cancer Institute (NCI) was formed. The federal government allocated $700,000 for cancer research and another $750,000 to build the National Cancer Institute in Bethesda, Maryland. Today the NCI is the world's largest research institute devoted solely to cancer research. By the mid–1900's, several scientific advances led to a greater understanding of the cell biology and biochemistry of cancer. Watson and Crick's discovery in 1953 that DNA is the genetic material of life began the modern era of biological research. As further genetic experiments clarified the roles of DNA, RNA, and proteins, modern molecular biology emerged. And within the past twenty years, phenomenal

acceleration of research has occurred fueled by the tools of recombinant DNA technology.

1995

An estimated 1/5 of all deaths in the U.S. are due to cancer. The number one type of fatal cancer among both men and women is lung cancer. Prostate cancer is the second most fatal cancer among men; while breast cancer is the second most fatal among women. Colo–rectal cancer is the third most fatal cancer for both sexes.

The American Cancer Society estimates that 1,252,000 new cancer cases will be diagnosed in the United States in 1995. 500,000 (about 40%) will survive for at least 5 years. After 5 cancer–free years, former cancer patients are considered to have the same life expectancy as someone who has never had cancer. This "cure" rate is a tremendous improvement over survival rates for cancer patients at the turn of this century. The steady improvement in the war against cancer is due to scientific research, public education, and early detection of tumors.

Marvelous research strides have contributed greatly to cures for some types of cancer. The ACS reports that "acute lymphocytic leukemia in children, Hodgkin's disease, Burkitt's lymphoma, Ewing's sarcoma (a form of bone cancer), Wilm's tumor (a kidney cancer in children), rhabdomyosarcoma (a cancer in certain muscle tissue), testicular cancer, and osteogenic (bone) sarcoma" have all been successfully treated in some patients.

Cell biology

Normal cells have specialized roles in multi–cellular organisms. They begin as stem cells, the infants in cellular society. (These stem cells are often named using the suffix –blast. Hence, a neuroblastoma is a neuronal stem cell cancer.) Stem cells are undifferentiated, not yet educated to perform a specific task for the organism of which they are part. With maturity, a neuronal cell transmits signals in the brain and communicates with other neuronal cells via specific neurotransmitters. This maturation is analogous to the way a human baby learns to speak in words, phrases, sentences, paragraphs, and then stories.

All mature cells receive and send environmental signals to and from other cells. One signal tells a cell to stop dividing; another informs a cell when it has come into contact with another cell. Like neighbors who must respect a common property–line, these neighboring cells must respect other cell's space so that they can live harmoniously. Cells which have lost these controls are said to be "transformed." Transformed cells can stack up on top of each other and grow rampant.

Sherwin Nuland has called cancer cells "the juvenile delinquents of cellular society." Advanced tumor cells rob neighboring cells of essential nutrients and continue multiplying at the expense of normal tissue. Late stage tumors can even send out chemical messengers into their environment which direct the formation of new blood vessels to them. The formation of new vessels is called angiogenesis. The new vessels import additional food and supplies for the disruptive tumor and allow it to grow even more wantonly in complete disregard for normal cells which begin to starve.

Cancer works by turning a cell's sophisticated molecular machinery against the cell itself. The genetic information which a cell requires to perform its specific function are kept on; whereas, the genes it does not need are turned off. A mutation which alters this off/on status or tampers with the functional balance of a cell's genes can lead to changes which cause transformation. Whether a mutation is due to a genetic defect, a carcinogen, or a virus, the end result is that a cell begins to misbehave.

Neoplastic transformation is a phrase sometimes used to mark the beginning of this misbehavior. Neoplastic ("new form") simply describes an altered tissue growth. Neoplasm refers to a pattern of growth, whereas a tumor is the actual mass of tissue. However, these terms are used somewhat interchangeably.

One transformed cell can eventually yield an entire tumor; however, multiple mutations within that single cell are usually required to progress into a tumor. Although tumor initiation is due to a mutation, some initiators only weaken the cell to further attacks by non–mutagens. Tumor promoters are non–mutagenic substances which can trigger an eventual transformation. The initial cellular defect can occur years or decades before exposure to the tumor promoters. It is this aspect of cancer which makes it a disease of age. Most cancers occur after age 50 with the highest percentage of first cancers detected after age 65.

Types of cancer/tumors

There can be more than 200 different types of cancer named according to their original organ or tissue location. Leukemia refers to cancer of white blood cells, and lymphoma is cancer of the lymphatic system which carries fluids around the body. In addition, melanomas are cancers which begin in melanocytes (skin pigment cells). Melanomas usually appear as a change in a mole and result from excessive exposure to sunlight.

Cancers are further subdivided on the basis of whether they originate in epithelial or connective tissues. Epithelial tissues include cells which line cavities such as the stomach or lung. Connective tissues include bones and cartilage. Cancers which begin in epithelial tissue are called carcinomas; and cancers starting in connective tissues or muscle are called sarcomas.

Characterization of a tumor as benign or malignant is closely related to the effect of a tumor on the host. In general, malignant cells are more likely to metastasize. But benign and malignant tumor cells have some clear visible differences as well. Benign cells resemble their parent cell. Whereas, malignant cells may have grown and divided so rapidly and haphazardly that they no longer resemble their parent cells. Rapidly dividing cells are most likely to perpetuate a mutation. At particular risk are cells which divide often to replenish themselves; these include bone marrow, stem, lung, and intestinal cells.

Causes of cancer

Cancer is attributed to three main causes. They are carcinogenic exposure, heredity, and viruses. The same genetic mutation could be due to any of these three. (Researchers can use tests to determine the causative agent in some cancers.) Although stress has received much attention as a contributor to health problems, stress alone can not cause cancer.

Carcinogens

Carcinogens are mutagens which can cause neoplastic transformations. Since most cancers are caused by carcinogens, knowledge of what is carcinogenic can enable people to avoid exposure to these substances. Carcinogens fall into several chemical categories. The major classes of carcinogens are: polycyclic aromatic hydrocarbons, aromatic amides, azo dyes, nitrosamines, halogenated hydrocarbons, alkylating agents, and metal ions.

Carcinogens can alter DNA directly or indirectly. Some carcinogens directly bind to DNA and change the sequence coding for cellular events. Others are metabolized by the body into substances which cause genetic aberrations.

One of the most carcinogenic substances known is tobacco smoke which contains several mutagens, toxins, and poisons. Tobacco smoke is the number one cause of lung cancer and increases risk for developing other cancers. People who smoke at least 2 packs per day have more cases of larynx, esophagus, oral cavity, urinary bladder, kidney, and pancreas cancer than non–smokers.

Not all carcinogens are chemicals, however. Any mutagen which leads to cancer is carcinogenic. Ultraviolet (uv) light, a normal component of sunlight, is a physical carcinogen. Uv light can cause faulty bonds to form within DNA. Uv light is one of the carcinogens people can minimize their exposure to.

Ionizing radiation is another physical carcinogenic. At sufficient levels, it can break chromosomes. Particles emitted from an atomic bomb are an example of ionizing radiation which lead to increases in the incidence of cancers in their vicinity. This type of radiation is also used in some scientific research, industrial work, and medical diagnostics. Federal laws require that individuals exposed to ionizing radiation be monitored with exposure not allowed to exceed set amounts.

The Ames test is the foremost test used to assess the mutagenicity of a substance. A culture of a growth deficient strain of Salmonella bacteria is exposed to possible carcinogens. In order for the bacteria to grow, they must somehow be mutated. If the substance added to the culture is carcinogenic, then the bacteria grow. The Ames test has positively identified many carcinogens.

Heredity

Susceptibility to specific cancers can be hereditary. Chromosomal flaws in genes for specific cell types can make a person more likely to develop a particular cancer. A number of mutations in genes regulating breast cells can lead to breast cancer. However, mutations are only hereditary when they are acquired at conception from the sperm and egg which each contributed half of the new organism's genetic material. A mutation which occurred in an individual's non–sex cells will not be carried on to the next generation. Although cancer patterns vary in different countries, these differences are thought to have more to do with exposure differences than with heredity.

Some inherited and chemically–induced mutations occur in proto–oncogenes, genes responsible for orchestrating cellular development in multi–cellular organism. Proto–oncogenes are particularly active in embryogenesis and child development. Hence, these genes must be tightly regulated with regard to when they are turned on and when they are turned off. A mutated proto–oncogene is called an oncogene. Oncogenes lead to cancer by turning on a cellular signal that should have laid dormant. This type of mutation will lead to transformation if only one of a cell's two copies

(alleles) of this gene is altered. Thus, this mutation is called a dominant mutation.

Other mutations can turn off a control which suppresses a cellular function. Genes which normally inhibit are called tumor suppressor genes. Mutations in tumor suppressor genes are recessive in nature. In other words, they require that both alleles be mutated for transformation to occur.

Viruses

Some viruses cause cancer by infecting a host with DNA for an oncogene. Such oncogenic viruses insert an activated form of the proto–oncogene into the host cell's DNA. Some viruses contain RNA instead of DNA. RNA tumor viruses can use the cellular mechanisms in the host nucleus to make viral DNA which can then transform the cell. The normal flow of cellular genetic information is from DNA to RNA to protein. RNA tumor viruses which reverse this process by producing DNA from viral RNA are referred to as retroviruses, because they operate in reverse of regular activity. The viral DNA can have drastic effects on its host cell depending on how and where it inserts into the host DNA. Retroviruses cause most possible types of cancer including leukemia, AIDS, and sarcomas.

Diagnosis

There are several early warning signs that may indicate the presence of cancer. They include bloody sputum, stools, or genital discharge; a lump or change in shape of breasts, testes, or moles; persistent abdominal pain; rapid weight loss; a sore that does not heal; swallowing or speaking difficulty; and severe recurrent headaches. People with these symptoms should see their physician.

Confirmation of cancer is accomplished through a cellular analysis. Cells for testing are obtained from normal sloughing as in salvia or biopsy using a needle. The cells are then observed under a microscope by a pathologist who determines whether they are malignant or benign. Transformed cells usually appear abnormal compared to normal cells of the same type. Myosarcoma cells differ from healthy muscle cells in architecture.

An x ray, computerized axial tomography (CAT) scan, or magnetic resonance imaging (MRI) can then be used to assess the extensiveness of cancer. A plain x ray is a short, painless procedure which can visualize tumors. CAT scans use x rays and computers to examine visual cross–sections of an area. CAT scans can be used diagnostically or to follow the progression of a known tumor. MRI uses a magnetic field and radio waves to depict an image of a region. MRI's give a highly detailed image; however, they do take 30 to 60 minutes and can be uncomfortable for that reason.

Surgery is used both diagnostically and as a form of treatment. Sometimes the surgery is exploratory, meaning that the surgeon does not know the extent of possible damage. During surgery, biopsies are usually obtained for additional analysis. Benign, non–cancerous, tumors are also surgically removed. For malignant cases, surgery is often followed by other therapies to give the patient the best chance for a cure. Fortunately, a diagnosis of cancer is not a death sentence; almost half of cancer patients recover their health.

Treatment

Various treatments are used for various reasons. Treatments can alleviate the pain or complications resulting from cancer, slow tumor progression, or cure different cancers. The treatment course varies based on the specific type and the extent of cancer. Surgery or radiation or both are often used to treat or remove localized tumors. Whereas, chemotherapy is more often used to treat cancers which have spread.

Radiation

Radiation therapy uses ionizing radiation such as x rays and other radioactive sources to kill transformed cells. Radiation has the advantage of focusing on a defined anatomical region such as the throat or cervix; hence, it can spare normal cells in other sites. This therapy can also reach areas which are surgically unavailable. It can effectively kill transformed cells in cancers of the mouth, larynx, cervix, and uterus. It also can cure Hodgkin's disease, basal and squamal cell carcinomas, and leukemia.

Radiation is usually administered on an out–patient basis and takes only a few minutes several times a week. A linear accelerator machine aims an x–ray beam directly at the tumor. Patients usually lie on a table, and the x–ray beam angle is altered to create the best results. The radiation room is designed to prevent radiation leakage and exposure to individuals not undergoing treatment.

Radiation can also be used in a palliative, or pain–reducing, manner. In this condition, the radiation can reduce a tumor's size enough to provide a patient with esophageal cancer enough room to swallow or restore some of a paralyzed brain cancer patient's ability to move. Radiation is also used to kill any remaining cancerous cells after surgical removal of a tumor.

Chemotherapy

Chemotherapy is a course of drug therapy which specifically targets the cellular mechanism of the disease being treated. Some drugs are synthetic hormones. Some inhibit DNA synthesis and can halt or slow cell division in cancer cells. Major advantages of chemotherapy its ability to reach cancer cells anywhere in the body and that it can be taken by mouth or injected. However, chemotherapy has the drawback that it does not distinguish well between normal and transformed cells. Since DNA synthesis inhibitors act on dividing cells regardless of their status, healthy dividing cells lining the stomach, lungs, and hair follicles can also be effected.

Chemotherapy is most effective against leukemia and Hodgkin's disease. It is also used in combination with other treatments for uterine, breast, ovarian, bladder, and other advanced stage cancers and is being investigated as a means of treating oral and colo–rectal cancers.

Chemotherapy often lasts longer than equivalent radiation therapy. Another difficulty that arises with chemotherapy is the high number of drug–resistant cells which can emerge. Because cancer cells naturally divide and mutate rapidly, a gradual selection process can promote survival of those cells resistant to a drug being used. For this reason, a chemotherapeutic approach sometimes employs multiple drugs at the same time to outwit potentially resistant mutants. This can, in turn, lead to greater toxicity to normal cells causing adverse effects such as nausea in patients. Several anti–nausea drugs are given to chemotherapy recipients to help them combat this discomfort. However, not all chemotherapy is so debilitating.

Immunotherapy

Another approach to treatment is to boost the immune system to fight the cancer. The human immune system kills a large number of naturally–occurring cancer cells every day, and our bodies have natural DNA–repair mechanisms which scout out and kill abnormal cells. Scientists have developed ways to boost these natural cancer–fighting properties. By injecting chemical signals into cancer patients, they have been able to improve some cancer patients' health. Interleukin–2 and interferons have given early promising results; however, they do not offer a cure. Because of the uniqueness of each cancer case, each cancer and its treatment require individual assessment and treatment plans.

Monoclonal antibodies (MoAb's) are another immunological tool used to counter some cancers. In this technique, a patient's own cancerous cells are combined with antibody producing cells. The resulting antibodies can recognize and destroy abnormal cells similar to the initial cancerous cells.

Genetic engineering also offers future promise for treating cancer. The more scientists learn about how normal and transformed cells differ, the closer they are to being able to develop specific weapons against the cancer cells. One hope is to engineer genes to replace mutated DNA in transformed cells. Inserting healthy genes into the location of the aberrant gene may cure cancers in the future. One immunological disorder, Adenosine Deaminase Deficiency (ADD), has already been successfully treated using genetic engineering. ADD is due to a single mutation in a single protein. While cancer is not currently treated with gene therapy, this approach may offer future hope for some patients.

A combination of the above treatments and a few alternative therapies are used to tackle cancers. Alternative therapies such as investigational drugs are recommended for people with extremely rare or untreatable cancers. The power of positive thinking and hope are also emphasized as important psychological factors in facing cancer.

When someone is responding to treatment, this means that their cancer is subsiding. Remission refers to a lack of detectable symptoms. Remission can be due to treatment or unknown factors. When a cancer is responding or in remission, then the person with that cancer may be on the road to being cured.

Prevention

A number of cancer cases each year could be prevented. People are not powerless in the cancer battle. Protection against excessive uv light, tobacco smoke, excessive alcohol, high–fat diets, and known carcinogens could prevent more than half of all cancer cases.

In addition, regular screening to detect cancer early gives people a chance to win the battle against cancer. Cancer screening is the search for disease in symptom–free individuals. The ACS recommends the following screening guidelines. To detect breast tumors, women over age 40 should have a mammogram every 1–2 years until age 50 after which they should have annual mammograms. A mammogram uses low–dose x rays to visualize breast tissue. For the early detection of colon or rectal cancer, an annual digital rectal exam after the age of 40 and annual stool blood test after the age of 50 is recommended. All women who are sexually active or over age 18 should have an annual pap smear to test for cervical cancers. Men over age 50 should have an annual digital rectal exam for prostate examination

---

KEY TERMS

Angiogenesis—Growth of blood vessels which supply nutrients to a specific area.

Carcinogen—A mutagen which can cause cancer.

Chromosome—Organized strands of DNA in the cellular nucleus.

DNA—Deoxyribonucleic acid, the genetic material of the cell.

Mutagen– A substance capable of increasing the mutation rate of cells.

Mutation—A change in the DNA in a cell.

Prognosis—The quality and extent of a person's life after being diagnosed with a disease.

RNA—Ribonucleic acid, a class of molecules with multiple functions in the expression of genetic material.

---

and a blood test for prostate–specific antigen. X–rays can also be used to screen for lung tumors in smokers. An educated public who routinely checks for early detection of cancers has the best protection from cancer.

See also Ames test; Interferons.

Further Reading:

Alberts, B., et al., eds. *Molecular Biology of the Cell* . New York: Garland Publishing, Inc., 1994.

The American Cancer Society. *Cancer Facts and Figures–1995*. Atlanta: The American Cancer Society, 1995.

Harpham, W. *Diagnosis Cancer: Your Guide through the First Few Months*. New York: W. W. Norton & Company, 1992.

Nuland, S. *How We Die: Reflections on Life's Final Chapter* . New York: Alfred A Knopf, 1994.

Ruddon, R., ed. *Cancer Biology*. 2nd ed. New York: Oxford University press, 1987.

Louise H. Dickerson

Canines

Canines are in the carnivore family canidae, dogs that includes wolves, foxes, coyotes, the dingo, jackals, and a number of species of wild dog. The family also includes the domesticated dog, which is believed to have descended from the wolf. The canidae includes from 10–14 genera with 30–35 species depending on taxonomic authority. There are two species of wolves, the gray wolf (*Canis lupus*) and the red wolf (*Canis rufus*), several species of jackals and foxes.

Canines originated in North America in the Eocene (38 to 54 million years ago), from where they spread throughout the world. The social behavior of canines varies from solitary habits to highly organized packs that exhibit considerable cooperation. Canines range in size from the Fennec fox, which is about 16 1/2 inches long (including the tail), and which weighs one pound (0.5 kg), to the Gray wolf, which is more than six feet (2 m) in length, and which weighs about 175 pounds (87.5 kg).

Canine skulls have a long muzzle, well–developed jaws and a characteristic dental formula of 42 teeth. Most canines live in packs, which offers several benefits including defense of group territory, the care of the young, and the ability to catch large prey species.

Wolves

Wolves are found in North America, Europe, and Asia. The gray or timber wolf, *Canis lupus*, is the largest member of the dog family weighing up to 175 lbs (87.5 kg) and is a widely distributed species. The gray wolf lives in a variety of habitats, including forests, plains, mountains, tundra, and deserts. The red wolf, *Canis rufus*, is found only in southeastern Texas and southern Louisiana. The red wolf is smaller than the gray wolf, and there is some evidence that it may be even a hybrid cross between the gray wolf and coyote (*Canis latrans*).

The gray wolf lives in packs and is a territorial species. Territories are scent marked, and range from 50–5,000 square miles. Pack size is usually small, about eight members, consisting of a mature male and female and their offspring and relatives. When the pack size becomes large, a system of dominance hierarchy is established. The dominant male leader of the pack is called the alpha male, and the dominant female is called the alpha female. Hierarchy is acknowledged among pack members through submissive facial expressions and body postures.

Only the dominant male and female breed. Gestation is about two months and the average litter size is from four to seven pups, who are born blind. The young are weaned within five weeks and reach physical maturity within the year, but do not become sexually mature until the end of their second year. The non–breeding members of a pack will help protect and feed the young. The prey species of the wolf include deer, moose, and elk, as well as beavers.

Besides scent marking, wolves communicate by howling. It is believed that howling lets dispersed pack members know each other's position, and warns off other packs from the territory. During the spring and summer the wolf pack has a stationary phase and remains within its territory. It is during this period that the pups are raised. During the nomadic phase in autumn and winter, the wolf pack travels widely, often following the migration of prey species.

In Africa, the Canidae is represented by the Fennec fox, sand fox, Ruppell's fox, cape fox and bat-eared fox, the golden jackal, black-backed jackal, side-striped jackal, simien jackal, and the cape wild dog. In South America the canidae includes the peaved wolf and the crab–eating fox. In North America, the Canidae include the gray wolf, red wolf, coyote, red fox, arctic fox, kit fox, swift fox and grey fox. In Europe and Asia the canidae are the grey wolf, Indian jackal, red fox, Corsac fox, and Indian wild dog. The only member of the canidae in Australia is the dingo.

Foxes

There are 21 species of fox in four genera. Foxes range in size from the 3 lb (15 kg) Fennec fox (*Fennecus cerda*) to the 20 lb (10 kg) red fox. The gray fox (*Urocyon cinereargenteus*) arctic or white fox (*Alopex lagopus*) are highly valued for their pelts. Color phases of the arctic fox include the silver fox and the blue fox. The other species are found in the USA–the kit fox (*Valpes macrotis*) and the swift for (*V. velox*), which live on the western plains, including, the vulpine fox, the crab-eating South American fox (*Dusicyon azarae*) the sand fox (*Vulpes ruppelli*), and the Corsac fox (*Vulpes corsac*).

Foxes have a pointed muzzle, large ears, a slender skull, and a long bushy tail. Foxes are territorial and scent-mark their territories. Foxes use stealth and dash-and-grab hunting techniques to catch their prey. Foxes are generally solitary hunters and most species feed on rabbits, rodents, and birds, as well as beetles, grasshoppers, and earthworms. The bat–eared fox of Africa eats mainly insects, as well as fruit and small animals. Foxes mate in winter, sharing an annual litter of one to six pups after a gestation period of 50–60 per day. Besides scent mallary, foxes by vocalizations such as yapping, howling, barking, whimpering, and screaming.

Foxes are heavily hunted for their pelts, and to prevent the spread of the viral disease rabies, which are

Two dingos hunting for mice, Australia.

often shot to prevent the spread of the disease. Some efforts at oral vaccination for rabies have been successful in Switzerland and Canada.

Coyotes, jackals, dingos, and a number species of wild dog comprise the rest of the canine family. The distribution of coyotes is from Alaska to Central America. Coyote populations have flourished as wolves have been eliminated. Coyotes have interbred with wolves and with domestic dogs. Coyotes prey on small animals, but coyotes are opportunistic predators and will feed on carrion, insects and fruit. Coyotes reach maturity within a year and produce a litter of six pups. While the basic social unit of coyotes is the breeding pair, some coyotes form packs similar to wolf packs and scent mark territory. In the United States, coyotes have been responsible for considerable losses of sheep.

There are four species of jackals which replace wolves in the warmer parts of the world. Jackals are found throughout Africa, southeastern Europe, and southern Asia as far east as Burma. The four species are the golden jackal (*Canis aureus*), the simien jackal (*Canis simensis*), the black–backed jackal (*Mesomelas*), and the sidestriped jackal (*C. adustus*). The golden jackal is the most widely distributed of the four species. The golden jackal prefers arid grasslands, the silver-backed jackal prefers brush woodlands, the simien jackal prefers the high mountains of Ethiopia, and the sidestriped jackal prefers moist woodland. Jackal have a varied diet of fruit, reptiles, birds, and small mammals.

Jackals are unusually stable in their breeding relationships, forming long–lasting partnerships. They also engage in cooperative hunting. Jackals are territorial and engage in scent marking, usually as a unified male and female pair. They also participate in raising their young together and tend to remain monogamous. Jackals communicate by howling, barking, and yelping. In

The endangered red wolf (*Canis rufus*).

KEY TERMS

Alpha male or female—The dominant male or female in a pack of wolves.

Dominance hierarchy—Rank ordering among animals, with dominant and submissive ranks.

Opportunistic predator—An animal that eats what is available, either killing its own prey stealing food from other predators, or eating plant material, such as fruit and berries.

Stationary or nomadic phase—Seasonal periods in which animals may remain within a specific area, usually during warmer seasons, as compared to nomadic periods when the group moves extensively to follow prey.

Ethiopia, the simien jackal is an endangered species because it has been killed for its fur.

Other wild canines include the Indian wild dog (*Cuon alpimus*) of southeast Asia and China, the maned wolf (*Hrysocyon subatis*), which looks like a long–legged fox, the bush dog (*Speothes venaticus*) of Central America and northern parts of South America, the dingo of Australia, and the raccoon dog (*Nyetereutes procyonoides*) of east Asia, Siberia, Manchuria, China, Japan, and the northern Indochinese peninsula. In Africa, the cape hunting dog (*Lycaon pictus*) with a black, yellow, and white coat and large ears hunts in packs which can overpower any game species.

Domestic dogs

Kennel societies in the United States recognize 130 breeds of domesticated dog while kennel societies in Great Britain recognize 170 breeds, and the Federation Cynologique. Internationale (representing 65 countries) recognizes 335 breeds. The size range of domestic dogs is from the 4 lbs (2 kg) to the 200 lbs (100 kg). Some breeds, such as the dachshund, have very short legs, while others, such as the greyhound, have very long legs.

For dog owners, these animals serve a number of different purposes. Pet dogs provide companionship and protection, while others herd sheep or cattle, or work as sled dogs. Police use dogs to sniff out illegal drugs and to help apprehend criminals. Dogs are also used for hunting and for racing. Guide dogs help blind people find their way around.

Female dogs reproduce at about the age of 7–18 months. Gestation lasts about two months, and the size

of a litter is from three to six puppies. Born unable to see, like other canines, domestic dog puppies develop all their senses by 21 days. Around the age of two months, puppies are less dependent on their mothers and begin to relate more to other dogs or people. Typical vocalizations of domestic dogs include barking and yelping.

About 5,000 years ago human civilization changed from a gatherer and hunter society to a farming culture, and the domestication of the dog began. It is believed that all breeds of domestic dogs, whether small or large, long–haired or short–haired, are descended from a wolflike animal over several millions of years. Domestic dog breeds have been produced through selective breeding. One distinguishing feature between domestic dogs and wolves is the orbital angle. Dogs have a larger angle, which is measured from lines at the top of the skull and at the side of the skull at the eye socket.

Unlike the wolf, the dog, known as "man's best friend," is treasured by humans. Dog stories abound in children's literature, from Lassie to Rin Tin Tin, and politicians, like Presidents Franklin D. Roosevelt and Richard Nixon, used dogs to enhance their images.

Hunting and the destruction of habitat have endangered some species of canines. Their reputation as predators has added to efforts to eradicate them from areas where livestock is raised or where they live too close to urban populations. Some of the rare wild dogs, for instance the jackal of Ethiopia, are few in number. The maned wolf (*Chrysocyon jubatus*) of Argentina and Brazil has a population of only 1,000–2,000 members. Efforts are being made to reintroduce the gray wolf into national parks in the United States, but this effort is opposed by many people, particularly ranchers.

Further Reading:

Carey, Alan. *Twilight Hunters: Wolves, Coyotes, and Foxes.* Flagstaff, Arizona: Northland Press, 1987.

Olsen, Stanley John. *Origins of the Domestic Dog: The Fossil Record.* Tucson, Arizona: University of Arizona Press, 1985.

Sheldon, Jennifer W. *Wild Dogs: The Natural History of the Non–Domestic Canidae.* San Diego: Academic Press, 1992.

Wolves. San Francisco: Sierra Club Books, 1990.

Vita Richman

Cannabis see **Marijuana**

Cantaloupe see **Gourd family**

Cantilever

A cantilever, also called a fixed end beam, is a beam supported only at one end. The beam cannot rotate in any direction; thus it creates a solid support. The cantilever is considered the third of the three great structural methods, the other two being post–and–beam construction and arch construction. The cantilever thrusts down which is different from the thrust of an arch which is outward against its supports.

Cantilevers did not become popular in architecture until the invention of steel and its widespread adoption in construction, because the combined strength of steel and cement is needed to create an effective cantilever system. A building using cantilevers has an internal skeleton, from which the walls hang very much like curtains. Unlike more traditional building methods where the walls are used as support for the ceiling and walls, here they are dividers of space. This allows the interior of the building to be designed for purpose and creative architecture, rather than on where columns and other structural supports must be. The most famous architect to use the cantilever system was Frank Lloyd Wright. He first used it in the 1906 construction of the Robie House in Chicago. With the use of steel and concrete, Wright was able to extend the roof 20 ft (6 m) beyond its support. With the cantilever and Wright's belief in the use of the nature in which the building resided, an entire new school of architecture was created called the Prairie School.

Before cantilevers were used in buildings, they were used to create bridges. The first cantilever bridge was built in the late 1800s by Heinrich Gerber in Germany. He based his ideas on ancient Chinese bridges which, much earlier, used the concept of the cantilever. By using the cantilever, bridges would no longer need supports in their middles and, thus, could span deep ravines or rivers. In addition, bridges could be built across extremely wide bodies of water, or valleys, because fewer supports are needed, and the supports which are used can be further apart. Thus, the incorporation of steel, cement, and cantilevers changed the world of architecture and civil engineering.

Canvasbacks see **Ducks**

Capacitance

Capacitance is an electrical effect that opposes change in voltage between conducting surfaces separated by an insulator. Capacitance stores electrical energy when electrons are attracted to nearby but separate surfaces. The voltage across an unchanging capacitance value will stay constant unless the quantity of charge stored is changed.

The Farad, the unit of capacitance

The unit of capacitance is the Farad, in honor of Michael Faraday's work with electrostatics. When a 1–Farad capacitance store 1 Coulomb the result will be 1 volt. The Coulomb is the basic unit of electrical charge, equal to 6.2422×10^{18} charges the size carried by an electron or by a proton.

An electrical component that introduces capacitance is called a capacitor. Practical capacitors may have as small a value as a few trillionths of a Farad or as large as several Farads.

Energy storage in capacitors

Work is performed to accumulate charge in a capacitor. Each additional electron stored must overcome the repelling force caused by the charge previously stored. Energy storage increases as the square of the voltage across a capacitor. This often considerable energy can be used later.

Capacitors used as energy reservoirs can deliver powerful pulses of energy. A capacitor can discharge quickly then slowly recharge until the next power demand. The power source needs only to be large enough to supply the average energy. Inexpensive audio amplifiers often use large capacitors to provide high power peaks required by occasional loud sounds. Quiet intervals allow the capacitor to recharge before the next power burst.

Capacitance and alternating current

A capacitor effectively conducts alternating current even though electrons do not cross from one plate to other plate. Alternating current that appears to pass through a capacitor is actually, the charge and discharge current resulting from the constantly–changing voltage across the capacitor.

An uncharged capacitor always appears as a short circuit because its voltage must equal zero when its stored charge is zero. A capacitor carrying an alternating current continually charges and discharges, spending much of the time in a near–zero charge state. The resulting low voltage across its terminals means that it is often less significant in limiting circuit than other components in the circuit.

A capacitor's opposition to alternating current is called reactance. Higher capacitance introduces less reactance and higher frequencies result in lower reactance.

Capacitance and direct current

In a direct–current circuit a series capacitor will permit only a single pulse of charging current when the circuit voltage is changed. The charging current in quickly falls to almost zero as a capacitor charges from a constant–voltage source. Capacitors are sometimes used in circuits to oppose direct current. They may block direct current while simultaneously passing a superimposed alternating currents. A blocking capacitor is commonly used to separate alternating and direct current components.

Dielectrics

Dielectrics are the insulating materials used between the conducting plates of capacitors. Dielectrics increase capacitance or provide better insulation between the plates. Dielectrics materials exhibit very little ability to conduct electric charge. Mylar, paper, mica, and ceramics are commonly–used dielectrics. When extremely–high capacitance is required, a thin film of aluminum oxide on etched aluminum plates is used as a dielectric.

Dielectrics have a property called polarizability. A dielectric placed within an electric field appears to have electric charge on its surfaces even though the insulator remains electrically neutral. Each of the dielectric's molecules is stretched when the electric field causes its negative charges to be pulled toward the positive–charged capacitor plate and the molecule's positive charges are pulled toward the negative plate. This polarization strain causes each dielectric molecule to act as a voltage source. These voltages add in series aiding as do the voltage from several cells making up the battery in a flashlight. A phantom charge appears on each surface of the dielectric canceling much of the electric field produced by the real charges. The greater the polarization developed by a dielectric the larger the quantity of real charge the capacitor must store to develop a given voltage. The capacitance appears to increase as a result of dielectric polarization.

The capacitance multiplier for any dielectric is called its dielectric constant. The dielectric constant of a perfect vacuum is defined as exactly 1. Common dielectrics have dielectrics constants in the range of 2–4. Using a higher quality dielectric increases the capacitance by a factor equal to the dielectric constant.

Dielectric strength

Dielectric strength is the measure of a dielectric's ability to resist electric stress without losing its insulating capabilities. A high dielectric constant does not always correspond to high dielectric strength. Distilled water has a fairly high dielectric constant but it has poor dielectric strength. Water, therefore, is not a useful dielectric for capacitors because it breaks down too easily. Some ceramics have dielectric constants as high as 10,000. These materials would be extremely valuable if they had better dielectric strength.

Working voltage

If the voltage across a capacitor is increased until charges jump from one plate to the other, the capacitor will probably fail, either momentarily or permanently. Capacitors are rated to specify the maximum continuous voltage that can be applied across the dielectric before the capacitor will fail.

Capacitors as a cause of electronics equipment failures

Failed capacitors are a common cause of electronic–equipment breakdowns. When a capacitor's dielectric is destroyed the resulting short circuit may

Bord, Donald J. and Vern J. Ostdiek. *Inquiry Into Physics*, 3rd ed. West Publishing Company, 1995.

Sear, Zemansky, and Young. *College Physics*, 6th ed. Addison–Wesley Publishing Company, 1985.

Donald Beaty

KEY TERMS

Alternating current—Current where the direction of charge flow reverse.

Direct current—Current where charges flow does not reverse.

Electric field—Measure of electrical force experienced by a given charge.

Electron—Negatively–charged particle present in atoms.

Farad—The unit of capacitance, equal to 1 Volt per Coulomb.

Neutral—No net charge, when positive and negative charges cancel.

Open circuit—A physical break in a circuit path that stops the current.

Polarizability—Possible asymmetrical charge distribution in a molecule.

Power supply—A source of electrical energy used to supply a circuit.

Proton—The positively–charged particle in atoms.

Short circuit—Unwanted bypass of the expected current path in a circuit.

Voltage—Ratio of electrical potential energy to the quantity of charge.

Capacitor

A capacitor stores electrical energy. It is charged by hooking into an electrical circuit. When the capacitor is fully charged a switch is opened and the electrical energy is stored until it is needed. When the energy is needed, the switch is closed and a burst of electrical energy is released.

A capacitor consists of two electrical conductors that are not in contact. The conductors are usually separated by a layer of insulating material, dielectric. The dielectric is not essential but it keeps the conductors from touching. When the capacitor is hooked into an electric circuit with a current, one conductor becomes positively charged and the other negative. The conductors are not in contact, so the current can't flow across the capacitor. The capacitor is now charged up and the switch can be opened. The capacitor is storing electrical energy. When the energy is needed the capacitor is connected to the circuit needing the energy. The current flows rapidly in the opposite direction, discharging the capacitor in a burst of electrical energy.

Capacitors take many shapes, but the simplest is a parallel plate capacitor. It consists of two flat conductors placed parallel to each other. Larger plates can store more charge and hence more energy. Putting the plates close together also allows the capacitor to store more energy. The capacitance of a capacitor is the charge on the conductor divided by the voltage and is used to measure the ability of a capacitor to store energy. The capacitance of a parallel plate capacitor is proportional to the area of the plates divided by the distance between them. This number must then be multiplied by a constant which is a property of the dielectric between the plates. The dielectric has the effect of increasing the capacitance.

Capacitors come in a wide range of sizes. Banks of large capacitors can store and rapidly release large bursts of electrical energy. Among other uses, engineers can use such devices to test a circuit's performance when struck by a bolt of lightning. On an intermediate

cause other components to fail. Capacitors also develop open circuits, causing the loss of the capacitance.

Electrolytic capacitors are generally less reliable than other types, a tradeoff made to secure very–high capacitance in a small package. They tend to fail if stored without a voltage across their terminals. The electrolytic paste may dry in time, causing a loss of capacitance. Experienced electronic technicians consider electrolytic capacitor failures as a likely cause of an equipment fault that is not otherwise immediately obvious.

The significance of capacitance

Capacitance, inductance, and resistance are the passive electrical properties affecting electrical circuits. Understanding capacitance is an essential part of the study of electricity and electronics.

Further Reading:

Asimov, Isaac. *Understanding Physics: Light, Magnetism, and Electricity*, vol. II. Signet Books, The New American Library.

scale, a camera flash works by storing energy in a capacitor and then releasing it to cause a quick bright flash of light. Electronic circuits use large numbers of small capacitors. For example, a RAM (Random Access Memory) chip uses hundreds of thousands of very small capacitors coupled with switching transistors in a computer memory. Computer information is stored in a binary code of ones and zeros. A charged capacitor is a one, and an uncharged is a zero. These are just a few example of the many uses of capacitors.

Capillaries see **Circulatory system**

Caprimulgids

The frogmouths, oilbird, potoos, owlet frogmouths, and nightjars are five unusual families of birds that make up the order Caprimulgiformes, and are collectively referred to as caprimulgids.

Caprimulgids have a large head, with a short but wide beak that can open with an enormous gape, fringed by long, stiff bristles. This apparatus is used by caprimulgids to catch their food of insects in flight.

Caprimulgids have long, pointed wings, and short, weak legs and feet. Most of these birds are crepuscular, meaning they are active in the dim light of dusk. Some species are nocturnal, or most active during the night. Caprimulgids have soft feathers and a subdued coloration, consisting of streaky patterns of brown, grey, and black. Caprimulgids are well camouflaged when they are at rest, and can be very difficult to detect when roosting or sitting on a nest.

Caprimulgids may nest on the ground, in a tree cavity, or in caves. The lay one to five eggs. The chicks are downy and helpless at first, and are fed and brooded by both parents.

The oilbird

The oilbird (*Steatornis caripensis*) of Trinidad and northern South America is the only species in the family Steatornithidae. This bird forages widely for its major food of oily palm nuts, and it roosts and nests in caves. The oilbird navigates inside of its pitch–black caves using echolocation, similar to bats. It rears two to four young, which are extremely fat, and at one stage are about 50% larger than their parents.

In the past, large numbers of fat, baby oilbirds were collected and boiled down (that is, rendered) as a source of oil for illumination and cooking. Dead young oilbirds were even sometimes impaled on a stick and used as a long–burning torch. Excessive exploitation soon threatened the oilbird, and it is now a managed or protected species over most of its range. However, the forest habitat of oilbirds is not well protected, and deforestation represents an important threat to the species over much of its range.

Frogmouths

Frogmouths are 12 species occurring in lowland and secondary forests, collectively making up the family Podargidae. Frogmouths occur from India, through Indochina, Southeast Asia, the Philippines, Australia, and many nearby Pacific Islands.

Frogmouths are rather large birds, with a body length of up to 20 in (50 cm). They have short, rounded wings and a long, pointed tail, and are relatively weak fliers. Their bill is very wide, flattened, and heavy. Unlike most caprimulgids, frogmouths do not feed aerially. Rather, these nocturnal birds pounce on their prey of invertebrates, small mammals, birds, and other small animals, on the ground and in tree branches. The cup–shaped or platform nest is usually built in a forked branch of a tree or on a horizontal branch, and depending on the species, contains one to four eggs.

The tawny frogmouth (*Podargus strigoides*) occurs in Australia and Tasmania. The Papuan frogmouth (*P. papuensis*) breeds in New Guinea. The large frogmouth (*Batrachostomus auritus*) occurs in lowland forests of Indochina, Sumatra, and Borneo.

Potoos

Potoos or tree–nighthawks are five species of birds that comprise the family Nyctibiidae. Potoos occur in open forests from southern Mexico and the West Indies to northern Argentina and Paraguay.

Potoos have long, pointed wings and a long tail. These birds have weak legs and feet, but long claws, and they perch in an upright, almost–invisible stance on tree limbs. Potoos are solitary birds, feeding nocturnally on insects in flycatcher–fashion, by making short sallies from a prominent perch. Potoos lay a single egg on a cup–like cavity atop a broken stub of a dead branch.

The common potoo (*Nyctibius griseus*) is a widespread species, occurring from southern Mexico to northern Argentina. The great potoo (*N. grandis*) occurs widely in forests of Central and northern South America.

Owlet frogmouths

Owlet frogmouths (or owlet nightjars) are eight species that make up the family Aegothelidae. These birds are Australasian, occurring in Australia, New Guinea, New Caledonia, and nearby islands. Their typical breeding habitat is open forests and brushlands.

Owlet frogmouths have long, pointed wings and a long, pointed tail. They are solitary, nocturnal animals that feed on insects in the air, and on the ground. Owlet frogmouths lay their clutch of three to five eggs in cavities in trees.

The owlet nightjar (*Aegotheles cristatus*) occurs in savannas and open woodlands in Tasmania, Australia, and New Guinea. The grey or mountain owlet frogmouth (*Aegotheles albertisi*) is widespread in mountain forests of New Guinea.

Goatsuckers and nighthawks

The goatsuckers, nightjars, and nighthawks are 70 species that make up the family Caprimulgidae. Most species in this family occur in Africa and Asia, but eight species breed in North America. These birds have extremely long, pointed wings, and are excellent fliers that feed aerially on flying insects.

The whip–poor–will (*Caprimulgus vociferous*) is a familiar species of forests in the eastern United States and southeastern Canada. Chuck–will's–widow (*C. carolinensis*) breeds in pine forests of the southeastern United States. The common poor–will (*Phalaenoptilus nuttallii*) occurs in the western United States. The common nighthawk (*Chordeiles minor*) is a familiar species over most of the United States and southern Canada, and sometimes nests on flat, gravelled roofs in cities. The lesser nighthawk (*C. acutipennis*) is a smaller species of the southwestern United States.

See also Goatsuckers.

Further Reading:

Brooke, M. and T. Birkhead. *The Cambridge Encyclopedia of Ornithology.* Cambridge, U.K.: Cambridge University Press, 1991.
Harrison, C. J. O., ed. *Bird Families of the World.* New York: H.N. Abrams Pubs., 1978.

Bill Freedman

Captive breeding and reintroduction

Since 1973, when the Endangered Species Act was passed in the United States to protect species that are rapidly declining due to human disturbance, attempts to halt or reverse the extinction of some species from the wild have resulted in attempts to breed those animals and plants in captivity, with the eventual goal of re–establishing them into their native wild habitat. Such programs are often carried out by zoos, aquaria, botanical gardens, and various conservation organizations, and have met with limited success. There are several complications involved with the captive breeding and reintroduction of endangered species, but they have also resulted in deepening our understanding of ecology, evolution, and the extinction process. Such knowledge can only benefit future attempts at impeding human–induced extinctions.

Captive breeding

The goal of captive breeding, also known as ex situ conservation, is to breed and maintain a population of a species such that the captive population is self–sustaining, without continual augmentation by newly captured individuals from the wild. Further, the captive population must be maintained at a size that will be able to exist and proliferate in the wild when eventually reintroduced.

Genetics of captive breeding

In addition to maintaining a target size in captivity, a critical goal of captive breeding programs is to maintain a level of genetic diversity that will allow the population to adapt in the wild to the adversities of its environment once released. The term genetic diversity refers to the maintenance in a population of several alleles, or forms of a gene, the unit that is inherited by offsprings from their parents. If all of the individuals in a captive population are offspring of the same parents, for example, then that captive population has very low genetic diversity because all of the alleles for all of the genes in it were inherited from the same two parents. If this population were reintroduced into the wild, there would be a relatively low chance of its survival and continued reproduction unless conditions in the wild were completely without adversities such as disease, predation, climatic fluctuations, and food shortage. In other words, unless conditions in the wild were just like the stable and protected conditions of the zoo that the population came from, there would likely not be enough genetic variation to ensure that at least some of the individuals would have critical alleles, such as those for disease resistance, that would allow them to persist under difficult conditions. However, a population with greater genetic diversity would, in contrast, maintain the potential to have at least some of its members survive adversity and reproduce, thus passing their genes on to the next generation. In essence, genetic diversity helps to ensure that the species will be able to survive, despite natural selection against some of its individuals.

Since captive breeding attempts to reestablish a species' continued existence in the long–term, such issues are of crucial importance. The population size plays a role here as well. Not only will a small population have a greater probability of extinction once reintroduced, simply because of deaths due to random environmental factors and flaws in the reintroduction process, but small populations frequently undergo a process known as random genetic drift. This phenomenon refers to the random chance of disappearance of certain alleles and complete fixation in the population of others. The process is a result of small population size, and results in a loss of genetic diversity. Another goal that must be kept in mind is that the alleles of the founder individuals, that is, the animals that are caught from the wild and brought into the breeding program, are to be maintained so that the "wild" alleles are not lost during the years of captive breeding. Since the ultimate aim is to reintroduce these animals into their native habitat, maintaining the original genetic stock can only act to increase the odds that some of those individuals will survive in the wild. Also, captive breeding over several generations may select for characteristics such as docility, which are not necessarily advantageous in the wild, but are advantageous in captivity.

A further potential problem involving genetic diversity involves inbreeding depression. This refers to the detrimental effects on offspring of matings between close relatives, and is due to an accumulation of deleterious alleles. Inbreeding depression may be manifested in several aspects of an individuals' biology, such as lowered fecundity, or numbers of offspring produced, altered male mating success, and decreased probability of survival after birth.

In order to address these potentially grave problems, the Minnesota Zoo initiated the International Species Inventory system to keep track of individuals in zoos around the world, and to maximize genetic diversity of captively bred populations by engineering exchanges of reproductive adults between these zoos. Information on the geographic origin of the animals being bred allows control of mating between potential relatives, and is a way of bringing new alleles into one captive population from another captive population.

A black-footed ferret in a release cage in Wyoming being observed by a researcher.

A number of methods are used to breed a maximum number of offspring from a fixed number of parents. Such methods include artificial insemination, that is the transfer of sperm by artificial means so that animals from different zoos may be mated without actually moving the individuals; increasing fecundity by egg removal in bird species that exhibit egg replacement so that more eggs are produced by a female than would be under natural conditions; and foster parenting of young by "parents" from a closely related species, thus ensuring the rearing of young in a non–human environment. An example of the latter involves whooping cranes, whose adult numbers in the wild are extremely low. Captively bred eggs are placed in the nests of the behaviorally and morphologically similar sandhill cranes, who then rear the young to adulthood.

Environmental effects in captive breeding

In addition to the obstacles presented by loss of genetic variation, captive breeding programs must address the issue of adequately preparing the animals behaviorally to live in their native environment. This is an especially formidable task with animals that form social groups, and whose mating, communication, foraging, predator avoidance, offspring rearing, migration, and/or other behaviors are learned by observation. The zoo environment cannot adequately simulate natural conditions and ensure that natural social hierarchies are formed properly to the degree necessary for the learning of these complex survival skills to occur.

To circumvent these problems, many programs have developed training programs to teach these skills to the animals before reintroduction. Some examples of this include teaching red wolves to hunt and kill their prey, and training golden lion tamarins to manipulate boxes which contain food to simulate their natural activity of opening fruit. An extremely important learned behavior that captive populations do not usually posses is the fear of potential predators, including humans. To this end, dummies are often used in situations that frighten the animals so that they learn to associate fear with the dummy. To avoid the problem of imprinting on humans (young animals learning their behaviors from and associating with people) puppets of an adult of the species are used to "interact" with the young. For example, young whooping crane chicks that are born and raised in captivity are fed by people wearing puppets of adult whooping cranes on their arms, and blocking the rest of their body from view with a partition of some sort. This way, the young never see the image of a human, and are fed by what looks and acts like their own parent species.

The most difficult problem may be that of teaching the animals about their own social hierarchy, mainly because the intricacies of these social interactions cannot be fully understood by humans. The most practical approach to this has been to let the animals teach each other by putting wild–caught individuals in with the captive ones, and releasing them all together. This method has been somewhat successful with primates, namely the golden lion tamarin reintroduction to the Brazilian Amazon rain forests.

Reintroduction

In order for a successful reintroduction to occur, not only do certain standards have to be met during the captive breeding phase, but the mechanisms that led to the decline in the first place must be understood and halted. Since by far the most common reason for endangerment of a species is habitat destruction or degradation, this usually means ensuring adequate habitat size and quality for the population being released, and an assurance of future preservation of that habitat. This is not an easily attained goal, as the reasons for habitat destruction often involve complex social, cultural, and economic factors. Such conflict has surrounded the reintroduction of the California condor, for example, as it is a large predatory bird that requires a large range size to exist. It in fact may forage over millions of hectares per bird. Early failure of the U. S. Department of Interior to acquire land to support the highly endangered bird, while simultaneously breeding them in captivity, sparked controversy over the ultimate goal of such breeding programs. The U. S. Fish and Wildlife Service did eventually purchase a large tract of land in 1986 to be used for the reintroduction, which has not yet taken place but is in the early stages of test releasing a pair of birds.

After release, the population must be monitored as to whether the individuals are able to adequately survive the stress of living in a wild habitat. Often release is somewhat gradual. For example, what is known as a "soft release" provides food for the animals at the release point until they are able to forage on their own. When early environmental conditions turn particularly stressful, such as during drought when water and food are scarce, a decision must be made as whether to intervene temporarily until conditions improve. Monitoring the released population is also necessary to assess survival and causes of death so that future releases may attempt to avoid pitfalls.

Although species reintroduction of animals has more public attention, attempts at reintroduction of plants are fairly common. Many of the same issues are involved, but plants also present unique problems due to their lack of mobility and somewhat specific requirements at the microsite level for seed germination. That is, the immediate area in the soil surrounding a seed must have just the right light, water, nutrient, temperature conditions, and must be free of seed predators, fungal disease spores. Therefore, even in native habitats, only a very small percentage of seed produced by any given plant germinates. Further requirements for germination often involve disturbance such as fire or light gaps created by tree falls. Such natural phenomena are often artificially prevented on preserved land. The land, then, must be managed to create these periodic disturbances in order to create as natural a habitat as possible. Higher success rates in germination are often achieved in a greenhouse, after which the seedlings are transplanted into the wild. This, however, requires a thorough understanding of germination requirements, and does not dismiss the necessity of managing the land for future reproduction and survival of the plant.

In a study that attempted to evaluate 79 different reintroductions of birds and mammals, it was found that some types of reintroduction conditions have a higher probability of success than others. The conclusions of the study were that the highest probability of failure occurs when: the species is a carnivore and not a herbivore, it is a rare species as opposed to a relatively common one, the land they are reintroduced to is peripheral or marginal habitat instead of core habitat, habitat is of poor quality, and when those individuals are reared in captivity instead of having been wild–caught and released within their lifetime. If these qualities are a true indicator of the likelihood of success, it is concluded, then by starting programs before certain species or habitats exhibit the critical characteristics such as rarity and poor quality, their chances of failure may be greatly reduced. Such foresight requires a vast body of knowledge on the biology of the species and habitat in question, and large planning efforts.

A final point involves the cost of maintaining such programs. They may be extremely expensive and limited in success due to the difficulties involved with addressing the ultimate cause of the species decline. Such efforts must always be accompanied by public education programs, because ultimately it will be the informed public that must decide whether it is more prudent and economical to attempt to reverse human–induced losses of biological diversity, or to take measures in advance of the crisis so that rates of extinction are halted, or if indeed it is better to simply live in a world that does not recognize the intrinsic value of other species.

See also Condors; Cranes; Endangered species; Genetics; Imprinting.

Further Reading:

Frazer, N. B. "Sea Turtle Conservation and Halfway Technology." *Conservation Biology* 6 (1992): 179–184.

Griffith, B., et al. "Translocation as a Species Conservation Tool: Status and Strategy." *Science* 245 (1989): 477–480.

Kleiman, D. G. "Reintroduction of Captive Mammals for Conservation." *Bioscience* 39 (1989): 152–161.

Primack, R. B. *Essentials of Conservation Biology.* Sunderland, MA: Sinauer, 1993.

Spellerberg, I. F., and S. R. Hardes. *Biological Conservation.* Cambridge: Cambridge University Press, 1992.

Puja Batra

Capuchins

Capuchins are New World monkeys characterized by a cap or crown patch of hair that resembles a hood, called a capuche, worn by Franciscan monks. Capuchins belong to the family Cebidae, which includes 31 species in 11 genera. The Cebidae is subdivided into seven subfamilies which include night monkeys, squirrel monkeys, titis, sakis, howlers, spider monkeys, and the capuchins.

Monkeys in the family Cebidae are thin animals with long legs and a prehensile tail, which is muscular and can be used to help the animal in climbing and swinging through trees. Most of these New World monkeys, including capuchins, are active during the day and sleep at night. Capuchins are medium–sized animals with a body and legs that are evenly proportioned, and have fingers and toes with nails. The nostrils of New World monkeys are round and set far apart while those of the Old World monkeys are set close together.

Physical characteristics

There are four species of capuchin monkeys found in South America. The brown capuchin (*Cebus apella*) lives in tropical and subtropical forests from Venezuela to Brazil. Capuchins are not found in the Andes Mountains along the western part of the continent. The brown capuchin has tufts of hair on the forehead and a dark cap which extends downward on his forehead into a triangle. Other distinctive markings of the brown capuchin are black sideburns, and a coarse coat that is usually paler on the abdomen, with black limbs. The hair on the face is sparser than the rest of the fur, and the facial skin is pale. The average weight is 6 lbs (3 kg) for females and 8 lbs (4 kg) for males.

The white–faced capuchin (*C. capucinus*) is found in Central America from the southern region of Mexico, south into Colombia. White–faced capuchins live in dry or wet forests, and in mangroves. The color of their fur is pale cream to white on their bellies and the upper parts of their arms and legs, with black fur on their backs and lower limbs. They have white fur on their faces and a black cap. Many older white–faced capuchins have a ruff (fringe) of hair on their foreheads and crowns. The average weight for males is 7 lbs (3.5 kg) and 5 lbs (2.5 kg) for females.

Weeper capuchins (*C. nigrivittatus*) are found north of the Amazon and north and east of the Rio Negro in Brazil, the Guianas, and central Venezuela. Females weigh less than 5 lbs (2.5 kg) and males weigh around 6 lbs (3 kg). Their colorings are like the white–faced

A white-fronted capuchin (*Cebus albifrons*).

capuchins but there is less contrast between the dark and light colors. They have a narrow crown patch that comes to a marked point on their foreheads. They also live in dry and wet forests and mangroves as do the white–faced capuchin.

The white–fronted capuchin (*C. albifrons*) is found in the moist forests of Venezuela, Brazil, Bolivia, Ecuador, Colombia, and on the island of Trinidad. This species is slightly smaller than other capuchin monkeys. The colors are similar to weeper and white–faced capuchins, with a pale and broad cap that covers most of the tops of their heads.

Capuchins are capable of running on two legs, as well as on all fours. They are very nimble and acrobatic in the treetops. The use of the tail as a fifth limb in capuchins is rather restricted. They do not spend all their time in trees, however, since they also find food on the forest floor. Fruit comprises 80% of capuchins' diet, the rest consisting mainly of leaves and insects. In laboratory studies capuchins will use tools to help them get food.

Social behavior

The social groups of capuchin monkeys vary in size from small groups with three members, to groups of 30 or more. There are usually more females in the group than males, and half of the members of these social groups are infants and adolescents. While there is a dominant male and female in each group, there is little evidence of any other hierarchy within the group, except that dominant males exhibit different degrees of tolerance among the various members of the group. This is particularly evident when the group is foraging for food.

The dominant male does not mingle much with other members of the group, but does play a role in defending the group from intruders. The dominant female establishes a special relationship with the dominant male and tries to keep others away from him.

Capuchins are polygamous, and it is the females who do the courting. Their methods of luring males include raising their eyebrows, gesturing, and making sounds. If a male is interested, he will mimic her gestures and sounds, follow her, and mate. Females give birth to one infant at a time, about every two years. Gestation is about five months, and infants are completely dependent on their mothers during the first three weeks of life.

A South American capybara (*Hydrochoerus hydrochoerus*).

Pastime activities among capuchins differ by age and gender. During the first few months, sisters especially take an interest in an infant sibling. After the third month of birth, the infant will also seek out the company of younger members of the group. A main social activity of male capuchins includes fighting games, while females spend a good deal of time sitting close together and in mutual grooming, particularly those parts of their bodies which are hard to reach or which they cannot see. Relationships among capuchins extend not only to siblings and their mothers, but to other relatives within the group as well.

See also New World monkeys.

Further Reading:
Loy, James and Peters, Calvin B. *Understanding Behavior: What Primate Studies Tell Us about Human Behavior.* New York: Oxford University Press, 1991.

Mason, William A. and Mendoza, Sally P.. *Primate Social Conflict.* Albany: State University of New York Press, 1993.

Vita Richman

Capybaras

Capybaras, carpinchos, or water hogs, are large South American rodents in the family Hydrochoeridae. *Hydrochoerus hydrochoerus* is the larger of the two species of capybaras and can reach a body weight of 110 lb (50 kg), a body length of 4.5 ft (1.3 m), and a height of 1.5 ft (50 cm), and is the largest living rodent. *Hydrochoerus isthmius* is about half this size. *Hydrochoerus hydrochoerus* has a wide distribution in South America, while *H. isthmius* (which is about half the size of its relative) has a relatively restricted distribution in Panama.

Capybaras have a large head with a blunt snout and small ears. The body is stout, robust, and almost tailless. The feet of capybaras are partially webbed and have four digits on the forefeet and three on the hind, and all have strong claws. The fur of capybaras is long, coarse, and rather sparse, so that naked skin can be readily seen. The body color is generally brownish or grayish. Capybaras have a strong physical resemblance to another group of much smaller South American rodents, the closely related guinea pigs (family Caviidae).

Capybaras are semiaquatic animals, occurring in a wide range of terrestrial habitats in the vicinity of fresh water, including the forested edges of streams, rivers, ponds, lakes, swamps, and marshes. Capybaras can run easily on land, and when disturbed near water they generally swim and dive to escape. These animals can swim with only their eyes and nostrils exposed to the atmosphere, or they can swim completely submerged.

Capybaras are herbivores, eating a wide range of aquatic, near–shore, and riparian plants. Capybaras sometimes feed with cattle and other domestic herbivores, and they are known to raid gardens for vegetables, fruits, and grains. Capybaras feed most actively during the moderate temperatures of dawn and dusk, spending the heat of the day in a cool, underground excavation. However, in places where they are frequently disturbed or hunted by people, capybaras generally develop a nocturnal habit.

Capybaras are peaceful, social animals, living in extended family groups containing as many as several tens of animals. They give birth once a year to two to eight offspring. Capybaras are known to live as long as 10 years in the wild.

Capybaras are hunted by various species of natural predators, including jaguar and large caimans. Capybaras are also hunted by humans, because they are often regarded as agricultural pests. The meat of capybaras is sometimes consumed, although it is not regarded as one of the higher–quality game species.

Bill Freedman

Caraway see **Carrot family**

Carbohydrate

Carbohydrates are naturally occurring compounds composed of carbon, hydrogen, and oxygen. The carbohydrate group includes sugars, starches, cellulose, and a number of other chemically related substances. For the most part, these carbohydrates are produced by green plants through the process known as photosynthesis. Countless varieties of plants use this process to synthesize a simple sugar (glucose, mostly) from the light energy absorbed by the chlorophyll in their leaves, water from the soil, and carbon dioxide from the air. Typically, plants use some of this simple sugar to form the more complex carbohydrate cellulose (which makes up the plant's supporting framework) and some to provide energy for its own metabolic needs; the rest is stored away for later use in the form of seeds, roots, or fruits.

Interestingly, the digestive and metabolic processes in animals and humans work almost in reverse fashion. When a fruit is eaten, for instance, the complex carbohydrates are broken down in the digestive tract to simpler glucose units. The glucose is then used primarily to produce energy in a process which involves oxidation and the excretion of carbon dioxide and water as waste products. In the mid–1800s, German chemist Justus von Liebig was one of the first to recognize that the body derived energy from the oxidation of foods recently eaten, and also declared that it was carbohydrates and fats that served to fuel the oxidation—not carbon and hydrogen as Antoine–Laurent Lavoisier had thought.

Carbohydrates are usually divided into three main categories. The first category, the monosaccharides, are simple sugars that consist of a single carbohydrate unit that cannot be broken down into any simpler sub-stances. The three most common sugars in this group are glucose (or dextrose), the most frequently seen sugar in fruits and vegetables (and, in digestion, the form of carbohydrate to which all others are eventually converted); fructose, associated with glucose in honey and in many fruits and vegetables; and galactose, derived from the more complex milk sugar, lactose. Each of these simple but nutritionally important sugars is a hexose, which means it contains six carbon atoms, twelve hydrogen atoms, and six oxygen atoms. All three require virtually no digestion but are readily absorbed into the bloodstream from the intestine.

Slightly more complex sugars are the disaccharides which contain two hexose units. The three most nutritionally important of these are sucrose (ordinary table sugar), maltose (derived from starch), and lactose, which is formed in the mammary glands and is the only sugar not found in plants. In the digestive tract, specific enzymes split all of these sugars into the more easily absorbed monosaccharides. If needed for future energy use, glucose units are typically squeezed together into larger, more slowly absorbed units and stored as polysaccharides, whose molecules often contain a hundred times the number of glucose units as do the simple sugars. These highly complex carbohydrates include dextrin, starch, cellulose, and glycogen. More efficient and more stable than the simple sugars, they are much easier to store. On the other hand, most of them need to be broken down by the digestive tract's enzymes before they can be absorbed. Some of them—cellulose, for instance—are almost impossible for humans to digest, but this indigestibility is useful since the colon needs a certain amount of bulk, or roughage, to perform at its best.

Glycogen is the form in which most of the body's excess glucose is stored. Both the liver and muscle are able to store glycogen, with muscle glycogen used primarily to fuel muscle contractions and liver glycogen used (when necessary) to replenish the bloodstream's dwindling supply of glucose.

Glycogen was named by French physiologist Claude Bernard, who in 1856 discovered a starchlike substance in the liver of mammals. This substance, he later showed, was not only built out of glucose taken from the blood, but could be broken down again into sugar whenever it was needed. In 1891, German physiologist Karl von Voit demonstrated that mammals could make glycogen even when fed sugars more complex than glucose. In 1919, Otto Meyerhof was able to show that glycogen is converted into lactic acid in working muscles . It wasn't until the 1930s, however, that the complicated process by which glycogen, stored in the liver and muscle, is broken down in the body and resynthesized was discovered by Czech–American biochemists Carl Cori and Gerty Cori. Building on their work, Fritz Lipmann was able a few years later to further clarify the way carbohydrates can be converted into the forms of chemical energy most usable by the body.

The chemical structure of the various sugars was worked out in great detail by German biochemist Emil Fischer, who began his Nobel Prize–winning work in 1884. Fischer not only was able to synthesize glucose and 30 other sugars, he also showed that the shape of their molecules was even more important than their chemical composition.

See also Photosynthesis.

Carbon

Carbon is the non–metallic chemical element of atomic number 6 in Group 14 of the periodic table, symbol C, atomic weight 12.01, specific gravity as graphite 2.25, as diamond 3.51. Its stable isotopes are ^{12}C (98.90%) and ^{13}C (1.10%). The weight of the ^{12}C atom is the international standard on which atomic weights are based. It is defined as weighing exactly 12.00000 atomic mass units.

Carbon has been known since prehistoric times. It gets its name from *carbo*, the Latin word for charcoal, which is almost pure carbon. In various forms, carbon is found not only on Earth, but in the atmospheres of other planets, in the Sun and stars, in comets and in some meteorites.

On Earth, carbon can be considered to be the most important of all the chemical elements, because it is the essential element in practically all of the chemical compounds in living things. Carbon compounds are what make the processes of life work. Beyond Earth, carbon–atom nuclei are an essential part of the nuclear fusion reactions that produce the energy of the Sun and of many other stars. Without carbon, the Sun would be cold and dark.

How carbon is found

In the form of chemical compounds, carbon is distributed throughout the world as carbon dioxide gas, CO_2, in the atmosphere and dissolved in all the rivers, lakes and oceans. In the form of carbonates, mostly calcium carbonate ($CaCO_3$), it occurs as huge rocky masses of limestone, marble and chalk. In the form of hydrocarbons, it occurs as great deposits of natural gas, petroleum and coal. Coal is important not only as a fuel, but because it is the source of the carbon that we dissolve in molten iron to make steel.

All plants and animals on Earth contain a substantial proportion of carbon. After hydrogen and oxygen, carbon is the most abundant element in the human body, making up 10.7% of all the body's atoms.

Carbon is found as the free (uncombined) element in three different allotropic forms—different geometrical arrangements of the atoms in the solid. The two crystalline forms (forms containing very definite atomic arrangements) are graphite and diamond. Graphite is one of the softest known materials, while diamond is one of the hardest.

There is also a shapeless, or amorphous, form of carbon in which the atoms have no particular geometric arrangement. Carbon black, a form of amorphous carbon obtained from smoky flames, is used to make rubber tires and inks black. Charcoal—wood or other plant material that has been heated in the absence of enough air to actually burn—is mostly amorphous carbon, but it retains some of the microscopic structure of the plant cells in the wood from which is was made. Activated charcoal is charcoal that has been steam–purified of all the gummy wood–decomposition products, leaving porous grains of pure carbon that have an enormous microscopic surface area. It is estimated that one cubic inch of activated charcoal contains 200,000 sq ft (18,580 m^2) of microscopic surface. This huge surface has a stickiness, called adsorption, for molecules of gases and solids; activated charcoal is therefore used to remove impurities from water and air, such as in home water purifiers and in gas masks.

Graphite

Graphite is a soft, shiny, dark gray or black, greasy-feeling mineral that is found in large masses throughout the world, including the U.S., Brazil, England, western Europe, Siberia and Sri Lanka. It is a good conductor of electricity and resists temperatures up to about 6,300° F (3,500° C), which makes it useful as brushes (conductors that slide along rotating parts) in electric motors and generators, and as electrodes in high–temperature electrolysis cells. Because of its slipperiness, it is used as a lubricant. For example, powdered graphite is used to lubricate locks, where oil might "gum up the works." The "lead" in pencils is actually a mixture of graphite, clay and wax. It is called "lead" because the metallic element lead (Pb) leaves gray marks on paper and was used for writing in ancient times. When graphite–based pencils came into use, they were called "lead pencils."

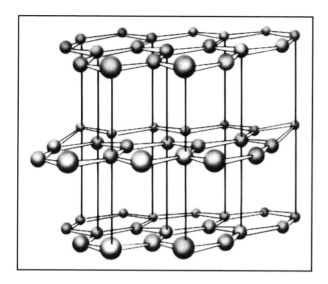

Figure 1. The structure of graphite.

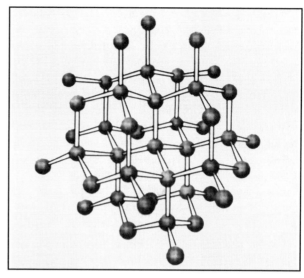

Figure 2. The structure of diamond. Each carbon atom is bonded to four others in the directions of the four corners of a tetrahedron.

The reason for graphite's slipperiness is its unusual crystalline structure. It consists of a stack of one-atom-thick sheets of carbon atoms, bonded tightly together into a hexagonal pattern in each sheet, but with only very weak attractions—much weaker than actual chemical bonds—holding the sheets together.

The sheets of carbon atoms can therefore slide easily over one another; graphite is slippery in the same way as layers of wet leaves on a sidewalk.

Diamond

Diamond, the other crystalline form of pure carbon, is the world's hardest natural material, and is used in industry as an abrasive and in drill tips for drilling through rock in oil fields and human teeth in dentists' offices. On a hardness scale of one to ten, which mineralogists refer to as the Moh scale of hardness, diamond is awarded a perfect ten. But that's not why diamonds are so expensive. They are the most expensive of all gems, and are kept that way by supply and demand. The supply is largely controlled by the De Beers Consolidated Mines, Inc. in South Africa, where most of the world's diamonds are mined, and the demand is kept high by the importance that is widely attributed to diamonds.

A diamond can be considered to be a single huge molecule consisting of nothing but carbon atoms that are strongly bonded to each other by covalent bonds, just as in other molecules. A one–carat diamond "molecule" contains 10^{22} carbon atoms.

The beauty of gem–quality diamonds—industrial diamonds are small, dark and cloudy—comes from their crystal clarity, their high refractivity (ability to bend light rays) and their high dispersion—their ability to spread light of different colors apart, which makes the diamond's rainbow "fire." Skillful chipping of the gems into facets (flat faces) at carefully calculated angles makes the most of their sparkle. Even though diamonds are hard, meaning that they can't be scratched by other materials, they are brittle—they can be cracked.

The chemistry of carbon

Carbon is unique among the elements because its atoms can form an endless variety of molecules with an endless variety of sizes, shapes and chemical properties. No other element can do that to anywhere near the degree that carbon can. In the evolution of life on Earth, Nature has always been able to "find" just the right carbon compound out of the millions available, to serve just about any required function in the complicated chemistry of living things.

Carbon–containing compounds are called organic compounds, and the study of their properties and reactions is called organic chemistry. The name organic was originally given to those substances that are found in living organisms—plants and animals. As we now know, almost all of the chemical substances in living things are carbon compounds (water and minerals are the obvious exceptions), and the name organic was eventually applied to the chemistry of all carbon compounds, regardless of where they come from.

Until the early nineteenth century, it was believed that organic substances contained a supernatural life force "that made them special, and that they were not susceptible to chemical experimentation. But in 1828, a German chemist named Friedrich Wöhler (1800–1882) apparently broke down the mysterious barrier between living and non–living things. By simply heating a non–organic, non–living chemical called ammonium cyanate (NH_4OCN), he converted it into a chemical called urea ($H_2N–CO–NH_2$), which was known to be a waste product in the urine of mammals and was therefore an "organic" substance. As Wöhler put it, he was amazed to be able to create an organic substance "without benefit of a kidney, a bladder or a dog."

What had happened in Wöhler's experiment was that the eight atoms in the ammonium cyanate molecule—two nitrogen atoms, four hydrogen atoms, one oxygen atom and one carbon atom—simply rearranged themselves into a molecule having a different geometry. In chemical language, the two molecules are isomers of one another.

After Wöhler, chemists boldly synthesized (made artificially) many of the chemical compounds that formerly had been observed only in living things. Today, biochemistry—living chemistry—is one of the most active and productive fields of scientific research. It has taught us more about the processes of life than could ever have been imagined.

Why carbon is special

There are now more than ten million organic compounds known by chemists. Many more undoubtedly exist in nature, and organic chemists are continually creating (synthesizing) new ones. Carbon is the only element that can form so many different compounds because each carbon atom can form four chemical bonds to other atoms, and because the carbon atom is just the right, small size to fit in comfortably as parts of very large molecules.

Having the atomic number six, every carbon atom has a total of six electrons. Two are in a completed inner orbit, while the other four are valence electrons—outer electrons that are available for forming bonds with other atoms.

The carbon atom's four valence electrons can be shared by other atoms that have electrons to share, thus forming covalent (shared–electron) bonds. They can even be shared by other carbon atoms, which in turn can share electrons with other carbon atoms and so on, forming long strings of carbon atoms, bonded to each other like links in a chain. Silicon (Si), another element in group 14 of the periodic table, also has four valence

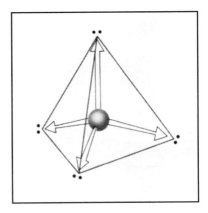

Figure 3. A carbon atom's four pairs of valence electrons stick out toward the corners of an imaginary tetrahedron.

electrons and can make large molecules called silicones, but its atoms are too large to fit together into as great a variety of molecules as carbon atoms can.

Carbon's ability to form long carbon–to–carbon chains is the first of five reasons that there can be so many different carbon compounds; a molecule that differs by even one atom is, of course, a molecule of a different compound. The second reason for carbon's astounding compound–forming ability is that carbon atoms can bind to each other not only in straight chains, but in complex branchings, like the branches of a tree. They can even join "head–to–tail" to make rings of carbon atoms. There is practically no limit to the number or complexity of the branches or the number of rings that can be attached to them, and hence no limit to the number of different molecules that can be formed.

The third reason is that carbon atoms can share not only a single electron with another atom to form a single bond, but it can also share two or three electrons, forming a double or triple bond. This makes for a huge number of possible bond combinations at different places, making a huge number of different possible molecules. And a molecule that differs by even one atom or one bond position is a molecule of a different compound.

The fourth reason is that the same collection of atoms and bonds, but in a different geometrical arrangement within the molecule, makes a molecule with a different shape and hence different properties. These different molecules are called isomers.

The fifth reason is that all of the electrons that are not being used to bond carbon atoms together into chains and rings can be used to form bonds with atoms of several other elements. The most common other element is hydrogen, which makes the family of compounds known as hydrocarbons. But nitrogen, oxygen, phosphorus, sulfur, halogens, and several other kinds of atoms can also be attached as part of an organic molecule. There is a huge number of ways in which they can be attached to the carbon–atom branches, and each variation makes a molecule of a different compound. It's just as if moving a Christmas tree ornament from one branch to another created a completely different tree.

Classes of carbon compounds

It is obviously impossible to summarize the properties of carbon's millions of compounds in one place. Introductory textbooks of organic chemistry generally run well over a thousand pages, and biochemistry textbooks run thousands more. But organic compounds can be classified into families that have similar properties, because they have certain groupings of atoms in common.

See also Alcohol; Aldehydes; Alkaloid; Amides; Amines; Amino acid; Barbiturates; Chemical bond; Calcium carbonate; Carbohydrate; Carbon cycle; Carboxylic acids; Ester; Ether; Fat; Fatty acids; Glycol; Halide, organic; Hydrocarbon; Isomer; Lipid; Natural gas; Petroleum; Polymer; Proteins.

Further Reading:

Loudon, G. Marc. *Organic Chemistry*. Menlo Park, CA: Benjamin/Cummings,1988.
Parker, Sybil P., ed. *McGraw–Hill Encyclopedia of Chemistry*. 2nd ed. New York: McGraw–Hill, 1993.
Sherwood, Martin, and Christine Sutton, eds. *The Physical World*. New York: Oxford University Press, 1991.

Robert L. Wolke

Carbon cycle

The carbon cycle describes the movement of carbon in the atmosphere where it is in the gaseous form carbon dioxide, through organisms, and then back into the atmosphere and the oceans. Carbon is an important element of organic chemicals found in all living things, such as sugars and other carbohydrates. Energy is contained in the chemical bonds that hold the carbon atoms together. Living things use chemical energy from organic compounds to carry out all the processes necessary to life.

How carbon is released into the atmosphere

Carbon is released into the atmosphere through three processes: cellular respiration, the burning of fossil fuels, and volcanic eruptions. In each of these processes, carbon is returned to the atmosphere or to the ocean.

Cellular respiration

Plants convert the carbon in atmospheric carbon dioxide into carbon–containing compounds, such as sugars, fats, and chemicals. Plants take in carbon dioxide through microscopic openings in their leaves, called stomata. They combine atmospheric carbon with water and manufacture organic compounds, using energy trapped from sunlight in a process called photosynthesis. The by–product of photosynthesis is oxygen, which plants release into the atmosphere through the stomata.

Animals that eat plants, or eat other animals that eat plants, incorporate the carbon in the sugars, fats, and proteins derived from plants into their bodies. Inside the cells energy is extracted from the food in a process called cellular respiration. Cellular respiration requires oxygen (which is the by–product of photosynthesis) and it produces carbon dioxide, which is used in photosynthesis.

In this way, photosynthesis and cellular respiration are linked together in the carbon cycle. Photosynthesis requires atmospheric carbon, while cellular respiration returns carbon to the atmosphere. The rates of photosynthesis and cellular respiration influence the amount of carbon dioxide in the atmosphere. In the summer, the high rate of photosynthesis uses up much of the carbon dioxide in the atmosphere, and the amount of atmospheric carbon dioxide falls. In the winter, when the rate of photosynthesis is low, the amount of atmospheric carbon increases.

Another way that cellular respiration releases carbon into the atmosphere is through the action of decomposers. Decomposers, such as bacteria and fungi, derive their nutrients by feeding on the remains of plants and animals. These bacteria and fungi use cellular respiration to extract the energy contained in the chemical bonds of the decomposing organic matter, and so release carbon dioxide into the atmosphere.

In some ecosystems, such as tropical rain forests, decomposition is accomplished quickly, and carbon dioxide is returned to the atmosphere at a fast rate. In other ecosystems, such as northern forests and tundra, decomposition proceeds more slowly. In aquatic environments carbon–containing compounds derived from photosynthesizing organisms are incorporated into the

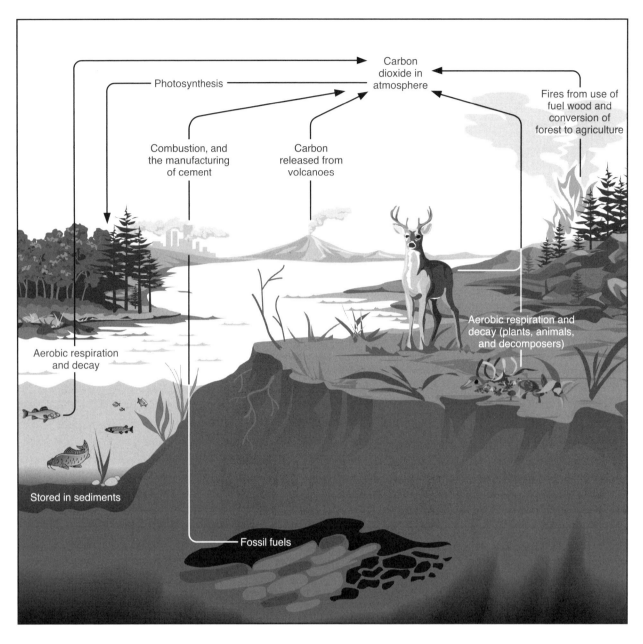

The carbon cycle.

shells, claws, and other carbon–rich hard parts of aquatic organisms. When these organisms die, the carbon–rich hard parts sink to the ocean bed. There they become buried in sediment, and decomposers cannot reach them. Slowly, over millions of years, these carbon–rich sediments are converted into other carbon–rich products, such as petroleum, natural gas, and coal. Fuels that are produced in this way are called fossil fuels.

The burning of fossil fuels

When fossil fuels are burned, the trapped carbon is released into the atmosphere. In the past 100 years, fos-

sil fuel consumption has increased dramatically, and this increase has led to an overabundance of carbon being released into the atmosphere. The high atmospheric carbon dioxide levels are a cause for great concern, since they may be responsible for global warming, an increase in the average world temperature and associated climate disruption.

Volcanic eruption

Another way that carbon is released into the atmosphere is through volcanic eruption. When a volcano erupts, it sends huge amounts of ash and soot high into the atmosphere. This ash and soot is ultimately derived from ancient buried carbon–rich sediments, and the cloud of debris that results from a volcanic eruption returns large amounts of carbon to the atmosphere.

The carbon cycle in land and sea

The cycling of carbon takes place in oceans and other water environments as well as in terrestrial environments. The world's oceans contain about 50% more carbon than does the atmosphere. The oceans may be able to absorb some of the carbon currently being released by the burning of fossil fuels, thus offsetting global warming.

In aquatic environments, carbon cycling is more complex because carbon interacts with water. When carbon dioxide is released by cellular respiration, it combines with water to form carbonic acid and bicarbonate. In aquatic environments, carbon is in the form of bicarbonate rather than carbon dioxide. Carbon dioxide from the atmosphere readily diffuses into water, and it is quickly converted to bicarbonate.

Importance of the carbon cycle

The carbon cycle is important in ecosystems because it moves carbon, a life–sustaining element, from the atmosphere and oceans into organisms and back again to the atmosphere and oceans. If the balance between these latter two reservoirs is upset, serious consequences, such as global warming and climate disruption, can result. Scientists are currently looking into ways in which humans can use other, non–carbon containing fuels for energy. Nuclear power, solar power, wind power, and water power are just a few alternative energy sources that are being investigated.

See also Alternative energy sources; Carbon; Greenhouse effect; Photosynthesis; Respiration.

Further Reading:

Dunnette, David A., and Robert J. O'Brien, eds. *The Science of Global Change: The Impact of Human Activities on the Environment.* Washington, DC: American Chemical Society, 1992.

Hileman, Bette. "New CO_2 Model Shows Whole Earth 'Breathing'." *Chemical and Engineering News* 72 (10 January 1994): 6.

Levi, Barbara Gross, David Hafemeister, and Richard Scribner. *Global Warming: Physics and Facts.* New York: American Institute of Physics, 1992.

Tolbert, N. E., and Jack Preiss, eds. *Regulation of Atmospheric Carbon by Photosynthetic Carbon Metabolism.* New York: Oxford University Press, 1994.

Vitousek, Peter M. "Beyond Global Warming: Ecology and Global Change." *Ecology* 75 (October 1994): 1861.

Volk, Tyler. "The Soil's Breath." *Natural History* 103 (November 1994): 48.

Zimmer, Carl. "The War Between Plants and Animals." *Discover* 14 (July 1993): 16.

Kathleen Scogna

Carbon dioxide

Carbon dioxide was the first gas to be distinguished from ordinary air, perhaps because it is so intimately connected with the cycles of plant and animal life. When we breathe air or when we burn wood and other fuels, carbon dioxide is released; when plants store energy in the form of food, they use up carbon dioxide. Early scientists were able to observe the effects of carbon dioxide long before they knew exactly what it was.

Around 1630, Flemish scientist Jan van Helmont discovered that certain vapors differed from air, which was then thought to be a single substance or element. Van Helmont coined the term gas to describe these vapors and collected the gas given off by burning wood, calling it gas sylvestre. Today we know this gas to be carbon dioxide, and van Helmont is credited with its discovery. He also recognized that carbon dioxide was produced by the fermentation of wine and from other natural processes. Before long, other scientists began to notice similarities between the processes of breathing (respiration) and burning (combustion), both of which use up and give off carbon dioxide. For example, a candle flame will eventually be extinguished when enclosed in a jar with a limited supply of air, as will the life of a bird or small animal.

Then in 1756, Joseph Black proved that carbon dioxide, which he called fixed air, is present in the atmosphere and that it combines with other chemicals to form compounds. Black also identified carbon dioxide in exhaled breath, determined that the gas is heavier than air, and characterized its chemical behavior as that of a weak acid. The pioneering work of van Helmont and Black soon led to the discovery of other gases by Henry Cavendish, Antoine–Laurent Lavoisier, Carl Wilhelm Scheele, and other chemists. As a result, scientists began to realize that gases must be weighed and accounted for in the analysis of chemical compounds, just like solids and liquids.

The first practical use for carbon dioxide was invented by Joseph Priestley, an English chemist, in the mid 1700s. Priestley had duplicated Black's experiments using a gas produced by fermenting grain and showed that it had the same properties as Black's fixed air, or carbon dioxide. When he dissolved the gas in water, he found that it created a refreshing drink with a slightly tart flavor. This was the first artificially carbonated water, soda water or seltzer. Carbon dioxide is still used today to make colas and other soft drinks. In addition to supplying bubbles and zest, the gas acts as a preservative.

The early study of carbon dioxide also gave rise to the expression to be a guinea pig, meaning to subject oneself to an experiment. In 1783, French physicist Pierre Laplace used a guinea pig to demonstrate quantitatively that oxygen from the air is used to burn carbon stored in the body and produce carbon dioxide in exhaled breath. Around the same time, chemists began drawing the connection between carbon dioxide and plant life. Like animals, plants breathe, using up oxygen and releasing carbon dioxide. But plants also have the unique ability to store energy in the form of carbohydrates, our primary source of food. This energy–storing process, called photosynthesis, is essentially the reverse of respiration. It uses up carbon dioxide and releases oxygen in a complex series of reactions that also require sunlight and chlorophyll (the green substance that gives plants their color). In the 1770s, Dutch physiologist Jan Ingen Housz established the principles of photosynthesis, which helped explain the age–old superstition that plants purify air during the day and poison it at night.

Since these early discoveries, chemists have learned much more about carbon dioxide. English chemist John Dalton guessed in 1803 that the molecule contains one carbon atom and two oxygen atoms (CO_2); this was later proved to be true. The decay of all organic materials produces carbon dioxide very slowly, and the Earth's atomophere contains a small amount of the gas (about 0.033 percent). In our solar system, the planets of Venus and Mars have atmospheres very rich in carbon dioxide. The gas also exists in ocean water, where it plays a vital role in marine plant photosynthesis.

In modern life, carbon dioxide has many practical applications. For example, fire extinguishers use CO_2 to control electrical and oil fires, which cannot be put out with water. Because carbon dioxide is heavier than air, it spreads into a blanket and smothers the flames. Carbon dioxide is also a very effective refrigerant. In its solid form, known as dry ice, it is used to chill perishable food during transport. Many industrial processes are also cooled by carbon dioxide, which allows faster production rates. For these commercial purposes, most carbon dioxide is obtained from natural gas wells, fermentation of organic material, and combustion of fossil fuels.

Recently, carbon dioxide has received negative attention as a greenhouse effect gas. When it accumulates in the upper atmosphere, it traps the Earth's heat, which could eventually cause global warming. Since the beginning of the industrial revolution in the mid 1800s, factories and power plants have significantly increased the amount of carbon dioxide in the atmosphere by burning coal and other fossil fuels. This effect was first predicted by Svante August Arrhenius, a Swedish physicist, in the 1880s. Then in 1938, British physicist G. S. Callendar suggested that higher CO_2 levels had caused the warmer temperatures observed in America and Europe since Arrhenius's day. Modern scientists have confirmed these views and identified other causes of increasing carbon dioxide levels, such as the clearing of the world's forests. Because trees extract CO_2 from the air, their depletion has contributed to upsetting the delicate balance of gases in the atmosphere.

In very rare circumstances, carbon dioxide can endanger life. In 1986, a huge cloud of the gas exploded from Lake Nyos, a volcanic lake in northwestern Cameroon, and quickly suffocated more than 1,700 people and 8,000 animals. Today, scientists are attempting to control this phenomenon by slowly pumping the gas up from the bottom of the lake.

See also Air pollution; Carbon; Carbon cycle; Chlorophyll; Combustion; Greenhouse effect; Photosynthesis; Planetary atmospheres.

Carbon monoxide

Carbon monoxide is a compound of carbon and oxygen with the chemical formula CO. It is a colorless, odorless, tasteless, toxic gas. It has a density of 1.250 g/L at 0°C and 760 mm Hg pressure. Carbon dioxide can be converted into a liquid at its boiling point of −191.5°C and then to a solid at its freezing point of −205.0°C.

History

The discovery of carbon monoxide is often credited to the work of the English chemist and theologian Joseph Priestley. In the period between 1772 and 1799, Priestley gradually recognized the nature of this compound and showed how it was different from carbon dioxide, with which it often appeared. Nonetheless, car-

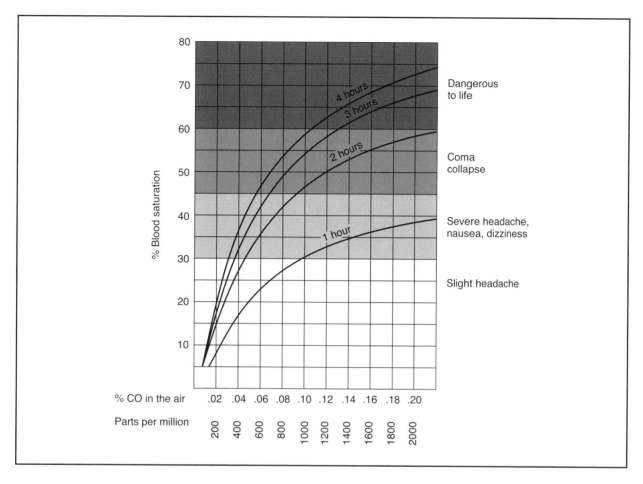

Figure 1. Effects of carbon monoxide on humans.

bon monoxide had been well known and extensively studied in the centuries prior to Priestley's work. As early as the late 1200s, the Spanish alchemist Arnold of Villanova described a poisonous gas produced by the incomplete combustion of wood that was almost certainly carbon monoxide.

In the five centuries between the work of Arnold and that of Priestley, carbon monoxide was studied and described by a number of prominent alchemists and chemists. Many made special mention of the toxicity of the gas. Johann (or Jan) Baptista van Helmont in 1644 wrote that he nearly died from inhaling *gas carbonum*, apparently a mixture of carbon monoxide and carbon dioxide.

An important milestone in the history of carbon monoxide came in 1877 when the French physicist Louis Paul Cailletet found a method for liquefying the gas. Two decades later, a particularly interesting group of compounds made from carbon monoxide—the carbonyls—were discovered by the French chemist Paul Sabatier.

Sources

Carbon monoxide is the twelfth most abundant gas in the atmosphere. It makes up about 1.2×10^{-5} percent of a sample of dry air in the lower atmosphere. The major natural source of carbon monoxide is the combustion of wood, coal and other naturally occurring substances on the Earth's surface. Huge quantities of carbon monoxide are produced, for example, during a forest fire or a volcanic eruption. The amount of carbon monoxide produced in such reactions depends on the availability of oxygen and the combustion temperature. High levels of oxygen and high temperatures tend to produce complete oxidation of carbon, with carbon dioxide as the final product. Lower levels of oxygen and lower temperatures result in the formation of higher percentages of carbon monoxide in the combustion mixture.

Commercial methods for producing carbon monoxide often depend on the direct oxidation of carbon under controlled conditions. For example, producer gas is made by blowing air across very hot coke (nearly pure carbon).

The final product consists of three gases, carbon monoxide, carbon dioxide, and nitrogen in the ratio of 6 to 1 to 18. Water gas is made by a similar process, by passing steam over hot coke. The products in this case are hydrogen (50 percent), carbon monoxide (40 percent), carbon dioxide (5 percent) and other gases (5 percent). Other methods of preparation are also available. One of the most commonly used involves the partial oxidation of hydrocarbons obtained from natural gas.

Physiological effects

The toxic character of carbon monoxide has been well known for many centuries. At low concentrations, carbon monoxide may cause nausea, vomiting, restlessness, and euphoria. As exposure increases, a person may lose consciousness and go into convulsions. Death is a common final result. The U.S. Occupational Safety and Health Administration has established a limit of 35 ppm (parts per million) of carbon monoxide in workplaces where a person may be continually exposed to the gas.

The earliest explanation for the toxic effects of carbon monoxide was offered by the French physiologist Claude Bernard in the late 1850s. Bernard pointed out that carbon monoxide has a strong tendency to replace oxygen in the respiratory system. Someone exposed to high concentrations of carbon monoxide may actually begin to suffocate as his or her body is deprived of oxygen.

Today we have a fairly sophisticated understanding of the mechanism by which carbon monoxide poisoning occurs. Normally, oxygen is transported from the lungs to cells in red blood cells. This process occurs when oxygen atoms bond to an iron atom at the center of a complex protein molecule known as oxyhemoglobin. Oxyhemoglobin is a fairly unstable molecule that decomposes in the intercellular spaces to release free oxygen and hemoglobin. The oxygen ins then available to carry out metabolic reactions in cells, reactions from which the body obtains energy.

If carbon monoxide is present in the lungs, this sequence is disrupted. Carbon monoxide bonds with iron in hemoglobin to form carbonmonoxyhemoglobin, a complex somewhat similar to oxyhemoglobin. Carbonmonoxyhemoglobin is, however, a more stable compound than is oxyhemoglobin. When it reaches cells, it has much less tendency to break down, but continues to circulate in the bloodstream in its bound form. As a result, cells are unable to obtain the oxygen they need for metabolism and energy production dramatically decreases. The clinical symptoms of carbon monoxide poisoning described above are manifestations of these changes.

Carbon monoxide poisoning—at least at moderate levels—is common in everyday life. Poorly vented charcoal fires, improperly installed gas appliances, and the exhaust from internal combustion vehicles are among the most common sources of the gas. In fact, levels of carbon monoxide in the air can become dangerously high in busy urban areas where automotive transportation is extensive. Cigarette smokers may also be exposed to dangerous levels of the gas. Studies have shown that the 1 – 2 pack–a–day smoker may have up to 7 percent of the hemoglobin in her or his body tied up in the form of carbonmonoxyhemoglobin.

Uses

Carbon monoxide is a very important industrial compound. In the form of producer gas or water gas, it is widely used as a fuel in industrial operations. The gas is also an effective reducing agent. For example, when carbon monoxide is passed over hot iron oxides, the oxides are reduced to metallic iron, while the carbon monoxide is oxidized to carbon dioxide.

In another application a mixture of metallic ores is heated to 122°–176° F (50–80° C) in the presence of producer gas. All oxides except those of nickel are reduced to their metallic state. This process, known as the Mond process, is a way of separating nickel from other metals with which it commonly occurs.

Yet another use of the gas is in the Fischer–Tropsch process for the manufacture of hydrocarbons and their oxygen derivatives from a combination of hydrogen and carbon monoxide. Carbon monoxide also reacts with certain metals, especially iron, cobalt, and nickel, to form compounds known as carbonyls. Some of the carbonyls have unusual physical and chemical properties that make them useful in industry. The highly toxic nickel tetracarbonyl, for example, is used to produce very pure nickel coatings and powders.

See also Carbon; Carbon dioxide; Combustion; Metallurgy.

Further Reading:

Boikess, Robert S., and Edward Edelson. *Chemical Principles*, 2nd edition. New York: Harper & Row Publishers, 1981, pp. 672 – 673.
Brown, Theodore L., and H. Eugene LeMay, Jr. *Chemistry: The Central Science*, 3rd edition. Englewood Cliffs, NJ: Prentice–Hall, 1985, pp. 390 – 392, 668 – 669.
Budavari, Susan, ed. *The Merck Index*, 11th edition. Rahway, NJ: Merck and Company, 1989, pp. 1821.
Greenwood, N. N., and A. Earnshaw. *Chemistry of the Elements*. Oxford: Pergamon Press, 1984, 1990, pp. 325 – 333.

KEY TERMS

· ·

Combustion—Oxidation that occurs so rapidly that noticeable heat and light are produced.

Hemoglobin—A iron–containing complex molecule that transports oxygen through the circulatory system.

Incomplete combustion—Combustion that occurs in such a way that fuel is not completely oxidized. The incomplete combustion of carbon–containing fuel, for example, always results in the formation of some carbon monoxide.

Intercellular spaces—The spaces between cells in tissue.

Reducing agent—A substance that removes oxygen or contributes electrons in a chemical reaction.

Toxicity—The extent to which a substance is poisonous.

Hill, John W., and Dorothy M. Feigl. *Chemistry and Life*, 2nd edition. Minneapolis: Burgess Publishing Company, 1978, pp. 168 – 170, 318 – 322.

Partington, J. R. *A Short History of Chemistry*, 3rd edition. London: Macmillan & Company, 1957, pp. 49, 116, 142, 151.

David E. Newton

Carbon tetrachloride

Carbon tetrachloride is an organic chemical that is commonly used as a solvent. It is also called tetra chloromethane and is composed of molecules that have one carbon atom and four chlorine atoms bonded together in the shape of a tetrahedron. It is made by combining elemental chlorine with simple carbon compounds like methane or carbon disulfide. It is a liquid at room temperature, with a freezing point of 9.4°F (–23° C) and a boiling point of 170.6° F(77° C). Carbon tetrachloride dissolves other organic materials such as oils, fats, and grease very well. This property makes carbon tetrachloride very useful for cleaning manufactured parts. Carbon tetrachloride was once used heavily in the dry–cleaning industry. Use in that industry has declined because it is toxic when inhaled or absorbed through the skin, and it is no longer used in products for the

home. Since carbon tetrachloride is a good solvent, it is used to dissolve things like oils, fragrances, and colors from flowers and seeds. Carbon tetrachloride is not flammable, so it can be used in fire extinguishers or as an additive to make other chemicals nonflammable. It is also very useful as a raw material in synthesizing larger, more complicated organic compounds. Because of the health hazards of long–term exposure to carbon tetrachloride, it should only be used where there is adequate ventilation present.

Carbonyl group

A carbonyl group is a group of atoms that consists of a carbon atom covalently attached to an oxygen atom by a double bond: C = O. The carbon atom, to satisfy its valence of 4, must also be attached by covalent bonds to two other atoms. The simplest type of molecule that contains a carbonyl group is a ketone. Other types of molecules that contain carbonyl groups are aldehydes, acids, esters, and amides.

Ketones

A ketone is a compound whose molecules contain a carbonyl group and have two other groups attached to the carbon atom of the carbonyl group. There are many molecules that belong to this classification, but the simplest one is acetone. A condensed structural formula for acetone looks like this.

$$CH_3 - \overset{\overset{\displaystyle O}{\|}}{C} - CH_3$$

In this formula, the C=O represents the carbonyl group, and the two CH_3 groups satisfy the carbon atom's valence of 4. In other molecules that contain the carbonyl group, the C=O is still present, but the two CH_3 groups are traded for other atoms or groups of atoms.

Sometimes we need to talk about the entire class of possible ketone molecules, and then we use a structural formula that looks like this.

$$R - \overset{\overset{\displaystyle O}{\|}}{C} - R'$$

In this picture, R and R' can stand for any hydrocarbon–containing group and as CH_3-, C_2H_5-, etc.

Properties of the carbonyl group

The carbonyl group is somewhat polar. That means that one end of it (the carbon atom) has a slight positive

$$R-\overset{\overset{\displaystyle O}{\|}}{C}-H \qquad R-\overset{\overset{\displaystyle O}{\|}}{C}-OH \qquad R-\overset{\overset{\displaystyle O}{\|}}{C}-O-R' \qquad R-\overset{\overset{\displaystyle O}{\|}}{C}-NH_2$$

aldehyde   acid   ester   amide

See also Acids and bases; Aldehydes; Amides; Ester.

Further Reading:

Mark, Herman F. *From Small Organic Chemicals to Large: a Century of Progress.* Washington DC: American Chemical Society, 1993.

Mauskopf, Seymour H. *Chemical Sciences in the Modern World.* Pennsylvania: University of Pennsylvania Press, 1993.

Smith, S. G. *Introduction to Organic Chemistry*, Wentworth, NH: Falcon Software, 1989. 5 1/4 in computer disks + user's manual.

G. Lynn Carlson

electric charge, and one end of it (the oxygen atom) has a slight negative charge. This makes the entire molecular a polar molecule.

The polar nature of the carbonyl part of the molecule affects the physical properties of the entire molecule. For instance, small ketone molecules, with fewer than 6 carbon atoms in all, are soluble in water, a very polar solvent. At the same time, small ketone molecules are themselves often good solvents for other compounds with polar groups. This is in contrast to small hydrocarbon molecules with no carbonyl group—they are insoluble in water, and they won't dissolve other polar molecules.

A carbonyl group in a molecule is often the most chemically reactive portion. When a molecule containing a carbonyl group undergoes a chemical reaction, it is often this polarity that controls which reaction will take place. Usually a chemical reaction in a molecule containing only a carbonyl group and hydrocarbon groups will take place at the carbonyl group.

Other molecules with carbonyl groups

In many molecules that contain a carbonyl group, the other two groups of atoms are not hydrocarbon groups. Molecules like this are so different chemically that they belong to entirely different classifications. There are four major classes of molecules like this. Again, R stands for any hydrocarbon group. There is more information about these kinds of carbonyl–containing molecules in their entries in this encyclopedia.

Carboxyl group

A carboxyl group, also called a carboxy group, is a characteristic group of atoms found in organic molecules. Organic compounds that contain carboxyl groups are called carboxylic acids.

The carboxyl group occurs on the end or side of a molecule. The group consists of a carbon atom that forms two chemical bonds to one oxygen atom and one chemical bond to a second oxygen atom. This second oxygen is also bonded to a hydrogen atom. The arrangement is written –COOH or –C(O)OH (which emphasizes the different chemical bonding between the carbon atom and one of the oxygen atoms). The name "carboxyl" is actually a combination of the words "carbonyl" and "hydroxyl," since the carboxyl group itself can be considered as a combination of carbonyl (CO) and hydroxyl (OH) groups.

Carboxylic acids

Carboxylic acids are chemical compounds that contain a carboxyl group, which is –COOH. The carboxyl group is attached to another hydrogen atom or to one end of a larger molecule. Examples include formic acid, which is produced by some ants and causes their bites to sting. (In fact, the scientific name for ants, Formica, is what gives formic acid its name.) Another example is acetic acid, which is found in vinegar. Many carboxylic acids dissolve in water. Solutions of many carboxylic acids have a sour taste to them, a characteristic of many acids. Carboxylic acids also react with alkalis, or bases. Generally, however, carboxylic acids are not as chemically active as the non–organic mineral acids such as hydrochloric acid or sulfuric acid.

Biological importance

Carboxylic acids are very important biologically. The drug aspirin is a carboxylic acid, and some people are sensitive to its acidity. The non–aspirin pain reliever ibuprofen is also a carboxylic acid. Carboxylic acids that have very long chains of carbon atoms attached to them are called fatty acids. As their name suggests, they are important in the formation of fat in the body. Many carboxylic acids are present in the foods and drinks we ingest, like malic acid (found in apples), tartaric acid (grape juice), oxalic acid (spinach and some parts of the rhubarb plant), and lactic acid (sour milk). Two other simple carboxylic acids are propionic acid and butyric acid. Propionic acid is partly responsible for the flavor and odor of Swiss cheese. Butyric acid is responsible not only for the smell of rancid butter, but also contributes to the odor of sweat. Lactic acid is generated in muscles of the body as the individual cells metabolize sugar and do work. A buildup of lactic acid, caused by overexertion, is responsible for the fatigue one feels in the muscles by such short–term use. When one rests, the lactic acid is gradually converted to water and carbon dioxide, and the feeling of fatigue passes. A form of Vitamin C is called ascorbic acid and is a carboxylic acid.

A special form of carboxylic acids are the amino acids, which are carboxylic acids that also have a nitrogen–containing group called an amine group in the molecule. Amino acids are very important because combinations of amino acids make up the proteins. Proteins are one of the three major components of the diet, the other two being fats and carbohydrates. Much of the human body, like skin, hair, and muscle, is composed of protein.

Industrial importance

Carboxylic acids are also very important industrially. Perhaps one of the most important industrial applications of compounds with carboxyl groups is the use of fatty acids (which are carboxyl groups attached to long carbon chains) in making soaps, detergents, and

---

KEY TERMS

Amino acid—Carboxylic acids that also have an amine group in them. Amino acids are the building blocks of proteins.

Carboxyl group—The –COOH group of atoms, whose presence defines a carboxylic acid.

Ester—A derivative of a carboxylic acid, where an organic group has been substituted for the hydrogen atom in the acid group. Esters contribute to tastes and smells.

Fatty acid—Carboxylic acids that have long carbon chains. They are important components in fats, and are used to make soaps.

Lactic acid—A carboxylic acid formed during the metabolism of sugar in muscle cells. A buildup of lactic acid leads to a feeling of fatigue.

Mineral acid—An acid that is not organic. Examples include hydrochloric acid and sulfuric acid.

Saponification—The reaction of fatty acids with glycerin to make soap.

---

shampoos. In some such compounds, the hydrogen atom in the carboxyl group is replaced with some metal cation. The modified carboxyl group is soluble in water, while the long chain of carbons remains soluble in fats, oils, and greases. This double solubility allows water to wash out the fat– and oil–based dirt. Many shampoos are based on lauric, palmitic, and stearic acids, which have long chains of 12, 16, and 18 carbon atoms, respectively. To make other cleansing agents, three molecules of fatty acid are combined with one molecule of a compound called glycerin in a reaction called saponification. This reaction also makes a soap molecule which has one end soluble in water and the other soluble in fat or grease or oil. Various fatty acids are used to make soaps and detergents that have different applications in society. Carboxylic acids are also important in the manufacture of greases, crayons, and plastics.

Compounds with carboxyl groups are relatively easily converted to compounds called esters, which have the hydrogen atom of the carboxyl group replaced with a group containing carbon and hydrogen atoms. Such esters are considered derivatives of carboxylic acids. Esters are important because many of them have characteristic tastes and odors. For example, methyl butyrate, a derivative of butyric acid, smells like apples. Benzyl acetate, from acetic acid, has a jasmine odor. Carboxylic acids are thus used commercially as raw materials for the production of synthetic odors and flavors. Other esters, derived from carboxylic acids, have different uses. For example, the ester ethyl acetate is a very good solvent and is a major component in nail polish remover.

See also Acetic acid; Acetylsalicylic acid; Acids and bases; Amino acid; Carboxyl group; Ester; Fatty acids; Lactic acid; Oxalic acid; Tartaric acid.

Further Reading:
Kitson, Trevor M. *Organic Chemistry: A Guide to Common Themes*. London: E. Arnold, Ltd., 1988.
Murray, Frank. "Hydroxycitric Acid." *Better Nutrition for Better Living* 56 (1994): 34 – 39.
Snyder, Carl H. *The Extraordinary Chemistry of Ordinary Things*. New York: John Wiley & Sons, 1992.

David W. Ball

Carcinogen

A carcinogen is a substance that causes a normal cell to change into a cancerous cell. The word "carcinogen" is derived from Greek and means in English, cancer–causing. Carcinogens fall into two broad categories, naturally occurring substances that are found in food or soil, or artificial substances created by chemists for various industrial purposes. Although the way carcinogens cause cancer is still not completely understood, cancer researchers believe that humans and other animals must be exposed to a carcinogen for a certain period of time and at a high enough concentration for cancer to occur.

What is cancer?

Cancer is a disease in which cells grow abnormally. Like all living things, normal cells grow, reproduce and die. These processes are controlled by chemicals and reactions within the cell, which are in turn controlled by the cell's genetic material within its nucleus. In a cancerous cell, the genetic material is altered, and the genes which encode and direct the chemical reactions within the cell are mutated, or changed. Cancerous cells grow uncontrollably, forming a large mass of cells called a tumor, which invades tissues and kills non–cancerous cells. Sometimes cancerous cells "break off" from a tumor and enter the bloodstream, traveling to other parts of the body and infecting other organs and tissues in a process known as metastasis. In this way, a cancer can spread from an isolated tumor to the entire body.

Several agents, such as viruses, medication, and synthetic carcinogens can cause mutations within a cell's genetic material. Some kinds of cancers are caused by viruses. For example, a special kind of virus called a retrovirus causes a rare form of leukemia (cancer of the white blood cells). Radiation from naturally–occurring radioactive substances (such as uranium) can disrupt a cell's genetic material and bring about cancer. Synthetic carcinogens are found in processed foods and industrial chemicals.

How carcinogens cause cancer

For a carcinogen to cause cancer a person must be exposed for a certain length of time to the carcinogen and at a high enough concentration. Repeated exposure to a carcinogen over an extended period (such as 20 years) increases the likelihood that a normal cell's genetic material will mutate and initiate cancer. Cigarette smoke contains potent carcinogens; it can take many years and many repeated exposure to the carcinogens in smoke for smoking to cause cancer. Smoking–related lung cancers typically develop between 10 and 20 years of continuous smoking. In Hiroshima and Nagasaki in Japan, where atomic bombs were dropped in 1945, the leukemia rates in the surviving population increased dramatically some five years after the bombs were detonated.

Some carcinogens are more powerful, cancer–causing agents, than others. Powerful carcinogens are called tumor promoters, and can cause genetic mutations directly within cells. Less powerful carcinogens are called tumor initiators and can cause latent changes in the cell's genetic material. These changes are not enough to actually cause cancer, but sensitize the tissue for later exposures to tumor promoters. If a tumor initiator has already wrought some damage to the cell's genetic material, the likelihood that a tumor promotor will cause the cell to become cancerous is increased.

Cancerous tumors develop over many stages, and it is rare that exposure to a carcinogen is the sole cause of most cancers. Exposure to a carcinogen must usually be combined with other environmental factors for a cancer to develop. Some environmental risk factors are difficult to identify, while others such as prolonged, heavy cigarette smoking have been easy to identify. Heredity, such as whether close relatives have developed cancer, is another risk factor that is not as easily characterized.

Some carcinogens such as cigarette smoke can be avoided. Other factors, such as a diet, can be modified.

Additional risk factors such as gender, immune status, metabolic rate, levels of certain enzymes, and age can neither be avoided nor modified.

Types of carcinogens

Carcinogens used in industry

The idea that chemicals could cause cancer was first promoted in 1775 by Percivall Pott, a London physician. Dr. Pott noted that young chimney sweeps had a high incidence of scrotal cancer. Because most sweeps began their careers very early in life and seldom washed or changed clothes, the sweeps were exposed to soot repeatedly and for long periods of time, leading to scrotal cancer in young adulthood. Not until 150 years later were the actual carcinogenic substances in soot identified, but Dr. Pott made his case for more humane treatment and better working conditions for the chimney sweeps by noting the connections between cancer and this profession.

With the advent of industrial development in the nineteenth century, other connections between certain cancers and chemicals were noticed. Shale oil and coal tar workers had a high incidence of skin cancer. Dye-stuff workers developed bladder cancer. And a chemical called vinyl chloride, used in the manufacture of leather goods, caused a rare liver tumor.

In response to growing concern about cancer in industrial workers, the International Agency for Research on Cancer and the National Toxicology Program formulated a system to classify chemicals according to their cancer–causing risk. A chemical could be classified either as a probable carcinogen, or as a non–carcinogen.

A problem with this and other classification systems is that much of the research is based on experiments on animals. If cancer can be induced in experimental animals with high levels of a chemical, it is sometimes assumed that humans could also be at risk even with lower exposure levels over a long period of time. The science of risk assessment investigates the possibility of developing cancer from very low levels of exposure to chemicals that cause cancer at very high levels.

Dioxin is a case in point. In the early 1980s, dioxin was sprayed on the roads of Times Beach, Missouri, to seal the pavement. Dioxin had been classified by the Environmental Protection Agency (EPA) as a probable carcinogen. When the townspeople discovered that dioxin had been sprayed on their roads, the town was abandoned and lawsuits against the road contractor were initiated which were challenged by the defendants.

Carcinogens in food

Some foods contain naturally–occurring carcinogens. Safrole, found in sassafras root; estragole, found in the herb tarragon; allyl isothiocynate, found in mustard seed; and benzene, found in eggs, fruits, vegetables, cooked meats, and fish are all carcinogens. However, these substances must be consumed in large amounts, over a long period to initiate cancer.

Processed foods such as bacon, sausages, and canned meats contain the preservative nitrite. Frying the cured bacon can convert some non–carcinogenic substances in the nitrites into potent carcinogens. Browning meats such as hamburger can also cause carcinogenic chemicals to be produced. However, in both cases, the amount of carcinogen is extremely small. Interestingly, microwave cooking does not release the carcinogens in beef.

Foods that involve fermentation in their production, such as beer, wine, bread, and yogurt, all contain mildly carcinogenic substances. Again, these foods must be eaten in large amounts over decades to cause the genetic mutations that can lead to cancer.

Other carcinogens

Radioactive substances found in rocks and soil are also considered potentially carcinogenic. While most people do not come in contact with radioactive chemicals on a day–to–day basis, these substances can emit radioactive particles that can be dangerous. Radon, a radioactive substance emitted by uranium, can seep from rocks into buildings. In some areas of the country, radon can be emitted in relatively large amounts into buildings which should be tested for radon. If the levels are found to be high, changes should be made to the building's ventilation system to reduce the amount of radon in the building.

In 1993, the EPA designated second–hand smoke from cigarettes to be a known human carcinogen. It is estimated that 2,000 lung cancer deaths a year are caused by second–hand smoke, which has led to the designation of many public areas as smoke–free zones.

Avoiding carcinogens

It is recommended that people eat a varied diet high in fresh fruits and vegetable and avoid excess consumption of foods high in nitrites. While it is not possible to completely eliminate one's exposure to carcinogens, it is possible to avoid the concomitant risk factors that

KEY TERMS

Cancer—A disease in which cells grow abnormally.

Carcinogen—A chemical that causes cancer.

Mutation—A change in the genetic material of a cell.

Risk assessment—The study of the risk of exposure to certain levels of an agent that may lead to the development of a disease, such as cancer.

Risk factor—Environmental factors that may increase the risk of initiating a disease, such as cancer.

may lead to cancer. Avoiding smoking, eating a varied, balanced diet that includes fiber, and limiting alcohol consumption are all associated with a lowered cancer risk.

See also Cancer; Cigarette smoke; Mutagen; Mutation; Radiation exposure; Virus.

Further Reading:

Ashby, John. "Change the Rules for Food Additives." *Nature* 368 (April 1994).

Begley, Susan. "Don't Drink the Dioxin." *Newsweek* 124 (September 1994): 57.

Boyle, Peter. "The Hazards of Passive—and Active—Smoking." *New England Journal of Medicine* 328 (June 1993): 1708.

Moolenaar, Robert J. "Overhauling Carcinogen Classification." *Issues in Science and Technology* 8 (Summer 1992): 70.

Nesnow, Stephen. "Breakthroughs in Cancer Risk Assessment." *EPA Journal* 19 (Jan/Mar 1993): 27.

"Second–hand Smoke Designated as a Known Human Carcinogen." *EPA Journal* 19 (2): 5. April/June 1993.

Kathleen Scogna

Cardinal number

A measure of the number of elements in a group or a set. For example, the number of books on a shelf can be described by a single cardinal number. Similarly, the set {2,4,6} can be assigned the cardinal number 3 because it has only 3 elements. Since cardinal numbers count the number of elements in a set, they are always positive whole integers. If the elements from two sets have a one–to–one relationship, namely each element can be paired together such that no elements are left over, then they can be represented by the same cardinal number.

Some sets have an infinite number of elements. However, not all infinite sets have a one–to–one relationship. Consider the following sets:

Set X $\{1,2,3,4,...,n..\}$ Set Y $\{1,4,9,16,...,n^2..\}$

Although both of these sets have an infinite number of elements, they can not be represented by the same cardinal number because set X contains all the elements of set Y, but it also contains additional elements. To solve this problem a 19th century mathematician named George Cantor (1845 – 1918) created a new numbering system to deal with infinite sets. He called these new numbers transfinite cardinal numbers and used the symbol $_0$ (aleph null) to represent the smallest one. He also developed an arithmetic system for manipulating these numbers.

Cardinals and grosbeaks

The cardinals and grosbeaks belong to the subfamilies Cardinalinae, of the finch family (Fringillidae), which is the largest of all North American bird families. (Some researchers include the cardinals and grosbeaks with the Emberizidae, the buntings and tanagers).

Cardinals and grosbeaks are New World birds, ranging from central Argentina as far north as central Canada. They live primarily in temperate zone woodlands, and have adapted to life around humans, whose help (in the form of birdseed) has helped cardinals extend their range north to Canada.

The name "grosbeak" is descriptive: these birds have thick, sturdy beaks, which help them crack open seeds. Their diet also includes blackberries, strawberries, insects, spiders, bees, corn, snails, slugs, and earthworms. Cardinals have been seen drinking maple sap from holes left by sapsuckers. The pine grosbeak has special throat pouches in which it transports food.

The males of cardinals and grosbeaks are brightly colored; females are duller. Pine grosbeaks (*Pinicola enucleator*) and evening grosbeaks (*Hesperiphona vespertina*)remain in their northern or high–mountain habitats year–round, but have been known to migrate out of these areas if food is in short supply. Three species of

North American grosbeak–the rose–breasted grosbeak (*Pheuctinus ludovicanus*), black–headed, and blue grosbeak (*Guiraca caerulea*)–prefer southern areas, and the rose–breasted will migrate as far south as Venezuela and Peru come winter.

In some species, including the cardinal (*Cardinais cardinalis*), the female builds the nest and incubates the eggs without help from the male. In others, males and females share in these efforts. Between 2–5 eggs are laid. Young cardinals fledge quickly, leaving the nest when 10 or 11 days old. This rapid development allows the cardinal to raise multiple clutches in a season, up to as many as four; the male cares for the hatchlings while the female incubates the next clutch.

Male cardinals and grosbeaks are renowned singers. The cardinal has at least 28 different songs. Male rose–breasted grosbeaks will compete for a female by hovering over her and singing a long, liquid, robin-like song; the winner of that courtship will sing while he is helping incubate the eggs.

Cardiology see **Heart diseases**

A reindeer bull in Finnish Lapland.

Caribou

The caribou or reindeer (*Rangifer tarandus*) is a northern species of deer occurring in the subarctic and arctic of North America and Eurasia. At one time caribou and reindeer were considered to be separate species, but these animals are fully interfertile and are now considered to be the same species. In North America they are called caribou, whereas in Eurasia they are known as reindeer. However, there are many well–differentiated, geographically distinct populations of these animals, which are designated as subspecies. Northern caribou are relatively small, while southern caribou are larger, with the biggest males (bucks) weighing up to 660 lb (300 kg).

Caribou are even–toed hoofed mammals in the order Artiodactyla and suborder Ruminanta. They are in the family Cervidae, along with other species of deer. Like other deer and cattle, caribou have four–chambered stomachs capable of digesting the tough, fibrous plant materials containing cellulose that comprise their diet. Caribou ruminate, which means that they re–chew forage that has previously fermented in the four pouches of the stomach.

Like other deer (family Cervidae), caribou have deciduous antlers, which are long, branching, bony outgrowths of the frontal bones of the skull. During their growth antlers are covered with a heavily vascularized tissue called velvet, which eventually dries and is peeled or rubbed off, leaving the bare bone exposed. Unlike other species of deer, both sexes of caribou can develop antlers. However, the antlers of mature male animals are much larger and more elaborate, and are used in jousting during the rutting season, when they attempt to assemble a harem of does. The antlers of adult bucks grow most rapidly from May to July, and are at their largest size in August. By October the antlers are hardest and velvet free, and are used in ritualized (or real) combat with other males. Soon after, the rut, the joint between the antler and the skull weakens, and the antler is shed, usually by early December. Antler growth in female caribou starts later (June to September), and shedding is delayed until April or May when the calves are born.

The newborn calves of caribou are very precocious, and are able to stand within one–half hour of birth. After only a few days calves are capable of running several kilometers an hour, and of keeping up with the moving herd. This rapid development is, of course, an adaptation to reducing the predation rate of young calves, the stage with the highest risk of mortality.

In North America, the most northerly subspecies is the Peary caribou (*Rangifer tarandus pearyi*). This relatively small, whitish subspecies is a resident of the high–arctic islands of northern Canada. Peary caribou gain weight during the warmest two to three months of the year, foraging on grasses and forbs (broadleaf herbs) in the relatively productive wet meadows and dwarf–shrub tundra. During most of the rest of the year, however, these animals must survive on the much sparser and less nutritious vegetation of upland, relatively snow–free ridges.

Farther to the south are woodland or barren–ground caribou (mostly *R. t. caribou* in the east, and *R. t. groenlandicus* in the west). These relatively large, brown–colored caribou tend to undertake long–distance, seasonal migrations, which can be more than 621 mi (1,000 km) in their circuitous passage. The caribou often swim across large rivers during those journeys. During the growing season these caribou move to open habitats such as northern tundra and muskeg (a peat bog or tussock meadow with a variety of woody vegetation), where they calve and feed on the lush growth of grasses, forbs, and young twigs of shrubs. At the end of the growing season, the barren–ground caribou migrate back to the boreal forest, where they feed largely on ground and arboreal lichens during the winter. More southerly caribou living in mountainous terrain undertake vertical migrations, to alpine tundra and meadows during the summer, and montane forest in winter.

In general, the winter diet of caribou consists of not very nutritious foods such as lichens, twigs, and dried grasses and forbs. Caribou tend to slowly lose weight on this poor quality diet, at times of greater metabolic demands for thermoregulation in cold temperatures and windy conditions. During summer, a much wider range of more nutritious foods is available, and caribou put weight on at that time. Summer foods include grasses, sedges, forbs, new twigs and foliage of shrubs, mushrooms, and berries. Caribou will also opportunistically eat lemmings and birds eggs.

Caribou are rather social animals, tending to occur in groups of various size. These assemblies are loosely segregated by sex and age–class, and their size can vary seasonally. The density of animals in the groups also varies, being more compact when caribou are harassed by predators such as wolves or humans, or sometimes if the animals are being severely bothered by biting flies. During the autumn migrations and the rutting period, woodland caribou occur in enormous herds of tens of thousands of animals, which disperse into much smaller herds at other times.

Caribou have an excellent sense of smell, but do less well visually. These animals can be closely approached

KEY TERMS

Ruminant—Animals in the order Artiodactyla, having a four–chambered stomach, and that chew a pre–digested cud.

Rutting season—A period of sexual excitement in an animal, for example, in bull caribou during the autumn.

Velvet—The soft, vascular skin that covers deer antlers during growth.

from upwind. Caribou can be quite curious, and humans can sometimes approach these animals while walking directly towards them and holding their arms straight up, simulating the silhouette of an oncoming caribou. When frightened, caribou usually run a short distance, circle around until they catch a confirming scent of the intruder, and then move to a safer distance.

Wolves are the most important natural predators of caribou, but grizzly bear, wolverine, and lynx also kill some animals. Caribou were also a staple food for aboriginal humans in North America, and they continue to be an important game species throughout their range. In some areas caribou have been overharvested, and they have been extirpated from most of the southern parts of their original North American range, for example in Maine, the Maritime Provinces, the Northwoods, and parts of the Rocky Mountains.

Reindeer (*R. t. tarandus*) have long been domesticated by northern peoples of Eurasia, such as the Lapps of northern Scandinavia. Reindeer have also been introduced to the western Arctic of North America, and to subarctic South Georgia Island in the Southern Hemisphere, in attempts to develop commercial enterprises. Domestic reindeer are husbanded for their meat, hide, and milk. In recent years, a large export market has developed in China and elsewhere in eastern Asia for reindeer or caribou horn in velvet, which is made into a medicinal powder. Domestic reindeer have also been used to pull small sleighs and wagons. Of course, the most famous usage of reindeer in this fashion occurs on a particular night each year, when a team of these animals led by an individual with a shiny red nose, carries Santa Claus around the world to bring presents to good little children.

See also Deer.

Further Reading:
Banfield, A. W. F. *The Mammals of Canada.* Toronto: University of Toronto Press, 1974.

Grzimek, B., ed. *Grzimek's Encyclopedia of Mammals*. London: McGraw Hill, 1990.

Wilson, D. E. and D. Reeder, comp. *Mammal Species of the World*. Washington, D.C.: Smithsonian Institution Press, 1993.

Bill Freedman

Carnivore

In the literal sense, a carnivore is any flesh–eating organism. However, in the ecological usage of the word, carnivores kill animals before eating them (that is, they are predators), as opposed to feeding on animals that are already dead (the latter are called scavengers or detritivores).

Trophic ecology deals with the feeding and nutritional relationships within ecosystems, and this field has developed some specialized terminology. Carnivores, for example, are heterotrophs, which means that they must ingest other organisms to obtain energy and nutrition. (In contrast, autotrophs such as green plants can fix their own energy and synthesize biochemicals utilizing diffuse sources such as sunlight and simple inorganic molecules). Animals that feed on plants are herbivores (or primary consumers), while animals that eat herbivores are known as primary carnivores (or secondary consumers), and carnivores that feed upon other carnivores are tertiary consumers. It is rare for an ecosystem to sustain carnivores of an order higher than tertiary. This is due to the pyramid–shaped structure of productivity in ecological food webs, which itself is caused by thermodynamic inefficiencies of energy transfer between levels. Therefore, the productivity of green plants is always much larger than that of herbivores, while carnivores sustain even less productivity. As a result of their trophic structure, ecosystems cannot sustain predators that feed upon, for example, lions, wolves, or killer whales.

Another consequence of the pyramidal structure of ecological webs is the tendency of top carnivores to bioconcentrate especially large residues of fat–soluble, persistent chemicals such as the chlorinated hydrocarbons, DDT, PCBs, and dioxins. This happens because organisms in successive levels of the trophic web absorb most of the chlorinated hydrocarbons that they ingest, storing these chemicals in fatty tissues. Consequently, top carnivores further concentrate the pre–concentrated residues of organisms lower in the ecological web. Therefore, the largest residues of these chemicals

A cougar (*Felis concolor*).

occur in peregrine falcons, polar bears, and seals, and these top predators have a disproportionate risk of being poisoned.

Almost all carnivores are animals. However, a few carnivores are specialized species of plants that trap, kill, and digest small animals, and then absorb some of their nutrients. Examples of these so–called carnivorous plants include Venus' flytrap, sundews, and pitcher plants.

See also Ecological pyramid; Food chain/web; Herbivore; Heterotroph; Omnivore; Predator; Scavenger; Trophic levels.

Carnivorous plants

Carnivorous plants are botanical oddities that supplement their requirement for nutrients by trapping, killing, and digesting small animals, mostly insects. Carnivorous plants are photosynthetic, and are therefore fundamentally autotrophic. Still, their feeding relationship with animals represents a reversal of the normal trophic connections between autotrophs and consumers.

Carnivorous plants have long been fascinating to humans. They have the subject of some captivating tales of science fiction, involving fantastic trees that consume large, unwary creatures in tropical forests. Tales have even been told about ritual sacrifices of humans to these awesome carnivores, presumably to appease evil, botanical spirits. Fortunately, fact involves much smaller predators than those of science fiction. Still, the few species of carnivorous plants that really exist are very curious variants on the usual form and function of plants. Scaled up, these carnivores would indeed be formidable predators.

A slender-leaved sundew (*Drosera linearis*) in Bruce National Park, Ontario.

All species of carnivorous plants are small, herbaceous plants, generally growing in nutrient poor habitats, such as acidic bogs and oligotrophic lakes. The usual prey of these green predators is not unwary deer, cattle, or humans, but insects and other small invertebrates, although a few of the larger species are capable of capturing tadpoles and small fish.

Ecology of carnivorous plants

Carnivorous plants are mostly herbaceous perennials with poorly developed root systems, and often propagate by vegetative means, such as stolons and rhizomes. Carnivorous plants are typically intolerant of competition, occurring in open, wet habitats subject to full sunlight. Carnivorous plants are often tolerant of a limited amount of disturbance, and in fact may benefit from a low intensity of trampling, which prepares a substrate suitable for the germination of their seeds and the establishment of new individuals. Some species are also tolerant of light fires, which also favor their reproduction.

Most carnivorous plants grow in acidic bogs, unproductive lakes, or sandy soils. These are all habitats that are poor in the nutrients that plants require for growth, particularly inorganic nitrogen, phosphorus, and calcium. The nutrients obtained through carnivory are important to these plants. In the absence of animal foods these plants grow less well, and they flower sparsely or not at all.

The types of traps

Contrary to some portrayals in science fiction, the flowers of carnivorous plants are not the organs that ensnare their prey. Rather, in all cases the deadly traps are modified leaves and stems. There are three basic types of trapping organs: active, adhesive, and passive.

A pitcher plant in Isle Royale National Park, Michigan.

Active traps of carnivorous plants attract their mostly arthropod prey using various machinations, including color, scent, and nectar. Once a victim is suitably within, the trap rapidly closes, preventing the escape of the prey. The active trap of the Venus flytrap (*Dionaea muscipula*) is modeled on a basic clamshell design. This species utilizes a fast–acting response to a mechanical stimulus caused when an insect triggers sensitive hairs in the trap, causing its clam–shell leaves to close. The fringing outer projectiles of the leaves rapidly enclose to form a barrier that prevents the trapped arthropod from escaping. At the same time, mechanical stimuli from the struggling victim trigger the synthesis and excretion of digestive enzymes onto the inner surface of the trap, which facilitate digestion of the prey.

Another design of active trap is based on a small, hollow chamber with a trap door. This design is utilized by the bladderworts (various species of *Utricularia*), small aquatic plants that form little bladders with diameters of several millimeters, that trap tiny aquatic invertebrates behind a rapidly closing trap door. The door of the bladderwort trap initially swings quickly into the bladder, triggered to respond in this way by motion sensed by fine, fringing bristles. The inward motion of the door develops a suction that can sweep invertebrates into the trap, where they are trapped by the re–closing door, and are digested for the nutrients they contain.

Adhesive, semi–active traps primarily rely on sticky, surface exudates to ensnare their prey. Once a victim is firmly entangled, the leaf slowly enfolds to seal the fate of the unlucky arthropod, and to facilitate the process of digestion. This manner of trap is typified by the most species–rich of the carnivorous plants, the genus of plants known as sundews (*Drosera* spp.). These plants develop relatively wide, modified leaves, that are densely covered with stalked glands that resemble tentacles several millimeters long. Each tentacle is tipped with a droplet of sticky mucilage. Unwary arthropods, lured by scent, color, and nectar, are caught by this gluey material and are then firmly entangled during their struggles. The leaf then slowly, almost imperceptibly, enfolds the prey, which is then digested by proteolytic enzymes secreted by special glands on the leaf surface.

Passive traps lie in deadly wait for their small victims, which are attracted by enticing scents, colors, and nectar. However, these seeming treats are located at the end of a fatal, usually one–way passage, from which the prey cannot easily exit. The passage terminates in a pit filled with water and digestive enzymes, where the victim drowns, or is attacked by predacious insects that live symbiotically with the carnivorous plant.

The ingenious design of the pitcher plant (*Sarracenia purpurea*) is a revealing example of passive traps. The pitcher plant has foliage modified into upright vessels, as much as 4–6 in (10–15 cm) tall. When mature, these are reddish–green in color, with ultraviolet nectar guides pointing into their interior, which also emits alluring scents. The fringing lip and upper part of the inside of the pitcher are rich in insect attracting nectaries (organs that secrete nectar), and are covered with stiff, downward pointing bristles. These bristles can be easily traversed by an insect walking into the trap, but they passively resist movement upwards and out of the trap. Beneath the zone of bristles is a very waxy, slippery zone, the surface of which is almost impossible for even the tiny feet of insects to grasp, so they fall to the bottom of the trap. There the victim encounters a pool of collected rainwater, replete with digestive enzymes and the floating corpses of drowned insects, in various stages of decay and digestion. The newest victim struggles for a while, then drowns, and is digested.

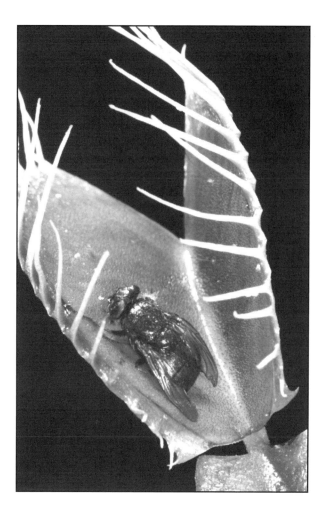

A venus fly trap, opening after having consumed its catch.

Interestingly, a few species of insects are capable of living happily in the water–filled vessels of the pitcher plant and related species, such as the cobra plant (*Darlingtonia californica*). These insects are resistant to the digestive enzymes of the carnivorous plants, and they utilize the pitchers as a micro–aquatic habitat. Some species of midges and flies that live in pitcher plants actually attack recently trapped insects, killing and feeding on them. Eventually, the carnivorous plant benefits from nutrients excreted by the symbiotic insects. These pitchers also support a rich microbial community, which are useful in the decay of trapped arthropods, helping to make nutrients available for uptake by the carnivorous plant.

Conservation and protection of carnivorous plants

Most species of carnivorous plants are rare, and many are endangered. The principle threats to these

CARP

species are habitat destruction caused by the drainage and infilling of wetlands and bogs to develop housing, and ecological conversions associated with agriculture and forestry. The mining of bog peat for horticultural materials or as a source of energy is another threat to some species of carnivorous plants. In addition, some species of carnivorous plants are actively collected in the wild to supply the horticultural trade, and this can seriously threaten the populations of those species.

Venus flytrap is a famous, North American example of a carnivorous plant that is endangered in the wild. The natural distribution of this species is restricted to a small area of the coastal plain of North and South Carolina, fringing inland as far as 124 mi (200 km) along about 186 mi (300 km) of the coast, on either side of Cape Fear. However, the Venus flytrap only occurs today in a few small, scattered remnants of its natural habitat, associated with open spots in acidic bogs and pine savannahs. To some degree this species has been endangered in the wild by excessive collecting in the past, but the modern threat is mostly associated with habitat losses to urbanization, agriculture, and forestry.

Fortunately, the Venus flytrap and many other species of carnivorous plants are fairly easy to propagate by vegetative means, usually by sowing leaf fragments onto moist sphagnum peat. For these species, there is no need to collect plants from the wild to supply the economic demands of horticulture.

However, some other species of carnivorous plants cannot be easily propagated in greenhouses, and the demand for these species by aficionados of these charismatic carnivores must be satisfied by collecting wild plants. In some cases, these demands are resulting in unsustainable harvests that are endangering wild populations, for example, of some of the species of the tropical Eurasian pitcher plant, *Nepenthes*.

However, even species that can be propagated in greenhouses may be collected from the wild for sale to horticulturalists, because quick and easy profits can be made in this way. So, if you decide to try to grow carnivorous plants as unusual pets, ensure that you are obtaining stock that was cultivated in a greenhouse, and not collected from the wild.

Further Reading:
Juniper, B. E., R. J. Robins, and D. M. Joel. *The Carnivorous Plants*. San Diego: Academic Press, 1989.
Lecoufle, M. *Carnivorous Plants: Care and Cultivation*. Blandford, U.K.: Sterling Publishing Co., 1991.
Schwartz, R. *Carnivorous Plants*. New York: Avon Books, 1975.

Bill Freedman

KEY TERMS

Carnivorous plant—Plants that supplement their nutrient requirements by trapping, killing, and digesting small animals, most commonly insects.

Oligotrophic—Refers to a waterbody or wetland with a restricted supply of nutrients and a small rate of productivity.

Carnot cycle see **Thermodynamics**

Carp

Carp (family Cyprinidae), one of the major groups of freshwater fish worldwide, include not only the common carp (*Cyprinus carpio*), but also more familiar species such as the goldfish, minnow, tench, bream, and suckers. The family is characterized by having no teeth in the jaws, although well–developed teeth occur on the pharyngeal bones (located behind the gill chamber) which grind food against a hard, rough pad in the roof of the pharynx.

The body of the carp is covered with scales. A single dorsal fin is present with 17–22 branched rays and a strong, toothed spine in front. The carp has four barbels—fleshy outgrowths that play a sensory role, for example, in the location of food—two long ones at the corners of the mouth and shorter ones on the upper lip. Mainly a vegetable feeder, it will also eat worms, shrimp, insects, and small fish. These are found by probing in the mud of the river bed. In color, the common carp is a dull green–brown on the flanks, darkening on the back. The underside may be a golden–yellow. Fins are a gray–green or dusky brown with a reddish tinge.

The carp is a hardy fish that can live and breed almost under any conditions. Their preferred habitat is lowland lakes and slow–flowing rivers with abundant vegetation for food and shelter. During periods of exceptionally cold weather, carp move into deep water and enter a resting phase when their body metabolism is slowed down. Breeding takes place during the spring and carp generally spawn from May–June, when water temperature reaches 68° F (20° C). Breeding takes place in shallow waters, and the eggs are laid directly onto plants. When the eggs hatch the tiny fry remain in the shallows for several weeks, concealed amongst the vegetation. The growth rates of carp varies considerably

A carp (*Cyprinus carpio*).

according to local conditions, but carp are renowned for the large size that they can attain: some fish weighing more than (30 kg) have been recorded. In general, however, these relatively long–lived fish average (50–60 cm) in length and weigh from (2–4.5 kg). In their natural environment, wild carp are thought to live for as many as 15 years; in captivity, however, far greater ages have been recorded with some even being credited with a life span of more than 200 years.

Of the many species that have been reared successfully from egg to maturity in captivity, the carp has probably been the most successful on a commercial basis. There is a long history of carp culture in the Far East, while this is also still widely practiced in parts of Europe. The Romans are probably responsible for bringing the carp into Europe sometime from the 14th–17th century. Carp have also been released in North America, Australia, and New Zealand both as a sport fish and as a commercial venture. A wide number of varieties of common carp are found, including one that is scaleless.

See also Minnows; Suckers.

Carpal tunnel syndrome

Carpal tunnel syndrome results from compression and irritation of the median nerve where it passes through the wrist. In the end, the median nerve is responsible for both sensation and movement. When the median nerve is compressed, an individual's hand will feel as if it has "gone to sleep," and the individual will experience numbness, tingling, and a prickly pin like sensation over the palm surface of the hand, and the individual may begin to experience muscle weakness, making it difficult to open jars and hold objects with the

affected hand. Eventually, the muscles of the hand served by the median nerve may begin to atrophy, or grow noticeably smaller.

Compression of the median nerve in the wrist can occur during a number of different conditions, particularly conditions that lead to changes in fluid accumulation throughout the body. Because the area of the wrist through which the median nerve passes is very narrow, any swelling in the area will lead to pressure on the median nerve, which will interfere with the nerve's ability to function normally. Pregnancy, obesity, arthritis, certain thyroid conditions, diabetes, and certain pituitary abnormalities all predispose to carpal tunnel syndrome. Furthermore, overuse syndrome, in which an individual's job requires repeated strong wrist motions (in particular, motions which bend the wrist inward toward the forearm) can also predispose to carpal tunnel syndrome. Women are known to experience carpal tunnel syndrome more frequently than do men.

Carpal tunnel syndrome is initially treated by splinting, which prevents the wrist from flexing inward into the position which exacerbates median nerve compression. When carpal tunnel syndrome is more advanced, injection of steroids into the wrist to decrease inflammation may be necessary. The most severe cases of carpal tunnel syndrome may require surgery to decrease the compression of the median nerve and restore its normal function.

Carpinchos see **Capybaras**

Carrot family (Apiaceae)

The carrot family (Apiaceae, or Umbelliferae) is a diverse group of about 3,000 species of plants, occurring in all parts of the world.

Most umbellifers are herbaceous, perennial plants, often with aromatic foliage. Some species have poisonous foliage or roots. The leaves are typically alternately arranged on the stem, and in many species they are compound and divided into lobes. The flowers are small and contain both female (pistillate) and male (staminate) organs. The individual flowers are aggregated into characteristic, flat–topped inflorescences (groups) called umbels, from which one of the scientific names of the family (Umbelliferae) is derived. The fruits are dry, two–seeded structures called schizocarps, which split at maturity into two one–seeded, vertically ribbed sub–fruits, known as mericarps.

Cow parsnip and beach rose plants at Napatree Pt., Rhode Island.

Edible species in the carrot family

Various species of the Apiaceae are grown as food or as flavorings. The best known of the food crops is the carrot (*Daucus carota*), a biennial plant native to temperate Eurasia. The cultivated carrot develops a large, roughly conical, orange–yellow tap root, which is harvested at the end of one growing season, just before the ground freezes. The color of carrot roots is due to the pigment carotene, a metabolic precursor for the synthesis of vitamin A. Carotene is sometimes extracted from carrots and used to color other foods, such as cheddar cheese, and sometimes butter and margarine. Carrots can be eaten raw, cooked as a vegetable, or added to stews and soups.

The parsnip (*Pastinaca sativa*) is another biennial species in which the whitish tap root is harvested and eaten, usually as a cooked vegetable. Both the carrot and parsnip are ancient cultivated plants, being widely used as a food and medicine by the early Greeks and Romans.

The celery (*Apium graveolens*) is native to moist habitats in temperate regions of Eurasia. Wild celery plants are tough, distasteful, and even poisonous, but domesticated varieties are harvested for their crisp, edible petioles (stalks). The most commonly grown variety of celery has been bred to have long, crunchy, juicy petioles. Until this variety was developed, the flavor of cultivated celery was commonly improved by a technique known as blanching, in which the growing plant is partially covered by mulch, paper, or boards to reduce the amount of chlorophyll that it develops. This practice is still used to grow "celery hearts." The celeriac or celery–root is a variety in which the upper part of the root and the lower part of the stem, a tissue known as a hypocotyl, are swollen, and can be harvested and used in soups or cooked as a nutritious vegetable. Celery seeds are sometimes used as a savory garnish for cooked foods, and to manufacture celery salt.

Parsley (*Petroselinum crispum*) is one of the most common of the garden herbs, and is often used as a savory, edible foliage, rich in vitamin C and iron. Parsley is most commonly used as a pleasing, but not–to–be–eaten visual garnish for well–presented, epicurean foods. This dark–green plant can be a pleasant food in itself and is used to flavor tabouleh, a North African dish made with bulgar wheat, tomatoes, and lots of chopped parsley.

The foliage of dill (*Anethum graveolens*) is commonly used to flavor pickled cucumbers, gherkins, and tomatos, and sometimes as a steamed garnish for fish or chicken. Chervil (*Anthriscus cerefolium*) leaves are also used as a garnish, and in salads.

Other species in the Apiaceae are cultivated largely for their tasty, aromatic seeds. The economically most important of these savory seeds are those of caraway (*Carum carvi*), which are widely used to flavor bread and cheese. An aromatic oil extracted from caraway seeds is used in the preparation of medicine and perfume, and to flavor the liquors kummel and aqua–vitae. The anise or aniseed (*Pimpinella anisum*) is one of the oldest of the edible, aromatic seeds. An oil extracted from the seeds of anise is used to flavor candies, cough medicines, and a liquor known as anisette. The seeds of fennel (*Foeniculum vulgare*) also contain anise oil, and are used in the preparation of medicines and liquorice, while the foliage is sometimes used as a garnish. The seeds of angelica (*Angelica archangelica*) are also a source of an aromatic oil, used to flavor vermouth and other liquors. Coriander (*Coriander sativum*) seeds yield another aromatic oil, used to flavor candy, medicine, and liquors. The seeds of cumin (*Cuminum cyminum*) are used to flavor breads, cheese, candy, soup, and pickles.

Ornamental species

A few species in the carrot family are grown as ornamentals, usually as foliage plants, rather than for their flowers. A variegated variety of goutweed (*Aegopodium podagraria*) is often cultivated for this reason, as are some larger species, such as angelica (*Angelica sylvestris*).

Wild species occurring in North America

A number of species of wildflowers in the carrot family occur naturally in North America, or have been introduced from elsewhere and have spread to natural habitats.

Some of the more familiar and widespread native species of Apiaceae in North America include black snake–root (*Sanicula marylandica*), sweet–cicely (*Osmorrhiza claytoni, O. divaricata*), Scotch or sea lovage (*Ligusticum scothicum*), golden Alexanders (*Zizia aurea*), marsh–pennywort (*Hydrocotyle umbellata*), and water hemlock (*Sium suave*).

Some wild species in the Apiaceae are deadly poisonous. The poison hemlock (*Conium maculatum*) is a native of Eurasia, but has spread in North America as an introduced weed. Poison hemlock may be the most poisonous of the temperate plants, and it can be a deadly

Fennel (*Foeniculum vulgare*).

forage for cattle. The famous Greek philosopher, Socrates, is thought to have been executed by being condemned in the courts to drink a fatal infusion prepared from the poison hemlock. Native species are similarly poisonous, for example, the water hemlock or cowbane (*Cicuta maculata*), and the bulb–bearing water hemlock (*Cicuta bulbifera*). Most cases of poisoning by these plants involve cattle or people eating the roots or the seeds, which, while apparently tasty, are deadly toxic.

Some other wild species, while not deadly, can cause a severe dermatitis in exposed people. These include wild parsnip (*Pastinaca sativa*) and cow-parsnip (*Heracleum lanatum*).

The wild carrot, also known as Queen Anne's–lace, or bird's–nest plant (*Daucus carota*) is a common, introduced species in North America. This is a wild variety of the cultivated carrot, but it has small, fibrous tap roots, and is not edible. The Queen Anne's–lace probably escaped into wild habitats in North America from cultivation. However, other Eurasian species in the Apiaceae appear to have been introduced through the dumping of ships' ballast. This happened when ships sailing from Europe to America carried incomplete loads of cargo, so they had to take on soil to serve as a stabilizing ballast at

KEY TERMS

. . . .

Biennial—A plant that requires at least two growing seasons to complete its life cycle.

Inflorescence—A grouping or arrangement of flowers into a composite structure.

Umbel—A flat–topped inflorescence, with flowers arranged at the end of supporting structures called pedicels, which are of roughly equal length, and originate from a single point.

Weed—Any plant that is growing abundantly in a place where humans do not want it to be.

sea. The soil ballast was usually dumped at an American port, serving as a means of entry for many species of Eurasian weeds, which had viable seeds in the material. Species of Apiaceae that are believed to have spread to North America in this way include the knotted hedge–parsley (*Torilis nodosa*), Venus'–comb or shepherd's–needle (*Scandix pecten–veneris*), and cow–parsnip (*Heracleum sphondylium*).

See also Herb.

Further Reading:

Conger, R. H. M., and G. D. Hill. *Agricultural Plants*. 2nd ed. Cambridge: Cambridge University Press, 1991.

Hartmann, H. T., et al. *Plant Science. Growth, Development, and Utilization of Cultivated Plants*. Englewood Cliffs, NJ: Prentice–Hall, 1988.

Hvass, E. *Plants That Feed and Serve Us*. New York: Hippocrene Books, 1975.

Klein, R. M. *The Green World. An Introduction to Plants and People*. New York: Harper & Row, 1987.

Woodland, D. W. *Contemporary Plant Systematics*. Englewood Cliffs, NJ: Prentice–Hall, 1991.

Bill Freedman

Carrying capacity

Carrying capacity refers to the maximum abundance of a species that can be sustained within a given area of habitat. When an ideal population is at equilibrium with the carrying capacity of its environment, the birth and death rates are equal, and size of the population does not change. Populations larger than the carrying capacity are not sustainable, and will degrade their habitat. In nature, however, neither carrying capacity or populations are ideal—both vary over time for reasons that may be complex, and in ways that may be difficult to predict. Nevertheless, the notion of carrying capacity is very useful because it highlights the ecological fact that, for all species, there are environmental limitations to the sizes of populations that can be sustained.

Carrying capacity is never static. It varies over time in response to gradual environmental changes, perhaps associated with climatic change or the successional development of ecosystems. More rapid changes in carrying capacity are caused by disturbances of the habitat occurring because of a fire or windstorm, or because of a human influence such as forest harvesting, pollution, or the introduction of an exotic competitor. Carrying capacity can also be decreased by overpopulation, which leads to exploitation and a degradation of the habitat's ability to support the species. Of course, birth and death rates of a species must respond to changes in carrying capacity along with changes in other factors, such as the intensities of disease or predation.

Carrying capacity for humans

Humans, like all organisms, can only sustain themselves and their populations through access to the products and services of their environment, including those of other species and ecosystems. However, humans are clever at developing and using technologies; as a result they have an unparalleled ability to manipulate the carrying capacity of the environment for their own activities. When prehistoric humans first discovered that crude tools and weapons allowed greater effectiveness in gathering wild foods and hunting animals, they increased their ability to exploit the resources of their environment. This increased the carrying capacity for their species, as have all subsequent improvements of agricultural systems. In recent centuries, even larger increases in carrying capacity have been achieved through discoveries in medicine and industrial technology.

Clearly, the cultural evolution of human socio-technological systems has allowed enormous increases in environmental carrying capacity to be achieved for our species. This increased effectiveness of environmental exploitation has allowed a tremendous multiplying of the human population to occur. In prehistoric times— that is, more than about 10,000 years ago—all humans were engaged in a primitive hunting and gathering lifestyle, and their global population probably amounted to several million individuals. Today, because humans have been so adept at increasing the carrying capacity of their environment, almost six billion individuals are sustained.

Humans have also increased the carrying capacity of the environment for a few other species, including those with which we live in a mutually beneficial symbiosis. Those companion species include more than about 20 billion domestic animals such as cows, horses, pigs, sheep, goats, dogs, cats, and chickens, as well as certain plants such as wheat, rice, barley, maize, tomato, and cabbage. Clearly, humans and their selected companions have benefitted greatly through active management of Earth's carrying capacity.

Of course, an enormously greater number of Earth's species have not fared as well, having been displaced or made extinct as a consequence of ecological changes associated with the use and management of the environment by humans, especially through loss of their habitat and over harvesting. In general, any increase in the carrying capacity of the environment for one species will negatively affect another species.

In addition, there are increasingly powerful indications that the intensity of environmental exploitation that is required to sustain the large populations of humans and our symbionts is causing important degradations of carrying capacity. Symptoms of this environmental deterioration include the extinction crisis, decreased soil fertility, desertification, deforestation, fishery declines, pollution, and increased competition among nations for scarce resources. Many reputable scientists believe that the sustainable limits of Earth's carrying capacity for the human enterprise may already have been exceeded. This is a worrisome circumstance, especially in the context of projections for future, large increases in the global population of humans. The degradation of Earth's carrying capacity for humans is associated with two integrated factors: (1) overpopulation and (2) intensity of resource use and pollution. In recent decades human populations have been growing most quickly in poorer countries, but the most intense lifestyles occur in the richest countries.

If it is true that the human enterprise has exceeded Earth's carrying capacity for our species, then compensatory adjustments will either have to be manmade, or they will occur naturally. Those managed or catastrophic changes will involve a combination of decreased per–capita use of environmental resources, decreased birth rates, and possibly, increased death rates.

See also Extinction; Population ecology; Sustainable development.

Further Reading:

Begon, M., J. L. Harper, and C. R. Townsend. *Ecology: Individuals, Populations and Communities.* 2nd ed. London: Blackwell Sci. Pub., 1990.

Freedman, B. *Environmental Ecology.* 2nd ed. San Diego: Academic Press, 1994.

Ricklefs, R. E. *Ecology.* New York: W.H. Freeman and Co., 1990.

Bill Freedman

Cartesian coordinate plane

The Cartesian coordinate system is named after Rene Descartes (1596–1650), the noted French mathematician and philosopher, who was among the first to describe its properties. However, historical evidence shows that Piere de Fermat (1601–1665), also a French mathematician and scholar, did more to develop the Cartesian system than did Descartes.

To best understand the nature of the Cartesian plane, it is desirable to start with the number line. Begin with line L and let L stand for a number axis (see figure 1). On L choose a point, O, and let this point designate the zero point or origin. Let the distance to the right of O be considered as positive; to the left as negative. Now choose another point, A, to the right of O on L. Let this point correspond to the number 1. We can use this distance between O and A to serve as a unit with which we can locate B, C, D, ... to correspond to the +1, +2, +3, +4, ... Now we repeat this process to the left of O on L and call the points Q, R, S, T, ... which can correspond to the numbers –1, –2, –3, –4, ... Thus the points A, B, C, D, ... , Q, R, S, T, ... correspond to the set of the integers (see figure 1). If we further subdivide the segment OA into d equal parts, the $1/d$ represents the length of each part. Also, if c is a positive integer, then c/d repre-

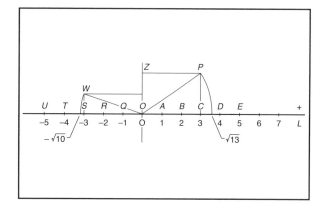

Figure 1.

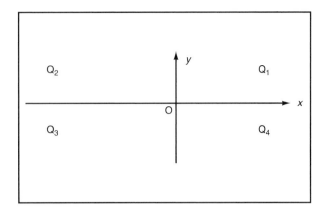

Figure 2. Cartesian Plane

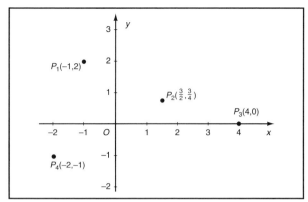

Figure 3. A plot of the points P₁(-1, 2); P₂(3/2,3/4); P₃(4,0); P₄(-2, -1).

sents the length of c of these parts. In this way we can locate points to correspond to rational numbers between 0 and 1.

By constructing rectangles with their bases on the number line we are able to find points that correspond to some irrational numbers. For example, in Figure 1, rectangle OCPZ has a base of 3 and a segment of 2. Using the Theory of Pythagorus we know that the segment OP has a length equal to $\sqrt{13}$. Similarly, the length of segment OW is $\sqrt{10}$. The real numbers have the following property: to every real number there corresponds one and only one point on the number axis; and conversely, to every point on the number axis there corresponds one and only one real number.

What happens when two number line, one horizontal and the other vertical, are introduced into the plane? In the rectangular Cartesian plane, the position of a point is determined with reference to two perpendicular line called coordinate axes. The intersection of these axes is called the origin, and the four sections into which the axis divide a given plane are called quadrants.

The vertical axis is real numbers usually referred to as the y axis or functions axis; the horizontal axis is usually known as the x axis or axis of the independent variable. The direction to the right of the y axis along the x axis is taken as positive; to the left is taken as negative. The direction above the x axis along the y axis is taken as positive; below as negative. Ordinarily, the unit of measure along the coordinate axes is the same for both axis, but sometimes it is convenient to use different measures for each axis.

The symbol P_1 (x_1, y_1) is used to denote the fixed point P_1. Here x_1 represents the x coordinate (abscissa) and is the perpendicular distance from the y axis to P_1; y_1 represents the y coordinate (ordinate) and is the perpendicular distance from the axis to P_1. In the symbol P_1 (x_1, y_1), x_1 and y_1 are real numbers. No other kind of

numbers would have meaning here. Thus, we observe that by means of a rectangular coordinate system we can show the correspondence between pairs of real numbers and points in a plane. For each pair of real numbers (x, y) there corresponds one and only one point (P), and conversely, to each point (P) there corresponds one and only pair of real numbers (x,y). We say there exists a one–to–one correspondence between the points in a plane and the pair of all real numbers.

The introduction of a rectangular coordinate system had many uses, chief of which was the concept of a graph. By the graph of an equation in two variables, say x and y, we mean the collection of all points whose coordinates satisfy the given equation. By the graph of the function f(x) we mean the graph of the equation y= f(x). To plot the graph of an equation we substitute admissible values for one variable and solve for the corresponding values of the other variable. Each such pair of values represents a point which we locate in the coordinate system. When we have located a sufficient number of such points, we join them with a smooth curve.

In general, to draw the graph of an equation we do not depend merely upon the plotted points we have at our disposal. An inspection of the equation itself yields certain properties which are useful in sketching the curve like symmetry, asymptotes, and intercepts.

Cartilage see **Connective tissues**

Cartilaginous fish

Cartilaginous fish such as sharks, skates, and rays are vertebrates whose internal skeleton is made entirely

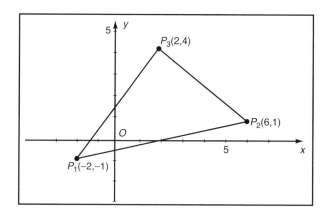

Figure 4. A graph of the triangle whose vertices are the points P_1(-2,-1), P_2(6,1), and P_3(2,4).

of cartilage and contains no ossified bone. Cartilaginous fish are also known as Chondrichthyes and have one or two dorsal fins, a caudal fin, an anal fin, and ventral fins which are supported by girdles of the internal skeleton.

Placoid scales, or dermal teeth, are characteristic of the skin of both sharks and rays. The touch of shark's skin is similar to the feel of sandpaper and was used as such for many years. The tiny teeth that protrude from the skin vary in each species of shark. The tooth tip is dentine with an overlay of dental enamel, while the lower part of the tooth is made of bone, which anchors the tooth to the skin.

The skin of rays is naked in places, that is, without dermal teeth, but on the back of or upper tail surface, the dermal teeth have developed large, strong spines.

The jaw teeth of both sharks and rays are in fact modified dermal teeth, which are lost when they become worn, and are replaced by rows of new teeth from the space behind. In some species of sharks, the jaw looks like an assembly line, with new teeth filling spaces immediately.

Both sharks and rays breathe through gills and have an opening called a spiracle on both sides of the head behind the eye. The spiracle enables the rays, which often bury in the sand, and seabed–resting sharks to take in water, pump it through the gill chamber, and release it through the gill slits without taking in large amounts of mud and sand. These fish usually take respiratory water in through the mouth, extract the oxygen from the water in the gills, and pass it out through the gill slits.

Cartilaginous fish are divided into two subclasses on the basis of gill slits and other characteristics. The first is the Elasmobranchs, which have at least five gill

slits and gills on each side, one spiracle behind each eye, dermal teeth on the upper body surface, a tooth jaw, and an upper jaw not firmly attached to the skull. Sharks (Selachii), rays, and skates (Rajiformes) belong to this group. The chimeras (Holocephali) have one gill opening on each side, tooth plates, and a skull with a firmly attached upper jaw.

Cartilaginous fish do not have swim bladders, so a swimming motion must be maintained continuously, even when sleeping, or they will sink to the bottom. The caudal fin of the shark provides the propellant force in swimming, the dorsal fin provides balance, and the pectoral fins are used for upward force and depth rudders.

The flattened body and the rear spine of the rays makes their swimming motion unique and completely different than that of sharks. The large flattened body of the rays has become fused with the pectoral fins, which produces vertical waves from front to rear, similar to that of a bird in flight.

The chimeras utilize their pectoral fins when swimming, beating these fins simultaneously for propulsion, or alternately, to change direction. This method is highly effective for this group of cartilaginous fish, but is seen most often in bony fish.

The pectoral fins in the male cartilaginous fish are also used for mating. The rear part of the pectoral fin is modified as a copulatory organ. All cartilaginous fish have internal fertilization. Some species are oviparous, or egg–layers, and some are ovoviviparous, hatching the eggs within the female and giving birth to live young. Still others may be viviparous, with the young developing in utero, similar to mammals, with the yolk sac developing into a yolk placenta providing nutrients to the embryo.

Only true rays, species of sharks which live near the sea bed, and the chimeras lay eggs. The eggs are often encased in a leathery shell with twisted tendrils which anchor the egg case to rocks or weeds. These leathery shells are known as the "mermaid's purse".

Cartilaginous fish are predatory, meaning that they feed on other animals, from zoo plankton to shellfish to whales. Cartilaginous fish themselves are sought after by humans as a food source. Shark meat, once marketed under the pseudonyms of "flake" and "steakfish" is now popular worldwide. Shark fins have long been popular in the Orient. Rays are considered delicacies in Great Britain and France, and thornback rays and flapper skates are often sold as sea trout.

F. C. Nicholson

Cartography

Cartography is the creation, production, and study of maps. It is considered a subdiscipline of geography, which is the study the of spatial distribution of various phenomena. Cartographers are often geographers who particularly enjoy the combination of art, science, and technology employed in the making and studying of maps.

Maps are studies as works of art as well as scientific documents. Many people focus on maps as tools: tourists, wildlife managers, geologists, backpackers, and city planners all use maps as tools. Cartographers, however, focus on the maps themselves. Some cartographers teach map–making skills and techniques, others design and produce maps, still others are curators of map libraries, but all focus on maps as the object of their study or livelihood.

What is a map?

A map is a generalized two–dimensional representation of the spatial distribution of one or more phenomenon. For example, a map may show the location of cities, mountain ranges, and rivers, or may show the types of rock in a given region. Maps are flat, making their production, storage, and handling relatively easy. Maps present their information to the viewer at a reduced scale. They are smaller than the area they represent, using mathematical relationships to maintain proportionally accurate geographic relationships between various phenomena. Maps show the location of selected phenomena by using symbols that are identified in a legend.

The history of cartography

References to surveying and mapping are found in ancient Egyptian and Mesopotamian writings. The oldest known map is of an area in northern Mesopotamia. The baked clay tablet, found near Nuzi, Iraq, dates from approximately 3800 B.C. Fragments of clay maps nearly 4,000 years old have been found in other parts of Mesopotamia, some showing city plans and others showing parcels of land. Over 3,000 years ago, the ancient Egyptians were surveying the lands in the Nile Valley. They drew detailed maps on papyrus to use for taxation purposes.

Chinese cartographers produced maps as early as 227 B.C. Following the invention of paper about 100 A.D., cartography flourished throughout the Chinese empire. Chinese cartography continued to have its own distinctive style until the 1500s, when it began to be influenced by European cartography.

Although Chinese cartography followed certain standards, it was not based on the same scientific principles as European cartography. The Greeks developed many of the basic principles of modern cartography, including latitude and longitude, and map projections. The maps of Ptolemy, a Greek astronomer and mathematician who lived in the first century A.D., are considered the high point of Greek cartography. Although his maps appear crude by current standards, they are amazingly accurate given the extent of geographic knowledge at the time.

Cartography came to a near–halt in Europe during the medieval period, when maps were little more than imaginative illustrations for theological texts. In Moslem countries, however, the science of cartography continued to grow, and various techniques were refined or improved by Arabic cartographers. Their knowledge and skills were introduced into Europe during the Renaissance.

The eras of exploration that followed the Renaissance supplied cartographers with a wealth of new information, which allowed them to produce maps and navigation charts of ever–increasing accuracy and detail. Europeans became fascinated with the idea of mapping the world. The French initiated the first national topographic survey during the 1700s, and soon other European countries followed suit. Today, most countries have an official organization devoted to cartographic research and production.

Types of maps

There are many different types of maps. So many, in fact, that it can be very difficult to classify them into groups. A common classification system divides maps into two categories, general and thematic. General maps are maps that show spatial relationships between a variety of geographic features and phenomena, emphasizing their location relative to one another. Thematic maps illustrate the spatial variations of a single phenomenon, or the spatial relationship between two particular phenomena, emphasizing the pattern of the distribution.

Many maps can be either general or thematic, depending on the intent of the cartographer. For example, a cartographer may produce a vegetation map, one that shows the distribution of various plant communities. If the cartographer shows the location of various plant communities in relation to a number of other geographic features, the map is properly considered a general map. The map is more likely to be considered thematic if the cartographer uses it to focus on something about the relationship of the plant communities to each other, or to another particular phenomenon or feature, such as the differences in plant communities associated with changes in elevation or changes in soil type.

Some examples of general maps include large–scale and medium–scale topographic maps, planometric maps, and charts. Topographic maps show all important physical and cultural features, including relief. Relief is the difference in elevation of various parts of the Earth's surface. Planometric maps are similar to topographic maps, but omit changes in elevation. Charts are used by the navigators of aircraft and seagoing vessels to establish bearings and plot positions and courses. World maps on a small– or medium–scale showing physical and cultural features, such as those in atlases, are also considered general maps.

Although the subject matter of thematic maps is nearly infinite, cartographers use common techniques involving points, lines, and aerial units to illustrate the structure of spatial distribution. Isarithmic maps use lines to connect points of equal value; these lines are called isopleths, or isolines. Isopleths used for a particular phenomenon may have a particular name; for example, isotherms connect points of equal temperature, isobars connect points of equal air pressure, and isohyets connect points of equal precipitation. Isopleths indicating differences in elevation are called contour lines. Isopleths are used to show how certain quantities change with location.

A topographic map is a good example of how isopleths are used to present information. Topographic maps use isopleths called contour lines to indicate variations in relief. Each contour line connects points of the same elevation. Adjacent lines indicate variations in relief; these variations are called contour intervals. The contour interval is indicated in the map legend. A contour interval of 20 ft (6.1 m) means that there is a 20 ft (6.1 m) difference in elevation between the points connected by one contour line and the points connected by the adjacent contour line. The closer the lines are to each other, the more dramatic the change in elevation.

Chloropleth maps are another type of thematic map. They use areas of graduated gray tones or a series of gradually intensifying colors to show spatial variations in the magnitude of a phenomenon. Greater magnitudes are symbolized by either darker gray tones or more intense colors; lesser magnitudes are indicated by lighter gray tones or less intense colors.

Geographic illustrations

There are many portrayals of geographic relationships which do not qualify as maps as we have defined them. Throughout human history, people have been illustrating geographic relationships between various elements of the physical and cultural environment. These geographic illustrations and representations are often very beautiful, and can serve as keys to understanding the world view of the culture that produced them. Some are extremely accurate in their representation of geographic relationships. Most geographic illustrations, however, are not considered true maps by modern cartographers because they do not use a scale based on distance. The development of the tools and techniques for accurately measuring distance requires a particular technical and scientific world view not shared by all cultures.

Many geographic illustrations or representations do not have a scale. Those that do, usually have a scale based on traveling times. Traveling times for the same distance can vary depending on the nature of the terrain, weather conditions, or other variables. For example, a four–mile journey across rugged mountains in a snow storm and a 12–mile journey across a relatively smooth plain on a pleasant spring day may both take eight hours. A geographic illustration using a time–based scale would show two equal intervals; a distance–based scale would show the twelve–mile journey as three times longer than the rugged four–mile trek. Clearly, for a nomadic or migratory society, a geographic representation with a scale based on traveling times would be extremely useful, whereas one with a scale based on a distance would be of little or no use.

Map making

Cartographers traditionally obtained their information from navigators and surveyors. Explorations that expanded the geographical awareness of a map–making culture also resulted in increasingly sophisticated and accurate maps. Today, cartographers incorporate information from aerial photography and satellite imagery in the maps they create.

Modern cartographers face three major design challenges when creating a map. First, they must decide how to accurately portray that portion of the Earth's surface that the map will represent; that is, they must figure out how to represent three dimensional objects in two dimensions. Second, cartographers must represent geographic relationships at a reduced size while maintaining their proportional relationships. Third, they must select which pieces of information will be included in the map, and develop a system of generalization, which will make the information presented by the map useful and accessible to its readers.

Showing three–dimensional relationships in two dimensions

When creating a flat map of a portion of the Earth's surface, cartographers first locate their specific area of interest using latitude and longitude. They then use map projection techniques to represent the three dimensional characteristics of that area in two dimensions. Finally, a grid, called a rectangular coordinate system, may be superimposed on the map, making it easier to use.

LATITUDE AND LONGITUDE

Distance and direction are used to describe the position of something in space, its location. In conversation, terms like right and left, up and down, or here and there are used to indicate direction and distance. These terms are useful only if you know the location of the speaker; in other words, they are relative. Cartographers, however, need objective terms for describing location, because maps are intended for use by many individuals in many different situations. The system of latitude and longitude, a geographical coordinate system developed by the Greeks, is used by cartographers for describing location.

The Earth is a sphere, rotating around an axis tilted approximately 23.5 degrees off the perpendicular. The two points where the axis intersects the Earth's surface are called the poles. The equator is an imaginary circle drawn around the center of the Earth, equidistant from both poles. A plane that sliced through the Earth at the equator would intersect the axis of the Earth at a right angle. Lines drawn around the Earth to the north and south of the equator and at right angles to the Earth's axis are called parallels. Any point on the Earth's surface is located on a parallel.

An arc is established when an angle is drawn from the equator to the axis and then north or south to a parallel. Latitude is the measurement of this arc in degrees. There are 90 degrees from the equator to each pole, and sixty minutes in each degree. Latitude is used to determine distance and direction north and south of the equator.

Meridians are lines running from the north pole to the south pole, dividing the Earth's surface into sections, like those of an orange. Meridians intersect parallels at right angles, creating a grid. Just as the equator acts as the line from which to measure north or south, a particular meridian, called the prime meridian, acts as the line from which to measure east or west. There is no meridian that has a natural basis for being considered the prime meridian. The prime meridian is established by international agreement; currently, it runs through the Royal Observatory in Greenwich, England. Longitude is the measurement in degrees of the arc created by an angle drawn from the prime meridian to the Earth's axis and then east or west to a meridian. There are 180 degrees west of the prime meridian and 180 degrees east of it. The international dateline lies approximately where the 180th meridian passes through the Pacific Ocean.

Using the geographical coordinate system of latitude and longitude, any point on the Earth's surface can be located with precision. For example, Buenos Aires, the capital of Argentina, is located 34 degrees 35 minutes south of the equator and 58 degrees 22 minutes west of the prime meridian; Anchorage, the capital of the state of Alaska, is located 61 degrees 10 minutes north of the equator and 149 degrees 45 minutes west of the prime meridian.

MAP PROJECTIONS

After locating their area of interest using latitude and longitude, cartographers must determine how best to represent that particular portion of the Earth's surface in two dimensions. They must do this in such a way that minimal amounts of distortion affect the geographic information the map is designed to convey.

In order to understand the difficulty of such a task, imagine an orange with lines similar to parallels and meridians inked onto its surface. Now imagine removing the peel from the orange in one piece. If the peel of an orange is laid out flat on a tabletop, the peel will crack and break in various places. The cracks and breaks will distort the original shape of the orange, and the inked lines will no longer bear the same spatial relationship to each other as they did when the peel was on the orange. If the peel is arranged so that there are no cracks, breaks, or distortions in the relationships between the lines on its surface, the peel will assume the shape of a hollow sphere. There are only two choices: a spherical, distortion–free arrangement or a flat, distorted arrangement.

Cartographers have developed map projections as a means for translating geographic information from a spherical surface onto a planar surface. A map projection is a method for representing a curved surface, such as the surface of the Earth, on a flat surface, such as a piece of paper, so that each point on the curved surface corresponds to only one point on the flat surface.

There are many types of map projections. Some of them are based on geometry, others are based on mathematical formulas. None of them, however, can accurately represent all aspects of the Earth's surface; inevitably there will be some distortion in shape, distance, direction or area. Each type of map projection is intended to reduce the distortion of a particular spatial element. Some projections reduce directional distortion, others try to present shapes or areas in as distortion–free a manner as possible. The cartographer must decide which of the many projections available will provide the most distortion–free presentation of the information to be mapped.

RECTANGULAR COORDINATES

Although the geographical coordinate system is useful for large areas, it can be awkward to use for small areas. Many city maps use rectangular coordinate systems. After the map is complete, a grid is superimposed over it. The horizontal lines of the grid are assigned one set of numbers or letters, the vertical lines are assigned another set of numbers or letters. An index of place names is generated, which lists the horizontal and vertical coordinates for each place shown on the map. Used in conjunction with an index of place names, the rectangular coordinate system makes it simple for map readers to locate particular places.

Reducing size while maintaining accurate proportions

Maps present various pieces of geographical information at a reduced scale. In order for the information to be useful to the map reader, the relative proportions of geographic features and spatial relationships must be kept as accurate as possible. Cartographers use various types of scales to keep those features and relationships in the correct proportion.

Scale is the mathematical relationship between a distance between two points on the map and the distance between two corresponding points on the ground. The relationship is expressed as a ratio, the first number being the distance between two points on the map and the second number being the actual distance represented. The number indicating map distance is always one. Thus, a map with a scale of 1:125,000 tells the map reader that every unit of distance on the maps equals 125,000 of the same units of distance on the ground. The units of distance used are not important as long as they are the same on both sides of the ratio. One centimeter on the map would equal 125,000 centimeters on the ground, one foot on the map would equal 125,000 feet on the ground, and one meter on the map would equal 125,000 meters on the ground.

Maps showing a large area are called "small–scale maps." This is because the ratio between map distance and actual distance is a small number. The number is small because one distance unit on the map represents a large number of distance units on the ground. For exam-

ple, a map showing North America at a scale of 1:40,000,000 shows the map reader one unit of distance on the map for every 40,000,000 units of actual distance. One centimeter on this maps equals 40 kilometers of actual distance, one inch on this map equals 631 miles. Such a map fits on a piece of paper only 23 cm by 21 cm (9 inches wide and 8.25 inches high).

Maps showing a small area are called "large–scale maps." The ratio between map distance and actual distance is a large number. It is large because each unit of distance on the map represents a relatively small number of distance units on the ground. City maps are good example of large–scale maps. A city map of Portland, Oregon with a scale of 1:38,000 fits on a piece of paper 106.5 cm by 90 cm (41.75 inches by 35.5 inches). One centimeter on this map equals .38 kilometers of actual distance, and one inch equals six tenths of a mile.

Every map has a statement of its scale, which is an expression of the ratio between map distance and actual distance. This statement can take many forms, and many maps express scale in more than one way. The scale may be indicated by a ratio, such as 1:100,000 or 1/100,000 (the latter is less common). This ratio is called the representative fraction. Representative fractions are not particularly easy to use in everyday situations, so cartographers have developed other ways to communicate the scale of a map to its users.

Sometimes cartographers use a graphic scale, also called a bar scale. A graphic scale is a line or bar subdivided to show how many actual miles fit into a particular measurement on the map. In most parts of the world the graphic scale shows how many actual miles or kilometers are represented by a particular number of inches or centimeters on the map.

Two other means for expressing scale are the area scale and the verbal statement. Area scales are used for maps based on equal–area projections, that is, maps that present all areas shown in the same proportion to one another as they occur on the Earth's surface. These scales tell the reader that one unit of area on the map represents a certain number of areal units on the ground. The scale can be written $1:250,000^2$, although 1:250,000 is more common. The latter expression assumes the reader is aware that the number represents a ratio of square units. A verbal statement of scale uses words, rather than numbers or graphic symbols. "1 inch equals 1 mile" is a verbal statement of scale equivalent to the representative fraction 1:63,360 (there are 63,360 inches in one mile).

Presenting geographic information effectively

No single map can accurately show every feature on the Earth's surface. There is simply too much spatial information at any particular point on the Earth's surface for all of the information to be presented in a comprehensible, usable format. In addition, the process of reduction has certain visual effects on geographic features and spatial relationships. Because every feature is reduced by the ratio of the reduction, the distance between features is reduced, crowding them closer together and lessening the clarity of the image. The width and length of individual features are also reduced.

When designing a map, cartographers strive for clarity and effective communication. In order to achieve this goal, cartographers use the technique of selection to determine which pieces of information to include in a map, and the techniques of cartographic generalization to overcome the difficulties presented by reduction.

A wide array of geographical information is available to mapmakers. When preparing a map, cartographers must choose only those pieces of information that are pertinent to the purpose of the map and then display those pieces of information in a way that effectively communicates their significance. Only information deemed significant or useful is selected for inclusion in the map.

Once cartographers have selected the information that will be portrayed on the map, the information must be displayed in an effective manner. Cartographers deal with this problem by applying the techniques of cartographic generalization. Both map geometry and map content are generalized.

Geometric generalization techniques change the placement and appearance of various map features in order to make the map easier to interpret and more pleasing to the eye. For example, not every twist and turn of a 15 mile stretch of river can be accurately portrayed at a 1:500,000 scale, where one inch equals 7.89 miles. The path of the river is simplified, reducing excessive detail and angularity. A railroad running 50 feet from the river would appear to run in the riverbed when shown at a 1:500,000 scale. Using cartographic generalization, the cartographer displaces the railroad, showing it next to the river, avoiding graphic interference and increasing the readability of the map. The numerous right–angle bends in a highway following rural property boundaries along the river would be smoothed by the cartographer, reducing their angularity and thereby making the line of the highway easier for the eye to follow. Although many of the river's smaller curves were initially simplified, the cartographer may

enhance its form, adding typical meander loops to increase map readability and to make the map more aesthetically pleasing.

Linear and areal features can be generalized using the techniques of simplification, displacement, smoothing, and enhancement. Additionally, the techniques of dissolution, segmentation, and aggregation are applied to areal features. Point features are generalized by displacement, graphic association, and abbreviation.

Map content is generalized using the technique of classification, in which similar features to be grouped together are represented by a single symbol. Campgrounds, for example, are often represented by a tent–shaped symbol, even when the facilities can accommodate trailers or large recreational vehicles. Categorization is another form of classification. Many maps use one point symbol for population centers of 1,000–10,000, another point symbol for population centers of more than 10,000 but less than 100,000, yet another point symbol for population centers of more than 100,000 but less than 500,000, and so on. Cartographers must carefully consider the implications of such classification schemes; this one implies that towns of 1,000 and towns of 9,000 have more in common than towns of 9,500 and towns of 10,500.

Cartographic production

For many centuries maps were produced entirely by hand. They were drawn or painted on paper, hide, parchment, clay tablets, and slabs of wood, among other things. Each map was an original work; the content may have been copied, but each map was executed by hand.

Once printing techniques were developed, many reproductions could be made from one original map. Chinese printmakers were producing maps on hand-made paper using wood block printing techniques over 1,800 years ago. The Europeans developed the printing press and movable type in the 1400s, and maps became more common and more accessible. The paper they were printed on was still handmade, however, and any colored areas on the map had to be painted by hand.

The introduction of the lithographic printing method in the late 1800s allowed multi–colored maps to be produced by machine. Various photographic techniques were integrated into the printing process during the last 200 years, increasing the variety of scales at which maps were produced. Despite these production advances, each original map was still drawn by cartographers, using technical pens, various lettering devices, straight edges and razor knives, the traditional tools of the trade.

During the last two decades, however, the cartographer has acquired another production tool, the computer. Advanced computer–assisted design programs allow cartographers to set aside their technical pens and their straight edges. They use the computer to conjure and produce map images, but computer–assisted design programs cannot replace cartographers. The various techniques for cartographic expression involve a sense of craft and artistry that has not yet been duplicated by electronic means.

Further Reading:

Greenhood, D. *Mapping*. Chicago: University of Chicago Press, 1964.

Hall, S. *Mapping the Next Millenium*. New York: Random House, 1992.

Harley, J. B., and D. Woodward, eds. *History of Cartography*. 6 vols. Chicago: University of Chicago Press, 1987.

Lobeck, A. K. *Things Maps Don't Tell Us: an Adventure into Map Interpretation*. Chicago: University of Chicago Press, 1984.

Monmonier, M. *How to Lie with Maps*. Chicago: University of Chicago Press, 1991.

Robinson, A., R. Sale, J. Morrison, and P. C. Muehrcke. *Elements of Cartography*. New York: John Wiley, 1994.

Turnbull, D. *Maps are Territories*. Chicago: University of Chicago Press, 1989.

Karen Lewotsky

Cashew family (Anacardiaceae)

The cashew family (Anacardiaceae) is a group of about 600 species of plants, most of which are tropical in distribution, although some occur in the temperate zone.

Almost all members of the cashew family are trees or shrubs, though some are vines. Many species have foliage, fruits or bark on the stems and roots that contain acrid, an often milky resin, and saps that are irritating or poisonous if touched or eaten. The leaves are typically compound, with at least three if not more leaflets per leaf. The flowers are small, five–parted, insect pollinated, and arranged in compact inflorescences. The fruits are either a one–seeded drupe or a many–seeded berry, and are generally eaten and dispersed by birds or small mammals.

The fruits of some species in the cashew family are an important source of food for people, while other species are used in horticulture. Many species are considered to be important weeds because they are poisonous, often causing a severe dermatitis (rash) in exposed people.

Edible species of the cashew family

Various nuts and other fruits are obtained from species in the cashew family.

The cashew (*Anacardium occidentale*) is the source of kidney–shaped cashew nuts. The cashew was originally from northeastern South America, but it is now planted widely throughout the humid tropics. The seedcoat of the fruit contains a toxic oil, and the raw cashew nut is also poisonous if eaten by people. However, the toxic chemical can be neutralized by roasting, and this richly delicious nut can be eaten safely.

Maturing pistachio (*Pistacia vera*) nuts on a tree in California.

Poison ivy growing on a tree trunk.

The pistachio or green almond (*Pistacia vera*) is native to Syria, but is now widely cultivated in the Mediterranean region, the southern United States, and elsewhere. These fruits are prepared for eating by roasting and are usually salted by a brief soaking in a brine solution. The natural color of the pistachio's shell is white, but they are sometimes dyed red to make them more attractive to consumers.

The mango (*Mangifera indica*) is an evergreen tropical tree that grows up to 98 ft (30 m) and is native to southern Asia. Its fruit is known as a mango, possessing a yellow–red skin with a large, flat seed surrounded by a tasty, juicy pulp, which can be yellow, red, or orange in color. However, there are numerous cultivated varieties of mangos varying greatly in the size, shape, and color of their fruits. The flavor of the mango is an exotic blend of sweet and acidic tartness, with an aromatic undercurrent. Mangos are an ancient, cultivated fruit, having been grown in tropical Asia for as many as 6,000 years, and achieving sacred status in some Indian cultures. Most mangos are eaten as a fresh fruit, but this food is also used to prepare sauces, jams, and chutney.

Other, less–well known tropical fruits in the cashew family include the ogplum, Jamaica plum, Otaheite apple (obtained from species of *Spondias*) and the kaffir plum (*Harpephyllum caffrum*) of southern Africa.

Other useful species

The lacquer tree (*Rhus verniciflua*) occurs in China and Japan, where the viscous, milky sap of this plant has long been collected and applied as a natural varnish to fine wood carvings and furniture. The sap turns dark after oxidation in the atmosphere, providing an attractive, glossy coating to oriental lacquerware. A lacquer finish is resistant to heat, moisture, acid, alkali, and alcohol, and is therefore an excellent protection for fine works of art. Lacquering is an old art form, although it reached its greatest expression in China during the Ming Dynasty of 1368–1644 and in Japan during the seventeenth century. The finest pieces of lacquerware received as many as hundreds of individual coatings, applied over a period of several years. Other minor sources of lacquer are the Burmese lacquer tree (*Melanorrhoea usitata*) and an Indonesian sumac (*Rhus succedanea*).

The leaves of some species in the cashew family are dried and processed as a source of tannins, chemicals that are useful for preparing leather. The Sicilian sumac (*Rhus coriaria*) of southern Italy is especially useful, as its leaves can have a tannin concentration of 20–35%. This species is actually cultivated as a source of tannins, and it produces a superior, soft leather with a pale color, considered especially useful for fine gloves and book–covers. The red quebracho (*Schinopsis lorentzii*) of South American temperate forests is another important source of tannins, which are obtained from the wood of this tree. The dried leaves of native sumacs (*Rhus* spp.) of North America have also been used as a minor source of tannins.

Chios mastic is a type of resin derived from the dried sap of *Pistacia lentiscus* of the Mediterranean region, while Bombay mastic is obtained from *P. cabulica* of southern Asia. These materials are used to manufacture a clear, high–grade varnish, which is sometimes used to coat metallic art and pictures, and in lithography.

The terebinth tree (*Pistacia terebinthus*) was the original source of artists' turpentine, but this solvent is now more commonly distilled from other types of trees. Another minor product is a yellow dye obtained from the twigs of the tropical South American tree, *Cotinus cuggygroa.*

702

Ornamental species

Various species of sumac are grown as ornamentals. The staghorn sumac (*Rhus typhina*) is cultivated for its attractive, purple–red foliage in the autumn and the interesting, reddish, horn–shaped fruiting inflorescences of female plants. This species is dioecious, meaning individual plants only bear female flowers (pistillate), or male flowers (staminate). The fragrant sumac (*R. aromatica*) is also commonly grown in horticulture.

The South American pepper–tree (*Schinus molle*) is also grown as an ornamental shrub. So are the smoke trees, *Cotinus obovatus* of North America, and the introduced *C. coggygria*, with their diffuse and fuzzy, smoke–like inflorescences, and attractive, purplish foliage in autumn.

Wild species occurring in North America

Various species in the cashew family are native to North America. One of the more familiar groups includes species of vines and shrubs in the genus *Toxicodendron*, many of which contain a toxic oil that causes a contact dermatitis in people exposed to crushed foliage, stems, or roots. It appears that some people develop an increased sensitivity to this toxic oil with increased exposure. Many people appear to not have been initially affected by contact with poison ivy and its relatives, but subsequent exposures then elicited sensitive responses. In contrast, others appear to progressively obtain an immunity to the toxic oil of these plants. Especially severe poisoning can be caused if smoke from the burning of *Toxicodendron* biomass is inadvertently inhaled—human deaths have been caused by this type of exposure resulting from severe blistering of the pharynx and lungs. The most widespread species is known as poison ivy (*T. radicans*, sometimes known as *Rhus radicans*), a plant with distinctive, shiny, compound leaves with three leaflets, and shiny, white berries. Poison ivy can grow as a perennial ground cover or as a vine that grows up trees. Other toxic species include poison oak (*T. toxicodendron*) and poison or swamp sumac (*T. vernix*), both of which are shrubs. The Florida poison tree or poisonwood (*Metopium toxiferum*) grows in southern Florida.

Various species of sumac (*Rhus* spp.) occur as shrubs in North America. One of the more familiar species is the staghorn sumac (*Rhus typhina*), the fruits of which are sometimes collected and used to prepare a lemonade–like drink. Other widespread species are the shining or mountain sumac (*Rhus copallina*), smooth or scarlet sumac (*R. glabra*), fragrant sumac (*R. aromatica*), and ill–scented sumac or skunkbush (*R. trilobata*).

KEY TERMS

Inflorescence—A grouping or arrangement of flowers into a composite structure.

Tannin—Chemicals that can be extracted from certain plants, and used to prepare leather from raw animal skins.

Weed—Any plant that is growing abundantly in a place where humans do not want it to be.

The wild smoke–tree (*Cotinus obovatus*) occurs in the southeastern United States and is sometimes grown as an ornamental shrub.

See also Poisons and toxins.

Further Reading:

Conger, R. H. M., and G. D. Hill. *Agricultural Plants*. 2nd ed. Cambridge: Cambridge University Press, 1991.

Hartmann, H. T., et al. *Plant Science. Growth, Development, and Utilization of Cultivated Plants*. Englewood Cliffs, NJ: Prentice–Hall, 1988.

Hill, A. F. *Economic Botany. A Textbook of Useful Plants and Plant Products*. New York: McGraw–Hill, 1937.

Jones, S. B., and A. E. Luchsinger. *Plant Systematics*. New York: McGraw–Hill, 1979.

Kostermans, A. J. G. H., and J. M. Bompard. *The Mangoes. Their Botany, Nomenclature, Horticulture, and Utilization*. London: Academic Press, 1993.

Woodland, D. W. *Contemporary Plant Systematics*. Englewood Cliffs, NJ: Prentice–Hall, 1991.

Bill Freedman

Catabolism

Catabolism is the breakdown of large molecules into small molecules. Its opposite process is anabolism, the combination of small molecules into large molecules. These two cellular chemical reactions are together called metabolism. Cells use anabolic reactions to synthesize enzymes, hormones, sugars, and other molecules needed to sustain themselves, grow and reproduce.

Energy released from organic nutrients during catabolism is stored within the molecule adenosine triphosphate (ATP), in the form of the high–energy chemical bonds between the second and third molecules of phosphate. The cell uses ATP for synthesizing cell components from simple precursors, for the mechanical work of contraction and motion, and for transport of substances across its membrane. ATP's energy is released when this bond is broken, turning ATP into adenosine diphosphate (ADP).

The cell uses the energy derived from catabolism to fuel anabolic reactions that synthesize cell components.

Although anabolism and catabolism occur simultaneously in the cell, their rates are controlled independently of each other. Cells separate these pathways because catabolism is a so–called "downhill" process during which energy is released, while anabolism is an energetically "uphill" process which requires the input of energy.

The different pathways also permit the cell to control the anabolic and catabolic pathways of specific molecules independently of each other. Moreover, some opposing anabolic and catabolic pathways occur in different parts of the same cell. For example, in the liver, the fatty acids are broken down to acetyl CoA inside mitochondria, while fatty acids are synthesized from acetyl CoA in the cytoplasm of the cell.

Both catabolism and anabolism share an important common sequence of reactions known collectively as the citric acid cycle, or Krebs cycle, which is part of a larger series of enzymatic reactions known as oxidative phosphorylation. Here, glucose is broken down to release energy, which is stored in the form of ATP (catabolism), while other molecules produced by the Krebs cycle are used as precursor molecules for anabolic reactions that build proteins, fats, and carbohydrates (anabolism).

Cells regulate the rate of catabolic pathways by means of allosteric enzymes, whose activity increases or decreases in response to the presence or absence of the end product of the series of reactions. For example, during the Krebs cycle, the activity of the enzyme citrate synthase is slowed by the buildup of succinyl CoA, a product formed later in the cycle.

See also Adenosine diphosphate; Adenosine triphosphate; Anabolism; Krebs cycle; Metabolism.

Further Reading:

Alberts, Bruce, et al. *Molecular Biology of The Cell.* 2nd ed. New York: Garland Publishing, 1989.

Lehninger, Albert L. *Principles of Biochemistry.* New York: Worth Publishers, 1982.

Catalyst and catalysis

Humans used the process known as catalysis long before, they understood what took place in that process.For example, soap–making, the fermentation of wine to vinegar, and the leavening of bread are all processes that involve catalysis. Ordinary people were using these procedures in their everyday lives without knowing that catalysis was involved.

The term catalysis was proposed in 1835 by the Swedish chemist Jons Berzelius. The term comes from the Greek words for down—*kata* and loosen—*lyein*. Berzelius explained that he meant by the term catalysis the property of exerting on other bodies an action which is very different from chemical affinity. By means of this action, they produce decomposition in bodies, and form new compounds into the composition of which they do not enter.

One of the examples of catalysis familiar to Berzelius was the conversion of starch to sugar in the presence of strong acids. In 1812, the Russian chemist Gottlieb Sigismund Constantin Kirchhof had studied this reaction. He found that when a water suspension of starch is boiled, no change occurs in the starch.

However, when a few drops of concentrated sulfuric acid are added to the same suspension before boiling, the starch breaks down into a simple sugar called glucose. The acid can be recovered unchanged from the reaction. Kirchhof concluded that it had played a helping role in the breakdown of the starch, without itself having undergone any change.

Berzelius had been able to draw on many other examples of catalysis. For example, both Humphry Davy and Johann Dîbereiner had studied the effect of platinum metal on certain organic reactions. They had concluded that the metal increased the rate at which these reactions occurred without undergoing any change itself. Davy's most famous protégé, Michael Faraday, also demonstrated the ability of platinum to bring about the recombination of hydrogen and oxygen that had been obtained by the electorlysis of water.

When Berzelius first defined catalysis, he had in mind some kind of power or force by which an agent (the catalyst) acted on a reaction. He imagined, for example, that platinum might exert an electrical force on gases with which it came into contact in order to bring about a change in reaction rates.

This kind of explanation works well for heterogeneous catalysis, in which the catalyst and the reaction are in different phases. In a platinum catalyzed reaction, for example the platinum is in a solid state and the reaction in a gaseous or liquid state.

Homogeneous catalysis, in which catalyst and reaction are in the same state, requires a different explanation. How does sulfuric acid in the liquid state, for example, bring about the conversion of a starch suspension with which it is intermixed?

The solution to this problem came in the early 1850s. Alexander William Williamson was carrying out research on the preparation of ethers from alcohols. Chemists knew that concentrated sulfuric acid was an effective catalyst for this reaction, but they did not know why. Williamson was able to demonstrate that the catalyst does break down in the first stage of this reaction, but is regenerated in its original form at the conclusion of the reaction.

The role of catalysts in living systems was first recognized in 1833. Anselme Payen and Jean Franáois Persoz isolated a material from malt that accelerated the conversion of starch to sugar. Payen called the substance diastase. A half century later, the German physiologist, Willy Kåhne, suggested the name enzyme for catalysts that occur in living systems.

Toward the end of the nineteenth century, catalysts rapidly became important in a variety of industrial applications. The synthesis of indigo became a commercial possibility in 1897 when mercury was accidentally found to catalyze the reaction by which indigo was produced. Catalysis also made possible the commercial production of ammonia from its elements (the Haber-Bosch process), of nitric acid from ammonia (the Ostwald process) and of sulfuric acid from sulfur oxides (the contact process).

See also Reaction, chemical.

Cataracts see **Vision disorders**

Catastrophism

Catastrophism is the belief that the Earth's features—including mountains, valleys, and lakes—are created suddenly rather than over a long period of time.

For example, the following are examples of how a catastrophist might interpret the origins of several well known landscapes. Upon observing the Rocky Mountains or the Alps, a catastrophist might think a huge earthquake lifted them quickly. When viewing the Yosemite Valley in California a catastrophist might not believe they were carved by glaciers, but rather the floor of the valley collapsed over a 1,000 ft (305 m) to its present position in one giant plunge. A catastrophist might think that a monstrous flood deposited the oceanic rock on top of Mt. Everest. In addition, a catastrophist would tend to believe that eons of inactivity follow such catastrophic events.

In terms of today's knowledge of Earth sciences, those explanations are difficult to accept. But catastrophism developed in the seventeenth and eighteenth centuries when, by tradition and even by law, scientists used the Bible as a scientific document.

When a prominent theologian, Bishop Ussher in the mid–1600's, counted the ages of people in the Bible and proclaimed that the Earth was created in 4004 B.C. (on the evening of October 22), geologists tried to work within a time frame that encompassed only around six thousand years. (Current research estimates the Earth at 4.5 billion years old.) Therefore, fossils of ocean–dwelling organisms discovered on mountain tops resulted from Noah's Flood. Receding flood waters carved valleys, pooled in lakes, and deposited huge boulders far from their sources. Even Georges Cuvier, the world–famous French anatomist of the early 1800's, announced that fossilized organisms became extinct in a series of big floods followed by new Genesis–style creations—flood, creation, flood, creation, and so on—with the latest flood being Noah's. Each flood not only killed the organisms but also deposited the large amount of sediment that solidified into the rock surrounding the fossils.

In its original form, catastrophism eventually fell from grace with the scientific community as they reasoned more logical explanations for natural history. A new concept, known as uniformitarianism, eventually replaced catastrophism. Uniformitarianism is the belief that mountains are uplifted, valleys carved, and sediments deposited over immense time periods by many kinds of forces.

However, catastrophism has made a slight comeback since the late 1970's with the theory that large objects from space periodically collide with the Earth, extinguishing life. Scientists speculate that when these objects strike, they clog the atmosphere with sunlight–blocking dust and gases, ignite forest fires, and trigger volcanism. There is a theory that holds that the most famous of these collisions killed off the dinosaurs roughly 65 million years ago. If a cosmic bombardment occurs again within the next million years, as some scientists suggest will happen, then eventually a majority of life on Earth will again vanish in a cloud of dust.

See also Uniformitarianism

Catbirds see **Mockingbirds and thrashers**

Catfish

Catfish include some 2500 species of fish characterized by two to four pairs of whiskers or barbels around the water. Many species of catfish have spines on the dorsal fins and near the gills. In some species these spines may contain poison.

Catfish belong to the bony fish order Siluriformes, and are mainly freshwater forms with representatives throughout the world. Most species of catfish lack scales although some species are covered with heavy scales or armor. Catfish tend to be very hardy and some can adapt to living out of water as long as their skin is kept moist by a layer of mucus.

A few species of the catfish live in the oceans, such as the sea catfishes of the family Aridae which are found in tropical and subtropical seas, and in temperate waters during the summer. Catfish vary in size from the pygmy corydoras (*Corydoras hastatus*), about 0.8 in long (5 mm), to *Pangasianodon giga* from southeastern Asia which exceeds 7 ft (2.3 m) and may weigh 250 lbs (125 kg). This group includes the aquarium fish *Physailla pellucida*, the glass catfish.

North American freshwater catfish are found from Canada to Guatemala. They are often caught by rod and reel, have considerable commercial importance, and are raised on fish farms. Catfish live in murky lakes and ponds, feeding on the bottom on both live and dead material. Catfish spawn around May and June. The parents prepare a nest in the mud or sand. After the eggs hatch the parents guard the nest and protect the young until they have developed enough to become independent.

Probably the most numerous North American catfish are the bullheads: the black bullhead (*Ictalurus melas*), the brown bullhead (*I. nebulosus*), and the yellow bullhead (*I. natali*).

Bullheads are plentiful in streams and ponds of North America from the Atlantic to the Pacific Oceans.

Bullheads were introduced to the west from the east, spreading naturally. Adhesive bullhead eggs sticking to the legs and feet of the wading birds wash off when the birds waded in another pond, thus establishing a new population of bullheads.

Rivalling the bullheads in commercial importance in some areas is the channel catfish (*I. punctatus*), the blue catfish (*I. punctatus*), the blue catfish (*I. furcatus*), the white catfish (*I. catus*), and flathead catfish (*Pylodictus olivaris*). These other species may reach 150 lbs (75 kg) while the channel catfish may weigh about 30 lbs (15 kg), although it averages under 5 lbs (2.5 kg).

The diet of the ictalurids is varied since they eat almost anything—dead or alive. Catfisherman use "stink bait," where the stinkier preparations are more effective in luring the fish. Such bait would be adequate to lure catfishes over a wide expanse. Catfish can detect this bait from great distances because most catfish have sense organs over an extensive surface of their body, and in their long sensory barbels.

Included in the North American catfish family are the madtoms in the genus *Noturus*, which are small fish under 5 in (2 cm) in length. Madtoms have glands associated with spines which can inflict extremely painful stab wounds.

The Eurasian catfish family Siluridae includes the wels (*Siluris glanis*) which grows over 12 ft (4 m) long and weighs hundreds of pounds. At the other extreme in this family is the glass catfish (*Kryptopterus bicirrhus*) from southeastern Asia which is only 4 in (10 cm). The skin of the glass catfish is transparent enough to display the viscera, rainbow colors.

The catfish family Clariidae includes labyrinthic fishes which have evolved a special air–breathing apparatus found anterior to the gills which is equipped with numerous blood vessels. These catfish can stay out of water for an extended period of time as long as their skin is kept moist with mucus. Air–breathing catfish can live in low–oxygen or stagnant water which would kill other species of fish.

The walking catfish (*Clarius batrachus*), from southeast Asia walks on dry land by performing snake-like movements with their pectoral fins as legs. In times of severe drought these catfish can move to ponds containing water, or they may dig into the bottom of a pool and wait there for the return of the rains.

The talking catfish (*Acanthodoras spinosissimus*, family Doradidae) makes a croaking sound, especially when captured. These sounds result from air forced in and out of the swim bladder due to changes in pressure when the pectoral fins flap.

In Africa, electric catfish (*Malapterurus electicus*, family Malapteruridae) range in size from 8 in (20 cm) to 4 ft (1.2 m) and reach a size of 50 lb (23 kg). These can produce a 100 volt shock followed by lesser shocks which stun large fish. In addition to predation and defense, electrical impulses are used to navigate in turbid water. The electric organs are found along the body and tail, and are derived from glandular cells in the epidermis, rather than from the muscles as found in other electric fish.

Nathan Lavenda

Catheters

Catheters are long, flexible tubes that are inserted into the body for various purposes, either to remove an unwanted substance or to instill nourishment or medication.

A relatively large catheter can be passed through the nose, down the throat and into the stomach to remove the contents of the stomach; for example, if someone has consumed a poisonous substance, a catheter can be used to remove a small sample of the stomach contents for laboratory testing. A catheter may also be used to pass liquid nourishment into the digestive tract, as in the case of someone unable to swallow for some reason. This catheter is called a nasogastric tube.

A smaller tube can be passed through the urethra into the bladder to empty its urine. Oftentimes after surgery or trauma an individual is unable to void and must have the bladder emptied. Sometimes these urinary catheters must be left in place; a small balloon near the end of the catheter is inflated to hold the catheter in the bladder.

Very long catheters are often passed through an incision in the thigh into an artery and into the heart; a doctor can then inject contrast agents into the patient to outline the coronary arteries. The physician can watch as the agent, which is visible on x–rays, is injected and courses through the heart's arterial system. In this way a doctor can see a blockage and take measures to bypass it or remove it. These catheters have now been fitted with devices to open clogged arteries. Small balloons mash obstructions out of the way, and laser tips or whirring blades cut stubborn blockages from the arterial passage. Since there are no pain receptors inside blood vessels, passing the cardiac catheter is done under local anesthetic with the patient fully awake.

Still other catheters can be inserted through the trachea into the lungs to remove fluid or mucus. Some two–channeled catheters are used to induce a chemical into an organ and remove the organ's contents at the same time. Others can be used for wound drainage or for measuring blood pressure in any of the heart's four chambers.

See also Surgery.

Cathode

The cathode is one of the two electrodes that are present in any system in which electricity is entering and leaving a region; the other electrode is called the anode. The electric current enters through one of the electrodes and leaves through the other.

Two general kinds of systems employ electrodes: vacuum tubes (also called gas discharge tubes) and electrochemical cells.

In a vacuum tube, the cathode is the negative electrode—the electrode that carries a negative potential with respect to the other one. The cathode is often heated to drive out electrons, which then fly through the vacuum toward the positive electrode, the anode. These streams of electrons are referred to as cathode rays. Cathode ray tubes are vacuum tubes that are widely used as oscilloscopes, television tubes, and computer monitors.

Electrochemical cells are of two types: voltaic cells (also called galvanic cells) and electrolytic cells. In a galvanic cell, such as an automobile battery, an electric current is produced by a chemical oxidation–reduction reaction. In an electrolytic cell, such as a cell designed for the electrolysis of water, the chemical oxidation–reduction reaction is produced by an externally–supplied electric current. In either case, the cathode is defined as the electrode at which the chemical reduction process is taking place in the cell—that is, the electrode at which electrons are being taken up by atoms, molecules, or ions. The anode, on the other hand, is the electrode at which the oxidation process is taking place—that is, the electrode at which electrons are being given off by atoms, molecules, or ions.

See also Anode; Cathode ray tube; Cell, electro-chemical; Electric current; Electricity; Vacuum tube.

Cathode ray see **Subatomic particles**

Cathode ray tube

A cathode ray tube is a device that uses a beam of electrons in order to produce an image on a screen. Cathode ray tubes are also known commonly as CRTs. Cathode ray tubes are widely used in a number of electrical devices, such as computer screens, television sets, radar screens, and oscilloscopes used for scientific and medical purposes. A cathode ray tube consists of five major parts: an envelope or container, an electron gun, a focusing system, a deflection system, and a display screen.

Envelope or container

Most people have seen a cathode ray tube or pictures of one. The "picture tube" in a television set is perhaps the most familiar form of a cathode ray tube. The outer shell that gives a picture tube its characteristic shape is called the envelope of a cathode ray tube. The envelope is most commonly made of glass, although tubes of metal and ceramic can also be used for special purposes. The glass cathode ray tube consists of a cylindrical portion that holds the electron gun and the focusing and deflection systems. At the end of the cylindrical portion farthest from the electron gun, the tube widens out to form a conical shape. At the flat wide end of the cone is the display screen.

Air is pumped out of the cathode ray tube to produce a vacuum with a pressure in the range of 10^{-2} to 10^{-6} pascal, the exact value depending on the use to which the tube will be put. A vacuum is necessary to prevent electrons produced in the CRT from colliding with atoms and molecules within the tube.

Electron gun

An electron gun consists of three major parts. The first is the cathode, a piece of metal which, when heated, gives off electrons. One of the most common cathodes in use is made of cesium metal, a member of the alkali family that loses electrons very easily. When a cesium cathode is heated to a temperature of about 1750°F (825°C), it begins to release a stream of electrons. These electrons are then accelerated by an anode (a positively charged electrode) placed a short distance away from the cathode. As the electrons are accelerated, they pass through a small hole in the anode into the center of the cathode ray tube.

The intensity of the electron beam entering the anode is controlled by the grid. The grid may consist of a cylindrical piece of metal to which a variable electrical charge can be applied. The amount of charge placed on the control grid determines the intensity of the electron beam that passes through it.

Focusing and deflection systems

Under normal circumstances, an electron beam produced by the electron gun described above would have a tendency to spread out to form a cone–shaped beam. However, the beam that strikes the display screen must be pencil–thin and clearly defined. In order to form the electron beam into the correct shape, an electrical or magnetic lens, similar to an optical lens, can be created adjacent to the accelerating electrode. The lens consists of some combination of electrical or magnetic fields that shapes the flow of electrons that pass through it, just as a glass lens shapes the light rays that pass through it.

The electron beam in a cathode ray tube also has to be moved about so that it can strike any part of the display screen. In general, two kinds of systems are available for controlling the path of the electron beam, an electrostatic system and a magnetic system. In the first case, negatively charged electrons are deflected by similar or opposite electrical charges and in the second case, they are deflected by magnetic fields.

In either case, two deflection systems are needed, one to move the electron beam in a horizontal direction, and the other to move it in a vertical direction. In a standard television tube, the electron beam completely scans the display screen about 25 times every second.

Display screen

The actual conversion of electrical to light energy takes place on the display screen when electrons strike a material known as a phosphor. A phosphor is a chemical that glows when exposed to electrical energy. A commonly used phosphor is the compound zinc sulfide. When pure zinc sulfide is struck by an electron beam, it gives off a greenish glow. The exact color given off by a phosphor also depends on the presence of small amounts of impurities. For example, zinc sulfide with silver metal as an impurity gives off a bluish glow and with copper metal as an impurity, a greenish glow.

The selection of phosphors to be used in a cathode ray tube is very important. Many different phosphors are known, and each has special characteristics. For example, the phosphor known as yttrium oxide gives off a red glow when struck by electrons, and yttrium silicate gives off a purplish blue glow.

The rate at which a phosphor responds to an electron beam is also of importance. In a color television set, for example, the glow produced by a phosphor has to last long enough, but not too long. Remember that the screen is being scanned 25 times every second. If the phosphor continues to glow too long, color will remain from the first scan when the second scan has begun, and the overall picture will become blurred. On the other hand, if the color from the first scan fades out before the second scan has begun, there will be a blank moment on the screen, and the picture will appear to flicker.

Cathode ray tubes differ in their details of construction depending on the use to which they will be put. In an oscilloscope, for example, the electron beam has to be able to move about on the screen very quickly and with high precision, although it needs to display only one color. Factors such as size and durability are also more important in an oscilloscope than they might be in a home television set.

In a commercial television set, on the other hand, color is obviously an important factor. In such a set, a combination of three electron guns is needed, one for each of the primary colors used in making the color picture.

Further Reading:

Keller, Peter A. *The Cathode–Ray Tube: Technology, History, and Applications.* Palisades Press, 1992.
Parr, Geoffrey, and O. H. Davie. *The Cathode–Ray Tube and Its Applications.* London: Chapman and Hall, 1959.

David E. Newton

Cation

A cation is any atom or group of atoms that has a net positive charge. While matter is electrically neutral overall, ionic compounds are matter that is composed of

positively–charged and negatively–charged particles called ions. An ion is any atom or group of atoms with an overall electrical charge. According to the laws of physics, opposite charges attract, so the oppositely-charged ions attract each other to form compounds that are, overall, electrically neutral. In such compounds, the number of positive charges on the cations is equal to the number of negative charges. Species that have an overall negative charge are called anions. Compounds that are composed of cations and anions are called ionic compounds. Examples include table salt (sodium chloride) and potash (potassium carbonate).

Cations are formed when an atom or group of atom loses one or more electrons. The resulting species has more protons than electrons, so it has an overall positive charge. (Each proton has a +1 charge, and each electron has a –1 charge. In normal atoms, the number of protons equals the number of electrons, so a normal atom has an overall charge of zero. We say it is electrically neutral.) On the other hand, anions are formed when an atom or group of atoms accepts one or more electrons, so it has more negative charges than positive charges. Most metallic elements react chemically to form cations, losing electrons. Most nonmetallic elements react chemically to gain electrons, thereby forming anions.

See also Anion; Ionization; Sodium chloride.

Cation-ratio dating see **Dating techniques**

Cats

Cats are mammals in the family Felidae of the order Carnivora, which includes all of the carnivores. Cats are in fact the most carnivorous of all meat–eating animals, and will eventually die if not fed regularly with meat which contains essential proteins. The predatory instinct in wild cats can be seen in the domestic cats, for even well fed domestic cats will hunt mice and birds.

The cat family includes both big cats (lions, tigers, and leopards) and small (lynx, servals, and ocelots) cats. Small cats purr but do not roar, whereas big cats roar but do not purr. The reason for this is that the tongue muscles of large cats are attached to a pliable cartilage at the base of the tongue, which allows roaring, while the tongue muscles of small cats are attached to the hyoid bone, which allows purring, but not roaring.

Most cats have 30 teeth, including large canine and carnassal teeth, and few cheek teeth, an arrangement suited to crushing bones and tearing, cutting, and gripping prey. Cats' jaws are limited to vertical movements, and their chewing action is aided by sharp projections on the tongue (papillae) which grip and manipulate food.

Members of the cat family occur naturally in all parts of the world, except Australia and Antarctica. There are 36 species of cats in four genera. The genus *Panthera* includes jaguars, leopards, lions, and tigers. The cheetah is the sole member of the genus *Acinonyx*, while the clouded leopard is in the genus *Neofelis*. The puma, lynx, and other small cats, including the wildcat and domestic cat, are all in the genus *Felis*.

Species of big cats

There are eight species of big cats, including the lion (*Panthera leo*), tiger (*P. tigris*), leopard (*P. pardus*), cheetah (*Acinonyx jubatus*), jaguar (*P. onca*), snow leopard (*Uncia uncia*), clouded leopard (*Neofelis nebulosa*), and cougar (*Puma concolor*). The onza is a possible undescribed species or subspecies from Mexico that resembles the cougar and has been seen only rarely. Sightings of the onza go back to the time of the Spanish conquest of Mexico, but the first specimen was collected only in 1986 by a Mexican rancher, who shot what he thought was a puma.

The lion

Lions were once distributed over much of Europe, Asia, and Africa. Today, lions are found only in sub-Saharan Africa and in the Gir Forest, a wildlife sanctuary in India. Lions prefer open grasslands to forest, but are also found in the Kalahari desert. Adult male lions weigh from 300–500 lbs (135–225 kg), while the female weighs about 300 lbs (135 kg). Lions are a light tawny color with black markings on the abdomen, legs, ears, and mane. Lions live up to 15 years, reaching sexual maturity in their third year. Male lions have been observed to kill cubs that they have not fathered.

Lions are the most social of the cats, living in family groups called prides, consisting of 4–12 related adult females, their young, and 1–6 adult males. The size of the pride usually reflects the amount of available food: where prey is abundant, lion prides tend to be larger, making them better able to protect their kills from hyenas and other scavengers. Most lion kills are made by the females, while the males defend the pride's territory, which may range from 8 sq mi (20 sq km) to more than 150 sq mi (385 sq km).

The tiger

The tiger is the largest member of the cat family, with males weighing from 400–600 lbs (180–275 kg)

Two cheetahs in Kenya.

and females 300–350 lbs (135–160 kg). Tigers range from a pale yellow to a reddish–orange color (depending on habitat) with characteristic vertical stripes. Tigers live in habitats with a dense vegetation cover, commonly forests and swamps in India, Southeast Asia, China, and Indonesia. A century ago, tigers inhabited areas as far north as Siberia, all of India and Southeast Asia, and regions along the eastern part of China. Today, all eight subspecies of tigers are endangered.

The tiger lives a solitary life and systematically protects its territory by marking its boundaries with urine, feces, glandular secretions, and scrape marks on trees. Tigers are solitary nocturnal hunters, approaching their prey stealthily in a semi–crouching position. When close enough, the tiger makes a sudden rush for the prey, attacking from the side or the rear. The prey is seized by the shoulder or neck with the tiger's front paws and jaws, while keeping its hind feet on the ground. The tiger applies a throat bite that usually suffocates its victim, which it carries into cover and consumes.

The leopard

Male leopards weigh about 200 lbs (90 kg), with females weighing about half that amount. Leopards are found in sub–Saharan Africa, India, and Southeast Asia.

A Canada lynx (*Lynx canadensis*) pouncing.

There are some small populations of leopards in Arabia and North Africa. Leopards have a distinctive coloring—black spots over a pale brown coat. Their habitat includes rain forest, dry savanna grassland, and cold mountainous areas.

Leopards feed on a variety of small prey, usually hunting at night by ambush. Leopards use trees as resting places and frequently drag their catches up into trees to eat them. The number of leopards is declining worldwide due to hunting and habitat destruction from human population pressures.

The cheetah

Cheetahs can reach speeds of up to 70 mph (112 kph), and are the fastest animals on land: over short distances, a cheetah can outrun any other animal. Cheetahs resemble leopards in that they have a black spotted pattern over a tawny coat, but are distinguished by large black "tear" stripes under their eyes, a long, lithe body, and a relatively small head. Cheetahs are the only members of the cat family that do not have retractable claws. Cheetahs are solitary hunters, feeding on gazelles and impala. They hunt mainly in the morning and early afternoon, when other large cats are usually sleeping, thereby enabling them to share hunting areas with other carnivores. Cheetahs are also found in North and East Africa and along the eastern regions of southern Africa, as well as in selected areas of the Middle East and southern Asia. There is a considerable trade in cheetah skins, and hunting, together with the loss of habitat, threatens their survival in the wild.

Other big cats

Among the other large cats are the jaguar, the snow leopard, and the clouded leopard. These three cats inhabit a forest wilderness, and all are solitary and nocturnal. Jaguars are found in Central and South America, while the snow leopard is found in Central Asia, and the clouded leopard in Southeast Asia. The average weight of the jaguar is about 125 lbs (55 kg). The snow leopard is found in the Himalayas at elevations from 9,000 ft (2,750 m) to nearly 20,000 ft (6,100 m). The clouded leopard and the snow leopard have a rigid hyoid bone in their throats which prevents them from roaring. The black panther is a black form of the jaguar; its spots are discernable within its black coat. The cougar, also known as the puma or mountain lion, is about the size of a leopard and ranges from western Canada to

Argentina. The cougar is found in mountains, plains, deserts, and forests, and preys on deer and other medium–sized herbivores.

The small wild cats

The small wild cats, such as the lynx and the bobcat, are considered to be the ancestors of the domestic cat, and are native to most areas of the world, except Australia and Antarctica. Other features small wild cats share with domestic cats include the inability to roar, retractable claws, and a hairless strip along the front of their noses. Small wild cats include the European wild cat (*Felis sylvestris*), the African wild cat (*F. lybica*), the sand cat (*F. margarita*) of the Sahara, the African tiger cat (*Profelis aurata*) of tropical forests, the golden cat (*P. temminckii*), and Pallas' cat (*Otocolobus manul*) of central Asia. Asian medium–sized cats include the African serval (*Leptailurus serval*) and the caracal or desert lynx (*Caracal caracal*) of the Sahara. Medium-sized cats of the New World include the ocelot (*Leopardus pardalis*) of South and Central America and the jaguarundi (*Herpailurus jaguarundi*).

The wildcat or bobcat (*Lynx rufus*) of North America is colored to blend into the rocky, densely vegetated background of its habitat. Bobcats rely more on hearing than on sight to catch their prey, and the tufts on their ears are thought to improve their hearing. The lynx (*Lynx lynx*) lives in cold climates and has long legs, to make trekking through deep snow easier, and foot pads covered with fur to protect them while walking in snow. (The bobcat's foot pads are bare.) The Canada lynx (*L. canadensis*) differs from the common lynx in that it is larger, has longer hair, and does not have a spotted coat.

The other 26 species of small wild cats live mainly in forests and feed on small prey, such as rodents, hares, lizards, small deer, fish, snakes, squirrels, insects, and birds. Most species have a spotted or striped coat and usually have a rounded head. Small wild cats are either solitary in habit or form groups, depending on the abundance of the food supply. Some species, such as the ocelot, are hunted for their spotted skin and are in danger of becoming extinct.

Senses

Cats have excellent binocular eyesight, which allows them to judge distances. Cats cannot see in complete darkness, but need at least dim light in order to distinguish objects at night. Cats' eyes have a special reflective layer behind the retina; because of this, light that has not been absorbed on its first pass through the retina stimulates the retina a second time, providing good vision in poor light. It is this tapetal layer that makes cats' eyes appear to glow in the dark when a light flashes on them.

The senses of smell and taste in cats are closely connected, as they are in all mammals. Distinctive to cats is the absence of response to sweets, and cats avoid foods that taste sweet. The taste buds of cats are located along the front and side edges of their tongues. Their vomeronasal organ, also known as Jacobson's organ, is a saclike structure, located in the roof of the mouth, that is believed to be involved in sensing chemical messages associated with sexual activity. When a male cat smells a female's urine which contains hormones indicating sexual receptiveness, he may wrinkle his nose and curl back his upper lip in a gesture known as flehmening . He will also raise his head and bare his teeth.

Cats have the ability to hear high–frequency sounds that humans are unable to hear. This ability is particularly helpful when cats are stalking prey such as mice, since the cats can detect the high–frequency sounds emitted by these rodents. The external ears of cats are flexible and can turn as much as 180 degrees to locate sounds precisely.

A cat's whiskers have a sensory function, helping it avoid objects in its path in the dimmest light. If a cat passes an object that touches its whiskers, it will blink, thus protecting the eyes from possible injury. Besides the long cheek whiskers, cats have thicker whiskers above their eyes. Cats use their nose to determine the temperature, as well as the smell, of food. The hairless paw pads of cats are an important source of tactile information gained from investigating objects with their paws.

Behavior

In the wild, most forest–living members of the cat family tend to be solitary hunters. Some species of cats live in pairs, while others, such as lions, live in family groups. Cats engage in daily grooming which not only keeps their fur in good condition, but also helps them regulate their body temperature (fur licking helps cool the cat), and keeps their coat waterproof.

Cats need a great deal of sleep, which is consistent with the large amounts of energy they expend during their hunting periods. They sleep intermittently almost two–thirds of the day. Because of a slight fall in their body temperatures when they sleep, they look for warm, sunny spots for dozing.

Cats are excellent climbers, great jumpers, and have remarkable balance. Except for the cheetah, cats have retractable claws that are curved, sharp, and sheathed. The claws are particularly useful to cats when climbing trees. The bones of their feet (like those of dogs) are arranged in a digitigrade posture, meaning that only their toes make contact with the ground, which increases their speed of running. Cats have the remarkable ability—called the righting reflex—to right themselves during a fall, when first a cat's head, then the rest of its body, turns toward the ground so that the cat lands on all four feet.

Cats follow a well–defined hunting sequence that begins with the sighting or smelling of prey. The hunting skills that cats display are in some aspects instinctual and in others learned. Cats begin learning how to hunt through the play they engage in when they are young. Mother cats are involved in teaching hunting skills to their young, first by bringing back dead prey, later by bringing back immobilized prey, allowing young cats to kill the prey themselves. Still later, the mother cat will take the young cat on a stalking and killing mission, so that it learns how to successfully hunt. Cats that do not have the opportunity to learn to hunt from their mothers do not become good hunters.

Cats are territorial, marking their territory by spraying the boundaries with urine. Cats will also scratch and rub against fixed objects to mark their territory. Within a male territorial boundary, there may be several female territories. During mating, the male will seek out or be lured to nearby females that are in heat (estrous). Females may vocalize loudly when they are ready to mate, thus attracting males. Frequent scenting and rubbing against trees also help the male cat know the female is ready to mate. In cats, frequent sexual contact during estrous is important to insure successful ovulation, which is induced during sexual intercourse.

The gestation (pregnancy) period in cats depends upon their body size. Domestic cats have a gestation period of about 60 days and an average litter size of about four kittens. In the wild, gestation ranges from slightly less than 60 days for the smaller species of cats to about 115 days for large cats, such as lions. The number in the litter varies from one to seven; the body size of the cat does not seem to be the factor that determines litter size. It may have more to do with the availability of food and the survival rate in the area the cat inhabits. With the exception of lions, the care and training of the young are left to the mother. Nursing continues until the cubs or kittens are gradually weaned and learn to eat meat.

Evolution and history

The emergence of modern cats began about 25 million years ago during the Miocene epoch. The saber–toothed tiger lived in Europe, Asia, Africa, and North America, and had long, upper canine teeth for stabbing its prey. The remains of saber–toothed tigers have been found to be as recent as 13,000 years old.

Cats were first domesticated in ancient Egypt about 5000 years ago. The Egyptians used cats to protect grain supplies from rodents; they also worshiped cats, and mummified large numbers of them along with their owners. Since that time, the domestic cat has spread throughout Europe, Asia, Africa, and the New World. Breeding of cats into specific pedigrees did not begin, however, until the middle of the 19th century.

Domestic cats

The breeding of domestic cats involves basic principles of heredity, with consideration of dominant and recessive traits. It was in England that cat breeding first became serious enough that so–called "purebred" cats were displayed at cat shows and a system of authenticating a cat's genetic lineage was begun by issuing a pedigree certificate. Special associations were established to regulate the validation of cat pedigrees and to sponsor the cat shows.

Cat breeds can be categorized as either long–haired breeds or short–haired breeds. Within each group, color, head and ear shape and size, body formation, hair color and length, eye color and shape, and special markings like stripes and color variations on the feet, tail, face, and neck distinguish the breeds from one another.

There are more than a hundred different breeds of cats recognized around the world, subdivided into five broad groups. One group includes Persian longhairs, another the rest of the long–haired cats, a third the British short–haired cats, a fourth the American short–haired cats, and a fifth the Oriental short–haired cats.

The Persian cat, highly prized among cat fanciers, has a round body, face, eyes, and head with a short nose and legs. Its fur is long and woolly, and its tail is fluffy and bushy. Persians vary from black to white, cream, blue, red, blue–cream, cameo, tortoiseshell, smoke, silver, tabby, calico, pewter, chocolate, and lilac. Other popular long–haired cats include the Balinese, the ragdoll, the Turkish angora, and the Maine coon cat. Among the short–haired cats, the Manx, British shorthair, American shorthair, Abyssinian, Burmese, and Siamese are popular. One unfortunate breed is hairless: the sphynx, bred from a mutant kitten in 1966, does not even have whiskers.

The domestic cat is rivaled only by the dog as a household pet, and in recent years has outnumbered the dog as an urban pet. Cats are more self–sufficient than dogs in that they self–groom, need little if any training to use the litter box, and don't have to be walked. Cats are generally quiet and aloof, but will display affection to their owners. They have the reputation of being fussy eaters, but will usually adapt quickly to a particular brand of cat food.

See also Marsupial cats.

Further Reading:

Alderton , David. *Wildcats of the World*. New York: Facts on File, 1993.

Bailey, Theodore N. *The African Leopard: Ecology and Behavior.* New York: Columbia University Press, 1993.

Loxton , Howard. *The Noble Cat: Aristocrat of the Animal World*. London: Merehurst , 1990.

Savage, R. J. G., and M. R. Long. *Mammal Evolution—An Illustrated Guide.* New York: Facts on File, 1986.

Taylor, David. *The Ultimate Cat Book*. New York: Simon and Schuster , 1989.

Turner, Dennis C., and P. P. G. Bateson . *The Domestic Cat: the Biology of Its Behaviour* . New York: Cambridge University Press, 1988.

Vita Richman

Cattails

Cattails or reedmaces are about 10 species of monocotyledonous plants in the genus *Typha*, compris-

Cattails gone to seed at Sespe Creek in Ventura County, California.

ing the family Typhaceae. Cattails are tall, herbaceous, aquatic plants, growing from stout rhizomes located in shallow sediments of wetlands. The leaves of cattails are long and strap–like, sheathing at the base of the plant, while the spike–like inflorescence is borne by a long cylindrical shoot. The typical habitat of cattails is productive marshes, the edges of shallow, fertile lakes, and ditches. Cattails occur in temperate and tropical regions but not in Australia or South America.

Cattail inflorescences are dense aggregations of numerous small separate female and male flowers, the latter occurring segregated at the top of the club–like flowering structure. Pollination is anemophilous, meaning the pollen is shed copiously to the wind which transports it to the stigmatic surfaces of female flowers. The small, mature fruits of cattails are shed late in the growing season or during the ensuing autumn or winter. The fruits have a white filamentous pappus that makes them aerodynamically buoyant so they can be easily dispersed by the wind.

Two familiar species of cattail in North America are the broad–leaved cattail (*Typha latifolia*) and the narrow–leaved cattail (*T. angustifolia*). Both occur commonly in a wide range of fertile, freshwater wetlands.

Cattail leaves are sometimes used for weaving mats, baskets, chair bottoms, and floor mats. Cattail pollen can be collected and used to make or include in protein–rich pancakes and breads. The rhizomes of cattails are sometimes collected and used as a starchy food. Sometimes the dried plants are collected, dried, and used for winter bouquets and other natural decorations.

The major importance of cattails, however, is ecological. These plants are a significant component of the vegetation of many productive marshes. As such, cattails help to provide critical habitat for many species of aquatic wild life such as waterfowl, waders, other species of birds, and mammals such as muskrats.

Because of their great productivity, cattails can take up large quantities of nutrients from water and sediment. This makes these plants rather efficient and useful at cleansing nutrients from both natural and waste waters. In this way cattails can help to alleviate eutrophication, an environmental problem associated with large rates of aquatic productivity caused by nutrient loading.

See also Eutrophication; Wetlands.

Cattle family

The cattle family, Bovidae, is a widespread group of animals which also includes the goat antelopes, goats, sheep, gazelles and antelopes. Of the 107 species currently recognized within this family, just 12 are wild cattle. Even the large musk ox (*Ovibos moschatus*), which looks quite cowlike, is more closely related to the goats than to cattle. Cattle are generally characterized by their large size and presence of one pair of non–branching horns that grow from the forehead. The horns, which are not shed, are largely hollow inside and differ considerably among species: some of the largest are seen in the wild yak (*Bos mutus*) and African buffalo (*Syncerus caffer*), the smallest in the anoas (*Bubalus* sp). Both males and females develop horns as they mature, but those of the male are usually much longer. Wild cattle vary considerably in appearance – from the brown–black colors of the anoas to the banteng (*Bos javanicus*) in which the females are a reddish–brown, the males a shiny black. Both sexes are adorned with white stockings, a white rump patch, a white patch over the eyes and a white band around the muzzle. The complete antithesis to these decorative cattle are wild yak, whose unkempt, shaggy appearance and unpredictable temperament is a prize example of

how one species has evolved to withstand extreme conditions which few other animals could exploit.

The precise origins of wild cattle are still unclear, but it is thought that they arose from species resembling the small four–horned antelope (*Tetracerus quadricornis*) and larger nilgai (*Boselaphus tragocamelus*) which today survive only in India. The ancestors of modern–day cattle have been traced back to a species known as the auroch (*Bos primigenius*), a wild ox of Europe and Asia which reached more than 7 ft (2m) at the shoulder. These were largely forest–dwelling cattle, feeding in open glades and around the fringes of woodlands. Adult males, or bulls, had long curving horns, a black coat with a white stripe down the middle of the back and a patch of short tufty white hair between the horns. Females, or cows, were smaller and a reddish–brown color. The last auroch is known to have died in Poland in 1627.

Wild cattle have evolved to survive in a wide range of habitats, from Arctic to tropical conditions. Wild yak are one example of a species that has adapted to living in a harsh climate with their thick shaggy outer hair and densely matted undercoat, features that provide insulation against the extreme cold in its native habitat, the high, wind– and snow–swept mountains of the Himalayas. Species that live in the tropics have other physiological problems to overcome, such as avoiding becoming too hot. These species are typically forest–dwelling, and have short hair which will not retain body heat. Some species, such as the kouprey (*Bos sauveli*), have extended dewlaps, large fat–filled folds of loose skin that hang below the neck and serve as heat–radiating surfaces. Other species, such as buffalos, cope with the heat and ever–present flies by immersing themselves in water. By frequent wallowing buffalo cover themselves with a layer of mud that also helps protect them from the piercing bites of insects. Most species are diurnal, often feeding at dawn and dusk in order to avoid the midday heat. Some of the shyer species, such as gaur, anoa, and tamaraw (*Bubalus mindorensis*) may feed at nighttime in order to avoid detection from predators, including humans.

Over the centuries, many species of wild cattle have been domesticated, including the yak, gaur, banteng, and water buffalo. For some people cattle are their most important possessions. In Africa, cattle are an important symbol of wealth and are used for trade purposes, as well as for their milk and blood, both of which feature in the diet of certain tribes. Their meat, of course, is also of importance, as are their valuable hides – but cattle are only butchered on special occasions. Even their dung is of considerable importance as it is dried and stored as an essential source of cooking fuel

A water buffalo during a monsoon in Nepal.

in many parts of the continent where tree cover is sparse. Domesticated yak are equally important for the people of Nepal and Tibet, in regions where roads are few and the climate extreme. Working at altitudes of up to 20,000 ft (6000 m), yak are capable of hauling heavy loads and surviving on a low quality diet. In addition, they provide people with an essential supply of milk, meat, wool and hides.

Cattle are grazing animals that feed mainly on grasses, leaves and herbs. Bovids feed by twisting grasses and stems around the tongue and cutting the vegetation off with the lower incisors, which protrude slightly forward. The jaw is designed to allow a circular grinding motion which allows the food to be thoroughly crushed and masticated between the animal's large teeth. Plants, however, are largely composed of cellulose, a tough carbohydrate that few animals are able to digest. Many animal species have evolved a means of overcoming this problem and are able to benefit from the relatively abundant sources of plant materials at their disposal. Cattle belong to a group of animals known as ruminants – species that have a specialized system of digestion which enables them to break down the cellulose fibers and extract the energy from the vari-

ous plants they eat. One of the most significant features of this system is a specialized stomach which, in ruminants, consists of four distinct chambers: the rumen, reticulum, omasum and abomasum. Another is the presence of large numbers of specialized bacteria that live within a sort of liquid broth in the stomach. Without these bacteria, no amount of chewing would render the plant material in a state from which nutrients might be absorbed.

Cattle are prodigious eaters; at any one feeding, large quantities of grasses are consumed and pass directly into the large rumen. Here they are moistened and mixed with the bacteria which begin to attack the tough plant fibers. From the rumen, partly digested materials pass onto the reticulum, where the same process continues. Most wild cattle have preferred feeding and resting grounds and, when not feeding or moving, they withdraw to cover to digest their food. At this time the animal will regurgitate this partly digested food once again into the mouth, where it is chewed a second time, mixed with salivary enzymes and the swallowed in a process commonly known as "chewing the cud." When it is swallowed again, the food passes through the upper stomach to the omasum and abomasum where normal digestive enzymes take over the process of breaking down the plant materials and freeing the nutrients which can then be absorbed and used by the cow. In total, food takes from 70 to 100 hours to pass through the digestive system of a cow – one of the slowest passage rates in the animals kingdom. Although it is slow, it is extremely effective. A thoroughly masticated food base permits an opportunity during which a maximum amount of proteins may be absorbed.

Wild cattle play an important ecological role through their grazing habits, in particular by keeping grasslands open from invading shrubs and coarse grasses and creating an environment favorable for many other smaller grazing animals such as deer and antelope. Their dung, which is widely scattered across the grasslands or throughout the forest ecosystem serves as an important fertilizer and is broken down by a wide range of beetles, fungi and bacteria who release essential nutrients and minerals that promote further plant growth.

Cattle are naturally social animals and form small herds, the composition of which varies according to the species. Some species like the anoa may be solitary or travel in groups of just 2–4 animals while at the other extreme, herds of several thousand buffalo once ranged across the vast fertile prairies of North America, each massive herd separated into sub–units of several hundred animals.

The African buffalo displays an advanced system of social behavior and the entire herd not only feeds and moves around as a colossal single unit, but individual animals will also gather around an injured or sick animal if it is threatened by predators. This is a non–territorial species that forms herds of 50–2000 animals, with an average size of about 350 animals. Within the herd a distinct social system is evident: dominant males breed with females and there is constant rivalry between these and other transient males who do not belong to the herd. Subordinate juvenile males are allowed to remain with the herd until they reach maturity at which stage they are driven out and may remain solitary or form small bachelor groups with other males. Juvenile females remain with the herd and establish a strong bond with their mothers.

Breeding is a frantic time for any species of wild cattle with adult males vying with other socially dominant males for the rights to mate with receptive females. Dominant males must also keep a vigilant eye on sexually mature transient males who may attempt to steal their cows and form their own herd. Adult bulls challenge others of similar status with loud roars and mock charges. On most occasions these displays of strength are sufficient to deter challenging males but, sometimes, the challenging male refuses to back down and the situation escalates to another level with fierce clashes taking place in which one bull pitches his strength and agility against the power of another. The bull's horns are one focus of attention in such battles as males interlock their horns and try to wrestle their opponents into a vulnerable position where they may strike other parts of the body with their pointed horns. The winner of such conflicts is almost certainly guaranteed the rights of dominant male within the herd, until he, in turn, is deposed by other challenging males.

The gestation period of wild cattle varies considerably, from 270 days to over 400 days. At the calving time approaches, most cows leave the herd, returning to join it once again some 7–10 days later with their offspring. Most cows give birth to a single calf which remains close to its mother until weaned. Following that, calves usually remain with the herd for a further three years until they reach sexual maturity. The fate of young cattle thereafter depends on the social system of the particular species, as described above.

Wild cattle have few natural predators, at least at the adult stage. Calves, however, are susceptible to predation from lions, tigers, leopards, and wild dogs in particular. Predation is thought to have been one of the main reasons why wild cattle developed a herding life style as the presence of large numbers of heavily armored animals is often enough to deter a predator from attacking. When feeding as a group, the animals are slightly spread apart and it is advantageous to have many eyes on the lookout – each animal takes its turn to scan the surrounding vegetation in between feeding bouts. Through the centuries, however, wild cattle have suffered considerably at the hands of humans, as they have been hunted for their meat, hides and sport. Widespread herds of auroch were decimated by the 16th century; the European bison (*Bison bonasus*) suffered a similar fate during the 19th century; while the once vast herds of American bison suffered heavily at the hands of European settlers in their quest to open up the American West.

The European bison is one example where the species was extirpated in the wild but its future has been secured as a result of animals held in captivity. A sedentary, woodland–dwelling species, the bison was reduced to a few scattered populations by the beginning of the 20th century. Many of these were destroyed during World War I and the last remaining wild herds died out in Lithuania and the Caucasus by the middle 1920s. Concentrated efforts by a few zoos led to the re–introduction of a small herd to the animal's natural habitat in the Bialowieza Forest in Poland. At first these animals were retained in semi–captive conditions but were later released to form free–living herds and replace part of the country's natural heritage. Although this species has been saved from extinction, present–day herds are closely inbred – the pure species being descended from just 17 animals. Additional conservation programs are underway to try and maximize the genetic exchange between breeding herds.

One of the least–known cattle species is the tamaraw, a small species that reaches just 3 ft (1 m) at the shoulder. This species inhabits forested parts of the island of Mindoro in the Philippines. It is thought to be nocturnal and quite aggressive, but almost nothing is known about its ecology. Over–hunting, as well as loss of habitat and human encroachment on this species' habitat has resulted in a serious population decline from an estimated 10,000 animals in the early 1900s to fewer than 400 animals today. The majority of these free–living animals are confined to Mount Ilgo National Park. In view of the level of forest loss on this island, the species is classified as endangered by conservation organizations. Several conservation initiatives have been attempted in the past, but these have met with little success so far.

Like the tamaraw, the kouprey is another highly endangered species. Once wide ranging throughout Indochina, it is now thought to be extinct in countries such as Thailand. The last remaining herds may survive in the forested border countries of Laos, Cambodia and Vietnam. A large species reaching a height of 6 ft (1.9 m) at the shoulder and measuring from 7–8 ft (2.1–2.3 m)in length, males of this species are much larger than females. Young calves and females are generally a gray color (the species is locally known as the "gray ox"), with the undersides a lighter hue and the neck, chest and forelegs slightly darker. Mature males are a rich dark brown color, with white or gray coloring on the lower legs. The species may be recognized by its dewlap which, in some older males, may even reach and drag along the ground. Apart from color differences, bulls are easily distinguished from cows by their horns: the latter generally have horns that spiral upwards, while those of a bull are more widely spaced and often frayed at the ends. The reason why these split at the ends is unknown, but some authorities believe that kouprey use their horns for digging in earth, perhaps in search of mineral salts.

Kouprey are animals of gently rolling hills in deciduous and semi–evergreen tropical forests that offer a wide range of open feeding and resting sites. They may, however, move to higher ground during the wettest periods of the year. Little is known about the ecology of this species. They are known to form small herds of cows and offspring, with separate bachelor herds of young males. Animals appear to be most active in the morning and again in late afternoon and frequently travel at night. Mixed herds of kouprey, banteng, and feral water buffalos have been reported. In 1949, there were thought to be around 1,000 animals surviving. This number is thought to have declined to 500 in 1951 and just 100 in 1969. No one is quite sure how many kouprey survive in the wild today, as this species' habitat is at the center of almost constant human warfare. Authorities fear for its survival in view of the heavy hunting pressure in the region. Major conservation efforts have been designed to undertake captive breeding programs in safe parts of Kampuchea and Laos if sufficient animals can be obtained from the wild.

Other species which are perhaps equally threatened are the anoas, of which two species have been recorded: the mountain (*Bubalus quartesi*) and lowland (*B. depressicornis*) anoa. Both species are only found in Sulawesi, Indonesia. In appearance anoas resemble dwarf buffalos, measuring just 2–3 ft (0.7–1 m) at the shoulder and 5–6 ft (1.6–1.7 m) in body length, and weighing about 300–600 lbs (150–300 kg). Adults are usually a dull brown color, but the shading pattern may vary, with some animals having lighter undersides. Calves are covered with woolly yellow–brown hair, but this is lost as they mature. Little is known about the ecology of these secretive cattle as few observations have been made in the wild. It is known that they are widely hunted for their meat, but another serious threat is continuing loss of forest habitat, which affects both species.

Wild cattle are of enormous importance for our present civilization, just as they have been in our past. They not only play a vital role in the local ecology of their diverse environments, but also represent an important genetic reservoir which may once again prove important for breeding purposes. Hybrids of cattle–yak origin are already of great importance in many parts of Nepal and China. Elsewhere in Asia, farmers in Laos and Kampuchea used to drive their cows into the forest in the hope that they would breed with wild kouprey bulls, as they found that such offspring were stronger than if the cows were mated with domestic cattle. All wild cattle therefore have considerable potential in the breeding arena since these species are often far better adapted to local climatic and forage conditions, as well as being stronger and more resistant to diseases, many of which are debilitating for certain domestic breeds.

If we are to save these remaining species in the wild, however, there is not much time to loose. Most species are now threatened by hunting as well as habitat loss. As the habitat range of these species continues to shrink in the face of human encroachment, all wild populations of cattle risk becoming isolated and susceptible to disease, as well as inbreeding, as there will no longer be a possibility of genetic exchange between other populations. Future conservation efforts must continue to focus on preserving natural feeding and breeding ranges, as well as essential migration corridors of these species, in order to ensure the continued viability of these wild herds.

See also Livestock.

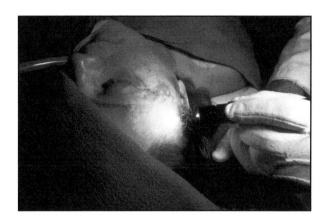

Birthmark removal by cauterization with an argon laser.

Cauterization

Cauterization is the application of heat, mechanically or chemically, to prevent or stop bleeding. It is widely used in surgery to hold bleeding to a minimum and speed the surgical process.

History

Searing areas of bleeding with a hot instrument, a hot iron or other metallic object, was practiced for many years for the treatment of wounded soldiers. Even thousands of years ago, all wounded were treated by pouring boiling oil into the wound to arrest bleeding. Of course, in this case the cure was nearly as harmful as the original injury. Many of the wounded, already in shock from their trauma, were plunged into deeper shock and death by the oil.

As surgery progressed and anesthesia was introduced to quiet the patient and prevent his feeling pain, more care and more time could be devoted to preventing bleeding. In making an incision the surgeon would cut across small blood vessels such as capillaries and arterioles that would begin to ooze blood. The surgeon then had to locate each point of bleeding and apply a clamp to stop it, and then go back and tie a suture around each bleeder, a long and exacting process.

The electric cautery, a form of scalpel, then was invented and introduced into the surgical suite. Using this instrument the surgeon could make his incision and the cautery seared and sealed off all sites of bleeding except the largest ones. This considerably reduced the time the surgeon spent in stanching the flow of blood into the surgical field. It was also a benefit to the patient who spent less time under the anesthetic and reduced the amount of blood loss.

Currently the ubiquitous laser has been introduced as a scalpel. The powerful beam cuts into tissue and opens the incision while at the same time heat–searing the small blood vessels.

Other applications

Chemical cauterization also is used in limited circumstances. For example, one means of stopping a nosebleed that has defied all other means of cure is to use an applicator with silver nitrate on one end. The silver nitrate is applied directly to the bleeding area and cauterizes it.

See also Surgery; Laser surgery.

Cave

A cave is a naturally occurring hollow area inside the earth. All caves are formed by some type of erosion process. The formation of caves depend upon geologic, topographic, and hydrologic factors. These factors determine where and how caves develop, as well as their structure and shape. The study of caves is called speleology. Some caves may be small hillside openings, while others consist of large chambers and interconnecting tunnels and mazes. Openings to the surface may be large gaping holes or small crevices.

Caves have provided shelter to prehistoric, ancient, and primitive contemporary people such as the Tasadays of the Philippine Islands. Human remains, artifacts, sculptures, and drawings found in caves have aided archeologists to learn about early humans. Caves are sites of many important archeological discoveries such as The Dead Sea Scrolls. Many religious traditions have

Stalactites and stalagmites in the Hams Caves, Spain.

regarded caves as sacred and have used them to perform rituals, ceremonies, and sacrifices. Some ancient traditions felt that caves led to the underworld. Caves have fascinated poets, artists, philosophers, and musicians.

Cave types

Most caves are formed by water erosion. Rivers running through canyons with steep walls erode the rock at points where the current is strong. Such caves usually have large openings and are not too deep. Caves of this type can be found in the southwestern United States and were at one time inhabited by prehistoric American Indians known as Cliff Dwellers. Sea caves are formed by waves continually crashing against cliffs or steep walls. Often these caves can only be entered at low tide. Ice caves are also formed in glaciers and icebergs by meltwater that drains down crevices in the ice.

Lava caves, which are often several miles long, form when the exterior of a lava flow hardens and cools

to form a tube, but inside the tube lava escapes to the surface leaving a cave. Wind or aeolian caves usually form in sandstone cliffs as wind–blown sand abrades the cliff face. They are found in desert areas, and occur in a bottle neck shape with the entrance much smaller than the chamber. Talus caves are formed by boulders that have piled up on mountain slopes. The most common, largest, and spectacular caves are solution caves.

Solution caves

Solution caves form by chemical weathering of the surrounding bedrock as groundwater moves along fractures in the rock. These caves produce a particular type of terrain called karst. Karst terrain consists primarily of calcium carbonate, or limestone, but can form in any soluble sedimentary rock such as dolomite, rock gypsum, or rock salt. The host rock extends from near the earth's surface to below the water table. Several distinctive karst features make this terrain easy to identify. The most common are sinkholes, circular depressions where the underlying rock has been dissolved away. Disappearing streams and natural bridges are also common clues. Entrances to solution caves are not always obvious, and their discovery is sometimes quite by accident.

Formation of karst involves the chemical interaction of air, soil, water, and rock. As water flows over and drains into the earth's surface, it mixes with carbon dioxide from the air and soil to form carbonic acid (H_2CO_3). The groundwater becomes acidic and dissolves the calcium carbonate in the bedrock, and seeps or percolates through naturally occurring fractures in the rock. With continual water drainage, the fractures become established passageways. The passageways eventually enlarge and often connect, creating an underground drainage system. Over thousands, perhaps millions of years, these passages evolve into the caves we see today.

During heavy rain or flooding in a well–established karst terrain, very little water flows over the surface, or runs off. Most water drains into the ground through enlarged fractures and sinkholes. This underground drainage system sometimes carries large amounts of water, sand, and mud through the passageways and further erodes the bedrock. Sometimes ceilings fall and passageways collapse, creating new spaces and drainage routes.

Not all solution caves form due to dissolution by carbonic acid. Some caves form in areas where hydrogen sulfide gas is released from the earth's crust or from decaying organic material. Sulfuric acid forms when the hydrogen sulfide comes in contact with water, and chemical weathers the limestone, similar to acid rain.

Cave environment and formations

The deep cave environment is completely dark, has a stable atmosphere, and the temperature is rather constant, varying only a few degrees throughout the year. The humidity in limestone caves is usually near 100%. Many caves contain unique life forms, underground streams and lakes, and have unusual mineral formations called speleothems.

When groundwater seeps through the bedrock and reaches a chamber or tunnel, it meets a different atmosphere. Whatever mineral is in solution reacts with the surrounding atmosphere, precipitates out, and is deposited in the form of a crystal on the cave ceiling or walls. Calcite, and to a lesser degree, aragonite, are the most common minerals of speleothems. The amount of mineral that precipitates out depends upon how much gas was dissolved in the water. For example, water that must pass through a thick layer of soil becomes more saturated with carbon dioxide than water that passes through a thin layer. This charges the water with more carbonic acid and causes it to dissolve more limestone from the bedrock, and later to form a thicker mineral deposit in the cave interior.

Water that makes its way to a cave ceiling hangs as a drop. When the drop of water gives off carbon dioxide and reaches chemical equilibrium with the cave atmosphere, calcite starts to precipitate out. Calcite deposited on the walls or floors in layers is called flowstone.

Sometimes the water runs down the slope of the wall, and as the calcite is deposited, a low ridge is formed. Subsequent drops of water follow the ridge, adding more calcite. Constant buildup of calcite in this fashion results in the formation of a big sheet hanging from the ceiling called a curtain. Curtain formations often have waves and folds in them and have streaks of various shades of off–white and browns. The streakiness reflects the mineral and iron content of the precipitating solution.

Often, the hanging drop falls directly to the ground. Some calcite is deposited on the ceiling before the drop falls. When the drop falls, another takes its place. As with a curtain formation, subsequent drops will follow a raised surface and a buildup of calcite in the form of a hanging drop develops. This process results in icicle–shaped speleothems called stalactites. The water that falls to the floor builds up in the same fashion, resembling an upside down icicle called a stalagmite.

Of course, there are variations in the shape of speleothems depending on how much water from a drop falls, how often the water drips, and how much mineral is deposited. They occur as tiered formations, cylinders, cones, some join together, and occasionally stalactites and stalagmites meet and form a tower. Sometimes, when a stalactite is forming, the calcite is initially deposited in a round ring. As calcite builds up on the rim and water drips through the center, a hollow tube called a straw develops. Straws are often transparent or opaque and their diameter is only that of a drop of water.

Stalactites and stalagmites occur in most solution caves and usually, wherever a stalactite forms, there is also a stalagmite. In caves where there is a great deal of seepage, there may be water dripping continually. Speleothems formed under a steady drip of water are typically smooth. Those formed in caves where the water supply is seasonal may reveal growth rings similar to those of a tree trunk. Stalactites and stalagmites grow by only a fraction of an inch or centimeter in a year, and since some are many yards or meters long, one can appreciate the time it takes for these speleothems to develop.

The most bizarre of speleothems are called helictites. Helictites are hollow, cylindrical formations that grow and twist in a number of directions and are not simply oriented according to the gravitational pull of a water drop. Other influences such as, crystal growth patterns and air currents influence the direction in which these speleothems grow. Helictites grow out from the side of other speleothems and rarely grow larger than 4 in (8.5cm) in length.

Speleothems called anthodites are usually made of aragonite. Calcite and aragonite are both forms of calcium carbonate, but crystallize differently. Anthodites grow as radiating, delicate, needle–like crystals. Pools of seepage water that drain leave behind round formations called cave popcorn. Cave pearls are formed in seepage pools by grains of sand encrusted with calcite; the grains move about gathering concentric layers of calcite.

Cave life

There are three main groups of animals that inhabit caves. These animals are classified by their degree of dependence on specific cave conditions such as amount of light, temperature, atmospheric conditions, and water. Animals that commonly use caves but depend on the outside world for survival are called trogloxenes. The best known trogloxenes are bats. Other examples include birds, bears, and crickets. Troglophiles are species that live their entire life cycle within a cave, generally near the entrance, but are also found living outside caves. Cockroaches, beetles, and millipedes are some examples of troglophiles. Certain fungi and algae are also classified as troglophiles. The third classification are troglobites. Troglobites are permanent cave dwellers and are found deep within the cave system in total darkness, and consequently lack color. These species are either white, transparent, or slightly pinkish. Troglobites have no need for eyes and have evolved into eyeless creatures, although some species have retained eye sockets. They rely on their sense of touch to get around. Some examples of troglobites are fish, shrimp, crayfish, salamanders, worms, snails, insects, bacteria, fungi, and algae. Each cave has a self–contained ecosystem, and it is thought that some have not changed for millions of years. As new caves are discovered, speleobiologists regularly find new species of animals.

Further Reading:

Jacobson, Don and Stral, Lee, *Caves and Caving*. Harbor House, 1987.

Mohr, C.E. and Poulson T., *Life of the Cave*. New York: McGraw–Hill, 1966.

Waltham, A.C. *The World of Caves*. New York: G.P. Putnams's Sons, 1976.

Waltham, Tony, *Caves*. New York: Crown Publisher, Inc., 1974.

Christine Miner Minderovic

Cave fish

Many species of fish have evolved to living under strange conditions, but few situations are perhaps as intriguing as those that have adapted to living in complete darkness. Some of these fish have developed a tendency to live at great depths in the ocean where no light penetrates, while others have found refuge in equally dim locations such as caves, wells and subterranean streams. This specialization to living in complete darkness has arisen many times during the course of evolution and the physical and behavioral attributes that these species have developed are not confined to a single taxonomic group of fish. Some 32 different species of fish have been observed to exhibit this cave–dwelling behavior. Most of these are small species, measuring some (7 cm) in length; the largest known species, the Kentucky blind fish (*Amblyopsis spelaea*), which lives in limestone caves, is one of the largest known cave–dwelling species, with adults reaching a length of almost (20 cm).

A few of these species have functional eyes but, for the vast majority, vision is of little use: some of them are even completely blind with the vestiges of eyes still visible beneath a thin layer of skin. In many species, functional eyes are present in the young fry, but these either disappear or are covered up by a layer of skin as they grow and mature. Many cave fish have little or no skin pigment as these species have no need for body coloring, a feature widely used for communication purposes among other fish. Some cave fish do, however, appear to be a pinkish color, but this is the result of the animal's blood vessels showing through the pale skin, rather than any pigmentation.

Apart from the specialized adaptations that these fish have developed, what is interesting to scientists is the fact that so many fish of different groups have evolved independently to living in perpetual darkness. In Africa, a group of Cyprinid fish (related to the carp) has adapted to living in underground streams and wells, while several species of catfish in Africa, the United States of America, and parts of South America have developed a similar habit. In Central America, the brotulid fish (Family Brotulidae) of Mexico and Cuba are typically cave–dwellers, lacking functional eyes and body pigment. Similar features have been detected among the Amblyopsidae, a group of five species of small freshwater fish that only occur in the United States. Some of these species actually live in slow–moving streams and swamps in the open air in southern Atlantic coastal plains, yet they are all blind and live amongst the rubble and vegetation in the lower water columns, well out of direct light.

To compensate for their lack of vision, all of these species have developed other means of locating food and finding a mate, two of the most essential features for survival. Many species have developed sensory organs that are capable of detecting prey either through chemical means or touch. Most are even thought to be sensitive to vibrations. Some of these species retain their body scales but, in others, these have been lost during the course of evolution, enabling them to develop additional sensory organs on the skin. In addition to this range of specialized adaptations, one feature that all of these fish have developed to a higher level that other ocean or freshwater species is an improved lateral line system—a series of grooves or canals that run along each side of the body and extend over the head to the eyes, snout, and jaws. These lines are well equipped with sensory organs known as neuromasts, each of which consists of a group of sensory cells with fine hairlike projections that extend beyond the body wall. They function not only in orientation and balance, but also perhaps in helping the fish locate potential food sources.

While many of these adaptations assist with the detection and gathering of food, it is also likely that some nourishment is obtained on a chance basis. Very little is known about the feeding behavior of cave fish, but they are known to eat a wide range of insects, small crustaceans, small fish, and probably some detritus. Some species are even thought to feed on fecal droppings from overhead bat roosts.

The reasons why species should evolve to living in total darkness are not immediately obvious, and there is probably no single explanation for this phenomenon. Cave environments are known to provide a relatively stable habitat in terms of temperature fluctuations, but the species living in caves and wells are totally reliant on food being brought to them by underground streams. As such they are highly vulnerable to external factors as subterranean aquifers are becoming increasingly tapped for irrigation purposes, and many sites may be at risk from drying out either temporarily or permanently. These species are also at risk from water–borne pollutants such as agricultural runoff and other waste products entering the underground water courses. On the other hand, these fish experience a reduced level of feeding competition as so few species have succeeded in colonizing these habitats. They are also relatively safe from predators, which is an obvious advantage provided they can obtain enough food in their immediate surroundings.

Scientists now believe that the colonization of caves and wells by these fish was a deliberate, rather than accidental, move. Many species are known to live in and around cave openings and pools near underground springs. It is therefore possible that these dim habitats were gradually explored by a few different species that may have already favored living in poorly lit conditions such as beneath rocks, or in the murky depths of swamps and lakes. Through a gradual progression and corresponding behavioral and anatomical changes, these fish could have eventually moved further into the cave system, exploiting the untapped food resources of these habitats.

Cavies see **Guinea pigs and cavies**

Cedar see **Pines**

Celebes ape see **Macaques**

Celery see **Carrot family**

Celestial coordinates

Celestial coordinates locate objects on the sky, which is considered to be an infinitely large (celestial) sphere. The four conventional celestial coordinate systems are defined.

Horizon coordinates

These refer to an observer on the Earth's surface at the center of the celestial sphere.

Altitude h, an object's arc distance along a vertical circle from the horizon, positive for objects above the horizon [between it and the zenith ($h=+90°$)] and negative for objects below it [between it and the nadir ($h=+90°$)].

Azimuth A, the arc distance from the North Point of the Horizon ($h=0°$, $A=0°$) eastward along it to where it meets the object's vertical circle, going from $0°$ to $360°$ from the North Point to full circle back to the North Point. Azimuth is undefined at the Earth's North and South Poles, where the North and South Celestial Poles (NCP and SCP) coincide with the zenith and nadir, and the celestial meridian become undefined.

Equatorial coordinates

These are based on the Earth's rotation, which produces an apparent westward rotation of the celestial sphere around the NCP and SCP.

Right Ascension α

Measured eastward along the celestial equator from the vernal equinox to where an object's hour circle meets the celestial equator, usually measured full circle in time units from 0^h to 24^h.

Declination δ

An object's arc distance along its hour circle from the celestial equator, positive north of the equator, negative south of it. $\delta=+90°$ for the NCP, and $\delta=+90°$ for the SCP.

Hour Angle

An object's Hour Angle t is the arc distance westward along the celestial equator from its intersection with the celestial meridian above the horizon to where the celestial equator meets the object's hour circle; its value increases with time from 0^h to 24^h.

Right ascension and declination on the celestial sphere are analogous to geographic longitude and lati-

KEY TERMS

. . . .

Celestial Equator—The intersection of the Earth's orbital plane with the celestial sphere.

Celestial Merdian—The circle passing through the zenith, zadir, North Celestial Pole, and South Celestial Pole.

Ecliptic—The intersection of the Earth's orbital plane with the celestial sphere.

Galactic Equator—The circle through the middle of our Milky Way galaxy's disk which passes through the direction from the solar system to the center of the Milky Way.

Horizon—The circle on the celestial sphere 90° from the zenith and nadir.

Hour Circles—Half circles from the North Celestial Pole to the South Celestial Pole.

Nadir—The point on the celestial sphere directly below (by downward extension of the plumb line through the Earth) the observer.

North Point of the Horizon—The intersection of the horizon and celestial meridian closer to the North Celestial Pole (NCP).

North (South) Celestial Poles (NCP, SCP)—The intersection(s) of the Earth's rotation axis extended beyond the North (South) geographic poles, respectively, with the celestial sphere.

Secondaries to the Galactic Equator—Half circles from the North Galactic Pole to the South Galactic Pole.

Secondaries to the Ecliptic—Half circles from the North Ecliptic Pole to the South Ecliptic Pole.

Vernal Equinox—The intersection of the celestial equator and ecliptic which the Sun appears to reach on or about March 21.

Vertical Circles—Half circles from the zenith to the nadir.

Zenith—The point on the celestial sphere directly above (by upward extension of the local direction of gravity (plumb line) the observer.

North (NEP) and South (SEP) Ecliptic Poles are $23°.5$ from the NCP and SCP, respectively, and are everywhere 90° from the ecliptic.

Celestial Longitude λ

The arc distance eastward along the ecliptic from the vernal equinox to where an object's secondary to the ecliptic meets the ecliptic; it is expressed in arc units form 0° to 360°.

Celestial latitude β

An object's arc distance from the ecliptic along its secondary to the ecliptic; it is positive north of the ecliptic, negative south of it. $\beta = +90°$ at the NEP and $\beta = 90°$ at the SEP. These coordinates may be either geocentric (Earth–centered) or heliocentric (Sun-centered).

Galactic Coordinates 1, the Galactic Equator is the basic circle and the direction from the solar system to the center of our Milky Way galaxy is the zero point for them. The North (NGP) and South (SGP) Galactic Poles are 90° from the galactic equator and are 62.6° from the NCP and SCP, respectively.

Galactic longitude

The arc distance eastward along the galactic equator from the direction to the center of our Milky Way galaxy to where an object's secondary to the galactic equator crosses the galactic equator; it increases from 0° to 360°.

Galactic latitude b, the arc distance of an object from the galactic equator along its secondary to the galactic equator. Values of b vary from +90° at the NGP to –90° at the SGP. Galactic coordinates of the direction to the center of the Milky Way galaxy are $1 = 0°$, $b = 0°$. Galactic coordinates are usually heliocentric but can also be centered at the center of our Milky Way galaxy.

Further Reading:

Berg, Rebecca M. and Laurence W. Frederick. *Descriptive Astronomy.* New York: Van Nostrand, 1978.

Bernhard, Hubert J., Dorothy A. Bennett, and Hugh S. Rice. *New Handbook of the Heavens.* New York: McGraw-Hill, 1948.

Motz, Lloyd and Anneta Duveen. *Essential of Astronomy.* Belmont, CA: Wadsworth, 1966.

tude, respectively, on Earth, but their measurement differs somewhat.

Ecliptic coordinate

The ecliptic is the basic circle and the vernal equinox is the zero point for these coordinates. The

Celestial mechanics

Modern celestial mechanics began with Isaac Newton's generalization of Kepler's Laws published in his

Principia in 1687. Newton used his three laws of motion and his Law of Universal Gravitation to do this. The three generalized Kepler's Laws are:

1) The orbits of two bodies around their center of mass (barycenter) are conic sections (ellipses, circles, parabolas or hyperbolas) with the center of mass at a focus of each conic section;

2) The line joining the center of the two bodies sweeps out equal areas in their orbits in equal time intervals. Newton showed that this is a consequence of conservation of angular momentum of an isolated two–body system unperturbed by other forces (Newton's Third Law of Motion);

3) From his Law of Universal Gravitation, which states that Bodies 1 and 2 of masses M_1 and M_2 whose centers are separated by a distance r experience equal and opposite attractive gravitational forces F_g of magnitudes

$$F_g = \frac{GM_1M_2}{r^2} \text{(Eq. 1)}$$

where G is the Newtonian gravitations factor, and from his Second Law of Motion, Newton derived the following general form of Kepler's Third Law for these bodies moving around the center of mass along elliptical or circular orbits:

$$P^2 = \left[\frac{4\pi^2}{G(M_1 + M_2)} \right] a^3 \text{ (Eq. 2)}$$

where P is the sidereal period of revolution of the bodies around the center of mass, π is the ratio of the circumference of a circle to its diameter, X, M_1 and M_2 are the same as in Equation 1 and a is the semi–major axis of the *relative* orbit of the center of the less massive Body 2 around the center of the more massive Body 1.

These three generalized Kepler's Laws form the basis of the two–body problem of celestial mechanics.

Astrometry is the branch of celestial mechanics which is concerned with making precise measurements of the positions of celestial bodies, then calculating precise orbits for them based on the observations. In theory, only three observations are needed to define the orbit of one celestial body relative to a second one. Actually, many observations are needed to obtain an accurate orbit.

However, for the most precise orbits and predictions, the vast majority of systems investigated are not strictly two–body systems but consist of many bodies (the solar system, planetary satellite systems, multiple star systems, star clusters, and galaxies).

Planetary perturbations

To a first approximation, the solar system consists of the Sun and eight major planets, a system much more complicated than a two–body problem. However, use of Equation 2 with reasonable values for the astronomical unit (a convenient unit of length for the solar system) and for G showed that the Sun is far more massive than even the most massive planet Jupiter (whose mass is 0.000955 the Sun's mass). This showed that the gravitational forces of the planets on each other are much weaker than the gravitational forces between the Sun and each of the planets, which enabled astronomers to consider the gravitational interactions of the planets as producing small changes with time perturbations) in the elliptical orbit of each planet around the center of mass of the solar system (which is always in or near the Sun). If the Sun and a planet (say the Earth or Jupiter) were alone in empty space, we would have an ideal two-body problem and we would expect the two–body problem as defined by the generalized Kepler's Laws to exactly describe their orbits around the systems center of mass. Then the seven orbital elements (of which a and y are two) of a planet's orbit should remain constant forever.

However, the gravitational forces of the other planets on a planet cause its orbit to change slightly over time; these changes can be accurately allowed for over limited time intervals by calculating the perturbations of its orbital elements over time that are caused by the gravitational forces of the other planets.

Historically, perturbation theory has been more useful than merely providing accurate predictions of future planetary positions. Only six major planets were known when Newton published his *Principia*. William Herschel (1738–1822) fortuitously discovered Uranus, the seventh major planet from the Sun, in March 1781. The initial orbital elements calculated for Uranus did not accurately allow prediction of its future position even after inclusion of the perturbations caused by the six other major planets. Before 1821, Uranus was consistently observed to be ahead of its predicted position in its orbit; afterwards, it lagged behind its predicted positions.

John Couch Adams (1819–1892) in England and Urbain Leverier (1811–1877) in France, hypothesized that Uranus had passed an undiscovered massive planet further than it was from the Sun in the year 1821. They both made detailed calculations to locate the position of the undiscovered planet perturbing the motion of Uranus. Johann Galle (1812–1910) in Berlin, Germany used Leverier's calculations to discover the unknown planet in September 1846, which was then named Neptune.

Further unexplained perturbations of the orbits of Uranus and Neptune led Percival Lowell (1855–1916) and several other astronomers to use them to calculate predicted positions for another undiscovered (trans–Neptunian) planet beyond Neptune's orbit. Lowell searched for the trans–Neptunian planet he predicted from 1906 until his death in November 1916 without finding it. The search for a trans–Neptunian Planet was resumed in 1929 at Lowell Observatory, where Clyde Tombaugh (1905–) who discovered Pluto in February 1930.

Lowell had predicted that a planet more massive than Earth produced the unexplained perturbations. During the years following Pluto's discovery, however, detailed studies of its perturbations of the orbits of Uranus and Neptune showed that Pluto is considerably less massive than the Earth. The discovery of Pluto's satellite, Charon, in 1978 allowed the determination of the total mass of Pluto and Charon from Equation 2 which is about 0.00237 the Earth's mass (about 0.2 the mass of the Earth's moon). There are two consequences of this discovery; Tombaugh's discovery of Pluto may have been fortuitous, and one may make the case that Pluto is not a major planet.

The discrepancy in mass between the masses predicted by Lowell and others for the trans–Neptunian planet and the mass of the Pluto–Charon double planet has led to a renewed search for one or more additional trans–Neptunian planet(s) that still continues. The opinion also exists that the unexplained perturbations of the orbits of Uranus and Neptune are caused by systematic errors in some early measurements of their positions and that no trans–Neptunian planets with masses on the order of the Earth's mass exist.

Resonance phenomena

Ceres, the first asteroid or minor planet, was discovered to orbit the Sun between the orbits of liars and Jupiter in 1801. Thousands of other asteroids have been discovered in that part of interplanetary space, which is now called the Main Asteroid Belt.

Daniel Kirkwood (1815–1895) noticed in 1866 that the periods of revolution of the asteroids around the Sun did not form a continuous distribution over the Main Asteroid Belt but showed gaps (now known as Kirkwood's gaps) at periods corresponding to 1/2 1/3, and 2/5 Jupiter's period of revolution (11.86 sidereal years). This phenomenon can be explained by the fact that, if

an asteroid is in one of Kirkwood's gaps, then every second, third, or fifth revolution around the Sun, it will experience a perturbation by Jupiter of the same direction and magnitude; over the course of millions of years, these perturbations move asteroids out of the Kirkwood's gaps. This is a resonance effect of planetary perturbations, and it is only one of several resonance phenomena found in the solar system.

Ratios between the periods of revolution of several planets around the Sun are another resonance phenomenon that is poorly understood. The periods of revolution of Venus, the Earth, and Mars around the Sun are nearly in the ratio is 5:8:15. The periods of revolution of Jupiter and Saturn are nearly in a 2:5 ratio, and for Uranus, Neptune, and Pluto they are nearly in a 1:2:3 ratio. The 2:3 ratio between the periods of revolution of Neptune and Pluto makes Pluto's orbit more stable. Due to the ellipticity of its orbit, near perihelion (the point on its orbit closest to the Sun) Pluto comes closer to the Sun than Neptune. Pluto last reached perihelion in September 1989; it has been closer to the Sun than Neptune since 1979 and will continue to be closer until 1998, when it will resume its usual place as the Sun's most distant known planet. However, Neptune will be the Sun's most distant known planet from 1995 to 1998! Recent calculations showed that, because of the 2:3 ratio of the orbital periods, the orientation of Pluto's orbit, and of the positions of Neptune and Pluto in their orbits , Neptune and Pluto have never been closer than 2,500,000,000 km in the last 10,000,000 years. Without the 2:3 ratio of their orbital periods, Pluto probably would have had a close encounter with Neptune which could have ejected Pluto and Charon into separate orbits around the Sun that are drastically different from the systems present orbit.

Let us now turn to resonance phenomena in planetary satellite systems. Jupiter's inner three Gallean satellites, Io, Europa, and Ganymede, have orbital periods of revolution around Jupiter that are nearly in the ratio 1:2:4. Five of Saturn's closest satellites, Pandora, Mimas, Enceladus, Tethys, and Dione, have orbital periods of revolution around Saturn that are nearly in the ratio 4:6:9:12:18. Resonance effects produced by some of these satellites, especially the 1.2 resonance with Mimas' period of revolution around Saturn, seem to have produced the Cassini Division between Saturn's A and B rings, which is analogous to the 1:2 Kirkwood's gap in the Main Asteroid Belt. A 3:4 orbital period resonance seems to exist between Saturn's largest satellite Titan and its next satellite out Hyperion.

Other resonances between the satellites and ring systems of Jupiter, Uranus, and Neptune are not clear because these ring systems are far less developed than that of Saturn.

Tidal effects

A tidal effect is produced when the gravitational pull of one body on a second one is appreciably greater on the nearer part of the second one than on its center, and in turn, the first body's pull on the second one's center is greater than its pull on the second one's most distant part. Unlike the gravitational force F_g, which varies as the inverse square of the distance r between the centers of the two bodies ($1/r_2$); see Equation 1, the tidal effect varies as the inverse cube ($1/r^3$) of the distance between their centers. Both the Moon and the Sun raise tides in the Earth's oceans, atmosphere, and solid body. The lag of the tides raised in the oceans behind the Moon's crossings of the celestial meridian causes a gravitational interaction between the Earth and Moon which slows the Earth's rotation and moves the Moon's orbit further from the Earth.

Tides raised in the Moon's solid body by the Earth have slowed its rotation until it has become tidally locked to the Earth (the Moon keeps the same hemisphere turned towards the Earth, and its periods of rotation and revolution around the Earth are the same, 27.32 mean solar days). Eventually the Earth's rotation will be slowed to where the Earth will be tidally locked to the Moon, and the durations of the sidereal day and sidereal month will both equal about 47 present mean solar days.

Tidal evolution has forced most planetary satellites to become tidally locked to their planets. This includes all of Jupiter's Galilean satellites and its four small satellites closer to Jupiter than Io, probably most of Saturn's satellites out to Iasetus (Titan, Saturn's largest satellite, is probably tidally locked to Saturn), the satellites of Uranus and Neptune, and the Pluto–Charon double planet. Tidal action in Io's interior produced by Jupiter (and to a lesser degree by its next satellite out Europa) powers volcanism on Io, making it the most volcanically active body in the solar systems Tidal effects also may have powered volcanic activity on Europa and Ganymede, Saturn's satellite Enceladus, and Uranus satellites Miranda and Ariel; all of them show some evidence of resurfacing. Some of the Earth's internal heat may have been produced by the Moon's tidal action.

The Sun's tidal action on Mercury at perihelion has tidally locked Mercury's rotation to its angular velocity near perihelion, which is 1.5 times Mercury's average orbital angular velocity; Mercury's rotation period is 58.6 days, 2/3 of its 87.9 day period of revolution around the Sun.

When two bodies are very close together, tidal forces tending to disrupt a body can equal or exceed the attractive gravitational forces holding it together. If the tidal stresses exceed the yield limits of the body's material, the body will gradually disintegrate into many smaller bodies. The mathematician E. Roche (1820–1885) studied the limiting separation of two bodies where the tidal and gravitational forces are equal; it usually between 2–3 times the radius of the more massive body and depends on the relative densities of the bodies and their state of motion. If two bodies approach closer than this Roche limit, one (usually the smaller, less massive body) or both bodies will begin to disintegrate. The rings of some of the Jovian planets may have formed from the tidal disintegration of one or more of their close satellites. Theory predicts that after the Earth's and Moon's rotations become tidally locked (see above), the Sun's tides raised on the Earth will cause the Moon to approach the Earth. If this effect lasts long enough, the Moon may get closer to the Earth than its Roche limit, be disintegrated by the Earth's tidal forces, and form a ring of small bodies which orbit the Earth.

Tidal effects act on close double stars, distorting their shapes, changing their orbits, and sometimes tidally locking their rotations. In some cases, tidal effects cause streams of gas to flow in a double star system and can transfer matter from one star to the other or allow it to escape into interstellar space. Tidal effects even seem to act between galaxies, with one galaxy distorting the form of its neighbor.

Precession

Rapidly rotating planets and satellites have appreciable equatorial bulges as a consequence of Newton's First Law of Motion. If the rotation axis of such a body is not perpendicular to its orbit, other bodies in the system will exert stronger gravitational attractions on the near part of the bulge than its far part. The effect of this difference is to tend to turn the body's rotation axis perpendicular to the plane of its orbit. Because the body is rotating rapidly, however, this does not happen, and, like the rotation axis of a spinning top, the body's rotation axis describes a cone in space whose axis is the perpendicular to the body's orbit (in a two–body system). This phenomenon is called precession, and it is important for the Earth, Mars, and the Jovian planets. For the Earth, precession causes its celestial poles to describe small circles of 23.°5 arc radii around its ecliptic poles and the equinoxes to move westward on the ecliptic. They require 25,800 years to make one 360 circuit around the ecliptic poles and the ecliptic. For liars, the estimated period of precession is about 175,000 years.

Non–gravitational effects

Twentieth century physics have found that photons of light possess momentum which, when they are absorbed or reflected by material bodies, transfers momentum to the bodies, producing a light pressure effect. The interaction of photon velocity of light with the orbital velocities of bodies orbiting the Sun produces a retarding effect on their orbits known as the Poynting–Robertson Effect. These effects are insignificant for large solar system bodies, but are important for bodies smaller than .394 in (1 cm) in diameter. The Poynting–Robertson Effect causes such small interplanetary particles to spiral inwards towards the Sun and to eventually be vaporized by heating from its radiation. Much smaller (micron–sized) particles will be pushed out away from the Sun by light pressure which, along with electromagnetic forces, are the dominant mechanisms for the formation of comet tails.

The three–body problem

No closed general solution has been found for the problem of systems of three or more bodies whose motions are controlled by their mutual gravitational attractions in a form analogous to the generalized Kepler's Laws for the two–body problem.

However, in 1772 Joseph Lagrange (1736–1813) found a special stable solution known as the Restricted Three-Body Problem. If the second body in the three–body system has a mass M_2 less than $0.04M_1$ where M_1 is the mass of the most massive Body 1, then there are five stability points in the orbital plane of Bodies 1 and 2. Three of these points, L_1, L_2, and L_3 lie on the line joining Bodies 1 and 2. The stability of particles placed at these points is minimal; slight perturbations will cause them to move away from these points indefinitely. The points L_4 and L_5, respectively 60° ahead of and 60° behind Body 2 in its orbit around the system's center of mass, are more stable; particles placed there will, if slightly perturbed, go into orbits around these points.

Lagrange's solution became relevant to the solar system in 1906 when Max Wolf (1863–1952) discovered the asteroid Achilles in Jupiter's orbit but about 60° ahead of it (near the L_4 point of the solution). Several hundred such asteroids are now known; they are called the Trojan asteroids, since they are named for heroes of the Trojan War. Following the three-body problem, the Sun is Body 1, Jupiter is Body 2, and the asteroids Achilles, Agamemnon, Ajax, Diomedes, Odysseus, and other asteroids named after Greek heroes cluster around the L_4 point of Jupiter's orbit, forming the "Greek camp." The asteroids Anchises, Patroclus, Priam, Aneas, that are named for Trojan heroes cluster around the L_5 point (60° behind Jupiter in its orbit), forming the "Trojan camp." The L_4 and L_5 points of the orbits of the Earth, Mars, and Saturn around the Sun and of the Moon's orbits around the Earth have been searched for the presence of small bodies ranging in size from asteroids to interplanetary dust without confirmed success. In Saturn's satellite system, with Saturn as Body 1 and its satellite Dione as Body 2, Saturn's small satellite Helene orbits Saturn in Dione's orbit near the L_4 point; with Saturn's satellite Tethys as Body 2, Saturn's satellites Telesto orbits in Tethys' orbit close to the leading L_4 point and Calypso orbits close to the–following L_5 point.

The n–body problem

For systems of n gravitationally interacting bodies where n=3 to thousands, that is, multiple stars and star clusters where the member stars are of comparable mass, the Virial Theorem, by working with a systems gravitational potential energy and the kinetic energies of the member stars, can give some insight into the system's stability and evolution. However, the theorem gives mainly information of a statistical nature about the system; it cannot define the space trajectory of a specific star in the system over an extended time interval, and therefore, it cannot predict close encounters of it with other stars nor whether or not this specific star will remain part of the system or will be ejected from it.

Recent developments

In the last 30 years high performance computers have been used to study the no body problem (n=3 to n=10 or more) by stepwise integration of the orbits of the gravitationally interacting bodies. Earlier computers were incapable of performing such calculations over sufficiently long time intervals. The study of the stability of Pluto's orbits over the last 10,000,000 years mentioned above was made for n=5 (the Sun and the Jovian planets) perturbing Pluto's orbit. Some other studies have treated the solar system as a n=9 system (the Sun and the eight major planets) over time intervals of several million years.

However, the finite increments of space and time used in stepwise integrations introduce small uncertainties in the predicted positions of solar system objects; these uncertainties increase as the time interval covered by the calculations increases. This has led to the application to celestial mechanics of a new concept in science, Chaos, which started to develop in the 1970s. Chaos studies indicate that, due to increasing inaccuracy of prediction from integration calculations and also due to incompleteness of the mathematical models integrated, meaningful predictions about the state or position of a system cannot be made beyond some finite time. One result is that Pluto's orbit is chaotic over times of about 800,000,000 years, so that its orbit and position in the early solar system or billions of years from now cannot be specified. Also the rotation of Saturn's satellite Hyperion appears to be chaotic. Chaos is now being applied to studies of the stability of the solar system, a problem which celestial mechanics has considered for centuries without finding a definite answer.

Chaos has also been able to show how certain orbits of main belt asteroids can, over billions of years, evolve into orbits which cross the orbits of Mars end the Earth, producing near–Earth asteroids (NEA), of which about 100 are now known. Computer predictions of NEA orbits are now being made to identify NEA which may collide with the Earth in the future; such collisions would threaten the very existence of our civilization. The prediction of such Earth–impacting asteroids may allow them to be dejected past the Earth or to be destroyed; the space technology to do this may be available soon.

High performance computers and the concept of chaos are now also being used to study the satellite systems of the Jovian planets. They have also been used to study the orbits of stars in multiple star systems and the trajectories of stars in star clusters and galaxies.

The search for planets around other stars is also a recent development. It uses the theory of the two–body problem, starting from earlier work on astrometric double stars. These are stars whose proper motions on the sky are not straight lines as are the case for single stars, but are wavelike curves with periods of some years. This indicates that they are actually double stars with the visible star moving around the system's center of mass (which has straight–line proper motion) with an unseen companion. The stellar companions of Airius A (Gliese 244A), Procyon A (Gliese 280A), Ross 614 A (Gliese 234A), and Mu Cassiopeiae (Gliese 53A) were first detected as astrometric double stars before being observed optically. Small departures of the proper motions of stars from straight lines have been used since 1940 to predict the presence of companions of substellar mass (less than 0.07 solar mass) around nearby stars.

Action of a star around a double star system's center of mass produces periodic variations of the Doppler shift of the star's spectral lines as the star first approaches the Earth, then recedes from it as seen from the system's center of mass. Since 1980, very precise spectroscopic observations have allowed searches for companions of substellar mass of visible stars to be made at several observatories.

These methods have allowed several dozen companions of substellar mass (so–called "brown dwarfs" and bodies of Jovian planet mass) to be suspected near stars other than the Sun. Unfortunately, as of late 1994 none of the suspected bodies of planetary mass associated with other stars has been confirmed by consistent observations at two or more observatories. Surprisingly, the two or three most reliably established planets have been detected orbiting a pulsar, which is a neutron star, a star that has used up its nuclear energy sources and has almost completed its evolution. The planets have been detected by apparent periodic variations in the period of the radio pulses from this neutron star pulsar PSR 1257 + 12, and moreover, they seem to have masses on the order of the Earth's mass or less. The search for planets orbiting normal stars continues; this is closely associated with the Search for Extra–Terrestrial Intelligence (the SETI Project).

Since 1957, the Space Age has accelerated the development of the branch of celestial mechanics called astrodynamics, which is becoming increasingly important. In addition to the traditional gravitational interactions between celestial bodies, astrodynamics must also consider (rocket) propulsion effects that are necessary for inserting artificial satellites and other spacecraft into their necessary orbits and trajectories. Aerodynamic effects must sometimes be considered for planets and satellites with appreciable atmospheres (Venus, Earth, Mars, the Jovian planets, Io, Titan, Neptune's satellite Britons and Pluto). Trajectory building is a new part of astrodynamics; it consists of combining different conic section orbits and propulsion segments along with planet and planetary satellite flybys to increase spacecraft payload on missions requiring very large propellant expenditures. The spacecraft *Voyagers 1* and *2*, *Magellan*, and *Galileo* have all used trajectory building, and future spacecraft such as the Cassini/Huygens mission to Saturn and Titan plan to use it to reach their destinations. Minor perturbations due to light pressure, the Poynting–Robertson Effect, and electromagnetic effects sometimes must also be considered. The solar sail is now being studied in spacecraft design as a way of using the light pressure from sunlight on solar sails to maneuver spacecraft and propel them through interplanetary space. Finally, the development of astrodynamics has increased the importance of hyperbolic orbits, since so far all flybys of planets and planetary satellites by spacecraft have occurred along hyperbolic orbits. The space-craft Pioneers 10 and 11 Voyagers 1 and 2 are leaving the solar system along hyperbolic orbits with respect to the Sun that will take them into interstellar trajectories around the center of our Milky Way galaxy. Their hyperbolic orbits are being checked by radio signals from their transmitters as they leave the solar system for perturbations that could be produced by the gravitational attractions of undiscovered trans–Neptunian planets.

See also Brown dwarf; Celestial coordinates; Kepler's laws; Gravity and gravitation; Laws of motion; Moon; Neutron star; Pluto; Precession of the equinoxes; Solar system; Stellar evolution; Tides.

Further Reading:

Brouwer, Kirk and G. M. Clemence. *Methods of Celestial Mechanics.* New York, New York: Academic Press, 1961.
Glelek, Jame. *Chaos: Making a New Science.* New York, New York: Viking Penguin, Inc. 1988.
Motz, Lloyd and Anneta Duveen. *Essentials of Astronomy.* Belmont, California: Wadsworth, 1966.
"Pulsar's Planets Confirmed." *Sky and Telescope* 87 (1994).

Celsius see **Temperature**

Cell

The cell is the smallest living component of organisms and is the basic unit of life. In multicellular living things, a collection of cells that work together to perform similar functions is called a tissue; various tissues that perform coordinated functions form organs; and organs that work together to perform general processes form body systems. The human digestive system, for example, is composed of various organs including the stomach, pancreas, and the intestines. The tissue that lines the intestine is called epithelial tissue. Epithelial tissue, in turn, is composed of special cells called epithelial cells. In the small intestine, these epithelial cells are specialized for their absorptive function: each epithelial cell is covered with thousands of small projections called microvilli. The numerous microvilli greatly increase the surface area of the small intestine through which nutrients can be absorbed into the bloodstream.

Types of cells

Multicellular organisms contain a vast array of highly specialized cells. Plants contain root cells, leaf cells, and stem cells. Humans have skin cells, nerve cells, and sex cells. Each kind of cell is structured to perform a highly specialized function. Often, examining a cell's structure reveals much about its function in the organism. For instance, as we have already seen, epithelial cells in the small intestine are specialized for absorption due to the numerous microvilli that crowd their surfaces. Nerve cells, or neurons, are another kind of specialized cell whose form reflects function. Nerve cells consist of a cell body and long processes, called axons, that conduct nerve impulses. Dendrites are shorter processes that receive nerve impulses.

Sensory cells—the cells that detect sensory information from the outside environment and transmit this information to the brain—often have unusual shapes and structures that contribute to their function. The rod cells in the retina of the eye, for instance, look like no other cell in the human body. Shaped like a rod, these cells have a light–sensitive region that contains numerous membranous disks. Within each disk is embedded a special light–sensitive pigment that captures light. When the pigment receives light from the outside environment, nerve cells in the eye are triggered to send a nerve impulse in the brain. In this way, humans are able to detect light.

Cells, however, can also exist as single–celled organisms. The organisms called protists, for instance, are single–celled organisms. Examples of protists include the microscopic organism called *Paramecium* and the single–celled alga called *Chlamydomonas*.

Prokaryotes and eukaryotes

Two types of cells are recognized in living things. Prokaryotes (literally, "before the nucleus") are cells that have no distinct nucleus. Most prokaryotic organisms are single–celled, such as bacteria and algae. Eukaryotic (literally, "true nucleus") organisms, on the other hand, have a distinct nucleus and a highly organized internal structure. Distinct organelles, the small structures that each perform a specific set of functions, are present within eukaryotes. These organelles are bound by membranes. Prokaryotes, in addition to their lack of a nucleus, also lack these membrane–bound organelles.

Cell size and numbers

It is estimated that an adult human body contains about 60 trillion cells. Most of these cells, with some exceptions, are so small that a microscope is necessary to see them. The small size of cells fulfills a distinct purpose in the functioning of the body. If cells were larger, many of the processes that cells perform could

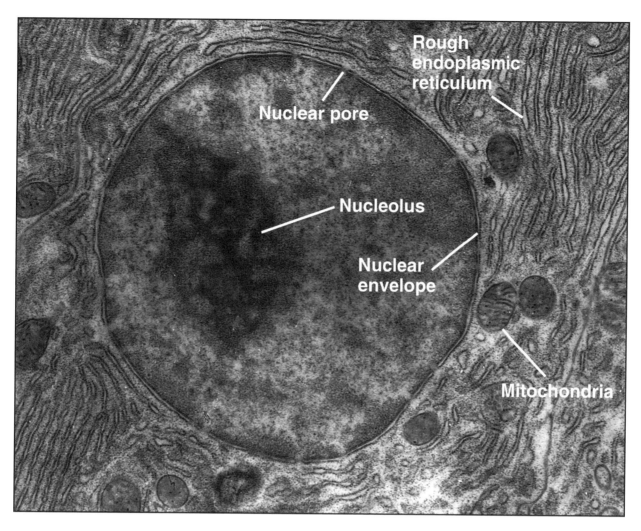

Rough endoplasmic reticulum

Nuclear pore

Nucleolus

Nuclear envelope

Mitochondria

Some features common to animal cells.

not occur efficiently. To visualize this concept, think about the intestinal epithelial cells discussed earlier. What if the intestinal epithelium were composed of one, large cell instead of thousands of small cells? A large cell has a large volume, or contents. The surface area, or membrane, of this large cell is the site through which nutrients enter the small intestine for delivery to the bloodstream. Because the volume of this large cell is so large, the surface area, by comparison, is relatively small. Large cells, therefore, have a small surface area to volume ratio. Only so many nutrients can pass through the limited membrane area of this large cell. With a small surface area to volume ratio, the amount of substances passing into and out of the cell is severely restricted.

However, if the intestinal epithelium is divided into thousands of smaller cells, the volume stays the same, but the surface area—the number of cell membranes— greatly increases. Many more nutrients can pass

through the intestinal epithelium cells. Small cells, therefore, have a large surface area to volume ratio. The large surface area to volume ratio of small cells makes the transport of substances into and out of cells extremely efficient.

Another reason for the small size of cells is that control of cellular processes is easier in a small cell than in a large cell. Cells are dynamic, living things. Cells transport substances from one place to another, reproduce themselves, and produce various enzymes and chemicals for export to the extracellular environment. All of these activities are accomplished under the direction of the nucleus, the control center of the cell. If the nucleus had to control a large cell, then this direction might break down. Substances transported from one place to another would have to traverse great distances to reach their destinations; reproduction of a large cell would be an extremely complicated endeavor; and products for export would not be as efficiently produced. Smaller cells, because of their more manageable size, are much more efficiently controlled than larger cells.

The structure and function of cells

The basic structure of all cells, whether prokaryote and eukaryote, is the same. All cells have a plasma membrane through which substances pass into and out of the cell. With the exception of a few minor differences, plasma membranes are the same in prokaryotes and eukaryotes. The interior of both kinds of cells is called the cytoplasm. Within the cytoplasm of eukaryotes are embedded the cellular organelles; the cytoplasm of prokaryotes contains no organelles. Finally, both types of cells contain small structures called ribosomes that function in protein synthesis. Composed of two protein subunits, ribosomes are not bounded by membranes; therefore, they are not considered organelles. In eukaryotes, ribosomes are either bound to an organelle, the endoplasmic reticulum, or exist as "free" ribosomes in the cytoplasm. Prokaryotes contain only free ribosomes.

The structure of prokaryotes

An example of a typical prokaryote is the bacterial cell. Bacterial cells can be shaped like rods, spheres, or corkscrews. All prokaryotes are bounded by a plasma membrane. Overlying this plasma membrane is a cell wall, and in some bacteria, a capsule consisting of a jelly–like material overlies the cell wall. Many pathogenic bacteria that cause illness in animals have capsules. The capsule provides an extra layer of protection for the bacteria, and often pathogenic bacteria with capsules cause much more severe disease than those without capsules.

Within the cytoplasm of prokaryotes is a nucleoid, a region where the genetic material (DNA) resides. This nucleoid is not a true nucleus because it is not bounded by a membrane. Also within the cytoplasm are numerous ribosomes. These ribosomes are not attached to any structure and are thus called "free" ribosomes.

Attached to the cell wall of some bacteria are flagella, whip–like structures that provide for movement. Some bacteria also have pili, which are short, finger–like projections that assist the bacteria in attaching to tissues. Bacteria cannot cause disease if they cannot attach to tissues. Bacteria that cause pneumonia, for instance, attach to the tissues of the lung. Bacterial pili greatly facilitates this attachment to tissues, and thus, like capsules, bacteria with pili are often more virulent than those without.

The structure of eukaryotes

The organelles found in eukaryotes include the membrane system consisting of plasma membrane, endoplasmic reticulum, Golgi body, and vesicles; the nucleus; cytoskeleton; and mitochondria. In addition, plant cells have special organelles not found in animals cells. These organelles are the chloroplasts, cell wall, and vacuoles(Figure 1).

The membrane system

The membrane system of a cell performs many important functions. This system controls the entrance and exit of substances into and out of the cell, and also provides for the manufacture and packaging of substances within the cell. The membrane system of the cell consists of the plasma membrane, which encloses the cell contents; the endoplasmic reticulum, which manufactures lipids and proteins; the Golgi body, which packages substances manufactured within the cell; and various vesicles, which perform different functions.

The plasma membrane

The plasma membrane of the cell is often described as "selectively permeable;" that is, the plasma membrane is designed so that only certain substances are allowed to traverse its borders. The plasma membrane is composed of two layers of molecules called phospholipids. Each phospholipid molecule consists of a phosphate "head" and two fatty acid chains that dangle from the head.

The orientation of these two sections of the phospholipid molecule is crucial to the function of the plasma membrane. The phosphate region is hydrophilic (literally, "water–loving") and attracts water. The fatty acid region is hydrophobic (literally, "water–hating") and repels water. In the phospholipid bilayer of the plasma membrane, the phospholipid layers are arranged so that the two phosphate hydrophilic regions face outward, towards the watery extracellular environment, and inward, towards the cellular cytoplasm, which also contains water. The two hydrophobic fatty acid portions of the chains face each other, forming a water–tight shield. The plasma membrane, then, is both water-proof and water–attracting. It functions both as a boundary between the cell's contents and the external cellular environment, yet also allows the transport of water-containing and other substances across its boundaries.

Embedded within the plasma membranes of eukaryotes are various proteins. These proteins serve several distinct functions in the cell. Some proteins are pumps or channels for the import and export of sub-

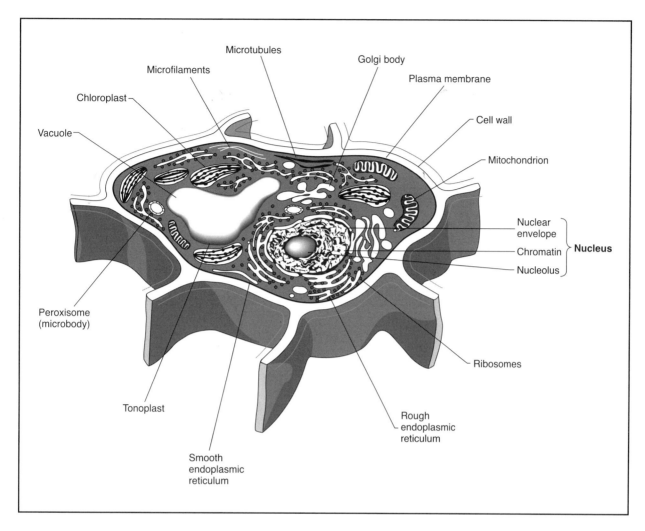

Figure 1. A plant cell.

stances. Other proteins, called antigens, serve as identification markers for the cell. Still other proteins help the cell form attachments with other cells. Because these membrane proteins often protrude out of the cell membrane into the extracellular environment, they too have hydrophobic and hydrophilic regions. Portions of the proteins that are embedded within the plasma membrane are hydrophobic, and portions of the proteins that extend outward into the extracellular environment are hydrophilic.

Scientists studying plasma membranes use the term "fluid–mosaic model" to describe the structure of plasma membranes. The "mosaic" portion of the model describes the way proteins are embedded within the plasma membrane. The "fluid" part of the model explains the fluid nature of plasma membranes. Rather than being fixed in one place within the plasma membrane, experiments have shown that the phospholipids exhibit some movement within the plasma membranes,

sometimes moving laterally, sometimes (although rarely), flip–flopping from one phospholipid layer to another. The membrane proteins also move within the plasma membrane, albeit more slowly than the phospholipids.

Endoplasmic reticulum

The endoplasmic reticulum (meaning "within the cytoplasm" and "net") consists of flattened sheets, sacs, and tubes of membrane that cover the entire expanse of a eukaryotic cell's cytoplasm. This internal system of membranes is continuous with the double membrane that surrounds the cell's nucleus. Therefore, the encoded instructions that the nucleus sends out for the synthesis of proteins flow directly into the endoplasmic reticulum. Within the cell, the endoplasmic reticulum synthesizes lipids and proteins. The proteins that the endoplasmic reticulum synthesizes, such as enzymes, are exported from the cell to perform various functions in the body.

Proteins that are made in the cell for use by the cell—for instance, as channels in the plasma membrane—are made by the free ribosomes that dot the cytoplasm.

Two types of endoplasmic reticulum are found in the eukaryotic cell. Rough endoplasmic reticulum is studded with ribosomes on its outer face. These ribosomes are the sites of protein synthesis. Once a protein is synthesized on a ribosome, it is enclosed within a vesicle, a small, membrane–bound "bubble." The vesicle travels to another organelle, the Golgi body. Within the Golgi body, the proteins within the vesicle are further modified before they are exported from the cell. Cells that specialize in protein secretion contain large amounts of rough endoplasmic reticulum. For instance, cells of the pancreas that produce the protein insulin, have abundant rough endoplasmic reticulum. Plasma cells, white blood cells that secrete immune proteins called antibodies, are so crowded with rough endoplasmic reticulum it is difficult to distinguish other organelles within the cytoplasm.

The other type of endoplasmic reticulum is smooth endoplasmic reticulum. Smooth endoplasmic reticulum does not have ribosomes and is the site of lipid metabolism. Here, macromolecules containing lipids are broken down into their constituent parts. In addition, smooth endoplasmic reticulum functions in the synthesis of lipid–containing macromolecules. Smooth endoplasmic reticulum is not as common in cells as rough endoplasmic reticulum. Large amounts of smooth endoplasmic reticulum are found in cells that specialize in lipid metabolism. For instance, liver cells remove alcohol and drugs from the bloodstream. Liver cells have an impressive network of smooth endoplasmic reticulum. Similarly, cells of the ovaries and testes, which produce the lipid–containing hormones estrogen and testosterone, contain large amounts of smooth endoplasmic reticulum.

The Golgi body

Named for its discoverer, the nineteenth century Italian scientist Camillo Golgi, the Golgi body is one of the most unusually shaped organelles. Looking somewhat like a stack of pancakes, the Golgi body consists of stacked, membrane–bounded, flattened sacs. Surrounding the Golgi body are numerous, small, membrane-bounded vesicles. The Golgi body and its vesicles function in the sorting, modifying, and packaging of macromolecules that are secreted by the cell or used within the cell for various functions.

The Golgi body can be compared to the shipping and receiving department of a large company. Each Golgi body within a cell has a *cis* face, which is analogous to the receiving division of the department. Here,

the Golgi body receives macromolecules synthesized in the endoplasmic reticulum encased within vesicles. The *trans* face of the Golgi body is analogous to the shipping division of the department, and is the site from which modified and packaged macromolecules are transported to their destinations.

Within the Golgi body, various chemical groups are added to the macromolecules so ensure that they reach their proper destination. In this way, the Golgi body attaches an "address" to each macromolecule it receives. For example, cells called goblet cells in the lining of the intestine secrete mucous. The protein component of mucous, called mucin, is modified in the Golgi body by the addition of carbohydrate groups. From the Golgi body, the modified mucin is packaged within a vesicle. The vesicle containing its mucous cargo fuses with the plasma membrane of the goblet cell, and is released into the extracellular environment.

Vesicles

Vesicles are small, membrane–bounded spheres that contain various macromolecules. Some vesicles, as we have seen, are used to transport macromolecules from the endoplasmic reticulum to the Golgi body, and from the Golgi body to various destinations. Special kinds of vesicles perform other functions as well. Lysosomes are vesicles that contain enzymes involved in cellular digestion. Some protists, for instance, engulf other cells for food. In a process called phagocytosis, the protist surrounds a food particle and engulfs it within a vesicle. This food containing vesicle is transported within the protist's cytoplasm until it is contiguous with a lysosome. The food vesicle and lysosome merge, and the enzymes within the lysosome are released into the food vesicle. The enzymes break the food down into smaller parts for use by the protist.

Lysosomes, however, are found in all kinds of cells. In all cells, lysosomes digest old, worn–out organelles. They also play a role in the self–destruction of old cells. Although scientists do not understand the trigger mechanism of this self–destruction, cells that are not functioning properly due to old–age apparently self–digest by means of lysosomes. Cell death is also a component of normal developmental processes. For instance, a human fetus has web–like hands and feet. As development progresses, the cells that compose these webs slowly self–destruct, freeing the fingers.

Peroxisomes, as their name implies, contain hydrogen peroxide. Peroxisomes function in the oxidation of many materials, including fats. In oxidation, oxygen is added to a molecule. When oxygen is added to fats, hydrogen peroxide is formed. As anyone who has treated a cut with hydrogen peroxide knows, this substance is lethal to cells. Therefore, the oxidation of fats takes place within the membranes of peroxisomes so that the harmful chemical does not leak out into the cell's cytoplasm.

The nucleus

The nucleus is the control center of the cell. Under a microscope, the nucleus looks like a dark blob, with a darker region, called the nucleolus, centered within it. The nucleolus is the site where the subunits of ribosomes are manufactured. Surrounding the nucleus is a double membrane called the nuclear envelope. The nuclear envelope is studded all over with tiny openings called nuclear pores.

The nucleus directs all cellular activities by controlling the synthesis of proteins. The nucleus contains encoded instructions for the synthesis of proteins in a helical molecule called deoxyribonucleic acid (DNA). The cell's DNA is packaged within the nucleus in a structural form called chromatin. Chromatin consists of DNA wound tightly around spherical proteins called histones. When the cell prepares to divide, the DNA unwinds from the histones and assumes the shape of chromosomes, the X–shaped structures visible within the nucleus prior to cell division. Chromatin packaging of DNA allows all of the cell's DNA to fit into the combined space of the nucleus. If DNA was not packaged into chromatin, it would spill out over a space about 100 times as large as the cell itself.

The first step in protein synthesis begins in the nucleus. Within the nucleus, DNA is translated into a molecule called messenger ribonucleic acid (mRNA). mRNA then leaves the nucleus through the nuclear pores. Once in the cytoplasm, mRNA attaches to ribosomes (either bound to endoplasmic reticulum or free in the cytoplasm) and initiates protein synthesis. Proteins made for export from the cell function as enzymes that participate in all the body's chemical reactions. Because enzymes are essential for all the body's chemical processes—from cellular respiration to digestion—direction of the synthesis of these enzymes in essence controls all the activities of the body. Therefore, the nucleus, which contains the instructions for the synthesis of these proteins, directs all cellular activities and thus all body processes.

The cytoskeleton

The cytoskeleton is the "skeletal" framework of the cell. Instead of bone, however, the cell's skeleton consists of three kinds of protein filaments that form networks. These networks give the cell shape and provide for cellular movement. The three types of cytoskeletal fibers are microtubules, actin filaments, and intermediate filaments.

Microtubules are 25 nanometers in diameter and consist of protein subunits called tubulin. Each microtubule is composed of eleven pairs of these tubulin subunits arranged in a ring. In animal cells, microtubules arise from a region of the cell called the microtubule organizing center (MTOC) located near the nucleus. From this center, microtubules fan out across the cell, forming a network of "tracks" over which various organelles move within the cell. Microtubules also form small, paired structures called centrioles within animal cells. These structures are not considered organelles because they are not bounded by membranes. Scientists once thought that centrioles formed the microtubules that pull the cell apart during cell division; now it is known that each centriole with the pair move apart during cell division and indicate the plan along which the cell divides.

Some eukaryotic cells move about by means of microtubules attached to the exterior of the plasma membrane. These microtubules are called flagella and cilia. Flagella and cilia both have the same structure: a ring of nine tubulin triplets arranged around two tubulin subunits. The difference between flagella and cilia lies in their movement and numbers. Flagella are attached to the cell by a "crank"–like apparatus that allows the flagella to rotate. Usually, a flagellated cell has only one or two flagella. Cilia, on the other hand, are not attached with a "crank," and beat back and forth to provide movement. Ciliated cells usually have hundreds of these projections that cover their surfaces. For example, the protist *Paramecium* moves by means of a single flagellum, while the protist *Didinium* is covered with numerous cilia. Ciliated cells also perform important functions in the human body. The airways of humans and other animals are lined with ciliated cells that sweep debris and bacteria upwards, out of the lungs and into the throat. There, the debris is either coughed from the throat or swallowed into the digestive tract, where digestive enzymes destroy harmful bacteria.

Actin filaments are 8 nanometers in diameter and consist of two strands of the protein actin that are wound around each other. Actin filaments are especially prominent in muscle cells, where they provide for the contraction of muscle tissue.

Intermediate filaments are 10 nanometers in diameter and are composed of fibrous proteins. Because of their relative strength, they function mainly to anchor organelles in place within the cytoplasm.

KEY TERMS

· ·

Actin filament—A type of cytoskeletal filament that has contractile properties.

Amyloplast—A plant cell plastid that stores starch.

Cell wall—A tough outer covering that overlies the plasma membrane of bacteria and plant cells.

Centriole—Paired structures consisting of microtubules; in animal cells, directs the plane of cell division.

Chloroplast—A plant cell plastid that performs photosynthesis.

Chromoplast—A plant cell plastid that contains yellow and orange pigments.

Cilia—Short projections consisting of microtubules that cover the surface of some cells and provide for movement.

***Cis* face**—The side (or "face") of the Golgi body that receives vesicles containing macromolecules.

Crista—pl., cristae, the folds of the inner membrane of a mitochondrion.

Cytoplasm—The intracellular space of a cell.

Cytoskeleton—The network of filaments that provide structure and movement of a cell.

Deoxyribonucleic acid—DNA; the genetic material of a cell that contains encoded instructions for the synthesis of proteins

Endoplasmic reticulum—The network of membranes that extends throughout the cell; involved in protein synthesis and lipid metabolism.

Endosymbiotic theory—A theory that proposes that mitochondria, chloroplasts, and other eukaryotic organelles originally arose within cells by symbiosis between a single–celled prokaryote and another prokaryote.

Eukaryotic cell—A cell that contains a distinct nucleus and organelles.

Flagellum—A whip–like structure that provides for movement in some cells.

Fluid–mosaic model—The model that describes the nature of the plasma membrane; the "mosaic" portion describes the proteins embedded within the plasma membrane, and the "fluid" portion describes the fluidity of the plasma membrane.

Golgi body—Organelle that sorts, modifies, and packages macromolecules.

Granum—Sacs within a chloroplast that contain photosynthetic enzymes.

Hydrophilic—"Water–loving;" describes the phosphate portion of a phospholipid.

Hydrophobic—"Water–hating;" describes the fatty acid portion of a phospholipid.

Intermediate filament—A type of cytoskeletal filament that anchors organelles.

Lysosome—A vesicle that contains digestive enzymes.

Matrix—The inner space of a mitochondrion formed by cristae.

Mitochondria

The mitochondria are the power plants of cells. Each sausage–shaped mitochondrion is covered by an outer membrane; the inner membrane of a mitochondrion is folded into compartments called cristae (meaning "box"). The matrix, or inner space created by the cristae, contains the enzymes necessary for the many chemical reactions that eventually transform food molecules into energy.

Cells contain hundreds to thousands of mitochondria. An interesting aspect of mitochondria is that they contain their own DNA sequences, although not in the profusion that the nucleus contains. The presence of this separate DNA, along with the resemblance of mitochondria to single–celled prokaryotes, has led to a the-ory of eukaryotic evolution called the endosymbiotic theory. This theory postulates that mitochondria were once separate prokaryotes that became engulfed within other prokaryotes. Instead of being digested, the mitochondrial prokaryotes remained within the engulfing cell and performed its energy–releasing functions. Over millions of years, this symbiotic relationship fostered the evolution of the eukaryotic cell.

Plant organelles

Plant cells have several organelles not found in animal cells. These are plastids, vacuoles, and a cell wall.

Plastids

Plastids are vesicle–type organelles that perform a variety of functions in plants. Amylopasts store starch,

KEY TERMS

. . . .

Microtubule—A type of cytoskeletal filament; the component of centrioles, flagella, and cilia.

Mitochondrion—The power–house of the cell; contains the enzymes necessary for the oxidation of food into energy.

Nuclear envelope—The double membrane that surrounds the nucleus.

Nuclear pore—Tiny openings that stud the nuclear envelope.

Nucleoid—The region in a prokaryote where the cell's DNA is located.

Nucleolus—The darker region within the nucleolus where ribosomal subunits are manufactured.

Nucleus—The control center of a cell; contains the DNA.

Organelle—A membrane–bounded cellular "organ" that performs a specific set of functions within a eukaryotic cell.

Peroxisome—A vesicle that oxidizes fats and other substances and stores hydrogen peroxide.

Phospholipid bilayer—The double layer of phospholipids that compose the plasma membrane.

Phospholipid—A molecule consisting of a phosphate head and two fatty acid chains that dangle from the head; the component of the plasma membrane.

Photosynthesis—In plants, the process in which carbon dioxide and water are converted to sugars.

Pili—Short projections that assist bacteria in attaching to tissues.

Plasma membrane—The membrane of a cell.

Plastid—A vesicle–like organelle found in plant cells.

Prokaryote—A cell without a true nucleus.

Protist—A single–celled eukaryotic organism.

Ribonucleic acid—RNA; the molecule translated from DNA in the nucleus that directs protein synthesis in the cytoplasm.

Ribosome—A protein composed of two subunits that functions in protein synthesis.

Stroma—The material that bathes the interior of chloroplasts in plant cells.

Surface area to volume ratio—The relationship between the surface area provided by the plasma membrane to the volume of the contents of a cell.

Thylakoid—A membranous structure that bisects the interior of a chloroplast.

Trans **face**—The side (or "face") of a Golgi body that releases macromolecule–filled vesicles for transport.

Tubulin—A protein that comprises microtubules.

Vacuole—A space–filling organelle of plant cells.

Vesicle—A membrane–bound sphere that contains a variety of substances in cells.

and chromoplasts store pigment molecules that give some plants their vibrant orange and yellow colors.

Chloroplasts are plastids that carry out photosynthesis, a process in which water and carbon dioxide are transformed into sugars. The interior of chloroplasts contains an elaborate membrane system. Thylakoids bisect the chlorplasts, and attached to these platforms are stacks of membranous sacs called grana. Each granum contains the enzymes necessary for photosynthesis. The membrane system within the chloroplast is bathed in a fluid called stroma, which also contains enzymes.

Like mitochondria, chloroplasts resemble some ancient single–celled prokaryotes and also contain their own DNA sequences. Their origin within eukaryotes is thought to have arisen from the endosymbiotic relationship between a photosynthetic single–celled prokaryote that was engulfed and remained within another prokaryotic cell.

Vacuoles

Plant vacuoles are large vesicles bound by a single membrane. In many plant cells, they occupy about 90% of the cellular space. They perform a variety of functions in the cell, including storage of organic compounds, waste products, pigments, and poisonous compounds, as well as digestive functions.

Cell wall

All plant cells have a cell wall that overlies the plasma membrane. The cell wall of plants consists of a tough carbohydrate substance called cellulose laid down in a matrix or network of other carbohydrates. The cell wall provides an additional layer of protection between the contents of the cell and the outside environment. The crunchiness of an apple, for instance, is attributed to the presence of these cell walls.

See also Cellular respiration; Chloroplast; Chromosome; Deoxyribonucleic acid; Enzyme; Eukaryotae; Flagella; Gene; Meiosis; Mitosis; Neuron; Nucleus, cellular; Organ; Prokaryote; Proteins; Ribonucleic acid (RNA); Tissue.

Further Reading:

Barritt, Greg J. *Communication within Animal Cells.* Oxford: Oxford University Press, 1992.
Bittar, F. Edward, ed. *Chemistry of the Living Cell.* Greenwich, CT: JAI Press, 1992.
Bray, Dennis. *Cell Movements.* New York: Garland Press, 1992.
Carroll, Mark. *Organelles.* New York: Guilford Press, 1989.
The Cell Surface. Plainview, NY: Cold Spring Harbor Laboratory Press, 1992.
Maddox, John. "Why microtubules grow and shrink." *Nature* 362 (18 March 1993): 201.
Pante, Nelly, and Ueli Aebi. "The nuclear pore complex." *The Journal of Cell Biology* 122 (September 1993): 5–6.

Kathleen Scogna

Cell, electrochemical

Electrochemical cells are devices based on the principle that when a chemical oxidation–reduction reaction takes place, electrons are being transferred from one chemical species to another. In one type of electrochemical cell called a voltaic or galvanic cell, these electrons are deliberately taken outside the cell and made to flow through an electric circuit to operate some kind of electrical device. A flashlight battery is an example of a voltaic electrochemical cell.

In the other type of electrochemical cell, called an electrolytic cell, the reverse process is taking place: electrons in the form of an electric current are deliberately being pumped through the chemicals in the cell in order to force an oxidation–reduction reaction to take place. An example of an electrolytic cell is the setup that is used to decompose water into hydrogen and oxygen by electrolysis.

Thus, a voltaic cell produces electricity from a chemical reaction, while an electrolytic cell produces a chemical reaction from electricity. Voltaic and electrolytic cells are considered separately below, following a general discussion of the relationship between chemistry and electricity.

Chemistry and electricity

In order to understand the intimate relationship between chemical reactions and electricity, we can consider a very simple oxidation–reduction reaction: the spontaneous reaction between a sodium atom and a chlorine atom to form sodium chloride:

$$Na + Cl \quad \text{R} \quad Na^+ + Cl^- + energy.$$

$$\underset{atom}{\underset{sodium}{Na}} \quad \underset{atom}{\underset{chlorine}{Cl}} \qquad \underset{ion}{\underset{sodium}{Na^+}} \quad \underset{ion}{\underset{chloride}{Cl^-}}$$

What happens in this reaction is that an electron is passed from the sodium atom to the chlorine atom, leaving the sodium atom positively charged and the chlorine atom negatively charged. (Under normal conditions, the chlorine atoms are paired up into diatomic chlorine molecules, Cl_2; but that doesn't change the present argument.)

When a large number of sodium atoms and chlorine atoms are mixed together and react, a large number of electrons move from sodium atoms to chlorine atoms. These moving electrons constitute a flow of electricity. The "push" or *potential* for this electron flow comes from the sodium atoms' eagerness to get rid of electrons and the chlorine atoms' relative eagerness to grab them.

Voltaic cells

The practical problem when large numbers of sodium and chlorine atoms react is that the electrons are flowing in every direction—wherever a sodium atom can find a chlorine atom. We therefore can't harness the electron flow to do useful electrical work. In order to use the electricity to light up a bulb, for example, we must make the electrons flow in a single direction through a wire; then we can put a bulb in their path and they'll have to push through the filament to get from the sodium atoms to the chlorine atoms, lighting the filament up in the process. In other words, we must separate the sodium atoms from the chlorine atoms, so that they can only transfer their electrons on our terms: through the wire that we provide. Such an arrangement constitutes a voltaic or galvanic cell. It has the effect of converting chemical potential energy—a chemical push—into electrical potential energy—an electrical push: in other words, a voltage.

The sodium–plus–chlorine reaction is difficult to use in practice, because chlorine is a gas and sodium is a highly reactive metal that is nasty to handle. But many other chemical reactions can be used to make voltaic cells for generating electricity. All that is needed is a reaction between a substance (atoms, molecules, or ions) that wants to give up electrons and a substance that wants to grab onto electrons: in other words, an oxidation–reduction reaction. Then it's just a matter of arranging the substances so that the passing of electrons from one to the other must take place through an external wire. Strictly speaking, the resulting devices are voltaic cells, but people generally call them batteries.

As an illustration of how a voltaic cell works, we can choose the metallic elements silver (Ag) and copper (Cu) with their respective ions in solution, Ag^+ and Cu^{++}. Because copper atoms are more eager to give up electrons than silver atoms are, the copper atoms will tend to force the Ag^+ ions to take them. Or to say it the other way, Ag^+ ions are more eager to grab electrons than Cu^{++} ions are, so they will take them away from copper atoms to become neutral silver atoms. Thus, the spontaneous reaction that will take place when all four species are mixed together is

$$Cu \quad + \quad 2Ag^+ \quad R \quad Cu^{++} \quad + \quad 2Ag$$

| copper | silver | copper | silver |
| metal | ions | ion | metal |

This equation says that a piece of copper metal dipped into a solution containing silver ions will dissolve and become copper ions, while at the same time silver ions "plate out" as metallic silver. (This isn't how silver plating is done, however, because the silver comes out as a rough and non–adhering coating on the copper. The silver plating of dinnerware and jewelry is done in an electrolytic cell.)

To make a useful voltaic cell out of the copper–silver system, we must put the Cu and Cu^{++} in one container, the Ag and Ag^+ in a separate container, and then connect them with a wire. Bars of copper and silver metal should be dipped into solutions of copper nitrate, $Cu(NO_3)_2$, and silver nitrate, $AgNO_3$, respectively. A *salt bridge* should be added between the two containers. It is a tube filled with an electrolyte—a solution of an ionic salt such as potassium nitrate KNO_3, which allows ions to flow through it. Without the salt bridge, electrons would tend to build up in the silver container and the reaction would stop because the negative charge has no place to go. The salt bridge allows the negative charge, this time in the form of NO_3^- ions, to complete the circuit by crossing the bridge from the silver container back into the copper container. Now the circuit is complete and the reaction can proceed, producing a steady flow of electrons through the wire and keeping the bulb lit until something runs out—either the copper

KEY TERMS

Anode—The positive electrode in an evacuated tube, or the electrode at which oxidation takes place in an electrochemical cell.

Cathode—The negative electrode in an evacuated tube, or the electrode at which reduction takes place in an electrochemical cell.

Electrode—A conductor, usually a piece of metal, used to lead electricity (electrons) into or out of a region.

Electrolysis—The process of causing a chemical reaction by passing an electric current through a substance or mixture of substances. This process often involves the decomposition of a compound into its elements.

Electrolyte—A substance that forms an electrically conducting solution when dissolved in water, because it forms ions in the solution.

Oxidation—The process in which an atom's oxidation state is increased, by its losing one or more electrons.

Oxidation–reduction reaction—A chemical reaction in which one or more atoms are oxidized, while one or more other atoms are reduced.

Oxidation state or oxidation number—A positive or negative whole number that expresses how many units of combining power an atom is exhibiting toward other atoms. For example, sodium in NaCl has an oxidation number of +1, while sulfur in Na_2S has an oxidation number of –2.

Reduction—The process by which an atom's oxidation state is decreased, by its gaining one or more electrons.

bar is all dissolved or the silver ions are all depleted: our "battery" is dead.

In principle, a voltaic cell can be made from the four constituents of any oxidation–reduction reaction: any two pairs of oxidizable and reducible atoms, ions, or molecules. For example, any two elements and their respective ions can be made into a voltaic cell. Examples: Ag/Ag^+ with Cu/Cu^{++} (as above), or Cu/Cu^{++} with Zn/Zn^{++} (zinc), or H_2/H^+ (hydrogen) with Fe/Fe^{+++} (iron), or Ni/Ni^{++} (nickel) with Cd/Cd^{++} (cadmium). The last cell is the basis for the rechargeable nickel–cadmium (nicad) batteries that are used to power many electrical devices from razors to computers. When voltaic cells are used for portable purposes, they are "dry cells': instead of a liquid solution, they contain a non–spillable paste. The lead storage battery in automobiles, however, does contain a liquid: a sulfuric acid solution.

Electrolytic cells

There are many chemical reactions that, unlike the sodium–chlorine and copper–silver reactions above, simply will not occur spontaneously. One example is the breakup of water into hydrogen and oxygen:

$$2H_2O \ + \ energy \ R \ 2H_2 \ + \ O_2$$
$$\text{water} \qquad\qquad \text{hydrogen} \quad \text{oxygen}$$
$$\text{gas} \qquad\quad \text{gas}$$

This won't happen all by itself (that is, without the added energy) because water is an extremely stable compound. We can force this reaction to go, however, by pumping energy into the water in the form of an electric current. When we do this— passing an electric current through a chemical system in order to make chemical reactions happen—we have what is called an electrolytic cell.

Electrolytic cells are used for a variety of purposes other than the electrolysis of water. They are used for obtaining metals such as sodium, magnesium, and aluminum from their compounds; for refining copper; for producing important industrial chemicals such as sodium hydroxide, chlorine, and hydrogen, and for electroplating metals such as silver, gold, nickel, and chromium onto jewelry, tableware, and industrial machine parts.

Sea also Bond, chemical; Electrolysis; Sodium.

Further Reading:

Chang, Raymond. *Chemistry*. New York: McGraw–Hill, 1991.
Ebbing, Darrell D. *General Chemistry*. Boston: Houghton Mifflin, 1990.
Umland, Jean B. *General Chemistry*. St. Paul: West, 1993.

Robert L. Wolke

Cell staining

Medical science depends on the staining of cells in tissues to make accurate diagnoses of a wide range of diseases from cholera to sexually transmitted diseases, to parasitic diseases and skin infections. Staining techniques performed routinely in microbiological laboratories include gram's stain, acid–fast stains, acridine orange, calcofluor white, toluidine blue, methylene blue, silver stains, and fluorescent stains. Stains are classified broadly as basic, acidic, or neutral stains. The chemical nature of the cells under examination determines which stain is selected for use.

Cell staining is important in the diagnosis of microorganisms because bacteria can be identified by the color differentiation of stains (dyes). Microscopic examination of stained cell samples allows examination of the size, shape, and arrangement of organelles, as well as external appendages such as the whip–like flagella, which are the cell's organs of motion. When sample cells are stained to show their chemical composition it is called differential staining.

Histochemistry is the specialty that studies the staining properties of cells. Histochemistry is used in other specialties such as histology (the study of tissues), biochemistry (the study of the chemical makeup of cells), cytology (the study of cells), and microbiology (the study of organisms that are too small to be seen without a microscope).

In 1880, Hans Christian Gram of Denmark noted the differences in the way bacteria react to stains. Those bacteria that retained a deep purple stain, even after they were washed, were termed "stain positive." Those that lost the stain and responded again to another stain, were termed "stain negative." Today, bacteria are classified as "gram–positive" or "gram–negative" to distinguish the two major groups of bacteria. This staining test highlights differences in the structure of the cell wall of the two types of bacteria.

Penicillin G is used to treat gram–positive infections, but it is ineffective against gram–negative bacteria. Other antibiotics are only effective against gram–negative bacteria. Chloromycetin, which was discovered in 1947, was the first antibiotic to be effective against both gram–positive and gram–negative bacteria.

Staining techniques

Bacteria are nearly colorless, so their features are difficult to distinguish when they are suspended in a fluid and viewed directly under a microscope. Stains are salts that color particular ions in the bacterial cell, and make more visible distinctions under the microscope. The chemical composition of the cell determines which stain is absorbed. Acidic parts of a cell absorb stains that are positively charged; alkaline parts of a cell combine with stains that are acidic or negatively charged.

Before tissues are stained a thin layer of cells that have been sliced from the specimen (a smear) is prepared by fixing. Fixing a specimen that has been placed on a slide is done by either allowing it to dry at room temperature, or by passing the specimen quickly over a flame. Next the specimen is stained: either a simple stain, a differential stain, a negative or indirect stain, a stain for reserve materials, or for microbial structures is used. Most staining dyes are prepared from coal tar and those used in microbiology come from aniline, an oily liquid.

In simple (or direct) staining only one dye is used, which is washed away after thirty to sixty seconds, before drying and examination. Gentian violet, crystal violet, safranin, methylene blue, basic fuchsin, and others are the dyes used in this method. In differential staining, the gram stain and the acid–fast stain are used to distinguish different microorganisms.

There are four steps involved in the gram stain method, which is considered the most valuable cell–staining technique used in bacteriological cell analysis. In the first step, the specimen is stained with crystal violet or gentian, and one minute later, the second step is taken which involves washing the dye off and flooding the solution with iodine. The third step involves washing the iodine off sixty seconds after it is applied and then washing the slide with an ethyl alcohol solution of 95 percent or a 50:50 mixture of acetone and ethyl alcohol fifteen to thirty seconds after this. The fourth and final step is to stain the slide for thirty seconds with a red or brown dye. The critical action in this process is the washing away of the stain, called decolorization stain, (sometimes called the Ziehl–Neelsen technique) is particularly useful in identifying the organism that causes tuberculosis. When these microorganisms are stained with a red dye (carbol fuchsin), the color remains even though the slide is washed with a strong solution of acid alcohol. Most organisms, other than the ones responding to acid–fast staining, would decolorize from this wash. Methylene blue is then used to differentiate any other organisms present in the smear.

Negative (or indirect) techniques stain the background of cell smears, rather than the organisms directly. In this technique, a drop of the stain is placed on a slide and organisms are added to the stain. After the specimen is smeared over the slide, it is allowed to air dry and is then examined under the microscope. Negative or indirect staining procedures are useful when examining the size and shape of microorganisms.

Staining for reserve materials in cells isolates specific structures in the cells of microorganisms (such as granules or other reserve substances in bacteria that

KEY TERMS

Acidic stains—Stains that adhere to microorganisms having a high lipid (fatty) content.

Decolorization—Washing away of the staining medium.

Differential staining—Staining technique that uses more than one stain to differentiate the structure of the microorganism.

Fixing—Preparing a cell specimen on a slide for examination under a microscope.

Gram–negative—Those cells that lose the color of the stain after they are washed with a 95 percent alcohol solution during the staining process.

Gram–positive—Those cells that retain the color of the stain after they are washed with a 95 percent alcohol solution during the staining process.

cause diseases such as diphtheria). In staining of microbial structures, the flagella, nuclear material of the cell, the cell wall, or capsule is stained for viewing under the microscope. These procedures use two or more stains.

Standardization of tests

Cell staining is one of a number of laboratory tests that are performed to aid in the analysis and diagnosis of disease. The work in these laboratories is performed for physicians as well as for government agencies involved in water purification and sewage treatment, and for industries such as the food industry involved in the manufacture of goods that need to adhere to strict health standards.

Standardization of these tests have been widely adopted throughout the microbiological laboratory community. The National Committee for Clinical Laboratory Standards (NCCLS), located in Villanova, Pennsylvania, continuously publishes standards for these laboratory tests. Among the factors that have been standardized in laboratory testing are temperature, pH (acidity or alkalinity), growth medium, antibiotics, quality control, and other factors.

See also Bacteria; Cell; Diagnosis; Microorganisms.

Further Reading:

Funke, Berdell R., and Christine L. Case. *Microbiology: An Introduction.* 3rd ed. Redwood City, CA: Benjamin/ Cummings Pub. Co., 1989.

Hunt, Tim. *The Cell Cycle: An Introduction*. New York: Oxford University Press, 1993.

Keynes, Milton. *Handling Laboratory Microorganisms*. Philadelphia: Open University Press, 1991.

Koneman, Elmer W. *Color Atlas and Textbook of Diagnostic Microbiology*. 4th ed. Philadelphia: J. B. Lippincott, 1992.

Postgate, John R. *The Outer Reaches of Life*. Cambridge, England: Cambridge University Press, 1994.

Vita Richman

Cellular respiration

Cellular respiration in the presence of oxygen (aerobic respiration) is the process by which energy–rich organic substrates are broken down into carbon dioxide and water, with the release of a considerable amount of energy in the form of adenosine triphosphate (ATP). Anaerobic respiration breaks down glucose in the absence of oxygen, and produces pyruvate, which is then reduced to lactate or to ethanol and CO_2. Anaerobic respiration releases only a small amount of energy (in the form of ATP) from the glucose molecule.

Respiration occurs in three stages. The first stage is glycolysis, which is a series of enzyme–controlled reactions that degrades glucose (a 6–carbon molecule) to pyruvate (a 3–carbon molecule) which is further oxidized to acetylcoenzyme A (acetyl CoA). Amino acids and fatty acids may also be oxidized to acetyl CoA as well as glucose.

In the second stage, acetyl CoA enters the citric acid (Krebs) cycle, where it is degraded to yield energy–rich hydrogen atoms which reduce the oxidized form of the coenzyme nicotinamide adenine dinucleotide (NAD^+) to NADH, and reduce the coenzyme flavin adenine dinucleotide (FAD) to $FADH_2$. (Reduction is the addition of electrons to a molecule, or the gain of hydrogen atoms, while oxidation is the loss of electrons or the addition of oxygen to a molecule.) Also in the second stage of cellular respiration, the carbon atoms of the intermediate metabolic products in the Krebs cycle are converted to carbon dioxide.

The third stage of cellular respiration occurs when the energy–rich hydrogen atoms are separated into protons [H^+] and energy–rich electrons in the electron transport chain. At the beginning of the electron transport chain, the energy–rich hydrogen on NADH is removed from NADH, producing the oxidized coenzyme, NAD^+ and a proton (H+) and two electrons (e–). The electrons are transferred along a chain of more than 15 different electron carrier molecules (known as the electron transport chain). These proteins are grouped into three large respiratory enzyme complexes, each of which contains proteins that span the mitochondrial membrane, securing the complexes into the inner membrane. Furthermore, each complex in the chain has a greater affinity for electrons than the complex before it. This increasing affinity drives the electrons down the chain until they are transferred all the way to the end where they meet the oxygen molecule, which has the greatest affinity of all for the electrons. The oxygen thus becomes reduced to H_2O in the presence of hydrogen ions (protons), which were originally obtained from nutrient molecules through the process of oxidation.

During electron transport, much of the energy represented by the electrons is conserved during a process called oxidative phosphorylation. This process uses the energy of the electrons to phosphorylate (add a phosphate group) adenosine diphosphate (ADP), to form the energy–rich molecule ATP.

Oxidative phosphorylation is driven by the energy released by the electrons as they pass from the hydrogens of the coenzymes down the respiratory chain in the inner membrane of the mitochondrion. This energy is used to pump protons (H^+) across the inner membrane from the matrix to the intermediate space. This sets up a concentration gradient along which substances flow from high to low concentration, while a simultaneous current of OH^- flows across the membrane in the opposite direction. The simultaneous opposite flow of positive and negative ions across the mitochondrial membrane sets up an electrochemical proton gradient. The flow of protons down this gradient drives a membrane–bound enzyme, ATP synthetase, which catalyzes the phosphorylation of ADP to ATP.

This highly efficient, energy conserving series of reactions would not be possible in eukaryotic cells without the organelles called mitochondria. Mitochondria are the "powerhouses" of the eukaryotic cells, and are bounded by two membranes, which create two separate compartments: an internal space and a narrow inter-membrane space. The enzymes of the matrix include those that catalyze the conversion of pyruvate and fatty acids to acetyl CoA, as well as the enzymes of the Krebs cycle. The enzymes of the respiratory chain are embedded in the inner mitochondrial membrane, which is the site of oxidative phosphorylation and the production of ATP.

In the absence of mitochondria, animal cells would be limited to glycolysis for their energy needs, which releases only a small fraction of the energy potentially available from the glucose.

The reactions of glycolysis require the input of two ATP molecules and produce four ATP molecules for a net gain of only two molecules per molecule of glucose. These ATP molecules are formed when phosphate groups are removed from phosphorylated intermediate products of glycolysis and transferred to ADP, a process called substrate level phosphorylation (synthesis of ATP by direct transfer of a high–energy phosphate group from a molecule in a metabolic pathway to ADP).

In contrast, mitochondria supplied with oxygen produce about 36 molecules of ATP for each molecule of glucose oxidized. Procaryotic cells, such a bacteria, lack mitochondria as well as nuclear membranes. Fatty acids and amino acids when transported into the mitochondria are degraded into the two–carbon acetyl group on acetyl CoA, which then enters the Krebs cycle. In animals, the body stores fatty acids in the form of fats, and glucose in the form of glycogen in order to ensure a steady supply of these nutrients for respiration.

While the Krebs cycle is an integral part of aerobic metabolism, the production of NADH and FADH$_2$ is not dependent on oxygen. Rather, oxygen is used at the end of the electron transport chain to combine with electrons removed from NADH and FADH$_2$ and with hydrogen ions in the cytosol to produce water.

Although the production of water is necessary to keep the process of electron transport chain in motion, the energy used to make ATP is derived from a different process called chemiosmosis.

Chemiosmosis is a mechanism that uses the proton gradient across the membrane to generate ATP and is initiated by the activity of the electron transport chain. Chemiosmosis represents a link between the chemical and osmotic processes in the mitochondrion that occur during respiration.

The electrons that are transported down the respiratory chain on the mitochondrion's inner membrane release energy that is used to pump protons (H$^+$) across the inner membrane from the mitochondrial matrix into the intermembrane space. The resulting gradient of protons across the mitochondrial inner membrane creates a backflow of protons back across the membrane. This flow of electrons across the membrane, like a waterfall used to power an electric turbine, drives a membrane-bound enzyme, ATP synthetase. This enzyme catalyzes the phosphorylation of ADP to ATP, which completes the part of cellular respiration called oxidative phosphorylation. The protons, in turn, neutralize the negative charges created by the addition of electrons to oxygen molecules, with the resultant production of water.

Cellular respiration produces three molecules of ATP per pair of electrons in NADH, while the pair of electrons in FADH$_2$ generate two molecules of ATP. This means that 12 molecules of ATP are formed for each acetyl CoA molecule that enters the Krebs cycle; and since two acetyl CoA molecules are formed from each molecule of glucose, a total of 24 molecules of ATP are produced from each molecule of this sugar. When added to the energy conserved from the reactions occurring before acetyl CoA is formed, the complete oxidation of a glucose molecule gives a net yield of about 36 ATP molecules. When fats are burned, instead of glucose, the total yield from one molecule of palmitate, a 16–carbon fatty, is 129 ATP.

See also Adenosine diphosphate; Adenosine triphosphate; Catabolism; Glycolysis; Krebs cycle; Respiration.

Further Reading:
Alberts, Bruce, et al. *Molecular Biology of The Cell.* 2nd ed. New York: Garland Publishing, 1989.
Lehninger, Albert L. *Principles of Biochemistry.* New York: Worth Publishers, 1982.

Marc Kusinitz

Cellulose

Cellulose is a substance found in the cell walls of plants. Although cellulose is not a component of the human body, it is nevertheless the most abundant organic macromolecule on Earth. The chemical structure of cellulose resembles that of starch, but unlike starch, cellulose is extremely rigid (Figure 1). This rigidity imparts great strength to the plant body and protection to the interiors of plant cells.

Structure of cellulose

Like starch, cellulose is composed of a long chain of at least 500 glucose molecules. Cellulose is thus a polysaccharide (Latin for "many sugars"). Several of these polysaccharide chains are arranged in parallel arrays to form cellulose microfibrils. The individual polysaccharide chains are bound together in the microfibrils by hydrogen bonds. The microfibrils, in turn, are bundled together to form macrofibrils (Figure 1).

The microfibrils of cellulose are extremely tough and inflexible due to the presence of hydrogen bonds. In fact, when describing the structure of cellulose microfibrils, chemists call their arrangement "crys-

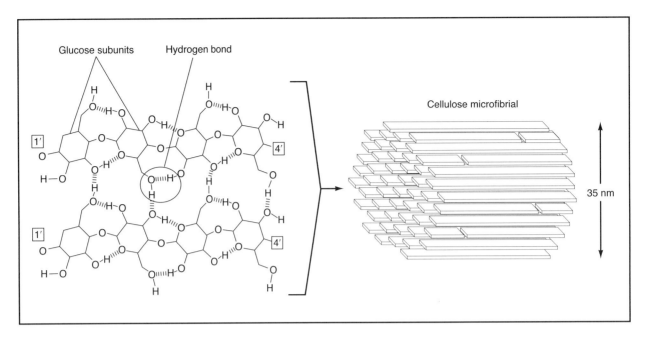

Figure 1. The structure of cellulose.

talline," meaning that the microfibrils have crystal–like properties. Although starch has the same basic structure as cellulose—it is also a polysaccharide—the glucose subunits are bonded in such a way that allows the starch molecule to twist. In other words, the starch molecule is flexible, while the cellulose molecule is rigid.

How cellulose is arranged in plant cell walls

Like human bone, plant cell walls are composed of fibrils laid down in a matrix, or "background" material. In a cell wall, the fibrils are cellulose microfibrils, and the matrix is composed of other polysaccharides and proteins. One of these matrix polysaccharides in cell walls is pectin, the substance that, when heated, forms a gel. Pectin is the substance that cooks use to make jellies and jams.

The arrangement of cellulose microfibrils within the polysaccharide and protein matrix imparts great strength to plant cell walls. The cell walls of plants perform several functions, each related to the rigidity of the cell wall. The cell wall protects the interior of the plant cell, but also allows the circulation of fluids within and around the cell wall. The cell wall also binds the plant cell to its neighbors. This binding creates the tough, rigid skeleton of the plant body. Cell walls are the reason why plants are erect and rigid. Some plants have a secondary cell wall laid over the primary cell wall. The secondary cell wall is composed of yet another polysaccharide called lignin. Lignin is found in

trees. The presence of both primary and secondary cell walls makes the tree even more rigid, penetrable only with sharp axes.

Unlike the other components of the cell wall, which are synthesized in the plant's Golgi body (an organelle that manufactures, sorts, and transports different macromolecules within the cell), cellulose is synthesized on the surface of the plant cell. Embedded within the plant's plasma membrane is an enzyme, called cellulose synthetase, which synthesizes cellulose. As cellulose is synthesized, it spontaneously forms microfibrils that are deposited on the cell's surface. Because the cellulose synthetase enzyme is located in the plasma membrane, the new cellulose microfibrils are deposited under older cellulose microfibrils. Thus, the oldest cellulose microfibrils are outermost on the cell wall, while the newer microfibrils are innermost on the cell wall.

As the plant cell grows, it must expand to accommodate the growing cell volume. However, because cellulose is so rigid, it cannot stretch or flex to allow this growth. Instead, the microfibrils of cellulose slide past each other or separate from adjacent microfibrils. In this way, the cell wall is able to expand when the cell volume enlarges during growth.

Cellulose digestion

Humans lack the enzyme necessary to digest cellulose. Hay and grasses are particularly abundant in cellulose, and both are indigestible by humans (although humans can digest starch). Animals such as termites and herbivores such as cows, koalas, and horses all digest cellulose, but even these animals do not themselves have an enzyme that digests this material. Instead, these animals harbor microbes that can digest cellulose.

The termite, for instance, contains protists (single–celled organisms) called mastigophorans in their guts that carry out cellulose digestion. The species of mastigophorans that performs this service for termites is called *Trichonympha*, which, interestingly, can cause a serious parasitic infection in humans.

Animals such as cows have anaerobic bacteria in their digestive tracts which digest cellulose. Cows are ruminants, or animals that chew their cud. Ruminants have several stomachs that break down plant materials with the help of enzymes and bacteria. The partially digested material is then regurgitated into the mouth, which is then chewed to break the material down even further. The bacterial digestion of cellulose by bacteria in the stomachs of ruminants is anaerobic, meaning that the process does not use oxygen. One of the by–products of anaerobic metabolism is methane, a notoriously foul–smelling gas. Ruminants give off large amounts of methane daily. In fact, many environmentalists are concerned about the production of methane by cows, because methane may contribute to the destruction of ozone in the Earth's stratosphere.

Although cellulose is indigestible by humans, it does form a part of the human diet in the form of plant foods. Small amounts of cellulose found in vegetables and fruits pass through the human digestive system intact. Cellulose is part of the material called "fiber" that dieticians and nutritionists have identified as useful in moving food through the digestive tract quickly and efficiently. Diets high in fiber are thought to lower the risk of colon cancer because fiber reduces the time that waste products stay in contact with the walls of the colon (the terminal part of the digestive tract)

See also Cell; Rumination.

Further Reading:

Benedict, C. R., et. al. "Crystalline Cellulose and Cotton Fiber Strength". *Crop Science* 24 (January–February 1994): 147.

Brett, C. T. *Physiology and Biochemistry of Plant Cell Walls.* London: Unwin Hyman, 1990.

Dunkle, Richard L. "Food Science Research: An Investment in Health." *Agricultural Research* 41 (December 1993): 2.

Dwyer, Johanna. "Dietary Fiber and Colorectal Cancer Risk." *Nutrition Reviews* 51 (May 1993): 147.

KEY TERMS

Anaerobic—Describes biological processes that take place in the absence of oxygen.

Cell wall—The tough, outer covering of plant cells composed of cellulose microfibrils held together in a matrix.

Cellulose synthetase—The enzyme embedded in the plasma membrane that synthesizes cellulose.

Colon—The terminal portion of the human digestive tract.

Golgi body—The organelle that manufactures, sorts, and transports macromolecules within a cell.

Lignin—A polysaccharide that forms the secondary cell wall in some plants.

Matrix—The material, composed of polysaccharides and protein, in which microfibrils of cellulose are embedded in plant cell walls.

Methane—A gas produced during the anaerobic digestion of cellulose by bacteria in certain animals.

Microfibril—Small fibrils of cellulose; consists of parallel arrays of cellulose chains.

Polysaccharide—A molecule composed of many glucose subunits arranged in a chain.

Ruminant—An animal with several stomachs.

Kleiner, Susan M. "Fiber Facts: How to Fight Disease with a High–fiber Diet." *The Physician and Sportsmedicine* 18 (October 1990): 19.

Slavin, Joanne L. "Dietary Fiber: Mechanisms or Magic on Disease Prevention?" *Nutrition Today* 25 (December 1990): 6.

Van Soest, Peter J. *Nutritional Ecology of the Ruminant.* 2nd ed. Ithaca: Comstock Press, 1994.

Young, Stephen. "How Plants Fight Back." *New Scientist* 130 (1 June 1991): 41.

Kathleen Scogna

Centipedes

Centipedes (phylum Arthropoda, class Chilopoda) occur throughout the world in both temperate and tropical regions where they live in soil and humus and beneath fallen logs, bark, and stones. Because they lack a hard outer skeleton, centipedes are confined to moist environments in order to maintain water balance. Many species are therefore active only at night, remaining sheltered during the day. Most centipedes are active on the surface, but some of the more slender species are capable of burrowing in loose soils.

Four main orders of centipedes have been recognized with some 3000 species described so far. Among these, there is considerable variation in size, color and behavior. One of the largest species that has been recorded is *Scolopendra gigantea* from Latin America, which reaches a length of 10 in (26 cm). Most tropical species are distinguished by their bright colors – red, yellow, green, blue or various combinations of these, while temperate–dwelling centipedes tend to be a reddish–brown color. Many of these bold colors have evolved to deter potential predators. Such vivid yet simple colors advertise one of the following: that the animals can sting, inflict a painful or poisonous bite, produce a foul taste if eaten, or may cause an irritation to the skin. In the case of centipedes, all of these hold true: an inquisitive animal may receive a small injection of poison from special claws on the head, a painful pinch from the last pair of legs, or may be covered in foul acids produced from a series of glands along the body.

All centipedes are instantly recognizable by their segmented body, each segment of which bears a single pair of legs. The number of legs varies considerably according to species—from 15 to as many as 170 pairs. The legs, however, are not always of similar length: in some Scutigeromorpha species the posterior legs may be twice as long as those nearer the head. With so many legs, people have often wondered how centipedes manage to coordinate their movements, especially when running. But centipedes are well adapted for walking and running, as rhythmic waves of leg movements alternate on either side of the body. Thus at any one time, the feet on one side of the body may be clustered together in movement, while those on the opposite side are spread apart to provide balance. Some burrowing species, such as those of the Geophilomorpha, have a different form of locomotion, with each foot being able to move independently of the others. These centipedes usually have quite short feet that are used more as anchors in the soil rather than digging tools. The main digging force in these species is provided by the strong muscular body trunk, which pushes the body through the soil, much in the same manner as an earthworm.

The head betrays the highly predatory nature of these animals: extended antennae constantly move to detect potential prey which, once detected, is seized by the front pair of legs and firmly held by other, smaller pairs of claws. The front legs are not only sharply pointed but are also modified as poison claws and can deliver a lethal injection of paralyzing fluid produced from special glands. The sense of vision is limited in most species – probably to the level of being able to differentiate between light and dark. Many species, however, lack eyes, especially the burrowing and cave-dwelling centipedes. Prey consists of small arthropods as well as earthworms, snails, and nematodes. Some of the larger tropical species have been known to eat frogs and small snakes.

Male and female centipedes are quite similar on the outside and the sexes are difficult to tell apart. Tropical species may breed throughout the year but temperate–dwelling centipedes breed in the spring and summer months, becoming less active during the cold winter period. Most species have a simple courtship routine, after which the pair may mate. Reproduction takes place outside of the body, with the male constructing a shallow web of silk–like strands on which he deposits a single package known as a spermatophore, which contains his sperm cells. The female then moves over the web and collects the spermatophore which is transferred to the ovary, where fertilization occurs. After carrying the eggs for some time the female may deposit them one by one in a protected place in the ground, for example, under a stone or in a rotten log. These eggs are covered with a glutinous secretion which helps them to adhere to soil particles or other substances. Not all species lay their eggs in such a scattered fashion however: some females create a simple nest in an enlarged cavity in a fallen log, or similar suitable chamber, where she remains to guard her eggs and even the larvae once they have hatched. The young later disperse and grow through a series of molt stages to reach adult size and sexual maturity.

Centrifuge

A centrifuge is a device for separating two or more substances from each other by using centrifugal force. Centrifugal force is the tendency of an object traveling around a central point to continue in a linear motion and fly away from that central point.

Centrifugation can be used to separate substances from each other because materials with different masses experience different centrifugal forces when traveling at the same velocity and at the same distance from the common center. For example, if two balls of different mass are attached to strings and swung around a common point at the same velocity, the ball with the greater mass will experience a greater centrifugal force. If the two strings are cut simultaneously, the heavier ball will tend to fly farther from the common center than will the lighter ball.

Centrifuges can be considered devices for increasing the effects of the Earth's gravitational pull. For example, if a spoonful of clay is mixed vigorously with a cup of water and then allowed to sit for a period of time, the clay will eventually settle out because it experiences a greater gravitational pull than does the water. If the same clay–water mixture is centrifuged, however, the separation will take place much more quickly.

Types of centrifuges

Centrifuges can be sub–divided into two major categories, stationary devices and rotating devices. Both types of centrifuge work on a common principle, however. A collection of particles of different mass is set into motion around a common center. The faster these particles move, the greater will be the difference with which they tend to escape from their common center, and the more easily they will be separated from each other.

In a stationary centrifuge, a fluid (a gas or liquid) consisting of two or more components is sprayed into a cylindrical or conical chamber at a high rate of speed. As the fluid travels around the inside of the chamber, it separates into its components, the heavier substance(s) traveling to the outside of the container, and the lighter substance(s) remaining closer to the center of the cylinder.

One application of the stationary centrifuge is in the separation of the isotopes of uranium isotope from each other. Naturally occurring uranium consists of a mixture of uranium–235, which will undergo fission, and uranium–238, which will not. A sample of uranium is first converted into the gaseous compound uranium hexafluoride and then injected into a stationary centrifuge. As the rapidly moving stream of uranium hexafluoride travels around inside the centrifuge, it begins to separate into two parts. The heavier uranium uranium–235–hexafluoride concentrates along the outer wall of the centrifuge, while the lighter uranium-238–hexafluoride is left toward the center of the stream. The heavier isotope can then be drawn out of the centrifuge, leaving behind a sample of uranium hexafluoride slightly richer in the desired uranium–235 isotope. This sample can then be re–centrifuged and made still richer in the lighter isotope.

Rotating centrifuges

Another type of centrifuge is one in which the fluid to be separated is introduced into a container, and the

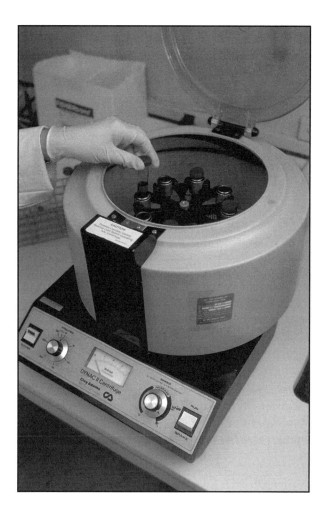

A centrifuge.

container is then set into rapid rotational motion. Most beginning chemistry students are familiar with this instrument. It is commonly used as a substitute for filtration in the separation of a solid precipitate from the liquid in which it is suspended.

In this kind of machine, hollow tubes about five centimeters in length are attached to arms radiating from the center of the machine. When the machine is turned on, the arms are spun around the center at a speed of about 30,000 revolutions per minute. The gravitational force experienced by materials inside the tubes—about 25,000 times that of gravity—causes the separation of materials much more efficiently than would a conventional filtration system.

Laboratory centrifuges have become invaluable tools in many kinds of scientific research. For example, today a widely used method of studying cells is to break apart a tissue sample and then centrifuge the resulting fluid. In this way, the discrete components of the cell can be separated and identified.

KEY TERMS

. . . .

Centrifugal force—The tendency of an object traveling in a circle around a central point to escape from the center in a straight line.

Gravitation—The pull of the Earth's mass on an object.

Revolutions per minute—The number of times per minute an object travels around some central point.

Rotation—The spinning of an object on its axis.

Applications of the rotating centrifuge

The basic centrifuge design described above can be adapted for use in many different settings. Industrial centrifuges, for example, tend to be quite large, ranging in size from 4in to 4ft (10 cm to 1.2 m) in diameter, with rotational velocities from 1,000 to 15,000 revolutions per minute. They can be designed so as to remove separated portions continuously, all at once after the machine has been stopped, or intermittently.

Large–scale centrifugation has found a great variety of commercial and industrial uses. For example, the separation of cream from milk has been accomplished by this process for well over a hundred years. Today, centrifuges are used to remove water from oil and from jet fuel and in the removal of solid materials from waste water during the process of water purification.

A centrifuge for use with very small particles of similar weight—the ultracentrifuge—was first developed by the Swedish chemist Theodor Svedberg in about 1923. In the ultracentrifuge, containers no more than about 0.2in (0.6 cm) in diameter are set into rotation at speeds of about 230,000 revolutions per minute. In this device, colloidal particles, not much larger than the size of molecules, can be separated from each other.

Centrifuge studies in the space sciences

Centrifuge studies have been very important in the development of manned space flight programs. Human volunteers are placed into very large centrifuges and then spun at high velocities. Inside the centrifuge, humans feel high gravitational velocities that correspond to high gravitational forces ("g forces") that occur during the launch of space vehicles. Such experiments help space scientists understand the limits of acceleration that humans can endure in such situations.

See also Gravity and gravitation; Subsurface detection; Ultracentrifuge.

Further Reading:

Centrifugation, McGraw–Hill Encyclopedia of Science & Technology, 6th edition. New York: McGraw–Hill Book Company, 1987, volume 3, pp. 392 – 398.

Centrifuge, The Illustrated Encyclopedia of Science and Technology, vol. 4, Westport, CT: H. S. Stuttman, 1982, pp. 539 – 540.

Dufour, John W., and W. Ed Nelson. *Centrifugal Pump Sourcebook.* New York: McGraw–Hill, 1992.

Lobanoff, Val S., and Robert R. Ross. *Centrifugal Pumps,* 2nd edition. Houston: Gulf Publications, 1992.

Weissberger, Arnold, and Hsien–wen Hsu. *Separations by Centrifugal Phenomena.* New York: Wiley–Interscience, 1981.

David E. Newton

Century tree see **Amaryllis family**

Ceramics

Ceramic materials are usually understood to be compounds of metallic and nonmetallic elements, though some are actually ionic salts, and others are insulators. These materials can be very complicated, as are for example clays, spinels, and common window glass. Many ceramic compounds have very high melting points.

Ceramics have a wide range of applications. They have been used as refractories, abrasives, ferroelectrics, piezoelectric transducers, magnets, building materials, and surface finishes.

Unlike metals, there are really no heat treatments that can be used to modify the properties of ceramics, but their properties can be altered by changes in chemical composition. By carefully considering the choice of chemical composition, purity, particle size and uniformity and arrangement, and packing of atoms, high quality ceramics can be synthesized in a wide variety.

Traditional Ceramics

Ceramics have been used by man since antiquity. The earliest ceramic articles were made from naturally occurring materials such as clay minerals. It was discovered in prehistoric times that clay materials become malleable when water is added to them, and that a

TABLE 1. TRADITIONAL CERAMICS	
Category	*Examples*
whitewares	dishes, plumbing materials, enamels, tiles
heavy clay products	brick, pottery, materials for the treatment and transport of sewage, water purification components
refractories	brick, cements, crucibles, molds
construction	brick, plaster, blocks, concrete, tile, glass, fiberglass

molded object can then be dried in the sun and hardened in a high temperature fire. The word ceramic comes from the Greek word for burnt material, *keramos.*

Many of the same raw materials that were used by the ancients are still used today in the production of traditional ceramics. Traditional ceramic applications include whitewares, heavy clay products, refractories, construction materials, abrasive products, and glass.

Clay minerals are hydrated compounds of aluminum oxide and silica. These materials have layered structures. Examples include kaolinite, halloysite, pyrophillite, and montmorillonite. They are all formed by the weathering of igneous rocks under the influence of water, dissolved CO_2, and organic acids. The largest sources of these clays were formed when feldspar was eroded from granite and deposited in lake beds, where it became altered to a clay.

Silica is a major ingredient in glass, glazes, enamels, refractories, abrasives, and whiteware. Its major sources include quartz, which is made up primarily of sand, sandstone, and quartzite.

Feldspar is also used in the manufacture of glass, pottery, enamel, and other ceramic products. Other naturally occurring minerals used directly in ceramic production include talc, asbestos, wollastonite, and sillimanite.

Hydraulic cement

Hydraulic cements set by interaction with water. Portland cement, the most common hydraulic cement, is primarily a water–free calcium silicate. It is slightly soluble in water and sets by a combination of solution precipitation and chemical reaction with water to form a hydrated composition. The ratio of water to cement in the initial mix greatly influences the strength of the final concrete: the lower the water–to–cement ratio, the higher the strength.

Glass

Glass is a ceramic material consisting of uniformly dispersed mixtures of silica, soda ash, and lime, that is often combined with metallic oxides of calcium, lead, lithium, cerium, etc. Glass is distinguished from solid ceramics by its lack of crystallinity. It is in fact a supercooled liquid. The atoms in glass remain disordered in the solid state, much as they are in the liquid state. Glasses are thus rigid structures whose atomic arrangements and properties depend on both composition and thermal history.

Group 16 elements (oxygen, sulphur, selenium, tellurium) are especially good candidates for glass formation. Oxygen is able to form stable bonds with silicon, boron, phosphorous, and arsenic and thereby form stable structures having oxygen atoms at the corners and one of the other atoms at the center. Pure oxide glasses are very stable because each oxygen atom is linked by electron bonds to two other atoms.

Various two–phase structures may exist as glasses. One such structure is a mixture of glass and crystal. These materials are converted into strong and durable ceramics that are part glass and part crystal by prolonged heat treatment.

Modern ceramics

In the twentieth century, scientists and engineers have acquired a much better understanding of ceramics and their properties. They have succeeded in producing ceramics with tailor–made properties. Modern ceramics include oxide ceramics, magnetic ceramics, ferroelectric ceramics, nuclear fuels, nitrides, carbides, and borides.

Aluminum oxide

Aluminum oxide (Al_2O_3) occurs naturally in the mineral corundum, which in gem–quality form is known as the precious stones ruby and sapphire. Ruby and sapphire are known for their chemical inertness and hard-

TABLE 2. MODERN CERAMICS	
Category	**Examples**
electronics	heating elements, dielectric materials, substrates, semiconductors, insulators, transducers, lasers, hermetic seals, igniters
aerospace and automotive	turbine components, heat exchangers, emission control
medical	prosthetics, controls
high-temperature structural	kiln furniture, braze fixtures, advanced refractories
nuclear	fuels, controls

ness. Al_2O_3 is produced in large quantities from the mineral bauxite. In the Bayer process, bauxite (primarily aluminum hydroxide mixed with iron hydroxide and other impurities) is selectively leached with caustic soda. Purified aluminum hydroxide is formed as a precipitate. This material is converted to aluminum oxide powder, which is used in the manufacture of aluminum–oxide–based ceramics. Aluminum oxide powder is used in the manufacture of porcelain, alumina laboratory ware, crucibles and metal casting molds, high temperature cements, wear–resistant parts (sleeves, tiles, seals), sandblast nozzles, etc.

Magnesium oxide

Magnesium oxide (MgO) occurs naturally in the mineral periclase, but not in sufficient quantity to meet commercial demand. Most MgO powder is produced from $MgCO_3$ or from seawater. MgO is extracted from sea water as a hydroxide, then converted to the oxide. MgO powder finds extensive use in high temperature electrical insulation and in refractory brick.

Silicon carbide

Silicon carbide (SiC) has been found to occur naturally only as small green hexagonal plates in metallic iron. The same form of silicon carbide has been manufactured synthetically, however. In this process, SiO_2 sand is mixed with coke in a large elongated mound in which large carbon electrodes have been placed at either end. As electric current is passed between the electrodes, the coke is heated to about 2200° C. The coke reacts with the SiO_2 to produce SiC plus CO gas. Heating continues until the reaction has completed in the mound. After cooling, the mound is broken up, and the green hexagonal SIC crystals, which are low in impurities and

suitable for electronic applications, are removed. The lower purity material is used for abrasives. The outer layer of the mound is reused in the next batch. SiC can be formed from almost any source of silicon and carbon. It has been produced in the laboratory from silicon metal powder and sugar, and from rice hulls. SiC is used for high–temperature kiln furniture, electrical resistance heating elements, grinding wheels and abrasives, wear–resistance applications, and incinerator linings.

Silicon nitride

Silicon nitride does not occur naturally. Most of the powder commercially available has been produced by reacting silicon metal powder with nitrogen at temperatures between 1250 and 1400° C. The powder that is removed from the furnace is not ready to use. It is loosely bonded and must be crushed and sized. The resulting powder contains impurities of Fe, Ca, and Al. Higher purity silicon nitride powder has been produced by reducing SiO_2 with carbon in a nitrogen environment, and by reaction of $SiCl_4$ with ammonia; these reactions produce a very fine powder. High purity silicon nitride powder has also been made by laser reactions in which a mixture of silane (SiH_4) and ammonia is exposed to laser light from a CO_2 laser. This produces spherical particles of silicon nitride of very fine size.

Processing

The raw materials for ceramics are chosen on the basis of desired purity, particle size distribution, reactivity, and form. Purity influences such high temperature properties as strength, stress rupture life, and oxidation resistance. Impurities may severely influence electrical, magnetic, and optical properties. Particle size distribution affects strength.

Binders may be added to the ceramic powder to add strength prior to densification. Lubricants reduce particle–tool friction during compaction. Other agents are added to promote flowability during shaping.

Forming processes

The ceramic powder along with suitable additives are placed in a die, to which pressure may be applied for compaction. Uniaxial pressing is often used for small shapes such as ceramics for electrical devices. Hydrostatic pressing (equivalent pressing from all sides) is often used for large objects.

Alternatively, the ceramic powder may be cast. Although molten ceramics may be cast into cooled metal plates and quenched to produce materials made up of very fine crystals with high material toughness, casting of ceramics is usually done at room temperature. The ceramic particles are first suspended in a liquid and then cast into a porous mold that removes the liquid, leaving a particulate compact in the mold.

Yet another method of shaping a ceramic involves plastic forming. In this process a mixture of ceramic powder and additives is deformed under pressure. In the case of pure oxides, carbides, and nitrides, an organic material is added in place of or in addition to water to make the ceramic mixture plastic. While forming the ceramic object, heat and pressure are usually applied simultaneously.

Sintering

Densification of the particulate ceramic compact is referred to as sintering. Sintering is essentially the removal of pores between particles, combined with particulate growth and strong bonding between adjacent particles. In order for sintering to occur, the particles must be able to flow, and there must be a source of energy to activate and sustain this material transport. Sintering can take place in the vapor, liquid, or solid phase, or in a reactive liquid.

Machining

The sintered material must frequently be machined to allow it to meet dimensional tolerances, to give it an improved surface finish, or to remove surface flaws. Machining must be done carefully to avoid brittle fracture. The machining tool must have a higher hardness than the ceramic. The ceramic material can be processed by mechanical, thermal, or chemical action.

Design considerations

When evaluating the suitability of a ceramic material for a particular application, it is first necessary to understand the requirements of the application. These

---

KEY TERMS

. . . .

Ceramic—A hard, brittle substance produced by strongly heating a nonmetallic mineral or clay.

Glass—A ceramic material consisting of a uniformly dispersed mixture of silica, soda ash, and lime; and often combined with metallic oxides.

Refractory—A ceramic material of low thermal conductivity that is able to withstand extremely high temperatures without essential change.

Sintering—The agglomeration of metal or ceramic powders at temperatures below the melting point.

---

requirements might typically be defined by the load that the material will experience, the stress distribution in the material, interface, frictional requirements, the chemical environment and range of temperatures that the material will experience, and restriction on the final cost of the materials. Usually, one or two material properties will dictate the choice of a material for a particular application.

Historically most ceramic designs have been developed by empirical, or trial–and–error investigation. Only since the advent of the digital computer has it been possible to predict the properties of a particular ceramic material prior to actually producing it.

Further Reading:

Richerson, David W., *Modern Ceramic Engineering*, New York, NY: Marcel Dekker, Inc., 1982.

Randall Frost

Cerebellum see **Brain**

Cerebral cortex see **Brain**

Cerebrospinal fluid see **Nervous system**

Cerebrum see **Brain**

Cerenkov effect

The Cerenkov effect is the emission of light from a transparent substance like water or glass when a charged particle, such as an electron, travels through the

---

material with a speed faster than the speed of light in that material.

The Cerenkov effect was discovered by Russian experimentalist P. A. Cerenkov in 1934 and explained by Russian theorists I. Y. Tamm and I. M. Frank. All three scientists received the Nobel prize in physics in 1958.

The electric field of a fast–moving charged particle shifts the electrons of the atoms of a nonconducting material as the particle passes through. When the particle travels at speeds faster than the speed of light in the material, the atoms respond by emitting light in a cone at an angle determined by the index of refraction of the material. The process can be compared to that of a shock wave of sound generated when an airplane exceeds the speed of sound in air.

The index of refraction is computed by dividing the speed of light in a vacuum (3×10^8 m/sec or 186,000 mi/sec) by the speed of light in the medium through which the particle passes. The speed of light in lucite or heavy lead glass, for example, is 2×10^8 m/sec; therefore the index of refraction for those substances is 1.5.

Cerenkov detectors use the properties of Cerenkov radiation in high energy physics and cosmic ray physics experiments. Since the radiation is only emitted when the velocity of the particle is above a predetermined speed, a "threshold" value for the particle velocity can be set on the detector to discriminate against slow particles. For a particle velocity above the threshold value, an angular measurement of the Cerenkov light relative to the particle direction determines the velocity of the particle.

See also Light.

James O'Connell

Cerium see **Lanthanides**
Cero see **Mackerel**
Cervical cap see **Contraception**
Cesium see **Alkali metals**

Cetaceans

Human contact with cetaceans—whales, dolphins, and porpoises—has a rich history, beginning with our very earliest civilizations. Although ancient people believed they were fish, cetaceans are aquatic mammals, which means that they bear live young, produce milk to feed their offspring, and have hair (albeit just a few sensory hairs). The Greek philosopher Aristotle (384–322 B.C.) was the first to record this fact; in his *Historia Animalium*, Aristotle noted that whales and dolphins breathe air through a blowhole, and therefore have lungs; and that instead of laying eggs like fishes, the animals deliver their offspring fully developed.

Modern biologists believe that life first appeared in the sea; from these marine beginnings, land–dwelling organisms such as mammals gradually evolved. Cetaceans have returned to the water after an ancestral period on the land. As evidence of their terrestrial pedigree, consider that a whale fetus possesses four limb buds, a pelvis, tail, and forelimbs with five fingers like any land mammal. Adult whales and dolphins have the streamlined, fish–like appearance befitting their watery existence, but they have maintained and modified key terrestrial features (e.g., a much–reduced pelvic girdle in the tail, and forelimbs now used as flippers for swimming). A blowhole atop the head—one in dolphins, two in whales—replaces the nostrils, and thus the passageways for food and air are completely separate, as opposed to the usual terrestrial condition, in which food and air share a common tube. Other anatomical changes include a reduced neck, sensory modifications, and the addition of a thick layer of blubber to insulate against the cold of the ocean depths and provide extra energy stores.

The order Cetacea is divided into three suborders. The Archaeoceti are a group of extinct cetaceans with elongated bodies, and are known only from fossils that are still being discovered and described. The living cetaceans are the Mysticeti or baleen whales, ten species restricted to the ocean, and the Odontoceti or toothed whales, whose many species (including dolphins and porpoises) are found in diverse habitats from deep ocean to fresh–water rivers many miles from sea. Cetologists—scientists who study cetaceans—still disagree about how many toothed whales may be distinguished, but at least 68 species are recognized.

Mysticeti: Baleen whales

Baleen whales include the great whales or rorquals, a word that comes from the Norse for "grooved whale," owing to the conspicuous grooves or pleats on the throat and belly of these huge animals. There are seven rorquals, including the blue whale *(Balaenoptera musculus)*, the largest creature that has ever lived. The largest blue whale ever recorded, according to the *Guiness Book of World Records,* was a female caught in 1926 off the Shetland Islands, measuring 109 ft, 4 in (33.2 m, 10 cm) Together with the fin whale *(B. physalus)*, sei whale *(B borealis)*, Bryde's whale *(B. edeni)*, minke whale *(B. acutorostrata)*, plus the humpback *(Megaptera novaeangliae)*, and grey *(Eschrictius robustus)* whales, the blue whale belongs to the family Balaenopteridae, a group that migrates from its summer feeding grounds in cold polar waters to breed in warmer waters in the fall and winter. Rounding out the baleen whales are the Balaenidae, three genera that include the right whale *(Balaena glacialis)*, the bowhead whale *(B. mysticetus)* and their elusive cousin, the pygmy right whale *(Caperea marginata)*. Many cetologists recognize three subspecific forms of the right whale, and some argue that the southernmost of these deserves recognition as a separate species, the southern right whale *(B. australis)*.

Although baleen whales are so very large, they subsist on some of the smallest creatures: tiny oceanic plankton, or krill. Mysticetes are filter feeders, straining the water to collect their microscopic food, swallowing them in vast numbers; one mouthful of water may net its owner tens or hundreds of thousands of these tiny prey, which are trapped on the baleen as the seawater rushes back out. The baleen are rows of flexible, horny plates suspended from the upper jaw, each one fringed with a mat of hair–like projections to create an effective filtering device. Baleen was used for many years in ladies' corsets and other fashions, and thus was given the misleading name 'whalebone'—it is not bone at all, but rather the tough, flexible protein called keratin. As a group, baleen whales are larger and slower moving than toothed whales, perhaps in part because they don't need to pursue their prey.

Odontoceti: Toothed whales

In contrast, the faster–moving, smaller–bodied toothed whales—including dolphins and porpoises—pursue squid, fishes of many sizes, and in the case of killer whales *(Orcinus orca),* sea birds and mammals, including other cetaceans. Many toothed whales travel in groups of from five to many dozens of animals, whose purpose seems to be in part to hunt cooperatively. Killer whales have been observed to gang up on and kill larger whales such as grey whales. They also collectively hunt seals resting on ice floes; once a seal is spotted, the killers will dive together, causing a great wave that upsets the ice, dumping the unfortunate seal into their midst. (Interestingly, there is no record of a killer whale having killed a human.)

Cooperative behavior has also been suggested for several dolphin species; bottlenose dolphins *(Tursiops truncatus)* have been observed to circle a school of fish, causing them to group more tightly together, and then take turns lunging through the school, grabbing mouthfuls of fish as they pass. Perhaps in these species, individuals hunting together can catch more food than each would hunting alone—probably not true of the plankton–eating baleen whales.

There are many solitary species of odontocetes, however, each with innovative "solo" feeding strategies. Odontocete teeth are generally conical in shape, except in porpoises; these animals have spade–shaped teeth, and they lack the dolphin's protruding rostrum or beak. However, the bouto *(Inia geoffrensis)* of the Amazon and Orinoco rivers in South America, has rear teeth that resemble molars, used for crushing the armored catfish which is among its favorite foods. The susu river dolphins *(Platanista minor* and *P. gangetica)* of the Indian subcontinent have long, pincer–like jaws for grabbing prey out in front of them. The largest odontocete, the sperm whale *(Physeter catodon)* is also the deepest diver: these animals have been observed diving to 4000 ft (1,219 m), and have been captured with squid inhabiting depths of 10,000 ft (3,048 m) within their stomachs; however, their average dives are probably around 1100 ft (335 m).

Anatomy and physiology

The sperm whale's deep dives raise interesting questions about cetacean anatomy and physiology. Even the shallower dives performed regularly by many cetaceans would jeopardize the health of a human diver without proper diving equipment. One important issue for a diving animal is keeping warm in the cold depths. All cetaceans have a thick layer of blubber insulating them from the frigid water; in addition, a diving cetacean is aided by the increasing pressure of the greater depths, which reduces blood circulation automatically. Blood flow to peripheral body areas is further reduced by proximity to the cold water, keeping the warm blood circulating to the internal organs. It is still a mystery that the cetacean brain can function normally at great depths; the heartbeat drops during a long dive, but somehow the brain maintains its normal temperature.

Another important issue to a diving animal is oxygen deprivation. Many rorquals routinely stay under for 30 minutes before surfacing for a breath. Longer dives are always followed by a certain amount of panting at the surface, so the whale can restore its depleted blood oxygen levels. This is not the whole story, of course, since no land animal could hope to match this feat of breath–holding. Cetacean muscle tissue contains much greater amounts of myoglobin, the oxygen–binding protein found in the muscles of all mammals. This means that ounce for ounce, cetacean muscle is capable of storing more oxygen where it is needed most, even when new oxygen is not being provided via the lungs. In addition, cetaceans apparently have a high tolerance for the waste products—lactic acid and carbon dioxide—that accumulate in working muscle in the absence of respiration.

Of special interest to people who dive for recreation is the dangerous phenomenon known as the bends. Human divers take to the depths with a tank of compressed air, whose pressure equals or exceeds that of the surrounding water—otherwise, our relatively feeble chests would collapse under the pressure of the surrounding water. The bends occurs when nitrogen gas present in the compressed air dissolves into our blood and tissues, forming bubbles when the pressure is reduced too rapidly upon ascending. How do cetaceans avoid this deadly condition? Upon diving, their remarkably flexible chests and small, elastic lungs collapse; the tiny pouches that absorb oxygen within the lungs— the alveoli—are forced shut and gas exchange ceases. This means that little or no nitrogen is transferred into the bloodstream, and the dangerous bubbling–up of dissolved gas does not occur upon resurfacing.

In a swimming cetacean, the tail is the main source of forward propulsion, pushing the animal forward by an up and down movement against the water (rather than side–to–side, like a fish). The tail is a flexible extension of the last vertebra, which supports the muscular flukes. Rolling and changing position in the water is accomplished by the flippers; the flippers and dorsal fin (which is not present in all species) act together as stabilizers. Cetacean bones are heavier than water, but the body floats easily owing to buoyant blubber, oil in the bones, and air in the lungs. Some great whale species have been observed to sleep for hours, usually at night, their heads passively rising clear of the water to expose the blowhole. Both eyes are closed, and the body floats motionless with tail and flippers hanging limply, while the whale breathes once or twice per minute with a brief, snorting exhale. Amazingly, the smaller dolphins, who have more to fear from sharks and other predators, appear to sleep with only half of their brain at a time; one eye remains open, enabling the animal to rouse itself should danger arise.

Sensory perception

Cetologists have been able to infer a good deal about the sensory powers of whales and dolphins. Their vision is good, but is limited to 15 yds (13.7 m) or so, even in the clearest water; the depths of the ocean are quite dark, and vision is of no use. Their sense of hearing is much more important, in part because water is such an excellent conductor of sound. In addition, many cetaceans navigate and find food using echolocation, or sonar.

An echolocating animal perceives objects in its path by listening for the reflected echoes of pulsed sounds that it produces. In keeping with this practice, the cetacean hearing range is much greater than ours; some species can hear sounds up to 180,000 Hz. The sound is produced in a complex chamber in the airway atop the head, and is conducted out through the melon, a waxy, lens–shaped structure in the forehead. The melon functions to focus the beam of sound the way a magnifying glass focuses a beam of light. We know that around a dozen toothed whales and dolphins use sound to find food items; for instance, blindfolded bottlenose dolphins can find fish swimming in their tanks. Baleen whales lack the sophisticated structures for true echolocation, but may use echoes from lower–frequency sounds for a more rudimentary echonavigation.

Scientists once believed that cetaceans had no sense of taste or smell. More recently, bottlenose dolphins have been shown to distinguish the four basic taste stimuli (sour, sweet, salty, and bitter); in addition, beluga whales have been observed to show alarm when swimming through areas where other belugas have been killed, and quantities of blood are present in the water. Several cetacean species are sensitive to substances found in mammalian urine and feces, which could provide information on the identity or status of other individuals. Most modern cetologists agree that taste and smell are important to many cetaceans.

The cetacean sense of touch is very keen, as becomes obvious to anyone who watches two familiar animals interacting: whales and dolphins large and small rub up against each other, stroking and petting one another with flukes or flippers. Such touching clearly feels good to the recipient, and captive dolphins have been trained to do various tricks using touch alone as the positive reinforcement.

Scientists have suggested the existence of a cetacean magnetic sense; this would help to explain their remarkable navigational powers during long migrations in the otherwise featureless marine environment. In support of this possibility, the mineral magnetite has been found in the brains of some species (including common dolphins, Dall's porpoise, humpback whales and beaked whales). A magnetic sense could help explain the bizarre phenomenon of live stranding; although rare, stranding is generally fatal to the whale, which is ultimately crushed by its own weight out of the supporting water. A magnetic sense might not be fool–proof, and could be upset by various disturbances from on shore, leading the animals to beach themselves. Others have proposed that mass strandings of cetaceans are the result of the intense social bonds that form among members of some species. Perhaps the urge to avoid the dangers of separation is stronger than that to avoid the fatal risk of stranding along with a sick or injured comrade seeking shallow water.

Social behavior

Social behavior in cetaceans runs the gamut from species that are largely solitary to those that are highly social. Baleen whales are rarely seen in groups of more than two or three; however, grey whales and other rorquals may form transient groups from five to fifty animals during migration. Among toothed whales, river dolphins and narwhals (Monodon menoceros) are examples of species that appear to have mainly solitary habits.

The most highly social species are found among the toothed whales. In bottlenose dolphins and killer whales, for instance, individuals typically have social bonds with many others, which may last for life. In these species, females form the core of the society: long–term bonds between females and their adult daughters are important in many aspects of life, including foraging, fending off predators and aggressive dolphins, and delivering and raising the young. For example, sperm whale mothers often leave their infants in the company of a "babysitter," while they make the deep dives for squid where a baby could not follow. In bottlenose dolphins, social alliances between adult males are a prominent feature of society. Trios of adult male bottlenose perform together in synchronous aggressive displays, herding a sexually receptive female, or attempting to dominate rival males from similar alliances.

Courtship and mating remains largely undescribed for many species, owing to the difficulty of observing events under water; systematic study of most species is simply lacking. The mating systems of many that have been studied are classified as promiscuous, meaning that individuals select a new mating partner each year, and both males and females may mate more than once in a given season.

Some cetacean species—for example, narwhals, killer whales, and sperm whales—exhibit rather pronounced sexual dimorphism in size, meaning that males are noticeably larger than females. Such a size difference is believed to indicate a relatively high degree of competition among males for a chance to mate. These species are assumed to be polygynous, meaning that a few males mate with most of the available females, excluding the rest of the males for mating opportunities. Male–male fights in the presence of a receptive female may become fierce, and adult males often bear the physical scars of such contests. Adult male narwhals have a long, spiral tusk made of ivory growing out from their heads, which they use in jousting and sparring with their competitors.

Pregnancy and birth

Most baleen whales first mate when they are four to ten years of age. Many toothed whales take longer to mature, and in sexually dimorphic species, males take longer still. Sperm whales require 7–12 years, killer whales 8–10, and false killer whales (Pseudorca crassidens) need up to 14 years to mature.

Gestation in mysticetes lasts 10–13 months on average. Many odontocetes have similar gestation times but some are longer: pilot, sperm, and killer whale pregnancies last up to 16 months. The birth of a baby has rarely been witnessed by humans—typically, a formerly pregnant female simply appears one day with her new infant at her side. On rare occasions, however, a human observer has been lucky enough to see a birth. One laboring grey whale spent the last ten minutes of her labor hanging vertical in the sea, head down, with her flukes held 6 ft (1.8 m) out of the water. As she lowered her flukes to a horizontal position, the calf's snout was seen to be emerging from her belly. The mother shifted to a belly–up position, just at the surface, as the calf continued emerging; then the mother submerged, and the calf popped up to the surface, separate from its mother. Bottlenose dolphins are thought usually to deliver their calves tail–first, but head–first deliveries have been observed in captivity. In a captive situation, the dolphin mother typically uses her tail and rostrum (beak) to guide the baby to the surface for its first breath of air.

In all species, the baby soon takes up the "infant" position below and to her side, near her mammary slits. The nipple of a nursing mother protrudes from this slit on her belly, and the milk is ejected into the baby's mouth by her mammary muscles with no effort on the part of the calf. Nursing bouts are relatively brief, since the calf must surface to breathe. Even so, the baby gains weight steadily; blue whale infants gain 200 lbs (90.8 kg) per day! Blue and grey whales nurse for a period of about seven months; bottlenose dolphins nurse for three to four years or more. The record must be for pilot and sperm whales, who are occasionally observed to be nursing at 10–15 years of age! Of course, these youngsters have been eating other foods as well.

Intelligence and communication

Lengthy juvenile periods are typical for animals of greater intelligence. In Greek myths and other ancient sources, whales and dolphins have been accorded the attributes of higher intelligence, congeniality, and kindness to humans. Observations of wild and captive dolphins supporting a dead baby dolphin at the surface for hours and days—probably an instinctive act by a naturally protective mother—are no doubt the source of long–standing anecdotes about dolphins saving injured human divers from drowning.

It is generally agreed that cetacean intelligence surpasses other mammals such as trained dogs, seals, and even many primates. Curiosity, affection, jealousy, self–control, sympathy, spite, and trick–playing are all common observations by human handlers of captive cetaceans. Their brains feature a sizeable and deeply convoluted cortex, suggesting considerable higher learning ability; dolphins in particular are known for their powers of innovation. An especially large supralimbic area of the brain explains their excellent powers of memory and social intelligence.

Greater communication skills often accompany greater powers of intelligence. An underwater listener in the vicinity of a group of cetaceans may be surprised by the great variety of sounds they produce, from the repetitive tonal pulses of fin whales, to the moans and knocks of grey whales, the whoops, purrs and groans of bowhead whales, and the elaborate, eerie songs of humpbacks. Cetaceans do not have vocal cords; odontocete vocalizations are produced in a group of air sacs in the region below the blowhole atop the head, and are projected out through the melon. Mysticete sounds seem to come from an area off the lower side of the larynx, but the exact origin is unclear. Many of the social odontocetes emit whistles, and intense whistling seems to accompany excitement surrounding feeding, sex, and the joy of riding a wave before a speeding boat. Individuals may recognize one other from their unique whistles and other sounds.

Male humpback whales, who sing primarily during the breeding season, are the greatest balladeers of all cetaceans. In addition to their melodic, haunting songs, humpback whales produce a harsh gurgling noise, something like the sound a drowning person might make; their vocalizations, which may go on for hours, were audible through the wooden hulls of old whaling vessels. Superstitious sailors, hearing these voices out of the deep below their ship, believed that they were the ghosts of drowned comrades, coming back to haunt their old vessel.

Commercial whaling and other threats

Cetaceans have been harvested on an individual basis by native peoples, including Eskimos, in many parts of the world since before recorded time. Commercial whaling was underway in earnest by the twelfth century, when the Basque people of the French and Spanish coasts harvested whales harpooned from small boats called shallops, in struggles lasting many hours. Such struggles were worth the risks, because a single whale yields enormous amounts of valuable commodities. The victorious whalers returned with huge quantities of meat and blubber, which was rendered down into valuable oil for fuel and lubricants. By the eighteenth century, commercial whaling was a burgeoning industry, notably for baleen, to be used in ladies' corsets.

Modern whaling methods are viewed by many outside the industry as grossly inhumane. Whales today are killed by a harpoon whose head has four claws and one or more grenades attached; when a whale is within range, the harpoon is fired into its body, where the head explodes, lacerating muscle and organs. The whale dives to escape, but is hauled to the surface with ropes and shot again. Death may not be swift, taking fifteen minutes or more.

Commercial whaling inflicted a devastating blow on the world's baleen whale populations until 1986; many populations have yet to recover. Public outcry resulted in reduced catch quotas during the 1970s, and finally in a 1982 International Whaling Commission moratorium on commercial whaling (to which all nations complied by 1989). Since then, however, Iceland, Norway and Japan have demanded resumption of whaling; when the IWC refused, Norway announced plans to resume anyway, and Iceland left the IWC. Commercial whaling continues.

Further dangers to cetacean populations include marine pollution and loss of food resources due to human activity. Drift nets hanging invisible in the water cause the death of cetaceans along with seals, seabirds and fish; nets that get torn free during storms may drift at sea for many years. Thus, although the use of drift nets was halted by 1992, their effects persist. Meanwhile, purse–seine fishing methods for tuna have killed an estimated 7 million dolphins since 1959.

Susan Andrew

CFCs see **Chlorofluorocarbon**

Chachalacas

Chachalacas, curassows, and guans are 42 species of birds that make up the family Cracidae. These birds are in the order Galliformes, which also includes the grouse, pheasants, quail, guineafowl, and turkey. Curassows, chachalacas, and guans (or cracids) are believed to represent a relatively ancient and primitive lineage within this order. Fossil members of this family are known from deposits in Europe, but modern birds only occur in the Americas, ranging from the lower Rio Grande Valley of south Texas to Paraguay and northern Argentina.

The cracids are relatively large birds, ranging in body weight from about 1 lb (0.5 kg) for chachalacas to as much as 10.5 lb (4.8 kg) in the great curassow (*Crax rubra*). These birds have large, bare legs and large feet, well adapted for running and scratching for food in the forest floor. Cracids have a long tail, and a fowl–like body and head. The coloration of the plumage of cracids is generally a relatively plain brown or black, with little patterning. However, many species have colorful wattles and bare skin about the face, likely important in species recognition and courtship.

Most species of cracids occur in dense forests and thickets, although some species occur in more open forests. The curassows and guans mostly feed on the ground on fruits, seeds, and other plant materials, as well as insects, but guans mostly feed in the canopy. When disturbed, the ground–feeding birds typically fly up into the forest canopy. Cracids are not migratory, spending the entire year in a local environment.

Cracids build a simple nest of sticks, located on a tree branch. The clutch is two to five eggs, which are incubated by the female. The young are able to walk and run soon after birth, and are tended only by the female.

The chachalaca (*Ortalis vetula*) is the only species in North America, breeding in woodlands and thickets in extreme southeastern Texas and eastern Mexico. Like many other birds, this species is named after the sound that it makes.

All of the ten species of chachalacas are in the genus *Ortalis*. The 20 species of guans occur in the genera *Pipile*, *Aburria*, *Chamaepetes*, and *Oreophasis*. The 13 species of curassows are in the genera *Pauxi*, *Mitu*, *Crax*, and *Nothocrax*.

Bill Freedman

Chameleons

Chameleons are small, strange–looking lizards in the family Chamaeleonidae. There are 86 species of chameleons, in four genera. The majority of species of chameleon are found in the tropics of Africa and Madagascar, but some species live in southern Spain, Crete, India, and Sri Lanka. Most species of chameleons spend their lives in trees and shrubs, but some occur in herbaceous, grassy vegetation, and a few can be found on the ground.

Biology of chameleons

Most chameleons are green, yellow, or brown colored. However, these animals are famous for their ability to rapidly change the color and pattern of their skin pigmentation among these colors, and almost black or white shades can be achieved. This is done by varying the amount of pigment displayed by specialized cells in the skin, known as chromatophores. This visual behavior is primarily performed in response to changes in temperature, sunlight, and mood, especially when a chameleon is interacting socially with other chameleons. Chameleons may change the color of their skin to blend in better with their surroundings, as a type of opportunistic camouflaging. Although it is often believed that camouflage is the most common reason for the color changes of chameleons, the primary reasons are actually related to the mood or motivation of the animal.

A chameleon catching an insect with its tongue.

Almost all chameleons are arboreal animals, moving slowly and deliberately in their habitat of trees and shrubs. The often imperceptible movements of these animals, coupled with their usual green or mottled color, makes chameleons difficult to detect among the foliage of their habitat. Chameleons have feet that grip twigs and branches well, with their toes fused in groups of two or three (a zygodactylous arrangement) that oppose each other to confer a strong grip.

The prehensile tail of most chameleons can be wrapped around twigs and other structures to give the animal stability while it is resting or moving around. In some respects, the tail serves as a fifth "leg" for these animals, because it is so useful for locomotion and securing their grip. The laterally compressed body of chameleons also appears to be an adaptation to a life in the trees, by conferring advantages related to the distribution of body weight, and perhaps in camouflage.

Chameleons have very unusual eyes, which extend rather far from the sides of the head within turret- or cone-like, fused eyelids. The eyes of chameleons can move and focus independently of each other. However, chameleons also have excellent binocular vision, which is necessary for sensing the distance of prey from the

animal, so that it can be accurately snared by the long, unfurled tongue.

The tongue of chameleons is very important for the method of feeding. The tongue of chameleons is very long, and it can be rapidly extended by inflating it with blood. The tongue is accurately and quickly extruded from the mouth to catch prey up to a body length away from the animal. The sticky, club-like tip of the tongue snares the arthropod prey securely. Chameleons commonly feed on insects of all sorts, as well as on spiders, and scorpions.

Like other lizards, chameleons also use their tongue as a sense organ. The tongue is especially useful as a chemosensory organ which detects chemical signals from the air, ground, or food. The chemicals are transported to a sensory organ on the roof of the mouth, which analyzes the chemical signature.

Male chameleons aggressively defend a breeding territory, interacting with other males through drawn-out, ritualized displays. Some species have horn- and crest-like projections from their forehead which are used by the males as visual displays during their territorial disputes, and for jousting, during which the animals push at each other with their horns, until one combatant loses its grip on the branch, and falls to the ground. Most species of chameleons lay eggs, but a few are ovoviviparous, meaning the eggs are retained within the body of the female, where they hatch, so that the young are born as miniature replicas of the adults.

Some populations of chameleons consist entirely or mostly of female animals. This is an unusual trait in animal populations, and it may be indicative of parthenogenesis in these chameleon species, that is, the production of fertile eggs by females that have not mated with a male animal.

Species of chameleons

There are two genera of chameleons: *Chamaeleo* with 70 species, and *Brookesia* with 16 species. Species *Chamaeleo* occur in Africa, Madagascar, southern Europe, and southern and southeast Asia. Species of *Brookesia* occur only in East and West Africa and on the island of Madagascar.

The European chameleon (*Chamaeleo chameleon*) is represented by a number of subspecies in a few places in southern Europe, and much more widely in northern Africa, southern Arabia, and India. The African chameleon (*C. africanus*) occurs from West Africa through Somalia and Ethiopia. The common chameleon (*C. dilepis*) occurs throughout subsaharan Africa.

Some Madagascan and African chameleons have long projections on their snout which are used by male animals during their territorial jousts. Examples of these unusual, horned chameleons are Fischer's chameleon (*C. fischeri*) and the mountain chameleon (*C. montium*). The most spectacular of the horned species is Owen's chameleon (*C. oweni*), which has three long, *Triceratops*–like horns. This species is only found in the lowlands of Cameroon.

Unlike *Chamaeleo*, species of *Brookesia* chameleons do not have a prehensile tail, and they do not undergo marked color changes. Examples of these stump–tailed chameleons are *Brookesia superciliaris*, *B. stumpfi*, and *B. tuberculata*, all found on Madagascar and several neighboring islands. *Brookesia spectrum* and *B. platyceps* occurs throughout subsaharan Africa.

Chameleons and people

In some regions local people have developed a fear of these unusual, bizarre–looking lizards, believing them to be poisonous or deadly in some other way. In other places, chameleons are believed to have medicinal value, and are sold dried for use in folk medicine.

Chameleons are striking and interesting animals, and they are sometimes kept as pets. Some chameleons are also sold internationally in the pet trade. However, chameleons are rather finicky creatures, and they usually do not survive very long in captivity. Not many people have the zoological skills needed to successfully keep chameleons alive.

As with so many other types of wild life, the greatest threat to populations of chameleons is through the loss of their natural habitat. Most chameleon species do not adapt well to habitats that are intensively managed by humans. As a result, the populations of chameleons generally decline markedly when their natural habitats are converted to agricultural or residential land uses.

See also Anoles.

Further Reading:
Goin, C. J., O. B. Goin, and G. R. Zug. *Introduction to Herpetology*. 3rd ed. San Francisco: Freeman, 1978.
Grzimek, B. *Grzimek's Animal Life Encyclopedia*. Vol. 6. New York: Van Nostrand, 1975.
Halliday, T. R., and K. Adler. *The Encyclopedia of Reptiles and Amphibians*. New York: Facts on File, 1986.

Bill Freedman

Chamomile see **Composite family (Compositaceae)**

Chaos

Chaos theory is the study of non–linear dynamic systems, that is, systems of activities (weather, turbulence in fluids, the stock market) that cannot be visual-

A head-on collision between two dipolar vortices entering a stratified fluid environment from the right and left sides of the picture. The original vortices have exchanged some of their substance to form two new mixed dipoles which are moving at roughly right angles to the original direction of travel (toward the top and bottom of the photo). Dipolar vortices are relevant to turbulence in large-scale geophysical systems like the Earth's atmosphere or oceans. Turbulence within a fluid is an example of a chaotic system.

ized in a graph with a straight line. Although dictionaries usually define "chaos" as "complete confusion," scientists who study chaos have discovered deep patterns that predict global stability in dynamic systems in spite of local instabilities.

Revising the Newtonian world view

Isaac Newton and the physicists of the 18th and 19th centuries who built upon his work showed that many natural phenomena could be accounted for in equations that would predict outcomes. If enough was known about the initial states of a dynamic system, then, all things being equal, the behavior of the system could be predicted with great accuracy for later periods, because small changes in initial states would result in small changes later on. For Newtonians, if a natural phenomenon seemed complex and chaotic, then it simply meant that scientists had to work harder to discover all the variables and the interconnected relationships involved in the physical behavior. Once these variables

and their relationships were discovered, then the behavior of complex systems could be predicted.

But certain kinds of naturally–occurring behaviors resisted the explanations of Newtonian science. The weather is the most famous of these natural occurrences, but there are many others. The orbit of the moon around the Earth is somewhat irregular, as is the orbit of the planet Pluto around the sun. Human heartbeats commonly exhibit minor irregularities, and the 24–hour human cycle of waking and sleeping is also irregular.

In 1961, Edward N. Lorenz discovered that one of the crucial assumptions of Newtonian science is unfounded. Small changes in initial states of some systems do not result in small changes later on. The contrary is sometimes true: small initial changes can result in large, completely random changes later. Lorenz's discovery is called the butterfly effect: a butterfly beating its wings in China creates small turbulences that eventually affect the weather in New York.

Lorenz, of MIT, made crucial discoveries in his research on the weather in the early 1960s. Lorenz had written a computer program to model the development of weather systems. He hoped to isolate variables that would allow him to forecast the weather. One day he introduced an extremely small change into the initial conditions of his weather prediction program: he changed one variable by one one–thousandth of a point. He found that his prediction program began to vary wildly in later stages for each tiny change in the initial state. This was the birth of the butterfly effect. Lorenz proved mathematically that long–term weather predictions based upon conditions at any one time would be impossible.

Mitchell Feigenbaum was one of several people who discovered order in chaos. He showed mathematically that many dynamic systems progress from order to chaos in a graduated series of steps known as scaling. In 1975 Feigenbaum discovered regularity even in orderly behavior so complex that it appeared to human senses as confused or chaotic. An example of this progression from order to chaos occurs if you drop pebbles in a calm pool of water. The first pebble that you drop makes a clear pattern of concentric circles. So do the second and third pebbles. But if the pool is bounded, then the waves bouncing back from the edge start overlapping and interfering with the waves created by the new pebbles that you drop in. Soon the clear concentric rings of waves created by dropping the first pebbles are replaced by a confusion of overlapping waves.

Feigenbaum and others located the order in chaos: apparently chaotic activities occur around some point, called an attractor because the activities seem attracted to it. Figure 1 illustrates an attractor operating in three–dimensional space. Even though none of the curving lines exactly fall one upon the other, each roughly circular set of curves to the left and right of the vertical line seems attracted to an orbit around the center of the set of circles. None of the curved lines in Figure 1 are perfectly regular, but there is a clear, visual structure to their disorder, which illustrates the structure of a simple chaotic system.

James Yorke applied the term "chaos" to non–linear dynamic systems in the early 1970s. But before Yorke gave non–linear dynamical systems their famous name, other scientists had been describing the phenomena now associated with chaos.

Current research

Chaos theory has a variety of applications. One of the most important of these is the stock market. Some researchers believe that they have found non–linear pat-

terns in stock indexes, unemployment patterns, industrial production, and the price changes in Treasury bills. These researchers believe that they can reduce to six or seven the number of variables that determine some stock market trends. However, the researchers concede that if there are non–linear patterns in these financial areas, then anyone acting on those patterns to profit will change the market and introduce new variables which will make the market unpredictable.

Population biology illustrates the deep structure that underlies the apparent confusion in the surface behavior of chaotic systems. Some animal populations exhibit a boom–and–bust pattern in their numbers over a period of years. In some years there is rapid growth in a population of animals, followed by a bust created when the population consumes all of its food supply and most members die from starvation. Soon the few remaining animals have an abundance of food because they have no competition. Since the food resources are so abundant, the few animals multiply rapidly, and some years later, the booming population turns bust again as the food supplies are exhausted from overfeeding. This pattern, however, can only be seen if many data have been gathered over many years. Yet this boom–and–bust pattern has been seen elsewhere, including disease epidemics. Large numbers of people may come down with measles, but in falling ill, they develop antibodies which protect them from future outbreaks. Thus, after years of rising cases of measles, the cases will suddenly decline sharply because so many people are naturally protected by their antibodies. After a period of reduced cases of measles, the outbreaks will rise again and the cycle will start over, unless a program of inoculation is begun.

Chaos theory can also be applied to human biological rhythms. The human body is governed by the rhythmical movements of many dynamical systems: the beating heart, the regular cycle of inhaling and exhaling air that makes up breathing, the circadian rhythm of waking and sleeping, the saccadic (jumping) movements of the eye that allow us to focus and process images in the visual field, the regularities and irregularities in the brain waves of mentally healthy and mentally impaired people as represented on electroencephalograms. None of these dynamic systems is perfect all the time, and when a period of chaotic behavior occurs, it is not necessarily bad. Healthy hearts often exhibit brief chaotic fluctuations, and sick hearts can have regular rhythms. Applying chaos theory to these human dynamic systems provides information about how to reduce sleep disorders, heart disease, and mental disease.

See also Mathematics; Weather.

KEY TERMS

. . . .

Antibodies—Proteins in the human immune system which help to fight foreign bodies, such as bacteria or viruses, and preserve health.

Boom–and–bust cycle—A recurring period of sharply rising activity (usually economic prosperity) which abruptly falls off.

Circadian—The rhythmical biological cycle of sleep and waking which, in humans, usually occurs every 24 hours.

Dynamics—The motion and equilibrium of systems which are influenced by forces, usually from the outside.

Electroencephalogram—An electronic medical instrument used to measure brain activity in the form of waves printed on a sheet of paper.

Newtonian World View—The belief that actions in the physical world can be predicted (within a reasonable margin of error) according to physical laws, which only need to be discovered, combined appropriately, and applied accurately to determine what the future motions of objects will be.

Nonlinear—Something that cannot be represented by a straight line: jagged, erratic.

Population biology—The branch of biology that analyses the causes and (if necessary) solutions to fluctuations in biological populations.

Quantum—Literally, quantum means amount. But in physics, quantum usually refers to the amount of radiant energy in the different orbits of an electron around the nucleus of an atom.

Scaling—A regular series or progression of sizes, degrees, or steps.

Further Reading:

Gleick, James. *Chaos: Making a New Science*. New York: Viking, 1987.

Gutzwiller, Martin C. "Quantum Chaos." *Scientific American* 266.1 (January 1992): 78–84.

Kneale, Dennis. "Market Chaos: Scientists Seek Pattern in Stock Prices." *The Wall Street Journal*, November 1987: 41.

Pool, Robert. "Chaos Theory: How Big an Advance?" *Science* 245 (July 1989): 26–28.

Patrick Moore

Charles' law see **Gases, properties of**

Cheetah see **Cats**

Chelate

A chelate is a type of coordination compound in which a single metallic ion is attached by coordinate covalent bonds to a molecule or an ion called a ligand. The term chelate comes from the Greek word *chela*, meaning "crab's claw." The term clearly describes the appearance of many kinds of chelates, in which the ligand surrounds the central atom in a way that can be compared to the grasping of food by a crab's claw.

Bonding in a chelate occurs because the ligand has at least two pairs of unshared electrons. These unshared pairs of electrons are regions of negative electrical charge to which are attracted cations such as the copper(I) and copper(II), silver, nickel, platinum, and aluminum ions. A ligand with only two pairs of unshared electrons is known as a bidentate ("two–toothed") ligand; one with three pairs of unshared electrons, a tridentate ("three–toothed") ligand, and so on.

The geometric shape of a chelate depends on the number of ligands involved. Those with bidentate ligands form linear molecules, those with four ligands form planar or tetrahedral molecules, and those with six ligands form octahedral molecules.

One of the most familiar examples of a chelate is hemoglobin, the molecule that transports oxygen through the blood. The "working part" of a hemoglobin molecule is heme, a complex molecule at whose core is an iron(II) ion bonded to four nitrogen atoms with coordinate covalent bonds.

Among the most common applications of chelates is in water softening and treatment of poisoning. In the former instance, a compound such as sodium tripolyphosphate is added to water. That compound forms chelates with calcium and magnesium ions, ions responsible for the hardness in water. Because of their ability to "tie up" metal ions in chelates, compounds like sodium tripolyphosphate are sometimes referred to as sequestering agents.

A typical sequestering agent used to treat poison victims is ethylenediaminetetraacetic acid, commonly known as EDTA. Suppose that a person has swallowed a significant amount of lead and begins to display the symptoms of lead poisoning. Giving the person EDTA allows that molecule to form chelates with lead ions, removing that toxic material from the bloodstream.

Electron-dot diagrams of some elements in the periodic table.

See also Blood; Coordination compound; Ethylenediaminetetraacetic acid (EDTA).

Chemical bond

A chemical bond is any force of attraction that holds two atoms or ions together. In most cases, that force of attraction is between one or more electrons held by one of the atoms and the positively charged nucleus of the second atom. Chemical bonds vary widely in their stability, ranging from relatively strong covalent bonds to very weak hydrogen bonds.

History

The concept of bonding as a force that holds two particles together is as old as the concept of ultimate particles of matter itself. As early as 100 B.C., for example, Asklepiades of Prusa speculated about the existence of "clusters of atoms," a concept that implies the existence of some force of attraction holding the particles together. At about the same time, the Roman poet Lucretius in his monumental work *De Rerum Natura* ("On the nature of things") pictured atoms as tiny spheres to which were attached fishhook-like appendages. Atoms combined with each other, according to Lucretius, when the appendages from two adjacent atoms became entangled with each other.

Relatively little progress could occur in the field of bonding theory, of course, until the concept of an atom itself was clarified. When John Dalton proposed the modern atomic theory in 1803, he specifically hypothe-

sized that atoms would combine with each other to form "compound atoms." Dalton's concept of bonding was essentially non–existent, however, and he imagined that atoms simply sit adjacent to each other in their compound form.

The real impetus to further speculation about bonding was provided by the evolution of the concept of a molecule, originally proposed by Amedeo Avogadro in 1811 and later refined by Stanislao Cannizzaro more than four decades later.

The origin of bond symbolism

Some of the most vigorous speculation about chemical bonding took place in the young field of organic chemistry. In trying to understand the structure of organic compounds, for example, Friedrich Kekulé suggested that the carbon atom is tetravalent; that is, it can bond to four other atoms. He also hypothesized that carbon atoms could bond with each other almost endlessly in long chains.

Kekulé had no very clear notion as to how atoms bond to each other, but he did develop an elaborate system for showing how those bonds might be arranged in space. That system was too cumbersome for everyday use by chemists, however, and it was quickly replaced by another system suggested earlier by the Scottish chemist Archibald Scott Couper. Couper proposed that the bond between two atoms (what the real physical nature of that bond might be) be represented by a short dashed line. Thus, a molecule of water could be represented by the structural formula: H – O – H.

That system is still in existence today. The arrangement of atoms in a molecule is represented by the symbols of the elements present joined by dashed lines that

	1A	2A		3A	4A	5A	6A	7A
								2.1 **H** Hydrogen
	1.0 **Li** Lithium	1.5 **Be** Beryllium	. . . .	2.0 **B** Boron	2.5 **C** Carbon	3.0 **N** Nitrogen	3.5 **O** Oxygen	4.0 **F** Fluorine
	0.9 **Na** Sodium	1.2 **Mg** Magnesium	. . . .	1.5 **Al** Aluminum	1.8 **Si** Silicon	2.1 **P** Phosphorus	2.5 **S** Sulfur	3.0 **Cl** Chlorine

Electronegativities of some elements in the periodic table.

show how the atoms of those elements are bonded to each other. Thus, the term chemical bond refers not only to the force of attraction between two particles, but also to the dashed line used in the structural formula for that substance.

Development of the modern theory of bonding

The discovery of the electron by J. J. Thomson in 1897 was, in the long run, the key needed to solve the problem of bonding. In the short run, however, it was a serious hindrance to resolving that issue. The question that troubled many chemists at first was how two particles with the same electrical charge (as atoms then seemed to be) could combine with each other.

An answer to that dilemma slowly began to evolve, beginning with the work of the young German chemist Richard Abegg. In the early 1900s, Abegg came to the conclusion that inert gases are stable elements because their outermost shell of electrons always contain eight electrons. Perhaps atoms combine with each other, Abegg said, when they exchange electrons in such as way that they all end up with eight electrons in their outer orbit. In a simplistic way, Abegg had laid out the principle of ionic bonding. Ionic bonds are formed when one atom completely gives up one or more electrons, and a second atom takes on those electrons.

Since Abegg was killed in 1910 at the age of 41 in a balloon accident, he was prevented from improving upon his original hypothesis. That work was taken up in the 1910s, however, by a number of other scientists, most prominently the German chemist Walther Kossel and the American chemists Irving Langmuir and Gilbert Newton Lewis.

Working independently, these researchers came up with a second method by which atoms might bond to each other. Rather than completely losing or gaining electrons, they hypothesized, perhaps atoms can share electrons with each other. One might imagine, for example, that in a molecule of methane (CH_4), each of the four valence electrons in carbon is shared with the single electron available from each of the four hydrogen atoms. Such an arrangement could provide carbon with a full outer shell of eight electrons and each hydrogen atom with a full outer shell of two. Chemical bonds in which two atoms share pairs of electrons with each other are known as covalent bonds.

In trying to illustrate this concept, Lewis developed another system for representing chemical bonds. In the Lewis system (also known as the electron–dot system), each atom is represented by its chemical symbol with the number of electrons in its outermost orbit, its bonding or valence electrons. The formula of a compound, then, is to be represented by showing how two or more atoms share electrons with each other. The formula for hydrogen iodide, therefore, can be represented using Lewis': symbols as : H : I : :.

Bond types

Credit for the development of the modern theory of chemical bonding belongs largely to the great American chemist Linus Pauling. Early in his career, Pauling learned about the revolution in physics that was taking place largely in Europe during the 1920s. That revolution had come about with the discovery of the relativity theory, quantum mechanics, the uncertainty principle, the duality of matter and energy, and other new and strikingly different concepts in physics.

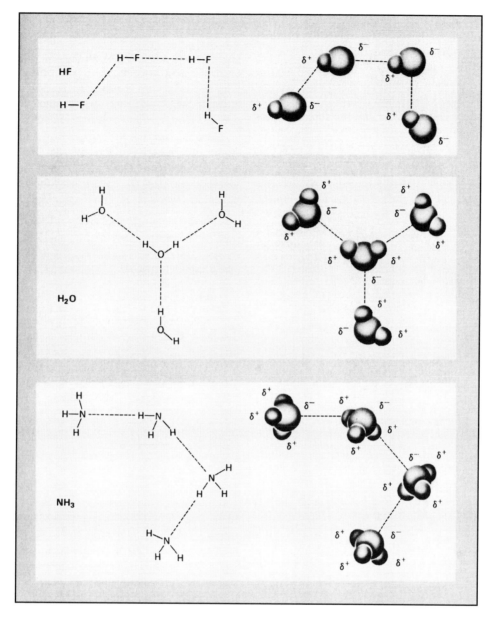

Hydrogen bonding in HF, H₂0, and NH₃.

Most physicists recognized the need to reformulate the fundamental principles of physics because of these discoveries. Relatively few chemists, however, saw the relevance of the revolution in physics for their own subject. Pauling was the major exception. By the late 1920s, he had already begun to ask how the new science of quantum mechanics could be used to understand the nature of the chemical bond.

In effect, the task Pauling undertook was to determine the way in which any two atoms might react with each other in such a way as to put them in the lowest possible energy state. Among the many discoveries he made was that, for most cases, atoms form neither a purely ionic nor purely covalent bond. That is, atoms typically do not completely lose, gain, or share equally the electrons that form the bond between them. Instead, the atoms tend to form hybrid bonds in which a pair of shared electrons spend more time with one atom and less time with the second atom.

Electronegativity

The term that Pauling developed for this concept is electronegativity. Electronegativity is, in a general sense, the tendency of an atom to attract the electrons in a covalent bond. The numerical values for the electronegativities of the elements range from a maximum of 4.0 for fluorine to a minimum of about 0.7 for cesium. A bond formed between fluorine and cesium would tend to be ionic because fluorine has a much stronger attraction for electrons than does cesium. On the other hand, a bond formed between cobalt (electronegativity = 1.9) and silicon (electronegativity = 1.9) would be a nearly pure covalent bond since both atoms have an equal attraction for electrons.

The modern concept of chemical bonding, then, is that bond types are not best distinguished as purely ionic or purely covalent. Instead, they can be envisioned as lying somewhere along a continuum between those two extremes. The position of any particular bond can be predicted by calculating the difference between the two electronegativities of the atoms involved. The greater that difference, the more ionic the bond; the smaller the difference, the more covalent.

Bond polarity

The preceding discussion suggests that most chemical bonds are polar; that is, one end of the bond is more positive than the other end. In the bond formed between hydrogen (electronegativity = 2.2) and sulfur (electronegativity = 2.6), for example, neither atom has the ability to take electrons completely from the other. Neither is equal sharing of electrons likely to occur. Instead, the electrons forming the hydrogen–sulfur bond will spend somewhat more time with the sulfur atom and somewhat less time with the hydrogen atom. Thus, the sulfur end of the hydrogen–sulfur bond is somewhat more negative (represented as Δ–) and the hydrogen end, somewhat more positive (Δ+).

Coordination compounds

Some chemical bonds are unique in that both electrons forming the bond come from a single atom. The two atoms are held together, then, by the attraction between the pair of electrons from one atom and the positively charged nucleus of the second atom. Such bonds have been called coordinate covalent bonds.

An example of this kind of bonding is found in the reaction between copper(II) ion and ammonia. The nitrogen atom in ammonia has an unshared pair of electrons that is often used to bond with other atoms. The copper(II) ion is an example of such an anion. It is positively charged and tends to surround itself with four ammonia molecules to form the cupric ammonium ion, $Cu(NH_3)_4^{2+}$. The bonding in this ion consists of coordinate covalent bonds with all bonding electrons supplied by the nitrogen atom.

Multiple bonds

The bonds described thus far can all be classified as single bonds. That is, they all consist of a single pair of electrons. Not uncommonly, two atoms will combine with each other by sharing two pairs of electrons. For example, when lead and sulfur combine to form a compound, the molecules formed might consist of two pairs of electrons, one electron from lead and one electron from sulfur in each of the pairs. The standard shorthand for a double bond such as this one is a double dashed line (=). For example, the formula for a common double–bonded compound, ethylene, is: $H_2C=CH_2$.

Compounds can also be formed by the sharing of three pairs of electrons between two atoms. The formula for one such compound, acetylene, shows how a triple bond of this kind is represented: $HC\equiv CH$.

Other types of bonds

Other types of chemical bonds also exist. The atoms that make up a metal, for example, are held together by a metallic bond. A metallic bond is one in which all of the metal atoms share with each other a cloud of electrons. The electrons that make up that cloud originate from the outermost energy levels of the atoms.

A hydrogen bond is a weak force of attraction that exists between two atoms or ions with opposite charges. For example, the hydrogen–oxygen bonds in water are polar bonds. The hydrogen end of these bonds are slightly positive and the oxygen ends, slightly negative. Two molecules of water placed next to each other will feel a force of attraction because the oxygen end of one molecule feels an electrical force of attraction to the hydrogen end of the other molecule. Hydrogen bonds are very common and extremely important in biological systems. They are strong enough to hold substances together, but weak enough to break apart and allow chemical changes to take place within the system.

Van der Waals forces are yet another type of chemical bond. Such forces exist between particles that appear to be electrically neutral. The rapid shifting of electrons that takes place within such molecules means that some parts of the molecule are momentarily charged, either positively or negatively. For this reason, very weak, transient forces of attraction can develop between particles that are actually neutral.

Further Reading:

Brown, Theodore L., and H. Eugene LeMay, Jr. *Chemistry: The Central Science*, 3rd edition. Englewood Cliffs, NJ: Prentice–Hall, 1985, Chapter 7.

Bynum, W. F., E. J. Browne, and Roy Porter. *Dictionary of the History of Science*. Princeton, NJ: Princeton University Press, 1981, pp. 433–435.

KEY TERMS

Coordinate covalent bond—A type of covalent bond in which all shared electrons are donated by only one of two atoms.

Covalent bond—A chemical bond formed when two atoms share one or more pairs of electrons with each other.

Double bond—A covalent bond consisting of two pairs of electrons.

Electronegativity—A quantitative method for indicating the relative tendency of an atom to attract the electrons that make up a covalent bond.

Ionic bond—A chemical bond formed when one atom gains and a second atom loses electrons.

Lewis symbol—A method for designating the structure of atoms and molecules in which the chemical symbol for an element is surrounded by dots indicating the number of valence electrons in the atom of that element.

Molecule—A collection of atoms held together by some force of attraction.

Multiple bond—A double or triple bond.

Polar bond—A covalent bond in which one end of the bond is more positive than the other end.

Structural formula—A collection of chemical symbols written in such a way as to show how the atoms in a compound are connected with each other in space.

Triple bond—A covalent bond consisting of three pairs of electrons.

Valence electrons—The electrons in the outermost energy level of an atom, those most likely to take part in a chemical reaction.

Masterson, William L., Emil J. Slowinski, and Conrad L. Stanitski. *Chemical Principles*. Philadelphia: Saunders, 1983, Chapter 8.
Partington, J. R. *A Short History of Chemistry*, 3rd edition. London: Macmillan & Company, 1957, pp. 366–377.
Pauling, Linus. *The Nature of the Chemical Bond and the Structure of Molecules and Crystals: An Introduction to Modern Structural Chemistry*, 3rd edition. Ithaca, NY: Cornell University Press, 1960.

Chemical compound, see **Compound, chemical**

Chemical element, see **Element, chemical**

Chemical equilibrium see **Equilibrium, chemical**

Chemical evolution

Chemical evolution describes chemical changes on the primitive Earth that gave rise to the first forms of life. The first living things on Earth were prokaryotes with a type of cell similar to present–day bacteria. Prokaryote fossils have been found in 3.4-million-year–old rock in the southern part of Africa, and in even older rocks in Australia, including some that appear to be photosynthetic. All forms of life are theorized to have evolved from the original prokaryotes, probably 3.5–4.0 billion years ago.

The primitive Earth

The chemical and physical conditions of the primitive Earth are invoked to explain the origin of life, which was preceded by chemical evolution of organic chemicals. Astronomers believe that 20–30 billion years ago, all matter was concentrated in a single mass, and that it blew apart with a "big bang." In time, a disk–shaped cloud of dust condensed and formed the Sun, and the peripheral matter formed its planets. Heat produced by compaction, radiation, and impacting meteorites melted the Earth. Then, as the planet cooled, the Earth's layers formed. The first atmosphere was made up of hot hydrogen gas, too light to be held by the Earth's gravity. Water vapor, carbon monoxide, carbon dioxide, nitrogen, and methane replaced the hydrogen atmosphere. As the Earth cooled, water vapor condensed and torrential rains filled up its basins, thereby forming the seas. Also present were lightning, volcanic activity, and ultraviolet radiation. It was in this setting that life began.

How life began

Obviously, any explanation of how life on Earth originated is theoretical. According to one theory, chemical evolution occurred in four stages.

In the first stage of chemical evolution, molecules in the primitive environment formed simple organic substances, such as amino acids. This concept was first proposed in 1936 in a book entitled, "The Origin of Life on Earth," written by the Russian scientist, Aleksandr Ivanovich Oparin. He considered hydrogen, ammonia, water vapor, and methane to be components in the early atmosphere. Oxygen was lacking in this chemically–

reducing environment. He stated that ultraviolet radiation from the Sun provided the energy for the transformation of these substances into organic molecules. Scientists today state that such spontaneous synthesis occurred only in the primitive environment. Abiogenesis became impossible when photosynthetic cells added oxygen to the atmosphere. The oxygen in the atmosphere gave rise to the ozone layer which then shielded the Earth from ultraviolet radiation. Newer versions of this hypothesis contend that the primitive atmosphere also contained carbon monoxide, carbon dioxide, nitrogen, hydrogen sulfide, and hydrogen. Present–day volcanoes emit these substances.

In 1957, Stanley Miller and Harold Urey provided laboratory evidence that chemical evolution as described by Oparin could have occurred. Miller and Urey created an apparatus that simulated the primitive environment. They used a warmed flask of water for the ocean, and an atmosphere of water, hydrogen, ammonia and methane. Sparks discharged into the artificial atmosphere represented lightning. A condenser cooled the atmosphere, causing rain that returned water and dissolved compounds back to the simulated sea. When Miller and Urey analyzed the components of the solution after a week, they found various organic compounds had formed. These included some of the amino acids that compose the proteins of living things. Their results gave credence to the idea that simple substances in the warm primordial seas gave rise to the chemical building blocks of organisms.

In the second stage of chemical evolution, the simple organic molecules (such as amino acids) that formed and accumulated joined together into larger structures (such as proteins). The units linked to each other by the process of dehydration synthesis to form polymers. The problem is that the abiotic synthesis of polymers had to occur without the assistance of enzymes. In addition, these reactions give off water and would, therefore, not occur spontaneously in a watery environment. Sydney Fox of the University of Miami suggested that waves or rain in the primitive environment splashed organic monomers on fresh lava or hot rocks, which would have allowed polymers to form abiotically. When he tried to do this his laboratory, Fox produced proteinoids—abiotically synthesized polypeptides.

The next step in chemical evolution suggests that polymers interacted with each other and organized into aggregates, known as protobionts. Protobionts are not capable of reproducing, but had other properties of living things. Scientists have successfully produced protobionts from organic molecules in the laboratory. In one study, proteinoids mixed with cool water assembled into droplets or microspheres that developed mem-

KEY TERMS

Abiogenesis—Origin of living organisms from non–living material.

Autotroph—Organism capable of synthesizing food from inorganic raw materials.

Heterotroph—Organism that requires food from the environment since it is unable to synthesize nutrients from inorganic raw materials.

Prokaryote—Type of cell that lacks a membrane-enclosed nucleus. Found solely in bacteria.

branes on their surfaces. These are protobionts, with semipermeable and excitable membranes, similar to those found in cells.

In the final step of chemical evolution, protobionts developed the ability to reproduce and pass genetic information from one generation to the next. Some scientists theorize RNA to be the original hereditary molecule. Short polymers of RNA have been synthesized abiotically in the laboratory. In the 1980s, Thomas Cech and his associates at the University of Colorado at Boulder discovered that RNA molecules can function as enzymes in cells. This implies that RNA molecules could have replicated in prebiotic cells without the use of protein enzymes. Variations of RNA molecules could have been produced by mutations and by errors during replication. Natural selection, operating on the different RNAs would have brought about subsequent evolutionary development. This would have fostered the survival of RNA sequences best suited to environmental parameters, such as temperature and salt concentration. As the protobionts grew and split, their RNA was passed on to offspring. In time, a diversity of prokaryote cells came into existence. Under the influence of natural selection, the prokaryotes could have given rise to the vast variety of life on Earth.

See also Amino acid; Evolution; Natural selection; Origin of life; Prokaryote; Ribonucleic acid.

Further Reading:

Franklin, Carl. "Did Life Have a Simple Start?" *New Scientist* (2 October 1993).

Keeton, William T., and James L. Gould. *Biological Science.* New York: W.W. Norton and Co., 1993.

Radetsky, Peter. "How Did Life Start?" *Discover* (November 1992).

Bernice Essenfeld

Chemical oxygen demand

Chemical oxygen demand (COD) is a measure of the capacity of water to consume oxygen during the decomposition of organic matter and the oxidation of inorganic chemicals such as ammonia and nitrite. COD measurements are commonly made on samples of waste waters or of natural waters contaminated by domestic or industrial wastes. Chemical oxygen demand is measured as a standardized laboratory assay in which a closed water sample is incubated with a strong chemical oxidant under specific conditions of temperature and for a particular period of time. A commonly used oxidant in COD assays is potassium dichromate ($K_2Cr_2O_7$) which is used in combination with boiling sulfuric acid (H_2SO_4). Because this chemical oxidant is not specific to oxygen–consuming chemicals that are organic or inorganic, both of these sources of oxygen demand are measured in a COD assay.

Chemical oxygen demand is related to biochemical oxygen demand (BOD), another standard test for assaying the oxygen–demanding strength of waste waters. However, biochemical oxygen demand only measures the amount of oxygen consumed by microbial oxidation and is most relevant to waters rich in organic matter. It is important to understand that COD and BOD do not necessarily measure the same types of oxygen consumption. For example, COD does not measure the oxygen–consuming potential associated with certain dissolved organic compounds such as acetate. However, acetate can be metabolized by microorganisms and would therefore be detected in an assay of BOD. In contrast, the oxygen–consuming potential of cellulose is not measured during a short–term BOD assay, but it is measured during a COD test.

See also Biochemical oxygen demand.

Chemical warfare

Chemical warfare involves the use of natural or synthetic substances to incapacitate or kill an enemy or to deny them the use of resources such as agricultural products or screening foliage. The effects of the chemicals may last only a short time, or they may result in permanent damage and death. Most of the chemicals used are known to be toxic to humans or plant life. Other normally benign chemicals have also been intentionally misused in more broadly destructive anti–environmental actions, called ecocide, and as a crude method of causing mayhem and damaging an enemy's economic system. The deliberate dumping of large quantities of crude oil on the land or in the ocean is an example.

Chemical warfare dates back to the earliest use of weapons. Poisoned arrows and darts used for hunting were also used as weapons in intertribal conflicts. In 431 B.C., the Spartans used burning sulfur and pitch to produce clouds of suffocating sulfur dioxide in their sieges against Athenian cities. When the Romans defeated the Carthaginians of North Africa in 146 B.C. during the last of a series of Punic Wars, they levelled the city of Carthage and treated the surrounding fields with salt to destroy the agricultural capability of the land, thereby preventing the rebuilding of the city.

The attraction of chemicals as agents of warfare was their ability to inflict mass casualties or damage to an enemy with only limited risk to the forces using the chemicals. Poisoning a town's water supply, for example, posed almost no threat to an attacking army, yet resulted in the death of thousands of the town's defenders. In many cases the chemicals were also not detectable by the enemy until it was too late to take action.

Chemical agents can be classified into several general categories. Of those that attack humans, some, like tear gas, cause only temporary incapacitation. Other agents cause violent skin irritation and blistering, and may result in death. Some agents are poisonous and are absorbed into the bloodstream through the lungs or skin to kill the victim. Nerve agents attack the nervous system and kill by causing the body's vital functions to cease. Still others cause psychological reactions including disorientation and hallucinations. Chemical agents which attack vegetation include defoliants that kill a plant's leaves, herbicides that kill the entire plant, and soil sterilants which prevent the growth of new vegetation.

Antipersonnel agents—chemicals used against people

The first large–scale use of poisonous chemicals in warfare occurred during World War I. More than 100,000 tons (90.744 tonnes) of lethal chemicals were used by both sides during several battles in an effort to break the stalemate of endless trench warfare. The most commonly used chemicals were four lung-destroying poisons: chlorine, chloropicrin, phosgene, and trichloromethyl chloroformate, along with a skin–blistering agent known as mustard gas, or bis(2-chloroethyl) sulfide. These poisons caused about 100,000 deaths and another 1.2 million injuries, almost all of which involved military personnel.

American troops wearing gas masks during World War I. The soldier at left, unable to don his mask, clutches his throat as he breathes in poisonous gas.

Despite the agreements of the Geneva Protocol of 1925 to ban the use of most chemical weapons, the United States, Britain, Japan, Germany, Russia and other countries all continued development of these weapons during the period between World War I and World War II. This development included experimentation on animals and humans. Although there was only limited use of chemical weapons during World War II, the opposing sides had large stockpiles ready to deploy against military and civilian targets.

During the war in Vietnam the United States military used a nonlethal "harassing agent" on many operations. About 9,000 tons (8,167 tonnes) of tear gas, known as CS or o–chlorobenzolmalononitrile, were sprayed over 2.5 million acres (1.0 million ha) of South Vietnam, rendering the areas uninhabitable for 15–45 days. Although CS is classified as nonlethal, several hundred deaths have been reported when CS has been used in heavy concentrations in confined spaces such as underground bunkers and bomb shelters.

Poisonous chemicals were also used during the Iran–Iraq War of 1981–1987, especially by Iraqi forces. During that war, both soldiers and civilians were targets of chemical weapons. Perhaps the most famous incident was the gassing of Halabja, a town in northern Iraq that had been overrun by Iranian–supported Kurds. The Iraqi military attacked Halabja with two rapidly acting neurotoxins, known as sabin and tabun, which cause rapid death by interfering with the transmission of nerve impulses. About 5,000 people, mostly civilians, were killed in this incident.

Use of herbicides during the Vietnam War

During the Vietnam War, the U.S. military used large quantities of herbicides to deny their enemies agricultural food production and forest cover. Between 1961 and 1971, about 3.2 million acres (1.3 million ha) of forest and 247,000 acres (100,000 ha) of croplands were sprayed at least once. This is an area equivalent to about one–seventh of South Vietnam.

The most commonly used herbicide was called agent orange, a 1:1 blend of two phenoxy herbicides, 2,4–D and 2,4,5–T. Picloram and cacodylic acid were also used, but in much smaller amounts. In total, this military action used about 25,000 tons of 2,4–D, 21,000 tons of 2,4,5–T, and 1,500 tons of picloram. Agent orange was sprayed at a rate of about 22.3 lb/acre (25 kg/ha), equivalent to about 10 times the rate at which those same chemicals were used for plant control purposes in forestry. The spray rate was much more intense during warfare, because the intention was to destroy the ecosystems through ecocide, rather than to manage them towards a more positive purpose.

The ecological damages caused by the military use of herbicides in Vietnam were not studied in detail. However, cursory surveys were made by some visiting ecologists. These scientists observed that coastal mangrove forests were especially sensitive to herbiciding. About 36% of the mangrove ecosystem of South Vietnam was herbicided, amounting to 272,000 acres (110,000 ha). Almost all of the plant species of mangrove forests proved to be highly vulnerable to herbicides, including the dominant species of tree, red mangrove. Consequently, mangrove forests were devastated over large areas, and extensive coastal barrens were created.

There were also severe ecological effects of herbicide spraying in the extremely biodiverse upland forests of Vietnam, especially rain forests. Mature tropical forests in this region have many species of hardwood trees. Because this forested ecosystem has such a dense and complexly layered canopy, a single spraying of herbicide killed only about 10% of the larger trees. However, subsequent resprays of upland forests were often made in order to achieve a greater and longer–lasting defoliation. To achieve this effect, about 34% of the herbicided area of Vietnam was treated more than once.

The effects on animals of the herbicide spraying in Vietnam were not well documented. However, there are many accounts of sparse populations of birds, mammals, reptiles, and other animals in the herbicided mangrove forests, and of large decreases in the yield of nearshore fisheries, for which an intact mangrove ecosystem provides important spawning and nursery habitat. More than a decade after the war, Vietnamese ecologists examined an inland valley that had been converted by herbiciding from a rich upland tropical forest,

into a degraded ecosystem dominated by grasses and shrubs. The secondary, degraded landscape only supported 24 species of birds and five species of mammals, compared with 145–170 birds and 30–55 mammals in nearby unsprayed forests.

The effects on wild animals were probably caused mostly by habitat changes resulting from herbicide spraying. However, there were also numerous reports of domesticated agricultural animals becoming ill or dying. Because of the constraints of warfare, the specific causes of these illnesses and deaths were never studied properly by veterinary scientists. However, these ailments were commonly attributed to toxic effects of exposure to herbicides, mostly ingested with their food.

Use of petroleum as a weapon during the Gulf War

Large quantities of petroleum are often spilled at sea during warfare, mostly through the shelling of tankers or other facilities, such as offshore production platforms. However, during the Iran–Iraq War of the 1980s and the brief Gulf War of 1991–1992, oil spills were deliberately used to gain tactical advantage, as well as being a method of inflicting economic damages on the postwar economy.

The world's all–time largest oceanic spill of petroleum occurred during the Gulf War, when the Iraqi military deliberately released almost 1.0 million tons (907,441 tonnes) of crude oil into the Persian Gulf from several tankers and an offshore facility for loading tankers. In part, the oil was spilled to establish a defensive barrier against an amphibious counterinvasion of Kuwait by coalition forces. Presumably, if the immense quantities of spilled petroleum could have been ignited, the floating inferno might have provided an effective barrier to a seaborne invasion. The spilled oil might also have conferred some military advantage by contaminating the seawater intakes of Saudi Arabian desalination plants, which supply most of that nation's fresh water, and therefore have great strategic value.

However, another view is that this immense spillage of petroleum into the ocean was simply intended to wreak economic and ecological havoc. Certainly, there was no other reason for the even larger spillages that were deliberately caused when Iraqi forces sabotaged and ignited the wellheads of 788 Kuwaiti oil wells on land. This act caused enormous releases of petroleum and combustion residues to land and air during the next year or so, and although the wells have been capped, there will be lingering pollution of the land for many decades.

KEY TERMS

. . . .

Defoliant—A chemical which kills the leaves of plants and causes them to fall off.

Ecocide—The deliberate carrying out of anti–environmental actions over a large area, as a tactical element of a military strategy.

Harassing agent—A chemical which causes temporary incapacitation of animals, including humans.

Herbicide—A chemical which kills entire plants, often selectively.

Nerve agent—A chemical which kills animals, including humans, by attacking the nervous system and causing vital functions, such as respiration and heartbeat, to cease.

Controls over the use of chemical weapons

The first treaty to control the use of chemical weapons was agreed upon in 1925, and subsequently signed by 132 nations. This Geneva Protocol was stimulated by the horrific uses of chemical weapons during the First World War, and it banned the use of asphyxiating, poisonous, or other gases, as well as bacteriological methods of warfare. However, in spite of their having signed this treaty, it is well known that all major nations subsequently engaged in research towards the development of new, more effective chemical and bacteriological weapons.

In 1993, negotiators for various nations finalized the Chemical Weapons Convention, which would require the destruction of all chemical weapons within 10–15 years of the ratification of the treaty. This treaty has been signed by 147 nations, but is not yet being enforced. The Chemical Weapons Convention is an actual pact to achieve a disarmament of chemical weapons. However, its effectiveness depends on its ratification by all countries having significant stockpiles of chemical weapons, their subsequent acting in good faith in terms of executing the provisions of the treaty, and the effectiveness of the associated international monitoring program to detect non–compliance.

It is important to understand that the destruction of existing chemical weapons will not be an inexpensive activity. It has been estimated that it could cost $16–20 billion just to safely destroy the chemical weapons of the United States and Russia.

See also Agent orange; Herbicides; Poisons and toxins.

Further Reading:

Dyer, G. "Environmental Warfare in the Gulf." *Ecodecision* (1991): 21–31.

Freedman, B. *Environmental Ecology*. 2nd ed. Academic Press, 1994.

Harris, Robert and Jeremy Paxman. *A Higher Form of Killing*. Hill and Wang, 1982.

Sivard, R. L. *World Military and Social Expenditures, 1993*. World Priorities, 1993.

Bill Freedman and Chris Cavette

Chemistry

Chemistry is the science that studies why materials have their characteristic properties, how these particular qualities relate to their simplest structure, and how these properties can be modified or changed. The term chemistry is derived from the word alchemist which finds its roots in the Arabic name for Egypt or the "black country," *al–Kimia*. The Egyptians are credited with being the first to study chemistry. They developed an understanding of the materials around them and became very skillful at making different types of metals, manufacturing colored glass, dying cloth, and extracting oils from plants. Today, chemistry is divided into four traditional areas: organic, inorganic, analytical, and physical. Each discipline investigates a different aspect of the properties and reactions of the substances in our universe. The different areas of chemistry have the common goal of understanding and manipulating matter.

Organic chemistry is the study of the chemistry of materials and compounds that contain carbon atoms. Carbon atoms are one of the few elements that bond to each other. This allows vast variation in the length of carbon atom chains and an immense number of different combinations of carbon atoms from which to form the basic structural framework of millions of molecules. The word organic is used because most natural compounds contain carbon atoms and are isolated from either plants or animals. Rubber, vitamins, cloth, and paper represent organic materials we come in contact with on a daily basis. Organic chemistry explores how to change and connect compounds based on carbon atoms in order to synthesize new substances with new properties. Organic chemistry is the backbone in the development and manufacture of many products produced commercially, such as drugs, food preservatives, perfumes, food flavorings, dyes, etc. For example, recently scientists discovered that chlorofluorocarbon containing compounds, or CFCs, are depleting the ozone layer around the earth. One of these CFCs is used in refrigerators to keep food cold. Organic chemistry was used to make new carbon atom containing compounds that offer the same physical capabilities as the chlorofluorocarbons in maintaining a cold environment, but do not deplete the ozone layer. These compounds are called hydrofluorocarbons or HFCs and are not as destructive to the earth's protective layer.

Inorganic chemistry is the study of the chemistry of all the elements in the periodic table except for carbon. Inorganic chemistry is a very diverse field because it investigates the properties of many different elements. Some materials are solids and must be heated to extremely high temperatures to react with other substances. For example, the powder that is responsible for the light and color of fluorescent light bulbs is manufactured by heating a mixture of various solids to thousands of degrees of temperature in a poisonous atmosphere. An inorganic compound may alternatively be very unreactive and require special techniques to change its chemical composition. Inorganic chemistry is used to construct electronic components such as transistors, diodes, computer chips, and various metal compounds. In order to make a new gas for refrigerators that does not deplete the ozone layer, inorganic chemistry was used to make a metal catalyst that facilitated the large scale production of HFCs for use throughout the world.

Physical chemistry is the branch of chemistry that investigates the physical properties of materials and relates these properties to the structure of the substance. Physical chemistry studies both organic and inorganic compounds and measures such variables as the temperature needed to liquefy a solid, the energy of the light absorbed by a substance, and the heat required to accomplish a chemical transformation. The computer is used to calculate the properties of a material and compare these assumptions to laboratory measurements. Physical chemistry is responsible for the theories and understanding of the physical phenomenon utilized in organic and inorganic chemistry. In the development of the new refrigerator gas, physical chemistry was used to measure the physical properties of the new compounds and determine which one would best serve its purpose.

Analytical chemistry is that area of chemistry that develops methods to identify substances by analyzing and quantitating the exact composition of a mixture. A material is identified by a measurement of its physical

KEY TERMS

Analytical chemistry—That area of chemistry that develops ways to identify substances and to separate and measure the components in a mixture.

Inorganic chemistry—The study of the chemistry of all the elements in the periodic table except for carbon.

Organic chemistry—The study of the chemistry of materials and compounds that contain carbon atoms.

Physical chemistry—The branch of chemistry that investigates the properties of materials and relates these properties to the structure of the substance.

properties, such as the boiling point (the temperature where the physical change of state from a liquid to a gas occurs) and the refractive index (the angle which light is bent as it shines though a sample), and the reactivity of the material with various known substances. These characteristics that distinguish one compound from another are also used to separate a mixture of materials into their component parts. If a solution contains two materials with different boiling points, then they can be separated by heating the liquid until one of the materials boils out and the other remains. By measuring the amount of the remaining liquid, the component parts of the original mixture can be calculated. Analytical chemistry develops instruments and chemical methods to characterize, separate, and measure materials. In the development of HFCs for refrigerators, analytical chemistry was used to determine the structure and purity of the new compounds tested.

Chemists are scientists who work in the university, the government, or the industrial laboratories investigating the properties and reactions of materials. These people research new theories and chemical reactions as well as synthesize or manufacture drugs, plastics, and chemicals. The chemist of today may have many "non–traditional" occupations such as a pharmaceutical salesperson, a technical writer, a science librarian, an investment broker, or a patent lawyer, since discoveries by a "traditional" chemist may expand and diversify into a variety of related fields which encompass our whole society.

Further Reading:

Castellan, G.W. *Physical Chemistry*. Addison–Werley, 1983.

Hargis, L. *Analytical Chemistry: Principles & Techniques.* Prentice–Hall, 1988.

Huheey, J. *Inorganic Chemistry.* New York: Harper & Row, 1983.

McMurry, J. *Organic Chemistry.* Pacific Grove, CA: Brooks/Cole Publishing Co., 1992.

Segal, B. *Chemistry, Experiment and Theory.* New York, NY: John Wiley & Sons, 1989.

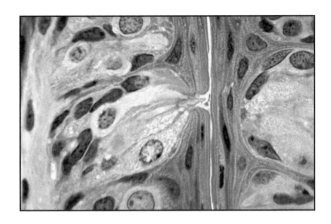

Taste buds on the tongue.

Chemoreception

Chemoreception is the biological recognition of chemical stimuli, by which living organisms collect information about the chemistry of their internal and external environments. Chemoreception has three sequential stages: detection, amplification, and signaling.

In detection, a molecule typically binds to a chemoreceptor protein on the surface of a cell, changing the shape of the chemoreceptor. All chemoreceptors therefore have some degree of specificity, in that they only bind to specific molecules or specific classes of molecules.

In amplification, the cell uses energy to transform the shape change of the chemoreceptor into biochemical or electrical signals within the cell. In many cases, amplification is mediated by formation of cAMP (cyclic adenosine monophosphate), which increases the cell's permeability to sodium ions, and this alters the electrical potential of the cell membrane.

In signaling, the amplified signal is transformed into a physiological or behavioral response. In higher animals the nervous system does the signaling, while in single–celled organisms signaling is intracellular, which may be manifested as chemotaxis, a directional movement in response to a chemical stimulus.

Detection, amplification, and signaling are often connected by feedback pathways. Feedback pathways allow adjustment of the sensitivity of the chemoreceptive system to different concentration ranges of the elicitor molecule. Thus, the sensitivity decreases as the background concentration of the molecule increases; the sensitivity increases as the background concentration of the molecule decreases.

Chemoreceptive systems detect chemical changes within an organism (interoreception) or outside an organism (exteroreception). The most familiar examples of exteroreception in humans are the senses of taste and smell.

Humans have chemoreceptor cells for taste in taste buds, most of which are on the upper surfaces of the tongue. Each human has about 10,000 taste buds and each taste bud consists of about 50 cells. An individual taste bud is specialized for detection of a sweet, sour, salty, or bitter taste. The sense of smell is important in discriminating among more subtle differences in taste.

Human chemoreceptors in the nasal cavity can discriminate thousands of different odors. One theory of odor perception in humans proposes that each chemoreceptive cell is connected to a single neuron and that an odorant molecule binds to many different chemoreceptors with different affinities. Thus, the neural signals from many different neurons can be integrated in many different ways to yield a rich panoply of odor sensations.

Many chemoreception systems also collect information about the internal environment of multicellular organisms. For example, the carotid body in the carotid artery of humans has chemoreceptive cells which respond to changes in the pH and oxygen levels in the blood. As the amount of dissolved oxygen in the blood decreases, chemoreceptive cells in the carotid body emit an electrical discharge, which stimulates specific neurons in the hind brain respiratory centers to increase the rate of breathing. The hypothalamus in the human brain has chemoreceptive cells which respond to changes in blood glucose levels. When blood glucose levels fall, the chemoreceptive system causes a person to feel hungry; when blood glucose levels rise, this chemoreceptive system causes a person to feel satiated. The endocrine and nervous systems also have many other chemoreceptive cells which signal different organs within the body to change their activity.

Cherenkov effect see **Cerenkov effect**

Cherry see **Rose family**

Chestnut see **Beech family (Fagaceae)**

Chickadees see **Tit family**

Chickarees see **Squirrels**

Chicken pox

Chicken pox, a disease characterized by skin lesions and low–grade fever, is common in the United States and other countries located in areas with temperate climates. The incidence of chicken pox is extremely high—almost everyone living in the United States contracts chicken pox, usually during childhood, but sometimes in adulthood. A highly contagious disease, chicken pox is caused by Varicella–Zoster virus (VZV), the same virus that causes the skin disease shingles. For most cases of chicken pox, no treatment besides pain relief and management of itching is necessary. In some cases, however, chicken pox may evolve into more serious conditions, such as bacterial infection of the skin lesions or pneumonia. These complications tend to occur in persons with weakened immune systems, such as children receiving chemotherapy for cancer or people with Acquired Immune Deficiency Syndrome (AIDS). A vaccine for chicken pox tested in the United States in 1995 showed promising results.

Despite its name, chicken pox has nothing to do with chickens. Its name has two possible origins. Some think that "chicken" comes from the French word *chiche* ("chick–pea") because at one stage of the disease, the lesions do indeed resemble chick–peas. Others think that "chicken" may have evolved from the Old English word *gigan* ("to itch"). Interestingly, the term "varicella" is a diminutive form of the term "variola," the Latin term for smallpox. Although both chicken pox and small pox are viral diseases that cause skin lesions, small pox is more deadly and its lesions cause severe scarring.

Symptoms of chicken pox

The incubation period—or the time from exposure to VZV to the onset of the disease—is about 14–15 days. The first sign of chicken pox in children is the appearance of the chicken pox rash. Adults may have a prodrome, or series of warning symptoms. This prodrome is typical of the flu, and includes headache, fatigue, backache, and a fever. The onset of the rash is quite rapid. First, small red "dots" appear on the skin. Soon, a vesicle containing clear fluid appears in the center of the dot. The vesicle rapidly dries, forming a crust. This cycle, from the appearance of the dot to the formation of the crust, can take place within eight to 12 hours. As the crust dries, it falls off, leaving a slight depression that eventually recedes. Scarring from chicken pox is rare.

The lesions occur in waves, with the first set of lesions drying up just as successive waves appear. The waves appear over two to four days. The entire disease runs its course in about a week, but the lesions continue to heal for about two to three weeks. The lesions first appear on the scalp and trunk. Most of the lesions in chicken pox are found at the center of the body; few lesions form on the soles and palms. Lesions are also found on the mucous membranes, such as the respiratory tract, the gastrointestinal tract, and the urogenital tract. Researchers think that the lesions on the respiratory tract may help transmit the disease. If a person with respiratory lesions coughs, they may spray some of the vesicle fluid into the atmosphere, to be breathed by other susceptible persons.

Although the lesions look serious, chicken pox in children is usually a mild disease with few complications and a low fever. Occasionally, if the rash is severe, the fever may be higher. Chicken pox is more serious in adults, who usually have a higher fever and general malaise. The most common complaint about chicken pox from both children and adults is the itching caused by the lesions. It is important not to scratch the lesions; scratching may cause scarring.

Treatment

Because chicken pox is usually a mild disease, no drug treatment is prescribed. Pain relief, in the form of acetaminophen (i.e. Tylenol) is recommended rather than salicylate, or aspirin. Salicylate may cause Reye syndrome, a very serious neurological condition that is especially associated with aspirin intake and chicken pox; in fact, 20–30% of the total cases of Reye syndrome occur in children with chicken pox. It is therefore important to control pain in children with chicken pox (or any other respiratory illness) with acetaminophen, not aspirin. Adults should also take acetaminophen if they have chicken pox.

The itching of the lesions can sometimes be controlled with calamine lotion or special preparations that are put into bath water. Antihistamines may also help relieve itching. The itching becomes less severe as the lesions heal; however, because children are more likely to scratch the lesions, the potential for scarring is greater in children than in adults.

Chicken pox, although not deadly for most people, can be quite serious in those who have weakened immune systems, and drug therapy is recommended for these cases. Antiviral drugs have been shown to lessen the severity of the disease, although some of the side effects, such as gastrointestinal upset, can be problematic.

Complications

If the lesions are severe and the person has scratched them, bacterial infection of the lesions can result. This complication is managed with antibiotic treatment. A more serious complication is pneumonia. Pneumonia is rare in otherwise healthy children and is more often seen in older patients or in children who already have a serious disease, such as cancer. Pneumonia is also treated with antibiotics. Another complication of chicken pox is shingles. Shingles are painful outbreaks of skin lesions that occur some years after a bout with chicken pox. Shingles are caused by VZV left behind in the body which then becomes reactivated. It is not clear why VZV is reactivated in some people and not in others, but many people with compromised immune systems develop shingles.

Pregnant women are more susceptible to chicken pox, which also poses a threat to both prenatal and newborn children. If a woman contracts chicken pox in the first trimester (first three months) of pregnancy, the fetus may be at increased risk for birth defects such as scarring and eye damage. A newborn may contract chicken pox in the uterus if the mother has chicken pox five days before birth. Newborns can also contract chicken pox if the mother has the disease up to two days after birth. Chicken pox can be a deadly disease for newborns—the fatality rate from chicken pox in newborns up to five days old is about 30%. For this reason, women contemplating pregnancy may opt to be vaccinated with the new VZV vaccine prior to conception if they have never had the disease.

Chicken pox and environmental factors

Researchers have long noted the seasonality of chicken pox. According to their research, chicken pox cases occur at their lowest rate during September. Numbers of cases increase throughout the autumn, peak in March and April, and then fall sharply once summer begins. This cycle corresponds to the typical school year in the United States. When children go back to school in the fall, they begin to spread the disease; when summer comes and school ends, cases of chicken pox diminish. A typical "mini–epidemic" within a school occurs when one child contracts chicken pox.

KEY TERMS

. . . .

Immunocompromised—A condition in which the immune system is weakened, as during chemotherapy for cancer or AIDS.

Reye syndrome—A neurological condition that usually occurs in children; associated with a respiratory illness and aspirin intake.

This child rapidly infects other susceptible children. Soon, all the children who had not had chicken pox contract the disease within two or three cycles of transmission. It is not uncommon for high numbers of children to be infected during one "mini–epidemic"—one school with 69 children reported that the disease struck 67 of these students.

Immunity and the new vaccine

Contrary to popular belief, it is possible to get chicken pox a second time. If a person had a mild case during childhood, his or her immunity to the virus may be weaker than that of someone who had a severe childhood case. In order to prevent chicken pox, especially in already–ill children and immunocompromised patients, researchers have devised a VZV vaccine. Tested in the United States, the vaccine consists of live, attenuated (modified) VZV. The vaccine provokes strong immunity against the virus. Although some side effects have been noted, including a mild rash and the reactivation of shingles, the vaccine is considered safe and effective. Researchers hope to begin vaccinating susceptible people in 1995 or 1996. In a few years, all children may be vaccinated against chicken pox.

See also Childhood diseases.

Further Reading:
Gorman, Christine. "Chicken Pox Conundrum." *Time* 142 (19 July, 1993): 53.
Kolata, Gina. "Curtailing Chicken Pox." *Reader's Digest* 137 (August 1990).
Kump, Theresa. "Chicken Pox Survival Guide." *Parents' Magazine* 69 (May 1994): 29.
Plotkin, Stanley A. "Vaccines for Chicken Pox and Cytomegalovirus: Recent Progress." *Science* 265 (2 September 1994): 1383.
"Vaccine Found to Be Effective on Chicken Pox; FDA Panel Still Has Questions to Resolve." *New York Times*, January 29, 1994.

Kathleen Scogna

Chickens see **Livestock; Pheasants**

Chicory see **Composite family**

Chiggers see **Mites**

Childhood diseases

Diseases that are more common among children than among adults are referred to as childhood diseases. That is not to say that adults cannot or will not contract these illnesses; but usually children contract these diseases and form the immunity against them that will protect them as adults. Some of these diseases can be life threatening to an adult, or can at least cause some permanent damage. Vaccines provide immunization against some of these diseases; others, however, can neither be prevented nor cured.

Although the first vaccination for any disease was administered in the late 18th century, the development of immunology proceeded slowly for the next hundred years. Dr. Edward Jenner, an English physician, noticed that milkmaids who developed cowpox from contact with cows were immune to the plague (smallpox). He correctly hypothesized that exposure to the cowpox somehow conferred protection on the milkmaids. Jenner withdrew some of the material from the skin pustules of the milkmaids and injected it under the skin of his own children, and they never developed smallpox. His methodology, however, was not accepted by the mainstream medical world of the time. Also, the means to develop, test, and produce vaccines were unknown. Physicians had not yet connected disease to the existence of microscopic organisms (bacteria).

Some childhood diseases are brought on by a bacterium or virus (chicken pox or measles, for example), others are inherited (Tay Sachs disease or sickle cell anemia), and still others are caused by heavy use of alcohol or drugs by the mother while she is pregnant.

Many of these diseases are contagious—that is, can be passed on from one person to another by transmission of the bacterium or virus. Children are brought together in school buses and classrooms, and these close quarters are ideal for the transmission of the etiologic agents that cause diseases. When one child contracts measles, usually several in the same bus or class will also get the disease before steps can be taken to slow the rate of transmission, because the disease usually is contagious before any outward symptoms appear. A child with mumps can infect a number of other children before he actually shows signs of being ill. This is particularly true of the common cold. The virus that causes the cold is especially numerous in the early stages of the cold, before the patient actually starts to sneeze and develop a fever.

Much research is directed toward developing vaccines and remedies for diseases which are presently incurable (e.g., the common cold or AIDS), but virus–borne diseases are much more difficult to cure or prevent than the bacterial diseases. A virus cannot be seen under the normal light microscope used in laboratories. A special electron microscope must be used to see a virus. Viruses also change or mutate to fend off any natural immunity that may develop against them. Some diseases, such as the common cold, are caused by more than one virus. A cold can be brought on by any one of some 200 viruses. A vaccine, if developed, would be effective against only one virus; many scientists feel such a vaccine would hardly be worth the trouble to develop. Even diseases that are caused by a single virus (such as AIDS) can defy the development of an effective vaccine.

Contagious diseases

The etiologic agents of contagious diseases can be passed from one person to another in any number of ways. They are present in droplets of saliva and mucus sprayed by sneezing and coughing. They can be conveyed by passing an object from the infected person to someone else. With the close proximity of children in classrooms, the agent can be passed quickly through the class.

Chicken pox

Chicken pox is one of the most easily transmitted childhood diseases; it is second only to measles. It is caused by the varicella–zoster virus, which in adults is responsible for the disease called shingles. After exposure to the virus, a three–to four–week period of incubation occurs before any symptoms appear. Chicken pox begins with a low fever and general feeling of tiredness. Soon a rash develops on the abdomen and chest, which may or may not spread to the extremities, but usually affects the scalp. The rash appears in successive stages; as a result, some of the bumps are mature while others are just appearing. The rash progresses from the initial red bumps through a vesicle stage, in which they are filled with liquid, to a mature, crusty stage. Itching is intense, but scratching can cause localized infection of the broken vesicles and may require antibiotics. Within a week after the appearance of the rash, the patient is no longer infectious.

There is no treatment for chicken pox, but the Food and Drug Administration approved a varicella–zoster vaccine in March 1995. The live–virus vaccine, developed from a strain of the virus isolated in Japan in 1981, is recommended for children between the ages of 12–18 months. A person also develops immunity to the virus if he has experienced an outbreak of chicken pox. The outbreak is usually harmless to children and passes within a week without any noticeable permanent effect. In adults the disease is much more serious; it can cause damage to the eyes and, in males, the testes. An adult with chicken pox also requires a longer period of rest than does a child.

Even when the infection has disappeared, however, the virus remains in the person's body and can cause shingles later in life. The chicken pox virus lies dormant in some nerve cells and can become active in an individual after the age of 50 years. In this case, the nerve root becomes inflamed, and the area of the body served by that nerve is affected. Again an eruption occurs, but in this case it is very painful. A rash may appear on the abdomen or any area of the arms or legs. The outbreak lasts for five to six days, unless the patient has an underlying cancer, in which case the rash may persist for two weeks or longer.

It is not possible to predict who will have shingles after they have had chicken pox as a child. There is no treatment for shingles, but usually an individual will have it only once and then be immune to any further outbreaks. If the virus infects certain facial nerves, care must be taken to prevent damage to the eyes. Unlike chicken pox, shingles is not contagious. The virus is confined to the nerve fiber and is not released into the air.

Measles

Measles generally refers to nine–day measles, also called rubeola, a highly contagious disease spread by a virus. A person who has the measles virus can pass it to others before he shows signs of the disease. Once exposed to the virus, it will be 7–14 days before the typical measles rash develops. The patient is infectious, however, for the two to four days immediately before the rash appears; thus he spreads the disease unknowingly. Present in mucus and saliva droplets from the nose and mouth, the virus is spread by coughing or sneezing.

The initial symptoms of measles include headaches, a low fever, tiredness, and itchy eyes. Spots appearing on the roof of the mouth look like white grains of sand surrounded by an inflamed area. A sore throat may also develop. The rash appears three to five days later: a bright red outbreak usually begins on the side of the head in front of the ears and spreads over the body within the next day or two. The temperature may climb to 104° F (40° C).

The disease is short lived; the rash fades within three to five days and the body temperature returns to normal. The disease, while active, renders the patient much more susceptible to bacterial infections and may worsen diseases such as tuberculosis, if present. Pneumonia and ear infections are common complications of measles, especially in infants and very young children. Also, the virus can penetrate the central nervous system and cause encephalitis (damage to brain tissue), which can lead to convulsions, coma, and even death. A person with measles should have bed rest during the active stage of the disease and be protected from exposure to any bacterial infections.

Fortunately, a vaccine has been developed against measles. The vaccine is a suspension of a live, attenuated (weakened) virus which is given to children at the age of approximately 15 months. The vaccine causes the formation of antibodies against the measles virus that will protect the child from future infections.

Another form of measles, known as three–day measles, German measles, or rubella, is also caused by a virus. Contagion is high because the infected person can transmit the virus to others for a week before showing any symptoms, and remains infectious for up to a week after the measles rash disappears.

Rubella is less infectious than the nine–day measles, and some infections may be so mild that the patient's case of rubella goes undetected. After exposure to the virus, an incubation period of 14–21 days passes before any symptoms appear. Usually the symptoms afflict only young children; teenagers and adults will not develop the typical rash.

The rubella rash is similar to that of nine–day measles but is less extensive; it appears on the face and neck and may spread to other areas. The rash lasts about three days before fading. No other symptoms, such as a sore throat, accompany the rash.

The most serious complication of three-day measles is its effect on a woman in the early stages of pregnancy. The virus can cause loss of the fetus or stillbirth, or it may result in congenital (birth) defects. A woman in the first three months of pregnancy should be protected from exposure to individuals who have measles. This form of measles can also be prevented by vaccination.

Mumps

Mumps, also called epidemic parotitis, is a viral infection of the salivary glands, especially the parotid glands. The mumps virus is spread in droplets of saliva sprayed during sneezing or coughing, and can be passed along on any object that has the infected saliva on it. The virus is present in the saliva of the infected person for up to six days before symptoms appear. Late winter and early spring are the peak periods of mumps epidemics, and children aged 5–15 years are most commonly infected. The disease is not as infectious as chicken pox or measles, and it is rare in children under two years of age.

The first symptom of mumps is pain during chewing or swallowing. The pain is worsened by acidic foods such as vinegar or lemon juice. The parotid gland, located in the area at the angle of the jaw, becomes sensitive to pressure. Body temperature increases to 103–104°F (40°C) once the inflammation of the parotid gland begins. The infected parotid gland becomes inflamed and swollen; the swelling may extend beyond the gland to the ear and the lower area of the jaw. The swelling reaches its maximum within two days and then recedes.

The mumps virus can also penetrate the central nervous system and cause abnormally high numbers of cells to accumulate in the spinal fluid. Usually this form of encephalitis has no residual effects, although rarely some facial paralysis or deafness due to auditory nerve damage may result. Mumps afflicting an adult male can cause atrophy of the testes and, in some cases, subsequent sterility. Patients should remain in bed until the fever accompanying the disease has subsided.

There is no treatment for mumps. Usually it is benign and will leave no residual effects other than a natural immunity against catching it again. During the illness, patients may take aspirin to ease the pain in the jaw and lower the fever. Eating soft food also helps to ease jaw pain. Anyone who has been in contact with a mumps patient should be watched closely for up to four weeks to see whether he or she will also develop the disease. A live–virus mumps vaccine is available for administration to children who are 15 months of age.

Other infectious childhood diseases

As recently as the early decades of the twentieth century, childhood was fraught with diseases that often entailed suffering and premature death. Many of those diseases were highly contagious; a child who contracted one of them was immediately isolated at home and a "quarantine" sign was posted conspicuously on the door to warn others. These once–perilous diseases included diphtheria, whooping cough (pertussis), and tetanus (lockjaw), which have been effectively controlled by vaccines; scarlet fever, another such disease, is now easily treated with antibiotics.

Diphtheria is caused by a toxin–producing bacterium, *Corynebacterium diphtheriae*, which infects the nervous tissue, kidneys, and other organs. The disease is spread by contact with the secretions of an infected person or objects that have the bacterium on them. Diphtheria develops rapidly after a short incubation period of one to four days. The bacterium usually lodges in the tonsils, where it multiplies and begins to produce a toxin. The toxic exudate, or secretion, is lethal to the cells around the infected area and can be carried to distant organs by the blood. Areas of infection and damage can be found in the kidneys, heart muscle, and respiratory tissues as well as in the brain. A membrane that is characteristic of the infection forms over the area affected by the toxin.

If left untreated, diphtheria can cause serious heart damage that can result in death, nerve damage resulting in a palsy, or kidney damage, which is usually reversible. A penicillin treatment and a diphtheria antitoxin are used to neutralize the bacterial secretions. One of the earliest vaccines now given to children is a combined vaccine for diphtheria, pertussis, and tetanus; as a result, diphtheria is rare now.

Pertussis, or whooping cough, is another highly infectious bacterial disease so named because of the characteristic high–pitched crowing sound of the breath between coughs. The etiologic agent is the bacterium *Bordetella pertussis.*

Pertussis is known throughout the world. It is transmitted in the saliva of coughing patients who have the bacterium, usually in the early stages of the disease. Patients are no longer infectious after eight weeks. The bacterium invades the nose, pharynx (back of the throat), trachea (windpipe), and bronchi. Symptoms appear after an incubation period of about one to two weeks. The earliest stage of the disease consists of sneezing, fatigue, loss of appetite, and a bothersome nighttime cough. This stage lasts for about two weeks, after which the coughs become rapid (paroxysmal) and are followed by the characteristic whoop, a few normal breaths, and another paroxysm of coughing. The coughing spells expel copious amounts of a thick mucus, which may cause gagging and vomiting. This stage of the disease can last up to four weeks, after which the patient begins a recovery; the coughing lessens and the mucus decreases.

Pertussis may be fatal in very young children; it is rarely serious in older children and adults. Fatalities in young children are usually caused by a subsequent bout of pneumonia. Infected individuals should be isolated, but do not necessarily need bed rest. Very young children should be hospitalized so that mucus may be suctioned from the throat area. A pertussis vaccine is available and is part of the early inoculation program in children. It is given with the vaccines for diphtheria and tetanus.

Poliomyelitis

Poliomyelitis, also called polio or infantile paralysis, is caused by a virus and once appeared in epidemic proportions. It occurs mostly in young children and appears primarily in the summer or fall. The poliovirus, the causative agent, is found in three forms—types I, II, and III. Type I is the most likely to cause paralysis.

Most people who host the poliovirus do not develop any symptoms but can still spread the virus. Because it is present in the throat of infected individuals, the virus is spread by saliva. Polio is known worldwide, and cases of it occur year round in tropical areas. Fortunately, only one of every 100 people who have the virus actually exhibits the symptoms of polio.

At one time polio was so widespread that young children developed an immunity to polio very early in life, because they would acquire the virus without fail. With the onset of hygienic sanitation, however, the disease began to appear as epidemics in developed countries. Since children no longer develop a natural immunity, as they did prior to the installation of modern sewage facilities, an outbreak of polio can quickly sweep through the younger population.

The onset of polio is divided into two phases: a minor illness and a major illness. The minor illness, experienced by about 90% of those who contract the virus, consists of vague symptoms such as headaches, nausea, fatigue, and a mild fever. These symptoms pass within 72 hours, and for most victims the minor illness is the extent of the disease. Those who acquire the major illness, however, combat a much more drastic form of the disease. It begins with severe headaches during the 7–35 days following exposure to the virus. A fever develops, and stiffness and pain in certain muscles appear. The affected muscles become weak and the nerve reflexes to those muscles are lost. This is the beginning of the paralysis, which results because the virus infects certain areas of the nervous system, preventing control of muscle groups.

A vaccine is available for the prevention of polio. The first polio vaccine was given by injection, but a later version, the one now used, is an oral vaccine. The polio vaccine is one of the earliest vaccines given to young children.

Noncontagious childhood diseases

Noncontagious childhood diseases are acquired by heredity—that is, passed from parents to offspring. In fact, neither of the parents may have any physical signs of the disease, but if they are carriers—people who have the recessive gene for the disease—they can pass it on to their children.

Some of these conditions are serious or even fatal; there is no cure for the person who has the disease. Some effective preventive measures can be taken to keep the disease in an inactive state, but even these measures are sometimes not effective.

Sickle–cell anemia

Sickle–cell anemia is named for the shape assumed by some of the red blood cells in persons who have this disease. It primarily affects people of African descent, but it can also be present in people of Mediterranean descent, such as Arabs and Greeks.

Some people carry the gene for sickle–cell anemia without having any active symptoms. For those in whom the disease is active, however, a "sickle–cell crisis" can be a painful and debilitating experience.

When the red blood cell undergoes changes that alter its shape from a disk to a sickle, the cells can no longer pass easily through the tiniest blood vessels, the capillaries. The sickle cells stick in these vessels and prevent the passage of normal cells; as a result, the organ or muscle dependent on blood flow through the affected capillaries is no longer getting oxygen. This causes a very painful crisis that may require the hospitalization of the patient.

No treatment exists for sickle–cell anemia, so the person who has the active disease must avoid infections and maintain a healthy lifestyle. Any activity that is strenuous enough to cause shortness of breath can also bring on a crisis.

Tay–Sachs disease

Tay–Sachs disease is an inherited, invariably fatal condition in which a missing enzyme allows certain toxic substances to accumulate in the brain. Under ordinary circumstances the enzyme, hexosaminidase A, breaks down these toxins, but without its presence the toxins accumulate.

The condition causes the development of red spots in the eye, retarded development, blindness, and paralysis. The child usually dies by the age of three or four. Tay–Sachs disease primarily affects Jews from eastern Europe.

Parents who carry the gene for Tay–Sachs can be counseled about having children. Statistically for parents who are both carriers of the gene, one in four children will have the active disease, two of the four will be unaffected carriers of the gene, and one of four will have neither the gene nor the disease.

Congenital diseases

Some conditions are passed from mother to child not as a result of an infection or a genetic malfunction, but because the mother has failed to provide an optimum prebirth condition for the developing baby. The placenta, which lines the womb and serves to nourish the developing infant, can be penetrated by substances such as alcohol, nicotine, cocaine, and heroin. Also, a mother who has AIDS can pass the virus to the child during gestation.

The mother who smokes, drinks alcohol, or uses drugs while pregnant can cause developmental problems for the child. The fetus is especially susceptible to these influences during the first three months (first trimester) of pregnancy. The organs are formed and the anatomy and physiology of the infant are established during the first trimester.

Fetal alcohol syndrome (FAS) is a well–recognized affliction brought about by the mother's heavy consumption of alcohol during pregnancy. Alcohol consumed very early in the pregnancy can cause brain damage by interfering with the fetus' brain development. Other features of a child with FAS are wide–set eyes, flattened bridge of the nose, and slowed growth and development.

A child born of a mother addicted to drugs will also be addicted. Often the baby will exhibit signs of withdrawal, such as shaking, vomiting, and crying with pain. These children usually have a low birth weight and are slow to begin to thrive. In time, once the drug is out of his system, the child will assume a normal life pattern.

See also Chicken pox; Diphtheria; Fetal alcohol syndrome; Poliomyelitis; Scarlet fever; Sickle–cell anemia; Tay–Sach's disease; Tetanus; Vaccine; Whooping cough.

Further Reading:

Schultz, D. "That Spring Fever May Be Chickenpox." *FDA Consumer* 27 (March 1993): 14–17.
Stix, G. "Immuno–Logistics." *Scientific American* 270 (June 1994): 102–103.
Ziegleman, David. *The Pocket Pediatrician.* New York: Doubleday Publishing, 1995.

Larry Blaser

Chimaeras

The chimaeras (order Chimaerae, class Bradyodonti) are a most peculiar looking group of fish that live near the sea bed off continental shelves and in deep offshore waters at a depth of 985–1640 miles (300–500 m). Collectively these species form a small, cohesive group of about 25 species. They are all exclusively marine species. Closely related to sharks, rays, and dogfish, chimaeras are characterized by their cartilaginous skeletons—in contrast to the bony skeletons of most fish. One feature that distinguishes them from rays and dogfish is the fact that the upper jaw is firmly attached to the cranium. They also have flattened teeth (two on the upper jaw and one on the lower) that are modified for crushing and grinding their food. There is one gill opening on either side of the head, each of which is covered with a fleshy flaplike cover.

Also known as rabbit fish, rat fish, or elephant fish, these species have large heads, a tapering body and a long, rat–like tail. Relatively large fish, they range from 2–6 ft (0.61–2 m) in length. Unlike their larger relatives–the sharks, for example they are all weak swimmers. The fins are highly modified: one striking feature is the presence of a strong, sharp spine at the front of the first dorsal fin. In some species this may be venomous. When the fin is relaxed, for example when the fish is resting, this spine folds into a special groove in the animal's back, but it may be quickly erected if disturbed. Chimaeras have a very reduced, elongated tail fin. The large pectoral fins, unlike those of sharks, play a major role in swimming, while additional propulsion is gained through lateral body movements.

Chimaeras have a smooth skin and one gill opening on either side a morphological change that lies between that of a shark and the bony fish. A series of mucussecreting canals occur on the head. The males of some species such as *Callorhinchus* have a moveable club-shaped growth on the head, the function of which is not known.

Little is known about the ecology of chimaeras. Most are thought to feed on a wide range of items, including seaweed, worms, crabs, shrimps, brittle stars, molluscs and small fish. Most rat fish are thought to be nocturnal–one explanation for their peculiarly large eyes. Male chimaeras have a small appendages known as claspers, used to retain their hold on females during copulation, this act is also observed in sharks and rays. Unlike the fertilized eggs of bony fishes, those of chimaeras are enclosed in toughened capsules. In some species these capsules may measure 6 in (15 cm) in length and are pointed to stick into the soft substrate, possibly to prevent the eggs from drifting too far.

Chimpanzees

Chimpanzees belong to the order Primates, which includes monkeys, apes, and humans. Chimpanzees are assigned to the ape family Pongidae, which includes gorillas, orang–utans, and gibbons. Apes are characteristically larger than monkeys, have no tails, and have longer arms and broader chests than monkeys. When apes stand upright, their long arms reach below their knees. Chimpanzees have a great deal of upper body strength that is needed for a life spent in the trees. Although chimpanzees have long powerful fingers, they have small weak thumbs. The big toes on their feet function like human thumbs, and so their feet, as well as their hands, can be used for grasping.

Physical characteristics

The height of chimpanzees varies from about 39.4 in (1 m) in males to about 35.5 in (90 cm) in females. An adult male of the common chimpanzee species weighs on average 132 lb (60 kg), but can grow larger in captivity up to 220 lb (100 kg). Female weights range from an average of 66 lb (30 kg) in the wild to about 190 lb (87 kg) in captivity. Pygmy chimpanzees are slightly smaller with a lighter body than the common chimps.

Chimpanzee coats are primarily black, turning gray on the back after about 20 years. Chimpanzees have a short white beard found in both sexes, and baldness is frequent in later years. The skin on the hands and feet is black, and the face ranges from pink to brown or black. The ears are large and the nostrils are small. Chimpanzees have heavy brows, a flattened forehead, large

protruding ears, and a short neck. The jaw is heavy and protruding, and the teeth are large. Male chimpanzees have larger canine teeth than females which are used in battle with other males.

The genitalia in both sexes are prominent, with areas of the female's genital skin becoming pink during estrus, a period that lasts about two to three weeks and occurs every four to six weeks. A chimpanzee's characteristic gait on the ground is the "knuckle–walk" that involves the use of the knuckles for support. Gorillas also walk in this manner. Chimps spend time climbing trees, which gorillas do not do much. Common chimpanzees live only about 40–45 years; the longevity of pygmy chimps is not known.

Researchers who have worked with chimpanzees contend that chimps experience a full range of emotions from joy to grief, fear, anger, and curiosity. It is also believed that chimps have a high level of ability to learn and understand concepts and some language.

Species and habitat

There are two species of chimpanzees, the common chimpanzee, *Pan troglodytes*, and the pygmy chimpanzee, or bonobo, *Pan paniscus*. The common chimpanzee is found in forested West and Central Africa from Senegal to Tanzania. Their habitat includes humid rain forest and deciduous woodland from sea level to above 6,000 ft (1,830 m). Common chimpanzees are rarely found in open areas, unless there is access to evergreen and fruit–producing trees. The pygmy chimp is found only in Central Africa, and is confined to Zaire between the Kasai and Zaire rivers. Their habitat is restricted to closed–canopy humid forests below 5,000 ft (1,525 m).

Chimpanzees sleep alone in leaf nests that they make with fresh leaves every day. A mother will sleep with her baby until her next infant is born. There are between 50 and 200,000 chimpanzees (both common and pygmy) living within the borders of some 15 African countries. Chimpanzees are threatened by habitat destruction, a low rate of reproduction, and by hunting for meat by humans.

Behavior

Chimpanzees have a sophisticated social organization in the wild. They band together in groups, varying in size and the age of its members. Between 15 and 120 individuals will form a community, with generally twice as many adult females as adult males in the group. The range and territory of a particular group depends on the number of sexually mature males.

Chimpanzees (*Pan troglodytes*) in Gombe National Park, Tanzania.

Chimps generally do not travel as an entire unit. Instead, they move together in smaller groups of three to six individuals. While moving about, these individuals may separate and join other chimpanzees. Bonds with other chimps are created by an abundant food source, or by a female in estrus. The strongest bond that is created is between a mother and her young. Offspring that are under eight years of age are always found with their mothers.

Parenting

A female's reproductive cycle averages 38 days, which includes two to four days of menstruation. When a female starts her estrus cycle, her genital area swells up for approximately ten days. It is during this time that a female is sexually attractive and receptive. The last three or four days of the estrus cycle is when the likelihood of conception is the highest. Mating is random and varied, and females are often mounted by most of the males in the community. A high–ranking male may also claim possession and prevent other males from mating with a female. All males, regardless of rank and social status in the community, do have a chance to pass on their genes, nonetheless.

On average, female chimpanzees give birth every five to six years. Gestation is 230–240 days or about seven and a half to eight months. Newborn chimps have a weak grasping reflex, and initially require full support from their mothers. After a few days, the new infant is able to cling to its mother's underside. About the age of five to seven months, the youngster will be able to ride on its mother's back. At the age of four years, a young chimp is able to travel by walking. Weaning occurs before its third year, but the youngster will stay with its mother until it is five to seven years old.

When a new chimp is born, the older sibling will start to become more independent. It will look for food and will build its own sleeping nest, but there is a close relationship that remains between siblings. Young males stay close to their family units until about the age of nine. At this time, they find an adult male to follow and watch his behavior. Thus begins the long struggle for male independence and his search for his place in his community.

Young females stay with their mothers until about ten years of age. After her first estrus, a young female will withdraw from the group and find members from a neighboring group, mating with the males there. At this time females may transfer out of groups to form families of their own. This type of exchange helps prevent inbreeding and increases diversity in the gene pool.

Eating habits

Chimpanzees are omnivorous, eating both meat and plant material. Their diet includes fruits, leaves, buds, seeds, pith, bark, insects, birds' eggs, and animals. Chimpanzees have been observed to kill baboons, monkeys, and young bush pigs, and they practice cannibalism. Chimps eat up to 200–300 species of plants, depending on availability.

Chimpanzees also seem to know the medicinal value of plants. In the Gombe National Forest in Tanzania, chimps have been seen to eat a plant that is a member of the sunflower family, *Apilia mossambicensis*. They look for this plant before breakfast to help get rid of parasites in their digestive systems. A new branch of science, zoopharmacognosy, has developed recently to study the medicinal use of plants by animals.

Fruit is the main component of the chimpanzee diet, for these animals spend at least four hours a day eating a variety of ripe fruits. In the afternoon chimps also spend another hour or two eating young leaves. They also eat quantities of insects that they collect by hand or with tools. Chimpanzees break open the hard shells of nuts with sticks or smash the shells open between two rocks. Animal prey is eaten less regularly than fruits and leaves. Chimpanzees (usually males) will eat young pigs, monkeys, or antelopes they happen upon.

Chimpanzees are able to devise tools to assist them in finding food and for other daily activities. They use stones as tools to smash open nuts, they use sticks for termite digging, and they peel leaves from bamboo shoots to use as wash cloths for wiping off dirt or blood, and for collecting rainwater from holes in tree trunks. The use of tools by chimpanzees seems to vary from region to region, which is a strong indication that it is a learned behavior. Young chimps have been seen to attempt to imitate their elders in the use of tools and fumble with the activity until they succeed after trial and error efforts.

Communication

Chimpanzees use a multitude of cries to communicate with one another, some of which seem very humanlike. After being separated, chimpanzees can be seen to embrace, kiss, touch, stroke, or even hold hands with each other. When fighting, the aggressor will strike his opponent with a flat hand, hit or kick, bite, stomp or drag him across the ground. Scratching and hair pulling

are favorite tactics with females. When the fighting is over, the loser will approach the winner and weep, crouch humbly, or hold out its hand. The victor responds by touching, stroking, embracing, or even grooming the defeated chimp.

Body contact is of utmost importance in maintaining social harmony in a chimpanzee community. Chimpanzees can groom each other for hours. Not only is this a way to maintain calmness and tranquility, but grooming also helps to preserve close relationships.

Chimpanzees also communicate through a combination of posture, gesture, and noise. In avoiding direct conflict, a male chimpanzee will charge over the ground and through the trees, swinging and pulling down branches. He will drag the branches on the ground, throw sticks and stones, and stomp on the ground. He is then able to give the impression that he is more dangerous and larger then he actually is. For younger males this behavior establishes the idea that the more impressive their display is, the better their position in the male ranking order will be.

Confrontations between members of different communities are often much more violent. Fighting is more ferocious and is conducted without restraint. It almost always results in serious injuries and on occasion in death. These encounters usually take place in areas where several communities overlap, areas in which chimpanzees behave cautiously. They often climb trees in order to survey the surrounding area and look for activity within the neighboring community.

When two chimpanzee groups meet, they first perform wild dances, show aggression by throwing rocks, beating tree trunks, and emitting fierce noises. This aggressive display is usually followed by retreat into their own territories. When a single stranger is met by a group, whether it is male or female, it is in danger of being attacked by the group of chimpanzees. This suggests that chimpanzees do not tolerate strangers of their own species. Chimpanzees have been seen to pull off flesh, twist limbs, and drink the blood of their victim in an aggressive attack.

Much of this hostile activity takes place when common chimpanzees are routinely involved in their so-called border patrols. Several males will take patrol duty for several hours, watching and listening for signs of activity nearby. It is not certain if the purpose of the patrols is to protect the food source of the group's members or if the males are engaged in competition for females.

Jane Goodall

In 1960, Jane Goodall, a young Englishwoman, set up camp in Gombe, Tanzania, to conduct a long–term study of chimpanzees. Dr. Louis Leakey helped Goodall start her research by providing the funding she needed for her project. Leakey is known for his important discoveries of pre–human fossils in Africa that have contributed to our knowledge of human evolution.

Although Goodall was not a trained scientist, Leaky felt that this was an advantage, since she would not bring any scientific bias into her research. The most difficult hurdle that Goodall had to overcome in the scientific community was to avoid making references to the idea that chimps have feelings. Projecting human emotions onto animals is referred to as anthropomorphic, and is a common scientific error.

Goodall made two significant discoveries early in her research. Her first chimpanzee friend was a male chimp that she named David Greybeard. One day she was sitting observing him when he walked over to a termite mound. David Greybeard proceeded to pick up a blade of grass, then he carefully trimmed it, and finally began to poke it into a hole in the termite mound. When he pulled the blade of grass out of the mound, there were termites on it, and he began to eat them. This discovery verified that chimps are toolmakers.

Goodall's second discovery also involved David Greybeard. She observed him eating the carcass of an infant bushpig. George Schaller, another field biologist who had been studying gorillas, had remarked to Jane Goodall that gorillas did not eat meat or use tools. If she could see chimpanzees doing both of those things it would be highly significant. Goodall saw that David Greybeard was not only eating meat, but that he was also sharing it with some companions, although he did keep the best parts for himself.

Bonobos (pygmy chimpanzees)

The common chimpanzee was first encountered by western science during the seventeenth century, when up to 14 different "species" were named, but today three subspecies are recognized. Several projects were begun in the early 1970s that were the first to study bonobos in the wild. The name pygmy chimp is inaccurate, since they are only slightly smaller than common chimpanzees. The reference has more to do with pedomorphic traits of bonobos, which means that they exhibit aspects of adolescence in early adulthood, such as a rounded head.

The one characteristic of the bonobo that differs from the common chimp is the joining of two digits in the foot. Additionally, the bonobo's body frame is thinner, its head is smaller, its shoulders are narrower, and its legs are longer and stretch while it is walking. Furthermore, the bonobo eyebrow ridges are slimmer, its lips are reddish with a black edge, its ears are smaller, and its nostrils are nearly as wide as a gorilla's. Bonobos have a flatter and broader face with a higher forehead than do common chimpanzees, and their hair is black and finer than the other species of chimpanzee.

Bonobos also have a complex social structure. Like common chimpanzees, bonobos belong to large communities and form smaller groups of 6–15 that will travel and forage together. Groups of bonobos have equal sex ratios, unlike those of the common chimpanzee. Among bonobos the strongest bonds are created between adult females and between the sexes. Bonds between adult males are weak. Bonobo society depends on females taking a more central position.

Sex is an important pastime among the bonobo chimpanzees. Female bonobos are almost always receptive and are willing to mate during most of their monthly cycle. The ongoing sexual exchanges within these communities help to maintain peace and to ease friction. Bonobos will avoid conflict at all cost, especially when it relates to food.

Bonobos are extremely acrobatic and enjoy spending time in the trees. They do not fear water and have been observed to become playful on rainy days, unlike common chimpanzees who hate the rain. It is believed that there are fewer than 100,000 bonobos in existence; they are threatened by hunting, both for food and for foreign trade, and by destruction of their natural forest habitat.

Language

Sign language has been used successfully for communication between human beings and chimpanzees. Sign language research has shown that some chimpanzees are able to create there own symbols for communication when none has been given for a specific object. Other studies of chimpanzees' use of language suggests they understand the syntax of language, that is, they understand the relationship of the words to the action and to the actor. Studies also suggest that bonobos learn the meanings of the symbols used in language training more quickly than do common chimpanzees. Chimpanzees also have pre–mathematical skills, and are able to differentiate and categorize, understanding, for example, the difference between fruits and vegetables. They are also able to divide an assemblage of sundry things into piles of similar objects.

Anthropomorphic—Ascribing human feelings or traits to animals.

Bipedal—The ability to walk on two legs.

Border patrol—A routine visit that common chimpanzees make to the edges of their communal areas to observe neighboring territories.

Estrus—In females, the period signaling ovulation and the readiness to conceive.

Pedomorphic—Having juvenile traits in adulthood.

Zoopharmacognosy—A field of research that studies the medicinal values of plants that animals eat.

Research value

The chimpanzee is our closest living relative. Genetically, the DNA of humans and chimpanzees differs by less than 2%. Because of this genetic closeness, chimps are good candidates for testing new vaccines or drugs in medical research. There are also similarities in the structure of the brain and nervous systems of chimpanzees and human beings.

Life in the wild presents many challenges for chimpanzees. They have complex social systems. On any normal day chimpanzees are forced to use their mental skills for their daily survival. They are presented with a multitude of choices in their natural habitats, and they exercise highly developed social skills. For instance, males aspire to attain high positions of dominance within the hierarchy of chimpanzee society, and consequently low–ranking males must learn the art of deception, doing things in secret to satisfy their own needs.

What interests scientists about bonobos particularly is the fact that they display three important elements of early human development. Female bonobos exhibit prolonged periods of sexual receptivity, and their sex life is varied. Bonobos are also more bipedal (able to walk on their hind legs) than other nonhuman primates. Chimpanzees can become infected by diseases that humans are susceptible to, such as colds, flu, AIDS and hepatitis B. Gorillas, gibbons, and orang–utans are the only other animals that show this same susceptibility to human diseases.

See also Apes; Primates.

Further Reading:

De Waal, Frans. *Peacemaking Among Primates.* Cambridge, MA: Harvard University Press, 1989.

Goodall, Jane. *Through a Window: My Thirty Years with the Chimpanzees of Gombe.* Boston: Houghton Mifflin, 1990.

Goodall, Jane, and Dale Peterson. *Visions of Caliban: On Chimpanzees and People.* Boston: Houghton Mifflin, 1993.

Grzimek, Bernhard. *Encyclopedia of Mammals.* Vol. 2. New York: McGraw–Hill, 1990.

Montgomery, Sy. *Walking with the Great Apes.* Boston: Houghton Mifflin, 1991.

Nichols, Michael. *The Great Apes Between Two Worlds.* Washington, D.C.: National Geographic Society, 1993.

Savage–Rumbaugh, Sue, and Roger Lewin. "Ape at the Brink," *Discover,* (September 1994): 91–98.

Small, Meredith F. "What's Love Got to Do with It?" *Discover,* (June 1992): 48–51.

Kitty Richman

Chinch bug see **True bugs**

Chinchilla

Chinchillas and viscachas are seven species of small, South American rodents in the family Chinchillidae. Chinchillas have a large head, broad snout, large eyes, rounded ears, and an extremely fine and dense fur. Their forelimbs are short and the paws small, while the hindlegs and feet are larger and relatively powerful, and are used for a leaping style of locomotion, as well as for running and creeping.

Two species of true chinchillas are recognized. The short–tailed chinchilla (*Chinchilla brevicaudata*) is native to Andean mountains of Argentina, Bolivia, and Peru, while the long–tailed chinchilla (*C. laniger*) occurs in the mountains of Chile. Chinchillas are alpine animals, living in colonies in rock piles and scree, basking at dawn and dusk, and feeding at night on vegetation and occasional arthropods.

Chinchillas have an extremely thick, warm, and soft pelage, considered to be perhaps the finest of any fur. When the commercial implications of this fact were recognized in the late nineteenth century, a relentless exploitation of the wild populations of both species of chinchillas ensued. The over–harvesting of these animals brought both species to the brink of extinction by the early twentieth century.

Fortunately, methods have been developed for breeding and growing chinchillas in captivity, and large numbers are now raised on fur ranches. This develop-

A long-tailed chinchilla (*Chinchilla lanigera*).

ment made it possible to stop most of the unregulated exploitation of wild chinchillas. Unfortunately, this happened rather late, and both species are widely extirpated from their original native habitats. The short–tailed chinchilla may, in fact, no longer be found in the wild, and this species is not commonly ranched on fur farms. The long–tailed chinchilla has fared much better, and although it remains rare in the wild, it is common in captivity, and is often kept as a pet. Attempts are being made to re–stock wild populations of chinchillas, but it is too soon to tell whether these efforts will be successful.

The plains viscacha (*Lagostomus maximus*) is another species in the Chinchillidae, occurring in the dry, lowland pampas of Argentina. These animals are much larger than the true chinchillas, and can reach a body length of 24 in (60 cm). Viscachas live in colonies of about 20–50 individuals, which inhabit complexes of underground burrows. The diggings from the burrows are piled in large heaps around the entrances, and the viscachas have a habit of collecting odd materials and placing them on those mounds. These can include natural objects such as bones and vegetation, but also things scavenged from people, such as watches, boots, and other unlikely items.

Viscachas are sometimes hunted as a source of wild meat. More importantly, viscachas have been widely exterminated because their diggings are considered to be a hazard to livestock, which can fall and break a leg if they break through an underground tunnel.

Four species of mountain viscachas (*Lagidium* spp.) occur in rocky habitats in the Andean tundra. Mountain viscachas live in colonies located in protective crevices, from which they forage during the day.

Mountain viscachas are eaten by local people, and their fur is used in clothing. Sometimes the hair is removed from the skin of trapped animals, and used to weave an indigenous Andean cloth.

Chipmunks

Chipmunks are small mammals in the order Rodentia, the rodents. Specifically, they are classified with the squirrel–like rodents, the Sciuridae. Chipmunks are divided into two genera: Gallos and Tamias.

North America is home to seventeen species of chipmunk, sixteen in the West and only one, *Tamias striatus*, the eastern chipmunk, in the East. The eastern chipmunk is about 5–6 in (12.7–15 cm) long, and the tail adds another 4 in (10 cm) or so to the animal's length. They have stripes on their faces and running the length of their body. In all species the tail is bushy, although not quite as much in the tree squirrels. Their eyes are large, their vision is excellent, and their sensitive whiskers give them a well–developed sense of touch.

Like other squirrels, chipmunks are opportunists, making a comfortable home where other animals would not dare. They are generally unafraid of human beings, and are frequent visitors to campgrounds. They are burrowers, digging holes among rocks, under logs, and within scrub, to make a burrow as long as 15 ft (4.6 m) and extend downward about 3 ft (0.9 m).

Like squirrels, chipmunks are active during the day. They emerge from their burrows in the morning to forage on mushrooms, fruits, seeds, berries, and acorns. The chipmunk will store food, particularly items with a long "shelf–life," in its cheek pouches for transport back to the burrow. The Siberian chipmunk can carry more than a quarter of an ounce of seed for half a mile. This food is stored in an underground larder, which can contain between 4 1/2 to 13 lbs (2–5.9 kg) of food. They do not hibernate like bears; instead they become more lethargic than normal during the winter months.

In the spring, the female bears a litter of pups, numbering up to eight, which are born naked, toothless, and with closed eyes. The young grow quickly and are weaned at five weeks, but stay with the female for several months.

Chipmunks can live as long as five years, providing they avoid predators such as weasels, owls, hawks, bobcats, pine martens, and coyotes. Many chipmunks die after eating rodenticide set out for rats; these poisons have effectively eliminated chipmunks in some locations.

See also Squirrels.

Chiropractic medicine see **Alternative medicine**

Chitons

Chitons are small mollusks, oval in outline, with a broad foot, and a mantle that secretes, and sometimes extends over, the shell. They live on rocky seashores in much the same life–style as limpets. They are easily distinguishable from limpets, however, by their shell made of eight plates (or valves) with transverse sutures. Also, unlike limpets and other snails, the chitons have no tentacles or eyes in the head region, just a mouth and a radula. The shell is so different from those of other mollusks that one might think chitons are segmented (or metameric), but contrary to the general rule, this is incorrect. Internally, there is no evidence of segmentation, and the eight valves are actually derived from a single embryonic shell.

Except for the color, the uniformity of external appearance tempts one to regard chitons as races of a single species, but the small variations are very important to other chitons and to chiton specialists, who like to count the notches and slits along the valve edges. The word chiton is a Greek word meaning a gown or tunic, usually worn next to the skin, and covered with a cloak on going outdoors. The chiton was worn by both men and women, just as the eight plates are worn by both male and female chitons. There are about 600 species of chitons in all, about 75 of them are on the U.S. Pacific Coast. Among the most common species are *Chaetopleura apiculata* of New England and *Mopalia muscosa* of California.

Chitons are classified as subclass Polyplacophora in the class Amphineura, one of the six classes of mollusks. The other subclass contains the Aplacophora, a group of wormlike mollusks lacking a shell, but possessing in some genera calcareous spicules embedded in the mantle. Amphineura means nerves on both sides, and Polyplacophora means bearing many plates; chitons have two pairs of parallel nerve cords running the length of the body. The nervous system is simple and straight, not twisted as in prosobranch snails. In spite of their anatomical simplicity, there is no reason to sup-

pose that chitons represent a form ancestral to all the mollusks. Rather the opposite, the fossil record suggests that they followed the gastropods and bivalves in evolution, and lost some structures or traits as they became adapted to a restricted niche. The lack of tentacles and eyes, for example, means that chitons cannot function as predators. The shell is obviously defensive. When pried loose from their preferred spot, chitons roll up in a ball, much like certain isopod crustaceans, called pill bugs, and like the armadillo, an armored mammal.

Most chitons are 0.8–1.2 in (2–4 cm) long, but there is a giant Pacific coast species, *Cryptochiton stelleri*, up to 11.8 in (30 cm) long. This species is unusual also for the mantle or girdle that completely covers the shell (crypto = hidden). Other surprises include a species of *Callochiton septemvalvis* (seven valves). Eggs are laid singly or in a jelly string, and are fertilized by sperm released into the sea water. The larvae of a few species develop within the female, but most larvae are planktonic.

The giant chiton *Cryptochiton stelleri* was included in a classic study of nucleotide sequences in RNA of a great variety of animals, in which the goal was to establish relations of the phyla. On the resultant phylogenetic tree, the chiton appeared at the end of a branch close to a polychaete worm and a brachiopod, and not far from two clams. Another analysis of the same data put *Cryptochiton* on a branch next to a nudibranch *Anisodoris nobilis* and ancestral to the two clams. There is reason to suspect that living chitons are highly evolved creatures, and not good subjects for deductions about the initial metazoan radiation in the pre–Cambrian. The reasoning is as follows: Many marine mollusks have oxidative enzymes that use an amino acid to produce products such as octopine, alanopine, etc. while serving to reoxidize coenzyme, and keep anaerobic metabolism going. These opine enzymes are most varied in archaeogastropods, which are regarded as primitive on numerous grounds. The trend in evolution has been to lose some or all of the opine enzymes, and come to depend entirely on lactic acid production for their function. This is what has happened in a few bivalves and polychaete worms, and in fishes and other vertebrates. It is also the case with the chitons *Chaetopleura apiculata* and *Mopalia muscosa*, which have only a lactate oxidase and no opine enzymes. The earliest chitons may have had a great variety of genes that modern species no longer possess, but this is something that would be difficult to investigate.

Further Reading:

Abbott, R.T. 1991. *Seashells of the northern hemisphere.* New York: Gallery Books.

Field, K.G., Olsen, G.J., Lane, D.J., Giovannoni, S.J., Ghiselin, M.T., Raff, E.C., Pace, N.R. & Raff, R.A. 1988. "Molecular phylogeny of the animal kingdom." *Science* 239, 748–753.

Hammen, C.S. and Bullock, R.C. 1991. "Opine oxidoreductases in brachiopods, bryozoans, phoronids, and molluscs." *Biochem. Syst. Ecol.* 19, 263–269.

Morton, J.E. 1960. *Molluscs.* New York: Harper.

Chlordane

Chlordane is an organochlorine insecticide, more specifically a chlorinated cyclic hydrocarbon within the cyclodiene group. The proper scientific name for chlordane is 1,2,4,5,6,7,8,8–Octachloro–3a,4,7,7a–tetrahydro–4,7–methanoindan. However, the actual technical product is a mixture of various chlorinated hydrocarbons, including isomers of chlordane and other closely related compounds.

The first usage of chlordane as an insecticide was in 1945. Its use was widespread up until the 1970s and included applications inside of homes to control insects of stored food and clothing, as well as usage to control termites, carpenter ants, and wood–boring beetles. An especially intensive use was to kill earthworms in golf–course putting greens and in prize lawns, for which more than 9 kg/ha might be applied. The major use of chlordane in agriculture was for the control of insect pests in soil and on plants. In 1971 about 25 million lb (11.4 million kg) of chlordane was manufactured in the United States, of which about 8% was used in agriculture, and most of the rest in and around homes. Today the use of chlordane is highly restricted, and limited to the control of fire ants.

Like other chlorinated hydrocarbon insecticides such as DDT, chlordane is virtually insoluble in water (5 ppm), but highly soluble in organic solvents and oils. This property, coupled with the persistence of chlordane in the environment, gives it a propensity to accumulate in organisms (i.e., to bioaccumulate), especially in animals at the top of food webs. Because of its insolubility in water, chlordane is relatively immobile in soil, and tends not to leach into surface or ground water.

The acute toxicity of chlordane to humans is considered to be high to medium by oral ingestion, and hazardous by inhalation. Chlordane causes damage to many organs, including the liver, testicles, blood, and the neural system. It also affects hormone levels and is a suspected mutagen and carcinogen. Chlordane is very toxic to arthropods and to some fish, birds, and mammals.

See also Bioaccumulation; DDT; Pesticides.

Chlorination

Chlorination is the process by which the element chlorine reacts with some other substance. Chlorination is a very important chemical reaction both in pure research and in the preparation of commercially important chemical products. For example, the reaction between chlorine and methane gas produces one or more chlorinated derivatives, the best known of which are trichloromethane (chloroform) and tetrachloromethane (carbon tetrachloride). The chlorinated hydrocarbons constitute one of the most commercially useful chemical families, albeit a family surrounded by a myriad of social, political, economic, and ethical issues. One member of that family, as an example, is dichlorodiphenyltrichloroethane (DDT). Although one of the most valuable pesticides ever developed, DDT is now banned in most parts of the world because of its deleterious effects on the environment.

The term chlorination is perhaps best known among laypersons in connection with its use in the purification of water supplies. Chlorine is widely popular for this application because of its ability to kill bacteria and other disease–causing organisms at relatively low concentrations and with little risk to humans. In many facilities, chlorine gas is pumped directly into water until it reaches a concentration of about one ppm (part per million). The exact concentration depends on the original purity of the water supply. In other facilities, chlorine is added to water in the form of a solid compound such as calcium or sodium hypochlorite. Both of these compounds react with water releasing free chlorine. Both methods of chlorination are so inexpensive that nearly every public water purification system in the world has adopted one or the other as its primary means of destroying disease–causing organisms.

Chlorine

Chlorine is the non–metallic chemical element of atomic number 17, symbol Cl, atomic weight 35.45, melting point −149.8°F (−101°C), and boiling point −29.02°F (−33.9°C). It consists of two stable isotopes, of mass numbers 35 and 37. Ordinary chlorine is a mixture of 75.77% chlorine–35 atoms and 24.23% chlorine–37 atoms.

Chlorine is a highly poisonous, greenish yellow gas, about two and a half times as dense as air, and with a strong, sharp, choking odor. It was, in fact, one of the first poisonous gases used in warfare—in 1915 during World War I. In spite of its disagreeable nature, there are so many everyday products that contain chlorine or are manufactured through the use of chlorine that it is among the top ten chemicals produced in the United States each year. In 1994, more than 24 billion pounds of chlorine were produced.

In nature, chlorine is widely distributed over the Earth in the form of the salt (sodium chloride) in sea water. At an average rate of 0.67 oz (19 g) of chlorine in each liter of sea water, it is estimated that there are some 10^{16} tons of chlorine in the world's oceans. Other compounds of chlorine occur as minerals in the Earth's crust, including huge underground deposits of solid sodium chloride.

Along with fluorine, bromine, iodine and astatine, chlorine is a member of the halogen family of elements in group 17 of the periodic table—the most non–metallic (least metallic) and most highly reactive group of elements. Chlorine reacts directly with nearly all other elements; with metals, it forms salts called chlorides. In fact, the name *halogen*, meaning salt producer, was originally invented for chlorine (in 1811 by J. S. C. Schweigger), and it was later applied to the rest of the elements in this family.

History of chlorine

The most common compound of chlorine, sodium chloride, has been known since ancient times; archaeologists have found evidence that rock salt was used as early as 3000 B.C. The first compound of chlorine ever made by humans was probably hydrochloric acid (hydrogen chloride gas dissolved in water), which was prepared by the Arabian alchemist Rhazes around 900 A.D. Around 1200 A.D., aqua regia (a mixture of nitric and hydrochloric acids) began to be used to dissolve gold; it is still the only liquid that will dissolve gold. When gold dissolves in aqua regia, chlorine is released along with other evil–smelling and irritating gases, but probably nobody in the thirteenth century paid much attention to them except to get as far away from them as possible.

The credit for first preparing and studying gaseous chlorine goes to Karl W. Scheele (1742–86) in 1774. Scheele was a Swedish chemist who discovered several other important elements and compounds, including barium, manganese, oxygen, ammonia and glycerin. Scheele thought that chlorine was a compound, which he called dephlogisticated marine acid air. All gases were called airs at that time, and what we now know as hydrochloric acid was called marine acid because it was made from sea salt. The word dephlogisticated came from a completely wrong theory that slowed the progress of chemistry for decades and which is best left unexplained.

It was not until 1811 that Sir Humphry Davy (1778–1829) announced to the Royal Society of London that chlorine gas was an element. He suggested the name chlorine because it is the same pale, yellowish green color that sick plants sometimes develop, a color that is known as *chloros* in Greek. (The sick plants are said to have chlorosis.)

Properties and uses of chlorine

Because it is so reactive, chlorine is never found alone—chemically uncombined—in nature. It is prepared commercially by passing electricity through a water solution of sodium chloride or through molten sodium chloride.

When released as the free element, chlorine gas consists of diatomic (two–atom) molecules, as expressed by the formula Cl_2. The gas is very irritating to the mucous membranes of the nose, mouth and lungs. It can be smelled in the air at a concentration of only 3 parts per million (ppm); it causes throat irritation at 15 ppm, coughing at 30 ppm, and is very likely to be fatal after a few deep breaths at 1,000 ppm.

Chlorine gas dissolves readily in water, reacting chemically with it to produce a mixture of hydrochloric acid (HCl) and hypochlorous acid (HOCl), plus some unreacted Cl_2. This solution, called chlorine water, is a strong oxidizing agent that can be used to kill germs or to bleach paper and fabrics. It is used to obtain bromine (another member of its halogen family) from sea water by oxidizing bromide ions to elemental bromine.

In organic chemistry, chlorine is widely used, not only as an oxidizing agent, but as a way of making many useful compounds. For example, chlorine atoms can easily replace hydrogen atoms in organic molecules. The new molecules, with their chlorine atoms sticking out, are much more reactive and can react with various chemicals to produce a wide variety of other compounds. Among the products that are manufactured by the use of chlorine somewhere along the way are antiseptics, dyes, explosives, foods, insecticides, medicines, metals, paints, paper, plastics, refrigerants, solvents and textiles.

Probably the most important use of chlorine is as a water purifier. Every water supply in the U.S. and in much of the rest of the world is rendered safe for drinking by the addition of chlorine. Several chlorine–releasing compounds are also used as general disinfectants.

Bleaching is another very practical use of chlorine. Until it was put to practical use as a bleach around 1785, bright sunlight was the only way people had to bleach out stains and undesired colors in textiles and paper. Today, in the form of a variety of compounds, chlorine is used almost exclusively. Here's how it works. Many colored compounds are colored because their molecules contain loose electrons that can absorb specific colors of light, leaving the other colors unabsorbed and therefore visible. An oxidizing agent such as chlorine water or a compound containing the hypochlorite ion OCl^- removes those electrons (an oxidizing agent is an electron remover), which effectively removes the substance's light–absorbing power and therefore its color. Ordinary laundry bleach is a 5.25% solution of sodium hypochlorite in water.

Among the important organic compounds containing chlorine are the chlorinated hydrocarbons—hydrocarbons that have had some of their hydrogen atoms replaced by chlorine atoms. A variety of chlorinated hydrocarbons have been used as insecticides. One of the earliest to be used was DDT, dichlorodiphenyltrichloroethane. Because it caused serious environmental problems, its use has largely been banned in the United States. Other chlorinated hydrocarbons that are used as pesticides include dieldrin, aldrin, endrin, lindane, chlordane, and heptachlor. Because all of these compounds are very stable and don't degrade easily, they also have serious environmental drawbacks.

Compounds of chlorine

Following are a few of the important compounds of chlorine.

Calcium hypochlorite, CaOCl: A white powder known as bleaching powder and used (obviously) for bleaching. It is also used as a swimming pool disinfectant. Both its bleaching and its disinfectant qualities come from its chemical instability: it decomposes to release chlorine gas.

Chlorates: Chlorates are compounds of metals with the anion ClO_3^-. An example is potassium chlorate, $KClO_3$. Chlorates can cause explosions when mixed with materials that can burn, because the chlorate ion decomposes under heat to release oxygen and the oxygen speeds up the combustion process to explosive levels. Potassium chlorate is used in fireworks.

Chlorides: Chlorides are the salts of hydrochloric acid, HCl. They are compounds of a metal with chlorine and nothing else. Some common examples are sodium chloride (NaCl), ammonium chloride (NH_4Cl), calcium chloride ($CaCl_2$), and magnesium chloride ($MgCl_2$). When dissolved in water, these salts produce chloride ions, Cl^-. Polyvinyl chloride, the widely used plastic known as PVC, is a polymer of the organic chloride, vinyl chloride.

Freons are hydrocarbons with fluorine and chlorine atoms substituted for some of the hydrogen atoms in their molecules. They have been widely used as the liquids in refrigerating machines and as propellants in aerosol spray cans. They have been implicated in destroying the ozone layer in the upper atmosphere, however, and their use is now severely restricted.

See also Bleach; Carbon tetrachloride; Chlordane; Chlorination; Chlorofluorocarbons; Chloroform; DDT; Dioxin; Halide, Organic; Halogenated hydrocarbons; Halogens; Hydrochlorofluorocarbons; Hydrogen chloride; Mercurous chloride; Pesticides; Polychlorinated biphenyls; Sodium chloride; Sodium hypochlorite.

Further Reading:

"Chlorine Industry Running Flat Out Despite Persistent Health Fears." *Chemical & Engineering News* (November 21, 1994).

Emsley, J. *The Elements*. 2nd ed. New York: Oxford University Press, 1991.

Greenwood, N. N. *Chemistry of the Elements*. New York: Pergamon Press, 1985.

Sconce, J. S. *Chlorine, Its Manufacture, Properties and Uses*. New York, Reinhold, 1962.

Robert L. Wolke

Chlorofluorocarbons (CFCs)

Chlorofluorocarbons (CFCs) are manufactured compounds containing carbon, chlorine, and fluorine atoms. CFCs are emitted in large quantities to the lower atmosphere, where they are very persistent. Consequently, CFCs slowly penetrate to the upper atmospheric layer known as the stratosphere, where they are degraded by intense exposures to highly energetic, short–wave solar radiation. This releases chlorine and fluorine atoms, which then consume ozone molecules in secondary reactions. The loss of stratospheric ozone is a serious ecological problem, because this gas is a critical component of the shield that protects Earth's surface from an intense exposure to solar ultraviolet radiation. Exposure to ultraviolet radiation causes biological damages by degrading plant pigments, increasing the risks of skin cancers, and depressing immune systems.

The nature and use of chlorofluorocarbons

CFCs are not naturally occurring chemicals, being first synthesized in the 1890s. The utility of CFC–12 was first recognized in 1928, after which it and other CFCs were rapidly developed as industrial products, initially as replacements for ammonia in refrigeration. The most common CFCs are: CFC–11 ($CFCl_3$), CFC–12 (CF_2Cl_2), CFC–113 ($CF_2ClCFCl_2$), and CFC–114 (CF_2ClCF_2Cl).

Because of their stability, low toxicity, low surface tension, ease of liquification, thermodynamic properties, and non–flammability, CFCs have been used as: refrigerants in heat pumps, refrigerators, freezers, and air conditioners; as propellants in aerosols; as blowing agents in the manufacture of plastic foam products and insulation, such as expanded polystyrene and polyurethane; as cleaning and de–greasing agents for metals and electronic equipment and components, especially circuit boards; as carrier gases for chemicals used in the sterilization of medical instruments; and as dry-cleaning fluids.

The most commonly used CFCs are CFC–11 and CFC–12. CFC–11 is mostly used in large, industrial air–conditioning equipment and centrifugal systems. CFC–12 is used for automobile, domestic, and commercial refrigeration and air–conditioning equipment. Other important CFCs include CFC–113 and CFC–114, mostly used in commercial air–conditioning equipment.

Depending on its size a typical domestic refrigerator contains about 0.4–0.6 lbs (0.2–0.3 kg) of CFCs, a freezer 0.6–1.1 lbs (0.3–0.5 kg), and a central air–conditioning unit about 65.5 lbs (13.5 kg). About 90% of new automobiles sold in the United States and 60% of those in Canada have air conditioning units, each containing 3–4 lbs (1.4–2.0 kg) of CFCs.

Emissions of CFCs to the atmosphere peaked in 1988, when 690 million lbs (315 million kg) of CFC–11 and 860 million lbs (392 million kg) of CFC–12 were released. At that time about 45% of the global use of CFCs was in refrigeration, 38% for the manufacture of foams, 12% as solvents, and 5% for aerosols and other uses. CFC production and use in the United States in 1988 involved about 5–thousand companies in 375–thousand locations, employing 700–thousand people, and generating $28 billion worth of goods and services. However, since 1988 the uses and emissions of CFCs have decreased substantially, and they will hopefully be largely eliminated by the turn of the century.

CFCs can be effectively recovered from used equipment after some of these uses, and they can then be degraded chemically and removed from the global stock of these chemicals. Some recovered CFCs may also be re–used in older, still serviceable equipment that cannot run on the available replacements for these chemicals.

There are alternatives to the use of CFCs for most purposes, especially in refrigeration, air conditioning, the manufacture of materials, and in aerosol propellants. Hydrochlorofluorocarbons (HCFCs) and hydrofluorocarbons (HFCs) can replace CFCs for many purposes, as can ammonia in some refrigeration applications. Because the HCFCs and HFCs contain some hydrogen atoms in their molecular structure, they are less durable than CFCs in the lower atmosphere. The shorter persistence of HCFCs and HFCs means that they have much less of an opportunity to diffuse into the stratosphere, where Earth's protective ozone layer occurs.

The first important restrictions on the use of CFCs occurred in the early 1980s, when their use as propellants in aerosol cans was prohibited. However, elimination of this use was more than offset by large increases in other uses of CFCs in refrigeration and the electronics industries.

The Montreal Protocol on Substances that Deplete the Ozone Layer was the first comprehensive, international agreement to regulate the production, use, and emissions of CFCs. This was done in order to achieve a rapid reduction in the apparent depletions of stratospheric ozone, and hence deal with this relatively new but important environmental problem. The Montreal Protocol was developed under the auspices of the United Nations Environment Program (UNEP), and is named after the city where the agreement was reached in 1987. The Montreal Protocol was revised in 1990, at which time it called for a 100% global phaseout of CFC use by the year 2000. However, some major industrial users of CFCs have committed to earlier phaseouts, as early as 1997. Because of the unusually rapid and effective international response to the problem of stratospheric ozone depletion caused by emissions of CFCs (described below), the Montreal Protocol and subsequent agreements on CFCs have been described as an environmental "success story."

Chlorofluorocarbons in the enviroment

CFCs are highly stable, essentially inert chemicals in the lower atmosphere (or troposphere), with correspondingly long residence times. For example, CFC–11 has an atmospheric lifetime of 60 years, CFC–12 120 years, CFC–113 90 years, and CFC–114 200 years. The present atmospheric concentration of total CFCs is about 0.7 ppb (parts per billion), but this is increasing at about 5–6% per year. Moreover, atmospheric concentrations of CFCs will continue to increase for many decades after their manufacture and new uses are stopped, because of continued releases from CFC–containing equipment and products already in use.

Because of their persistence in the troposphere, CFCs slowly wend their way into the higher atmospheric layer known as the stratosphere. There the CFCs are subject to intense exposures to ultraviolet and other short–wave radiation. This causes the CFCs to degrade, releasing highly reactive atoms of chlorine and fluorine, which then form simple compounds such as ClO. These secondary products of stratospheric degradation of CFCs react with ozone, resulting in a net consumption of this gas, and accounting for at least 80% of the total, stratospheric ozone depletion.

CFCs and the depletion of stratospheric ozone

Ozone (O_3) is a gas, naturally present in relatively large concentrations in the stratosphere, a layer of the upper atmosphere higher than 4.9–11 lbd (8–17 km). Stratospheric O_3 concentrations typically average 0.2-0.3 ppm, compared with <0.02–0.03 ppm in background situations in the troposphere. Stratospheric O_3 is formed naturally by photochemical reactions in which oxygen (O_2) interacts with ultraviolet radiation to form O atoms, which can then combine with O_2 to form O_3.

Stratospheric ozone can be consumed by various reactions, including a photodissociation caused by ultraviolet light, and reactions with trace chemicals, including ions or simple molecules of chlorine, bromine, and fluorine. Human activities have caused large increases in the emissions of some O_3–consuming chemicals or their precursors. As a result, there are concerns about upsets of the dynamic equilibria among stratospheric reactions involving ozone, which could result in potential decreases in O_3 concentration.

During the late 1970s, decreases in concentration of stratospheric O_3 (called ozone "holes") were observed at high latitudes. The holes are especially intense over Antarctica, where they develop under intensely cold conditions during the southern springtime of September to November. Between the late 1970s and the late 1980s, the decreases in stratospheric ozone in spring averaged 30–40%. However, in 1987

the decrease of stratospheric ozone over Antarctica was 50%, and 95% in the zone of greatest depletion at 9–12 mi (15–20 km). Ozone holes also develop over the Arctic, but they are smaller and the amount of depletion is less than in Antarctica.

The ozone depletions are believed to be caused by the presence of atoms or simple compounds of chlorine, especially ClO. As noted above, these have an indirect origin through the emissions of CFCs, which are inert in the troposphere, and are slowly transported to the stratosphere by large–scale, atmospheric mixing.

The ozone holes are seasonal and restricted to high latitudes. However, stratospheric concentrations of O_3 at lower latitudes can also be depleted. This occurs when the normal ozone concentrations are diluted by O_3–depleted air dispersing as the holes break up in late spring time.

Stratospheric O_3 absorbs most incoming solar ultraviolet (UV) radiation, thereby serving as a UV shield that protects organisms on Earth's surface from some of the deleterious effects of this high–energy radiation. If the ultraviolet radiation was not intercepted, it could disrupt the genetic material DNA, which is an efficient absorber of UV. Damage to DNA could result in greater incidences of skin cancers, including the often deadly melanoma. Other health effects of increased ultraviolet exposure could include increased incidences of cataracts and other eye damages such as snowblindness, and suppression of the immune system. Ecological damages could include an extensive inhibition of plant productivity in ultraviolet–stressed regions, possibly caused by UV–caused degradations of pigments such as chlorophyll.

CFCs and the greenhouse effect

Another potential consequence of increasing concentrations CFCs in Earth's atmosphere is an intensification of an existing physical process known as the "greenhouse effect." The greenhouse effect is a well–understood phenomenon that allows the planet's surface to be maintained at an average temperature of 77° F (25° C). This is approximately 33 degrees warmer than would be possible if certain gases and vapors did not interfere with cooling of the planet's surface by the emission of long–wave, infrared energy.

If the atmosphere was transparent to long–wave infrared energy emitted by Earth's surface, that energy would travel unobstructed to outer space. However, certain gases and vapors in the atmosphere absorb these infrared wavelengths, and thereby slow the rate of cooling of the planet. The most important of these so–called

KEY TERMS

. . . .

Greenhouse effect—This is a physical process that allows Earth's surface to be maintained at an average of 77° F (25° C), about 33° warmer than would otherwise be possible if certain gases and vapors, especially carbon dioxide and water, did not interfere with the rate of dissipation of absorbed solar radiation. CFCs are also active in this process.

Ozone holes—Decreased concentrations of stratospheric ozone, occurring at high latitudes during the early springtime. Ozone holes are most apparent over Antarctica, where they develop under intensely cold conditions during September and November, allowing a greater penetration of deleterious solar ultraviolet radiation to Earth's surface.

Stratosphere—A layer of the upper atmosphere above an altitude of 4.9–11 mi (8–17 km) and extending to about 31 mi (50 km), depending on season and latitude. Within the stratosphere, air temperature changes little with altitude, and there are few convective air currents.

Troposphere—The lower atmosphere, occurring below the stratosphere.

radiatively active constituents of the atmosphere are carbon dioxide and water, but trace gases such as chlorofluorocarbons, methane, nitrous oxide, and ozone are also active.

CFCs are very efficient absorbers of infrared energy. On a per–molecule basis, CFC–11 is 3-12-thousand times as efficient as carbon dioxide as a greenhouse gas, and CFC–12 is 7–15–thousand times as effective. The atmospheric concentrations of total CFCs have increased from zero several decades ago, to about 0.5 ppb today. Overall, CFCs are believed to account for about 12% of the enhancement of Earth's greenhouse effect caused by human influences.

See also Air pollution; Atmosphere, composition and structure of; Greenhouse effect; Halogenated hydrocarbons; Ozone; Ozone layer depletion.

Further Reading:

Anonymous. *The State of Canada's Environment.* Government of Canada, Ottawa, 1991.

Freedman, B. *Environmental Ecology, 2nd ed.* San Diego: Academic Press, 1994.

Manzer, L.E. *The CFC–ozone issue: Progress on the development of alternatives.* Science, 1990.

Bill Freedman

Chloroform

Chloroform is the common name of the organic compound whose chemical formula is $HCCl_3$. The molecule of trichloromethane, as it is also called, consists of a central carbon atom bonded to a hydrogen atom and three chlorine atoms. Chloroform is a nonflammable colorless liquid (boiling point 145–146° F (61–62° C) that has a heavy sweet odor and taste. The compound was first prepared in 1831 simultaneously by Justus von Liebig (1803–1873) in Germany and by Eugene Soubeirane (1797–1858) in France using different procedures. Samuel Guthrie (1782–1848), in the United States, also discovered chloroform in that same year.

Chloroform was originally used to calm people suffering from asthma. In 1847, James Y. Simpson, a Professor of Midwifery at the University of Edinburgh, began using chloroform as an anesthetic to reduce pain during childbirth. From this initial experiment, chloroform began to be used as general anesthesia in medical procedures throughout the world. The use of chloroform in this application was eventually abandoned because of its harmful side effects on the heart and liver.

Chloroform has commonly been used as a solvent in the manufacture of pesticides, dyes, and drugs. The use of the chemical in this manner was important in the preparation of penicillin during World War II. Chloroform was used as a sweetener in various cough syrups and to add flavor "bursts" to toothpastes and mouthwashes. Its pain relieving properties were incorporated into various liniments and toothache medicines. The chemical was also used in photographic processing and dry cleaning. All of these applications for chloroform were stopped by the Federal Drug Administration (FDA) in 1976, when the compound was discovered to cause cancer in laboratory mice. Today, chloroform is a key starting material for the production of chemicals used in refrigerators and air conditioners.

See also Anesthesia; Solvent.

Chlorophyll

Chlorophyll is a green pigment contained in the foliage of plants, giving them their notable coloration. This pigment is responsible for absorbing sunlight required for the production of sugar molecules, and ultimately of all biochemicals, in the plant.

Chlorophyll is found in the thylakoid sacs of the chloroplast. The chloroplast is a specialized part of the cell that functions as an organelle. Once the appropriate wavelengths of light are absorbed by the chlorophyll into the thylakoid sacs, the important process of photosynthesis is able to begin. In photosynthesis, the chloroplast absorbs light energy, and converts it into the chemical energy of simple sugars.

Vascular plants, which can absorb and conduct moisture and nutrients through specialized systems, have two different types of chlorophyll. The two types of chlorophyll, designated as chlorophyll *a* and *b*, differ slightly in chemical makeup and in color. These chlorophyll molecules are associated with specialized proteins that are able to penetrate into or span the membrane of the thylakoid sac.

When a chlorophyll molecule absorbs light energy, it becomes altered and goes into an excited state, which allows the initial chain reaction of photosynthesis to occur. The pigment molecules cluster together in what is called a photosynthetic unit. Several hundred chlorophyll *a* and chlorophyll *b* molecules are found in one photosynthetic unit.

A photosynthetic unit absorbs light energy. Red and blue wavelengths of light are absorbed. Green light cannot be absorbed by the chlorophyll and the light is reflected, making the plant appear green. Once the light energy penetrates these pigment molecules, the energy is passed to one chlorophyll molecule, called the reaction center chlorophyll. When this molecule becomes excited, the light reactions of photosynthesis can proceed. With carbon dioxide, water, and the help of specialized enzymes, the light energy absorbed creates chemical energy in a form the cell can use to carry on its processes.

In addition to chlorophyll, there are other pigments known as accessory pigments that are able to absorb light where the chlorophyll is unable to. Carotenoids, like B–carotenoid, are also located in the thylakoid membrane. Carotenoids give carrots and some autumn leaves their color. Several different pigments are found in the chloroplasts of algae, bacteria, and diatoms, coloring them varying shades of red, orange, blue, and violet.

See also Chloroplast; Photosynthesis; Plant pigment.

Chloroplast

Chloroplasts are organelles—specialized parts of a cell that function in an organ–like fashion. They are found in vascular plants, mosses, liverworts, and algae. Chloroplast organelles are responsible for photosynthesis, the process by which sunlight is absorbed and converted into fixed chemical energy in the form of simple sugars synthesized from carbon dioxide and water.

Chloroplasts are located in the mesophyll, a green tissue area in plant leaves. Four layers or zones define the structure of a chloroplast. The chloroplast is a small lens–shaped organelle which is enclosed by two membranes with a narrow intermembrane space, known as the chloroplast envelope. Raw material and products for photosynthesis enter in and pass out through this double membrane, the first layer of the structure.

Inside the chloroplast envelope is the second layer, which is an area filled with a fluid called stroma. A series of chemical reactions involving enzymes and the incorporation of carbon dioxide into organic compounds occur in this region.

The third layer is a membrane–like structure of thylakoid sacs. Stacked like poker chips, the thylakoid sacs form a grana. These grana stacks are connected by membranous structures. Thylakoid sacs contain a green pigment called chlorophyll. In this region the thylakoid sacs, or grana, absorb light energy using this pigment. Chlorophyll absorbs light between the red and blue spectrums and reflects green light, making leaves appear green. Once the light energy is absorbed into the final layer, the intrathylakoid sac, the important process of photosynthesis is able to begin.

Scientists have attempted to discover how chloroplasts convert light energy to the chemical energy stored in organic molecules for a long time. It has only been since the beginning of this century that scientists have begun to understand this process. The following equation is a simple formula for photosynthesis:

$$6CO_2 + 6H_2O \ R \ C_6H_{12}O_6 + 6O_2$$

Carbon dioxide plus water produce a carbohydrate plus oxygen. Simply, this means that the chloroplast is able to split water into hydrogen and oxygen.

Many questions still remain unanswered about the complete process and role of the chloroplast. Researchers

A transmission electron micrograph (TEM) of a chloroplast from a tobacco leaf (*Nicotiana tabacum*). The stacks of flattened membranes that can be seen within the chloroplast are grana. The membranes that run between the stacks are stroma. The faint white patches within the chloroplast are nucleoids, where chloroplast DNA is stored.

continue to study the chloroplast and its evolution. Based on studies of the evolution of early complex cells, scientist have devised the serial endosymbiosis theory. It is suspected that primitive microbes were able to evolve into more complex ones by incorporating other photosynthetic microbes into their cellular structures and allowing them to continue functioning as organelles. As molecular biology becomes more sophisticated, the origin and genetic makeup of the chloroplast will be more clearly understood.

See also Chlorophyll; Leaf; Photosynthesis.

Cholera

Cholera is one of the most devastating of all human diseases. Although endemic in some areas of the world, cholera is usually associated with massive migrations of people, such as those occurring during war or famine. If not treated, cholera has a fatality rate of over 60%. Death results from dehydration, a consequence of the severe diarrhea and vomiting that characterize this disease. In the last 15 years, treatment strategies have been devised that have cut the fatality rate of cholera to 1%. Preventive measures have also reduced the incidence of cholera outbreaks. These measures, however, require swift intervention, which is not always possible during the social upheavals that lead to cholera epidemics.

The cause of cholera

Cholera is caused by a bacteria called *Vibrio cholerae*, which secretes a toxin, or poison, that binds to the cells of the small intestine. One of the functions of the small intestine in humans is to regulate the amount of fluid that is absorbed by cells. Normally, small intestine cells absorb most of the fluid that is ingested; only a small amount of fluid is excreted in the feces. Under abnormal conditions, such as in response to a pathogen, cells do not absorb fluid, and as a result a lot of fluid enters the small intestine and is excreted in the feces. These frequent, watery stools are called diarrhea. Diarrhea can actually be helpful, as the rapid movement of fluid flushes the gastrointestinal tract of harmful bacteria and other pathogens. But if diarrhea is severe or long lasting, such as occurs in cholera, too much fluid is lost and the body becomes dehydrated. If fluids are not replaced, death can result.

Along with causing fluid loss, the binding of cholera toxin to small intestine cells also results in loss of electrolytes. Electrolytes are chemicals that the body needs to function properly, such as potassium chloride, sodium chloride (salt), and bicarbonate. Electrolytes are crucial in the control of blood pressure, excretion of metabolic wastes, and maintenance of blood sugar levels. If the amount of electrolytes in the body deviates even slightly, these crucial body functions are imperiled. Cholera toxin prompts the small intestine cells to secrete large amounts of electrolytes into the small intestine. These electrolytes are then excreted in the watery diarrhea.

The cholera toxin consists of two subunits, the A subunit and the B subunit. The B subunit is a ring, and the A subunit is suspended within it. By itself, the B subunit is nontoxic; the A subunit is the poisonous part of the toxin. The B subunit binds to the small intestine cell and creates a channel within the cell membrane through which the A subunit enters. Once inside the small intestine cell, the A subunit disrupts the cascade of reactions that regulates the cell's fluid and electrolyte balance. Fluid and electrolytes leave the cell and enter the small intestine. The resultant diarrhea may cause a fluid loss that exceeds 1 qt (1 liter) per hour.

V. cholerae lives in aquatic environments, and especially favors salty or brackish waters. *V. cholerae* frequently colonize shellfish; in fact, cholera cases in the United States are almost always traced to eating raw or undercooked shellfish. Interestingly, *V. cholerae* can also cause skin and other soft tissue infections. Cases of such infection with these bacteria have been found in persons who have sustained injuries in marine environments; apparently, *V. cholerae* in water can penetrate broken skin and cause infection.

Transmission of cholera

Cholera is endemic in several areas of the world, including parts of India and Bangladesh. From these areas, cholera has been disseminated throughout the world during several pandemics, or worldwide outbreaks. In the United States, a cholera pandemic that lasted from 1832–49 killed 150,000 people; in 1866, another cholera pandemic killed 50,000 U.S. citizens. The most recent pandemic, which began in the 1960s and lasted until the early 1980s, involved Africa, Western Europe, the Philippines, and Southeast Asia. Smaller outbreaks, such as the Rwanda epidemic of 1994, are characteristic of wartime and famine conditions, in which large numbers of people concentrate in one place where sanitary conditions are poor to nonexistent.

Because of the nature of *V. cholerae* infection, past epidemics can lead to future epidemics. People recovering from cholera continue to shed the organism in their feces for weeks to months after the initial infection. These people are called convalescent carriers. Another kind of carrier, called a chronic carrier, continues to shed the bacteria for years after their recovery. In both carrier types, no symptoms are present. With the ease of worldwide transportation, carriers can travel throughout the world, spreading *V. cholerae* wherever they go. If a carrier visits an area with less–than–ideal sanitary conditions or does not wash his or her hands after using the bathroom, the deadly *V. cholerae* bacteria can be easily transmitted.

Symptoms and treatment of cholera

Cholera is characterized by sudden onset. Within several hours or days after ingesting *V. cholerae*, severe diarrhea and vomiting occur. Fluid losses can be up to 4–5 gal (15–20 liters) per day. As a consequence of this severe fluid loss, the eyes and cheeks can appear sunken, and the skin loses its pliancy.

Treatment of cholera involves the rapid replacement of fluid and electrolytes coupled with a course of powerful antibiotics. In severe cases, intravenous infusions of electrolytes and fluids may be necessary. Once fluid and electrolyte balance is restored, rapid reversal of symptoms occurs. Treatment with antibiotics, typically tetracycline, neutralizes the *V. cholerae.*

Prevention

In the United States, sewage treatment and water purification plants are ubiquitous, and consequently, the

KEY TERMS

Electrolyte—Compounds that ionize in a solution; electrolytes dissolved in the blood play an important role in maintaining the proper functioning of the body.

Endemic—Belonging to a particular area or among a particular group of people.

Pandemic—Occurring on a worldwide scale or spread over an entire country or nation.

Toxin—Chemical produced by an organism as a result of metabolism that acts as a poison within the host.

incidence of cholera is low. Almost all cases of cholera in the U.S. are caused by improperly cooked shellfish. Experts recommend that all shellfish be boiled for 10 minutes; steaming does not kill *V. cholerae*. Raw shellfish should be avoided.

Another way to prevent cholera is to identify and treat cholera carriers in areas where cholera is endemic. Treating carriers would eliminate a major route of cholera transmission.

Currently, several cholera vaccines are being developed, but only one is likely to be effective. Injectable vaccines are impractical in many areas. Oral vaccines are more easily delivered to the population, but are not nearly as effective. A genetically engineered vaccine that consists of an altered *V. cholerae* organism appears to stimulate an immune response in a small number of volunteers. Larger vaccine trials in endemic populations are necessary, however, to determine the efficacy of this vaccine.

See also Vaccine.

Further Reading:

Besser, R. E., D. R. Feiken, and P. N. Griffin. "Diagnosis and Treatment of Cholera in the United States: Are We Prepared?" *Journal of the American Medical Association* 272 (19 October 1993): 1203.

Delaporte, François. *Disease and Civilization: The Cholera in Paris, 1832.* Cambridge: MIT Press, 1986.

Royal, Louis and Iain McCoubrey. "International Spread of Disease by Air Travel." *American Family Physician* 40 (1 November 1989): 129.

Spangler, Brenda D. "Structure and Function of Cholera Toxin and the Related *Escherichia coli* Heat–Labil Enterotoxin." *Microbial Reviews* 56 (1 December 1992): 622.

Van Heyningen, Willian Edward and John R. Seal. *Cholera: The American Scientific Experience, 1947–1980*. Boulder, CO: Westview Press, 1983.

Cholesterol

Cholesterol is a complex organic compound with the molecular formula $C_{27}H_{46}O$. It is a member of the biochemical family of compounds known as the lipids. Other lipids, such as the waxes, fats, and oils, share not a structural similarity (as is the case with most families of compounds), but a physical property—they are all insoluble in water, but are soluble in organic liquids.

Cholesterol belongs more specifically to a class of compounds known as the steroids. Most steroids are naturally occurring compounds that play critical roles in plant and animal physiology and biochemistry. Other steroids include the sex hormones, certain vitamins, and the adrenocorticoid hormones. All steroids share a common structural unit, a four–ring structure known as the perhydrocyclopentanophenanthrene ring system or, more simple, the steroid nucleus.

History

Although cholesterol had been isolated as early as 1770, productive research on its structure did not begin until the twentieth century. Then, in about 1903, a young German chemist by the name of Adolf Windaus decided to concentrate on finding the molecular composition of the compound. Windaus, sometimes referred to as the Father of Steroid Chemistry, eventually worked out a detailed structure for cholesterol, an accomplishment that was partially responsible for his earning the 1928 Nobel Prize in chemistry.

Late research showed that the structure proposed by Windaus was in error. By the early 1930s, however, additional evidence from x–ray analysis allowed Windaus' long–time colleague Heinrich Wieland (among others) to determine the correct structure for the cholesterol molecule.

The next step in understanding cholesterol, synthesizing the compound was not completed for another two decades. In 1951, the American chemist Robert B. Woodward completed that line of research when he synthesized cholesterol starting with simple compounds. For this accomplishment and his other work in synthesizing large molecule compounds, Woodward was awarded the 1965 Nobel Prize in chemistry.

Properties and occurrence

Cholesterol crystallizes from an alcoholic solution as pearly white or pale yellow granules or plates. It is waxy in appearance and has a melting point of 300°F (148.5°C) and a boiling point of 680°F (360°C) (with some decomposition). It has a specific gravity of 1.067. Cholesterol is insoluble in water, but slightly soluble in alcohol and somewhat more soluble in ether and chloroform.

Cholesterol occurs in almost all living organisms with the primary exception of microorganisms. Of the cholesterol found in the human body, about 93% occurs in cells and the remaining 7% in the circulatory system. The brain and spinal cord are particularly rich in the compound. About 10% of the former's dry weight is due to cholesterol. An important commercial source of the compound is spinal fluid taken from cattle. Cholesterol is also found in myelin, the material that surrounds nerve strands. Gallstones are nearly pure cholesterol.

The concentration of cholesterol in human blood varies rather widely, from a low of less than 200 mg/dL (milligrams per deciliter) to a high of more than 300 mg/dL. It is also found in bile, a source from which, in fact, it gets its name: chole (Greek for bile) + stereos (Greek for solid).

Cholesterol in the human body

Cholesterol is a critically important compound in the human body. It is synthesized in the liver and then used in the manufacture of bile, hormones, and nerve tissue.

But cholesterol is also a part of the human diet. A single egg yolk for example, contains about 250 mg of cholesterol. Organ meats are particularly rich in the compound. An 3 oz (85 g) serving of beef liver, for example, contains about 372 mg of cholesterol and a similar–size serving of calves' brain, about 2,700 mg of the compound. Because diets differ from culture to culture, the amount of cholesterol an individual consumes differs widely around the world. The average European diet includes about 500 mg of cholesterol a day, but the average Japanese diet, only about 130 mg a day. The latter fact reflects a diet in which fish rather than meat tends to predominate.

The human body contains a feedback mechanism that keeps the serum concentration of cholesterol approximately constant. The liver itself manufactures about 600 mg of cholesterol a day, but that output changes depending on the intake of cholesterol in the daily diet. As a person consumes more cholesterol, the liver reduces it production of the compound. If one's

798

intake of cholesterol greatly exceeds the body's needs, excess cholesterol may then precipitate out of blood and be deposited on arterial linings.

Cholesterol and health

Some of the earliest clues about possible ill effects of cholesterol on human health came from the research of Russian biologist Nikolai Anitschow in the 1910s. Anitschow fed rabbits a diet high in cholesterol and found that the animals became particular susceptible to circulatory disorders. Post mortem studies of the animals found the presence of plaques (clumps) of cholesterol on their arterial walls.

Since Anitschow's original research, debate has raged over the relationship between cholesterol intake and circulatory disease, particular atherosclerosis (the blockage of coronary arteries with deposits of fatty material). Over time, it has become increasingly obvious that high serum cholesterol levels do have some association with such diseases. A particularly powerful study in forming this conclusion has been the on–going Framingham Study, conducted since 1948 by the National Heart Institute in the Massachusetts town that has given its name to the research. Among the recommendations evolving out of that study has been that a reduced intake of cholesterol in one's daily diet is one factor in reducing the risk of heart disease.

The cholesterol–heart disease puzzle is not completely solved. One of the remaining issues concerns the role of lipoproteinsin the equation. Since cholesterol is not soluble in water, it is transported through the blood stream bound to molecules containing both fat and protein components, lipoproteins. These lipoproteins are of two kinds, high density lipoproteins (HDLs) and low density lipoproteins (LDLs). For some time, researchers have thought that LDL is particularly rich in cholesterol and, therefore, "bad," while HDL is low in cholesterol and, therefore, "good." While this analysis may be another step in the right direction, it still does not provide the final word on the role of cholesterol in the development of circulatory diseases.

See also Circulatory system; Heart diseases; Lipid; Nervous system.

Further Reading:

Byrne, Kevin P. *Understanding and Managing Cholesterol: A Guide for Wellness Professionals.* Champaign, IL: Human Kinetics Books, 1991.
Davis, Goode P., Jr., Edwards Pak, and the editors of U.S. News Books. *The Heart: Living Pump.* Washington, DC: U.S. News Books, 1981.
Fisher, Arthur, and the editors of Time–Life books. *The Healthy Heart.* Alexandria, VA: Time–Life Books, 1981.

KEY TERMS

Bile—A greenish–yellow liquid secreted by the liver that aids in the digestion of fats and oils in the body.

Circulatory system—The part of an animal body that includes the heart, arteries, veins, and capillaries, through which blood circulates.

Lipid—A family of biochemical compounds soluble in many organic solvents, but not in water.

Steroids—A group of organic compounds that belong to the lipid family and that include many important biochemical compounds including the sex hormones, certain vitamins, and cholesterol.

Synthesis—Any chemical reaction or series of reactions by which a large molecule is built up from small, basic molecules.

National Cholesterol Education Program. *Second Report of the Expert Panel on Detection, Evaluation, and Treatment of High Blood Cholesterol in Adults (Adult Treatment Panel II).* Bethesda MD: National Institute of Health, National Heart, Lung, and Blood Institute, 1993.

David E. Newton

Chordates

Chordates are a diverse group of animals that comprise the phylum Chordata. There are approximately 44,000 species of chordates, ranging in size from several millimeters to 105 feet (32 m) long. The simplest and earliest chordates are pre–vertebrate animals such as ascidians, tunicates, and *Amphioxus.* The major group of chordates are the sub–phylum Vertebrata, the vertebrates. Listed more–or–less in the order of their first appearance in the fossil record, vertebrates include sharks, lampreys, bony fishes, amphibians, reptiles, birds, and mammals.

Chordates exhibit bilateral symmetry, and they have a body cavity (the coelom), which is enclosed within a membrane (the peritoneum), and which develops from the middle tissue layer known as the mesoderm. A defining feature of chordates is a structure known as the notochord. This is a rod–like, flexible structure that runs along the upper, mid–line of chordates, and a notochord is present for at least some part of the life of all chordates. In the earliest chordates, the notochord stiffens the body against the pull of muscles. This function is less important in the more advanced vertebrate chordates, whose bodies are supported by the cartilaginous and bony elements of the skeleton. In vertebrates, the notochord is only present during the embryonic, developmental stages.

Other defining features of chordates are the presence of pharyngeal gill slits (which are precursors of the gill arches in fish and amphibians), a hollow nerve cord on the upper surface of the animal (that eventually develops into the spinal cord in vertebrates), and a tail extending beyond the anal opening. As with the notochord, these features may only occur during a part of the life of the animal, especially in the more recently evolved chordates, such as the vertebrates.

Chordate animals have a closed circulatory system, in which blood is transported around the body inside veins and arteries of various sizes. The blood is circulated by the pumping action of the heart; the respiratory gases in the blood diffuse across the thin walls of the smallest vessels (capillaries) in the tissues. The most recently evolved vertebrates have a four–chambered heart, and a double circulation of the blood, which involves a separate circulation for the heart and the lungs, and for the heart and the rest of the body (systemic circulation).

Most chordates have two sexes, and the male and female individuals tend to be different in many aspects of their form and function (dimorphic). Fertilization is external in the earlier–evolved groups of chordates (fish and amphibians), and internal in later groups (reptiles, birds, and mammals). Many chordates lay eggs, or are oviparous, while others give birth to live young (viviparous).

Chordates utilize a wide range of habitats. The earliest evolved chordates and some of the more recent groups are aquatic, while others are primarily terrestrial.

See also Sea squirts and salps.

Chorionic villus sampling

Chorionic villus sampling (CVS) is a prenatal test done early in pregnancy to check for genetic defects in the fetus. Chorionic villi are tiny hair–like projections extending from the fetal structure that eventually develop into the placenta. By inserting a thin plastic tube into the uterus a physician can suction off a small sample of villi. This sample is analyzed for chromosomal defects. CVS can be performed much earlier in pregnancy than amniocentesis, another prenatal test. However CVS carries a slightly higher risk of causing miscarriage and if done too early in pregnancy it increases the chance of a baby born with missing fingers or toes.

The procedure

Chorionic villus sampling is performed during the first trimester of pregnancy at 9–12 weeks. CVS is a relatively quick and painless procedure done without any anesthesia. To retrieve the small sample of villi the physician inserts a thin plastic tube called a catheter through the pregnant woman's vagina and into her uterus. The catheter is placed between the uterine lining and the chorion, the membrane surrounding the fetus. From here a tiny sample of chorionic villi is suctioned. The doctor relies upon an ultrasound image of the uterus to position the catheter accurately. (Ultrasound produces an image of the fetus and uterus by bouncing sound waves off of them.) Sometimes villi are collected with a needle inserted through the abdomen and into the uterus.

Once the villi are gathered, a geneticist examines cells taken from the sample. Although the villi are not part of the developing fetus they share its genetic makeup because the chorionic villi, the placenta, and the fetus developed from the same fertilized egg. Studying the villi's cells is the same as studying the fetus's cells.

During a certain stage in cell division the geneticist can take a photograph of the chromosomes in a cell through a microscope. From this photograph the chromosomes can be sorted and organized by pairs into a complete set, a karyotype. Humans normally have 23 pairs of chromosomes. With karyotyping, geneticists can determine quickly whether a developing fetus has an abnormal number of chromosomes.

For example, people with Down's Syndrome have three copies of chromosome 21. Down's Syndrome is marked by mental retardation and a distinctive physical appearance. The older a woman is when she becomes pregnant the greater her likelihood of having a Down's Syndrome baby. Many couples undergo CVS to learn whether they are expecting a Down's Syndrome baby.

Karyotype results from CVS are available in 1–14 days. The majority of expectant couples undergoing CVS learn that their fetus has a normal karyotype. Although CVS does not test for many kinds of birth defects including neural–tube defects it offers important genetic information to couples. In cases where CVS shows a fetus with severe chromosomal abnormalities, many couples chose to abort it.

Advantage of CVS over amniocentesis

First developed in China then introduced in the United States in 1983, CVS has an important advantage over another prenatal test, amniocentesis. In amniocentesis, amniotic fluid is removed from the uterus with a needle and fetal cells in the fluid are studied for the presence of genetic defects. Amniocentesis has been available since the 1970s.

The problem with amniocentesis is that it must be done relatively late in pregnancy at 16 weeks. It also may take several weeks to obtain results from the test since the fetal cells must be grown in a lab dish before karyotyping is possible. By this time the pregnancy is well established. The pregnant woman feels the fetus kick. She may look pregnant and wear maternity clothes. If the amniocentesis shows that the fetus is abnormal and the couple chooses to abort, a second-trimester abortion is far more emotionally and physically difficult than a first–trimester abortion.

Risks and benefits of CVS

The clear advantage of CVS over amniocentesis is that results are available earlier in pregnancy. The test conveys the same information regarding chromosomal defects as amniocentesis though it also provides additional information on a few other birth defects. But CVS carries a slightly higher risk of miscarriage than amniocentesis.

A 1989 study sponsored by the National Institutes of Health concluded that 0.8% more women undergoing CVS will lose their pregnancies as a result of the test than those who undergo amniocentesis. Amniocentesis is known to cause miscarriage in 0.5% of patients. For many women, especially those over 35, these are risks worth taking.

Several studies have also shown an increase in limb defects, particularly missing fingers or toes, in babies whose mothers underwent CVS during pregnancy. A 1994 study reported by the Centers for Disease Control and Prevention stated that babies born after CVS testing are six times as likely to have missing or malformed fingers or toes as a baby whose mother had amniocentesis or no prenatal testing. Some medical researchers theorize that CVS can damage fingers or toes by blocking the blood supply to the developing extremities. Most physicians agree that this risk can be reduced by performing the procedure after the 10th week of preg-

---

KEY TERMS

Amniocentesis—Amniotic fluid is removed from the pregnant uterus with a needle so that fetal cells in the fluid can be studied for the presence of certain genetic defects.

Chromosomal defects—Abnormalities caused by an unusual number of chromosomes.

Down's Syndrome—A syndrome characterized by mental retardation and a distinctive physical appearance. It is caused by the presence of three copies of chromosome 21.

Karyotype—A photograph of a complete organized set of an individual's chromosomes.

Prenatal test—Procedure done to determining the presence of disease or defect in a fetus.

Ultrasound—A picture of a fetus produced by bouncing sound waves on the tissue.

---

nancy. It is also important that CVS be carried out by a person skilled in the procedure.

See also Birth defects; Embryo and embryonic development.

Further Reading:

Edelson, Edward. *Birth Defects.* New York and Philadelphia: Chelsea House Publishers, 1992.

Edelson, Edward. *Genetics and Heredity.* New York and Philadelphia: Chelsea House Publishers, 1990.

Fackelman, Kathy A. "Setting Odds on Extremity Defects After CVS." *Science News,* 146 (9 July 1994): 21.

Kolata, Gina. *The Baby Doctors.* New York: Delacorte Press, 1990.

Reuben, Carolyn. *The Health Baby Book.* New York: Jeremy P. Tarcher/Perigee Books, 1992.

Rosenthal, Elisabeth. "A New Prenatal Test." *Glamour,* 88 (June 1990).

Seligmann, Jean. "Is My Baby All Right?" *Newsweek,* 120 (22 June 1992): 62.

Liz Marshall

Chromatin

Chromatin is the masses of fine fibers comprising the chromosomes in the nucleus of a eukaryotic cell in a nondividing state. During cell division (mitosis or meiosis) the chromatin fibers pull together into thick shortened bodies which are then called chromosomes. Chromatin is present only in cells with a nuclear membrane; it is not found in prokaryotic cells (e.g. bacteria) which lack a nucleus.

Chromatin earned its name from early biologists who examined cells using light microscopes. These scientists found that in cells stained with a basic dye, the granular material in the nucleus turned a bright color. They named this material "chromatin," using the Greek word *chroma,* which means color. When the chromatin condensed during cell division, the researchers called the resulting structures chromosomes, which means "colored bodies." Chromatin granules which form the chromosomes are known as chromomeres, and these may correspond to genes.

Chemically, chromatin fibers consist of DNA (deoxyribonucleic acid) and two types of proteins found in the cell nucleus (nucleoproteins): histones and nonhistones. The histones are simple proteins found in chromosomes bound to the nucleic acids. Histones may be important in switching off gene action. While all cells of the body contain the same DNA instructions for every type of body cell, the specialized cells do not use all of these instructions. The unneeded DNA is put into storage, by binding with proteins, forming a complex called a nucleosome. Histones link the nucleosomes, forming large pieces of chromatin. DNA contains the genetic material that determines heredity. That chromatin contains DNA is to be expected, since chromosomes are made of chromatin. The compact structure of chromatin chromomeres, where DNA is wrapped around protein balls, is an efficient means of storing long stretches of DNA.

The discovery in 1949 of a condensed X chromosome of sex (termed the Barr body) which was visible at interphase (nondividing) in body cells of female mammals, provided physicians with a new means of determining the genetic sex of hermaphrodites. The sex chromatin test has now given way to direct M chromosomal analysis.

The Barr (X chromosome) is the inactive partner of the two X sex chromosomes in female mammals, including humans. Its dense, compact form led researcher M. F. Lyon to hypothesize in 1962 that it was inactive. In effect, then, both sexes have only one active X chromosome. Males (XY) have the sex chromosomes X and Y, while females (XX) have one functional almost inactive X chromosome. The influence of the inactive X chromosome expression in offspring is known as "lyonization," and is responsible for female tortoiseshell cats.

See also Chromosome; Deoxyribonucleic acid; Eukaryotae; Gene; Nucleus, cellular.

Chromatography

Chromatography is a family of laboratory techniques for separating mixtures of chemicals into their individual compounds. The basic principle of chromatography is that different compounds will stick to a solid surface, or dissolve in a film of liquid, to different degrees.

To understand chromatography, suppose that all the runners in a race have sticky shoe soles, and that some runners have stickier soles than others. The runners with the stickier shoes will not be able to run as fast. All other things being equal, then, the runners will cross the finish line in the exact order of their shoe stickiness—the least sticky first and the stickiest last. Even before the race is over, they will spread out along the track in order of their stickiness.

Similarly, different chemical compounds will stick to a solid or liquid surface to varying degrees. When a gas or liquid containing a mixture of different compounds is made to flow over such a surface, the molecules of the various compounds will tend to stick to the surface. If the stickiness is not too strong, a given molecules will become stuck and unstuck hundreds or thousands of times as it is swept along the surface. This repetition exaggerates even tiny differences in the various molecules' stickiness, and they become spread out along the "track," because the stickier compounds move more slowly than the less–sticky ones do. After a given time, the different compounds will have reached different places along the surface and will be physically separated from one another. Or, they can all be allowed to reach the far end of the surface—the "finish line"—and be detected or measured one at a time as they emerge.

Using variations of this basic phenomenon, chromatographic methods have become an extremely powerful and versatile tool for separating and analyzing a vast variety of chemical compounds in quantities from picograms (10^{-12} gram) to tons.

Chromatographic methods all share certain characteristics, although they differ in size, shape, and configuration. Typically, a stream of liquid or gas (the mobile phase) flows constantly through a tube (the column) packed with a porous solid material (the stationary phase). A sample of the chemical mixture is injected into the mobile phase at one end of the column, and the compounds separate as they move along. The individual separated compounds can be removed one at a time as they exit (or "elute from") the column.

Because it usually does not alter the molecular structure of the compounds, chromatography can provide a non–destructive way to obtain pure chemicals from various sources. It works well on very large and very small scales; chromatographic processes are used both by scientists studying micrograms of a substance in the laboratory, and by industrial chemists separating tons of material.

The technology of chromatography has advanced rapidly in the past few decades. It is now possible to obtain separation of mixtures in which the components are so similar that they only differ in the way their atoms are oriented in space: they are isomers of the same compounds. It is also possible to obtain separation of a few parts per million of a contaminant from a mixture of much more concentrated materials.

The development of chromatography

The first paper on the subject appeared in 1903, written by Mikhail Semyonovich Tsvet (1872–1919), a Russian–Italian biochemist, who also coined the word chromatography. Tsvet had managed to separate a mixture of plant pigments, including chlorophyll, on a column packed with finely ground calcium carbonate, using petroleum ether as the mobile phase. As the colored mixture passed down the column, it separated into individual colored bands. (The term chromatography comes from the Greek words chroma, meaning color, and graphein, meaning writing, or drawing.)

Although occasionally used by biochemists, chromatography as a science lagged until 1942, when A. J. P. Martin and R. L. M. Synge developed the first theoretical explanations for the chromatographic separation process. Although they eventually received the Nobel Prize in chemistry for this work, chromatography did not come into wide use until 1952, when Martin, this time working with A. T. James, described a way of using a gas instead of a liquid as the mobile phase, and a highly viscous liquid coated on solid particles as the stationary phase.

Gas–liquid chromatography (now called gas chromatography) was an enormous advance. Eventually, the stationary phase could be chemically bonded to the solid support, which improved the temperature stability of the column's packing. Gas chromatographs could then be operated at high temperature, so even large molecules could be vaporized and would progress through the column without the stationary phase vaporizing and

bleeding off. Additionally, since the mobile phase was a gas, the separated compounds were very pure; there was no liquid solvent to remove. Subsequent research on the technique produced many new applications.

The shapes of the columns themselves began to change, too. Originally vertical tubes an inch or so in diameter, columns began to get longer and thinner when it was found that this increased the efficiency of separation. Eventually, chemists were using coiled glass or fused silica capillary tubes less than a millimeter in diameter and many yards long. Capillaries cannot be packed, but they are so narrow that the stationary phase can simply be a thin coat on the inside of the column.

A somewhat different approach is the set of techniques known as "planar" or "thin layer" chromatography (TLC), in which no column is used at all. The stationary phase is thinly coated on a glass or plastic plate. A spot of sample is placed on the plate, and the mobile phase migrates through the stationary phase by capillary action.

In the mid–1970s, interest in liquid mobile phases for column chromatography resurfaced when it was discovered that the efficiency of separation could be vastly improved by pumping the liquid through a short packed column under pressure, rather than allowing it to flow slowly down a vertical column by gravity alone. High pressure liquid chromatography, also called high performance liquid chromatography (HPLC), is now widely used in industry. A variation on HPLC is Supercritical Fluid Chromatography (SFC). Certain gases (carbon dioxide, for example), when highly pressurized above a certain temperature, become a state of matter intermediate between gas and liquid. These "supercritical fluids" have unusual solubility properties, some of the advantages of both gases and liquids, and appear to very promising for chromatographic use.

Most chemical compounds are not highly colored, as were the ones Tsvet used. A chromatographic separation of a colorless mixture would be fruitless if there were no way to tell exactly when each pure compound eluted from the column. All chromatographs thus must have a device attached, and some kind of recorder to capture the output of the detector—usually a chart recorder or its computerized equivalent. In gas chromatography, several kinds of detectors have been developed; the most common are the thermal conductivity detector, the flame ionization detector, and the electron capture detector. For HPLC, the UV detector is standard. to the concentration of the separated compound. The sensitivity of the detector is of special importance, and research has continually concentrated on increasing this sensitivity, because chemists often need to detect and quantify exceedingly small amounts of a material.

Within the last few decades, chromatographic instruments have been attached to other types of analytical instrumentation so that the mixture's components can be identified as well as separated. (This takes the concept of the "detector" to its logical extreme.) Most commonly, this second instrument has been a mass spectrometer, which allows identification of compounds based on the masses of molecular fragments that appear when the molecules of a compound are broken up. Currently, chromatography as both science and practical tool is intensively studied, and several scientific journals are devoted exclusively to chromatographic research.

Types of chromatographic attraction

Adsorption chromatography (the original kind) depends on physical forces such as dipole attraction to hold the molecules onto the surface of the solid packing. In gas chromatography and HPLC, however, the solubility of the mixture's molecules in the stationary phase coating determines which ones progress through the column more slowly. Polarity can have an influence here as well. In gel filtration (also called size–exclusion or gel permeation) chromatography, the relative sizes of the molecules in the mixture determine which ones exit the column first. Large molecules flow right through; smaller ones are slowed down because they spend time trapped in the pores of the gel. Ion exchange chromatography depends on the relative strength with which ions are held to an ionic resin. Ions that are less strongly attached to the resin are displaced by more strongly attached ions. Hence the name ion–exchange: one kind of ion is exchanged for another. This is the same principle upon which home water softeners operate.

Chemists choose the mobile and stationary phases carefully, because it is the relative interaction of the mixture's compounds with those two phases that determines how efficient the separation can be. If the compounds have no attraction for the stationary phase at all, they will flow right through the column without separating. If the compounds are too strongly attracted to the stationary phase, they may stick permanently inside the column.

Industrial applications of chromatography

Chromatography of many kinds is widely used throughout the chemical industry. Environmental testing laboratories look for trace quantities of contaminants such as PCBs in waste oil, and pesticides such as

KEY TERMS

Chromatography—The separation of chemical mixtures into their individual compounds utilizing some version of a technique in which two phases—one mobile, one stationary—flow past one another. The mixture separates as it interacts with the two phases.

Column—In chromatography, the tube which holds the stationary phase, and through which the mobile phase passes. If the column is narrow enough, the stationary phase is coated on the inside walls. Larger columns are packed with a finely divided solid on which the stationary phase is either coated or chemically bonded.

Detector—A device that can detect the presence of a chemical. In chromatography, the detector is usually positioned at the end of the column, and detects and quantifies chemicals as they elute.

Elution—The process of a chemical exiting a chromatography column, after being separated.

Mobile Phase—The chromatographic phase—gas or liquid—that flows past the stationary phase. It interacts with the materials undergoing separation.

Stationary Phase—The chromatographic phase—viscous liquid coating, chemically bonded coating, or solid material—that remains in place as the mobile phase flows past it. The stationary phase interacts with the materials undergoing separation.

DDT in groundwater. Pharmaceutical companies use chromatography both to prepare large quantities of extremely pure materials, and also to analyze the purified compounds for trace contaminants.

A growing use of chromatography in the pharmaceutical industry is for the separation of chiral compounds. These compounds have molecules that differ slightly in the way their atoms are oriented in space. Although identical in almost every other way, including molecular weight, element composition, and physical properties, the two different forms—called optical isomers, or enantiomers—can have enormous differences in their biological activity. The compound thalidomide, for example, has two optical isomers. One causes birth defects when women take it early in pregnancy; the other isomer does not cause birth defects. Because this compound looks promising for the treatment of certain drug–resistant illnesses, it is important that the benign form be separated completely from the dangerous isomer.

Chromatography is used for quality control in the food industry, by separating and analyzing additives, vitamins, preservatives, proteins, and amino acids. It can also separate and detect contaminants such as aflatoxin, a cancer–causing chemical produced by a mold on peanuts. Chromatography can be used for purposes as varied as finding drug compounds in urine or other body fluids, to looking for traces of flammable chemicals in burned material from possible arson sites.

See also Calcium carbonate; Compound, chemical; Dipole; Ion exchange; Isomer; Mixture, chemical.

Further Reading:

Ebbing, Darrell. *General Chemistry.* 3d ed. Boston: Houghton Mifflin, 1990.
Poole, F., and S. A. Schuette. *Contemporary Practice of Chromatography.* Amsterdam: Elsevier, 1984.

Gail B. C. Marsella

Chromium see **Element, chemical**

Chromosomal abnormalities

Chromosome abnormalities describe alterations in the normal number of chromosomes or structural problems within the chromosomes themselves. Both kinds of chromosome abnormalities may result from an egg or sperm with the incorrect number of chromosome or a structurally faulty chromosome uniting with a normal egg or sperm during conception. Some chromosome abnormalities may occur shortly after conception. In this case, the zygote, the cell formed during conception that eventually develops into an embryo, divides incorrectly. Chromosomal abnormalities can cause serious mental or physical disabilities. Down's syndrome, for instance, is caused by an extra chromosome 21. People with Down's syndrome are mentally retarded and have a host of physical defects, including heart disorders. Other abnormalities may lead to death of the embryo. Zygotes that receive a full extra set of chromosomes, for instance, a condition called polyploidy, usually do not survive inside the uterus, and are spontaneously aborted (a process sometimes called a miscarriage).

Normal number and structure of human chromosomes

A chromosome consists of the body's genetic material, the deoxyribonucleic acid, or DNA, along with a small amount of protein. Within the chromosomes, the DNA is tightly coiled and takes up a small space within the nucleus of the cell. When a cell is not dividing, the chromosomes are invisible within the cell's nucleus. Just prior to cell division, the chromosomes uncoil and begin to replicate. As they uncoil, the individual chromosomes look somewhat like a fuzzy "X."

Chromosomes contain the genes, or segments of DNA that encode for proteins, of an individual. When a chromosome is structurally faulty, or if a cell contains an abnormal number of chromosomes, the types and amounts of the proteins encoded by the genes changes. When proteins are altered in the human body, the result can be serious mental and physical defects.

Humans have 22 pairs of chromosomes and one pair of sex chromosomes, for a total of 46 chromosomes. These chromosomes can be studied by constructing a karyotype, or photograph, of the chromosomes. To construct a karyotype, a technician stops cell division of a cell just after the chromosomes have replicated; the chromosomes are visible at this point within the nucleus. The chromosomes are photographed, and the technician cuts up the photograph and matches the chromosome pairs according to size and shape.

Normal cell division

In most animals, two types of cell division exist. In mitosis, cells divide to produce two identical daughter cells. Each daughter cell has exactly the same number of chromosomes. This preservation of chromosome number is accomplished through the replication of the entire set of chromosomes just prior to mitosis.

Sex cells, such as eggs and sperm, undergo a different type of cell division called meiosis. Because sex cells each contribute half of a zygote's genetic material, sex cells must carry only half the full complement of chromosomes. This reduction in the number of chromosomes within sex cells is accomplished during two rounds of cell division, called meiosis I and meiosis II. Prior to meiosis I, the chromosomes replicate, and chromosome pairs are distributed to daughter cells. During meiosis II, however, these daughter cells divide without a prior replication of chromosomes. It is easy to see that mistakes can occur during either meiosis I and meiosis II. Chromosome pairs can be separated during meiosis I, for instance, or fail to separate during meiosis II.

Meiosis produces four daughter cells, each with half of the normal number of chromosomes. These sex cells are called haploid cells (haploid means "half the number"). Non–sex cells in humans are called diploid (meaning "double the number").

Alterations in chromosome number

Two kinds of chromosome number defects can occur in humans: aneuploidy, or an abnormal number of chromosomes, and polyploidy, or more than two complete sets of chromosomes.

Aneuploidy

Most alterations in chromosome number occur during meiosis. During normal meiosis, chromosomes are distributed evenly among the four daughter cells. Sometimes, however, an uneven number of chromosomes are distributed to the daughter cells. As noted in the previous section, chromosome pairs may not move apart in meiosis I, or the chromosomes may not separate in meiosis II. The result of both kinds of mistakes (called nondisjunction of the chromosomes) in that one daughter cell receives an extra chromosome, and another daughter cell does not receive any chromosome.

When an egg or sperm that has undergone faulty meiosis and has an abnormal number of chromosomes unites with a normal egg or sperm during conception, the zygote that is formed will have an abnormal number of chromosomes. This condition is called aneuploidy. There are several types of aneuploidy. If the zygote has an extra chromosome, the condition is called trisomy. If the zygote is missing a chromosome, the condition is called monosomy.

If the zygote survives and develops into a fetus, the chromosomal abnormality is transmitted to all of its cells. The child that is born will have symptoms related to the presence of an extra chromosome or absence of a chromosome.

Examples of aneuploidy include trisomy 21, also known as Down's syndrome, and trisomy 13, also called Patau syndrome. Trisomy 13 occurs in 1 out of every 5000 births, and its symptoms are more severe than those of Down's syndrome. Children with trisomy 21 have cleft palates, hare lips, and severe brain and eye defects. Trisomy 18, known as Edwards' syndrome, results in severe multi–system defects. Children with trisomy 13 and trisomy 18 usually survive less than a year after birth (Figure 1).

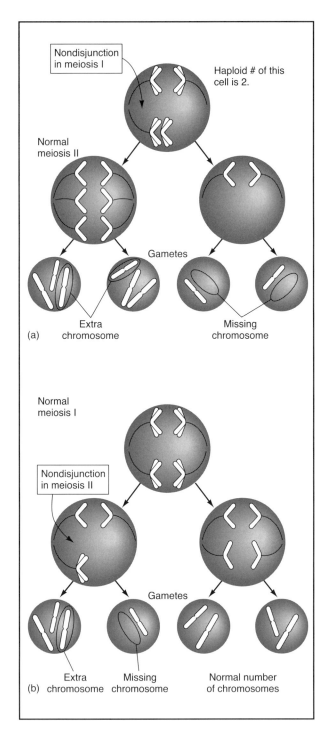

Figure 1. Karyotype from a child with trisomy 13 (a) or trisomy 18 (b).

Aneuploidy of sex chromosomes

Sometimes, nondisjunction occurs in the sex chromosomes. Humans have one set of sex chromosomes. These sex chromosomes are called "X" and "Y" after their approximate shapes in a karyotype. Males have both an X and a Y chromosome, while females have

Klinefelter's syndrome	XXY
Extra Y	XYY
Metafemale	XXX
Turner's syndrome	XO

Figure 2.

two X chromosomes. Remarkably, abnormal numbers of sex chromosomes usually result in less severe defects than those that result from abnormal numbers of the other 22 pairs of chromosomes. The lessened severity may be due to the fact that the Y chromosome carries few genes, and any extra X chromosomes become inactivated shortly after conception. Nevertheless, aneuploidy in sex chromosomes causes changes in physical appearance and in fertility (Figure 2).

In Klinefelter's syndrome, for instance, a male has two X chromosomes (XXY). This condition occurs in 1 out of every 2000 births. Men with Klinefelter's syndrome have small testes and are usually sterile. They also have female sex characteristics, such as enlarged breasts. Males who are XXY are of normal intelligence. However, males with more than two X chromosomes, such as XXXY, XXXXY, or XXXXXY are mentally retarded.

Males with an extra Y chromosome (XYY) have no physical defects, although they may be taller than average. XYY males occur in 1 out of every 2000 births.

Females with an extra X chromosome (XXX) are called metafemales. This defect occurs in 1 out of every 1000 births. Metafemales have lowered fertility, but their physical appearance is normal.

Females with only one X chromosome (XO) have Turner's syndrome. Turner's syndrome is also called monosomy X and occurs in 1 out of every 5000 births. People with Turner's syndrome have sex organs that do not mature at puberty and are usually sterile. They are of short stature and have no mental deficiencies.

Polyploidy

Polyploidy is lethal in humans. Normally, humans have two complete sets of chromosomes. Normal human cells, other than sex cells, are thus described as diploid. In polyploidy, a zygote receives more than two complete chromosome sets. Examples of polyploidy include triploidy, in which a zygote has three sets of chromosomes, and tetraploidy, in which a zygote has four sets of chromosomes. Triploidy could result from the fertilization of an abnormally diploid sex cell with a normal sex cell. Tetraploidy could result from the failure of the zygote to divide after it replicates its chromosomes. Human zygotes with either of these conditions usually die before birth, or soon after. Interestingly, polyploidy is common in plants and is essential for the proper development of certain stages of the plant life cycle.

Alterations in chromosome structure

Another kind of chromosomal abnormality is alteration of chromosome structure. Structural defects arise during the replication of the chromosomes just prior to a meiotic cell division. Replication is a complex process that involves the chromosomes exchanging segments with each other. If the process is faulty, the structure of the chromosomes changes. Sometimes these structural changes are harmless to the zygote; other structural changes, however, can be lethal.

Four types of general structural alterations occur during replication of chromosomes (Figure 3).

All four types begin with the breakage of a chromosome during replication. In a deletion, the broken segment of the chromosome is "lost." Thus, all the genes that are present on this segment are also lost. In a duplication, the segment joins to the other chromosome of the pair. In an inversion, the segment attaches to the original chromosome, but in a reverse position. And in a translocation, the segment attaches to an entirely different chromosome.

Because chromosomal alterations in structure cause the loss or misplacement of genes, the effects of these defects can be quite severe. Deletions are usually fatal to a zygote. Duplications, inversions, and translocations can cause serious defects, as the expression of the genes changes due to its changed position on the chromosomes.

Examples of structural chromosomal abnormalities include *cri du chat* syndrome. *Cri du chat* means "cat cry" in French. Children with this syndrome have an abnormally developed larynx that makes their cry sound like the mewing of a cat in distress. They also have a small head, misshapen ears, and a rounded face, as well as other systemic defects. These children usually die in infancy. *Cri du chat* is caused by a deletion of a segment of DNA in chromosome 5.

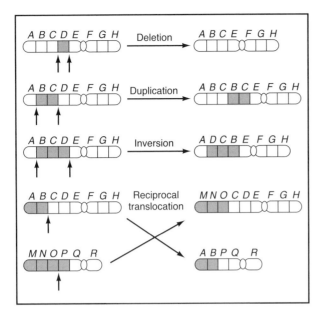

Figure 3. The four types of chromosome structure alterations.

A structural abnormality in chromosome 21 occurs in about 4% of people with Down's syndrome. In this abnormality, a translocation, a piece of chromosome 21 breaks off during meiosis of the egg or sperm cell and attaches to chromosome 13, 14, or 22.

Some structural chromosomal abnormalities have been implicated in certain cancers. For instance, myelogenous leukemia is a cancer of the white blood cells. Researchers have found that the cancerous cells contain a translocation of chromosome 22, in which a broken segment switches places with the tip of chromosome 9.

Some unusual chromosomal abnormalities include Prader–Willi syndrome, Angelman's syndrome, and fragile X syndrome. These structural defects are unusual because the severity or type of symptoms associated with the defect depend on whether the child receives the defect from the mother or the father.

Both Prader–Willi syndrome and Angelman's syndrome are caused by a deletion in chromosome 5. Prader–Willi syndrome is characterized by mental retardation, obesity, short stature, and small hands and feet. Angelman's syndrome is characterized by jerky movements and neurological symptoms. People with this syndrome also have an inability to control laughter, and may laugh inappropriately at odd moments. If a child inherits the defective chromosome from its father, the result is Prader–Willi syndrome. But if the child inherits the defective chromosome from its mother, the child will have Angelman's syndrome. Researchers believe

that genes from the deleted region function differently in offspring depending on whether the genes come from the mother or father, but they are not sure about the exact nature of these differences.

Another condition that depends on whether the defect is inherited from the mother or father is fragile X syndrome. In fragile X, an extra X chromosome hangs off the normal X by a thin "thread" of genetic material. The syndrome occurs in 1 out of 1000 male births and 1 out of 2000 female births. Males are affected more severely than females, and thus the syndrome is more pronounced if the child inherits the defect from its mother. To understand why this is so, remember that a male is XY and a female is XX. A male child receives a Y chromosome from the father and an X chromosome from the mother. A female child, however, can receive an X from either the mother or the father. Again, researchers believe this difference in fragile X symptoms between boys and girls stems from a difference in gene function that depends on whether they come from the mother or father.

Genetic counseling

Currently, no cures exist for any of the syndromes caused by chromosomal abnormalities. For many of these conditions, the age of the mother carries an increased risk for giving birth to a child with a chromosomal abnormality. The risk for Down's syndrome, for instance, jumps from 1 in 1000 when the mother is age 15–30 to 1 in 400 at age 35.

People at high risk for these abnormalities may opt to know whether the fetus they have conceived has one of these abnormalities. Amniocentesis is a procedure in which some of the amniotic fluid that surrounds and cushions the fetus in the uterus is sampled with a needle placed in the uterus. The amniotic fluid contains some of the fetus's skin cells, which can be tested for chromosomally–based conditions. Another test, called chorionic villi sampling, involves taking a piece of tissue from a part of the placenta. If a chromosomal defect is found, the parents can be advised of the existence of the abnormality. Some parents opt to abort the pregnancy; others can prepare before birth for a child with special needs.

In addition to amniocentesis and chorionic villi sampling, researchers are working on devising easier tests to detect certain abnormalities. A new test for Down's syndrome, for instance, measures levels of certain hormones in the mother's blood. Abnormal levels of these hormones indicate an increased risk that the fetus has Down's syndrome. These enzyme tests are safer and less expensive than the sampling tests and

Amniocentesis—A method of detecting genetic abnormalities in a fetus; in this procedure, amniotic fluid is sampled through a needle placed in the uterus; fetal cells in the amniotic fluid are then analyzed for genetic defects.

Aneuploidy—An abnormal number of chromosomes.

Angelman's syndrome—A syndrome caused by a deletion in chromosome 5 inherited from the mother.

Chorionic villi sampling—A method of detecting genetic abnormalities in a fetus; in this procedure, a piece of placental tissue is analyzed for genetic defects.

Chromosome—Structures that consist of deoxyribonucleic acid (DNA) and protein.

***Cri du chat* syndrome**—A syndrome caused by a deletion in chromosome 5; characterized by a strange cry that sounds like the mewing of a cat.

Deletion—Deletion of a segment of DNA from a chromosome.

Deoxyribonucleic acid (DNA)—The cell's genetic material.

Diploid—Means "double number;" describes the normal number of chromosomes for all cells of the human body, except for the sex cells.

Down's syndrome—A syndrome caused by trisomy 13; characterized by distinct facial characteristics, mental retardation, and several physical disorders, including heart defects.

Duplication—A type of chromosomal defect in which a broken segment of a chromosome attaches to the chromosome pair.

Edwards' syndrome—A syndrome caused by trisomy 18; characterized by multi–system defects; is usually lethal by age 1.

Fragile X syndrome—A condition in which an extra X chromosome hangs from the X chromosome by a "thread" of genetic material.

Gene—A segment of DNA that encodes for a protein.

Haploid—Means "half the number;" the number of chromosomes in a sex cell.

Inversion—A type of chromosomal defect in which a broken segment of a chromosome attaches to the same chromosome, but in reverse position.

Klinefelter's syndrome—A syndrome that occurs in XXY males; characterized by sterility, small testes, and female sex characteristics.

Meiosis—Cell division that results in four haploid sex cells.

Metafemale—An XXX female.

Mitosis—Cell division that results in two diploid cells.

Monosomy—A form of aneuploidy in which a person receives only one chromosome of a particular chromosome pair, not the normal two.

Patau's syndrome—A syndrome caused by trisomy 13; characterized by a hare lip, cleft palate, and many other physical defects; usually lethal by age 1.

Polyploidy—A condition in which a cell receives more than two complete sets of chromosomes.

Prader–Willi syndrome—A syndrome caused by a deletion in chromosome 5 inherited from the father.

Tetraploidy—A form of polyploidy; four sets of chromosomes.

Translocation—A type of chromosomal defect in which a broken segment of a chromosome attaches to a different chromosome.

Triploidy—A form of aneuploidy; three sets of chromosomes.

Trisomy—A form of aneuploidy in which a person receives an extra chromosome of a particular chromosome pair, not the normal two.

Turner's syndrome—A syndrome that occurs in X0 females; characterized by sterility, short stature,small testes, and immature sex organs.

Zygote—The cell formed by the uniting of egg and sperm.

may be able to diagnose chromosomally–based conditions in more women.

See also Chromosome.

Further Reading:
Bos, A. P., et. al. "Avoidance of emergency surgery in new-born infants with trisomy 18." *The Lancet* 339 (8798): 913–6. April 11, 1992.
D'Alton, Mary E., et. al. "Prenatal diagnosis." *New England Journal of Medicine* 328 (2): 114–21, January 14, 1995.
Day, Stephen. "Why genes have a gender." *New Scientist* 138 (1874): 34–39, Mary 22, 1993.
Harper, Peter S. *Practical Genetic Counseling.* Boston: Butterworth–Heineman, 1993.
Hoffman, Michelle. "Unraveling the genetics of fragile X syndrome." *Science* 252 (5010): 1070, May 24, 1991.
Money, John. "Specific neurological impairments associated with Turner and Kline–felter syndromes: a review." *Social Biology* 40 (1–2): 147–152, Spring–Summer 1993.
Nicolaides, K.H., et. al. "Ultrasonographically detectable markers of fetal chromosomal abnormalities." *The Lancet* 340 (8821): 704–8, September 19, 1992.
Therman, Eeva. *Human Chromosomes: Structure, Behavior, and Effects.* New York: Springer–Verlag, 1993.
Solomon, Ellen, et. al. "Chromosome aberrations and cancer." *Science* 254 (5035): 1153–61, November 22, 1991.

Kathleen Scogna

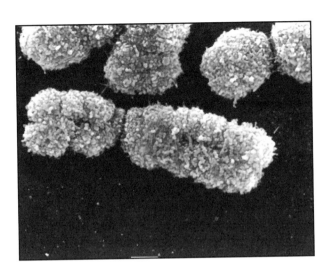

A scanning electron micrograph (SEM) of a human X-chromosome.

nucleotides. The nucleotides in DNA have four kinds of nitrogen–containing bases: adenine, guanine, cytosine, and thymine. Within DNA, each strand of nucleic acid is partnered with the other strand by bonds that form between these nucleotides, adenine pairs only with thymine, and guanine pairs only with cytosine. Thus, by knowing the sequence of bases in one strand of the DNA helix, you automatically know the sequence of bases in the other strand. For instance, if the sequence in one strand of DNA were ATTCG, the other strand's sequence would be TAAGC.

DNA functions in the cell by providing a template by which another nucleic acid, called ribonucleic acid (RNA), is formed. Like DNA, RNA is also composed of nucleotides. Unlike DNA, RNA is single stranded and does not form a helix. In addition, the RNA bases are the same as in DNA, except that uracil replaces thymine. RNA is transcribed from DNA in the nucleus of the cell. RNA is formed when the DNA "unzips," and nucleotides fall into place on the exposed DNA strand. If the exposed DNA sequence of bases is, for example, ATTCG, the new RNA sequence would be UAAGC.

This RNA molecule, called a messenger RNA (mRNA) molecule, then leaves the nucleus through the nuclear pore and enters the cytoplasm. There, the mRNA molecule attaches to a ribosome (also composed of RNA) and initiates protein synthesis. Each block of three nucleotides on the mRNA molecule encodes for an amino acid, the building blocks of a protein. The amino acids are brought to the mRNA and placed in position by yet another kind of RNA, the transfer RNA (tRNA) molecule. The parts of both tRNA and rRNA molecules are synthesized in the nucleus from the DNA

Chromosome

A chromosome is a structure that houses the cell's deoxyribonucleic acid (DNA), the cell's genetic material. In prokaryotes, or cells without a nucleus, the chromosome is merely a circle of DNA. In eukaryotes, or cells with a distinct nucleus, chromosomes are much more complex in structure. The function of chromosomes is to package the extremely long DNA molecule—which within one chromosome can be as long as 0.6–3.3 in (1.7–8.5 cm)—into the small space of the nucleus. If DNA were not coiled within chromosomes, the total DNA in a typical eukaryotic cell would extend thousands of times the length of the cell nucleus.

The DNA molecule and a review of protein synthesis

DNA is the genetic material of all cells and directs the synthesis of proteins. DNA is composed of two strands of nucleic acids arranged in a helix. The nucleic acid strands, in turn, are composed of a sequence of template, but these parts are put together to form complete molecules in the cytoplasm.

Genes

Genes are the parts of DNA that, transcribed into an mRNA molecule, encode for a protein or form a tRNA or mRNA molecule. Surprisingly, much of the DNA molecule does not encode for anything at all. Out of the 3 billion base pairs that exist in the human DNA, only about 500,000–100,000 of these pairs code for proteins. The noncoding sections of DNA are called introns, while the coding sections of DNA are called exons. During transcription of mRNA from DNA, these introns are snipped out of the newly formed mRNA molecule before it leaves the nucleus.

Chromosome numbers

As we have noted, chromosomes are essential in packaging the extremely long DNA molecules into a structure that fits into the cell's nucleus. The human genome (the total amount of DNA in a typical human cell) numbers about 3×10^9 nucleotide pairs. If these nucleotide pairs were letters, the genome "book" would number over a million pages.

The DNA of the human genome is parceled out to 23 pairs of chromosomes, for a total number of 46 chromosomes. One pair of chromosomes in the 23 are the sex chromosomes, X and Y. Males have both an X and a Y chromosome, while females have two X chromosomes.

All human cells have 23 pairs of chromosomes, except for the sex cells (eggs and sperm). The sex cells have half this number of chromosomes. Sex cells are haploid ("half the number") because during fertilization, the sex cell of the father combines with the sex cell of the mother to form a new cell, the zygote, which eventually develops into an embryo. If the sex cells had the full complement of chromosomes (a condition called "diploid," or "double the number"), then the zygote would have two full sets of chromosomes instead of one complete set. Sex cells are formed in a special kind of cell division called meiosis. During meiosis, two rounds of cell division ensure that the sex cells receive the haploid number of chromosomes.

Other species have different numbers of chromosomes in their nuclei. The mosquito, for instance, has 6 chromosomes. Lilies have 24, earthworms 36, chimps 48, and horses 64. The most number of chromosomes are found in the Adder's tongue fern, which has more than 1,000 chromosomes. Most species have, on average, 10–50 chromosomes. With 46 chromosomes, humans fall well within this average.

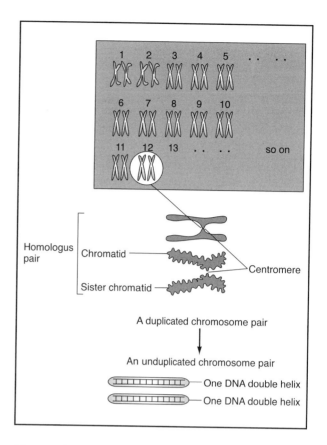

Figure 1. A human karyotype.

Chromosome shape

In photos, chromosomes resemble the letter "X" in structure. However, the chromosomes that appear in photos are duplicated chromosomes. The only time that chromosomes are visible to the camera is just prior to cell division, when the DNA within the nucleus uncoils as it replicates. By "freezing" a body cell with chemicals at this precise moment, researchers can take pictures of the duplicated chromosomes. Researchers then match and number the pairs of chromosomes from 1 to 23, using the characteristic patterns of bands that appear on the chromosomes. The resulting arrangement is called a karyotype (Figure 1).

Karyotypes are useful in diagnosing some chromosomally–based genetic conditions, because the karyotype reveals any aberration in chromosome number. For instance, Down's syndrome is caused by an extra chromosome 21. A karyotype of a child with Down's syndrome would clearly reveal this extra chromosome.

An unduplicated chromosome resembles a long, slender rod and contains one double helix, or one molecule, of DNA. Pairs of chromosomes are called homologues. In the duplicated state, the duplicated chromo-

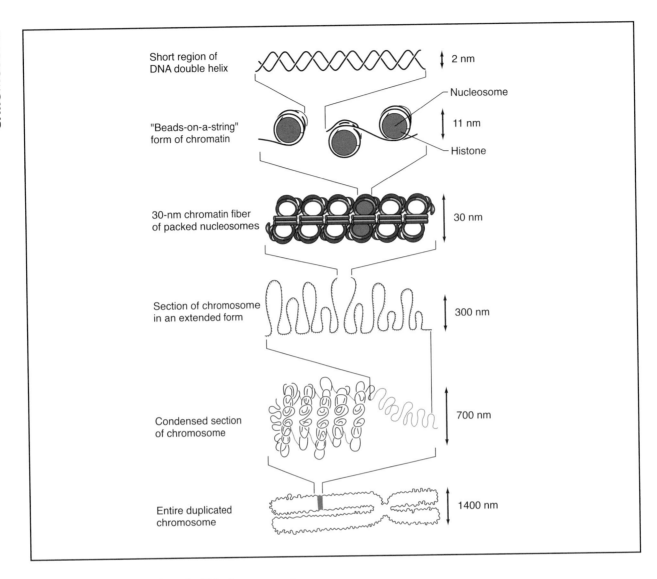

Short region of
DNA double helix
↕ 2 nm

Nucleosome

"Beads-on-a-string"
form of chromatin
↕ 11 nm

Histone

30-nm chromatin fiber
of packed nucleosomes
30 nm

Section of chromosome
in an extended form
300 nm

Condensed section
of chromosome
700 nm

Entire duplicated
chromosome
1400 nm

Figure 2. How DNA is packaged within chromosomes.

some resembles the letter "X." Each separate chromosome within the duplicate is called a sister chromatid. The sister chromatids are attached to each other by a structure called the centromere, forming the familiar X shape. When looking at the chromosome 12 pair in a karyotype, for instance, you are seeing a homologous pair of duplicated chromosomes, or two "Xs." Within each "X" are two sister chromatids. The spot in the middle of the X holding the two chromatids together is the centromere. You might notice that the X is lopsided. The longer portion of the X is called the long arm of the chromosome, and the shorter arm is called the short arm of the chromosome.

If somehow it were possible to photograph unduplicated chromosomes, you would see at the chromosome 12 pair two long, slender rods. The unduplicated chromosomes would not look like "Xs."

How DNA is packaged within chromosomes

With so much DNA within the nucleus, packaging the long helical molecules into such a small space requires that the DNA be intricately folded and arranged within the chromosomes (Figure 2).

The DNA molecule is assisted with this folding by proteins. In fact, the material that makes up the chromosomes is not DNA only; it is chromatin, a material that consists of both DNA and protein.

The role of proteins in packaging DNA in chromosomes

Several kinds of proteins are found within chromosomes. Some proteins initiate DNA replication when the cell prepares to divide; other proteins control gene transcription in the preliminary stages of protein synthesis. Still other proteins, called structural proteins, help the DNA fold into the intricate configurations within the chromosomes.

Histones are structural proteins that are abundant within chromosomes. In fact, the mass of histones in a chromosome is almost equal to that of DNA. Chromosomes contain five types of these small proteins: H1, H2A, H2B, H3, and H4. The last four types of histones in this list form a structure called the octomeric histone core. The H1 histone is larger than the other histones, and performs a structural role separate from the octomeric histone core in organizing DNA within the chromosome.

The octomeric histone core functions as a spool around which DNA is wound twice. Each histone–DNA spool is called a nucleosome. Nucleosomes occur at intervals of every 200 nucleotide pairs. In photographs taken with the help of powerful microscopes, DNA wrapped around nucleosomes resembles beads (the nucleosome) threaded on a string (the DNA molecule). The DNA that exists between nucleosomes is called linker DNA. Chromosomes can contain some very long stretches of linker DNA. Often, these long linker DNA sequences are the regulatory portions of genes. These regulatory portions switch genes on when certain molecules bind to them.

Nucleosomes are only the most fundamental organizing structure in the chromosome. Nucleosomes themselves are packed into structures called a 30 nanometer chromatin fiber. The H1 histone functions in forming this fiber: looking somewhat like a horizontal hook, this histone gathers together DNA in clusters of eight or more histones. The 30 nanometer fibers are then further folded into a larger chromatin fiber sometimes as much as 100 nanometers thick.

But the chromatin fibers are still not the ultimate organizational structure in chromosomes. The chromatin fibers are formed into loops by yet another structural protein. Each loop contains 20,000–30,000 nucleotide pairs. These loops are then arranged within the chromosomes, held in place by still more structural proteins.

Chromosomes and mitosis

Chromosomes in eukaryotes perform a useful function during mitosis, the process in which cells replicate their genetic material and then divide into two new cells, or daughter cells. Because the DNA is packaged within chromosomes, the distribution of the correct amount of genetic material to the daughter cells is maintained during the complex process of cell division.

Before a cell divides, the chromosomes are replicated within the nucleus. During this stage, the chromosomes take on the "X" shape familiar to us in karyotypes. In a human cell, the nucleus just prior to cell division contains 46 pairs of chromosomes. When the cell divides, the sister chromatids from each duplicated chromosome separate. Each daughter cell ends up with 23 pairs of chromosomes, the correct diploid number for human cells.

In meiosis, the type of cell division that leads to the production of sex cells, the division process is more complicated. Two rounds of cell division occur in meiosis. Before meiosis, the chromosomes replicate, and the nucleus has 46 pairs of chromosomes. In the first round of meiotic cell division, the homologous pairs—not the sister chromatids, as in mitosis—of the chromosomes separate. In the second round of cell division, which is not preceded by chromosomal replication, the sister chromatids separate, so that each of the four daughter cells receives the haploid number of chromosomes.

Protein synthesis and chromosomes

Because DNA is bound up within chromosomes, how does protein synthesis proceed? In order for an mRNA molecule to be transcribed from a DNA template, the DNA needs to be "freed" from its chromosome structure so that the RNA molecule can form on its exposed strands. Some evidence exists that RNA transcription can take place through histones. However, most often the genes on the DNA that have been activated by the binding of regulatory molecules to the regulatory sections separate out from the chromosomal structure. This "loosened," active DNA is seen as "puffs" on chromosomes. These puffs represent genes that are being actively transcribed into RNA molecules. When RNA transcription concludes, the puffs receded and the chromosome resumes its somewhat smooth contours.

See also Chromatin; Deoxyribonucleic acid; Eukaryotae; Gene; Genetics; Meiosis; Mendelian laws of inheritance; Mitosis; Nucleus, cellular; Prokaryote; Proteins; Ribonucleic acid (RNA).

Further Reading:
Adolph, Kenneth W. *Chromosomes: Eukaryotic, Prokaryotic, and Viral.* Boca Raton, FL: CRC Press, 1990.
Drlica, Karl, and Monica Riley, eds. *The Bacterial Chromosome.* Washington, DC: American Society for Microbiology, 1990.
Heslop–Harrison, J. S., and R. B. Flavell, eds. *The Chromosome.* Oxford, UK: BIOS Scientific Publishers, 1993.

KEY TERMS

30 nanometer chromatin fiber—The fiber that is formed by the gathering of nucleosomes by H1 histones.

Chromatin—The material that comprises chromosomes; consists of DNA and proteins.

Chromosome puffs—The regions of active DNA that are transcribing RNA; appear as puffed regions in a chromosome.

Deoxyribonucleic acid—DNA; the genetic material of cells that are packed into chromosomes.

Eukaryote—A cell with a distinct nucleus.

Exons—The regions of DNA that code for a protein or form tRNA or rRNA.

Genome—The full amount of an organism's genetic material.

Histone—A kind of structural protein that functions in packaging DNA in chromosomes.

Homologue—The partner of a chromosome in a chromosome pair.

Introns—The sections of DNA that do not code for proteins or RNA's.

Karyotype—An arrangement of photographs of chromosomes according to number.

Linker DNA—The sections of DNA between nucleosomes.

Meiosis—The process of sex cell division; results in four haploid daughter cells.

Messenger RNA—The RNA that is transcribed from DNA in the nucleus; functions in protein synthesis.

Mitosis—The process of body cell division; results in two diploid daughter cells.

Nitrogen–containing base—Part of a nucleotide; in DNA, the bases are adenine, guanine, thymine, and cytosine; in RNA, the bases are adenine, guanine, uracil, and cytosine.

Nucleic acid—The chemical component of DNA and RNA.

Nucleosome—DNA wrapped around a histone core.

Nucleotide—The building blocks of nucleic acids.

Octomeric histone core—The "spool" in a nucleosome; consists of four small histones.

Ribonucleic acid—RNA; single stranded nucleic acid transcribed from DNA in the nucleus; functions in protein synthesis.

Ribosomal RNA—A type of RNA that functions in protein synthesis.

Sister chromatid—One complete chromosome in a duplicated chromosome.

Transcription—The process in which an RNA molecule is produced from a template of DNA.

Transfer RNA—A type of RNA that functions in protein synthesis; brings amino acids to mRNA.

Rothwell, Norman W. *Understanding Genetics: A Molecular Approach.* New York: Wiley–Liss, 1993.

Therman, Eeva. *Human Chromosomes: Structure, Behavior, and Effects.* 3rd ed. New York: Springer–Verlag, 1993.

Wolffe, A. *Chromatin: Structure and Function.* London; San Diego: Academic Press, 1992.

Kathleen Scogna

Chub see **Suckers**

Chubsucker see **Suckers**

Chuck-will's-widow   see **Caprimulgids**

Chulengo see **Camels**

Cicadas

Cicadas are insects in the order Homoptera, family Cicadidae. Male cicadas make a well–known, loud, strident, buzzing sound during the summer, so these unusual insects are often heard, but not necessarily seen. Species of cicadas are most diverse in closed and open forests of the temperate and tropical zones.

Biology of cicadas

Cicadas are large dark–bodies insects, with a body length of 2 in (5 cm), membranous wings folded tent–like over the back, and large eyes.

Male cicadas have a pair of small drum–like organs (tymbals), located at the base of their abdomen. These

A cicada on a person's hand on the coast of Kenya.

structures have an elastic, supporting ring, with a membrane extending across it (the tymbal membrane). The familiar very loud, buzzing noises of cicadas are made by using powerful muscles to move the tymbal membrane rapidly back and forth, as quickly as several hundred times per second. The actual sound is made in a manner similar to that by which a clicking noise is made by moving the center of the lid of a metal can back and forth. The loudness of the cicada song is amplified using resonance chambers, known as opercula. Each species of cicada makes a characteristic sound.

Cicadas are herbivorous insects, feeding on the sap of the roots of various types of perennial plants, most commonly woody species. Cicadas feed by inserting their specialized mouth parts, in the form of a hollow tube, into a plant root, and then sucking the sap.

Life cycle of cicadas

Cicadas have prolonged nymphal stages, which are spent within the ground, sucking juices from the roots of plants, especially woody species. Most cicada species have overlapping generations, so that each year some of the population of subterranean nymphs emerges from the ground and transforms into a fairly uniform abundance of adults, as is the case of the dog–day or annual cicada (*Tibicen pruinosa*).

Other species of cicadas have non–overlapping generations, so there are periodic events of the great abundance of adults and their noisy summer renditions, interspersed with much longer periods during which the adult animals are not found in the region. The irruptive adult phase occurs at intervals as long as 17 years, in the case of northern populations of the periodical cicada

(*Magicicada septendecum*), which has the longest generation time of any plant–sucking insect. Southern populations of the periodical cicada gave generation times as short as 13 years, and are usually treated as a different species.

The periodical cicada spends most of its life in the ground, in its developmental nymph stages. During years of irruption or peak emergence, the ground in late spring and early summer can be abundantly pock–marked with the emergence holes of the mature nymphs of this species, at a density greater than one thousand per square meter. The stout–bodied nymphs emerge from the ground and then climb up upon some elevated object, where they metamorphose into the adult form, which lives for about one month. During years when periodical cicadas are abundant, the strange–looking, cast exoskeletons of their mature nymphs can be found in all manner of places.

The adult periodic cicada is black or dark brown, with large, membranous wings folded over its back, and large, red eyes. The females have a strong, chisel–like ovipositor, which is used to make incisions in small branches and twigs, into which her eggs are deposited. The incisions severely injure the affected twigs, which generally die from the point of the incision to the tip. Soon after hatching, the small nymphs drop to the ground and burrow in, ready for a relatively long life of 17 years. The subterranean nymph excavates a chamber beside the root of a woody plant, into which the cicada inserts its beak and feeds on sap.

Cicadas and people

When they are breeding in abundance, some species of cicadas cause economic damage by the injuries that result when the females lay their eggs in the branches and twigs of commercially important species of trees. The periodical cicada is the most important species in this respect in North America. This species can cause a great deal of damage in hardwood–dominated forests in parts of eastern North America. The damage is not very serious in mature forests, but can be important in younger forests and nurseries.

Although cicadas are not often seen, their loud buzzing noises are a familiar noise of hot, sunny days in many regions. As such, cicadas are appreciated as an enjoyable aspect of the outdoors.

Bill Freedman

Cigarette smoke

As of 1990, 46.3 million adults throughout the world smoked. Of these, 24 million were men, and 22 million were women. The prevalence of smoking is highest in the 25–44 age category. Smoking has been linked to a variety of diseases, such as lung cancer, cardiovascular disease, and chronic lung ailments. In the United States alone, 1 in 5 of all deaths is attributable to smoking, and in the 35–64 age category, smoking is responsible for 1 in 4 deaths. In developed countries, smoking causes 30% of all deaths, and in the 35–69 age category, smoking is the single largest cause of premature death.

Cigarette smoke is called mainstream smoke when it is inhaled directly from a cigarette. Sidestream smoke is the smoke that is emitted from the burning cigarette and that is exhaled from a smoker's lungs. Sidestream smoke is also called environmental tobacco smoke (ETS) or secondhand smoke. Passive smoking, or the inhaling of sidestream smoke by nonsmokers, has recently been identified by the Environmental Protection Agency (EPA) as a significant health risk, which can lead to all the negative health consequences that mainstream smoking causes.

Components of cigarette smoke

Over 4,000 different chemicals are present in cigarette smoke. Among these, many are carcinogenic, or capable of causing the cellular genetic mutations that can lead to cancer. Cigarette smoke contains nicotine, an addictive chemical. Cigarette smoke also contains tars, nitrosamines, and polycyclic hydrocarbons—all carcinogenic substances. In addition, cigarettes produce carbon monoxide when they are smoked. When inhaled, carbon monoxide interferes with oxygen transport and utilization.

Environmental tobacco smoke

Interestingly, ETS may be more carcinogenic than mainstream smoke. ETS contains more particles of car-cinogenic materials with smaller diameters. These smaller particles are more likely to lodge in the lungs than the larger particles in mainstream smoke. More carbon monoxide is generated while a cigarette is smoldering than when it is smoked directly. In recent studies of passive smoking, researchers found that no safe threshold exists for exposure to ETS, and that nonsmokers are placed at an increased risk for the same problems and complications recognized in smokers. In 1993, the EPA classified ETS as a known human carcinogen, its highest carcinogenic category. With this information, many municipal governments and workplaces have banned cigarette smoking altogether.

The health consequences of smoking

Smoking causes a variety of health problems. Cigarette smoke is inhaled into the lungs, where the large surface area of the lung tissues and alveoli quickly absorb the chemical components and nicotine. Within one minute of inhaling cigarette smoke, the chemicals in cigarette smoke are distributed by the bloodstream to the brain, heart, kidneys, liver, lungs, gastrointestinal tract, muscle, and fat tissue. In pregnant women, cigarette smoke crosses the placenta and may effect fetal growth.

Cardiovascular disease

Cardiovascular disease, or diseases of the blood vessels and heart, include stroke, heart attack, peripheral vascular disease, and aortic aneurysm. In 1990 in the United States, one fifth of all deaths due to cardiovascular disease were linked to smoking. Specifically, 179,820 deaths from general cardiovascular disease, 98,921 deaths from heart disease, and 23,281 deaths from cerebrovascular disease (stroke) were directly linked to smoking. In addition, researchers have noted a strong dose–response relationship between the duration and extent of smoking and the death rate from heart disease in men under 65. The more one smokes, the more one is likely to develop heart disease. Researchers have also seen a similar trend in women.

Cigarette smoking leads to cardiovascular disease in a number of ways. Smoking damages the inside of the blood vessels, initiating changes that lead to atherosclerosis, a disease characterized by blood vessel blockage. Smoking also causes the coronary arteries (the arteries that supply the heart muscle with oxygen) to constrict. In this way, smoking increases the vulnerability of the heart to heart attack (when heart muscle dies as a result of lack of oxygen) and cardiac arrest (when the heart stops beating). Smoking also raises the levels of low–density lipoproteins (the so–called "bad" cho-

A normal lung (left) and the lung of a cigarette smoker (right).

lesterol in the blood) and lowers the levels of high–density lipoproteins (the so–called "good" cholesterol). Too much cholesterol in the blood has been linked to atherosclerosis. Finally, smoking increases the risk of stroke by 1.5 to 3 times the risk that nonsmokers have.

ETS also causes cardiovascular disease. An estimated 53,000 deaths are caused by passive smoking, and 37,000 of these deaths are due to heart disease. In a study of nonsmoking spouses living with smoking spouses, researchers found that the nonsmokers had a 30% greater risk of death from heart disease or heart attack than spouses who lived with nonsmokers. In addition, researchers also found that the coronary arteries constrict more as a result of inhaling ETS than inhaling mainstream smoke.

Cancer

Smoking causes 85% of all lung cancers, but also causes other cancers, among them cancers of the mouth, pharynx (throat), larynx (voice–box), esophagus, stomach, pancreas, cervix, kidney, ureter, and bladder.

Other environmental factors may contribute to the development of cancer when a person smokes. Alcohol consumption, for instance, when combined with smok-ing, accounts for three–quarters of all oral and pharyngeal cancers. Esophageal cancer is caused by the direct contact of the cigarette smoke with the delicate esophageal tissues. Persons predisposed genetically to certain cancers may develop cancer more quickly if they smoke.

Lung disease

Smoking is the leading cause of lung disease in the United States, resulting in many deaths each year. Among the direct causes of death are pneumonia, influenza, bronchitis, emphysema, and chronic airway obstruction. Smoking increases mucus production in the airways and deadens the respiratory cilia, the tiny hairs that sweep debris out from the lungs. Without the action of the cilia, bacteria and the inhaled particles from the cigarette smoke can damage the lungs.

In the smaller airways of the lungs—the tiny bronchioles that branch off from the larger bronchi—chronic inflammation is present in smokers. This inflammation causes airway constriction. Symptoms that many smokers notice include a cough, mucus production, and shortness of breath. Eventually, this inflammation can lead to chronic obstructive pulmonary disease (COPD), a condition in which little oxygen is absorbed by the lungs to be transported to body tissues.

ETS can be a serious health problem for children of smokers. These children have an increased risk of bronchitis and pneumonia. If they also have asthma, ETS can cause more severe attacks and more frequent attacks.

Other health problems

Women who smoke also have a higher risk of developing cardiovascular disease. Other effects include an increased risk of osteoporosis (a disease in which bones become brittle and vulnerable to breakage), cervical cancer, and decreased fertility. Pregnant women who smoke have increased risk for spontaneous abortion, premature separation of the placenta from the uterine wall (a life–threatening complication for mother and fetus), placenta previa (in which the placenta implants much lower in the uterus than normal, which may lead to hemorrhage), bleeding during pregnancy, and premature rupture of the placental membranes (which can lead to infection). Infants born to women who smoke during pregnancy are at increased risk for low birth weight and other developmental problems.

In men, smoking lowers testosterone levels in the bloodstream, and studies are currently taking place to measure the effects of smoking on male fertility. Preliminary results show an association between low birth weight and paternal smoking.

Various other health problems are caused by smoking. Poor circulation in the extremities caused by the constriction of blood vessels leads to constantly cold hands and feet. Smoking deadens the taste buds and the receptors in the nasal epithelium, interfering with the senses of taste and smell. Smoking may also contribute to periodontal disease.

How is nicotine addictive?

In 1992, the Surgeon General of the United States declared nicotine to be as addictive as cocaine. When a smoker smokes the first cigarette in the morning, nicotine levels in the blood are at their lowest point of the day. However, it is important to note that nicotine does not leave the body over a 24–hour period. It takes about three days without smoking for the last traces of nicotine to be eliminated. As the smoker smokes the first cigarette, nicotine levels rise dramatically in the blood. As the smoker smokes more cigarettes during the day, nicotine levels continue to rise until a threshold level is reached. The smoker must maintain this threshold level to avoid feelings of deprivation. If the nicotine levels begin to drop, the smoker experiences a craving for a

cigarette. He or she may become anxious, impatient, and unable to concentrate. Smoking immediately acts on the brain and alleviates these feelings, and the cycle of dependence on cigarettes is established.

The physical effects of cigarette smoke include several neurological responses. Serotonin, a neurotransmitter, is released in response to nicotine. Neurotransmitters are substances that nerve cells use to transmit nerve impulses. When more serotonin is released from nerve cells, a person feels more alert. When a person smokes a cigarette, he or she associates this good feeling with the cigarette. Soon, serotonin release from nerve cells is slow and sluggish without the boost from nicotine. This interaction between serotonin and nicotine is the essence of nicotine addiction. A smoker becomes dependent on nicotine to prompt the release of serotonin from nerve cells.

Other substances that are released in response to nicotine include opioids, naturally–occurring pain-killing substances, and various hormones. All of these substances have powerful effects on brain function. Although cigarette smoking affects all body systems, its effects on the brain are perhaps the most potent, since the brain effects of smoking leads to addiction.

Nicotine is actually a stimulant, not a depressant, although many smokers experience feelings of relaxation. This effect may be attributed to the relaxation of skeletal muscle that accompanies smoking. Smoking also increases heart rate and blood pressure and constricts blood vessels throughout the body, and it may also interfere with sleep patterns.

The effects of quitting

Quitting smoking can significantly lower the risk of cancer and cardiovascular disease. In fact, the risk of lung cancer decreases from 18.83 at 1–4 years after quitting, to 7.73 at 5–9 years, to below 5 at 10–19 years, to 2.1 at 20–plus years. The risk of lung cancer for nonsmokers is 1.

Weight gain is a common side effect of quitting, since smoking interferes with pancreatic function and carbohydrate metabolism, leading to a lower body weight in some people. However, not all people experience this lowered body weight from smoking, and thus, not all people who quit gain weight. Taste buds and smell are reactivated in nonsmokers, which may lead to increased food intake.

Methods of treatment

About 80% of people trying to quit smoking relapse within the first two weeks of stopping smoking.

KEY TERMS

· ·

Carcinogen—A substance that causes cancer.

Cardiovascular disease—Diseases that affect the blood vessels and heart.

Environmental tobacco smoke—Also called sidestream smoke; the smoke emitted from a burning cigarette and exhaled from a smoker.

Mainstream smoke—The smoke inhaled by a smoker from a cigarette.

Nicotine—The addictive substance in cigarettes.

It is therefore important that a smoker be highly motivated to quit. An ambivalent quitter or a person who is quitting under pressure from friends and family may not succeed. Some people are able to quit alone, while others find group smoking cessation programs helpful. Some people may also enlist the help of their physicians and families in the quitting effort. One method of treatment is to introduce small amounts of nicotine into the body. Nicotine gum and nicotine patches are currently being prescribed to help smokers quit. Both maintain nicotine at a steady level in the blood. The quitter then switches to lower–dose patches or cuts down on the number of pieces of gum throughout a set time period. This method—especially the patches—have met with considerable success, especially in people who are highly addicted to nicotine. Experts stress, however, that the patches and gum should be combined with group meetings or other support systems for maximum effectiveness.

See also Addiction; Nicotine; Respiratory system.

Further Reading:
Bertrecchi, Carl E., et. al. "The Human Costs of Tobacco Use, Part I" *New England Journal of Medicine* 330 (March 1994): 907.

Boyle, Peter. "The Hazards of Passive—and Active—Smoking." *New England Journal of Medicine* 328 (June 1993): 1708.

Brownlee, Shannon. "The Smoke Next Door." *U.S. News and World Report* 116 (June 1994): 66.

MacKenzie, Thomas D., et. al. "The Human Costs of Tobacco Use, Part II" *New England Journal of Medicine* 330 (April 1994): 975.

Hurt, Richard D., et. al. "Nicotine Patch Therapy for Smoking Cessation Combined with Physician Advice and Nurse Follow–Up: One Year Outcome and Percentage of Nicotine Replacement." *Journal of the American Medical Association* 271 (February 1994): 595.

Rogge, Wolfgang F. "Cigarette Smoke in the Urban Atmosphere." *Environmental Science and Technology* 28 (July 1994): 1375.

Sekhon, Harmanjatinder S., et. al. "Cigarette Smoke Causes Rapid Cell Proliferation in Small Airways and Associated Pulmonary Arteries." *American Journal of Physiology* 267 (November 1994): L557.

Kathleen Scogna

Cinchona see **Quinine**

Cinematography see **Motion picture**

Cinnamon see **Laurel family (Lauraceae)**

Circadian rhythm see **Biological rhythms**

Circle

In the language of geometry, a circle is the locus of points in a plane that are all at an equal distance from a single point, called the center of the circle. The fixed distance is called the radius of the circle. A line segment with each of its endpoints on the circle, that passes through the center of the circle, is called a diameter of the circle. The length of a diameter is twice the radius. The distance around a circle, called its circumference, is the length of the line segment that would result if the circle were broken at a point and straightened out. This length is given by $2\pi r$, where r is the radius of the circle and π (the Greek letter pi, pronounced "pie") is a constant equal to approximately 3.14159. Points lying outside the circle are those points whose distance from the center is greater than the radius of the circle, and points lying in the circle are those points whose distance from the center is less than the radius of the circle. The area covered by a circle, including all the points within it, is called the area of the circle. The area of a circle is also related to its radius by the formula $A = \pi r^2$, where A is the area, r is the radius, and π is the same constant as that in the formula for the circumference. In the language of algebra, a circle corresponds to the set of ordered pairs (x,y) such that $(x - a)^2 + (y - b)^2 = r^2$, where the point corresponding to the ordered pair (a,b) is the center of the circle and the radius is equal to r.

See also Locus.

Circuit see **Electrical circuit**

Circulatory system

Living things require a circulatory system to deliver food, oxygen, and other needed substances to all cells, and to take away waste products. Materials are transferred between individual cells and their internal environment through the cell membrane by diffusion, osmosis, and active transport. During diffusion and osmosis, molecules move from a higher concentration to a lower concentration. During active transport, carrier molecules push or pull substances across the cell membrane, using adenosine triphosphate (ATP) for energy. Unicellular organisms depend on passive and active transport to exchange materials with their watery environment. More complex multicellular forms of life rely on transport systems that move material–containing liquids throughout the body in specialized tubes. In vascular plants, tubes transport food and water. Some invertebrates rely on a closed system of tubes, while others have an open system. Humans and other higher vertebrates have a closed system of circulation.

Circulation in vascular plants

Water and dissolved minerals enter a plant's roots from the soil by means of diffusion and osmosis. These substances then travel upward in the plant in xylem vessels. The transpiration theory ascribes this ascending flow to a pull from above, caused by transpiration, the evaporation of water from leaves. The long water column stays intact due to the strong cohesion between water molecules. Carbohydrates, produced in leaves by photosynthesis, travel downward in plants in specialized tissue, phloem. This involves active transport of sugars into phloem cells and water pressure to force substances from cell to cell.

Circulation in invertebrates

Animal circulation depends on the contraction of a pump—usually a heart that pumps blood in one direction through vessels along a circulatory path. In a closed path, the network of vessels is continuous. Alternately, an open path has vessels that empty into open spaces in the body. The closed system in the earthworm uses five pairs of muscular hearts (the aortic arches), to pump blood. Located near the anterior or head end of the animal, the aortic arches contract and force blood into the ventral blood vessel that runs from head to tail. Blood then returns back to the hearts in the dorsal blood vessel. Small ring vessels in each segment connect dorsal and ventral blood vessels. As blood circulates throughout the body, it delivers nutrients and oxygen to cells and picks up carbon dioxide and other wastes.

Most arthropods and some advanced molluscs such as squid and octopuses have an open circulatory system. In the grasshopper, a large blood vessel runs along the top of the body, and enlarges at the posterior or tail end to form a tubelike heart. Openings in the heart (ostia) have valves that permit only the entry of blood into the heart. The heart contracts, forcing blood forward in the blood vessel and out into the head region. Outside the heart, the blood goes into spaces that surround the insect's internal organs. The blood delivers food and other materials to cells and picks up wastes. Animals with open circulatory systems depend on the respiratory system to transport oxygen and carbon dioxide. The blood moves slowly from the head to the tail end of the animal. At the posterior, the blood re–enters the heart through the openings. Contraction of muscles helps speed up the blood flow.

Human circulatory system

The human circulatory system is termed the cardiovascular system, from the Greek word *kardia*, meaning heart, and the Latin *vasculum*, meaning small vessel. The basic components of the cardiovascular system are the heart, the blood vessels, and the blood. The work done by the cardiovascular system is astounding. Each year, the heart pumps more than 1,848 gal (7,000 l) of blood through a closed system of about 62,100 mi (100,000 km) of blood vessels. This is more than twice the distance around the equator of the earth. As blood circulates around the body, it picks up oxygen from the lungs, nutrients from the small intestine, and hormones from the endocrine glands, and delivers these to the cells. Blood then picks up carbon dioxide and cellular wastes from cells and delivers these to the lungs and kidneys, where they are excreted. Substances pass out of blood vessels to the cells through the interstitial or tissue fluid which surrounds cells.

The human heart

The adult heart is a hollow cone–shaped muscular organ located in the center of the chest cavity. The lower tip of the heart tilts toward the left. The heart is about the size of a clenched fist and weighs approximately 10.5 oz (300 g). Remarkably, the heart beats more than 100,000 times a day and close to 2.5 billion times in the average lifetime. A triple–layered sac, the pericardium, surrounds, protects, and anchors the heart. A liquid pericardial fluid located in the space between two of the layers, reduces friction when the heart moves.

The heart is divided into four chambers. A partition or septum divides it into a left and right side. Each side is further divided into an upper and lower chamber. The upper chambers, atria (singular atrium), are thin–walled. They receive blood entering the heart, and pump it to the ventricles, the lower heart chambers. The walls of the ventricles are thicker and contain more cardiac muscle than the walls of the atria, enabling the ventricles to pump blood out to the lungs and the rest of the body. The left and right sides of the heart function as two separate pumps. The right atrium receives oxygen–poor blood from the body from a major vein, the vena cava, and delivers it to the right ventricle. The right ventricle, in turn, pumps the blood to the lungs via the pulmonary artery. The left atrium receives the oxygen–rich blood from the lungs from the pulmonary veins, and delivers it to the left ventricle. The left ventricle then pumps it into the aorta, a major artery that leads to all parts of the body. The wall of the left ventricle is thicker than the wall of the right ventricle, making it a more powerful pump able to push blood through its longer trip around the body.

One–way valves in the heart keep blood flowing in the right direction and prevent backflow. The valves open and close in response to pressure changes in the heart. Atrioventricular (AV) valves are located between the atria and ventricles. Semilunar (SL) valves lie between the ventricles and the major arteries into which they pump blood. The "lub–dup" sounds that the physician hears through the stethoscope occur when the heart valves close. The AV valves produce the "lub" sound upon closing, while the SL valves cause the "dup" sound. People with a heart murmur have a defective heart valve that allows the backflow of blood.

The rate and rhythm of the heartbeat are carefully regulated. We know that the heart continues to beat even when disconnected from the nervous system. This is evident during heart transplants when donor hearts keep beating outside the body. The explanation lies in a small mass of contractile cells, the sino–atrial (SA) node or pacemaker, located in the wall of the right atrium. The SA node sends out electrical impulses that set up a wave of contraction that spreads across the atria. The wave reaches the atrio–ventricular (AV) node, another small mass of contractile cells. The AV node is located in the septum between the left and right ventricle. The AV node, in turn, transmits impulses to all parts of the ventricles. The bundle of His, specialized fibers, conducts the impulses from the AV node to the ventricles. The impulses stimulate the ventricles to contract. An electrocardiogram, ECG or EKG, is a record of the electric impulses from the pacemaker that direct each heartbeat. The SA node and conduction system provide the primary heart controls. In patients with disorganized electrical activity in the heart, surgeons implant an artifi-

cial pacemaker that serves to regulate the heart rhythm. In addition to self–regulation by the heart, the autonomic nervous system and hormones also affect its rate.

The heart cycle refers to the events associated with a single heartbeat. The cycle involves systole, the contraction phase, and diastole, the relaxation phase. In the heart, the two atria contract while the two ventricles relax. Then, the two ventricles contract while the two atria relax. The heart cycle consists of a systole and diastole of both the atria and ventricles. At the end of a heartbeat all four chambers rest. The rate of heartbeat averages about 75 beats per minute, and each cardiac cycle takes about 0.8 seconds.

Heart disease is the number one cause of death among people living in the industrial world. In coronary heart disease (CHD), a clot or stoppage occurs in a blood vessel of the heart. Deprived of oxygen, the surrounding tissue becomes damaged. Education about prevention of CHD helps to reduce its occurrence. We have learned to prevent heart attacks by eating less fat, preventing obesity, exercising regularly, and by not smoking. Medications, medical devices and techniques also help patients with heart disease. One of these, the heart–lung machine, is used during open–heart and bypass surgery. This device pumps the patient's blood out of the body, and returns it after having added oxygen and removed carbon dioxide. For patients with CHD, physicians sometimes use coronary artery bypass grafting (CABG). This is a surgical technique in which a blood vessel relocated from another part of the body is grafted into the heart. The relocated vessel provides a new route for blood to travel as it bypasses the clogged coronary artery. In addition, cardiologists can also help CHD with angioplasty. Here, the surgeon inflates a balloon inside the aorta. This opens the vessel and improves the blood flow. For diagnosing heart disease, the echocardiogram is used in conjunction with the ECG. This device uses high frequency sound waves to take pictures of the heart.

Blood vessels

The blood vessels of the body make up a closed system of tubes that carry blood from the heart to tissues all over the body and then back to the heart. Arteries carry blood away from the heart, while veins carry blood toward the heart. Capillaries connect small arteries (arterioles) and small veins (venules). Large arteries leave the heart and branch into smaller ones that reach out to various parts of the body. These divide still further into smaller vessels called arterioles that penetrate the body tissues. Within the tissues, the arterioles branch into a network of microscopic capillaries. Substances move in and out of the capillary walls as the blood exchanges materials with the cells. Before leaving the tissues, capillaries unite into venules, which are small veins. The venules merge to form larger and larger veins that eventually return blood to the heart. The two main circulation routes in the body are the pulmonary circulation, to and from the lungs, and the systemic circulation, to and from all parts of the body. Subdivisions of the systemic system include the coronary circulation, for the heart, the cerebral circulation, for the brain, and the renal circulation, for the kidneys. In addition, the hepatic portal circulation passes blood directly from the digestive tract to the liver.

The walls of arteries, veins, and capillaries differ in structure. In all three, the vessel wall surrounds a hollow center through which the blood flows. The walls of both arteries and veins are composed of three coats. The inner coat is lined with a simple squamous endothelium, a single flat layer of cells. The thick middle coat is composed of smooth muscle that can change the size of the vessel when it contracts or relaxes, and of stretchable fibers that provide elasticity. The outer coat is composed of elastic fibers and collagen. The difference between veins and arteries lies in the thickness of the wall of the vessel. The inner and middle coats of veins are very thin compared to arteries. The thick walls of arteries make them elastic and capable of contracting. The repeated expansion and recoil of arteries when the heart beats creates the pulse. We can feel the pulse in arteries near the body surface, such as the radial artery in the wrist. The walls of veins are more flexible than artery walls and they change shape when muscles press against them. Blood returning to the heart in veins is under low pressure often flowing against gravity. One–way valves in the walks of veins keep blood flowing in one direction. Skeletal muscles also help blood return to the heart by squeezing the veins as they contract. Varicose veins develop when veins lose their elasticity and become stretched. Faulty valves allow blood to sink back thereby pushing the vein wall outward. The walls of capillaries are only one cell thick. Of all the blood vessels, only capillaries have walls thin enough to allow the exchange of materials between cells and the blood. Their extensive branching provides a sufficient surface area to pick up and deliver substances to all cells in the body.

Blood pressure is the pressure of blood against the wall of a blood vessel. Blood pressure originates when the ventricles contract during the heartbeat. In a healthy young adult male, blood pressure in the aorta during systole is about 120 mm Hg, and approximately 80 mm Hg during diastole. The sphygmomanometer is an instrument that measures blood pressure. A combination of nervous carbon and hormones help regulate blood pressure around a normal range in the body. In addition, there are local controls that direct blood to tissues according to their need. For example, during exercise, reduced oxygen and increased carbon dioxide stimulate blood flow to the muscles.

Two disorders that involve blood vessels are hypertension and atherosclerosis. Hypertension, or high blood pressure, is the most common circulatory disease. For about 90% of hypertension sufferers, the blood pressure stays high without any known physical cause. Limiting salt and alcohol intake, stopping smoking, losing weight, increasing exercise, and managing stress help reduce blood pressure. Medications also help control hypertension. In atherosclerosis, the walls of arteries thicken and lose their elasticity. Fatty material such as cholesterol accumulates on the artery wall forming plaque that obstructs blood flow. The plaque can form a clot that breaks off, travels in the blood, and can block a smaller vessel. For example, a stroke occurs when a clot obstructs an artery or capillary in the brain. Treatment for atherosclerosis includes medication, surgery, a low– fat, high–fiber diet, and exercise. The type of cholesterol carried in the blood indicates the risk of atherosclerosis. Low density lipoproteins (LDLs) deposit cholesterol on arteries, while high density lipoproteins (HDLs) remove it.

Blood

Blood is liquid connective tissue. It transports oxygen from the lungs and delivers it to cells. It picks up carbon dioxide from the cells and brings it to the lungs. It carries nutrients from the digestive system and hormones from the endocrine glands to the cells. It takes heat and waste products away from cells. The blood helps regulate the body's base–acid balance (pH), temperature, and water content. It protects the body by clotting and by fighting disease through the immune system.

When we study the structure of blood, we find that it is heavier and stickier than water, has a temperature in the body of about 100.4° F (38° C), and a pH of about 7.4. Blood makes up approximately 8% of the total body weight. A male of average weight has about 1.5 gal (5–6 l) of blood in his body, while a female has about 1.2 gal (4–5 l). Blood is composed of a liquid portion (the plasma), and blood cells.

Plasma is composed of about 91.5% water which acts as a solvent, heat conductor, and suspending medium for the blood cells. The rest of the plasma includes plasma proteins produced by the liver, such as albumins, which help maintain water balance, globulins, which help fight disease, and fibrinogen, which aids in blood clotting. The plasma carries nutrients, hormones, enzymes, cellular waste products, some oxygen, and carbon dioxide. Inorganic salts, also carried in the plasma, help maintain osmotic pressure. Plasma leaks out of the capillaries to form the interstitial fluid (tissue fluid) that surrounds the body cells and keeps them moist, and supplied with nutrients.

The cells in the blood are erythrocytes (red blood cells), leukocytes (white blood cells), and thrombocytes (platelets). More than 99% of all the blood cells are erythrocytes, or red blood cells. Red blood cells look like flexible biconcave discs about 8 µm in diameter that are capable of squeezing through narrow capillaries. Erythrocytes lack a nucleus and therefore are unable to reproduce. Antigens, specialized proteins on the surface of erythrocytes, determine the ABO and Rh blood types. Erythrocytes contain hemoglobin, a red pigment that carries oxygen, and each red cell has about 280 million hemoglobin molecules. An iron ion in hemoglobin combines reversibly with one oxygen molecule, enabling it to pick up, carry and drop off oxygen. Erythrocytes are formed in red bone marrow, and live about 120 days. When they are worn out, the liver and spleen destroy them and recycle their breakdown products. Anemia is a blood disorder characterized by too few red blood cells.

Leukocytes are white blood cells. They are larger than red blood cells, contain a nucleus, and do not have hemoglobin. Leukocytes fight disease organisms by destroying them or by producing antibodies. Lymphocytes are a type of leukocyte that bring about immune reactions involving antibodies. Monocytes are large leukocytes that ingest bacteria and get rid of dead matter. Most leukocytes are able to squeeze through the capillary walls and migrate to an infected part of the body. Formed in the white/yellow bone marrow, a leukocyte's life ranges from hours to years depending on how it functions during an infection. In leukemia, a malignancy of bone marrow tissue, abnormal leukocytes are produced in an uncontrolled manner. They crowd out the bone marrow cells, interrupt normal blood cell production, and cause internal bleeding. Treatment for acute leukemia includes blood transfusions, anticancer drugs, and, in some cases, radiation.

Thrombocytes or platelets bring about clotting of the blood. Clotting stops the bleeding when the circulatory system is damaged. When tissues are injured, platelets disintegrate and release the substance thromboplastin. Working with calcium ions and two plasma proteins, fibrinogen and prothrombin, thromboplastin converts prothrombin to thrombin. Thrombin then changes soluble fibrinogen into insoluble fibrin. Finally, fibrin forms a clot. Hemophilia, a hereditary

KEY TERMS

Artery—Vessel that transports blood away from the heart.

Atherosclerosis—Abnormal narrowing of a coronary artery that generally originates from the buildup of fatty plaque on the wall.

Atrium—Receiving chamber of the heart.

Capillary—Vessel that connects artery to vein.

Phloem—Plant tissue that transports food.

Pulmonary route—Circuit that transports blood to and from the lungs.

Systemic route—Circuit that transports blood to and from all parts of the body except the lungs.

Vein—Vessel that transports blood to the heart.

Ventricle—Pumping chamber of the heart.

Xylem—Plant tissue that transports water and minerals upward from the roots.

blood disease in which the patient lacks a clotting factor, occurs mainly in males. Hemophiliacs hemorrhage continuously after injury. They can be treated by transfusion of either fresh plasma or a concentrate of the deficient clotting factor.

The lymphatic system and the circulatory system

The lymphatic system is an open transport system that works in conjunction with the circulatory system. Lymphatic vessels collect intercellular fluid (tissue fluid), kill foreign organisms, and return it to the circulatory system. The lymphatic system also prevents tissue fluid from accumulating in the tissue spaces. Lymph capillaries pick up the intercellular fluid, now called lymph, and carry it into larger and larger lymph vessels. Inside the lymph vessels, lymph passes through lymph nodes, where lymphocytes attack viruses and bacteria. The lymphatic system transports lymph to the large brachiocephalic veins below the collarbone where it is re–enters the circulatory system. Lymph moves through the lymphatic system by the squeezing action of nearby muscles, for there is no pump in this system. Lymph vessels are equipped with one–way valves that prevent backflow. The spleen, an organ of the lymphatic system, removes old blood cells, bacteria, and foreign particles from the blood.

See also Adenosine triphosphate; Blood; Heart; Heart diseases; Lymphatic system.

Further Reading:

Berne, R. M., and M. N. Levy. *Cardiovascular Physiology*. St. Louis: C. V. Mosby, 1992.

Fackelmann, K. A. "Immune Cell Triggers Attack on Plaque." *Science News* (22 October 1994).

Kapit, Wynn, and Lawrence M. Elson. *The Anatomy Coloring Book*. New York: Harper & Row, 1995

Two Hearts That Beat as One. Films for Humanities and Science, 1995. Videocassette.

Vogel, Steven. "Nature's Pumps." *American Scientist* (September/October 1994).

Bernice Essenfeld

Circumscribed and inscribed

The terms circumscribed and inscribed refer, respectively, to geometric figures that have been drawn around the outside of or within some other geometric figure. For example, imagine that a circle is drawn around a triangle so that the circle passes through all three vertices of the triangle. Then the circle is said to be circumscribed around the triangle, and the triangle is said to be inscribed within the circle.

Many combinations of figures could be substituted for the triangle and circle described above. For example, a circle circumscribed about any kind of polygon is one that passes through all of the vertices of the polygon. Then the polygon itself is said to be inscribed within the circle. Conversely, a polygon can be circumscribed around a circle if all of the sides of the polygon are tangent to the circle. Then the circle is inscribed within the polygon.

Three–dimensional figures can be circumscribed around and inscribed within each other also. For example, a cone can be circumscribed around a pyramid if the vertices of the cone and pyramid coincide with each other, and the base of the cone circumscribes the base of the pyramid. In such a case, the pyramid is inscribed within the cone. As another example, a sphere can be inscribed within a cylinder if all parts of the cylinder are tangent to the sphere's surface. Then the cylinder is circumscribed around the sphere.

Cirrhosis

Cirrhosis is a degenerative liver disease in which the lobes of the liver become infiltrated with fat and fibrous tissue (fibrous tissue is a type of connective tissue composed of protein fibers called collagen). The word "cirrhosis" is derived from the Greek words *kirrhos*, meaning "yellowish–orange" and *osis*, meaning "condition," and connotes the appearance of the liver of a patient with cirrhosis. The infiltration of these substances within the liver disrupts liver functions, including the conversion of the storage carbohydrate glycogen into glucose; detoxification of drugs and other substances; vitamin absorption; gastrointestinal functions; and hormone metabolism. Because the blood vessels of the liver are affected by fibrous tissue formation, blood flow through the liver is impaired, leading to increased blood pressure within the liver. Impaired blood flow in the liver also causes a condition called esophageal varices, in which blood vessels in the esophagus bleed due to increased blood pressure. In addition, patients with cirrhosis are often weakened by hypoglycemia, or low blood sugar.

Complications of cirrhosis include coma, gastrointestinal hemorrhage, and kidney failure. No definitive treatment for cirrhosis is available besides management of symptoms and complications. The mortality rate of cirrhosis ranges from 40% to 63%, and it is the ninth leading cause of death in the United States.

Causes of cirrhosis

Cirrhosis is most often caused by excessive ingestion of alcohol. In the United States, 90% of all cases of cirrhosis are related to alcohol overconsumption. Although researchers still do not have a clear understanding of how alcohol damages the liver, it is thought that consuming more than 1 pint of alcohol (86 proof) daily for 10 years increases the risk of cirrhosis by 10%. The risk of cirrhosis increases to 50% if this consumption lasts 25 years. Women may be more susceptible to alcoholic cirrhosis than men. Women have lower levels of the enzyme alcohol dehydrogenase, which breaks down alcohol in the stomach. Lower levels of this enzyme leads to higher blood alcohol levels.

Researchers believe that the main cause of alcohol–induced cirrhosis is acetaldehyde, the first product created when alcohol is broken down in the stomach. Acetaldehyde combines with proteins in the body and damages the liver cells, leading to fat accumulation and fibrous tissue formation. Further damage to liver cells may be caused by a secondary effect of alcohol on the liver: the acetaldehyde may make the liver cells vulnerable to the potentially damaging effects of substances such as acetaminophen (a common over–the–counter pain reliever), industrial solvents, and certain anesthetics on the liver cells.

Although excessive alcohol intake is considered the leading cause of cirrhosis, there are numerous other causes of the disease. These include several types of viral hepatitis, nutritional factors, genetic conditions, and others. In addition, these are often contributing factors in alcoholic cirrhosis. Chronic infection with hepatitis B virus (HBV) can lead to cirrhosis and is also related to liver cancer.

Progression of cirrhosis

Cirrhosis is a progressive disease. In cases of alcoholic cirrhosis, it begins with a condition called alcoholic fatty liver. In this condition, fat accumulates in the liver. The liver enlarges, sometimes to as much as 10 lb (5000 g), and appears yellow and greasy. Patients with this condition often have no symptoms beyond low blood sugar or some digestive upset. Some patients have more severe symptoms, such as jaundice (a condition caused by the accumulation of a yellowish bile pigment in the blood; patients with jaundice have yellow–tinged skin) and weight loss. Complete recovery is possible at this stage of liver disease if the patient abstains from alcohol.

The next stage in the progression of cirrhosis is often a condition called hepatitis. Hepatitis is a general term meaning inflammation of the liver. Hepatitis may be caused by alcohol, a virus, or other factors. In acute alcoholic hepatitis, the inflammation is caused by alcohol. Fibrous tissue is deposited in the liver, the liver cells degenerate, and a type of connective tissue called hyaline infiltrates the liver cells. Regardless of the cause, patients with hepatitis have serious symptoms, including general debilitation, loss of muscle mass, jaundice, fever, and abdominal pain. The liver is firm, tender, and enlarged. Vascular "spiders," or varicose veins of the liver, are present. Again, no definitive treatment is available, although some patients respond well to corticosteroids. General treatment for this condition includes treatment of symptoms and complications.

Acute alcoholic hepatitis often progresses to cirrhosis. In cirrhosis, the fibrous tissue and fat accumulation is prominent. Collagen is deposited around the veins of the liver, leading to impairment of blood flow. The liver cells degenerate further and die, leading to formation of nodules in the liver, and the liver atrophies (shrinks). Symptoms of cirrhosis include nausea, weight loss, jaundice, and esophageal varices. Gastrointestinal symptoms, such as diarrhea and gastric distention, are also features of cirrhosis. The mortality rate of cirrhosis is high. Five year survival of patients with cirrhosis is 64% for patients who stop drinking, and 40% for patients

KEY TERMS

Acute alcoholic hepatitis—Inflammation of the liver caused by excessive alcohol consumption.

Collagen—A type of protein that comprises connective tissue; infiltrates the liver in cirrhosis.

Fatty liver—A condition in which the liver accumulates fat due to excessive alcohol consumption.

Fibrous tissue—Connective tissue composed primarily of collagen.

Hepatitis—General inflammation of the liver; may be caused by viral infection or by excessive alcohol consumption.

Jaundice—A condition in which a yellowish bile pigment increases in the blood; patients with jaundice have a characteristic yellow tinge to their skin.

who continue to drink. Death results from kidney failure, coma, malnutrition, and cardiac arrest.

Treatment of cirrhosis depends on the type and cause. For patients with alcoholic cirrhosis, it includes general support, treatment of complications, a nutritious diet, and abstention from alcohol consumption. In selected patients, liver transplant may be indicated. Although the liver has a remarkable ability to regenerate, the damage that cirrhosis inflicts on the liver may be so severe that recovery is not possible. In cirrhosis caused by viral hepatitis, the use of experimental drugs has had some success.

Further Reading:

Cohen, Carl et. al. "Alcoholics and Liver Transplantation." *Journal of the American Medical Association* 265 (March 1991): 1299.

Hegarty, Mary. "The good news (preventing cirrhosis of the liver)." *Health* 5 (March–April 1991): 11.

Mann, Robert E.G. and Smart, Reginald G. "Alcohol and the Epidemic of Liver Cirrhosis." *Alcoholic Health and Research World* 16 (Summer 1992): 217.

Parrish, Kiyoko M. et. al. "Average daily alcohol consumption during adult life among descendants with and without cirrhosis: the 1986 National Mortality Followback Survey." *Journal of Studies on Alcohol* 54 (July 1993): 450.

Poynard, Thierry et. al. "Evaluation of efficacy of liver transplantation in alcoholic cirrhosis by a case control study and simulated controls." *The Lancet* 344 (August 1994): 502.

Kathleen Scogna

Figure 1. Citric acid

Citric acid

Citric acid is an organic (carbon based) acid found in nearly all citrus fruits, particularly lemons, limes, and grapefruits. It is widely used as a flavoring agent, preservative, and cleaning agent. The structure of citric acid is shown below. The COOH group is a carboxylic acid group, so citric acid is a tricarboxylic acid, possessing three of these groups.

Citric acid is produced commercially by the fermentation of sugar by several species of mold. As a flavoring agent, it can help produce both a tartness [caused by the production of hydrogen ions (H^+)] and sweetness (the result of the manner in which citric acid molecules "fit" into "sweet" receptors on our tongues). Receptors are protein molecules that recognize specific other molecules.

Citric acid helps to provide the "fizz" in remedies such as Alka–Seltzer™. The fizz comes from the production of carbon dioxide gas which is created when sodium bicarbonate (baking soda) reacts with acids. The source of the acid in this case is citric acid, which also helps to provide a more pleasant taste.

Citric acid is also used in the production of hair rinses and low pH (highly acidic) or slightly acidic shampoos and toothpaste. As a preservative, citric acid helps to bind (or sequester) metal ions that may get into food via machinery used in processing. Many metals ions speed up the degradation of fats. Citric acid prevents the metal ions from being involved in a reaction with fats in foods and allows other preservatives to function much more effectively. Citric acid is also an intermediate in metabolic processes in all mammalian cells. One of the most important of these metabolic pathways is called the citric acid cycle (it is also called the *Krebs cycle*, after the man who first determined the role of this series of reactions). Some variants of citric acid containing fluorine have been used as rodent poisons.

See also Carboxylic acid; Krebs cycle; Metabolism.

Citron see **Gourd family**

Citrus trees

Citrus trees are various species of trees in the genus Citrus, in the rue family, or Rutaceae. There are 60 species in the genus *Citrus,* of which about 10 are used in agriculture. The center of origin of most species of *Citrus* is southern and southeast Asia. Citrus trees are widely cultivated for their edible fruits in sub–tropical and tropical countries around the world. The sweet orange (*Citrus sinensis*) is the most common species of citrus in cultivation, and is one of the most successful fruits in agriculture.

The rue family consists of about 1,500 species and 150 genera. Most species in this family are trees or shrubs. The greatest richness of species occurs in the tropics and subtropics, especially in South Africa and Australia. However, a few species occur in the temperate zone. Several species native to North America are the shrubs known as prickly ash (*Zanthoxylum americanum*), southern prickly ash (*Z. clava–herculis*), and three–leaved hop tree (*Ptelea trifoliata*).

Biology of citrus

Citrus trees are species of sub–tropical and tropical climates. They are intolerant of freezing, and their foliage and fruits will be damaged by even a relatively short exposure to freezing temperatures for just a few hours. Colder temperatures can kill the entire tree.

Species of citrus trees range in size from shrubs to trees. Most species have thorny twigs. The leaves are alternately arranged on the twigs, and the foliage is dark green, shiny, aromatic, leathery, and evergreen. The roots of citrus trees do not develop root hairs, and as a result citrus trees are highly dependent for their mineral nutrition on a mutualistic symbiosis with soil fungi called mycorrhizae.

Citrus trees have small white or purplish flowers, which are strongly scented and produce nectar. Both scent and nectar are adaptations for attracting insects, which are the pollinators of the flowers of citrus trees. Some species in the genus *Citrus* will easily hybridize with each other. This biological trait can make it easier for plant breeders to develop profitable agricultural

Grapefruit ready to pick.

varieties using controlled hybridization experiments to incorporate desirable traits from one species into another. However, the occurrence of hybrid *Citrus* plants makes it difficult for plant taxonomists to designate true species. As a result, there is some controversy over the validity of some *Citrus* species that have been named.

The ripe fruit of citrus trees is properly classified as a hesperidium, which is a type of berry, or a fleshy, multi–seeded fruit. The fruits of citrus trees have a relatively leathery, outer shell, with a more spongy rind on the inside. The rind of citrus fruits is very rich in glands containing aromatic oils, which can be clearly detected by smell when these fruits are being peeled. The interior of the fruit is divided into discrete segments, which contain the seeds, surrounded by a large–celled, juicy pulp. The seeds of citrus trees are sometimes called "pips."

Edible fruits like those of citrus trees are an adaptation to achieve dispersal of their seeds. The attractive and nutritious fruits are sought out by many species of animals, who eat the pulp and seeds. However, the citrus seeds generally survive the passage through the gut of the animal, and are excreted with the feces. In the meantime, the animal has likely moved somewhere, and the seeds have been dispersed far from the parent tree, ready to germinate, and hopefully, develop into a new citrus plant.

Cultivation and economic products of citrus trees

The fruits of citrus trees contain large concentrations of sour–tasting citric acid. Nevertheless, the fruits of some species can be quite sweet because they contain large concentrations of fruit sugar. Plant breeders have developed various sorts of cultivated varieties, or culti-

vars, from the wild progenitors of various species of citrus trees. This has resulted in the selective breeding of varieties with especially sweet fruits, others which peel relatively easily, and yet others that are seedless and therefore easier to eat or process into juice.

Once plant breeders discover a desirable cultivar of a species of citrus tree, it is thereafter propagated by rooting stem cuttings or by grafting. The latter procedure involves taking a stem of the cultivar, and attaching it to the rootstock of some other, usually relatively hardy, variety. The graft is carefully wrapped until a protective callus tissue is formed. Because the attributes of the cultivar are genetically based, these methods of propagation avoid the loss of desirable genetic attributes of the new variety that would inevitably occur through sexual cross–breeding.

Citrus trees can also be propagated using relatively new techniques by which small quantities of cells can be grown and induced to develop into fully–formed plants through specific hormone treatments. These relatively new techniques, known as micro propagation or tissue culture, allow for the rapid and inexpensive production of large numbers of trees with identical genetic qualities.

The most important economic products of cultivated citrus trees are, of course, their fruits. In agriculture, the fruits of oranges and grapefruits are commonly picked when they are ripe or nearly so, while those of lemons and limes are usually picked while they are still unripened, or green.

The fruits of the sweet orange can be eaten directly after peeling, or they may be processed into a juice, which can be drunk fresh. It may also be concentrated by evaporating about three–quarters of its water content, and then frozen for transport to far–away markets. This is a more economical way of moving orange juice around, because removal of much of the water means that much less weight must be transported. In addition, juice concentrates can also be used to manufacture flavorings for various types of drinks.

The juice of citrus fruits is relatively rich in ascorbic acid, or vitamin C. For example, a typical orange contains about 40 mg of vitamin C, compared with only 5 mg in an apple. Vitamin C is an essential nutrient for proper nutrition of animals. However, animals cannot synthesize their own vitamin C and must obtain the micronutrient from their diet. In the absence of a sufficient dietary supply of vitamin C, a debilitating and eventually lethal disease known as scurvy develops. In past centuries scurvy often afflicted mariners on long oceanic voyages, during which foods rich in vitamin C or its biochemical precursors could not be readily obtained. Because they stored relatively well, lemons were an important means by which sailors could avoid scurvy, at least while the supply of those fruits lasted.

At one time, citric acid was commercially extracted from the fruits of citrus trees, mostly for use in flavoring drinks. Today, citric acid is used in enormous quantities to flavor carbonated soft drinks and other beverages. However, most of this industrial citric acid is synthesized by fungi in huge fermentation vats.

In addition, the shredded peel and juice of citrus fruits can be sweetened and jelled for use in such sweet spreads as marmalade.

The major economic value of oranges lies in their fruits, but several fragrant oils can also be extracted from their flowers, or more usually, their peel as a by–product of the orange–juice industry. These essences can be used to manufacture so–called Neroli and Portugal oils. These fragrances were originally used in the manufacturing of perfumes and to scent potpourri, and they are still used for these purposes. In addition, many household products, such as liquid detergents, shampoos, and soaps, are pleasantly scented using the aromatic oils extracted from citrus trees.

Pomanders, which are oranges studded with cloves, are an archaic use of the fruit. Originating in Spain, pomanders were worn around the neck for several purposes—as perfumery, to ward off infections, or to attract a person of the opposite sex. Today pomanders are more commonly used to pleasantly scent closets and drawers.

In regions with a warm climate, citrus trees are sometimes grown as ornamental shrubs and trees. The citron was reputedly grown in the ancient Hanging Gardens of Babylon in what is now Iraq. During those times the citron was used in scenting toilet water and in making an aromatic ointment known as pomade.

The sweet orange

The sweet orange (*Citrus sinensis*) is a 16–46 ft (5–14 m) tall tree with evergreen foliage, white flowers, and spherical fruits. This species is originally from southern China or perhaps Southeast Asia. However, the original range is somewhat uncertain, because wild plants in natural habitats are not known. The sweet orange has been cultivated in China and elsewhere in southern Asia for thousands of years, being mentioned in dated Chinese scripts from 2200 B.C. The sweet orange reached Europe as a cultivated species sometime before the fourteenth century. Sweet oranges are now grown around the world wherever the climate is suitably subtropical or tropical.

The sweet orange tends to flower and fruit during periods of relatively abundant rainfall, and becomes dormant if a pronounced drier period occurs during the summer. The sweet orange is commonly cultivated in plantations or groves. These are widely established in subtropical parts of the southern United States, particularly in southern Florida and California. Oranges are also widely grown in Mexico, Spain, the Middle East, North Africa, and many other countries, for both local use and for the export market. The global production of sweet oranges is more than 34 million tons (35 million metric tonnes) per year.

Orange fruits are very tasty and nutritious, containing 5–10% sugar, 1–2% citric acid, along with vitamin C and beneficial fiber and pulp. Most sweet oranges have an orange–colored rind when they are ripe as well as an orange interior and juice. However, some cultivated varieties of sweet oranges have a yellow or green rind, while still others have a deep–red interior and juice. Some varieties have been bred to be seedless, including, navel, Jaffa, and Malta oranges.

Oranges were a scarce and expensive fruit in past centuries, and many children were delighted to find a precious orange in their Christmas stocking. Today, however, oranges are grown in enormous quantities and are readily available as an inexpensive fruit at any time of the year.

The tangerine or mandarin orange

The tangerine and mandarin (*Citrus reticulata*) are a species of small tree native to southern China. The fruits of this species are similar to those of the sweet orange, but they are generally smaller, their rind is much easier to separate from the interior pulp, and the segments separate more readily.

Compared with the sweet orange, the tangerine and mandarin do not store very well. As a result, these citrus fruits tend to be sold fairly close to where they are grown, and less of a long–distance export market exists for these crops. However, in some countries a tradition has developed of eating mandarin oranges at certain festive times of year. For example, North Americans and many western Europeans often eat mandarins around Christmas time. Because a premium price can be obtained for these fruits during the Christmas season, there is a well organized market that keys on about a one–or–two month export market for mandarins during that festive season.

The grapefruit

The grapefruit or pomelo (*Citrus paradisi*) is a variety of cultivated citrus tree whose geographic origin is not known, but is likely native to Southeast Asia. The fruit of the grapefruit has a yellowish rind, and is relatively large, as much as 1 lb (0.5 kg) in weight. The pulp and juice of the grapefruit are rather bitter and acidic and are often sweetened with cane sugar before being eaten.

The lemon

The lemon (*C. limon*) is an evergreen tree native to Indochina and cultivated there for thousands of years. The lemon was later imported to the basin of the Mediterranean Sea, where it has been cultivated for at least 2,000 years. Lemon trees are very attractive, especially when their fragrant white or yellow flowers are in bloom. However, the fruits of lemons are quite tart and bitter, containing about 5% citric acid, but only 0.5% sugar.

The fruits of lemons are picked when they are not yet ripe and their rinds are still green. This is done because lemon fruits deteriorate quickly if they are allowed to ripen on the tree. Commercial lemons develop their more familiar, yellow–colored rinds some time after they are harvested while they are being stored or transported to markets.

Although few people have the fortitude to eat raw lemons, the processed juice of this species can be used to flavor a wide range of sweetened drinks, including lemonade. Lemon flavoring is also used to manufacture many types of carbonated beverages, often in combination with the flavoring of lime. A bleaching agent and stain remover can also be made from lemon juice.

The lime

The lime is native to Southeast Asia and is very susceptible to frost. More sour than the lemon, the lime (*C. aurantifolia*) cannot be eaten raw. However, the lime can be used to make a sweetened beverage known as limeade, and an extract of its juice is widely used to flavor commercially prepared soft drinks.

Other citrus trees

The Seville, sour, or bitter orange (*C. media*) is derived from a wild progenitor that grows in the foothills of the Himalayan Mountains of south Asia. The flowers of this species are exceedingly fragrant and have been used to produce aromatic oils for perfumery. The large orange–red fruits of the sour orange are rather bitter and acidic. These are not often eaten, but are used to make flavorings, marmalades, candied peels, aromatic oils, and to flavor a liquor known as curacao.

KEY TERMS

Cultivar—A distinct variety of a plant that has been bred for particular agricultural or culinary attributes. Cultivars are not sufficiently distinct in the genetic sense to be considered a subspecies.

Cutting—A section of a stem of a plant, which can be induced to root and can thereby be used to propagate a new plant that is genetically identical to the parent.

Grafting—A method of propagation of woody plants whereby a shoot, known as a scion, is taken from one plant and inserted into a rootstock of another plant. The desired traits of the scion for horticultural or agricultural purposes are genetically based. Through grafting, large numbers of plants with these characteristics can be readily and quickly developed.

Scurvy—A disease of humans that is caused by an insufficient supply of ascorbic acid, or vitamin C, in the diet. The symptoms of scurvy include spongy, bleeding gums, loosening and loss of teeth, and subcutaneous bleeding. It can ultimately lead to death.

Tissue culture—This is a relatively recently developed method of growing large numbers of genetically identical plants. In tissue culture, small quantities of undifferentiated cells are grown on an artificial growth medium, and are then caused to develop into small plantlets by subjecting them to specific treatments with growth-regulating hormones.

The citron (*C. medica*) is another species native to the southern Himalayas, probably in northern India. This may be the oldest of the cultivated citrus trees, perhaps going back as far as 6,000 years. The fruit of this species is very large in comparison to those of other citrus trees, weighing as much as 6.5 lb (3 kg). The rind of the citron is thick and has a lumpy surface, and the pulpy interior is bitter. The peel of the citron is soaked in salty water, which removes much of the bitter taste. It is then candied with sugar and used to flavor cakes, pastries, and candies.

The shaddock or pomelo (*C. maxima*) is probably native to Southeast Asia. This species is mostly used to manufacture candied rind. The pomelo develops a large, spherical, thick–rinded fruit, weighing as much as 13 lb (6 kg), and having a diameter of up to 6 in (16 cm). The name shaddock comes from the name of a sea captain who first introduced this species to the West Indies.

Other relatively minor species of citrus trees include the Panama orange or calamondin (*C. mitis*) and the bergamot (*C. bergamia*).

See also Citric acid; Graft; Mycorrhiza; Vitamin.

Further Reading:

Hvass, E. *Plants That Serve and Feed Us*. New York: Hippocrene Books, 1975.

Klein, R. M. *The Green World. An Introduction to Plants and People*. New York: Harper and Row, 1987.

Woodland, D. W. *Contemporary Plant Systematics*. Upper Saddle River, NJ: Prentice–Hall, 1991.

Bill Freedman

Civets

Small to medium–sized carnivores, civets are in the Viverridae family which includes genets, linsangs, and mongooses. There are 35 species of civets and gentes in 20 genera. Their natural distribution is restricted to the warmer regions of the Old World, and they occupy a niche similarly filled by the weasels and their relatives found in temperate deciduous forests. Civets vary in size, form, but most present a catlike appearance with long noses, slender bodies, pointed ears, short legs and generally a long furry tail.

Civets with a spotted or striped coat have five toes on each foot. There is webbing between the toes and the claws are totally or semi–retractile. The pointed ears extend above the profile of the head. The ear flaps have pockets or bursae on the outside margins, similar to domestic cats. Their teeth are specialized for an omnivorous diet, including shearing carnassial teeth and flat–crowned molars in both upper and lower jaws. Teeth number from 38–40, depending on the species.

Primarily nocturnal foragers with semiarboreal and arboreal habits, civets typically ambush their prey. During the day, civets usually rest in a hollow tree, rock crevice or empty, shallow burrow. They are solitary animals maintaining a wide home range (250 acres) by scent marking trees on the borders of their territory. The term "civet" is derived from an Arabic word describing the oily fluid and its odor secreted by the perineal glands. Scent marking is important in civet communication, but the method differs among species from passively passing the scent when moving about causing the gland to rub

vegetation to squatting and then wiping or rubbing the gland on the ground or some prominent object.

Civet oil has been used in the perfume industry for centuries and has been recorded as being imported from Africa by King Solomon in the 10th century B.C. Once refined, civet oil is prized for its odor and long lasting properties. Civet oil is also valued for its medicinal uses which include the reduction of perspiration, a cure for some skin disorders and claims of aphrodisiac powers. Although the development of sensitive chemical substitutes have decreased the value of civet oil, it is still a part of some East African and Oriental economies.

The Viverridae family can be broken into six subfamilies. There are seven southern Asian and one African species of palm civets (subfamily Paradoxurinae). The African palm civet, also known as the two–spotted palm civet, spends most of its time in the forest canopy where it feeds primarily on fruit occasionally supplemented with small mammals, birds, insects, and lizards. It is distinguished by its semi–retractile claws and perineal gland covered by a single fold of skin. All other species of palm civets live in the forests of Asia. Their semiarboreal life style is supported by sharp, curved retractile claws, hairless soles, and partially fused third and fourth toes which add to a more sure–footed grasp. Although skillful climbers, they spend considerable time foraging on the ground for animals and fallen fruits. The broad–faced binturong, or bear cat, has a strong muscular long–haired tail that is prehensile at the tip. This characteristic is unique among viverrids. The body hair is long and coarse. The ears have long black tufts of hair with white margins. Nearly four feet long, it is the largest member of the civet family. Despite its mostly vegetarian diet, binturongs have been reported to swim in rivers and prey on fish. The celebes, giant, or brown palm civet may be fairly common in certain limited areas (known by its tracks and feces, rather than by actual sightings). It is quite adept at climbing and has a web of thin skin between the toes.

There are five species of banded palm civets and otter civets (subfamily Hemigalinae), all living in the forests of Southeast Asia. Perhaps best known is the banded palm civet, named for the dark brown markings on its coat. The general coat color ranges from pale yellow to grayish–buff. The face is distinctly marked by several dark longitudinal stripes. The coloration of the body is broken by about five transverse bands stretching midway down the flank. The tail is dark on its lower half, with two broad dark rings at the base. Foraging at night on the ground and in trees, the banded palm civet searches for rats, lizards, frogs, snails, crabs, earthworms and ants.

KEY TERMS

. . . .

Aphrodisiac—Stimulating or intensifying sexual desire.

Arboreal—Living in trees.

Bursae—Pockets; a saclike body cavity.

Carnassial—The last upper premolar and the first lower molar teeth in carnivorous mammals.

Niche—The area within a habitat occupied by an organism.

Omnivorous—Eating all kinds of food.

Perineal—The region between the scrotum and the anus in males and between the posterior vulva junction and the anus in females.

Prehensile—Adapted for seizing or holding, especially by wrapping around an object.

Retractile—Able to pull back in; withdraw.

Terrestrial—Of or pertaining to the earth and its inhabitants.

Otter civets could be mistaken for long–nosed otters. Similar in habit and appearance, otter civets are excellent swimmers and capable of climbing trees. Their toes are partially webbed, but their dense water repellant fur, thick whiskers, and valve–like nostrils are effective adaptations for living in water and preying on fish. There are two species which show differences in their coat coloration and number of teeth. Otter civets have smaller ears, blunter muzzles, shorter tails and more compact bodies than most banded palm civets.

There are 19 species of true civets and genets classified in the subfamily Viverrinae. One of the best known is the African civet. A rather large, heavily built, long–bodied and long–legged carnivore, it is the most doglike viverrid. Preferring to be near water, it lives in a variety of habitats ranging from moist tropical forest to dry scrub savannah. It is considered terrestrial, climbing trees only in an emergency such as when hunted. The African civet hunts exclusively on the ground at night, resting in thickets or burrows during the day. An opportunistic and omnivorous predator, it will eat carrion, but prefers small mammals. Birds, eggs, amphibians, reptiles, invertebrates, fruit, berries, and vegetation round out its diet. African civets deposit their droppings in one place creating middens or "civetries." Although typically found at territorial boundaries, they also mark their territory using their perineal gland.

Betsy A. Leonard

Clams see **Bivalves**

Classical mechanics see **Newton's laws of motion**

Clay see **Sediment and sedimentation**

Clay minerals see **Minerals**

Climatology see **Weather**

Climax (ecological)

Climax is a theoretical, ecological notion intended to describe a relatively stable community that is in equilibrium with environmental conditions, and occurring as the terminal, end–point of succession.

One of the early proponents of the concept of climax was the American ecologist, Frederic Clements. In an important publication in 1916, he theorized that there was only one true climax community for any given climatic region. This so–called climatic climax would be the eventual end–point of all successions, whether they started after fire, deglaciation, or other disturbances, or even from a pond or lake filling in, and regardless of soil type. This monoclimax theory was criticized as too simple, and was challenged by other ecologists. A.G. Tansley proposed a more realistic polyclimax theory that accommodated the important successional influences of local soil type, topography, and disturbance history. In the early 1950s, R.H. Whittaker suggested that there were gradually varying climax types on the landscape, associated with continuous gradients of environmental variables. According to Whittaker, ecological communities vary continuously, and climax communities cannot be objectively divided into discrete types.

In a practical sense, it is not possible to identify the occurrence of a climax community. The climax condition may be suggested by relatively slow rates of change in the structure and function of old–growth communities, compared with earlier, more dynamic stages of succession. However, change in ecological communities is a universal phenomenon, so the climax state cannot be regarded as static. For example, even in old–growth communities microsuccession is always occurring, associated perhaps with the death of individual trees. Moreover, if the frequency of return of stand–level disturbance events is relatively short, the old–growth or climax condition will not be reached.

See also Old–growth forest; Succession.

Clingfish

Clingfish are about 100 species of small, ray-finned bony fish found primarily in tropical marine waters. They belong to the family Gobiesocidae in the order Gobiesociformes. Clingfish are shaped like a tadpole with a wide, flattened head; they have no scales and are covered with a thick coating of slime that makes them very slippery. Clingfish are characterized by a large suction disc formed by the union of the pelvic fins and adjacent folds of flesh. This disc allows clingfish to attach themselves to the bottom and, in this way, they are able to withstand strong currents. Clingfish have a single dorsal fin and no spines. Most species of clingfish are small, about 4 in (10 cm) or less in length, but the rocksucker (*Chorisochismus dentex*) clingfish of South Africa may grow as large as 12 in (30 cm) long.

Clingfish are most commonly found in the intertidal zone of oceans worldwide. A number of species inhabit Caribbean waters, and about 20 species are found along the Pacific coast of North America. Among these North American species is the northern clingfish (*Gobiesox meandricus*) which is found from California to Alaska; this species averages 6 in (15 cm) in length. Six other species of *Gobiesox* inhabit the North American coastal waters of the Atlantic Ocean. The most common of these species is the skilletfish (*G. strumosus*), a drab, dusky fish measuring 4 in (10 cm) in length.

Clone and cloning

A clone is a cell, group of cells, or organism produced by asexual reproduction which contains genetic information identical to the parent cell or organism. Although some organisms reproduce asexually naturally, the first artificial cloning by humans were plants developed from grafts and stem cuttings. Cloning involving complex laboratory techniques is a relatively recent scientific advance that is at the forefront of modern biology. Among these techniques is the ability to isolate and make copies of (clone) individual genes that direct an organism's development. Cloning has many promising applications in medicine, industry, and basic research.

History of cloning

Humans have manipulated plant asexual reproduction through methods like grafting and stem cuttings for more than 2,000 years. The modern era of laboratory cloning began in 1958 when F. C. Steward cloned carrot plants from mature single cells placed in a nutrient culture containing hormones. The first cloning of animal cells took place in 1964 when John B. Gurdon took the nuclei from intestinal cells of toad tadpoles and injected them into unfertilized eggs whose nuclei containing the original parents' genetic information had been destroyed with ultraviolet light. When the eggs were incubated, Gurdon found that 1–2% of the eggs developed into fertile, adult toads.

The first successful cloning of mammals was achieved nearly 20 years later when scientists in both Switzerland and the United States successfully cloned mice using a method similar to Gurdon's approach; but, their method required one extra step. After the nuclei was taken from the embryos of one type of mouse, they were transferred into the embryos of another type of mouse who served as a surrogate mother that went through the birthing process to create the cloned mice. The cloning of cattle livestock was achieved in 1988 when embryos from prize cows were transplanted to unfertilized cow eggs whose own nuclei had been removed.

The cloning process

Simple organisms are relatively easy to clone. In some cases entire cells can be inserted into bacteria or a yeast culture that reproduce asexually. As these cultures multiply, so do the inserted cells.

The cloning of animal cells in laboratories has been achieved through several methods, including inserting the nucleus of an animal cell into a fertilized egg cell with its own nucleus removed. Another method is to divide embryo tissues and insert them into surrogate mothers where they then develop normally.

In 1993, the first human embryos were cloned using a technique that placed individual embryonic cells (blastomeres) in a nutrient culture where the cells then divided into 48 new embryos. These experiments were conducted as part of some studies on in vitro (out of the body) fertilization aimed at developing fertilized eggs in test tubes which could then be implanted into the wombs of women having difficulty becoming pregnant. However, these fertilized eggs did not develop to a stage that was suitable for transplantation into a human uterus.

The cloning of specific genes can provide large numbers of copies of the gene for use in genetics, medical research, and systematics. Gene cloning begins by separating a specific length of DNA that contains the target gene. This fragment is then placed into another

DNA molecule, called the vector, which is then called a recombinant DNA molecule. The recontainment DNA molecule is then used to transport the gene into a host cell, such as a bacterium, where the vector DNA multiplies through cell division, to produce many copies, or clones, of the target gene.

The benefits of cloning

Cloning cells promises to produce many benefits in farming, medicine, and basic research. In the realm of farming, the goal is to clone plants that contain specific traits that make them superior to naturally occurring plants. For example, in 1985 field tests were conducted using clones of plants whose genes had been altered in the laboratory (by genetic engineering) to produce resistance to insects, viruses, and bacteria. New strains of plants resulting from the cloning of specific traits could also lead to fruits and vegetables with improved nutritional qualities and longer shelf lives, or new strains of plants that can grow in poor soil or even under water. A cloning technique known as twinning could induce livestock to give birth to twins or even triplets, thus reducing the amount of feed needed to produce meat. Cloning also holds promise for saving certain rare breeds of animals from extinction.

In the realm of medicine and health, gene cloning has been used to produce vaccines and hormones. Cloning techniques have already led to the inexpensive production of the hormone insulin for treating diabetes and of growth hormones for children who do not produce enough hormones for normal growth. The use of monoclonal antibodies in disease treatment and research involves combining two different kinds of cells (such as mouse and human cancer cells), to produce large quantities of specific antibodies, which are produced by the immune system to fight off disease. These cloned antibodies when injected into the blood stream seek out and attack disease causing cells anywhere in the body. By attaching a tracer element to the cloned antibodies, scientists can locate hidden cancers. By attaching specific cancer–fighting drugs to the cloned antibody, the treatment dose can be transported directly to the cancer cells.

The ethics of cloning

Despite the benefits of cloning and its many promising avenues of research, certain ethical questions concerning the possible abuse of cloning have been raised. At the heart of these questions is the idea of humans tampering with life in a way that could harm society, either morally or in a real physical sense.

KEY TERMS

Blastomeres—Individual embryonic cells.

Chromosome—Threadlike structures in the cell that carry most of the genetic material in the form of DNA and genes.

Cell cycle—A cycle of growth and cellular reproduction which includes nuclear division (mitosis) and cell division (cytokinesis).

Genetic engineering—The process of combining specific genes to attain desired traits.

DNA (deoxyribonucleic acid)—The specific molecules that make up chromosomes and house genes.

Embryo—The earliest stage of animal development in the uterus before the animal is considered a fetus (which is usually the point at which the embryo takes on the basic physical form of its species).

Genetics—The study of hereditary traits passed on through the genes.

Genes—Specific biological components that carry the instructions for the formation of an organisms and its specific traits, such as eye or hair color.

Heredity—Characteristics passed on from parents to offspring.

Hybrid—The offspring resulting from combination of two different varieties of plants.

Nucleus (plural nuclei)—The part of the cell that contains most of its genetic material, including chromosomes and DNA.

Despite these concerns, there is little doubt that cloning will continue to be used. Many countries, such as Germany, are already developing laws governing cloning procedures, hoping to assure that cloning is used solely for the benefit of society.

See also Asexual reproduction; Gene splicing; Genetic engineering.

Further Reading:

Adler, Jerry. "Clone Hype (Controversy Over Advances in In–Vitro Fertilization." *Newsweek* (8 November 1993): 60.

Brown, T. A. *Gene Cloning: An Introduction.* New York: Chapman and Hall, 1990.

Ellstrand, Norman C. "The Cloning of America." *Omni* (October 1988): 49.

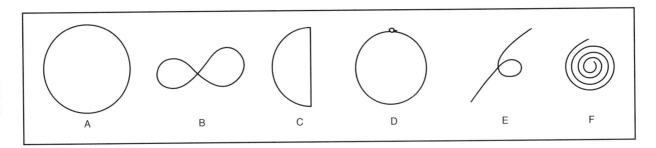

Figure 1.

Fackelmann, Kathy A. "Cloning Human Embryos: Exploring the Science of a Controversial Experiment." *Science News* (5 February 1994): 88.

"Hunting Down Genes that Say 'No' to Disease." *Business Week* (13 December 1993): 113.

Hyde, Margaret O., and Lawrence E. Hyde. *Cloning and the New Genetics.* Springfield, NJ: Enslow Publishers, 1984.

David Petechuk

Closed curves

A closed curve is one which can be drawn without lifting the pencil from the paper and which ends at the point where it began. In Figure 1, A, B, and C are closed curves; D, E, and F are not.

Curve A is a circle. Although the starting point is not indicated, any of its points can be chosen to serve that purpose. Curve B crosses itself and is therefore not a "simple" closed curve, but it is a closed curve. Curve C has a straight portion, but "curve" as used in mathematics includes straight lines as well as those that bend. Curve D, in which the tiny circle indicates a single missing point, fails for either of two reasons. If the starting point is chosen somewhere along the curve, then the one–point gap is a discontinuity. One cannot draw it without lifting the pencil. If one tries instead to start the curve at the point next to the gap, there is no point "next to" the gap. Between any two distinct points on a continuous curve there is always another point. Whatever point one chooses, there will always be an undrawn point between it and the gap—in fact an infinitude of such points. Curve E has a closed portion, but the tails keep the curve as a whole from being closed. Curve F simply fails to end where it began.

Curves can be described statically as sets of points. For example, the sets {P: PC = r, where C is a fixed point and r a positive constant} and {(x,y): $x^2 + y^2 = r^2$} describe circles. The descriptions are static in the way a pile of bricks is static. Points either belong to the sets or they don't; except for set membership, there is no obvious connection between the points.

Although such descriptions are very useful, they have their limitations. For one thing it is not obvious that they describe curves as opposed, say, to surfaces (in fact, the first describes a sphere or a circle, depending on the space in which one is working). For another, they omit any sense of continuity or movement. A planet's path around the sun is an ellipse, but it doesn't occupy every point on the ellipse simultaneously, and it doesn't hop from point to point. It moves continuously along the curve as a function of time. A dynamic description of its path is more useful than a static one. Curves are therefore often described as paths, as the position of a point, P(t), which varies continuously as a function of time (or some analogous variable) which increases from some value a to a value b. If the variable t does not represent time, then it represents a variable which increases continuously as time does, such as the angle formed by the earth, the sun, and a reference star.

However it is described, a curve is one–dimensional. It may be drawn in three–dimensional space, or on a two–dimensional surface such as a plane, but the curve itself is one–dimensional. It has one degree of freedom.

A person on a roller coaster experiences this. The car on which he is riding loops, dives, and twists, but it does not leave the track. As time passes, it makes its way from the starting point, along the track, and finally back to the starting point. Its position is a function of a single variable, called a "parameter," time.

A good way to describe a circle as a path is to use trigonometric functions: P(t) = (r cos t, r sin t), where P(t) is a point on the coordinate plane. This describes a circle of radius r with its center at the origin. If t is mea-

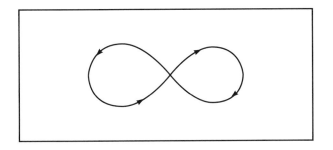

Figure 2.

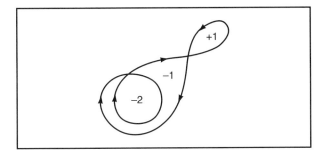

Figure 3.

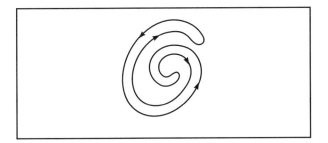

Figure 4.

sured in degrees, varying over the closed interval [90,450], the curve will start at (0,1) and, since the sine and cosine of 90° are equal to the sine and cosine of 450°, will end there. If the interval over which t varies is the open interval (90,450), it will be the circle with one point missing shown in Figure 1, and will not be closed.

Not all curves can be represented as neatly as circles, but from a topological point of view, that doesn't matter. There are properties which certain closed curves share regardless of the way in which P(t) is represented.

One of the properties is that of being a "simple" closed curve. In Figure 1, curve B was not a simple curve; it crossed itself. There were two values of t, call them t_1 and t_2, for which $P(t_1) = P(t_2)$. If there are no

such values—if different values of t always give different points, then the curve is simple.

Another property is a sense of direction along the curve. On the roller coaster, as time passes, the car gets closer and closer to the end of the ride (to the relief of some of its passengers). On the circle described above, P(t) moves counterclockwise around it. If, in Figure 2, a toy train were started so that it traversed the left loop in a counterclockwise direction, it would traverse the other loop in a clockwise direction. This can be indicated with arrowheads.

Associated with each closed part of a closed curve is a "winding number." In the case of the circle above, the winding number would be +1. A person standing inside the circle watching P(t) move around the circle would have to make one complete revolution to keep the point in view. Since such a person would have to rotate counterclockwise, the winding number is arbitrarily considered positive.

In the same way, a person standing inside the left loop of Figure 2 would rotate once counterclockwise. Watching the point traverse the right loop would necessitate some turning first to the left and then to the right, but the partial revolutions would cancel out. The winding number for the left loop is therefore +1. The winding number for the right loop, based on the number of revolutions someone standing inside that loop would have to make, would be –1.

In Figure 3 the winding numbers are as shown.

The reader can check this. In Figure 4, although the curve is quite contorted, the winding number is +1.

This illustrates a fundamental fact about simple closed curves: their winding numbers are always +1 or –1.

Being or not being closed is a propery of a curve that can survive a variety of geometrical transformations. One can rotate a figure, stretch it in one direction or two, shrink it, shear it, or reflect it without breaking it open or closing it. One transformation that is a notable exception to this is a projection. When one projects a circle, as with a slide projector, one can, by adjusting the angle of the screen, turn that circle into an open parabola or hyperbola.

Further Reading:

Chinn, W. G., and Steenrod, N. E. *First Concepts of Topology*, Washington, D.C.: The Mathematical Association of America, 1966.

J. Paul Moulton

Closed interval see **Interval**

Closure property

"Closure" is a property which a set either has or lacks with respect to a given operation. A set is closed with respect to that operation if the operation can always be completed with elements in the set.

For example, the set of even natural numbers, 2, 4, 6, 8, ..., is closed with respect to addition because the sum of any two of them is another even natural number. It is not closed with respect to division because the quotients 6/2 and 4/8, for instance, cannot be computed without using odd numbers of fractions.

Knowing the operations for which a given set is closed helps one understand the nature of the set. Thus one knows that the set of natural numbers is less versatile than the set of integers because the latter is closed with respect to subtraction, but the former is not. Similarly one knows that the set of polynomials is much like the set of integers because both sets are closed under addition, multiplication, negation, and subtraction, but are not closed under division.

Particularly interesting examples of closure are the positive and negative numbers. In mathematical structure these two sets are indistinguishable except for one property, closure with respect to multiplication. Once one decides that the product of two positive numbers is positive, the other rules for multiplying and dividing various combinations of positive and negative numbers follow. Then, for example, the product of two negative numbers must be positive, and so on.

The lack of closure is one reason for enlarging a set. For example, without augmenting the set of rational numbers with the irrationals, one cannot solve an equation such as $x2 =2$, which can arise from the use of the pythagorean theorem. Without extending the set of real numbers to include imaginary numbers, one cannot

solve an equation such as $x^2 + 1=0$, contrary to the fundamental theorem of algebra.

Closure can be associated with operations on single numbers as well as operations between two numbers. When the Pythagoreans discovered that the square root of 2 was not rational, they had discovered that the rationals were not closed with respect to taking roots.

Although closure is usually thought of as a property of sets of ordinary numbers, the concept can be applied to other kinds of mathematical elements. It can be applied to sets of rigid motions in the plane, to vectors, to matrices, and to other things. For example, one can say that the set of three–by–three matrices is closed with respect to addition.

Closure, or the lack of it, can be of practical concern, too. Inexpensive, four–function calculators rarely allow one to use negative numbers as inputs. Nevertheless, if one subtracts a larger number from a smaller number, the calculator will complete the operation and display the negative number which results. On the other hand, if one divides 1 by 3, the calculator will display .333333, which is close, but not exact. If an operation takes a calculator beyond the numbers it can use, the answer it displays will be wrong, perhaps significantly so.

Cloud chamber see **Particle detectors**

Clouds

All clouds are a form of water. Clouds are condensed atmospheric moisture in the form of minute water droplets or ice crystals. The creation of a cloud begins at ground level. The sun heats the earth's surface, the warm ground heats the air, which rises. The air contains variable amounts of water, as vapor, that has evaporated from bodies of water and plants. Air at ground level is denser than air higher up, and as the warm air rises, it expands and becomes less dense. Expansion cools the air and as the air cools, the water vapor that is present in the air, condenses into tiny microscopic droplets. Cloud formation depends on how much water is in the atmosphere, the temperature, the air current, and topography. If there is no water, no clouds can form. If condensation occurs below the freezing point, the cloud is made of ice crystals. Warm and cold air fronts, as well as topography can control how air rises. Clouds that form during vigorous uplift of

Cirrus clouds (top) and cumulus clouds (bottom).

air have a tall, stacked appearance and clouds formed by gentle uplift of air currents have a flat or stratified appearance. One can make short–term forecasts by observing clouds, as any change in the way a cloud looks indicates a change in the weather.

Classification

A couple of hundred years ago clouds were not identified by name. Luke Howard, an English pharmacist and amateur naturalist, developed a system of classification (from Latin) for clouds in 1803. Howard categorized clouds into three major groups: cumulus (accumulate or piled up heaps and puffs), cirrus (fibrous and curly), and stratus (stretched out and layered). To further describe clouds, he combined those terms and used other descriptive words such as, alto (high), and nimbus (rain). Today, the International Cloud Classification is based on Howard's system.

There are three basic forms of clouds: cirrus, cumulus, and stratus. All clouds are either purely these forms, or a combination or modification of the basic forms. Since there is more water vapor at lower elevations, lower clouds appear denser than higher, thin clouds.

Cloud categories

Today, there are 10 characteristic forms or genera of clouds recognized by the International Cloud Classification, and there are three height categories with an established altitude range for each category. Low–level clouds range from the surface to 6,500 ft (2,000 m), mid–level from 6,500–23,000 ft (2,000–7,000 m) and high–level, generally above 20,000 ft (6,000 m). Below is a brief description of each category and their genera.

Nimbus category

There are two genera of rain clouds, cumulonimbus and nimbostratus. Nimbostratus clouds are usually mid level clouds, thick, dark, gray, and sometimes seen with "virga" or skirts of rain trailing down. These clouds are made of water droplets that produce either rain or snow. Cumulonimbus clouds are thunderstorm clouds, and arise from cumulus clouds that have reached a great height. When the cloud normally reaches the height of the tropopause above, it flattens out, resembling an anvil. All phases of water, gas, liquid, and solid, are contained in these clouds. There are powerful updrafts and downdrafts that can create violent storms.

High clouds

The altitude range for these clouds is 16,500-45,000 ft (5,032–13,725 m) but they usually form between 20,000–25,000 ft (6,000–7,500 m). There are three genera of high level clouds and they are all labeled with the term cirrus. Cirrus clouds are the highest clouds, forming around 30,000 ft (9,150 m). They are totally made of ice crystals (or needles of ice) because they form where freezing temperatures prevail. Pure cirrus clouds look wispy, with a slight curl, and very white. Because of their appearance, they are often called mares' tails. Cirrocumulus clouds, the least common cloud, are small, white or pale gray, with a rippled appearance. Sometimes they appear like a sky full of fish scales; this effect is called a mackerel sky. These clouds usually cover a large area. They form around 20–25,000 ft (6,000–7,500 m) and are made of either supercooled water droplets or ice crystals. Cirrostratus also form at 20–25,000 ft, but are made completely of ice crystals. They usually cover the sky as a thin veil or sheet of white. These clouds are responsible for the halos that occur around the sun or moon. The term "on cloud nine" (feeling of euphoria) is derived from the fact that the highest clouds are labeled category nine.

Middle level clouds

The mid level clouds 6,500–23,000 ft (2,000–7,000 m) typically have the prefix "alto" added to the two genera in this category. Altostratus clouds appear as a uniform bluish or gray sheet covering all, or large areas of the sky. The sun or moon may be totally covered or shine through very weakly. These clouds are complex as they are usually layered, with ice crystals at the higher, top layers, ice and snow in the middle, and water droplets in the lower layers. Altostratus clouds often yield precipitation. Altocumulus are elliptical, dense, fluffy balls. They are seen as singular units or as closely bunched groups in a clear sky. When the sun or moon shines through these clouds, one can sometimes see the "sun's rays" or corona.

Low level clouds

There are three genera in the low level (surface to 6,500 ft [2,000 m]). Stratus clouds are usually the lowest of the three genera. Stratus clouds blanket the sky and usually appear gray. They form when a large mass of air rises slowly and the water vapor condenses as the air becomes cooler, or when cool air moves in over an area close to ground level. These clouds often produce mist or drizzle. Fog is a stratus cloud at ground level. Cumulus clouds have flat bases, are vertically thick, and appear puffy. Inside a cumulus cloud are updrafts that create the cloud's appearance. They form when a column of warm air rises, expands, cools, and condenses. Cumulus clouds occur primarily in warm weather. They consist of water droplets and appear white because the sunlight reflects off the droplets. Thick clouds appear darker at the bottom because the sunlight is partially blocked. Cumulus clouds can develop into cumulonimbus clouds. Stratocumulus clouds are large, grayish masses, spread out in a puffy layer. Sometimes they appear as rolls. These clouds appear darker and heavier than the altocumulus cloud. They can transform into nimbostratus clouds.

Unusual clouds

Beside the basic cloud types, there are subgroups and some unusual cloud formations. Terms such as humulus (fair weather), and congestus (rainshower) are used to further describe the cumulus genus. Fractus (jagged), castellanus (castle shaped), and uncinus (hook shaped) are other descriptive terms used together with some basic cloud types. In mountainous regions, lenticular clouds are a common sight. They form only over mountain peaks and resemble a stack of different layers of cloud matter. Noctilucent clouds form only between sunset and sunrise, and are only seen in high latitude countries. Contrails (condensation trails) are artificial clouds formed from the engine exhaust of high altitude aircraft.

See also Precipitation; Weather forecasting; Weather modification.

Further Reading:

Hobbs, Peter V. and A. Deepak. *Clouds: Their Formation. Optical Properties and Effects.* New York: Academic Press, Inc., 1981.
Roth, Charles E. *The Sky Observer's Guidebook.* New York: Prentice Hall Press, 1986.
Rubin, Louis D. Sr., and Jim Duncan. *The Weather Wizard's Cloud Book.* Chapel Hill: Algonquin Books of Chapel Hill, 1984.
Shafer, Vincent J., and John A Day. *A Field Guide to the Atmosphere.* Boston: Houghton Mifflin Co., 1981.

Christine Minderovic

Cloud seeding see **Weather modification**

Clover see **Legumes**

Clove tree see **Myrtle family**

Club mosses

Club mosses, also called lycophytes, are flowerless and seedless plants in the family Lycopodiaceae, which belongs to an ancient group of plants of the division Lycophyta. The lycophytes were one of the dominant plants during the Coal Age (360–286 million years ago) and many were shrubs or large trees. By 250 million years ago, most of the woody species had died out. Between 10 and 15 living genera have been recognized, consisting of about 400 species. Lycopodiaceae are cosmopolitan, occurring in arctic to tropical regions. Nowhere do they dominate plant communities today as they did in the past. In arctic and temperate regions, club mosses are terrestrial; whereas in the tropics, they are mostly epiphytes near the tops of trees and seldom seen. The classification of club mosses has changed radically in recent years. Most temperate species were grouped within the genus *Lycopodium*, from the Greek *lycos*, meaning wolf, and *pous* meaning foot, in an imaginative reference to the resemblance in some species of the densely–leaved branch tips to a wolf's foot. However, it is now clear that fundamental differences exist among the club mosses with respect to a variety of important characters. Seven genera and 27 species have been recognized in the flora of North America. Four of the common genera, formerly all within the genus *Lycopodium*, are *Lycopodium*, the tree club mosses (6 species), *Diphasiastrum*, the club mosses (5 species), *Huperzia*, the fir mosses (7 species), and *Lycopodiella*, the bog club mosses (6 species); all are terrestrial. The sole epiphytic member of the club moss family in North America is the hanging fir moss (*Phlegmariurus dichotomus*), which is common in subtropical and tropical Central and South America. In North America it is known only from Big Cypress Swamp, Florida.

Unlike some of the other ancient plants, such as liverworts, the sporophytes of club mosses are clearly differentiated into root, stem, and leaves. All living club mosses are perennial herbs that typically possess underground stems that branch and give rise to shoots that rarely exceed 7.9 in (20 cm) in height. Although the photosynthetic organs of club mosses are commonly called leaves, technically speaking they are microphylls and differ from true leaves in that they contain only one unbranched strand of conducting tissue. The "micro" in the name does not necessarily mean that these photosynthetic organs are small, in fact some microphylls of extinct tree lycophytes were 3.3 ft (1 m) long. Micro refers to the evolution of the structure from an initially very small flap of tissue that grew along the stem of primitive leafless plants, and that eventually, through

KEY TERMS

Gametophyte—Individual plant containing only one set of chromosomes per cell that produces gametes i.e. reproductive cells that must fuse with other reproductive cells to produce a new individual.

Sporophyte—Individual plant containing two sets of chromosomes per cell that produces spores, which on germination give rise to gametophytes.

evolution, grew larger and had a strand of conducting tissue enter it to produce the modern type of microphyll. Microphylls are generally needle–like, spear–shaped, or ovate and arranged spirally along the stem, but occasionally appear opposite or whorled. The habit of evergreen leaves on stems that in some species run along the ground has given rise to the common name of ground or running pines. Stems have a primitive vascular tissue composed of a solid, central column.

Spores, all of one type, are produced in sporangia that occur either singly on fertile leaves (sporophylls) that look much like non–fertile leaves or on modified leaves that are tightly appressed on the tip of a branch producing a cone or club–like structure, hence the name club moss. The cones may or may not be stalked. The spores germinate to produce bisexual gametophytes that are either green and photosynthetic on the soil surface or are underground and non–photosynthetic, in the latter case deriving some of their nourishment from mycorrhyzae. The maturation of a gametophyte may require 6–15 years. Biflagellated sperm are produced in an antheridium (male reproductive organ) and an egg is produced in a flask–shaped archegonium (female reproductive organ). Water is required for the sperm to swim to another gametophyte and down the neck of an archegonium to reach the egg at the bottom. The young sporophyte produced after fertilization may remain attached for many years, and in some species the gametophyte may continue to grow and produce a succession of young sporophytes.

Club mosses are ecologically minor components of all the ecosystems in which they occur. Their economic importance is also slight. Many club mosses produce masses of sulpher–colored spores that are highly inflammable and were therefore once used as a constituent of flash powder in early photography and in fireworks. The spores were also formerly used by pharmacists to coat pills. In parts of eastern North America, local cottage industries have sprung up to collect club mosses in order to make the most elegant of Christmas wreaths. Spores of common club moss (*Lycopodium clavatum*) are used by paleoecologists to calibrate the number of fossil pollen grains in samples of lake mud. Some Druid sects considered club mosses to be sacred plants and had elaborate rituals to collect club mosses and display them on their alters for good luck.

See also Liverwort; Spore.

Further Reading:

Flora of North America Editorial Committee, eds. *Pterido-phytes and Gymnosperms*. Vol. 2 of *Flora of North America*. New York: Oxford University Press, 1993.

Raven, P. H., R. F. Evert, and S. E. Eichhorn. *Biology of Plants*. 5th ed. New York: Worth Publishers, 1992.

Les C. Cwynar

Cnidarians see **Corals**

Coal

Coal is a naturally occurring combustible material consisting primarily of the element carbon, but with low percentages of solid, liquid, and gaseous hydrocarbons and other materials, such as compounds of nitrogen and sulfur. Coal is usually classified into the sub–groups known as anthracite, bituminous, lignite, and peat. The physical, chemical, and other properties of coal vary considerably from sample to sample.

Origins of coal

Coal forms primarily from ancient plant material that accumulated in surface environments where the complete decay of organic matter was prevented. For example, a plant that died in a swampy area would quickly be covered with water, silt, sand, and other sediments. These materials prevented the plant debris from reacting with oxygen and decomposing to carbon dioxide and water, as would occur under normal circumstances. Instead, anaerobic bacteria (bacteria that do not require oxygen to live) attacked the plant debris and converted it to simpler forms: primarily pure carbon and simple compounds of carbon and hydrogen (hydrocarbons). Because of the way it is formed, coal (along with petroleum and natural gas) is often referred to as a fossil fuel.

The initial stage of the decay of a dead plant is a soft, woody material known as peat. In some parts of

A coal seam in northwest Colorado.

the world, peat is still collected from boggy areas and used as a fuel. It is not a good fuel, however, as it burns poorly and with a great deal of smoke.

If peat is allowed to remain in the ground for long periods of time, it eventually becomes compacted as layers of sediment, known as overburden, collect above it. The additional pressure and heat of the overburden gradually converts peat into another form of coal known as lignite or brown coal. Continued compaction by overburden then converts lignite into bituminous (or soft) coal and finally, anthracite (or hard) coal. Coal has been formed at many times in the past, but most abundantly during the Carboniferous Age (about 300 million years ago) and again during the Upper Cretaceous Age (about 100 million years ago).

Today, coal formed by these processes is often found in layers between layers of sedimentary rock. In some cases, the coal layers may lie at or very near the earth's surface. In other cases, they may be buried thousands of feet or meters under ground. Coal seams range from no more than 3–197 ft (1–60 m) or more in thickness. The location and configuration of a coal seam determines the method by which the coal will be mined.

Composition of coal

Coal is classified according to its heating value and according to its relative content of elemental carbon. For example, anthracite contains the highest proportion of pure carbon—about 86%–98%—and has the highest heat value—13,500–15,600 Btu/lb (British thermal units per pound)—of all forms of coal. Bituminous coal generally has lower concentrations of pure carbon (from 46%–86%) and lower heat values (8,300–15,600 Btu/lb). Bituminous coals are often sub–divided on the basis of their heat value, being classified as low, medium, and high volatile bituminous and sub–bituminous. Lignite, the poorest of the true coals in terms of heat value (5,500–8,300 Btu/lb) generally contains about 46%–60% pure carbon. All forms of coal also contain other elements present in living organisms, such as sulfur and nitrogen, that are very low in absolute numbers, but that have important environmental consequences when coals are used as fuels.

Properties and reactions

By far the most important property of coal is that it combusts. When the pure carbon and hydrocarbons found in coal burn completely only two products are formed, carbon dioxide and water. During this chemical reaction, a relatively large amount of energy is released. The release of heat when coal is burned explains the fact that the material has long been used by humans as a source of energy, for the heating of homes and other buildings, to run ships and trains, and in many industrial processes.

Environmental problems associated with the burning of coal

The complete combustion of carbon and hydrocarbons described above rarely occurs in nature. If the temperature is not high enough or sufficient oxygen is not provided to the fuel, combustion of these materials is usually incomplete. During the incomplete combustion of carbon and hydrocarbons, other products besides carbon dioxide and water are formed, primarily carbon monoxide, hydrogen, and other forms of pure carbon, such as soot.

During the combustion of coal, minor constituents are also oxidized. Sulfur is converted to sulfur dioxide and sulfur trioxide, and nitrogen compounds are converted to nitrogen oxides. The incomplete combustion of coal and the combustion of these minor constituents results in a number of environmental problems. For example, soot formed during incomplete combustion may settle out of the air and deposit an unattractive coating on homes, cars, buildings, and other structures. Carbon monoxide formed during incomplete combustion is a toxic gas and may cause illness or death in humans and other animals. Oxides of sulfur and nitrogen react with water vapor in the atmosphere and then are precipitated out as acid rain. Acid rain is thought to be responsible for the destruction of certain forms of plant and animal (especially fish) life.

In addition to these compounds, coal often contains a few percent of mineral matter: quartz, calcite, or perhaps clay minerals. These do not readily combust and so become part of the ash. The ash then either escapes into the atmosphere or is left in the combustion vessel

and must be discarded. Sometimes coal ash also contains significant amounts of lead, barium, arsenic, or other compounds. Whether air borne or in bulk, coal ash can therefore be a serious environmental hazard.

Coal mining

Coal is extracted from the Earth using one of two major techniques, sub–surface or surface (strip) mining. The former method is used when seams of coal are located at significant depths below the Earth's surface. The first step in sub–surface mining is to dig vertical tunnels into the Earth until the coal seam is reached. Horizontal tunnels are then constructed laterally off the vertical tunnel. In many cases, the preferred method of mining coal by this method is called room–and–pillar mining. In this method, vertical columns of coal (the pillars) are left in place as coal around them is removed. The pillars hold up the ceiling of the seam preventing it from collapsing on miners working around them. After the mine has been abandoned, however, those pillars may often collapse, bringing down the ceiling of the seam and causing subsidence in land above the old mine.

Surface mining can be used when a coal seam is close enough to the Earth's surface to allow the overburden to be removed economically. In such a case, the first step is to strip off all of the overburden in order to reach the coal itself. The coal is then scraped out by huge power shovels, some capable of removing up to 100 cubic meters at a time. Strip mining is a far safer form of coal mining, but it presents a number of environmental problems. In most instances, an area that has been strip mined is terribly scarred, and restoring the area to its original state is a long and expensive procedure. In addition, any water that comes in contact with the exposed coal or overburden may become polluted and require treatment.

Resources

Coal is regarded as a non–renewable resource, meaning that it was formed at times during the Earth's history, but significant amounts are no longer forming. Therefore, the amount of coal that now exists below the Earth's surface is, for all practical purposes, all the coal that humans have available to them for the foreseeable future. When this supply of coal is used up, humans will find it necessary to find some other substitute to meet their energy needs.

Large supplies of coal are known to exist (proven reserves) or thought to be available (estimated resources) in North America, the former Soviet Union, and parts of Asia, especially China and India. According to the most recent data available, China produces the largest amount of coal each year, about 22% of the world's total, with the United States 19%, the former members of the Soviet Union 16%, Germany 10% and Poland 5% following. China is also thought to have the world's largest estimated resources of coal, as much as 46% of all that exists. In the United States, the largest coal–producing states are Montana, North Dakota, Wyoming, Alaska, Illinois, and Colorado.

Uses

For many centuries, coal was burned in small stoves to produce heat in homes and factories. Today, the most important use of coal, both directly and indirectly, is still as a fuel. The largest single consumer of coal as a fuel is the electrical power industry. The combustion to coal in power generating plants is used to make steam which, in turn, operates turbines and generators. For a period of more than 40 years beginning in 1940, the amount of coal used in the United States for this purpose doubled in every decade. Coal is no longer widely used to heat homes and buildings, as was the case a half century ago, but it is still used in industries such as paper production, cement and ceramic manufacture, iron and steel production, and chemical manufacture for heating and for steam generation.

Another use for coal is in the manufacture of coke. Coke is nearly pure carbon produced when soft coal is heated in the absence of air. In most cases, one ton of coal will produce 0.7 ton of coke in this process. Coke is of value in industry because it has a heat value higher than any form of natural coal. It is widely used in steel making and in certain chemical processes.

Conversion of coal

A number of processes have been developed by which solid coal can be converted to a liquid or gaseous form for use as a fuel. Conversion has a number of advantages. In a liquid or gaseous form, the fuel may be easier to transport, and the conversion process removes a number of impurities from the original coal (such as sulfur) that have environmental disadvantages.

One of the conversion methods is known as gasification. In gasification, crushed coal is reacted with steam and either air or pure oxygen. The coal is converted into a complex mixture of gaseous hydrocarbons with heat values ranging from 100 Btu to 1000 Btu. One suggestion has been to construct gasification systems within a coal mine, making it much easier to remove the coal (in a gaseous form) from its original seam.

KEY TERMS

Anthracite—Hard coal; a form of coal with high heat content and high concentration of pure carbon.

Bituminous—Soft coal; a form of coal with less heat content and pure carbon content than anthracite, but more than lignite.

British thermal unit (Btu)—A unit for measuring heat content in the British measuring system.

Coke—A synthetic fuel formed by the heating of soft coal in the absence of air.

Combustion—Burning, or oxidation.

Gasification—Any process by which solid coal is converted to a gaseous fuel.

Lignite—Brown coal; a form of coal with less heat content and pure carbon content than either anthracite or bituminous coal.

Liquefaction—Any process by which solid coal is converted to a liquid fuel.

Peat—A primitive form of coal with less heat content and pure carbon content than any form of coal.

Strip mining—A method for removing coal from seams that are close to the Earth's surface.

In the process of liquefaction, solid coal is converted to a petroleum–like liquid that can be used as a fuel for motor vehicles and other applications. On the one hand, both liquefaction and gasification are attractive technologies in the United States because of our very large coal resources. On the other hand, the wide availability of raw coal means that new technologies have been unable to compete economically with the natural product.

During the last century, coal oil and coal gas were important sources of fuel for heating and lighting homes. However, with the advent of natural gas, coal distillates quickly became unpopular, since they were somewhat smoky and foul smelling.

See also Air pollution; Carbon; Hydrocarbon; Petroleum.

Further Reading:

Anderson, Larry L., and David A. Tillman. *Synthetic Fuels from Coal: Overview and Assessment.* New York: Wiley, 1979.

Gorbaty, Martin L., John W. Larsen, and Irving Wender, eds. *Coal Science*. New York: Academic Press, 1982.

David E. Newton

Coast and beach

The coast and beach, where the continents meet the sea, are dynamic environments where agents of erosion vie with processes of deposition to produce a set of features reflecting their complex interplay and the influences of changes in sea level, climate, sediment supply, etc. "Coast" usually refers to the larger region of a continent or island which is significantly affected by its proximity to the sea, whereas "beach" refers to a much smaller region, usually just the areas directly affected by wave action.

Observing erosion and deposition

The Earth is constantly changing. Mountains are built up by tectonic forces, weathered, and eroded away. The erosional debris is deposited in the sea. In most places these changes occur so slowly that they are barely noticeable, but at the beach we can often watch them progress.

Most features of the beach environment are temporary, steady state features. To illustrate this, consider an excavation in soil, where groundwater is flowing in, and being pumped out by mechanical pumps. The level of the water in the hole is maintained because it is being pumped out just as fast as it is coming in. It is in a steady state, but changing either rate will promptly change the level of the water. A casual observer may fail to notice the pumps, and erroneously conclude that the water in the hole is stationary. Similarly, a casual observer may think that the sand on the beach is stationary, instead of in a steady state. The size and shape of a spit, which is a body of sand stretching out from a point, parallel to the shore, is similar to the level of the water in this example. To stay the same, the rate at which sand is being added to the spit must be exactly balanced by the rate at which it is being removed. Failure to recognize this has often led to serious degradation of the coastal environment.

Sea level is the point from which we measure elevation, and for good reason. A minor change in elevation high on a mountain is undetectable without sophisticated surveying equipment. The environment at 4,320

The coast of Long Island, New York.

feet above sea level is not much different from that at 4,310 feet. The same ten foot change in the elevation of a beach would expose formerly submerged land, or inundate formerly exposed land, making it easy to notice. Not only is the environment different, but the dominant geologic processes are different: Erosion occurs above sea level, deposition occurs below sea level. As a result, coasts where the land is rising relative to sea level (emergent coasts) are usually very different from those where the land is sinking relative to sea level (submergent coasts).

Emergent coasts

If the coast rises, or sea level goes down, areas which were once covered by the sea will emerge and form part of the landscape. The erosive action of the waves will attack surfaces which previously lay safely below them. This wave attack occurs right at sea level, but its effects extend from there. Waves may undercut a cliff, and eventually the cliff will fail and fall into the

A coastal area in Oregon.

sea, removing material from higher elevations. In this way the cliff retreats, while the beach profile is extended at its base . The rate at which this process continues depends on the material of the cliff and the profile of the beach. As the process continues, the gradual slope of the bottom extends farther and farther until most waves break far from shore and the rate of cliff retreat slows, resulting in a stable profile which may persist for long periods of time. Eventually another episode of uplift is likely to occur, and the process repeats.

Emergent coasts, such as the coast along much of California, often exhibit a series of terraces, each consisting of a former beach and wave cut cliff. This provides evidence of both the total uplift of the coast, and its incremental nature.

Softer rocks erode more easily, leaving resistant rock which forms points of land called headlands jutting out into the sea. Subsurface depth contours mimic

that of the shoreline, resulting in wave refraction when the change in depth causes the waves to change the direction of their approach. This refraction concentrates wave energy on the headlands, and spreads it out across the areas in between. The "pocket beaches" separated by jagged headlands, which characterize much of the scenic coastline of Oregon and northern California were formed in this way. Wave refraction explains the fact that waves on both sides of a headland may approach it from nearly opposite directions, producing some spectacular displays when they break.

Submergent coasts

If sea level rises, or the elevation of the coast falls, formerly exposed topography will be inundated. Valleys carved out by rivers will become estuaries like Chesapeake Bay. Hilly terrains will become collections of islands, such as those off the coast of Maine.

The ability of rivers to transport sediment depends on their velocities. When they flow into a deep body of water they slow down and deposit their sediment in what will eventually become a delta. Thus, the flooding of estuaries causes deposition further inland. As the estuary fills in with sediment the depth of the water will decrease, and the velocity of the water flowing across the top of the delta will increase. This permits it to transport sediment further, and the delta builds out toward, and eventually into, the sea. The additional load of all the sediment may cause the crust of the Earth to deform, submerging the coast further.

The sand budget

Wave action moves incredible amounts of sand. This may seem strange, if you think about waves out at sea, where a cork will bob around in a circle without going anywhere. As waves approach shallow water, however, they slow down because of friction with the bottom, get steeper and finally break. It is during this slowing and breaking that sand gets transported. When waves reach the shore they approach it almost straight on, so that the wave front is nearly parallel to the shore as it breaks. Usually not exactly parallel, though, and it is this difference which moves sand along the beach.

When a breaking wave washes up onto the beach at a slight angle it moves sand on the beach with it. This movement is mostly towards shore, but also slightly down the beach. When the water sloshes back, it goes directly down the slope, without any oblique component. As a result, sand moves in a zigzag path with a net motion parallel to the beach. This is called "longshore drift." Although most easily observed and understood in the swash zone, the area of the beach which gets alternately wet and dry with each passing wave, longshore drift is active in any water shallow enough to slow waves down.

Many features of sandy coasts are the result of longshore drift. Spits build out from projecting land masses, sometimes becoming hooked at their end, as sand moves parallel to the shore. At Cape Cod, Mass. glacial debris, deposited thousands of years ago, is still being eroded and redistributed by wave action.

An artificial jetty or "groin" can trap sand on one side of it, broadening the beach there. On the other side, however, wave action will transport sand away. Because of the jetty it will not be replenished, and erosion of the beach will result.

The magnitude and direction of transport of longshore drift depends on the strength and direction of approach of waves, and these may vary with the season.

A beach with a very gentle slope, covered with fine sand every July may be a steep pebble beach in February.

Barrier islands

Long, linear islands parallel to the shore are common along the Atlantic coast. Attractive sites for resorts and real estate developments, these barrier islands are in flux. A hurricane can drive storm waves over low spots, cutting islands in two. Conversely, migration of sand can extend a spit across the channel between two islands, merging them into one.

Interruptions in sand supply can result in erosion. This has happened off the coast of Maryland, where Assateague Island has gotten thinner and moved shoreward since jetties were installed at Ocean City, just to the north.

Society and the beach environment

Often, the steady state nature of the beach environment has not been properly respected.

At higher elevations, where rates of erosion and deposition are so much slower, we can construct huge hills to support interstate highways, level other hills to make parking lots, etc., expecting the results of our work to persist for centuries, or at least decades. But in a beach environment our modifications are ephemeral. Maintaining a parking lot where winds would produce a dune requires removal of tons of sand—every year!

Even more significantly, because the flow of sediment is so great, modifications intended to have only a local, beneficial effect may influence erosion and deposition far down the beach, in ways which are not beneficial. Tossing a drain plug into a bucket of water raises the level of the water by just a tiny amount. Putting the same drain plug into the drain of a bathtub, into which water is flowing steadily, will change the level in the tub in very substantial ways! Similarly, you may be able to protect the beach in front of your beach house by installing a concrete barrier, but this might result in eroding the supports to the highway giving you access to your beach house.

See also Barrier islands; Erosion; Ocean; Sea level; Tides.

Further Reading:

Bird, E.C.F. *Submerging Coasts: The Effects of a Rising Sea Level on Coastal Environments.* Chichester, New York: John Wiley & Sons, 1993.

Carter, R. W. G. *Coastal Environments: An Introduction to the Physical, Ecological, and Cultural Systems of Coastlines.* London; San Diego: Academic Press, 1988.

Carter, R.W.G., and C.D. Woodroffe. *Coastal Evolution.* Cambridge: Cambridge University Press, 1994.

Commission on Geosciences, Environment, and Resources, National Research Council. *Environmental Science in the Coastal Zone: Issues for Further Research.* Washington: National Academy Press, 1994

Davis, Richard A. *The Evolving Coasts.* New York: Scientific American Library, Distributed by W.H. Freeman and Co., 1994

Press, Frank, and Raymond Siever. *Understanding Earth.* New York: W.H. Freeman and Co., 1994.

Otto H. Muller

Coatis

Coatis are raccoon–like mammals in the family Procyonidae, coatis which have a long ringed tail, typically held perpendicular to the body, and a flexible, upturned, elongated snout. Coatis are also distinctive socially. The females live together in highly organized groups called bands, composed of 5–12 allied individuals, while adult males are solitary. The difference in the social patterning of the sexes initially confused biologists who described the males as a separate species. The use of the name "coatimundi" for this species, meaning "lone coati" in Guarani, reflects this error.

There are four species of coatis in two genera, all fairly similar in appearance. Coatis are versatile animals found in a variety of vegetation ranging from thorn scrub, moist tropical forest, and grassland areas stretching from southwestern North America through Central and South America to northern Argentina. The ringtailed coati (*Nasua nasua*) is a common species. Its coat is tawny red in color with a black face. Patches of white accentuate the coat above and below each eye and one on each cheek. The throat and belly are also white, while the feet and the rings on the tail are black, and the ears are short and heavily furred. The head–to–tail length ranges from 32–51 in (80–130 cm) with a little more than half the length being tail. Other species of coati vary slightly in size, coat color, and markings.

Coatis have strong forelimbs that are shorter than the hind legs. Despite a plantigrade foot posture the animal is arboreal as well as terrestrial. The long, strong claws are nonretractile, and the long tail is used for balance. Coatis can reverse the direction of their ankles, facilitating a head–first descent from the trees. The upper mandible is longer than the lower contributing to the flexible use of the snout. The coati has 38–40 teeth with long, slender and sharp canines.

Contrary to other members of the family Procyonidae, coatis are primarily diurnal searching for their omnivorous diet by probing their sensitive snout in the leaf litter and rotting logs on the forest floor. Predominately insectivorous, eating such things as beetles, grubs, ants and termites, coatis also eat a considerable amount of fruit when it is in season, foraging both on the ground and high in trees. Additionally, they are opportunistic predators on vertebrates, occasionally catching frogs, lizards, and mice. Coatis have been known to unearth and eat turtle and lizard eggs. Foraging alone, male coatis typically catch more lizards and rodents than the females and young, who forage in small groups.

Most of the day is spent foraging for food. During rest periods, coatis will groom each other. They curl up and sleep in trees at night. Coatis are highly vocal and use a variety of communication calls. They make a wide diversity of grunts, whines and shrieks, including a sharp whistle. When enraged, coatis will produce a chittering sound.

In the larger Ringtailed and White–nosed coatis, females mature in their second year; males mature in their third year. During most of the year, females chase males away from the band because they often will kill juveniles. However, around February and March females become more tolerant and allow a dominant male to interact with the band. The male wins favor with the band females by submissively grooming them. Actual mating occurs in trees. Soon after the male has bred with all the females, he is expelled from the group by the once again aggressive females.

About four weeks before birth, females leave their bands to build stick platform nests in trees. After a 77

A coati.

day gestation period, females bear a litter of three to five poorly developed young, weighing only 100–180 g (3.5–6.4 oz). For the next five to six weeks, females care for the young in the nest. Once the females and youngsters return to the band, young coatis will join their mothers in search of food, but they also play much of the time, wrestling and chasing each other among the trees.

Home ranges of bands of coatis cover about 0.6 mi (1 km), though there is considerable overlapping of range territory of neighboring bands. Despite friendly relations among bands, coatis maintain stable and distinct band membership.

Coatis have little interaction with humans in the wild, however, they are hunted for their fur and meat. Coatis have been kept in captivity, both as pets and as exhibit animals. They typically live about seven years, but have been known to survive fourteen years in captivity.

Further Reading:

Burton, Maurice, ed. *The New Larousse Encyclopedia of Animal Life*. New York: Bonanza Books, 1984.

Farrand, Jr. John, ed. *The Audubon Society Encyclopedia of Animal Life*. New York: Clarkson N. Potter, Inc./Publishers, 1982.

Macdonald, Dr. David, ed. *The Encyclopedia of Mammals*. New York: Facts on File Publications, 1984.

Mares, Michael A., Ojeda, Ricardo A., & Barquez, Rubén M. *Guide to the Mammals of Salta Province, Argentina*. Norman: University of Oklahoma Press, 1989.

National Geographic Society, ed. *Book of Mammals, Volume One*. Washington, D.C.: National Geographic Society, 1981.

Redford, Kent H. and Eisenberg, John F. *Mammals of the Neotropics: The Southern Cone, Volume 2*. Chicago: University of Chicago Press, 1989.

Vaughan, Terry A. *Mammalogy*. New York: Saunders College Publishing, 1986.

Betsy A. Leonard

The leaves and fruit of a coca plant (*Erythroxylum coca*) in Costa Rica, the plant from which cocaine is extracted.

Cobalt see **Element, chemical**

Cobras see **Elapid snakes; Snakes**

Coca

The coca plant, genus *Erythroxylum*, family Erythroxylaceae, order Linales, is native to the Andean slopes of South America. The genus *Erythroxylum* comprises approximately 250 species, of which the most cultivated species are *Erythroxylum coca* (southern Peru and Bolivia) and *Erythroxylum novogranatense* (Colombia and northern coastal Peru). The coca plant is a shrub, growing to about 15 ft (5 m). Cultivated plants are pruned to about 6 ft (2 m). The leaves are oval, smooth–edged, dark green, and 1.6–3.1 in (4–8 cm) long, 1–1.6 in (2.5–4 cm) wide. Unlike other short term crops such as maize and rice, or other mountain grown commodities such as coffee, coca plants require little care. Coca plants can thrive in poor soil, have few pests or predators—an ideal crop for the bleak growing conditions in the Andes. After planting, leaves can be harvested by 6–12 months. Coca plants can yield 4–5 crops per year for 30–40 years.

The coca plant is the source of cocaine, one of about 14 alkaloids obtained from the leaves. The concentration of cocaine in the leaves varies from about 23% to 85%, depending on the species and growing conditions. The cocaine alkaloid was first extracted from the leaves in the 1840s. It soon became a popular addition to powders, medicines, drinks, and potions. The popular American soft drink Coca–Cola, introduced in 1885 by John Pemberton, uses coca leaves in its preparation. Since 1906, when the Pure Food and Drug Law was passed, Coca–Cola has been made with decocainized coca leaves. Today, some species of *Erythroxylum* are grown in other regions of the world, such as India and Indonesia, where the climate is similar to the Andean tropics, and cultivated primarily for cocaine extraction. Before cocaine became a popular street drug, coca was grown mainly for traditional consumption among the Andean peoples, and for legal industrial medicinal use.

The indigenous people of the Andean mountain range have been chewing the leaves of the coca plant for thousands of years. Archeological evidence indicates that Peruvians were chewing coca as early as 1800 B.C. Ancient sculptures show the heads of warriors with the characteristic "bulge" in the cheek, depicting coca chewing. The coca plant was one of the first cultivated and domesticated plants in the New World. During the reign of the Incas, coca was regarded as sacred and it was used only by chieftains, priests, or privileged classes. Coca was the link between man and the supernatural. It was used for various social and religious rituals, ceremonies, and fortune telling. Leaves of the coca plant were buried with the dead to help with the journey to the afterworld. Coca leaves were used in traditional medical practices, aiding in diagnosis and treatment. When the leaves are chewed with an alkaline substance such as lime, or plant ash, the active ingredients that stimulate the central nervous system are released. Stamina was increased, hunger depressed, pain eased—a feeling of well being and strength was achieved.

After the Spanish conquered the Incas in the sixteenth century, coca was given to the peasants, or working classes. The Spanish realized that coca enabled the peasants to work harder, longer, and that they needed less food. What was once exclusive to the ruling class was made available to the common people. Thus chewing coca leaves became a way of life for an entire peasant nation. The Indians, then and now, chew the leaves with other substances and never ingest the cocaine alkaloid alone, and apparently do not experience the addictive mind altering effects associated with cocaine. Coca leaf chewing is still identified with religious practices, social rituals, traditional medicine, and work situations. The leaves are used for bartering or, as a form of currency, to obtain other goods such as food items. In the past few decades however, growing coca has become associated with obtaining material goods and becoming rich. An entirely new economy, mostly illegal or underground, has developed around coca. Many plantation owners have changed their focus from leaf production to the extraction of the cocaine alkaloid in paste form. Coca production is now the most lucrative industry in Peru and Bolivia, the world's leading producers. The coca industry is heavily scrutinized by several international governmental groups. Realizing the cultural significance of coca chewing among certain sectors of people living in the Andes, the Peruvian government developed a separate agency to protect and supervise legal trade. Most of the annual production of coca however, goes to the black market.

See also Cocaine.

Christine Miner Minderovic

Cocaine

Cocaine is a colorless or white narcotic crystalline alkaloid derived from the leaves of the South American coca plant—*Erythroxylum coca*. Aside from its use as a local anesthetic, which has largely been supplanted by safer drugs, its medical applications failed to live up to the hopes of physicians and chemists of the late nineteenth century. They administered cocaine to themselves and others in the hope that it would be a cure–all wonder drug. After about two decades of wide use in prescription and patented medicine, the harmful effects of cocaine became manifest, and its use as a drug in medical practice was eventually banned.

It subsequently became an illegal drug used for its mood–altering effects, which include euphoria and bursts of short–lived physical energy. The "high" produced by cocaine lasts for a short time. The "crash" that follows leaves the user in need of another "fix" to get back to the former high. But each encounter produces diminished highs, so that increasing doses are required to recapture the initial experience. The physical and social consequences of cocaine addiction are devastating both to the individual and society. It leads to impoverishment and the destruction of the individual's health. When young people begin to use cocaine, communities begin to feel the effects of increased crime, violence, and social decay.

In the late 1970s cocaine was "snorted," or sniffed through the nose, in its crystalline form, then known as "snow." Because of its high cost, the number of users was limited. In order to get a faster and stronger high, cocaine was also taken by injection with a hypodermic needle. By the 1980s a cheaper version of pure cocaine made its appearance on the illegal market in the form of "crack," which is smoked, primarily in the "crack houses" where it is produced. In the form of crack, cocaine has reached a larger population, making it one of the chief drug problems of the present.

History

Coca plants, which are the source for cocaine, are indigenous to Central and South America. The name of the plant is derived from the Inca word *Kuka*. Archaeological evidence points to the use of coca plants in South America as early as seven thousand years ago. They were used for many centuries by the Incas as part of their religious ceremonies. To help the dead in the afterworld, mounds of stored coca leaves were left at burial sites in the area of modern Peru. These sites are estimated to be about 4,500 years old. The Incas may also have been using liquid coca leaf compounds to perform brain surgery 3,500 years ago. Inca records dating from the thirteenth through the sixteenth century indicate that coca was revered as a sacred object with magical powers. The magic plant of the Incas was chewed by priests to help induce trances that led them into the spirit world to determine the wishes of their gods. Artifacts dating back thousands of years to the earliest Incan periods show the cheeks of their high priests distended with what in all probability were the leaves of the coca plant.

Even before the Spanish conquest, Indians working in silver mines of the northern Andes chewed the coca leaf to help overcome pain, fatigue, and the respiratory problems common at high altitudes. Early European

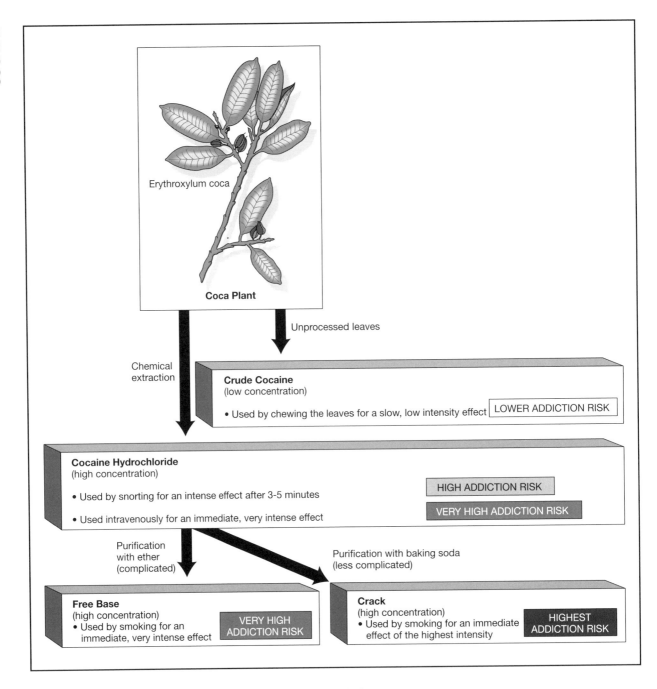

Erythroxylum coca

Coca Plant

Unprocessed leaves

Chemical extraction

Crude Cocaine
(low concentration)

• Used by chewing the leaves for a slow, low intensity effect | LOWER ADDICTION RISK

Cocaine Hydrochloride
(high concentration)

• Used by snorting for an intense effect after 3-5 minutes | HIGH ADDICTION RISK

• Used intravenously for an immediate, very intense effect | VERY HIGH ADDICTION RISK

Purification with ether (complicated)

Purification with baking soda (less complicated)

Free Base
(high concentration)
• Used by smoking for an immediate, very intense effect | VERY HIGH ADDICTION RISK

Crack
(high concentration)
• Used by smoking for an immediate effect of the highest intensity | HIGHEST ADDICTION RISK

Various forms of cocaine and the addiction risks associated with them.

explorers in the fifteenth century compared the common sight of Indians they saw chewing the coca leaves to cattle chewing cud. After the Spanish conquest the Church sought to ban the practice of chewing the coca leaf, mainly because of its association with Incan religious ceremonies. When the ban failed, the Spanish allowed the Incan survivors to continue their ancient practice of coca leaf chewing in order to maintain mining production. South American farmers, who are descendants of the Incas, continue the practice to the present day.

Introduction to the West

The main alkaloid in the leaves of the coca plant was extracted in 1859 by Albert Niemann, a German scientist, who gave it the name cocaine. Reports soon followed of therapeutic benefits of cocaine in the treatment of a number of physical and mental disorders. These reports also praised cocaine for being a highly effective stimulant, able to conquer the most severe cases of fatigue.

Sigmund Freud, two decades after Niemann's work, began experimenting with cocaine, thinking it could be used to treat "nervous fatigue," an ailment many upper– and middle–class Viennese were diagnosed with. He gave his fiancée cocaine and also administered it to himself. Then he wrote a paper praising the curative powers of cocaine in the treatment of such problems as alcohol and morphine addiction, gastrointestinal disorders, anxiety, depression, and respiratory problems. In this paper, Freud completely dismissed the powerful addictive properties of the drug, insisting that the user would develop an aversion to, rather than a craving for, its continued use.

Freud shortly afterwards became aware of his mistake when he attempted to cure a friend's morphine addiction with the use of cocaine. At first the treatment seemed to work, but he soon saw that the friend developed an addiction to cocaine instead. Soon afterwards Freud's friend suffered a complete nervous breakdown.

Unfortunately, there were other physicians and chemists who misjudged the properties of cocaine in the same way Freud had done. For example, a neurologist and former surgeon general of the United States, William Hammond, also praised the healing powers of cocaine and pronounced it no more addictive than coffee or tea.

Coca–Cola

In the 1880s, John Pemberton, a pharmacist from Atlanta, concocted a drink called Coca–Cola from a prescription syrup that had been used to treat headache, hysteria, and depression. Pemberton's elixir drink contained coca leaves, kola nuts, and a small amount of cocaine in a sugary syrup. His secret formula was picked up by Asa Chandler, who formed the Coca–Cola company. The drink was praised by the *New York Times* as the new wonder drug. At about the same time, cocaine was sold in a cigarette produced by the Parke–Davis pharmaceutical company. The cigarettes were marketed as a cure for infections of the throat.

Early drug laws

From all the nineteenth–century hopes for the possible medical uses of cocaine, the only practical application that held up was its use as a local anesthetic. All the other efforts to prove that cocaine was a wonder drug were dismal failures in light of the powerful addictive effects of the drug. By the early twentieth century, it had become clear that cocaine posed a serious hazard to any user.

In 1904 the cocaine was removed from the Coca–Cola syrup. In 1906 the Pure Food and Drug Act was enacted to stop the sale of patent medicines containing substances such as cocaine. Before that date, manufacturers were not required to list the ingredients of their patent medicines. The 1906 act made truthful labeling of patent medicines sold across state borders mandatory, but it did not stop the sale of cocaine products. New York State tried to curtail cocaine sales by passing a law in 1907 that limited the right to distribute cocaine to physicians. That law merely paved the way for the illicit street traffic. Dealers obtained cocaine from physicians and then sold it on the street.

The cocaine drug problem continued to rise until 1914, when the Harrison Act was passed. This legislation used the federal Treasury Department to levy taxes on all phases of cocaine trafficking and imposed further strict measures on the sale and distribution of cocaine. From that time to the 1960s, cocaine use dwindled, in part because of the rising popularity of amphetamines on the illegal market. The medical use of cocaine as a topical anesthetic and as an ingredient in cough medicines continued, while its illegal use was largely confined to the very rich.

After the 1960s

By the 1970s, when illegal drug use became more widespread in the general population, middle– and upper–class groups began to use cocaine in its white crystalline form. A mythology of its effectiveness as an aphrodisiac (a substance supposed to enhance the sex drive), a mental energizer, and a self–esteem booster began to develop. Along with benefits that active and ambitious middle–class people hoped for in their drug of choice, came reports of the relative safety of cocaine use in comparison to other drugs. The harsh lessons learned around the turn of the century were all but forgotten.

Crack

By the late 1970s, cocaine addiction in the United States had reached epidemic proportions. In the mid–1980s people started smoking cocaine after "freebasing" it, that is, dissolving the cocaine alkaloid from its white powder base to create a smokable form of pure cocaine. Ether is used to remove the hydrochloride base, which does not burn. The smoked cocaine goes straight into the bloodstream and gives a quicker and stronger high. Freebasing with ether can be dangerous because if any ether remains in the freebase cocaine, it can quickly ignite into flames when smoked. The comedian Richard Pryor, to mention one of the more famous cases, was severely burned when he freebased cocaine.

Besides freebase cocaine, there is another form of smokable cocaine, called "crack," which also gives a fast and potent high. Crack is safer and easier to obtain than freebase cocaine because baking soda is used instead of ether to remove the hydrochloride. The baking soda produces pure forms of cocaine in small pellets that can be smoked in a pipe (where it makes the crackling sound that gave this form of cocaine its name). The cost of crack is so low that anybody, even a child, can afford it, and the drug soon began to wreak its devastations on the working classes. The widespread use of crack cocaine has led most visibly to rising crime rates, with gang wars erupting over control of territory and with users resorting to theft, prostitution, and other crimes to support their habits. Other consequences have been impaired workplace performance, new public health problems including such phenomena as crack babies, and a host of other social and economic evils.

Biochemistry

Used as a local anesthetic, cocaine constricts the blood vessels, thereby slowing down blood circulation. It also reduces the sensitivity of nerve endings, especially in the skin, eyes, and areas of the mouth. Because cocaine is a stimulant, it increases the heart and pulse rate and raises blood pressure, causing alertness, insomnia, loss of appetite, and dilated pupils.

Several theories have been proposed to explain the addictive effects of cocaine, which differs from other stimulants in its ability to trap the user in a cycle of continued use. Experiments using animals who are able to self–administer cocaine show that, once the need for cocaine is established, an animal will neglect its hunger and sex drives in order to satisfy the craving for the drug. Rats took cocaine until they died, while monkeys indulged until they exhibited such behaviors as paranoia, hyperactivity, convulsions, and heart failure.

Cocaine, like the opioids morphine and heroin, causes addiction by arousing an intense sense of pleasure. Certain parts of the brain induce pleasurable sensations when stimulated. Unlike the opioids, though, cocaine appears to have a greater access to those parts of the brain known as the limbic system, which controls the emotions. Cocaine stimulates the release of the neurotransmitter dopamine, which is responsible for the stimulation of the limbic system. The drug is therefore more potent than other drugs in being more psychologically rewarding. According to a recent theory, most of the mood and behavior changes brought about by cocaine use is due to the release of excess amounts of dopamine

KEY TERMS

Alkaloid—A member of a group of chemicals containing nitrogen, which is the active ingredient in drugs that affect the nervous system.

Amphetamines—Stimulant drugs discovered in the 1930s that were widely prescribed as diet pills and became a staple in the illegal drug traffic.

Aphrodisiac—A drug that is supposed to stimulate sexual impulses.

Coca leaves—Leaves of the coca plant that were chewed by the Incas and are still used by farmers of certain regions in South America.

Crack—A smokable and inexpensive form of pure cocaine sold in the form of small pellets, or "rocks."

Dopamine—The neurotransmitter believed to be responsible for the cocaine high.

Euphoria—A state of heightened pleasure and feelings of well–being that arises independently of any external events when drugs such as cocaine are used.

Freebasing—Processes used to free drugs such as cocaine from their hydrochloride base.

Local anesthetic—A pain killer that acts on a particular site of the body without affecting other sites or causing unconsciousness.

Snow—The white powder of cocaine hydrochloride that is inhaled through the nostrils. This way of taking cocaine is called "snorting" and was popular in the 1970s before the advent of crack cocaine.

in the reward centers of the brain. The ensuing depression and craving for the drug are caused by dopamine depletion after the effects of the drug wear off.

Treatment and prevention

Breaking a cocaine dependency is difficult, and treatment is costly and prolonged, involving treatment centers and support groups. Since addiction is a chronic disorder, the detoxification process is just the first step, and there is no final cure. Remissions can be expected, and the goal of treatment may have to be the control and reduction of use and dependency.

Prevention efforts in the United States have for a long time been focused primarily on stopping cocaine imports from South America, mainly Peru and Columbia, and these efforts have had some success in breaking up the powerful and wealthy cartels that control the cultivation and trade of the coca leaf. However, these producers are still sending coca to the United States and continue to seek other markets worldwide for their deadly crop.

Studies have shown that a recent decline of cocaine usage in the United States is directly correlated to educational programs targeting young people and aiming to enhance their understanding of the dangers of cocaine use. Such educational programs are more likely to lead to results than interdiction efforts and provide the best hope of curtailing the current epidemic of cocaine abuse and preventing similar epidemics in the future.

See also Addiction.

Further Reading:

Flynn, John C. *Cocaine*. New York: Carol Publishing, 1991.
Gold, Mark S. *Cocaine*. New York: Plenum Publishing, 1993.
Rice–Licare, Jennifer and Katharine Delaney–McLaughlin. *Cocaine Solutions*. Binghamton: Haworth Press, 1990.
Washton, Arnold M. and Mark S. Gold. *Cocaine: A Clinician's Handbook*. New York: Guilford Press, 1987.

Jordan P. Richman

Coccids see **Scale insects**

Cochlea see **Ear**

Cockatoos.

Cockatoos

Cockatoos are species of birds in the family Cacatuidae, in the order Psittaciformes, which also contains the typical parrots (family Psittacidae).

Parrots and cockatoos all have powerful, curved bills, short legs, and strong, dexterous feet with two toes pointing forward and two backward. These birds also have specialized feathers known as powder down, which disintegrates into a powder that is used for dressing the feathers during preening. Parrots and cockatoos are colorful, intelligent birds. They mostly eat fruits and seeds.

Cockatoos are relatively simply colored birds, with a crest on the top of the head that can be erected at will. Species in this family mostly occur in Australia, New Guinea, and nearby islands, with species occurring as far north as the Philippines. Cockatoos usually nest in holes in trees. They feed on a wide range of fruits and seeds, as well as flowers, roots, rhizomes, palm shoots, and beetle and moth larvae.

The best–known species is the sulfur–crested cockatoo (*Cacatua galerita*), which occurs widely in eastern Australia and New Guinea. This large bird has a pure–white body, with a yellow–colored crest, and a black beak and feet. The galah (*Cacatua roseicapilla*) has a rosy breast and face, and a grey back and wings. This species occurs widely in woodlands, savannahs, grasslands, and parks throughout most of Australia. The pink cockatoo (*Cacatua leadbeateri*) has white wings, a salmon–colored belly and head, and occurs in woodlands of western and central Australia. The little corella (*C. sanguinea*) is a smaller species, with a white body, dark eye–patch, and yellow under the wings. This species occurs widely in Australia and southern New Guinea.

The palm cockatoo (*Probosciger aterrimus*) is a large, dark–grey bird, with orange–pink facial skin, and a long and erectile, black crest. This cockatoo occurs in tropical rainforests and eucalyptus woodlands of northeastern Australia and New Guinea. The red–tailed black cockatoo (*Calyptorhynchus magnificus*) is a sooty black bird with red streaks on the tail, occurring in woodlands of northern Australia, and in scattered places elsewhere on that continent.

Cockatoos are sometimes kept as highly entertaining, rather intelligent, and chatty, sometimes "talking" pets. The sulfur–crested cockatoo is the species most commonly kept in this way. Some species of cockatoos are hunted as food by aboriginal peoples in Australia and New Guinea.

See also Parrots.

Cockles see **Bivalves**

Cockroaches

Cockroaches are insects in the order Blattaria. They are somewhat flat, oval shaped, leathery in texture, and are usually brown or black in color. Cockroaches range in body size from 0.1–2.3 in (2.5–60 mm), and are rampant pest insects in human inhabited areas, as well as common outdoor insects in most warm areas of the world.

These insects were formerly classified in the order Orthoptera, which consists of the grasshoppers and katydids. Now they are often classified along with the mantises in an order referred to as Dictyoptera. The separate order Blattaria, however, is the more common classification for them, and this order is placed in the phylogeny, or evolutionary history, of the class Insecta between the orders Mantodea, the mantids, and Isoptera, the termites.

The primitive wood–boring cockroaches in the family Cryptocercidae, a family in which there is only a single species in the United States, *Cryptocercus punctulatus*, are thought to have shared a common ancestor with termites. The evidence for this is a close phylogenetic relationship between the two groups' obligate intestinal symbionts, single–celled organisms called protozoans which break down the wood that the insects eat into a form that is useful to the insect, and in turn receive nutrition from the matter which is not nutritive to the insect. There are also behavioral similarities between these wood–boring cockroaches and termites, including the fact that they both live gregariously in family groups, a characteristic not shared by any of the other types of cockroaches. Finally, the relationship between the two orders is evidenced by the resemblance between *Cryptocercus* nymphs, and adult termites.

Interesting morphological characteristics of these insects are their chewing mouthparts and large compound eye. The pronotum, or segment of the thorax that is closest to the head, conceals the head, and in most species, both male and female are winged, although they rarely fly. They exhibit many fascinating behaviors, such as the ability to stridulate, that is, produce sound by rubbing a comb–like structure with a scraper. Other species, however, communicate by producing sound by drumming the tip of their abdomen on a substrate. An important developmental feature of these insects is their paurometabolous life–history. Paurometabolism is a type of simple metamorphosis in which there are definite egg, immature or nymph, and adults stages, but no larval or pupal stages and in which the nymphs resemble the adults except in size, development of wings, and body proportions. Habitat requirements of nymphs and adults do not vary in paurometabolous insects, a fact which helps cockroaches to thrive under a rather generalized set of environmental conditions at all stages of their lives.

Cockroaches are saprophagous insects, or scavengers, feeding on a great variety of dead and decaying plant and animal matter such as leaf litter, rotting wood, and carrion, as well as live material. They are, thus, very flexible in their diet, and this flexibility allows them to exist under a wide range of conditions. In fact, the habitat types of this order span such areas as wood rat nests, grain storage silos, forest leaf litter, and nests of leaf cutter ants. They thrive in areas with moisture and warmth.

Cockroaches produce oothecae, sacs in which the eggs are held and protected by secretions produced by the female. These egg sacs may be carried by the female externally until the time of hatching, or internally until the female gives birth to live young, or they may simply be deposited on a suitable substrate and left to hatch without any care from the female.

Besides being rather fast runners, many cockroaches have other adaptations that allow them to escape from predation. One such defensive adaptation is the ability to produce an offensive odor which they emit when disturbed. Other species, such as the Madagascaran cockroach, *Gromphadorhina laevigata*, force air out through their spiracles, thus producing an intimidating hissing sound.

Cockroaches are worldwide in distribution, although most of this order's approximately 4,000 species occur in the tropics. In the United States and

KEY TERMS

Obligate intestinal symbiont—An organism that lives in the intestinal tract of another organism, and whose presence is necessary for the survival of the host. Intestinal symbionts are usually bacteria or protozoans.

Oothecae—Egg sacs produced by some insects including cockroaches.

Paurometabolism—A type of simple metamorphosis in which the nymph, or immature, stage of the insect resembles the adult except in size, proportion, and wing length, and whose habitat requirements are the same as those of the adult.

Phylogeny—A hypothesized shared evolutionary history between members of a group of organisms based on shared traits of the organisms; also known as "evolutionary trees."

Saprophagous—Refers to decomposer organisms that eat dead and decaying plant and animal matter.

Simple metamorphosis—A type of developmental change in insects which does not involve a larval or pupal stage, but instead only has the egg, nymph, and adult stages.

has contributed greatly to our general understanding of physiology due to its use as a model study organism in biological research investigating nutrition, neurophysiology, and endocrinology. Medical knowledge has expanded as a result of the data gained from such studies of the cockroach.

Further Reading:

Arnett, R. H.,Jr. *American Insects: A Handbook of the Insects of America North of Mexico.* Gainesville, FL: Sandhill Crane Press, 1993.

Borror, D. J., C. A. Triplehorn, and N. F. Johnson. *An Introduction to the Study of Insects,* 6th ed. Orlando, FL: Harcourt Brace College Publishers, 1989.

Cornell, P. B. *The Cockroach.* London: Hutchinson, 1968.

Chapman, R. F. *The Insects: Structure and Function.* 3rd ed. Cambridge, MA: Harvard University Press, 1982.

Elzinga, R. J. *Fundamentals of Entomology.* 3rd ed. Englewood Cliffs, NJ: Prentice–Hall, 1987.

Roth, L. M. "Evolution and Taxonomic Significance of Reproduction in Blattaria." *Annual Review of Entomology* 15 (1970): 75–96.

Puja Batra

Coconut see **Palms**

Canada, there are some 29 different genera, and about 50 species. Most of these species occur in the southern United States.

Due to their preference for moist, warm places, flexible diet, and nocturnal activity, cockroaches are very successful at living uncontrolled in human areas. Although annoying and often feared by people, they are not known to be significant disease carriers, crop pests, or agents of other large–scale damage to human areas. There are four species in North America which are common as household insects. They are the German cockroach (*Blattella germanica*), the American cockroach (*Periplaneta americana*), the brown–banded cockroach (*Supella longipalpa*, and the oriental cockroach (*Blatta orientalis*). The oothecae of these indoor species are often deposited on common household items such as cardboard boxes, and in this way may be transported from place to place before they actually hatch, thereby spreading to new areas.

In contrast to its image as a fearsome, although relatively harmless pest, the cockroach has for many years actually benefitted humans—a benefit that has resulted from its abundance and often large size. The cockroach

Codfishes

Codfish (Gadidae) are a family of bottom–feeding fish that live in cool or cold seas, mostly in the Northern Hemisphere. There are about 21 genera and 55 species of codfishes. The most common marine habitats are inshore waters and continental shelves, generally in depths of less than 100 m, but sometimes considerably deeper. Codfishes are voracious predators of smaller species of fish and invertebrates. Some species of codfish are of great economic importance, supporting very large fisheries.

The Gadidae family is divided into two subfamilies. The Gadinae includes cod (e.g., Atlantic cod, *Gadus morhua*) and haddock (*Melanogrammus aeglefinus*), while the Lotinae includes hake (e.g., silver hake, *Merluccius bilinearis*), rockling (e.g., silver rockling, *Gaidropsarus argentatus*), and burbot (e.g., the freshwater American burbot, *Lota lota).*

Atlantic cod and its fishery

The economically most important species of codfish is the Atlantic cod, which supports one of the

A black cod.

world's largest fisheries. This species is common on both sides of the Atlantic. The Atlantic cod extends from Novaya Zemlya and Spitzbergen in the northeastern Atlantic, to Baffin Island and central Greenland in the northwestern Atlantic. The Atlantic cod is found as far south as the Bay of Biscay in western Europe and coastal North Carolina in North America. In the western Atlantic, the Atlantic cod is most abundant on the Grand Banks, a large region of open–ocean shelf east of Newfoundland.

The Atlantic cod are ravenous feeders on a wide variety of prey found on the sea bottom or in the water column. Fry and juvenile cod eat smaller invertebrates and fish larvae. While the most common prey of adult Atlantic cod are small species of fish, cannibalistic feeding on smaller size classes of its own species is known to occur.

The Atlantic cod has long been the target of European fishermen, and this species was one of the first natural resources to be heavily exploited by European settlers in the Americas. The extraordinarily large cod populations of the Grand Banks and the northern Gulf of Saint Lawrence were noted during the exploratory voyages of the Cabot brothers, who sailed on behalf of

England during the late 1490s. By 1505, many Portuguese and Basque fishers were exploiting the bountiful cod resources of the New World. By 1550, hundreds of ships departed every year from European ports for the northwest Atlantic in search of cod, which were taken in large quantities, preserved by salting or drying, and transported to the kitchens of western Europe. By 1620, there were more than 1,000 fishing vessels in the waters off Newfoundland, and about 1,600 in 1812.

During this early stage of the cod fishery in the northwest Atlantic, fish were typically very large, commonly 1–2 m (3–6 ft) long and weighing more than 100 kg (220 lb). However, because of the long history of heavy exploitation of Atlantic cod, such large fish are very rare today.

During the 18th and 19th centuries the cod fishery on the banks off Newfoundland was an unregulated, open–access enterprise, involving large numbers of ships sailing from Europe, Newfoundland, Canada, and New England. In addition, flotillas of smaller, local boats were exploiting near–shore populations of cod. Most of the fishing during these times was done using hand lines and long lines, which are not very efficient methods. Still, the substantial fishing effort caused noticeable depletions of many of the near–shore cod stocks.

During the 20th century, especially its second half, the new technologies have allowed a much more intensive exploitation of the stocks of Atlantic cod. A variety of highly efficient trawls, seines, and gill nets have been developed, and their effective deployment is aided by fish–finding devices based on sonar technology. Moreover, storage and processing capacities of ships have significantly increased, which permits large vessels to stay at sea for long periods of time.

The 1960s saw the largest harvests of cod in the northwest Atlantic, as a result of efficient technology and open–access and unregulated fishery. The total catch in this region in 1968 was more than 2 million tons. These huge catches were unsustainable by the cod population, and the stocks of Atlantic cod began to collapse by the 1970s.

In 1977, the Canadian government began to manage fisheries within a 320–km–wide zone around its coast. This was mostly accomplished by controlling access and allocating quotas of fish, especially cod, the most important species in the fishery. These conservation efforts led to small increases in cod stocks and catches. However, during the late 1980s and 1990s, the cod stocks suffered a much more serious collapse. Because the populations of mature cod capable of reproducing the species are small, the stocks will probably recover quite slowly, despite the huge reductions in fishing beginning in 1991, and a ban on cod fishing in 1992. The fishing moratorium recognizes the sad fact that one of the world's greatest renewable resources, the stocks of cod in the northwest Atlantic, had been overfished to commercial extinction.

Undoubtedly, the collapse of cod stocks was mostly caused by overfishing, that is, exploitation by humans at a rate considerably exceeding the cod population growth. The overfishing occurred because of economic greed, unrealistic fish–population models that predicted quotas too large to be sustained by the cod population, and because politicians often set fishing quotas exceeding those recommended by their fishery scientists. Moreover, this overfishing occurred along with other environmental changes that may have exacerbated the effects of the excessive harvesting. In particular, several years of unusually cold waters off Newfoundland and Labrador may have greatly reduced spawning success, so the heavily fished population was not being replenished. Other factors have also been suggested, including a rapidly increasing population of seals. However, this particular seal species does not consume much cod and is therefore not considered a significant factor in the collapse of cod stocks. Unregulated fishing is clearly a major factor. For example, since the Canadian moratorium on fishing did not extend to those portions of the Banks that are beyond Canada's territorial waters, large European fleets continued to catch fish in those waters, further depleting the stocks of cod.

Fortunately, Atlantic cod populations, while low, are by no means threatened with extinction. In 1994, large spawning schools of fish were once again observed in the waters off Newfoundland. If the regulating authorities maintain the moratorium on cod fishing, and if they subsequently regulate and monitor the fishery, then there is hope that this great natural resource will again provide food for humans, but this time in a sustainable fashion.

Further Reading:

Freedman, B. *Environmental Ecology.* 2nd ed. San Diego: Academic Press, 1994.

Scott, W. B., and M. G. Scott. *Atlantic Fishes of Canada.* Toronto: University of Toronto Press, 1988.

Bill Freedman

Codeine

Codeine is a type of medication belonging to a class of drugs known as opioid analgesics, which are derived from the *Papaver somniferum,* a type of poppy flower, or are manufactured to chemically resemble the products of that poppy. In Latin, *Papaver* refers to any flower of the poppy variety, while *somniferum* translates to mean "maker of sleep." The plant has been used for over 6,000 years, beginning with the ancient cultures of Egypt, Greece, Rome, and China, to cause sleep. Analgesics are drugs which provide relief from pain. Codeine, an opioid analgesic, decreases pain while causing the user to feel sleepy. At lower doses, codeine is also helpful for stopping a cough.

Although codeine is present in nature within the sticky substance latex which oozes out of the opium poppy's seed pod, it is present in only small concentrations (less than 0.5). However, morphine, another opioid analgesic, is present in greater concentrations (10) within the opium poppy's latex, and codeine can be made from morphine via a process known as methylation, which is the primary way that codeine is prepared.

Codeine is a centrally acting drug, meaning that it goes to specific areas of the central nervous system (in the brain and spinal cord) to interfere with the transmission of pain, and to change your perception of the pain. For example, if you have your wisdom teeth removed and your mouth is feeling very painful, codeine will not go to the hole in your gum where the tooth was pulled and which is now throbbing with pain, but rather will act with the central nervous system to change the way you are perceiving the pain. In fact, if you were given codeine after your tooth was pulled, you might explain its effect by saying that the pain was still there, but it just wasn't bothering you anymore.

Codeine's anti–tussive (cough stopping) effects are also due to its central actions on the brain. It is believed that codeine inhibits an area of the brain known as the medullary cough center.

Codeine is not as potent a drug as is morphine, so it tends to be used for only mild–to–moderate pain, while morphine is useful for more severe pain. An advantage to using codeine is that a significant degree of pain relief can be obtained with oral medication (taken by mouth), rather than by injection. Codeine is sometimes preferred over other opioid analgesics because it has a somewhat lower potential for addiction and abuse than do other drugs in that class.

Scientists are currently trying to learn more about how codeine and other opioid analgesics affect the brain. It is interesting to note that there are certain chemicals (endorphins, enkephalins, and dynorphins) which are made within the brains of mammals, including humans, and which closely resemble opioid analgesics. In fact, the mammalian brain itself actually produces tiny amounts of morphine and codeine! Some of these chemicals are produced in the human brain in response to certain behaviors, including exercise. Exploring how and when human brains produce these chemicals could help scientists understand more about ways to control pain with fewer side effects, as well as helping to increase the understanding of addictive substances and behaviors.

See also Narcotic.

Further Reading:

Berkow, Robert, and Andrew J. Fletcher. *The Merck Manual of Diagnosis and Therapy.* Rahway, NJ: Merck Research Laboratories, 1992.

Ganong, William F. *Review of Medical Physiology.* Norwalk, CT: Appleton & Lange, 1993.

Katzung, Bertram G. *Basic & Clinical Pharmacology.* Norwalk, CT: Appleton & Lange, 1992.

Rosalyn Carson–DeWitt

Coefficient

A coefficient is any part of a term, except the whole, where term means an adding of an algebraic expression (taking addition to include subtraction as is usually done in algebra.) Thus, in the expression

$$3xy^2 \frac{x}{2} + \frac{4x}{3y}$$

the possible coefficients for the term $3xy^2$ would include 3, which is the coefficient of xy^2, and x, which is the coefficient of $3y^2$; for the term $-x-2$, the coefficients include -1 as a coefficient of x and -1 as a coefficient of X-2; finally the term

$$\frac{4x}{3y}$$

has 4 as a coefficient of

$$\frac{x}{3y}$$

and Y-3 as a coefficient of X-Y.

Most commonly, however, the word coefficient refers to what is, strictly speaking, the numerical coefficient. Thus, the numerical coefficients of the expression $5xy^2 - 3x + 2y - 4\text{-}X$ are considered to be 5, -3, $+2$, and -4.

In many formulas, especially in statistics, certain numbers are considered coefficients, such as correlation coefficients in statistics or the coefficient of expansion in physics.

Coelacanth

The coelacanth (*Latimeria chalumnae*) is the only known living representative of an order of fishes thought to have become extinct 70 million years ago, at about the same time as the dinosaurs.

The coelacanth is a sarcoptergian, or lobe–finned fish, related to the lungfish. Unlike most bony fish, its pectoral and pelvic fins are muscular, even leglike. (The ancestor of amphibians, and thus of all land–dwelling animals, had such fins.) Able to move 180°, these fins allow it to swim forwards, backwards, and even upside down. While swimming, the coelacanth moves its fins like a land animal moves its legs while walking: the

A coelacanth (*Latimeria chalumnae*).

front left and right rear fins advance together, and front right and left rear doing the same.

Its bluish body is covered with thick scales unique to the order. Its jaws are strong. A few specimens have been found with lanternfish in their stomachs, proof that the fish is predatory.

It is found in the cold, dark waters 1,313–1,970 ft (400–600 m) deep off the Comoro Islands, which lay in the Mozambique Channel near the northern tip of Madagascar. The retinas of its eyes include a reflective layer (similar to that of a cat) that helps it see in the dimly lit waters.

Most of what we know about coelacanths has come from the study of dead specimens. Upon dissection, some females were found to contain huge, nearly base-ball–sized eggs that lacked shells or hard egg cases. The question was, How did the fish protect these eggs? Did it nest? Although it had been hypothesized that fossil forms had bore their young alive, the question was not answered until 1975, when a female specimen at the American Museum of Natural History was dissected, five perfectly shaped fetuses were discovered. Each was about 14 in (35 cm) long, and had a yolk sac attached to its stomach. The coelacanth is ovoviviparous, that is, the female keeps the eggs inside her body to protect them as they develop to the hatchling stage.

Little is known at present about the coelacanth's ecology. In 1987, marine biologist Hans Fricke of Germany's Max Planck Institute for Comparative Physiology, managed to film coelacanths in their deep water environments. Not only did they observe the unusual swimming motion described above, but also saw the coelacanths doing "headstands." When the researchers triggered an electronic lure, they could initiate this behavior. The coelacanth has an organ between its nostrils called the rostral organ, which is believed to detect prey's electrical fields, as the ampullae of Lorenzini do in sharks. Fricke's research strengthened the evidence that the rostral organ is indeed an electrical sensor.

A rare find

The coelacanth first came to the attention of science in 1938. At the time, a young scientist named Majorie Courteney–Latimer was curator of a small natural history museum in East London, South Africa. Because the museum was new, Courteney–Latimer had been given the right to decide the direction the collections would take, and she had chosen to focus on marine life. Local fishermen often brought her unusual fish from their catches.

Capt. Hendrik Goosen contacted her, saying that he had several fish she might be interested in. When she got to the dock, she found a pile of sharks waiting for her. But buried in the pile was a blue fish unlike any she'd ever seen. This one she would take.

It was large, nearly five feet in length—far too big to fit in the museum's freezer. Desperate to preserve the fish against the hot South African weather, she asked the local hospital if she could keep it in their morgue and was refused. Finally, she managed to get it to a taxidermist.

Knowing the fish was unique, Courteney–Latimer wrote to L. B. J. Smith, an expert on South African fish. Smith recognized the fish as a coelacanth from Courteney–Latimer's sketch and was able to learn a great deal of information from the mounted specimen (dissecting one side of it). He published a notice in the journal *Nature* (CK) that told the world that the coelacanths still existed.

This notice also gave Smith the right to name the new species. He chose *Latimeria* in honor of Courteney–Latimer, and *chalumnae* after the river near which Goosen had caught the fish.

Fourteen years passed before another coelacanth turned up, despite Smith's blanketing the eastern coast of Africa with posters describing the coelacanth in French, Portuguese and English and offering a reward. As it was caught near the Comoro Islands in the Indian Ocean, many miles from where the first specimen was caught, Smith thought it represented another species, which he named *Malania anjouanae*. However, later scientists deduced that *Malania* was actually another *Latimeria*.

Since that 1952 specimen, 200 more coelacanths have been caught and have been included in research collections. Many are in France, which had ruled the Comoros as a colonial power. Most are caught by local fishermen, using handlines from dugout canoes, who tow the fish back to shore with a hook. The fish is usually dying by the time it reaches the surface, because of the great pressure difference between its home and the surface.

Some people have thought that catching a live coelacanth to display in an aquarium would be a very good idea. Others, including Hans Fricke, have objected, arguing that the number of coelacanths that have been taken from the small population have already adversely affected the species. Part of the problem is that animals that bear live young produce fewer offspring than those that release their eggs into the environment; thus, the coelacanth population would not bounce back as quickly from the loss of a breeding female as would, for example, a trout that produces thousands of eggs at one time.

Were one aquarium to obtain a coelacanth, they argue, others would want one, too. The American and British aquariums that had been considering an expedition to capture a breeding pair changed their minds, and an Asian aquarium that did mount such an expedition came up empty.

The coelacanth is protected under the Convention on International Trade in Endangered Species (CITES) . However, the interest continues and may have spawned a black market in coelacanths. Unless the government of the Comoro Islands decides to preserve instead of exploit the coelacanth, the future is not encouraging: the government uses prepared specimens as official gifts.

F.C. Nicholson

Coffee plant

The coffee tree, genus *Coffea*, family Rubiaceae (Madder family), is native to Ethiopia. The name coffee also refers to the fruit (beans) of the tree and to the beverage brewed from the beans. Coffee is one of the world's most valuable agricultural crops.

There are about 30 species of *Coffea*, but only two species provide most of the world market for coffee. *Coffea arabica* is indigenous to Ethiopia and was the first cultivated species of coffee tree. *C. arabica* provides 75% of the world's supply of coffee. *Coffea robusta*, also known as *Coffea canephora*, was first discovered growing wild in what is now Zaire. This species was not domesticated and cultivated until the

A coffee plant in Costa Rica.

turn of the twentieth century, and now supplies about 23% of the world's coffee. *Coffea liberica* is also an important source of coffee beans, but is mostly consumed locally and does not enter the world market in great quantity. *C. robusta* and *C. liberica* were developed because of their resistance to insects and diseases.

Cultivation and harvesting

The coffee tree or shrub grows to 15–30 ft (3–9 m). The tree has shiny, dark green, simple, ovate leaves that grow opposite each other in an alternate fashion, and reach 3 in (7.5 cm) in length. Fragrant, white flowers that bloom for only a few days grow where the leaves join the branches. Clusters of fruit, called cherries, follow the flowers. The cherries are green while developing and growing. The green berries change to yellow, and then to red when the cherries are mature, and deep crimson when ripe and ready for picking. The cherries do not all ripen at once and trees that grow in lower, hotter regions often hold multicolored berries, flowers, and leaves all at once. Each cherry has two chambers or locules that hold two beans. The beans are oval and flat on one side with a lengthwise groove. They are covered by papery skin that must be removed before roasting. A soft, fleshy pulp surrounds the beans. Cherries with one bean, usually round, are called peaberries. Coffee trees raised from seeds generally flower the third or fourth year, and produce a good crop at five years. The trees can produce crops for about 15–20 years. Coffee trees can yield from about 1–8 lb (0.5–3.6 kg) in a year, with 1.5–2 lb (0.7–0.9 kg) being the average. It takes 5 lb (2.3 kg) of cherries to produce 1 lb (0.5 kg) of beans.

Coffee grows best in regions located between the Tropic of Cancer and the Tropic of Capricorn (25° north and south of the equator), also called the "coffee belt." Coffee trees do not produce well in extremely hot weather, nor can they tolerate frost. Ideally, the annual mean temperature should be around 70°F (21.1°C). There should be adequate rainfall 70 in (178 cm) per year especially when the fruit is developing. *C arabica* grows best at higher altitudes 2,000–6,000 ft (610–1,830 m) and because the fruit of this species takes about 6–7 months to ripen after flowering, only one crop is harvested per year. *C. robusta* grows best at lower altitudes around 3,000 ft (915 m), and depending on the climate and soil, the fruit can be harvested 2–3 times per year. Coffee trees grow best in rich, well drained, organic soil, particularly in regions with disintegrated volcanic ash. The dangers for growing coffee trees are frost, the coffee bean borer, coffee leaf miner, and the fungus *Hemileia vastatrix*.

There are two methods of harvesting and processing the cherries. The wet method, used only where water is abundant, involves picking only the ripe cherries. The cherries are soaked in water to soften the skin and the skin and pulp are removed, leaving a sticky film. The cherries are put into tanks to ferment for about 24 hours and then washed to remove the sticky covering on the bean. The beans are spread out to dry, and put into hulling machines that remove the papery skin on the bean. Coffee beans processed by the wet method tend to be more expensive. They are considered to have a better flavor, probably because only ripe cherries are picked. The dry method involves stripping all the cherries from the branches. The cherries are thoroughly dried and put into machines that remove the dry outer covering, pulp, and papery skin. The dry method is the oldest type of processing and is currently used for about two–thirds of the world's coffee. Both processes result in a dried, green coffee bean. Dried, processed beans are then sorted, and graded for quality, type, and size. The beans are packed for transport into bags of 132 lb (60 kg) each. Coffee is exported all over the world and is usually roasted after it reaches its destination.

History

The first cultivated coffee, *C. arabica*, is native to Ethiopia. In Africa, coffee beans were consumed as food and later made into wine. The coffee plant made its way to neighboring Arabia around 1000 A.D. where it was made into and consumed as a beverage. Coffee beans were introduced to Europe during the spice trade (fifteenth century). The first coffee tree was brought to Europe by Jussieu and planted in the Jardin des Plantes, Paris in 1714. This tree was to become the source of all Latin American coffees. This same tree was stolen and later replanted (after a treacherous sea voyage) in Martinique. This species spread to the West Indies and later, Brazil. Until the late part of the seventeenth century, all coffee came from Arabia. The West Indian colonies of Spain and France became major world suppliers. Later, the Dutch successfully cultivated the coffee tree in Indonesia, and eventually became the leading coffee producer. The fungus, *Hemileia vastatrix*, wiped out most of the coffee trees in Asia, allowing the West Indian and Brazilian industry to gain dominance. By the late nineteenth century, Brazil had vast coffee plantations and was the leading coffee producer. This status fluctuated with the emancipation of its slaves, incoming European immigrant workers, the start of many small farms, and overproduction. Today, Brazil and Colombia are the world's leading producers of coffee beans.

Further Reading:

Clarke, R. C., and R. Macrae, eds. *Coffee.* 5 vol. New York: Elsevier, 1988.

Lewington, Anna. *Plants for People.* New York: Oxford University Press, 1990.

Christine Miner Minderovic

Cogeneration

Cogeneration is the simultaneous generation of two forms of energy, usually heat and electricity, from one energy source. Traditional energy generating systems produce only heat or electricity by burning a fuel source. In both cases, burning the fuel generates a lot of heat and the exhaust gases can be hotter than 932°F (500°C). Traditionally, this "waste heat" would be vented into the environment for disposal. Cogeneration facilities capture some of that waste heat and use it to produce steam or more electricity. Both systems produce the same amount of energy but cogeneration uses about 35% less fuel because it is designed to be a highly efficient process.

Cogeneration is widely used in some European countries, such as Denmark and Italy, where fuel costs are particularly large. In the United States, where fuel costs are relatively small, cogeneration produces about 5% of the energy supply. Some researchers estimate that if all large U. S. industrial plants used cogeneration technology, there would be enough energy–generating capacity to last until 2020 without building any new power plants.

Why cogenerate?

There are several reasons why cogeneration is a beneficial technology. Cogeneration is an excellent method of improving energy efficiency, which has positive environmental and economic results. It also buys time to find new energy sources, and is a reliable, well–understood process.

The most important environmental reason to cogenerate is that vast amounts of precious, non-renewable resources are being wasted by inefficient uses. For example, in the United States, only 16% of the energy used for industrial processes creates useful energy or products. About 41% of the waste is unavoidable because some energy is always lost whenever energy is transformed. However, 43% of the wasted energy could potentially be used in a more energy–efficient process. Cogeneration is an excellent way to increase energy efficiency, which reduces both environmental impacts and operating costs.

Another benefit of cogeneration is that it is an off–the–shelf technology. It has been used in some forms for over a century and therefore most technical problems have been solved. Because cogeneration is a reliable, proven technology, there are fewer installation and operating problems compared with new, untested technology.

History of cogeneration

At the beginning of the twentieth century, steam was the main source of mechanical power. However, as electricity became more controllable, many small "power houses" that produced steam realized they could also produce and use electricity, and they adapted their systems to cogenerate both steam and electricity. Then from 1940–1970, the concept developed of a centralized electric utility that delivered power to the surrounding area. Large utility companies quickly became reliable, relatively inexpensive sources of electricity, so the small power houses stopped cogenerating and bought their electricity from the utilities.

During the late 1960s and early 1970s, interest in cogeneration began to revive, and by the late 1970s the need to conserve energy resources became clear. In the United States, legislation was passed to encourage the development of cogeneration facilities. Specifically, the Public Utilities Regulatory Policies Act (PURPA) of 1978 encouraged this technology by allowing cogenerators to connect with the utility network to purchase and sell electricity. PURPA allowed cogenerators to buy electricity from utility companies at fair prices, in times of shortfall, while also allowing them to sell their electricity based on the cost the utility would have paid to produce that power, the so–called "avoided cost." These conditions have encouraged a rapid increase in cogeneration capacity in the United States.

In Europe, there has been little government support because cogeneration is not seen as new technology and therefore is not covered under "Thermie," the European Community's (EC) energy program. Under Thermie, 40% of the cost for capital projects is covered by the EC government. However, some individual European countries, like Denmark and Italy, have adopted separate energy policies. In Denmark, 27.5% of their electricity is produced by cogeneration, and all future energy projects must involve cogeneration or some form of alternative energy. In Italy, low–interest loans are provided to cover up to 30% of the cost of building new cogeneration facilities.

Barriers to cogeneration

There are several barriers to the large–scale implementation of cogeneration. Although the operating costs of cogeneration facilities are relatively small, the initial costs of equipment and installation are large. Also, multinational oil companies and central utility companies have substantial political influence in many countries. These companies emphasize their own short–term profits over the long–term environmental costs of inefficient use of non–renewable resources. Other barriers to cogeneration are the falsely low costs of fossil fuels, relative to their true, longer–term costs and future scarcity. In a world of plentiful, seemingly inexpensive energy, there is little incentive to use fuel wisely. In addition, national energy policies can have a tremendous effect, like the EC's Thermie policy which does not support cogeneration, and the recent cutbacks in the U. S. energy conservation policies and research, the effects of which remain to be seen.

In the United States, much of the energy research dollar is devoted to developing new energy sources, despite the fact that most of the country's current energy sources are wasted due to inefficient uses. In fact, energy efficiency has not increased much since 1985. As the world's largest user and waster of energy, the United States has a substantial impact on many forms of worldwide pollution, and therefore has a special responsibility to use its resources efficiently.

Current research

Current cogeneration research is examining ways of improving the old technology. One improvement involves steam–injected gas turbines, which would increase the electric output capacity of the turbines, and thereby increase the energy efficiency of cogeneration. Other improvements are making cogeneration more feasible for smaller plants. Currently, this technology is feasible only in larger facilities. Smaller cogeneration

---

KEY TERMS

Avoided cost—Under PURPA, this is the price that the utility company must pay to buy electricity from a cogenerating company. It is calculated as the amount the utility would have paid if the utility company had generated the electricity itself.

Public Utilities Regulatory Policies Act (PURPA)—This is U. S. federal legislation that is designed to encourage the development of cogenerating plants.

Waste heat—This is heat that is released as fuels are burned but is not used.

---

units would allow a more widespread application of this energy efficient technology.

See also Electrical power supply; Energy efficiency.

Further Reading:

Ganapathy, V. "Recovering Heat When Generating Power." *Chemical Engineering* (February 1993): 94–98.

Miller, G. T., Jr. *Environmental Science: Sustaining the Earth*. Belmont, CA: Wadsworth Publishing Company, 1991.

Orlando, J. A. *Cogeneration Planner's Handbook*. Lilburn, GA: Fairmont Press, 1991.

Payne, F. W., ed. *Cogeneration Sourcebook*. Atlanta, GA: Fairmont Press, 1985.

Shelley, S., and K. Fouhy. "All Fired Up About Cogeneration." *Chemical Engineering* (January 1992): 39–45.

Jennifer LeBlanc

Cognition

Cognition is a complex mental process whereby an individual gains knowledge and understanding of the world. While cognition cannot be neatly dissected into constitutive processes, psychologists point out that it reveals the interplay of such critical psychological mechanisms such as perception, attention, memory, imagery, verbal function, judgment, problem–solving, decision–making, with the admixture of other factors, including physical health, educational background, socio–economic status, and cultural identity. A dynamic process, since both the world and the individual are subject to change, cognition is a vital function which enables an individual to exist in the world as an independent and active participant.

Historical background

Before psychology existed as a scientific discipline, the study of cognition was the domain of philosophy. There are two fundamental scientific paradigms—with many variations—regarding cognition in Western philosophy: idealism and empiricism. According to idealistic view, represented by such thinkers as Plato (c. 427–347 B.C.) and René Descartes (1596–1650), innate ideas are the crucial component in cognition; in other words, knowledge is determined by what has been in an individual's mind since—or before—birth. The opposing, empiricist view, is succinctly expressed by John Locke's (1632–1704) dictum that, without sense–perceptions, the mind is an empty slate, a *tabula rasa*. While certain psychologists struggled to determine which of the two paradigms was dominant, the celebrated Swiss cognitive psychologist Jean Piaget (1896–1980) developed a theoretical model of cognition which recognized the importance of both the innate/ genetic and the empirical components of cognition. It could be said that cognition depends on both components, just as the successful operation of a computer program requires both the hardware and the software.

How cognition works

Cognition starts with perception. Perception, which occurs in space and time, provides the general framework for cognition; perception is also the process of becoming aware of a stimulus, which can be external or internal. The next step is conceptualization: after realizing the existence of something we try to figure out what it is: the percept becomes a concept. For example, cognition happens at the instance when the perception "something coming our way" crystallizes as the concept "dog." If the dog is unfriendly, we will use judgment to evaluate our newly acquired knowledge of the situation in an effort to avoid injury. Fortunately, while problem–solving is a key application of the power of judgment in everyday life, not all problems are unpleasant. Working on a mathematical problem, for instance, can be a pleasant, one could say esthetic, experience; the same could be said for any problems requiring creativity and ingenuity, abilities of a higher order than simpler methods, such as the trial–and–error approach. In the realm of the scientific imagination, cognition can, in rare moments, occur as an unexpected flash of illumination. The problem appears to solve itself. One such extraordinary experience is an often quoted mathematical discovery by the French mathematician and philosopher Henri Poincaré (1854–1912). Unable to fall asleep one night, Poincaré thought about a tough problem that he had been grappling with: "Ideas rose in crowds; I felt them collide until pairs interlocked, so to speak, making a stable combination. By the next morning I had established the existence of a new class of Fuchian functions."

Varieties of cognition

Poincaré's experience shows that cognition, while originally stemming from less complex psychological mechanisms, such as perception, is not literally tied to the world of sense–perception. Without contradicting the statement about perception providing the spatio-temporal context of cognition, we can say that cognition also operates in the seemingly unlimited expanses of imaginary space (as in art and mathematics) and inner space (as in introspection) . In addition, while cognition is traditionally defined as rational and conceptual, it can contain such non–intellectual components as feelings, intuitions, and physical acts. The process of learning to play a musical instrument, for example, although a rationally structured endeavor, contains many repetitive, mechanical operations that could be defined as elements of unconscious learning. When the source of new knowledge is unknown, when we do not know why we know something, we are probably dealing with the hidden, silent, non–conceptual dimensions of cognition. A new skill, insight, ability, or perspective suddenly appears "out of nowhere." But this "nowhere" is not really outside the realm of cognition. As in the case of perception, conceptual thinking provides a framework but does not limit cognition. While cognition is certainly limited by human biology, it has no limits of its own. Finally, cognition is also never complete; despite repeated attempts, throughout the history of thought, to create closed intellectual systems postulating absolute knowledge as a theoretical goal, the human mind—as evidenced, for example, by the tremendous development of science since the Scientific Revolution—inevitably finds a way to widen the horizons of knowledge. That cognition is an open-ended process is also demonstrated by the seemingly unlimited human capacity for learning, introspection, change, and adaptation to a changing world.

See also Brain; Memory; Perception; Psychology; Scientific revolution.

Further Reading:

Matlin, K. M. *Cognition*. 3d ed. San Diego: Harcourt Brace Jovanovich, 1994.

KEY TERMS

. . . .

Concept—A mental construct, based on experience, used to identify and separate classes of phenomena. The perceived distinctions between cats and dogs allow us to formulate the concepts "cat" and "dog."

Creativity—The ability to find solutions to problems and answers to questions without relying on established methods.

Empiricism—Scientific thinking based on the primacy of sense-experience.

Idealism—Scientific thinking based on the view that ultimate reality is immaterial.

Imagination—The ability to create alternate worlds without losing contact with reality.

Judgment—The ability to evaluate events and statements.

Percept—The mental representation of a single perceived event or object.

Scientific paradigm—A general view shared by groups of scientists.

Morris, Charles G. *Psychology: An Introduction.* 7th ed. Englewood Cliffs, NJ: Prentice Hall, 1990.

Piaget, Jean. *Psychology and Epistemology: Towards a Theory of Knowledge.* New York: Viking, 1971.

Polanyi, Michael. *The Tacit Dimension.* Magnolia, MA: Peter Smith, 1983.

Sheldrake, Rupert. *The Presence of the Past: Morphic Resonance and the Habits of Nature.* New York: Random House, 1988.

Zoran Minderovic

Coherence see **Interference**

Cold, common

The common cold, also called acute coryza or upper respiratory infection, is caused by any of some 200 different viruses and has defied both cure and vaccine for centuries. The United States alone will have about a half a billion colds a year, or two for each man, woman, and child.

Dedicated researchers have searched for a cure or even an effective treatment for years. The pharmaceutical company that discovers the antiviral agent that will kill the cold viruses will reap a great return. Discovering or constructing the agent that will be universally lethal to all the cold-causing viruses has been fruitless. A drug that will kill only one or two of the viruses would be of little use since the patient would not know which of the viruses was the one that brought on his cold. So at present, as the saying goes, if you treat a cold you can get rid of it in about a week. Left untreated it will hang around for about seven days.

The common cold differs in several ways from influenza or the flu. Cold symptoms develop gradually and are relatively mild. The flu has a sudden onset and has more serious symptoms the usually put the sufferer to bed, and the flu lasts about twice as long as the cold. Also influenza can be fatal, especially to elderly persons, though the number of influenza viruses is more limited than the number of cold viruses and vaccines are available against certain types of flu.

Rhinoviruses, adenoviruses, influenza viruses, parainfluenza viruses, syncytial viruses, echoviruses, and coxsackie viruses—all have been implicated as the agent that causes the runny nose, cough, sore throat, and sneezing that advertise that you have a cold. More than 200 viruses, each with its own favored method of being passed from one person to another, its own gestation period, each different from the others, wait patiently to invade the mucous membranes that line the nose of the next cold victim.

Passing the cold-causing virus from one person to the next can be done by sneezing onto the person or shaking hands or by an object handled by the infected person and picked up by the next victim. Oddly, direct contact with the infected person, as in kissing, is not an efficient way for the virus to spread. Only in about 10 percent of such contacts does the uninfected person get the virus. Walking around in a cold rain will not cause a cold. Viruses like warm, moist surroundings so they will thrive indoors in the winter and people spend more time indoors then than they do outdoors. However, being outdoors in cold weather can dehydrate the mucous membranes in the nose and make them more susceptible to infection by a rhinovirus.

In addition, the viruses mutate with regularity. Each time it is passed from one person to the next the virus changes slightly, so it is not the virus the first person had. Viruses are tiny creatures considered to be alive, though they hover on the brink of life and lifelessness. They are obligate parasites, meaning that they can carry out their functions only when they invade another living thing, plant or animal.

The virus is a tough envelope surrounding its nucleic acid, the genetic structure for any living thing. Once it invades the body the virus waits to be placed in the location in which it can function best. Once there it attaches to a cell by means of receptor areas on its envelope and on the cell membrane. The viral nucleic acid then is inserted into the cell nucleus and it takes over the functions of the nucleus, telling it to reproduce viruses.

Taking regular doses of vitamin C will not ward off a cold. However, high doses of vitamin C once a person has a cold may help to alleviate the symptoms to the point that discomfort is less. Over–the–counter drugs to treat colds treat only the symptoms. True, they may dry up the patient's runny nose, but after a few days the nose will compensate and overcome the effects of the medication and begin to drip again. The runny nose is from the loss of plasma from the blood vessels in the nose. Some researchers believe the nose drip is a defensive mechanism to prevent the invasion of other viruses. Antibiotics such as penicillin are useless against the cold because they do not affect viruses.

Scientists agree that the old wives' remedy of chicken soup can help the cold victim, but so can any other hot liquid. The soup or tea or herb tea helps to liquify the mucus in the sinus cavities and let them drain, reducing the pressure and making the patient feel better. The remedy is temporary and has no effect on the virus.

Clearing out the virus, easing the symptoms of the cold are the functions of the body's immune system. An assortment of white blood cells, each type with a differ-

ent function, marshals at the site of invasion and heaviest viral population and wages a life and death struggle against the invaders. It will take about a week, but the body's defenses will prevail.

See also Influenza.

Further Reading:

Huntington, D. "How to stop the family cold before it stops you." *Parents*, 69 (February, 1994): 26–28.
Menagh, Melanie. "Cold comforts." *Mademoiselle*, 100 (January, 1994): 120–121.
Poppy, J. "How to make colds less common." *Men's Health* 9 (January/February, 1994): 30–31

Larry Blaser

Colies see **Mousebirds**

Collagen

Collagen is a protein found abundantly throughout the bodies of animals, including humans. In fact, collagen makes up about one–third of the total body weight. Collagen is an important component of the body's connective tissues, which perform a variety of functions in the body. These tissues provide the framework, or internal scaffolding, for various organs such as the kidneys and lymph nodes. Connective tissues also impart great support and strength to structures such as the bones and tendons. Blood, an important type of connective tissue, transports oxygen and nutrients throughout the body.

Connective tissue is composed of a nonliving, gel–like material called a matrix, in which living cells are embedded. The matrix is composed of different kinds of protein fibers, the most common of which is collagen.

Structure of collagen

Collagen is a fibrous protein; that is, it is composed of many fibers. Each fiber consists of three microscopic ropes of protein wrapped around each other. The fibers in collagen are arranged parallel to each other, and are often grouped together in bundles. The bundling of collagen fibers gives the fibers greater strength than if they occurred individually. Collagen fibers are extremely tough and can resist a pulling force, but because they are not taut, they allow some flexibility.

Locations and functions of collagen

Collagen is a primary component of the connective tissue located in the dermis, the tough inner layer of the skin. This kind of connective tissue is also found in mucous membranes, nerves, blood vessels, and organs. Collagen in these structures imparts strength, support, and a certain amount of elasticity. As the skin ages, it loses some of its elasticity, resulting in wrinkles. Recently, injections of animal collagen given under the surface of the skin have been used to "plump up" the skin and remove wrinkles. However, this treatment is controversial. Many people develop allergic reactions to the collagen, and the procedure must be performed by a qualified physician.

Collagen is also a component of a kind of connective tissue that surrounds organs. This connective tissue encases and protects delicate organs like the kidneys and spleen.

Other locations where collagen fibers are prominent are in the tendons and ligaments. Tendons are straps of tough tissue that attach muscles to bones, allowing for movement. Ligaments are structures that hold the many bones of a joint, such as the knee joint, in proper position. Tendons and ligaments differ slightly in structure. In ligaments, the collagen fibers are less tightly packed than in tendons; in some ligaments, the fibers are not parallel.

Collagen adds strength to tendons and ligaments, and it imparts some stretch to these structures by allowing for some flexibility. However, collagen is not extremely elastic. If tendons and ligaments are stretched too far, these structures will tear, which may lead to problems in movement and bone position. Many athletes tear tendons and ligaments. When tearing occurs, the joint or bone in which the structures occur must be immobilized to allow for proper healing.

Cartilage is a connective tissue found in various places throughout the body, including the tip of the nose, the outside of the ears, the knees, and parts of the larynx and trachea. Cartilage consists of collagen fibers and cartilage cells. At these locations, collagen provides flexibility, support, and movement. Cartilage soaks up water like a sponge and is therefore somewhat "springy" and flexible. If the tip of the nose is pushed in and let go, it springs immediately back into place.

Examples of collagen in the animal kingdom

In vertebrates, which include all animals with a backbone, connective tissues are highly organized and developed. In invertebrates, which include the animals without backbones, connective tissues are not as well organized. However, in nematodes, also known as roundworms (an invertebrate animal), collagen plays a role in movement. The outer covering of the nematode, called the cuticle, consists primarily of collagen. The collagen helps the nematode move and also imparts some longitudinal elasticity. Because the collagen fibers crisscross each other and are not parallel in the nematode cuticle, nematodes are limited in side–to–side movement.

See also Connective tissue; Muscular system.

Further Reading:

Ayad, Shirley, et al. *The Extracellular Matrix Factsbook.* San Diego: Academic Press, 1994.
Fackelmann, Kathy A. "Chicken Collagen Soothes Aching Joints." *Science News* 144 (25 September 1993): 198.
Hay, Elizabeth D., ed. *The Cell Biology of Extracellular Matrix.* New York: Plenum Press, 1991.
Kucharz, Eugene. *The Collagens: Biochemistry and Pathophysiology.* New York: Springer–Verlag, 1992.
Johnstone, Iain L. "The Cuticle of the Nematode *Caenorhabditis elegans.*" *BioEssays* 16 (March 1993): 171.
Young, Crain M., et al. "Smart Collagen in Sea Lilies." *Nature* 366 (9 December 1993): 519.

Kathleen Scogna

Colloid

A colloid is a type of particle intermediate in size between a molecule and the type of particles we normally think of, which are visible to the naked eye. Colloidal particles are usually from 1 to 1,000 nanometers in diameter. When a colloid is placed in water, it forms a mixture which is similar in some ways to a solution, and similar in some ways to a suspension. Like a solution, the particles never settle to the bottom of the container. Like a suspension, the dispersion is cloudy.

The size of colloidal particles accounts for the cloudiness of a colloidal dispersion. A true solution, such as you might obtain by dissolving table salt in water, is transparent, and light will go through it with no trouble, even if the solution is colored. A colloidal dispersion, on the other hand, is cloudy. If it is held up to the light, at least some of the light scatters as it goes through the dispersion. This is because the light rays bounce off the larger particles in the colloid, and bounce away from your eye.

A colloidal dispersion doesn't ever settle to the bottom of the container. In this way, it is like a solution. The particles of the dispersion, though relatively large, are not large and heavy enough to sink. The solvent molecules support them for an indefinite time.

Everyone has seen what looks like dust particles moving about in a beam of sunlight. What you see is light reflected from colloid–sized particles, in motion because of tiny changes in air currents surrounding the suspended particles. This type of motion, called *Brownian motion*, is typical of colloids, even those in suspension in solution, where the motion is actually caused by bombardment of the colloidal particles by the molecular of the liquid. This constant motion helps to stabilize the suspension, so the particles don't settle.

Another commonly visible property of a colloidal dispersion is the *Tyndall effect*. If you shine a strong light through a translucent colloidal dispersion that will let at least some of the light through, the light beam becomes visible, like a column of light. This is because the large particles of the dispersed colloid scatter the light, and only the most direct beams make it through the medium.

Milk is the best known colloidal dispersion, and it shows all these properties. They can be seen by adding several drops of milk to a glass of water. Most of its cloudiness is due to fat particles that are colloidal in size, but there is also a significant amount of protein in it, and some of these are also in the colloidal size range.

See also Brownian motion; Solution.

Colobus monkeys

Colobus monkeys and the closely related langurs and leaf monkeys are Old World monkeys in the sub-

family Colobinae of the family Cercopithecidae. The primates in this subfamily share a common trait—they lack thumbs or have only small, useless thumbs.(The name *colobus* comes from a Greek word meaning mutilated.) However, lack of a thumb does not stop them from nimbly moving among the branches. They just grasp a branch between the palm of the hand and the other fingers. The Colobinae are distinguished from the other subfamily of Old World monkeys, the Cercopithecinae, by their lack of cheek pouches, their slender build, and their large salivary glands. They live throughout equatorial Africa, India, and Southeast Asia.

Unlike most monkeys, which are fairly omnivorous, eating both plant and animal foods, many colobus monkeys eat primarily leaves and shoots. In the tropical and subtropical regions in which these leaf–eaters live, they have an advantage over other monkeys in that they have a year–round supply of food. Leaf–eaters also have an advantage in that they can live in a wider variety of habitats than fruit–eaters, even in open savanna. Fruit–eaters, on the other hand, must keep on the move in forests to find a fruit supply in season. Most colobus monkeys also eat fruits, flowers, and seeds when they can find them.

Like all Old World monkeys, colobus monkeys have tough hairless pads, called ischial callosities, on their rear ends. There are no nerves in these pads, a fact that allows them to sit for long periods of time on tree branches without their legs "going to sleep." Some colobus monkeys have loud, raucous calls that they use particularly at dawn. Apparently these signals tell neighboring troops of monkeys where a particular group is going to be feeding that day.

Leaves do not have much nourishment, so colobus monkeys must eat almost continuously, up to a quarter of their body weight each day. Their leafy diet requires them to have stomachs specially adapted for handling hard–to–digest materials. The upper portion of the stomach contains anaerobic bacteria that break down the cellulose in the foliage. These bacteria are also capable of digesting chemicals in leaves that would be poisonous to other primates. Colobus monkeys have large salivary glands which send large amounts of saliva into the fermenting food to help its passage through the digestive system.

Black and white colobus monkeys

The black and white colobus monkeys of central Africa (genus *Colobus*) have the least visible thumb of any genus in the subfamily Colobinae, although what little thumb remains has a nail on it. These monkeys have slender bodies, bare faces, and long tails with a

A black and white colobus monkey in Lake Nakuru National Park, Kenya.

where the trees are more widely spaced. When they sit still in the trees, these monkeys are well camouflaged because their black and white color blends with the patches of sunlight and shadow. When moving in the trees, colobus monkeys tend to walk along branches, either upright or on all fours, instead of swinging beneath them, and they often make amazingly long leaps from tree to tree. Their long hair apparently acts as a parachute to slow them down.

Black and white colobus monkeys often live in small social groups, consisting of both males and females. For example, *C. guereza* lives in groups of 3–15 individuals; most groups have a single adult male and several adult females with their young. The female membership in these groups seems stable, but adult males are sometimes ousted by younger males. Relations among members of the same group are generally friendly and are reinforced by mutual grooming.

Black and white colobus monkeys can apparently breed at any time of the year. Females become sexually mature at about four years of age, while males reach sexual maturity at about six years of age. Each pregnancy results in a single offspring. Infants are born with all white fur, which is shed before the regular coloring comes in. Child rearing seems to be shared among the females in the group.

All species of black and white colobus monkeys have declined over the last 100 years due to hunting for meat and the fur trade, the rapid expansion of human populations, and habitat destruction by logging or agriculture. The skins of black–and–white colobus monkeys were often used for clothing in Europe during the nineteenth century. They were still available as rugs in the early 1970s. The pelts of as many as 50 animals might have been used to make a single rug. The black colobus *(C. satanus)* is classified as vulnerable by IUCN–The World Conservation Union—its continued survival is threatened by hunting and habitat disturbance and destruction.

Red colobus monkeys

Red colobus monkeys (genus *Procolobus* or *Piliocolobus*) live along the equator in Africa. They come in many different colors in addition to the reddish black that gives them their name. They often have whitish or grayish faces and chests, with the deep red color appearing only on their back, crown of the head, paws, and tip of the tail. This color variety has made these monkeys difficult to classify, and there is considerable disagreement in their grouping. Red colobus monkeys have a head and body length of 17.7–26.4 in (45–67 cm), a tail length of 20.5–31.5 in (52–80 cm),

puff of long fur on the end. Head and body length is 17.7–28.3 in (45–72 cm), tail length is 20.5–39.3 in (52–100 cm), and weight is 11.9–31.9 lb (5.4–14.5 kg).

The five species in this genus are distinguished by the amount of white markings and by the placement of long silky strands of fur in different locations. The black colobus *(C. satanus)* has a completely black, glossy coat. *Colobus polykomos* has a white chest and whiskers and a white, tuftless tail; *C. vellerosus* has white thigh patches, a white mane framing its face, and a white, tuftless tail; *C. guereza* has a flat black cap over a white beard and "hairline," a long white mantle extending from the shoulders to the lower back, and a large white tuft on its tail; *C. angolensis* has long white hairs around the face and on the shoulders, and a white tuft on the end of its tail.

Black and white colobus monkeys are typically highly arboreal (tree–dwelling) inhabitants of deep forests, but some species feed and travel on the ground and weigh 11.2–24.9 lb (5.1–11.3 kg). These monkeys have no thumb at all, lacking even the small vestigial thumb seen in black and white colobus monkeys.

Red colobus monkeys are also arboreal. Most populations are found in rain forests, but they also inhabit savanna woodland, mangrove swamps, and floodplains. Red colobus monkeys also form stable groups, but the groups are much larger than those formed by black and white colobus monkeys—ranging in size from 12–82 with an average size of 50. These groups usually include several adult males and 1.5–3 times as many adult females. There is a dominance hierarchy within the group maintained by aggressive behavior, but rarely by physical fighting. Higher ranking individuals have priority access to food, space, and grooming.

Red colobus monkeys also seem to breed throughout the year. A single offspring is born after a gestation period of 4.5–5.5 months. The infant is cared for by the mother alone until it reaches 1–3.5 months old.

Most red colobus species are coming under increased pressure from timber harvesting. This activity not only destroys their rain forest habitat, but also makes them more accessible to hunters. At least one authority considers red colobus monkeys to be the easiest African monkeys to hunt. Several species and subspecies are considered endangered, vulnerable, or rare by international conservation organizations. For example, the Zanzibar red colobus (Procolobus kirkii) is seriously endangered—in 1981 less than 1,500 animals were estimated to survive.

Grouped with the red colobus monkeys because of its four–chambered stomach is the olive colobus, Procolobus verus, of Sierra Leone and central Nigeria. This monkey is actually more gray than olive or red. Its head and body length is 16.9–35.4 in (43–90 cm) and it weighs 6.4–9.7 lb (2.9–4.4 kg). This species is also arboreal and is restricted to rain forests. It forms small groups of 10–15 individuals usually with more than one adult male in each group. In a practice unique among monkeys and apes, mothers of this species carry newborns in their mouths for the first several weeks of the infant's life. This species is threatened by intensive hunting and habitat destruction; it is considered vulnerable by IUCN–The World Conservation Union.

See also Langurs and leaf monkeys.

Further Reading:

Emanoil, Mary, ed. *Encyclopedia of Endangered Species.* Detroit: Gale Research, 1994.

Kerrod, Robin. *Mammals: Primates, Insect–Eaters and Baleen Whales.* New York: Facts on File, 1988.

Napier, J. R., and P. H. Napier. *The Natural History of the Primates.* Cambridge, MA: The MIT Press, 1985.

Nowak, Ronald M., ed. *Walker's Mammals of the World.* 5th ed. Baltimore: Johns Hopkins University Press, 1991.

Peterson, Dale. *The Deluge and the Ark: A Journey Into Primate Worlds.* Boston: Houghton Mifflin, 1989.

Preston–Mafham, Rod and Ken. *Primates of the World.* New York: Facts on File, 1992.

Jean F. Blashfield

Colon see **Digestive system**

Color

Color is a complex and fascinating subject. Several fields of science are involved in explaining the phenomenon of color. The physics of light, the chemistry of colorants, the psychology and physiology of human emotion are all related to color. Since the beginning of history, people of all cultures have tried to explain why there is light and why we see colors. Some people have regarded color with the same mixture of fear, reverence, and curiosity with which they viewed other natural phenomena. In recent years scientists, artists, and other scholars have offered interpretations of the sun, light, and color differences.

Color perception plays an important role in our lives and enhances the quality of life. This influences what we eat and wear. Colors help us to understand and appreciate the beauty of sunrise and sunset, the artistry of paintings, and the beauty of a bird's plumage. Because the sun rises above the horizon in the East, it gives light and color to our world. As the sun sets to the West, it gradually allows darkness to set in. Without the sun we would not be able to distinguish colors. The energy of sunlight warms the earth, making life possible; otherwise, there would be no plants to provide food. We are fortunate to have light as an essential part of our planet.

Light and color

Colors are dependent on light, the primary source of which is sunlight. It is difficult to know what light really is, but we can observe its effects. An object appears colored because of the way it interacts with light. A thin line of light is called a ray; a beam is made up of many rays of light. Light is a form of energy that travels in waves. Light travels silently over long distances at a speed of 190,000 mi (300,000 km) a second. It takes about eight minutes for light to travel from the sun to the earth. This great speed explains why light from shorter distances seems to reach us immediately.

When we talk about light, we usually mean white light. When white light passes through a prism (a triangular transparent object) something very exciting happens. The colors that make up white light disperse into seven bands of color. These bands of color are called a spectrum (from the Latin word for image). When a second prism is placed in just the right position in front of the bands of this spectrum, they merge to form invisible white light again. Isaac Newton (1642–1727) was a well known scientist who conducted research on the sun, light, and color. Through his experiments with prisms, he was the first to demonstrate that white light is composed of the colors of the spectrum.

Seven colors constitute white light: red, orange, yellow, green, blue, indigo, and violet. Students in school often memorize acronyms like ROY G BIV, to remember the seven colors of the spectrum and their order. Sometimes blue and indigo are treated as one color. In any spectrum the bands of color are always organized in this order from left to right. There are also wavelengths outside the visible spectrum, such as ultraviolet.

Rainbows

A rainbow is nature's way of producing a spectrum. One can usually see rainbows after summer showers, early in the morning or late in the afternoon, when the sun is low. Rain drops act as tiny prisms and disperse the white sunlight into the form of a large beautiful arch composed of visible colors. To see a rainbow one must be located between the sun and raindrops forming an arc in the sky. When sunlight enters the raindrops at the proper angle, it is refracted by the raindrops, then reflected back at an angle. This creates a rainbow. Artificial rainbows can be produced by spiraling small droplets of water through a garden hose, with one's back to the sun. Or, indoors, diamond-shaped glass objects, mirrors, or other transparent items can be used.

Refraction: the bending of light

Refraction is the bending of a light ray as it passes at an angle from one transparent medium to another. As a beam of light enters glass at an angle, it is refracted or bent. The part of the light beam that strikes the glass is slowed down, causing the entire beam to bend. The more sharply the beam bends, the more it is slowed down.

Each color has a different wavelength, and it bends differently from all other colors. Short wavelengths are slowed more sharply upon entering glass from air than are long wavelengths. Red light has the longest wavelength and is bent the least. Violet light has the shortest wavelength and is bent the most. Thus violet light travels more slowly through glass than does any other color.

Like all other wave phenomena, the speed of light depends on the medium through which it travels. As an analogy, think of a wagon that is rolled off a sidewalk onto a lawn at an oblique angle. When the first wheel hits the lawn, it slows down, pulling the wagon toward the grass. The wagon changes direction when one of its wheels rolls off the pavement onto the grass. Similarly, when light passes from a substance of high density into one of low density, its speed increases, and it bends away from its original path. In another example, one finds that the speed and direction of a car will change when it comes upon an uneven surface like a bridge.

Sometimes while driving on a hot sunny day, we see pools of water on the road ahead of us, which vanish mysteriously as we come closer. As the car moves towards it the pool appears to move further away. This is a mirage, an optical illusion. Light travels faster through hot air than it does through cold air. As light travels from one transparent material to another it bends with a different refraction. The road's hot surface both warms the air directly above it and interacts with the light waves reaching it to form a mirage. In a mirage, reflections of trees and buildings may appear upside down. The bending or refraction of light as it travels through layers of air of different temperatures creates a mirage.

Diffraction and interference

Similar colors can be seen in a thin film of oil, in broken glass and on the vivid wings of butterflies and other insects. Scientists explain this process by the terms, diffraction and interference. Diffraction and refraction both refer to the bending of light. Diffraction is the slight bending of light away from its straight line of travel when it encounters the edge of an object in its path. This bending is so slight that it is scarcely noticeable. The effects of diffraction become noticeable only when light passes through a narrow slit. When light waves pass through a small opening or around a small object, they are bent. They merge from the opening as almost circular, and they bend around the small object and continue as if the object were not there at all. Diffraction is the sorting out of bands of different wavelengths of a beam of light.

When a beam of light passes through a small slit or pin hole, it spreads out to produce an image larger than the size of the hole. The longer waves spread out more than the shorter waves. The rays break up into dark and light bands or into colors of the spectrum. When a ray is diffracted at the edge of an opaque object, or passes through a narrow slit, it can also create interference of one part of a beam with another.

Interference occurs when two light waves from the same source interact with each other. Interference is the reciprocal action of light waves. When two light waves meet, they may reinforce or cancel each other. The phenomenon called diffraction is basically an interference effect. There is no essential difference between the phenomena of interference and diffraction.

Light is a mixture of all colors. One cannot look across a light beam and see light waves, but when light waves are projected on a white screen, one can see light. The idea that different colors interfere at different angles implies that the wavelength of light is associated with its colors. A spectrum can often be seen on the edges of an aquarium, glass, mirrors, chandeliers or other glass ornaments. These colored edges suggest that different colors are deflected at different angles in the interference pattern.

The color effects of interference also occur when two or more beams originating from the same source interact with each other. When the light waves are in phase, color intensities are reinforced; when they are out of phase, color intensities are reduced.

When light waves passing through two slits are in phase there is constructive interference, and bright light will result. If the waves arrive at a point on the screen out of phase, the interference will be destructive, and a dark line will result. This explains why bubbles of a nearly colorless soap solution develop brilliant colors before they break. When seen in white light, a soap bubble presents the entire visible range of light, from red to violet. Since the wavelengths differ, the film of soap cannot cancel or reinforce all the colors at once. The colors are reinforced, and they remain visible as the soap film becomes thinner. A rainbow, a drop of oil on water, and soap bubbles are phenomena of light caused by diffraction, refraction, and interference. Colors found in birds such as the blue jay are formed by small air bubbles in its feathers. Bundles of white rays are scattered by suspended particles into their components colors. Interference colors seen in soap bubbles and oil

on water are visible in the peacock feathers. Colors of the mallard duck are interference colors and are iridescent changing in hue when seen from different angles. The wings of iridescent beetles, dragonflies, and butterflies are as varied as the rainbow and are produced in a number of ways, which are both physical and chemical. Here, the spectrum of colors are separated by thin films and flash and change when seen from different angles.

Light diffraction has the most lustrous colors of mother of pearl. Light is scattered for the blue of the sky which breaks up blue rays of light more readily than red rays.

Transparent, translucent and opaque

Materials like air, water, and clear glass are called transparent. When light encounters transparent materials, almost all of it passes directly through them. Glass, for example, is transparent to all visible light. The color of a transparent object depends on the color of light it transmits. If green light passes through a transparent object, the emerging light is green; similarly if red light passes through a transparent object, the emerging light is red.

Materials like frosted glass and some plastics are called translucent. When light strikes translucent materials, only some of the light passes through them. The light does not pass directly through the materials. It changes direction many times and is scattered as it passes through. Therefore, we cannot see clearly through them; objects on the other side of a translucent object appear fuzzy and unclear. Because translucent objects are semi–transparent, some ultraviolet rays can go through them. This is why a person behind a translucent object can get a sunburn on a sunny day.

Most materials are opaque. When light strikes an opaque object none of it passes through. Most of the light is either reflected by the object or absorbed and converted to heat. Materials such as wood, stone, and metals are opaque to visible light.

Mixing colors

We do not actually see colors. What we see as color is the effect of light shining on an object. When white light shines on an object it may be reflected, absorbed, or transmitted. Glass transmits most of the light that comes into contact with it, thus it appears colorless. Snow reflects all of the light and appears white. A black cloth absorbs all light, and so appears black. A red piece of paper reflects red light better than it reflects other colors. Most objects appear colored because their chemical structure absorbs certain wavelengths of light and reflects others.

The sensation of white light is produced through a mixture of all visible colored light. While the entire spectrum is present, the eye deceives us into believing that only white light is present. White light results from the combination of only red, green, and blue. When equal brightnesses of these are combined and projected on a screen, we see white. The screen appears yellow when red and green light alone overlap. The combination of red and blue light produces the bluish–red color of magenta. Green and blue produce the greenish–blue color called cyan. Almost any color can be made by overlapping light in three colors and adjusting the brightness of each color.

Color vision

Scientists today are not sure how we understand and see color. What we call color depends on the effects of light waves on receptors in the eye's retina. The currently accepted scientific theory is that there are three types of cones in the eye. One of these is sensitive to the short blue light waves; it responds to blue light more than to light of any other color. A second type of cone responds to light from the green part of the spectrum; it is sensitive to medium wavelengths. The third type of light sensitive cone responds to the longer red light waves. If all three types of cone are stimulated equally our brain interprets the light as white. If blue and red wavelengths enter the eye simultaneously we see magenta. Recent scientific research indicates that the brain is capable of comparing the long wavelengths it receives with the shorter wavelengths. The brain interprets electric signals that it receives from the eyes like a computer.

Nearly 1,000 years ago, Alhazen, an Arab scholar recognized that vision is caused by the reflection of light from objects into our eyes. He stated that this reflected light forms optical images in the eyes. Alhazen believed that the colors we see in objects depend on both the light striking these objects and on some property of the objects themselves.

Color blindness

Some people are unable to see some colors. This is due to an inherited condition known as color blindness. John Dalton (1766–1844), a British chemist and physicist, was the first to discover color blindness in 1794. He was color blind and could not distinguish red from green. Many color blind people do not realize that they do not distinguish colors accurately. This is potentially dangerous, particularly if they cannot distinguish between the colors of traffic lights or other safety signals. Those people who perceive red as green and green as red are known as red–green color blind. Others are completely color blind; they only see black, gray, and white. It is estimated that seven percent of men and one percent of women on earth are born color blind.

Color effects in nature

We often wonder why the sky is blue, the water in the sea or swimming pools is blue or green, and why the sun in the twilight sky looks red. When light advances in a straight line from the sun to the earth, the light is refracted, and its colors are dispersed. The light of the dispersed colors depends on their wavelengths. Generally the sky looks blue because the short blue waves are scattered more than the longer waves of red light. The short waves of violet light (the shortest of all the light waves) disperse more than those of blue light. Yet the eye is less sensitive to violet than to blue. The sky looks red near the horizon because of the specific angle at which the long red wavelengths travel through the atmosphere. Impurities in the air may also make a difference in the colors that we see.

Characteristics of color

There are three main characteristics for understanding variations in color. These are hue, saturation, and intensity or brightness. Hue represents the observable visual difference between two wavelengths of color. Saturation refers to the richness or strength of color. When a beam of red light is projected from the spectrum onto a white screen, the color is seen as saturated. All of the light that comes to the eye from the screen is capable of exciting the sensation of red. If a beam of white light is then projected onto the same spot as the red, the red looks diluted. By varying the intensities of the white and red beams, one can achieve any degree of saturation. In handling pigments, adding white or gray to a hue is equivalent to adding white light. The result is a decrease in saturation.

A brightly colored object is one that reflects or transmits a large portion of the light falling on it, so that it appears brilliant or luminous. The brightness of the resulting color will vary according to the reflecting quality of the object. The greatest amount of light is reflected on a white screen, while a black screen would not reflect any light.

Mixing colorants, pigments, dyes & printing

Color fills our world with beauty. We delight in the golden yellow leaves of Autumn and the beauty of

Spring flowers. Color can serve as a means of communication, to indicate different teams in sports, or, as in traffic lights, to instruct drivers when to stop and go. Manufacturers, artists, and painters use different methods to produce colors in various objects and materials. The process of mixing of colorants, paints, pigments and dyes is entirely different from the mixing of colored light.

Colorants are chemical substances that give color to such materials as ink, paint, crayons and chalk. Most colorants consist of fine powders that are mixed with liquids, wax or other substances that facilitate their application to objects. Dyes dissolve in water. Pigments do not dissolve in water, but they spread through liquids. They are made up of tiny, solid particles, and they do not absorb or reflect specific parts of the spectrum. Pigments reflect a mixture of colors.

When two different colorants are mixed, a third color is produced. When paint with a blue pigment is mixed with paint that has yellow pigments the resulting paint appears green. When light strikes the surface of this paint, it penetrates the paint layer and hits pigment particles. The blue pigment absorbs most of the light. The same color looks different against different background colors. Each pigment subtracts different wavelengths.

Additive and subtractive

All color is derived from two types of light mixture, an additive and a subtractive process. Both additive and subtractive mixtures are equally important to color design and perception. The additive and subtractive elements are related but different. In a subtractive process, blended colors subtract from white light the colors that they cannot reflect. Subtractive light mixtures occur when there is a mixture of colored light caused by the transmittance of white light. The additive light mixture appears more than the white light.

In a subtractive light mixture, a great many colors can be created by mixing a variety of colors. Colors apply only to additive light mixtures. Mixing colored light produces new colors different from the way colorants are mixed. Mixing colorants results in new colors because each colorant subtracts wavelengths of light. But mixing colored lights produces new colors by adding light of different wavelengths.

Both additive and subtractive mixtures of hues adjacent to each other in the spectrum produce intermediate hues. The additive mixture is slightly saturated or mixed with light, the subtractive mixture is slightly darkened. The complimentary pairs mixed subtractively do not give white pigments with additive mixtures.

Additive light mixtures can be used in a number of slide projectors and color filters in order to place different colored light beams on a white screen. In this case, the colored areas of light are added to one another. Subtractive color mixing takes place when a beam of light passes through a colored filter. The filter can be a piece of colored glass or plastic or a liquid that is colored by a dye. The filter absorbs and changes part of the light. Filters and paints absorb certain colors and reflect others.

Subtractive color mixing is the basis of color printing. The color printer applies the colors one at a time. Usually the printer uses three colors: blue, yellow, and red, in addition to black for shading and emphasis. It is quite difficult for a painter to match colors. To produce the resulting colors, trial and error, as well as experimenting with the colors, is essential. It is difficult to know in advance what the resulting color will be. It is interesting to watch a painter trying to match colors.

People who use conventional methods to print books and magazines make colored illustrations by mixing together printing inks. The color is made of a large number of tiny dots of several different colors. The dots are so tiny that the human eye does not see them individually. It sees only the combined effects of all of them taken together. Thus, if half of the tiny dots are blue and half are yellow, the resulting color will appear green.

Dying fabrics is a prehistoric craft. In the past, most dyes were provided solely from plant and animal sources. In antiquity, the color purple or indigo, derived from plants, was a symbol of aristocracy. In ancient Rome, only the emperor was privileged to wear a purple robe.

Today, many dyes and pigments are made of synthetic material. Thousands of dyes and pigments have since been created from natural coal tar, from natural compounds, and from artificially produced organic chemicals. Modern chemistry is now able to combine various arrangements and thus produce a large variety of color.

The color of a dye is caused by the absorption of light of specific wavelengths. Dyes are made of either natural or synthetic material. Chemical dyes tend to be brighter than natural dyes. In 1991 a metamorphic color system was created in a new line of clothes. The color of these clothes changes with the wearer's body temperature and environment. This color system could be used in a number of fabrics and designs.

Sometimes white clothes turn yellow from repeated washing. The clothes look yellow because they reflect more blue light than they did before. To improve the color of the faded clothes a blue dye is added to the wash water, thus helping them reflect all colors of the spectrum more evenly in order to appear white.

Most paints and crayons use a mixture of several colors. When two colors are mixed, the mixture will reflect the colors that both had in common. For example, yellow came from the sap of a tree, from the bark of the birch tree, and onion skins. There were a variety of colors obtained from leaves, fruits, and flowers.

Primary, secondary and complimentary

Three colorants that can be mixed in different combinations to produce several other colors are the primary colorants. In mixing red, green, and blue paint the result will be a muddy dark brown. Red and green paint do not combine to form yellow as do red and green light. The mixing of paints and dyes is entirely different from the mixing of colored light.

By 1730, a German engraver named J. C. LeBlon discovered the primary colors red, yellow, and blue are primary in the mixture of pigments. Their combinations produce orange, green, and violet. Many different three colored combinations can produce the sensation of white light when they are superimposed. When two primary colors such as red and green are combined, they produce a secondary color. A color wheel is used to show the relationship between primary and secondary colors. The colors in this primary and secondary pair are called complimentary. Each primary color on the wheel is opposite the secondary color formed by the mixture of the two primary colors. And each secondary color produced by mixing two primary colors lies half–way between them on a color wheel. The complimentary colors produce white light when they are combined.

Colors are everywhere

Color influences many of our daily decisions, consciously or unconsciously from what we eat and what we wear. Color enhances the quality of our lives, it helps us to fully appreciate the beauty of colors. Colors are also an important function of the psychology and physiology of human sensation. Even before the ancient civilizations in prehistoric times, color symbolism was already in use.

Different colors have different meanings which are universal. Colors can express blue moods. On the other hand, these could be moods of tranquility or moods of conflict, sorrow or pleasure, warm and cold, boring or stimulating. In several parts of the world, people have specific meanings for different colors. An example is how Eskimos indicate the different numbers of snow

---

KEY TERMS

Beams—Many rays of light.

Colorant—A chemical substance that gives color to such materials as ink, paint, crayons and chalk.

Diffraction—The bending of light.

Hue—The observable visual different between two wavelengths of color.

Light—A form of energy that travels in waves.

Mirage—An optical illusion.

Pigment—A substance which becomes paint or ink when it is mixed with a liquid.

Ray—A thin line of light.

Reflection—The change in direction of light when it strikes a substance but does not pass through it.

Refraction—The bending of a ray of light.

Spectrum—A band of colors that disperses when passed through a prism.

---

conditions. They have seventeen separate words for white snow. In the west the bride wears white, in China and in the Middle East area white is worn for mourning. Of all colors, that most conspicuous and universal is red.

The color red can be violent, aggressive, and exciting. The expression "seeing red" indicates one's anger in most parts of the world. Red appears in more national and international colors and red cars are more often used than any other color. Homes can be decorated to suit the personalities of the people living in them. Warm shades are often used in living rooms because it suggests sociability. Cool shades have a quieting effect, suitable for study areas. Hospitals use appropriate colors depending on those that appeal to patients in recovery, in surgery, or very sick patients. Children in schools are provided bright colored rooms. Safety and certain color codes are essential. The color red is for fire protection, green is for first aid, and red and green colors are for traffic lights.

Human beings owe their survival to plants. The function of color in the flowering plants is to attract bees and other insects—to promote pollination. The color of fruits attract birds and other animals which help the distribution of seeds. The utmost relationship between humans and animals and plants are the chlorophylls. The green coloring substance of leaves and the yellowish–green chlorophyll is associated with the production of carbohydrates by photosynthesis in plants. Life and the quality of the earth's atmosphere depends on photosynthesis.

Further Reading:

Birren, Faber. *Color—A Survey in Words and Pictures.* New Hyde Park, N.Y.: University Books, Inc, 1963.

Birren, Faber. *History of Color in Painting.* New York: Reinhold Publishing Corporation, 1965.

Birren, Faber. *Principles of Color.* New York: Van Nostrand Reinhold Co., 1969.

Cunningham, James and Norman Herr. "Waves," and "Light." In *Hands on Physics Activities with Real Life Applications.* West Nyack, N.Y.: Center for Applied Research Education, 1994.

Englert, Berthold–Georg, Marlan O. Scully and Herbert Walther. "The Duality of Matter and Light," *Scientific American*, 1994.

Hewitt, Paul G. "Color." In *Conceptual Physics: The High School Physics Program.* (Chapter 28) New York: Addison Wesley Publishing Co., 1992.

Kosvanec, Jim."Mixing Grayed Color," *American Artist*, 1994.

Meadows, Jack. *The Great Scientists.* New York: Oxford University Press, 1992.

Suding, Heather and Jeanne Bucegross."A Simple Lab Activity to Teach Subtractive Color and Beer's Law," *Journal of Chemical Education*, 1994.

Verity, Enid. *Color Observed.* New York: Van Nostrand Reinhold Co., 1990.

Nasrine Adibe

Color blindness

The condition known as color blindness is a defect in vision that causes problems in distinguishing between certain colors. The condition is usually passed on genetically, and is more common in men than in women. About 6% of all men and about .6% of women inherit the condition. Individuals can also acquire the condition through various eye diseases. There is no treatment for color blindness.

Reds and greens

The first study of color blindness was published in 1794 by physicist John Dalton, who was color–deficient himself. The condition Dalton described is not actually any sort of blindness. Color blindness does not affect the overall visual acuity of individuals with the condition. A small number of people can not distinguish between any color and see all things in shades of gray.

People who are color blind often are not aware they have a problem until they are asked to distinguish between reds and greens. This is the most common problem among individuals who are color blind. Some people who are color blind also have trouble telling the difference between green and yellow.

Color blindness stems from a problem in the cone cells of the retina. Light rays enter the eye in some combination of red, green, or blue. Normal cone cells contain light–sensitive molecules sensitive to one of the color spectrum's band of colors. Short–wave cone cells absorb blue, middle–wave cone cells absorb green, and long–wave cone cells absorb red.

Individuals with a color defect do not have a normal complement of these substances, and may be missing one or more of them. Some people who are color blind have trouble distinguishing between reds and greens when the light is dim, but are capable of seeing the difference between the two colors in good light. A less common type of color blindness makes distinguishing between reds and greens difficult regardless of the light quality.

A simple test for color blindness involves the use of cards with dots in different colors. Individuals who are color blind see different numbers or words than those who have a complete range of color vision.

Inherited or acquired defect

Most individuals who are color blind inherit the trait. Men are more likely to be color blind because of the way color blindness is inherited. The gene for the trait is located on the X chromosome. Men have one X chromosome and women have two. If a man inherits the gene for the trait, he will have a color vision defect. If a woman inherits a single gene for the trait, she will not, because the normal gene on her other X chromosome will dominate over the defective gene. Women must inherit the defective trait from both parents to be color blind.

Color blindness is a so–called sex–linked characteristic. This means it is a gene that occurs only on the X chromosome, which is passed to the child by the mother. The Y chromosome, which is passed to the child by the father, does not carry the defective gene. This means that children inherit color blindness only from their mothers. Children can inherit color blindness from a mother who is color blind or from a mother who is a carrier of the gene but is not color blind herself. Daughters of men who are color blind will carry the trait, but sons will not.

A more unusual way to become color blind is through disease. Cataracts are the most common cause of acquired color deficiency. In one of the most common eye diseases, cataracts, a cloudy layer in the lens or eye capsule develops. The condition can cause vision to worsen in bright sunlight. Other conditions that may cause acquired color deficiency are retinal and optic nerve diseases.

Medications such as digitalis, a common medication for heart disease, and quinine, medicine for malaria, can also make color perception change. Alcohol has also been known to change the way people see color.

Adapting to a different world

Color blindness generally does not cause a great deal of hardship. However, there is evidence that individuals who are color blind may face higher risks on the road. A German study found that men who were color blind were twice as likely to have rear–end collisions as were men who had normal vision. About 7 million North American drivers can not distinguish easily between red and green lights.

Designers of traffic signals are working to make driving easier for color–deficient motorists. Traffic lights are generally made in a standard format today, with red on top, amber in the middle and green at the bottom. One improvement would be changing the shape of each of the different signals, so that color–deficient drivers could more easily distinguish between stop and go. Another possible change would involve altering the color of brake lights. Experts bemoan the fact that people who are color–deficient can not see the red in brake lights clearly.

There is no cure or treatment for color blindness. However, there is an abundant amount of research concerning the nature of vision in people with normal and limited color discrimination. As researchers become more knowledgeable about the process of sight, correction of color blindness may become a possibility.

See also Eye; Vision disorders.

Further Reading:

Chandler, David G. "Diabetes Problems Can Affect Color Vision." *Diabetes in the News.* May–June 1993. 42.
"Color Blindness Misconceptions." *USA Today,* February 1992. 16.
Donn, Anthony. "The Eye and How it Works." in *The Columbia University College of Physicians and Surgeons Complete Home Medical Guide.* Edition 2, 1989. 694.

Kunz, Jeffrey R.M.; Finkel, Asher J. "Color Blindness." *The American Medical Association Family Medical Guide.* New York: Random House. 1987.
Mollon, John. "Worlds of Difference." *Nature.* Vol. 356. April 2, 1992. 378—379.
"Not Seeing Red." *The University of California, Berkeley Wellness Letter.* August 1993. 2.

Patricia Braus

Colugos

A colugo is a furry mammal with a thin neck, a slender body, and large eyes. It is about the size of an average house cat, measuring between 15–16 1/2 in (38–41 cm) long with a tail adding another 8–10 in (20–25 cm). Also known as a flying lemur, the colugo neither truly flies nor is it a lemur. A gliding mammal, it is able to give the appearance of flight with the help of a membrane that stretches completely around its body starting behind its ears, going down its neck to its wrists and ankles and ending at the tip of its tail. Colugos have characteristics of lemurs, bats, prosimians, and insectivores; recent studies suggest that their closest relatives are primates.

Because of its varying characteristics, colugos have been classified in their own order, the order Dermoptera. Belonging to the Cynochephalidae family, the only two species of colugo are the Malayan or Temminck colugo (*Cynocephalus temminckii*) and the Philippine colugo (*Cynocephalus volans*). Colugos inhabit the rain forests and rubber plantations in Southeast Asia, Thailand, Malaysia, Java, Borneo, Vietnam, Kampuchea, and the Philippines.

Characteristics

Colugos differ greatly in terms of their basic coloring. Their backs are usually shades of brown, brownish–gray, or gray sprinkled with light yellow spots. Their undersides can be bright orange, brownish–red, or yellow. In general, they have very thick, soft fur on their slender bodies. Their necks are long and their heads can be described as "doglike."

Colugos females are slightly bigger than males. The Malayan colugo is the larger of the two species, weighing approximately 4 lbs (1.8 kg) and measuring about 25 in (63.5 cm) from head to tail. Colugos have large eyes and very good eyesight, traits essential in judging the distances between trees. They have interesting teeth as well; for reasons unknown, their lower incisors are made up of ten thin prongs each, similar to the structure of a comb.

Flightskin

Many animals inhabiting rain forests evolve special mechanisms to enable them to move easily among the trees; thus, they avoid exposing themselves to predators living on the ground. In the colugo's case, this has been accomplished by the development of a membrane surrounding almost all of its body. On each colugo, there are three separate sections of this "parachute–skin." In the first section (called the propatagium), the skin comes out of both sides of the colugo's neck, down its shoulders to completely attached to the entire span of its arm all the way to its fingertips. The second section (called the plagiopatagium) begins on their underside of the colugos' arms and spans its entire body, thus connecting the animal's front and rear legs. The final section of this skin (uropatagium) connects the hind legs to the tail on both sides all the way to its tip.

Interestingly, the colugo is the only mammal that has developed the rearmost uropatagium section of its flightskin. The tails of all of the other mammals with the capacity to glide—such as honey gliders and flying squirrels—are free of the membrane; thus, they use their tails as steering mechanisms.

Covered in hair on both sides, this "parachute-skin" enables these animals to glide long distances—reportedly up to 426 feet—while losing very little altitude. Although colugos have strong claws with which to grip branches, they are not skilled climbers. In fact, colugos are almost helpless on the ground.

Behavior

Colugos have never lived more than a few months in captivity; thus, there is only limited knowledge of their behavior. One fact that is known is that they are strict vegetarians. Specifically, they feed on shoots, fruit, buds, young seed pods, and flowers from multiple kinds of forest trees. They pull the vegetation out of trees using their very powerful tongues. Colugos get their water by licking it from leaves and tree hollows.

Colugos are nocturnal; when the sun goes down, they move quickly, skirting the underside of branches. To get the height they need to glide from tree to tree, they scramble up tree trunks with few powerful jumping motions. According to observation, colugos often reuse the their routes when traveling from location to location. In the Philippines, the inhabitants seize on the easy hunting that this behavior presents; Philippine locals often wait on known colugo paths with weapons or traps ready.

During the daytime, colugos rest, hanging from the undersides of branches, in tree hollows, or in the shade of palm stalks using all four of their feet. Hanging in such a way makes colugos hard to see. Their brownish coloring helps to camouflage them further in the shady rain forest.

Reproduction

Colugos of the Philippines generally mate in February, although the mating behavior of colugos throughout Southeast Asia can occur from January to March. After a two month pregnancy, the female gives birth to a single offspring. (Although, on rare occasions, colugo females have twins.) Interestingly, because females cannot nurse more than one young at a time, they have the ability to give birth in rapid succession to stabilize the population. Thus, the female is able to become pregnant again before her young are weaned.

When born, the baby colugo measures about 10 inches long and is fairly undeveloped; in fact, some authorities describe these young as "semi–fetal." After a baby's birth, the female carries it in a pouch which she creates by folding the flightskin under her tail. She holds her young tightly against her as she feeds; as she travels, the baby fastens itself to one of its mother's nipples. The female generally carries the baby around everywhere she goes, reducing the baby's vulnerability to predators. This relationship continues, until the young is too large and heavy for the mother to carry.

Threats to colugos

The main natural predator of the colugo is the Philippine monkey–eating eagle, which eats colugos almost to the exclusion of all other types of food. Humans also pose a significant threat to these animals. People operating rubber and coconut plantations often shoot colugos because they view them as pests. Furthermore, colugos are hunted for their meat. Most importantly, colugo habitats are continually shrinking due to deforestation. While neither species is endangered, their numbers will shrink as their habitats disappear.

Further reading:

Grzimek, H.C. Bernard, Dr., ed. *Grzimek's Animal Life Encyclopedia*. New York: Van Nostrand Reinhold Company, 1993.
Pearl, Mary Corliss, Ph.D. Consultant. *The Illustrated Encyclopedia of Wildlife*. London: Grey Castle Press, 1991.
Gunderson, Harvey L. *Mammalogy*. New York: McGraw Hill, 1976.

Kathryn Snavely

Coma

Coma, from the Greek word *koma*, meaning deep sleep, is a state of extreme unresponsiveness in which an individual exhibits no voluntary movement or behavior. In a deep coma, stimuli, even painful stimuli, are unable to effect any response. Normal reflexes may be lost.

Coma lies on a spectrum with other alterations in consciousness. The level of consciousness which you, the reader, are currently enjoying is at one end of the spectrum, while complete brain death is at the other end of the spectrum. In between are such states as obtundation, drowsiness, and stupor, which all allow the individual to respond to stimuli, though such response may be brief and require a stimulus of greater than normal intensity.

Consciousness

In order to understand the loss of function suffered by a comatose individual, consider the important characteristics of the conscious state. Consciousness is defined by two fundamental elements: awareness and arousal.

Awareness allows us to receive and process information communicated by the five senses and thereby relate to ourselves and the rest of the world. Awareness has psychological and physiological components. The psychological component is governed by an individual's mind and its mental processes. The physiological component refers to the functioning—the physical and chemical condition—of an individual's brain. Awareness is regulated by areas within the cerebral hemispheres, the outermost layer of the brain, which separates humans from other animals because it allows greater intellectual functioning.

Arousal is regulated solely by physiological functioning. Its primitive responsiveness to the world is demonstrated by predictable reflex (involuntary) responses to stimuli. Arousal is maintained by the reticular activating system (RAS). This is not an anatomical area of the brain but rather a network of structures (including the brainstem, the medulla, and the thalamus) and nerve pathways which function together to produce and maintain arousal.

Causes of coma

Coma is the result of something which interferes with the functioning of the cerebral cortex and/or the functioning of the structures which make up the RAS. The number of conditions which could result in coma is mind–boggling. A good way of categorizing these conditions is to consider the anatomic and the metabolic causes of coma. Anatomic causes of coma are those conditions which disrupt the normal physical architecture of the brain structures responsible for consciousness. Metabolic causes of coma consist of those conditions which change the chemical environment of the brain and thereby adversely affecting function.

Anatomic causes of coma include brain tumors, infections, and head injuries. All three types of condition can affect the brain's functioning by actually

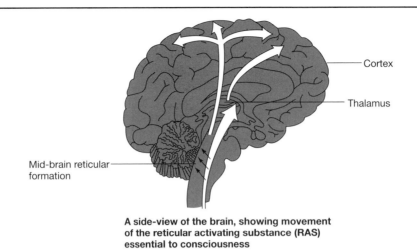

A side-view of the brain, showing movement of the reticular activating substance (RAS) essential to consciousness

Cortex

Thalamus

Mid-brain reticular formation

Diffuse and bilateral damage to the cerebral cortex (relative preservation of brain-stem reflexes)

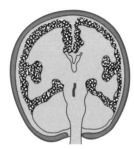

Possible causes
- Damage due to lack of oxygen or restricted blood flow, perhaps resulting form cardiac arrest, an anaesthetic accident, or shock
- Damage incurred from metabolic processes associated with kidney or liver failure, or with hypoglycemia
- Trauma damage
- Damage due to a bout with meningitis, encephalomyelitis, or a severe systemic infection

Mass lesions in this region resulting in compression of the brain-stem and damage to the reticular activating substance (RAS)

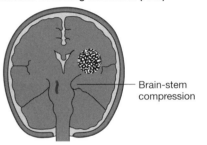

Brain-stem compression

Structural lesions within this region also resulting in compression of the brain-stem and damage to the reticular activating substance (RAS)

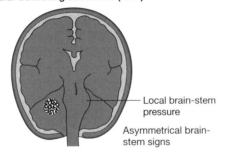

Local brain-stem pressure

Asymmetrical brain-stem signs

Possible causes • Cerebellar tumors, abscesses, or hemorrhages

Lesions within the brain-stem directly suppressing the reticular activating substance (RAS)

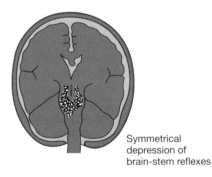

Symmetrical depression of brain-stem reflexes

Possible causes • Drug overdosage

The four brain conditions that result in coma.

destroying brain tissue. They may also affect the brain's functioning by taking up too much space within the skull. The skull is a very hard, bony structure which is unable to expand in size. If something within the skull begins to require more space (for example an expanding tumor or an injured/infected area of the brain which is swelling) other areas of the brain are compressed against the hard surface of the skull, which results in damage to these areas.

There are many metabolic causes of coma, including the following: (1) A decrease in the delivery of substances necessary for appropriate brain functioning, such as oxygen, glucose, and sodium. (2) The presence of certain substances disrupting the functioning of neurons. Drugs or alcohol in toxic quantities can result in neuronal dysfunction, as can some substances normally found in the body, but which accumulate at toxic levels due to some disease state. Accumulated substances which might cause coma include ammonia due to liver disease, ketones due to uncontrolled diabetes, or carbon dioxide due to a severe asthma attack. (3) The changes in chemical levels in the brain due to the electrical derangements caused by seizures.

Outcome

It is extremely important for a physician to quickly determine the cause of a coma, so that potentially reversible conditions are treated immediately. For example, an infection may be treated with antibiotics, a brain tumor may be removed, brain swelling from an injury can be reduced with certain medications. Furthermore, various metabolic disorders can be addressed by supplying the individual with the correct amount of oxygen, glucose, or sodium, by treating the underlying disease in liver disease, asthma, or diabetes, and by halting seizures with medication.

Some conditions which cause coma can be completely reversed, restoring the individual to his or her original level of functioning. However, if areas of the brain have been sufficiently damaged because of the severity or duration of the condition which led to the coma, the individual may recover from the coma with permanent disabilities, or may never regain consciousness. Take the situation of someone whose coma was caused by brain injury in a car accident. Such an injury can result in one of three outcomes. In the event of a less severe brain injury, with minimal swelling, an individual may indeed recover consciousness and regain all of his or her original abilities. In the event of a more severe brain injury, with swelling which resulting in further pressure on areas of the brain, an individual may regain consciousness, but with some degree of impair-

ment. The impairment may be physical, such as paralysis of a leg, or result in a change in the individual's intellectual functioning and/or personality. The most severe types of brain injury result in states in which the individual loses all ability to function and remains deeply unresponsive. An individual who has suffered such a brain injury may remain in a coma indefinitely.

Outcome from a coma depends on its cause and duration. In drug poisonings, extremely high rates of recovery can be expected, following prompt medical attention. Patients who have suffered head injuries tend to do better than patients whose coma was caused by other types of medical illnesses. Excluding drug poisoning–induced comas, only about 15% of patients who remain in a coma for more than a few hours make a good recovery. Adult patients who remain in a coma for more than four weeks have almost no chance of regaining their previous level of functioning. However, children and young adults have regained functioning after two months in a coma.

Glasgow Coma Scale

The Glasgow Coma Scale, a system of examining a comatose patient, can be helpful for evaluating the depth of the coma, tracking the patient's progress, and possibly predicting ultimate outcome of the coma. The Glasgow Coma Scale assigns a different number of points for exam results in three different categories: opening the eyes, verbal response (using words or voice to respond), and motor response (moving a part of the body). Fifteen indicates the highest level of functioning. An individual who spontaneously opens his or her eyes, gives appropriate answers to questions about his or her situation, and can follow a command (such as "move your leg," "nod your head") has the highest level of functioning. Three is the smallest possible number of points, and would be given to a patient who is unresponsive to a painful stimulus. In the middle are those patients who may be able to respond, but who require an intense or painful stimulus, and whose response may demonstrate some degree of brain malfunctioning. When performed as part of the admission examination, a Glasgow score of three to five points suggests that the patient likely has suffered fatal brain damage, while eight or more points indicates that the patient's chances for recovery are good.

The ethical dilemma presented by persistent coma

When a patient has not suffered brain death (the complete absence of any electrical activity within the brain) but has been in a deep coma for some time, a change in condition may occur. This condition is called a persistent vegetative state. The patient may open his or her eyes and move his or her limbs in a primitive fashion, demonstrating some degree of arousal. However, the patient lacks any element of awareness and is unable to have any measurably meaningful interactions with the surrounding world. This condition may last for years. The care of these patients has sparked some of the most heated debates within the field of medical ethics. The discovery of medical advances which allow various disease states to be arrested, without restoration of lost brain function, and the fact that medical resources are limited, have led to debates regarding when medical help should be withdrawn from an individual who has no hope of recovery.

See also: Brain; Nervous system; Neuron; Psychology; Stimulus.

Further Reading:

Guberman, Alan. *An Introduction to Clinical Neurology.* Boston: Little, Brown, 1994.

Isselbacher, Kurt J. et al. *Harrison's Principles of Internal Medicine.* New York: McGraw–Hill, 1994.

Liebman, Michael. *Neuroanatomy Made Easy and Understandable.* Baltimore: University Park Press, 1991.

Rosalyn Carson–DeWitt

Comatulids see **Feather stars**

Combinations see **Combinatrics**

Combinatorics

Combinatorics is the study of combining objects by various rules to create new arrangements of objects. The objects can be anything from points and numbers to apples and oranges. Combinatorics, like algebra, numerical analysis and topology, is a important branch of mathematics. Examples of combinatorial questions are whether we can make a certain arrangement, how many arrangements can be made, and what the best arrangement for a set of objects is.

Combinatorics has grown rapidly in the last two decades making critical contributions to computer science, operations research, finite probability theory and cryptology. Computers and computer networks operate with finite data structures and algorithms which makes them perfect for enumeration and graph theory applications. Leading edge research in areas like neural networking rely on the contribution made by combinatorics.

Combinatorics can be grouped into two categories. Enumeration, which is the study of counting and arranging objects, and graph theory, or the study of graphs.

History of combinatorics

Leonhard Euler (1701–1783) was a Swiss mathematician who spent most of his life in Russia. He was responsible for making a number of the initial contributions to combinatorics both in graph theory and enumeration. One of these contributions was a paper he published in 1736. The people of an old town in Prussia called Königsberg (now Kaliningrad in Russia) brought to Euler's attention a stirring question about moving along bridges. Euler wrote a paper answering the question called "The Seven Bridges of Königsberg." The town was on an island in the Pregel river and had seven bridges. A frequently asked question there at the time was "Is it possible to take a walk through town, starting and ending at the same place, and cross each bridge exactly once?" Euler generalized the problem to points and lines where the island was represented by one point and the bridges were represented by lines. By abstracting the problem, Euler was able to answer the question. It was impossible to return to the same place by only crossing each bridge exactly once. The abstract picture he drew of lines and points was a graph, and the beginnings of graph theory. The study of molecules of hydrocarbons, a compound of hydrogen and carbon atoms, also spurred the development of graph theory.

Enumeration

To enumerate is to count. In combinatorics, it is the study of counting objects in different arrangements. The objects are counted and arranged by a set of rules called equivalence relations.

One way to count a set of objects is to ask, "how many different ways can the objects be arranged?" Each change in the original arrangement is called a permutation. For example, changing the order of the songs to be played on a compact disc (CD) player would be a permutation of the regular order of the songs. If there were only two songs on the CD, there would be only two orders, playing the songs in the original order or in reverse order, song two and then song one. With three songs on the CD, there are more than just two ways to play the music. There is the original order, or songs one, two and three (123) and in reverse order, 321. There are two orders found by flipping the first two songs or the last two songs to get 213 or 132 respectively. There are another two orders, 312 and 231, found by rotating the songs to the right or left. This gives a total of six ways to order the music on a CD with three songs. By just trying different orders, it was intuitively seen how many combinations there were. If the CD had twelve or more songs on it, then this intuitive approach would not be very effective. Trying different arrangements would take a long time, and knowing if all arrangements were found would not be easy. Combinatorics formalizes the way arrangements are found by coming up with general formulas and methods that work for generic cases.

The power of combinatorics, as with all mathematics, is this ability to abstract to a point where complex problems can be solved which could not be solved intuitively. Combinatorics abstracts a problem of this nature in a recursive way. Take the CD example, with three songs. Instead of writing out all the arrangements to find out how many there are, think of the end arrangement and ask, "for the first song in the new arrangement, how many choices are there?" The answer is any three of the songs. There are then two choices for the second song because one of the songs has already been selected. There is only one choice for the last song. So three choices for the first song times two songs for the second choice gives six possibilities for a new arrangement of songs. Continuing in this way, the number of permutations for any size set of objects can be found.

Another example of a permutation is shuffling a deck of playing cards. There are 52 cards in a deck. How many ways can the cards be shuffled? After tearing off the plastic on a brand new deck of cards, the original order of the cards is seen. All the hearts, spades, clubs, and diamonds together and, in each suit, the cards are arranged in numerical order. To find out how many ways the cards can be shuffled, start by moving the first card to any of the 52 places in the deck. Of course, leaving the card in the first place is not moving it at all, which is always an option. This gives 52 shuffles only by moving the first card. Now consider the second card. It can go in 51 places because it can not go in the location of the first card. Again, the option of not moving the card at all is included. That gives a total of 52×51 shuffles which equals 2,652 already. The third card can be placed in 50 places and the fourth in 49 places. Continuing this way find to the last card gives a total of $52 \times 51 \times 50.... \times 4 \times 3 \times 2 \times 1$ possible shuffles which equals about 81 with sixty–six zeros behind it. A huge number of permutations. Once 51 cards were placed, the last card had only one place it could go, so the last number multiplied was one. Multiplying all the numbers from 52 down to one together is called 52 factorial and is written 52!.

Binomial coefficients

The importance of binomial coefficients comes from another question that arises. How many subsets are contained in a set of objects? A set is just a collection of objects like the three songs on the CD. Subsets are the set itself, the empty set, or the set of nothing, and any smaller groupings of the set. So the first two songs alone would be a subset of the set of three songs. Intuitively, eight subsets could be found on a three song CD by writing out all possible subsets, including the set itself.

Unfortunately, the number of subsets also gets large quickly. The general way to find subsets is not as easily seen as finding the total number of permutations of a deck of cards. It has been found that the number of subsets of a set can be found by taking the number of elements of the set, and raising the number two to that power. So for a CD with three songs, the number of subsets is just two to the third power, $2 \times 2 \times 2$, or eight.

For a deck of 52 cards, the number of subsets comes to about 45 with fourteen zeros behind it. It would take a long time to write all of those subsets down. Binomial coefficients represent the number of subsets of a given size. Binomial coefficients are written C(r;c) and represent "the number of combinations of r things taken c at a time." Binomial coefficients can be calculated using factorials or with Pascal's triangle as seen below (only the first six rows are shown.) Each new row in Pascal's triangle is solved by taking the top two numbers and adding them together to get the number below.

row 0				1		
row 1			1		1	
row 2		1		2		1
row 3	1		3		3	1
row 4	1	4		6	4	1
row 5	1	5	10	10	5	1

Pascal's Triangle

The triangle always starts with one and has ones on the outside.

So for our three song CD, to find the number of two song subsets we want to find C(3,2) which is the third row and second column, or three. The subsets being songs one and two, two and three, and one and three. Binomial coefficients come up in many places in algebra and combinatorics and are very important when working with polynomials. The other formula for calculating C(r;c) is r! divided by c! × (r–c)!.

Equivalence relations

Equivalence relations is a very important concept in many branches of mathematics. An equivalence relation is a way to partition sets into subsets and equate elements with each other. The only requirements of an equivalence relation are that it must abide by the reflexive, symmetric and transitive laws.

Relating cards by suits in the deck of cards is one equivalence relation. Two cards are equivalent if they have the same suit. Card color, red or black, is another equivalence relation. In algebra, "equals," "greater than" and "less than" signs are examples of equivalence relations on numbers. These relations become important when we ask questions about subsets of a set of objects.

Recurrence relations

A powerful application of enumeration to computers and algorithms is the recurrence relation. A sequence of numbers can be generated using the previous numbers in a sequence by using a recurrence relation. This recurrence relation either adds to, or multiplies one or more previous elements of the sequence to generate the next sequence number. The factorial, n!, is solved using a recurrence relation since n! equals n × (n–1)! and (n–1)! equals (n–1) × (n–2)! and so on. Eventual one factorial is reached, which is just one. Pascal's triangle is also a recurrence relation. Computers, being based on algorithms, are designed to calculate and count numbers in this way.

Graph theory

Graphs are sets of objects which are studied based on their interconnectivity with each other. Graph theory began when people were seeking answers to questions about whether it was possible to travel from one point to another, or what the shortest distance between two points was.

A graph is composed of two sets, one of points or vertices, and the other of edges. The set of edges represents the vertices that are connected to each other. Combinatorally, graphs are just a set of objects (the vertex set) and a set of equivalence relations (the edge set) regarding the arrangement of the objects. For example, a triangle is a graph with three vertices and three edges. So the vertex set may be (x,y,z) and the edge set (xy,yz,zx). The actual labeling of the points is not as important as fundamental concepts which differentiate graphs.

Sometimes graphs are not easy to tell apart because there are a number of ways we can draw a graph. The graph (x,y,z) with edges (xy,yz,zx) can be drawn as a circle with three points on the circumference. The lines do not have to be straight. The vertex and edge sets are the only information defining the graph. So a circle with three distinct points on the circumference, and a triangle, are the same graph. Graphs with hundreds of vertices and edges are hard to tell apart. Are they the same?

One of a number of ways to tell graphs apart is to look at their connectivity and cycles, inherent properties of graphs.

A graph is connected if every vertex can be reached to every other vertex by traveling along an edge. The triangle is connected. A square, thought of as a graph with four vertices, (x,y,z,w) but with only two edges (xy,zw) is not connected. There is no way to travel from vertex x to vertex z. A graph has a cycle if there is a path from a vertex back to itself where no edge is passed over twice. The triangle has one cycle. The square, as defined above, has no cycles. Graphs can have many cycles and still not be connected. Ten disconnected triangles can be thought of as a graph with ten cycles. The two properties, connectivity and cycles, do not always allow for the differentiation of two graphs. Two graphs can be both connected and have the same number of cycles but still be different.

Another four properties for determining if two graphs are different is explained in a very nice introduction to the subject, *Introduction to Graph Theory* by Richard Trudeau.

Computer networks are excellent examples of a type of graph that demonstrates how important graphs are to the computer field. Networks are a type of graph that has directions and weights assigned to each edge. An example of a network problem is how to find the best way to send information over a national computer network. Should the information go from Washington,

D.C. through Pittsburgh, a high traffic point, and then to Detroit, or should the information be sent through Philadelphia and then through Toledo to Detroit? Is it faster to go through just one city even if there is more traffic through that city?

A simular issue involving networks is whether to have a plane make a stop at a city on the way to Los Angeles from Detroit, or should the trip be non–stop. Adding factors like cost, travel time, number of passengers, etc. along with the number of ways to travel to Los Angles leads to an interesting network theory problem.

A traditional problem for the gasoline companies has been how to best determine their truck routes for refilling their gas stations. The gasoline trucks typically drive around an area, from gas station to gas station, refilling the tanks based on some route list, a graph. Driving to the nearest neighboring gas stations is often not the best route to drive. Choosing the cheapest path from vertex to vertex is known as the greedy algorithm. Choosing the shortest route based on distance between locations is often not the most cost effective route. Some tanks need refilling sooner than others because some street corners are much busier than others. Plus, like the Königsberg Bridge problem, traveling to the next closest station may lead to a dead end and a trucker may have to back track. The list of examples seems endless. Graph theory has applications to all professions.

Trees

Trees are yet another type of graph. Trees have all the properties of graphs except they must be connected with no cycles. A computer's hard drive directory structure is set up as a tree, with subdirectories branching out from a single root directory. Typically trees have a vertex labeled as the root vertex from which every other vertex can be reached from a unique path along the edges. Not all vertices can be a root vertex. Trees come into importance for devising searching algorithms.

Further Reading:

Berman, Gerald and Fryer, K.D. *Introduction to Combinatorics,* Academic Press, 1972.

Bogard, Kenneth P. *Introductory Combinatorics,* Harcourt Brace Jovanovic Incorporated, 1990.

Bose R.C and Manvel B *Introduction to Combinatorial Theory,* John Wiley & Sons, 1984.

Trudeau, Richard J. *Introduction to Graph Theory,* Dover, 1993.

Tucker, Alan. *Applied Combinatorics,* John Wiley & Sons, 1984.

Jackson, Bradley and Thoro, Dmitri. *Applied Combinatorics with Problem Solving,* Addison–Wesley, 1990.

David Gorsich

KEY TERMS

Binomial coefficients—Numbers which stand for the number of subsets of equal size within a larger set.

Combinatorics—The branch of mathematics concerned with the study of combining objects (arranging) by various rules to create new arrangements of objects.

Cycles—A graph has a cycle if there is a path from a vertex back to itself where no edge is passed over twice. The triangle has one cycle.

Enumeration—The methods of counting objects and arrangements.

Equivalence Relations—A way to relate two objects which must abide by the reflexive, symmetric and transitive laws.

Factorial—The factorial of a positive integer is the positive integer multiplied by all the lesser positive integers.

Graphs—A graph is a finite set of vertices or points and a set of finite edges.

Trees—Graphs which have no cycles.

Königsberg Bridge Problem—A common question in the Königsberg town on how to travel through the city and over all the bridges without crossing one twice.

Network—A term used in graph theory to mean a graph with directions and weights assigned to each edge.

Permutations—Changing the order of objects in a particular arrangement.

Recurrence relation—A means of generating a sequence of numbers by using one or more previous numbers of the sequence and multiplying or adding terms in a repetitive way. Recurrence relations are especially important for computer algorithms.

Combustion

Combustion is the chemical term for a process known more commonly as burning. It is certainly one of the earliest chemical changes noted by humans, at least partly because of the dramatic effects it has on materials. Today, the mechanism by which combustion takes place is well understood and is more correctly defined as a form of oxidation that occurs so rapidly that noticeable heat and light are produced.

History

Probably the earliest reasonably scientific attempt to explain combustion was that of Johann (or Jan) Baptista van Helmont, a Flemish physician and alchemist who lived from 1580 to 1644. Van Helmont observed the relationship among a burning material, smoke and flame and said that combustion involved the escape of a "wild spirit" (*spiritus silvestre*) from the burning material. This explanation was later incorporated into a theory of combustion—the phlogiston theory—that dominated alchemical thinking for the better part of two centuries.

According to the phlogiston theory, combustible materials contain a substance—phlogiston—that is emitted by the material as it burns. A non–combustible material, such as ashes, will not burn, according to this theory, because all phlogiston contained in the original material (such as wood) had been driven out. The phlogiston theory was developed primarily by the German alchemist Johann Becher and his student Georg Ernst Stahl at the end of the seventeenth century.

Although scoffed at today, the phlogiston theory satisfactorily explained most combustion phenomena known at the time of Becher and Stahl. One serious problem was a quantitative issue. Many objects weigh more after being burned than before. How this could happen when phlogiston escaped from the burning material? One possible explanation was that phlogiston had negative weight, an idea that many early chemists thought absurd, while others were willing to consider. In any case, precise measurements had not yet become an important feature of chemical studies, so loss of weight was not an insurmountable barrier to the phlogiston concept.

Modern theory

As with so many other instances in science, the phlogiston theory fell into disrepute only when someone appeared on the scene who could reject traditional thinking almost entirely and propose a radically new view of the phenomenon. That person was the great French chemist Antoine Laurent Lavoisier (1743-1794). Having knowledge of some recent critical discoveries in chemistry, especially the discovery of oxygen by Karl Wilhelm Scheele (1742–1786) in 1771 and Joseph Priestley (1733–1804) in 1774, Lavoisier framed a new definition of combustion. Combustion, he said, is the process by which some material combines with oxygen. By making the best use of precise quantitative experiments, Lavoisier provided such a sound basis for his new theory that it was widely accepted in a relatively short period of time.

Lavoisier initiated another important line of research related to combustion, one involving the amount of heat generated during oxidation. His earliest experiments involved the study of heat lost by a guinea pig during respiration, which Lavoisier called "a combustion." In this work, he was assisted by a second famous French scientist, Pierre Simon Laplace (1749–1827). As a result of their research, Lavoisier and Laplace laid down one of the fundamental principles of thermochemistry, namely that the amount of heat needed to decompose a compound is the same as the amount of heat liberated during its formation from its elements. This line of research was later developed by the Swiss–Russian chemist Henri Hess (1802–1850) in the 1830s. Hess' development and extension of the work of Lavoisier and Laplace has earned him the title of father of thermochemistry.

Combustion mechanics

From a chemical standpoint, combustion is a process in which chemical bonds are broken and new chemical bonds formed. The net result of these changes is a release of energy, the heat of combustion. For example, suppose that a gram of coal is burned in pure oxygen with the formation of carbon dioxide as the only product. In this reaction, the first step is the destruction of bonds between carbon atoms and between oxygen atoms. In order for this step to occur, energy must be added to the coal/oxygen mixture. For example, a lighted match must be touched to the coal.

Once the carbon–carbon and oxygen–oxygen bonds have been broken, new bonds between carbon atoms and oxygen atoms can be formed. These bonds contain less energy than did the original carbon–carbon and oxygen–oxygen bonds. That energy is released in the form of heat, the heat of combustion. The heat of combustion of one mole of carbon, for example, is about 94 kcal.

Applications

Humans have been making practical use of combustion for millennia. Cooking food and heating homes have long been two major applications of the combustion reaction. With the development of the steam engine by Denis Papin, Thomas Savery, Thomas Newcomen, and others at the beginning of the eighteenth century, however, a new use for combustion was found: performing work. Those first engines employed the combustion of some material, usually coal, to produce heat that was used to boil water. The steam produced was then able to move pistons and drive machinery. That concept is essentially the same one used today to operate fossil–fueled electrical power plants.

Before long, inventors found ways to use steam engines in transportation, especially in railroad engines and steam ships. However, it was not until the discovery of a new type of fuel—gasoline and its chemical relatives and a new type of engine—the internal combustion engine—that the modern face of transportation was achieved. Today, most forms of transportation depend on the combustion of a hydrocarbon fuel such as gasoline, kerosene, or diesel oil to produce the energy that drives pistons and moves the vehicles on which modern society depends.

When considering how fuels are burned during the combustion process, "stationary" and "explosive" flames are treated as two distinct types of combustion. In stationary combustion, as generally seen in gas or oil burners, the mixture of fuel and oxidizer flows toward the flame at a proper speed to maintain the position of the flame. The fuel can be either premixed with air or introduced separately into the combustion region. An explosive flame, on the other hand, occurs in a homogeneous mixture of fuel and air in which the flame moves rapidly through the combustible mixture. Burning in the cylinder of a gasoline engine belongs to this category. Overall, both chemical and physical processes are combined in combustion, and the dominant process depends on very diverse burning conditions.

Environmental issues

The use of combustion as a power source has had such a dramatic influence on human society that the period after 1750 has sometimes been called the Fossil Fuel Age. Still, the widespread use of combustion for human applications has always had its disadvantages. Pictorial representations of England during the Industrial Revolution, for example, usually include huge clouds of smoke emitted by the combustion of wood and coal in steam engines.

Today, modern societies continue to face environmental problems created by the prodigious combustion of carbon–based fuels. For example, one product of any combustion reaction in the real world is carbon monoxide, a toxic gas that is often detected at dangerous levels in urban areas around the world. Oxides of sulfur, produced by the combustion of impurities in fuels, and oxides of nitrogen, produced at high temperature, also have deleterious effects, often in the form of acid rain

KEY TERMS

Chemical bond—Any force of attraction between two atoms.

Fossil fuel—A fuel that is derived from the decay of plant or animal life; coal, oil, and natural gas are the fossil fuels.

Industrial Revolution—That period, beginning about the middle of the eighteenth century, during which humans began to use steam engines as a major source of power.

Internal combustion engine—An engine in which the chemical reaction that supplies energy to the engine takes place within the walls of the engine (usually a cylinder) itself.

Thermochemistry—The science that deals with the quantity and nature of heat changes that take place during chemical reactions and/or changes of state.

and smog. Even carbon dioxide itself, the primary product of combustion, is suspected of causing global climate changes because of the enormous concentrations it has reached in the atmosphere.

See also Air pollution; Chemical bond; Heat; Internal combustion engine; Oxidation-reduction reaction.

Further Reading:
Bradley, John N. *Flame and Combustion Phenomena*. London: Methuen, 1969.
Gilpin, Alan. *Dictionary of Fuel Technology*. New York: Philosophical Library, 1969.
Joesten, Melvin D., et al. *World of Chemistry*. Philadelphia: Saunders, 1991.
Olah, George A., ed. *Chemistry of Energetic Materials*. San Diego: Academic Press, 1991.
Partington, J. R. *A Short History of Chemistry*. 3rd ed. London: Macmillan & Company, 1957, passim.

David E. Newton

Comets

A comet is a body in the solar system with a dark, solid nucleus (core) surrounded by a gigantic, glowing mass (coma). Together, the nucleus and coma comprise the comet's head, seen as a glowing ball shooting through space and from which streams a long, luminous tail. Visible comets rotate on an axis following either an elliptic (eccentric, elongated circle) or almost parabolic (extremely elongated ellipse) orbit of the Sun. This orbit may be prograde, in the same direction as the planets; or retrograde, in the opposite direction. Perhaps among the most primitive bodies in the solar system, comets are probably debris from the formation of our Sun and planets some 4.5 billion years ago. The most popular theory about their source is the Oort cloud, a dense "shell" of debris at the frigid, outer edge of the solar system. Occasionally, disruptive gravitational forces (perturbations) from interstellar space hurl a piece of debris from the cloud into the gravitational pull of one of the large planets, like Jupiter, where it is "captured" and ultimately pulled into orbit around the Sun. Comets are either short–period (periodic) with orbits of less than 200 years and which seldom leave the solar system; or long–period, having enormous elliptical, nearly parabolic orbits of more than 200 years and which often travel far beyond our planets into interstellar space. Of the 710 individual comets recorded from 1680 to mid–1992, 121 were short–period and 589 long–period.

Age–old fascination

Fascination with the night sky goes back as far as human history. Etchings on clay tablets unearthed in the ancient city of Babylon dating to at least 3000 B.C. and rock carvings found in prehistoric sites in Scotland dating to 2000 B.C. depict unexplained astronomical phenomena that may have been comets. Until the Arabic astronomers of the eleventh century, the Chinese were by far the most astute sky–watchers in the world. By 400 B.C. their intricate cometary classification system included sketches of 29 comet forms, each associated with a past event and predicting a future one. Comet type 9 was named Pu–Hui, meaning "Calamity in the state, many deaths." Another comet appearing in that form supposedly foretold a similar calamity. In fact, from Babylonian civilization right up until the seventeenth century and across cultures, comets were viewed with superstition and as omens portending human disasters and terrestrial catastrophes.

Of all the Greek and Roman theories on comets—a Greek word meaning "long–haired one"—the most influential, though entirely incorrect, was that of Greek philosopher, Aristotle (384–322 B.C.). His geocentric view of the solar system put Earth at the center circled by the Moon, Mercury, Venus, Sun, Mars, Jupiter and Saturn. Stars were stationary, and temporary bodies like comets traveled in straight lines. Aristotle believed

Comet West above Table Mountain in California shortly before sunrise in March, 1976. The bright head of the comet is seen just above the mountains, while its broad dust tail sweeps up and back from the nucleus, pushed outward by the pressure of sunlight. The comet passed within 73 million miles (118 million kilometers) of Earth and will not return for another 560,000 years.

comets were fires in the dry, sublunar "fiery sphere," a combustible atmosphere "exhaled" from Earth which accumulated between Earth and the Moon. Comets were therefore considered terrestrial—originating from Earth, rather than celestial—heavenly bodies. They were God's warning to, or vengeance upon, humans.

Aristotle's model left many unexplained questions about the movement of bodies through the solar system. His theory became so strongly supported by the Christian church, however, that those who challenged it were often called heretics. His theory remained sacred for over 2,000 years, bringing European investigations into comets virtually to a halt. Fortunately, because of their immense value to modern astronomical science, prolific and accurate cometary records were kept by the Chinese during this entire period.

Sporadic scientific investigations into comets had some influence, however. Although the church held his theory in check, Copernicus (1473–1543) hinted that a heliocentric (Sun–centered) solar system would help explain motions of the planets and other "temporary" celestial bodies. Through astute observation of the "Great Comet" of 1577, Danish astronomer Tycho Brahe calculated that it must be four times further away from Earth than the Moon, strongly refuting Aristotle's sublunar positioning. Also, even though we now know Chinese astronomers noted it hundreds of years previously, Tycho found the comet's tail pointed away from the Sun and its orbit may be oval.

The study of the Great Comet by Tycho and his contemporaries was the turning point for astronomical science. Throughout the seventeenth and eighteenth centuries, now famous mathematicians and astronomers proposed conflicting ideas on the origin, formation, movement, shape of orbit, and meaning of comets. In the early 1600s, Isaac Newton built on theories from the likes of Johannes Kepler, who developed the three laws of planetary motion; Johannes Hevelius, who suggested comets move on a parabola (U–shape) around the Sun; and Robert Hooke, who introduced the possibility of a universal gravitational influence. Newton developed an astounding mathematical model for the parabolic motion of comets, published in 1687 in *Principia*, one of the "most influential scientific works ever written." By now, comets were viewed as celestial rather than terrestrial, and the focus turned from superstition to science.

However, comets were still viewed as singular. In 1687, English astronomer Edmond Halley suggested to Newton that comets may be periodic, following an elliptical path. Newton did not agree. Using Newton's mathematical model, Halley predicted that the comets of 1531, 1607, and 1682—the latter observed by both he and Newton—were one and the same, and should return late in 1758. It did, and was subsequently named Halley's comet.

By the end of the eighteenth century, comets were believed to be permanent, astronomical bodies composed of solid material, the movement of which could be calculated using Newton's laws of planetary motion, and the return of two more comets in 1822 and 1832 was accurately predicted. The first, comet Enke, did not follow Newton's law of planetary motion, however, as its orbit size and period of recurrence were decreasing. In 1835, Friedreich Bessel accurately suggested this was because gases given off by the comet as it flew through the atmosphere acted like a rocket, thrusting the comet either closer to or further away from the Sun, thus affecting its orbital length. The second predicted periodic comet, comet Biela, with a periodic orbit of 6.75 years, upset Newton's permanency proposal when, in 1846, it split in two. The twin comet reappeared in 1852 for the last time. Earlier in the century, scientists speculated that meteor showers may be flying debris from disintegrating comets. In November 1872, when Biela should have returned, the meteor shower predicted by some astronomers did indeed appear, strengthening the connection between meteors and dying comets.

Stargazing and discovering comets

The first observation of a comet through a telescope was made in 1618. Until the twentieth century, comets were discovered and observed with the naked eye or through telescopes. Today, most new discoveries are made from photographs of our galaxy and electronic detectors, although many discoveries are still made by amateur astronomers with a passion for gazing into the heavens. The long focal–length, refracting telescope, the primary astronomical observation tool of the 1800s, worked well for viewing bright objects but did not collect sufficient light to allow astronomical photography. In 1858, an English artist named Usherwood used a short focal–length lens to produce the first photograph of a comet. In 1864, by using a spectroscope, an instrument which separates the wave lengths of light into spectral bands, Italian astronomer Giovanni Donati first identified a chemical component in a comet's atmosphere. The first cometary spectrogram (spectral photograph) was taken by amateur astronomer William Huggins of London in 1881. The early twentieth century saw the development of short focal–length spectrographs which, by the 1950s, allowed identification of several different chemical components in a comet's tail. Infrared spectrography was introduced in the 1960s and, in 1983, the Infrared Astronomy Satellite (IRAS) gathered information on cometary dust particles unattainable from ground–based technology. Observations are also made by radio wave detection and ultraviolet spectrography.

Composition, origin, and extinction

The birth, source, composition, and death of comets is an extremely complex topic which still defies definitive answers. Increasing knowledge and advancing twentieth–century technology brought many and, as usual, conflicting theories.

Composition of the nucleus

Two major theories on the composition of the nucleus have developed over time. The "flying sandbank" model, first proposed by Richard Proctor in the mid 1800s and again in the mid 1900s by Raymond Lyttleton, conjectured swarms of tiny solid particles bound together by mutual gravitational attraction. In 1950, Fred Whipple introduced the "icy–conglomerate" model, which described a comet as a solid nucleus of meteoric rock particles and dust frozen in ice. Observations of Halley's comet by spacecraft in 1986 strongly support this model. Noone knows the exact composition of the nucleus, but rocks and dust are held together with ices from water, methane, ammonia, and carbon monoxide, as well as other ices containing carbon and sulphur. The 1986 encounter showed Halley's nucleus as peanut or potato–shaped, 9 mi (15 km) long, and 5.5 miles (8 km) wide. However, probing beneath its dark, solid surface proved impossible. Also, nuclei have been seen to produce sudden, bright flares and some even split into two, three, four, or five pieces, but the reason is not yet known. Comet nuclei are among the smallest bodies in the Solar system—too small, in fact, for observation even through a telescope. As they approach the Sun, however, they produce one of the largest, most spectacular sights in the solar system—a magnificent, glowing coma often visible even to the naked eye.

Creation of the coma

As the nucleus approaches the Sun, beginning at about the distance of the astroid belt and much further out than the orbit of Mars, its ices begin to vaporize and sublimate (purify), releasing gases of hydrogen, carbon, oxygen, nitrogen and other molecules, as well as dust particles. Streaming away at several hundred meters per second, they create an enormous coma hundreds of thousands of kilometers long, completely hiding the nucleus. The Sun's ultraviolet light electrically charges the gaseous molecules, ionizing and exciting them, causing them to fluoresce and shine like a fluorescent light. Microscopic mineral particles in the dust reflect and scatter the Sun's light. Only in 1970, during the first spacecraft observation of a comet, was a gigantic hydrogen cloud discovered surrounding the coma. Depending on the size of the nucleus and its proximity to the Sun, this cloud can be much larger than the Sun itself.

Configuration of the tails

As the comet swings around the Sun on its elliptical orbit, the gas and dust particles stream from the coma creating two types of tails: the gaseous ion tail, or Type I; and the dust tail, or Type II. In Type I, ionized gases form a thin, usually straight tail, sometimes millions of kilometers long. (The tail of the Great Comet of 1843 was more than 136 million mi/220 million km long!) The ion tail, glowing with incredible brightness, does not trail behind but is blown away from the head in a direction almost opposite the Sun by the "solar wind," a continual flow of magnetized plasma emitted by the Sun. The head collides with this plasma, which wraps around the nucleus, pulling the ionized particles with it. Depending on its position to the Sun, the tail may even be traveling almost ahead of the nucleus. A Type II tail is usually shorter and wider, and curves slightly because the heavier dust particles are carried away at a slower rate. The Great Comet of 1744 actually displayed six brilliant tails fanning above the horizon like peacock feathers.

Birth of a comet

A decade–old debate continues today—Do comets originate from within or outside the solar system?

Solar system origin and the Oort cloud

In 1950, Dutch astronomer Jan Oort proposed a primordial "cloud" of debris left over from the formation of the solar system. This immense band of comets would begin well outside the orbit of Pluto, the planet furthest from the Sun, about 50,000 astronomical units (AU) from the Sun and extend 150,000 AU into space. One AU is the mean distance from the Sun to Earth—93 million mi (150 million km). Shrink our entire solar system to the size of a dime with its edge being Pluto's orbit. The Oort cloud would reach from 36–108 ft (11–33 m) from the center of the dime. Oort suggested that occasionally, perturbations of passing stars knock debris out of this cloud, hurling it outward to interstellar space or inward to the realm of the planets where it is captured and begins orbiting the Sun. At about three AU from the Sun, the comet's icy components vaporize, making it visible.

This theory was widely accepted as the source of long–period comets, but did not address the origin of short–period comets (because of their different orbital shapes). Slight theory modifications point to a belt of comets beginning outside the orbit of Neptune—the Kuiper Belt—extending outward to a gigantic "inner cloud." This densely populated inner cloud spreads out to the less dense Oort cloud. Independent studies in the 1980s support this theory; it resolves some questions about the source of short–period comets, unusual cometary orbits, and even about the evolution of the solar system.

But questions remain. Estimates suggest that 65% of outer Oort cloud comets are knocked into interstellar space by perturbations from Jupiter. The cloud is also depleted by stellar perturbations and galactic tides—waves of gravity flowing through the galaxy caused by the distribution of matter within the galaxy. Also, as the solar system moves slowly through the center of the galaxy, it encounters gigantic molecular gas clouds, heavily populated with comets which, under certain velocity–related circumstances, strip comets from the Oort cloud. How, then, is the Oort cloud replenished? One theory is that stellar and galactic tide perturbations hurl comets into the Oort cloud from the dense inner cloud. A second theory proposes "capture" of comets from interstellar space.

Interstellar origin

The popularity of the interstellar theory waxes and wanes like the galactic tide, and new hypotheses are again being proposed. One suggests the presence of comets in high–density clouds within the galaxy's inner spiral arms. The Sun may capture comets while passing through one of these arms, which happens once every

100 million years. Also, comets may be captured from the very same molecular gas clouds which, under other circumstances, so severely deplete the Oort cloud population. Mathematical calculations and known chemical composition of comets and stars indicate the possibility of interstellar origins.

Death of a comet

Although vaporization diminishes the nucleus, it is not believed to be enough to cause a comet's extinction. Two phenomena—splitting, which may result in deterioration and ultimately a meteor shower; and flaring, bright explosions visible in the coma—are the most commonly accepted reasons for a comet's death. Another theory postulates that asteroids may be extinct comets.

Comets to Earth

The paths of comets and asteroids actually cross the orbital path of the planets and are believed to be the cause of impact craters, including those on Earth and the Moon. In 1979, United States Air Force space–test satellite P78–1 took the first photograph of a comet colliding with the Sun. Late in 1994, several comets collided with Jupiter. Cometary impact on Earth may have caused extinction of many species, including the dinosaurs, while making the development of entirely new species possible. For millennia, humans have predicted the "end of the world" from the impact of a giant comet. However, many scientists, even some in the late part of this century, believe molecules released by comets' vaporized gases may have supplied important molecules in Earth's early atmosphere. When exposed to the Sun's radiation, these molecules began the formation of biochemical compounds which actually began the process of life on Earth and from which new species developed.

Bright objects keep us in the dark

Despite spaceships probing the outer limits of our solar system, gigantic telescopes in deserts, atop mountains, and floating in space probing its secrets, and satellites designed specifically to capture meteor dust hurtling through Earth's atmosphere from interstellar space, the ancient mystery of the comet—that dark, icy, rocky, debris blazing brilliantly as it flies around the Sun—remains unsolved. Unraveling this mystery presents an exciting challenge for stargazers of the future, and may even reveal how life on Earth began.

See also Halley's comet; Meteors and meteorites.

Further Reading:

Bailey, M. E., S. V. M. Clube, and W. M. Napier. *The Origin of Comets*. Oxford: Pergamon Press, 1990.

KEY TERMS

Astronomical Unit (AU)—Mean distance from the center of the Sun to Earth.

Coma—Glowing cloud of mass surrounding the nucleus of a comet.

Ellipse—An eccentric or elongated circle, or oval.

Galactic tide—Tides of gravity moving through the Galaxy caused by the overall distribution of matter within the Galaxy.

Ion—Electrically–charged group of atoms.

Nucleus—Core, or center.

Parabola—Open–ended, elongated ellipse; U-shaped.

Perturbation—Change in the orbit of an astronomical body by the gravitational influence of a body other than the one around which the object orbits.

Retrograde orbit—From east to west, the opposite direction to the planets.

Solar wind—Magnetized plasma continually flowing from the Sun composed primarily of protons and electrons.

Spectrograph—Instrument for dispersing light into its spectrum of wavelengths then photographing that spectrum.

Sublimation—Purification of a solid by heating to a gaseous state and condensing the vapor back into solid form.

Gibilisco, Stan. *Comets, Meteors & Asteroids—How They Affect Earth*. Blue Ridge Summit, PA: Tab Books, 1985.

Levy, David H. *The Quest for Comets, An Explosive Trail of Beauty and Danger*. New York: Plenum Press, 1994.

Yeomans, Donald K. *Comets, A Chronological History of Observation, Science, Myth, and Folklore*. New York: John Wiley & Sons, 1991.

Marie L. Thompson

Commensalism

Commensalism is a type of symbiosis, specifically, a biological relationship in which one species benefits from an interaction, while the host species is neither positively or negatively affected to any tangible degree.

For example, epiphytic plants (which grow on other plants but are not parasitic) gain an enormous ecological benefit from living on larger plants, because they gain access to a substrate upon which to grow relatively high in the canopy. The host trees, however, are not affected in any significant way by this relationship, even in cases when they are supporting what appears to be a large population of epiphytes. Some plants are specialized as epiphytes, for example, many species of air–plants or bromeliads (family Bromeliaceae), orchids (Orchidaceae), and ferns (Pterophyta). Many lichens, mosses, and liverworts are also epiphytes on trees. There are also animal analogues of this relationship. Sometimes sea anemones (order Actiniaria) will gain a benefit in terms of food availability by growing on the upper carapace of a hermit crab (crustacean infraorder Anomura) which is apparently unaffected by the presence of the epiphyte.

Another commensal relationship, known as phoresy, is a type of biological hitch–hiking in which one organism benefits through access to a mode of transportation while the animal providing this service is not significantly affected by its role. For example, many plants produce fruits that adhere to fur and are thereby dispersed by the movement of mammals. Some North American examples of such animal–dispersed plants are the burdock (*Arctium lappa*), beggar–tick or stick–tight (*Bidens frondosa*), and tick–trefoil (*Desmodium canadense*). The fruits of these plants have special anatomical adaptations for adhering to fur—in fact, those of the burdock are the botanical model from which the idea for the very useful fastening material known as velcro was developed. In a few cases, individual animals may become heavily loaded with these sorts of sticky fruits causing their fur to mat excessively, perhaps resulting in a significant detriment. This is not common, however, and usually this biological relationship is truly commensal.

See also Symbiosis.

Commutative property

"Commutativity" is a property which an operation between two numbers (or other mathematical elements) may or may not have. The operation is commutative if it does not matter which element is named first.

For example, because addition is commutative, 5 + 7 has the same value as 7 + 5. Subtraction, on the other hand, is not commutative, and the difference 5 – 7 does not have the same value as 5 – 7.

Commutativity can be described more formally. If * stands for an operation and if A and B are elements from a given set, then * is commutative if, for all such elements A * B = B * A.

In ordinary arithmetic and algebra, the commutative operations are multiplication and addition. The non–commutative operations are subtraction, division, and exponentiation. For example, x + 3 is equal to 3 + x; xy is equal to yx; and (x + 7)(x – 2) is equal to (x – 2)(x + 7). On the other hand, 4 – 3x is not equal to 3x – 4; 16/4 is not equal to 4/16; and 5^2 is not equal to 2^5.

The commutative property can be associated with other mathematical elements and operations as well. For instance, one can think of a translation of axes in the coordinate plane as an "element," and following one translation by another as a "product." Then, if T_1 and T_2 are two such translations, T_1T_2 and T_2T_1 are equal. This operation is commutative. If the set of transformations includes both translations and rotations, however, then the operation loses its commutativity. A rotation of axes followed by a translation does not have the same effect on the ultimate position of the axes as the same translation followed by the same rotation.

When an operation is both commutative and associative (an operation is associative if for all A, B, and C, (A * B) * C = A * (B * C), the operation on a finite number of elements can be done in any order. This is particularly useful in simplifying an expression such as $x^2 + 5x + 8 + 2x^2 + x + 9$. One can combine the squared terms, the linear terms, and the constants without tediously and repeatedly using the associative and commutative properties to bring like terms together. In fact, because the terms of a sum can be combined in any order, the order need not be specified, and the expression can be written without parentheses. Because ordinary multiplication is both associative and commutative, this is true of products as well. The expression $5x^2y^3z$, with its seven factors, requires no parentheses.

Compact disc

In 1978, Philips and Sony together launched an effort to produce an audio compact disc (CD) technology as a method of delivering digital sound and music to consumers. The two companies continued to cooperate through the 1980s, and eventually worked out standards for using the CD technology to store computer data. These recommendations evolved into the CD–ROM technology of today.

The CD–ROM (compact disc–read only memory) is a read–only optical storage medium capable of holding 600 megabytes of data (approximately 500,000 pages of text), 70 minutes of high fidelity audio, or some combination of the two. Legend has it that the size of the compact disc was chosen so that it could contain a slow–tempo rendition of Beethoven's Ninth Symphony. As can be seen from Table 1, compact discs afford very low data storage and delivery costs compared to those for more traditional media.

The first users of CD–ROMs were owners of large databases: library catalogs, reference systems, and parts lists, but typical applications of CD–ROMs as storage media now include storage of such information as the following:

- every listing from all of the Yellow Pages in the United States
- maps of every street in the country
- facsimile numbers for all publicly held businesses and government institutions
- a 21–volume encyclopedia

CD–ROMs are expected to achieve significant impact in the storage of

- Business reference materials
- Interactive education for schools
- Scholarly publications
- Government archives
- Home–based reference materials

What is a CD–ROM?

A compact disc is a thin wafer of clear polycarbonate plastic and metal measuring 4.75 in (120 mm) in diameter with a small hole in its center. The metal layer is usually pure aluminum that is sputtered onto the polycarbonate surface in a layer that is few molecules thick. The metal reflects light from a tiny infrared laser as the disc spins in the CD player. The reflections are transformed into electrical signals, and then further converted to meaningful data for use in digital equipment.

Information is stored in pits on the CD–ROM that are 1–3 microns long, about 0.5 microns wide, and 0.1 microns deep. There may be more than 3 miles of these pits wound about the center hole on the disc. The CD–ROM is coated with a layer of lacquer that protects the surface. By convention, a label is usually silkscreened on the backside.

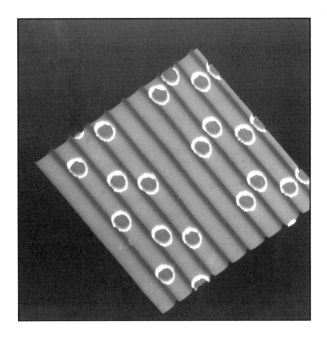

An atomic force microscope image of marks (data) burned into a write-once optical disc (WORM). The write laser burns holes in an ablative material that is part of the disc. The marks cannot be erased, hence "write-once."

Compact discs are made in a multistep process. First a glass master is made using photolithographic techniques. An optically ground glass disc is coated with a layer of photoresist material 0.1 microns thick. A pattern is produced the disc using a laser; then the exposed areas on the disc are then washed away, and the disc is silvered to produce the actual pits. The master disc is next coated with single molecular layers of nickel, one layer at a time, until the desired thickness has been achieved. The nickel layer is next separated from the glass disc and used as a metal negative.

In the case of low production runs, the metal negative is used to make the actual discs. Most projects require that several positives be produced by plating the surface of the metal negative. Molds or stampers are then made from the positives and used in injection molding machines.

Plastic pellets are heated and injected into the molds, where they form the disc with pits in it. The plastic disc is coated with a thin aluminum layer for reflectance and with a protective lacquer layer. The disc is then given its silkscreened label and packaged for delivery. Most of these operations take place in a cleanroom because a single particle of dust larger than a pit can destroy data. Mastering alone takes about 12 hours of work.

TABLE 1. COSTS OF INFORMATION STORAGE		
Medium	*Capacity*	*Cost per megabyte*
Hard disc	100 megabytes	~$7.00
Paper	2 kilobytes per page	~$5.00
Magnetic tape	60 megabytes	<$1.00
Floppy disc	1.44 megabytes	<$0.50
CD-ROM	650 megabytes	~$0.01

How does it work?

The primary unit of data storage on a compact disc is a sector, which is 1/75 second long. Each sector on a CD contains 2352 bytes of data, and each sector is followed by 882 bytes of error detecting and correcting information and timing control data. Thus, a CD actually requires 3234 bytes to store 2352 bytes of data.

The disc spins at a constant linear velocity, which means that the rotational speed of the disc may vary from about 200 rpm when the data being read are near the outer of the disc, to about 530 rpm when the data are located near the center of the disc. (This is because rotational speed = linear velocity x radius of sector.)

The CD is read at a sustained rate of 150K per second, which is sufficient for good audio but very slow for large image files, motion video, and other multimedia resources. Newer drives spin at twice, or even three, four or six times this rate. Still, CD access speeds and transfer rates are much slower than those from a hard disc. This is expected to change as discs are made to spin faster and different types of lasers are employed.

The surface of the CD-ROM is essentially transparent. It must allow a finely focused beam of laser light to pass through it twice, first to the metallic layer beneath the plastic where the data reside, and then back to the receptors. Dirt, scratches, fingerprints, and other imperfections interfere with retrieval of the stored data.

CD–ROM drives

Each CD-ROM drive for a personal computer may be characterized according to the following:
- drive specifications
- formats the drive reads
- interface the drive requires to connect the computer

Drive specifications

The drive specifications tell the drive's performance capabilities. Commonly included in these specifications are the following:

- The data transfer rate, which specifies how much data the drive can read from a data CD and transfer to the host computer when reading one large, sequential chunk of data.
- The access time, which is the delay between the drive receiving the command to read and its actual first reading of the data.
- The buffer size, which is the size of the cache of memory stored in the drive. Not all drives are equipped with memory buffers.

Drive formats

The data on compact discs need to be organized if the CD–ROM drive and computer are to make sense of the data. The data are therefore encoded to conform to certain standards. Although advanced CD–ROM standards are still evolving, most drives today comply with earlier CD–ROM formats (see Table 2).

Interfaces

The CD–ROM interface is the physical connection of the drive to the PC's expansion bus. Interfaces typically include:

SCSI Standard Interfaces

Small Computer System Interface (SCSI) refers to a group of adapter cards that conform to a set of common commands. These adapter cards allow you to string along a chain of devices from a single adapter. Consequently, SCSI interfaces are preferred for connecting a CD–ROM drive to a personal computer.

SCSI–2 and ASPI Interfaces

SCSI–2 and Advanced SCSI Programming Interface (ASPI) take into account rapid enhancements of computer interface technology. SCSI–2 incorporates several enhancements, including greater data throughput, and improved read and write technologies. ASPI provides a standard software interface to the host adapter hardware.

TABLE 2. COMPACT DISC AND DRIVE FORMATS

Format name	Description	Notes
CD-ROM ISO 9660	Read-only memory	Applies to MS-DOS and Macintosh files. This standard evolved from the Yellow Book specifications of Philips and Sony. Defined the Volume Table of Contents that tells the CD reader where and how the data are laid out on the disc.
CD-ROM High Sierra	Read-only memory	Based on a standard worked out in 1985 to resolve differences in leading manufacturers' implementations of ISO 9660.
CD-DA	Digital audio	Data drives that can read data and audio are called CD-DA.
PhotoCD	Compressed images	KODAK multisession XA system. Customers present an exposed 35 mm roll of color film for wet processing, and purchase a Photo CD for an additional charge. The negatives are then processed by a technician who scans each image at an imaging workstation. The images are written onto the Photo CD write-once media, color thumbnails of all of the images are printed, and the Photo CD is returned to the consumer in a CD jewel case with the index sheet inserted as a cover. The customer may return the same Photo CD to have more images written onto it, with the result that a multisession disc is produced. A Photo CD can hold 125 or more high resolution images. Photo CDS may be viewed using a Kodak Photo CD player connected to a television at the customer's home. Photo CD images can also be viewed using a CD-ROM/XA player attached to a computer. Photo CD images can be converted to other formats for incorporation into multimedia applications.

Nonstandard SCSI Interfaces

Nonstandard SCSI interfaces may not let you install multiple SCSI devices; in cases where this is not a problem, they may prove acceptable.

Care of CD–ROMs

Audio CDs tend to be more forgiving than CDs that will be read by computers. The audio CD player can fill in any missing data on the disc because audio data are

TABLE 2. COMPACT DISC AND DRIVE FORMATS (cnt'd)

Format name	Description	Notes
CD-ROM/XA	Read-only memory	Extended architecture. Data are read off a disc in alternating pieces, and synchronized at play-back. The result is a simultaneous presentation of graphics and audio. CD-ROM/XA defined a new sector format to allow computer data, compressed audio data, and video/image information to be read and played back apparently simultaneously. Special enabling hardware is required on CD-ROM/XA players because the audio must be separated from the interleaved data, decompressed, and sent to speakers, at the same time the computer data are being sent to the computer.
CD-R (CD-WO or CD-WORM)	Write-once	May use multiple sessions to fill disc. Instead of burning pits into a substrate, the CD-R uses differences in reflectivity to fool the reader into believing that a pit actually exists. This format allows you to write your own CDS.
CD-ROM HFS	Read-only memory	The Macintosh Hierarchical File System (HFS) is Apple's method for managing files and folders on the Macintosh desktop. The HFS driver provides Macintosh users with the expected and familiar Apple desktop. This is the preferred format for delivery to Macintosh platforms, even though it does not conform to the ISO 9660 standard.
CD-I or CD-RTOS	Interactive	Philips Interactive motion video. CD-I discs are designed to work with Philips CD-I players, but the CD-I system also hooks up to the customer's TV or stereo. It can play audio CDS, and can also read Kodak PhotoCD discs. The CD-I is marketed for education, home, and business use.
CD-I Ready	Interactive/Ready	CD-Audio with features for CD-I player.
CD-Bridge	Bridge	Allows XA track to play on CD-I player.

TABLE 2. COMPACT DISC AND DRIVE FORMATS (cnt'd)		
Format name	*Description*	*Notes*
CD-MO	Magneto-optical	Premastered area readable on any CD player.
CD+G	Mixed mode	CD+G stands for CD audio plus graphics. This format allows the customer to play CD audio along with titles, still pictures, and song lyrics synchronized to the music. This CD may be best suited to karaoke-style discs, i.e., music playing along with on-screen lyrics.
CDTV	ISO 9660 variant	Commodore proprietary system.

easily interpolated, with the result that scratches do not have much effect on the quality of the sound produced when the CD is played.

Computer data are less predictable than audio data. Consequently, it is not as easy to interpolate when data are missing. Because computer data are digital (either 0s or 1s), the computer cannot represent missing data by an "average" value lying somewhere between 0 and 1. Because small scratches are inevitable, the CD–ROM incorporates a scheme that makes it possible to reconstruct any bit from the surrounding data. This scheme is called Error Correction Code (ECC). ECC permits the CD–ROM to undergo some surface damage and still remain usable, but it does not replace the need to exercise care when handling a disc.

Multimedia

Multimedia is a computer application that employs more than one medium to convey information. Examples of multimedia include

- text with graphics
- text with photos
- text with sound
- text with animation
- text with video
- graphics with sound
- photos with sound
- animation with sound
- video with sound

As indicated in Table 3, some multimedia combinations require very large amounts of disc storage space. To date, most multimedia applications have been text–based with multimedia features added. Many multimedia applications, however, make heavy use of memory–intensive features such as video and sound. Although the CD–ROM is not a requirement for multimedia on the personal computer, its impressive storage capacity makes it a logical choice for delivering multimedia documentation.

See also Computer, digital; Laser.

TABLE 3. MULTIMEDIA STORAGE REQUIREMENTS	
One Minute Of...	*Storage Space Required*
audio, mono	700 kilobytes
audio, stereo	more than 1.5 megabytes
animation	2.5 to 5.5 megabytes
video	20 to 30 megabytes, compressed

Further Reading:

Bosak, S,. J. Sloman, and D. Gibbons, *The CD–ROM Book,* Indianapolis, IN: Que Corporation, 1994.

Vaughan, T., *Multimedia: Making It Happen,* Berkeley, CA: Osborne–McGraw Hill, 1994.

Randall Frost

Competition

Competition is a biological interaction among organisms of the same or different species associated with the need for a common resource that occurs in a limited supply relative to demand. In other words, competition occurs when the capability of the environment to supply resources is smaller than the potential biological requirement so that organisms interfere with each other. Plants, for example, often compete for access to a limited supply of nutrients, water, sunlight, and space.

Intraspecific competition occurs when individuals of the same species vie for access to essential resources, while interspecific competition occurs between different species. Stresses associated with competition are said to be symmetric if they involve organisms of similar size and/or abilities to utilize resources. Competition is asymmetric when there are substantial differences in these abilities, as occurs in the case of large trees interacting with plants of a forest understory.

Competition as an ecological and evolutionary factor

Individuals of the same species have virtually identical resource requirements. Therefore, whenever populations of a species are crowded, intraspecific competition is intense. Intraspecific competition in dense populations results in a process known as self–thinning, which is characterized by mortality of less–capable individuals and relative success by more–competitive individuals. In such situations, intraspecific competition is an important regulator of population size. Moreover, because individual organisms vary in their reproductive success, intraspecific competition can be a selective factor in evolution.

Interspecific competition can also be intense if individuals of the various species are crowded and have similar requirements of resources. One ecological theory, known as the competitive exclusion principle, states that species with ecologically identical life styles and resource needs cannot coexist over the longer term; the competitively less–fit species will be displaced by the better fit species. Although it is debatable that different species could have identical ecological requirements, it is not difficult to comprehend that intense competition must occur among similar species living in the same, resource–limited habitat. In such situations, interspecific competition must be important in structuring ecological communities and as an agent of natural selection. There are many indications that this is the case.

For example, disturbance or some other environmental changes may change competitive relationships within an ecological community. The term competitive release refers to a situation in which an organism or species is relieved of the stresses associated with competition allowing it to become more successful and dominant in its habitat. For example, by the early 1950s the American chestnut (*Castanea dentata*) had been eliminated as a dominant canopy species in deciduous forests of eastern North America by the accidental introduction of a fungal pathogen known as chestnut blight (*Endothia parasitica*). Other tree species took advantage of their sudden release from competition with the chestnut by opportunistically filling in the canopy gaps that were left by the demise of mature chestnut trees. Similarly, competitively suppressed plants may be released when a mature forest is disturbed, for example, by wildfire, a windstorm, or harvesting by humans. If the disturbance kills many of the trees that formed the forest canopy but previously suppressed plants survive, then these understory plants will gain access to an abundance of environmental resources such as light, moisture, and nutrients, and they will be able to grow relatively freely.

Competitive displacement is said to occur when a more competitive species causes another to utilize a distinctly sub–optimal habitat. A number of interesting cases of competitive displacement have been described by ecologists, many involving interactions of plant species. For example, in eastern North America, the natural habitat utilized by the tree, the silver maple (*Acer saccharinum*) is almost entirely restricted to forested wetlands, or swamps. However, the silver maple is more productive of biomass and fruits if it grows on well–drained, upland sites, and for this reason it is commonly cultivated in cities and towns. In spite of this habitat preference, the silver maple does not occur in the natural forest community of well drained sites. It appears that the silver maple is not sufficiently competitive to co–occur in well–drained sites with more vigorous tree species such as the sugar maple (*Acer saccharum*), basswood (*Tilia americana*), or the red oak (*Quercus rubra*). Consequently, the silver maple is displaced to swamps, a distinctly sub–optimal habitat in which there is frequent physiological stress associated with flooding.

Over long periods of time, competitive displacement may lead to evolutionary changes. This happens as species that are displaced to marginal environments evolve to become better adapted to those conditions, and they may eventually become new species. Competitive displacement is believed to be the primary force leading to the evolution of species swarms on isolated islands such as those of fruit flies (*Drosophila* spp.) and honeycreepers (Drepaniidae) on the Hawaiian Islands and Darwin's finches (Geospizinae) on the Galapagos Islands.

In the cases of the honeycreepers and Darwin's finches, the islands are believed to have been colonized by a few individuals of a species of finch. These founders then developed a large population which saturated the carrying capacity of the common habitats so that intraspecific competition became intense. Some individuals that were less competitive in the usual means of habitat exploitation were relegated to marginal habitats or to unusual means of exploiting resources within a common habitat. Natural selection would have favored genetically based adaptations that allowed a more efficient exploitation of the marginal habitats or lifestyles of the populations of displaced birds, leading to evolutionary changes. Eventually, a condition of reproductive isolation would have developed, and a new species would have evolved from the founder population. Competitive displacements among species of finches could then have further elaborated the species swarms. The various species of Darwin's finches and Hawaiian honeycreepers are mostly distinguished on the basis of differences in the size and shape of their bills and on behavioral differences associated with feeding styles.

It must be understood that not all environments are resource limited, and in such situations competition is not a very important process. There are two generic types of non–competitive environments—recently disturbed and environmentally stressed. In habitats that have recently been subjected to a catastrophic distur-

bance, the populations and biomass of organisms is relatively small, and the biological demand for resources is correspondingly not very intense. Species that are specialized to take advantage of the resource–rich and competition–free conditions of recent disturbances are known as ruderals. These species are adapted to rapidly colonizing disturbed sites where they can grow freely and are highly fecund. However, within several years the ruderals are usually reduced in abundance or eliminated from the community by slower growing, but more competitive species that eventually take over the site and its resources and dominate later successional stages.

Some habitats are subject to intense environmental stress such as physical stress associated with climate or toxic stress associated with nutrient deficiency or pollution. Because of the severe intensity of environmental stress in such habitats, the productivity of organisms is highly constrained, and there is little competition for resources. The arctic tundra, for example, is an ecosystem that is highly stressed by climate. If the density of individual plants of the tundra is experimentally decreased by thinning, the residual plants do not grow better because their productivity was not constrained by competition. However, the intensity of environmental stress can be experimentally alleviated by enclosing an area of tundra in a greenhouse and by fertilizing with nutrients. In such a situation, competition among arctic plants can become a significant ecological interaction, and this change can be experimentally demonstrated.

See also Evolution; Natural selection; Stress, ecological.

Further Reading:

Begon, M., J. L. Harper, and C. R. Townsend. *Ecology: Individuals, Populations and Communities.* 2nd ed. London: Blackwell Sci. Pub., 1990.
Ricklefs, R. E. *Ecology.* New York: W. H. Freeman, 1990.

Bill Freedman

Complex numbers

Complex numbers are numbers which can be put into the form a + bi, where a and b are real numbers and $i^2 = -1$.

Typical complex numbers are 3 – i, 1/2 + 7i, and –6 – 2i. If one writes the real number 17 as 17 + 0i and the imaginary number –2.5i as 0 – 2.5i, they too can be considered complex numbers.

Complex numbers are so called because they are made up of two parts which cannot be combined. Even though the parts are joined by a plus sign, the addition cannot be performed. The expression must be left as an indicated sum.

Complex numbers are occasionally represented with ordered pairs, (z,b). Doing so shows the two–component nature of complex numbers but renders the operations with them somewhat obscure and hides the kind of numbers they are.

Inklings of the need for complex numbers were felt as early as the sixteenth century. Cardan, in about 1545, recognized that his method of solving cubic equations often led to solutions with the square root of negative numbers in them. It was not until the seventeenth and early eighteenth centuries that de Moivre, the Bernoullis, Euler, and others gave formal recognition to imaginary and complex numbers as legitimate numbers.

Arithmetic

Complex numbers can be thought of as an extension of the set of real numbers to include the imaginary numbers. These numbers must obey the laws, such as the distributive law, which are already in place. This they do with two exceptions, the fact that the "sum" a + bi must be left uncombined, and the law $i^2 = –1$, which runs counter to the rule that the product of two numbers of like sign is positive.

Arithmetic with complex numbers is much like the "arithmetic" of binomials such as 5x + 7 with an important exception. When such a binomial is squared, the term $25x^2$ appears, and it doesn't go away. When a + bi is squared, the i^2 in the term b^2i^2 does go away. It becomes $–b^2$. These are the rules:

Equality: To be equal two complex numbers must have equal real parts and equal imaginary parts. That is a + bi = c + di if and only if a = c and b = d.

Addition: To add two complex numbers, add the real parts and the imaginary parts separately. The sum of a + bi and c + di is (a + c) + (b + d)i. The sum (3 + 5i) + (8 – 7i) is 11 – 2i.

Subtraction: To subtract a complex number, subtract the real part from the real part and the imaginary part from the imaginary part. The difference (a + bi) – (c + di) is (a – c) + (b – d)i; (6 + 4i) – (3 – 2i) is 3 + 6i.

Zero: To equal zero, a complex number must have both its real part and its imaginary part equal to zero: a + bi = 0 if and only if a = 0 and b = 0.

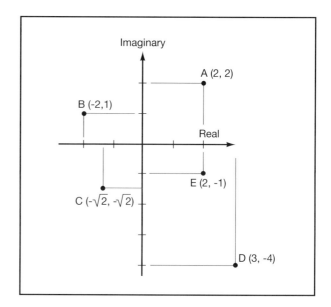

Figure 1.

Opposites: To form the opposite of a complex number, take the opposite of each part: –(a + bi) = –a + (–b)i. The opposite of 6 – 2i is –6 + 2i.

Multiplication: To form the product of two complex numbers multiply each part of one number by each part of the other: (a + bi)(c + di) = ac + adi + bci + bdi^2, or (ac – bd) + (ad + bc)i. The product (5 – 2i)(4 – 3i) is 14 – 23i.

Conjugates: Two numbers whose imaginary parts are opposites are called "complex conjugates." These complex numbers a + bi and a – bi are conjugates. Pairs of complex conjugates have many applications because the product of two complex conjugates is real: (6 – 12i)(6 + 12i) = 36 – $144i^2$, or 180.

Division: Division of complex numbers is an example. Except for division by zero, the set of com-

$$\frac{5 - i}{6 + 2i} = \frac{(5 - i)(6 - 2i)}{(6 + 2i)(6 - 2i)}$$
$$= \frac{28 - 16i}{36 + 4}$$
$$= 7/10 - 2/5i$$

plex numbers is closed with respect to division: If a + bi is not zero, then (c + di)/(a + bi) is a complex number. To divide c + di by a + bi, multiply them both by the conjugate a – bi, which eliminates the need to divide by a complex number. For example

While the foregoing rules suffice for ordinary complex–number arithmetic, they must often be coupled with ingenuity for non–routine problems. An example

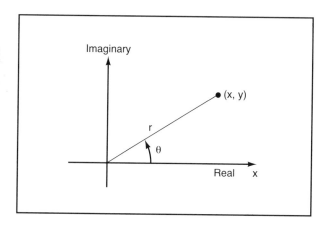

Figure 2.

of this can be seen in the problem of computing a square root of 3 – 4i.

On starts by assuming that the square root is a complex number a + bi. Then 3 – 4i is the square of a + bi, or $a^2 - b^2 + 2abi$.

For two complex numbers to be equal, their real and imaginary parts must be equal

$$a^2 - b^2 = 3$$
$$2ab = -4$$

Solving these equations for a yields four roots, namely 2, –2, i, and –i. Discarding the imaginary roots and solving for b gives 2 – i or –2 + i as the square roots of 3 – 4i. These roots seem a little weird, but their squares are in fact 3 – 4i.

Graphical representation

The mathematicians Wessel, Argand, and Gauss, separately, devised a graphical method of representing complex numbers. (Figure 1) Real numbers have only a real component and can be represented as points on a one–dimensional number line. Complex numbers, on the other hand, with their real and imaginary components, require a two–dimensional complex–number plane. Figure 1 shows such a plane. The real axis is horizontal, the imaginary axis vertical. Point A in the first quadrant represents 2 + 2i; point B, –2 + i; point C, $\sqrt{2} - \sqrt{2}i$ int D, 3 – 4i; and point E, 2 – i.

The complex number plane can also by represented with polar coordinates. The relation between these coordinates (Figure 2) and rectangular coordinates are given by the equations

$$x = r \cos \theta$$
$$y = 4 \sin \theta$$
$$r = \sqrt{x^2 + y^2}$$
$$\theta = \text{arc tan } y/x$$

Thus the complex number x + iy can also be written in polar form r cos θ + ir sin θ or r(cos θ + i sin θ), abbreviated r cis θ. When written in polar form, r is called the "modulus" or "absolute value" of the number. When the point is plotted on a Gauss–Argand diagram, r represents the distance from the point to the origin.

The angle θ is called the "argument" or the "amplitude" of the complex number, and represents the angle shown in Figure 2. Because adding or subtracting 360° to θ will not change the position of the ray drawn to the point, r cis θ, r cis (θ + 360°), r cis (θ – 360°), and others all represent the same complex number. When θ is measured in radians, adding or subtracting a multiple of 2π will change the representation of the number, but not the number itself.

In polar form the five points shown in Figure 1 are A: $\sqrt{\theta}$ (cos 45° + i sin 45°) or $\sqrt{\theta}$ cis 45°. B: $\sqrt{5}$ cis 153.4°. C: 2 cis 225°. D: 5 cis 306.9°. E: $\sqrt{5}$ cis 333.4°. Except for A and C, the polar forms seem more awkward. Often, however, it is the other way about. 1 cis 72°, which represents the fifth root of 1 is simple in its polar form, but considerably less so in its rectangular form: .3090 + .9511 i, and even this is only an approximation.

The polar form of a complex number has two remarkable features which the rectangular form lacks. For one, multiplication is very easy. The product of r_1 cis θ_1 and r_2 cis θ_2 is simply $r_1 r_2$ cis ($\theta_1 + \theta_2$). For example, (3 cis 30°) (6 cis 60°) is 18 cis 90°. The other feature is known as de Moivre's theorem: (r cis $\theta)^n$ = r^n cis nθ, where n is any real number (actually any complex number). This is a powerful theorem. For example, if one wants to compute (1 + i)^n, multiplying it out can take a lot of time. If one converts it to polar form, $\sqrt{2}$ cis 45°, however, ($\sqrt{2}$ cis 45°)^5 is $\sqrt{32}$ cis 225° or –4 – 4i.

One can use de Moivre's theorem to compute roots. Since the n–th root of a real or complex number z is $z^{1/n}$, the n–th root of r cis θ is $r^{1/n}$ cis θ/n.

It is interesting to apply this to the cube root of 1. Writing 1 as a complex number in polar form one has 1 cis 0°. Its cube root is $1^{1/3}$ cis 0/3°, or simply 1. But 1 cis 0° is the same number as 1 cis 360° and 1 cis 720°. Applying de Moivre's theorem to these alternate forms yields 1 cis 120° and 1 cis 240°, which are not simply 1. In fact they are –1/2 + $\sqrt{2}$ /2 i and –1/2 – $\sqrt{3}$/2 i in rectangular form.

Uses of complex numbers

Complex numbers are needed for the fundamental theorem of algebra: Every polynomial equation, P(x) = 0, with complex coefficients has a complex root. For example, the polynomial equation $x^2 + 1 = 0$ has no real roots. If one allows complex numbers, however, it has two: $0 + i$ and $- i$.

Complex numbers are also used in the branch of mathematics known as "functions of complex variables." Such functions can often describe physical situations, as in electrical engineering and fluid dynamics, which real–valued functions cannot.

Further Reading:

Birkhoff, Garrett, and Mac Lane, Saunders, *A Survey of Modern Algebra.* New York: The Macmillan Co. 1947.

Boyer, Carl B., *A History of Mathematics.* New York: John Wiley and Sons, 1968.

Jourdain, Philip E. B., "The Nature of Mathematics", *The World of Mathematics.* Newman, James, editor. New York: Simon and Schuster, 1956.

Stein, Sherman K. *Mathematics, the Man–made Universe.* San Francisco: W. H. Freeman and Co., 1969.

J. Paul Moulton

Composite family

The composite or aster family (Asteraceae) is one of the largest families of plants, containing about 20,000 species, distributed among more than 1,000 genera, and occurring widely on all continents, except Antarctica. This family is commonly regarded by modern botanists as the most advanced of the plant families, because of the complex, highly evolved structure of its multi–flowered, composite reproductive structures.

The members of the composite family display a remarkable range of growth forms, ranging from tiny, herbaceous annual plants, to vine–like lianas, and tall, tree–like perennials. For example, some species in the genus *Senecio* are small, annual plants, such as the widespread common groundsel (*Senecio vulgaris*). In

Artichokes in Salinas, California.

contrast, the giant senecio (*S. adnivalis*) species found on a mountain in Uganda, is a perennial plant that grows as tall as 26 ft (8 m).

The most species–rich genera in the aster family are *Senecio* (about 1,500 species), *Vernonia* (900 species), *Hieracium* (800 species), and *Eupatorium* (600 species). Various members of the aster family are familiar species in natural habitats, while others are cultivated plants in gardens, and some are grown as foods. Some species in the aster family are considered to have negative values as weeds of agriculture or lawns.

Characteristics of the asteraceae

Members of the Asteraceae are most readily characterized by their unique floral structure. The flowers of members of this family are aggregated within a composite grouping known as an inflorescence, which in this family is known as a head. In the head, the small, individual flowers, called florets, are attached to a basal structure known as a receptacle. The latter is surrounded by one or more rows of bracts, that make up the involucre.

The heads may be present singly, or they may occur in various sorts of aggregated groupings. Typically, each head gives the visual impression of being a single, large flower, even though the structure is actually a composite of several to many, small florets. This visual display is best developed in insect–pollinated species of the Asteraceae, and is ultimately designed to attract pollinators.

In many cases, the individual flowers may occur as disk florets that have functional stamens and pistils but lack petals, or as ray florets that have an elongate, strap–shaped petal known as a ligule or ray. In some species, the head is entirely composed of disk florets, and is known as a discoid head. Discoid heads occur,

Late goldenrod (*Solidago gigantea*).

for example, in the tansies (*Tanacetum* spp.). In other species the head is entirely made up of ray florets, and is referred to as a ligulate head, for example, in the dandelions (*Taraxacum* spp.).

In other species, the disk florets occur in the center of the head, and ray florets on the periphery, giving a particularly striking resemblance to a single, large flower. The ray florets of these latter, relatively complex inflorescences are commonly sterile, and are only designed to aid in attracting pollinating insects. One familiar example of this head structure is the ox–eye daisy (*Chrysanthemum leucanthemum*), which has a central packing of bright–yellow disc florets, and a white fringe of long, ray florets. The ox–eye daisy is the species of wildflower that love–struck young people use to tell whether their adoration is returned by their sweetheart—the petals are picked off one by one, to determine whether "he/she love me, or loves me not."

The seeds of plants in the aster family are borne in dry fruits known as achenes. In many cases, the achenes of these plants are small, and have a fine, filamentous attachment known as pappus, which serves to give the fruits aerodynamic qualities that favor their dispersal by the wind. This seed form and dispersal method can be illustrated by the familiar dandelion, whose fruiting heads develop as whitish puffs of pappus–bearing seeds, which eventually disintegrate and blow about on the wind.

In some other cases, such as the sunflowers (*Helianthus* spp.), the seeds are encased in a relatively hard coat, and are only dispersed locally. The seeds of some other plants in the composite family are specialized to stick to the fur of mammals, and are dispersed in this way. Two common examples of this hitch–hiking strategy are the beggar ticks (*Bidens* spp.) and the burdock (*Arctium* spp.).

Horticultural species

Many species in the aster family have very attractive inflorescences, and some of these are commonly grown as ornamentals in parks and gardens.

Many of the ornamental species in the aster family are annuals, and are used as bedding plants, in annual gardens, and in self–seeding gardens. Some common examples include the cosmos (*Cosmos bipinnatus*), sunflower (*Helianthus annuus*), summer chrysanthemum (*Chrysanthemum coronarium*), blanket flower (*Gaillardia pulchella*), strawflower (*Helichrysum bracteatum*), iceplant or living–stone daisy (*Mesembryanthemum criniflorum*), marigolds (*Tagetes patula, T. erecta*, and *T. tenuifolia*), and zinnia (*Zinnia elegans*).

A few horticultural species are biennials, or species that can complete their life cycle in two years. Two examples are the daisy (*Bellis perennis*) and ox–eye daisy (*Chrysanthemum leucanthemum*).

Many other horticultural species in the composite family are longer–lived, herbaceous perennials, and can be used in perennial gardens. Some common examples include various species of asters (*Aster* spp., such as New England aster, *A. novae–angliae*), black–eyed Susan (*Rudbeckia hirta*), shasta daisy (*Chrysanthemum maximum*), hemp agrimony (*Eupatorium purpureum*), Scotch thistle (*Onopordum acanthium* and *O. arabicum*), yarrow (*Achillea* spp., such as *A. filipendulina*), yellow chamomile (*Anthemis tinctoria*), knapweed (*Centaurea montana*), blanket flower (*Gaillardia aristata*), and goldenrods (*Solidago* spp., such as Canada goldenrod, *S. canadensis*).

Wormwoods (*Artemisia* spp.) have rather unattractive, greenish inflorescences, but are commonly cultivated for their attractive foliage.

Agricultural species of composites

A few species of composites have been domesticated for agricultural purposes. The cultivated sunflower (*Helianthus annuus*) is an annual plant native to Mexico and South America that is now widely grown for its seeds, which are eaten roasted or raw. Sunflower seeds contain about 40–50% oil, which can be extracted as a fine edible oil, the remaining cake being used as animal fodder. This sunflower grows as tall as 11.5 ft (3.5 m), and can have enormous flowering heads, up to 14 in (35 cm) in diameter. The long ray florets make this sunflower very attractive, and it is often grown as an ornamental. Safflower (*Carthamus tinctorius*) is another species that is sometimes grown as a source of edible oil.

The Jerusalem artichoke (*Helianthus tuberosus*) is a perennial sunflower, native to the prairies of North America. The Jerusalem artichoke has underground rhizomes, on which grow starchy and nutritious tubers. The tubers can be eaten as a vegetable, or may be processed into alcohol.

The globe artichoke (*Cynara scolymus*) is another perennial composite, originally from the Mediterranean region. The pre–flowering heads of this species are cut off before they begin to expand. These are boiled or steamed, and the thick, fleshy material of the involucral leaves of the receptacle (that is, the base of the flowering structure) are eaten, commonly by peeling them between the teeth. The fleshy interior of the receptacle itself, known as the artichoke heart, is also eaten.

The lettuce, or cabbage lettuce (*Lactuca sativa*) originated in southern Europe, and is grown for its greens, which are mostly used in salads, or as a green decoration for other foods.

Chicory (*Cichorium intybus*) is grown for its roots, which can be roasted and used as a substitute for coffee. A leafy variety of chicory is used as a salad green. Endive (*Cichorium endivia*) is a related species, also used as a salad green. These plants are originally from western Europe. Species of dandelions are also used as salad greens, for example, the common dandelion (*Taraxacum officinalis*).

Other useful species of composites

Several species of composites have minor uses in medicine. Chamomile (*Anthemis nobilis*) is an annual European species that is collected and dried, and brewed into an aromatic tea that has a calming effect. The dried leaves and flowers of common wormwood (*Artemisia absinthium*) of Europe are used to make a tonic known as bitters, while the flower buds are used to flavor a liquor known as vermouth. The seeds of the wormwoods *Artemisia cina* and *A. maritima*, species native to the steppes of central Asia, are given as a treatment against several types of intestinal parasites.

Some other species in the aster family have been erroneously ascribed medicinal qualities. This occurred as a result of a theory of medicine that was developed during the Middle Ages, known as the "Doctrine of Signatures." According to this ideology, the potential medicinal usefulness of plants was revealed through some sort of sign, such as a similarity between their shape, and that of a part of the human anatomy. In the case of the herbaceous plant known as boneset (*Eupatorium perfoliatum*), the leaves are arranged opposite each other on the stem, and they lack a petiole, and are fully joined to each other by a band of leafy tissue that broadly clasps the stem. This unusual growth form, or signature, was interpreted by herbalists to suggest that boneset must have therapeutic properties in helping broken bones to heal. As a result, boneset was spread as a moist poultice over a broken bone, which was then encased within a bandage, plaster, or splint.

Several species of chrysanthemums are used to manufacture an organic insecticide known as pyrethrum. *Chrysanthemum roseum*, *C. coccinium*, and *C. cinerariaefolium* of southern regions of Asia have been widely cultivated for the production of these chemicals. Sometimes, living chrysanthemums are inter–cultivated with other plants in gardens, in order to deter some types of herbivorous insects.

The latex of the rubber dandelion (*Taraxacum bicorne*) contain 8–10% rubber latex, and is potentially useful for the commercial production of rubber.

Composites as weeds

Some members of the aster family have become regarded as important weeds. In many cases, these are aesthetic weeds, because they occur abundantly in places where people, for whatever reason, do not want to see these plants. For example, the common dandelion (*Taraxacum officinale*), originally from Europe but now widely distributed in North America and elsewhere, is often regarded to be a weed of lawns and landscapes. This is largely because many people only want to see certain species of grasses in their lawns, so that any dicotyledonous plants, such as dandelions, are considered to be weeds. As a result, many people put a great deal of time and effort into manually digging dandelions out of their lawns, or they may use a herbicide such as 2,4–D to rid themselves of these perceived weeds.

Interestingly, many other people consider the spectacular, yellow displays that dandelion flowers can develop in lawns and pastures in the springtime to be very pleasing. Dandelions are also favored by some people as a food, especially the fresh leaves that are collected in the early springtime. Clearly, the judgement of a plant as an aesthetic weed is substantially a matter of perspective and context.

However, a few species in the aster family are weeds for somewhat more important reasons. Some species are weeds because they are poisonous to livestock. For example, the ragwort or stinking–Willie (*Senecio jacobea*) has alkaloids in its foliage that are toxic to liver of cattle. The natural range of the ragweed is Eurasia, but it has become an important weed in pastures in parts of North America and elsewhere, possibly having been introduced as an ornamental plant. Recently, several insect species that are herbivores of ragweed in its native habitats have been introduced to some of its invasive range, and these are showing promise as agents of biological control of this important pest.

Some other species in the aster family are important weeds of pastures because they are very spiny, and livestock cannot eat them. These inedible plants can become abundant in pastures, displacing valuable forage species. Some examples of these sorts of weeds in North America include various thistles introduced from Europe, such as bull thistle (*Cirsium vulgare*), field thistle (*C. arvense*), nodding thistle (*Carduus nutans*), and Scotch thistle (*Onopordum acanthium*).

Some species in the aster family have anatomical mechanisms of attaching their seeds to the fur of mammals, for the purposes of dispersal. Animals with large numbers of these seeds in their fur can become very irritated by the matting, and they may scratch themselves so much that wounds develop, with a risk of infection. Examples of weeds that stick to animals, and to the clothing of humans, include the beggar-ticks (for example, *Bidens frondosa*), and several introduced species known as burdock (for example, the greater burdock, *Arctium lappa*). Interestingly, the finely hooked bristles of the globular fruits of burdock were the inspiration for the development of the well-known fastening material known as velcro.

The several species that are known as ragweed (*Ambrosia artemesiifolia* and *A. trifida*) are the major causes of hay-fever during the summer and early autumn. The ragweeds are wind pollinated, and to achieve this function they shed large quantities of tiny, spiny-surfaced pollen grains to the wind. Many people have an allergy to ragweed pollen, and they may suffer greatly from hay-fever caused by ragweeds.

Interestingly, at about the same time that ragweeds are shedding their abundant pollen to the air, some other, more conspicuous species in the aster family are also flowering prolifically. For example, pastures, fields, and other habitats may develop spectacular shows of yellow goldenrods (*Solidago* spp.) and white, blue, or purple asters (*Aster* spp.) at that time of year. Because people notice these brightly colored plants, but not the relatively small and drab ragweeds, the asters and goldenrods are commonly blamed for hay-fever. For this reason, fields of these attractive plants may be mowed or herbicided to deal with this perceived weed-management problem. However, the asters and goldenrods are insect-pollinated, and they do not shed their pollen to the wind. Therefore, these plants are not

---

KEY TERMS

. . . .

Achene—A dry, one-seeded fruit, such as those of members of the aster family.

Bract—A small, scale-like, modified leaf that is associated with a flower or inflorescence.

Floret—A small flower, generally of a dense cluster, such as the head of a species in the aster family, and often with some reduced or missing parts.

Head—A dense cluster of flowers attached to a common receptacle. This is the characteristic arrangement of the flowers of members of the aster family.

Inflorescence—A grouping or arrangement of flowers into a composite structure.

Pappus—A distinctive tissue of members of the aster family, attaching to the top of the achene, and resembling small scales or fine hairs, sometimes intricately branched to achieve aerodynamic buoyancy. The pappus is derived from modified tissues of the calyx.

Receptacle—The extended, enlarged end of a stalk, which bears the flowers or florets of a compound flowering structure, such as that of the aster family.

Weed—Any plant that occurs in a situation where people regard it as a pest.

---

the cause of hay-fever—they are merely implicated by their association in time with the guilty but inconspicuous ragweed. Indeed, even people who suffer badly from hay-fever, often do not recognize the rather plain-green, unobtrusive-looking ragweeds as the cause of their allergy.

Many medicines that are sold for treating the symptoms of hay-fever, such as antihistamine drugs, feature brilliant illustrations of goldenrods and asters in their advertising in magazines, on billboards, and on television. However, this is clearly a botanical mistake.

Further Reading:

Hvass, E. *Plants That Serve and Feed Us*. New York: Hippocrene Books, 1975.

Klein, R. M. *The Green World. An Introduction to Plants and People*. New York: Harper and Row, 1987.

Woodland, D. W. *Contemporary Plant Systematics*. New York: Prentice-Hall, 1991.

Bill Freedman

Composite materials

A composite material is a microscopic or macroscopic combination of two or more distinct materials with a recognizable interface between them. For structural applications, the definition can be restricted to include those materials that consist of a reinforcing phase such as fibers or particles supported by a binder or matrix phase. Other features of composites include the following: 1) The distribution of materials in the composite is controlled by mechanical means; (2) The term composite is usually reserved for materials in which distinct phases are separated on a scale larger than atomic, and in which the composite's mechanical properties are significantly altered from those of the constituent components; (3) The composite can be regarded as a combination of two or more materials that are used in combination to rectify a weakness in one material by a strength in another. (4) A recently developed concept of composites is that the composite should not only be a combination of two materials, but the combination should have its own distinctive properties. In terms of strength, heat resistance, or some other desired characteristic, the composite must be better than either component alone.

Composites were developed because no single, homogeneous structural material could be found that had all of the desired characteristics for a given application. Fiber–reinforced composites were first developed to replace aluminum alloys, which provide high strength and fairly high stiffness at low weight but are subject to corrosion and fatigue.

An example of a composite material is a glass-reinforced plastic fishing rod in which glass fibers are placed in an epoxy matrix. Fine individual glass fibers are characterized by their high tensile stiffnesses and a very high tensile strengths, but because of their small diameters, have very small bending stiffnesses. If the rod were made only of epoxy plastic, it would have good bending stiffness, but poor tensile properties. When the fibers are placed in the epoxy plastic, however, the resultant structure has high tensile stiffness, high tensile strength, and high bending stiffness.

The discontinuous filler phase in a composite is usually stiffer or stronger than the binder phase. There must be a substantial volume fraction of the reinforcing phase (~10%) present to provide reinforcement. Examples do exist, however, of composites where the discontinuous phase is more compliant and ductile than the matrix.

Natural composites include wood and bone. Wood is a composite of cellulose and lignin. Cellulose fibers are strong in tension and are flexible. Lignin cements these fibers together to make them stiff. Bone is a composite of strong but soft collagen (a protein) and hard but brittle apatite (a mineral).

Particle–reinforced composites

A particle has no long dimension. Particle composites consist of particles of one material dispersed in a matrix of a second material. Particles may have any shape or size, but are generally spherical, ellipsoidal, polyhedral, or irregular in shape. They may be added to a liquid matrix that later solidifies; grown in place by a reaction such as age–hardening; or they may be pressed together and then interdiffused via a powder process. The particles may be treated to be made compatible with the matrix, or they may be incorporated without such treatment. Particles are most often used to extend the strength or other properties of inexpensive materials by the addition of other materials.

Fiber–reinforced composites

A fiber has one long dimension. Fiber–reinforced materials are typified by fiberglass in which there are three components: glass filaments (for mechanical strength), a polymer matrix (to encapsulate the filaments); and a bonding agent (to bind the glass to the polymer). Other fibers include metal, ceramics, and polymers. The fibers can be used as continuous lengths, in staple–fiber form, or as whiskers (short, fine, perfect, or nearly perfect single crystals). Fiber–reinforcement depends as much on fabrication procedure as on materials.

Laminar composites

Platelets or lamina have two long dimensions. Laminar composites include plywood, which is a laminated composite of thin layers of wood in which successive layers have different grain or fiber orientations. The result is a more–or–less isotropic composite sheet that is weaker in any direction than it would be if the fibers were all aligned in one direction. The stainless steel in a cooking vessel with a copper–clad bottom provides corrosion resistance while the copper provides better heat distribution over the base of the vessel.

Mechanical properties

The mechanical properties of composite materials usually depend on structure. Thus these properties typically depend on the shape of inhomogenities, the volume fraction occupied by inhomogenities, and the interfaces between the components. The strength of composites depends on such factors as the brittleness or ductility of the inclusions and matrix.

For example, failure mechanisms in fiber–filled composites include fracture of the fibers; shear failure of the matrix along the fibers; fracture of the matrix in tension normal to the fibers or failure of the fiber–matrix interface. The mechanism responsible for failure depends on the angle between the fibers and the specimen's axis.

If a mechanical property depends on the composite material's orientation, the property is said to be anisotropic. Anisotropic composites provide greater strength and stiffness than do isotropic materials. But the material properties in one direction are gained at the expense of the properties in other directions. For example, silica fibers in a pure aluminum matrix produce a composite with a tensile strength of about 110,000 psi along the fiber direction, but a tensile strength of only about 14,000 psi at right angles to the fiber axis. It therefore only makes sense to use anisotropic materials if the direction that they will be stressed is known in advance.

Isotropic material are materials properties independent of orientation. Stiff platelet inclusions are the most effective in creating a stiff composite, followed by fibers, and then by spherical particles.

High performance composites

High performance composites are composites that have better performance than conventional structural materials such as steel and aluminum alloys. They are almost all continuous fiber–reinforced composites, with organic (resin) matrices.

Fibers for high performance composites

In a high–performance, continuous fiber-reinforced composite, fibers provide virtually all of the load–carrying characteristics of the composite, i.e., strength and stiffness. The fibers in such a composite form bundles, or filaments. Consequently, even if several fibers break, the load is redistributed to other fibers, which avoids a catastrophic failure.

Glass fibers are used for nonstructural, low–performance applications such as panels in aircraft and appliances to high–performance applications such as rocket-motor cases and pressure vessels. But the sensitivity of the glass fiber to attack by moisture poses problems for other applications. The most commonly used glass fiber is a calcium aluminoborosilicate glass (E–glass). High silica and quartz fibers are also used for specialized applications.

Carbon fibers are the best known and most widely used reinforcing fiber in advanced composites. The earliest carbon fibers were produced by thermal decomposition of rayon precursor materials. The starting material is now polyacrylonitrile.

Aramid fibers are aromatic polyamide fibers. The aramid fiber is technically a thermoplastic polymer like nylon, but it decomposes when heated before it reaches its projected melting point. When polymerized, it forms rigid, rod–like molecules that cannot be spun from a melt. Instead they have to be spun from a liquid crystalline solution. Early applications of aramid fibers included filament–wound motor cases, and gas pressure vessels. Aramid fibers have lower compressive strengths than do carbon fibers, but their high specific strengths, low densities, and toughness keep them in demand.

Boron fibers were the first high–performance reinforcement available for use in advance composites. They are, however, more expensive and less attractive for their mechanical properties than carbon fibers. Boron filaments are made by the decomposition of boron halides on a hot tungsten wire. Composites can also be made from whiskers dispersed in an appropriate matrix.

Continuous silicon carbide fibers are used for large–diameter monofilaments and fine multifilament yarns. Silicon carbide fibers are inherently more economical than boron fibers, and the properties of silicon carbide fibers are generally as good or better than those of boron.

Aluminum oxide (alumina) fibers are produced by dry spinning from various solutions. They are coated with silica to improve their contact properties with molten metal.

There is usually a size effect associated with strong filaments. Their strengths decrease as their diameter increases. It turns out that very high strength materials have diameters of about 1 micrometer. They are consequently not easy to handle.

Matrices for high performance composites

The matrix binds fibers together by virtue of its cohesive and adhesive characteristics. Its purpose is to transfer load to and between fibers, and to protect the fibers from hostile environments and handling. The matrix is the weak link in the composite, so when the composite experiences loading, the matrix may crack, debond from the fiber surface, or break down under far lower strains than are usually desired. But matrices keep the reinforcing fibers in their proper orientation and position so that they can carry loads, distribute loads evenly among fibers, and provide resistance to crack propagation and damage. Limitations in the matrix generally determine the overall service temperature limitations of the composite.

Polyester and vinyl ester resins are the most widely used matrix materials in high performance continuous–fiber composites. They are used for chemically resistant piping and reactors, truck cabs and bodies, appliances, bathtubs and showers, automobile hoods, decks, and doors. These matrices are usually reinforced with glass fibers, as it has been difficult to adhere the matrix suitably to carbon and aramid fibers. Epoxies and other resins, though more expensive, find applications as replacements for polyester and vinyl ester resins in high performance sporting goods, piping for chemical processing plants, and printed circuit boards.

Epoxy resins are used more than all other matrices in composite materials for structural aerospace applications. Epoxies are generally superior to polyesters in their resistance to moisture and other environmental influences.

Bismaleimide resins, like epoxies, are fairly easy to handle, relatively easily processed, and have excellent composite properties. They are able to withstand greater fluctuations in hot/wet conditions than are epoxies, but they have worse failure characteristics.

Polyimide resins release volatiles during curing, which produces voids in the resulting composite. However, these resins do withstand even greater hot/wet temperature extremes than bismaleimide matrices, and work has been underway to minimize the void problem.

The thermoplastic resins used as composite matrices such as polyether etherketone, polyphenylene sulfide, and polyetherimide are very different from the commodity thermoplastics such as polyethylene and polyvinyl chloride. Although used in limited quantities, they are attractive for applications requiring improved hot/wet properties and impact resistance.

Other composites

In addition to the examples already given, examples of composites materials also include: (1) Reinforced and prestressed concrete, which is a composite of steel and concrete. Concrete is itself a composite of rocks (coarse aggregate), sand (fine aggregate), hydrated Portland cement, and usually, voids. (2) Cutters for machining made of fine particles of tungsten carbide, which is extremely hard, are mixed with about 6% cobalt powder and sintered at high temperatures. (3) Ordinary grinding wheels, which are composites of an abrasive with a binder that may be plastic or metallic.

KEY TERMS

. . . .

Fiber—In terms of composite fillers, a fiber is a filler with one long dimension. More specifically, a fiber is a complex morphological unit with an extremely high ratio of length to diameter (typically several hundred to one) and a relatively high tenacity.

Lamina (platelet)—In terms of composite fillers, a lamina is a filler with two long dimensions.

Matrix—The part of the composite that binds the filler by virtue of its cohesive and adhesive characteristics.

Particle—In terms of composite fillers, a particle is a filler with no long dimension. Particles may have any shape or size, but are generally spherical, ellipsoidal, polyhedral, or irregular in shape.

---

(4) Walls for housing, which have been made of thin aluminum sheets epoxied to polyurethane foam. The foam provides excellent thermal insulation. This composite has a higher structural rigidity than aluminum sheets or polyurethane foam alone. The polyurethane foam is itself a composite of air and polyurethane. (5) Underground electrical cables composed of sodium metal enclosed in polyethylene. (6) Superconducting ribbons made of Nb_3Sn deposited on copper. (7) Synthetic hard superconductors made by forcing liquid lead under pressure into porous glass fibers. (8) Microelectronic circuits made from silicon, which are oxidized to form an insulating layer of SiO_2. This insulating layer is etched away with hydrofluoric acid, and phosphorous is diffused into the silicon to make a junction. Aluminum or another metal can be introduced as a microconductor between points. The microelectronic circuit is thus a tailored composite. (9) Ceramic fiber composites including graphite or pyrolytic carbon reinforced with graphite fibers; and borosilicate glass lithium aluminum silicate glass ceramics reinforced with silicon carbide fibers. It was possible to drive a tungsten carbide spike through such a composition without secondary cracking in much the same way that a nail can be driven through wood.

Further Reading:

Reinhart, Theodore J., *Introduction to Composites*, in Engineered Materials Handbook, Metals Park, OH: ASM International, 1987. Vol. 1.

Smith, Charles O., *The Science of Engineering Materials*. Englewood Cliffs, NJ: Prentice–Hall, Inc. 1969.

Sperling, L.H. *Introduction to Physical Polymer Science.* New York, NY: John Wiley & Sons, Inc. 1992.

Randall Frost

Composting

Composting is the process of arranging and manipulating organic wastes so that they are gradually broken down, or decomposed, by soil microorganisms and animals. The resulting product is a black, earthy–smelling, nutritious, crumbly mixture called compost or humus. Compost is usually mixed with other soil to improve the soil's structural quality and to add nutrients for plant growth. Composting and the use of compost in gardening are important activities of gardeners who prefer not to use synthetic fertilizers.

Nature itself composts materials by continually recycling nutrients from dead organic matter. Living things take in inorganic nutrients to grow. They give off waste, die, and decompose. The nutrients contained in the plant or animal body become available in soil for plants to take up again. Composting takes advantage of this natural process of decomposition, usually speeding up the process, by the creation of a special pile of organic materials called a compost heap.

The major benefit of compost is its organic content. Humus added to soil changes its structure, its ability to hold oxygen and water, and its capacity to adsorb certain nutrient ions. It improves soils that are too sandy to hold water or contain too much clay to allow oxygen to penetrate. Compost also adds some mineral nutrients to the soil. Depending on the organic material of the compost and microorganisms present, it can also balance the pH of an acidic or alkaline soil.

History

Prehistoric farming people discovered that if they mixed manure from their domesticated animals with straw and other organic waste, such as crop residues, the mixture would gradually change into a fertile soil–like material that was good for crops. Composting remained a basic activity of farming until the twentieth century, when various synthetic fertilizers were found to provide many of the nutrients occurring naturally in compost.

The steadily increasing population of the world has come to require large supplies of food. In order to increase productivity, farmers have come to depend on synthetic fertilizers made in factories from nonrenewable resources. However, regular use of these fertilizers does not improve the structure of the soil, and can, in fact, gradually harm the soil. Also, synthetic fertilizers are expensive, an important consideration to farmers in less developed countries.

It was in an underdeveloped country—India—that modern composting got its big start. Sir Albert Howard, a government agronomist, developed the so–called Indore method, named after a city in southern India. His method calls for three parts garden clippings to one part manure or kitchen waste arranged in layers and mixed periodically. Howard published his ideas on organic gardening in the 1940 book *An Agricultural Testament.*

The first articulate advocate of Howard's method in the United States was J.I. Rodale (1898–1971), founder of *Organic Gardening* magazine. These two men made composting popular with gardeners who prefer not to use synthetic fertilizers.

Why compost?

People are attracted to composting for a variety of reasons. Many wish to improve their soil or help the environment. Compost mixed with soil makes it darker, allowing it to warm up faster in the spring. Compost adds numerous naturally occurring nutrients to the soil. It improves soil quality by making the structure granular, so that oxygen is retained between the granules. In addition, compost holds moisture. This is good for plants, of course, but it is also good for the environment because it produces a soil into which rain easily soaks. When water cannot soak directly into soil, it runs across the surface, carrying away soil granules and thus eroding the soil. In addition, the use of compost limits the use of natural gas, petrochemicals, and other nonrenewable resources that are used in making synthetic fertilizers. Composting also recycles organic materials that might otherwise be sent to landfills.

Despite its many benefits, making and using compost does have its disadvantages. Composting releases methane, a greenhouse gas which traps solar heat in the earth's atmosphere and may contribute to global warming. The kitchen wastes and warmth of compost heaps may attract pests such mice, rats, and raccoons.

Composting on any scale

Composting can be done by anyone. A homeowner can use a small composting bin or a hole where kitchen wastes (minus meats and fats) are mixed with grass

Backyard composting in Livonia, Michigan. This system includes a 16 cubic foot (0.5 cubic meter) composting bin made from chicken wire and plywood, a soil screen made from 1/2 inch galvanized mesh wire and 1x6 boards, a wheelbarrow, and a digging fork. The system produces about 10 cubic feet (0.3 cubic meters) of compost per year.

clippings, small branches, shredded newspapers, or other coarse, organic debris.

Communities may have large composting facilities to which residents bring grass, leaves, and branches to be composted. Such communities often have laws against burning garden waste and use composting as an alternative to disposal in a landfill. Sometimes sewage sludge, the semisolid material from sewage treatment plants, is added. The heat generated in the heap kills any disease–causing bacteria in the sludge. The materials are usually arranged in long rows, called windrows, which may be covered by roofs. The resulting humus is used to condition soil on golf courses, parks, and other municipal grounds.

The largest scale of composting is done commercially by companies that collect organic materials, including paper, from companies and private citizens. Commercial composting is usually mechanized, using large machines called composters. Raw solid waste is loaded onto a slow–moving belt, then is dumped into a device which turns the waste, and compost comes out

the other end within a few days or weeks. This in–vessel or container process allows careful control of moisture and air. Some communities are looking toward such mechanized digesters as a way of helping to solve the municipal solid waste problem as more and more landfills close in the future.

Materials to compost

Most organic materials can be used in a compost heap—shredded paper, hair clippings, food scraps from restaurants (omitting meats), coffee grounds, eggshells, fireplace ashes, chopped–up Christmas trees, seaweed, anything that originally came from a living thing. Meat is omitted because it can putrefy, giving off bad odors. It can also attract rats and other pests. Soil or finished humus is added to supply the microorganisms needed to make the heap work. To work most efficiently, the materials are layered, with woody materials, grasses, kitchen waste, and soil alternating. Farmyard or zoo manure mixed with straw makes an excellent addition to compost. However, feces from household pets may carry diseases.

A ratio of approximately 25 parts carbon to 1 part nitrogen should be available in the compost heap. If the ratio is quite different, ammonia smells can be given off, or the process may not work efficiently. Chopped–up tree branches, fallen leaves, and sawdust are good sources of carbon. Alfalfa is a good nitrogen source.

How it works

A compost heap needs to have both water and oxygen to work efficiently. In dry weather it may need to be watered. More importantly, however, the compost heap must be turned regularly. The more often it is turned, the more the compost materials are exposed to oxygen, which raises their temperature and increases the efficiency of the process.

A compost heap needs to be at least 3 ft (0.9 m) in diameter and about 3 ft (0.9 m) high to work properly. The heap can be just piled on the ground or layered within a shallow hole. It can also be placed inside a small fenced enclosure or even in a large plastic or metal tub with holes cut into it. A smaller compost heap will probably be unable to achieve the high internal temperature—about 120–140°F (55–60°C)—necessary to work efficiently.

The chemical process

The processes that occur within a compost heap are microbiological, chemical, and physical. Microorganisms break down the carbon bonds of organic materials in the presence of oxygen and moisture, giving off heat in the process.

High temperatures can be achieved most easily in a compost heap that is built all at once and tended regularly. Enclosed bins, often used by city gardeners, may produce humus within a month. An open heap, such as in the back corner of a garden, will probably achieve lower temperatures, but it will still eventually decompose. However, a year or more may be required to produce humus, and it will contain some undecomposed materials. In northern winters, the composting process will slow down and almost stop except at the core of a large, well–arranged heap.

The byproducts of composting can also be used. Some composters run water pipes through their compost heaps and utilize the heat generated to warm greenhouses and even houses. The methane given off can also be collected and used as a fuel called biogas for cooking.

The organisms

The most heat is given off at the beginning of the composting process, when readily oxidized material is decomposing. Digestion of the materials by bacteria is strongest at that time. Later, the temperature within the pile decreases, and the bacterial activity slows down, though it continues until all the waste is digested. Other microorganisms take over as the heap cools.

Microorganisms, such as bacteria, protozoa, fungi, and actinomycetes (the latter resemble both bacteria and fungi), work to change the chemistry of the compost. They produce enzymes that digest the organic material. Bacteria are most important initially and fungi later. If the pile is not turned regularly, the decomposition will be anaerobic and produce foul–smelling odors. By turning the pile, a gardener creates conditions for aerobic decomposition, which does not produce odors.

Some organisms work on the compost pile physically instead of chemically. They tend to arrive only after the pile has cooled to normal air temperature. These organisms include mites, millipedes, sowbugs and pillbugs (isopods), snails and slugs, springtails, and beetles. Finally, the worms—nematodes, flatworms, and earthworms—do their part. These animals eat and digest the organic materials, adding their nutrient–filled excrement to the humus. In addition, they give off substances that bind the material in granules or clumps. The movement of these animals, especially earthworms, through the material helps to aerate it.

The nutrients

During the composting process, the material oxidizes, breaking down into proteins and carbohydrates. The proteins break down into peptides and amino acids, then into ammonium compounds. These compounds are changed by certain bacteria into nitrates, a form of nitrogen which can be used by plants to make chlorophyll and essential proteins. The carbohydrates break down into simple sugars, organic acids, and carbon dioxide.

Nutrients in humus enter plant tissues by a process called base exchange. In this process, hydrogen ions in the fine root hairs of plants are exchanged for the nutrient ions in the soil moisture. The nutrients are then free to move up into the plant.

Composting with worms

Some composters use a somewhat different form of composting, especially during winter. Called vermicomposting, it consists of maintaining worms (preferably redworms, or *Eisenia foetida*) in a container filled with a plant–based material (such as shredded corrugated paper, manure, or peat moss) that they gradually consume.

KEY TERMS

Aerobic—Requiring or in the presence of oxygen.

Anaerobic—Functioning in the absence of oxygen.

Decomposition—The natural breakdown of complex organic materials into simple substances; decay.

Microorganism—Any living thing that can only be seen through a microscope.

Nutrient—Any substance required by a plant or animal for energy and growth.

Organic—Made of or requiring the materials of living things. In pure chemistry, organic refers to compounds that include carbon.

Vermicomposting—Using the digestive processes of worms to compost organic materials.

Kitchen waste is pushed into the soil and digested by the worms. Their excrement, called castings, along with partially decomposed waste, can be "harvested" in about four months and used as a nutrient–laden addition to soil. Worm castings are even more nutrient–filled than garden compost.

See also Fertilizers; Humus; Recycling; Waste management.

Further Reading:

Appelhof, Mary. *Worms Eat My Garbage.* Kalamazoo, MI.: Flower Press, 1982.

Appelhof, Mary. *Worms Eat Our Garbage: Classroom Activities for a Better Environment.* Kalamazoo, MI.: Flower Press, 1993.

Blashfield, Jean F., and Wallace B. Black. *Recycling.* Saving Planet Earth series. Chicago: Childrens Press, 1991.

Campbell, Stu. *Let It Rot! The Gardener's Guide to Composting.* Rev. ed. Pownal, VT: Storey Communications, 1990.

Logsdon, Gene. *The Gardener's Guide to Better Soil.* Emmaus, PA: Rodale Press, 1975.

Martin, Deborah L., and Grace Gershuny, eds. *The Rodale Book of Composting.* Rev. ed. Emmaus, PA: Rodale Press, 1992.

Whitehead, Bert. *Don't Waste Your Wastes—Compost 'Em: The Homeowner's Guide to Recycling Yard Wastes.* Sunnyvale, TX: Sunnyvale Press, 1991.

Jean F. Blashfield

Compound, chemical

A compound is a substance composed of two or more elements chemically combined with each other. Historically, the distinction between compounds and mixtures was often unclear. Today, however, the two can be distinguished from each other on the basis of three primary criteria. First, compounds have constant and definite compositions, while mixtures may exist in virtually any proportion. A sample of water always consists of 88.9% oxygen and 11.1% hydrogen. However, a mixture of hydrogen and oxygen gases can have any composition whatsoever.

Second, the elements that make up a compound lose their characteristic elemental properties when they become part of the compound, while the elements that make up a mixture retain those properties. In a mixture of iron and sulfur, for example, black iron granules and yellow sulfur crystals can often be recognized. Also, the iron can be extracted from the mixture by means of a magnet, or the sulfur can be dissolved out with carbon disulfide. One part of the compound is called iron(II) sulfide, however, both iron and sulfur lose these properties.

Third, the formation of a compound is typically accompanied by the evolution of light and heat, while no observable change is detectable in the making of a mixture. A mixture of iron and sulfur can be made simply by stirring the two elements together. But the compound iron(II) sulfide is produced only when the two elements are heated. Then, as they combine with each other, they give off a glow.

Non–chemical definitions

The term compound is often used in fields of science other than chemistry, either as an adjective or a verb. For example, medical workers may talk about a compound fracture in referring to a broken bone that has cut through the flesh. Biologists use a compound microscope, one that has more than one lens. Pharmacologists may speak of compounding a drug, that is, putting together the components of which that medication consists. In the case of the last example, a compounded drug is often one that is covered by a patent.

History

Prior to the 1800s, the term compound had relatively little precise meaning. When used, it was often unclear as to whether one was referring to what scientists now call a mixture or to what they now know as a compound. During the nineteenth century, the debate as to the meaning of the word intensified, and it became one of the key questions in the young science of chemistry.

A critical aspect of this debate focused on the issue of constant composition. The issue was whether all compounds always had the same composition, or whether their composition could vary. The primary spokesman for the latter position was the French chemist Claude Louis Berthollet. Berthollet pointed to a considerable body of evidence that suggested a variable composition for compounds. For example, when some metals are heated, they form oxides that appear to have a regularly changing percentage composition. The longer they are heated, the higher the percentage of oxygen found in the oxide. Berthollet also mentioned alloys and amalgams as examples of substances with varying composition.

Berthollet's principal antagonist in this debate was his countryman Joseph Louis Proust. Proust argued that Dalton's atomic theory required that compounds have a constant composition, a position put forward by Dalton himself. Proust set out to counter each of the arguments set forth by Berthollet. In the case of metal oxides, for example, Proust was able to show that metals often form more than one oxide. As copper metal is heated, for example, it first forms copper(I) or cuprous oxide and then, copper(II) or cupric oxide. At any one time, then, an experimenter would be able to detect some mixture of the two oxides varying from pure copper(I) oxide to pure copper(II) oxide. However, each of the two oxides itself, Proust argued, has a set and constant composition.

Working in Proust's favor was an argument that nearly everyone was willing to acknowledge, namely that quantitative techniques had not yet been developed very highly in chemistry. Thus, it could be argued that what appeared to be variations in chemical composition were really nothing other than natural variability in results coming about as a result of imprecise techniques.

Proust remained puzzled by some of Berthollet's evidence, the problem of alloys and amalgams as an example. At the time, he had no way of knowing that such materials are not compounds but are in fact mixtures. These remaining problems notwithstanding, Proust's arguments eventually won the day and by the end of the century, the constant composition of compounds was universally accepted in chemistry.

Early theories of compounds

It is difficult for a reader in the 1990s to appreciate the challenge facing a chemist in 1850 who was trying

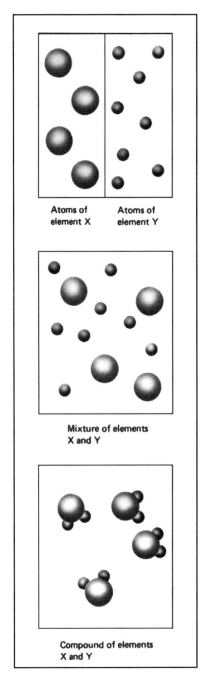

Atoms of element X **Atoms of element Y**

Mixture of elements X and Y

Compound of elements X and Y

A mixture versus a compound.

to understand the nature of a compound. Today it is clear that atoms of elements combine with each other to form, in many cases, molecules of a compound. Even the beginning chemistry student can express this concept with facility by using symbols and formulas, as in the formation of iron(II) sulfide from its elements:

$$Fe + S \text{ R } FeS.$$

Name of family	Characteristic group of atoms (functional group)	Example	
		Structure	Name
Halides	—F, —Cl, —Br, or —I	$H-\overset{\overset{\displaystyle Cl}{\mid}}{\underset{\underset{\displaystyle Cl}{\mid}}{C}}-Cl$	Chloroform
Alcohols	—OH	CH_3-CH_2-OH (or C_2H_5-OH)	Ethyl alcohol
Ethers	—O—	$CH_3-CH_2-O-CH_2-CH_3$ (or $C_2H_5-O-C_2H_5$)	Diethyl ether
Amines	$-\overset{\mid}{\underset{\mid}{N}}-$	$CH_3-CH_2-\overset{\overset{\displaystyle H}{\mid}}{N}-CH_2-CH_3$ (or $C_2H_5-NH-C_2H_5$)	Diethyl amine
Aldehydes	$-\overset{\overset{\displaystyle O}{\parallel}}{C}H$	$CH_3-\overset{\overset{\displaystyle O}{\parallel}}{C}H$	Acetaldehyde
Ketones	$-\overset{\overset{\displaystyle O}{\parallel}}{C}-$	$CH_3-\overset{\overset{\displaystyle O}{\parallel}}{C}-CH_3$	Dimethyl ketone (acetone)
Acids	$-\overset{\overset{\displaystyle O}{\parallel}}{C}-OH$	$CH_3-\overset{\overset{\displaystyle O}{\parallel}}{C}-OH$	Acetic acid
Esters	$-\overset{\overset{\displaystyle O}{\parallel}}{C}-O-C-$	$CH_3-\overset{\overset{\displaystyle O}{\parallel}}{C}-O-CH_2-CH_3$ (or $CH_3-\overset{\overset{\displaystyle O}{\parallel}}{C}-O-C_2H_5$)	Ethyl acetate
Amides	$-\overset{\overset{\displaystyle O}{\parallel}}{C}-N\big\langle$	$CH_3-\overset{\overset{\displaystyle O}{\parallel}}{C}-N\overset{\diagup H}{\diagdown H}$	Acetamide

Some families of organic compounds.

The chemist of 1850 was just barely comfortable with the idea of an atom and had not yet heard of the concept of a molecule. Moreover, the connection between ultimate particles (such as atoms and molecules) and materials encountered in the everyday work of a laboratory was not at all clear. As a result, early theories about the nature of compounds were based on empirical data (information collected from experiments), not from theoretical speculation about the behavior of atoms.

One of the earliest theories of compounds was that of the Swedish chemist Jons Jakob Berzelius. Berzelius argued that all compounds consist of two parts, one

charged positively and one, negatively. The theory was at least partially based on Berzelius' own studies of electrolysis, studies in which compounds would often be broken apart into two pieces by the passage of an electrical current. Thus, he pictured salts as being composed of a positively charged metal oxide and a negatively charged non–metallic oxide. According this theory, sodium sulfate, Na_2SO_4 could be represented as $Na_2O \cdot SO_3$.

Other theories followed, many of them developed in an effort to explain the rapidly growing number of organic compounds being discovered and studied. According to the radical theory, for example, compounds were viewed as consisting of two parts, one of which was one of a few standard radicals, or groups of atoms. Organic compounds were explained as being derived from the methyl, ethyl, benzyl, cyanogen, or some other radical.

The type theory, proposed by Charles Gerhardt in the 1840s, said that compounds could be understood as derivatives of one or more basic types, such as water or ammonia. According to this theory, bases such as sodium hydroxide (NaOH) were thought to be derivatives of water (HOH) in which one hydrogen atom is replaced by a metal.

Modern theory of compounds

The most fundamental change that has taken place in chemistry since the nineteenth century is that atomic theory now permits an understanding of chemical compounds from the particle level rather than from purely empirical data. That is, as our knowledge of atomic structure has grown and developed, our understanding of the reasons that atoms (elements) combine with each other has improved. For example, the question of how and why iron and sulfur combine with each other to form a compound is now approached in terms of how and why an iron atom combines with a sulfur atom to form a molecule of iron(II) sulfide.

A key to the solution of that puzzle was suggested by the German chemist Albrecht Kossel in 1916. In considering the unreactivity of the inert gases, Kossel came to the conclusion that the presence of eight electrons in the outermost energy level of an atom (as is the case with all inert gases) conferred a certain stability on a substance. Perhaps, Kossel said, the tendency of atoms to exchange electrons in such a way as to achieve a full octet (eight) of electrons could explain chemical reactions in which elements combine to form compounds.

Although Kossel had hit on a key concept, he did not fully develop this theory. That work was left to the American chemist Gilbert Newton Lewis. At about the same time that Kossel was proposing his octet theory, Lewis was developing a comprehensive explanation showing how atoms can gain a complete octet either by the gain and loss or by the sharing of pairs of electrons with other atoms. Although Lewis' theory has undergone many transformations, improvements, and extensions (especially in the work of Linus Pauling), his explanation of compound formation still constitutes the heart of such theory today.

Types of compounds

Most of the ten million or so chemical compounds that are known today can be classified into a relatively small number of subgroups or families. More than 90% of these compounds are, in the first place, designated as organic compounds because they contain the element carbon. In turn, organic compounds can be further subdivided into a few dozen major families such as the alkanes, alkenes, alkynes, alcohols, aldehydes, ketones, carboxylic acids, and amines. Each of these families can be recognized by the presence of a characteristic functional group that strongly determines the physical and chemical properties of the compounds that make up that family. For example, the functional group of the alcohols is the hydroxyl group (–OH) and that of the carboxylic acids, the carboxyl group (–COOH).

An important subset of organic compounds are those that occur in living organisms, the biochemical compounds. Biochemical compounds can largely be classified into four major families: the carbohydrates, proteins, nucleic acids, and lipids. Members of the first three families are grouped together because of common structural features and similar physical and chemical properties. Members of the lipid family are so classified on the basis of their solubility. They tend not to be soluble in water, but soluble in organic liquids.

Inorganic compounds are typically classified into one of five major groups: acids, bases, salts, oxides, and others. Acids are defined as compounds which ionize or dissociate in water solution to yield hydrogen ions. Bases are compounds that ionize or dissociate in water solution to yield hydroxide ions. Oxides are compounds whose only negative part is oxygen. Salts are compounds whose cations are any ion but hydrogen and whose anions are any ion but the hydroxide ion. Salts are often described as the compounds formed (other than water) when an acid and a base react with each other.

This system of classification is useful in grouping compounds that have many similar properties. For example, all acids have a sour taste, impart a pink color to litmus paper, and react with bases to form salts. One drawback of the system, however, is that it may not give a sense of the enormous diversity of compounds that exist within a particular family. For example, the element chlorine forms at least five common acids, known as hydrochloric, hypochlorous, chlorous, chloric, and perchloric acids. For all their similarities, these five acids also have important distinctive properties.

The "others" category of compound classification includes all those compounds that don't fit into one of the other four categories. Perhaps the most important group of compounds contained in this "others" category is the coordination compounds. Coordination compounds are different from acids, bases, salts, and oxides

KEY TERMS
. . . .

Alloy—A mixture of two or more metals with properties distinct from the metals of which it is made.

Amalgam—An alloy that contains the metal mercury.

Coordination compounds—Compounds formed when metallic ions or atoms are joined to other atoms, ions, or molecules by means of coordinate covalent bonds.

Empirical—Evidence that is obtained from some type of experimentation.

Family—A group of chemical compounds with similar structure and properties.

Functional group—A group of atoms that give a molecule certain distinctive chemical properties.

Mixture—A combination of two or more substances that are not chemically combined with each other and that can exist in any proportion.

Molecule—A particle made by the chemical combination of two or more atoms; the smallest particle of which a compound is made.

Octet rule—An hypothesis that atoms that have eight electrons in their outermost energy level tend to be stable and chemically unreactive.

Oxide—An inorganic compound whose only negative part is the element oxygen.

Radical—A group of atoms that behaves as if it were a single atom.

primarily because of their method of bonding. Members of the last four groups are formed when atoms give or take electrons to form ionic bonds, share pairs of electrons to form covalent bonds, or exchange electrons in some fashion intermediary between these cases to form polar covalent bonds. Coordination compounds, on the other hand, are formed when one or more ions or molecules contributes both electrons in a bonding pair to a metallic atom or ion. The contributing species in such a compound is (or are) known as ligands and the compound as a whole is often called a metal complex.

See also Element, chemical; Mixture, chemical.

Further Reading:

Brown, William H., and Elizabeth P. Rogers. *General, Organic and Biochemistry*. Boston: Willard Grant, 1980, Chapters 4 and 9.

Masterson, William L., Emil J. Slowinski, and Conrad L. Stanitski. *Chemical Principles*. Philadelphia: Saunders, 1983, Chapter 3.

Partington, J. R. *A Short History of Chemistry*, 3rd edition. London: Macmillan & Company, 1957, passim.

Williams, Arthur L., Harland D. Embree, and Harold J. DeBey. *Introduction to Chemistry*, 3rd edition. Reading, MA: Addison–Wesley Publishing Company, 1986, Chapter 11.

David E. Newton

Compton effect

The Compton effect (sometimes called Compton scattering) occurs when an x ray collides with an electron. In 1923, Arthur H. Compton did experiments bouncing x rays off the electrons in graphite atoms. Compton found the x rays that scattered off the electrons had a lower frequency (and longer wavelength) than they had before striking the electrons. The amount the frequency changes depends on the scattering angle, the angle that the x ray is deflected from its original path. Why?

Imagine playing pool. Only the cue ball and 8 ball are left on the table. When the cue ball strikes the 8 ball, which was initially at rest, the cue ball is scattered at some angle. It also loses some of its momentum and kinetic energy to the 8 ball as the 8 ball begins to move. The x–ray photon scattering off an electron behaves similarly. The x ray loses energy and momentum to the electron as the electron begins to move. The energy and frequency of light and other electromagnetic radiation are related so that a lower frequency x–ray photon has a lower energy. The frequency of the x ray decreases as it loses energy to the electron.

In 1905, Albert Einstein explained the photoelectric effect, the effect that causes solar cells to produce electricity, by assuming light can occur in discrete particles, photons. This photon model for light still needed further experimental confirmation. Compton's x ray scattering experiments provided additional confirmation that light can exhibit particle–like behavior. Compton received the 1927 Nobel Prize in physics for his work. Additional experiments show that light can also exhibit wave–like behavior and has a wave particle duality.

Compulsion

The main concern of psychiatrists and therapists who treat people with compulsions is the role they play in a mental illness called obsessive–compulsive disorder (OCD). Compulsions need to be distinguished from obsessions in order to understand how they interconnect with compulsive behavior and reinforce this debilitating illness.

In psychiatric literature, compulsions are defined as repetitive behavior, such as hand washing, counting, touching, and checking and rechecking an action (like turning the light off and on again and again to be sure it is off or on). Performing the specific act relieves the tension of the obsession that the light may not be on or off. The person feels no pleasure from the action. On the contrary, the compulsive behavior and the obsession cause a great deal of distress for the person.

Compulsive behavior also needs to be distinguished from excessive or addictive behaviors where the person feels pleasure from the activity, such as in compulsive eating or compulsive gambling.

Obsessive–compulsive disorder (OCD)

Obsessive–compulsive disorder is classified as an anxiety disorder. Other anxiety disorders are panic attacks, agoraphobia (the fear of public places), phobias (fear of specific objects or situations), and certain stress disorders. This illness becomes increasingly more difficult to the patient and family because it tends to consume more and more of the individual's time and energy. While a person who is suffering from an obsessive–compulsive disorder is aware of how irrational or senseless the fear is, he or she is overwhelmed by the need to carry out compulsive behavior in order to avoid anxiety that is created if the behavior is not carried out.

Therapists categorize compulsions into motor compulsions and ideational or mental compulsions. A motor compulsion involves the need to use physical action. Touching or hand washing would be classified as motor compulsions. An ideational compulsion involves thinking processes. Examples of ideation or mental compulsions are counting, following a ritualized thought pattern, such as picturing specific things, or repeating what someone is saying in the mind.

Obsessive–compulsive personality disorder

People with personality traits, like being a perfectionist or rigidly controlling, may not have OCD, but may have obsessive–compulsive personality disorder. In this illness, the patient may spend excessive amounts of energy on details and lose perspective about the overall goals of a task or job. They become compulsively involved with performing the details but disregard larger goals.

Like obsessive–compulsive disorder, obsessive-compulsive personality disorder can be time–consuming. The compulsive personality may be able to function successfully in a work environment but may make everyone else miserable by demanding excessive standards of perfection.

Treatments for obsessive–compulsive illnesses

The problem for treatment of obsessive–compulsive illnesses must follow careful diagnosis of the specific nature of the disorder.

Methods used to treat these illnesses include a careful physical and psychological diagnosis, medications, and therapies. Besides the compulsive behavior symptoms a person with OCD exhibits, he or she may also have physical symptoms, such as tremors, dry mouth, stammering, dizziness, cramps, nausea, headaches, sweating, or butterflies in the stomach. Since these and the major symptoms are found in other illnesses, a careful diagnosis is important before treatment is prescribed.

In behavior therapy, the patient is encouraged to control behavior, which the therapist feels can be accomplished with direction. The patient is also made to understand that thoughts cannot be controlled, but that when compulsive behavior is changed gradually through modified behavior, obsessive thoughts diminish. In this therapy, patients are exposed to the fears that produce anxiety in them, called flooding, and gradually learn to deal with their fears.

Cognitive therapists feel it is important for OCD patients to learn to think differently in order to improve their condition. Because OCD patients are rational, this type of therapy can sometimes be useful. Most professionals who treat obsessive–compulsive illnesses feel that a combination of therapy and medication is helpful. Some antidepressants, like Anafranil (clomipramine) and Prozac (fluoxetine), are prescribed to help alleviate the condition.

When patients exhibit compulsive slowness, prompting and shaping techniques are used. Persons who are compulsively slow work with a helper who prompts them along gradually until they can perform actions in a more reasonable time frame, such as reduc-

KEY TERMS

· ·

Anxiety disorder—An illness in which anxiety plays a role.

Behavior therapy—A therapeutic program that emphasizes changing behavior.

Compulsive behavior—Behavior that is driven by an obsession.

Cognitive therapy—A therapeutic program that emphasizes changing a patient's thinking.

Diagnosis—A careful evaluation by a medical professional or therapist to determine the nature of an illness or disorder.

Flooding—Exposing a person with an obsession to their fears as a way of helping them face and overcome them.

Ideational or mental compulsions—Compulsions of a mental nature, such as counting or repeating words.

Motor compulsions—Compulsions where a specific, ritualized act is carried out.

Obsessive–compulsive disorder—A mental illness in which a person is driven to compulsive behavior to relieve the anxiety of an obsession.

Obsessive–compulsive personality disorder—The preoccupation with minor details to the exclusion of larger issues; exhibiting overcontrolling and perfectionistic attitudes.

Prompting and shaping—A therapeutic technique that involves using a helper to work with a person suffering from compulsive slowness.

ing a two–hour morning grooming period to half an hour. The shaping aspect is the reduction of time.

Further Reading:

Amchin, Jess. *Psychiatric Diagnosis: A Biopsychosocial Approach Using DSM–III–R.* Washington, D.C.: Psychiatric Press, 1991.

Baer, Lee. *Getting Control.* Boston: Little, Brown, 1991.

Green, Stephen A. Green. *Feel Good Again.* Mt. Vernon, N.Y.: Consumers Union, 1990.

Jamison, Kay Redfield. *Touched with Fire.* New York: Free Press, 1993.

Neziroglu, Fugen and Yaryura–Tobias, Jose A.. *Over and Over Again.* Lexington, Mass.: D.C. Heath, 1991.

Vita Richman

Computer-aided design see
CAD/CAM/CIM

Computer-aided manufacture see
CAD/CAM/CIM

Computer, analog

Unlike a digital computer which performs calculations strictly upon numbers or symbols, an analog computer translates continuously varying quantities such as temperature, pressure, weight, or speed into corresponding voltages or gear movements. It then performs calculations by comparing, adding or subtracting voltages or gear motions in various ways, finally directing the result to an output device such as a cathode–ray tube or pen plotter on a roll of paper. Common devices like thermostats and bathroom scales are actually simple analog computers: they compute one thing by measuring another; they do not count.

The earliest known analog computer is an astrolabe. Built in Greece during the 1st century B.C., the device used pointers and scales on its face and a complex arrangement of bronze gears to predict the motions of the sun, planets, and stars.

Other early measuring devices were also analog computers. Sundials traced a shadow's path to show the time of day. Springweight scales, which have been used for centuries, convert the pull on a stretched spring to avoirdupois. The slide rule was invented about 1620 and is still used, although it has been almost completely superseded by the electronic caluclator.

In 1905 Rollin Harris and E. G. Fisher of the United States Coast and Geodetic Survey started work on a calculating device that would forecast tides. Dubbed the "Great Brass Brain," it was 11 ft (3 m) long, 7 ft (2 m) high, and weighed 2,500 lb (1135 kg). It contained a maze of cams, gears, and rotating shafts. Completed in 1910, the machine worked as follows: an operator set 37 dials (each representing a particular geological or astronomical variable), turned a crank, and the computer drew up tidal charts for as far into the future as the operator wished. It made accurate predictions and was used for 56 years before being retired in 1966.

Vannevar Bush, an electrical engineer at the Massachusetts Institute of Technology, created what is considered to be the first modern computer in the 1930s. He and a team from MIT's electrical engineering staff, discouraged by the time–consuming mathematical computations, called differential equations, required to solve certain engineering problems, began work on a device to solve these equations automatically. In 1935, the incredible second version of their device, dubbed the differential analyzer was unveiled: it weighed 100 tons, contained 150 motors, and hundreds of miles of wires connecting relays and vacuum tube. Three copies of the machine were built for military and research use. Over the next 15 years, MIT built several new versions of the computer. By present standards the machine was slow, only about 100 times faster than a human operator using a desk calculator.

In the 1950s RCA produced the first reliable design for a fully electronic analog computer, but by this time, many of the most complex functions of analog computers were being assumed by faster and more accurate digital computers. Analog computers are still used today for some applications such as scientific calculation, engineering design, industrial process control, and spacecraft navigation.

Computer, digital

The digital computer is a programmable electronic device that processes numbers and words accurately and at enormous speed. It comes in a variety of shapes and sizes, ranging from the familiar desktop microcomputer to the minicomputer, mainframe, and supercomputer. The supercomputer is the most powerful in this hierarchy and is used by organizations such as NASA to process upwards of 100 million instructions per second. The impact of the digital computer on society has been tremendous; in its various forms, it is used to run everything from spacecraft to factories, healthcare systems to telecommunications, banks to household budgets.

The story of how the digital computer evolved is largely the story of an unending search for labor–saving devices. Its roots go back beyond the calculating machines of the 1600s to the pebbles (in Latin, *calculi*) that the merchants of Rome used for counting, to the abacus of the fifth century B.C. Although none of these early devices were automatic, they were useful in a world where mathematical calculations, laboriously performed by human beings, were riddled with human error.

By the early 1800s, with the Industrial Revolution well underway, errors in mathematical data had assumed new importance; faulty navigational tables, for example, were the cause of frequent shipwrecks. Such errors were a source of irritation to Charles Babbage, a

brilliant young English mathematician. Convinced that a machine could do mathematical calculations faster and more accurately than humans, Babbage in 1822 produced a small working model of his difference engine. The difference engine's arithmetic functioning was limited, but it could compile and print mathematical tables with no more human intervention needed than a hand to turn the handles at the top of the model. Although the British government was impressed enough to invest £17,000 in the construction of a full-scale difference engine, it was never built; the project came to a halt in 1833 in a dispute over payments between Babbage and his workmen.

By that time, Babbage had already started to work on an improved version—the analytical engine, an automated programmable machine that could perform all types of arithmetic functions. The analytical engine had all the essential parts of the modern computer: an input device, a memory, a central processing unit, and a printer. For input and programming, Babbage used punched cards, an idea borrowed from Joseph Jacquard, who had used them in his revolutionary weaving loom in 1801.

Although the analytical engine has gone down in history as the prototype of the modern computer, a full–scale version was never built. Among the deterrents were lack of funding and a technology that lagged well behind Babbage's vision. Even if the analytical engine had been built, it would have been powered by a steam engine, and given its purely mechanical components, its computing speed would not have been great. Less than twenty years after Babbage's death in 1871, an American by the name of Herman Hollerith was able to make use of a new technology—electricity—when he submitted to the United States government a plan for a machine that could compute census data. Hollerith's electromechanical device tabulated the results of the 1890 U.S. census in less than six weeks, something of an improvement over the seven years it had taken to tabulate the results of the 1880 census. Hollerith went on to found the company that ultimately emerged as IBM.

World War II was the movitation for the next significant stage in the evolution of the digital computer. Out of it came the Colossus, a special–purpose electronic computer built by the British to decipher German codes; the Mark I, a gigantic electromechanical device constructed at Harvard University under the direction of Howard Aiken; and the ENIAC, another huge machine, but one that was fully electronic and thus much faster that the Mark I. Built at the University of Pennsylvania under the direction of John Mauchly and J. Presper Eckert, the ENIAC operated on some 18,000 vacuum tubes. If its

A possible future direction for computer technology is the optical computer. The Bit-Serial Optical Computer (BSOC) shown here is the first computer that both stores and manipulates data and instructions as pulses of light. To enable this, the designers developed bit-serial architecture. Each binary digit is represented by a pulse of infrared laser light 13 ft (4 m) long. The pulses circulate sequentially through a tightly wound 2.5 mile (4 km) loop of optical fiber some 50,000 times per second. Other laser beams operate lithium niobate optical switches which perform the data processing. This computer was developed by Harry Jordan and Vincent Heuring at the University of Colorado and was unveiled on January 12, 1993.

electronic components had been laid side by side two inches apart, they would have covered a football field.

The ENIAC was a general purpose computer in theory, but to switch from one program to another meant that a part of the machine had to be disassembled and rewired. To circumvent this tedious process, John von Neumann, a Hungarian–born American mathematician, proposed the concept of the stored program—that is, coding the program in the same way as the stored data and keeping it in the computer for as long as needed. The computer could then be instructed to change programs, and the programs themselves could even be written to interact with each other. For coding, Neumann proposed using the binary numbering system—0 and 1—rather than the 0 to 9 of the decimal system. Because 0 and 1 correspond to the on or off states of electric current, computer design was greatly simplified.

Neumann's concepts were incorporated in the British–built EDSAC and the University of Pennsylvania's EDVAC in 1949, and in the UNIVAC and other first–generation computers that followed in the 1950s. All these machines were large, plodding dinosaurs by today's standards. Since then, advances in programming languages and electronics (such as the transistor, the integrated circuit, and the microprocessor) have led to computing power in the forms we know it today, ranging from the supercomputer to far more compact models.

See also Computer, analog; Computer software.

Computerized axial tomography

Computerized axial tomography (CAT) is a diagnostic procedure that employs x rays in a unique manner. The CAT scan machine is computer controlled to assure accuracy in placement of the x–ray beam. Axial refers to the fact that the x–ray tubes are arranged in an arc about an axis. Tomography is a combination of *tomo*, from the Greek meaning "to cut", and graph, "to draw", a reference to the fact that the CAT scan image reveals a cross–section of the body or body part.

The tomograph was developed in England in 1972. After a number of years of fine tuning the apparatus, it became a part of clinical medicine that is widely relied on now. Prior to the development of the CAT, x rays were done on the familiar table by a single x–ray tube that passed the rays through a given part of the body and exposed a plate of x–ray film. That film had to be developed and then viewed by a physician. This form of x ray was displayed on a film plate that offered a one–dimensional view of the body part under the x–ray tube. If a different angle was needed, the patient had to be turned over. The CAT offers a number of improvements over the old method.

The CAT scan machine, often referred to as the CT machine, consists of a horizontal pad on which the patient lies. Sandbags are placed around him to insure that he lies motionless. At one end of the pad is a circular structure that contains an array of x–ray tubes. The patient lies on the pad which is advanced into the circle until the desired area of the body is under the x–ray tubes. The x–ray tubes are focused to provide a very narrow angle of exposure, approximately 0.4 inches (1 cm). The first x rays are made after which the array of tubes rotates and another exposure is made, the tubes rotate again, and so on until x rays have been made from all angles around the body.

Each x–ray tube is connected to the controlling computer. As the x rays pass through the patient's body they fall upon a sensitive window. The image from each tube is fed into the computer, and this is repeated whenever the x–ray tube fires, which is from a different angle each time.

In this way, the x–ray image is projected into the computer from different angles. The computer constructs a cross–sectional image of the body each time the array of x–ray tubes has completed a revolution around the patient.

Following each x–ray exposure the patient is advanced another centimeter into the machine and the process repeats. X rays are made and the patient is advanced until exposures have been made in 1–cm increments for the length of the organ being examined.

The images from each x–ray tube are fed through a computer, giving numerical values to the density of tissue through which the beam passed. The computer uses the numerical values to reconstruct an image of the

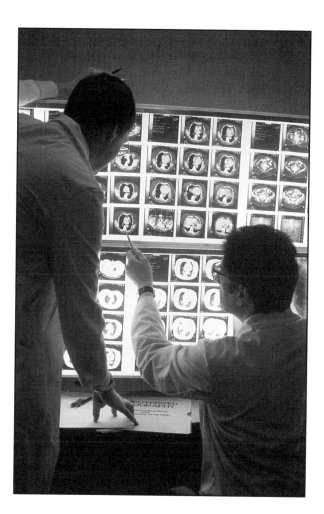

Doctors examining CAT scan x rays.

cross–section of the body at the level the x rays passed through. The image is printed onto a screen for the physician to see and on a panel of x–ray film.

The differences in tissue density give the CT scan its definition. The liver is more dense than the pancreas, bone is more dense than liver, and so forth. The structures appear in different shades of gray on the screen and the film. The film is printed as a series of cross sectional images showing, for example, the liver from top to bottom. Any of the images can be called up on the computer screen for closer evaluation if the physician needs to do so.

A CT scan as described is a noninvasive procedure; that is, nothing is inserted into the body. At times the physician may want more contrast or definition to a given organ and may resort to injecting a contrast medium to accomplish this. A contrast medium is a substance that is visible on x rays. The medium, injected into the blood, will concentrate in an organ and will outline the organ or a cavity within it. In this way, the size of a kidney tumor may be determined, for example, as may other forms of pathology.

Obviously, the CAT scan is a specialized form of diagnosis and is not practical for such cases as bone fractures. The procedure requires more time to complete than does the ordinary, one–dimensional x ray and is not cost–effective for simpler procedures.

For diagnosis of soft–tissue tumors, which are difficult to print on an ordinary x ray, the CAT scan is superior.

All x rays rely on differences in tissue density to form the x–ray image. Bone resists the passage of the x–ray beam more than muscle, which resists more than a softer tissue, such as liver. Thus, the x–ray image from a single x–ray beam is a plate somewhat like a film negative showing various tones of gray. Small differences in tissue density, as would be seen with a tumor in the liver, where both tissues are nearly the same density, would not be seen as two separate structures. The liver would appear as a uniformly dense organ.

The CAT scan, however, takes x rays from different angles and the machine is capable after several exposures to determine the slight difference in densities of nearly similar tissues. The liver will appear as an organ of a certain shade of gray, and a tumor within it will be

discernable as a spot of slightly lighter gray because of the minute variation in density. Also, by finding the panel on which the tumor first appears and following it through to the panel on which it disappears, the radiologist can determine the size of the tumor.

See also Radioactive tracers.

Further Reading:

Cukier, Daniel and McCullough, Virginia E. *Coping With Radiation Therapy*. Los Angeles: Lowell House, 1993.
"Finding the brain's autopilot." *USA Today* 122 (April 1994): 13.
Nadis, S.J. "Kid's brainpower: Use it or lose it." *Technology Review* 96 (November–December 1993): 19–20.

Larry Blaser

Computer languages

A computer language is any means of transmitting instructions and data to computers. Computer languages are the interface between man and machine. While humans can communicate with computers in binary language (ones and zeros), people find it far more efficient to communicate with computers in a higher level language.

First–generation languages

With machine languages (first–generation language and the lowest level computer language), the programmer feeds information into the computer as binary instructions, the equivalent of the on/off (zeros and ones) signals used by computers to carry out operations. The first computers were programmed by scientists sitting before control panels equipped with toggle switches so that they could input instructions as strings of ones and zeros. Machine language is the most difficult language to move from one type of computer to another.

Example 1. In machine language, the sequence 011011 000000 000000 000000 000001 000000 might mean place the contents of storage 64 in the accumulator.

Second–generation languages

Assembly or assembler language (second–generation language; in wide use by the late 1950s) renders instructions as simple combinations of alphabet letters for programming convenience. With assembly language, there is a one–to–one correspondence between a language statement and the machine instruction issued to the computer. Assembly language makes use of mnemonics, or memory aids, that are easier for the human programmer to recall than are numerical codes. Assembly language is easier to move across computer platforms than is machine language. Use of assembly language requires an understanding of the computer's architecture and the operating system under which the code will run.

Example 2. In assembly language, the sequence CLA 0 0 0 64 might have the same meaning as the machine language string given in Example 1, i.e., place the contents of storage 64 in the accumulator.

Third–generation languages

The introduction of the compiler in 1952 marked the advent of third–generation computer languages. With a third–generation language, the programmer with the aid of a text editor creates a file containing language statements that he or she can still makes sense of. Third–level computer languages have become the major means of communication between a person with a problem and the digital computer used to solve it.

Most computer programming is still done in third–generation languages such as COBOL (Common Business–Oriented Language), FORTRAN (Formula Translator), Algol (Algorithmic Language), LISP (List Processor), BASIC (Beginner's All–purpose Symbolic Instruction Code), or PASCAL (named for the French mathematician and theologian Blaise Pascal, who built the first mechanical calculating machine in the seventeenth century). Programs written in third–generation computer languages can be moved from one computer to another with relative ease; they are therefore said to be portable.

Characteristics of third–generation languages include the following:

- The user does not need to know any machine code.
- The programming language must have some significant amount of machine independence; it should run on different types of computers.
- When the programming language is translated into machine code; there is normally more than one machine instruction created for each statement in the programming language.
- The programming language must have a notation that is somewhat closer to the specific problem being solved than is normal machine code.

Advantages of working with higher level languages include:

- Ease of learning
- Ease of coding and understanding
- Ease of debugging
- Ease of maintaining and documenting
- Ease of moving across computer platforms
- Reduced elapsed time for problem solving

Disadvantages include:

- Time required for compiling
- Inefficient machine code
- Difficulties in debugging without learning machine language
- Inability of a language to express all needed operations

The actual program written in the third–generation language is called the source program. This is the material that the programmer puts into the computer to obtain results. The source program can usually be translated into an object program. The term object program strictly relates only to the final binary form that the computer can execute, but may in fact refer to the source program translated down to the assembly level.

An interpreter or compiler takes this source code and turns it into machine code, i.e., language understandable by the computer. The price for this convenience is that the programs written in third–generation languages require more memory and run more slowly than those written in lower level languages.

Interpreters

An interpreter is a program that executes a source program, usually on a step–by–step, line–by–line, or unit–by–unit basis. An interpreter will usually execute the smallest possible meaningful unit in the programming language. The output of the interpreter is an actual answer, i.e., the result of performing the actions designated in the program.

An interpreted language is one in which each source code statement is parsed before execution. Interpreters provide immediate feedback: you can make a change to a source code statement and immediately see the result of the change. Interpreted languages are less efficient than compiled languages because they (interpreted languages) do not allow for optimization. With interpreters, certain phases of the work and analysis must be done repeatedly.

Compilers

A compiler is a program that translates a source program written in a particular programming language to an object program that a particular computer can run. The compiler is both language and machine dependent. The output of the compiler is a program in some form or another, and not an answer of any kind.

With compiled languages, the compiler examines the generated code. It then may perform several kinds of optimization. At the simplest level, the compiler will move repeated instructions in a loop instruction to the outside of the loop. This speeds up execution of the code because the expression is evaluated once instead of each time through the loop.

Compiler writers have many ways to optimize the generated source code.

BLOCK–STRUCTURED LANGUAGES

Block–structured languages grew out of research leading to the development of structured programming. Structured programming is based on the premise that any computer program can be reduced to three blocks: sequential, selection, and iteration. In sequential blocks, each statement is executed one after the other. In selection blocks, choices are typically made with an IF...THEN...ELSE structure. Iteration, also known as loop structure, is the third block. Loop structures specify how many times a loop will be executed. The loop structure usually specifies a beginning value, how much the counter is to be incremented at each iteration, and the termination value for the loop counter.

The programmer should be familiar with how each source code statement will be rendered into machine language by the compiler he or she is using. Compiler developers may have different priorities. One may optimize source–code compilation speed, another may optimize generated code size or execution speed.

Languages such as Pascal, Algol, and Modula–2 were designed to provide the modularity required to take advantage of block structuring. These languages competed with nonblock structured languages such as BASIC, FORTRAN, and LISP.

Block–structured languages rely on modular construction. Each module in a block–structured language typically begins with a "BEGIN" statement and ends with an "END" statement. The block looks like a black box to the calling module that it feeds data into and takes transformed data from.

Most modern languages are block structured. Even languages that began as unstructured languages have become more structured. Examples included FORTRAN

and BASIC. COBOL is a semi–block–structured language that relies on the programmer to modularize it.

LINE–ORIENTED LANGUAGES

Computer languages may be classified according to whether they are line–oriented or not. COBOL and FORTRAN were first developed in the days when programs were punched onto computer cards. Meaning was assigned to the card columns; for example, the line number might be specified in columns one through six.

Languages developed since the development of interactive terminals do not tend to be line oriented. Each statement in a FORTRAN statement is separated by an end–of–line token; but the white space in a PASCAL statement conveys no information to the computer. Still, the white space conveys meaning to the programmer by allowing him to recognize separate statements.

Computer languages have unique syntaxes. The statement a = b in PASCAL is an enquiry whether variable a is equal to variable b. But the same statement in a C program means that the value contained in the variable b is placed in the variable a. The C language has the characteristics of both second– and third–generation languages. A C program requires more statements than a COBOL program but is just as portable; it requires fewer statements than an assembly language program but runs almost as quickly. These features make C a very popular language among programmers and software developers.

Computer–aided software engineering (CASE) tools are now being used to generate language source codes. Programmers spend less time writing individual language source instructions and more time analyzing the job the program is to perform. The programmer uses a graphical environment to create an abstract picture of the overall job to be performed by the system being created. Using the CASE tool, the programmer employs a graphical description of the task to create a functional description of how the program is organized. With this approach, the programmer first explores what the program or system will accomplish (analysis), and then translates what is derived in the preceding phase into an abstract description of how the system will perform the task defined in the analysis phase (design).

Fourth–generation languages

Fourth–generation languages attempt to make communicating with computers as much like the processes of thinking and talking to other people as possible. The problem is that the computer still only understands ones and zeros, so a compiler and interpreter must still con-

KEY TERMS

Binary digit—Either of two digits (0 or 1) used to express numbers in binary scale. In binary scale, the base is two, and successive places denote units, twos, fours, etc. Thus, 10 in the binary scale represents the number 2 in base ten, and 100 the number 4.

Compiler—A program that translates a source program written in a particular programming language to an object program.

Computer language—Any of numerous systems of rules, words, and symbols for writing computer programs or representing instructions.

Interpreter—A program that executes a source program, usually on a step-by-step, line-by-line, or unit-by-unit basis.

Source program—A computer program written in a third-generation language.

Object program—The final binary program that the computer can execute, but sometimes also used to refer to a source program translated down to the assembly level.

vert the source code into code that the computer can understand, i.e., machine language.

Fourth–generation languages typically consist of English–like words and phrases. When they are implemented on microcomputers, some of these languages include graphic devices such as icons and on–screen push buttons for use during programming and when running the resulting application.

Many fourth–generation languages uses Structured Query Language (SQL) as the basis for operations. SQL was developed at IBM to develop information stored in relational databases. Eventually it was adopted as an American National Standards Institute (ANSI) and later International Standards Organization (ISO) standard for managing structured, factual data. Many database companies offer an SQL–type database because purchasers of such databases seek to optimize their investments by buying open databases, i.e., those offering the greatest compatibility with other systems. This means that the information systems are relatively independent of vendor, operating system, and computer platform.

Examples of fourth–generation languages include PROLOG, an artificial intelligence language that applies rules to data to arrive at solutions; and Occam

and PARLOG, both parallel–processing languages. Newer languages may combine SQL and other high–level languages.

See also Artificial intelligence; Computer software.

Further Reading:

Hall, Sheldon T. "Very High Level Languages." In *MacMillan Encyclopedia of Computers*, edited by Gary G. Bitter. New York, MacMillan, 1992.

Keuffel, Warren. "Computer Languages." In *MacMillan Encyclopedia of Computers*, edited by G. Bitter. New York: MacMillan, 1992.

Sammet, Jean E. *Programming Languages: History and Fundamentals*. Englewood Cliffs, NJ: Prentice–Hall, 1969.

Randall S. Frost

Computer software

Computer software is a package of instructions that tells a computer what to do and how to do it. It is the "brains" that tells the hardware or "body" of a computer what to do. Hardware is anything you can touch in a computer system, things like the electrical connections, silicon chips, disk drives, monitor, and printer. The hardware is driven by the procedures in a software program every time a person commands a computer to perform a specific job. The instructions in computer software are a convenient collection of highly detailed and specific commands written in a defined order. Software is written by computer programmers and is recorded on disks or tapes. It is always available and does not have to be entered by the user every time he or she wants to use the computer. Without software, a computer can do nothing; it is only a collection of circuits and metal in a box.

History

One of the first sophisticated calculating machines, an ancestor of modern computers, was designed by Charles Babbage (1792–1871), an English Professor of mathematics. Babbage called his planned calculator an "Analytical Engine." It was never completed, unfortunately, but Babbage's design contained all the crucial parts of modern computers. Although it did not use electricity, it included an input device for entering information, a processing device (called "The Mill" by Babbage) for calculating answers, a memory unit for storing answers and even an output device, an automated printer, for reporting results.

One of Babbage's financial backers for his "Analytical Engine" was the daughter of poet Lord Byron, Ada Augusta, also known as Lady Lovelace. Augusta was an amateur mathematician. She also became the first computer programmer when she wrote instructions for the "Analytical Engine." Her programs were sequences of steps that would have turned the gears and cranks of the machine to allow it to compute or perform calculations. Augusta wrote her instructions on punch cards, cards with holes in them. Punch cards had been used as early as the 1750s by human weavers who read them for instruction on what pattern of cloth to weave. By the turn of the century, a loom had been invented that could read the cards by itself. Punch cards were used for years by many computer users right up until a generation ago.

Babbage's machine, like the automatic loom, was designed to sense where the holes were in the cards. Different combinations of holes told the computer what settings to adopt. Depending on where the holes were in the card, and what cards were in a sequence, the computer would perform different calculations by translating the instructions into physical movements of the machines' calculating mechanical parts.

Augusta invented many basic programming techniques still used by computer programmers: "subroutines," a series of instructions that could be used over and over for different purposes; "conditional jumps," an instruction for the machine to jump to different cards for instruction if certain criteria were met; "looping," the ability to repeat the instructions on a set of cards repeatedly to satisfy the demands of a task.

The first modern computers were developed by the United States military during World War II to calculate the paths of artillery shells and bombs. These computers used vacuum tubes that had on–off switches. The settings had to be reset by hand for each operation. This was time–consuming and difficult for the programmers.

John von Neumann (1903–1957), a Princeton math professor, suggested that computers would be more efficient if they stored their programs in memory, rather than getting every single instruction from settings provided by programmers each time a different problem had to be solved. This suggestion and others by von Neumann helped transform the computer from a fancy adding machine or calculator into a machine capable of simulating many complex situations found in the real world.

The development of computer languages

The first modern computer was named ENIAC for Electronic Numerical Integrator And Calculator. It was finally assembled in 1946. Most programming was done by and for military and scientific users. That began to change after Grace Hopper, an American computer scientist and Naval officer, developed FLOW–MATIC, the first computer language useful for solving problems for commercial users. FLOW–MATIC used a language slightly closer to English than the on–off switch language the computer understood. This was an important step toward developing "user–friendly" computer software. FLOW–MATIC was one of the first "high–level" computer languages. A high–level computer language is one that is easier for humans to use but can still be translated by another program (called a compiler) into language a computer can interpret and act on.

By 1957, IBM had created FORTRAN, a language specifically designed for scientific work involving complicated mathematical formulas. FORTRAN stands for FORmula TRANslater. It became the first high–level programming language to be used by many computer users. (Computer scientists sometimes called high–level programs "source code" and machine language translations "object code.")

In 1958, ALGOL (ALGOrithmic Language), became available. It was designed to do some tasks better than FORTRAN. COBOL (COmmon Business Oriented Language) was developed to help businesses organize records and manage data files.

During the first half of the 1960s, scientists at Dartmouth College in New Hampshire developed BASIC (Beginner's All–purpose Symbolic Instruction Code). This was the first widespread computer language designed for and used by nonprofessional programmers. It was extremely popular throughout the 1970s and 80s. Its popularity was increased by the development and sale of personal computers, computers small and cheap enough to attract people from all walks of life. Two reasons explain the wide-spread use and popularity of BASIC. One, it is a very easy programming language to learn and to use (although some programmers do not like it because they consider it slow, awkward and unsophisticated compared to other computer languages). Second, BASIC was included in many personal computers, and thus available to everyone who purchased or used such a machine.

Some other popular programming languages among the hundreds that have been developed since the 1960s include PASCAL, first developed as a teaching tool; LISP, a language used by computer scientists interested in writing programs they hoped would give computers some abilities usually associated with intelligence in humans; and C, a language used to create systems programs, a name given to all the programs that enable the computer to use higher–level language programs like store–bought software.

Types of computer software

Computers can do nothing by themselves. They must receive instructions to complete every task they perform. Some microcomputers, such as hand–held calculators, wristwatches, and newer automobile engines contain built–in operating instructions. These devices can be called "dedicated" computers. Personal computers found in businesses, homes and schools, however, are general–purpose machines because they can be programmed to do many different types of jobs. They contain enough built–in programming to enable them to interpret and use commands provided by a wide range of external software packages which can be loaded into their memory.

The instructions computers receive from software are written in a computer language, a set of symbols that convey information. Like spoken languages used by humans, computer languages come in many different forms.

Computers use a very basic "language" to perform their jobs. The language ultimately can be reduced to a pattern of "on–or–off" responses, called binary digital information or Machine Language. Computers work using nothing but electronic "switches" that are either on or off. Computer scientists represent on by "1" and off by "0." (Check the nearest personal computer. On many machines the on/off switch is labeled "1/0.")

Human beings have trouble writing complex instructions using binary, "1 or 0" language. A simple command to a computer might look something like this: 00010010 10010111001 010101000110. Because such code is tedious and time consuming to write, programmers invented Assembly Language. It allows programmers to assign a separate code "word" (actually the "word" is often a few letters long) to different machine language commands. It is easier for humans to work with lettered codes than with lots of 1s and 0s. Another, special program called a Compiler translates the codes back into 1s and 0s for the computer. One problem with Assembly Language was that it only worked with computers that had the same type of "computer chip" or microprocessor, an electrical component that controls the main operating parts of the computer.

The development of high–level languages helped to make computers common objects in work places and homes. They allowed instructions to be written in languages that many people and their computers could recognize and interpret. For the first time recognizable words like READ, LIST and PRINT could be used by people writing instructions for computers. Each word may represent hundreds of instructions in the 1s and 0s language of the machine.

Computers of course must have the high–level language command translated back into machine language before they can act on it. The programs needed to translate high–level language back into machine language are called Translator Programs. They represent another type of computer software.

Operating System software is yet another type of software that must be in a computer before it can read and use commercially available software packages. Before a computer can use application software, such as a word processing or a game-playing package, the computer must run the instructions through the operating system software. This contains many built in instructions, so that each piece of application software does not have to repeat simple instructions, like telling the computer how to print something out. DOS, Disk Operating System, is a popular Operating System software program for many personal computers used today.

Once Operating System software is loaded into a computer, the computer can load and understand many other types of software (providing the software was written for the same type of computer it is loaded into. IBM–compatible machines can all run the same type of software, but Macintosh computers can not). There are now thousands of computer software packages that can program computers to help people perform hundreds of specific tasks from writing a letter to balancing a checkbook to playing a game of chess.

Application software

Software can tell computers how to create documents, to solve simple or complex calculations for business people and scientists, to play games, to create images, to maintain and sort files, and to complete hundreds of other tasks. Word–processing software, for example, makes writing, rewriting, editing, correcting, arranging, and rearranging words convenient.

Database software enables computer users to organize and retrieve lists, facts and inventories, each of which may include thousands of items. Spreadsheet software allows users to keep complicated and related figures straight, to graph the results and to see how a change in one entry affects others. It is useful for financial and mathematical calculations. Each entry can be connected, if necessary, to other entries by a mathematical formula. Let's say you have a spreadsheet that keeps track of your earnings and the taxes you owe on them. When you add more earnings to the part of the spreadsheet that keeps track of them, (called a "register") the spreadsheet can be set up, or programmed, to automatically adjust the amount of taxes you owe. Once you program the spreadsheet, all you have to do is enter your earnings and the spreadsheet will immediately recalculate your taxes.

Graphics software lets you draw and create images. Desktop publishing software allow publishers to arrange photos, pictures and words on a page before any printing is done. With desktop publishing and word processing software, there is no need for cutting and pasting layouts. Today, thanks to this type of computer software, anyone with a computer, a good quality printer and the right software package can create professional looking documents at home. Entire books can be written and formatted by the author. The printed copy or even just a computer disk with the file can be delivered to a traditional printer without the need to reenter all the words on a typesetting machine.

Software for games can turn a computer into a space ship, a battlefield, or an ancient city. Game software like "Myst," "Doom," and "King's Quest" have earned big profits for their manufacturers. As computers get more powerful, computer games get more realistic and sophisticated.

Communications software allows people to send and receive computer files and faxes over phone lines. Education and Reference software makes tasks such as learning spoken languages and finding information easier. Dictionaries, encyclopedias, and other reference books can all be searched quickly and easily with the correct software.

Utility programs help computer users use their computers more efficiently by helping allowing them to search for information and inspecting computer disks for flaws.

Future developments

Current trends in computer science make it possible to predict future developments with some degree of confidence. Already, large software programs are written by groups of programmers. It is safe to predict that software will continue to get more complex and more powerful as computers are sold with more memory and power.

Computer designers and manufacturers will continue to pack more electrical circuits into smaller com-

---

KEY TERMS

. . . .

Computer hardware—The physical equipment used in a computer system.

Computer program—Another name for computer software, a series of commands or instructions that a computer can interpret and execute.

---

puter chips that will help to make systems more powerful. To make computers faster, some researchers are experimenting with extreme cold. Electrical signals, which carry information in a computer, are slowed by electrical resistance. Scientists have observed that some electrical conductors lose resistance as temperatures get colder and colder. This is called "superconductivity." Perhaps someday computers will come with coolant systems to exploit superconductivity and take advantage of faster processing speeds.

Today's computers work on several problems at once while constantly checking on the progress of each separate task. They are able to use the intermediate results of one task to influence ongoing work on a separate, but related, task and vice versa. This is called parallel–processing, and may one day enable computers to develop artificial intelligence, which has been an elusive goal for computer scientists.

Sophisticated software called CAD, for computer–aided design, helps architects, engineers, and other professionals develop complex designs for buildings and machines. The software uses high–speed calculations and high–resolution graphic images to let designers try out different ideas for a project. Each change is translated into the overall plan, which is modified almost instantly. This system helps designers create structures and machines such as buildings, airplanes, scientific equipment, and even other computers.

Further Reading:

Gookin, Dan and Rathbone, Andy. *PCS for Dummies*. San Mateo, CA: IDG Books, 1992.

Gornick, Larry. *The Cartoon Guide to The Computer*. New York: Harper/Perennial, 1991.

Rubin, Charles. *The Little Book of Computer Wisdom*. Boston: Houghton Mifflin Company, 1995.

White, Ron. *How Software Works*. Emeryville, CA: Ziff–Davis Press, 1993.

Dean Allen Haycock

Concentration

Concentration is a ratio of how much of one ingredient is present in a mixture, compared to the whole mixture or compared to the main ingredient, often the solvent. The amounts of each substance can be expressed in mass or volume units, and many different units can be used. The components of the mixture can be gases, liquids, or solids.

The Earth's atmosphere, for example, is a mixture of gases, and 78% of the total volume is nitrogen gas. (Percentages are the number of parts of a certain substance per hundred parts of the mixture.) Different types of steel are mixtures of iron with other elements. For example, stainless steel has close to 20%, by weight, of chromium. Sometimes a combination of mass and volume measurements are used; vinegar can be said to be a 5% solution of acetic acid, meaning 0.18 oz (5 g) of acetic acid per 0.21 pints (100 mL) of solution. Because it is not usually practical to analyze the whole substance in question, (the earth's atmosphere, for example) only samples are taken. Getting a true representation of the whole is crucial, or the concentration determined will not be accurate. For example, the concentration of nitrogen in the atmosphere changes slightly with altitude.

Many commonly used mixtures are liquid solutions. For chemical reactions, molarity is a useful unit of concentration. It is the number of moles of solute per liter of solution. Concentrated hydrochloric acid is 12 M, meaning that there are 12 moles of hydrogen chloride per liter of water solution. Other useful units of concentrations are molality, or the number of moles of solute per kilogram of solvent; mole fraction, which is the ratio of the numbers of moles of solute and solution; and normality, which is the number of chemical equivalents per liter of solution.

When very small amounts of a substance are present, parts per million or parts per billion may be used. A sample of tap water may contain 35 parts per million of dissolved solids. The concentration of a radioactive gas such as radon in air can be reported in picocuries per liter, or the amount of radioactivity per unit volume of air. For homes that are tested for the presence of radon, the safe limit is about 4 picocuries per liter. Exposure levels of dust or vapors in air may be given in units of mass of substance per volume of air. The maximum acceptable level for human exposure to ammonia vapor, for example, is 94.5 oz (27 mg) per cubic meter of air for short term exposure, that is, during a 15–minute period. Because modern analytical instruments require only small samples, results are often reported in milligrams per milliliter or nanograms per milliliter. Clinical laboratory reports of substances in blood or urine may be reported as milligrams per deciliter.

Concentration also refers to the process of removing solvent from a solution to increase the proportion of solute. The Dead Sea becomes more concentrated in salts as water evaporates from the surface. Ores are produced by the concentration of valuable minerals, such as those containing gold or silver, in small region of the earth's crust.

See also Mole; Solution.

Conch see **Snails**

Concrete

Concrete, from the Latin word *concretus* meaning "having grown together", generally consists of Portland cement, water, and a relatively unreactive filler called aggregate. The filler is usually a conglomerate of gravel, sand, and blast–furnace stony matter known as slag.

Portland cement consists of finely pulverized matter produced by burning mixtures of lime, silica, alumina, and iron oxide at about 2,640° F (1450° C). Chemically, Portland cement is a mixture of calcium aluminum silicates, typically including tricalcium silicate ($3CaO \cdot SiO_2$), dicalcium silicate ($2CaO \cdot SiO_2$), and tricalcium aluminate ($3CaO \cdot Al_2O_3$); it may also contain tetracalcium aluminoferrate ($4CaO \cdot Al_2O_3 \cdot Fe_2O_3$). Small amounts of sulfur, potassium, sodium, and magnesia may also be present. The properties of the Portland cement may be varied by changing the relative proportions of the ingredients, and by grinding the cement to different degrees of fineness.

When Portland cement is mixed with water, the various ingredients begin to react chemically with the water. For a short time, the resultant mix can be poured or formed, but as the chemical reactions continue, the mix begins to stiffen, or set. Even after the mix has finished setting, it continues to combine chemically with the water, acquiring rigidity and strength. This process is called hardening.

Ordinarily, an excess of water is added to the concrete mix to decrease its viscosity so that it can be poured and shaped. When the chemical reactions have more or less finished taking place, the excess water, which is only held by secondary chemical bonds, either escapes, leaving behind voids, or remains trapped in tiny capillaries.

Concrete supports being cast in place for road construction in Phoenix, Arizona.

It is important to recognize that setting and hardening result from chemical reactions between the Portland cement and the water. They do not occur as the result of the mixture drying out. In the absence of water, the reactions stop. Likewise, hardening does not require air to take place, and will take place even under water.

The strength of concrete is determined by the extent to which the chemical reactions have taken place by the filler size and distribution, the void volume, and the amount of water used.

Concrete is usually much stronger in compression than in tension.

Concrete may be modified with plastic (polymeric) materials to improve its properties. Reinforced concrete is made by placing steel mesh or bars into the form or mold and pouring concrete around them. The steel adds strength.

Concrete is used in buildings, bridges, dams, aqueducts, and road construction. Concrete is also used as radiation shielding.

See also Bond energy.

Condensation see **Gases, properties of**

Condensed matter physics see **Physics**

Conditioning

Conditioning is a term used in psychology to refer to two specific types of associative learning as well as to the operant and classical conditioning procedures which produce that learning. Very generally, operant conditioning involves administering or withholding reinforcements based on the performance of a targeted response, and classical conditioning involves pairing a stimulus that naturally elicits a response with one that does not until the second stimulus elicits a response like the first. Both of these procedures enabled the scientific study of associative learning, or the forming of connections between two or more stimuli. The goal of conditioning research is to discover basic laws of learning and memory in animals and humans.

Historical roots

Theories of conditioning and learning have a number of historical roots within the philosophical doctrine of associationism. Associationism holds that simple associations between ideas are the basis of human thought and knowledge, and that complex ideas are combinations of these simple associations. Associationism can be traced as far back as Aristotle (384–322 B.C.), who proposed three factors—contrast, similarity, and contiguity, or nearness in space or time of occurrence—that determine if elements, things, or ideas will be associated together.

British associationist–empiricist philosophers of the 1700s and 1800s such as Locke, Hume, and Mills, held that the two most fundamental mental operations are association and sensation. As empiricists, they believed all knowledge is based on sensory experience, and complex mental processes such as language, or ideas such as truth, are combinations of directly experienced ideas. This school of thought differs from nativist views which generally stress inherited genetic influences on behavior and thought. According to these views, we are born with certain abilities or predispositions that actively shape or limit incoming sensory experience. For example, Plato (c. 427–347 B.C.) believed we are born with certain pre–formed ideas as did Rene Descartes (1596–1650). Many contemporary psychologists believe we are born with certain skill–based potentials and capacities such as those involved in language. In the 1880s the German psychologist Hermann Ebbinghaus brought this philosophical doctrine within the realm of scientific study by creating experimental methods for testing learning and memory that were based on associationistic theory. Associationist ideas are also at the root of behaviorism, a highly influential school of thought in psychology that was begun by John B. Watson in the 1910s. And conditioning experiments enabling the standardized investigation of associations formed, not between ideas, but between varying stimuli, and stimuli and responses, are also based on associationism.

Classical and operant conditioning

The systematic study of conditioning began with the Russian physiologist Ivan P. Pavlov. Working in the late 1800s, Pavlov developed the general procedures and terminology for studying classical conditioning wherein he could reliably and objectively study the conditioning of reflexes to various environmental stimuli.

Pavlov initially used a procedure wherein every few minutes a hungry dog was given dry meat powder that was consistently paired with a bell tone. The meat powder always elicited salivation, and after a few experimental trials the bell tone alone was able to elicit salivation. In Pavlov's terminology, the meat powder is

an unconditional stimulus because it reliably or unconditionally lead to salivation. The salivation caused by the meat powder is an unconditional response because it did not have to be trained or conditioned. The bell tone is a conditional stimulus because it was unable to elicit salivation until it had been conditioned to do so through repeated pairings with the unconditional stimulus. The salivation that eventually occurred to the conditional stimulus alone (the bell tone) is now called a conditional response. Conditional responses are distinctly different from unconditional responses even though they are superficially the same behavior. Conditioning is said to have occurred when the conditional stimulus will reliably elicit the conditional response, or when reflexive behaviors have come under the control of a novel stimulus.

In line with his physiological orientation, Pavlov interpreted his findings according to his hypotheses about brain functioning. He believed that organism responses are determined by the interaction of excitatory and inhibitory processes in the brain's cerebral hemispheres.

There are a number of different classical conditioning experimental designs. Besides varying the nature of the unconditional stimulus, many involve varying the timing of the presentation of the stimuli. Another type of experiment involves training a subject to respond to one conditional stimulus and not to any other stimuli. When this occurs it is called discrimination.

American psychologist Edward L. Thorndike developed the general procedures for studying operant conditioning (also referred to as instrumental conditioning) in the late 1800s. Thorndike's experimental procedure typically involved placing cats inside specially designed boxes from which they could escape and obtain food located outside only by performing a specific behavior such as pulling on a string. Thorndike timed how long it took individual cats to gain release from the box over a number of experimental trials and observed that the cats behaved aimlessly at first until they seemed to discover the correct response as if by accident. Over repeated trials the cats began to quickly and economically execute the correct response within just seconds. It seemed the initially random behaviors leading to release had become strengthened or reinforced by their positive consequences. It was also found that responses decreased and might eventually cease altogether when the food reward or reinforcement was no longer given. This is called extinction.

In the 1930s and 1940s, the American psychologist Burrhus F. Skinner modified Thorndike's procedures by, for instance, altering the box so that food could be delivered automatically. In this way the probability and rate of responding could be measured over long periods of time without needing to handle the animal. Initially, Skinner worked with rats but he eventually altered the box for use with pigeons.

In these procedures the response being conditioned, pressing the lever, is called the operant because it operates on the environment. The food reward or any consequence that strengthens a behavior is termed a reinforcer of conditioning. In operant conditioning theory, behaviors cease or are maintained by their consequences for the organism (Thorndike's "Law of Effect").

In most operant conditioning experiments, a small number of subjects are observed over a long period of time, and the dependent variable is the response rate in a given period of time. In traditional operant conditioning theory, physiological or biological factors are not used to explain behavior as they are in traditional classical conditioning theory.

Variations in operant conditioning experimental designs involve the nature of the reinforcement and the timing or scheduling of the reinforcers with respect to the targeted response. Reinforcement is a term used to refer to the procedure of removing or presenting negative or positive reinforcers to maintain or increase the likelihood of a response. Negative reinforcers are stimuli whose removal, when made contingent upon a response, will increase the likelihood of that response. Negative reinforcers then are unpleasant in some way, and they can range from uncomfortable physical sensations or interpersonal situations, to severe physical distress. Turning off one's alarm clock can be seen as a negative reinforcer for getting out of bed, assuming one finds the alarm unpleasant. Positive reinforcers are stimuli that increase the likelihood of a response when its presentation is made contingent upon that response. Giving someone pizza for achieving good grades is using pizza as a positive reinforcer for the desired behavior of achieving good grades (assuming the individual likes pizza). Punishment involves using aversive stimuli to decrease the occurrence of a response.

Reinforcement schedules are the timing and patterning of reinforcement presentation with respect to the response. Reinforcement may be scheduled in numerous ways, and because the schedule can affect the behavior as much as the reinforcement itself, much research has looked at how various schedules affect targeted behaviors. Ratio and interval schedules are two types of schedules that have been studied extensively. In ratio schedules, reinforcers are presented based on the number of responses made. In interval schedules, reinforcements are presented based on the length of time between reinforcements. Thus the first response to occur after a given time interval from the last reinforcement will be reinforced.

Conditioning and theory thrived from approximately the 1940s through the 1960s, and many psychologists viewed the learning theories based upon conditioning as one of psychology's most important contributions to the understanding of behavior. Psychologists created numerous variations on the basic experimental designs and adapted them for use with humans as well.

Comparison

Operant and classical conditioning have many similarities but there are important differences in the nature of the response and of the reinforcement. In operant conditioning, the reinforcer's presentation or withdrawal depends on performance of the targeted response, whereas in classical conditioning the reinforcement (the unconditional stimulus) occurs regardless of the organism's response. Moreover, whereas the reinforcement in classical conditioning strengthens the association between the conditional and unconditional stimulus, the reinforcement in operant conditioning strengthens the response it was made contingent upon. In terms of the responses studied, classical conditioning almost exclusively focuses on reflexive types of behavior that the organism does not have much control over, whereas operant conditioning focuses on non–reflexive behaviors that the organism does have control over.

Whether the theoretical underlying conditioning processes are the same is still an open question that may ultimately be unresolvable. Some experimental evidence supports an important distinction in how associations are formed in the two types of conditioning. Two–process learning theories are those that see classical and operant conditioning processes as fundamentally different.

Current research/Future developments

How findings from conditioning studies relate to learning is an important question. But first we must define learning. Psychologists use the term learning in a slightly different way than it is used in everyday language. For most psychologists, learning at its most general is evidenced by changes in behavior due to experience. In traditional theories of conditioning learning is seen in the strengthening of a conditional reflex, and the creation of a new association between a stimulus and a response. Yet more recent and complex conditioning

KEY TERMS

Associationism—A philosophical doctrine which holds that simple associations between ideas are the basis of all human thought and knowledge, and complex ideas are built upon combinations of the simple.

Behaviorism—A highly influential school of thought in psychology, it holds that observable behaviors are the only appropriate subject matter for psychological research.

Conditional—Term used in classical conditioning to describe responses that have been conditioned to elicit certain responses. It also describes the stimuli that elicit such responses

Classical conditioning—A procedure involving pairing a stimulus that naturally elicits a response with one that does not until the second stimulus elicits a response like the first.

Empiricism—A general philosophical position holding that all knowledge comes from experience, and that humans are not born with any ideas or concepts independent of personal experience.

Operant conditioning—A procedure involving administering or withholding reinforcements based on the performance of a targeted response.

Unconditional—Term used in classical conditioning to describe responses that are naturally or unconditionally elicited, they do not need to be conditioned. It also describes the stimuli that elicit such responses.

experiments indicate that conditioning involves more than the strengthening of stimulus–response connections or new reflexes. It seems conditioning may be more accurately described as a process through which the relationship between events or stimuli and the environment are learned about and behavior is then adjusted.

In addition, research comparing normal and retarded children, and older children and adults, suggests that people have language– or rule–based learning forms that are more efficient than associative learning, and these types of learning can easily override the conditioning process. In sum, conditioning and associative learning seem to explain only certain aspects of human learning, and are now seen as simply another type of learning task. So, while conditioning had a central place in American experimental psychology from approxi-

mately the 1940s through the 1960s, its theoretical importance for learning has diminished. On the other hand, practical applications of conditioning procedures and findings continue to grow.

See also Memory; Psychology; Reinforcement, positive and negative; Stimulus.

Further Reading:

Hearst, E. "Fundamentals of learning and conditioning." *Stevens' Handbook of Experimental Psychology, Volume 2*, 2nd Ed, eds. R.C. Atkinson, R.J. Herrnstein, G. Lindzey, and R. D. Luce. New York: John Wiley & Sons, 1988.

Mackintosh, N.J. "Classical and operant conditioning." In *Companion Encyclopedia of Psychology*, ed. A.W. Colman, 379–396. New York: Routledge, 1994.

Schwartz, B. *Psychology of Learning and Behavior*, 3rd ed. New York: W.W. Norton & Co., Inc., 1988.

Marie Doorey

Condom see **Contraception**

Condors

Condors are New World vultures that are among the largest of flying birds. There are only two species, the Andean condor (*Vultur gryphus*) and the almost extinct California condor (*Gymnogyps californianus*). They are related to the king vulture (*Sarcoramphus papa*) and turkey vulture (*Cathartes aura*), which also belong to family Cathartidae. In the same family as the condors, but long extinct, was the largest flying bird that ever lived. *Teratornis incredibilis* was a vulture found in Nevada that had a wingspan of at least 16 ft (4.9 m).

The combined head and body length of the living condors is about 50 in (127 cm). Each species weighs 20–25 lb (9–11.4 kg). They have black or dark brown plumage with white patches on the wings. The California condor has a wing span of 9 ft (2.7 m), while the Andean condor's wing span is 10 ft (3.1 m). Both species have a ruff of feathers around the neck, black on the California condor and a startling white on the Andean. Both condors have bald heads with short, sharply hooked beaks. The Andean condor's naked skin is red, while the California condor's is pinkish orange. The Andean male has an extra fleshy growth, rather like a rooster's comb, on top of its head. The California condor does not have this growth.

A California condor.

The Andean condor's range extends throughout the Andean Mountains, and much of this habitat remains wild. It can fly over the highest peaks, but it may also land on a low–lying field to scavenge for baby animals. This species still exists in large numbers.

The California condor, however, is one of the most seriously endangered animals on Earth. Historically, the range of this species extended over much of North America. At one time, these birds foraged for large Ice Age mammals, but the condors began to decline at the same time that these large mammals became extinct. By the time of European settlement, the California condor's range was restricted to the western coast and mountains. As human populations in the region grew, the condor population declined. By the 1950s its range was restricted to an area of central California surrounding the southern end of the San Joaquin valley. In recent decades, condor habitat has been disrupted by oil drilling, planting of citrus groves, and real estate developments. Rangeland, where dead cattle might have been available, has been converted to fields of alfalfa and other crops.

Habitat destruction is not the only threat to the survival of the California condor. Hunting and lead poisoning suffered by condors who ingest lead shot in carrion as well as DDT and other pesticides and poisons have also negatively affected this species. The condor's own life cycle also adds to the precariousness of its position. It takes six years for a California condor to attain sexual maturity. Then it lays only a single egg. If the egg does hatch, it takes the young condor 18 months to develop wings for flight. During that time, the chick remains vulnerable. The farther the parents have to fly to hunt for food, the longer the chick is exposed to cold or hunger, and the less likely it is to survive.

Return to the wild

It became obvious as much as 50 years ago that California condors were in danger of extinction. But the debate over what actions to take continued for decades. In 1978, there were about 30 birds left in the wild. Seven years later, the number was down to nine. At that time, all wild condors were captured and taken to the San Diego Zoo, where several other condors were already in residence. The zoo began a captive breeding program for the California condor. By 1992, 52 condors were living in captivity, and scientists felt the time had come to release some of these birds back into the wild.

In order to test the theories about how best to return condors to the wild, several Andean condors were brought to the United States and released in a national forest. It quickly became apparent that there were too many human artifacts and activities in the area for the birds to be reintroduced successfully. They would have to be taken farther from civilization. First two, then more, California condors were released at Sespe Condor Sanctuary. When several birds were poisoned by bullets in the carrion they ate, it became clear that the reintroduced birds would have to be provided with safe food until their numbers increased. Additional birds will be released, probably on an annual basis, with the goal of establishing two separate populations of at least 150 birds each. Although the California condor has received a temporary reprieve from extinction, its future survival depends on continued intensive management efforts and the conservation of sufficient habitat to sustain a viable breeding population.

See also Vultures.

Further Reading:

Caras, Roger A. *Source of the Thunder: The Biography of a California Condor.* Lincoln, NE: University of Nebraska Press, 1991.
Peters, Westberg. *Condor.* New York: Crestwood House, 1990.

Jean F. Blashfield

Conenose see **True bugs**

Cones see **Eye; Vision**

Congenital

The term congenital is used to describe a condition or defect that exists at birth. Congenital disorders are inborn. They are present in the developing fetus. Sickle cell disease, Down's syndrome, and congenital rubella syndrome are three examples of congenital conditions in humans. Congenital disorders result from abnormalities in the fetus's genetic inheritance, conditions in the fetal environment, or a combination of the two. Two to three percent of babies in the United States are born with a major congenital defect. Prenatal testing can detect some congenital conditions.

Many congenital conditions are caused by chromosomal disorders. A human fetus inherits 23 chromosomes from its mother and 23 chromosomes from its father, making a total of 23 pairs. An extra chromosome or a missing chromosome creates havoc in fetal development. Down's syndrome, marked by mental retardation and a distinctive physical appearance, is caused by an extra chromosome.

Each chromosome carries many genes. Like chromosomes, genes are present in pairs. Genes are responsible for many inherited traits, including eye color and blood type. Genetic disorders are caused by abnormal genes. Sickle cell disease, a blood disorder, occurs when a fetus inherits an abnormal gene from each parent. Polydactyly, the presence of extra fingers or toes, occurs when an abnormal gene is inherited from one parent.

Some congenital disorders are caused by environmental factors. It may be that certain genetic combinations leave some fetuses more vulnerable to the absence or presence of certain nutrients or chemicals. Spina bifida, also known as "open spine," occurs when embryo development goes awry and part of the neural tube fails to close. Adequate amounts of folic acid, a vitamin, help prevent spina bifida. Cleft palate, a hole in the roof of the mouth, is another congenital defect that seems to be caused by multiple factors. Congenital rubella syndrome, marked by mental retardation and deafness, is present in newborns whose mothers contracted rubella (German measles) during pregnancy.

Prenatal testing can diagnose certain congenital disorders. Ultrasound, which uses sound waves to produce an image of the fetus, can discover some defects of the heart and other organs. Amniocentesis and chorionic villi sampling are procedures that remove fetal cells from the pregnant uterus for genetic testing. These tests can determine the presence of Down's syndrome, sickle cell anemia, cystic fibrosis, and other genetic diseases. Couples may choose to terminate the pregnancy if serious abnormalities are discovered.

See also Birth; Birth defects; Embryo and embryonic development.

Further Reading:

Davis, Joel. *Mapping the Code.* New York: John Wiley & Sons, 1990.

Edelson, Edward. *Birth Defects.* New York: Chelsea House Publishers, 1992.

Marshall, Liz. *The Human Genome Project: Cracking the Code Within Us.* Brookfield, CT: Millbrook Press, 1995.

Planning for Pregnancy, Birth, and Beyond, Washington, D.C.: American College of Obstetricians and Gynecologists, 1990.

Wills, Christopher. *Exons, Introns, and Talking Genes,* New York: Basic Books, 1991.

Congruence (triangle)

Two triangles are congruent if they are alike in every geometric respect except, perhaps, one. That one possible exception is in the triangle's "handedness."

There are only six parts of a triangle that can be seen and measured: the three angles and the three sides. The six features of a triangle are all involved with congruence. If triangle ABC is congruent to triangle DEF, then

$$\angle A = \angle D \qquad AB = DE$$
$$\angle B = \angle E \qquad BC = EF$$
$$\angle C = \angle F \qquad CA = FD$$

(The symbol for "is congruent to" is "≅.") Thus triangles ABC and DEF in Figure 1 are (or appear to be) congruent.

The failure of congruence to include handedness usually doesn't matter. If triangle DEF were a mirror, however, it would not fit into a frame in the shape of triangle ABC.

The term *congruent* comes from the Latin word *congruere*, meaning "to come together." It therefore carries with it the idea of superposition, the idea that one of two congruent figures can be picked up and

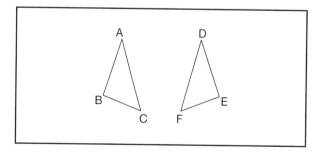

Figure 1.

placed on top of the other with all parts coinciding. In the case of congruent triangles the parts would be the three sides and the three angles.

Some authors prefer the word "equal" instead of "congruent." Congruence is usually thought of as a relation between two geometric figures. In most practical applications, however, it is not the congruence of two triangles that matters, but the congruence of the triangle with itself at two different times.

There is a remarkably simple proof, for instance, that the base angles of an isosceles triangle are equal, but it depends on setting up a correspondence of a triangle ABC with the triangle ACB, which is, of course, the same triangle.

Two triangles are congruent if two sides and the included angle of one are congruent to two sides and the included angle of the other. This can be proven by superimposing one triangle on the other. They have to match. Therefore the third side and the two other angles have to match. Modern authors typically make no attempt to prove it, taking it as a postulate instead.

Whatever its status in the logical structure, side–angle–side congruence (abbreviated S.A.S) is a very useful geometric property. The compass with which one draws circles works because it has legs of a fixed length and a tight joint between them. In each of the positions the compass takes, the spacing between the legs—the third side of the triangles—is unchanging. Common shelf brackets support the shelf with two stiff legs and a reinforced corner joining them. A builder frames a door with measured lengths of wood and a carpenter's square to make the included angle a right angle. In all these instances, the third side of the triangle is missing, but that doesn't matter. The information

is sufficient to guarantee the length of the missing side and the proper shape of the entire triangle.

Two triangles are congruent if two angles and the included side of one are congruent respectively to two angles and the included side of the other. This is known as angle–side–angle (A.S.A.) congruence, and is usually proved as a consequence of S.A.S. congruence.

This is also a very useful property. The range finders, for example, which photographers, golfers, artillery observers, and others use are based on A.S.A. congruence. In Figure 2, the user sights the target C along line AC, and simultaneously adjusts angle B so that C comes into view along CB (small mirrors at B and at A direct the ray CB along BA and thence into the observer's eye). The angle CAB is fixed; the distance AB is fixed; and the angle CAB, although adjustable, is measurable. By A.S.A. congruence there is enough information to determine the shape of the triangle.

Although A.S.A. congruence calls for an included side, the side can be an adjacent side as well. Since the sum of the angles of a triangle is always a straight angle, if any two of the angles are given, then the third angle is determined. The correspondence has to be kept straight, however. The equal sides cannot be an included side in one triangle and an adjacent side in the other or adjacent sides of angles which are not the equal angles.

Two triangles are congruent if its three sides of one triangle are equal, respectively, to the three sides of the other triangle . This is known as side–side–side (S.S.S.) congruence.

This is probably the most widely exploited case of congruence. a folding ladder is kept steady by a locking brace. It is only the lengths of the three sides AB, AC, and AB (see Figure 3), that are fixed. The angles at A,

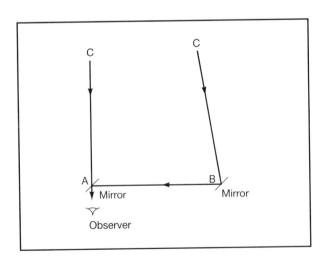

Figure 2.

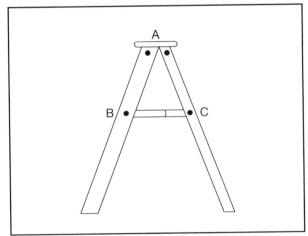

Figure 3.

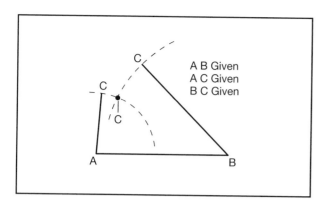

Figure 4.

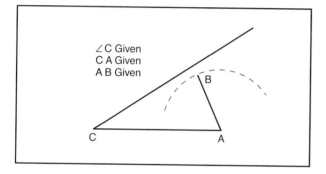

Figure 5.

B, and C are free to vary, and do so when the brace is unlocked and the ladder folded.

The draftsman can replicate a triangle easily and accurately with only a T–square, compass, and scale. Figure 4 shows the technique which he or she would use. A contractor, with nothing more than a tape, some pegs, and some string, can lay out a rectangular foundation.

One set of criteria for congruence that can be used with caution is side–side–angle congruence. Figure 5 illustrates this. Here the lengths AB and AC are given. So is the size of angle C, which is not an included angle. With AB given, the vertex B can lie anywhere on a circle with center at A. If the second side of angle C misses the circle, no triangle meeting the specifications is possible. If it is tangent to the circle, one triangle is possible; if it cuts the circle, two are. This type of congruence comes into play when using the law of sines

$$\frac{\text{sine of angle B}}{\text{side opposite B}} \qquad \frac{\text{sine of angle C}}{\text{side opposite C}}$$

to find an unknown angle, say angle B, by solving for sin B. If sin B is greater than 1, no such angle exists.

If it equals 1, then B is a right angle. If it is less than 1, then sin B = sin (180 – B) gives two solutions.

Further Reading:
Birkoff, George David, and Beatley, Ralph. *Basic Geometry.* New York: Chelsea Publishing Co. 1959.
Coxeter, H. S. M. and Greitzer, S. L. *Geometry Revisited.* Washington, D. C.: The Mathematical Association of America, 1967.
Euclid. *Elements.* translated by Heath, Sir Thomas L. New York: Dover Publications, 1956.
Hilbert, D. and Cohn–Vossen, S. *Geometry and the Imagination.* New York: Chelsea Publishing Co. 1952.
Moise, Edwin E. *Elementary Geometry from an Advanced Standpoint.* Reading, Massachusetts: Addison–Wesley Publishing Co., 1963.

J. Paul Moulton

Conic sections

A conic section is the plane curve formed by the intersection of a plane and a right–circular, two–napped cone. Such a cone is shown in Figure 1.

The cone is the surface formed by all the lines passing through a circle and a point. The point must lie on a line, called the "axis," which is perpendicular to the plane of the circle at the circle's center. The point is called the "vertex," and each line on the cone is called a "generatrix." The two parts of the cone lying on either side of the vertex are called "nappes."

When the intersecting plane is perpendicular to the axis, the conic section is a circle (Figure 2).

When the intersecting plane is tilted and cuts completely across one of the nappes, the section is an oval called an ellipse (Figure 3).

When the intersecting plane is parallel to one of the generatrices, it cuts only one nappe. The section is an open curve called a parabola (Figure 4).

When the intersecting plane cuts both nappes, the section is a hyperbola, a curve with two parts, called "branches" (Figure 5).

All these sections are curved. If the intersecting plane passes through the vertex, however, the section will be a single point, a single line, of a pair of crossed lines. Such sections are of minor importance and are known as "degenerate" conic sections.

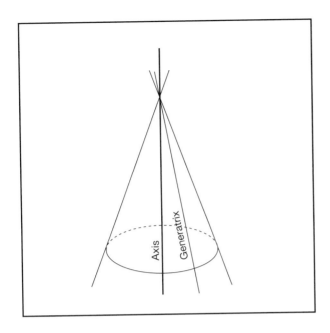

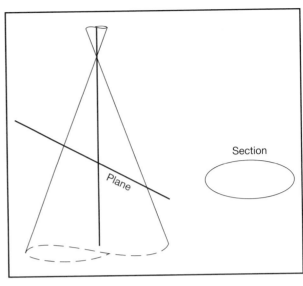

Figure 3.

Figure 1.

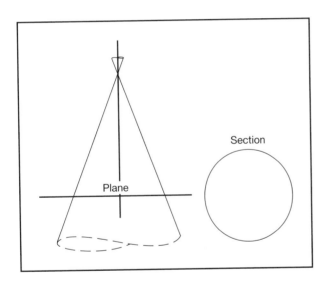

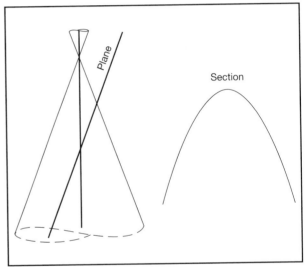

Figure 4.

Figure 2.

Since ancient times, mathematicians have known that conic sections can be defined in ways that have no obvious connection with conic sections. One set of ways is the following:

Ellipse: The set of points P such that $PF_1 + PF_2$ equals a constant and F_1 and F_2 are fixed points called the "foci" (Figure 6).

Parabola: The set of points P such that PD = PF, where F is a fixed point called the "focus" and D is the foot of the perpendicular from P to a fixed line called the "directrix" (Figure 7).

Hyperbola: The set of points P such that $PF_1 - PF_2$ equals a constant and F_1 and F_2 are fixed points called the "foci" (Figure 8).

If P, F, and D are shown as in Figure 7, then the set of points P satisfying the equation PF/PD = e where e is a constant, is a conic section. If $0 < e < 1$, then the section is an ellipse. If e = 1, then the section is a parabola. If e > 1, then the section is a hyperbola. The constant e is called the "eccentricity" of the conic section.

Because the ratio PF/PD is not changed by a change in the scale used to measure PF and PD, all conic sections having the same eccentricity are geometrically similar.

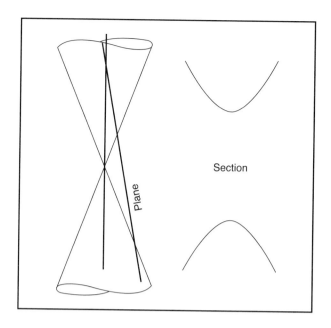

Figure 5.

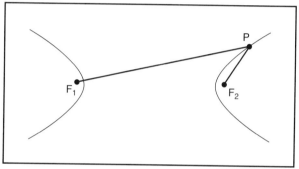

Figure 7.

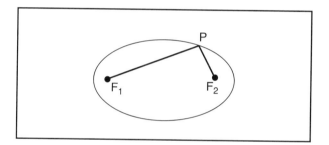

Figure 6.

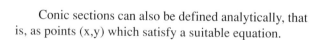

Figure 8.

Conic sections can also be defined analytically, that is, as points (x,y) which satisfy a suitable equation.

An interesting way to accomplish this is to start with a suitably placed cone in coordinate space. A cone with its vertex at the origin and with its axis coinciding with the z–axis has the equation $x^2 + y^2 - kz^2 = 0$. The equation of a plane in space is $ax + by + cz + d = 0$. If one uses substitution to eliminate z from these equations, and combines like terms, the result is an equation of the form $Ax^2 + Bxy + Cy^2 + Dx + Ey + F = 0$ where at least one of the coefficients A, B, and C will be different from zero.

For example if the cone $x^2 + y^2 - z^2 = 0$ is cut by the plane $y + z - 2 = 0$, the points common to both must satisfy the equation $x^2 + 4y - 4 = 0$, which can be simplified by a translation of axes to $x^2 + 4y = 0$. Because, in this example, the plane is parallel to one of the generatrices of the cone, the section is a parabola (see Figure 9).

One can follow this procedure with other intersecting planes. The plane $z - 5 = 0$ produces the circle $x^2 + y^2 - 25 = 0$. The planes $y + 2z - 2 = 0$ and $2y + z - 2 = 0$ produce the ellipse $12x^2 + 9y^2 - 16 = 0$ and the hyperbola $3x^2 - 9y^2 + 4 = 0$ respectively (after a simplifying translation of the axes). These planes, looking down the x–axis are shown in figure 10.

As these examples illustrate, suitably placed conic sections have equations which can be put into the following forms:

Circle: $x^2 + y^2 = r^2$

Ellipse: $A^2x^2 + B^2y^2 = C^2$

Parabola: $y = Kx^2$

Hyperbola: $A^2x^2 - B^2y^2 = +C^2$

The equations above are "suitably placed." When the equation is not in one of the forms above, it can be hard to tell exactly what kind of conic section the equation represents. There is a simple test, however, which can do this. With the equation written $Ax^2 + Bxy + Cy^2$

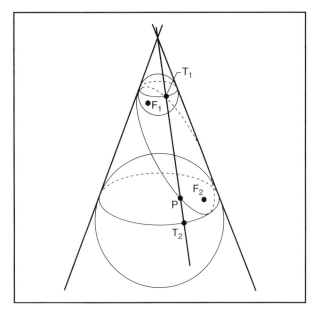

Figure 9.

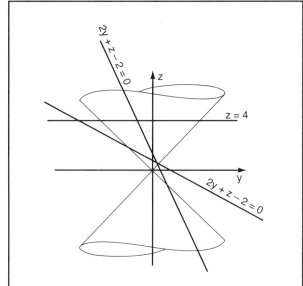

Figure 11.

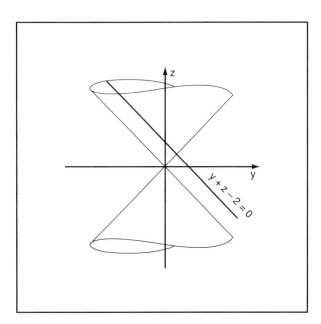

Figure 10.

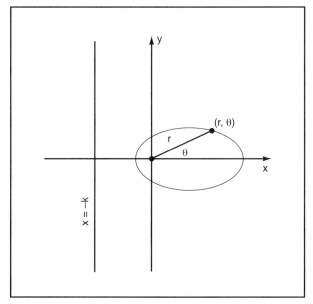

Figure 12.

$+ Dx + Ey + F = 0$, the discriminant $B^2 - 4AC$ will identify which conic section it is. If the discriminant is positive, the section is a hyperbola; if it is negative, the section is an ellipse; if it is zero, the section is a parabola. The discriminant will not distinguish between a proper conic section and a degenerate one such as $x^2 - y^2 = 0$; it will not distinguish between an equation that has real roots and one, such as $x^2 + y^2 + 1 = 0$, that does not.

Students who are familiar with the quadratic formula

$$x = \frac{-b \pm \sqrt{b^2 - 4ac}}{2a}$$

will recognize the discriminant, and with good reason. It has to do with finding the points where the conic section crosses the line at infinity. If the discriminant is negative, there will be no solution, which is consistent with the fact that both circles and ellipses lie entirely within the finite part of the plane. Parabolas lead to a single root and are tangent to the line at infinity. Hyperbolas lead to two roots and cross it in two places.

Conic sections can also be described with polar coordinates. To do this most easily, one uses the focus–directrix definitions, placing the focus at the origin and the directrix at $x = -k$ (in rectangular coordinates). Then the polar equation is $r = Ke/(1 - e \cos \theta)$ where e is the eccentricity (Figure 11).

The eccentricity in this equation is numerically equal to the eccentricity given by another ratio: the ratio CF/CV, where CF represents the distance from the geometric center of the conic section to the focus and CV the distance from the center to the vertex. In the case of a circle, the center and the foci are one and the same point; so CF and the eccentricity are both zero. In the case of the ellipse, the vertices are end points of the major axis, hence are farther from the center than the foci. CV is therefore bigger than CF, and the eccentricity is less than 1. In the case of the hyperbola, the vertices lie on the transverse axis, between the foci, hence the eccentricity is greater than 1. In the case of the parabola, the "center" is infinitely far from both the focus and the vertex; so (for those who have a good imagination) the ratio CF/CV is 1.

Further Reading:

Eves, Howard. *An Introduction to the History of Mathematics.* New York: Holt, Rinehart and Winston, 1976

Finney, Ross L., et al. *Calculus: Graphical, Numerical, Algebraic of a Single Variable.* Reading, Mass.: Addison Wesley Publishing Co., 1994

Hilbert, D. and Cohn–Vossen, S. *Geometry and the Imagination.* New York: Chelsea Publishing Co., 1952

Kazarinoff, Nicholas D. *Geometric Inequalities.* Washington, D.C.: The Mathematical Association of America, 1961

Zwikker, C. *The Advanced Geometry of Plane Curves and Their Applications.* New York: Dover Publications, Inc., 1963

J. Paul Moulton

Conies see **Lagomorphs**

Conifer

Conifer (common name for phylum Pinophyta) is a type of tree that thrives in temperate and boreal climates. Characterized by seed–bearing cones, conifers typically have narrow, needle–like leaves covered with a waxy cuticle, and straight trunks with horizontal branches. These trees are usually evergreen, meaning they do not shed their leaves all at once, and can photosynthesize continually. There are two orders of conifer, Pinales and Taxales.

There are two major seed–producing plants: gymnosperms (meaning naked seed) and angiosperms (meaning enclosed seed). These two groups get their names from their female reproductive characteristics: the gymnosperms have egg cells or seeds on the scales of the cone, while the angiosperm seeds are enclosed within ovaries, which, if fertilized, eventually turn into fruit. Conifers are one of the three groups of gymnosperms, which also include the cycads (tropical plants with palm-like leaves) and a group consisting of four plants having both gymnosperm and angiosperm features.

The female cones and male cones grow separately on the same tree. The female cones are larger and grow on the upper branches, while the male cones tend to grow on the lower branches. Both female and male cones have a central shaft with scales or leaflike projections called sporophylls that are specially shaped to bear sporangia (a reproductive unit). Each female sporophyll has an area where two ovules (each containing a group of fertile eggs) develop within a protective tissue called the nucellus. Male sporangia contain thousands of microspores, which divide (through meiosis) into more microspores, which eventually turn into grains of yellow pollen. The dispersal of pollen is dependent on air currents, and with dry, windy conditions, a grain of pollen can travel miles from where it was released. The pollen enters the female cone through an opening in the nucellus and sticks to the ovule. After fertilization, a little conifer seedling, complete with a root, develops within a seed coat. The seed is still attached to the scale of the cone, which, when caught by the wind, acts as a wing to carry the seed.

Some conifers can be shrublike while others grow very tall, like the giant sequoia (*Sequoia sempervirens*). Through fossils, it has been learned that conifers have existed since the Carboniferous Period, some 300 million years ago. Most species no longer exist. Currently there are approximately 550 known species. In North America, firs (*Abies*), larches (*Larix*), spruces (*Picea*), pines (*Pinus*), hemlocks (*Tsuga*), and junipers (*Juniperus*) are most common in mountain ranges of the Pacific Northwest and the Rocky Mountains. Conifers also extend through the northern regions of the United States and Canada, as well as into mountain ranges closer to the tropics. Some pine species grow in lowland areas of the southeastern United States.

Conifers are an important renewable resource; they provide the majority of wood for building as well as pulp for paper. Resins, oleoresins, and gums are important materials for the chemical industry for products such as soaps, hard resins, varnishes, and turpentine.

See also Firs; Gymnosperm; Juniper; Pines; Sequoia; Spruce; Yew.

Further Reading:
Wilkins, Malcolm. *Plantwatching*. New York: Facts On File, 1988.

Christine Miner Minderovic

Conjuntiva see **Eye**

Connective tissue

Connective tissue is found throughout the body and includes fat, cartilage, bone and blood. The main functions of the different types of connective tissue include providing support, filling in spaces between organs, protecting organs and aiding in the transport of materials around the body.

General structure of connective tissue

Connective tissue is composed of living cells and protein fibers suspended in a gel–like material called matrix. Depending on the type of connective tissue, the fibers are either collagen fibers, reticular fibers, or

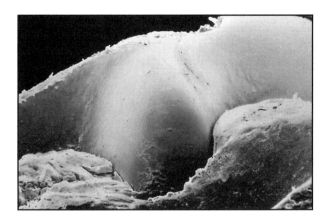

A scanning electron micrograph (SEM) of hyaline articular cartilage covering the end of a long bone. The smooth, slippery surface of the cartilage enables movement of the joint.

elastin fibers or a combination of two or more types. The type and arrangement of the fibers gives each type of connective tissue its particular properties.

Overview of connective tissue matrix

Of the three types of protein fibers in connective tissue collagen is by far the most abundant, and accounts for almost one third of the total body weight of humans. Under the microscope, collagen looks like a rope, with three individual protein fibers twined around each other. Collagen is extremely strong, but has little flexibility. Reticular fibers are composed of very small collagen fibers, but are shorter than collagen fibers, and they form a net–like supporting structure that gives shape to various organs. Elastin fibers have elastic properties and can stretch and be compressed, importing flexibility in the connective tissues where it is found.

Types of connective tissue

Two main types of fibrous connective tissue are found in the body: dense and loose. In dense connective tissue, almost all the space between the cells is filled by large numbers of protein fibers. In loose connective tissue, there are fewer fibers between the cells which imparts a more open, loose structure.

Dense connective tissue contains large numbers of collagen fibers, and so it is exceptionally tough. Dense regular connective tissue has parallel bundles of collagen fibers and forms tendons that attach muscles to bone and ligaments that bind bone to bone. Dense irregular connective tissue, with less orderly arranged collagen fibers, forms the tough lower layer of the skin known as the dermis, and encapsulates delicate organs such as the kidneys and the spleen.

Loose connective tissue has fewer collagen fibers than dense connective tissue, and therefore is not as tough. Loose connective tissue (also known as areolar connective tissue) is widely distributed throughout the body and provides the loose packing material between glands, muscles, and nerves.

Two other connective tissues with fibers are adipose tissue and reticular tissue. Adipose tissue is composed of specialized fat cells and has few fibers: this tissue functions as an insulator, a protector of delicate organs and as a site of energy storage. Reticular connective tissue is composed mostly of reticular fibers that form a net–like web, which forms the internal framework of organs like the liver, lymph nodes, and bone marrow.

Connective tissue composed of ground substance and protein fibers

Connective tissue composed of ground substance and protein fibers differs from fibrous connective tissue in that it contains more ground substance. Two main types of this kind of connective tissue are found in the body: cartilage and bone.

Cartilage is composed of cartilage cells, and collagen fibers or a combination of collagen and elastin fibers. An interesting characteristic of cartilage is that when it is compressed it immediately springs back into shape.

Hyaline cartilage is rigid yet flexible, due to evenly–spaced collagen fibers. Hyaline cartilage is found at the ends of the ribs, around the trachea (windpipe), and at the ends of long bones that form joints. Hyaline cartilage forms the entire skeleton of the embryo, which is gradually replaced by bone as the newborn grows.

Fibrocartilage contains densely–packed regularly arranged collagen fibers which impact great strength to this connective tissue. Fibrocartilage is found between the bones of the vertebrae as discs that act as a cushion.

Elastic cartilage contains elastin fibers and is thus more flexible that either hyaline cartilage or fibrocartilage. Elastic cartilage is found in the pinnas of the external ear.

Bone is composed of bone cells (osteocytes), suspended in a matrix consisting of collagen fibers and minerals. The mineral portion imparts great strength and rigidity to bone. Osteocytes are located in depressions called lacunae connected by canals called Haversian canals.

Two types of bone form the mammalian skeleton: cancellous bone and compact bone. Cancellous bone is more lattice–like than compact bone, and does not contain as many collagen fibers in its matrix. Cancellous bone is light–weight, yet strong, and is found in the skull, the sternum and ribs, the pelvis and the growing ends of the long bones. Compact bone is densely packed with fibers, and forms the outer shell of all bones and the shafts of the long bones of the arms and legs. Compact bone is heavier than cancellous bone, and provides great strength and support.

Mostly fluid connective tissue

Blood is a liquid connective tissue composed of a fluid matrix and blood cells. The blood cells include white blood cells, which function in the immune system, and red blood cells, which transport oxygen and carbon dioxide. The fluid part of the blood (the plasma) transports hormones, nutrients, and waste products, and plays a role in temperature regulation.

See also Blood; Collagen; Skeletal system.

Further Reading:

Brittberg, Mats, et. al. "Treatment of Deep Cartilage Defects in the Knee with Autologous Chondrocyte Transplantation." *New England Journal of Medicine* 331 (October 1994).

Couzens, Gerald Seor, and Paula Derrow. "Weak in the Knees: New Ways to Protect—and Prevent—this Fragile Joint." *American Health* 12 (June 1993): 70.

Gagliardi, Nancy. "The New Way to Fight Fat." *McCall's* 120 (June 1993): 56.

Larkin, Marilynn. "Coping with Connective Tissue Diseases." *FDA Consumer* 26 (November 1992): 28.

Urry, Dan W. "Elastic Biomolecular Machines: Synthetic Chains of Amino Acids, Patterned After Those in Connective Tissue, Can Transform Heat and Chemical Energy Into Motion." *Scientific American* 272 (January 1995): 64.

Kathleen Scogna

Conservation laws

Conservation laws refer to physical quantities that remain constant throughout the multitude of processes which occur in nature. If these physical quantities are carefully measured, and if all known sources are taken into account, they will always yield the same result. The validity of the conservation laws is tested through experiments. However, many of the conservation laws are suggested from theoretical considerations. The conservation laws include: the conservation of linear momentum, the conservation of angular momentum, the conservation of energy and mass, and the conservation of electric charge. In addition, there are many conservation laws that deal with subatomic particles, that is, particles that are smaller than the atom.

Conservation of linear momentum

A rocket ship taking off, the recoil of a rifle, and a bank–shot in a pool are examples which demonstrate the conservation of linear momentum. Linear momentum is defined as the product of an object's mass and its velocity. For example, the linear momentum of a 100 kilogram (220 lb) football–linebacker traveling at a speed of 10 miles (16 km) per hour is exactly the same as the momentum of a 50 kilogram (110 lb) sprinter traveling at 20 miles (32 km) per hour. Since the velocity is both the speed and direction of an object, the linear momentum is also specified by a certain direction.

The linear momentum of one or more objects is conserved when there are no external forces acting on those objects. For example, consider a rocket–ship in deep outer space where the force of gravity is negligible. Linear momentum will be conserved since the external force of gravity is absent. If the rocket–ship is initially at rest, its momentum is zero since its speed is zero (Fig . 1a). If the rocket engines are suddenly fired, the rocket–ship will be propelled forward (Fig. 1b). For linear momentum to be conserved, the final momentum must be equal to the initial momentum, which is zero. Linear momentum is conserved if one takes into account the burnt fuel which is ejected out the back of the rocket. The positive momentum of the rocket–ship going forward is equal to the negative momentum of the fuel going backward (Note that the direction of motion is used to define positive and negative). Adding these two quantities yields zero. It is important to realize that the rocket's propulsion is not achieved by the fuel pushing on anything. In outer space there is nothing to push on! Propulsion is achieved by the conservation of linear momentum. An easy way to demonstrate this type of propulsion is by propelling yourself on a frozen pond. Since there is little friction between your ice skates and the ice, linear momentum is conserved. Throwing an object in one direction will cause you to travel in the opposite direction.

Even in cases where the external forces are significant, the concept of conservation of linear momentum can be applied to a limited extent. An instance would be the momentum of objects which are affected by the

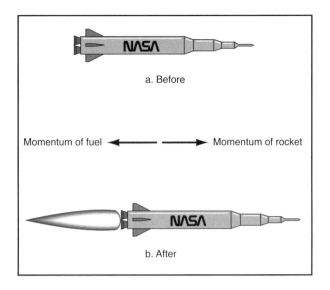

a. Before

Momentum of fuel ⟵   ⟶ Momentum of rocket

b. After

Figure 1.

external force of gravity. For example, a bullet is fired at a clay pigeon that has been launched into the air. The linear momentum of the bullet and clay pigeon at the instant just before impact (Fig. 2a) is equal to the linear momentum of the bullet and hundreds of shattered clay pieces at the instant just after impact (Fig. 2b). Linear momentum is conserved just before, during, and just after the collision. The reason this is true is because the external force of gravity does not significantly affect the momentum of the objects within this narrow time period. Many seconds later, however, gravity will have had a significant influence and the total momentum of the objects will not be the same as just before the collision.

There are many examples that illustrate the conservation of linear momentum. When we walk down the road, our momentum traveling forward is equal to the momentum of the Earth traveling backward. Of course, the mass of the Earth is so large compared to us that its velocity will be negligible. (A simple calculation using the 100 kilogram linebacker shows that as he travels forward at 10 miles per hour. The Earth travels backward at a speed of 9 trillionths of an inch per century!) A better illustration is to walk forward in a row–boat and you will notice that the boat travels backward relative to the water. When a rifle is fired, the recoil you feel against your shoulder is due to the momentum of the rifle which is equal but in the opposite direction to the momentum of the bullet. Again, since the rifle is so much heavier than the bullet, its velocity will be correspondingly less than the bullet's. Conservation of linear momentum is the chief reason that heavier cars are safer than lighter cars. In a head on collision with two cars traveling at the same speed, the motion of the two cars

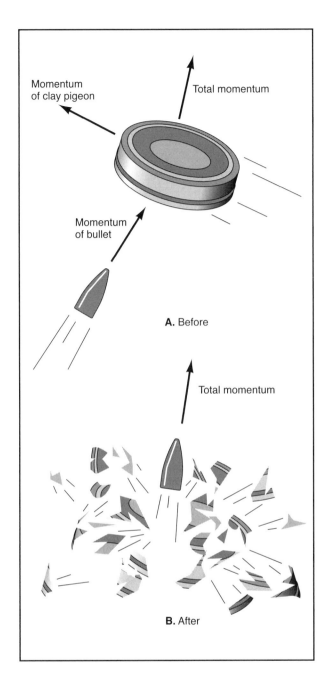

Momentum of clay pigeon

Total momentum

Momentum of bullet

A. Before

Total momentum

B. After

Figure 2.

Conservation of angular momentum

Just as there is the conservation of motion for objects traveling in straight lines, there is also a conservation of motion for objects traveling along curved paths. This conservation of rotational motion is known as the conservation of angular momentum. An example is shown in Figure 3 of an object which is traveling at a constant speed in a circle (compare this to a race car on a circular track). The angular momentum for this object is defined as the product of the object's mass, its velocity, and the radius of the circle. For example, a 1000 kilogram car traveling at 30 miles per hour on a 2 mile radius track, a 2000 kilogram truck traveling at 30 miles per hour on a 1 mile radius track, and a 1000 kilogram car traveling at 60 miles per hour on a 1 mile radius track will all have the same value of angular momentum. In addition, objects which are spinning, such as a top or an ice skater, have angular momentum which is defined by their mass, their shape, and the velocity at which they spin.

In the absence of external forces that tend to change an object's rotation, the angular momentum will be conserved. Close to Earth, gravity is uniform and will not tend to alter an object's rotation. Consequently, many instances of angular momentum conservation can be seen every day. When an ice skater goes from a slow spin with her arms stretched into a fast spin with her arms at her sides, we are witnessing the conservation of angular momentum. With arms stretched, the radius of the rotation circle is large and the rotation speed is small. With arms at her side, the radius of the rotation circle is now small and the speed must increase to keep the angular momentum constant.

An additional consequence of the conservation of angular momentum is that the rotation axis of a spinning object will tend to keep a constant orientation. For example, a spinning Frisbee thrown horizontally will tend to keep its horizontal orientation even if tapped from below. To test this, try throwing a Frisbee without spin and see how unstable it is. A spinning top remains vertical as long as it keeps spinning fast enough. The earth itself maintains a constant orientation of its spin axis due to the conservation of angular momentum.

As is the case for linear momentum, there has never been a violation of the law of conservation of angular momentum. This applies to all objects, large and small. In accordance with the Bohr model of subatomic particles, the electrons that surround the nucleus of the atom are found to possess angular momentum of only certain discrete values. Intermediate values are not found. Even with these constraints, the angular momentum is always conserved.

after the collision will be along the original direction of the larger car due to its larger momentum. Conservation of linear momentum is used to give space probes an extra boost when they pass planets. The momentum of the planet as it circles the sun in its orbit is given to the passing space probe, increasing its velocity on its way to the next planet. In all the experiments ever attempted, there has been never been a violation of the law of conservation of linear momentum. This applies to all objects ranging in size from galaxies to subatomic particles.

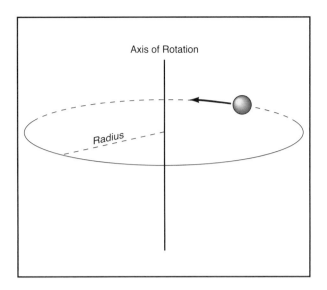

Figure 3.

Conservation of energy and mass

Energy is found in many forms. The most basic form of energy is kinetic energy, which is the energy of motion. A moving object has energy solely due to the fact that it is moving. However, many non–moving objects contain energy in the form of potential or stored energy. A boulder on the top of a cliff has potential energy. This implies that the boulder could convert this potential energy into kinetic energy if it were to fall off the cliff. A stretched bow and arrow have potential energy also. This implies that the stored energy in the bow could be converted into the kinetic energy of the arrow, after it is released. Stored energy may be more complicated than these mechanical examples, however, as in the stored electrical energy in a car battery. We know that the battery has stored energy because this energy can be converted into the kinetic energy of a cranking engine. There is stored chemical energy in many substances, for example gasoline. Again we know this because the energy of the gasoline can be converted into the kinetic energy of a car moving down the road. This stored chemical energy could alternately be converted into thermal energy by burning the gasoline and using the heat to increase the temperature of a bath of water. In all these instances, energy can be converted from one form to another, but it is always found that the total energy remains constant.

In certain instances, even mass can be converted into energy. For example, in a nuclear reactor the nucleus of the uranium atom is split into fragments. The sum of the masses of the fragments is always less than the original uranium nucleus. What happened to this original mass? This mass has been converted into ther-mal energy which heats the water to drive steam turbines which ultimately produces electrical energy. As first discovered by Albert Einstein (1879 – 1955), there is a precise relationship defining the amount of energy that is equivalent to a certain amount of mass. In instances where mass is converted into energy, or visa versa, this relationship must be taken into account.

In general, therefore, there is a universal law of conservation of energy and mass that applies to all of nature. The sum of all the forms of energy and mass in the universe is a certain amount which remains constant. As is the case for angular momentum, the energies of the electrons that surround the nucleus of the atom can possess only certain discrete values. And again, even with these constraints, the conservation of energy and mass is always obeyed.

Conservation of electric charge

Electric charge is the property that makes you experience a spark when you touch a metal door knob after shuffling your feet across a rug. It is also the property that produces lightning. Electric charge comes in two varieties, positive and negative. Like charges repel, that is, they tend to push one another apart, and unlike charges attract, that is, they tend to pull one another together. Therefore, two negative charges repel one another and, likewise, two positive charges repel one another. On the other hand, a positive charge will attract a negative charge. The net electric charge on an object is found by adding all the negative charge to all the positive charge residing on the object. Therefore, the net electric charge on an object with an equal amount of positive and negative charge is exactly zero. The more net electric charge an object has, the greater will be the force of attraction or repulsion for another object containing a net electric charge.

Electric charge is a property of the particles that make up an atom. The electrons that surround the nucleus of the atom have a negative electric charge. The protons which partly make up the nucleus have a positive electric charge. The neutrons which also make up the nucleus have no electric charge. The negative charge of the electron is exactly equal and opposite to the positive charge of the proton. For example, two electrons separated by a certain distance will repel one another with the same force as two protons separated by the same distance and, likewise, a proton and electron separated by this same distance will attract one another with the same force.

The amount of electric charge is only available in discrete units. These discrete units are exactly equal to the amount of electric charge that is found on the electron or the proton. It is impossible to find a naturally occurring amount of electric charge that is smaller than what is found on the proton or the electron. All objects contain an amount of electric charge which is made up of a combination of these discrete units. An analogy can be made to the winnings and losses in a penny ante game of poker. If you're ahead, you have a greater amount of winnings (positive charges) than losses (negative charges), and if you're in the hole you have a greater amount of losses than winnings. Note that the amount that you're ahead or in the hole can only be an exact amount of pennies or cents, as in 49 cents up or 78 cents down. You cannot be ahead by 32 and 1/4 cents. This is the analogy to electric charge. You can only be positive or negative by a discrete amount of charge.

If one were to add all the positive and negative electric units of charge in the universe together, one would arrive at a number that never changes. This would be analogous to remaining always with the same amount of money in poker. If you go down by 5 cents in a given hand, you have to simultaneously go up by 5 cents in the same hand. This is the statement of the law of conservation of electric charge. If a positive charge turns up in one place, a negative charge must turn up in the same place so that the net electric charge of the universe never changes. There are many other subatomic particles besides protons and electrons which have discrete units of electric charge. Even in interactions involving these particles, the law of conservation of electric charge is always obeyed.

Other conservation laws

In addition to the conservation laws already described, there are conservation laws that describe reactions between subatomic particles. Several hundred subatomic particles have been discovered since the discovery of the proton, electron, and the neutron. By observing which processes and reactions occur between these particles, physicists can determine new conservation laws governing these processes. For example, there exists a subatomic particle called the positron which is very much like the electron except that it carries a positive electric charge. The law of conservation of charge would allow a process whereby a proton could change into a positron. However, the fact that this process does not occur leads physicists to define a new conservation law restricting the allowable transformations between different types of subatomic particles.

Occasionally, a conservation law can be used to predict the existence of new particles. In the 1920s, it

---

KEY TERMS

Angular momentum—For objects in rotational motion, it is the product of an object's mass, its speed and its distance from the axis of rotation.

Conserved quantities—Physical quantities, the amount of which remains constant before, during, and after some physical process.

Linear momentum—The product of an object's mass and its velocity.

Mass—A measure of the quantity of matter, more specifically the ratio of the force on an object to the acceleration produced by that force.

Subatomic particles—Particles that include protons, neutrons, and electrons which are smaller than an atom.

---

was discovered that a neutron could change into a proton and an electron. However, the energy and mass before the reaction was not equal to the energy and mass after the reaction. Although seemingly a violation of energy and mass conservation, it was instead proposed that the missing energy was carried by a new particle, unheard of at the time. In 1956, this new particle named the neutrino was discovered. As new subatomic particles are discovered and more processes are studied, the conservation laws will be an important asset to our understanding of the universe.

Further Reading:
Feynman, Richard. *The Character of Physical Law*. Cambridge, MA: MIT Press, 1965.
Feynman, Richard. *Six Easy Pieces*. Reading, MA: Addison–Wesley, 1995.
Giancoli, Douglas. *Physics*. Englewood Cliffs, NJ: Prentice Hall, 1995.
Schwarz, Cindy. *A Tour of the Subatomic Zoo*. New York: American Institute of Physics, 1992.
Young, Hugh. *University Physics*. Reading, MA: Addison–Wesley, 1992.

Kurt Vandervoort

Conservation tillage see **Contour plowing**

Constellation

A constellation is a group of stars that form a long–recognized pattern in the sky. The names of many constellations are Greek in origin and are related to ancient mythology. The stars that make up a constellation may be at very different distances from the earth and from one another. The pattern is one that we as humans choose to see and has no physical significance.

Novice stargazers are often taught that the pattern of stars in a constellation resembles an animal or a person engaged in some activity. For example, Sagittarius is supposed to be an archer, Ursa Major a large bear, and Ursa Minor a small bear. However, most people locate Sagittarius by looking for a group of stars that resemble an old–fashioned coffee pot. Ursa Major is more commonly seen as a Big Dipper and Ursa Minor as a Little Dipper. In fact, it is more likely that ancient stargazers named constellations to honor people, objects, or animals that were a part of their mythology and not because they thought the pattern resembled the honoree.

Today's modern stars divide the sky into 88 constellations that are used by astronomers to identify regions where stars and other objects are located in the celestial sphere (sky). Just as you might tell someone that Pike's Peak is near Colorado Springs, Colorado, so an astronomer refers to nebula (M 42) as the Orion Nebula, or speaks of galaxy M 31 in Andromeda and the globular cluster M 13 in Hercules.

The constellations that you see in the Northern Hemisphere's winter sky–Orion, Taurus, Canis Major, and others–gradually move westward with time, rising above the eastern horizon approximately four minutes earlier each evening. By late spring and early summer, the winter constellations are on the western horizon in the early evening and Leo, Bootes, Cygnus, and Sagittarius dominates the night sky. In the fall, Pegasus, Aquila, and Lyra brighten the heavens. A number of polar constellations (Cephus, Cassiopeia, and Ursa Minor in the north and Crux, Centaurus, and Pavo in the south) are visible all year as they rotate about points directly above the North and South Poles.

The westward movement of the constellations is the result of the earth's motion along its orbit. With each passing day and month, we see a different part of the celestial sphere at night. From our frame of reference on a planet with a tilted axis, the sun, moon and planets follow a path along the celestial sphere called ecliptic, which makes an angle of 23.5° with the celestial equator. As the sun moves along the ecliptic, it passes through 12 constellations, which ancient astronomers referred to as the Signs of the

The constellation Orion, the Great Hunter. The three closely placed stars just left of center in this photo are Alnilam, Alnitak, and Mintaka, and they mark Orion's belt. The short line of less brilliant stars beneath the belt are his scabbard. In the upper left, at Orion's right shoulder, is the star Betelgeuse. His left shoulder is the star Bellatrix. His left foot is the star Rigel, and the bright stars to the right of top center are an animal skin that he carries as a shield.

Zodiac–Aries, Taurus, Gemini, Cancer, Leo, Libra, Scorpius, Sagittarius, Capricorn, Aquarius, and Pisces. The planets also move along the ecliptic, but because they are much closer to us than the stars constellations along the zodiac their paths change with respect to the constellations. These wanderers, which is what the ancients called the planets, led to astrology–the belief that the motion of the sun, moon, and planets along the zodiac has some influence on human destiny. While there is no evidence to support such belief, the careful observations of early astronomers owes much to the pseudoscience of astrology.

See also Celestial coordinates; Milky Way; Star

Constructions

Much of Euclidean geometry is based on two geometric constructions: the drawing of circles and the drawing of straight lines. To draw a circle with a compass, one needs to know the location of the center and some one point on the circle. To draw a line segment with a straightedge, one needs to know the location of its two end points. To extend a segment, one must know the location of it or a piece of it.

Three of the five postulates in Euclid's *Elements* say that these constructions are possible:

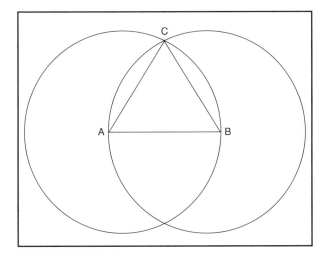

Figure 1. Construction of an equilateral triangle.

To draw a line from any point to any point.

To produce a finite straight line in a straight line.

To describe a circle with any center and distance.

The constructions based on these postulates are called "straightedge and compass" constructions.

The *Elements* does not explain why these tools have been chosen, but one may guess that it was their utter simplicity which geometers found, and continue to find, appealing. These tools are certainly not the only ones which the Greeks employed, and they are not the only ones upon which modern draftsmen depend. They have triangles, french curves, ellipsographs, T–squares, scales, protractors, and other drawing aids which both speed the drawing and make it more precise.

These tools are not the only ones on which contemporary geometry courses are based. Such courses will often include a protractor postulate which allows one to measure angles and to draw angles of a given size. They may include a ruler–placement postulate which allows one to measure distances and to construct segments of any length. Such postulates turn problems which were once purely geometric into problems with an arithmetic component. Nevertheless, straightedge and compass constructions are still studied.

Euclid's first proposition is to show that, given a segment AB, one can construct an equilateral triangle ABC. (There has to be a segment. Without a segment, there will not be a triangle.) Using A as a center, he draws a circle through B. Using B as a center, he draws a circle through A. He calls either of the two points where the circles cross C. That gives him two points, so he can draw segment AC. He can draw BC. Then ABC is the required triangle (Figure 1).

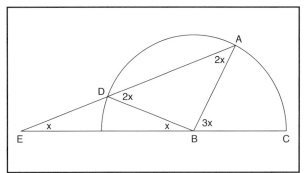

Figure 2. Illustration of Archimedes method for trisecting an arbitrary angle ABC.

Once Euclid has shown that an equilateral triangle can be constructed, the ability to do so is added to his tool bag. He now can draw circles, lines, and equilateral triangles. He goes on to add the ability to draw perpendiculars, to bisect angles, to draw a line through a given point parallel to a given line, to draw equal circles, to transfer a line segment to a new location, to divide a line segment into a specified number of equal parts, and so on.

There are three constructions which, with the given tools, neither Euclid nor any of his successors were able to do. One was to trisect an arbitrary angle. Another was to draw a square whose area was equal to that of a given circle. A third was to draw the edge of a cube whose volume was double that of a given cube. "Squaring the circle," as the second construction is called, is equivalent to drawing a segment whose length is π times that of a given segment. "Duplicating the cube" requires drawing a segment whose length is the cube root of 2 times that of the given segment.

In about 240 B. C., Archimedes devised a method of trisecting an arbitrary angle ABC. The figure shows how he did it. Angle ABC is the given angle. ED is a movable line with ED = AB. It is placed so that E lies on BC extended; D lies on the circle; and the line passes through A. Then ED = DB = AB, so triangles EDB and ABD are isosceles. Because the base angles of an isosceles triangle are equal and because the exterior angle of a triangle is equal to the sum of the two non–adjacent interior angles, the sizes, in terms of x, of the various angles are as marked. Angle E is, therefore, one third the size of the given angle ABC; ABC has been trisected (Figure 2).

Why is this ingenious but simple construction not a solution to the problem of trisecting an angle? Line ED has to be movable. It requires a straightedge with marks on it. Simple as marking a straightedge might be, the Euclidean postulates don't make provision for doing so.

Archimedes' technique for trisecting an angle is by no means the only one which has been devised. Eves, in his *History of Mathematics,* describes several others, all ingenious. He also describes techniques for squaring the circle and duplicating the cube. All the constructions he describes, however, call for tools other than a compass and straightedge.

Actually doing these constructions is not just difficult with the tools allowed; it is impossible. This was proved using algebraic arguments in the nineteenth century. Nevertheless, because the goals of the constructions are so easily stated and understood, and because the tools are so simple, people continue to work at them, not knowing, or perhaps not really caring, that their task is a Sisyphean one.

The straightedge and compass are certainly simple tools, yet mathematicians have tried to get along with even simpler ones. In the tenth century Abul Wefa, a Persian mathematician, based his constructions on a straightedge and a rusty compass—one that could not be adjusted. Nine centuries later it was proved by mathematicians Poncelet and Steiner that, except for drawing circles of a particular size, a straightedge and rusty compass could do everything a straightedge and ordinary compass could do. They went even further, replacing the rusty compass with one already–drawn circle and its center.

In 1797, the Italian mathematician Mascheroni published a book in which he showed that a compass alone could be used to do anything that one could do with a compass and straightedge together. He could not draw straight lines, of course, but he could locate the two points that would determine the undrawn line; he could find where two undrawn lines would intersect; he could locate the vertices of a pentagon; and so on. Later, his work was found to have been anticipated more than 100 years earlier by the Danish mathematician Mohr. Compass–only constructions are now known as Mohr–Mascheroni constructions.

Further Reading:

Birkhoff, George David, and Beatley, Ralph. *Basic Geometry.* New York: Chelsea Publishing Co., 1959

Euclid. *Elements* translated by Heath, Sir Thomas L. New York: Dover Publishing Co., 1956.

Eves, Howard. *An Introduction to the History of Mathematics.* New York: Holt, Rinehart and Winston, 1976.

Gardner, Martin. *Mathematical Circus.* New York: Alfred A. Knopf, 1979.

KEY TERMS

. . . .

Compass—A device for drawing circles having a given center and radius.

Construction—A drawing of a geometrical figure made with the use of certain specified tools.

Straightedge—An unmarked ruler which can be used to draw lines through two given points.

Moise, Edwin E. *Elementary Geometry from an Advanced Standpoint.* Reading, Massachusetts: Addison–Wesley Publishing Co., 1963.

J. Paul Moulton

Contamination

Contamination generally refers to the occurrence of some substance in the environment. The contaminant may be present in a larger concentration than normally occurs in the ambient environment. However, contamination is only said to occur when the concentration is smaller than that at which measurable biological or ecological damages can be demonstrated. Contamination is different from pollution, which is judged to occur when a chemical is present in the environment at a concentration greater than that required to cause damages to organisms. Pollution results in toxicity and ecological changes, but contamination does not cause these effects, because it involves sub–toxic exposures.

Chemicals that are commonly involved in toxic pollution include the gases sulfur dioxide and ozone, elements such as arsenic, copper, mercury, and nickel, pesticides of many kinds, and some naturally occurring biochemicals. In addition, large concentrations of nutrients such as phosphate and nitrate can cause eutrophication, another type of pollution. All of these pollution causing chemicals can occur in the environment in concentrations that are smaller than those required to cause toxicity or other ecological damages. Under these circumstances the chemicals would be regarded as contaminants.

Modern analytical chemistry has become extraordinarily sophisticated. As a result, trace contaminations by potentially toxic chemicals can often be measured in amounts that are much smaller than the thresholds of exposure, or dose, that are required to demonstrate physiological or ecological damages.

Toxic chemicals

An important notion in toxicology is that any chemical can poison any organism, as long as a sufficiently large dose is experienced. In other words, all chemicals are potentially toxic, even water, carbon dioxide, sucrose (table sugar), sodium chloride (table salt), and other substances that are routinely encountered during the course of the day. However, exposures to these chemicals, or to much more toxic substances, do not necessarily result in a measurable poisonous response, if the dose is small enough. Toxicity is only caused if the exposure exceeds physiological thresholds of tolerance. According to this interpretation of toxicology, it is best to refer to "potentially toxic chemicals" in any context in which the actual environmental exposure to chemicals is unclear, or the effects of small doses of particular chemicals are not known.

However, it is important to understand that there is scientific controversy about this topic. Some scientists believe that even exposures to single molecules of certain chemicals could be of toxicological significance, and that dose–response relationships can therefore be extrapolated in a linear fashion to a zero dosage. This might be especially relevant to some types of cancers, which could theoretically be induced by genetic damages occurring in a single cell, and potentially caused by a single molecule of a carcinogen. This is a very different view from that expressed above, which suggests that there are thresholds of physiological tolerance that must be exceeded if toxicity is to be caused.

The notion of thresholds of tolerance is supported by several lines of scientific evidence. It is known, for example, that cells have some capability of repairing damages caused to nuclear materials such as DNA (deoxyribonucleic acid), suggesting that minor damages caused by toxic chemicals might be tolerated because they could be repaired. However, major damages could overwhelm the physiological repair function, so that there would be a threshold of tolerance.

In addition, organisms have physiological mechanisms of detoxifying many types of poisonous chemicals. Mixed–function oxidases (MFOs), for example, are a class of enzymes that are especially abundant in the livers of vertebrate animals, and to a lesser degree in the bloodstream. Within limits, these enzymes can detoxify certain potentially toxic chemicals, such as chlorinated hydrocarbons, by rendering them into simpler, less toxic substances. Mixed–function oxidases are inducible enzymes, meaning that they are synthesized

in relatively large quantities when there is an increased demand for their metabolic services, as would occur when an organism is exposed to a large concentration of toxic chemicals. However, the ability of the mixed-function oxidase system to deal with toxic chemicals can be overwhelmed if the exposure is too intense, a characteristic that would be represented as a toxicological threshold.

Organisms also have some ability to deal with limited exposures to potentially toxic chemicals by partitioning them within tissues that are not vulnerable to their poisonous influence. For example, chlorinated hydrocarbons such as the pesticides DDT and dieldrin, the industrial fluids known as polychlorinated biphenyls (PCBs), and the dioxin TCDD are all very soluble in fats, and therefore are mostly found in the fatty tissues of animals. Within limits, organisms can tolerate exposures to these chemicals by immobilizing them in fatty tissues. However, toxicity may still result if the exposure is too great, or if the fat reserves must be mobilized in order to deal with large metabolic demands, as might occur during migration or breeding. Similarly, plants have some ability to deal with limited exposures to toxic metals, by synthesizing certain proteins, organic acids, or other metal–binding biochemicals that bind with the ionic forms of metals, rendering them much less toxic.

Moreover, all of the chemicals required by organisms as essential nutrients are toxic at larger exposures. For example, the metals copper, iron, molybdenum, and zinc are required by plants and animals as micronutrients. However, exposures that exceed the therapeutic levels of these metals are poisonous to these same organisms. The smaller, sub–toxic exposures would represent a type of contamination.

Some chemicals are ubiquitous in the environment

An enormous variety of chemicals occurs naturally in the environment. For example, all of the natural elements are ubiquitous, occurring in all aqueous, soil, atmospheric, and biological samples in at least a trace concentration. If the methodology of analytical chemistry has sufficiently small detection limits, this ubiquitous presence of all of the elements will always be demonstrable. In other words, there is a universal contamination of the living and non–living environment with all of the natural elements. This includes all of the potentially toxic metals, most of which occur in trace concentrations.

Similarly, the organic environment is ubiquitously contaminated by a class of synthetic, persistent chemicals known as chlorinated hydrocarbons, including such chemicals as DDT, PCBs, and TCDD. These chemicals are virtually insoluble in water, but they are very soluble in fats. In the environment, almost all fats occur in the biomass of living or dead organisms, and as a result chlorinated hydrocarbons have a strong tendency to bioaccumulate in organisms, in strong preference to the non–organic environment. Because these chemicals are persistent and bioaccumulating, they have become very widespread in the biosphere, and all organisms contain their residues, even in remote places such as Antarctica. The largest residues of chlorinated hydrocarbons occur in predators at the top of the ecological food web. Some of these top predators, such as raptorial birds and some marine mammals, have suffered toxicity as a result of their exposures to chlorinated hydrocarbons. However, toxicity has not been demonstrated for most other species, even though all are contaminated by various of the persistent chlorinated hydrocarbons.

One last example concerns some very toxic biochemicals that are synthesized by wild organisms, and are therefore naturally occurring substances. Saxitoxin, for example, is a biochemical that is produced by a few species of marine dinoflagellates, a group of unicellular algae. Saxitoxin is a very potent toxin of the vertebrate nervous system. When these dinoflagellates are abundant, filter–feeders such as mollusks can accumulate saxitoxin to a large concentration, and these can then be poisonous to birds and mammals, including humans, that eat the shellfish. This toxic syndrome is known as paralytic shellfish poisoning. Other species of dinoflagellates synthesize the biochemicals responsible for diarrhetic shellfish poisoning, while certain diatoms produce domoic acid, which causes amnesic shellfish poisoning. The poisons produced by these marine phytoplankton are commonly present in the marine environment as a trace contamination, but when the algae are very abundant the poisons occur in large enough amounts to poison animals in their food web, causing a type of natural, toxic pollution.

See also Biomagnification; Eutrophication; Poisons and toxins; Pollution; Red tide; Toxicology.

Further Reading:

Freedman, B. *Environmental Ecology.* 2nd ed. San Diego: Academic Press, 1994.

Hemond, H. F., and E. J. Fechner. *Chemical Fate and Transport in the Environment.* San Diego: Academic Press, 1994.

Bill Freedman

Continental drift

Once explorers returned to their home countries from their travels around the world and constructed global maps, people noticed that the shapes of the continents, particularly South America and Africa, appeared to fit together like pieces on a colossal jigsaw puzzle. Not until around the early twentieth century did scientists propose that these continents fit together because they were joined in the distant past. Two Americans, Frank Taylor and Howard Baker, provided evidence that the Americas separated from Europe and Africa. However, Alfred Wegener, a German meteorologist, is generally credited with originating the Continental Drift theory, which states that all continents were once joined together in one supercontinent named Pangaea (Pangea) and drifted apart to the spots they now occupy.

History of Wegener's theory

In Wegener's 1915 book, *The Origin of Continents and Oceans,* he cited the following evidence (mostly from Gondawana, the southern half of the supercontinent) that Pangaea (meaning "All Earth") existed: glacially gouged rocks in southern Africa, South America, and India; the fit of the coastlines and undersea shelves of the continents, especially eastern South America into western Africa and eastern North America into northwestern Africa; fossils in South America that match fossils in Africa and Australia, mountain ranges that start in Argentina and continue into South Africa and Australia; other mountains (Appalachians) that begin in North America and trend into Europe. He even measured Greenland's distance from Europe over many years to show that the two drift slowly apart.

Although compelling today, scientists for decades dismissed Wegener's Continental Drift theory because he could not satisfactorily explain how the continents moved. His assertion that continents plowed through oceanic rock riding tides in the Earth like an icebreaker through sea ice brought derision from the world's geophysical community, responsible for studies of the Earth's movement. Harold Jeffreys, a leading British geophysicist of the 1920s, calculated that if continents did ride these Earth tides, mountain ranges would collapse and the Earth would stop spinning within a year.

Additionally, a widely–held belief that defunct land bridges (now sunken below sea level) connected current continents, countered much of Wegener's fossil arguments. These bridges allowed the small fossil reptiles Lystrosaurus and Mesosaurus discovered on opposite sides of the Atlantic to roam freely across what is now

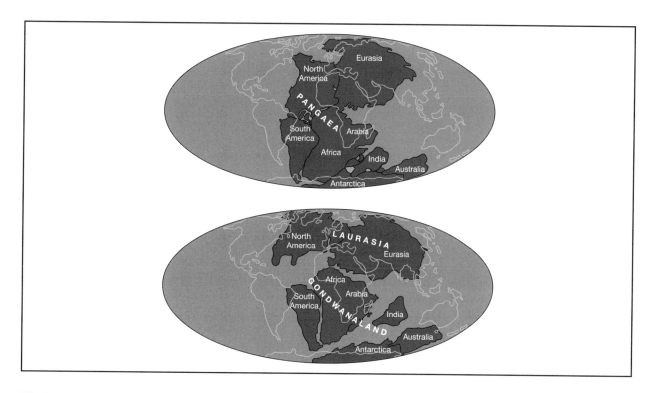

The Pangaea supercontinent (top) and its break up into Laurasia and Gondwanaland (bottom). Contemporary continental outlines are shown in gray.

an ocean too wide to swim. The cooling and shrinking of the Earth since its formation supposedly caused the flooding of the bridges. Furthermore, critics explained that Wegener's fossil plant evidence from both sides of the Atlantic resulted from wind–blown seeds and plant–dispersing ocean currents.

The Greenland measurements proved too imprecise for the equipment available to Wegener at that time. The fit of continents could be dismissed as coincidence or by a counter theory explaining that the Earth expands. Like shapes drawn on an expanding balloon, the continents move farther from each other as the earth grows wider.

Evidence of the theory

Technological improvements after World War II vindicated many of Wegener's ideas about continental drift. New methods of dating and drilling for rock samples, especially from deep–sea drilling ships like the Glomar Challenger, allowed for more precise matching of Pangaea's rocks and fossils. Magnetometers measuring the magnetism of the iron in sea floor rocks demonstrated the spreading of the sea floor since Pangaea's breakup. Even satellites have clocked continental movement.

For the 100 million years of Pangea, geologists assume the climatic zones operating today were the

same as then: cold at the poles, temperate to desert–like at the mid–latitudes, and tropical at the equator. The rocks and fossils deposited in early Pangaea–time show the equator crossed a clockwise–tilted North America form roughly southern California through the mid–Atlantic United States and into Northwestern Africa. Geological and archaeological evidence from the Sahara desert indicate the remains of a tropical world beneath the sands. Rock layers in southern Utah point to a warm sea that gradually altered into a large sandy desert as the west coast of the North American section of Pangaea slid north into an arid latitude. Global climates changed as Pangaea rotated and slowly broke up over those 100 million years.

Meanwhile, dinosaurs, mammals, and other organisms evolved as they mingled across the connected Earth for millions of years, responding to the changing climates created by the shifting landmass. Fossil dinosaurs unearthed in Antarctica proved that it connected to the rest of Pangaea, and dinosaur discoveries in the Sahara desert indicate that the last connection between Laurasia (the northern half of Pangaea) and Gondwana severed as recently as 130 million years ago.

All these discoveries helped develop plate tectonics, the study of moving plates (sections of the earth's outer shell, or crust). These plates constantly smash into, split from, and grind past each other creating and destroying themselves. Wegener had no knowledge of plate tectonics. He dealt only with drifting continents not knowing the ocean floor drifts as well, with only the knowledge and technology available to him in the early 1900's. Parts of his Continental Drift theory proved wrong (e.g. – his argument that continental movement would cause the average height of land to rise), and parts proved correct. The Continental Drift theory and plate tectonics, although demonstrating many similar ideas, are not synonymous.

Laurasia and Gondwana

With the improved technology, geologists ascertained that nearly 300 million years ago, Laurasia (what is now Eurasia, Greenland, and North America) drifted from the north and crashed into Gondwana (also called Gonwanaland and composed of South America, Africa, Australia, Antarctica, India, and New Zealand), creating Pangaea. The C–shaped Pangaea, united along Mexico to Spain/Algeria, was separated by Tethys, an ancient sea to the east, whose remnants include the Mediterranean, Black, Caspian, and Aral Seas. Panthalassa, the superocean ("All Ocean"), covered the side of the globe split into Laurasia and Gondwana again and later divided into the present continents.

Pangaea splits

The collision of North America and northwestern Africa around 300 million years ago uplifted a mountain range 621 miles (1000 km) long and as tall as the Himalayas, whose much–eroded roots can still be traced from Louisiana to Scandinavia. The Appalachians are remnants of these mountains, the tallest of which centered over today's Atlantic Coastal Plain and over the continental shelf. Pangaea's crushing closure shortened the eastern margin of North America by at least 161 miles (260 km).

Once Pangaea completed its collision, most of the colliding shifted from the east coast of North America to the western edge of the continent. As Pangaea drifted northward before the breakup, it plowed into the Panthalassa ocean floor and created some of today's western mountains. However, the splitting of Pangaea 200 million years ago forced up most of the mountain ranges from Alaska to southern Chile as North and South America sailed west into and over more ocean floor.

The tearing apart of Pangaea produced long valleys that ran roughly parallel to the east coasts of the Americas and the west coasts of Europe and Africa. The floors of these valleys dropped down. One of the valleys filled

KEY TERMS

Continental Drift theory—Alfred Wegener's idea that all the continents once formed a giant continent called Pangaea and later shifted to their present positions.

Gondwana (Gondwanaland)—The southern half of Pangaea that included today's South America, Africa, India, Australia, Antarctica, and New Zealand.

Laurasia—The northern half of Pangaea that included today's North America, Greenland, Europe, and Asia.

Pangaea (Pangea)—The supercontinent from approximately 200–300 million years ago which was composed of all today's landmasses.

Panthalassa—The ocean covering the opposite site of the globe from Pangea. Panthalassa means "All Ocean."

Wegener, Alfred—German meteorologist (1880-1930), inventor of the Continental Drift theory, and coiner of the term "Pangaea." He died researching glaciers in Greenland decades before his ideas became accepted.

with seawater and became the Atlantic Ocean, which still grows larger every year. Other valleys gradually choked with sediment eroded off the ridges on either side. Today many of these former low spots lie buried beneath thousands of feet of debris. The formation of the valleys did not occur along the same line as the collision 100 million years before; a chunk of Gondwana now sits below the eastern United States.

Pangaea began to break up around 200 million years ago with the separation of Laurasia from Gondwana, and with the separation of what is now India, Antarctica, and Australia from South America/Africa. The Atlantic zippered open northward for the next few tens of millions of years until Greenland eventually tore from northern Europe. By about 65 million years ago, all the present continents had split and were sliding toward their current locations while India hurried north to smack the south side of Asia.

Current Pangaea research no longer focuses on whether or not it existed but hones the matching of the continental margins.

See also Plate tectonics.

Further Reading:

Lessem, Don. *Kings of Creation.* New York: Simon & Schuster, 1992.

Menard, H.W. *The Ocean of Truth: A Personal History of Plate Tectonics.* Princeton, NJ: Princeton University Press, 1986.

Miller, Russell, and editors of Time–Life Books. *Planet Earth: Continents in Collision.* Alexandria, VA: Time–Life Books, 1983.

Raymo, Chet. *The Crust of Our Earth.* New York: Prentice Hall Press, 1986

Redfern, Ron. *The Making of a Continent.* New York: Times Books, 1983.

Trefill, James. *Meditations at 10,000 Feet: A Scientist in the Mountains.* New York, Charles Scribner's Sons, 1986.

Ed Fox

Continental margin

The continental margin is that portion of the ocean that separates the continents from the deep ocean floor. For purposes of study, the continental margin is usually subdivided into three major sections: the continental shelf, the continental slope, and the continental rise. In addition to these sections, one of the most important features of the continental margin is the presence of very large submarine canyons that cut their way through the continental slope and, less commonly, the continental shelf.

Continental shelf

The continental shelf is a portion of the continent to which it is adjacent, and not actually part of the ocean floor. As a result of continual earth movement, the shelf is continuously exposed and covered by water. Even when covered by water, as it is today, it shows signs of once having been dry land. Fossil river beds, for example, are characteristic of some slopes. Remnants of glacial action can also be found in some regions of the continental shelf.

The continental shelf tends to be quite flat, with an average slope of less than two meters for each kilometer of distance. It varies in width from a few kilometers to more than 932 mi (1,500 km) with a worldwide average of about 27 mi (70 km). Some of the widest continental slopes are to be found along the northern coastline of Russia and along the western edge of the Pacific Ocean, from Alaska to Australia. Very narrow continental slopes are to be found along the western coastline of

South America and the comparable coasts of west Africa. The average depth at which the continental shelf begins to fall off toward the ocean floor (the beginning of the continental slope) is about 135 meters (440 feet).

Materials washed off the continents by rivers and streams gradually work their way across the continental shelf to the edge of the continental slope. In some instances, the flow of materials can be dramatically abrupt as, for example, following an earthquake. At the outer edge of the continental shelf, eroded materials are dumped, as it were, over the edge of the shelf onto the sea floor below.

The continental shelf is one of the best studied portions of the ocean bottom. One reason for this fact, of course, is that it is more accessible to researchers than are other parts of the sea floor. More than that, however, the waters above the continental shelf are the richest fishing grounds in the world. A number of nations have declared that their national sovereignty extends to the end of the continental shelf around their territory— often a distance of 200 kilometers (120 miles)—to protect their marine resources.

Included among those resources are extensive mineral deposits. Many nations now have offshore wells with which they extract oil and natural gas from beneath the continental shelf.

The continental slope

At the seaward edge of the continental shelf, the ocean floor drops off abruptly along the continental slope. The break point between the shelf and slope is sometimes known as the continental shelf break. The continental slopes are the most dramatic cliffs on the face of the Earth. They may drop from a depth of 200 meters to more than 3,000 meters in a distance of about 100 kilometers. In the area of ocean trenches, the drop–off may be even more severe, from 200 meters to more than 10,000 meters.

The average slope of sea floor along the continental slope is about 4°, although that value may range from as little as 1° to as much as 25°. In general, the steepest slopes tend to be found in the Pacific Ocean, and the least steep slopes in the Atlantic and Indian Oceans. Sedimentary materials carried to the continental slope from the continental shelf do not remain along the slope (because of its steep sides), but flow downward into the next region, the continental rise.

Submarine canyons

The most distinctive features of the continental slopes are the submarine canyons. These are V–shaped features, often with tributaries, similar to canyons found on dry land. The deepest of the submarine canyons easily rivals similar landforms on the continents. The Monterrey Canyon off the coast of northern California, for example, drops from a water depth of 108 meters (354 feet) below sea level near the coastline to 2,034 meters (6,672 feet) below sea level. That vertical drop is half again as great as the depth of the Grand Canyon.

There seems little doubt that the submarine canyons, like their continental cousins, have been formed by erosion. But, for many years, oceanographers were puzzled as to the eroding force that might be responsible for formation of the submarine canyons. Today, scientists agree that canyons are produced by the flow of underwater rivers that travel across the continental slopes (and sometimes the continental shelf) carrying with them sediments that originated on the continents. These rivers are known as turbidity currents.

Evidence for the turbidity current theory of canyon formation was obtained in 1929 when an earthquake struck the Grand Banks region of the Atlantic Ocean off Newfoundland. An enormous turbidity current was set in motion that traveled at a speed ranging from 40 to 100 kilometers per hour (25 to 60 miles per hour), breaking a sequence of transatlantic telegraph cables along the way. The pattern of cable destruction was what made it possible, in fact, for scientists to track so precisely the movement of the giant turbidity current.

The continental rise

Sediments eroded off continental land, after being carried across the shelf and down the continental slope, are finally deposited at the base of the slope in a region of the ocean known as the continental rise. By some estimates, half of all the sediments laid down on the face of the planet are found in the continental rise.

In many regions, the continental rise looks very much like a river delta such as the one found at the mouth of the Mississippi River. In fact, these underwater deltas may also include a network of channels and natural levees similar to those found in the area of New Orleans. One of the most thoroughly studied sections of the continental rise is the Amazon Cone located northeast of the coast of Brazil. The Amazon Cone has a total width of about 50 kilometers (30 miles) and a depth of about 300 meters (1,000 feet). It is bisected by a primary channel that is 250 meters (800 feet) deep and as much as 3 kilometers (2 miles) wide.

See also Ocean; Ocean zones

Further Reading:

Duxbury, Alyn C., and Alison Duxbury. *An Introduction to the World's Oceans*. Reading:, MA: Addison–Wesley Publishing Company, 1984, Chapter 2.

KEY TERMS

....

Continental rise—A region at the base of the continental slope in which eroded sediments are deposited.

Continental shelf—A gently–sloping stretch of the ocean adjacent to the continents.

Continental shelf break—The outer edge of the continental shelf, at which the ocean floor drops off quite sharply in the continental slope.

Continental slope—A steeply–sloping stretch of the ocean that reaches from the outer edge of the continental shelf to the continental rise and deep ocean bottom.

Submarine canyon—A steep V–shaped feature cut out of the continental slope by underwater rivers known as turbidity currents.

Turbidity current—An underwater movement of water, mud, and other sediments.

Golden, Fred, Stephen Hart, Gina Maranto, and Bryce Walker. *How Things Work: Oceans*. Alexandria, VA: Time–Life Books, 1991.

Larson, Edwin E., and Peter W. Birkeland. *Putnam's Geology*, 4th edition. New York: Oxford University Press, 1982, Chapter 15.

The Ocean: A Scientific American Book. San Francisco: W. H. Freeman, 1969.

Ross, David A. *Introduction to Oceanography*, 2nd edition. Englewood Cliffs, NJ: Prentice–Hall, 1977, Chapter 8.

Thurman, Harold V. *Introductory Oceanography*, 4th edition. Columbus, OH: Charles E. Merrill Publishing Company, 1985, Chapter 3.

David E. Newton

Continental rise see **Continental margin**

Continental shelf

The continental shelf is a gently sloping and relatively flat extension of a continent that is covered by the oceans. Seaward, the shelf ends abruptly at the shelf break, the boundary that separates the shelf from the continental slope.

The shelf occupies only 7% of the total ocean floor. The average slope of the shelf is about 1.9 meters per kilometer (10 ft per mile). That is, for every one kilometer of distance, the shelf drops 1.9 m in elevation until the shelf break is reached. The average depth of the shelf break is 135 m (440 ft). The greatest depth is found off Antarctica [350 m (1,150 ft)], where the great weight of the ice on the Antarctic continent pushes the crust downward. The average width of the shelf is 70 kilometers (43 miles) and varies from tens of meters to approximately 1,300 kilometers (800 miles) depending on location. The widest shelves are in the Arctic Ocean off the northern coasts of Siberia and North America. Some of the narrowest shelves are found off the tectonically active western coasts of North and South America.

The shelf's gentle slope and relatively flat terrain are the result of erosion and sediment deposition during the periodic fall and rise of the sea over the shelf in the last 1.6 million years. The changes in sea level were caused by the advance and retreat of glaciers on land over the same time period. During the last glacial period (approximately 18,000 years ago), sea level was 300–400 feet lower than present and the shoreline was much farther offshore, exposing the shelf to the atmosphere. During lowered sea level, land plants and animals, including humans and their ancestors, lived on the shelf. Their remains are often found at the bottom of the ocean. For example, 12,000 year old bones of mastodons, extinct relatives of the elephant, have been recovered off the coast of northeastern United States.

Continental shelves contain valuable resources, such as oil and gas and minerals. Oil and gas are formed from organic material that accumulates on the continental shelf. Over time the material is buried and transformed to oil and gas by heat and pressure. The oil and gas moves upward and is concentrated beneath geologic traps. Oil and gas is found on the continental shelf off the coasts of California and Louisiana, for example. Minerals come from rocks on land and are carried to the ocean by rivers. The minerals were deposited in river channels and beaches on the exposed continental shelf and sorted (concentrated) by waves and river currents, due to their different densities. Over time as the sea level rose, these minerals were again sorted by waves and ocean currents and finally deposited. The different colored bands of sand that one can see on a beach are an example of density sorting by waves. The concentrated minerals are often in sufficient enough quantities to be minable. Examples of important minerals on the shelf are diamonds, chromite (chromium ore), ilmenite (titanium ore), magnetite (iron ore), platinum, and gold.

Continental slope see **Continental margin**

Continuity

Continuity expresses the property of being uninterrupted. Intuitively, a continuous line or function is one that can be graphed without having to lift the pencil from the paper; there are no missing points, no skipped segments and no disconnections. This intuitive notion of continuity goes back to ancient Greece, where many mathematicians and philosophers believed that reality was a reflection of number. Thus, they thought, since numbers are infinitely divisible, space and time must also be infinitely divisible. In the 5th century B.C., however, the Greek mathematician Zeno pointed out that a number of logical inconsistencies arise when assuming that space is infinitely divisible, and stated his findings in the form of paradoxes. For example, in one paradox Zeno argued that the infinite divisibility of space actually meant that all motion was impossible. His argument went approximately as follows: before reaching any destination a traveler must first complete one–half of his journey, and before completing one–half he must complete one–fourth, and before completing one–fourth he must complete one–eighth, and so on indefinitely. Any trip requires an infinite number of steps, so ultimately, Zeno argued, no journey could ever begin, all motion was impossible. Zeno's paradoxes had a disturbing effect on Greek mathematicians, and the ultimate resolution of his paradoxes did not occur until the intuitive notion of continuity was finally dealt with logically .

The continuity of space or time, considered by Zeno and others, is represented in mathematics by the continuity of points on a line. As late as the 17th century, mathematicians continued to believe, as the ancient Greeks had, that this continuity of points was a simple result of density, meaning that between any two points, no matter how close together, there is always another. This is true, for example, of the rational numbers. However, the rational numbers do not form a continuum, since irrational numbers like $\sqrt{2}$ are missing, leaving holes or discontinuities. The irrational numbers are required to complete the continuum. Together, the rational and irrational numbers do form a continuous set, the set of real numbers. Thus, the continuity of points on a line is ultimately linked to the continuity of the set of real numbers, by establishing a one–to–one correspondence between the two. This approach to continuity was first established in the 1820s, by Augustin–Louis Cauchy, who finally began to solve the problem of handling continuity logically. In Cauchy's view, any line corresponding to the graph of a function is continuous at a point, if the value of the function at x, denoted by f(x), gets arbitrarily close to f(p), when x

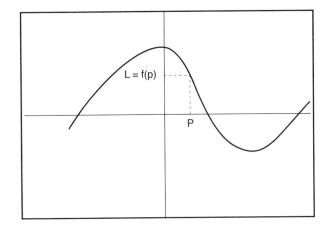

Figure 1.

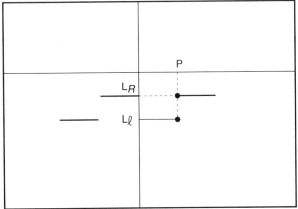

Figure 2.

Figure 3.

Figure 4.

gets close to a real number p . If f(x) is continuous for all real numbers x contained in a finite interval, then the function is continuous in that interval. If f(x) is continuous for every real number x , then the function is continuous everywhere.

Cauchy's definition of continuity is essentially the one we use today, though somewhat more refined versions were developed in the 1850's, and later in the 19th century. For example, the concept of continuity is often described in relation to limits. The condition for a function to be continuous, is equivalent to the requirement that the limit of the function at the point p be equal to f(p), that is:

$$\lim_{x \, R \, p} f(x) = f(p).$$

In this version, there are two conditions that must be met for a function to be continuous at a point. First, the limit must exist at the point in question, and, second, it must be numerically equal to the value of the function at that point. For instance, polynomial functions are continuous everywhere, because the value of the function f(x) approaches f(p) smoothly, as x gets close to p , for all values of p (see figure 1).

However, a polynomial function with a single point redefined (see figure 2) is not continuous at the point x = p if the limit of the function as x approaches p is L , and not f(p) . This is a somewhat artificial example, but it makes the point that when the limit of f(x) as x approaches p is not f(p) then the function is not continuous at x = p . More realistic examples of discontinuous functions include the square wave (see figure 3), which illustrates the existence of a right and left hand limits that differ; and functions with infinite discontinuities, that is, with limits that do not exist (see figure 4).

These examples serve to illustrate the close connection between the limiting value of a function at a point, and continuity at a point.

There are two important properties of continuous functions. First, if a function is continuous in a closed interval, then the function has a maximum value and a minimum value in that interval. Since continuity implies that f(x) cannot be infinite for any x in the interval, the function must have both a maximum and a minimum value, though the two values may be equal. Second, the fact that there can be no holes in a continuous curve implies that a function, continuous on a closed interval [a,b], takes on every value between f(a) and f(b) at least once. The concept of continuity is central to isolating points for which the derivative of a function does not exist. The derivative of a function is equal to the slope of the tangent to the graph of the function. For some functions it is not possible to draw a unique tangent at a particular point on the graph, such as any endpoint of a step function segment. When this is the case, it is not possible to determine the value of the derivative at that point. Today, the meaning of continuity is settled within the mathematics community, though it continues to present problems for philosophers and physicists.

Further Reading:
Allen, G.D., C. Chui, and B. Perry. *Elements of Calculus*, 2nd ed. Pacific Grove, California: Brooks/Cole Publishing Co, 1989.
Boyer, Carl B. *A History of Mathematics*, 2nd ed. Revised by Uta C. Merzbach. New York: John Wiley and Sons, 1991.
McLaughlin, William I. "Resolving Zeno's Paradoxes." *Scientific American* 271 (1994): 84–89.
Paulos, John Allen. *Beyond Numeracy, Ruminations of a Numbers Man.* New York: Alfred A. Knopf. 1991.
Silverman, Richard A. *Essential Calculus With Applications.* New York: Dover, 1989.
Thomas, George B., Jr. and Ross L Finney. *Elements of Calculus and Analytic Geometry*, 6th ed. Reading MA: Addison Wesley, 1989.

J. R. Maddocks

Contour plowing

One of the earliest methods of conservation tillage came to be known as contour plowing, or "plowing on the contour." Tilling the soil along the gentle slopes of a piece of crop land, instead of up and down the gradient, prevents fertile topsoil from being carried downhill by flowing rainwater. This preventive measure is most important in areas which are prone to violent storms or heavy rains. Not only is the topsoil kept in place, minerals like salt or additives such as fertilizers, insecticides or weed control agents, as well as bacteria from animal waste are not swept away to pollute bodies of potable water.

In Thomas Jefferson's time, contour plowing was called more simply "horizontal plowing." Jefferson had won a coveted medal from the major agricultural society in France for his design of the moldboard plow, but he began to notice drawbacks to the heavy use of that instrument. One of his relatives, a politically active farmer named Thomas Mann Randolph, was inspired to develop a new plowing technique in order to salvage the hilly areas in Virginia. Instead of funneling water down, like shingles on the roof of a house, it caught the rain in little ridges of upturned earth. Jefferson commented on a noticeable improvement, specifying that the horizontal furrows retained surplus rainwater and allowed it to evaporate back into the soil.

Even after this successful experiment, later versions of the moldboard plow caused damage to the delicate topsoil of the great plains and prairies of the Midwest United States. The most dramatic evidence of soil erosion took the form of huge dust storms and crop failures during the Great Depression. Since then, contour plowing and other forms of conservation tillage have been reinstituted.

Contour rice farming in Arkansas.

Drawbacks to contour plowing have caused it to be less widely used than conventional tillage methods. Some farmers may not have been fully aware of erosion damage and prevention. Lack of access to equipment, funding, or training sometimes take their toll. One of the main limitations of contour plowing results from its contribution of pockets of untilled land. These untended spots eventually develop weeds, which require extra herbicides. Killing off the weeds sometimes destroys surrounding grasses, which in turn leaves another opportunity for rainwater runoff to arise. To combat this possibility, contour plowing is often applied in combination with other soil conservation techniques, such as terracing.

See also Terracing.

Contraception

Efforts to prevent the conception of children through contraception have been attempted since ancient times and in many cultures. These methods range from the use of tampons treated with herbal spermicide by the Egyptians in 1550 B.C. to the use of animal membrane condoms in the eighteenth century. The introduction of the oral contraceptive pill in 1960 launched a new era, making contraception easier and more effective than earlier methods. Sterilization is the contraceptive method used most frequently.

In the United States, about 60% of American women 15–44 used contraception in 1988, a total of about 35 million women. Worldwide, contraceptive use increased 10–fold from 1963 to 1993. Although widespread, contraceptive use remains controversial, with some religious and political groups opposed to distribution of contraceptives.

An ancient interest

A survey of early contraceptive methods reflects an odd combination of human knowledge and ignorance. Some methods used by ancient people sound absurd to modern observers, such as the suggestion by the ancient Greek Discordies that the wearing of cat testicles or asparagus would inhibit contraception. Yet some early methods of contraception draw on techniques still used today.

The Egyptian contraceptive tampon, described in the Ebers Papyrus of 1550 B.C., was made of lint and soaked in honey and tips from the acacia shrub. The acacia shrub contains gum arabic, the substance from which lactic acid is made, a spermicidal agent used in modern contraceptive jellies and creams.

Aristotle was one of many ancient Greeks to write about contraception. He advised women to use olive oil or cedar oil in the vagina, a method which helps inhibit contraception by slowing the movement of sperm. Other Greeks recommended the untrue contention that obesity was linked to reduced fertility.

Roman birth control practices varied from the use of woolen tampons to the practice of sterilization, which was typically performed on slaves. Another common Ancient practice, still in use today, was the prolonged nursing of infants. This practice makes conception less likely, though it remains possible.

Ancient Asian cultures also drew from a wide range of birth control methods. Women in China and Japan used bamboo tissue paper discs which had been oiled as barriers to the cervix. These were precursors of the modern diaphragm contraceptive device. The Chinese believed that behavior played a role in fertility, and that women who were passive during sex would not become pregnant. They suggested that women practice a total passivity beginning as early as 1100 B.C.. In addition, they suggested that men practice intercourse without ejaculating.

The Chinese were not alone in promoting contraceptive methods based on men's ejaculation practices. The practice of withdrawal of the man's penis before ejaculation during intercourse, also known as coitus interruptus, has been called the most common contraceptive method in the world. While it was believed that coitus interruptus prevented conception, contemporary researchers have proven that pre–ejaculatory fluid can be released prior to ejaculation, resulting in pregnancy. A 1990 study found that 18% of women who depended on withdrawal as a contraceptive method became pregnant accidentally within their first year of using the method.

Magical potions were also used extensively throughout the world as contraceptives, including a wide range of herbal and vegetable preparations. Some of these substances may have actually caused abortions.

A controversial practice

Respectable physicians advocated contraceptive methods in ancient Greek and Roman society. By the Middle Ages, contraception had become a controversial practice, in large part due to opposition to contraception by the Church. Early Christians were not outspoken about contraception. The first clear statement about sin and contraception was made in the fifth century by Saint Augustine. Saint Augustine and others wrote that contraception was a mortal sin, a pronouncement that continues to resonate in modern culture. Since the fifth Century, the Catholic Church has retained its opposition to all forms of birth control except abstinence and the so–called rhythm method, a calendar–based method involving timely abstinence.

As Christian influence took precedence during the Medieval period, contraceptive knowledge was suppressed. One measure of the primitive level of this knowledge was the writing of Albert the Great (1193–1280), a Dominican bishop. Albert the Great's writing about sciences included contraceptive recipes. To avoid conception, readers were advised to wear body parts of a dead fetus around the neck or to drink a man's urine.

Many scholars suggest that couples continued to practice contraception during the Middle Ages, in spite of the limited level of official contraceptive knowledge. Even when religious authorities condemned contraception, women passed knowledge of such practices to one another.

In addition, other religious and cultural traditions maintained support for certain types of contraception during the Middle Ages. Most Jewish authorities supported women's use of contraceptive devices. Islamic physicians were not limited by the Christian opposition to birth control, and medical writings from the Middle Ages included a wide range of contraceptive information. The Koran, the holy book for Muslims, supported the use of prolonged nursing to prevent conception, and did not oppose other contraceptive methods. While European Christians condemned contraception, the practice continued in other countries and among other cultures.

Evolution of the condom

Prior to the modern era, many of the most effective contraceptives evolved, rather than appearing suddenly as the result of an invention. The development and evolution of the condom is an example of a device that was present for hundreds of years, changing in function and manufacture to fit the times and needs of its users.

Contemporary condoms are used widely as contraception and to prevent the spread of sexually transmitted disease. Initially, condoms were developed for other reasons. Among the earliest wearers of condoms were the ancient Egyptians, who wore them as protection against *Schistosoma,* a type of parasite spread through water. Condoms were also worn as decoration or signs of rank in various cultures.

Condoms emerged as weapons against sexually transmitted disease in Renaissance Europe of the sixteenth century, when epidemics of a virulent form of syphilis swept through Europe. Gabriele Fallopio (1523–1562), an Italian anatomist who discovered the Fallopian tube, advised men to use a linen condom to protect against venereal disease.

By the eighteenth century, condoms were made of animal membrane. This made them waterproof and more effective as birth control devices. Condoms acquired a host of nicknames, including the English riding coat, instruments of safety, and prophylactics. The great lover Casanova (1725–1798) described his use of condoms "to save the fair sex from anxiety."

The Industrial Revolution transformed the condom once again. In 1837, condom manufacturers took advantage of the successful vulcanization of rubber, a process in which sulfur and raw latex were combined at a high temperature. This enabled manufacturers to make a cheaper yet durable product.

In the 1980s, after many women had turned to modern medical contraceptives, condoms experienced another resurgence. This was due to the emergence of Acquired Immune Deficiency Syndrome (AIDS), and the discovery that condoms were most effective in preventing its transmission.

Currently, condoms are among the most common contraceptive used by Americans. A 1988 survey of the 57.9 million American women using contraceptives reported that 13.2% depended on condoms for contraception. A total of 12% of women who used condoms for contraception experienced accidental pregnancy in the first year of use in 1990.

Modern times

For centuries, limited knowledge of women's physiology slowed the development of effective contraceptives. There was no understanding of the accurate relationship between menstruation and ovulation until the early twentieth century. Yet contraceptive developers did make progress in the nineteenth century.

One major area was in updating the vaginal pessary. The rubber diaphragm and the rubber cervical cap, two types of pessary developed in the nineteenth century, are still in use today. The vaginal diaphragm was a disc–shaped object, designed to prevent conception by preventing the passage of sperm. The cervical cap fit over the cervix and was designed also to prevent the movement of sperm.

Spermicides, substances developed to kill sperm, were mass produced by the late 1880s for use alone or for greater effectiveness with other devices such as the diaphragm. Vaginal sponges were also developed for contraceptive use in the late 1800s. Another popular nineteenth century method of contraception was douching, the use of a substance in the vagina following intercourse to remove sperm.

Contemporary use of these methods yields varying pregnancy rates. The diaphragm was used by 5% of American women who used contraceptives in 1988. A total of 18% of women who used diaphragms with spermicide experienced accidental pregnancy in 1990 in their first year of using the contraceptive. Women who depended on spermicides, who made up 0.7% of women using contraceptives, experienced a 21% accidental pregnancy rate in their first year of use.

Although similar use figures were not available for the cervical cap or the sponge, the cap had an accidental pregnancy rate of 18% in 1990, and the sponge had a first–year accidental pregnancy rate of 18% among women who had never given birth.

While types of birth control increased in the nineteenth century, the topic of contraception was still considered sordid and unsuitable for public discourse. In the United States, the Comstock Law of 1873 declared all contraceptive devices obscene. The law prevented the mailing, interstate transportation, and importation of contraceptive devices. One effect of this was to eliminate contraceptive information from medical journals sent through the mail.

The social movement to make birth control legal and available challenged the Comstock Law and other restrictions against contraception. By the 1930s, the movement lead by Margaret Sanger (1883–1966) had successfully challenged the Comstock Law, and the mailing and transportation of contraceptive devices was no longer illegal. Sanger was also instrumental in developing clinics to distribute birth control devices.

Advances in medical knowledge generated new contraceptive methods. The first intrauterine device (IUD), designed to be placed in the uterus for contraceptive use, was described in 1909. The IUD was not used widely in the U.S. until the 1960s, when new models were introduced. The copper IUD and the IUD with progesterone made the IUD more effective. A 1990 study found the typical accidental pregnancy rate in the first year of use was 3%.

The IUD works by causing a local inflammatory reaction within the uterus. This reaction results in an increase in leukocytes, white blood cells, in the area. The product which results when the leukocytes break down is deadly to spermatozoa cells, greatly reducing the risk of pregnancy. The IUD devices available in the United States must be inserted by a health provider and typically must be replaced after one to four years, depending on the type. Possible dangers of the IUD include bleeding, perforation of the uterus and infection.

International use of the IUD is far higher than use in the United States. For example, in Scandinavia, 21% of married women used IUDs in 1987, compared to 5% in the United States and Canada. One reason for this may be fear of complications in the United States, where government officials pulled the Dalkon Shield IUD off the market in 1974, following reports of pelvic infections and other problems in women using the device. A second explanation may stem from the decision by two major IUD manufacturers to pull back from the U.S. market in the 1980s.

Another contraceptive method which emerged in the early twentieth century was the rhythm method, which was approved for use by Catholics by Pope Pius XII in 1951. For centuries, various experts on birth control had speculated that certain periods during a woman's cycle were more fertile than others. But they often were wrong. For example, Soranos, a Greek who practiced medicine in second century Rome, believed a woman's fertile period occurred during her menstrual period.

As researchers learned more about female reproductive physiology in the early twentieth century, they learned that ovulation usually takes place about 14 days before a woman's next menstrual period. They also learned that an egg could only be fertilized within 24 hours of ovulation. The so–called calendar rhythm method calculates "safe" and "unsafe" days based on a woman's average menstrual cycle, and calls for abstinence during her fertile period. The method is limited by the difficulty of abstinence for many couples and the irregularity of menstrual cycles.

Contemporary methods of contraception include methods referred to as natural family planning techniques. These methods incorporate knowledge of the rhythm method with factors such as basal body temperature, which varies depending on time of ovulation; and cervical mucus, which tracks the ovulation cycle based on the way a woman's cervical mucus looks. Accidental pregnancy rates for these methods were 20% in the first

year of use. A total of 2.1% of Americans used these methods in 1988.

As birth control became more acceptable in the twentieth century, controversy grew about the social uses of contraception. A series of mixed court decisions in the twentieth century considered whether it is right to force an individual who is mentally deficient to be sterilized. In the 1970s, national controversy erupted over evidence that low–income women and girls had been sterilized under the federal Medicaid program. Federal regulations were added to prohibit the forced sterilization of women under the Medicaid program. Legal debates also continue on the issue of whether certain individuals, such as convicted child abusers, should be required to use contraceptives.

The pill and its offspring

The development of oral contraceptives has been credited with helping to launch the sexual revolution of the 1960s. Whether oral contraceptives, also known as "the pill," should take credit for broadening sexual activity or not, their development changed the contraceptive world dramatically. In 1988, oral contraceptives were the most popular reversible contraceptive in the United States, with 27.7% of all women who used birth control using them, second only to sterilization. Internationally, more than 60 million women use oral contraceptives. The accidental pregnancy rate among women using oral contraceptives is less than 1%.

The development of oral contraceptives incorporated great advances in basic scientific knowledge. These included the finding in 1919 that transplanted hormones made female animals infertile, and the isolation in 1923 of estrogen, the female sex hormones.

For years, the knowledge that hormones could make animals infertile could not be applied to humans because of the expense of obtaining naturally–occurring estrogen. Until chemist Russell Marker developed a technique for making estrogen from plant steroids in 1936, estrogen had to be obtained from animal ovaries. Scientists needed ovaries taken from 80,000 sows to manufacture a "fraction of a gram" of estrogen.

Once synthetic hormones were available, the creation of oral contraceptives was limited by a lack of interest in the development of new birth control devices among drug companies and other, conventional funding sources. Gregory Pincus (1903–1967), who developed the oral contraceptive, obtained only limited funding from a drug company for his research. The bulk of his funding was from Katherine McCormick, a philanthropist, suffragist and Massachusetts Institute of Technology graduate who was committed to broadening birth control options.

The birth control pill, approved for use in the United States in 1960, uses steroids to alter the basic reproductive cycle in women. Pincus knew that steroids could interrupt the cyclic release of a woman's eggs during ovulation. Most pills use a combination of synthetic estrogen and progestin, although some only contain progestin. The steady levels of estrogen and progestin, obtained through daily oral contraceptive doses, prevent the release from the hypothalamus of gonadotrophin, a hormone which triggers ovulation. The pill also changes the cervical mucus so it is thicker and more difficult for sperm to penetrate.

Oral contraceptives can cause weight gain, nausea and headaches. In addition, women who smoke and are over 35 are advised not to take oral contraceptives due to risk of stroke. Oral contraceptives slightly increase the risk of cervical cancer, but they decrease the risk of endometrial and ovarian cancers.

Other contraceptives have drawn from oral contraceptive technology, including several contraceptives which work for a long period of time and do not require daily doses of hormones. Norplant, which was approved for use in the United States in 1991, is a hormone–based contraceptive which is surgically implanted in the arm. Norplant, which lasts approximately five years, distributes a steady dose of the hormone progestin. This hormone inhibits ovulation and alters cervical mucus to reduce movement of the sperm. The implant is highly effective, with an accidental pregnancy rate of less than .05%. However, the side affects include excess bleeding and discomfort, which sometimes force removal of the device.

Several long–term contraceptives are injectable and also use progestin to inhibit ovulation. The most widely used is Depo–Medroxyprogesterone Acetate, also known as Depo–Provera or DMPA. The method is used in more than 90 countries but not used widely in the United States. The drug, which is given every three months, is popular internationally, with as many as 3.5 million users worldwide. Fewer than 0.5% of women taking DMPA get pregnant accidentally. Most women who take DMPA for long periods of time stop having a regular menstrual cycle. The drug also causes temporary infertility after use.

Permanent contraception

Sterilization, the surgical alteration of a male or female to prevent them from bearing children, is an increasingly popular option. While sterilization can be reversed in some cases, it is not always possible, and sterilization should be considered permanent. In 1988, 39% of all contraceptive users ages 15–44 used sterilization, an increase from 34% in 1982. Among married contraceptive users, 49% used sterilization in 1988, up from 42% in 1982 and 23.5% in 1973. Internationally, sterilization is also extremely common, with 70 million women and men sterilized in China alone, according to the Population Council.

Sterilization of women is more popular than sterilization of men, even though the male operation, called vasectomy, is simpler and takes less time than the female operation, called tubal ligation. In 1988, a total of 27.5% of U.S. women ages 15–44 used sterilization as their birth control method, compared to 11.7% of men.

Tubal ligation, which takes about an hour, calls for sealing the tubes that carry eggs to the uterus. The incision to reach the oviducts can either be made conventionally or by using laparoscopy, a technique which uses fiber optic light sources to enable surgeons to operate without making a large incision. Women continue to produce eggs following a tubal ligation, but the eggs can no longer be fertilized.

Vasectomy, which takes about 20 minutes, involves cutting the vas deferens to prevent sperm from reaching the male semen. Men continue to produce semen following a vasectomy, but the semen no longer carries spermatozoa. Vasectomy and tubal ligation are considered to be safe procedures with few complications.

Challenges of contraception

Birth control policies and practices are controversial in the developed and the developing worlds. In developed countries, such as the United States, contraceptive methods fail frequently. Many of the types of contraceptives used commonly by Americans, such as condoms, spermicide, and the contraceptive sponge, have well documented rates of failure.

One measure of the number of unwanted pregnancies is the rate of abortion, the surgical termination of pregnancy. Although all individuals who receive abortions do not practice birth control, it is clear that many women do become pregnant when contraceptive methods fail. Abortion rates typically are highest in countries where contraceptives are difficult to obtain. For example, in the Soviet Union in the early 1980s, when contraceptives were scarce, 181 abortions were performed annually for every 1,000 women aged 15–44. This means 1 in 6 women had an abortion every year.

The abortion rate in the United States is typically higher than in many other developed countries. A 1990 study found that 28 per 1,000 women in the United States received an abortion annually, or 1 in 36 women. The rate in Great Britain was less than half—13 per 1000 women, and the rate in the Netherlands was 5.6 per 1,000. A study of 20 Western Democracies found that countries with lower abortion rates tended to have contraceptive care made easily available through primary care physicians.

Some experts believe that more access to contraceptive services would result in lower rates of accidental pregnancy and abortion. However, vigorous debate concerning programs to deliver contraceptives through school–based clinics and in other public settings have polarized the United States. Groups such as the Roman Catholic Church have opposed funding for greater accessibility of contraceptive services because they believe the use of any contraceptives is wrong.

Internationally, use of contraceptives has increased dramatically from the years 1960–1965, when 9% of married couples used contraceptives in the developing countries of Latin America, Asia, and Africa. By 1990, over 50% of couples in these countries used contraceptives.

The number of people in developing countries has also increased—and continues to increase—dramatically. For example, the developing nations of the mid–East and North Africa are expected to increase their population size by 76% within the next 25 years.

China has taken an aggressive policy to limit population growth which some experts have deemed coercive. Couples who agree to have one child and no more receive benefits ranging from increased income and better housing to better future employment and educational opportunities for the child. In addition, the Chinese must pay a fine to the government for each "extra" child.

Numerous problems exist which prevent the great demand for contraceptive services in developing countries from being met. Currently, contraceptive services are not available as extensively as they might be in developing countries, due in part to the general difficulty of providing medical care to poor people. In addition, some services remain too expensive to offer to all those who could use them, such as sterilization. Experts call for more money and creativity to be applied to the problem in order to avoid a massive population increase.

Future contraceptive methods

The high cost in time and money of developing new contraceptive methods in the United States creates a barrier to the creation of new methods. In the early

---

KEY TERMS

Estrogen—Female sex hormones produced in men and women. Substance used in birth control pills, to reduce menopausal discomfort, and in osteoporosis.

Hormone—Chemical substance produced by the body which helps to regulate specific organs.

Ovary—Female sex gland in which ova, eggs used in reproduction, are generated.

Progestin—Synthetic form of progesterone, the hormone which prepares the uterus for development of the fertilized egg.

Sperm—Substance secreted by the testes during sexual intercourse. Sperm includes spermatozoon, the mature male cell which is propelled by a tail and has the ability to fertilize the female egg.

Steroid—A group of lipids containing a particular chemical configuration. Steroids include hormones produced by the gonads, progesterone, and sterols such as cholesterol.

Uterus—Muscular female organ in which embryo and fetus develop.

1990s, a new contraceptive device could take as long as 17 years and up to $70 million to develop.

Yet new methods of contraception are being explored and tested by researchers. One device in clinical trials is a biodegradable progestin implant which would last from 12 to 18 months. The device is similar to Norplant but dissolves on its own. Another device being explored in countries outside the U.S. is a vaginal ring, impregnated with progestin, which provides contraception for three months.

Another approach is to target human chorionic gonadotrophin, (hCG), a substance produced in early pregnancy. This substance maintains the corpus luteum, a glandular mass formed in the ovary in early pregnancy which secretes progesterone and helps maintain the pregnancy. Researchers hope to target hCG early in pregnancy, causing loss of the embryo as menstruation occurs.

Other research focuses on male contraceptive methods. Many researchers are exploring the potential of a male "pill." The goal of a male contraceptive pill is to use hormones to temporarily stop the production of sperm. Various substances are being used in clinical trials.

Another approach involves the use of chemical agents to stop the production of sperm. One method which was tested in China involves the use of Gossypol, a substance found in cottonseed oil. Chinese testing found the substance effective but dangerous in some men who experienced heart problems.

Throughout history, contraceptive methods have been practiced. For much of Western history, the subject of contraception has been controversial. Although discussion of contraception is no longer banned from medical journals and other respectable literature, there is still disagreement concerning how widely contraception should be made available and how much public money should be spent on birth control. While the future form of contraception is uncertain, it seems likely that the topic will continue to generate vigorous debate about the meaning of efforts to limit reproduction.

See also Fertilization; Sexual reproduction.

Further Reading:
Drife, J.O. "Contraceptive problems in the developed world." *British Medical Bulletin*. Vol. 49, No. 1 (1993): 17–26.

Gordon, Linda. Woman's Body, Woman's Right. *A Social History of Birth Control in America*. New York: Grossman Publishers, 1976.

Hatcher, Robert A.; Stewart, Felicia; Trussell, James; Kowal, Deborah; Guest, Felicia; Stewart, Gary K.; Cates, Willard. *Contraceptive Technology 1990–1992*. 15th Revised Edition. New York: Irvington Publishers, Inc. 1990.

Herbst, Arthur L.; Mishell, Daniel R. Jr.; Stenchever, Morton A.; Droegemueller, William. "Contraception, Sterilization, and Pregnancy Termination," *Comprehensive Gynecology*. St. Louis: Mosby Year Book, 1992.

Lincoln, D.W. "Contraception for the year 2020." *British Medical Journal* Vol. 49, No. 1 (1993): 222–236.

Reed, James. *The Birth Control Movement and American Society*. Princeton: Princeton University Press. 1983.

Schenker, Joseph G.; and Rabenou, Vicki. "Family Planning: cultural and religious perspectives." *Human Reproduction*. Vol. 8, No. 6 (1993): 969–976.

Waites, G.M.H. "Male fertility regulation: The challenges for the year 2000." *British Medical Journal* Vol. 49, No. 1 (1993): 210–221.

Patricia Braus

Coordinate covalent bond see **Bond, chemical**

Coordinate geometry see **Analytic geometry**

Coordination compound

A coordination compound is formed when groups of atoms, ions, or molecules chemically bond with each other by donating and accepting pairs of electrons. Groups donating electron pairs are called ligands. They are usually Lewis bases. Groups accepting electron pairs are often transition metal cations.

They are usually Lewis acids. Chemical bonds formed in this way are called coordinate–covalent, or dative bonds. As in any covalent bond, two electrons are shared between transition metal and ligand. But in a coordination compound, both electrons come from a pair found on the ligand (See Figure l).

The metal cation simply acts as the electron pair acceptor, itself donating no electrons to the bond. Because of the complicated nature of these arrangements, coordination compounds are often called coordination complexes or simply complexes.

It is most common to find six ligands coordinated to a single metal cation. The coordination number is then six. Think of ligands as bees swarming about and stinging a victim. The ligand–bee's stinger is its lone pair or non–bonding pair of electrons. These special ligand–bees attack their victim in groups of six, although ligand groups of four and other numbers do occur. Six coordination produces the shape of a eight–sided figure or octahedron. Four coordination produces one of two shapes, a flat square planar or a four sided tetrahedron.

While nearly all cations can form coordination compounds with ligands, those listed in Table 1 are especially common.

Ligands come in all shapes and sizes, though they are usually non–metals from the right side of the periodic table. Those listed in Table 2 are typical.

TABLE 1. TYPICAL TRANSITION METAL CATIONS, M_T^{N+}			
Iron(II)	Fe^{2+}	Iron(III)	Fe^{3+}
Cobalt(II)	Co^{2+}	Cobalt(III)	Co^{3+}
Nickel(II)	Ni^{2+}		
Copper(II)	Cu^{2+}		

In this context Iron(II) is read or spoken as 1, iron two. Cobalt(III) is referred to as "cobalt three," and so on.

TABLE 2. TYPICAL LIGANDS, L

	Name As Ligand	Ordinary Name
Electrically Neutral	:NH_3 ammine	ammonia
	:OH_2 aqua	water
	:C=O carbonyl	carbon monox-ide
Negatively Charged	:Cl:- chloro	chloride
	:CN- cyano	cyanide
	:NCS:- thiocyanato	thiocyanate

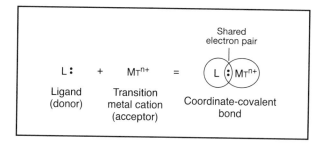

Figure 1. Formation and representations of a Coordinate–Covalent Bond.

The Swiss chemist Alfred Werner (1866–1919) is called the Father of Coordination Chemistry for his work in clarifying how coordination compounds are assembled. Figure 2 names and explains most of the parts.

Several theories help explain the nature of coordination compounds.

Effective atomic number theory matches the total number of electrons of the transition metal cation plus donated pairs of electrons from the ligands with the stable electron count of a noble gas atom. In $[Co^{III}(NH_3)_6]^{3+}$ above the central ion Co^{3+} contains 24 electrons. (A neutral cobalt atom has 27 electrons.) Each ammine ligand donates 2 electrons for a total of 12 electrons coming from the six ligands.

$$Co^{3+} + 6\,NH_3 = [Co(NH_3)_6]^{3+} = Krypton$$

24 electrons	+	6 x 2 electrons	=	36 electrons	=	36 electrons

If the total number of electrons associated with a coordination compound is the same as a noble gas, the compound will frequently have increased stability.

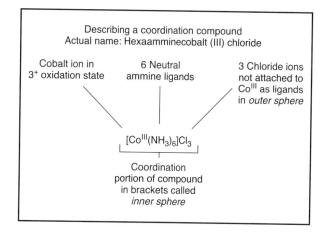

Figure 2.

Valence Bond Theory locates and creates empty orbitals on the transition metal cation. The empty orbitals will accept electron pairs from the ligands. A neutral cobalt atom contains 27 electrons: $1s^2\,2s^2\,2p^6\,3s^2\,3p^6 4s^2\,3d^7$. The 4s, 3d, and empty 4p orbitals are the

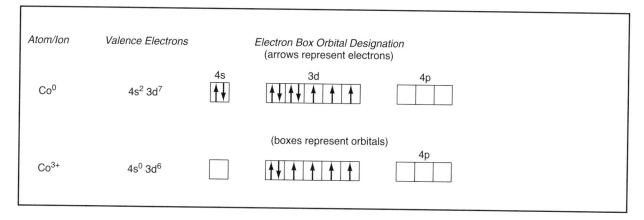

Figure 3. Electron boxes representing orbitals.

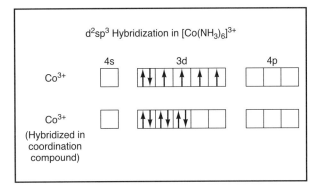

Figure 4. Six empty orbitals for six ligands.

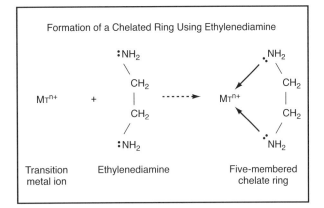

Figure 5.

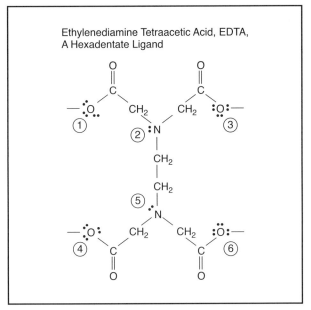

Figure 6.

valence orbitals containing the metal's valence electrons.

When forming cations, the 4s electrons are lost first, ahead of the 3d electrons (See Figure 3).

When Co^{3+} forms a coordination compound with six electron pair donating ammine ligands, it must have six empty receiving orbitals. But Co^{3+} only shows four empty orbitals, the one 4s and the three 4p. However, if two electrons in the 3d orbitals of Co^{3+} move over and pair up (See Figure 4), two additional empty 3d orbitals are created. Co^{3+} now has the required six empty orbitals, two 3ds, one 4s, and three 4ps.

This process is called hybridization, specifically $d^2s^1p^3$ or simply d^2sp^3 here.

An important magnetic phenomenon is associated with the Valence Bond Theory. Whenever at least one unpaired electron is present, that substance will be very weakly drawn towards a powerful magnetic. This is know as paramagnetism. Co^{3+} by itself has four unpaired electrons and is paramagnetic. But Co^{3+} in $[Co(NH_3)_6]^{3+}$ has no unpaired electrons. Most sub-

stances in nature do not have unpaired electrons and are said to be diamagnetic. These substances are very weakly repelled by a powerful magnetic. It is possible to measure paramagnetic and diamagnetic effects in a chemical laboratory.

Theories such as the Valence Bond Theory can thus be tested experimentally.

Crystal Field Theory is yet another approach to coordination compounds. It treats ligands as negatively charged anions, attracted to the positively charged transition metal cation.

This is what happens when a chloride anion, Cl^-, is attracted to the sodium ion, Na^+, in forming the ionic, crystalline compound, table salt, Na^+Cl^-. A crystal "field" is thus the electronic "field," produced in any ionic compound. Positive charges are attracted to negative charges and vice versa.

According to crystal field theory, when six negative ligands surround a transition metal cation, the energies of the metal's 3d electron orbitals are split up. Some 3d orbitals are stabilized and some are energized. The amount of stabilization energy predicted by the theory correlates well with that observed in laboratory experiments.

Many coordination compounds have vivid colors (See Table 3).

Crystal field theory predicts that these colors are due to metal 3d electrons jumping from stabilized to

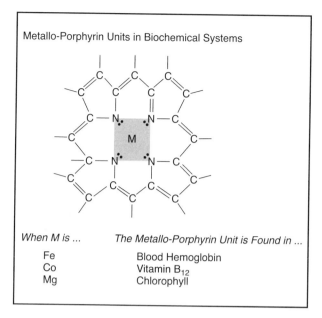

Metallo-Porphyrin Units in Biochemical Systems

When M is ...   The Metallo-Porphyrin Unit is Found in ...

Fe   Blood Hemoglobin
Co   Vitamin B$_{12}$
Mg   Chlorophyll

Figure 7.

energized orbitals when visible light or daylight shines on them.

The bright colors of coordination compounds make them good candidates for dyes, paint pigments, and coloring agents of all sorts.

A very special application of coordination compounds occurs in what is called the chelate effect. Chelation takes place when ligands "bite" or "bee sting" the metal in more than one place at a time. Using dental "biting" terminology, if a ligand has two "teeth" to bite a transition metal, it is called a bidentate (two teeth) ligand. One example of this is called ethylenediamine, $NH_2 CH_2 CH_2 NH_2$. Figure 5 shows simultaneous donation of two electrons each from the two nitrogen atoms of ethylenediamine. A five membered ring is produced involving the metal, two nitrogen atoms, and two carbon atoms.

A hexadentate ligand such as ethylenediamine tetraacetic acid, EDTA, bites a metal cation in six places simultaneously by wrapping itself around the

cation. This produces an extremely strong chelated compound. Using EDTA, such ions as calcium, Ca^{2+}, can be extracted from and tested in drinking water (See Fiure 6).

Chelated transition metal ions are also found in a wide variety of biochemical situations. A basic structural unit called metalloporphyrin is shown in Figure 7. It can be thought of as several ethylenediamine–like units fused and blended together into a single tetradentate (4 teeth) chelating ligand. Changing the central metal, M, changes the biochemical activity of the chelated coordination compound.

Research in this area is opening up a new field of chemistry called bio–inorganic chemistry.

See also Chemical bond, Ligand.

Copepods

Copepods are pale or translucent crustaceans, measuring between 0.04 mm to several millimeters long. They have adapted to many different habitats; while they usually live in salt water, copepods can live in lakes and ponds as well. Furthermore, they have different modes of locomotion: some can swim purposefully but others are planktonic, floating with the current. Scientists generally distinguish between two basic forms of copepods, free–living and parasitic.

The phylum Arthropoda is the largest phylum in the animal kingdom, containing more than one million species. Within this phylum, the subphylum Crustacea contains some 35,000 species and can be broken down into eight classes. Copepods belong to the class Maxillopoda and the subclass Copepoda, containing seven orders and more than 7,500 species. Three of these orders—Calanoida, Cyclopoida, and Harpacticoida—are primarily free–living and are present in huge numbers. The other orders are: Misophrioida, Monstrilloida, Siphonostomatoida, and Poecilostomatoida.

Characteristics of free–living copepods

Given the incredible number of species, the physical structure of copepods varies greatly. However, the free–living forms of copepods have certain physical traits in common. For instance, the body is usually short and cylindrical, composed of a head, thorax, and abdomen. The lower part of the copepods' head is generally fused with its thorax; the front of its head often juts forward, like a tiny beak. Its thorax is divided into

TABLE 3: EXAMPLES OF HIGHLY COLORED COORDINATION COMPOUNDS

$[Co(NH_3)_6]^{3+}$	$[Fe^{II}(CN)_6]^{3-}$	$[Cu(NH_3)_4]^{2+}$	$[Fe(H_2O)_5(SCN)]^{2+}$
Yellow-Orange	Deep Blue	Deep Blue	Blood-Red
	Coordination unit found in blue print ink	Used to identify copper as	Used to identify iron as
		Cu^{2+} ions	Fe^{3+} ions

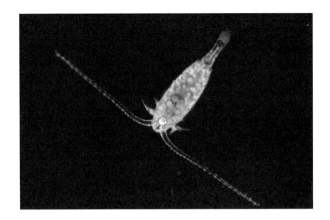

A copepod (*Diaptomus* sp.).

about six segments; each segment is connected to two appendages.

Generally, a free–living copepod has two pair of antennae and a single eye. The first pair of antennae is larger and has bristles. The male copepod can be distinguished from female because its antennae are slightly different from those of the female, modified for holding her during copulation. The free–living copepods' limbs are used for movement, sometimes with the help of its antennae. Its thin abdomen lacks limbs, except for the caudal furca – an appendage akin to a tail. Its tail has bristles similar to those found on its primary antennae. Some tropical forms of copepods actually use their bristles to facilitate flotation.

The parasites

There are over 1,000 species of parasitic copepods. As larva—or nauplia—most look and act like typical copepods. It is only later, when the parasites reach various stages in their development, that they begin to attach themselves to a host creature and radically change in appearance. In fact, many of the adult parasitic copepods are incredibly deviant in physical structure from their free–living relatives. Indeed, it is nearly impossible to find a single trait that is common to all copepods, both free–living and parasitic. One of the only characteristics that they tend to share is that the females have egg sacs which secrete a sticky liquid when the eggs are laid, gluing them together.

Furthermore, parasitic copepods are vastly different in appearance from other crustaceans. In general, adult parasitic copepods are shapeless, having neither limbs nor antennae and sometimes no body segments. Because these creatures start their lives as free–living animals, scientists infer that their ancestors were free–living and that they only evolved parasitic behavior after their environments dictated it.

Parasitic copepods can inflict severe damage on their hosts. This damage is often worsened by the presence and infestation of accompanying fungi.

Place in the food chain

Free–living copepods form a crucial link in the food chain and are often assigned the role of "primary consumers." Although some large forms of copepods are predators, free–living copepods are generally herbivores, feeding only on plant plankton which they filter from the water. Specifically, they eat small plant plankton and are, in turn, eaten by larger animals, like herring or mackerel. More fish and other aquatic animals feed on copepods than any other kind of animal in existence. One of the dominant forms of animal plankton, some scientists estimate that there are more copepods on the planet than all other multicellular animals combined.

Order Calanoida

Calanoids are of major importance to the commercial fishing industry. Like other copepods, this species filters minute animal algae from the water and eats it in large clumps. In turn, these copepods are eaten in large numbers by fish, such as herring and salmon. Calanoids thrive close to the surface of large expanses of water, both seas and lakes. Anatomically, they are easy to recognize. The fused head and thorax of an individual calanoid is oval and clearly separated from its abdomen. The multisegmented first antennae are long, about the same length as its body. The abdomen is much slimmer than its thorax.

Like other animal plankton, calanoids allow themselves to float with the current, although they can use their first antennae to swim upward in the water. Unlike most other genera of copepods, calanoids move from the surface to the depths of the water each day. At dawn, they sink to several hundred feet in the water; at dusk they rise to the surface again. There are several theories explaining this activity. The most likely reason is that they are escaping the dangerous ultraviolet rays of the sun. Another theory is that they are avoiding predators. In any case, this activity facilitates their fairly even distribution in the sea, since currents at various depths often run in different directions.

Order Cyclopoida

All of the free–living cyclopoida are almost identical to each other in physical appearance. Their antennae are shorter than those of the calanoids, growing about half of the length of their bodies. Their bodies, relatively pair–shaped, have two clearly divided regions: the head and thorax in the front; and the last segment of the thorax fused with the abdomen in the rear. Their front portions narrow slowly into their abdomens. This order contains many marine forms and numerous freshwater representatives. They are rarely planktonic, rather they tend to swim near the bottom of the water, never migrating upwards. They thrive in small pools of water with large amounts of aquatic vegetation. Some of the larger species are carnivores, eating insects and other crustaceans.

There are also twelve or more families living in relation to other animals: either as hosts to parasites or as parasites themselves. Some freshwater species are important as temporary hosts to certain forms of worms that are parasitic to man. Other species are parasites on mollusks, sea anemones, or sea–squirts. One specific group of parasitic cyclopoids live in the mouths or on the gills of certain fish, like frog–mouths. While the female can grow to 0.8 inches long, the male never surpasses about .04 inches. The jaws of the female are shaped like sickles, enabling her to cling to her host and eat it.

Order Harpacticoida

Harpacticoid bodies, which rarely exceed 0.07 in (2 mm) in length, are not clearly divided into three distinct regions, and they vary dramatically in shape. Some harpacticoids are long and snake–like, while others are flat. Their antennae are very short and forked.

Harpacticoids are planktonic, generally living in the muddy or sandy areas. Instead of swimming, these copepods hop, using the appendages on their thoraxes in combination with a rocking motion of their bodies. While most harpacticoids feed on organic waste or algae, some species are predators, swarming over small fish and immobilizing them by eating their fins.

Order Monstrilloida

Some of the most advanced species of parasitic copepods are found in this order. These copepods are worm parasites. Their nauplii appear quite typical, but have no stomach. When they find a suitable host, they shed their outer skeleton and all of their appendages and become a mass of cells. In this simple structure, they are able to reach the worms' body cavity. Once inside their host, these creatures form a thin outer skeleton; the copepods spend most of their lives without a mouth, intestines, or an anus. When they mature, they look like free–living copepods.

See also Zooplankton.

Further Reading:

George, David and Jennifer. *Marine Life: An Illustrated Encyclopedia of Invertebrates in the Sea.* New York: John Wiley and Sons, 1979.

KEY TERMS

Caudal furca—An appendage on the free–living copepod, resembling a tail, that is attached to its abdomen.

Free–living copepod—The copepods that does not attach itself to a living host but, instead, feeds on algae or small forms of animal life.

Nauplia—Larva of either free–living or parasitic copepods; both kinds of larvae are similar in appearance.

Planktonic—Free–floating; not using limbs for locomotion.

Thorax—The area just below the head and neck; the chest.

Grzimek, H.C. Bernard, Dr., ed. *Grzimek's Animal Life Encyclopedia.* New York: Van Nostrand Reinhold Company, 1972.

McGraw–Hill Encyclopedia of Science and Technology, 6th ed. New York: McGraw Hill Book Company, 1987.

The New Larousse Encyclopedia of Animal Life. New York: Bonanza Books, 1987.

Pearl, Mary Corliss, Ph.D. Consultant. *The Illustrated Encyclopedia of Wildlife.* London: Grey Castle Press, 1991.

Schmitt, Waldo L. *Crustaceans.* Ann Arbor: The University of Michigan Press, 1965.

Street, Philip. *The Crab and Its Relatives.* London: Faber and Faber Limited, 1966.

Kathryn Snavely

Copper

Copper is the metallic chemical element of atomic number 29, symbol Cu, atomic weight 63.55, specific gravity 8.96, melting point 1,985°F (1,085°C), and boiling point 4,645.4°F (2,563°C). It consists of two stable isotopes, of mass numbers 63 (69.1%) and 65 (30.9%).

Copper is one of only two metals that are colored, Copper is reddish brown, while gold is...gold—a unique color that is sometimes loosely described as yellow. All other metals are silvery, with various degrees of brightness or grayness. Almost everybody handles copper just about every day in the form of pennies. But because a piece of copper the size of a penny has become more valuable than one cent, today's pennies are made of zinc, with just a thin coating of copper. Take a file to one, and you'll see.

Copper is in group 11 of the periodic table, along with silver and gold. This trio of metals is sometimes referred to as the coinage metals, because they are relatively valuable, corrosion–free and pretty, which makes them excellent for making coins. Strangely enough, the penny is the only American coin that is *not* made from a copper alloy. Nickels, dimes, quarters and half dollars are all made from alloys of copper with other metals. In the case of nickels, the main metal is of course nickel.

Copper is one of the elements that are essential to life in tiny amounts, although larger amounts can be toxic. About 0.0004% of the weight of the human body is copper. It can be found in such foods as liver, shellfish, nuts, raisins and dried beans. Instead of the red hemoglobin in human blood, which has an iron atom in its molecule, lobsters and other large crustaceans have blue blood containing hemocyanin, which is similar to hemoglobin but contains a copper atom instead of iron.

History of copper

Copper gets its chemical symbol Cu from its Latin name, *cuprum*. It got that name from the island of Cyprus, the source of much of the ancient Mediterranean world's supply of copper.

But copper was used long before the Roman Empire. It is one of the earliest metals known to humans. One reason for this is that copper occurs not only as ores (compounds that must be converted to metal), but occasionally as native copper—actual metal found that way in the ground. In prehistoric times an early human could simply find a chunk of copper and hammer it into a tool with a rock. (Copper is very malleable, meaning that it can be hammered easily into various shapes, even without heating.)

Native copper was mined and used in the Tigris–Euphrates valley (modern Iraq) as long as 7,000 years ago. Copper ores have been mined for at least 5000 years because it is fairly easy to get the copper out of them. For example, if a copper oxide ore (CuO) is heated in a wood fire, the carbon in the charcoal can reduce the oxide to metal:

$2CuO$	+	C	R	$2Cu$	+	CO_2
copper		charcoal		copper		carbon
ore				metal		dioxide

Making pure copper

Extremely pure copper (greater than 99.95%), called electrolytic copper, can be made by electrolysis.

The high purity is needed because most copper is used to make electrical equipment, and small amounts of impurity metals in copper can seriously reduce its ability to conduct electricity. Even 0.05% of arsenic impurity in copper, for example, will reduce its conductivity by 15%. Electric wires must therefore be made of very pure copper, especially if the electricity is to be carried for many miles through high–voltage transmission lines.

To purify copper electrolytically, the impure copper metal is made the anode (the positive electrode) in an electrolytic cell. A thin sheet of previously purified copper is used as the cathode (the negative electrode). The electrolyte (the current–carrying liquid in between the electrodes) is a solution of copper sulfate and sulfuric acid. When current is passed through the cell, positively charged copper ions (Cu^{2+}) are pulled out of the anode into the liquid, and are attracted to the negative cathode, where they lose their positive charges and stick tightly as neutral atoms of pure copper metal. As the electrolysis goes on, the impure copper anode dissolves away and pure copper builds up as a thicker and thicker coating on the cathode. Positive ions of impurity metals such as iron, nickel, arsenic and zinc also leave the anode and go into the solution, but they remain in the liquid because the voltage is purposely kept too low to neutralize them at the cathode. Other impurities, such as platinum, silver and gold, are also released from the anode, but they are not soluble in the solution and simply fall to the bottom, where they are collected as a very valuable sludge. In fact, the silver and gold sludge is usually valuable enough to pay for the large amount of electricity that the electrolytic process uses.

Uses of copper

By far the most important use of copper is in electrical wiring; it is an excellent conductor of electricity (second only to silver), it can be made extremely pure, it corrodes very slowly, and it can be formed easily into thin wires—it is very ductile.

Copper is also an important ingredient of many useful alloys—combinations of metals, melted together. Brass is copper plus zinc. If it contains mostly copper, it is a golden yellow color; if it is mostly zinc, it is pale yellow or silvery. Brass is one of the most useful of all alloys; it can be cast or machined into everything from candle sticks to cheap, gold–imitating jewelry that turns your skin green. (When copper reacts with salt and acids in the skin, it produces green copper chloride and other compounds.) Several other copper alloys are common: bronze is mainly copper plus tin; German silver and sterling silver are silver plus copper; silver tooth fillings contain about 12% copper.

Probably the first alloy ever to be made and used by humans was bronze. Archaeologists broadly divide human history into three periods; the Bronze Age is the second one, after the Stone Age and before the Iron Age. During the bronze age, both bronze and pure copper were used for making tools and weapons.

Because it resists corrosion and conducts heat well, copper is widely used in plumbing and heating applications. Copper pipes and tubing are used to distribute hot and cold water through houses and other buildings.

Because copper is an extremely good conductor of heat, as well as of electricity (the two usually go together), it is used to make cooking utensils such as saute and fry pans. An even temperature across the pan bottom is important for cooking, so the food doesn't burn or stick to hot spots. The insides of the pans must be coated with tin, however, because too much copper in our food is toxic.

Copper corrodes only slowly in moist air—much more slowly than iron rusts. First it darkens in color because of a thin layer of black copper oxide, CuO. Then as the years goes by it forms a bluish green patina of basic copper carbonate, with a composition usually given as $Cu_2(OH)_2CO_3$. (The carbon comes from carbon dioxide in the air.) This is the green color of the Statue of Liberty, which is made of 300 thick copper plates bolted together. Without traveling to New York you can see this color on the copper roofs of old buildings such as churches and city halls.

Compounds of copper

In its compounds, copper can have a valence of either +1 (cuprous compounds) or +2 (cupric compounds). Cuprous compounds are not stable in water, and when dissolved they turn into a mixture of cupric ions and metallic copper.

Copper compounds and minerals are often green or blue. The most common minerals include malachite, a bright green carbonate, and azurite, a blue–green basic carbonate. Among the major copper ores are cuprite, CuO, chalcopyrite, $CuFeS_2$, and bornite, Cu_5FeS_4. Large deposits of copper ores are found in the United States, Canada, Chile, central Africa, and Russia.

Cupric sulfate, $CuSO_4 \cdot 5H_2O$, is also called blue vitriol. These poisonous blue crystals are used to kill algae in the purification of water, and as an agricultural dust or spray for getting rid of insects and fungi.

See also Alloy; Electric conductor; Electrolysis; Metal.

Further Reading:

Emsley, J. *The Elements.* New York: Oxford University Press, 1991.
Greenwood, N. N. *Chemistry of the Elements.* New York: Pergamon Press, 1985.
Kirk–Othmer Encyclopedia of Chemical Technology. New York: Wiley, 1992.
Parker, Sybil P., ed. *McGraw–Hill Encyclopedia of Chemistry,* 2nd ed. New York: McGraw–Hill, 1993.

Robert L. Wolke

Copperhead see **Snakes**

Copperheads see **Squirrels**

Coral reef

Coral reefs are very diverse, having more than one–third of the fish species occurring in this type of ecosystem. The reefs themselves are complex ecosystems. The spectacular beauty and biodiversity of coral reefs attracts divers, tourists, fishers, and scientists. Coral reefs are located in warm, shallow, tropical waters where there is sufficient light to stimulate growth of the reef. Besides warm, shallow water, coral reefs need wave action and favorable levels of salinity. The organisms that create the calcium carbonate of reefs are animals known as corals, along with coralline algae, which serve as the cement of the reef structure.

There are three kinds of coral reefs: atolls, barrier reefs, and fringing reefs. Atolls are rings of coral that surround a shallow lagoon and are found in the vicinity of sea mounts and atoll islands. Fringing reefs are located close to shore, and the water between them and the nearby land is shallow. Barrier reefs are located farther from the shoreline, and the depth of water in the lagoon between the reef and shore is around 30 ft (9 m) deep.

Theories about the formation of coral reefs were developed by Charles Darwin during his voyage to the Pacific islands on the Beagle in the early nineteenth century. Darwin believed that the first stage of development of an atoll was the creation of a fringing reef around an island. Later, as the island sank, the reef became a barrier reef, and finally, when the island completely sank into the ocean depths, an atoll was left. In the twentieth century Reginald Daly, a geologist, developed his theory around the concept of glaciated mountain peaks and involved the concept that the newer reefs around Hawaii were built on older ones that had been worn down through the ages.

Kayangel atoll, Belau.

Location of coral reefs

Coral reefs cover a total area of 68 million square miles (176 million sq km), an area larger than the continents of Asia, Africa, and Europe combined. Coral reefs are found in the Atlantic, Pacific, and Indian Oceans and wherever shallow, warm–water habitats are found. Coral reefs can also be found around Africa, the Atlantic Ocean, Caribbean, the Florida Keys, Central America, Mexico, the Persian Gulf and the Red Sea.

The Great Barrier Reef

The Great Barrier Reef, the world's largest reef, lies off the eastern coast of Australia. About 30% of the coral reefs of the world are found scattered around the islands and mainland of southeast Asia. The world's largest and most famous coral reef is the Great Barrier Reef that stretches along the continental shelf off the northeastern coast of Australia for more than 1,300 mi (2,093 km). The Great Barrier Reef covers 80,000 square miles (207,200 sq km). Despite its name, the Great Barrier is not one single, large reef but is composed of a network of nearly 3,000 barrier reefs, atolls, patch reefs, shoals, dunes, islets, and islands. The development of this gigantic system has been shaped by

millions of years of geological and ecological history, including the northward movement of Australia in a continental drift, changing sea levels associated with several ice ages, ocean currents, and hundreds of thousands of years of erosion and rebuilding.

There are considerable differences in the formations of the Great Barrier Reef from one end to the other. The warmest waters around the reef are located in its northern section where it is composed of narrow ribbon reefs tightly connected to form a wall of coral. In the middle sections of the reef, large platform reefs along the inside of the continental shelf can be found. Farther from shore, smaller and shorter reefs separated by shallow channels are scattered around the waters. The southern section of the reef is broken up into groups of atolls, where the channels between them are deep enough to navigate.

Formation and growth

Life within a coral reef is symbiotic, having many plants and animals living together mutually benefiting from one another. Remarkably, all coral reefs around the world have similar plants and animals which are vital to the formation and growth of the reef. Coral reefs are complex ecosystems in which diverse species of organisms have established balanced relationships. The main builders of coral reefs are the corals themselves, coralline algae, hydrozoans, and in some instances certain types of sponges.

Cementing the structure is accomplished mainly by the coralline algae, which act as the glue for dead coral skeletons, sand, shells, and debris. During storms when there is heavy wave motion, pieces of the reef may break off and may later become part a different reef in another location. The structure of the reef is also subject to erosion by organisms which create open spaces within the reef structure. Among the organisms that help create open spaces are bacteria, fungi, algae, sponges, worms, sea urchins, and clams. It is within these open spaces that some marine life can evade its predators, and some light–sensitive ones can protect themselves from the light. The amount of open space within a coral reef is estimated to range from 40–70%.

Environmental factors

While many of the creatures living within a coral reef benefit from its dark nooks and crannies, the reef itself is dependent on light for its growth since the algae eaten by corals need light to accomplish photosynthesis. The amount of light and the depth of the water help to develop the various shapes of the coral structure. Where there is a great deal of light, the reef grows in mounds or into boulder shapes. Where there is less light, the coral structure tends to take a somewhat flatter or branched shape.

Water temperature is another important environmental factor in the growth of coral reefs. The annual water temperature ranges from 74–78°F (23–25°C) which is ideal for coral reef building. Another factor in coral reef growth is submersion under water, although some reefs survive the temporary exposure of low tides. The salt content of the water needs to range between 35–38 parts per thousand. The concentration of oxygen and the acidity of sea water are other important factors in the growth of coral.

Coral reefs thrive in waters that do not contain large concentrations of phosphates, ammonia, and nitrate. Evidence of disease can be seen in corals that are subjected to nutrient–rich waters. Water circulation helps supply the nutrients that the coral and algae need for survival and to remove waste materials. Too much sediment in the water can also suffocate reef organisms and harm the growth of a coral reef.

The builders

The main players in reef–building are hermatypic coral polyps, flower–like animals once thought to be plants, and zooxanthellae, a single–celled algae that lives within the tissues of the corals. There are chemical exchanges between the coral polyps and the zooxanthellae that makes it possible for them to both thrive in a symbiotic relationship while building a reef.

Coral polyps have two tissue layers. The outer layer contains a funnel that leads into the digestive cavity, and the inner layer lines the stomach. The corals that build the reef are scleractinian animals and they secrete a hard, cup–like skeleton that becomes the framework of the reef. The polyps can reproduce asexually through a budding process that forms duplicate daughter polyps. One polyp has the potential of forming a limestone boulder more than 30 ft (9 m) across. Coral polyps are also able to reproduce sexually, which allows their offspring to be carried to other parts of the ocean floor to do their reef–building in other locations.

The zooxanthellae algae are able to supply coral polyps with more than 90% of their daily food nutrients on sunny days. In exchange for proteins and carbohydrates from the algae, the coral polyps supply the algae with a habitat and essential minerals. Corals also feed on microscopic organisms, invertebrates, zooplankton, and tiny fish that drift by. This additional feeding takes place at night when the corals do not receive nutrition from the algae, since the sun is necessary for photosynthesis to take place.

Red coralline algae also contribute to the framework of reefs by supplying it with calcite material that helps build up its crust. Coralline algae are usually referred to as the "cementer" in coral reef building. Other reef–building organisms are sponges, bryozoans (plant–like animals), and the skeletons of tube worms, oysters, and snails. In deep parts of a reef, hard sponges are especially important in reef building.

Life in coral reefs

As an underwater environment, coral reefs offer safe habitats for plants and animals that are not attached to the reef the way the corals are. Microscopic marine plants, plankton, are at the bottom of the food chain under water. Other algae and bacteria live at the bottom of the reef where they supply food for many other fish and sea urchins, which come in green, brown, gold, and red colors. Unlike higher plants, algae do not have leaves, stems, or roots with conductive tissue.

Turtle grass, a vascular plant, benefits coral reefs by forming a thick grassy meadow in open spaces of the reef. The meadows of turtle grass filter nutrients from the water, bind sediments together, and provide a baffle against the ocean current by forming banks that prevent erosion in the reef. Many animals shelter their offspring within these turtle grass meadows. Fish, snails, clams, sea turtles, sea horses, and sea urchins are found grazing in these meadows.

Besides the plankton drifting through a coral reef, there are jellyfish and similar large invertebrates floating around the reef. Among the animals swimming around and within a reef are fish, marine reptiles and mammals, cuttlefish, squid, and octopus. There may be as many as 500 species of fish that inhabit a specific coral reef, including the 50 ft (15 m) long whale shark. Porpoises, sea turtles, sea snakes, and manatees have been seen feeding around coral reefs. Some of the fish in the reef defend a specific territory for themselves, while others travel in large schools and may sound a chemical alarm when they encounter a threat from a predator.

There is an assortment of life at the bottom of the reef that includes barnacles, oysters, molluscs, clams, lamp shells, and a variety of worms. It is estimated that as many as 150,000 species are in some way attached to parts of reefs. Together they contribute to the varied forms and colors seen within a coral reef structure.

Predators

Destruction from the crown–of–thorns starfish has occurred in Pacific coral reefs. Large populations of crown–of–thorn starfish have infested reefs, eaten their way through many miles of reef, and destroyed nearly all the corals. This has been documented on reefs off of Guam and on the Great Barrier Reef of Australia, where almost one–fourth of it was destroyed by crown-of-thorn infestations. When corals have been destroyed by starfish, algae and bacteria grow over the surface and can prevent new coral from growing. Scientists believe that an increase in frequency of outbreaks of starfish infestations has been caused by enriched nutrient levels from coastal runoff during heavy rains. The enriched nutrient content of runoff may be related to nearby agricultural use of fertilizers, but this theory is controversial.

A different threat to coral reefs in the Caribbean and along the Florida Keys came from a blight in 1983 that nearly destroyed the spiny sea urchin population there. These creatures are important to the reefs because they limit the amount of algae that can grow. With the destruction of the sea urchins, algae overgrew the reef. As more fish graze, they contributed more erosion of the reef.

Destruction of coral reefs from natural causes, like rain storms, hurricanes, earthquakes, and thermal stress (radical weather changes) also contribute to the destruction of coral reefs. Fortunately, these natural conditions do not usually destroy the whole reef, and the ecosystem is able to recover over time.

A condition known as bleaching of coral has been related to high temperature conditions. When bleaching occurs, the coral polyps discharge the zooxanthellae, and the coral becomes pale or white in patches. Without the benefit of the algae, the coral becomes weak or dies. Major bleaching events took place during the 1980s in both the Caribbean Sea and the Pacific Ocean. The elements in common in the cases of bleaching have been periods of unusually calm weather, high water temperatures, and exposure to rather high levels of light.

Speculation over the causes of coral bleaching includes theories involving abnormally warm ocean currents and global warming from the "greenhouse effect" and increased ultraviolet light exposure. Pollution from oil spills and other water–polluting sources are also cited as possible causes of coral bleaching.

Uses

Coral reefs are a natural laboratory for marine scientists to study not only the life of the different organisms forming and living in the structure, but also as an area to study the complexities of an ecosystem. Many research institutes around the world are engaged in research and collect data used to advise governments about the conservation of natural resources. Other useful research of coral reefs can supply information about changes in the sea level.

Geologists are interested in living coral reefs because some of the largest oil and gas fields have been found in ancient reefs. They are interested in learning more about the entrapment of oil in ancient reefs. Some of the atolls in the South Pacific, where atomic and nuclear weapons were tested after World War II, are useful for biologists to study how radioactive fallout affects the fish in the coral reefs and the reef ecosystem itself.

Both the plant and animal life in coral reefs continue to contribute to world food supplies, including significant quantities of lobsters, shrimp, crabs, clams, squid, and fish. In medicine, more than 1,200 compounds have been extracted from coral reef dwellers. These compounds are being used in the treatment of diseases such as AIDS, multiple sclerosis, cancer, cardiovascular disease, asthma, ulcers, rheumatoid arthritis, and pain.

See also Corals; Hydrozoa; Ocean; Sea urchins; Sponges; Starfish.

KEY TERMS

Atoll—A ring–like coral formation surrounding a lagoon.

Barrier reef—A linear coral formation near the shoreline, usually along the seaward edge of an ocean shelf and separated from the land by a lagoon.

Biodiversity—Referring to the presence of a wide variety of life forms within a particular environment.

Bleaching—White or pale patching on a reef from the loss of zooxanthellae algae.

Ecosystem—The interrelationships of all living organisms and environmental factors within a biological community.

Fringing reef—A coral reef that runs parallel to the shore, closer to it than a barrier reef and with a shallower lagoon.

Hermatypic—Reef–building corals.

Patch reef—A small reef formation that grows on the floor of the lagoon.

Plankton—Microscopic marine plants and animals.

Symbiotic—A relationship between several organisms that benefits one or both.

Further Reading:

Gray, William. *Coral Reefs and Islands*. Devon, England: David and Charles, 1993.

Roessler, Carl. *Coral Kingdoms*. New York: Harry N. Abrams, 1986.

Strykowski, Joe, and Rena Bonem. *Palaces Under the Sea*. Crystal River, FL: Star Thrower Foundation, 1993.

Thorne–Miller, Boyce, and John Catena. *The Living Ocean*. Washington, DC: Island Press, 1991.

Vita Richman

Corals

Corals are a group of small, colonial, tropical marine animals in the subclass Hexacorallia, phylum Cnidaria, that attach themselves to the seabed and form extensive reefs. Corals have a planktonic stage in their life history, during which dispersal over a wide area is possible. Adult corals, on the other hand, are sessile animals, usually occurring in discrete, single–species colonies. Extensive coral reefs commonly develop in shallow, warm–water seas. These reefs are made up of the dead calcium–carbonate encasing structures of the coral animals. These coral reefs form the basis of complex marine food webs that are richer in species than any other ecosystem. Because corals build extensive shallow–water tropical reefs, these animals play a critically important role in their ecosystem.

Biology of corals

Hard corals, or cnidarians, are mostly colonial animals that grow upon the dead, calcareous remains of the previously living network of individuals, or polyps, in their colony. Therefore, the living coral polyps occur on the outside of the colony, while underneath are the dead skeletons of their predecessors.

The various species of corals form distinctively shaped colonies. Some species, such as the stag–head coral, are intricately branched, while large brain corals are almost spherical in outline.

Coral polyps occur in a close, mutually beneficial symbiosis with single–celled algae known as zooxanthellae. These microorganisms are dinoflagellate algae that provide the coral with biochemicals fixed through their photosynthesis and metabolism in return for shelter and inorganic nutrients.

Corals typically occur in shallow, warm seas where water temperatures are consistently warmer than about 67° F (18° C), and in water depths less than about 164 ft (50 m). Corals also prefer a relatively stable salinity, and clear, nonturbid waters. Nutrient concentrations must also be small to prevent the corals from becoming overgrown with free–living algae.

Corals are predators of tiny planktonic animals. Their prey is paralyzed by stinging cells (nematocysts), and then collected with tentacle–like appendages. Some corals feed by creating a weak current with cilia, which draws food into their mouths, or by producing a sticky mucus to trap planktonic animals.

Coral "bleaching" refers to rare events during which corals lose their zooxanthellae, which sometimes leads to the death of the colony. This syndrome appears to be induced by a variety of environmental stresses, including abnormally warm or cool water temperatures, changes in salinity, or excessive exposure to direct sunlight or shading.

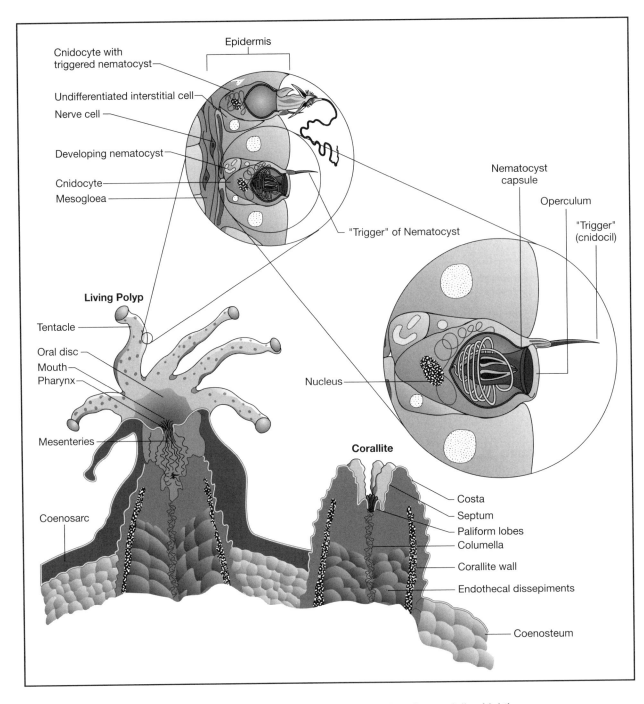

Epidermis

Cnidocyte with triggered nematocyst

Undifferentiated interstitial cell

Nerve cell

Developing nematocyst

Cnidocyte

Mesogloea

"Trigger" of Nematocyst

Nematocyst capsule

Operculum

"Trigger" (cnidocil)

Living Polyp

Tentacle

Oral disc

Mouth

Pharynx

Nucleus

Mesenteries

Corallite

Coenosarc

Costa

Septum

Paliform lobes

Columella

Corallite wall

Endothecal dissepiments

Coenosteum

The anatomy of a hard coral (left) and the skeletal corallite that remains after the coral dies (right).

Ecology of coral reefs

Coral reefs develop mainly from the hard calcareous substrate manufactured by corals, although the calcium–carbonate deposits of other marine animals, such as bivalves and certain algae, are also important. Coral reefs typically occur in water depths of less than about 190–230 ft (50–70 m), and they occur in tropical and subtropical waters, between about latitudes 30° N and 30° S.

Coral reefs are of three forms: fringing reefs occurring on the seaward edge of a larger landmass; barrier reefs occurring farther out to sea, with a deep channel between the reef and land; and atolls, or ring– or crescent–shaped islands developed as a fringe around submarine mountains or islands. The world's largest coral reef system is the Great Barrier Reef of eastern Australia, more than 1240 miles (2000 km) long, and up to 89 miles (144 km) from the mainland.

Coral reefs are highly developed natural ecosystems which sustain a great richness of species and a tremendous complexity of ecological interactions. Coral reefs develop under environmental conditions characterized by a highly restricted supply of nutrients. Nevertheless, coral reefs maintain a high rate of ecological productivity, because of the great efficiency of use, and because they recycle the small quantities of nutrients that are available. Because coral reefs have a high biodiversity and great ecological complexity, ecologists believe that these ecosystems are the most highly developed of all marine ecosystems.

Some ecologists believe that the high biodiversity of coral reefs is maintained in response to a stable, little–disturbed environment which allows for the accumulation of species over time. The most competitive species are prevented from completely dominating the ecosystem, while a shifting mosaic of relatively young habitats is maintained for colonization by less competitive species. The natural disturbances to which coral reefs are adapted include intense windstorms such as hurricanes, volcanic eruptions, events of sediment deposition, events of unusually low tides, and unusual temperature variations. Sometimes, events of unusual abundance of certain species of the coral reef ecosystem may also cause substantial ecological damage. Examples of these biological disturbances include blooms of toxic algae known as red tides and irruptive population of certain destructive animals such as the crown-of-thorns starfish (*Acanthaster planci*), which can degrade coral reefs by consuming much of the living, reef-building coral.

People and corals

Corals and the reefs they develop provide extremely valuable ecological services for humans, including the protection of shorelines from the full onslaught of storm–driven waves. Some of these services provided by coral reefs are of direct economic benefit, and they can potentially be used on a sustained yield basis—for example, through tourism, or a controlled fishery.

Regrettably, however, many human uses of coral reefs cause substantial degradations of their physical and ecological structure. The most devastating damage is caused by the mining of coral reefs, to provide calcium–based materials for the construction of buildings, including the manufacturing of cement.

Although fishing is a potentially sustainable activity, it has not been practiced in moderation or with care. The most destructive fishing practice used in coral reef ecosystems involves the use of dynamite to stun or kill fish, which are then gathered. Dynamiting is extremely wasteful of fish, many of which are not collected after they are killed, and also of the coral reef ecosystem, which suffers serious longer–term damage from the explosions. Dynamiting is also dangerous for the fishermen, many of whom are injured or killed while engaged in this livelihood.

Other physically destructive fishing practices involve large numbers of fishermen forming a drive–line in shallow waters and moving forward together to force fish towards a large net. The fishermen strike the bottom with poles and weights, scaring the fish forward, but also causing great destruction to the coral reef. Sometimes, poisons are used by divers to intoxicate fish, which can then be collected by hand. This method is used to catch fish as food for local people and also for the international aquarium trade.

Coral reefs are also highly vulnerable to pollution of various types. Pollution by nutrients is most commonly associated with the dumping of sewage effluents into the marine ecosystem, either as runoff from cities, carried to the vicinity of coral reefs through discharge pipes or river flows, or through the local effluents of smaller coastal villages. Inputs of nutrients such as nitrate and phosphate can cause phytoplankton to become highly productive and abundant, and their biomass can prevent sunlight from penetrating to the corals in sufficient intensity to sustain their zooxanthellae. Nutrients can also cause the free–living algae on the reef surface to become highly productive, and in some cases these can smother the corals, causing a degradation of the coral reef ecosystem. Changes in the availability and ratios of nutrients can also disrupt the finely–tuned balance between the corals and their zooxanthellae and can degrade this important symbiosis.

Many species of corals and their zooxanthellae are highly sensitive to toxic contaminants, such as pesticides, metals, and other chemicals. Coral reefs can be easily degraded by pollution involving substantial inputs of these sorts of chemicals, for example, through agricultural runoff into the near–shore environment.

Sometimes, coral reefs are severely damaged by oil spills from wrecked tankers, or from smaller but more frequent discharges from coastal refineries or urban runoff. Corals and their associated species can suffer damage from exposure to toxic hydrocarbons, and from the physical effects of smothering by dense, viscous residues of oil spills.

KEY TERMS

Calcareous—Composed of calcite or calcium carbonate ($CaCO_3$), a hard mineral.

Polyp—An individual animal in a coral colony.

Mutualism—A mutually beneficial interaction or symbiosis between two different species.

Zooxanthellae—The single–celled, dinoflagellate algae that live in a mutualistic symbiosis with corals.

Sedimentation is another type of pollution that occurs when large quantities of fine soil materials are eroded from nearby terrestrial ecosystems and are then carried to near–shore marine waters where they settle out of the water and smother coral reefs. Corals are tolerant of a certain amount of sedimentation. However, these animals can be killed when the rate of material deposition is greater than what the corals can cope with through their natural cleansing abilities. These are associated with polyp movements and ciliary action and the outward growth of the colony. Sedimentation may also cause damage if its associated turbidity excessively reduces the availability of light required by the symbiotic zooxanthellae.

Even tourism can be extremely damaging to coral reefs. Damage can be caused when boats anchor on the reef, resulting in physical disturbance of the coral, especially under windy conditions when the anchor may drag. Even people walking on shallow reefs may cause significant damages, because the more intricate species of corals are easily damaged. Also, some divers like to collect pieces of coral as souvenirs, a practice that can contribute to the degradation of frequently visited reefs. In many places in the tropics, coral reefs that support heavy recreational usage by ecotourists are in a relatively degraded condition, compared with more remote reefs that are used less intensively visited.

Coral reefs are wonderfully diverse and complex ecosystems. However, they are highly vulnerable to suffering damage from a wide range of human influences. It is critical that the future use and abuse of coral reefs be better controlled than in the past, or these marvelous ecosystems and their many species will become much more rare and endangered than they already are.

Further Reading:

Bakus, G. J. *Coral Reef Ecosystems*. Rotterdam: Balkema, 1994.

Dubinsky, Z., ed. *Coral Reefs*. Ecosystems of the World, no. 25. New York: Elsevier, 1991.

Bill Freedman

Coral snakes see **Elapid snakes**

Coreid bugs see **True bugs**

Coriander see **Carrot family**

Coriolis effect see **Wind**

Cork

Cork is the outer, regenerative bark of the cork oak tree, *Quercus suber,* family Fagaceae. Unlike other oak species, the cork oak is an evergreen tree and dates from the Oligocene epoch of the Tertiary period. The oldest cork fossil, dating 10 million years old, was found in Portugal and is identical to modern cork. Today cork oak trees grow exclusively around the edge of the Mediterranean, primarily in Portugal, Spain, and Algeria, and to a lesser extent in Morocco, Tunisia, Italy, Sicily, and France.

A cross section of the tree trunk or large branch of *Q. suber* reveals three distinct layers: (1) the inner and largest area, the xylem (woody tissue), (2) a thin layer covering the xylem called the inner bark, and (3) the outer cork layer, also known as phellogen or cork–cambium. When the tree is about 10 years old, it is stripped of its outer bark (the cork) for the first time. Cork from the first stripping is called virgin cork. Strippers make vertical and horizontal cuts into the bark and lift the planks off. Care is taken not to damage the living, inner bark, which cannot replenish the cork if it is damaged. Stripping takes place during spring or summer when new cork cells are developing near the inner bark, making the cork easier to strip off. Within three months after stripping, growth of the cork layer resumes. The cork layer stops growing when cold weather begins.

A cork oak is stripped about every 10 years. The second and subsequent strippings are called reproduction cork and are of better quality than virgin cork. A healthy tree can live for 150 years. An old tree with a large girth and branches can yield more than 1,000 lb (455 kg) of cork in a single harvest. Cork oaks aged between 35 and 45 years typically yield about 200 lb (91 kg) per year, and trees aged 50 or 60 years can yield 330 lb (150 kg) of cork.

The cork planks are seasoned for about six months in the open air. Exposure to rain, wind, and sun during seasoning cause chemical transformations in the cork, improving its quality. After the planks are seasoned, they are boiled to remove tannic acid and resins, to soften the cork, and to make the outermost, rough surface easier to remove. The cork planks are sorted according to quality. The highest quality cork is used for bottle stoppers. The rest of the cork is either cut into sections or granulated to make agglomerated cork. Agglomerated cork consists of small pieces (granules) of cork that are agglutinated (glued or adhered together) with either the cork oak's own resin, or with products such as rubber, asphalt, or synthetic resins, and then heat treated under pressure to solidify the composite material.

The cork consists of suberose tissue formed by the phellogen, a tissue between the inner bark and cork, from which cork develops. Suberin is a waxy, waterproof substance in the cell wall (suberose tissue), made of fatty acids and organic alcohols, and making cork impermeable to liquids and gases. Although cork is the bark of a living tree, it is actually a conglomeration of dead cells. Each cell is a multi-sided polyhedron, only 30–40 microns in diameter, and is filled with a gas almost identical to the normal atmosphere. One cubic centimeter of cork contains about 40 million cells. Cork is made up of more gas (90%) than solid material, making its density very low. Cork floats and does not rot. It is also fire resistant, compressible, and does not conduct heat or sound very well. These characteristics make cork a useful material for diverse purposes. Cork is used, for example, in the fishing industry, the electrical and building industries, automobile and aeronautic industries, the manufacture of sporting goods and home furnishings, shoes, and musical instruments. Some examples of cork products are floor and wall tiles, expansion or compression joints in concrete structures, insulation, safety helmets, several types of sporting good balls, heat shields, gaskets, shoe soles, and fishing tackle.

Today, Portugal is the leading producer of cork. In Portugal, the cork oak tree is protected by stringent laws regarding the growing, pruning, and stripping of the tree. Cork cultivators are given technical and financial assistance, and cork products are highly regulated to maintain high standards of quality.

See also Oaks.

Christine Miner Minderovic

Corm

A corm is modified, upright, swollen, underground stem base of a herbaceous plant. Corms serve as a perennating organ, storing energy and producing new shoots and flowering stems from one or more buds located in the axils of the scale–like leaves of the previous year. Corms differ from superficially similar bulbs in that their leaves are thin rather than fleshy, and they are entirely composed of stem tissues.

Herbaceous plants are perennials, meaning that they have a lifespan of several to many years. However, after each growing season the above–ground parts of herbaceous plants die back to the ground, and new growth must issue from below ground to begin the following season. In the case of cultivated species such as gladiolus (*Gladiolus communis*), crocus (*Crocus sativus*), and water chestnut (*Eleocharis tuberosa*), the new herbaceous growth develops from underground corms. In fact, the corm of the water chestnut is eaten.

Horticulturalists usually propagate these species using corms, which develop small "cormels" from lateral buds on the sides of the parent corm. A relatively vigorous production of cormels can be stimulated by wounding the parent corm, for example, by making some sharp but shallow cuts on its base. To cultivate these plants, the cormels are split off and individually planted, right–side up, and a new plant will develop. The use of corms to propagate new plants in these ways does not involve any exchange of genetic information, and is referred to as vegetative propagation because the parent and progeny are genetically identical.

Cormorants

Cormorants or shags are long–necked, generally black or dark grey, aquatic birds in the family Phalacrocoracidae. These birds occur in most temperate and tropical marine coasts, and on many large lakes. There are 29 species of cormorants with fewer species occurring at higher latitudes.

The plumage of cormorants is not completely waterproof, since these birds lack an oil gland for preening, so their feathers get waterlogged when they swim under water. As a result, after swimming, cormorants spend time drying their feathers by standing with their wings spread to the sun and breeze.

Cormorants, like this double-crested cormorant (*Phalacrocorax auritus*), are sometimes mistaken for geese in flight, but unlike geese, which flap steadily and honk as they fly, cormorants flap for a while and then glide, and they are silent in flight.

The diet of cormorants is mostly small- to medium-sized species of fish. Cormorants dive for their prey, which they catch underwater in their bills. Cormorants power their swimming using their webbed feet, employing their wings and tails to assist with steering.

Cormorants are colonial breeders. They usually build their rather bulky nests of twigs and other debris in trees, and sometimes on artificial platforms such as old pilings. The young birds are initially without feathers and are fed by their parents by regurgitation. Cormorant colonies are loud, raucous places. These birds commonly kill the stand of trees that they nest in, mostly through the caustic influence of their copious defecations.

The most widespread species is the common or great cormorant (*Phalacrocorax carbo*), which occurs in North America, Eurasia, and Australia. This species

and the double-crested cormorant (*P. auritus*) are the only cormorants on the coast of eastern North America. The double–crested cormorant also breeds abundantly on large, inland lakes.

The west coast of North America also has Brandt's cormorant (*P. penicillatus*) and the pelagic cormorant (*P. pelagicus*). The olivaceous cormorant (*P. olivaceous*) occurs on the southern coast of the Gulf of Mexico and off western Mexico, while the red–faced cormorant (*P. urile*) is a Eurasian species that occurs in the Aleutian islands of western Alaska.

The Peruvian cormorant (*P. bougainville*) breeds in enormous colonies on offshore islands of Chile and Peru, where its guano has long been mined as a source of phosphorus–rich fertilizer. This species is subject to occasional mass die–offs, caused by starvation resulting from periodic collapses of the stocks of its most important prey, the Peruvian anchovy. One unusual species, the Galapagos cormorant *Nannopterum harrisi*), which lives on the remote and predator–free Galapagos Islands is flightless.

Captive cormorants in Japan and coastal China have been trained for fishing. When used for this purpose, the birds are tethered by tying a line to one of their feet, and their neck is constricted by a ring, so the cormorant can catch fish but not swallow them.

Cormorants are considered to be a pest in many places, because they may eat species of fish that are also sought by human fishers. In some cases, cormorants are killed in large numbers for this reason. Sometimes, they are also considered to be pests because they kill vegetation in their nesting colonies.

Double–crested cormorants breeding on some of the Great Lakes of North America (eg., Lake Michigan) have rather large concentrations of polychlorinated biphenyls (PCBs) and other chlorinated hydrocarbons in their body fat and eggs. This effect of pollution has been blamed for apparent increases in the incidence of developmental deformities in some colonies of cormorants, especially the crossed–bill syndrome. However, in spite of this toxic stress, colonies of double-crested cormorants have been increasing rapidly on the Great Lakes during the past decade or so.

One species of cormorant, *P. perspicillatus,* bred on Bering Island in the Bering Sea, but was rendered extinct by humans.

Further Reading:

Brooke, M. and T. Birkhead, *The Cambridge Encyclopedia of Ornithology.* Cambridge, U.K.: Cambridge University Press, 1993.

Harrison, C.J., ed. *Bird Families of the World.* New York: Abrams Pubs., 1978.

Harrison, Peter. *Seabirds: An Identification Guide.* Beckenham, U.K.: Croom Helm, 1983.

Harrison, Peter. *A Field Guide to Seabirds.* New York: Viking/Penguin, 1987.

Mackenzie, John P. *Seabirds.* Minocqua, WI: NorthWord, 1987.

Perkins, Simon. *Audubon Society Pocket Guide to North American Birds of Sea and Shore.* New York: Random House, 1994.

Bill Freedman

Corollary see **Algebra**

Corpus callosum see **Brain**

Correlation (geology)

In geology, the term correlation refers to the methods by which the age relationship between various strata of the Earth's crust is established. Such relationships can be established, in general, in one of two ways: by comparing the physical characteristics of strata with each other (physical correlation); and by comparing the type of fossils found in various strata (fossil correlation).

Correlation is an important geological technique because it provides information with regard to changes that have taken place at various times in Earth history. It also provides clues as to the times at which such changes have occurred. One result of correlational studies has been the development of a geologic time scale that separates Earth history into a number of discrete time blocks known as eras, periods, and epochs.

The nature of sedimentary strata

Sedimentary rocks provide information about Earth history that is generally not available from igneous or metamorphic rocks. To understand why this is so, imagine a region in which sediments have been laid down for millions of years. For example, suppose that for many millions of years a river has emptied into an ocean, laying down, or depositing, sediments eroded from the land. During that period of time, layers of sediments would have collected one on top of the other at the mouth of the river.

These layers of sediments are likely to be very different from each other, depending on a number of factors, such as the course followed by the river, the climate of the area, the rock types exposed along the river course, and many other geological factors in the region. One of the most obvious differences in layers is thickness. Layers of sedimentary rock may range in thickness from less than an inch to many feet.

Sedimentary layers that are identifiably different from each other are called beds or strata. In many places on the Earth's surface, dozens of strata are stacked one on top of each other. Strata are often separated from each other by relatively well–defined surfaces known as bedding planes.

In 1669, the Danish physician and theologian Nicolaus Steno made a seemingly obvious assertion about the nature of sedimentary strata. Steno stated that in any sequence of sedimentary rocks, any one layer (stratum) is older than the layer below it and younger than the layer above it. Steno's discovery is now known as the law of superposition.

The law of superposition applies only to sedimentary rocks that have not been overturned by geologic forces. Igneous rocks, by comparison, may form in any horizontal sequence whatsoever. A flow of magma may force itself, for example, underneath, in the middle or, or on top of an existing rock stratum. It is very difficult to look back millions of years later, then, and determine the age of the igneous rock compared to rock layers around it.

Physical correlation

Using sedimentary rock strata it should be possible, at least in theory, to write the geological history of the continents for the last billion or so years. Some important practical problems, however, prevent the full realization of this goal. For example, in many areas, erosion has removed much or most of the sedimentary rock that once existed there. In other places, strata are not clearly exposed to view but, instead, are buried hundreds or thousands of feet beneath the thin layer of soil that covers most of the Earth's surface.

A few remarkable exceptions exist. A familiar example is the Grand Canyon, where the Colorado River has cut through dozens of strata, exposing them to view and making them available for study by geologists. Within the Grand Canyon, a geologist can follow a particular stratum for many miles, noting changes within the stratum and changes between that stratum and its neighbors above and below.

One of the characteristics observable in such a case is that a stratum often changes in thickness from one edge to another. At the edge where the thickness approaches zero, the stratum may merge into another stratum. This phenomenon is understandable when one considers the way the sediment in the rocks was laid down. At the mouth of a river, for example, the accumulation of sediments is likely to be greatest at the mouth itself, with decreasing thickness at greater distances into the lake or ocean. The principle of lateral continuity describes this phenomenon, namely that strata are three–dimensional features that extend outward in all directions, merging with adjacent deposits at their edges.

Human activity also exposes strata to view. When a highway is constructed through a mountainous (or hilly) area, for example, parts of a mountainside may be excavated, revealing various sedimentary rock strata. These strata can then be studied to discover the correlation among them and with strata in other areas.

Another problem is that strata are sometimes disrupted by earth movements. For example, an earthquake may lift one block of the Earth's crust over an adjacent block or may shift it horizontally in comparison to the second block. The correlation between adjacent strata may then be difficult to determine.

Physical correlation is accomplished by using a number of criteria. For example, the color, grain size, and type of minerals contained within a stratum make it possible for geologists to classify a particular stratum quite specifically. This allows them to match up portions of that stratum in regions that are physically separated from each other. In the American West, for example, some strata have been found to cover large parts of two or more states although they are physically exposed in only a few specific regions.

Interpreting earth history within a stratum

Imagine that geologists a million years from now began studying the Earth's surface within a 3 mile (5 kilometer) radius of your home. What would they find? They would probably discover considerable variation in the sediment deposits that are accumulating in your region today. They might find the remains of a river bed, a swamp, a lake, and other features. Geologists living today who study strata laid down millions of years ago make similar discoveries. As they follow an individual stratum for many kilometers, they find that its characteristics change. The stratum tends to have one set of characteristics in one region, which gradually changes into another set of characteristics farther along in the stratum. Those characteristics also change, at some distance farther along, into yet another set of characteristics.

Rocks with a particular set of characteristics are called a facies. Facies changes, changes in the charac-

teristics of a stratum or series of strata, are important clues to Earth history. Suppose that a geologist finds that the facies in a particular stratum change from a limestone to a shale to a sandstone over a distance of a few miles. The geologist knows that limestone is laid down on a sea bottom, shale is formed from compacted mud, and sandstone is formed when sand is compressed. The limestone to shale to sandstone facies pattern may allow an astute geologist to reconstruct what the Earth's surface looked like when this particular stratum was formed. For example, knowing these rocks were laid down in adjacent environments, the geologist might consider that the limestone was deposited on a coral reef, the shale in a quiet lagoon or coastal swamp, and the sandstone in a nearby beach. So facies changes indicate differences in the environments in which adjacent facies were deposited.

Fossil correlation

One of the most important discoveries in the science of correlation was made by the English surveyor William Smith in the 1810s. One of Smith's jobs involved the excavation of land for canals being constructed outside of London. As sedimentary rocks were exposed during this work, Smith found that any given stratum always contained the same set of fossils. Even if the stratum were physically separated by a relatively great distance, the same fossils could always be found in all parts of the stratum.

In 1815, Smith published a map of England and Wales showing the geologic history of the region based on his discovery. The map was based on what Smith called his law of faunal succession. That law says simply that it is possible to identify the sequence in which strata are laid down by examining the fossils they contain. The simplest fossils are the oldest and, therefore, strata that contain simple fossils are older than strata that contain more complex fossils.

The remarkable feature of Smith's discovery is that it appears to be valid over very great distances. That is, suppose that a geologist discovers a stratum of rock in southwestern California that contains fossils A, B, and C. If another stratum of rock in eastern Texas is also discovered that contains the same fossils, the geologist can conclude that it is probably the same stratum—or at least of the same age—as the southwestern California stratum.

Absolute vs. relative ages of strata

The correlational studies described so far allow scientists to estimate the relative ages of strata. If stratum

KEY TERMS

. . . .

Bedding plane—The top of a layer of rock.

Deposition—The accumulation of sediments after transport by wind, water, ice, or gravity.

Facies—A body of sedimentary rock with distinctive characteristics.

Fossil correlation—The matching of sedimentary strata based on fossils present in the strata.

Lateral continuity—The principle that sedimentary strata are three–dimensional features that extend horizontally in all directions and that eventually terminate against the margin of other strata.

Physical correlation—The matching of sedimentary strata based on the physical characteristics of rocks that make up the strata.

Radiometric dating—A process by which the age of a rock can be determined by studying the relative concentrations of a radioactive isotope and the products formed by its decay.

Superposition—The principle that a layer of rocks is older than any other layer that lies above it and younger than any other layer that lies below it.

B lies above stratum A, B is the younger of the two. However determining the actual, or absolute, age of strata (for example, 3.5 million years old) is often difficult since the age of a fossil cannot be determined directly. The most useful tool in dating strata is radiometric dating of materials. A radioactive isotope such as uranium–238 decays at a very regular and well–known rate. That rate is known as its half–life, the time it takes for one–half of a sample of the isotope to decay. The half–life of uranium–238, for example, is 4.5 billion years. By measuring the concentration of uranium–238 in comparison with the products of its decay (especially lead–206), a scientist can estimate the age of the rock in which the uranium was found. This kind of radioactive dating has made it possible to place specific dates on the ages of strata that have been studied and correlated by other means.

A serious complication in applying radiometric dating is that when you date a sedimentary rock, you learn the age of formation for its parent rock, not the age of the sedimentary rock's deposition. For example, if you radiometrically date a sandstone, you will determine the age of the sand grains that form it. These grains may have formed a billion years ago, or even two or three billion, and been part of half a dozen different sedimentary rocks before being incorporated into the most recent one, the sandstone that you dated. Therefore, radiometric dating must be used on things like volcanic ash beds that form when a volcano erupts and deposits a layer of ash. Volcanic ash layers can sometimes be found in an exposure of rock and they provide an absolute age for the eruption event and for the strata directly above and below.

See also Dating techniques; Deposit; Fossil and fossilization; Geologic time; Sediment and sedimentation; Strata.

David E. Newton

Correlation (mathematics)

Correlation refers to the degree of correspondence or relationship between two variables. Correlated variables tend to change together. If one variable gets larger, the other one systematically becomes either larger or smaller. For example, we would expect to find such a relationship between scores on an arithmetic test taken three month's apart. We could expect high scores on the first test to predict high scores on the second test, and low scores on the first test to predict low scores on the second test.

In the above example the scores on the first test are known as the independent or predictor variable (designated as "X") while the scores on the second test are known as the dependent or response variable (designated as "Y"). The relationship between the two variables X and Y is a positive relationship or positive correlation when high measures of X correspond with high measures of Y and low measures of X with low measures of Y. It is also possible for the relationship between variables X and Y to be an inverse relationship or negative correlation. This occurs when high measures of variable X are associated with low measures of variable Y and low measures on variable X are associated with high measures of variable Y. For example, if variable X is school attendance and variable Y is the score on an achievement test we could expect a negative correlation between X and Y. High measures of X (absence) would be associated with low measures of Y (achievement) and low measures of X with high measures of Y.

The correlation coefficient tells us that a relationship exists. The + or – sign indicates the direction of the relationship while the number indicates the magnitude of the relationship. This relationship should not be interpreted as a causal relationship. Variable X is related to variable Y, and may indeed be a good predictor of variable Y, but variable X does not cause variable Y although this is sometimes assumed. For example, there may be a positive correlation between head size and IQ or shoe size and IQ. Yet no one would say that the size of one's head or shoe size causes variations in intelligence. However, when two more likely variables show a positive or negative correlation, positive, see correlation>correlation many interpret the change in the second variable to have been caused by the first.

Further Reading:

Freedman, David, Robert Pisani, and Roger Purves. *Statistics*. New York: W. W. Norton, 1991.

Gonick, Larry, and Woollcott Smith. *The Cartoon Guide to Statistics*. New York: Harper Row, 1993.

Moore, David, and George McCabe. *Introduction to the practice of Statistics*. New York: W. H. Freeman, 1989.

Selma Hughes

Cosmetic surgery see **Plastic surgery**

Cosmic background radiation

In 1965, Arno Penzias and Robert Wilson announced the discovery of microwave radiation which uniformly filled the sky and had a black body temperature of about 3.5K. They had been testing a new radio amplifier which was supposed to be exceptionally quiet. What better way to do such a test than to tune the radio so that it should hear nothing at all? After many attempts to account for all extraneous sources of radio noise, they came to the conclusion that there was a general background of radiation at the radio frequency they were using. After discussions with a group led by Robert Dicke at nearby Princeton University it became clear that they had in fact detected remnant radiation from the origin of the universe. Although neither Dicke's group or Penzias and Wilson realized it at the time they had confirmed a prediction made 17 years earlier by Alpher, Bethe, and Gamow. Although the temperature which characterized that radiation was somewhat different, the difference can be accounted for by changes to the accepted structure of the universe discovered between 1948 and 1965. The detection of this radiation and its subsequent verification at other frequencies was taken as confirmation of a central prediction of a cosmology known as the Big Bang.

The interpretation of the red–shifts of spectral lines in distant galaxies by Edwin Hubble 40 years earlier suggested a universe that was expanding. One interpretation of that expansion was that the universe had a specific origin in space and time. Such a universe would have a very different early structure from the present one. However, it was George Gamow and colleagues who suggested that the early phases of the universe would have been hot and dense enough to sustain nuclear reactions. Following these initial phases, the expansion of the universe would eventually cool to the point where dominant material, hydrogen, would become relatively transparent to light and radio waves. We know that for hydrogen, this will occur when the gas has reached a temperature of between 5,000K-10,000K. From that point on in the evolution of the universe, the light and matter would go their separate ways.

As every point in the universe expands away from every other point, any observer in the universe sees all objects receding from him or her. The faster moving objects will appear at greater distances by virtue of their greater speed. Indeed, their speed will be directly proportional to their distance which is what one expects for material ejected from a particular point in space and time. However, this expansion results from the expansion of space itself and should not be viewed simply as galaxies rushing headlong away from one another through some absolute space. The space itself expands. As it does, light traveling through it is stretched, becoming redder and appearing cooler. If one samples that radiation at a later date it will be characteristic of radiation from a much cooler source. From the rate of expansion of the universe it is possible to predict what that temperature ought to be. Current values of the

KEY TERMS

. . . .

Microwave radiation—Electromagnetic radiation that occurs in the wavelength region of about 1 cm to 1 meter.

Black Body—A Black Body (not to be confused with a Black hole) is any object which absorbs all radiant energy which falls upon it and subsequently re–radiates that energy. The radiated energy can be characterized by a single dependant variable, the temperature. That temperature is known as the black body temperature.

Doppler shift—The change in frequency or wavelength resulting from the relative motion of the source of radiation and the observer. A motion of approach between the two will result in a compression of the waves as they pass the observer and a rise in "pitch" in the frequency of the wave and a shortening of the relative wavelength called a "blue shift." A relative motion of recession leads to a lowering of the "pitch" and a shift to longer "redder" wavelengths.

expansion rate are completely consistent with the current measured temperature of about 2.7K. The very existence of this radiation is strong evidence supporting the expanding model of the universe championed by Gamow and colleagues and disparagingly named the "Big Bang" cosmology by Sir Fred Hoyle.

Since its discovery in 1965, the radiation has been carefully studied and found to be a perfect black body as expected from theory. Since, this radiation represents fossil radiation from the initial Big Bang, any additional motion of the earth around the sun, the sun around the galactic center, and the galaxy through space should be reflected in a slight asymmetry in the background radiation. The net motion of the earth in some specific direction should be reflected by a slight Doppler shift of the background radiation coming from that direction toward shorter wavelengths.

This is the same effect that the police use to ascertain the velocity of approaching vehicles. Of course there will be a similar shift toward longer wavelengths for light coming from the direction from which we are receding. This effect has been observed indicating a combined peculiar motion of the earth, sun and galaxy on the order of 600 km/sec.

Finally, small fluctuations in the background radiation are predicted which eventually led to the formation

of galaxies, clusters of galaxies. Such fluctuations have been found by the CO(smic) B(ackground) E(xplorer) Satellite. COBE finds these fluctuations at about 1 part in 105 which is right near the detection limit of the satellite. The details of these fluctuations are crucial to deciding between more refined models of the expanding universe. It is perhaps not to much of an exaggeration to suggest that the Cosmic Microwave Background has elevated cosmology from enlightened speculative metaphysics to an actual science. We may expect developments of this emerging science to lead to a definitive description of the evolutionary history of the universe in the near future.

See also Big Bang theory; Cosmology.

George W. Collins, II

Cosmic ray

The term cosmic ray refers to tiny particles of matter that travel through space. Cosmic rays generally possess an electromagnetic charge and are highly energetic. Physicists divide cosmic rays into two categories: primary and secondary. Primary cosmic rays originate far outside the Earth's atmosphere. Secondary cosmic rays are particles produced within the Earth's atmosphere as a result of collisions between primary cosmic rays and molecules in the atmosphere.

Discovery of cosmic rays

The existence of cosmic radiation was first discovered in 1912, in experiments performed by the physicist Victor Hess. His experiments were sparked by a desire to better understand phenomena of electric charge. A common instrument of the day for demonstrating such phenomena was the electroscope. An electroscope contains thin metal leaves or wires that separate from one another when they become charged, due to the fact that like charges repel. Eventually the leaves (or wires) lose their charge and collapse back together. It was known that this loss of charge had to be due to the attraction by the leaves of charged particles (called ions) in the surrounding air. The leaves would attract those ions having a charge opposite to that of the leaves, due to the fact that opposite charges attract; eventually the accumulation of ions in this way would neutralize the charge that had been acquired by the leaves, and they would cease to repel each other. Scientists wanted to know where

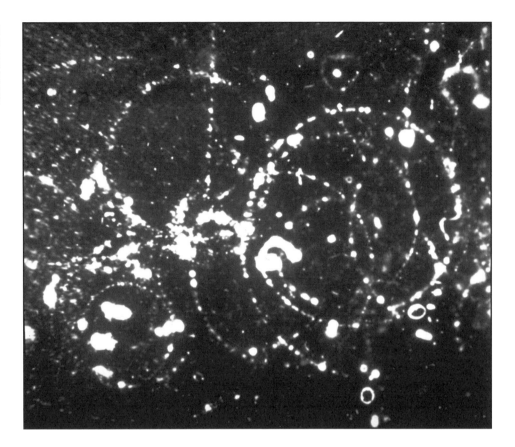

One of the first cloud chamber photographs showing the track of a cosmic ray; it was taken by Dmitry Skobeltzyn in his laboratory in Leningrad in 1927. Skobeltzyn was studying electrons knocked from atoms by gamma rays. He subjected his cloud chamber to a powerful magnetic field which causes the tracks of electrons to curve tightly (as demonstrated by most of the tracks in the picture). But a few photographs had straight tracks (like the one at top center) left by electrons that had momentum and energy enormously greater than those from any known source. Skobeltzyn concluded that they were fast-moving electrons knocked from atoms by cosmic gamma rays traversing his chamber.

these ions came from. It was thought that they must be the result of radiation emanating from the Earth's crust, since it was known that radiation could produce ions in the air. This led scientists to predict that there would be fewer ions present the further one traveled away from the Earth's surface. Hess's experiments, in which he took electroscopes high above the Earth's surface in a balloon, showed that this was not the case. At high altitudes, the electroscopes lost their charge even faster than they had on the ground, showing that there were more ions in the air and thus that the radiation responsible for the presence of the ions was stronger at higher altitudes. Hess concluded that there was a radiation coming into our atmosphere from outer space.

As physicists became interested in cosmic radiation, they developed new ways of studying it. The Geiger–Muller counter consists of a wire attached to an electric circuit and suspended in a gaseous chamber. The passage of a cosmic ray through the chamber produces ions in the gas, causing the counter to discharge an electric pulse. Another instrument, the cloud chamber, contains a gas which condenses into vapor droplets around ions when these are produced by the passage of a cosmic ray. In the decades following Hess's discovery, physicists used instruments such as these to learn more about the nature of cosmic radiation.

The nature and origin of cosmic rays

An atom of a particular element consists of a nucleus surrounded by a cloud of electrons, which are negatively charged particles. The nucleus is made up of protons, which have a positive charge, and neutrons, which have no charge. These particles can be further broken down into smaller constituents; all of these particles are known as subatomic particles. Cosmic rays consist of nuclei and of various subatomic particles. Almost all of the primary cosmic rays are nuclei of various atoms. The great majority of these are single protons, which are nuclei of hydrogen atoms. The next most common primary cosmic ray is the nucleus of the helium atom, made up of a proton and a neutron. Hydrogen and helium nuclei make up about 99% of the primary cosmic radiation. The rest consists of nuclei of other elements and of electrons.

When primary cosmic rays enter the earth's atmosphere, they collide with molecules of gases present there. These collisions result in the production of more high–energy subatomic particles of different types; these are the secondary cosmic rays. These include photons, neutrinos, electrons, positrons, and other particles. These particles may in turn collide with other particles, producing still more secondary radiation. If the energy of the primary particle that initiates this process is very high, this cascade of collisions and particle production can become quite extensive. This is known as a shower, air shower, or cascade shower.

The energy of cosmic rays is measured in units called electron volts (abbreviated eV). Primary cosmic rays typically have energies on the order of billions of electron volts. Some are vastly more energetic than this; a few particles have been measured at energies in excess of 1019 eV. This is in the neighborhood of the amount of energy required to lift a weight of 2.2 lb (1 kg) to a height of 3.3 ft (1 m). Energy is lost in collisions with other particles, so secondary cosmic rays are typically less energetic than primary ones. The showers of particles described above diminish as the energies of the particles produced decrease. The energy of cosmic rays was first determined by measuring their ability to penetrate substances such as gold or lead.

Since cosmic rays are mostly charged particles (some secondary rays such as photons have no charge), they are affected by magnetic fields. The paths of incoming primary cosmic rays are deflected by the Earth's magnetic field, somewhat in the way that iron filings will arrange themselves along the lines of force emitted by a magnet. More energetic particles are deflected less than those having less energy. In the 1930s it was discovered that more particles come to the Earth from the West than from the East. Because of the nature of the earth's magnetic field, this led scientists to the conclusion that most of the incoming cosmic radiation consists of positively charged particles. This was an important step towards the discovery that the primary cosmic rays are mostly bare atomic nuclei, since atomic nuclei carry a positive charge.

The ultimate origin of cosmic radiation is still not completely understood. Some of the radiation is believed to have been produced in the "big bang" at the origin of the universe. Other cosmic rays are produced by our sun, particularly during solar disturbances such

KEY TERMS

Electron—A negatively charged particle, ordinarily occurring as part of an atom. The atom's electrons form a sort of cloud about the nucleus.

Electron volt (eV)—The unit used to measure the energy of cosmic rays.

Electroscope—A device for demonstrating the presence of an electric charge, which may be positive or negative.

Ion—A molecule that has acquired a positive or negative electric charge as a result of the loss or gain of electrons.

Neutron—Particle found in the nucleus of an atom, possessing no charge.

Nucleus—The central mass of an atom. The nucleus is composed of neutrons and protons.

Primary cosmic ray—Cosmic ray originating outside the Earth's atmosphere.

Proton—Positively charged particle composing part of the nucleus of an atom. Primary cosmic rays are mostly made up of single protons.

Secondary cosmic ray—Cosmic ray originating within the Earth's atmosphere as a result of a collision between another cosmic ray and some other particle or molecule.

Shower (also air shower or cascade shower)—A chain reaction of collisions between cosmic rays and other particles, producing more cosmic rays.

as solar flares. Exploding stars, called supernovas, are also a source of cosmic rays.

The fact that cosmic ray collisions produce smaller subatomic particles has provided a great deal of insight into the fundamental structure of matter. The construction of experimental equipment such as particle accelerators has been inspired by a desire to reproduce the conditions under which high–energy radiation is produced, in order to gain better experimental control of collisions and the production of particles.

See also Big Bang theory; Particle detectors.

Further Reading:

Friedlander, Michael. *Cosmic Rays.* Cambridge (Mass.): Harvard University Press, 1989.
Longair, M.S. *High Energy Astrophysics.* Cambridge: Cambridge University Press, 1981.

Millikan, Robert Andrews. *Electrons (+ and −), Protons, Photons, Neutrons, and Cosmic Rays.* Chicago: University of Chicago Press, 1935.
Rossi, Bruno. *Cosmic Rays.* New York: McGraw–Hill, 1964.

John Bishop

Cosmology

Since the earliest days of history man has struggled to understand the world in which he lives. Over the last two thousand years that "world" has expanded to include the starry heavens as well as the earth itself. We now use the term universe to mean all that was, is, and will be available to observation and measurement. In the 20th century the scale of the universe has been pushed beyond our local galaxy of about 100 billion stars to include similar galaxies flung across space to the most distant reaches observable with the largest telescopes. Cosmology is an attempt to describe the large scale structure and order of the universe. To that end, one does not expect cosmology to deal with the detailed structure such as planets, stars, or even galaxies. Rather it attempts to describe the structure of the universe on the largest of scales and to determine its past and future.

Early attempts at such a description were generally statements of faith or philosophy supported by only the most meager objective data. One of the earliest constraints on any description of the universe is generally attributed to Heinreich Olbers in 1826. However, more careful study traces the idea back to Thomas Digges in 1576 and it was thoroughly discussed by Edmund Halley at the time of Isaac Newton. The notion, still called Olbers' paradox, is concerned with why the night sky is dark. At the time of Newton it was understood that if the universe was finite then Newton's Law of Gravity would require that all the matter in the universe should pull itself together to that point equidistant from the boundary of the universe. Thus, the prevailing wisdom was that the universe was infinite in extent and therefore had no center. However, if this were true, then the extension of any line of sight should sooner or later encounter the surface of a star. The night sky should then appear to have the brightness of the average star. The sun is an average star, thus one would expect the sky to be everywhere as bright as the sun. It is not, so there must be a problem with the assumptions. An alternative explanation, pointed out in 1964 by Ed Harrison, is that the universe had a finite beginning and the light from distant stars had not yet had time to arrive and that is why the night sky is dark.

At the turn of the 20th century cosmology placed the sun and its solar system of planets near the center of the Milky Way Galaxy which comprised the full extent of the known universe. However, early in the century information began to be complied that would change the popular view that the universe was static and made of primarily stars. On April 26, 1920 there was a historic debate between H. D. Curtis and Harlow Shapley concerning the nature of some fuzzy clouds of light which were called nebulae. Shapley thought they were objects within the galaxy while Curtis believed them to be "island universes" lying outside the Milky Way. As is often the case, most agreed that Shapley had won the debate, but as it turned out Curtis was right. Within a few years Edwin Hubble detected a type of star, whose distance could be independently determined, residing within several of these fuzzy clouds. These stars clearly placed the "clouds" beyond the limits of the Milky Way. While Hubble continued to use the term "Island universe," extragalactic nebulae became more common and they are now simply known as galaxies. In the span of a quarter of a century the scale for the universe had been grown dramatically.

About the same time V. M. Slipher, at the Lowell Observatory, had been acquiring spectra of these fuzzy clouds. By breaking the light of astronomical objects into the various "colors" or wavelengths which make up that light, astronomers can learn much about the composition, temperature, and pressure of the material that emitted that light. The familiar spectrum of hydrogen so common to so many astronomical objects didn't fall at the expected wavelengths, but appeared shifted to longer wavelengths. We now refer to such a change in wavelength as a redshift. Slipher noted that the fainter galaxies seemed to have larger redshifts and he sent his collection of galactic spectra off to Hubble.

Hubble interpreted the redshift as being caused by the Doppler effect and representing motion away from us. The increasing faintness was related to distance so that in 1929 Hubble turned Slipher's redshift–brightness relation into a velocity–distance relation and the concept of the expanding universe was born. Hubble found that the velocity of distant galaxies increased in direct proportion to their distance. The constant of proportionality is denoted by the symbol H_0 and is known as Hubble's constant. Although the historical units of Hubble's constant are (km/s/mpc), both kilometers and megaparsecs are lengths so that the actual units are inverse time (i.e. 1/sec). The reciprocal of the constant basically gives a value for the time it took distant galaxies to arrive at their present day positions. It is the same time for all galaxies. Thus, the inverse of Hubble's constant provides an estimate for the age of the expanding universe called the Hubble age. Due to its importance the determination of its correct value has been a central preoccupation of many astronomers from the time of Hubble to the present. Since the gravitational pull of the matter in the universe on itself should tend to slow the expansion, values of Hubble's constant determined by hypothetical astronomers billions of years ago would have yielded a somewhat larger number and hence a somewhat younger age. Therefore the Hubble age is an upper limit to the true age of the universe which depends on how much matter is in the universe.

The notion of a Heavens (i.e. universe) that was dynamic and changing was revolutionary for the age. Einstein immediately modified the equations of the General Theory of Relativity which he applied to the universe as a whole do deal with a dynamic universe. William de Sitter and quite independently Alexandre Friedmann expanded on Einstein's application of General Relativity to a dynamically expanding universe. The concept of a universe that is changing in time suggests the idea of predicting the state of the universe at earlier times by simply reversing the present dynamics. This is much like simply running a motion picture backwards to find out how the movie began. A Belgian priest by the name of Georges Lemaitre carried this to its logical conclusion by suggesting that at one time the universe must have been a very congested place with matter so squeezed together that it would have behaved as some sort of primeval atom.

The analysis of Einstein–de Sitter, Friedmann, Lemaitre, and others showed that the dynamical future of the expanding universe depended on the local density. Simply put, if the density of the universe were sufficiently high, then the gravitational pull of the matter in any given volume on itself would be sufficient to eventually stop the expansion. Within the description given by the General Theory of Relativity, the matter would be said to warp space to such an extent that the space would be called closed. The structure of such a universe would allow the expansion to continue until it filled the interior of a black hole appropriate for the mass of the entire universe at which point it would begin to collapse. A universe with less density would exhibit less space warping and be said to be open and would be able to expand forever. There exists a value for the density between these extremes where the matter of the universe can just stop the expansion after an infinite time. Such a universe is said to be flat. One of the central questions for observational cosmology continues to be which of these three cases applies to our universe.

George Gamow concerned himself with the early phases of an expanding universe and showed that Lemaitre's primeval atom would have been so hot that it would explode. After the World War II, a competing cosmology developed by Hermann Bondi, Thomas Gold, and Fred Hoyle was put forth in order to avoid the ultimate problem with the expanding universe, namely, it must have had an origin. The Steady State Cosmology of Bondi, Gold, and Hoyle suggested that the universe has existed indefinitely and that matter is continuously created so as to replace that carried away by the observed expansion. This rather sophisticated cosmology replaced the origin problem of the expanding universe by spreading the creation problem out over the entire history of the universe and making it a part of its continuing existence. It is somewhat ironic that the current name for the expanding universe cosmology as expressed by Gamow is derived from the somewhat disparaging name, Big Bang, given to it by Fred Hoyle during a BBC interview.

Gamow and colleagues noted that a very hot primeval atom should radiate like a Black Body (i.e. a perfect thermal radiator), but that radiation should be extremely red–shifted by the expansion of the universe so that it would appear today like a very cold Black Body. That prediction, made in 1948, would have to wait until 1965 for its confirmation. In that year Arno Penzias and Robert Wilson announced the discovery of microwave radiation which uniformly filled the sky and had a black body temperature of about 2.7 K (–270.3°C). While Gamow's original prediction had been forgotten, the idea had been re–discovered by Robert Dicke and his colleagues at Princeton University. Subsequent observation of this background radiation showed it to fit all the characteristics required by radiation from the early stages of the Big Bang. Its discovery spelled the end to the elegant Steady State Cosmology which could not easily accommodate the existence of such radiation.

After the Second World War, the science of nuclear physics developed to a point that it was clear that nuclear reactions would have taken place during the early phases of the Big Bang. Again scientists ran the motion picture backwards through an era of nuclear physics attempting to predict what elements should have been produced during the early history of the universe. Their predictions were then compared to the elemental abundances of the oldest stars and the agreement was amazingly good. The detailed calculations depended critically on whether the calculated model was for an 'open' or 'closed' universe. If the universe were open, then the era of nuclear reactions would not last long enough to produce elements heavier than hydrogen and helium. In such models some deuterium is formed, but the amount is extremely sensitive to the initial density of matter. Since deuterium tends to be destroyed in stars, the current measured value places a lower limit on the initial amount made in the Big Bang. The best present estimates of primordial deuterium suggest that there is not enough matter in the universe to stop its expansion at any time in the future.

In the last quarter of the 20th century some problems with the standard picture of the Big Bang emerged. The extreme uniformity of the cosmic background radiation, which seemed initially reasonable, leads to a subtle problem. Consider the age of elements of the cosmic background radiation originating from two widely separated places in the sky. The distance between them is so great that light could not travel between them in an amount of time less than their age. Thus the two regions could never have been in contact during their existence. Why then, should they show the same temperature? How was their current status coordinated? This is known as the horizon problem. The second problem has to do with the remarkable balance between the energy of expansion of the universe and the energy associated with the gravitational forces of the matter opposing that expansion. By simply counting the amount of matter we see in the universe, we can account for about 1% of the matter required to stop the expansion and close the universe. Because the expansion causes both the expansion energy and the energy opposing the expansion to tend to zero, the ratio of their difference to either one tends to get larger with time. So one can ask how good the agreement between the two was, say, when the cosmic background radiation was formed. The answer is that the agreement must have been good to about 1 part in a million. If one extends the logic back to the nuclear era where our physical understanding is still quite secure, then the agreement must be good to about thirty digits. The slight departure between these two fundamental properties of the universe necessary to produce what we currently observe is called the "Flatness Problem." There is a strong belief among many cosmologists that agreement to thirty digits suggests perfect agreement and there must be more matter in the universe than we can see. This matter is usually lumped under the name dark matter since it escapes direct visible detection. It has become increasingly clear that there is indeed more matter in the universe than is presently visible. Its gravitational effect on the rotation of galaxies and their motion within clusters of galaxies suggests that we see perhaps only a tenth of the matter than is really there. However, while this amount is still compatible with the abundance of deuterium, it is not enough to close the universe and solve the flatness problem.

In an attempt to 'run the motion picture' further backwards before the nuclear era requires physics which, while less secure, is plausible. This led to a modification of the Big Bang by Alan Guth called inflation. Inflation describes an era of very rapid expansion where the space containing the matter–energy that would eventually become galaxies spread apart faster than the speed of light for a short period of time. This solved the horizon problem in that it allowed all matter in the universe to be in contact with all other matter at the beginning of the inflation era. It also requires that the balance between expansion energy at that opposed to the expansion be balanced exactly thereby solving the flatness problem. This exact balance requires that there be an additional component to the dark matter which did not take part in the nuclear reactions that determined the initial composition of the universe. The search for such matter is currently the source of considerable effort.

Finally, one wonders how far back one can reasonably expect to run the movie. In the earliest microseconds of the universe's existence the conditions would have been so extreme that the very forces of nature would have merged together. Physical theories that attempt to describe the merger of the strong nuclear force with the electro–weak force are called Grand Unified Theories of GUTs for short. There is currently much effort being devoted to testing those theories. At sufficiently early times even the force of gravity should become tied to the other forces of nature. The conditions which lead to the merging of the forces of nature are far beyond anything achievable on the earth so that the physicist must rely on predictions from the early universe to test these theories. Ultimately quantum mechanics suggests that there comes a time in the early history of the universe where all theoretical descriptions of the universe must fail. Before a time known as the Planck Time, the very notions of time and space become poorly defined and one should not press the 'movie' further. Beyond this time science becomes ineffective in determining the structure of the universe and one must search elsewhere for its origin.

See also Big Bang theory; Blackbody radiation; Dark matter; Doppler effect; Galaxy; Redshift; Relativity, general.

Further Reading:

Arny, T.T. *Explorations—an Introduction to Astronomy*. St. Louis, Boston: Mosby, 1994.

Guth, A.H., and Steinhardt, P.J. "The Inflationary Universe," *Scientific American* 250, no.5 (1984): 116–28.

Harrison, E.R. *Cosmology: The Science of the Universe*. Cambridge England: Cambridge University Press, 1981.

KEY TERMS

Grand Unified Theory—Any theory which brings the description of the forces of electromagnetism, weak and strong nuclear interactions under a single representation.

Hubble constant—The constant of proportionality in Hubble's Law which relates the recessional velocity and distance of remote objects in the universe whose motion is determined by the general expansion of the universe.

Inflation Cosmology—A modification to the early moments of the Big Bang Cosmology which solves both the flatness problem and the horizon problem.

Megaparsec—A unit of distance used in describing the distances to remote objects in the universe. One megaparsec (i.e. a million parsecs) is approximately equal to 3.26 million light years or approximately ten trillion trillion centimeters.

Olbers' paradox—A statement that the dark night sky suggests that the universe is finite in either space or time.

Planck Time—An extremely short interval of time (i.e. 10^{-43} sec) when the conventional laws of physics no longer apply.

Primeval atom—The description of the very early expanding universe devised by Abbe Lemaitre.

Spectra—The representation of the light emitted by an object broken into its constituent colors or wavelengths.

Steady state cosmology—A popular cosmology of the mid 20th century which supposed that the universe was unchanging in space and time.

Seeds, M.A. *Horizons—Exploring the Universe.* Belmont CA: Wadsworth Pub. Co., 1995.

Weinberg, S. *The First Three Minutes.* New York: Basic Books, 1977.

George W. Collins, II

Cotingas

Cotingas are a highly diverse group of birds that make up the family Cotingidae. Species of cotingas occur widely in tropical forests of South and Central America. Cotingas are fly–catching birds, and are similar in many respects to species of tyrant flycatchers (family Tyrannidae), although these families are not closely related.

Species of cotingas are extremely variable in size, shape, color, behavior, and natural history, and the family is therefore difficult to characterize. As a result, estimates of the number of species range from about 70 to 80, depending on the taxonomic treatment that is consulted.

The largest cotinga is the crow–sized, umbrella-bird (*Cephalopterus ornatus*). This is a slate gray, 16 in (40 cm) long bird with a large crest over the top of the head, and an inflatable orange throat–sac, which is used to give resonance to the low–pitched, bellowing calls of this species. The smallest species is the kinglet calyptura (*Calyptura cristata*), only 3 in (7.5 cm) long. Some cotingas are rather drab in color, while others are extraordinarily beautiful, with hues of deep red, orange, purple, and yellow occurring in some species.

The feeding habits of cotingas are also highly varied. Some cotingas are exclusively fruit–eaters, while others are insectivorous, but most have a mixed diet of both of these types of foods. The insect–hunting species tend to glean their prey from the surfaces of foliage or branches. Alternatively, they may "fly–catch," that is sit motionless while scanning for large, flying insects, which, when seen, are captured in the beak during a brief aerial sally.

Perhaps the most famous species in the cotinga family are the cocks–of–the–rock (*Rupicola* spp.). For example, males of the Guianan cock–of–the–rock (*Rupicola rupicola*) are colored a beautiful golden orange, with an extraordinary semi–circular, flattened crest over the entire top of the head, long plumes over the wings, and delicate black–and–white markings. Male cocks–of–the–rock have a spectacular courtship display in which several cocks gather at a traditional strutting ground. Each bird clears a small area, known as a "court," in which to perform his display. When a female appears, the cocks fly down to their individual court, where they assume a still pose, designed to maximize the visual impact of their charismatic, orange crest on the female. Although all of the cocks seem spectacularly attractive to any human observer, the female is able to discern one that is even more–so, and she chooses him as her mate.

Other cotingas are noted for their extremely loud calls, which can resonate through even the densest tropical rain forest. Male bell–birds (*Procnias* spp.) advertise themselves to females with their bell–like calls, while male pihas (*Lipaugus* spp.) make extremely loud, piercing sounds to proclaim their virility.

The only cotinga to occur in the United States is the rose–throated becard (*Platypsaris aglaiae*), which is present in local populations close to the Mexican border in Arizona, New Mexico, and Texas.

Cotton

Cotton is a fiber obtained from various species of plants, genus *Gossypium,* family Malvaceae (Mallow), and is the most important and widely used natural fiber in the world. Cotton is primarily an agricultural crop, but it can also be found growing wild. Originally cotton species were perennial plants, but in some areas cotton has been selectively bred to develop as an annual plant. There are more than 30 species of *Gossypium*, but only four species are used to supply the world market for cotton. *Gossypium hirsutum*, also called New World or upland cotton, and *G. barbadense*, the source of Egyptian cotton and Sea Island Cotton, supply most of the world's cotton fiber. *G. barbadense* was brought from Egypt to the United States around 1900. A hybrid of these two cotton species known as Pima cotton, is also an important source of commercial cotton. These species have relatively longer fibers and greater resistance to the boll weevil, the most notable insect pest of cotton plants. Asian cotton plants, *G. arboreum* and *G. herbaceum* grow as small shrubs and produce relatively short fibers. Today, the United States produces one-sixth of the world's cotton. Other leading cotton producing countries are China (the world's biggest producer), India, Pakistan, Brazil, and Turkey. The world production of cotton in the early 1990s was about 18.9 million metric tons per year. The world's largest consumers of cotton are the United States and Europe.

History

Cotton was one of the first cultivated plants. There is evidence that the cotton plant was cultivated in India as long as 5,000 years ago. Specimens of cotton cloth as old as 5,000 years have been found in Peru, and scientists have found ancient specimens of the cotton plant dating 7,000 years old in caves near Mexico City. Cotton was one of the resources sought by Columbus, and while he did not manage to find a shorter route to India, he did find species of cotton growing wild in the West Indies.

Cotton plant

The cotton plant grows to a height of 3–6 ft (0.9–1.8 m), depending on the species and the region where it is grown. The leaves are heart–shaped, lobed, and coarse veined, somewhat resembling a maple leaf. The plant has many branches with one main central stem. Overall, the plant is cone or pyramid shaped.

After a cotton seed has sprouted (about four to five weeks after planting), two "seed" leaves provide food for the plant until additional "true" leaves appear. Flower buds protected by a fringed, leafy covering develop a few weeks after the plant starts to grow, and then bloom a few weeks later. The flower usually blooms in the morning and then withers and turns color within two to three days. The bloom falls off the plant, leaving a ripening seed pod.

Pollination must occur before the flower falls off. Pollen from the stamens (male part) is transferred to the stigma (female part) by insects and wind, and travels down the stigma to the ovary. The ovary contains ovules, which become seeds if fertilized. The ovary swells around the seeds and develops into a boll. The cotton boll is classified as a fruit because it contains seeds. As the bolls develop, the leaves on the plant turn red.

About four months are needed for the boll to ripen and split open. A cotton boll contains 27–45 seeds and each seed grows between 10,000 and 20,000 hairs or fibers. Each fiber is a single cell, 3,000 times longer than wide. The fibers develop in two stages. First, the fibers grow to their full length (in about three weeks). For the following three to four weeks, layers of cellulose are deposited in a crisscross fashion, building up the wall of the fiber. After the boll matures and bursts open, the fibers dry out and become tiny hollow tubes that twist up, making the fiber very strong. The seed hairs or fibers grow in different lengths. The outer and longer fibers grow to 2.5 in (6.4 cm) and are primarily used for cloth. These fibers are very strong, durable, flexible, and retain dyes well. The biological function of the long seed hairs is to help scatter the seeds around in the wind. The inner, short fibers are called linter.

Growing, harvesting, processing

Cotton requires a long growing season (from 180–200 days), sunny and warm weather, plenty of water during the growth season, and dry weather for harvest. Cotton grows near the equator in tropical and semitropical climates. The Cotton Belt in the United States reaches from North Carolina down to northern Florida and west to California. A crop started in March

Cotton plants in cultivation in North Carolina.

or April will be ready to harvest in September. Usually, cotton seeds are planted in rows. When the plants emerge, they need to be thinned. Herbicides, rotary hoes, or flame cultivators are used to manage weeds. Pesticides are also used to control bacterial and fungal diseases, and insect pests.

Harvesting

For centuries, harvesting was done by hand. Cotton had to be picked several times in the season because bolls of cotton do not all ripen at the same time. Today, most cotton is mechanically harvested. Farmers wait until all the bolls are ripe and then defoliate the plants with chemicals, although sometimes defoliation occurs naturally from frost.

Processing

Harvested cotton needs to be cleaned before going to the gin. Often, the cotton is dried before it is put through the cleaning equipment which removes leaves, dirt, twigs, and other unwanted material. After cleaning, the long fibers are separated from the seeds with a cotton gin and then packed tightly into bales of 500 lb (227 kg). Cotton is classified according to its staple (length

of fiber), grade (color), and character (smoothness). At a textile mill, cotton fibers are spun into yarn and then woven or knitted into cloth. The seeds, still covered with linter, are sent to be pressed in an oil mill.

Cotton by–products

Cotton seeds are valuable by–products. The seeds are delinted by a similar process to ginning. Some linter is used to make candle wicks, string, cotton balls, cotton batting, paper, and cellulose products such as rayon, plastics, photographic film, and cellophane. The delinted seeds are crushed and the kernel is separated from the hull and squeezed. The cottonseed oil obtained from the kernels is used for cooking oil, shortening, soaps, and cosmetics. A semi–solid residue from the refining process is called soap stock or foots, and provides fatty acids for various industrial uses such as insulation materials, soaps, linoleum, oilcloth, waterproofing materials, and as a paint base. The hulls are used for fertilizer, plastics, and paper. A liquid made from the hulls called furfural is used in the chemical industry. The remaining mash is used for livestock feed.

See also Natural fibers.

Further Reading:

Collins, Herbert R. *Threads of History: Americana, Recorded on Cloth—1775 to the Present.* Washington, DC: Smithsonian Institution Press, 1979.

Hamby, D. S. *American Cotton Handbook.* 3rd ed. New York: Wiley, 1965–66.

Lewington, Anna. *Plants for People.* New York: Oxford University Press, 1990.

Potter, M., and B. Corbman. *Textiles: Fiber to Fabric.* 4th ed. New York: McGraw–Hill, 1967.

Christine Miner Minderovic

Cotton fleahopper see **True bugs**

Cottonmouths see **Snakes**

Coulomb

A coulomb (abbreviation: C) is the standard unit of charge in the metric system. It was named after the French physicist Charles A. de Coulomb (1736–1806) who formulated the law of electrical force that now carries his name.

History

By the early 1700s, Sir Isaac Newton's law of gravitational force had been widely accepted by the scientific community, which realized the vast array of problems to which it could be applied. During the period 1760–1780, scientists began to search for a comparable law that would describe the force between two electrically charged bodies. Many assumed that such a law would follow the general lines of the gravitational law, namely that the force would vary directly with the magnitude of the charges and inversely as the distance between them.

The first experiments in this field were conducted by the Swiss mathematician Daniel Bernoulli around 1760. Bernoulli's experiments were apparently among the earliest quantitative studies in the field of electricity, and they aroused little interest among other scientists. A decade later, however, two early English chemists, Joseph Priestley and Henry Cavendish, carried out experiments similar to those of Bernoulli and obtained qualitative support for a gravitation–like relationship for electrical charges.

Conclusive work on this subject was completed by Coulomb in 1785. The French physicist designed an ingenious apparatus for measuring the relatively modest force that exists between two charged bodies. The apparatus is known as a torsion balance. The torsion balance consists of a non–conducting horizontal bar suspended by a thin fiber of metal or silk. Two small spheres are attached to opposite ends of the bar and given an electrical charge. A third ball is then placed adjacent to the ball at one end of the horizontal rod and given a charge identical to those on the rod.

In this arrangement, a force of repulsion develops between the two adjacent balls. As they push away from each other, they cause the metal or silk fiber to twist. The amount of twist that develops in the fiber can be measured and can be used to calculate the force that produced the distortion.

Coulomb's law

From this experiment, Coulomb was able to write a mathematical expression for the electrostatic force between two charged bodies carrying charges of q_1 and q_2 placed at a distance of r from each other. That mathematical expression was, indeed, comparable to the gravitation law. That is, the force between the two bodies is proportional to the product of their charges ($q_1 \times q_2$) and inversely proportional to the square of the distance between them ($1/r^2$). Introducing a proportionality constant of k, Coulomb's law can be written as: $q_1 \times q_2$ F =

kr^2 What this law says is that the force between two charged bodies drops off rapidly as they are separated from each other. When the distance between them is doubled, the force is reduced to one–fourth of its original value. When the distance is tripled, the force is reduced to one–ninth.

Coulomb's law applies whether the two bodies in question have similar or opposite charges. The only difference is one of sign. If a positive value of F is taken as a force of attraction, then a negative value of F must be a force of repulsion.

Given the close relationship between magnetism and electricity, it is hardly surprising that Coulomb discovered a similar law for magnetic force a few years later. The law of magnetic force says that it, too, is an inverse square law. In other words: p_1 x p_2 F = kr^2 where p_1 and p_2 are the strengths of the magnetic poles, r is the distance between them, and k is a proportionality constant.

Applications

Coulomb's law is absolutely fundamental, of course, to any student of electrical phenomena in physics. However, it is just as important in understanding and interpreting many kinds of chemical phenomena. For example, an atom is, in one respect, nothing other than a collection of electrical charges, positively charged protons, and negatively charged electrons. Coulombic forces exist among these particles. For example, a fundamental problem involved in a study of the atomic nucleus is explaining how the enormous electrostatic force of repulsion among protons is overcome in such a way as to produce a stable body.

Coulombic forces must be invoked also in explaining molecular and crystalline architecture. The four bonds formed by a carbon atom, for example, have a particular geometric arrangement because of the mutual force of repulsion among the four electron pairs that make up those bonds. In crystalline structures, one arrangement of ions is preferred over another because of the forces of repulsion and attraction among like-charged and oppositely–charged particles respectively.

Electrolytic cells

The coulomb (as a unit) can be thought of in another way, as given by the following equation: 1 coulomb = 1 ampere x 1 second. The ampere (amp) is the metric unit used for the measurement of electrical current. Most people know that electrical appliances in their home operate on a certain number of "amps." The ampere is defined as the flow of electrical charge per

second of time. Thus, if one multiplies the number of amps times the number of seconds, the total electrical charge (number of coulombs) can be calculated.

This information is of significance in the field of electrochemistry because of a discovery made by the British scientist Michael Faraday in about 1833. Faraday discovered that a given quantity of electrical charge passing through an electrolytic cell will cause a given amount of chemical change in that cell. For example, if one mole of electrons flows through a cell containing copper ions, one mole of copper will be deposited on the cathode of that cell. The Faraday relationship is fundamental to the practical operation of many kinds of electrolytic cells.

See also Electric charge.

Further Reading:

Gerald Holton and Duane H. D. Roller. *Foundations of Modern Physical Science.* Reading, MA: Addison–Wesley Publishing Company, 1958.
Jerry D. Wilson. *Physics: Concepts and Applications,* 2nd edition. Lexington, MA: D. C. Heath and Company, 1981.
James E. Brady and John R. Holum. *Fundamentals of Chemistry,* 2nd edition. New York: John Wiley and Sons, 1984.
Morris H. Shamos, ed. *Great Experiments in Physics.* New York: Holt, Rinehart and Winston, 1959.

David E. Newton

KEY TERMS

Electrolytic cell—An electrochemical cell in which an electrical current is used to bring about a chemical change.

Inverse square law—A scientific law that describes any situation in which a force decreases as the square of the distance between any two objects.

Magnetic pole—Either of the two regions within a magnetic object where the magnetic force appears to be concentrated.

Proportionality constant—A number that is introduced into a proportionality expression in order to make it into an equality.

Qualitative—Any measurement in which numerical values are not considered.

Quantitative—Any type of measurement that involves a mathematical measurement.

Torsion—A twisting force.

Countable

Every set that can be counted is countable, but this is no surprise. The interesting case for countable sets comes when we abandon finite sets and consider infinite ones.

An infinite set of numbers, points, or other elements is said to be "countable" (also called *denumerable*) if its elements can be paired one–to–one with the natural numbers, 1, 2, 3, etc. The term countable is somewhat misleading because, of course, it is humanly impossible actually to count infinitely many things.

The set of even numbers is an example of a countable set, as the pairing in table 1 shows.

Of course, it is not enough to show the way the first eight numbers are to be paired. One must show that no matter how far one goes along the list of even natural numbers there is a natural number paired with it. In this case this is an easy thing to do. One simply pairs any even number 2n with the natural number n.

What about the set of integers? One might guess that it is uncountable because the set of natural numbers is a proper subset of it. Consider the pairing in table 2.

Remarkably it works.

The secret in finding this pairing was to avoid a trap. Had the pairing been that which appears in table 3, one would never reach the negative integers. In working with infinite sets, one considers a pairing complete if there is a scheme that enables one to reach *any* number or element in the set after a finite number of steps. (Not everyone agrees that that is the same thing as reaching them *all*.) The former pairing does this.

Are the rational numbers countable? If one plots the rational numbers on a number line, they seem to fill it up. Intuitively one would guess that they form an uncountable set. But consider the pairing in table 4, in which the rational numbers are represented in their ratio form.

The listing scheme is a two–step procedure. First, in each ratio, the denominator and numerator are added. All those ratios with the same total are put in a group, and these groups are listed in the order of increasing totals. Within each group, the ratios are listed in order of increasing size. Thus the ratio 9/2 will show up in the group whose denominators and numerators total 11, and within that group it will fall between 8/3 and 10/1. The list will eventually include any positive rational number one can name.

Unfortunately, there are two flaws. The list leaves out the negative numbers and it pairs the same rational

number with more than one natural number. Because 1/1, 2/2, and 3/3 have different numerators and denominators, they show up at different places in the list and are paired with different natural numbers. They are the same rational number, however. The first flaw can be corrected by interleaving the negative numbers with the positive numbers, as was done with the integers. The second flaw can be corrected by throwing out any ratio which is not in lowest terms since it will already have been listed.

Correcting the flaws greatly complicates any formula one might devise for pairing a particular ratio a/b with a particular natural number, but the pairing is nevertheless one–to–one. Each ratio a/b will be assigned to a group a + b, and once in the group will be assigned a specific place. It will be paired with exactly one natural number. The set of rational numbers is, again remarkably, countable.

Another countable set is the set of algebraic numbers. Algebraic numbers are numbers which satisfy polynomial equations with integral coefficients. For instance, $\sqrt{2}$, I, and $(-1 + \sqrt{5})/2$ are algebraic, satisfying $x^2 - 2 = 0$, $x^2 + 1 = 0$, and $x^2 + x - 1 = 0$ respectively.

Are all infinite sets countable?

The answer to this question was given around 1870 by the German mathematician George Cantor. He showed that the set of numbers between 0 and 1 represented by infinite decimals was uncountable. (To include the finite decimals, he converted them to infinite decimals using the fact that a number such as .3 can be represented by the infinite decimal $.2\overline{9}$ where the 9s repeat forever.) He used a reductio ad absurdum proof, showing that the assumption that the set *is* countable leads to a contradiction. The assumption therefore has to be abandoned.

He began by assuming that the set *was* countable, meaning that there was a way of listing its elements so that, reading down the list, one could reach any number in it. This can be illustrated with an example. Suppose table 5 were such a listing.

From this list he constructs a new decimal. For its first digit, he uses a 1, which is different from the first digit in the first number in the list. For its second digit, he uses a 3, which is different from the second digit in the second number. For its third digit, he uses a 3 again, since it is different from the third digit in the third number.

He continues in this fashion, making the n–th digit in his new number different from the n–th digit in the n–th number in the list. In this example, he uses 1s and 3s, but he could use any other digits as well, as long as they differ from the n–th digit in the n–th number in the

TABLE 1								
Even Nos.	2	4	6	8	10	12	14	16 ...
Nat. Nos.	1	2	3	4	5	6	7	8 ...

TABLE 2									
Integers	0	1	-1	2	-2	3	-3	4	...n	-n ...
Nat. Nos.	1	2	3	4	5	6	7	8	...2n	2n + 1 ...

TABLE 3									
Integers	0	1	2	3	4	5	6	7	8 ...
Nat. Nos.	1	2	3	4	5	6	7	8	9 ...

TABLE 4												
Rat. Nos.	0/1	1/1	1/2	2/1	1/3	2/2	3/1	1/4	2/3	3/2	4/1	1/5	2/4 ...
Nat. Nos.	1	2	3	4	5	6	7	8	9	10	11	12	13 ...

TABLE 5	
1	.31754007...
2	.11887742...
3	.00037559...
4	.39999999...
5	.14141414...
6	.44116798...

list. (He avoids using 9's because the finite decimal .42 is the same number as the infinite decimal .4199999... with 9's repeating.)

The number he has constructed in this way is .131131... Because it differs from each of the numbers in at least one decimal place, it differs every number in the assumed complete list. If one chooses a number and looks for it in a listing of a countable set of numbers, after a finite number of steps he will find it (assuming that list has been arranged to demonstrate that the countability of the set). In this supposed listing he

won't. If he checks four million numbers, his constructed number will differ from them all in at least one of the first four million decimal places.

Thus the assumption that the set of infinite decimals between 0 and 1 is countable is a false assumption. The set has to be uncountable. The infinitude of such a set is different from the infinitude of the natural numbers.

Cantor gave the name $\aleph_0$ (Aleph null) to the infinitude of the natural numbers, and c to the number of infinite decimals between 0 and 1. This latter number represents the number of points on the number line lying in that interval and is therefore called the "cardinal number of the continuum" or the "power of the continuum." Mathematicians have struggled ever since Cantor's time to find out whether or not there is an infinity which is bigger than $\aleph_0$ but smaller than c, but have not been able to do so.

See also Natural numbers; Rational number.

Further Reading:

Eves, Howard. *An Introduction to the History of Mathematics.* New York: Holt, Rinehart and Winston, 1976.
Friedrichs, K. O. *From Pythagoras to Einstein.* Washington, D. C.: Mathematical Association of America, 1965.
Zippin, Leo. *Uses of Infinity.* Washington, D.C.: The Mathematical Association of America, 1962.

J. Paul Moulton

Counting number see **Natural numbers**

Coursers and pratincoles

Coursers and the closely related pratincoles are 17 species of birds that comprise the family Glareolidae, in the order Charadriiformes, which also contains the plovers, sandpipers, and other families of waders and shorebirds. The pratincoles occur in southern Europe and Asia, Africa, Southeast Asia, and Australasia, but coursers only occur in Africa, the Middle East, and India.

Coursers and pratincoles breed in sandy or stony deserts, in grassy plains, or in savannas, but always near water. Both types of birds fly gracefully, using their long, pointed wings.

Coursers have relatively long legs, three toes on their feet, a square tail, and a relatively long, thin, somewhat down–curved beak. Coursers are nomadic during their non–breeding season, undertaking wanderings in unpredictable directions, as is the case of many other bird species that breed in deserts.

Pratincoles have shorter legs, four toes, a deeply forked tail, and a short bill with a wide gape. Pratincoles undertake long–distance migrations during the non–breeding season, usually in flocks. The sexes are similar in both of these types of birds.

Pratincoles largely predate on flying insects, much in the manner of swallows (an alternate common name for these birds is swallow–plover). They also feed on the ground, running after their prey with rapid, short bursts of speed. Coursers are also insectivorous, but they feed exclusively on terrestrial insects, which are caught on the run. Coursers will also eat seeds when they are available.

Pratincoles occur in groups and nest in large, loosely structured colonies. Coursers are less social than this and do not nest in colonies. The nests of coursers and pratincoles are simple scrapes made in the open. In most species there are two eggs in a clutch, which are incubated by both the female and the male parents. These birds mostly nest in hot habitats, so the purpose of incubation is often to keep the eggs cool, rather than warm as in most birds. Some species moisten their eggs to keep them cooler.

Young coursers and pratincoles are precocious, hatching with their eyes open and are able to walk one day after birth. However, they are led to a sheltering bush or other hiding place as soon as they are mobile, and they shelter there while the parents bring them food. The young birds are well camouflaged to blend in with their surroundings.

If a predator is near the nest or babies, adult pratincoles will perform injury–feigning distraction displays meant to lure the animal away. Both coursers and pratincoles also have startle displays that they deploy under these conditions, in which the wings and tail are raised suddenly to reveal bold patterns of coloration in an attempt to unnerve the predator.

Species of coursers

The double–banded courser (*Rhinoptilus africanus*) of Africa lays only one egg, and the nest is commonly located near antelope dung as an aid to camouflage. The nest of the three–banded courser (*R. cinctus*) of Africa is a relatively deep scrape in which the clutch of two eggs is two–thirds buried in sand during incubation. The Egyptian plover (*Pluvialis aegyptius*) is a courser that breeds along large rivers in central and northeastern Africa. This species also buries its eggs and even its babies, and it also regurgitates water to cool these down on especially hot afternoons.

Species of pratincoles

The collared pratincole, red–winged pratincole, or swallow plover (*Glareola pratincola*) is highly unusual in having migratory populations in both the southern and northern hemispheres. Northern birds breed in open steppes, savannas, and dry mudflats in southern Europe and southeastern Asia, and winter in Africa. Birds that breed in southern Africa, migrate to northern Africa to spend their non–breeding season. The black–winged pratincole (*G. nordmanni*) is a widespread species that breeds from southeastern Europe through central Asia, and winters on tropical shores in south and southeast Asia. The oriental pratincole (*G. maldivarum*) breeds in central and southern Asia, and migrates as far south as Australia.

The Australian pratincole (*Stiltia isabella*) breeds widely across much of that island continent, including the semi–arid interior. This species migrates north to spend its non–breeding season in the coastal tropics, from northern Australia to Indonesia. This is the only species in its genus, and it is rather intermediate in form to the coursers and pratincoles. Like the coursers, the Australian pratincole has a relatively long beak and long legs, a short tail, and no hind toe. In addition, this species does not have comb–like structures called pectinations on the claw of the middle toe, a characteristic that all other pratincoles and the coursers exhibit.

See also Plovers.

Further Reading:

Brooke, M. and T. Birkhead. *The Cambridge Encyclopedia of Ornithology.* Cambridge, U.K.: Cambridge University Press, 1991.

Harrison, C. J. O., ed. *Bird Families of the World.* New York: H.N. Abrams Pubs., 1978.

Hayman, P., J. Marchant, and T. Prater. *Shorebirds: An Identification Guide to the Waders of the World.* London: Croom Helm, 1986.

Bill Freedman

Courtship

Courtship is a complex set of behaviors in animals that leads to mating. Courtship behavior communicates to each of the potential mates that the other is not a threat. It also reveals information to each animal that the species, gender, and physical condition of the other are suitable for mating. Pre–mating activities are for the most part ritualistic. They consist of a series of fixed action patterns that are species–specific. Each fixed action triggers an appropriate fixed reaction by the partner, with one action stimulating the next. Courtship allows one or both sexes to select a mate from several candidates. Usually, the females do the choosing. In some species of birds, males display in a lek, a small communal area, where females select a mate from the displaying males. Males, generally, compete with each other for mates, and females pick the best quality male available. The danger of courtship is that it can attract predators instead of mates.

Several basic factors influence a female's choice of mate. First, if a female provides parental care, she chooses as competent a male as possible. For example, in birds such as the common tern, the female selects a good fish catcher. As part of courtship, the male birds display fish to the female, and may even feed them to her. This demonstrates his ability to feed the young. In addition, females tend to select males with resources such as food or shelter which help a mating pair to produce more offspring that survive. In the long–jawed longhorned beetle that lives in the Arizona desert, males battle each other for saguaro cactus fruit. The females mate in exchange for access to the fruit. A male endowed with large mandibles can defeat other males, take over the fruit, and thus attract females. Genetic fitness is another important factor in mate selection. In species that lack parental care, offspring rely for survival on qualities that they inherit from their parents. During courtship, energetic displays and striking appearance indicate good health. Vigorous, attractive parents generally pass immunities to their offspring. Attractiveness may depend on the intensity of secondary sex characteristics, which in birds, for example, include colorful plumage and long tails. Another advantage is that inherited attractive features make offspring desirable to mates.

Courtship in insects

Insect courtship is ritualistic and has evolved over time. Male balloon flies of the family Empididae spin oval balloons of silk. Then they fly in a swarm, carrying their courtship objects aloft. Females approach the swarm and select their mates. As a female pairs off with a male, she accepts his balloon. In some species of balloon flies, the male brings the female a dead insect to eat during copulation. This may prevent her from eating him. In other species, the male carries a dead insect inside a silk balloon. Apparently, in the course of evolution, the suitor's gift–giving began with "candy," then a "box of candy," and finally just the empty "box."

A male peacock displays his plumage as part of the courtship ritual.

Other courtship strategies in insects include female moths that release a scent signal (or pheromone) that males of the same species recognize. When a male detects the signal, he flies upstream to the female. In queen butterflies, courtship is complex and requires steps that must occur in the proper order. First, the female flaps her wings and draws the male's attention and pursues her. As he hovers nearby his hairpencils (brushlike organs) release a pheromone. Then the receptive female lands on a nearby plant. Next, the male brushes his hairpencils on her antennae. She responds by closing her wings. This signals the male to land on her and begin mating. In other courtship behavior, male crickets rub their forewings together and produce a pulsed courtship song. In fireflies, the male's flashing light and the female's flashing answer is another type of courtship behavior. In fireflies, both sexes respond to a specific set of intervals between flashes.

Courtship in fish

In 1973, Niko Tinbergen won a Nobel prize for his work on animal behavior. One of the topics he studied was courting in stickleback, small freshwater fish. At breeding time, the male stickleback changes color from dull brown, to black and blue above and red underneath. At this time, he builds a tunnel–shaped nest of sand. Females swollen with unfertilized eggs cruise in schools through the male territory. The male performs his zigzag courtship dance toward and away from the female fish. Attracted to the red color on the male's belly, a female ready to lay eggs displays her swollen abdomen. The male leads her to the nest. He pokes the base of her tail with his snout, and the female lays her eggs and then swims away. The male enters the nest and fertilizes the eggs. In this manner, he may lead three or four females to his nest to lay eggs. Tinbergen showed in his studies that seeing the color red caused increased aggressiveness in males and attraction in females.

Courtship in birds

Adult birds generally return to their nesting grounds each mating season. A male claims a territory by singing a distinctive song. He then sings a song that attracts a female. Birds have different courtship rituals. Some use song, while others display colorful plumage. Woodcocks fly upward in a spiral, and birds of paradise do somersaults. Male frigatebirds—large birds with wings that spread wider than 6.6 ft (2 m)—breed in late

Davies, Nicholas B. "Backyard Battle of the Sexes." *Natural History* (April 1995).

Dennis, Jerry. "Mates for Life." *Wildlife Conservation* (May–June 1993).

Fernald, Russell D. "Cichlids in Love." *Sciences* (July-August 1993).

Films for the Humanities and Sciences. *Mating Signals.* Princeton, 1994–5.

Films for the Humanities and Sciences. *The Rituals of Courtship.* Princeton, 1994–5.

Hancock, Leah. "Whose Funny Valentine?" *Natural Wildlife* (February–March 1995).

Jackson, Robert. "Arachnomania." *Natural History* (March 1995).

Robert, Daniel, and Ronald R. Hoy. "Overhearing Cricket Love Songs." *Natural History* (June 1994).

Bernice Essenfeld

Covalent bond see **Chemical bond**

Cowfish see **Boxfish**

Coyote see **Canines**

KEY TERMS

Display—Showy exhibition by an animal that reveals information to others.

Lek—Communal area used by birds and insects for courtship and mate selection.

Pheromone—Chemical odorant that provides communication between animals.

Ritual—Species–specific behavior pattern or ceremony used for communication between animals.

---

winter on the coast of tropical islands in the western Atlantic and Pacific Oceans. The male perches in a low tree or brush and his red throat pouch inflates like a balloon. Its red color attracts females hovering overhead. Then the male spreads his wings, shakes them, and makes a whinnying sound. Finally, the pair come together, mate, and build a nest.

Courtship in mammals

Mammals use various strategies in courtship. Pheromones act as sexual lures that bring members of the opposite sex together. These attractants are so powerful that a male dog can smell a female in estrus more than half a mile (1 km) away. The fact that at puberty humans begin to produce odorous sweat suggests the role of pheromones in primate courtship. Sex selection also exists in primates. Females usually choose their male partners, but sometimes the reverse occurs. Recent research reveals that male lion–tailed macaques remain aloof during the day. At night, however, they seek out sleeping estrous females for mating. Until this study, biologists thought that it was the females who initiated mating. In humans, various cultures determine the customs of courtship. For example, in some societies, marriages are arranged by relatives. In these cases, a woman is matched to a man with the appropriate resources. Just as other female animals select mates with resources, humans tend to select mates with wealth and status. Further, even if a woman has no say in the selection of her husband, she will help arrange the marriage of her offspring. This merely delays female mate choice by a generation.

See also Behavior; Sexual reproduction.

Further Reading:

Batten, Mary. *Sexual Strategies.* New York: G.P. Putnam's Sons, 1992.

Coypu

The coypu or nutria (*Myocastor coypu*) is a species of semi–aquatic, dog–sized rodent in the family Capromyidae. These animals are native to central and southern South America, but they have become widely established elsewhere, mostly as a result of animals that have escaped from fur farms or that have been deliberately released.

Coypus have a stout, 17–25 in (43–64 cm) long body, with a roughly triangular–shaped head, and a round, scaly, sparsely–haired tail, which is 10–17 in (25–43 cm) long. Adult animals weight 15–20 lb (7–9 kg), with males being somewhat larger than females. The eyes and ears of coypus are small, and the legs are short. The forelegs are much larger than the hind and have four webbed toes as well as a single free toe used for grooming the fur. The toes have prominent claws. The fur is soft, dense, and lustrous, consisting of long guard hairs over a velvety underfur. The color of the guard hairs ranges from yellow–brown to red–brown, while the underfur is blackish.

Coypus are semi–aquatic animals, and are excellent swimmers. They typically live in the vicinity of slow–moving rivers and streams, or near the edges of shallow lakes, marshes, and other wetlands. Coypus mostly live in freshwater habitats, but in some places they occur in brackish and saltwater wetlands as well. Coypus den in burrows dug into banks, or in mounds of reedy vegetation that are constructed when ground suitable for digging is not available. Coypus live in pairs or small family groups and sometimes in larger colonies.

Coypus typically forage during twilight hours over a distance of up to several hundred yards, travelling along well–worn pathways through the usually grassy habitat. Coypus are shy and wary when foraging, and flee quickly to their burrow when any hint of danger is perceived. Coypus are mainly vegetarian in their feeding, although they will also eat molluscs.

The fur of coypus is a valued product, and this species has been introduced as a fur–bearing species into various parts of the United States and Europe. Coypus are also cultivated on fur farms, where they will breed continuously, and can be quite productive. Cultivated coypus can have a white or yellowish fur, in addition to the darker colors of the wild animals.

Coypus are considered to be pests in many of the places where they have become naturalized because they damage irrigation ditches and earthen dams with their burrows, compete with native fur–bearers, and, when abundant, can significantly deplete the abundance of forage.

See also Beavers.

Crabs

Crabs are some of the best known arthropods—a terms that means jointed foot (Greek: *arthron*, joint; *pous*, foot). They are among the most successful of all living species (about 4,500 species have been described), with members adapted to living on land and in water; some species even succeed in living in both habitats. The majority, however, live in the marine environment. Unlike lobsters (to which they are closely related), which have a long and cylindrical body with an extended abdomen, crabs have a broad, flattened body and a short, symmetrical abdomen—adaptations that enable them to squeeze beneath rocks and into crevices for feeding purposes as well as concealment.

The bulk of the body is taken up by the abdomen. Attached to this is a small head which bears long eye stalks that fit into special sockets on the carapace. There are also several pairs of antennae of unequal length and feeding mouthparts known as maxillipeds. The first pair of walking legs are large in comparison with the remainder of the body and end in pinching claws. These are usually referred to as chelipeds. In most species, the tips of the remaining four pairs of legs terminate in pointed tips. When feeding, food is picked up by the chelipeds, torn apart, and passed to the maxillipeds in small portions, from where it is pushed towards the pharynx. While some species are active predators of small fish, others are detritus feeders and scoop large volumes of mud towards the mouth region using the chelipeds as spades. These species then filter out any food particles and reject the remainder of the materials. Some species of burrowing crabs, which remain concealed in the soft sea bed, create a water current down into their burrows and filter out food particles in a similar manner. Their chelipeds are also fringed with tiny hair–like structures known as setae, which help extract the largest unwanted materials from the water current before other parts are ingested.

When moving on land or on the sea bed, crabs usually move in a sideways manner: the leading legs pull the body forward and those on the opposite side assist by pushing. Some species may use just two or three pairs of legs when moving quickly, stopping occasionally to turn around and reverse the order in which the legs move. Contrary to popular opinion, few crabs actually swim. One group of specialized swimming crabs (the family Portunidae) have an oval shaped body and the last pair of walking legs are flattened and act as paddles that propel the animal. Examples of these swimming crabs include the common blue crab (*Callinectes sapidus*), the green crab (*Carcinides maenas*) and the lady, or calico crab (*Ovalipes ocellatus*).

The remaining species, the "true crabs" vary considerably in size and behavior. Some of the largest of these are the spider crabs (family Maiidae). These are all marine species that live in the littoral zone, frequently skulking around on the sea bed in harbors and estuaries. This group contains the largest known arthropod, the giant Japanese crab (*Macrocheira kaempferi*) which can measure up to 13 ft (4 m) in diameter when fully extended. Most members of this family are scavenging animals. Many elect to carry a range of small sponges and other marine organisms on their outer carapace for concealment.

The aptly named fiddler crabs (family Ocyopidae), are easily recognized by the massively enlarged front claw of the male. The claw is usually carried horizontally in front of the body and has been likened to a fiddle; the smaller opposing claw is known as the bow. When males are trying to attract females, they wave these large claws two and fro; crabs with larger claws seem to attract more suitors than those with tiny claws. These crabs are usually a light brown color with mot-

A hermit crab.

tled purple and darker brown patches on the carapace—a pattern that helps to conceal them on the dark sands and mud flats on which they live.

Unlike all other crabs, the tiny hermit crab has a soft body which is inserted in the shell of a marine snail for protection. Hermit crabs never kill the original occupant of the shell and frequently change "homes" as they grow, slipping out of one shell and into another. House hunting is a demanding task, and hermit crabs spend considerable time inspecting new prospective pieces of real estate, checking for size and weight. The shell is held on through a combination of modified hind limbs, which grasp some of the internal rings of the shell, and the pressure of the body against the shell wall. When resting, the crab can withdraw entirely inside the shell, blocking the opening with its claws. Hermit crab shells are commonly adorned with sea anemones and hydroids, the reason seeming to be that these provide some protection against small predators on account of the battery of specialized stinging cells that these organisms possess. In return for this service, the anemones and hydroids may benefit from the guarantee that they will always be in clean water and the possibility of obtaining food scraps from the crab when

it is feeding. The importance of this relationship for the crab is seen when a hermit crab changes its shell, as they usually delicately remove the anemones and hydroids from their former home to their new abode.

Of the terrestrial species, one of the most distinctive groups are the robber, or coconut, crabs which live in deep burrows above the high water mark. These crabs rarely venture into the sea, apart from when they lay their eggs. They have overcome the problem of obtaining oxygen by converting their gill chambers to modified chambers lined with moisture, enabling them to breathe atmospheric oxygen. Closely related to the hermit crab, robber crabs have developed a toughened upper surface on their abdomen which means that have no need of a shell for protection. Coconut crabs—so called because of their habit of digging in the soft soils of coconut plantations—occasionally climb trees and sever the stems attaching young coconuts, on which they feed.

Crabs have a complicated life history. Mating is usually preceded by a short period of courtship. The eggs are laid shortly after copulation and are retained on the female's body until the larvae emerge. The tiny "zoea" larvae, as they are known, are free–living and grow through a series of body molts to reach a stage known as the "megalops" larvae, at which stage the first resemblance to the parent crabs is visible. Further development leads to the immature and mature adult form.

Cracids see **Chachalacas**

Cranberry see **Heath family**

Crane

An invention of ancient origin, the crane is used for the loading and unloading of heavy objects and as an aid in the construction of tall buildings. One common forerunner of the crane was the *shaduf*, prevalent in Egypt and India around 1500 B.C. Employed by a single person for lifting water, the *shaduf* consisted of a vertical support, a long, pivoting beam, and a counterweight.

The first true cranes, founded on principles governing the use of levers and counterweights, employed a pulley system affixed to a single mast (or boom). Lifting power was provided by humans or draft animals operating a treadmill or large wheel. Eventually, a second mast and guy wires were added to increase the strength and stability of this early form of crane.

One of the most significant developments in crane design, which probably occurred during Medieval times with the advent of Gothic architecture, was the jib crane, which featured a pivoting horizontal arm that projected outward from the top of the boom. The addition of hinged movement to the outermost section of the jib allowed for even further versatility and movement.

Jib–cranes are also known as derrick cranes, derrick being the term originally applied to gallows structures when Englishman Godfrey Derrick became a prominent hangman. Today, the derrick is a large hoisting machine similar in most respects to the crane, save for its typically stationary foundation. Oil derricks, for example, are specialized steel towers used for raising and lowering equipment for drilling oil wells. One of the most powerful cranes, a barge derrick, is a double–boomed structure capable of lifting and moving ships weighing up to 3,000 tons.

Other cranes with specialized uses include the cantilever crane (featuring a suspended horizontal boom and used in shipyards), the overhead traveling crane (guided by rails and a trolley–suspended pulley system and used for indoor work), and the tractor–mounted crawler crane (a hydraulic–powered crane with a telescoping boom). A simple example of a small-scale crane

A crane being used to lay decking on a bridge.

is the fork-lift truck. Like its much larger relatives, the fork-lift is limited not so much by the size of its hoisting apparatus as by the force of its rear counterweight.

Cranes

Cranes are tall birds known for their beauty, elaborate courtship dances, and voices that boom across the wetlands. They are among the oldest birds on Earth. Today 15 crane species in the family Gruidae are found throughout the world, except South America and Antarctica. Two species, the whooping crane (*Grus americana*) and the sandhill crane (*G. canadensis*), are found in North America. Cranes belong to order Gruiformes, which also includes rails, coots, trumpeters, and the limpkin.

Cranes have long legs, long necks, and narrow, tapered bills. Most of them have a featherless spot on the top of the head that exposes colored skin. Some have wattles, or flaps of flesh, growing from the chin. The wattled crane (*Bugeranus carunculatus*) of eastern and southern Africa has very large wattles. This bird looks more like a chunky stork than most cranes do. Although cranes do look rather like storks and herons, those birds have a toe that points backward, enabling them to grasp a tree branch. Cranes have a backward toe, but in all except the crowned cranes (*Balearica*) it is raised up off the ground and of no use in grasping branches. Crowned cranes are able to perch in trees like storks.

Most cranes migrate fairly long distances to their nesting sites. Their large, strong wings allow them, once airborne, to glide on air currents, taking the strain out of the trip. When flying, they stretch their necks and legs straight out, making a long straight line. They can cruise at speeds of about 45 mph (72 kph).

Cranes are very vocal birds. They make many different sounds, from a low, almost purring sound, apparently of contentment, to a loud, high–pitched call that announces to the other birds that one is about to take flight. Mating pairs of cranes will often point their beaks to the sky and make long, dramatic calls that have been called unison calls or bonding calls. Many cranes have extra long windpipes that give volume to their calls.

Cranes eat grains, especially liking the corn found in cornfields, as well as small invertebrates that they catch in the water. Those cranes with long, thin beaks that are most adapted to obtaining food in very wet areas are the species that are now threatened as their wetland habitats are destroyed. Both in water and on land, cranes often stand on one foot, tucking the other under a wing.

Dancing and mating

Cranes are most noted for their amazing dances that bond individual males and females together. These dances are very elaborate and ballet–like, and are probably the most intricate and beautiful in the animal kingdom. The cranes bow, leap high into the air, and twirl with their wings held out like a skirt. However, this wonderful dance is not only a courtship dance because once a pair has bonded, they are mated for life. Cranes dance at other times, too, possibly as a way of relieving frustration which might otherwise erupt into aggression. They also dance for pleasure. Very young cranes start dancing with excitement.

A pair of cranes construct a raised nest of dried grasses by water. Either one might start incubating as soon as the first egg is laid, although they usually lay two eggs. Crowned cranes often lay three. The eggs hatch after about 28–31 days. Both parents feed the

A sandhill crane at Big Marsh Lake, Michigan. The call of this bird is audible for more than a mile.

chicks and take care of them long past the time that they grow their adult feathers. The young are yellowish tan or grayish and very fuzzy. Once they reach adult size, their parents drive them away to establish lives of their own. The life spans of cranes vary considerably. Sandhill cranes rarely live more than 20 years. One Siberian crane (*Bugeranus leucogeranus*) was known to live 82 years, but 30–40 years is more likely.

While in their nesting sites, most cranes go through a period of molting, or losing their feathers. Some of them even have a period of up to a month during which so many feathers have been shed that they are completely flightless.

Varieties of cranes

The largest crane, and the rarest Asian crane, is the red–crowned or Japanese crane (*Grus japonicus*). This bird that can weigh up to 25 lb (11.4 kg). It has vivid red feathers on the top of its head, but its body is snowy white. It appears to have a black tail, but actually these feathers are the ends of its wings. Although formerly widespread, the red–crowned crane is now reduced to small populations in Japan, Russia, and China (these birds winter in Japan, China, North Korea, and South Korea). In 1952, this crane became Japan's national bird. There are probably not more than 1,800 of these birds left in the wild.

The smallest crane is the demoiselle crane (*Anthropoides virgo*) of Europe and north Africa. It has white ear tufts that stretch from its eyes backward and hang off the back of the head. Demoiselle cranes live on drier ground than other cranes. The blue crane (*A. paradisea*) of Africa has wingtip feathers that reach backward and to the ground, like a bustle. These two cranes do not nest by water, but in grasslands or even semiarid land. The blue crane is the national bird of South Africa. It has the surprising ability when excited of puffing out its cheeks until its head looks frightening.

The tallest crane is the sarus crane (*G. antigone*) of India, Nepal, Vietnam, Cambodia, and northern Australia. Standing 6 ft (almost 2 m) tall, it is a gray bird with a head and throat of vivid red. The red color ends abruptly in a straight line around the white neck. This species is among the least social of cranes, and it becomes aggressive when nesting.

A frequent resident of zoos is the crowned crane (*Balearica pavonina*) of Africa, which has a beautiful puff of golden feathers coming from the back of the head. It has a red wattle beneath its black and white head, a light gray neck, dark gray back and tail, and white, sometimes yellowish, wings. The West African subspecies has a black neck instead of gray and lacks the red wattle.

The rare black–necked or Tibetan crane (*Grus nigricollis*) of the Himalayas breeds on the high plateau of Tibet. It migrates to the valleys of southwest China and Bhutan to spent the winter. The black–necked crane is a medium–sized crane with a stocky appearance; it has a larger body and shorter neck and legs than related species, perhaps as an adaptation to the cold climate of the Tibetan plateau. This crane has a black neck and head, plus a striking black trailing edge to its wings. A golden circle around the eye makes the eye look enormous against the black feathers. It is estimated that a minimum of 5,500 black–necked cranes survive in the wild.

The seriously endangered Siberian crane is as beautiful as it is rare, with long reddish pink legs, a red–orange face, and a snowy white body with black areas on its wings. This crane breeds only at two loca-tions in Siberia and winters in India, Iran, and China. Only a few thousand of these birds are left.

Whooping cranes

Whooping cranes (*Grus americana*) are the rarest cranes and the tallest American bird. This crane stands 5 ft (1.5 m) tall and has a wing span of 7 ft (2.1 m). Adolescent birds have a golden yellow neck, back, and beak, with golden edges to the black–tipped wings. By adulthood, only the black wing tips remain. The rest of the bird is white except for the crown of the head and cheeks and part of the long, pointed beak, all of which are red.

The population of these North American birds was down to 16 in 1941. But this decline wasn't completely human–caused. Cranes evolved in the grassy wetlands that once covered much of the central part of the continent. As these wet regions gradually filled in naturally and created the American prairie, little crane habitat remained and their numbers shrank. Then, a 1940 hurricane killed half of the remaining whooping cranes.

The last normal nest was seen in 1932. In 1937, the birds' wintering area on the coast of Texas was protected as Aransas National Wildlife Refuge. It was another 32 years before another nest was found. In the meantime, the few remaining whooping cranes had all been taken into captivity. Each egg that was laid was carefully incubated, but few of the young survived. Then, a nesting area inside Wood Buffalo National Park in Canada was found.

Whoopers generally lay two olive–colored eggs, but only one of them hatches. Canadian wildlife experts began removing one egg from every nest with two eggs and taking it to safety to hatch. Some are hatched in incubators. Others are slipped into the nests of smaller sand-hill cranes. Gradually whooping crane numbers have increased and birds are being returned to the wild. By 1995, several hundred whooping cranes existed. However, it is not yet certain that the species will survive.

Sandhill cranes

Sandhill cranes are smaller than whooping cranes. They are generally light gray in color, with a red crown, black legs, and white cheeks. There are large breeding populations in Siberia and Alaska through the western and central United States. There are six subspecies of sandhill crane. Three of them—the greater, lesser, and Canadian sandhill cranes—are migratory birds. The other three—Florida, Mississippi, and Cuban—do not migrate. The lesser sandhill, which is the smallest subspecies (less than 4 ft/1.2 m tall and weighing no more than 8 lb/3.6 kg) migrates the greatest distance. Many birds that winter in Texas and northern Mexico nest in Siberia.

The populations of sandhill cranes were greatly reduced in the 1930s and 1940s. However, wherever protected, they have been making a good comeback. One population in Indiana increased from 35 to 14,000 over a 40–year period. In one of the most amazing sights in nature, perhaps half a million sandhill cranes land on the sandbars of the Platte River in Nebraska while they are migrating.

Further Reading:

Friedman, Judy. *Operation Siberian Crane: The Story Behind the International Effort to Save an Amazing Bird.* New York: Dillon Press, 1992.

Grooms, Steve. *The Cry of the Sandhill Crane.* Minocqua, WI: NorthWord Press, 1992.

Horn, Gabriel. *The Crane.* New York: Crestwood House, 1988.

Katz, Barbara. *So Cranes May Dance: A Rescue from the Brink of Extinction.* Chicago: Chicago Review, 1993.

Kerrod, Robin. *Birds: The Waterbirds.* New York: Facts on File, 1989.

Jean Blashfield

Crappies see **Bass**

Crayfish

Crayfish are freshwater crustaceans, (encased in a shell) of the order Decapoda (ten legged animals) which includes crabs, shrimp, lobsters, and hermit crabs. Crayfish are nocturnally active, live in shallow fresh waters, and feed on aquatic plant and animal life. Natural predators include wading birds, otters, fish, and turtles. Crayfish are particularly vulnerable to predation during their periodic molts, when their exoskeleton is shed to permit growth. Aggressive behavior usually occurs over resources such as habitat, food, or offspring. Crayfish are a popular culinary delicacy, and crayfish are also used as live fish bait.

A crayfish at the Fish Point State Wildlife Area, Michigan.

History and habitat

Crayfish evolved from saltwater ancestors which date back some 280 million years. There are over 300 species of crayfish worldwide which are classified in the three families: the Astacidae, the Cambridae, found only in the Northern Hemisphere, and the Parastacidae, which are indigenous to the Southern Hemisphere. A few species have adapted to tropical zones but most live in temperate regions. None exist in Africa and the Indian subcontinent, although there is a single species found in Madagascar. Crayfish live in water, hiding beneath rocks, logs, sand, mud, and vegetation. Crayfish also dig burrows, constructing little chimneys from moist soil excavated from their tunnels and carried to the surface. Some terrestrial species spend their whole life below ground in burrows emerging only to find a mate. Other species of crayfish live both in their tunnels as well as often venturing into open water. Many species live mostly in open water, retreating to their burrows during pregnancy and for protection from predators and cold weather.

Appearance

Crayfish are usually colored in earth tones of muted greens and browns. The body has three primary sections: the cephalothorax (the fused head and thorax), which is entirely encased by a single shell, the carapace; a six–segmented abdomen; and a five–sectioned, fan–shaped tail, the telson. Five pairs of strong, jointed, armored legs (pereiopods) on the cephalothorax are used for walking and digging. The first pair of legs known as the chelipeds, end in large pinchers (chelae) which are used for defense and food gathering. Two pairs of small antennae (the antennae and antennules) are specialized chemical detectors used in foraging and finding a mate. The antennae project on either side of the tip of the rostrum, which is a beak–like projection at the front of the head. A third and longer pair of antennae are tactile, or touch, receptors. Two compound eyes provide excellent vision, except in some cave–dwellers which live in perpetual dark and which are virtually blind. Below the rostrum are two pair of mandibles (the jaws) and three pair of maxillipeds, which are small appendages which direct food to the mouth. The second pair of maxillipeds facilitate gill ventilation by swishing water through the banks of gills located at the base of each pereiopod on the sides of the carapace in the gill chambers. The strong, long, muscular abdomen has ten tiny appendages (the pleopods) which aid in swimming movements. When threatened, the crayfish propels itself backward at lightning speed with a few quick flips of the telson, located at the tip of the abdomen.

Breeding habits

Crayfish usually mate in the fall. Females excrete pheromones which are detected by the antennules of males. The openings of the sex organs are located on the front end of abdomen just below the thorax. In the male the first two pairs of abdominal pleopods are used as organs of sperm transfer. Using his first set of pleopods, the male deposits sperm into a sac on the female's abdomen. The female stays well hidden as ovulation draws near, lavishly grooming her abdominal pleopods which will eventually secure her eggs and hatchlings to her abdomen. Strenuous abdominal contractions signal the onset of egg extrusion. Cupping her abdomen, the female crayfish collects her eggs as they are laid (which can number 400 or more) securing them with her pleopods, fastidiously cleaning them with thoracic appendages and discarding any diseased eggs.

Young crayfish hatchlings emerge from the eggs in the spring, and closely resemble adult crayfish. The hatchlings cling tightly to their mother's pleopods, eventually taking short foraging forays and scurrying

---

KEY TERMS

Antennule—Small antenna on the front section of the head.

Carapace—Shell covering the cephalothorax.

Cephalothorax—The head and thorax (upper part of the body) combined.

Chela—Pinchers on first pair of legs used for defense and food gathering.

Chelipeds—First pair of pereiopods ending with large pinchers.

Mandibles—Jaws.

Maxillipeds—Small leg–like appendages beneath the cephalothorax which aid in feeding.

Pereiopods—Ten jointed, armor–plated legs attached to the cephalothorax.

Pleopods—Small, specialized appendages below the abdomen which aid in swimming.

Rostrum—Beak–like projection at the front of the head.

Telson—Fan–shaped tail composed of five segments.

---

back for protection at the slightest disturbance. During this time, the mother remains relatively inactive and is extremely aggressive in protecting her young from other non–maternal crayfish, which cannibalistically prey on the young. Mother and young communicate chemically via pheromones; however, the young cannot differentiate between their own mother and another maternal female.

See also Crabs; Crustacea; Lobsters; Shrimp.

Further Reading:

Felgenhauer, Bruce E., Les Watling and Anne B. Thistle, *Functional Morphology of Feeding and Grooming in Crustacea*. Rotterdam/Brookfield: A.A. Balkema, 1989.

Hobbs, Horton H., Jr. *The Crayfishes of Georgia*. Washington: Smithsonian Institution Press, 1981.

Rebach, Steve, and Dunham, David W., ed. *Studies In Adaptation, The Behavior of Higher Crustacea*. New York, Chichester, Brisbane, Toronto, Singapore: John Wiley & Sons, 1983.

Marie L. Thompson

Cream of tartar see **Potassium hydrogen tartrate**

Crestfish

Crestfish, also called unicornfish, are a small family (Lophotidae) of deepwater, marine bony fish in the order Lampridiformes. These rare fish have unusual boxlike heads with protruding foreheads and ribbon–shaped silvery bodies with crimson fins. The prominent dorsal fin extends from the tip of the head to beyond the tail; the first rays of this fin form a crest above the head, giving these fish their common name. Crestfish also have a short anal fin, but the pelvic fin is absent. At least one species of crestfish (*Lophotus capellei*) has no scales, and another species (*L. lacepede*) has tiny, cycloid scales that are easily rubbed off.

Some crestfish can be quite large. Specimens as large as 6 ft (1.8 m) long have been found off the coast of southern California, although smaller fish (about 3.5 ft/1 m) are more typical. Crestfish are related to ribbonfish (family Trachipteridae) and oarfish (family Regalecidae), but are distinguished from these related families by having high foreheads and anal fins.

See also Opah.

Creutzfeldt–Jakob disease

Creutzfeldt–Jakob disease is a rare encephalopathy, or brain disease, that usually affects middle–aged men and women. It was first described by German psychiatrist Alfons Maria Jakob (1884–1931) in 1921. He gave credit to Hans Gerhard Creutzfeldt (1885–1964), also a German psychiatrist, for describing the syndrome first without realizing he had stumbled onto a repeating set of symptoms which constitute a syndrome. Although it is now known that what Creutzfeldt described was not the same syndrome that Jakob had discovered, the disease retains its compound name.

Creutzfeldt–Jakob disease is the more common of two known human spongiform encephalopathies, the other being kuru. Both encephalopathies are thought to be caused by prions, infectious agents made up of gene-lacking proteins.

The early stages of Creutzfeldt–Jakob disease include symptoms similar to those of Alzheimer's disease. Disturbances in vision and other senses, confusion, and inappropriate behavior patterns are the usual early signs. During the following months the patient will invariably progress first to dementia and then into a coma. Jerking movements of the arms and legs are common, and convulsions are less normative. Muscle spasms and rigidity are common in the late stages of the disease. Usually, the patient will deteriorate and die in less than a year, although some will live for as long as two years.

From its first description in 1921 until 1968, only 150 cases of Creutzfeldt–Jakob disease had been documented in medical literature. By the mid–1990s, more than 2,000 cases had been recorded, perhaps because of improved diagnosing techniques.

Creutzfeldt–Jakob disease occurs throughout the world, usually equally among middle–aged men and women. Rarely do young people get the disease. Because the disease sometimes appears to run in families it has been thought to be genetic, but this is not the case. Only 10% of Creutzfeldt–Jakob patients in the United States have a family history of presenile dementia (dementia occurring in non–elderly individuals).

There are no laboratory tests to help diagnose Creutzfeldt–Jakob disease. A brain scan using magnetic resonance imaging (MRI) will usually show the degeneration of the cerebrum and enlargement of the brain ventricles (fluid–filled openings in the center of the brain) which characterize encephalopathy. A definitive diagnosis can be made only when a specimen of the brain tissue is stained and studied under a microscope. (This study of tissue at the microscopic level is called histology.) Other neurological measurements are less directly correlated to diagnosing the disease. The electroencephalogram (which monitors the pattern of electric brain waves) may show certain repeated signs, but not always. The cerebrospinal fluid (which fills spaces in the brain and surrounds the spinal cord) may have an elevated level of protein when tested; this measurement is currently being investigated to determine whether the presence or elevation of specific proteins is diagnostic of this disease. The changes seen in brain tissue are not found in any organ outside the central nervous system. The etiologic agent that causes the disease can be found in other organs, but evidently it has no effect on their structure or function.

The etiologic agent of Creutzfeldt–Jakob disease has unique characteristics. The agent can withstand heat, ionizing radiation, and ultraviolet light—immunities that documented viruses do not possess. Some scientists consider the agent to be a unique, nonviral pathogen that does not contain any DNA or RNA, the nucleic acids containing the reproductive code for any organism. While other theories have been advanced, none has achieved acceptance; the causal agent for this disease has yet to be sufficiently described.

The means of transmitting this disease is unknown. A case has been documented in which a patient who received a transplanted cornea from the eye of a person with Creutzfeldt–Jakob disease also developed the disease. Another person contracted the disease when electrodes previously used on an infected patient were used in an electroencephalogram. Even the spread of the disease within families is the result of a mysterious mechanism. It is not always seen and may be the result of more than one family member having a genetic predisposition to the disease.

There is no cure for Creutzfeldt–Jakob disease. Symptoms are treated to make the patients more comfortable, but nothing has been found that will interfere with the progress of the disease or kill the causal agent. In fact, very special precautions are required around these patients because the means of spreading the disease is not known. Only three means of sterilization of instruments or other objects that have touched the patient are known—lye, bleach, and intense heat. It is recommended that clothing and bed linens of the patient be burned as washing will not kill the etiologic agent.

Creutzfeldt–Jakob disease, though rare, remains a medical mystery, since scientists do not yet know its means of transmission, its cure, or its prevention.

See also Brain; Kuru; Prion.

Larry Blaser

Crevalles see **Jacks**

Crickets

Crickets (order Orthoptera, family Grillidae) are found throughout the world except for the polar regions.

More than 900 species have been described. Often heard, but more seldom seen, at first glance crickets are quite similar to grasshoppers and bush crickets—also known as long–horned grasshoppers or katydids—but may be distinguished from these insects by their much longer, thread–like antennae. Crickets can also be easily identified by long hindlegs used for jumping. Most species are black or brown in appearance, which helps to conceal them and therefore reduce the risk of detection from predatory small mammals and birds.

A cricket's body is divided into three sections: the head, which bears the large eyes, antennae and mouthparts; the thorax, which is separated into three segments (each of which bears one pair of segmented legs and efficient claws) and supports the wings; and the abdomen. There are typically two pairs of wings, of which the front pair are thicker. At rest, the wings are held flat over the insect's back with the edges bent down along the sides of the body. Some species, however, may just have one pair of wings, while others still have lost all power of flight. Among the latter are some of the smallest members of the Orthoptera, the ant–loving crickets that measure less than an inch (3–5mm) and live in underground ant nests. Despite the presence of wings on some species, none of the crickets are exceptionally good fliers; most rely on a combination of short flights and jumps to move to new feeding patches.

Crickets are active during the day and night, depending on the species; some prefer the warmth of full sunlight, others prefer the twilight hours of dusk, while quite a few species are only active at nighttime. Most species live in open grassland or woodlands, but others such as the mole crickets (family Gryllotalpidae) spend much time underground, only emerging occasionally to fly from one site to another. Mole crickets are easily distinguished from all other insects by their broad, spade–like front legs which have evolved as powerful digging tools. Armed with these and strong bladelike teeth, the mole cricket is well equipped to dig shallow tunnels in moist soils.

Crickets are versatile insects and are capable of feeding off a wide range of organisms. Largely vegetarian, they eat great variety of young leaves, shoots, and stems but may also eat other insects (adults and larvae), as well as a range of dead or decaying matter, including household wastes. Like other orthopterans such as grasshoppers and locusts, their mouthparts are designed for biting and chewing.

Sound is important to all orthopterans, and crickets have specialized hearing organs (called tympanum) on their front legs, by which they are able to detect vibrations. Living in dense forests or rugged, tall grasslands can pose certain problems for small insects when it comes to finding a suitable mate. Crickets have solved this problem through an elaborate system of singing, which advertises their presence. Only male crickets are able to "sing" by a process known as stridulation. When he is ready to perform, the male chooses his auditorium carefully and, with both wings held above the body, begins to slowly rub one against the other. The right forewing bears a special adaptation which has been described as a toothed rib, or file; when this is rubbed against the hind margin of the left forewing, it produces a musical sound. In order to avoid confusion between different species, each cricket has its own distinct song, which varies not only in duration, but also in pitch. Among the songs commonly used are those used to attract females from a wide area around the male, while others serve as a courtship song once the ardorous male has succeeded in gaining the interest of a passing female.

As the courtship ritual proceeds—either within a short burrow or amongst vegetation—the male deposits a number of small capsules (spermatophores) containing sperm cells. These are then collected by the female and used to fertilize her eggs. Female crickets lay their eggs singly in the ground and in plant tissues, sometimes using their long, needle–like ovipositors, specialized egg–laying organs, to make an incision in the plant stem. When the eggs hatch, a small nymph–like replica of the adult cricket emerges and immediately begins to feed. As the nymphs grow, they molt, casting off their outer skeleton, perhaps as many as 10 times before they finally reach adult size. Depending on when the eggs were laid, the young nymphs or eggs themselves may have to spend the winter in a dormant state underground, emerging the following spring and summer to develop and breed.

Among the exceptions to this general pattern of reproduction is the parental nature of the mole crickets. Females may lay up to 300 eggs in an underground nest where, unlike most other insects, she guards them from potential predators and remains with the young nymphs for several weeks after they hatch, sometimes until just before they begin to disperse. As with other crickets, these nymphs then pass through many stages of growth and do not reach full adult size until the year after hatching.

Although widely conceived as major crop pests, most crickets are thought to cause relatively little harm. Some species, such as the house cricket (*Acheta domestica*) which has unwittingly been transported all around the world by humans, are considered a pest and health hazard on account of their liking for garbage heaps. In contrast, mole crickets are now being increasingly viewed as beneficial to many horticulturalists as they feed on a wide range of soil–dwelling larvae that cause considerable damage to crops. They, and other grassland species, have, however, suffered heavily through hanging agricultural practices, as well as the increased and often excessive use of pesticides and inorganic fertilizer which reduces the natural diversity of other insects (many of which are eaten by crickets) and plants in agricultural areas.

David Stone

Critical habitat

All species have particular requirements for their ecological habitat. These specific needs, known as critical habitat, must be satisfied if the species is to survive. These decisive necessities can involve specific types of food, a specific habitat required for breeding (as is the case with species that nest in cavities in trees), or some other crucial environmental requirement.

Some critical habitat features are obvious, and they affect many species. For example, although some species that live in desert regions are remarkably tolerant of drought, most have a need for regular access to water. As a result, the few moist habitats that occur in larger desert landscapes sustain a relatively great richness of species, all of which are dependent on this critical habitat feature. Such moist habitats in the desert are called oases, and in contrast to more typical, drier landscapes, they are renowned for the numbers of species that can be supported at relatively large population densities.

Salt licks are another critical habitat feature for many large species of mammalian herbivores. Herbivores consume enormous quantities of plant biomass, but this food source is generally lacking in sodium, resulting in a significant nutritional deficiency and intense cravings for salt. Salt licks are mineral–rich places to which large herbivores may gravitate from a very wide area, sometimes undertaking long–distance movements of hundreds of miles to satisfy their need for sodium. Because of their importance in alleviating the scarcity of minerals, salt licks represent a critical habitat feature for these animals.

Many species of shorebirds, such as sandpipers and plovers, migrate over very long distances between their wintering and breeding habitats. Many species of the Americas, for example, breed in the arctic tundra of

North America but winter in South America, some as far south as Patagonia. For some of these species, there are a few places along their lengthy migration route that provide critical staging habitats where the animals stop for a short time to feed voraciously. These critical habitats allow the animals to re–fuel after an arduous, energetically demanding part of their migration and to prepare for the next, similarly formidable stage.

For example, parts of Chesapeake Bay and the Bay of Fundy are two famous critical habitats for migrating shorebirds on the east coast of North America. Chesapeake Bay is most important for birds migrating north to their breeding grounds, because at that time horseshoe crabs (*Limulus* sp.) spawn in the bay, and there is an enormous, predictable abundance of their nutritious eggs available for the shorebirds to eat. The Bay of Fundy is most important during the post–breeding, southern migration, because at that time its tidal mudflats support a great abundance of small crustaceans that can be eaten by these birds, which can occur there in flocks of hundreds of thousands of individuals. There are other places on the east coast of North America that provide important staging habitat for these birds during their migrations, but none support such large populations as Chesapeake Bay and the Bay of Fundy which represent critical habitats that must be preserved if the shorebirds are to be sustained in large populations.

Another critical habitat feature for many species that live in forests is large dimension, that is, dead wood, either lying on the ground as logs or as standing snags. Many species of birds, mammals, and plants rely on dead wood as a critical habitat feature which may provide cavities for nesting or resting, feeding substrates, places from which to sing or search the surrounding habitat for food and enemies, or in the case of some plants, suitable places for seedlings to establish and grow. Woodpeckers, for example, have an absolute need for snags or living trees with heart–rotted interiors in which they excavate cavities that they use for breeding or roosting. Many other animals are secondary users of woodpecker cavities.

Sometimes, different species develop highly specific relationships to the degree that they cannot survive without their obligate partners which therefore represent critical, biological components of their habitat. For example, the dodo (*Raphus cucullatus*) was a flightless, turkey–sized bird that used to live on the island of Mauritius in the Indian Ocean. The dodo was quickly made extinct by overhunting and introduced predators after the island was discovered by Europeans. However, this bird lived in an intimate relationship with a species of tree, the tambalacoque (*Calvaria major*), that like the dodo only occurs on Mauritius. The large, tough fruits of this tree were an important food source for dodos. The fruits were found on the forest floor, ingested whole, ground up in the bird's gizzard, and the fleshy parts were then digested in the stomach as nutrition. However, the hard seeds were not digested but were defecated by the dodos and prepared for germination in a process that botanists call scarification. Dodos were the only animals on Mauritius that could perform this function, and since the dodo became extinct in the early 1600s, no seeds of tambalacoque were able to germinate although mature trees managed to persist. Several decades ago the need of tambalacoque for this sort of scarification was discovered, and seeds can now be germinated after they have been eaten and scarified by domestic turkeys. Seedlings of this species are now being planted in order to preserve this unique species of tree.

Because so many species and natural ecosystems are now endangered by human influences, it is very important that critical habitat needs be identified and understood. This knowledge will be essential to the successful preservation of those many endangered species which now must depend on the goodwill of humans for their survival. An important aspect of the strategy to preserve those species will be the active management and preservation of critical habitat.

See also Endangered species; Habitat; Symbiosis.

Further Reading:

Freedman, B. *Environmental Ecology*. 2nd ed. San Diego: Academic Press, 1994.

Bill Freedman

Critical mass see **Nuclear fission**

Critical temperature see **Gases, properties of**

Crocodiles

The crocodile order (Crocodylia) consists of several families of large, unmistakable, amphibious reptiles: the crocodiles (Crocodylidae), gavials (Gavialidae), and the alligators and caimans (Alligatoridae). Although these animals look superficially like lizards, they are different in many important respects, and are believed by biologists to be the most highly evolved of the living reptiles.

Crocodilians are amphibious animals, spending most of their time in water, but emerging onto land to bask in the sun and lay their eggs. Their usual habitat is in warm, tropical or subtropical waters. Most species occur in freshwaters, with only the saltwater crocodile being partial to marine habitats. Fish are the typical food of most adult crocodilians, but the biggest species will also eat large mammals, including humans. Younger crocodilians eat insects and other small invertebrates, as well as small fishes.

Crocodilians are economically important for their thick, attractive hides, which are used to make fine leathers for expensive consumer goods, such as shoes, handbags, and other luxury items. Wild crocodilians are hunted for their hides wherever they occur, and in some areas they are also raised on ranches. Crocodilian meat is also eaten, often as a gourmet food.

Most populations of wild crocodilians have been greatly reduced in size because of overhunting and habitat loss, and numerous species are endangered.

Biology of crocodilians

Among the more distinctive characteristics of the crocodilians are their almost completely four–chambered heart, teeth that are set into sockets in the jaw, a palate that separates the mouth from the nasal chambers, and spongy lungs. These animals also have a protective covering of partially calcified, horny plates on their back. The plates are not connected with each other, and are set into the thick, scaly skin, allowing a great freedom of movement. Crocodilians have a heavy body with squat legs and a large, strong, scale–ridged tail.

Sinusoidal motions of the powerful tail are used to propel the animal while swimming. The tail is also a formidable weapon, used to subdue prey and also for defense. Although they appear to be ungainly and often spend most of their time lying about, crocodilians can actually move quite quickly. Some crocodilians can even lift their body fully above the ground, and run quickly using all four legs—a human cannot outrun a crocodile over a short distance on open land.

Crocodilians have numerous adaptations for living in water. They have webbed feet for swimming slowly and their nostrils, eyes, and ears are set high on the head so that they can be exposed even while most of the body and head are below the surface. When a crocodilian is totally submerged, its eye is covered by a semi–transparent nictitating membrane, and flaps of skin seal its nostrils and ears against water inflow. Crocodilians often float motionless in the water, commonly with the body fully submerged and only the nostrils and eyes exposed. To accomplish this behavior, crocodilians regulate their body density by varying the amounts of air held in the lungs. Also, the stomachs of most adult crocodiles contain stones, to as much as 1% of the animal's total body weight. These stones are thought to be used as buoyancy–regulating ballast.

Crocodilians are poikilothermic, meaning they do not regulate their body temperature by producing and conserving metabolic heat. However, these animals are effective at warming themselves by basking in the sun, and they spend a great deal of time engaged in this activity. Crocodilians commonly bask through much of the day, often with their mouths held open to provide some cooling by the evaporation of water. Only when the day is hottest will these animals re–enter the water to cool down. Most species of crocodilians are nocturnal predators, although they will also hunt during the day if prey are available.

Stories exist of birds entering the open mouths of crocodiles to glean leeches and other parasites. This phenomenon has not been substantiated scientifically, although it is well known that crocodiles will tolerate certain species of birds picking external parasites from their skin, but not necessarily inside of their mouth.

Male crocodilians are territorial during the breeding season, and chase other males away from places that have good nesting, basking, and feeding habitat. The male animals proclaim their territories by roaring loudly, and sometimes by snapping their jaws together. Intruders are aggressively chased away, but evenly matched animals may engage in vicious fights. Territory–holding males do not actively assemble females into a harem—they focus on chasing other males away. Females will enter the defended territory if they consider it to be of high quality.

All crocodilians are predators, and they have large, strong jaws with numerous sharp teeth for gripping their prey. Crocodiles do not have cutting teeth, and if they capture a prey that is larger than can be eaten in a single gulp, it is dismembered by gripping strongly with the teeth, and rolling the body along its longitudinal axis to tear the carcass. Some of the larger crocodiles will opportunistically cooperate in subduing a large mammal, and then in tearing it into bits small enough to be swallowed. However, very large animals with tough skin, such as a dead hippopotamus, will be left to rot for

The endangered Orinoco crocodile (*Crocodylus intermedius*).

some time, until the carcass softens and can be torn apart by the crocodiles.

All crocodilians are oviparous, laying hard, white–shelled eggs. The nests may be a pit dug into a beach above high water, or the nests may be made of heaps of aquatic vegetation, which help to incubate the eggs through heat produced during decomposition. Often, a number of females will nest close to each other, but each builds a separate nest. The nesting grounds are used by the same females, year after year. In many species the nests are carefully guarded and tended by the mother. Fairly open, sandy beaches are generally preferred as sites upon which to build the nests or nest mounds.

Typically, 20–40 eggs are laid at a time, but this varies with species and size of the female. Incubation times vary with species and incubation temperature, but range, for example in the case of the Nile crocodile, from 11 to 14 weeks. Predators as diverse as monitor

lizards, mongooses, dogs, raccoons, and even ants regularly seek out crocodile nests to eat the eggs and newly hatched young.

An infant crocodilian has a small, so–called "egg tooth" at the end of its snout, which helps it to break out of the shell when it is ready to hatch. All of the baby crocodilians hatch within a short time of each other, synchronized in part by the faint peeping noises they make during the later stages of incubation while they are still in the eggs. In some crocodilians, the mother assists her babies in hatching, by gently taking eggs in her mouth and cracking them with her teeth. The mother also may guard her offspring for some time after hatching, often allowing them to climb onto her body and head. Female crocodiles are very aggressive against intruders while their eggs are hatching and newborn babies are nearby, and under these circumstances they will even emerge from the water to chase potential predators on land. Nevertheless, young crocodilians are vulnerable to being killed and eaten by many predators, and this is a high–risk stage of the life cycle.

Potentially, crocodilians are quite long–lived animals. Individuals in zoos have lived for more than 50 years, and the potential longevity of some species may be as great as a century.

Species of crocodilians

The gavial or gharial (family Gavialidae) is a single species, *Gavialus gangeticus*, which lives in a number of sluggish, tropical rivers in India and Indochina. Gavials have a long, slender snout, and are almost exclusively fish eaters, catching their prey with sideways sweeps of the open–mouthed head. Gavials can attain a length of about 20 ft (6 m). Gavials have long been considered holy in the Hindu religion, and this has afforded these animals a measure of protection in India. Unfortunately, this is not sufficiently the case anymore, and gavials have become severely endangered as a result of overhunting for their hide.

The true crocodiles (family Crocodylidae) include about 16 species that live in tropical waters. Crocodiles are large, stout animals, with a much heavier snout than that of the gavial. The main food of crocodiles is fish, but some species can catch and subdue large mammals that venture close to their aquatic habitat, or attempt to cross rivers in which the crocodiles are living. Perhaps the most famous species is the Nile crocodile (*Crocodylus niloticus*) of Africa, which can grow to a length of 23 ft (7 m). This crocodile can be a predator of unwary humans, although its reputation in this respect far exceeds the actual risks, except in certain places. This species used to be very abundant and widespread in Africa, but unregulated hunting, and to a lesser degree habitat losses, have greatly reduced its populations.

The most dangerous crocodilian to humans is the estuarine or salt–marsh crocodile (*Crocodylus porosus*), which lives in salt and brackish waters from northern Australia and New Guinea, through most of Southeast Asia, to southern India. This species can achieve a length of more than 23 ft (7 m). Individuals of this crocodile species sometimes occur well out to sea.

Other species are the mugger crocodile (*Crocodylus palustris*) of India, Bangladesh, and Ceylon; the Australian crocodile (*C. johnsoni*) of northern Australia; and the New Guinea crocodile (*C. novaeguineae*) of New Guinea and parts of the Philippines.

The American crocodile (*Crocodylus acutus*) is a rare and endangered species of brackish estuaries in southern Florida, occurring more widely in central and

The endangered false gavial (*Tomistoma schlegelii*).

northwestern South America and the Caribbean. This species can achieve a length of 20 ft (6 m). The Orinoco crocodile (*C. intermedius*) occurs in the Orinoco and Amazon Rivers of South America.

The false gavial (*Tomistoma schlegelii*) is a slender–snouted species of Southeast Asia.

The alligators and caimans (family Alligatoridae) are seven species that occur in fresh waters, with a broader head and more rounded snout than crocodiles. The American alligator (*Alligator mississipiensis*) can achieve a length of 13 ft (4 m), and occurs in the southeastern United States, as far north as South Carolina and Alabama. This species was endangered by unregulated hunting for its hide. However, strict conservation measures have allowed for a substantial recovery of the species, and it is now the subject of a regulated hunt.

The Chinese alligator (*Alligator sinensis*) occurs in the lower reaches of the Yangtze and Kiang Rivers in southern China, and it is the only member of this family to occur outside of the Americas. The Chinese alligator can grow as long as 6.5 ft (2 m).

Caimans are animals of very slowly flowing, freshwater habitats in South and Central America. The black caiman (*Melanosuchus niger*) can achieve a length of 16 ft (5 m). The spectacled caiman (*Caiman crocodilus*) and the broad–nosed caiman (*C. latisrostris*) of eastern Brazil can both grow somewhat longer than 6.5 ft (2 m). The dwarf caiman (*Paleosuchus palpebrosus*) and the smooth–fronted caiman (*P. trigonatus*) live in more swiftly flowing streams and rivers and are relatively small species that do not exceed about 5 ft (1.5 m) in length.

Crocodilians and people

The larger species of crocodilians are fierce predators. In particular, crocodiles have posed a long–standing risk to domestic livestock that try to drink from their aquatic habitat as well as to unwary humans. For this reason, crocodiles are commonly regarded as dangerous pests, and they are sometimes killed to reduce the risks associated with their presence.

Because some species of crocodilians are so dangerous, they are greatly feared in many places. This fear is certainly justified in some cases, at least in places where large human–eaters are abundant. In some cultures, the deep fear and revulsion that people have for dangerous crocodilians has transformed into an attitude of reverence. For example, a pool near Karachi, Pakistan, contains a number of large mugger crocodiles, which are venerated as priest–like entities, and worshipped by pilgrims. In other places, human sacrifices have been made to crocodiles to pacify animist spirits.

In addition, the skins of crocodilians can be used to make a very tough and beautiful leather. This valuable product is widely sought for use in the making of expensive shoes, handbags, wallets, belts, suitcases, and other items. Crocodilians are readily hunted at night, when they can be easily found using searchlights that reflect brightly off the eyes of these animals, which are then shot. In almost all parts of the range of crocodilians, they have been hunted to endangerment or extirpation. Almost all species in the crocodile family are endangered.

In a few places, however, strict conservation regulations have allowed the populations of crocodilians to increase from historically depleted lows. This has been particularly true of the American alligator, which was considered to be an endangered species only a few decades ago, but has now recovered sufficiently to allow for a carefully regulated sport and market hunt.

Some species of crocodilians are also ranched, usually by capturing young animals in the wild, and feeding them in confinement until they reach a large enough size to slaughter for their hides. The meat of crocodilians is also a saleable product, but it is secondary in importance to the hide.

Crocodilians are sometimes used to entertain people, and some species are kept as pets. The Romans, for example, sometimes displayed Nile crocodiles in their

circuses. To amuse the masses of assembled people, the crocodiles would be killed by humans, or alternatively, humans would be killed by the crocodiles.

In more modern times, alligator wrestling is popular in some places, for example, in parts of Florida. The key to successful alligator wrestling is to hold the jaws of the animal shut, which can be accomplished using only the hands (but watch out for the lashing tail). Crocodilians have very powerful muscles for closing their jaws, but their muscles to open the mouth are quite weak.

KEY TERMS

. . . .

Endangered—Refers to species or populations of organisms that are so small that there is a likelihood of imminent local extirpation, or even global extinction over its entire range.

Extirpated—A situation in which a species is elimated from a specific geographic area of its habitat.

Nictitating membrane—An inner eyelid.

Overhunting—Hunting of an animal at a rate that exceeds its productivity, so that the population size decreases, often to the point of endangerment.

Oviparous—This refers to an animal that lays eggs, from which the young hatch after a period of incubation.

Poikilotherm—Animals that have no physiological mechanism for the regulation of their internal body temperature. These animals are also known, less accurately, as "cold–blooded". In many cases, these animals bask in the sun or engage in other behaviors to regulate their body temperature.

Further Reading:

Alderton, D. *Crocodiles and Alligators of the World.* U.K.: Blandford Press, 1991.

Goin, C. J., O. B. Goin, and G. R. Zug. *Introduction to Herpetology,* 3rd ed. San Francisco: Freeman & Co. 1978.

Grenard, S. *Handbook of Alligators and Crocodiles.* New York: Krieger, 1991.

Halliday, T. R. and K. Adler. *The Encyclopedia of Reptiles and Amphibians.* New York: Facts on File, 1986.

Messel, H., F. W. King, and J. P. Ross, eds. *Crocodiles: An Action Plan for Their Conservation.* Gland, Switzerland: International Union for the Conservation of Nature (IUCN), 1992.

Webb, G., S. Manolis, and P. Whitehead, eds. *Crocodiles and Alligators.* Australia: Surrey Beatty, 1988.

Bill Freedman

Crocus see **Lily family**

Crop rotation

When a farmer grows two or more crops alternately on the same land, he or she is rotating crops. Farmers rotate crops to control erosion, promote the fertility of the soil, contain plant diseases, and to prevent or correct some of the problems associated with monocultures, including persistent weeds, insect infestations, and disease.

History

For 2,000 years, since the Roman army spread its farming practices throughout the areas it occupied, European farmers followed a Roman cropping system called "food, feed, and fallow." Farmers divided their land into sections and grew a food grain such as wheat one year, and barley or oats as feed for livestock the next year. After two years of cultivation, a field's fertility was depleted, so the farmer planted no crops there in the third year, letting it lie fallow, and the soil recovered some of its nutrients and organic matter. Following a year of rest, the field was again sown with wheat.

Farmers following this system harvested very little grain, often only 6 to 10 times as much seed as they had sown, and they had to save a sixth to a tenth of that harvested seed to sow the following year. During years of flood, drought, or pest infestation, crops failed and people often starved.

Around 1800, European farmers newly interested in scientific farming methods introduced a 4–year crop rotation cycle, which included one year of a root crop as feed for domestic animals, and one year of a nitrogen–fixing crop like clover, which improved the fertility of the soil. Using this new method, farmers could support more animals with the additional feed they grew, and so had more manure with which to fertilize the fields.

With the advent of chemical fertilizers following World War II, crop rotation fell out of favor somewhat. Farmers could provide their crops with nutrients without leaving some of their lands fallow each year. But over the past few decades, farmers have begun to return

KEY TERMS

. . . .

Fallow—Cultivated land that is allowed to lie idle during the growing season so that it can recover some of its nutrients and organic matter.

Nutrients—The portion of the soil necessary to plants for growth, including nitrogen, potassium, and other minerals.

Organic matter—The carbonaceous portion of the soil that derives from once living matter, including, for the most part, plants.

to the practice of rotating crops as a way to improve the structure and health of their soils.

Current crop rotation practices

Because climate, soil types, and extent of erosion vary from place to place around the globe, the kinds of crops appropriate for rotation vary as well. In the American Midwest, a typical rotation might include first a crop that helps build the structure of the soil: alfalfa, sweet clover, or red clover. This is followed by a feed grain, either corn or grain sorghum, then turnips, alfalfa, clovers. In rotating crops, farmers should alternate crops with different characteristics—sod–base crops with row crops, weed–suppressing crops with those that do not suppress weeds, crops susceptible to specific insects with those that are not, and soil enhancing crops with those that do not enhance soils.

Farmers rotate crops to assure that the soil is covered for as much of the year as possible to protect it from exposure to the elements that cause erosion—water, wind, etc. Cover crops are grown during the seasons that are unfriendly to cash crop, such as dry or cold seasons. These crops can either be started at the same time as the cash crop if they are slow starting crops that will take off when the cash crop is harvested, or, if they are fast–growing crops that will take off quickly when the cash crop is harvested, farmers plant them later. Examples of slow–starting crops include legumes such as sweet clover, red clover, crimson clover, and vetch. Fast–growing crops include Austrian winter peas, rye, oats, and ryegrass. Planting legumes as cover crops may help the soil accumulate high levels of nitrogen, the nutrient necessary for most plants, which will benefit the subsequent cash crop.

Sloping lands may experience excessive soil loss if row crops or small–grain crops are grown on them for too many years in a row. Farmers can keep soil loss

Adjacent fields of rice and wheat, Sacramento Valley, California.

within tolerable limits if they grow those crops on the same land in rotation with forage crops. Under row crops like corn and wheat, the organic matter content of the soil may decline and soil structure deteriorate, but these will improve under forage crops in rotation. Increasing the number of years of grass (forage) crops in the rotation usually increases the overall stability of the soil and its permeability to air and water.

Farmers can plow cover crops into the soil as "green manure," which benefits the soil by increasing its organic content, as well as its structure and permeability. Young, succulent growth contains the highest levels of nutrients and decomposes more quickly than older growth, and so is a more beneficial green manure.

Farmers can control weeds through crop rotation because if the same crop is not grown in the same field one year after another the reproductive cycles of insects preying on a specific plant are interrupted. By not growing soybeans on the same field year after year, a farmer can help control cyst nematodes, a parasite. As a farmer rotates a larger variety of crops, the size of the fields rotated decreases, and with smaller fields, it is possible to contain insect infestations more successfully. A greater variety of crops and greater complexity

of their placement on the land allows a farmer to place certain crops next to each other to control insects. For example, a wheat field infested with chinch bugs will not spread its infestation as easily if a crop such as soybeans is planted next to it, rather than a natural chinch bug host such as forage sorghum.

Farmers undertaking crop rotations must plan their planting more carefully than those who plant the same crop year after year. Using a simple principle, that there are the same number of fields or groups of fields as there are years in the rotation, farmers can assure that they produce consistent amounts of each crop each year even though the crops shift to different fields.

Further Reading:

Bender, Jim. *Future Harvest: Pesticide Free Farming.* Lincoln, NB: University of Nebraska, 1994.

Troeh, Frederick R. and Louis M. Thompson. *Soils and Soil Fertility.* New York: Oxford University Press, 1993.

Troeh, Frederick R., J. Arthur Hobbs, Roy L. Donahue. *Soil and Water Conservation.* Englewood Cliffs, NJ: Prentice Hall, 1991.

Beth Hanson

Crops

Crops are any organisms that humans utilize as a source of food, materials, or energy. Crops may be utilized for subsistence purposes, to barter for other goods, or to sell for a cash profit.

In addition, crops may be harvested from wild, unmanaged ecosystems, or they may be carefully husbanded and managed, as occurs with domesticated species in agriculture. However, there is a continuum of intensity of management systems. Some essentially wild and free–ranging species may also be managed to some degree. This occurs, for example, in some types of forestry, and in the management of some species of hunted animals. In general, the purpose of management is to increase the amount of crop productivity that is available for use by humans.

Most crops are species of plants, but animals can also be crops, as can microorganisms. In general, unmanaged, free–ranging crops are little modified genetically or morphologically from their non–crop progenitors. However, many modern, domesticated crops that are intensively managed are remarkably different from their wild ancestors. In many cases the domesticated species no longer exists outside of cultivation.

Hunting and gathering—crops obtained from unmanaged ecosystems

Humans can only be sustained by eating other organisms and by utilizing other species as sources of materials and energy. Humans have always had an absolute requirement for the goods and services provided by other species, and this will always be so.

Prior to the discovery of the first agricultural technologies about 9,000 to 11,000 years ago, almost all human societies were sustained by extensively gathering edible or otherwise useful products of wild plants and by hunting wild animals.

The plant foods that were gathered as crops by these early humans included the starchy tubers of certain plants and the fruits and seeds of others. Other plants were harvested as sources of fuel energy or to provide materials such as wood and bark, useful for the construction of shelters, canoes, and other tools or weapons. At the same time that plant crops were being gathered, animals may have been hunted for their edible meat, and for their useful hides and bones. Prior to the development of agriculture, these cropping activities were undertaken in essentially natural ecosystems, which in general were not intensively modified by the hunting and gathering activities of people.

Humans are rather eclectic in their choices of crops—selecting a wide range of useful species of plants, animals, and microorganisms from among the usually vast diversity of species that are available in particular places or regions. Humans are considered to be omnivorous, because they feed at all levels of ecological food webs, that is, on plants, animals, and other types of organisms, both living and dead.

Human societies that subsist only by the hunting and gathering of wild crops are now virtually extinct. However, modern human societies continue to obtain some important plant and animal crops from essentially unmanaged ecosystems. Some of these wild crops are discussed below.

Plants

Among the plants, species of trees are among the most notable crops that humans continue to obtain from natural ecosystems. In the parlance of forestry, the terms "virgin" and "primary" are used to refer to older, natural forests from which wild, unmanaged trees have not yet been harvested by humans. "Secondary" forests have sustained at least one intensive harvest of their resource of trees. In general, the ecological characteristics of secondary forests are very different from those of the more natural, primary forests that used to occur on the same sites.

Trees have always been an important crop for humans, being useful as sources of edible fruits, and of wood needed to manufacture tools, homes, canoes, and for burning as a source of energy. Even today, trees harvested from natural forests are extremely important crops in most countries. Tree biomass is the most important source of energy for cooking and heating for more than one–half of the world's people, almost all of them living in relatively poor tropical countries. Trees are also an important crop for people living in richer countries, mostly as a source of lumber for the construction of buildings and furniture, and as a source of pulpwood for the manufacturing of paper.

In many places, the original natural forests have been extensively depleted by the harvesting of trees, which was often followed by conversions of the land to agriculture and urban land–uses. This pattern has been quite common in great regions of North America, Europe, and elsewhere. To compensate to some degree for the losses of natural forests in those regions, efforts have been made to establish managed forests, so that tree crops will always be available for use by people.

Managed forests are discussed in more detail in a later section in this entry.

Trees are not the only plant crops that are gathered from wild, unmanaged ecosystems. In particular, people who are living subsistence lifestyles in tropical forests continue to obtain much of their food, medicine, and materials from wild plants, usually in combination with hunting and subsistence agriculture. Even in North America, small crops of a few wild food plants continue to be gathered. Some examples include harvests of wild rice (*Zizania aquatica*), strawberry (*Fragaria virginiana*), low–bush blueberry (*Vaccinium angustifolium*), and fiddleheads (from the ostrich fern, *Matteucia struthiopteris*). Other minor wild crops include various species of edible mushrooms and marine algae.

Terrestrial animals

Wild animals have always been an important source of food and useful materials for humans. Most people who live in rural areas in poorer countries supplement their diet with meat obtained by hunting wild animals. Hunting is also popular among many rural people living in wealthier countries. For example, each year in North America, millions of deer are killed by hunters as food and a source of hide, especially white–tailed deer (*Odocoileus virginianus*), mule deer (*O. hemionus*), and elk (*Cervus canadensis*). There are also large hunts of upland game birds such as ruffled grouse (*Bonasa umbellus*), and of wild ducks and geese, especially mallard (*Anas platyrhynchos*), Canada goose or honker (*Branta canadensis*), and snow goose (*Chen hyperboreus*).

Aquatic animals

Aquatic animals have also provided important wild meat crops for people living in places where there is access to the natural bounties of streams, rivers, lakes, and marine shores. Important food crops harvested from fresh–water ecosystems of North America include species of salmon, trout, and other fish, as well as crayfish, fresh–water mussels, and other invertebrates. Most of the modern marine fisheries also rely on harvesting the productivity of unmanaged populations of fish, invertebrates, seals, and whales as wild crops.

Agriculture—crops from managed ecosystems

As considered here, agricultural crops are managed relatively intensively for the sustained productivity of species useful to humans. In this sense, agricultural systems can involve the cultivation of plants and livestock on farms, as well as the cultivation of fish and invertebrates in aquaculture, and the growing of trees in agroforestry plantations.

Agricultural systems can vary tremendously in the intensity of their management systems. For example, species of terrestrial crop plants may be grown in mixed populations, a system known as *polyculture*. These systems are often not weeded or fertilized very intensively. Mixed–cropping systems are common in non–industrial agriculture, for example, in subsistence agriculture in many tropical countries.

In contrast, some monocultural systems in agriculture attempt to grow crops in single–species populations. Such intensively managed systems usually have a heavy reliance on the use of fertilizers, irrigation, and pesticides such as insecticides, herbicides, and fungicides. Of course, heavy, sophisticated, energy–requiring machinery is also required in intensive agricultural systems, to plow the land, apply agrochemicals, and harvest the crops. The intensive–management techniques are used in order to substantially increase the productivity of the desired species of crop plants. However, these gains are expensive in terms of dollar–costs, and sometimes, environmental damages.

Agricultural plants

Hundreds of species of plants are cultivated by humans under managed, agricultural conditions. However, most of these species are tropical crops of relatively minor importance, that is, in terms of their contribution to the global production of all agricultural plants. In fact, a remarkably small number of species of plants contribute disproportionately to the global harvest of plant crops in agricultural systems.

Ranked in order of their annual production (measured in millions of metric tons per year), the world's 15 most important food crops are:

1) sugar cane; 740; 2) wheat; 390; 3) rice; 370; 4) corn or maize; 350; 5) white potato; 300; 6) sugar beets; 260; 7) barley; 180; 8) sweet potato; 150; 9) cassava; 110; 10) soybean; 80; 11) wine grapes; 60; 12) tomato; 45; 13) banana; 40; 14) beans and peas; 40; 15) orange; 33.

Note that some care should be taken in interpreting these data in terms of yield of actual foodstuffs. The production data for sugar cane, for example, reflect the entire harvested plant, and not just the refined sugar that is the major economic product of this crop. In contrast, the data for wheat and other grain crops reflect the actual harvest of seeds, which are much more useful nutritionally than whole sugar cane.

Most agricultural crops are managed as annual plants, that is, they are cultivated over a cycle of one year or less, with a single rotation involving sowing, growth, and harvesting. This is true of all of the grains and legumes and most vegetables. Other agricultural species, however, are managed as perennial crops, which once established are capable of yielding crops on a sustained basis. This is typically the manner in which tree–fruit crops such as oranges are managed and harvested, as are certain tropical species such as oil palm (*Elaeis guineensis*) and para rubber (*Hevea brasiliensis*).

It should be pointed out that some extremely valuable crops are not utilized for conventional purposes, that is, as food, materials, or energy. Some crops are used for the production of important medicines, as is the case of the rosy periwinkle (*Catharantus roseus*), which produces several chemicals that are extremely useful in treatment of certain types of cancers. Other crops are used to produce extremely profitable but illegal drugs for illicit markets. Examples of these sorts of felonious crops include marijuana (*Cannabis sativa*), cocaine (*Erythroxylon coca*), and opium poppy (*Papaver somniferum*).

Agricultural animals

Enormous numbers of domesticated animals are cultivated by people as food crops. In many cases the animals are used to continuously produce some edible product which can be harvested without killing the animals. For example, milk can be continuously collected from various species of mammals, especially from cows, but also goats, sheep, horses, and even camels. Similarly, chickens can produce eggs regularly. However, all of the above animals plus many other domesticated species are also routinely slaughtered for their meat, which provides a high–quality, protein–rich food for humans.

The populations of some of these domesticated animals are enormously large. In addition to almost 6 billion people, the world today supports about 1.7 billion sheep and goats (*Ovis aries* and *Capra hircus*), 1.3 billion cows (*Bos taurus* and *B. indica*), 0.9 billion pigs (*Sus scrofa*), and 0.3 billion horses, camels, and water buffalo (*Equus caballus*, *Camelus dromedarius*, and *Bubalus bubalis*). In addition, there are about 10–11 billion domestic fowl, most of which are chickens (*Gallus gallus*). These populations of domesticated animals are much larger than those maintained by any wild large animals. For example, no wild mammals of a comparable size to those listed above have populations greater than about 50 million, which is equivalent to less than

1% of the populations maintained by humans and our large–animal domesticates.

Aquaculture

Aquaculture is an aquatic analogue of terrestrial agriculture. In aquaculture, animals or less commonly, plants, are cultivated under controlled, sometimes very intensively–managed conditions, to be eventually harvested as food for humans. Increasingly, aquaculture is being viewed as an alternative to the exploitation of wild stocks of aquatic animals and plants.

The best opportunities to develop aquaculture occur in inland regions where there are many ponds and small lakes, and in protected, coastal locations on the oceans. Fresh–water aquaculture is especially important in Asia, where various species of fish are cultivated in artificial ponds, especially carp (*Cyprinus carpio*) and tilapia (*Aureochromis niloticus*). In North America, various species of fish are grown in inland aquaculture in small ponds, most commonly rainbow trout (*Salmo gairdneri*) and catfish (*Ictalurus* spp.).

Aquaculture is also becoming increasingly important along sheltered, marine coastlines in many parts of the world. In the tropics, extensive areas of mangrove forest are being converted into shallow ponds for the cultivation of prawns (*Penaeus monodon*) and, to a lesser degree, giant prawns (*Macrobrachium rosenbergii*). In North America and Western Europe, the cultivation of Atlantic salmon (*Salmo salar*) has become an extensive industry in recent decades, using pens floating in shallow, coastal embayments, and sometimes in the open ocean. Intensive research is being undertaken into the potential domestication of other important and productive marine crops, including species of fish and seaweeds that are now harvested from unmanaged ecosystems.

Agroforestry

Agroforestry is a forest–related analogue of agriculture. In agroforestry, trees are cultivated under sometimes quite intensively managed conditions, to eventually be harvested as a source of lumber, pulpwood, or fuelwood. In many regions, this sort of intensive forestry is being developed as a high–yield alternative to the harvesting of natural forests.

The most important trees that are grown in plantations in the temperate zones and harvested as agroforestry crops are species of pines (*Pinus* spp.), spruces (*Picea* spp.), larch (*Larix* spp.), and poplar (*Populus* spp.). Depending on the species, site conditions, and

KEY TERMS
. . . .

Agroforestry—The cultivation of crops of trees under intensively managed conditions, usually in single–species plantations.

Domestic—This refers to crop species that live in an intimate association with humans, often with a significant co–dependence between the species.

Monoculture—The cultivation of an exclusive population of a particular species of crop.

Polyculture—The agricultural cultivation of mixed populations of different crop species.

economic product that is desired, intensively managed plantations of these trees can be harvested after a growth period of only 10 to 40–60 years, compared with 60 to more than 100 years for natural, unmanaged forests in the same regions. Increasingly, these temperate species of trees are being selectively bred and hybridized to develop high–yield varieties, in parallel with the ways in which food crops have been culturally selected from their wild progenitors, as part of the process of domestication.

Fast–growing, high–yield species of trees are also being grown under agroforestry systems in the tropics, for use locally as a source of fuelwood, but also for animal fodder, lumber, and pulpwood. Various tree species are being grown in this way, including species of pine, eucalyptus (*Eucalyptus* spp.), she–oak (*Casuarina* spp.), and tree–legumes (such as *Albizia procera* and *Leucaena leucocephala*). Plantations of slower–growing tropical hardwoods are also being established for the production of high–value lumber, for example, of mahogany (*Swietenia mahogani*) and teak (*Tectona grandis*).

See also Blue revolution; Forestry; Livestock; Old–growth forest.

Further Reading:

Conger, R.H.M. and G.D. Hill. 1991. *Agricultural Plants, 2nd ed.* Cambridge University Press, Cambridge, U.K.

Freedman, B. 1994. *Environmental Ecology, 2nd ed.* Academic Press, San Diego, CA.

Klein, R.M. 1987. *The Green World. An Introduction to Plants and People.* Harper & Row, New York.

Bill Freedman

Crossbills see **Finches**

Cross multiply

If two fractions are equal, say

$$\frac{a}{b} = \frac{c}{d}$$

then it is always true that the products of the numbers given by

$$\frac{a}{b} \bowtie \frac{c}{d}$$

are also equal or ad = bc. This is the most common form of cross multiplication. That

$$\frac{a}{b} = \frac{c}{d}$$

implies ad = bc can be shown by multiplying both sides of

$$\frac{a}{b} = \frac{c}{d}$$

by the common denominator bd and canceling.

Cross multiplying is a common first step in solving proportions.

$$\frac{3}{x} = \frac{7}{21}$$

is equivalent to

$3 \times 21 = x \times 7$ or $7x = 63$

Therefore, x = 9.

Adding fractions can also be done with cross multiplication.

$$\frac{a}{b} \bowtie \frac{c}{d} \quad \text{has the sum} \quad \frac{ad + bc}{bd}$$

Note that the cross product of two vectors does not involve cross multiplying.

See also Vector.

Cross section

In solid geometry, the cross section of a three–dimensional object is a two–dimensional figure obtained by slicing the object perpendicular to its axis and viewing it end on. Thus, a sausage has a circular cross section, a 4×4 fence post has a square cross section, and a football has a circular cross section when sliced one way and an elliptical cross section when sliced another way. More formally, a cross section is the locus of points obtained when a plane intersects an object at right angles to one of its axes, which are taken to be the axes of the associated rectangular coordinate system. Since we are free to associate a coordinate system relative to an object in any way we please, and because every cross section is one dimension less than the object from which it is obtained, a careful choice of axes provides a cross section containing nearly as much information about the object from which it is obtained, a careful choice of axes provides a cross section containing nearly as much information about the object as a full–dimensional view.

Often choosing an axis of symmetry provides the most useful cross section. An axis of symmetry is a line segment about which the object is symmetric, defined as a line segment passing through the object in such a way that every line segment drawn perpendicular to the axis having endpoints on the surface of the object is bisected by the axis. Examples of three–dimensional solids with an axis of symmetry include: right parallelepipeds (most ordinary cardboard boxes), which have rectangular cross sections; spheres (basketballs, baseballs, etc.), which have circular cross sections; and pyramids with square bases (such as those found in Egypt), which have square cross sections.

Other times, the most useful cross section is obtained by choosing an axis parallel to the axis of symmetry. In this case, the plane that intersects the object will contain the axis of symmetry. This is useful for picturing such things as fancy parfait glasses in two dimensions.

Finally, there are innumerable objects of interest that have no axis of symmetry. In this case, care should be taken to choose the cross section that provides the most detail.

The great usefulness of a properly chosen cross section comes in the representation of three–dimensional objects using two–dimensional media, such as paper and pencil or flat computer screens. The same idea helps in the study of objects with four or more dimensions. A three–dimensional object represents the cross section of one or more four–dimensional objects. For instance, a cube is the cross section of a four–dimensional hypercube. In general, one way to define the cross section of any N–dimensional object as the locus of points obtained when any (N–1) dimensional "surface" intersects an N–dimensional "solid" perpendicular to one of the solid's axes. Again, the axes of an N–dimensional object are the N axes of the associated rectangular coordinate system. While this concept is impossible to represent geometrically, it is easily dealt with algebraically, using vectors and matrices.

Crows and jays

The members of the crow family (Corvidae) are among the world's most intelligent birds. The family has recently undergone taxonomic expansion, brought about by evidence gathered through genetic testing, and now includes such diverse species as birds–of–paradise, orioles, and drongos. Crows and jays belong to the subfamily Corvinae. The corvids comprise 113 species in 25 genera, which include ravens, crows, jays, magpies, rooks, nutcrackers, and jackdaws. Corvids are passerine or perching birds and count among their numbers the largest of the passerines. Corvids vary considerably in size, ranging from the tiny Hume's ground jay, which is 7.5 in (19 cm) long and weighs 1.5 oz (45 g), to the thick–billed raven, which is 25 in (64 cm) long and weighs 53 oz (1.5 kg).

Corvids originated in the northern and tropical areas of the Old World. From there they spread to their current geographic range; they are found around the world and are found everywhere except in the high Arctic, Antarctic, the southern part of South America, and New Zealand. Corvids vary widely in size and appearance, particularly those species found in the forests of Central and South America and Southeast Asia. There are 27 oriental genera, which experts consider strong evidence that the corvids first evolved in Asia and then spread north and east, across the Bering land–bridge, into North America and, eventually, to Central and South America.

General characteristics

Crows are large to very large, robustly built birds, with tails that are short or medium length. The tail and primary feathers are stiff. The bill varies in shape from species to species, but is relatively long, although it can be stout or slender. The feet and legs are very strong, with scales on the front of the toes and smooth skin on the back. Among the crows the plumage is black, black and white, black and gray or sooty brown, while jays can also be green, blue, gray, and chestnut. The males and females appear similar; that is, there is not the sexual dimorphism found in other birds such as pheasants and ducks, where the male is brilliantly colored and the female has dull plumage. Some species of jays and magpies have crests. Common to all the corvids is a tuft of bristles at the base of the beak, just above the nostrils and there are more bristles fringing the mouth.

The personality of crows and jays can be described as aggressive, intelligent, quarrelsome, and sometimes playful. The voice of a corvid, once heard, is not easily forgotten. They produce an astounding range of harsh or more musical calls, which are part of languages, researchers also discovered. The repertoire of the blue jay (*Cyanocitta cristata*), for example, includes high–pitched shrieks (usually aimed at intruders such as cats, owls, or humans; a cry of *jeer–jeer*; a ringing, bell–like *tull–ull*; a call that sounds like the word "teacup'; a rapid clicking call; a soft, lisping song; a sound like a rusty gate; and imitations of the red–tailed hawk, the black–capped chickadee, the northern oriole, the grau catbird, the American goldfinch, and eastern wood pewee. Some species can even imitate human speech.

This range of imitative ability is common to several members of the crow family, and is both evidence of the family's intelligence and part of the reason these birds figure so prominently in human fiction. Experiments with captive common, or American, crows (*Corvus brachyrhynchos*) have proved the birds have excellent puzzle–solving abilities, can count up to three or four, have good memories, and can quickly learn to equate certain sounds or symbols with food. Caged jackdaws that were exposed to a 10–second burst of light accompanied by a four–minute recording of jackdaw distress calls, followed by two minutes of silence and darkness, soon learned to peck a key that shut off the light and the recording. A captive blue jay used a tool (a scrap of newspaper from the bottom of its cage) to reach a pile of food pellets that lay outside the cage, just out of reach of its beak. Most interesting, several other captive jays who watched this one method of problem solving soon used it too.

Although these captive experiments provide much information, observations of wild corvids provide even better evidence of the corvids' intelligence. In Norway and Sweden, springtime fishermen make holes in the ice and drop their fishing lines through them into the water. Hooded crows have been seen picking up the line and walking backward as far as they can, pulling the line out of the hole. The crow will do this as often as it needs to bring the end of the line to the surface, as well as the bait or the hooked fish–which the crow then devours.

The corvids are wary as well as smart. One bird researcher noted that blue jays' intelligence is the key to their not falling victim to the prowling cats that kill so many other species of bird. Crows also show signs of coming to one another's aid; the cawing of a common crow will bring crows from everywhere around, ready to mob the predator.

Crows live in varied habitats, including forests, grasslands, deserts, steppes, farms, and urban areas.

A Steller's jay (*Cyanocitta stelleri*) in California.

They are mostly tree–dwelling, but the ground–jays have adapted to a life on the ground so much that they will run from a threat rather than fly.

They are highly gregarious birds. A flock may consist of as few as six to as many as a few hundred birds. Within the flock is a social hierarchy, particularly among the crows, the pinyon jays, scrub jays, and Mexican jays. However, mated pairs nest on their own. Corvids are generally aboreal nesters, building a nest of twigs lined with soft materials, although some species nest in holes or build domed nests. The female incubates the eggs (2–8, depending on the species) alone for 16 to 22 days (again, the length of incubation depends on the species), and her mate feeds her while she does so and helps feed the young after they are born. Corvids do not carry food in their beaks, but rather in their throat or in a small pouch within the chin, under the tongue. Although the members of the crow family are known to be raucous, they become secretive near their nests, drawing as little attention as possible to themselves and their nestlings.

Young common crows fledge between 28 and 35 days old; among the family the nestling period ranges from 20 to 45 days. Although captive crows have been known to live 20 years or more, most wild corvids do not live that long.

The diet of crows and jays is varied both among and within species. The American, or common, crow eats insects, spiders, crustaceans, snails, salamanders, earthworms, snakes, frogs, the eggs and chicks of other birds, and carrion. The crows will crack the shells of clams, mussels, and other bivalve mollusks by picking them up, flying with them to a height, and then dropping them to rocks below (herring gulls and crows were seen practicing this tactic at the same time, but the gulls dropped the mollusks onto the mud; the crows figured out much sooner that aiming for the rock was a better, more certain, method). The corvids are not solely carnivorous, however; the blue jay eats about three times as much vegetable matter–including acorns, corn, berries, currants, sorrel, and even cultivated cherries–as it does animal matter. Blue jays have been known to eat mice, small fish, and even bats. Another common North American crow, the fish crow of the eastern United States, also eats shrimp, fiddler crabs, crawfish, and turtle eggs.

Most wild corvids that have been studied have been seen hiding food for future use. Small prey items, such as insects and earthworms, are not usually hidden, but unexpected "bonuses" are hidden away in small holes or under fallen leaves, although hiding places in trees or buildings will also be used. The Canada jay would be unable to recover ground–buried food during the harsh northern winter, so instead hides food in pine and fir trees, sticking it to the branches with saliva (this species has developed accordingly large salivary glands for this task).

Ravens and crows have both been reported to hide some of a large amount of food before settling down to eat the remainder. The apparently excellent memories of crows serve them well in rediscovering these food caches, although success varies among species. Many of the acorns hidden by blue jays in the fall are never recovered. The nutcrackers, on the other hand, have been known to recover 70% of the seeds they store.

Their natural enemies include owls, eagles, and buzzards, and they have had a long–running battle with human beings. In the United States, common crows are fond of corn and other cultivated crops, and as a result have been shot at and poisoned. The house crow of India—a tremendously successful commensal species which has tied its life so tightly with that of man that its survival alone would be unlikely—has been destroyed in several places because its large flocks caused it to be considered a health threat.

Despite this animosity, most cultures have tales to tell about the corvids. Raven figures prominently in Inuit legend. Two ravens, Huginn and Munnin, were the companions of the Norse god Odin. A legendary Celtic warrior god named Bran was also accompanied by a raven, and the bird is known by his name (Cigfran) in Celtic Welsh, Cornish, and Breton. In Cornwall, legend has it that the raven and another corvid, the red–billed chough, hold the spirit of King Arthur, and woe to he who harms either of these birds! From far back the raven has been associated with death, particularly with foretelling it–perhaps because of its close association with the Vikings, this raven–death association was particularly strong in western Europe.

And the legends are not all just in the past: even in the late twentieth century captive ravens are kept in the Tower of London. The belief is that when the last raven leaves it, the Tower will crumble.

Despite the success of the family as a whole, at least 22 species of corvids are endangered, including the Hawaiian crow (*Corvus tropicus*) and the Marianas crow (*C. kubaryi*).

F. C. Nicholson

Crustacea

The crustacea (subphylum Mandibulata, class Crustacea) are a diverse group of animals. This class includes some of the more familiar arthropods, including barnacles, copepods, crabs, prawns, lobsters, and wood lice. More than 30,000 species have been identified, the majority of which are marine–dwelling. Terrestrial species such as wood lice and pill bugs are believed to have evolved from marine species. Most crustaceans are free–living but some species are parasitic—some even on other crustaceans. Some species are free–swimming, while others are specialised at crawling or burrowing in soft sediments.

Despite such an extraordinary diversity of species, many crustaceans have a similar structure and way of life. The distinctive head usually bears five pairs of appendages: two pairs of antennae that play a sensory role in detecting food as well as changes in humidity and temperature; a pair of mandibles that are used for grasping and tearing food; and two pairs of maxillae that are used for feeding purposes. The main part of the body is taken up with the thorax and abdomen, both of which are often covered with a toughened outer skeleton, or exoskeleton. Attached to the trunk region are a number of other appendages which vary both in number and purpose in different species. In crabs, for example, one pair of appendages may be modified for swimming, another for feeding, another for brooding eggs and yet another for catching prey.

Crustacea exhibit a wide range of feeding techniques. The simplest of these are those species that practise filter feeding such as the copepods and tiny shrimps. Feeding largely on plankton and suspended materials, the animal creates a mini water current towards the mouth by the rhythmic beating of countless number of fine setae that cover the specialised feeding limbs of these species. Food particles are collected in special filters and then transferred to the mouth. Larger species such as crabs and lobsters are active hunters of small fish and other organisms, while some species adopt a scavenging role, feeding on dead animals or plants and other waste materials.

Apart from the smaller species, which rely on gas exchange through the entire body surface, most crustaceans have special gills that serve as a means of obtaining oxygen. Simple excretory organs ensure the removal of body wastes such as ammonia and urea. Most crustaceans have a series of well–developed sensory organs that include not only eyes, but also a range of chemical and tactile receptors. All crustaceans are probably capable of detecting a light source but in some of the more developed species, definite shapes and movements may also be detected.

Breeding strategies vary considerably amongst the crustacea. Most species are dioecious (being either male or female), but some, such as the barnacles, are hermaphrodite. Fertilization is usually internal through direct copulation. The fertilized eggs then mature either in a specialised brood chamber in some part of the female's body, or attached directly to some external appendage such as a claw. Most aquatic species hatch into a free–swimming larvae that progresses through a series of body moults until finally arriving at the adult size.

See also Crabs; Zooplankton.

Cryobiology

Cryobiology is the study of the effects of very low temperatures on living things. Cryobiology can be used to preserve, store, or destroy living cells. At very low temperatures, cellular metabolism is virtually nonexistent. Freezing technology is used for food preservation, blood storage at hospitals and blood banks, sperm and egg storage, preservation of some transplant tissues, and certain delicate surgeries. Cryopreservation, the freezing and eventual thawing of viable (living) material, is the most advanced use of this technology.

History

Ice has been used to slow the decay of food for centuries, but the widespread industrial use of freezing has occurred only in about the last 100 years with advances in refrigeration and cryotechnology. By the

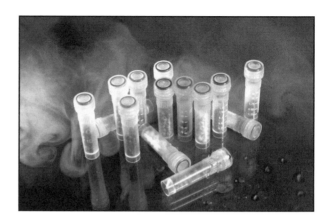

Cryotubes used to store strains of bacteria at low temperature. Bacteria are placed in the little holes in the beads inside the tubes and then stored in liquid nitrogen.

1940s, red blood cells (erythrocytes) were being frozen to provide blood supplies as needed during wartime. And not long afterwards, farmers began freezing bovine sperm to impregnate cows at distant locations, since transporting a tube of frozen sperm is much easier than moving a bull.

The cryopreservation of single cells or small clumps of cells has been used to the present day. However, preservation of whole live organs by freezing is more complex and has been largely unsuccessful. Freezing of sperm and blood has also raised some legal and ethical questions.

Cellular cryopreservation

Cryopreservation involves keeping cells at extremely low temperatures until they are needed. Careful steps must be taken to insure that the frozen cells will be viable and in good condition when they are thawed. One of the most important variables is the cell's initial health, since freezing will not improve an unhealthy cell's condition; in fact, freezing places additional stress on cells, such that even some healthy cells do not recuperate from the freezing and thawing process.

One of the major roadblocks to successful freeze-thawing is the water present on the inside of a frozen cell. Frozen water crystallizes into ice which can cause the cell to expand and crack. Because of this, scientists use a chemical treatment to remove as much water as possible from the cells prior to freezing. Chemicals which replace water inside the cell and facilitate its departure from the cell are called cryoprotectants. The two most widely used cryoprotectants are glycerol and dimethyl sulfoxide (DMSO).

Treatment with a cryoprotectant is the first step in cryopreservation. The glycerol or DMSO is allowed to penetrate the cells for a set period of time. Then, the cells are cooled at a set rate of freezing to allow the cells to acclimate to the new colder temperatures. The samples are frozen to successively colder temperatures until they reach about -321°F (-196°C). At this temperature, cellular metabolism becomes suspended until the cells are thawed. Cryopreserved samples are usually stored in liquid nitrogen tanks. Liquid nitrogen has a boiling point of -321°F (-196°C). Since nitrogen becomes gas at such a low temperature, it must be replaced on a periodic (often weekly) basis to maintain cryogenic conditions. However, most modern cryogenic freezers are designed to automatically add liquid nitrogen as needed.

Once a cryopreserved sample is removed from the freezer, it must be thawed under carefully controlled conditions. Experience has shown that samples which were frozen slowly must be thawed slowly, and samples which were frozen rapidly must be thawed rapidly. The thawing process is carried out in a medium which allows cells to reacquire water and other essential nutrients. The glycerol or DMSO leaves the cell, and the cell reacclimates to normal temperatures.

Cellular applications

The most successful medical applications of cryopreservation are in blood storage and the field of fertility. Blood banks can freeze rare and individual blood types for up to 10 years. Leukemia patients who must undergo radiation treatments can have their sperm and bone marrow cells, which are radiation sensitive, frozen and stored for later use. Some men undergoing a vasectomy store sperm to keep the option of having another child. In addition, fertilized eggs (up to about the 8-cell stage) have been successfully frozen and thawed for implantation.

Although red blood cells can be frozen and stored at -112°F (-80°C) for up to 10 years, most blood is not frozen, but merely refrigerated at 33.8-42.8°F (1-6°C) for 21-42 days. If blood is frozen, the process of removing cryoprotectant and washing red blood cells to remove incompatible residues of cryopreservation can take hours, and in an emergency, a patient can not wait hours for a transfusion. Plasma, the non-cellular liquid part of blood, can be stored at -0.4°F (-18°C) for up to a year.

Human sperm can be frozen at -292°F – -321°F (-180 – -196°C) indefinitely. The seminal fluid is separated from the sperm, and the sperm is preserved using the cryoprotectant glycerol in a rich egg yolk medium.

Ova (eggs) can be frozen in a similar manner. Within the last 10 years, the technology has also emerged to cryopreserve fertilized human eggs-early stage embryos. Embryos at the one- to ten-cell stage (2-3 days after fertilization) are cryopreserved with a variety of cryoprotectants. Current embryo cryopreservation has been achieved using glycerol and a less common cryoprotectant, propanediol. These embryos have shown a high implantation success rate.

Surgical cryobiology

Medical scientists can also use freezing technology during surgical procedures to improve a patient's outcome. In transplant surgery, some cornea and skin grafts are frozen prior to use. However, temperatures used to preserve most transplant tissues, which are multilayered, are not as low as freezing, since organs and tissues are more difficult to freeze than populations of single cells such as sperm and red blood cells.

Cold temperatures are also sometimes used to cool patients undergoing surgery and surgical instruments. When the brain and heart are cooled to about 80.6°F (27°C), their oxygen requirements decrease, allowing for longer surgery. When surgical patients are cooled, they are said to be in medical hypothermia. During this cooling, the body's natural warming response is pharmacologically blocked.

Cryosurgery—the freezing of surgical instruments—is also used to destroy or remove unwanted tissue. Cryosurgery can remove malignant tumors or superficial skin warts. A major advantage of cryosurgery is that it scars less than comparable noncryosurgery.

See also Blood supply; Cryogenics; Food preservation.

Further Reading:

Davenport J. *Animal Life at Low Temperatures.* New York: Chapman & Hall, 1992.

Fahning, M., and M. Garcia. "Status of Cryopreservation of Embryos from Domestic Animals." *Cryobiology* 29, No. 1 (1992).

Wolf, D., R. Stouffer, and R. Brenner, eds. *In Vitro Fertilization and Embryo Transfer in Primates.* New York: Springer-Verlag, 1993.

Louise H. Dickerson

Cryogenics

Cryogenics is the science of producing and studying low–temperature environments. The word cryogenics comes from the Greek word "cryos," meaning cold; combined with a shortened form of the English verb "to generate," it has come to mean the generation of temperatures well below those of normal human experience. More specifically, a low–temperature environment is termed a cryogenic environment when the temperature range is below the point at which permanent gases begin to liquefy. Permanent gases are elements that normally exist in the gaseous state and were once believed impossible to liquefy. Among others, they include oxygen, nitrogen, hydrogen, and helium. The origin of cryogenics as a scientific discipline coincided with the discovery by nineteenth century scientists, that the permanent gases can be liquefied at exceedingly low temperatures. Consequently, the term cryogenic applies to temperatures from approximately –148° F (–100° C) down to absolute zero.

The temperature of a sample, whether it be a gas, liquid, or solid, is a measure of the energy it contains, energy that is present in the form of vibrating atoms and moving molecules. Absolute zero represents the lowest attainable temperature and is associated with the complete absence of atomic and molecular motion. The existence of absolute zero was first pointed out in 1848 by William Thompson (later to become Lord Kelvin), and is now known to be –459° F (–273° C). It is the basis of an absolute temperature scale, called the Kelvin scale, whose unit, called a kelvin rather than a degree, is the same size as the Celsius degree. Thus, –459° F corresponds to –273° C corresponds to 0 K (note that by convention the degree symbol is omitted, so that 0 K is read "zero kelvin"). Cryogenics, then, deals with producing and maintaining environments at temperatures below about 173 K.

In addition to studying methods for producing and maintaining cold environments, the field of cryogenics has also come to include studying the properties of materials at cryogenic temperatures. The mechanical and electrical properties of many materials change very dramatically when cooled to 100 K or lower. For example, rubber, most plastics, and some metals become exceedingly brittle, and nearly all materials contract. In addition, many metals and ceramics lose all resistance to the flow of electricity, a phenomenon called superconductivity, and very near absolute zero (2.2 K) liquid helium undergoes a transition to a state of superfluidity, in which it can flow through exceedingly narrow passages with no friction.

History

The development of cryogenics as a low temperature science is a direct result of attempts by nineteenth century scientists to liquefy the permanent gases. One of these scientists, Michael Faraday, had succeeded, by 1845, in liquefying most of the gases then known to exist. His procedure consisted of cooling the gas by immersion in a bath of ether and dry ice and then pressurizing the gas until it liquefied. Six gases, however, resisted every attempt at liquefaction and were known at the time as permanent gases. They were oxygen, hydrogen, nitrogen, carbon monoxide, methane, and nitric oxide. The noble gases, helium, neon, argon, krypton, and xenon, were yet to be discovered. Of the known permanent gases, oxygen and nitrogen, the primary constituents of air, received the most attention. For many years investigators labored to liquefy air. Finally, in 1877, Louis Cailletet in France and Raoul Pictet in Switzerland, succeeded in producing the first droplets of liquid air, and in 1883 the first measurable quantity of liquid oxygen was produced by S.F. von Wroblewski at the University of Cracow. Oxygen was found to liquefy at –297° F (90 K), and nitrogen at –320 °F (77 K).

Following the liquefaction of air, a race to liquefy hydrogen ensued. James Dewar, a Scottish Chemist, succeeded in 1898. He found the boiling point of hydrogen to be a frosty –423° F (20 K). In the same year, Dewar succeeded in freezing hydrogen, thus reaching the lowest temperature achieved to that time, –434° F (14 K). Along the way, argon was discovered (1894) as an impurity in liquid nitrogen, and krypton and xenon were discovered (1898), during the fractional distillation of liquid argon. (Fractional distillation is accomplished by liquefying a mixture of gases each of which

	Boiling Point		
Cryogen	**° F**	**° C**	**° K**
Oxygen	-297	-183	90
Nitrogen	-320	-196	77
Hydrogen	-423	-253	20
Helium	-452	-269	4.2
Neon	-411	-246	27
Argon	-302	-186	87
Krypton	-242	-153	120
Xenon	-161	-107	166

TABLE 1

has a different boiling point. When the mixture is evaporated, the gas with the highest boiling point evaporates first, followed by the gas with the second highest boiling point, and so on.) Each of the newly discovered gases condensed at temperatures higher than the boiling point of hydrogen, but lower than 173 K (see Table 1). The last element to be liquefied was helium gas. First discovered in 1868 in the spectrum of the sun, and later on earth (1885), helium has the lowest boiling point of any known substance. In 1908, the Dutch Physicist Kamerlingh Onnes finally succeeded in liquefying helium at a temperature of –452° F (4.2 K).

Methods of producing cryogenic temperatures

There are essentially only four physical processes that are used to produce cryogenic temperatures, and cryogenic environments: heat conduction, evaporative cooling, cooling by rapid expansion (the Joule–Thompson effect), and adiabatic demagnetization. The first two are well known in terms of everyday experience. The third is less well known but is commonly used in ordinary refrigeration and air conditioning units, as well as cryogenic applications. The fourth process is used primarily in cryogenic applications and provides a means of approaching absolute zero.

Heat conduction is familiar to everyone. When two bodies are in contact, heat flows from the higher temperature body to a lower temperature body. Conduction can occur between any and all forms of matter, whether gas, liquid, or solid, and is essential in the production of cryogenic temperatures and environments. For example, samples may be cooled to cryogenic temperatures by immersing them directly in a cryogenic liquid or by placing them in an atmosphere cooled by cryogenic refrigeration. In either case, the sample cools by conduction of heat to its colder surroundings.

The second physical process with cryogenic applications is evaporative cooling, which occurs because atoms or molecules have less energy when they are in the liquid state than when they are in the vapor, or gaseous state. When a liquid evaporates, atoms or molecules at the surface acquire enough energy from the surrounding liquid to enter the gaseous state. The remaining liquid has relatively less energy, so its temperature drops. Thus, the temperature of a liquid can be lowered by encouraging the process of evaporation. The process is used in cryogenics to reduce the temperature of liquids by continuously pumping away the atoms or molecules as they leave the liquid, allowing the evaporation process to cool the remaining liquid to the desired temperature. Once the desired temperature is reached, pumping continues at a reduced level in order to maintain the lower temperature. This method can be used to reduce the temperature of any liquid. For example, it can be used to reduce the temperature of liquid nitrogen to its freezing point, or to lower the temperature of liquid helium to approximately –458° F (1 K).

The third process makes use of the Joule–Thompson effect, and provides a method for cooling gases. The Joule–Thompson effect involves cooling a pressurized gas by rapidly expanding its volume, or, equivalently, creating a sudden drop in pressure. The effect was discovered in 1852 by J.P. Joule and William Thompson, and was crucial to the successful liquefaction of hydrogen and helium. A valve with a small orifice (called a Joule–Thompson valve) is often used to produce the effect. High pressure gas on one side of the valve drops very suddenly, to a much lower pressure and temperature, as it passes through the orifice. In practice, the Joule–Thompson effect is used in conjunction with the process of heat conduction. For example, when Kamerlingh Onnes first liquefied helium he did so by cooling the gas, through conduction, to successively lower temperatures, bringing it into contact with three successively colder liquids: oxygen, nitrogen, and hydrogen. Finally, he used a Joule–Thompson valve to expand the cold gas, and produce a mixture of gas and liquid droplets. Today, the two effects together comprise the common refrigeration process. First, a gas is pressurized and cooled to an intermediate temperature by contact with a colder gas or liquid. Then, the gas is expanded, and its temperature drops still further. Ordinary household refrigerators and air conditioners work on this principle, using freon, which has a relatively high boiling point. Cryogenic refrigerators work on the same principle but use cryogenic gases such as helium, and repeat the process in stages, each stage having a successively colder gas until the desired temperature is reached.

The fourth process, that of adiabatic demagnetization, involves the use of paramagnetic salts to absorb heat. This phenomenon has been used to reduce the temperature of liquid helium to less than a thousandth of a degree above absolute zero in the following way. A paramagnetic salt is much like an enormous collection of very tiny magnets called magnetic moments. Normally, these tiny magnets are randomly aligned so the collection as a whole is not magnetic. However, when the salt is placed in a magnetic field, say by turning on a nearby electromagnet, the north poles of each magnetic moment are repelled by the north pole of the applied magnetic field, so many of the moments align the same way, that is, opposite to the applied field. This process decreases the entropy of the system. Entropy is a measure of randomness in a collection; high entropy is associated with randomness, zero entropy is associated with perfect alignment. In this case, randomness in the alignment of magnetic moments has been reduced, resulting in a decrease in entropy. In the branch of physics called Thermodynamics, it is shown that every collection will naturally tend to increase in entropy if left alone. Thus, when the electromagnet is switched off, the magnetic moments of the salt will tend to return to more random orientations. This requires energy, though, which the salt absorbs from the surrounding liquid, leaving the liquid at a lower temperature. Scientists know that it is not possible to achieve a temperature of absolute zero, however, in their attempts to get ever closer, a similar process called nuclear demagnetization has been used

to reach temperatures just one millionth of a degree above absolute zero.

Applications

Following his successful liquefaction of helium in 1908, Kamerlingh Onnes turned his attention almost immediately to studying the properties of other materials at cryogenic temperatures. The first property he investigated was the electrical resistance of metals, which was known to decrease with decreasing temperature. It was presumed that the resistance would completely disappear at absolute zero. Onnes discovered, however, that for some metals the resistance dropped to zero very suddenly at temperatures above absolute zero. The effect is called superconductivity and has some very important applications in today's world. For example, superconductors are used to make magnets for particle accelerators and for magnetic resonance imaging (MRI) systems used in many hospitals.

The discovery of superconductivity led other scientists to study a variety of material properties at cryogenic temperatures. Today, physicists, chemists, material scientists, and biologists study the properties of metals, as well as the properties of insulators, semiconductors, plastics, composites, and living tissue. In order to chill their samples they must bring them into contact with something cold. This is done by placing the sample in an insulated container, called a dewar, and cooling the inner space, either by filling it with a cryogenic liquid, or by cooling it with a cryogenic refrigerator. Over the years, this research has resulted in the identification of a number of useful properties. One such property common to most materials that are subjected to extremely low temperatures is brittleness. The recycling industry takes advantage of this by immersing recyclables in liquid nitrogen, after which they are easily pulverized and separated for reprocessing. Still another cryogenic material property that is sometimes useful is that of thermal contraction. Materials shrink when cooled. To a point (about the temperature of liquid nitrogen), the colder a material gets the more it shrinks. An example is the use of liquid nitrogen in the assembly of some automobile engines. In order to get extremely tight fits when installing valve seats, the seats are cooled to liquid nitrogen temperatures, whereupon they contract and are easily inserted in the engine head. When they warm up, a perfect fit results.

Cryogenic liquids are also used in the space program. For example, cryogens are used to propel rockets into space. A tank of liquid hydrogen provides the fuel to be burned and a second tank of liquid oxygen is provided for combustion. A more exotic application is the use of liquid helium to cool orbiting infrared telescopes. Any object warmer than absolute zero radiates heat in the form of infrared light. The infrared sensors that make up a telescope's "lens" must be cooled to temperatures that are lower than the equivalent temperature of the light they are intended to sense, otherwise the telescope will literally be blinded by its own light. Since temperatures of interest are as low as −454° F (3 K), liquid helium at −456° F (1.8 K) is used to cool the sensors.

Finally, the production of liquefied gases has itself become an important cryogenic application. Cryogenic liquids and gases such as oxygen, nitrogen, hydrogen, helium, and argon all have important applications. Shipping them as gases is highly inefficient because of their low densities. This is true even at extremely high pressures. Instead, liquefying cryogenic gases greatly increases the weight of cryogen that can be transported by a single tanker.

Further Reading:

Asimov, Isaac. *Asimov's Chronology of Science and Discovery*. New York: Harper and Row, 1989.

Donnelly, R.J., and Arthur W. Francis, ed. *Cryogenic Science and Technology: Contributions by Leo I. Dana*. Union Carbide Corporation, 1985.

Haines, Gail Kay. *Super Cold Super Hot*. New York: Franklin Watts, 1976.

Mendelssohn, K. *The Quest for Absolute Zero*. New York: McGraw–Hill, 1966.

Newman, R.J. "Chilling prostate Cancer." *U.S. News and World Report*. 113 (1992) 84–85.

Stamm, D.M., and D.A.Franz. "Hot and Cold Running Methane." *J. Chem Educ*. 69 (1992) 762–763.

Van Sciver, S.W. *Helium Cryogenics*. New York: Plenum Press, 1986.

J. R. Maddocks

Crystal

A crystal is a solid in which the particles that make up the solid take up a highly ordered, definite, geometric arrangement that is repeated in all directions within the crystal.

Crystals have always attracted the curiosity of humans. Archaeologists have unearthed shells, claws, teeth, and other crystalline solids dating to 25,000 B.C. that have holes, as though worn as necklaces, and that are engraved with symbols of magic. The treasures of the ancient Egyptian king, Tutankhamen, abound with crystals in the forms of gems and jewels. These were not only intended for personal adornment, but were designed in symbolic fashion and believed to possess mystical and religious powers. Healers used crystals in their magical rites and cures.

In ancient Greece, Archimedes made a study of regular solids, and Plato and Aristotle speculated on the relationship between regular solids and the elements. In the sixteenth century, the German naturalist, Giorgius Agricola, classified solids by their external forms, and Johann Kepler observed that snowflakes were always six–sided (circa 1611), commenting on geometrical shapes and arrangements that might produce this effect. In the seventeenth century, noted philosophers and mathematicians, including René Descartes, Robert Hooke, and Christian Huyghens followed and expanded Kepler's postulates.

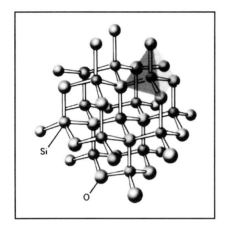

The structure of quartz.

In 1671, an English translation of a study by a Danish–born scientist, Nicolaus Steno, was published in London. It described his investigative work on crystals of quartz, which consists of silicon and oxygen. An Italian scientist, Domenico Guglielmini, developed a structural theory of crystals over the years 1688–1705. Later, measurements of crystals by the French scientist, Jean Baptiste Louis Romé Delisle, were published between 1772–1783. In 1809, the British scientist, William Hyde Wollaston, described an improved goniometer instrument for making accurate measurements on small crystals.

The study of crystals has led to major advances in our understanding of the chemistry of biological processes. In 1867, Louis Pasteur discovered two types of tartaric acid crystals which were related as the left hand is to the right; that is, one was the mirror image of the other. This led to the discovery that most biomolecules, molecules upon which living systems are based, exhibit this same type of "handedness." In fact, scientists have speculated on the possibility of life having evolved from crystals.

Detailed analyses of crystal structures are carried out by X–ray diffraction. In 1912, Max von Laue predicted that the spacing of crystal layers is small enough to cause diffraction (breaking of light, when it hits an opaque surface, into colored bands). William Henry Bragg and his son, William Lawrence Bragg, were awarded the Nobel Prize in chemistry (1915) for their development of crystal structure analysis using X–ray diffraction. In 1953, James Watson and Francis Crick deduced the double helix structure of DNA (deoxyribonucleic acid, one of the nucleic acids which controls heredity in living organisms) partly from the results of X–ray diffraction analysis of DNA. In recognition of this advancement in the study of the processes of life, they were awarded the Nobel prize in 1962.

Throughout the twentieth century the study of crystalline molecules has continued to expand our knowledge by providing detailed structures of vitamins, proteins (enzymes, myoglobin, bacterial membranes), liquid crystals, polymers, organic and inorganic compounds.

Today, crystals are still worn for decorative purposes in the form of gems and jewels; there are still believers in the mystical powers of crystals, but there is no scientific basis for any of the many claims made for them by "New Age" promoters. Crystals are used in modern technological applications, such as lasers.

Common classes of crystalline solids

The standard classes of crystalline solids are the metals, ionic compounds, molecular compounds, and network solids.

The metals are those elements occurring on the left side of the periodic table (a classification of elements based on the number of protons in their nuclei), up to the diagonal that connects boron and astatine. The nuclei of metal atoms take up highly ordered, crystalline arrangements; the atomic electrons are relatively free to move throughout the metal, making metals good conductors of electricity.

When a metallic element combines with a nonmetal (an element which is on the right side of the boron–astatine diagonal) an ionic compound is obtained. Ionic compounds do not consist of molecules, but are made up of ordered arrays of ions. An ion is a charged atom or molecule; a positive ion (or cation) is produced when an atom gives up an electron, and a negative ion (or anion) is the result when an atom gains an electron. The attraction of opposite charges of cations and anions (electrostatic attraction) keeps them in close proximity to each other. In compounds, the ions assume the ordered arrangements characteristic of crystals. The strong electrostatic forces between oppositely charged ions make it very difficult to separate the ions and break down the crystal structure; thus, ionic compounds have very high melting points [generally higher than $1,742°$ F $(800°C)$]. Because the electrons in ionic compounds are not free to move throughout the crystal, these compounds do not conduct electricity unless the ions themselves are released by heating to high temperatures or by dissolving the compound.

When nonmetallic elements combine in reactions, the resulting compound is a molecular compound. Within such compounds the atoms are linked by shared electrons, so that ions are not present. However, partial charges arise in individual molecules because of uneven distribution of electrons within each molecule. Partial positive charges in one molecule can attract partial negative charges in another, resulting in ordered crystalline arrangements of the molecules. The forces of attraction between molecules in crystals of covalent compounds are relatively weak, so these compounds require much less energy to separate the molecules and break down the crystals; thus, the melting points of covalent compounds are usually less than 300° C. Because charged particles are not present, covalent compounds do not conduct electricity, even when the crystals are broken down by melting or by dissolving.

Network solids are substances in which atoms are bonded covalently to each other to form large networks of molecules of nondefinite size. Examples of network solids include diamond and graphite, which are two crystalline forms of carbon, and silicates, such as sand, rock, and minerals, which are made up of silicon and oxygen atoms. Because the atoms occupy specific bonding sites relative to each other, the resulting arrangement is highly ordered and, therefore, crystalline. Network solids have very high melting points because all the atoms are linked to their neighbors by strong covalent bonds. Thus, the melting point of diamond is 6,332°F (3,500° C). Such solids are insoluble because the energy required to separate the atoms is so high.

Internal structures of metallic crystals

A complete description of the structure of a crystal involves several levels of detail. Metallic crystals are discussed first for simplicity, because the atoms are all of the same type, and can be regarded as spherical in shape. However, the basic concepts are the same for all solids.

If the spheres are represented by points, then the pattern of repeating points at constant intervals in each direction in a crystal is called the lattice. Fourteen different lattices can be obtained geometrically (the Bravais lattices). If lines are drawn through analogous points within a lattice, a three–dimensional arrangement of structural units is obtained. The smallest possible repeating structural unit within a crystal is called the unit cell, much like a brick is the smallest repeating unit (the unit cell) of a brick wall.

The fourteen unit cell types are based on seven types of crystal systems. These are the cubic, triclinic, monoclinic, orthorhombic, trigonal, tetragonal, and hexagonal systems. The specific crystal system and type of unit cell observed for a given solid is dependent on several factors. If the particles that make up the solid are approximately spherical, then there is a tendency for

them to pack together with maximum efficiency. Close–packed structures have the maximum packing efficiency, with 74% of the crystal volume being occupied by the particles. Close–packing occurs in two different ways: cubic close–packing (ccp), which gives rise to cubic unit cells (the face–centered cube), and hexagonal close–packing (hcp), which gives hexagonal unit cells.

The placement of atoms that produces each of these arrangements can be described in terms of their layering. Within each layer, the most efficient packing occurs when the particles are staggered with respect to one another, leaving small triangular spaces between the particles. The second layer is placed on top of the first, in the depressions between the particles of the first layer. Similarly, the third layer lies in the depressions of the second. Thus, if the particles of the third layer are also directly over depressions of the first layer, the layering pattern is ABCABC, in which the fourth layer is a repeat of the first. This is called cubic close–packing, and results in the face–centered cubic unit cell. Such close–packed structures are common in metals, including calcium, strontium, aluminum, rhodium, iridium, nickel, palladium, platinum, copper, silver, and gold. If the third layer particles are also directly over particles of the first, the repeating layer pattern is ABAB. This is called hexagonal close–packing, and produces the hexagonal unit cell. This packing arrangement also is observed for many metals, including beryllium, magnesium, scandium, yttrium, lanthanum, titanium, zirconium, hafnium, technetium, rhenium, rubidium, osmium, cobalt, zinc, and cadmium.

Other layering patterns in which the particles are not close–packed occur frequently. For example, particles within a layer might not be staggered with respect to one another. Instead, if they align themselves as in a square grid, the spaces between the particles also will be square. The second layer fits in the depressions of the first; the third layer lies in depressions of the second, and over particles of the first layer, giving the layering pattern (ABAB) with a space–filling efficiency of 68%. The resulting unit cell is a body–centered cube. Metals which have this arrangement of atoms include the alkali metals, barium, vanadium, niobium, tantalum, chromium, molybdenum, tungsten, manganese, and iron.

Common internal structures of crystals of ionic solids

Although ionic solids follow similar patterns as described above for metals, the detailed arrangements are more complicated, because the positioning of two

TABLE 1. COMMON CRYSTAL STRUCTURES OF IONIC COMPOUNDS

Compound	Structure Name	Radius Ratio and C.N. of cation and anion	Packing and layering
halides of lithium, sodium, potassium, rubidium; ammonium halides; silver halides; oxides and sulfides of magnesium, calcium, strontium, and barium	sodium chloride	0.41 to 0.75 6:6	chloride ccp, sodium in every octahedral hole
zinc sulfide, copper(I) chloride, cadmium (II) sulfide, mercury (II) sulfide	sphalerite	0.23 to 0.41 4:4	sulfide ccp, zinc in half the tetrahedral holes
zinc sulfide, zinc oxide, beryllium oxide, manganese (II) sulfide, silver iodide, silicon carbide, ammonium fluoride	wurtzite	0.23 to 0.41 4:4	sulfide hcp, zinc in half the tetrahedral holes
calcium fluoride, barium chloride, mercury (II) fluoride, lead (IV) oxide, barium fluoride, strontium fluoride	fluorite	0.72 and up 8:4	calcium ccp, fluoride in all tetrahedral holes
cesium chloride, calcium sulfide, cesium cyanide	cesium chloride	0.72 and up 8:8	chloride in primitive cubes, cesium at the centers

different types of ions, cations and anions, must be considered. In general, it is the larger ion (usually, the anion) that determines the overall packing and layering, while the smaller ion fits in the holes (spaces) that occur throughout the layers.

Two types of holes occupied by cations exist (in close–packed ionic structures.). These are named tetrahedral and octahedral. An ion in a tetrahedral site would be in contact with four ions of opposite charge, which, if linked by imaginary lines, produces a tetrahedron. An ion in an octahedral site would be in contact with six ions of opposite charge, producing an octahedron. The number of oppositely charged ions in contact with a given ion is called its coordination number (CN). Therefore, an ion in a tetrahedral site has a coordination number of four; an ion in an octahedral site has a coordination number of six. The total number of octahedral holes is the same as the number of close–packed ions, whereas there are twice as many tetrahedral holes as close–packed atoms. Because tetrahedral holes are

smaller, they are occupied only when the ratio of the smaller ion's radius to the radius of the larger ion is very small. As the radius ratio of the smaller ion to the larger ion becomes greater, the smaller ion no longer fits into tetrahedral holes, but will fit into octahedral holes.

These principles can be illustrated by several examples. The repeating structural unit of crystalline sodium chloride (table salt) is the face–centered cubic unit cell. The larger chloride ions are cubic close–packed (ABCABC layering pattern). The radius ratio of sodium ion to chloride ion is about 0.6, so the smaller sodium ions occupy all the octahedral sites. Chloride and sodium ions both have coordination numbers of six. This structure occurs frequently among ionic compounds (see Table 1) and is called the sodium chloride or rock salt structure.

In the sphalerite (or zinc blende) crystalline form of zinc sulfide, the larger sulfide ions are cubic close–packed (ABCABC layering), giving a face–centered cubic unit cell. The small zinc ions occupy tetrahedral sites. However, the number of tetrahedral holes is twice the number of sulfide ions, whereas the number of zinc ions is equal to the number of sulfide ions. Therefore, zinc ions occupy only half of the tetrahedral holes. In the wurtzite structure, another crystalline form of zinc sulfide, the sulfide ions are hexagonally close–packed, (ABAB layering), giving a hexagonal unit cell. Again, the zinc ions occupy half the tetrahedral sites.

Another common structure, the fluorite structure, is often observed for ionic compounds which have twice as many anions as cations, and in which the cations are larger than the anions. The structure is named after the compound, calcium fluoride, in which the calcium ions are cubic close–packed, with fluoride in all the tetrahedral sites.

As discussed for metals, many compounds have structures that do not involve close–packing. For example, in the cesium chloride structure, the larger chloride ions are arranged in primitive cubes, with cesium ions occupying positions at the cube centers.

Many other structures are observed for ionic compounds. These involve similar packing arrangements as described above, but vary in number and types of occupied holes, and the distribution of ions in compounds having more than two types of cation and/or anion.

Crystal structures of molecular compounds and network solids

The molecules that make up molecular compounds may not be approximately spherical in shape. Therefore, it is difficult to make detailed generalizations for molecular compounds. They exhibit many crystal structures that are dependent on the best packing possible for a specific molecular shape.

The most common network solids are diamond, graphite, and silicates. Diamond and graphite are two crystalline forms of carbon. In diamond, each carbon atom is covalently bonded to all four of its nearest neighbors in all directions throughout the network. The resulting arrangement of atoms gives a face–centered cubic unit cell. In graphite, some of the covalent bonds are double bonds, forcing the carbon atoms into a planar arrangement of fused six–membered rings, like a chicken–wire fence. Sheets of these fused rings of carbon lie stacked upon one another.

Silicates, present in sand, clays, minerals, rocks, and gems, are the most common solid inorganic materials. In the arrays, four oxygen atoms bond to one silicon atom to give repeating tetrahedral units. Silicate units can share oxygen atoms with adjacent units, giving chain silicates, sheet silicates, and framework silicates.

Crystallinity in macromolecules

Macromolecules are giant polymer molecules made up of long chains of repeating molecular units and bonded covalently to one another. Macromolecules occur widely in nature as carbohydrates, proteins, and nucleic acids. Polymers, plastics, and rubber also are macromolecules.

Macromolecules may be likened to a plate of spaghetti, in which the individual strands of the macromolecules are entangled. Notably, there is a lack of order in this system, and a lack of crystallinity. However, a marked degree of order does exist in certain regions of these entanglements where segments of neighboring chains may be aligned, or where chain folding may promote the alignment of a chain with itself. Regions of high order in macromolecules, called crystallites, are very important to the physical and chemical properties of macromolecules. The increased forces of attraction between chains in these regions give the polymer strength, impact resistance, and resistance to chemical attack. Polymers can be subjected to some form of heat treatment followed by controlled cooling and, sometimes, stretching, in order to promote greater alignment of chains, a higher degree of crystallinity, and a consequent improvement in properties.

Crystal defects and growth of crystals

The growth and size of a crystal depends on the conditions of its formation. Temperature, pressure, the presence of impurities, etc., will affect the size and perfection of a crystal. As a crystal grows, different imperfections may occur, which can be classified as either point defects, line defects (or dislocations), and plane defects.

Point defects occur: a) if a particle site is unoccupied (a Schottky defect); b) if a particle is not in its proper site (which is vacant) but is in a space or hole (a Frenkel defect); or c) if an extra particle exists in a space or hole, with no corresponding vacancy (an anti–Schottky defect). Line defects occur: a) if an incomplete layer of particles occurs between other, complete layers (an edge dislocation); or b) if a layer of particles is not planar, but is out of alignment with itself so that the crystal grows in a spiral manner (a screw dislocation). Plane defects occur; a) if two crystallites join to form a larger crystal in which the rows and planes of the two crystallites are mismatched (a grain boundary);

TABLE 2. GEMS

Name	Composition	Impurity	Common Color	Crystal System
Diamond	carbon		colorless and other	cubic
Ruby	aluminum oxide	chromium	red	hexagonal
Sapphire	aluminum oxide	titanium, iron	blue and other	hexagonal
Emerald	beryllium-aluminum silicate	chromium	green	hexagonal
Jade	calcium-magnesium-iron silicate	iron	green and other	monoclinic
Opal	silicon oxide hydrates	(scattered light)	various	none
Topaz	aluminum fluoride-hydroxide-silicate	unknown	colorless and other	orthorhombic
Turquoise	copper-aluminum-hydroxide-phosphate	copper	blue and other	none
Zircon	zirconium silicate	iron	colorless and other	tetragonal

or b) if a layer in an ABCABC pattern occurs out of sequence (a stacking fault).

Sometimes, imperfections are introduced to crystals intentionally. For example, the conductivity of silicon and germanium can be increased by the intentional addition of arsenic or antimony impurities. This procedure is called "doping," and is used in materials, called semiconductors, that do not conduct as well as metals under normal conditions. The additional electrons provided by arsenic or antimony impurities (they have one more electrons in their outermost shells than do silicon or germanium) are the source of increased conductivity.

Experiments in decreased gravity conditions aboard the space shuttles and in Spacelab I demonstrated that proteins formed crystals rapidly, and with fewer imperfections, than is possible under regular gravitational conditions. This is important because macromolecules are difficult to crystallize, and usually will form only crystallites whose structures are difficult to analyze. Protein analysis is important because many diseases (including Acquired Immunity Deficiency Syndrome, AIDS) involve enzymes, which are the highly specialized protein catalysts of chemical reactions in living organisms. The analysis of other biomolecules may also benefit from these experiments. It is interesting that similar advantages in crystal growth and degree of perfection have also been noted with crystals grown under high gravity conditions.

Gemstones

Although the apparent perfection of gems is a major source of their attraction, the rich colors of many gemstones are due to tiny impurities of colored metal ions within the crystal structure. Table 2 lists some common gemstones and their crystalline structures.

The value and desirable properties of crystals promote scientific attempts to synthesize them. Although methods of synthesizing larger diamonds are expensive, diamond films can be made cheaply by a method called chemical vapor deposition (CVD). The technique

KEY TERMS

. . . .

Close–packing—The positioning of atoms, ions, or molecules in a crystal in such a way that the amount of vacant space is minimal.

Covalent bonds—The linking of atoms by sharing of electrons.

Diffraction—A wave–like property of light: when a ray of light passes through a tiny opening it spreads out in all directions, as though the opening is the light source.

Electrostatic attraction—The force of attraction between oppositely charged particles, as in ionic bonding.

Ionic compounds—Compounds consisting of positive ions (usually, metal ions) and negative ions (nonmetal ions) held together by electrostatic attraction.

Lattice—A pattern obtained by regular repetition of points in three dimensions.

Liquid crystal—A compound consisting of particles which are highly ordered in some directions, but not in others.

Macromolecule—A giant molecule consisting of repeating units of small molecules linked by covalent bonds.

Periodic Table—A classification of the known elements, based upon their atomic numbers (the numbers of protons in the nuclei).

Unit cell—The simplest three–dimensional repeating structure in a crystal lattice.

involves methane and hydrogen gases, a surface on which the film can deposit, and a microwave oven. Energy from microwaves breaks the bonds in the gases, and, after a series of reactions, carbon films in the form of diamond are produced. The method holds much promise for: a) the tool and cutting industry (because diamond is the hardest known substance); b) electronics applications (because diamond is a conductor of heat, but not electricity); and c) medical applications (because it is tissue–compatible and tough, making it suitable for joint replacements, heart valves, etc.).

See also Diffraction.

Further Reading:

I. Amato, *Science*, 1992, v. 258, p.736.

A. G. Cairns–Smith; Edinburgh, *The Life Puzzle*: Oliver and Boyd, 1971.

S. W. Depp and W. E. Howard, *Scientific American*, March 1993, p. 90.

C. L. Hallmark, *Lasers, the Light Fantastic*; Ch. 7; Blue Ridge Summit, PA: Tab Books Inc., 1979.

J. Lima–de–Faria, ed., *Historical Atlas of Crystallography*; Published for The International Union of Crystallography by Dordrecht: Kluwer Academic Publishers, 1990.

R. J. Ondris–Crawford, G. P. Crawford, and J. W. Doane, *The Scientific Teacher*, 1993, v. 60, p.22.

R. Pool, *Science*, 1989, v. 246, p. 580.

P. Yam, *Scientific American*, March 1993, p. 138.

Massimo D. Bezoari

Cubic equations

A cubic equation is one of the form

$$ax^3+bx^2+cx+d = 0$$

where a,b,c and d are real numbers. For example, $x^3-2x^2-5x+6 = 0$ and $x^3-3x^2+4x-2 = 0$ are cubic equations. The first one has the real solutions, or roots, -2, 1, and 3, and the second one has the real root 1 and the complex roots $1+i$ and $1-i$.

Every cubic equation has either three real roots as in our first example or one real root and a pair of (conjugate) complex roots as in our second example.

There is a formula for finding the roots of a cubic equation that is similar to the one for the quadratic equation but much more complicated. It was first used by Geronimo Cardano in 1545, even though he had obtained the formula from Niccolo Tartaglia under the promise of secrecy.

Further Reading:

Garrett Birkhoff and Saunders MacLane. *A Survey of Modern Algebra* (Fourth Edition), Macmillan Publishing Company, 1977.

Burton W. Jones. *An Introduction to Modern Algebra*. Macmillan Publishing Company, 1975.

Roy Dubisch

Cuckoos

Cuckoos, coucals, anis, malkohas, and roadrunners are approximately 127 species of birds that make up the family Cuculidae. These birds are mostly tropical in distribution, but some species also breed in the temperate zones. Many species are parasitic breeders, laying their eggs in the nests of other species of birds. Species of the cuckoo family occupy a great diversity of habitats, ranging from desert to temperate and tropical forests.

The cuckoos vary greatly in size, with the range of body length being about 6–27.5 in (16–70 cm). These birds tend to have an elongated body, a rather long neck, a long tail, rounded wings, and a stout, down–curved beak. The basal coloration of the body is generally a brown, grey, or black hue, often with barring of the underparts or a white breast. Males and females are similarly colored, but juveniles are generally different.

A large number of species in the cuckoo family are nest–parasites. Instead of constructing their own nests, these parasitic birds seek out and discover nests of other species, and then lay an egg inside. If the host is of a similar size as the parasitizing cuckoo, then several eggs may be laid in the nest, but on separate days. Only one egg is laid if the cuckoo is substantially larger than the host, as is often the case. The female cuckoo may also remove any pre–existing eggs of the host species.

The host birds commonly do not recognize the foreign egg, and incubate it as if it was their own. The host then cares for the parasitic hatchling until it fledges, and often afterwards as well. In most cases, the host species is much smaller than the parasite, and it is quite a chore to feed the voracious young cuckoo. The young cuckoo commonly hatches quite quickly and ejects the unhatched eggs of the host from the nest, or it ejects or otherwise kills the babies of the host. Once their nest is discovered by a female cuckoo, the parasitized hosts are rarely successful in raising any of their own young under these sorts of circumstances.

Male cuckoos maintain a breeding territory, largely using a loud and distinctive, often bell–like call. Interestingly, females of the nest–parasitic species of cuckoos also maintain a territory, independent of that of males of their species. In this case, the defended area involves foraging habitat for the discovery of nests of other species, rather than for access to females, as in the case of the male cuckoos.

Many species of cuckoos that breed in the temperate zones undertake a long–distance migration between their breeding and non–breeding ranges. This is true of species breeding in the Northern Hemisphere, which winter to the south, and also of species breeding in the Southern Hemisphere, which winter to the north. For example, the shining cuckoo (*Chalcites lucidus*) of temperate New Zealand migrates across open waters of the

A roadrunner.

Pacific Ocean, to winter in tropical habitats of the Bismarck Archipelago and Solomon Islands off New Guinea.

Most species in the cuckoo family feed mostly on insects and other arthropods. Some of the smaller species of cuckoos will eat the hairy caterpillars of certain types of moths and butterflies. Hairy caterpillars are often an abundant type of food, in part because they are rejected by most other types of birds, which find the hairs to be irritating and distasteful. Some of the larger species of cuckoos will also feed on lizards, snakes, small mammals, and other birds.

Species of cuckoos

The best–known species in the Cuculidae is the Eurasian cuckoo (*Cuculus canorus*), which breeds widely in forests and thickets of Europe and Asia. This species is the best–studied of the nest–parasites, laying single eggs in the nests of a wide range of smaller species. Although the egg of the Eurasian cuckoo is usually larger than those of the parasitized host, it is often colored in a closely similar way to the host species. Individual Eurasian cuckoos are known to have laid single eggs in as many as 20 nests of other species in one season. The call of the male Eurasian cuckoo is the famous, bi–syllabic: "cuck–coo," a sound that has been immortalized in literature and, of course, in cuckoo–clocks. Northern populations of this species migrate to Africa or southern Asia to spend their non–breeding season.

Two familiar cuckoos of North America are the yellow–billed cuckoo (*Coccyzus americanus*) and the black–billed cuckoo (*C. erythrophthalmus*). Both of these species breed in open woodlands and brushy habi-

KEY TERMS

. . . .

Nest–parasite—A bird that lays its eggs, usually singly, in the nests of other species. The hosts incubate the parasitic egg along with their own, and also rear the baby parasite.

Further Reading:

Harrison, C. J. O., ed. *Bird Families of the World.* New York: H.N. Abrams Pubs., 1978.

Meinzer, W. *The Roadrunner.* Austin, TX: Texas Tech University Press, 1993.

Bill Freedman

tats. The yellow–billed cuckoo ranges over almost all of the United States, southern Ontario, and northern Mexico, and winters in South America. The black–billed cuckoo ranges over southeastern North America, and winters in northwestern South America. This species is most abundant in places where there are local outbreaks of caterpillars. Both of these species build their own nests and raise their two to four babies. However, both species are occasional nest–parasites on other species, including each other.

A much larger American species is the greater roadrunner (*Geococcyx californianus*), a terrestrial bird of dry habitats in the southwestern United States and Central America. The greater roadrunner is the largest cuculid in North America. This species commonly feeds on lizards and snakes, including poisonous rattlesnakes. The greater roadrunner is not a nest–parasite. Roadrunners are fast runners, although not so fast and intelligent as the one that always gets the better of Wile E. Coyote in the famous Warner Bros. cartoons.

Two species of anis breed in North America, the smooth–billed ani (*Crotophaga ani*) of southern Florida, and the groove–billed ani (*C. sulcirostris*) of southern Texas. These species also occur widely in Central and South America, and on many Caribbean islands. Anis build communal, globular, stick–nests in trees. Each of the several cooperating pairs of anis has its own nesting chamber, and incubate their own eggs. Both parents share in the brooding of the eggs and raising of the young, although there is some degree of cooperative feeding of young birds within the commune. Anis have home ranges, but because of their communal nesting, they do not appear to defend a territory.

The coucals are relatively large birds of Africa, South and Southeast Asia, and Australasia. Rather weak flyers, coucals are skulking birds that occur near the edges of scrubby and wooded habitats. The greater coucal or crow–pheasant (*Centropus sinensis*) of southern and southeastern Asia is a large (20 in [53 cm] body length), black, widespread species. Coucals build their own large globular nest of grasses and leaves near the ground in dense vegetation. The male and female share the incubation and rearing of the three to five babies.

Cucumber see **Gourd family**

Cultural eutrophication see **Eutrophication**

Curare

Curare (pronounced cue–rah'–ree) is a general term for certain chemical substance found in different plants throughout the world's rain forests. These plants produce a harmless sap which for centuries the natives of the rain forests have refined into a deadly poison. The way of refining and delivering the poison from certain types of plants is similar for natives occupying equatorial regions from South America, Africa, and Southeast Asia. Animals are hunted with blowguns loaded with darts that have been prepared with lethal doses of the curare preparations.

The word curare is derived from *woorari*, a word of native American origin from the Amazon and Orinoco basins meaning poison. There are different plants used to produce the poisons for the tips of the darts used in hunting. The blowgun is particularly effective against arboreal animals, such as monkeys and birds. The hunters final curare preparation is composed of "curares" or poisons from various plants. Curares from these plants share the same chemical composition. They are all alkaloids. An alkaloid is an organic compound containing nitrogen and usually oxygen. They are found in seed plants and are usually colorless and bitter like codeine or morphine.

The plant *Strychnos toxifera* produces the strongest type of curare for the hunters of the rain forests. Other curare type plants, however, have been used in western medicine as anesthetics after it was discovered that curares can have non–lethal effects as skeletal muscle relaxants. Tubocurarine, an anesthetic muscle relaxant introduced into medical practice in the early 1940s contains a curare alkaloid from the chondrodendron plant family.

History

Early eighteenth and nineteenth century researchers studied the effects of curare. In 1780 Abbe Felix Fontana found that its action was not on the nerves and heart but on the ability of the voluntary muscles to respond to stimuli. In British experiments, several English researchers showed that animals injected with curare would recover if their respiration was artificially continued. Laboratory experiments were continued throughout the nineteenth century using curare to find out more about the relationship between the nervous and skeletal muscle system. In 1850 Claude Bernard using curare identified the neuromuscular junction where the curare interferes with the acceptance of the neural impulse. Earlier in that century Squire Waterton had conjectured that curare could be used in the treatment of tetanus.

The first use of curare in surgery was in 1912. A German physician and physiologist, Arthur Lawen, wrote about his use of curare in surgery on a patient. He was able to relax the patients abdominal muscles with a small amount of regular anesthesia after administering curare. In order to control the curare he also learned how to intubate (insert a tube into the patient's trachea) and then ventilate the lungs, that is add air through the tube to control breathing. His reports, which were published only in German, were ignored largely because anesthesiologists at that time had not learned the techniques of intubation and ventilation.

In 1938 Richard and Ruth Gill returned from a trip to South America to New York with a large stock of crude curare. They collected these plants from their Ecuadorian ranch for the Merck Company. At that time there was some interest in using curare for the treatment of a friend who had multiple sclerosis. Merck lost interest in the project, but some of the Gill's curare stock passed on to Squibb & Co. Early use of the drug for anesthetic purposes, however, were not successful, and interest was dropped at that time for further clinical experimentation.

Interest in curare resumed in 1939 when psychiatrists from the American midwest began to use it to treat certain categories of patients. Children with spastic disorders were injected with curare but when no long range improvement was observed, these psychiatric researchers passed it on to those who were using Metrazol, a drug that was a precursor to electroconvulsive therapy (ECT), formerly referred to as shock treatment. The curare appeared to absorb some of the intense muscle responses or seizures, thus helping to avoid seizure induced fractures to the bones. Other psychiatrists

began to experiment with the drug after its successful application to ECT.

Shortly afterwards a Canadian physician, Harold Griffith, began to prepare to use curare for surgery after he saw the positive results of its use in psychiatric patients. He first utilized curare in an operation on January 23, 1942. Then he reported on the successful use of curare as a muscle relaxant for this operation, which was an appendectomy. He administered the curare after the patient's trachea was anesthetized and intubated early in the operation. The muscles of the abdominal wall became relaxed by the curare to help in the performance of the operation. Twenty–five other patients received similar treatment, After Griffith's report of his work, the use of curare and other synthetic type curare muscle relaxants became the standard practice for surgical procedures requiring muscle relaxation.

Tubocurarine

Since 1942 there have been about fifty different relaxants used in clinical anesthesia. Tubocurarine, whose chemical structure was determined 1935, is the prototype of a muscle relaxant that still contains the alkaloid constituent of curare and produces a similar physiological effect. Another semisynthetic derivative of tubocurarine is even more potent. It is given intravenously since it is not active when taken orally.

Anesthetic muscle relaxants block nerve impulses between the junctions of the nerve and muscle. It is believed they accomplish this task preventing the acceptance of acetylcholine, which is a chemical neurotransmitter, by the muscle fiber. In addition to the main clinical use of curare is as an accessory drug in surgical anesthesia to obtain relaxation of skeletal muscle, it is also used to facilitate diagnostic procedures, such as laryngoscopy and endoscopy. It is also used in cases of tetanus and myasthenia gravis, an autoimmune disorder.

See also Muscle relaxants.

Further Reading:

Barash, Paul G., Bruce F. Cullen, and Robert K. Stoelting. *Clinical Anesthesia.* Philadelphia, Lippincott, 1992.

Dripps, Robert D., James E. Eckenhoff, and Leroy D. Vandam. *Introduction to Anesthesia.* Philadelphia: Saunders, 1988.

Gold, Mark and Michael Boyette. *Wonder Drugs: How They Work.* New York: Simon & Schuster, 1987.

Jordan P. Richman

Curie (Ci) see **Radioactivity**

Curium see **Element, transuranium**

Curlews

Curlews are large, brownish shorebirds (family Scolopacidae) with long legs and lengthy, downward curving bills, adapted for probing into sediment and soil for their food of invertebrates.

Although neither species of curlew is common, the most abundant curlews in North America are the long–billed curlew (*Numenius americanus*) and the whimbrel or Hudsonian curlew (*N. phaeopus*). The long–billed curlew breeds in wet meadows and grassy habitats in the western United States and southwestern Canada, and winters on mud flats and beaches in southern California and parts of the Gulf of Mexico. This species appears to be declining in abundance, likely as a result of the loss of its natural habitat, and possibly because of damage caused by pesticides.

The whimbrel breeds further to the north in two subarctic populations, one in coastal Alaska and northwestern Canada, and the other around the west coast of Hudson Bay. The whimbrel also breeds in northern Eurasia. The winter range of this species is very broad, ranging from the southern coastal United States to the coasts of Central and South America, and some Pacific islands.

The bristle–thighed curlew (*N. tahitiensis*) is a rare species with a total population of fewer than ten–thousand individuals. The bristle–thighed curlew breeds in montane habitat in western Alaska, and migrates directly south, to winter on widely scattered islands of the Pacific Ocean, including the Hawaiian Islands. The 4,968–5,589 mile (8,000–9,000 km) migration of this species is an extraordinary feat of non–stop flight while navigating over trackless water, in search of its scattered wintering islands.

The Eskimo curlew (*N. borealis*) is the smallest of the North American species, only 11 in (28 cm) in body length. This species was once very abundant during its migration. However, the Eskimo curlew was decimated by market hunting during the nineteenth century, and is now exceedingly rare, and on the verge of extinction. The Eskimo curlew is one of many examples of once abundant species that have become extinct or endangered as a result of uncontrolled, unscrupulous exploitation. Such tragedies represent lessons to be learned, so that similar calamities in the future can be avoided.

See also Sandpipers; Shore birds.

Currant see **Saxifrage family**

Current see **Electric current**

Currents

Currents are steady, smooth movements of water following a specific course; they proceed either in a cyclical pattern or as a continuous stream. In the Northern Hemisphere, currents generally move in a clockwise direction, while in the Southern Hemisphere, they move counterclockwise. There are three basic types of ocean currents: surface currents; currents produced by long wave movements or tides; and deep water currents. Furthermore, turbidity currents play a role in shaping underwater topography. Measured in a variety of ways, currents are responsible for absorbing solar heat and redistributing it throughout the world.

Surface currents

Perhaps the most obvious type of current, surface currents are responsible for the major surface circulation patterns in the world's oceans. They are the result of the friction caused by the movement of atmosphere over water; they owe their existence to the winds that form as a result of the warming air masses at the sea surface near the equator and in temperate areas. When wind blows across the water surface, it set the water in motion. If the wind is constant and strong enough, the currents may persist and become permanent components of the ocean's circulation pattern; if not, they may be merely temporary. Surface currents can extend to depths of about 656 ft (200 m). They circle the ocean basins on both sides of the Equator in elliptical rotations.

There are several forces that affect and sustain surface currents, including the location of land masses, wind patterns, and the Coriolis Effect. Located on either side of the major oceans (including the Atlantic, Indian, and Pacific), land masses affect currents because they act as barriers to their natural paths. Without land masses, there would be a uniform ocean movement from west to east at intermediate latitudes and from east to west near the equator and at the poles. The Antarctic Circumpolar Current can illustrate the west to east movement. Because no land barriers obstruct the prevailing current traveling between the southern tips of South America and Africa and the northern coast of Antarctica, the Antarctic Circumpolar Current consistently circles the globe in a west to east direction. Interestingly, this current is the world's greatest, flowing at one point at a rate of 9.5 billion cubic feet per second.

Other than the presence of land barriers, two other factors that work together to affect the surface currents are wind patterns and the Coriolis Effect. The basic wind patterns that drive the currents in both hemispheres are the trade and westerly winds. The Coriolis Effect is a force which displaces particles, such as water, traveling on a rotating sphere, such as the earth. Thus, currents occur as water is deflected by the turning of the earth. At the equator, the effect is nonexistent, but at greater latitudes the Coriolis effect has a stronger influence. As a result, these winds combine with the Coriolis Effect to form elliptical circulating currents, called gyres. There are two large subtropical gyres dominating each side of the equator. In the Northern Hemisphere, the gyre rotates in a clockwise direction; in the Southern Hemisphere, it rotates counterclockwise. At the lower latitudes of each hemisphere, there are smaller, tropical gyres which move in the opposite direction of the subtropical gyres.

A good illustration of a surface current is the Gulf Stream, also called the Gulf Current. This current is moved by the trade winds in the Atlantic Ocean near the equator flowing in a northwesterly direction. Moving along the coasts of South and North America, the Gulf Stream circles the entire Atlantic Ocean north of the equator. Currents similar to this exist in the Pacific Ocean and in the Atlantic south of the equator.

One of the major consequences of surface currents is their ability to help moderate the earth's temperatures. As surface currents move, they absorb heat in the tropical regions and release it in colder environments. This process is referred to as a net poleward energy transfer because it moves the solar radiation from the equator to the poles. As a result, places like Alaska and Great Britain are warmer than they otherwise would be.

Tidal currents

Tidal currents are horizontal water motions associated with the sea's changing tides. Thus, in the ocean, wave tides cause continuous currents that change direction 360 degrees every tidal cycle, which typically lasts six to twelve hours. These tides can be very strong—reaching speeds of 15 centimeters per second and moving sediment long distances—or they can be weak and slow. Of interest to swimmers, rip currents are outward–flowing tidal currents, moving in narrow paths out to sea. The flow is swift in order to balance the consistent flow of water toward the beach brought by waves. In general, tidal currents are of minimal effect beyond the continental shelf.

Deep water (or density) currents

Deep water currents move very slowly, usually around two or three centimeters per second. They dominate approximately 90% of the oceans' circulation. Water circulation of this type is called thermohaline circulation. Basically, these currents are caused by variations in water density, which is directly related to temperature and salt level, or salinity. Colder and saltier water is heavier than warmer, fresher water. Water gets denser in higher latitudes due to (1) the cooling of the atmosphere and (2) the increased salt levels which result from the freezing of surface water. (Frozen water normally contains mostly freshwater, leaving higher concentrations of salt in the water that remains liquid.) Differences in water density generate slow moving currents, due to the sinking of the colder, saltier water into deeper parts of the oceans' basins and the displacement of lighter, fresher currents.

Turbidity currents

Turbidity currents are local, rapid–moving currents which travel along the ocean floor and are responsible for shaping its landscape. These currents result from water, heavy with suspended sediment, mixing with lighter, clearer water. Causes of turbidity currents are earthquakes or when too much sediment piles up on a steep underwater slope. They can move like avalanches.

KEY TERMS

· ·

Coriolis Effect—Generically, this force affects particles traveling on a rotating sphere. As it pertains to currents, it is a deflection of water caused by the turning of the earth. At the equator, the effect is nonexistent but it gets stronger toward the poles. Water tends to swirl to the right in the Northern Hemisphere and to the left in the Southern Hemisphere.

Gyre—Typically elliptical in shape, a gyre is a surface ocean current that results from a combination of factors, including: the Coriolis effect, the earth's rotation, and surface winds.

Rip Currents—Narrow areas in the ocean where water flows rapidly out to sea. The flow is swift in order to balance the consistent flow of water toward the beach brought by waves.

Thermohaline Circulation—The flow of water caused by variations in water density rather than caused by the wind. In certain situations, colder water from the sea floor mixes upward with the warmer water. As it does this, it rotates faster, moving toward the two poles.

Turbidity Currents—Local, rapid–moving currents that result from water heavy with suspended sediment mixing with lighter, clearer water. Causes of turbidity currents are earthquakes or when too much sediment piles up on a steep underwater slope. They can move like avalanches.

Turbidity currents often obscure the visibility of the ocean floor.

Measuring currents

Oceanographers measure currents in a variety of ways using a variety of equipment, yielding results that range from crude to sophisticated. Currents can be measured directly, by clocking the water movement itself, or indirectly, by looking at some characteristic closely related to water movement. Two common direct ways to measure currents are the Lagrangian and the Eulerian methods. Lagrangian measurements monitor the movement of water by watching objects that are released into the current. These objects are monitored and recollected at a later time. Eulerian measurements look at the movement of water past a designated fixed location and usually include an anchored current meter.

See also Ocean; Oceanography; Tides

Further Reading:

Black, John A. *Oceans of Coasts, An Introduction to Oceanography.* Dubuque, Iowa: William C, Brown Publishers, 1985.

Davis, Richard A., Jr. *Oceanography, An Introduction to the Marine Environment.* Dubuque, Iowa: William C, Brown Publishers, 1991.

Duxbury, Alison B. and Alyn C. Duxbury. *Fundamentals of Oceanography.* Dubuque, Iowa: William C, Brown Publishers, 1993.

Goudie, Andrew, ed. *The Encyclopaedic Dictionary of Physical Geography.* New York: Blackwell Reference, 1985.

Groves, Donald G. and Lee M. Hunt. *Ocean World Encyclopedia.* New York: McGraw–Hill Book Company, 1980.

Hendrickson, Robert. *The Ocean Almanac.* Garden City, New York: Doubleday and Company, 1984.

Ocean Science. San Francisco: W. H. Freeman and Company, 1977.

Curve

Informally, one can picture a curve as either a line, a line segment, or a figure obtained from a line or a line segment by having the line or line segment bent, stretched, or contracted in any way. A plane curve, such as a circle, is one that lies in a plane; a curve in three dimensional space, such as one on a sphere or cylinder, is called a skew curve.

Plane curves are frequently described by equations such as y = f(x) or F(x,y) = 0. For example, y = 3x + 2 is the equation of a line through (1,5) and (2,8) and

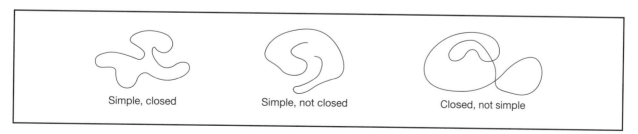

Simple, closed   Simple, not closed   Closed, not simple

Figure 1.

$x^2 + y^2 - 9 = 0$ is the equation of a circle with center at (0,0) and radius 3. Both of the curves described by the equations $y = 3x + 2$ and $x^2 + y^2 - 9 = 0$ are examples of algebraic curves. On the other hand, a curve described by an equation such as $y = \cos x$ is an example of a transcendental curve since it involves a transcendental function.

Another way of describing a curve is by means of parametric equations. For example, the parabola $y = x^2$ can be described by the parametric equations $x = t$, $y = t^2$ and the helix by $x = a \cos \theta$, $y = a \sin \theta$, $I = b\theta$.

A closed curve is a curve with no endpoints such as a circle or a figure eight. A curve that does not cross itself is a simple curve. So a circle is a simple closed curve whereas a figure eight is closed but not simple. Figure 1 shows another simple closed curve, a curve that is simple but not closed, and a curve that is closed but not simple.

Cuscuses see **Phalangers**

Cushing's syndrome

Early in the twentieth century, American surgeon Harvey Cushing described a set of symptoms that he labeled as a syndrome. At that time the cause of the syndrome remained a mystery, but since then, increased knowledge about the endocrine system in the body has led to an understanding of the underlying causes of Cushing's syndrome.

The endocrine glands are called ductless glands because they secrete their products directly into the bloodstream. The endocrine glands produce hormones that regulate various bodily functions, such as blood pressure, sugar metabolism, calcium metabolism, and gamete production, among other things. Malfunction of any of the endocrine glands can have serious consequences and may be fatal. The pituitary gland, located at the base of the brain, is the control center for the other endocrine glands. It secretes hormones that increase or cease production of hormones by other glands.

Cushing's syndrome is a condition that develops as a result of the presence of excess cortisol, a hormone produced in the adrenal gland cortex. The adrenal glands rest like limp, triangular caps atop each kidney. The adrenal cortex is the outer layer of the gland, covering the adrenal medulla. The adrenal gland produces a number of hormones, including epinephrine, also called adrenalin.

Excess cortisol secretion by the adrenal gland may result from the release of too much ACTH (adrenal corticotropic hormone) by the pituitary gland, which may be malfunctioning because of a tumor. ACTH is a hormone that causes a change in the adrenal cortex. Excess cortisol can also result from an adrenal tumor or from the medical administration of cortisone for the treatment of another condition. Certain tumors in other structures, such as the lungs, also can stimulate production of excess cortisol.

Normally the pituitary gland secretes ACTH when it is alerted to low levels of cortisol; the ACTH secretion, in turn, stimulates the adrenal cortex to secrete more cortisol. But the adrenal activity is carefully controlled to prevent overproduction of cortisol. Hormones are secreted in minute amounts because they are very potent.

Cortisol serves a number of essential functions in the body. It influences the metabolism of carbohydrates, fats, and proteins. High levels of cortisol cause sodium and water retention. Excess cortisol also can affect heart functions, muscle movements, blood cell formations, and other necessary bodily functions.

Certain tumors and other conditions can upset the balance between the pituitary gland and the adrenal gland, causing excess cortisol secretion. If the malfunctioning adrenal gland is the result of ACTH overproduction by the pituitary, the condition sometimes is referred to as Cushing's disease. If the condition exists from other causes, such as a tumor in the adrenal gland itself or the administration of cortisol doses, then it is called Cushing's syndrome.

Cushing's syndrome affects mostly females, for reasons unknown. The patient develops a rounded, moon–shaped face, a large fat pad below the neck and on the back between the shoulders—called a buffalo hump—and an accumulation of fat on the abdomen. The volume of abdominal fat develops dramatically, often hanging over the beltline. Sometimes vertical purplish stripes or striations will appear on the abdomen. Weakness and wasting away of the muscles occur. The skin bruises easily and wounds heal slow. Women develop a bone brittleness, called osteoporosis, rendering them vulnerable to fractures, especially in the pelvis and spine. The beginning stages of diabetes sometimes appear, such as glucose intolerance, but fully developed diabetes seldom develops with the syndrome. Psychiatric symptoms in the form of mood swings may appear as well. Excess hair growth often is seen in women, and high blood pressure may develop. If the syndrome occurs in children, they will cease to grow.

The first step in treatment is locating the source of the excess ACTH. It may be the pituitary, a tumor else-

Larson, D. E., ed. *Mayo Clinic Family Health Book.* New York: William Morrow and Company, Inc., 1990.

Larry Blaser

KEY TERMS

Cortisol—A hormone secreted by the adrenal gland that regulates or influences metabolism of a number of substances such as fat, protein, and water.

Endocrine—A system of glands that secrete hormones to regulate certain body functions such as growth and development of sex characteristics.

Hydrocortisone—An artificial form of cortisol that is administered medically for a number of conditions.

Syndrome—A collection of symptoms that appear together or progressively as the result of a given illness.

where in the body, the adrenal cortex itself, or a medical dosage of cortisone taken by the patient. Obviously, if the excess cortisone is coming from the medical treatment of another condition, the cortisone dose can be reduced or stopped, and the Cushing's syndrome will reverse itself.

A tumor of the pituitary gland may require surgery to remove it if other medical steps are unsuccessful. Removal of the adrenal gland is necessary if the tumor lies within it. Removal of one adrenal gland will not affect the endocrine balance since the other gland will naturally compensate. If both glands are removed, however, the patient must be given cortisol and other hormones to compensate for the lack of adrenal gland function.

An individual without an adrenal gland will not be able to react adequately in a crisis situation, however. The adrenal hormone epinephrine, or adrenalin, readies the body for fight or flight when it is faced with a dangerous situation. The pupils dilate, blood is diverted from the abdomen to the limbs, and the bladder will signal that it wants to empty itself. All of this is the result of a sudden release of epinephrine or adrenalin, a defensive mechanism.

Without treatment, Cushing's syndrome can be fatal. Medical or surgical treatment is usually effective in reversing the progression of symptoms and returning the patient to normal.

Further Reading:

Griffith, H. Winter. *Complete Guide to Symptoms, Illnesses and Surgery for People Over 50.* New York: The Body Press/Perigee, 1992.

Cuttlefish

Cuttlefish are squid–like cephalopod molluscs of the family Sepiidae, in the order Sepioidea. Cephalopod literally means "head–footed animal" and is the name given to advanced mollusks (such as cuttlefish, squid and octopus) whose heads are circled with tentacles. Cuttlefish have a relatively well developed brain, sensitive organs of smell and hearing, highly developed eyes, and a relatively advanced reproductive system.

There are more than 100 species of cuttlefish common in the warmer waters of the Mediterranean, the European Atlantic coast, and abundant in the Indian Ocean, and western Pacific. Cuttlefish are found in shallow, sandy, coastal waters, where they feed upon their usual diet of shrimp. Cuttlefish are not found in the oceans around the United States. The smallest species of cuttlefish (*Hemisepies typicus*), grows to about 3 in (7.5 cm) long, while the largest species (*Sepia latimanus*) can reach up to 5.5 ft (1.6 m) in length. The best known species of cuttlefish *Sepia officinalis*, or common cuttlefish, grows up to about 3 ft (91 cm) long, including its tentacles.

Cuttlefish have ten feet or tentacles (decapod), eight of which are short and have rows of suckers at their ends. The other two tentacles are longer and are retractable tentacles that can be used to catch prey. These tentacles have club–shaped ends with suckers, which can catch prey faster than the tongue of a lizard or frog, and can retract into sockets beside each eye. The cuttlefish mouth bears a strong beak–like structure that can bite and tear the prey, and cuttlefish salivary glands can secrete an immobilizing poison with the saliva.

The skin of a cuttlefish has pigment cells (chromatophores) that are under nervous and hormonal control, which enables the animal to become red, orange, yellow, brown or black. Cuttlefish are often colored brownish–green with white, irregular stripes that provide a perfect camouflage among seaweed. Cuttlefish also have a purple ribbon–like fin running the length of the body, and they are iridescent in sunlight. Cuttlefish can change their color and pattern at will, in a fraction of a second, a behavior which is thought to be a form of communication. They can become invisible by taking

Sepia latimanus, a cuttlefish, off Mota Island, Vanuatu.

on the colors and designs of their surrounding environment, including other cuttlefish.

The body of a cuttlefish is a flattened oval and supported by a shield shaped, internal, calcareous (calcium) shell that contains a number of tiny, gas filled chambers. The cuttlebone has a hydrostatic function–it can change the proportion of gas and liquid it contains, thus controlling its specific gravity. Cuttlebones are used in bird cages as a good source of calcium, and to help keep the bird's beak trimmed. Cuttlefish bone is also pulverized and used in polish.

These mollusks swim by undulating their side fins and by using a funnel in the mantle cavity to maintain a stationary position in the water and to propel itself backward with a great deal of speed if necessary. The cuttlefish can control the direction of the funnel, and so control the force with which the water is expelled. Another defense capability of the funnel is a brownish–black ink (called sepia) that is ejected when danger is sensed. The pigment in the ink is made of copper and iron, which are extracted from the cephalopod's blood. The sepia ink is the original India ink and is used by artists and industries as a pigment for paints, inks, and dyes.

See also Mollusks; Octopus; Squid.

Cybernetics

Cybernetics is the study of "intelligent" systems that interact with their environment, learn from their actions, and make decisions that help them to adapt to the environment, or to achieve some specified goal. These systems may be human beings, animals, machines, or organizations. The term cybernetics, derived from the Greek word meaning "to steer," was coined in 1947 by Norbert Wiener who was the first to suggest that control and communication functions may be similar in animals and machines. A simple example of a control system is a thermostat which measures the temperature of its environment and accordingly adjusts its action, of turning the heating system on or off, to maintain the desired temperature. A woman driving a car behaves as a very complicated cybernetic system as she watches the road and constantly changes the movements of her hands on the steering wheel in order to stay on track. Cybernetics is not a single discipline; it is rather a "way of reasoning" that can be applied to a variety of systems in diverse fields such as biology, engineering, and social sciences. In recent years cybernetics has been associated largely with artificial intelligence and robotics which try to duplicate some of the physical and mental functions of human beings through machines. Since this involves the control of machines through computers, cybernetics has become associated in the popular imagination with computers, giving rise to terms such as "cyberspace."

Control through feedback is one of the central ideas of cybernetics. Feedback is the information that helps people, machines or organizations to control their actions by telling them whether they are proceeding in the right direction. Students taking a course are often asked to fill out evaluation forms. This tells the instructor and the school how the course materials and teaching methods are affecting the students' learning. The school then uses this feedback to modify and improve the course. This closed loop, which involves giving a course, getting feedback, modifying the course, and giving the course again, is called a feedback loop. It helps the school to progressively improve the course and to achieve its goal of providing the students with the best possible instruction. The human being is such a complex system that the simplest action involves complicated feedback loops. A hand picking up a cup of tea is guided continually by the brain which receives feedback from the eyes and hand and decides where to grasp the cup and which path to follow in order to avoid collisions and prevent spillage. The constant temperatures and sugar levels in our bodies are maintained through feedback loops.

Although human beings and thermostats have very different degrees of control over themselves, it is the existence of some element of self–control that makes them both, and any kind of automation, cybernetic systems. The automated systems that have most fascinated people throughout history are those that recreate human behavior. In recent years, arm, hand, and leg movements of robots have achieved a very high degree of sophistication and humanness. Most fascinating of all is the attempt to duplicate the sensing and thinking processes of human beings. Robots are being taught to 'see', 'hear', 'touch', and maybe even 'taste' by chemical analysis of materials. They are being equipped with the ability to scan their memories, classify information, recognize patterns, use language, and learn from feedback. Greater sensing and thinking abilities are giving robots increasing degrees of self–control. NASA is testing a remote–controlled robot designed to explore volcanoes. This eight–legged walking robot called Dante is

equipped with a navigation system, physical and chemical sensors, laser sensing ability, and path planning ability. Similar robots, controlled from earth, could be sent into space to explore and conduct experiments. While many researchers are trying to make robots as intelligent as possible, some researchers have taken a complementary path and are exploiting the teamwork capabilities of robots that are not very smart. Bees and ants, rather than humans, are providing the biological model for these simple robots which could provide cheaper and more reliable ways of carrying out different tasks.

Although these developments are still at a very rudimentary stage, it is the stupendous increase in computational capability, along with new ways of computing, that has made this at all possible. Traditional computers faithfully follow a set of rigid instructions. New computing methods, such as neural networks, try to teach computers to learn from examples just as human beings do. Instead of being provided with a fixed set of rules, the system is allowed to recognize and generate its own set of rules based on information feedback. Knowledge–based computer programs, called *expert systems*, imitate the decision–making processes of humans using large amounts of stored information and a given set of rules used for processing that information. A variety of new intelligent systems are being created by combining knowledge–based systems with other technologies such as neural networks. Such "learning" systems constantly update their knowledge base and operating rules and are very effective in providing services, such as automated customer support, for firms with constantly evolving and changing products.

In the past few years, the concept of self–organization has become at least as important as that of control. Control focuses more on the external sensing and activity of the cybernetic system. Self–organization shifts the focus from the outside to the inside of the system. A present–day robot is a cybernetic system whose internal structure remains fixed as it senses and acts to achieve some fixed goal. A self–organizing social or biological system, on the other hand, is much more fluid and changes both its internal structure and its immediate goals in order to survive or to achieve some higher goal. Biological evolution provides some of the best examples of this kind of self–organization. During tens of thousands of years of adaptation to a hostile environment, the human brain has evolved into a massive organ, with over ten billion nerve cells, capable of coordinating the muscles and the senses through nerve fibers that transmit signals at speeds over 200 miles an hour. The principles of cybernetics are also being applied to the dynamics of social and political interaction. The new cybernetics, focused on communication

KEY TERMS

. . . .

Automatic control system—A system which incorporates some decision–making ability.

Feedback—Information that tells a system what the results of its actions are.

Artificial Intelligence (AI)—The science that attempts to imitate human intelligence with computers.

Robotics—The science that deals with the design and construction of robots.

Neural networks—A method of computation which imitates the human brain in employing parallel operations and learning by example.

Expert systems—Systems that mimic decision-making by human experts by using vast amounts of stored information and a set of rules for processing that information.

Self–organization—The changes that a system makes within itself in order to survive and adapt to the external environment.

and interactive adaptation, has great potential for helping our species survive by fostering cooperation rather than conflict in human affairs.

Since the days of Norbert Wiener, cybernetics has followed two different paths. One has led to concrete applications in robotics and artificial intelligence. The other has led to asking and answering basic questions, about perception, knowledge, thinking, language, complexity, and organization, by philosophers, mathematicians, and social scientists. Interestingly, the concrete applications have reached a level of such sophistication, that it would be very difficult for them to proceed much further without some answers to the very basic philosophical questions.

Further Reading:

Porter, Arthur. *Cybernetics Simplified.* London: The English Universities Press, 1969.

Rheingold, Howard. *Virtual Reality.* New York: Summit Books, 1991.

Rosheim, Mark E. *Robot Evolution.* New York: John Wiley & Sons, 1994.

Dane, Abe. "Robots Team Up." *Popular Mechanics* (August 1993): 88.

Freedman, David H. "The Robot Farm." *Discover* (March 1993): 24.

Sreela Datta

Cycads

The cycads are a relatively small phylum of plants (Cycadophyta) in the kingdom Plantae. The cycads are considered to be gymnosperms, because they bear their seeds naked on modified leaves called sporophylls. In contrast, the evolutionarily more advanced angiosperms (flowering plants) bear their seeds inside of ovaries. Cycads grow in tropical and subtropical regions of the world. Cycads are sometimes referred to as "living fossils" because they are very similar to extinct species that were much more abundant several hundred million years ago. The foliage of many species of cycads resembles that of palm trees, and plants in the genus *Cycas* are commonly called "Sago Palms." However, cycads are only distantly related to the palms, and their similarity is only superficial.

General characteristics

Many cycad species are shrub–sized in stature, but some species are 20–60 ft (6–18 m) tall at maturity. The cycads typically have an unbranched central stem, which is thick and scaly. Most species grow relatively slowly and have a large, terminal rosette of leaves. The leaves of most species are compound, in that they are composed of numerous small leaflets. Cycad leaves remain green for 3–10 years, so they can be considered to be "evergreen."

Many cycad species, though short in stature, have a thick tap root which can extend as much as 30–40 ft (9–12 m) beneath the soil surface. The function of the tap root is to take up water from deep beneath the surface. Cycads also produce coralloid (coral–like) roots, which grow near the surface and are associated with symbiotic cyanobacteria. In a process known as nitrogen fixation, the cyanobacteria take in atmospheric nitrogen gas (N_2) and transform it to ammonia (NH_4), a chemical form that can be used by the plant. In reciprocation, the plant provides habitat and carbohydrates to the cyanobacteria. The cycads are the only gymnosperms known to form symbiotic relationships with cyanobacteria.

There are about 200 species of cycads in the world. They are endemic to tropical and subtropical regions, and are found in Central America, South America, Africa, Asia, and Australia. The greatest richness of cycad species is in Mexico and Central America. *Zamia integrifolia* is the only species of cycad native to the United States and is found in Florida and Georgia. Several foreign cycad species are grown as ornamental plants in Florida and elsewhere in the southern United States.

A cycad in Hawaii.

The stems and seeds of most cycads are very rich in starch. In earlier times, the Seminole Indians of Florida used *Zamia* as an important food source. In particular, they dried and then ground up the starchy stem of *Zamia* to make a flour which they called "coontie." In India, the stem of another cycad, *Cycas circinalis*, is still used to make Sago flour. However, cycads are of little economic importance today, except as ornamental plants.

Life cycle

Cycads, like all seed–producing plants, have a dominant diploid sporophyte phase in their life cycle, and this is the large, familiar, green plant seen in nature. Cycads and other gymnosperms do not have true flowers and their seeds are borne naked. In the more evolutionarily advanced angiosperms (flowering plants) the seed is enveloped by a fruit which originates from the ovary.

All species of cycads are dioecious, meaning the male and female reproductive structures are borne on separate plants. The male reproductive structure, known as an androstrobilus, superficially looks like a large pine cone, though it is much simpler in structure. It consists of many densely packed, modified leaves, known as microsporophylls. Each microsporophyll produces a large quantity of pollen grains on its dorsal surface. The pollen grain is the small, multicellular, male haploid gametophyte phase of the cycad life cycle. The pollen is dispersed by wind or by insects to the gynostrobilus, or the female reproductive structure.

The gynostrobilus of cycads also looks like a large pine cone, but it has a morphology different from the androstrobilus. When a pollen grain lands on the gynostrobilus, it germinates and grows a pollen tube, a long tubular cell that extends to deep within the multicellular, female haploid gametophyte. Then a sperm cell of the pollen grain swims through the pollen tube using its whip–like tail, or flagella, and fertilizes the egg to form a zygote. The zygote eventually develops into an embryo, and then a seed. The cycad seeds are rich in starch and have a pigmented, fleshy outer layer known as the sarcotesta. The seeds are often dispersed by birds or mammals, which eat them for the nutritious sarcotesta, and later defecate the still–viable seed.

It is significant that the cycads have flagellated sperm cells, a primitive characteristic. Other evolutionarily primitive plants, such as mosses, liverworts and ferns, also have flagellated sperm cells. More evolutionarily advanced plants, such as the flowering plants, do not. In fact, other than the cycads, only one species of gymnosperm, the maidenhair tree (*Ginkgo biloba*), has flagellated sperm cells. In other gymnosperms and angiosperms, the sperm is transported directly to the female ovule by a sperm tube.

Evolution

The earliest cycad fossils are from the Permian period (about 300 million years ago). Paleobotanists believe that cycads evolved from the seed ferns, a large group of primitive, seed–bearing plants with fern–like leaves. The seed ferns originated at least 350 million years ago, and became extinct more than 200 million years ago.

Although cycads are considered to be gymnosperms because they bear naked seeds which are not enclosed by a fruit, fossil evidence suggests they are not closely related to other gymnosperms, such as the conifers. Therefore, many paleobotanists consider the gymnosperms to be an unnatural grouping of unrelated plants.

KEY TERMS

. . . .

Cyanobacteria—Photosynthetic bacteria, commonly known as blue–green alga.

Diploid—Nucleus or cell containing two copies of each chromosome, generated by fusion of two haploid nuclei.

Gametophyte—Haploid gamete–producing generation in a plant's life cycle.

Haploid—Nucleus or cell containing one copy of each chromosome.

Sporophyte—Diploid spore–producing generation in a plant's life cycle.

Sporophyll—Evolutionarily modified leaf which produces spores.

Rosette—Radial cluster of leaves, often on a short stem.

Cycads were particularly abundant and diverse during the Mesozoic era, so paleobotanists often refer to the Mesozoic as "the age of cycads." This is also the era during which dinosaurs were the dominant animals, so zoologists refer to this as "the age of dinosaurs." Consequently, museum drawings and dioramas which depict re–creations of dinosaur life typically show cycads as the dominant plants.

The cycads are no longer a dominant group of plants, and there are only about 200 extant species. The flowering plants essentially replaced the cycads more than 100 million years ago.

See also Ginkgo; Gymnosperm; Paleobotany; Seed ferns.

Further Reading:

Jones, D. C. *Cycads of the World*. Washington, DC: Smithsonian Institute Press, 1993.

Margulis, L., and K. V. Schwartz. *Five Kingdoms*. New York: W. H. Freeman and Company, 1988.

Peter A. Ensminger

Cyclamate

Cyclamate (chemical formula $C_6H_{13}NO_3S$) is an artificial, noncaloric sweetener with approximately 30 times the sweetness of ordinary table sugar. It is cur-

rently sold in more than 50 countries. In the United States, however, the Food and Drug Administration (FDA) has not allowed its sale since 1970.

University of Illinois graduate student Michael Sveda first synthesized cyclamate in 1937. Some say that he discovered its sweet taste by chance when he accidentally got some on the cigarette he was smoking. The university eventually transferred patent rights to Abbott Laboratories, which brought the sweetener to market in 1950.

Most cyclamate sales were as a 10–1 mixture with saccharin, marketed under the brand name Sucaryl®. (Since saccharin is about 10 times as sweet as cyclamate, each compound contributed roughly half the mixture's sweetening power.) The mixture was attractive because the two compounds together are sweeter and better–tasting than either alone. Cyclamate alone becomes relatively less sweet as its concentration increases—that is, raising the concentration ten–fold increases the total sweetness only six–fold. Thus, if cyclamate were used alone in very sweet products such as soft drinks, manufacturers would have to use large amounts. Besides cost, this risks development of the "off" flavors sometimes encountered at high cyclamate concentrations.

Another reason for combining saccharin with cyclamate is that the sweet taste of cyclamate develops slowly, although it lingers attractively on the tongue. On the other hand, saccharin has a bitter aftertaste that is much less noticeable in the mixture than when saccharin is used alone. Indeed, cyclamate is better than sugar at masking bitter flavors.

Unlike more recent low–calorie sweeteners, cyclamate is extremely stable. It can be used in cooking or baking and in foods of any level of acidic or basic character. Scientists have found no detectable change in Sucaryl tablets stored for seven years or more.

Regulatory controversary

Cyclamate's regulatory problems began in 1969, when a small number of rats fed very large amounts of Sucaryl for two years (virtually their entire lives) developed bladder cancer. This led the FDA to ban use of cyclamate—but not of saccharin, the mixture's other ingredient—the following year. The issue was far from settled, however. In 1973, Abbott Laboratories filed what the FDA calls a Food Additive Petition—that is, a request to allow use of cyclamate in foods. (A fine legal point is that this was the first such request for cyclamate. The law requiring FDA permission for use of food additives was not passed until 1958, so cyclamate and other additives used before that time were exempt.) This request was accompanied by a number of additional studies supporting the compound's safety. The FDA considered and debated this petition for seven years before finally rejecting it in 1980.

In 1982, Abbott Laboratories filed another Food Additive Petition, this time joined by an industry group called the Calorie Control Council. As of 1995, the FDA still has not acted. With the passage of so many years, however, the issue has become almost purely one of principle: Since the patent on cyclamate has expired, few believe Abbott Laboratories would manufacture and market the sweetener if allowed to do so. Possibly, though, another company might choose to offer it.

Does cyclamate cause cancer?

The idea that cyclamate may cause cancer rests on one study: When scientists fed 80 rats a cyclamate/saccharin mixture at a level equal to 5% of their diets, 12 of them developed bladder cancer within two years. Since then, there have been more than two dozen studies in which animals were fed similar levels of cyclamate for their entire lives; none has given any indication that the sweetener causes cancer.

As a result, the Cancer Assessment Committee of the FDA's Center for Food Safety and Applied Nutrition concluded in 1984 that, "the collective weight of the many experiments . . . indicates that cyclamate is not carcinogenic (not cancer causing)." The results of the 1969 study that led to banning of cyclamate, the committee says, "are . . . not repeatable and not explicable." The following year, the National Academy of Sciences added that, "the totality of the evidence from studies in animals does not indicate that cyclamate . . . is carcinogenic by itself." A joint committee of the World Health Organization (WHO) and the Food and Agriculture Organization (FAO) has similarly concluded that cyclamate is safe for human consumption. Unlike the two United States groups, the WHO/FAO panel addressed issues of genetic damage as well as cancer.

One of the most peculiar aspects of the entire regulatory situation is that, although the apparently incriminating study used a mixture of cyclamate and saccharin, only cyclamate was banned. We now know—although we did not in 1969—that saccharin itself produces occasional bladder cancers. So if the rats' diets did indeed cause their cancers (which some scientists doubt), most people today would assume that the saccharin was at fault.

Despite strong evidence for cyclamate's safety— the WHO/FAO committee commented, "one wonders

how may common foodstuffs would be found on such testing to be as safe as that"—future United States use of the sweetener remains uncertain on both regulatory and economic grounds. Nevertheless, many people hope that the FDA will soon clear this 25–year–old case from its docket. Whether manufacture of cyclamate will then resume remains to be seen.

Further Reading:

Lecos, Chris W. "Sweetness Minus Calories = Controversy." *FDA Consumer*. February 1985: 18–23.
Nabors, Lyn O'Brien and William T. Miller. Cyclamater–A Toxicological Review. *Comments Toxicology*, 1989.

W. A. Thomasson

Cycloalkane see **Hydrocarbon**

Cyclone and anticyclone

The terms cyclone and anticyclone are used to describe areas of low and high atmospheric pressure, respectively. Air flowing around one or the other of these areas is said to be moving cyclonically in the first case and anticyclonically in the second. In the northern hemisphere, cyclonic winds travel in a counterclockwise direction and anticyclonic winds, in a clockwise direction. When a cyclone or anticyclone is associated with a wave front, it is called a wave, a frontal, or a mid–latitude cyclone or anticyclone.

Vertical air movements are associated with both cyclones and anticyclones. In the former case, air close to the ground is forced inward, toward the center of a cyclone, where pressure is lowest, and then begins to rise upward. At some height, the rising air begins to diverge outward away from the cyclone center.

In an anticyclone, the situation is reversed. Air at the center of an anticyclone is forced away from the high pressure that occurs there and is replaced by a downward draft of air from higher altitudes. That air is replaced, in turn, by a convergence of air from higher altitudes moving into the upper region of the anticyclone.

Distinctive weather patterns tend to be associated with both cyclones and anticyclones. Cyclones and low pressure systems are generally harbingers of rain, clouds, and other forms of bad weather, while anticyclones and high pressure systems are predictors of fair weather.

One factor in the formation of cyclones and anticyclones may be the development of irregularities in a jet stream. When streams of air in the upper atmosphere begin to meander back and forth along an east–west axis, they may add to cyclonic or anticyclonic systems that already exist in the lower troposphere. As a result, relatively stable cyclones (or anticyclones) or families of cyclones (or anticyclones) may develop and travel in an easterly or northeasterly direction across the continent.

On relatively rare occasions, such storms may pick up enough energy to be destructive of property and human life. Tornadoes and possibly hurricanes are examples of such extreme conditions.

See also Atmospheric pressure; Tornado; Weather; Wind.

Cyclosporine

Cyclosporines are drugs used in the field of immunosuppressant medicine to prevent the rejection of transplanted organs. They were discovered by Jean F. Borel in 1972. The cyclosporine used for transplant surgery is called cyclosporine A (CsA) and in 1984 it was added to the group of medicines used to prevent transplant rejection. Cyclosporine A is the most common form of the Norwegian fungus *Tolypocladium inflatum.*

The discovery of cyclosporine has led to a significant rise in the number of organ transplant operations performed as well as the rate of success. Cyclosporine has increased both the short– and long–term survival rates for transplant patients, especially in heart and liver operations. The rejection of grafted tissues occurs when white blood cells (lymphocytes) called T–helper cells stimulate the activity of cell–destroying (cytotoxic) T–killer cells. It is believed that cyclosporine interferes with the signals sent by the T–helper cells to the T–killer cells. These T–cells, along with other white blood cells like monocytes and macrophages, cause the tissue rejection of the implanted organs.

Cyclosporine has proven to be the most effective medicine used to combat the body's own immune system, which is responsible for the rejection of transplanted organs. In addition to curtailing the activity of T–helper cells, cyclosporine is also able to fight the infectious illnesses that often occur after a transplant operation and can lead to death.

Cyclopsporine must be administered very carefully, since it can produce a number of toxic side effects, including kidney damage. Many clinical trials have been conducted using other drugs in combination with cyclosporine in an effort to reduce these side effects.

Immunosuppression

There are two types of immunosuppression: specific suppression and nonspecific suppression. In specific suppression, the blocking agent restricts the immune system from attacking one or a specific number of antigens (foreign substances). In nonspecific immunosuppression, the blocking agent prevents the immune system from attacking any antigen. Nonspecific immunosuppression, therefore, breaks down the ability of the body to defend itself against infections.

In the case of organ transplants, the recipient's body responds to the donor's organ tissues as if they were infecting foreign tissues. A drug that is a specific suppressing agent could block the immune system's antigenic response to the newly implanted organ. While specific suppression has been accomplished in animal transplants, it has not succeeded in human trials. So far, all the drugs used to suppress the immune system after an organ transplant are nonspecific suppressants.

In administering nonspecific immunosuppressants, a balance has to be maintained between the need for protecting the new organ from the immune system's attack (rejection) and the immune system's normal functioning, which protects the individual from infectious diseases. As time passes after the transplant operation, the body slowly begins to accept the new organ and the amount of immunosuppressant drugs can be decreased. If, however, the immunosuppressant is suddenly decreased shortly after the operation, larger doses may have to be given several years later to avoid rejection of the transplanted organ.

All the immunosuppressant drugs have side effects and individuals react to them in different ways. One strategy often used is to create a mix of the different drugs—usually azathioprine, cyclosporine, and prednisone—for the transplant patient. For example, a patient whose blood pressure is elevated by cyclosporine could take less of that drug and be introduced instead to prednisone. If an adverse reaction takes place with azathioprine, cyclosporine could replace it.

Administration

Cyclosporine can be taken either orally or by intravenous injection. While the injection reduces the amount of a dose by two–thirds, it can also produce side effects like kidney damage and other neural disturbances. As an oral preparation, it can be taken mixed

Further Reading:

Auchinloss, Hugh, Jr., et al. *Organ Transplants: A Patient's Guide.* Cambridge, Mass: H. F. Pizer, 1991.

Barrett, James T. *Textbook of Immunology.* St. Louis: Mosby, 1988.

Joneja, Janice V., and Leonard Bielory. *Understanding Allergy, Sensitivity, and Immunity.* New Brunswick: Rutgers University Press, 1990.

Sell, Stewart. *Basic Immunology.* New York: Elsevier, 1987.

Weiner, Michael A. *Maximum Immunity.* Boston: Houghton Mifflin, 1986.

Jordan P. Richman

KEY TERMS

Antigen—A protein or other substance foreign to the body's immune system.

Donor organ—An organ transplanted from one person (often a person who is recently deceased) into another.

Macrophage—A large cell in the immune system that engulfs foreign substances to dispose of them.

Organ recipient—A person into whom an organ is transplanted.

T–helper cells—Immune system cells that signal T–killer cells and macrophages to attack a foreign substance.

with other liquids or in capsules. It is most effective when taken with a meal, since the digestive process moves it toward the smaller intestine, where it is absorbed.

In order to prevent rejection, many doses of cyclosporine have to be taken, usually starting with high dosages and then reducing them over time. The size of the dose is determined by the weight of the individual. Dosages also vary from one individual to another depending on the patient's ability to withstand organ rejection. Frequent blood tests are done on the patient to monitor all the factors that go into successful drug therapy.

Another problem for transplant patients is the cost of cyclosporine; a year's supply can cost as much as $6,000. Although medical insurance and special government funds are available to pick up the cost of this drug, the expense of the medication still poses a problem for many transplant patients.

Side effects

Aside from potential damage to the kidneys, there are a number of other side effects of cyclosporine. They include elevated blood pressure, a raise in potassium levels in the blood, an increase in hair growth on certain parts of the body, a thickening of the gums, problems with liver functioning, tremors, seizures, and other neurological side effects. There is also a small risk of cancer with cyclosporine as well as with the other immunosuppressant drugs.

See also Antibody and antigen; Immune system; Transplant, surgical.

Cyclotron

A cyclotron is an early type of particle accelerator. It was designed to speed protons and ions to high velocities then release them to impact a target, yielding information about the nature of atomic particles. In contrast to the enormous particle accelerators used in particle physics today, the first cyclotron, built in 1930 by E.O. Lawrence, measured just 4.5 in (12 cm) in diameter.

Physics tells us that a charged particle moving at right angles to a magnetic field will be forced into a circular path. In a cyclotron, a pair of hollow, D–shaped pieces of metal are mounted above a powerful electromagnet, with their flat sides facing one another. One of the Ds is given a negative charge and the other is given a positive charge. Now a charged particle, say a proton, is injected into this environment. With its positive charge, the proton is attracted by the negative D and repelled by the positive D, which starts it into motion toward and through the negatively charged D. Once the particle is moving, the magnetic field deflects it into a curved path, and it circles the cyclotron again and again. The charges, or polarities, of the Ds are switched at a precisely calculated frequency so that the particle is constantly getting an extra push from the electric field. As the particle gains more speed, or energy, the size of the circle it is traveling increases. At the outer edge of the Ds, it is propelled out of the cyclotron by a bending magnet and directed toward a target.

The cyclotron was a revolutionary device for its time, but the design has since been outmoded. Cyclotrons are not capable of accelerating particles to the high speeds required for today's experiments in subatomic physics. As Einstein showed us, mass is proportional to energy. When an atomic particle moves at a

Cyprinid fish see **Cave Fish**

The first successful cyclotron, built in 1930 by Ernest Lawrence at Berkeley, California. Only 12 cm in diameter, it accelerated protons to 80 keV. The protons originated from a radioactive source at the center of the cyclotron and then circled round within the hollow chamber, which was subdivided into 2 D-shaped hemispheres; as they crossed the gaps between the two Ds, they were accelerated by an electric field.

high enough speed, it has considerable energy of motion and its mass increases significantly. To continue to boost the speed of the particle at this point, the polarities of the Ds must be switched at a gradually lower frequency. A more sophisticated version of the cyclotron, the synchrocyclotron, includes the complicated electronics necessary to do this.

The most efficient method of compensating for the increased mass of high energy particles is to increase the applied magnetic field as the particle speed increases. This class of device is called a synchrotron, and includes the most powerful particle accelerators in existence today. These installations have rings more than 1.2 mi (2 km) in diameter, a far cry from Lawrence's first cyclotron, but that first 4.5 in (12 cm) ring was the start of it all.

Cypress see **Swamp cypress family**

Cystic fibrosis

Cystic fibrosis is a genetic disorder that causes a thick mucus to build up in the respiratory system and in the pancreas, a digestive organ. People with cystic fibrosis are highly susceptible to respiratory infections and are typically malnourished due to the malfunctioning of the pancreas. The disease affects about one in 2,500 people worldwide; currently 300,000 Americans are afflicted with this disease. The genetic defect that causes cystic fibrosis is most common in people of northern European descent. It is estimated that one in 25 Americans carries the gene for cystic fibrosis. No cure for cystic fibrosis exists and the disease is invariably fatal. Only 10% of people with the disease survive into their 30s. Ninety–five percent of cystic fibrosis deaths are caused by lung complications; the other 5% are due to liver failure.

Recently researchers have located the defective gene that is responsible for the majority of cystic fibrosis cases. Knowing the location of this gene makes it possible to test for carriers of the gene. This genetic discovery may lead to a genetic treatment in which a normal gene is inserted into the cells of cystic fibrosis patients. This kind of treatment, called gene therapy, is currently being tested in several research centers around the world.

The genetic basis of cystic fibrosis

Cystic fibrosis is a homozygous recessive genetic disorder. In this type of disorder two defective alleles, or copies, of the gene, one from each parent, must combine to produce the defective gene. If two people who each carry the defective allele have a child chances are one in four that the child will have cystic fibrosis.

In 1989 a team of researchers located the defective cystic fibrosis gene on the long arm of chromosome 7. Genes are segments of deoxyribonucleic acid (DNA) that code for certain proteins. If the sequence of DNA mutates in a gene the protein for which it encodes also changes. In cystic fibrosis an infinitesimal change in the DNA sequence leads to the production of a defective version of an important protein.

This protein is called the CF transmembrane conductance regulator (CFTCR) and apparently performs a crucial function in airway and pancreas cells. The protein works as a pump within the cell membrane regulating the movement of sodium and chloride (the components of salt) in and out of cells. In people with cystic fibrosis this pump does not work. As a result water is retained within the cells depriving the tissues of much–needed moisture. A dry, sticky mucus builds up in the airway and the pancreas obstructing breathing and interfering with digestive processes. The mucus also clogs sweat glands and salivary glands.

An estimated 10–15% of people with cystic fibrosis have a different genetic disorder other than the mutation found by the researchers in 1989. Some of these mutations cause a less severe disease; others cause a more severe disease. Scientists currently are searching for all the mutations linked to cystic fibrosis.

Symptoms of cystic fibrosis

Most of the symptoms of cystic fibrosis are related to the sticky mucus that clogs the lungs and pancreas. People with cystic fibrosis have trouble breathing and are highly susceptible to bacterial infections of the lungs. Normally bacteria are expelled from the lungs by coughing and the movement of thin mucus up the airways to the throat where the bacteria are expelled. But in people with cystic fibrosis the mucus is too thick to be moved and bacteria are able to inhabit the lungs and cause infection. Children with cystic fibrosis often become infected with bacteria such as *Streptococcus pneumoniae, Hemophilus pneumoniae,* and *Staphylococcus aeureus.* Adults are most susceptible to *Pseudomonas aeurginosa.* A rare type of bacteria called *Pseudomonas cepacia* currently infects people with cystic fibrosis at alarming rates. *P. cepacia* causes a severe infection and hastens lung damage leading to earlier death.

In addition to lung disease people with cystic fibrosis have digestive disorders due to thick mucus that clogs the pancreas. The pancreas secretes enzymes during digestion that break food into smaller pieces so that the body can absorb nutrients. But with cystic fibrosis, this function is impaired. People with the disease are typically thin and malnourished due to malabsorption of nutrients. Liver disease and diabetes may also occur with cystic fibrosis.

The sweat of people with cystic fibrosis is typically saltier than usual due to the build–up of sodium and chloride in the fluid that bathes the cells. Testing for cystic fibrosis involves analyzing sweat for elevated levels of salt. This increase in the salt levels is not dangerous and causes no systemic effects.

Treating cystic fibrosis

Currently no definitive cure for cystic fibrosis exists. Treatment of the disease focuses on alleviating symptoms caused by the build–up of mucus.

To combat the lung infections that accompany cystic fibrosis many people with the disease periodically take courses of antibiotics as a preventive measure. Some people undergo a course of antibiotics four times a year. Mucus in the lungs also can be broken down by drugs called mucolytic agents. These agents can be taken as pills but some drugs are inhaled as aerosols.

Clearing the thick mucus from the lungs can also be accomplished by physiotherapy. Physiotherapy includes breathing exercises and percussion, the administration of blows to the back and chest to loosen the mucus. Some people with cystic fibrosis perform percussion on themselves but it is most effective when performed by someone else. In patients who can tolerate it vigorous exercise has been shown to improve fitness and well–being as it also loosens the thick secretions.

To control the malabsorption of nutrients people with cystic fibrosis take pancreatic enzymes in pill form with every meal. A diet high in fat, protein, and carbohydrates is also recommended to boost the nutrients that a cystic fibrosis sufferer receives. Multi–vitamins can also help prevent deficiencies of certain vitamins. When these methods do not result in adequate weight gain some people supplement their diets with tube feedings in which a nutrient–rich solution is infused through a tube placed in the stomach.

Gene therapy for cystic fibrosis

Researchers hope that the discovery of the gene responsible for cystic fibrosis will lead to a genetic approach to curing the disease. In gene therapy a normal gene is inserted into cells to replace the defective gene. The lung and pancreas cells are most affected by the disorder and must receive the new gene. Once inside these cells the normal gene encodes for the correct protein.

In most gene therapy experiments cells from an affected organ are removed from the body and infected with a virus that has been induced to carry the normal gene. The newly infected cells are then put back into the body. In cystic fibrosis this method has failed. Researchers are working on an approach in which the cystic fibrosis inhales the gene–carrying virus directly.

In 1994 researchers successfully transferred a virus containing the normal CFTCR gene into four cystic fibrosis patients. The patients inhaled the virus into the nasal passages and lungs. An adenovirus, the virus used to carry the gene is considered relatively harmless to human beings. Nevertheless one patient in this experiment developed viral–infection symptoms including headache, fatigue, and fever. Data are currently being collected on whether the experiment affected the mucus production in the lungs of the experimental subjects.

Before gene therapy is perfected researchers must overcome several obstacles. The most important obstacle is the use of viruses as carriers for the normal genes. Some scientists feel that using viruses is simply too dangerous especially for patients who already have a chronic debilitating disease. Furthermore the genetic material of viruses is small compared to human genetic material and thus can mutate quickly. If a virus undergoes a mutation a small chance exists that the mutation could result in an extremely dangerous disease such as cancer. In the future the genes might be transferred within liposomes, spheres consisting of a fatty–substance called lipid.

A test for the cystic fibrosis gene

Currently the test for the cystic fibrosis gene is 85% effective in detecting the gene in a person's blood, cheek scrapings, or saliva. Some researchers feel that this effectiveness rate is still too low and that testing be performed only on persons who have a familial history of cystic fibrosis. Others argue that because the test is relatively inexpensive, easy to perform, and the effectiveness rate acceptable, the test should be offered to everyone. At this time testing for the gene responsible for cystic fibrosis remains controversial.

See also Gene therapy; Genetic disorders.

Further Reading:

"Gene therapy for CF reaches Human Lungs." *Science News* 146 (3 September 1994): 149.

Johnson, Larry G. "Gene Therapy for Cystic Fibrosis." *Chest* 107 (February 1995): 775–815.

Koch, Christian and Holby Niels. "Pathogenesis of Cystic Fibrosis." *The Lancet* 3341 (24 April 1993): 1065.

Samuelson, Wayne M. "Cystic Fibrosis: A Newer Outlook." *Medicine* 74 (January 1995): 58–63.

Webb, A.K., and T.J. David. "Clinical Management of Children and Adults with Cystic Fibrosis." *British Medical Journal* 308 (12 February 1994): 459–63.

Kathleen Scogna

Cytochrome

Cytochromes are electron–transporting protein pigments concerned with cell respiration that contain an iron–containing molecule called heme, allied to that of hemoglobin. When the iron of heme accepts an electron, it changes from the oxidized ferric (Fe III) state to the reduced ferrous (Fe II) state. The oxidation of cytochromes to molecular oxygen and their subsequent reduction by oxidizable substances in the cell is the main way in which atmospheric oxygen enters into the metabolism of the cell. About 90% of all oxygen consumed is mediated by the cytochromes.

Cytochromes make up two of the three large enzyme complexes that together comprise the electron transport or respiratory chain. This chain represents the end of oxidative phosphorylation, the process by which many organisms synthesize the energy–rich molecules of adenosine triphosphate (ATP) needed for life processes.

The source of the electrons to drive the respiratory chain is from the metabolic breakdown (catabolism) of food molecules. Two major pathways of metabolism—glycolysis and the Krebs cycle—break down glucose molecules and provide the electrons for the third pathway, the respiratory chain.

Glycolysis is the preliminary process during which the 6–carbon sugar molecule glucose is split into 3–carbon products, a process that renders only a few electrons for the respiratory chain. The more efficient Krebs cycle, which uses the 2–carbon products of glycolysis as raw materials for a cyclic series of enzymatic reactions, produces many more electrons.

The electron transport chain extends from the initial electron donor, nicotinamide adenine dinucleotide (NADH), to oxygen, the final electron acceptor.

The exchange of electrons begins at the NADH dehydrogenase complex, which passes electrons to ubiquinone (coenzyme Q). Ubiquinone, in turn, passes electrons to the cytochrome b–c_1 complex, which is composed of cytochromes and iron–sulfur proteins. The last cytochrome in this complex (cytochrome c) passes electrons to the cytochrome oxidase complex, composed of both cytochromes and copper atoms. Finally, the cytochrome oxidase complex passes electrons to oxygen.

The exchange of electrons along the respiratory chain generates a gradient of protons across the membrane in which the chain is located. When the protons flow back across the membrane, they activate the enzyme ATP synthetase, which produces ATP from adenosine diphosphate (ADP).

Cells that use the respiratory chain produce most of the supply of high–energy molecules of ATP needed for life. Many bacteria do not use oxygen (i.e., they are anaerobic), and consequently lack respiratory chain enzymes. These bacteria must rely on the less efficient glycolysis to produce ATP.

Cytochromes occur in organisms as varied as bacteria, yeasts, humans, and insects. Indeed, beginning in 1925, researcher David Keilin made the first observations of cytochrome activity by studying the change in the wavelengths of light absorbed by cytochromes of flight muscles of living insects as the cytochromes underwent oxidation and reduction. He correctly postulated that these pigments underwent reduction and oxidation as they accepted electrons and then transferred them along the chain to the final electron acceptor, oxygen.

The heme group of cytochromes consists of a carbon–based ring called porphyrin, in which the iron atom is tightly bound by nitrogen atoms at each corner of a square. Related porphyrin molecules include hemoglobin, the oxygen–carrying molecule in blood, and chlorophyll, the green pigment of photosynthetic plants.

See also Adenosine triphosphate; Respiration.

Cytoplasm see **Cell**

Dams

Dams are structures which hold back water in a stream or river, thus forming a pond, lake, or reservoir behind the wall. Dams are used as flood control devices and as sources of hydrelectric power and water for crops. Of course, dams do not control all flooding. Extreme floods can, and do, overwhelm dams; however, even these extreme floods can sometimes be managed because the dam slows down the water, thus allowing people and animals a chance to escape. The dam is designed to resist the force of the water against it —the force of standing water, not a running stream.

Dam construction

There are five main types of dams: arch, buttress, earth, gravity, and rock-filled. Arch dams use arches and cantilevers to move the water. They are typically built in narrow canyons. A dome dam is similar, but its curves are on the vertical and horizontal planes, while the arch dam is only curved on the horizontal plane. In addition, dome dams are much thinner than arch dams.

A buttress dam uses the force of the water to support it. A slab of concrete is tilted at a 45° angle and has buttresses on the opposite face as the water. The water pushes down on the slab and the buttresses push up against the water. These counter forces makes sure the slab does not topple over. Because of the number of steel beams needed in construction, these dams are no longer popular—steel and labor are too expensive.

An earth dam uses the locally available supplies (gravel, sand, clay, etc.) in construction. These dams have a slope which is determined by the dam construction and materials, though it rarely is steeper than a 2:1 ratio. The slope helps the dam resist the water's pressure.

The gravity dam withstands the force of the water behind it with its weight. It accomplishes this by having

Hoover dam from downstream looking toward the east at the face of the dam. The Colorado river is in the foreground. The dam is 726 ft (221 m) high and impounds enough water in Lake Mead to cover the state of New York to one foot deep.

the profile width of the base at least two-thirds of its height. The dam wall is typically given a slight curve; this adds extra strength and watertightness. Made of cement or masonry, this type of dam is used in flood areas so the flood crest will pass over the top of the dam without causing damage. The strongest gravity dams are those whose length is at least five times the width.

Rock-filled dams are piles of rocks covered with rubble and then a facing, or covering. Often, when the lake first fills, the dam settles. If the surface is not flexible it will crack. Often a temporary facing is installed until this settling has finished.

Impact of dams

Building a dam changes the ecology of the surrounding area. While dams can help save lives, irrigate farm land, and provide hydroelectric power, the effects can also be damaging to farmers and the environment. Currently, before a dam is built a full-scale environmental impact study is completed. One of the early studies was done after the Cree of Ottawa, Canada, took Hydro-Québec (a hydroelectric power company) to court. The Cree had learned that the decaying plants in other areas where dams were built were poisoning the fish, which in turned poisoned the people eating the fish. The study took over two years and involved the Cree, Inuit, and local and federal officials.

See also Irrigation.

Further Reading:

Dunar, Andrew J., and Dennis McBride. *Building Hoover Dam: An Oral History of the Great Depression.* New York: Twayne Pub, 1993.

Keller, Edward A. *Environmental Geology.* 6th ed. New York: Macmillan Publishing Co., 1992.

Pearce, Fred. *The Dammed: Rivers, dams, and the coming world water crisis.* London: Bodley Head, 1992.

Water: The Power, Promise, and Turmoil of North America's Fresh Water. National Geographic Special Edition. November 1993.

Mara W. Cohen Ioannides

Damselflies

Damselflies are the smaller and more delicate members of the insect order Odonata, which includes the dragonflies. The damselfly suborder Zygoptera is characterized by similar fore and hind wings, which are both narrow at the base. Most damselflies can be easily distinguished from their larger and heavier dragonfly relatives in the field by their fluttering flight, and when at rest by their holding their wings up vertically or in a V-position when at rest.

Damselflies are usually found sitting on overhanging branches or other objects near water. They feed on small flying insects such as mosquitoes and gnats, which they catch in flight.

Although most damselflies are small and very slender, many have brightly colored bodies. The males are usually more colorful than the females, and often have spots or markings of vivid blue, green, or yellow.

Damselflies have a worldwide distribution. One of the larger and more conspicuous species in North America, found on shaded bushes overhanging small streams, is the black-winged damselfly (*Calopterix maculata*). The male of this species has all-black wings and a metallic-green body, whereas the female has gray wings with a small white dot (stigma) near the tip.

Damselflies mate on the wing in the same unusual fashion as dragonflies, and lay their eggs in the water. The eggs hatch into wingless larvae, called naiads, that remain on the bottom of the pond or stream. The damselflies larvae feed on smaller insect larvae and other aquatic animals. Damselfly larvae resemble dragonfly larvae except for the three leaf-like gills at the end of the body.

These beautiful, delicate animals neither sting nor bite. Indeed, damselflies help to control the disease-carrying mosquitoes and biting midges.

See also Dragonflies.

Dandelion see **Composite family**

Dandy fever see **Dengue fever**

Dark matter

Dark matter is the term astronomers use to describe material in the Universe that is non-luminous—that is, material that does not emit or reflect light and that is therefore invisible. Everything you can see when you look through a telescope is luminous. Stars, nebulae, and galaxies are examples of luminous objects. However, luminous matter appears to make up only a small fraction of all the matter in the Universe, perhaps only a few percent. The rest of the matter is cold and dark, hidden from our direct view.

Since dark matter is invisible, we can only detect it through indirect means, primarily by analyzing its effect on material we *can* see. Although dark matter does not shine, it still exerts a gravitational force on the matter around it. For example, stars in a galaxy orbit its center, and we understand very well the laws of physics that govern orbits. It is possible to obtain accurate

A composite image of a cluster of galaxies NGC 2300 (seen at optical wavelengths) and the recently discovered gas cloud (seen in x-ray emission) in which they are embedded. The cloud is considered to be strong evidence for the existence of dark matter because the gravitational pull of the cluster is not strong enough to hold it together. Some astronomers have suggested that dark matter (so-called because it does not emit detectable radiation) is preventing the cloud from dispersing into space.

velocities of stars in our Galaxy as well as in other galaxies, and often we find that the velocities of the stars are not what we expect. Something else must be out there, tugging on the stars and giving them unexpected motions. Many galaxies, including our own, appear to have massive dark "halos" of material that may account for most of their mass. If every galaxy is like this, this cold, dark matter may be the most important constituent of the universe.

What *is* dark matter? There are several possibilities. As mentioned above, galaxies may have a diffuse, dark "halo" of gas in and around them that increases their mass well beyond that which is apparent in the luminous objects in them. There may be *supermassive*

black holes at the centers of galaxies, contributing several hundred million or even a billion solar masses to the galaxy. Orbiting the stars in a galaxy may be multitudes of non-luminous *brown dwarfs*—blobs of gas not massive enough to initiate fusion reactions at their centers and thereby become stars. An intriguing possibility is that subatomic particles called *neutrinos* may have a very small mass. At present, neutrinos are thought to be massless, like photons, but it is possible that they may have a tiny mass. Neutrinos exist in vast quantities. Even if their mass is tiny, the combined mass of countless trillions of them could be a significant contributor to the mass of the universe.

Dark matter may turn out to be one or more of these possibilities, but in any event it plays a critical role in determining the fate of the universe. The most widely accepted theory regarding the origin and evolution of the universe is the Big Bang theory, which provides an elegant explanation for the well-documented expansion of the universe. The big question is whether the universe will expand forever, or whether it will eventually stop expanding and begin to contract under its own gravity, just as a ball thrown into the air will eventually stop and begin to descend. Clearly, the deciding factor is the amount of mass in the universe: the more mass there is, the stronger the overall gravity. There is a critical mass threshold above which the universe will eventually "turn around" and begin to contract (the so-called "closed" universe). Below this threshold the expansion will continue forever (the "open" universe). It turns out that the luminous material currently observed does not amount to nearly enough mass to halt the expansion. But what if there is a huge quantity of unseen mass out there, invisible but with a profound gravitational effect on the universe? The dark matter could supply the "missing gravity" necessary to halt the universe's expansion. At present, no one knows whether the universe is open or closed.

Date see **Palms**

Dating techniques

Dating techniques are procedures used by scientists to determine the age of a specimen. Relative dating methods tell only if one sample is older or younger than another; absolute dating methods provide a date in years. The latter have generally been available only for the last few decades. Many absolute dating techniques take advantage of radioactive decay, whereby a radioactive form of an element is converted into a non-radioactive product at a regular rate. Others, such as amino acid racimization and cation-ratio dating, are based on chemical changes in the organic or inorganic composition of a sample. In recent years a few of these methods have come under close scrutiny as scientists strive to develop the most accurate dating techniques possible.

Relative dating

Relative dating methods determine whether one sample is older or younger than another. They do not provide an age in years. Before the advent of absolute dating methods, nearly all dating was relative. The main relative dating method is stratigraphy.

Stratigraphy

Stratigraphy is the study of layers of rocks or the objects embedded within those layers. It is based on the assumption (which nearly always holds true) that deeper layers were deposited earlier, and thus are older, than more shallow layers. The sequential layers of rock represent sequential intervals of time. Although these unites may be sequential, they are not necessarily continuous due to erosional removal of some intervening units. The smallest of these rock units that can be matched to a specific time interval is called a bed. Beds that are related are grouped together into members, and members are grouped into formations. Stratigraphy is the principle method of relative dating, and in the early years of dating studies was virtually the only method available to scientists.

Seriation

Seriation is the ordering of objects according to their age. It is a relative dating method. In a landmark study, archaeologist James Ford used seriation to determine the chronological order of American Indian pottery styles in the Mississippi Valley. Artifact styles such as pottery types are seriated by analyzing their abundances through time. This is done by counting the number of pieces of each style of the artifact in each stratigraphic layer and then graphing the data. A layer with many pieces of a particular style will be represented by a wide band on the graph, and a layer with only a few pieces will be represented by a narrow band. The bands are arranged into battleship-shaped curves, with each style getting its own curve. The curves are then compared with one another, and from this the relative ages of the styles are determined. A limitation to this method is that it assumes that all differences in artifact styles are the result of different periods of time, and are not due to the immigration of new cultures into the area of study.

Dendrochronology is a dating technique that makes use of tree growth rings.

Faunal dating

The term faunal dating refers to the use of animal bones to determine the age of sedimentary layers or objects such as cultural artifacts embedded within those layers. Scientists can determine an approximate age for a layer by examining which species or genera of animals are buried in it. The technique works best if the animals belonged to species which evolved quickly, expanded rapidly over a large area, or suffered a mass extinction. In addition to providing rough absolute dates for specimens buried in the same stratigraphic unit as the bones, faunal analysis can also provide relative ages for objects buried above or below the fauna-encasing layers.

Pollen dating (palynology)

Each year seed-bearing plants release large numbers of pollen grains. This process results in a "rain" of pollen that falls over many types of environments. Pollen that ends up in lake beds or peat bogs is the most likely to be preserved, but pollen may also become fossilized in arid conditions if the soil is acidic or cool. Scientists can develop a pollen chronology, or calendar, by noting which species of pollen were deposited earlier in time, that is, residue in deeper sediment or rock layers, than others. The unit of the calendar is the pollen zone. A pollen zone is a period of time in which a particular species is much more abundant than any other species of the time. In most cases, this tells us about the climate of the period, because most plants only thrive in specific climatic conditions. Changes in pollen zones can also indicate changes in human activities such as massive deforestation or new types of farming. Pastures for grazing livestock are distinguishable from fields of grain, so changes in the use of the land over time are recorded in the pollen history. The dates when areas of North America were first settled by immigrants can be determined to within a few years by looking for the introduction of ragweed pollen.

Pollen zones are translated into absolute dates by the use of radiocarbon dating. In addition, pollen dating provides relative dates beyond the limits of radiocarbon (40,000 years), and can be used in some places where radiocarbon dates are unobtainable.

Absolute dating

Absolute dating is the term used to describe any dating technique that tells how old a specimen is in years. These are generally analytical methods, and are carried out in a laboratory. Absolute dates are also relative dates, in that they tell which specimens are older or younger than others. Absolute dates must agree with dates from other relative methods in order to be valid.

Amino acid racimization

This dating technique was first conducted by Hare and Mitterer in 1967, and was popular in the 1970s. It requires much less sample than radiocarbon dating, and has a longer range, extending up to a few hundred thousand years. It has been used to date coprolites (fossilized feces) as well as fossil bones and shells. These types of specimens contain proteins embedded in a network of minerals such as calcium.

Amino acid racimization is based on the principle that amino acids (except glycine, which is a very simple amino acid) exist in two mirror image forms called stereoisomers. Living organisms (with the exception of some microbes) synthesize and incorporate only the L-form into proteins. This means that the ratio of the D-form to the L-form is zero (D/L=0). When these organisms die, the L-amino acids are slowly converted into D-amino acids in a process called racimization. This occurs because protons (H^+) are removed from the amino acids by acids or bases present in the burial environment. The protons are quickly replaced, but will return to either side of the amino acid, not necessarily to the side from which they came. This may form a D-amino acid instead of an L-amino acid. The reversible reaction eventually creates equal amounts of L- and D-forms (D/L=1.0).

The rate at which the reaction occurs is different for each amino acid; in addition, it depends upon the moisture, temperature, and pH of the postmortem conditions. The higher the temperature, the faster the reaction occurs, so the cooler the burial environment, the greater the dating range. The burial conditions are not always known, however, and can be difficult to estimate. For this reason, and because some of the amino acid racimization dates have disagreed with dates achieved by other methods, the technique is no longer widely used.

Cation-ratio dating

Cation-ratio dating is used to date rock surfaces such as stone artifacts and cliff and ground drawings. It can be used to obtain dates that would be unobtainable by more conventional methods such as radiocarbon dating. Scientists use cation-ratio dating to determine how long rock surfaces have been exposed. They do this by chemically analyzing the varnish that forms on these surfaces. The varnish contains cations, which are positively-charged atoms or molecules. Different cations move throughout the environment at different rates, so the ratio of different cations to each other changes over time. Cation ratio dating relies on principle that the cation ratio ($K^+ + Ca^{2+})/Ti^{4+}$ decreases with increasing age of a sample. By calibrating these ratios with dates obtained from rocks from a similar microenvironment, a minimum age for the varnish can be determined. This technique can only be applied to rocks from desert areas, where the varnish is most stable.

Although cation-ratio dating has been widely used, recent studies suggest that it has many problems. Many of the dates obtained with this method are inaccurate due to improper chemical analyses. In addition, the varnish may not actually be stable over long periods of time. Finally, some scientists have recently suggested that the cation ratios may not even be directly related to the age of the sample.

Thermoluminescence dating

Thermoluminescence dating is very useful for determining the age of pottery. Electrons from quartz and other minerals in the pottery clay are bumped out of their normal positions (ground state) when the clay is exposed to radiation. This radiation may come from radioactive substances such as uranium that are present in the clay or burial medium, or from cosmic radiation. When the ceramic is heated to a very high temperature (over 932°F or 500°C), these electrons fall back to the ground state, emitting light in the process and resetting the "clock" to zero. The longer the exposure to the radiation, the more electrons that are bumped into an excited state, and the more light that is emitted upon heating. The process of displacing electrons begins again after the object cools. Scientists can determine how many years have passed since a ceramic was fired by heating it in the laboratory and measuring how much light is given off. Thermoluminescence dating has the advantage of covering the time interval between radiocarbon and potassium-argon dating, or 40,000-200,000 years ago. In addition, it can be used to date materials that cannot be dated with these other two methods.

Tree-ring dating

This absolute dating method is also known as dendrochronology. It is based on the fact that trees produce one growth ring each year. Narrow rings grow in cold and/or dry years, and wide rings grow in good years. The rings form a distinctive pattern, which is the same for all members in a given species and geographical area. The patterns from trees of different ages (including ancient wood) are overlapped, forming a master pattern that can be used to date timbers thousands of years old with a resolution of one year. Timbers can be used to date buildings and archaeological sites. In addition, tree rings are used to date changes in the climate such as sudden cool or dry periods. Dendrochronology has a range of 1-10,000 years or more.

Radioactive decay dating

As previously mentioned, radioactive decay refers to the process in which a radioactive form of an element is converted into a nonradioactive product at a regular rate. Radioactive decay dating is not a single method of absolute dating but instead a group of related methods for absolute dating of samples.

Potassium-argon dating

When volcanic rocks are heated to extremely high temperatures, they release any argon gas that is trapped in them. As the rocks cool, argon-40 (^{40}Ar) begins to accumulate. Argon-40 is formed in the rocks by the radioactive decay of potassium-40 (^{40}K). The amount of ^{40}Ar formed is proportional to the decay rate (half-life) of ^{40}K, which is 1.3 billion years. In other words, it

takes 1.3 billions years for half of the ^{40}K originally present to be converted into ^{40}Ar. This method is generally only applicable to rocks greater than three million years old, although with sensitive instruments rocks several hundred thousand years old may be dated. The reason such old material is required is that it takes a very long time to accumulate enough ^{40}Ar to be measured accurately. Potassium-argon dating has been used to date volcanic layers above and below fossils and artifacts in east Africa.

Radiocarbon dating

Radiocarbon is used to date charcoal, wood, and other biological materials. The range of conventional radiocarbon dating is 30,000-40,000 years, but with sensitive instrumentation this range can be extended to 70,000 years. Radiocarbon (^{14}C) is a radioactive form of the element carbon. It decays spontaneously into nitrogen-14 (^{14}N). Plants get most of their carbon from the air in the form of carbon dioxide, and animals get most of their carbon from plants (or from animals that eat plants). Atoms of ^{14}C and of a non-radioactive form of carbon, ^{12}C, are equally likely to be incorporated into living organisms—there is no discrimination. While a plant or animal is alive, the ratio ^{14}C/^{12}C in its body will be nearly the same as the ^{14}C/^{12}C ratio in the atmosphere. When the organism dies, however, its body stops incorporating new carbon. The ratio will then begin to change as the ^{14}C in the dead organism decays into ^{14}N. The rate at which this process occurs is called the half-life. This is the time required for half of the ^{14}C to decay into ^{14}N. The half-life of ^{14}C is 5730 years. Scientists can tell how many years have elapsed since an organism died by comparing the ^{14}C/^{12}C ratio in the remains with the ratio in the atmosphere. This allows us to determine how much ^{14}C has formed since the death of the organism.

A problem with radiocarbon dating is that diagenic (after death) contamination of a specimen from soil, water, etc. can add carbon to the sample and affect the measured ratios. This can lead to inaccurate dates. Another problem lies with the assumptions associated with radiocarbon dating. One assumption is that the ^{14}C/^{12}C ratio in the atmosphere is constant though time. This is not completely true. Although ^{14}C levels can be measured in tree rings and used to correct for the ^{14}C/^{12}C ratio in the atmosphere at the time the organism died, and can even used to calibrate some dates directly, radiocarbon remains a more useful relative dating technique than an absolute one.

Uranium series dating

Uranium series dating techniques rely on the fact that radioactive uranium and thorium isotopes decay into a series of unstable, radioactive "daughter" isotopes; this process continues until a stable (non-radioactive) lead isotope is formed. The daughters have relatively short half-lives ranging from a few hundred thousand years down to only a few years. The "parent" isotopes have half-lives of several thousand million years. This provides a dating range for the different uranium series of a few thousand years to 500,000 years. Uranium series have been used to date uranium-rich rocks, deep-sea sediments, shells, bones, and teeth, and to calculate the ages of ancient lake beds. The two types of uranium series dating techniques are daughter deficiency methods and daughter excess methods.

In daughter deficiency situations, the parent radioisotope is initially deposited by itself, without its daughter (the isotope into which it decays) present. Through time, the parent decays to the daughter until the two are in equilibrium (equal amounts of each). The age of the deposit may be determined by measuring how much of the daughter has formed, providing that neither isotope has entered or exited the deposit after its initial formation. Carbonates may be dated this way using, for example, the daughter/parent isotope pair protactinium-231/uranium-235 ($^{231}Pa/^{235}U$). Living mollusks and corals will only take up dissolved compounds such as isotopes of uranium, so they will contain no protactinium, which is insoluble. Protactinium-231 begins to accumulate via the decay of ^{235}U after the organism dies. Scientists can determine the age of the sample by measuring how much ^{231}Pa is present and calculating how long it would have taken that amount to form.

In the case of a daughter excess, a larger amount of the daughter is initially deposited than the parent. Non-uranium daughters such as protactinium and thorium are insoluble, and precipitate out on the bottoms of bodies of water, forming daughter excesses in these sediments. Over time, the excess daughter disappears as it is converted back into the parent, and by measuring the extent to which this has occurred, scientists can date the sample. If the radioactive daughter is an isotope of uranium, it will dissolve in water, but to a different extent than the parent; the two are said to have different solubilities. For example, ^{234}U dissolves more readily in water than its parent, ^{238}U, so lakes and oceans contain an excess of this daughter isotope. This excess is transferred to organisms such as mollusks or corals, and is the basis of $^{234}U/^{238}U$ dating.

Fission track dating

Some volcanic minerals and glasses such as obsidian contain uranium-238 (^{238}U). Over time, these substances become "scratched." The marks, called tracks, are the damage caused by the fission (splitting) of the uranium atoms. When an atom of ^{238}U splits, two "daughter" atoms rocket away from each other, leaving in their wake tracks in the material in which they are embedded. The rate at which this process occurs is proportional to the decay rate of ^{238}U. The decay rate is measured in terms of the half-life of the element, or the time it takes for half of the element to split into its daughter atoms. The half-life of ^{238}U is 4.47×10^9 years.

When the mineral or glass is heated, the tracks are erased in much the same way cut marks fade away from hard candy that is heated. This process sets the fission track clock to zero, and the number of tracks that then form are a measure of the amount of time that has passed since the heating event. Scientists are able to count the tracks in the sample with the aid of a powerful microscope. The sample must contain enough ^{238}U to create enough tracks to be counted, but not contain too much of the isotope, or there will be a jumble of tracks that cannot be distinguished for counting. One of the advantages of fission track dating is that it has an enormous dating range. Objects heated only a few decades ago may be dated if they contain relatively high levels of ^{238}U; conversely, some meteorites have been dated to over a billion years old with this method.

See also Pollen analysis; Strata.

Further Reading:

Geyh, Mebus A., and Helmut Schleicher. *Absolute Age Determination. Physical and Chemical Dating Methods and Their Application.* New York: Springer-Verlag, 1990.
Göksu, H.Y., M. Oberhofer, and D. Regulla, Eds. *Scientific Dating Methods.* Boston: Kluwer Academic Publishers, 1991.
Wagner, Günther, and Peter Van Den Haute. *Fission-Track Dating.* Boston: Kluwer Academic Publishers, 1992.

Kathryn M. C. Evans

DDT (Dichlorodiphenyl-trichloroacetic acid)

Dichlorodiphenyl-trichloroacetic acid (DDT) is a chlorinated hydrocarbon that has been widely used as an insecticide. DDT is virtually insoluble in water, but it is freely soluble in the fat of organisms. DDT is also persistent in the environment. The combination of persistence and lipid solubility means that DDT biomagnifies, occurring in organisms in preference to the non-living environment, especially in predators at the top of ecological food webs. Environmental contamination by DDT and related chemicals is a widespread problem, including the occurrence of residues in wildlife, in drinking water, and in humans. Ecological damages have included the poisoning of wildlife, especially predators.

DDT and other chlorinated hydrocarbons

Chlorinated hydrocarbons are a diverse group of synthetic compounds of carbon, hydrogen, and chlorine, used as pesticides and for other purposes. DDT is a particular chlorinated hydrocarbon with the formula 2,2-bis-(*p*-chlorophenyl)-1,1,1-trichloroethane.

The insecticidal relatives of DDT include DDD, aldrin, dieldrin, heptachlor, and methoxychlor. DDE is a related non-insecticidal chemical but an important, persistent, metabolic-breakdown product of DDT and DDD that is accumulated in organisms. Residues of DDT and its relatives are persistent in the environment, for example, having a typical half-life of 5-10 years in soil.

A global contamination with DDT and related chlorinated hydrocarbons has resulted from the combination of their persistence and a tendency to be widely dispersed with wind-blown dusts. In addition, their selective partitioning into fats and lipids causes these chemicals to bioaccumulate. Persistence, coupled with bioaccumulation, results in the largest concentrations of these chemicals occurring in predators near or at the top of ecological food webs.

Uses of DDT

DDT was first synthesized in 1874. Its insecticidal qualities were discovered in 1939 by Paul Muller, a Swiss scientist who won a Nobel Prize in medicine in 1948 for his research on the uses of DDT. The first important use of DDT was for the control of insect vectors of human diseases during and following World War II. At about that time the use of DDT to control pests in agricultural and forestry also began.

The peak production of DDT was in 1970 when 385.9 million lbs (175 million kg) was manufactured globally. The greatest use of DDT in the United States was 79.4 million lbs (36 million kg) in 1959, but the maximum annual production was 198.5 million lbs (90 million kg) in 1964, most of which was exported. Because of the discovery of a widespread environmental contamination with DDT and its breakdown products and associated ecological damages, most industri-alized countries banned its use in the early 1970s. Use of DDT continued elsewhere, however, mostly for control of insect vectors of human and livestock diseases in less developed tropical countries. Largely because of the evolution of resistance to DDT by many pest insects, its effectiveness for these purposes has decreased. Some previously well-controlled diseases such as malaria have even become more common in a number of countries (reduced effectiveness of some of the prophylactic pharmaceuticals used to threat malaria is also importance in the resurgence of this disease). Ultimately, the remaining uses of DDT will be curtailed and it will be replaced by other insecticides, largely because of its increasing ineffectiveness.

Until its use was widely discontinued because of its non-target, ecological damages, DDT was widely used to kill insect pests of crops in agriculture and forestry and to control some human diseases that have specific insect vectors. The use of DDT for most of these pest-control purposes was generally effective. To give an indication of the effectiveness of DDT in killing insect pests, it will be sufficient to briefly describe its use to reduce the incidence of some diseases of humans.

In various parts of the world, species of insects and ticks are crucial as vectors in the transmission of disease-causing pathogens of humans, livestock, and wild animals. Malaria, for example, is a debilitating disease caused by the protozoan *Plasmodium* and spread to people by mosquitoes, *Anopheles* spp. Yellow fever and related viral diseases such as encephalitis are spread by other species of mosquitoes. The incidence of these and some other important diseases can be greatly reduced by the use of insecticides to reduce the abundance of their arthropod vectors. In the case of mosquitoes, this can be accomplished by applying DDT or another suitable insecticide to the aquatic breeding habitat, or by applying a persistent insecticide to the walls and ceilings of houses which serve as resting places for these insects. In other cases, infestations of body parasites such as the human louse can be treated by dusting people with DDT.

The use of DDT has been especially important in reducing the incidence of malaria which has always been an important disease in warmer areas of the world. Malaria is a remarkably widespread disease, affecting more than 5% of the world's population each year during the 1950s. For example, in the mid-1930s an epidemic in Sri Lanka affected one-half of the population, and 80,000 people died as a result. In Africa, an estimated two to five million children died of malaria each year during the early 1960s.

The use of DDT and some other insecticides resulted in large decreases in the incidence of malaria by greatly reducing the abundance of the mosquito vectors. India, for example, had about 100 million cases of malaria per year and 0.75 million deaths between 1933 and 1935. In 1966, however, this was reduced to only 0.15 million cases and 1,500 deaths, mostly through the use of DDT. Similarly, Sri Lanka had 2.9 million cases of malaria in 1934 and 2.8 million in 1946, but because of the effective use of DDT and other insecticides there were only 17 cases in 1963. During a vigorous campaign to control malaria in the tropics in 1962, about 130 million pounds (59 million kg) of DDT was used, as was 7.9 million pounds (3.6 million) kg of dieldrin and one million pounds (0.45 million kg) of lindane. These insecticides were mostly sprayed inside of homes and on other resting habitat of mosquitoes rather than in their aquatic breeding habitat. More recently, however, malaria has resurged in some tropical countries, largely because of the development of insecticide resistance by mosquitoes and a decreasing effectiveness of the pharmaceuticals used to treat the actual disease.

Environmental effects of the use of DDT

As is the case of many actions of environmental management, there have been both benefits and costs associated with the use of DDT. Moreover, depending on socio-economic and ecological perspectives, there are large differences in the perceptions by people of these benefits and costs. The controversy over the use of DDT and other insecticides can be illustrated by quoting two famous persons. After the successful use of DDT to prevent a potentially deadly plague of typhus among Allied troops in Naples during the Second World War, Winston Churchill praised the chemical as "that miraculous DDT powder." In stark contrast, Rachael Carson referred to DDT as the "elixir of death" in her ground-breaking book *Silent Spring*, the first public chronicle of the ecological damages caused by the use of persistent insecticides, especially DDT.

DDT was the first insecticide to which large numbers of insect pests developed resistance. This is an evolutionary process occurring because of the selection for resistant individuals that occurs when large populations are exposed to a toxic pesticide. Resistant individuals are rare in unsprayed populations, but after spraying they become dominant because the insecticide does not kill them and they survive to reproduce and pass along their genetically based tolerance. More than 450 insects and mites now have populations that are resistant to at least one insecticide. Resistance is most common in the flies (Diptera), with 156 resistant species,

including 51 resistant species of malaria-carrying mosquito, 34 of which are resistant to DDT.

As mentioned previously, the ecological effects of DDT are profoundly influenced by certain of its physical/chemical properties. First, DDT is persistent in the environment because it is not readily degraded to other chemicals by microorganisms, sunlight, or heat. Moreover, DDE is the primary breakdown product of DDT, being produced by enzymatic metabolism in organisms or by inorganic de-chlorination reactions in alkaline environments. The persistences of DDE and DDT are similar, and once released into the environment these chemicals are present for many years.

Another important characteristic of DDT is its insolubility in water, which means that it cannot be "diluted" into this ubiquitous solvent, so abundant in Earth's environments and in organisms. In contrast, DDT is highly soluble in fats and oils (together known as lipids), a characteristic shared with other chlorinated hydrocarbons. In ecosystems, most lipids occur in the tissues of living organisms. Therefore, DDT has a strong affinity for organisms because of its lipid solubility, and it tends to biomagnify tremendously. Furthermore, top predators have especially large concentrations of DDT in their fat, a phenomenon known as food-web accumulation.

In ecosystems, DDT and related chlorinated hydrocarbons occur in very small concentration in water and air. Concentrations in soil may be larger because of the presence of organic matter containing some lipids. Larger concentrations occur in organisms, but the residues in plants are smaller than in herbivores, and the largest concentrations occur in predators at the top of the food web such as humans, predatory birds, and marine mammals. For example, DDT residues were studied in an estuary on Long Island where DDT had been sprayed onto salt marshes to kill mosquitoes. The largest concentrations of DDT occurred in fish-eating birds such as ring-billed gull (76 ppm), and double-crested cormorant, red-breasted merganser, and herring gull (range of 19-26 ppm).

Lake Kariba, Zimbabwe, is a tropical example of food-web bioconcentration of DDT. Although Zimbabwe banned DDT use in agriculture in 1982, it is still used to control mosquitoes and tsetse fly (a vector of diseases of cattle and other large mammals). The concentration of DDT in water of Lake Kariba was extremely small, less than 0.002 ppb, but larger in sediment of the lake (0.4 ppm). Algae contained 2.5 ppm, and a filter-feeding mussel contained 10 ppm in its lipids. Herbivorous fish contained 2 ppm, while a bottom-feeding species of fish contained 6 ppm. The tigerfish and cormorant (a bird) feed on small fish, and these contained 5 ppm and 10 ppm, respectively. The top predator in Lake Kariba is the Nile crocodile, and it contained 34 ppm. Lake Kariba exhibits a typical pattern for DDT and related chlorinated hydrocarbons—a large bio-concentration from water, and to a lesser degree from sediment, as well as a food-web magnification from herbivores to top predators.

Global contamination with DDT

Another environmental feature of DDT is its distribution everywhere in the biosphere in at least trace concentrations. This global contamination with DDT and related chlorinated hydrocarbons such as PCBs occurs because they enter into the atmospheric cycle and thereby become very widely distributed. This results from: (1) a slow evaporation of DDT from sprayed surfaces; (2) off-target drift of DDT when it is sprayed; and (3) entrainment by strong winds of DDT-contaminated dust into the atmosphere.

This ubiquitous contamination can be illustrated by the concentrations of DDT in animals in Antarctica, very far from places where it has been used. DDT concentrations of 5 ppm occur in fat of the southern polar skua, compared with less than 1 ppm in birds lower in the food web of the Southern Ocean such as the southern fulmar and species of penguin.

Much larger concentrations of DDT and other chlorinated hydrocarbons occur in predators closer to places where the chemicals have been manufactured and used. The concentration of DDT in seals off the California coast was as much as 158 ppm in fat during the late 1960s. In the Baltic Sea of Europe residues in seals were up to 150 ppm, and off eastern Canada as much as 35 ppm occurred in seals and up to 520 ppm in porpoises.

Large residues of DDT also occur in predatory birds. Concentrations as large as 356 ppm (average of 12 ppm) occurred in bald eagles from the United States, and up to 460 ppm in western grebes, and 131 ppm in herring gulls. White-tailed eagles in the Baltic Sea have had enormous residues—as much as 36,000 ppm of DDT and 17,000 ppm PCBs in fat, and eggs with up to 1900 ppm DDT and 2600 ppm PCBs.

Ecological damages

Some poisonings were directly caused by exposure to sprays of DDT. There were numerous cases of dying or dead birds being found after spraying of DDT, for example, after its use in residential areas to kill the beetle vectors of Dutch elm disease in North America.

Spray rates for this purpose were large, about 1.5 to 2.8 lbs (0.7 to 1.4 kg) of DDT per tree, and resulted in residues in earthworms of 33-164 ppm. Birds that fed on DDT-laced invertebrates had intense exposures to DDT, and many were killed.

Sometimes, detailed investigations were needed to link declines of bird populations to the use of organochlorines. One such example occurred at Clear Lake, California, an important waterbody for recreation. Because of complaints about the nuisance of a great abundance of a non-biting aquatic insects called midges, Clear Lake was treated in 1949 with DDD at 1 kg/ha. Prior research had shown that this dose of DDD would achieve control of the midges but have no immediate effect on fish. Unfortunately, the unexpected happened. After another application of DDD in 1954, 100 western grebes were found dead as were many intoxicated birds. Eventually, the breeding population of these birds on Clear Lake decreased from about 2,000 to none by 1960. The catastrophic decline of grebes was linked to DDD when an analysis of fat of dead birds found residues as large as 1,600 ppm. Fish were also heavily contaminated. The deaths of birds on Clear Lake was one of the first well documented examples of a substantial mortality of wildlife caused by organochlorine insecticides.

Damages to birds also occurred in places remote from sprayed areas. This was especially true of raptorial (that is, predatory) birds, such as falcons, eagles, and owls. These are top predators, and they food-web accumulate chlorinated hydrocarbons to large concentrations. Declines of some species began in the early 1950s, and there were extirpations of some breeding populations. Prominent examples of predatory birds that suffered population declines from exposure to DDT and other organochlorines include the bald eagle, golden eagle, peregrine falcon, prairie falcon, osprey, brown pelican, double-crested cormorant, and European sparrowhawk, among others.

Of course, birds and other wildlife were not only exposed to DDT. Depending on circumstances, there could also be significant exposures to other chlorinated hydrocarbons, including DDD, aldrin, dieldrin, heptachlor, and PCBs. Scientists have investigated the relative importance of these chemicals in causing the declines of predatory birds. In Britain, the declines of raptors did not occur until dieldrin came into common use, and this insecticide may have been the primary cause of the damages. However, in North America DDT use was more common, and it was probably the most important cause of the bird declines.

The damage to birds was mainly caused by the effects of chlorinated hydrocarbons on reproduction and not by direct toxicity to adults. Demonstrated effects of these chemicals on reproduction include: (1) a decrease in clutch size (i.e., the number of eggs laid); (2) the production of a thin eggshell which might break under the incubating parent; (3) deaths of embryos, unhatched chicks, and nestlings; and (4) pathological parental behavior. All of these effects could decrease the numbers of young successfully raised. The reproductive pathology of chlorinated hydrocarbons caused bird populations to decrease because of inadequate recruitment.

This syndrome can be illustrated by the circumstances of the peregrine falcon, a charismatic predator whose decline attracted much attention and concern. Decreased reproductive success and declining populations of peregrines were first noticed in the early 1950s. In 1970, a North American census reported almost no successful reproduction by the eastern population of peregrines, while the arctic population was declining in abundance. Only a local population in the Queen Charlotte Islands of western Canada had normal breeding success and a stable population. This latter population is non-migratory, inhabiting a region where pesticides are not used and feeding largely on non-migratory seabirds. In contrast, the eastern peregrines bred where chlorinated-hydrocarbon pesticides were widely used, and its prey was generally contaminated. Although the arctic peregrines breed in a region where pesticides are not used, these birds winter in sprayed areas in Central and South America where their food is contaminated, and their prey of migratory ducks on the breeding grounds is also contaminated. Large residues of DDT and other organochlorines were common in peregrine falcons (except for the Queen Charlottes). Associated with those residues were eggshells thinner than the pre-DDT condition by 15-20% and a generally impaired reproduction.

In 1975, another North American survey found a virtual extirpation of the eastern peregrines, while the arctic population had declined further and was clearly in trouble. By 1985 there were only 450 pairs of arctic peregrines, compared with the former abundance of 5,000-8,000. However, as with other raptors that suffered from the effects of chlorinated hydrocarbons, a recovery of peregrine populations has begun since DDT use was banned in North America and most of Europe in the early 1970s. In 1985, arctic populations were stable or increasing compared with 1975 as were some southern populations, although they remained small. This recovery has been enhanced by a captive-breeding and release program over much of the former range of the eastern population of peregrine falcons.

It is still too soon to tell for certain, but there are encouraging signs that many of the severe effects of

KEY TERMS

Drift—Movement of sprayed pesticide by winds beyond the intended place of treatment.

Ecotoxicology—The study of the effects of toxic chemicals on organisms and ecosystems. Ecotoxicology considers both direct effects of toxic substances and also the indirect effects caused, for example, by changes in habitat structure or the abundance of food.

Vector—A mobile animal that transports a pathogen among hosts. For example, certain species of mosquito are vectors between the malaria-causing *Plasmodium* parasite and humans.

DDT and other chlorinated hydrocarbons on wildlife are becoming less severe. Hopefully, in the future these toxic damages will not be important.

See also Biomagnification.

Further Reading:

Freedman, B. *Environmental Ecology,* 2nd ed. San Diego, CA: Academic Press, 1994.
Smith, R.P. *A Primer of Environmental Toxicology.* Philadelphia, PA: Lea & Febiger, 1992.

Bill Freedman

Deafness see **Hearing disorders**

Decimal fraction

A decimal fraction is a numeral that uses the numeration system, based on ten, to represent numbers that are not necessarily whole numbers. The numeral includes a dot, called the decimal point.

The digits to the right of the decimal point extend the place-values to tenths, hundredths, thousandths, and so forth. For example, the decimal fraction 5.403 means "5 ones, 4 tenths, 0 hundredths, and 3 thousandths." The same number can also be represented by a common fraction, such as 5403/1000, or as a mixed number, 5 403/1000.

See also Fraction, common.

Deer

Deer are members of the order Artiodactyla, the even-toed ungulates, the same order that includes the antelopes, bovines, and giraffes. Deer are generally slender and long-legged, and their most striking characteristic is the presence of antlers, which are often used to differentiate species.

The deer family, Cervidae, includes about 45 species, which are divided among 17 genera and five subfamilies: the Hydropotinae, the Chinese water-deer; the Muntiacinae, the muntjacs of Asia; the Cervinae, the Eurasian deer; the Odocoleinae, the New World deer, moose, and caribou; and the Moschinae, the musk deer of China, Southeast Asia, and the Himalayas. Some taxonomists argue that the Moschinae should not be a subfamily of the Cervidae, but an entirely separate family (Moshidae), based in part on the differences between *Mochus* and other deer. Unlike other deer, *Mochus* has a gall bladder, and where the females of other species have two pairs of teats, *Mochus* it has only one pair.

Deer have short hair ranging color from yellowish to dark brown. The underbelly and throat are lighter colored, and many species have a distinctive rump patch, an area of light hair fringed with darker hair. (A startled deer will lift its tail and flash the white of its rump patch as an alarm for other deer nearby.) The head of deer is angular, with the eyes set well on the side, the ears are oblong and the nose is usually covered with soft hair. The senses of hearing and smell are excellent. Vision is less so, as far as giving the animal an accurate picture of the world around it, yet although a deer cannot accurately perceive form at distances greater than 200 ft (60 m), it can detect the slightest movement up to 990 ft (300 m) away.

Besides the flash of the rump patch, deer communicate through sound and smell, and they produce a variety of vocalizations, from the roar of the red deer to the bark of the muntjac. Deer also have scent glands near their eyes, with which they use to mark territories on branches and twigs. Dung is also used as a marker. Males will also sniff a female's urine to learn if she is in estrus.

Deer's legs are long and slender, suited for fast running to escape their many predators. Over time, the leg bones lengthened, and the weight of the animal became supported entirely on the third and fourth toes, resulting in cloven hooves. The second and fifth toes are short and positioned up, as dewclaws. The first digit has vanished and the bones of the palm (metacarpals and metatarsals) have been forged into a single bone, the cannon bone.

This evolutionary change is common among herbivores that run to escape predators, such as horses.

Deer range in size from *Pudu* (two species, standing 10-17 in (25-43 cm) at the shoulder and weighing 13-29 lbs/5.8-13.4 kg) to *Alces*, the moose, which stands 56-94 in (140-235 cm) at the shoulder and weighs 440-1,870 lbs (200-850 kg). Most species of deer have antlers (usually found on the males, but in *Rangifer*, the caribou, on both sexes). Other species, such as the Chinese water-deer and the tufted deer, have tusks. Tusked deer are generally considered to be more primitive than those with antlers, because tusks are characteristic of the primitive chevrotains, or mouse deer. More advanced species of deer are generally considered to have larger bodies, larger and more complex antlers, and a more gregarious social system.

Deer originated in Eurasia in the Oligocene, and were present in North America in the Miocene, and in South America in the Pleistocene. Perhaps the most well-known fossil species is the Irish elk (*Megaloceros gigantus*). Although not as large as the modern moose, *Megaloceros* carried a rack of antlers that had a spread of six feet and weighed more than the rest of the animal's entire skeleton. Analysis of fossil specimens suggests that it was well-suited for life in the open and able to run quickly for long distances. The common name is misleading, for *Megaloceros* was neither an elk nor exclusively Irish, although the first specimens were found in Irish peat bogs. (Long before *Megaloceros* came to the attention of science, the Irish were using its great antlers as gateposts and, in County Tyrone, even as a temporary bridge.)

Deer occur naturally throughout most of the world, with the exception of sub-Saharan Africa, Australia, and Antarctica. As an introduced species deer have thrived in Australia, New Zealand, Cuba, New Guinea, and other sites. For large herbivores, they are remarkably adaptable. Most fond of wooded areas, deer have adapted to semiaquatic habitats (the Chinese water-deer and moose), open areas (the Pampas deer of South America), and the arctic tundra (the caribou). Slowly, deer are returning to areas frequented by humans; in suburban America white-tail deer are becoming a common backyard sight, and throughout the mountains of New Hampshire and Maine roadsigns warn of moose crossing.

Deer are herbivores. Lacking upper incisors, they bite off forage by pressing their lower incisors against a callous pad on the upper gum. Their teeth have low crowns, well-suited to their diet that, depending on the species, includes twigs, leaves, aquatic plants, fruits, lichens, and grass. During hard winters, white-tail deer

A wapiti (*Cervus elaphus*), or red deer, in Yellowstone National Park, Wyoming. Wapiti is a Native American word for "white" and refers to the light colored rump of this subspecies of deer.

have been known to strip the bark from trees and eat it. Furthermore, some temperate species, such as the white-tail deer, actually alter their metabolisms during the winter, lessening their need for food and therefore decreasing the likelihood of starvation. Even in captivity these species will eat less in the winter although the amount of food available remains constant, so strong is this natural adaptation.

Like other artiodactyls, deer are ruminants with a four-chambered stomach. When food is first eaten, it is stored in the first chamber, the rumen, where bacteria begin to break it down. It is later regurgitated into the mouth and, as a cud, is chewed again and mixed with saliva. When swallowed a second time, the food bypasses the rumen and goes into the second stomach chamber, the reticulum, and then passes into the third chamber, the omasum, and then into the fourth chamber, the abomasum. Food then moves into the small intestine, where nutrients are absorbed. Although this entire process takes about eighty hours, it converts about 60% of the cellulose in the food into usable sugars and thus is remarkably effective.

Deer vary their diet depending on the available seasonal forage and their nutritional needs. Seasonal variation in the availability of food results in changes in the deer's diet. Fallow deer, for instance, eat a great deal of grass; it comprises about 60% of their diet during the summer. In the fall, there is less grass and more fruit, such as acorns, available. As the grass proportion of their diet declines, the deer turn to fruit, which at the height of fall makes up almost 40% of their food intake. The winter diet consists of browse, that is, plants such as ivy and holly.

A three-year study of moose living on Isle Royale, Michigan, determined three major limiting factors on what moose could eat to satisfy their nutritional requirements. First was the capacity of the rumen, second was the time available for feeding, and third was the need for sodium, an important nutrient that is difficult to obtain on this glacier-scrubbed island in Lake Superior. Researchers calculated that to meet their bodies' needs, the moose would have to eat particular amounts of both terrestrial plants and higher-sodium aquatic plants each day. Remarkably, the observed diet of the moose in the study matched the scientists' predictions.

Like all herbivores, deer must spend a great deal of time eating in order to obtain sufficient nutrition from their food. Studies of wild red deer in Scotland found that females without calves spent 9.8 hours foraging each summer day, while the larger males spent 10.4 hours. Lactating females with calves spent 11.08 hours per day feeding. Spending large amounts of time feeding makes deer particularly vulnerable to predators, but the tendency to herd, and the ability to eat fast and store food in the rumen, help make it less vulnerable.

In North America, predators of adult deer include brown bears, wolves, cougars, bobcats, wolverines, and packs of roving domesticated dogs, while golden eagles sometimes take young deer. In South America, deer are taken by jaguars. Eurasian deer must deal with dholes (wild dogs), tigers, and wolves. One reptilian predator, the Komodo dragon of Indonesia, depends largely on the Timor hog deer (*Cervus rusak timoensis*). Deer have long been hunted by humans as well. Other causes of death include fighting between males, automobile and train accidents, falling through ice and drowning, becoming entangled in fences or stuck in the crotches of trees when reaching high for browse, being caught in forest fires, becoming stuck in swampy areas, and falling over snow-covered banks or cliffs. Many of the deer shot by hunters escape only to die of their wounds later. Particularly harsh winters also decimate deer populations.

Deer antlers are found primarily in the males and are a social and sexual symbol as well as a weapon. The huge antlers of the Irish elk may be the result of sexual selection, whereby females consistently breed with males that have the largest antlers, and may explain has the gene for larger and larger antlers was passed down through generations until the tremendous 6 ft (1.8 m) span was reached.

Antlers differ from horns. Horns are a permanent outgrowth of the skull and are covered by a layer of keratin. Antlers, on the other hand, are grown and shed annually. They consist of a bare bony core supported on bony disks, called pedicles, that are part of the skull. There is a tremendous investment of energy in the regrowth of antlers, which regrow to be more elaborate with each year as the deer ages, adding more prongs, or "points."

Antlers are often damaged during mating-season fights, which seriously curtail a male's reproductive success. A study of red deer males with damaged antlers showed that they had less mating success than did males with intact racks. However, the experimental removal of the antlers of a dominant male showed it to be only a temporary setback; despite the loss, the male retained his status and his females.

The antlers of temperate region species of deer begin to grow during early summer. The growing antlers are covered by a thin layer of skin that is covered by short, fine hairs. Aptly called velvet, this skin nourishes the antlers with a plentiful supply of blood until they reach full growth in late summer. The blood supply ceases, and the velvet dries up. The deer rubs off the velvet to reveal fresh new—and, for a short time after shedding the velvet, gory—antlers.

Those species of deer considered to be more evolutionarily advanced are generally more gregarious, but the diet of these species may also be related to social organization. Those deer that primarily browse, such as roe deer, live in small groups or alone, for a their food is generally found only in small patches. On the other hand, caribou, who graze on lichen over large open areas, are found in large herds of several thousand animals. Such grazers may find an extra benefit in their herding behavior, with extra eyes and ears alert for predators.

Mating strategies

During the mating season for temperate species, males use one of three strategies to obtain access to receptive females. They may defend a territory that overlaps the ranges of females, as does the muntjac. They may defend a single doe against all suitors, as do the white-tail deer. Or they may attempt to assemble and hold a harem of females, as do the red deer (*Cervus elaphus*). The males and females of this gregarious species spend most of the year in single-sex herds, which generally have particular ranges. Come September, the females gather in rutting areas, and are soon joined by the males, who compete for the females through displays of roaring, spraying urine, and fighting.

Fighting begins when the challenger appears, and he and the holder of the harem roar at each other. After several minutes of vocalizing, they walk parallel to each other, tense and alert, until one of them turns toward the other and lowers his antlers. They lock antlers and begin shoving each other. When one succeeds in pushing the other backwards, the loser runs off.

The fights are dangerous. Almost a quarter of the males in a Scottish study were injured during the rut, 6% permanently. A male between ages 7-10 has the best chance of winning such an encounter, which a harem holder must face about five times during the mating season. There is another danger besides injury; young males often lurk at the fringes of a harem, waiting until the harem holder is distracted and then spiriting away a female or two. The apparent benefits of holding a harem are deceiving; although there may be as many as 20 females in the harem, the male will father only about four or five calves.

Females of tropical species of deer come into estrus several times a year. Gestation lasts from 176 days in the Chinese water-deer to 294 days in the roe deer. The female deer delivers from one to six young (six in *Hydropotes*), but one or two is the norm. The young of most deer are born spotted.

The males of the Cervinae (such as the red deer) are called stags, the females, hinds, and the young, calves. Among the Odocoileinae, the male deer are called bucks, the females does, and the young fawns—with the exception of *Alces* (moose) and *Rangifer* (caribou), where the males are bulls, the females, cows, and the young, calves.

Besides the moose, other North American species include the white-tail deer (*Odocoileus virginianus*) found from southern Canada, throughout most of the United States, Mexico, down to Bolivia and northeastern Brazil. The mule deer (*O. hemionus*), named for its large ears, ranges from the southern Yukon and Manitoba to northern Mexico. The tiny Key deer (*O. v. clavium*) is an endangered species subspecies, only about 250 remain in the western Florida Keys.

F. C. Nicholson

Deer mouse

The deer mouse (*Peromyscus maniculatus*) is a small, native rodent with an almost ubiquitous distribution in North America. The deer mouse ranges from the subarctic boreal forest, through wide areas of more southern conifer and mixed-wood forests, to drier habitats as far south as some regions of Mexico.

The deer mouse is highly variable in size and color over its range, with a range of body length of 2.8-3.9 in (7-10 cm), a tail of 1.97-5.1 in (5-13 cm), and weighing 0.63-1.2 oz (18-35 g). Many geographic variants of the deer mouse have been described as subspecies. The color of the deer mouse ranges from greyish to reddish brown, with the body being dark above and white beneath. The bicolored coat of these mice gives rise to its common name, a reference to a superficial resem-

blance to the coloration of white-tailed and mule deer (*Odocoileus* spp.). The deer mouse can be difficult to distinguish from some closely related species, such as the white-footed mouse (*P. leucopus*), another widely distributed, but more eastern species.

The deer mouse occurs in a very wide range of habitat types. This species occurs in deserts, prairies, and forests, but not in wetlands. The deer mouse is often quite tolerant of certain types of disturbance, and its populations may be little affected by light wildfires or the harvesting of trees from its habitat.

The deer mouse nests in burrows dug in the ground, or in stumps or rotting logs. This species also sometimes nests in buildings. Deer mice can climb well, and they do so regularly in certain habitats. The deer mouse is a nocturnal feeder on a wide range of nuts and seeds, and when this sort of food is abundant it is stored for leaner times, because deer mice are active all winter. Deer mice also feed on insects when they are available.

The home range of deer mice can vary from about 0.5-3 acres (0.2-1.2 hectares), but this varies with habitat quality and also over time, because the abundance of these rodents can be somewhat irruptive if food supply is unusually large. Within any year, deer mice are generally most abundant in the late autumn, and least so in the springtime. Deer mice are quite tolerant of each other, and during winter they may sleep huddled in groups to conserve heat. The typical longevity of a wild animal is two years, but deer mice can live for eight years in captivity.

Depending on latitude, the deer mouse breeds from February to November, raising as many as four litters per year of typically three to five young each. Young deer mice are capable of breeding once they are older than 5-6 weeks. Adult males often assist with rearing their progeny.

When they are abundant, deer mice are important prey for a wide range of small predators, such as snakes, owls, hawks, weasels, foxes, and other species. In this sense, deer mice and other small mammals are critical links in ecological food webs.

Deer mice are sometimes a problem in forestry, in situations where they eat large quantities of tree seeds and thereby inhibit the natural regeneration of harvested stands. However, deer mice also provide a service to forestry, by eating large numbers of potentially injurious insects, such as sawflies and budworms .

Deer mice may also be considered to be pests when they occur in homes, because they raid stored foods and may shred fabrics and furnishings to get material with which to build their nests. However, when closely viewed, deer mice prove to be inquisitive and interesting creatures. Deer mice are readily tamed, and they make lively pets.

See also Mice.

Bill Freedman

Deforestation

Strictly speaking, deforestation should refer to longer-term conversions of forest to some other type of ecosystem, such as agricultural land. Sometimes, however, deforestation is used to refer to any situation in which forests are harvested, even if another forest subsequently regenerates on the same site. Various human activities result in net losses of forest area and therefore contribute to deforestation. The most important causes of deforestation are the creation of new agricultural lands and unsustainable harvesting of trees. In recent decades, deforestation has been proceeding most rapidly in underdeveloped countries of the tropics and subtropics. The most important ecological consequences of deforestation are the depletion of the economically important forest resource, losses of biodiversity through the clearing of tropical forests, and effects on global climate through an enhancement of Earth's greenhouse effect.

Historical deforestation

Ever since the development of agriculture and settlements, humans have converted forests into agroecosystems of various sort, or into urban lands. There are numerous references in historical, religious, and anthropological literature to forests that became degraded and were then lost through overharvesting and conversion. For example, extensive forests existed in regions of the Middle East that are presently deforested. This can be evidenced by reference in the Bible to such places as the Forest of Hamath, the Wood of Ziph, and the Forest of Bethel, the modern locations of which are now desert. The cedars of Lebanon were renowned for their abundance, size, and quality for construction of buildings and ships, but today they only survive in a few endangered groves of small trees. Much of the deforestation of the Middle East occurred thousands of years ago. However, even during the Crusades of the eleventh century through the thirteenth century, extensive pine forests stretched between Jerusalem and Bethlehem, and some parts of Lebanon had cedar-dominated forests into the nineteenth century. These are all now gone.

Similar deforestations have occurred in many regions of the world, including most of the Mediterranean region, much of Europe, south Asia, much of temperate North and South America, and, increasingly, many parts of the sub-tropical and tropical world.

Deforestation today

From earliest times to the present, the global extent of deforestation has been about 12%. This loss included a 19% loss of closed forest in temperate and boreal latitudes, but only a 5% loss of tropical and subtropical forests.

However, in recent decades the dynamics of deforestation have changed greatly. The forest cover in wealthier countries at higher latitudes has been relatively stable. In fact, regions of Western Europe, the United States, and Canada have experienced an increase in forest coverage as large areas of abandoned, poorer-quality agricultural land have regenerated to forest. Although these temperate regions support large forest industries, post-harvest regeneration generally results in new forests, so that ecological conversions to agriculture and other non-forested ecosystems do not generally occur.

In contrast, the rates of deforestation in tropical regions of Latin America, Africa, and Asia have increased alarmingly in recent decades. This deforestation is driven by the rapid growth in size of the human population of these regions, with the attendant needs to create more agricultural land to provide additional food and to harvest forests as fuel. In addition, globalization of the economy has caused large areas of tropical forest to be converted to agriculture to grow crops for an export market in wealthier countries, often to the detriment of local peoples.

In 1990, the global area of forest was 4.23 billion acres (1.71 billion ha), equivalent to 91% of the forest area in 1980. This represents an annual rate of change of about -0.9% per year, which if projected into the future would result in the loss of another one-half of Earth's remaining forest in only 78 years. During this period of time deforestation (indicated as % loss per year) has been most rapid in tropical regions, especially West Africa (2.1%), Central America and Mexico (1.8%), and Southeast Asia (1.6%). Among nations, the most rapid rates of deforestation are: Ivory Coast (5.2%/year), Nepal (4.0%), Haiti (3.7%), Costa Rica (3.6%), Sri Lanka (3.5%), Malawi (3.5%), El Salvador

Deforestation in the jungle in Brazil.

(3.2%), Jamaica (3.0%), Nicaragua (2.7%), Nigeria (2.7%), and Ecuador (2.3%).

These are enormously large rates of national deforestation. A rate of forest loss of 2% per year translates into a loss of one-half of the woodland area in only 35 years, while at 3%/year the half-life is 23 years, and at 4%/year it is 18 years.

Loss of a renewable resource

Potentially, forests are a renewable natural resource that can be sustainably harvested to gain a number of economically important products, including lumber, pulp for the manufacture of paper, and fuelwood to produce energy. Forests also provide habitat for game and the great diversity of animals not hunted for sport or food. In addition, they sustain important ecological services related to clean air and water and the control of erosion.

Any net loss of forest area detracts from these important benefits and represents the depletion of an important natural resource. Forest harvesting and management can be conducted in ways that encourage the regeneration of another forest after a period of recovery. However, this does not happen in the cases of agricul-

tural conversion and some types of unsustainable forest harvesting. In such cases, the forest is "mined" rather than treated as a renewable natural resource, and its area is diminished.

Deforestation and biodiversity

At the present time, most of Earth's deforestation involves the loss of tropical forests, which are extremely rich in species. Many of the species known to occur in tropical forests have local distributions, so they are vulnerable to extinction if their habitat is lost. In addition, these forests are thought to contain millions of additional species of plants, animals, and microorganisms as yet undiscovered by scientists.

Tropical deforestation is mostly caused by various sorts of conversions, especially to subsistence agriculture, and to market agriculture for the production of export commodities. Tropical deforestation is also caused by unsustainable logging and fuelwood harvesting (about two thirds of tropical people use wood fuels as their major source of energy, particularly poorer peoples). Less important causes of tropical deforestation include hydro-electric developments that flood large reservoirs and the production of charcoal as an industrial fuel. Because these extensive conversions cause the extinction of innumerable species, tropical deforestation is the major cause of the global biodiversity crisis.

Deforestation and the greenhouse effect

Mature forests contain large quantities of organic carbon, present in the living and dead biomass of plants, and in organic matter of the forest floor and soil. The quantity of carbon in mature forests is much larger than in younger, successional forests, or in any other type of ecosystem, including human agroecosystems. Therefore, whenever a mature forest is disturbed or cleared for any purpose, it is replaced by an ecosystem containing a much smaller quantity of carbon. The difference in carbon content of the ecosystem is balanced by an emission of carbon dioxide (CO_2) to the atmosphere. This CO_2 emission always occurs, but its rate can vary. The CO_2 emission is relatively rapid, for example, if the biomass is burned, or much slower if resulting timber is used for some years and then disposed into an anaerobic landfill, where biological decomposition is very slow.

Prior to any substantial deforestation caused by human activities, Earth's vegetation stored an estimated 914 billion tons (900 billion metric tons) of carbon, of which 90% occurred in forests. Mostly because of deforestation, only about 569 billion tons (560 billion metric tons) of carbon are presently stored in Earth's vegetation, and that quantity is further diminishing with time. It has been estimated that between 1850 and 1980, CO_2 emissions associated with deforestation were approximately equal to emissions associated with the combustion of fossil fuels. Although CO_2 emissions from the use of fuels has been predominant in recent decades, continuing deforestation remains an important source of atmospheric CO_2.

The CO_2 concentration in Earth's atmosphere has increased from about 270 ppm prior to about 1850, to 355 ppm today, and it continues to increase. Many atmospheric scientists hypothesize that these larger concentrations of CO_2 will cause an increasing effectiveness of an important process, known as the greenhouse effect, that interferes with Earth's cooling. If this theory proves to be correct, then a climatic warming could result, which would have great implications for agriculture, natural ecosystems, and human civilization.

Clearly, deforestation is an important problem because of its implications for the availability of natural resources, for biodiversity, and for Earth's greenhouse effect.

See also Rain forest; Slash-and-burn agriculture.

KEY TERMS

. . . .

Conversion—A longer-term change in character of the ecosystem at some place, as when a natural forest is harvested and the land developed into an agroecosystem.

Further Reading:

Freedman, B. *Environmental Ecology,* 2nd ed. San Diego, CA Academic Press, 1994.

Ponting, C. *A Green History of the World.* Middlesex: Penguin Books, 1991.

World Resources Institute. *World Resources 1992-93.* Oxford, UK: Oxford University Press, 1992.

Bill Freedman

Degree

The word "degree" as used in algebra refers to a property of polynomials. The degree of a polynomial in one variable (a monomial), such as $5x^3$, is the exponent, 3, of the variable. The degree of a monomial involving more than one variable, such as $3x^2y$, is the sum of the exponents; in this case, $2 + 1 = 3$. The degree of a polynomial with more than one term is the highest degree among its monomial terms. Thus the degree of $5 x^2y + 7 x^3y^2z^2 + 8x^4y$ is $3 + 2 + 2 = 7$.

The degree of a polynomial equation is the highest degree among its terms. Thus the degree of the equation $5x^3 - 3x^2 = x + 1$ is 3.

See also Algebra; Polynomials.

Delta see **Alluvial systems**

Dementia

Dementia is a decline in a person's ability to think and learn. To distinguish true dementia from more limited difficulties due to localized brain damage, the strict medical definition requires that this decline affect at least two distinct spheres of mental activity; examples of such spheres include memory, verbal fluency, calculating ability, and understanding of time and location.

Some definitions of dementia also require that it interfere with a person's work and social life. However, this may be difficult to show when a person's work and social life is already limited, either by choice or by another mental or physical disorder. As a result, the most recent and most authoritative definition (that developed jointly by the National Institute for Neurological and Communicative Disorders and Stroke—part part of the National Institutes of Health—and the Alzheimer's Disease and Related Disorders Association) does not include this criterion. The NINCDS-ADRDA definition focuses strictly on a decline from a previously higher level of mental function.

The term dementia goes back to antiquity, but was originally used in the general sense of being "out of one's mind." Identification specifically with difficulties in thinking and learning occurred in the late eighteenth and early nineteenth centuries. Even then, however, the term was used for almost any sort of thinking, learning, or memory problem, whether temporary or permanent and without regard to cause. The most typical picture was of a young adult suffering from insanity or a disease affecting the brain.

This picture changed later in the nineteenth century, as psychiatrists (then called alienists) sought to group disorders in ways that would help reveal their causes. Temporary stupor, dementia associated with insanity, and memory problems resulting from damage to a specific area of the brain were all reclassified. The central core of what was left was then senile dementia: the substantial, progressive loss of mental function sometimes seen in older people and now recognized as resulting from one or more specific, identifiable diseases. Current definitions still recognize the existence of dementia in younger people, however.

Diagnosis

The first step in diagnosing dementia is to show that the person's ability to think and learn has in fact declined from its earlier level. His or her current ability in different spheres of mental activity can be measured by any of a variety of mental status tests. The difficulty comes in comparing these current ability levels with those at earlier times. A patient's own reports cannot be relied upon, since memory loss is typically part of dementia. Frequently, however, family members' descriptions of what the person once could do will establish that a decline has occurred. In other cases, comparison with what a person has accomplished throughout his or her life is enough to show that a decline has occurred. If neither source of information provides a clear answer, it may be necessary to readminister the mental status test several months later and compare the two results.

Is any decline, no matter how small, sufficient to establish a diagnosis of dementia? The answer is not entirely clear. Research has shown that most older people suffer a small but measurable decrease in their mental abilities. For example, one recent study followed 5,000 people, some for as many as 35 years. This study found that scores on tests of mental abilities did not change between ages 25 and 60, but declined about 10% between ages 60 and 70. More significantly, people in their late eighties had scores more than 25% below those seen earlier.

Since none of the people tested were considered demented, one might assume that these declines are normal. It is still possible, however, that some tested individuals were in the early stages of dementia; these people's results may then have pulled down the average scores for the group as a whole and created a false impression of a sizable "normal" drop in IQ. This ambiguity is particularly unfortunate because it has significant implications at the individual level: No one knows whether, if an older person's mental sharpness starts to decline, this a normal part of aging or a possible signal of approaching dementia.

Once the existence of dementia has been established, the next question is: What is causing the condition? Alzheimer's disease is by far the most common cause of dementia, especially in older adults. One recent study found that it directly caused 54% of dementias in people over 65, and may have been partially responsible for up to 12% more.

Unfortunately, there is no direct way to diagnose Alzheimer's disease in a living person; only microscopic examination of the brain after death can conclusively establish that a person had this disorder. The same is true for the second most common cause, multi-infarct dementia. Both diagnoses are made by excluding other causes of dementia.

It is particularly crucial to exclude causes for which appropriate treatment might prove helpful. Among the most common and important of these are side effects of medications an individual may be taking—for example, sleeping pills, antidepressants, certain types of high blood pressure medications, or others to which a person may be particularly sensitive. Medications are particularly likely to be responsible when the affected person is not only confused and forgetful, but also is not alert to what is going on around him or her.

Older individuals—the group most likely to suffer dementia from other causes—are particularly likely to be taking multiple drugs for their various disorders. Sometimes these drugs interact, producing side effects such as dementia that would not occur with any single drug at the same dosage. Drug side effects, including dementia, may also be more common in older people because their body's ability to eliminate the drug often declines with age. Reduced speed of elimination calls for a corresponding reduction in dosage that does not always occur.

Another common, but treatable, cause of dementia—or of what looks like dementia—is depression. Some psychiatrists refer to the slowed thinking and confusion sometimes seen in people with major depression as pseudodementia because of its psychological origin. Others believe the distinction does not reflect a meaningful difference. In any case, effective treatment of the depression will relieve the dementia it has produced.

Causes

Dementia can result from a wide variety of disorders and conditions. Some are quite rare, while others are moderately common. In some cases—measles, for example—dementia may be a rare complication of an otherwise common disease; in other cases, such as infection with Human Immunodeficiency Virus (HIV), an impact on mental function well known to medical specialists may not be widely recognized by the general public.

Non-Alzheimer degenerative dementias

In addition to Alzheimer's disease, dementia may result from several other conditions characterized by progressive degeneration of the brain. The three most common of these are Pick's disease, Parkinson's disease, and Huntington's disease (Huntington's chorea).

Like Alzheimer's disease, Pick's disease affects the brain's cortex—that is, the outer part where most of the higher mental functions take place. In other respects, however, the disorders are quite different. In Pick's disease, for example, microscopic examination of the brain reveals dense inclusions (Pick bodies) within the nerve cells, while the cells themselves are inflated like blown-up balloons. This does not at all resemble the neurofibrillary tangles and ß-amyloid plaques seen in Alzheimer's disease. However, since microscopic examination of a living person's brain is rare, symptoms are used to distinguish the two diseases in practice.

Typically, Pick's disease affects different parts of the cortex than does Alzheimer's disease. This influ-

ences the order in which symptoms appear. The earliest symptoms of Pick's disease include personality changes such as loss of tact and concern for others, impaired judgement, and loss of the ability to plan ahead. Loss of language skills occurs later, while memory and knowledge of such things as where one is and the time of day are preserved until near the end. In contrast, memory and time-space orientation are among the first things lost in Alzheimer's disease, while personality changes and loss of language skills are late symptoms.

Both Parkinson's disease and Huntington's chorea initially affect deeper brain structures, those concerned with motor functions (that is, movement of the voluntary muscles). Indeed, most descriptions of Parkinson's disease focus on the muscular rigidity that the disorder produces. In the later stages, however, nearly all patients with the disease will develop some degree of dementia as well.

Shortly after appearance of the choreiform movements that typify Huntington's disease, most patients will begin to have trouble thinking clearly and remembering previous events. By the time they die, Huntington patients are intellectually devastated.

Vascular dementias

Although degenerative disorders account for the majority of dementia cases, a respectable minority result from interference with blood flow in or to the brain. Most such cases are due to a series of small strokes. Each stroke in the series may be unnoticeable, but the long-term result is a continuing and eventually severe decline in mental function.

(A stroke, known technically as an *infarct*, is a failure of blood flow beyond a certain point in an artery. Usually this is due to a blood clot at that point, but sometimes it results from a break in the artery allowing much or all of the blood to escape. Although the fundamental causes are almost diametrically opposite—a clot at the wrong place versus no clot where one is needed—the effects are virtually the same.)

Unlike the degenerative dementias, which follow a relatively predictable course, vascular dementias can be quite variable. When and precisely where the next stroke occurs will determine both how quickly the dementia progresses and the extent to which different mental abilities are affected. Typically, however, vascular dementias are characterized by sudden onset, stepwise progression, and occurrence of motor symptoms early in the disorder. High blood pressure is usually present as a predisposing factor. Most, but not all, physicians believe that other heart attack risk factors, such as diabetes, cigarette smoking, and high cholesterol, also increase the risk of developing vascular dementia.

Traditionally, physicians have distinguished two major types of vascular dementia. In multiple-infarct dementia, examination of the brain after death shows a number of small but individually identifiable areas where strokes have destroyed the brain tissue. In Binswanger's disease, individual areas of destruction cannot be identified: Almost the entire "white matter" of the brain—the portion occupied primarily by axons rather than nerve cell bodies—is affected to some degree. There is no sharp line between the two disorders, however, just as there is none between multiple-infarct dementia and the effect of two or three large strokes.

Dementia may also result from a reduction in blood flow to the brain as a whole. The most common cause is a severe narrowing of the carotid arteries in the neck. This may be considered analogous to partial plugging of an automobile's fuel line, whereas the local damage resulting from a stroke is more like knocking out a piston. Most other dementias similarly represent damage to the engine itself. (Alzheimer's disease might perhaps be likened to cylinder-wall deposits causing the pistons to stick, although we do not know enough about the origin of the disease to be sure this analogy is entirely accurate.)

Infectious dementias

Many infections either attack the brain as their primary target or can spread to it. If enough brain tissue is destroyed as a result, the outcome may be dementia. Brain infections can be due to viruses, bacteria, fungi, or parasites. For example, the measles virus will occasionally attack the brain, producing a condition known as subacute sclerosing panencephalitis that causes dementia and eventually death. The herpes (cold sore) virus can also cause dementia if it attacks the brain.

Infection by mosquito-borne encephalitis viruses may leave survivors with significantly reduced mental function. The frequency with which this occurs depends, however, both on the particular virus involved and the age of the individual. Dementia is rare following infection with Western encephalitis virus, but is found in more than half those under five years of age who survive an Eastern encephalitis virus attack. Similarly, equine encephalitis virus produces severe illness, often leading to serious brain damage or death, in children under 15; in older people, however, the disease is typically quite mild and causes no lasting problems.

Nevertheless, serious viral infections of the brain are relatively uncommon. The one exception is infection with the human immunodeficiency virus (HIV)—the virus that causes AIDS (see the article "AIDS"). This is the most common infectious cause of dementia In the United States today, and the number of people affected continues to grow.

Although popular accounts of HIV infection focus on the damage it causes to the immune system, the virus also typically attacks the brain: Nearly all HIV-infected people will develop dementia at some time during their illness. However, how soon this dementia occurs and how severe it may become varies widely. About 20% of people with HIV infection develop dementia before they develop the opportunistic infections that define progression to full-blown AIDS.

Over the past half-century, antibiotics have greatly reduced the threat from bacterial infection of the brain or the meninges that surround it. In one respect, however, the situation may be said to have worsened: Formerly, 95% of those with acute bacterial meningitis died; today, most survive, but the disease often leaves them with reduced mental capacities or other central nervous system problems.

On the other hand, tuberculous meningitis—which once accounted for up to 5% of children's hospital admissions—has now been almost eliminated. There has also been a major reduction in syphilis of the central nervous system, a disease whose effects once resulted in 15-30% of mental hospital admissions. Unfortunately, both disease are undergoing resurgences: The incidence of tuberculosis has increased 20% since 1985, while estimates suggest that 50,000 undetected and untreated new cases of syphilis occur each year. In the absence of treatment, 25-30% of syphilis cases will spread to the brain or meninges and result, over the course of years, in paralysis and dementia.

Fungal infections of the brain and meninges are generally rare except in people with weakened immune systems. Parasitic infections are also rare in this country. Elsewhere, however, the well-known African sleeping sickness—spread by a type of biting fly found only in equatorial Africa—is due to a parasite known as a trypanosome. Malaria, a mosquito-born parasitic disease, may also at times attack the brain and result in dementia.

Two infectious dementias that are quite rare but of tremendous scientific interest are Creutzfeldt-Jakob disease and kuru. The probable cause of these diseases are prions, infectious agents made up of gene-lacking proteins.

Miscellaneous Causes

The dementia that can result from medication side effects or overdoses has been discussed in connection with diagnosis. Certain vitamin deficiencies may also cause dementia. The only one that is not extremely rare in developed countries, however, is Korsakoff's syndrome. This results from thiamine deficiency produced by intense, prolonged alcohol abuse. Yet another potential cause of dementia is deficiency of thyroid hormone; unlike many other dementias, this is usually reversible once adequate amounts of the hormone are available.

In yet other cases, diseases of the kidney or liver may lead to build-up of toxic materials in the blood; dementia then becomes one symptom that these materials have reached poisonous levels. Chronic hypoglycemia (low blood sugar), often due to disorders of the pancreas, may also impair mental function.

Although both head injuries and brain tumors usually affect only a single sphere of mental activity—and thus, by definition, do not produce dementia—this is not always the case. Prize fighters in particular are likely to have experienced multiple blows to the head, and as a result often suffer from a generalized dementia. Conditions such as near-drowning, in which the brain is starved of oxygen for several minutes, may also result in dementia.

Almost 3% of dementia cases are due to hydrocephalus (literally "water on the brain"; more precisely, an accumulation within the brain of abnormal amounts of cerebrospinal fluid). This usually results from an injury that makes it difficult for the fluid to reach the areas where it is supposed to be reabsorbed into the bloodstream. In the most common form, and the one most easily overlooked, pressure within the brain remains normal despite the fluid build-up. The extra fluid nevertheless distorts the shape of the brain and impairs its function. Installing shunts that allow the fluid to reach its proper place usually cures the dementia.

See also AIDS; Alzheimer's disease; Creutzfeldt-Jakob disease; Encephalitis; Huntington's chorea; Hydrocephalus; Korsakoff's syndrome; Kuru; Meningitis; Nervous system; Parkinson's disease; Prion; Stroke.

Further Reading:

Cummings, Jeffrey L., and Benson, D. Frank, eds. *Dementia: A Clinical Approach*, 2nd ed. Boston: Butterworth-Heinemann, 1992.

Kra, Siegfried J. *Aging Myths: Reversible Causes of Mind and Memory Loss.* New York: McGraw-Hill, 1985.

Mace, Nancy L., and Rabins, Peter V. *The 36-Hour Day: A Family Guide to Caring for Persons with Alzheimer's Disease, Related Dementing Illnesses, and Memory Loss in Later Life.* Baltimore: Johns Hopkins University Press, 1981.

Safford, Florence. *Caring for the Mentally Impaired Elderly: A Family Guide.* New York: Henry Holt, 1987.

KEY TERMS

Pick's disease—A degenerative brain disorder causing progressive dementia.

Vascular dementias—Loss of mental function due to a number of small, individually unnoticeable, strokes or to some other problem with the blood vessels in or supplying blood to the brain.

Whitehouse, Peter J., ed. *Dementia*. Philadelphia: F.A. Davis Company, 1993.

W. A. Thomasson

Dengue fever

Dengue, also called breakbone or dandy fever, is endemic (always present) in the tropics. It is caused by an arbovirus transmitted by the bite of a mosquito of the *aedes* genus. The term arbovirus is a derivative for arthropod borne, meaning a virus that is transmitted by an insect.

The incubation period to develop dengue is usually 5-8 days, but may be as few as 3 or as many as 15 days. Once the virus has had a sufficient incubation, the onset of the disease is sudden and dramatic. The first symptom is usually the development of sudden chills. A headache follows and the patient feels pain when he moves his eyes. Within hours he is debilitated by extreme pain in the legs and joints. Body temperature may rise to 104° F (40°C). A pale rash may appear, usually on the face, but it is transient and soon disappears.

These symptoms persist for up to 96 hours, following which there is a rapid loss of fever accompanied by profuse sweating. The patient begins to feel better for about a day, and then a second bout of fever overtakes him. This temperature rise is rapid, but peaks at a lower level than did the first episode. A rash appears on the extremities and spreads rapidly to the trunk and face. Palms of the hands and soles of the feet may turn bright red and swollen.

Individuals usually recover completely from dengue after a convalescent period of several weeks with general weakness and lack of energy.

There is no cure for dengue. Treatment is palliative, that is, intended to ease the symptoms of the disease. Aspirin is given to fight the elevated temperature. Once a patient has recovered from dengue he has immunity to it for up to a year, after which he is susceptible to getting it again.

No vaccine exists to prevent the disease. The only preventive measure that can be taken is to eradicate the aedes mosquitoes. Patients who have the disease should be kept under mosquito netting to prevent their being bitten by a mosquito which can then spread the virus.

See also Mosquitoes; Virus.

Denitrification

Denitrification is a microbial process by which fixed nitrogen is lost from soil or aquatic systems to the atmosphere. This loss occurs when bacteria convert nitrogen-containing molecules, in particular, nitrate (NO_3^-) and nitrite (NO_2^-), to gaseous nitrous oxide (N_2O) and dinitrogen (N_2).

The biology of denitrification

Respiration is a chemical process in which energy is released when electrons are passed from a donor molecule to an acceptor molecule. In addition to energy being released, the respiratory process results in the donor molecule being converted to an oxidized molecule, meaning it has lost electrons, and the acceptor molecule being converted to a reduced molecule, meaning it has gained electrons. Typically, the acceptor molecule is oxygen, but in anaerobic environments, which lack oxygen, bacteria may reduce molecules other than oxygen that have high reduction potentials or ability to accept electrons in a process known as anaerobic respiration. Denitrification occurs when bacteria reduce nitrate or nitrite by this process. In a sequence of four reductions, nitrate is converted to dinitrogen gas, the molecular form in which nitrogen escapes from soils and aquatic systems. The four-step sequence is: 1. Nitrate is reduced to nitrite. 2. Nitrite is reduced to nitric oxide. 3. Nitric oxide (NO) is reduced to nitrous oxide. 4. Nitrous oxide is reduced to dinitrogen. Depending on its physiological capabilities, a single organism may carry out all of these reductions, or it may carry out only a few.

In addition to dinitrogen, small amounts of nitrous oxide leave aquatic and soil systems. This happens because not all bacteria that produce nitrous oxide can subsequently reduce it to dinitrogen. Therefore, some nitrous oxide can leak out of cells into the atmosphere, if it is not first reduced to dinitrogen by other organisms. Nitric oxide is also a gas, but organisms that have the ability to reduce nitrite to nitric oxide always have the ability to reduce nitric oxide to nitrous oxide. For this reason, nitric oxide is not an important product of denitrification.

In aquatic and soil systems fixed nitrogen primarily exists as a component of three inorganic molecules; nitrate, nitrite, and ammonium (NH_4^+), and in the proteins and other types of organic molecules that comprise living and dead organisms. Although only nitrogen from the molecules nitrate and nitrite is converted to a gaseous form and removed from these systems, nitrogen from proteins and ammonium can also be removed if it is first oxidized to nitrate or nitrite. This conversion begins in a process termed ammonification, when nitrogen is released from the biomass dead organism's, which produces ammonium. Ammonium can then be converted to nitrate in an aerobic respiratory reaction called nitrification, in which the ammonium serves as an electron donor, and oxygen an electron acceptor.

Importance

Along with dinitrogen fixation, ammonification, and nitrification, denitrification is a major component of the nitrogen cycle. Estimates of nitrogen fluxes from terrestrial and marine ecosystems to the atmosphere as a result of microbial denitrification range from 90×10^{12} to 243×10^{12} grams per year for terrestrial systems and 25×10^{12} to 179×10^{12} grams per year for marine systems. Scientist generally agree that less than 10% of these fluxes occur with nitrogen as a component of nitrous oxide. The range in these estimates reflects the difficulty researchers face in measuring denitrification and extrapolating the measurements to a global scale.

Humans are primarily interested in denitrification because this process is responsible for fixed nitrogen being removed from sewage and lost from cropland. Environmentally harmful nitrate concentrations in sewage discharge can be reduced by storing wastes under denitrifying conditions before releasing them into the environment. Although denitrification is a beneficial process in sewage treatment, it is considered a problem in agriculture. Farmers increase their crop yields by applying nitrogen containing fertilizers to their land. As a result of denitrification, crop yields may be reduced because much of the added nitrogen is lost to the atmosphere. This loss of fixed nitrogen may have

KEY TERMS

Aerobic respiration—Respiration in which oxygen serves as the electron acceptor.

Anaerobic respiration—Respiration in which a molecule other than oxygen serves as the electron acceptor.

Dinitrogen fixation—Process in which dinitrogen reacts to from a new nitrogen compound such as ammonium or ammonia. Most nitrogen is fixed as a result of microbial dinitrogen fixation, chemical synthesis by humans and lightning.

Fixed nitrogen—Nitrogen that occurs in molecular forms other than dinitrogen such as that found in ammonium, nitrite, nitrate, organic molecules, and nitrous oxide.

global consequences. Increased denitrification from cropland is responsible for increased amounts of nitrous oxide in the atmosphere. Although nitrous oxide is not the major end product of denitrification, it is highly reactive and may contribute to the depletion of ozone in the stratosphere.

See also Nitrogen cycle.

Further Reading:

Bitton, Gabriel. *Wastewater Microbiology*. New York: Wiley-Liss, Inc., 1994.

Kupchella, Charles, and Margaret Hyland. *Environmental Science: Living Within the System of Nature*. 2nd ed. Boston: Allyn and Bacon, 1989.

Steven MacKenzie

Density

The density of an object is defined simply as the mass of the object divided by the volume of the object. For a concrete example, imagine you have two identical boxes. You are told that one is filled with feathers and the other is filled with cement. You can tell when you pick up the boxes, without looking inside, which is the box filled with cement and which is the box filled with feathers. The box filled with cement will be heavier. It would take a very large box of feathers to equal the weight of a small box of cement because the box of cement will always have a higher density.

Density is a property of the material that does not depend on how much of the material there is. One pound of cement has the same density as one ton of cement. Both the mass and the volume are properties that depend on how much of the material an object has. Dividing the mass by the volume has the effect of canceling the amount of material. If you are buying a piece of gold jewelry, you can tell if the piece is solid gold or gold plated steel by measuring the mass and volume of the piece and computing its density. Does it have the density of gold? The mass is usually measured in kilograms or grams and the volume is usually measured in cubic meters or cubic centimeters, so the density is measured in either kilograms per cubic meter or in grams per cubic centimeter.

The density of a material is also often compared to the density of water to give the material's specific gravity. Typical rocks near the surface of the Earth will have specific gravities of 2 to 3, meaning they have densities of two to three times the density of water. The entire Earth has a density of about five times the density of water. Therefore the center of the Earth must be a high density material such as nickel or iron. The density provides an important clue to the interior composition of objects, such as the Earth and planets, that we can't take apart or look inside.

See also Mass.

Dentistry

Dentistry is the medical activity focused on treating the teeth, the gums and the oral cavity. This includes treating teeth damaged due to accidents or disease, filling teeth damaged due to tooth decay, and replacing damaged or injured teeth with replacement teeth. Major disciplines of dentistry include orthodontics, which focuses on the correction of tooth problems such as gaps between the teeth, crowded teeth and irregular bite; and periodontics, which addresses gum problems. Dentistry is considered an independent medical art, with its own licensing procedure. Medical doctors are not licensed to treat teeth; likewise dentists are not licensed to treat other parts of the body.

Skill and superstition

Ancient, medieval and early Renaissance dental practice can be seen as a stew of the sensible and the outrageous. In each era, stories of practitioners with wisdom and skill coexist with outrageous tales of superstition and myth connected to teeth. In the Ancient and Islamic worlds, doctors often performed dental work. The cleaning and extracting of teeth was often performed by individuals with little or no medical training.

Ancient men and women worked hard to alleviate dental pain. As early as 1550 B.C., the Ancient Egyptians documented their interest in dentistry in the *Ebers Papyrus*, a document discovered in 1872. The Papyrus listed various remedies for toothache, including such familiar ingredients as dough, honey, onions, incense and fennel seeds.

The Egyptians also turned to superstition for help preventing tooth pain. The mouse, which was considered to be protected by the Sun and capable of fending off death, was often used by individuals with a toothache. A common remedy involved applying half of the body of a dead mouse to the aching tooth while the body was still warm.

The Greeks offered a variety of conventional and unconventional dental therapy. One of the more illustrious dental pioneers was Hippocrates (460-375 B.C.), whose admonition to do no harm continues to be a central goal of medical practice. Hippocrates said that food lodged between teeth was responsible for tooth decay, and suggested pulling teeth that were loose and decayed.

Hippocrates also offered advice for bad breath. He suggested a mouth wash containing oil of anise seed and myrrh and white wine. Other Ancient Greeks took a more superstitious approach, with some depending on the mythical power of the mouse to protect their teeth. A recipe for bad breath from the 5th century B.C. called for a range of ingredients including the bodies of three mice, including one whose intestines had been removed, and the head of a hare. The ingredients were burned and mixed with dust and water before consumption.

The Etruscans, who lived in Tuscany, Italy, between approximately 1000 and 400 B.C., also made great advances in dentistry. They are often cited for the sophistication of their gold crowns and bridges. One bridge which has been preserved included three artificial teeth attached to gold bands, which hooked around the natural teeth. The artificial teeth were actually real teeth taken from an immature calf, then divided in two.

The Romans built upon the Etruscan knowledge of dentistry and took seriously the challenge of keeping teeth healthy. Celsus, a Roman writer who lived about 100 B.C., wrote about toothache, dental abscesses and other dental ailments. For toothache, which he called "among the worst of tortures," he suggested the use of hot poultices, mouthwash, and steam. He also suggested using pain-killers such as opium. The Romans also made bridgework.

Clean teeth were valued by the Romans, and affluent families had slaves clean their mouths using small sticks of wood and tooth powder. Such powders could include burned eggshell, bay-leaves and myrrh. These powders could also include more unusual ingredients, such as burned heads of mice and lizard livers. Earth worms marinated in vinegar were used for a mouth wash, and urine was thought of as a gum strengthener.

The Romans, like individuals in many other cultures, believed that worms in the teeth caused pain. A vast well of superstition can also be found concerning the premature appearance of teeth. Babies born with one or more teeth were considered dangerous in Africa, Madagascar, and India, and were at one point killed. In contrast, the Ancient Romans considered children born with teeth to be special, and children were often given a name, "Dentatus" in reference to their early dental development.

Non-western advances

Cultures outside Western civilization also focused on the teeth. The Chinese were the first to develop a silver amalgam filling, which was mentioned in medical texts as early as 659 A.D. The Chinese also developed full dentures by the 12th century A.D. and invented the toothbrush model for our contemporary toothbrushes in the 15th century. Dental advances also flourished in the Islamic culture, which emerged around the spiritual and political power of Muhammad (570-632) and his followers. Innovators drew from the translated works of Aristotle, Plato and Hippocrates, whose work was translated by Egyptians with links to Greece.

Mohammed's teaching called explicitly for the maintenance of clean teeth. Clean teeth were seen as a way of praising God, and he was reported to say "a prayer which is preceded by the use of the toothpick is worth seventy-five ordinary prayers." Dental powders, mouth wash and polishing sticks were used to keep teeth clean.

Dental surgery advanced greatly with the teaching of Albucasis (936-1013), a surgeon whose extensive writing about surgery in the *Al-Tasrif* influenced Islamic and Medieval European medical practitioners. He described surgery for dental irregularities, the use of gold wire to make teeth more stable, and the use of artificial teeth made of ox-bone. Albucasis also was one of the first to document the size and shape of dental tools, including drawings of dental saws, files and extraction forceps in his book.

As the Islamic world moved ahead in dentistry, European dental practice was overwhelmed by the superstition, ignorance, and religious fervor of the Middle Ages. Scientific research was discouraged during the Medieval era, which stretched from the 5th to the 15th century. Suffering and illness were widely considered to be punishment from God. Knowledge of dental anatomy and treatment did not advance during the Middle Ages, though the range of superstitious dental treatments flowered.

One fourteenth century therapy called for eating the brains of a hare to make lost teeth grow again. Charms made of stone, wood or paper devoted to a religious figure were believed to ward off disease. Religious officials suggested prayer as the best protector.

The practice of dentistry during the Middle Ages was generally limited to the pulling of teeth that were decayed or destroyed. This task initially fell to barbers, who also performed minor surgery in England in the 15th century and were called barber-surgeons. Transient tooth-pullers, who traveled from place to place, also made money extracting teeth.

From counting teeth to replacing them

By the end of the 15th century, the emphasis on obedience to authority was changing, in part under the influence of advances such as the discovery of the printing press in 1436. Dentistry benefitted from the new spirit of inquiry. Contemporary thinkers, such as anatomist Andreas Vassalius (1514-1564) challenged classical ideas about dentistry. One indication of the stagnation of independent thinking was Vassalius' successful challenge of Aristotle's belief that men had more teeth than women.

Ambrose Pare, (1510-1590), a Frenchman trained as a barber surgeon, gained fame as one of the great medical and dental surgeons of the era. His work resembled the work of a contemporary oral surgeon, focusing on the removal of teeth, the setting of fractured jaws and the draining of dental abscesses. He published extensively, documenting methods for transplanting teeth and for creating devices that held artificial teeth made of bone in place using silver or gold wire.

The eighteenth century saw many significant advances in dentistry, many of them inspired by the work of Pierre Fauchard (1678-1761). By the year 1700, Parisian dentists such as Fauchard were considered members of a distinct profession, complete with an examining board for new dentists. Fauchard's work is best known through his writing about the profession in the 1728, two-volume, *Le Chirurgien Dentiste*, a 863-page tome. In the book, Fauchard explained how to fill teeth with lead or gold leaf tin foil, and various types of

dentures. He also told how to make crowns from ivory or human teeth, how to straighten teeth, and how to protect teeth against periodontal damage.

Fauchard also took aim at some of the dental superstitions of the day, which included the erroneous belief that worms in the mouth played a role in tooth decay. His information was not all accurate, however, and Fauchard did suggest the use of urine as a mouth wash.

Another great 18th century finding was the development of porcelain, glazed white clay, as a substance for false teeth. Prior to this time, ivory was commonly used. Carving ivory was time consuming and difficult. The first porcelain teeth were developed by M. DeChateau, a French druggist, and M. Dubois De Chamant, a dentist.

DeChateau was frustrated that his teeth had discolored due to the chemicals he tasted while mixing substances for customers. After noticing that the chemicals never discolored his porcelain mortar and pestle, DeChateau decided that porcelain teeth would save him embarrassment and unhappiness. Gaining the help of DeChamant, the two men discovered a way to effectively fit and create a pair of false teeth made of porcelain, gaining a patent on the teeth in 1788.

The 19th century saw the development of many dental tools and practices which would be the bedrock for 20th century dentistry. Many of the great advances were made by Americans, who emerged as great dental innovators. The world's first dental school, the Baltimore College of Dentistry, opened in 1847, providing an organized curriculum to replace the apprenticeship system.

At the start of the century, false teeth were available to only the affluent. They were made of porcelain, which was not expensive. But they needed to be fastened to plates made of gold or silver, which were costly. The successful vulcanization of rubber in 1830 by American Charles Goodyear brought cheap false teeth to the masses. Now false teeth could be attached to vulcanized rubber, and dental laboratories emerged everywhere to keep up with the demand.

The development of anesthesia in the United States was a technological breakthrough which revolutionized surgical and dental practice. Many innovators experimented with the use of gases in the 18th and 19th centuries. Joseph Priestley, a British cleric, invented nitrous oxide, or laughing gas, in 1772. The substance caused euphoria, then sedation and unconsciousness.

Though researchers explored the application of nitrous oxide and ether in the early 19th century, the gases were not used for anesthetic purposes until the

1840s. Physician Crawford Williamson Long, a Georgia physician, first used ether to remove a tumor from a patient in 1842. Dentist Horace Wells used nitrous oxide on patients having their teeth pulled in 1844.

But dentist William Thomas Green Morton is widely credited with the first public display of anesthesia, in part because of the great success of his public demonstration and in part because of his canny alliance with influential physicians. Morton successfully extracted a tooth from a patient anesthetized with ether in 1846 in Boston.

Ether, nitrous oxide and chloroform were all used successfully during tooth extraction. But these gases were not effective for many other procedures, particularly those which took a long period of time to complete.

A breakthrough came in the form of the drug cocaine, an addictive drug derived from coca leaves which was highly valued in the nineteenth and early twentieth centuries for its pain-killing power. In 1899, cocaine was first used in New York as a local anesthetic to prevent pain in the lower jaw. Cocaine was effective but habit-forming and sometimes harmful to patients. The development of procaine, now known as novocaine, in 1905 provided dentists with a safer anesthetic than cocaine. Novocaine could be used for tooth grinding, tooth extraction and many other dental procedures.

Development of a drill powered by a footpedal in 1871 and the first electric drill in 1872 also changed the practice of dentistry.

Another major discovery of the era was the x ray by William Conrad Roentgen of Germany in 1895. The first x ray of the teeth was made in 1896. At the time, there was some skepticism about x rays. The *Pall Mall Gazette* of London railed in 1896 about the "indecency" of viewing another person's bones. William Herbert Rollins of New England reported as early as 1901 that x rays could be dangerous and should be housed properly to prevent excess exposure. Contemporary dentists continue to use x rays extensively to determine the condition of the teeth and the roots.

Modern dentistry

Cavities and fillings

The great nineteenth century advances in dentistry provided dentists with the tools to repair or remove damaged teeth with a minimum of pain. The hallmarks of dentistry in the twentieth century have been advances in the preservation of teeth.

The success of these efforts can be seen in the fact that more older Americans retain their teeth. For example, the number of Americans without teeth was 18 million in 1986, according to the Centers for Disease Control. By 1989, the number had dropped to 16.5 million. Children also have fewer dental caries, the technical name for cavities. While nearly three quarters of all 9-year-olds had cavities in the early 1970s, only one-third of 9-year-olds had cavities in the late 1980s, according to the Centers for Disease Control.

But many dental problems and challenges still exist. The two most common types of oral disease are dental caries and periodontal disease, Rowe reports. Dental caries stem from the destruction of the tooth by microbial activity on the surface. Dental caries occur when bacteria forms a dental plaque on the surface of the tooth. Plaque is a deposit of bacteria and their products which is sticky and colorless. After the plaque is formed, food and the bacteria combine to create acids that slowly dissolve the substance of the tooth. The result is a hole in the tooth which must be filled or greater damage may occur, including eventual loss of the tooth.

Many different strategies exist to prevent dental caries. These include the reduction of sugar consumption. While some foods, such as starches, do not digest completely in the mouth, other foods, such as sugars, break down quickly in the mouth and are particularly harmful. Tooth brushing also helps reduce plaque. Other preventive techniques, such as the use of fluoride and sealants, are also helpful.

Fluoride was recognized as early as 1874 as a protector against tooth decay. Great controversy surrounded the addition of fluoride to the public water supply in many communities in the 1950s and 60s, as concerns were raised about the long-term health affects of fluoride. While controversy on the issue remains in some areas, public health experts suggest that fluoride has greatly improved dental health in young and old people. The number of cavities are reduced 65% in areas in which water is fluoridated.

Another advance was the development of sealants for children in the late 1960s. These sealants, made of a clear plastic material, are typically added to an etched tooth surface to protect the tooth from decay. They can protect teeth from cavities for up to 15 years. They are generally used on the chewing surfaces of back teeth, which are most prone to tooth decay. Sealants are currently recommended for all children by the American Dental Association.

Regular dental check-ups are used to monitor teeth and prevent dental caries from growing large. Contempo-

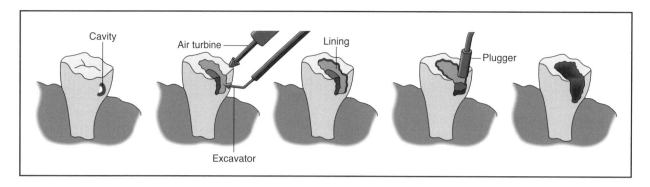

Figure 1. Teeth damaged by dental caries can be excavated and filled with an amalgam.

rary dentists typically examine teeth using dental equipment to poke and probe teeth and x rays to see potential dental caries before they can be seen easily without aid. To detect problems, x ray beams are focused on special photographic film placed in the mouth. The x rays create a record of the tooth, with the film documenting dental caries or other problems in the tooth.

The process of fixing dental caries can be a short procedure depending on the size of the cavity. Small cavities may require no anesthesia and minimal drilling, while extensive dental caries may require novocaine or nitrous oxide to dull the pain and extensive drilling. Typically the process of filling a cavity begins with the dentist using a drill or a hand tool to grind down the part of the tooth surrounding the dental carry. The dentist then shapes the cavity, removes debris from the cavity, and dries it off. At this point a cement lining is added as to insulate the inside of the tooth. The cavity is filled by inserting an amalgam or some other substance in small increments, compressing the material soundly.

Teeth are usually filled with an amalgam including silver, copper, tin, mercury, indium and palladium. Other materials may be used for front teeth where metallic fillings would stand out. These include plastic composite material, which can be made to match tooth color.

Controversy about the possible safety hazards of mercury in amalgam fillings lead some Americans to have their amalgam fillings removed in the early 1990s. While mercury is a proven toxic chemical, there is no proof that mercury in amalgam fillings causes disease, according to the American Dental Association. Still, some experts suggest that dentists seek alternatives to mercury to combat potential problems and fear linked to mercury exposure.

Tooth replacement

Teeth that have large cavities, are badly discolored, or badly broken often are capped with a crown, which covers all or part of the crown, or visible portion, of the tooth. This can be made of gold or dental porcelain. Dental cement is used to keep the crown in place.

Bridges are created when individuals need some tooth replacement but not enough to warrant dentures, which offer more extensive tooth replacement. These devices clasp new teeth in place, keep decayed teeth strong, and support the teeth in a proper configuration. Missing or damaged teeth may lead to difficulty speaking and eating. Like bridges for rivers or streams, dental bridges can be constructed many different ways, depending on the need and the area that needs bridging. There are cantilever dental bridges and many other types. Some are removable by the dentist, and may be attached to the mouth by screw or soft cement. Others, called fixed bridges, are intended to be permanent.

Dentures, a set of replacement teeth, are used when all or a large part of the teeth must be replaced. New teeth can be made of acrylic resin or porcelain. Creating a base to set the teeth in is an ambitious undertaking, requiring the development of an impression from the existing teeth and jaws and the construction of a base designed to fit the mouth exactly and not add errors. Contemporary dentists generally use acrylic plastics as the base for dentures. Acrylic plastic is mixed as a dough, heated, molded, and set in shape.

Gum disease and bad breath

Gum disease is an immense problem among adults. The more common gum diseases, gingivitis, can be found in about 44% of all employed Americans 18-64. Periodontitis can be found in at least 14% of this group, though it and gingivitis is far more common among older people. Gingivitis is the inflammation of gum tissue, and is marked by bleeding, swollen gums. Periodontitis involves damage to the periodontal ligament, which connects each tooth to the bone. It also involves damage to the alveolar bone to which teeth are attached.

Untreated periodontal disease results in exposure of tooth root surfaces and pockets between the teeth and supporting tissue. This leaves teeth and roots more susceptible to decay and tooth loss.

Periodontitis and gingivitis are caused primarily by bacterial dental plaque. This plaque includes bacteria which produce destructive enzymes in the mouth. These enzymes can damage cells and connective tissue. To prevent gum disease from forming, experts suggest regular brushing, flossing and removal of bacterial plaque using various dental tools. Regular mechanical removal of plaque by a dentist or hygienist is also essential.

Periodontal surgery is necessary when damage is too great. During this procedure, gums are moved away from bone and teeth temporarily to allow dentists to clean out and regenerate the damaged area.

Another less serious dental problem is halitosis, or bad breath. Bad breath can be due to normal body processes or to illness. Halitosis early in the morning is normal, due to the added amount of bacteria in the mouth during sleep and the reduced secretion of saliva, which cleanses the mouth. Another normal cause of bad breath is when one is hungry. This occurs because the pancreatic juice enters the intestinal tract when one has not eaten for some time, causing a bad smell. Certain foods also cause bad breath, such as garlic, alcohol, and fatty meat, which causes halitosis because the fatty acids are excreted through the lungs.

Halitosis can also be caused by a wealth of illnesses, ranging from diabetes to kidney failure and chronic lung disease. Dental problems such as plaque and dental caries can also contribute to bad breath. Treatment for the condition typically involves treating the illness, if that is causing the problem, and improving oral hygiene. This means brushing the tongue as well as the teeth.

Orthodontics: the art of moving teeth

The practice of orthodontics depends on the fact that the position of teeth in the mouth can be shaped and changed gradually using pressure. Orthodontia is used to correct problems ranging from a bite that is out of alignment, to a protruding jaw, to crowded teeth. Typically orthodontia begins when individuals are in their early teens, and takes about two years. However, with the development of clear plastic braces, adults are increasingly likely to turn to orthodontia to improve their appearance, and make eating and talking more comfortable.

The process may require some teeth to be pulled. The removal of teeth allows for the growth of other teeth to fill the newly-vacant area. Braces are made up

---

KEY TERMS

Abscess—A gathering in the tissue of the body of pus, often caused by bacteria.

Bridge—Replacement for a missing tooth or teeth which is supported by roots or natural teeth.

Gingivitis—Gum inflammation.

Vulcanization—A process in which sulfur and raw latex are combined at a high temperature to make rubber more durable.

---

of a network of wires and bands made of stainless steel or clear plastic. The tubes are often anchored on the molars and the wires are adjusted to provide steady pressure on the surface of the teeth. This pressure slowly moves the tooth to a more desirable location in the mouth and enables new bone to build up where it is needed. Orthodontia can also be used to help move the jaw by anchoring wires to the opposing jaw.

A look forward

Laser beams are already used in dentistry and in medical practice. But lasers are currently not used for everyday dentistry, such as the drilling of teeth. In the future, as laser technology becomes more refined, lasers may take the place of many conventional dental tools. Using lasers instead of dental tools would cut down on the opportunity to be exposed to blood-borne illness, and reduce damage to surrounding tissue.

Researchers also are exploring new ways to treat periodontal disease, such as more specific antibacterial therapy and stronger antibacterial agents. Many researchers also see a stronger role for fluoride in the future, in addition to its current presence in many public water supplies. Some dentists advocate the use of fluoride in sealants. A 1991 study reported that a sealant including fluoride reduced tooth irritation for some individuals with sensitive teeth.

While dentistry has made immense progress since days when a dead mouse was considered high dental technology, there is still progress to be made. Future challenges for the dental profession include continuing to reduce tooth loss and decay due to neglect and the aging process.

Further Reading:

Embery, G.; Rolla, G. *Clinical and Biological Aspects of Dentifrices.* Oxford: Oxford Medical Publications, 1992.

Gift, Helen C.; Corbin, Stephen B.; Nowjack-Raymer, Ruth E. "Public Knowledge of Prevention of Dental Disease." *Public Health Reports.* vo. 109, 397 (May-June 1994).

"What Will the Future Bring?" *Journal of the American Dental Association* 123. (April 1992): 40-46.

Patricia Braus

Denumerable see **Countable**

Deoxyribonucleic acid (DNA)

Deoxyribonucleic acid (DNA), "the master molecule," is a natural polymer which encodes the genetic information required for the growth, development, and reproduction of an organism. Found in all cells, it consists of chains of units called nucleotides. Each nucleotide unit contains three components: the sugar deoxyribose, a phosphate group, and a nitrogen-containing amine or base with a ring-type structure. The base component can be any of four types: adenine, cytosine, guanine or thymine.

DNA molecules are very long and threadlike. They consist of two polymeric strands twisted about each other into a spiral shape known as a double helix, which resembles two intertwined circular staircases. DNA is found within the cell nucleus in the chromosomes, which are extremely condensed structures in which DNA is associated with proteins. Each species contains a characteristic number of chromosomes in their cells. In humans every cell contains 46 chromosomes (except for egg and sperm cells which contain only 23). The total genetic information in a cell is called its genome.

The fundamental units of heredity are genes. A gene is a segment of a DNA molecule that encodes the information necessary to make a specific protein. Proteins are the "workhorses" of the cell. These large, versatile molecules serve as structural components: they transport molecules in and out of cells, catalyze cellular reactions, and recognize and eliminate invaders. Imagine a community in which the trash collectors, goods distributors, manufacturers, and police are all on strike, and you get an idea of the importance of proteins in the life of a cell.

DNA not only encodes the "blueprints" for cellular proteins but also the instructions for when and where they will be made. For example, the oxygen carrier hemoglobin is made in red blood cells but not in nerve cells, though both contain the same total genetic content. Thus, DNA also contains the information necessary for regulating how its genetic messages are used.

Human cells are thought to contain between 50,000 and 100,000 genes. Except in the case of identical twins, a comparison of the genes from different individuals always reveals a number of differences. Therefore, each person is genetically unique. This is the basis of DNA "fingerprinting", a forensic procedure used to match DNA collected from a crime scene with that of a suspect.

Through the sum of their effects, genes direct the function of all organs and systems in the body. Defects in the DNA of just one gene can cause a genetic disorder which results in disease because the protein encoded by the defective gene is abnormal. The abnormal hemoglobin produced by people afflicted with sickle cell anemia is an example. Defects in certain genes called oncogenes, which regulate growth and development, give rise to cancer. Only about 100 genes are thought to be oncogenes. Therefore, defects in DNA can affect the two kinds of genetic information it carries, messages directing the manufacture of proteins and information regulating the expression, or carrying out, of these messages.

History

Prior to the discovery of the nucleic acids, the Austrian monk Gregor Mendel (1822-1884) worked out the laws of inheritance by the selective breeding of pea plants. As early as 1865 he proposed that "factors" from each parent were responsible for the inheritance of certain characteristics in plants. The Swiss biochemist Friedrich Miescher (1844-1895) discovered the nucleic acids in 1868 in nuclei isolated from pus cells scraped from surgical bandages. However, research on the chemical structure of nucleic acids lagged until new analytical techniques became available in the mid twentieth century. With the advent of these new methods came evidence that the nucleic acid we now know as DNA was present in the nuclei of all cells and evidence about the chemical structure of its nucleotide components.

Despite knowledge of the chemical structure of nucleotides and how they were linked together to form DNA, the possibility that DNA was the genetic material was regarded as unlikely. As late as the mid twentieth century, proteins were thought to be the molecules of heredity because they appeared to be the only cellular components diverse enough to account for the large variety of genes. In 1944 Oswald Avery (1877-1955) and his colleagues showed that non-pathogenic strains of *pneumococcus*, the bacterium that causes pneumonia, could become pathogenic (disease-causing) if

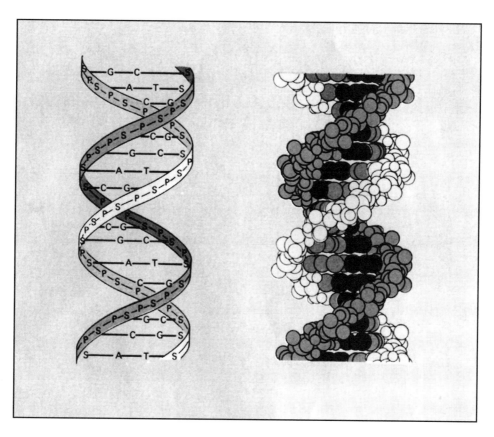

The structure of the DNA molecule.

treated with a DNA-containing extract from heat-killed pathogenic strains. Based on this evidence, Avery concluded that DNA was the genetic material. However, widespread acceptance of DNA as the bearer of genetic information did not come until a report by other workers in 1952 that DNA, not protein, enters a bacterial cell infected by a virus. This showed that the genetic material of the virus was contained in its DNA, confirming Avery's hypothesis.

Shortly afterwards in 1953, James Watson (1928-) and Francis Crick (1916-) proposed their double helix model for the three-dimensional structure of DNA. They correctly deduced that the genetic information was encoded in the form of the sequence of nucleotides in the molecule. With their landmark discovery began an era of molecular genetics in biology. Eight years later investigators cracked the genetic code. They found that specific trinucleotide sequences—sequences of three nucleotides—are codes for each of 20 amino acids, the building blocks of proteins.

In 1970 scientists found that bacteria contained restriction enzymes-molecular "scissors" that recognize a particular sequence of 4-8 nucleotides and will always cut DNA at or near that sequence to yield specific (rather than random), consistently reproducible DNA fragments. Two years later it was found that the bacterial enzyme DNA ligase could be used to rejoin these fragments. This permitted scientists to construct "recombinant" DNA molecules; that is, DNA molecules composed of segments from two different sources, even from different organisms. With the availability of these tools, genetic engineering became possible and biotechnology began.

By 1984 the development of DNA fingerprinting allowed forensic chemists to compare DNA samples from a crime scene with that of suspects. The first conviction using this technique came in 1987. Three years later doctors first attempted to treat a patient unable to produce a vital immune protein using gene therapy. This technique involves inserting a portion of DNA into a patient's cells to correct a deficiency in a particular function. The Human Genome Project also began in 1990. The aim of this project is to determine the nucleotide sequence in DNA of the entire human genome, which consists of about three billion nucleotide pairs.

Structure

Deoxyribose, the sugar component in each nucleotide, is so called because it has one less oxygen atom than ribose, which is present in ribonucleic acid (RNA). Deoxyribose contains five carbon atoms, four of which lie in a ring along with one oxygen atom. The fifth carbon atom is linked to a specific carbon atom in the ring. A phosphate group is always linked to deoxyribose via a chemical bond between an oxygen atom in the phosphate group and the carbon atom in deoxyribose by a chemical bond between a nitrogen atom in the base and a specific carbon atom in the deoxyribose ring.

The nucleotide components of DNA are connected to form a linear polymer in a very specific way. A phosphate group always connects the sugar component of a nucleotide with the sugar component of the next nucleotide in the chain. Consequently, the first nucleotide bears an unattached phosphate group, and the last nucleotide has a free hydroxyl group. Therefore, DNA is not the same at both ends. This directionality plays an important role in the replication of DNA.

DNA molecules contain two polymer chains or strands of nucleotides and so are said to be double-stranded. (In contrast, RNA is typically single-stranded). Their shape resembles two intertwined spiral staircases in which the alternating sugar and phosphate groups of the nucleotides compose the sidepieces. The steps consist of pairs of bases, each attached to the sugars on their respective strands. The bases are held together by weak attractive forces called hydrogen bonds. The two strands in DNA are antiparallel, which means that one strand goes in one direction (first to last nucleotide from top to bottom) and the other strand goes in the opposite direction (first to last nucleotide from bottom to top).

Because the sugar and phosphate components which make up the sidepieces are always attached in the same way, the same alternating phosphate-sugar sequence repeats over and over again. The bases attached to each sugar may be one of four possible types. Because of the geometry of the DNA molecule, the only possible base pairs that will fit are adenine (A) paired with thymine (T), and cytosine© paired with guanine (G).

The DNA in our cells is a masterpiece of packing. The double helix coils itself around protein cores to form nucleosomes. These DNA-protein structures resemble beads on a string. Flexible regains between nucleosomes allows these structures to be wound around themselves to produce an even more compact fiber. The fibers can then be coiled for even further compactness. Ultimately, DNA is paced into the highly condensed chromosomes. If the DNA in a human cell is stretched, it is approximately 6 ft (1.82 m) long. If all 46 chromosomes are laid end-to-end, their total length

is still only about eight-thousandths of an inch. This means that DNA in chromosomes is condensed about 10,000 times more than that in the double helix. Why all this packing? The likely answer is that the fragile DNA molecule would get broken in its extended form. Also, if not for this painstaking compression, the cell might be mired in its own DNA.

Function

DNA directs a cell's activities by specifying the structures of its proteins and by regulating which proteins and how much are produced, and where. In so doing, it never leaves the nucleus. Each human cell contains about 6 ft (2 m) of highly condensed DNA which encodes some 50,000-100,000 genes. If a particular protein is to be made, the DNA segment corresponding to the gene for that protein acts as a template, a pattern, for the synthesis of an RNA molecule in a process known as transcription. This messenger RNA molecule travels from the nucleus to the cytoplasm where it in turn acts as the template for the construction of the protein by the protein assembly apparatus of the cell. This latter process is known as translation and requires an adaptor molecule, transfer RNA, which translates the genetic code of DNA into the language of proteins.

Eventually, when a cell divides, its DNA must be copied so that each daughter cell will have a complete set of genetic instructions. The structure of DNA is perfectly suited to this process. The two intertwined strands unwind, exposing their bases, which then pair with bases on free nucleotides present in the cell. The bases pair only in a certain combination; adenine (A) always pairs with thymine (T) and cytosine (c) always pairs with guanine (G). The sequence of bases along one strand of DNA therefore determines the sequence of bases in the newly forming complementary strand. An enzyme then joins the free nucleotides to complete the new strand. Since the two new DNA strands that result are identical to the two originals, the cell can pass along an exact copy of its DNA to each daughter cell.

Sex cells, the eggs and sperm, contain half the number of chromosomes as other cells. When the egg and sperm fuse during fertilization, they form the first cell of a new individual with the complete complement of DNA—46 chromosomes. Each cell (except the sex cells) in the new person carries DNA identical to that in the fertilized egg cell. In this way the DNA of both parents is passed from one generation to the next. Thus, DNA plays a crucial role in the propagation of life.

Replication of DNA

DNA replication, the process by which the double-stranded DNA molecule reproduces itself, is a complicated process, even in the simplest organisms. DNA synthesis—making new DNA from old—is complex because it requires the interaction of a number of cellular components and is rigidly controlled to ensure the accuracy of the copy, upon which the very life of the organism depends. This adds several verification steps to the procedure. Though the details vary from organism to organism, DNA replication follows certain rules that are universal to all.

DNA replication (duplication, or copying) is always semiconservative. During DNA replication the two strands of the parent molecule unwind and each becomes a template for the synthesis of the complementary strand of the daughter molecule. As a result both daughter molecules contain one new strand and one old strand (from the parent molecule), hence the term semi-conservative. The replication of DNA always requires a template—an intact strand from the parent molecule. This strand determines the sequence of nucleotides on the new strand. Wherever the nucleotide on the template strand contains the base A, then the nucleotide to be added to the daughter strand at that location must contain the base T. Conversely, every T must find an A to pair with. In the same way, Gs and Cs will pair with each other and with no other bases.

Replication begins at a specific site called the replication origin when the enzyme DNA helicase binds to a portion of the double stranded helix and "melts" the bonds between base pairs. This unwinds the helix to form a replication fork consisting of two separated strands, each which serve as templates. Specific proteins then bind to these single strands to prevent them from re-pairing. Another enzyme, DNA polymerase, proceeds to assemble the daughter strands using a pool of free nucleotide units which are present in the cell in an "activated" form.

High fidelity in the copying of DNA is vital to the organism and, incredibly, only about one error per one trillion replications ever occurs. This high fidelity results largely because DNA polymerase is a "self-editing" enzyme. If a nucleotide added to the end of the chain mismatches the complementary nucleotide on the template, pairing does not occur. DNA polymerase then clips off the unpaired nucleotide and replaces it with the correct one.

Occasionally errors are made during DNA replication and passed along to daughter cells. Such errors are called mutations. They have serious consequences because they can cause the insertion of the wrong amino acid into a protein. For example, the substitution of a T for an A in the gene encoding hemoglobin causes an amino acid substitution which results in sickle cell anemia. To understand the significance of such mutations requires knowledge of the genetic code.

The genetic code

Genetic information is stored as nucleotide sequences in DNA (or RNA) molecules. This sequence specifies the identity and position of the amino acids in a particular protein. Amino acids are the building blocks of proteins in the same way that nucleotides are the building blocks of DNA. However, though there are only four possible bases in DNA (or RNA), there are twenty possible amino acids in proteins. The genetic code is a sort of "bilingual dictionary" which translates the language of DNA into the language of proteins. In the genetic code the letters are the four bases A, C, G and T (or U instead of T in RNA). Obviously, the four bases of DNA are not enough to code for twenty amino acids. A sequence of two bases is also insufficient, because this permits coding for only 16 of the 20 amino acids in proteins. Therefore, a sequence of three bases is required to ensure enough combinations or "words" to code for all 20 amino acids. Since all words in this DNA language, called codons, consist of three letters, the genetic code is often referred to as the triplet code.

Each codon specifies a particular amino acid. Because there are 64 possible codons (for example 4^3 = 64 different 3-letter "words" can be generated from a 4-letter "alphabet") and only twenty amino acids, several different codons specify the same amino acid, so the genetic code is said to be degenerate. However, the code is unambiguous because each codon specifies only one amino acid. The sequence of codons are not interrupted by "commas" and are always read in the same frame of reference, starting with the same base every time. So the "words" never overlap.

Since DNA never leaves the nucleus, the information it stores is not transferred to the cell directly. Instead, a DNA sequence must first be copied into a messenger RNA molecule which carries the genetic information from the nucleus to protein assembly sites in the cytoplasm. There it serves as the template for protein construction. The sequences of nucleotide triplets in messenger RNA are also referred to as codons.

Four codons serve special functions. Three are stop codons that signal the end of protein synthesis. The fourth is a start codon which establishes the "reading frame" in which the message is to be read. For example, suppose the message is PAT SAW THE FAT RAT. If we overshoot the reading frame by one "nucleotide," we obtain ATS AWT HEF ATR AT, which is meaningless.

The genetic code is essentially universal. This means that a codon which specifies the amino acid tryptophan in bacteria also codes for it in man. The only exceptions occur in mitochondria and chloroplasts and in some protozoa. (Mitochondria and chloroplasts are subcellular compartments which are the sites of respiration in animals and plants, respectively, and contain some DNA.)

The structure of the genetic code has evolved to minimize the effect of mutations. Changes in the third base of a codon do not necessarily result in a change in the specified amino acid during protein synthesis. Furthermore, changes in the first base in a codon generally result in the same or at least a similar amino acid. Studies of amino acid changes resulting from mutations have shown that they are consistent with the genetic code. That is, amino acid changes resulting from mutations are consistent with expected base changes in the corresponding codon. These studies have confirmed that the genetic code has been deduced correctly by demonstrating its relevance in actual living organisms.

Expression of genetic information

Genetic information flows from DNA to RNA to protein. Ultimately, the linear sequence of nucleotides in DNA directs the production of a protein molecule with a characteristic three dimensional structure essential to its proper function. Initially, information is transcribed from DNA to RNA. The information in the resulting messenger RNA is then translated from RNA into protein by small transfer RNA molecules.

In some exceptional cases the flow of genetic information from DNA to RNA is reversed. In retroviruses, such as the AIDS virus, RNA is the hereditary material. An enzyme known as reverse transcriptase makes a copy of DNA using the virus' RNA as a template. In still other viruses which use RNA as the hereditary material, DNA is not involved in the flow of information at all.

Most cells in the body contain the same DNA as that in the fertilized egg. (Some exceptions to this are the sex cells, which contain only half of the normal complement of DNA, as well as red blood cells which lose their nucleus when fully developed.) Some "housekeeping" genes are expressed in all cells because they are involved in the fundamental processes required for normal function. (A gene is said to be expressed when its product, the protein it codes for, is actively produced in a cell.) For example, since all cells require ribo-

somes, structures which function as protein assembly lines, the genes for ribosomal proteins and ribosomal RNA are expressed in all cells. Other genes are only expressed in certain cell types, such as genes for antibodies in certain cells of the immune system. Some are expressed only during certain times in development. How is it that some cells express certain genes while others do not, even though all contain the same DNA? A complete answer to this question is still in the works. However, the main way is by controlling the start of transcription. This is accomplished by the interaction of proteins called transcription factors with DNA sequences near the gene. By binding to these sequences transcription factors may turn a gene on or off.

Another way is to change the rate of messenger RNA synthesis. Sometimes the stability of the messenger RNA is altered. The protein product itself may be altered, as well as its transport or stability. Finally, gene expression can be altered by DNA rearrangements. Such programmed reshuffling of DNA is the means of generating the huge assortment of antibody proteins found in immune cells.

Genetic engineering and recombinant DNA

Restriction enzymes come from microorganisms. Recall that they recognize and cut DNA at specific base pair sequences. They cleave large DNA molecules into an assortment of smaller fragments ranging in size from a few to thousands of base pairs long, depending on how often and where the cleavage sequence appears in the original DNA molecule. The resulting fragments can be separated by their size using a technique known as electrophoresis. The fragments are placed at the top of a porous gel surrounded by a solution which conducts electricity. When a voltage is applied, the DNA fragments move towards the bottom of the gel due to the negative charge on their phosphate groups. Because it is more difficult for the large fragments to pass through the pores in the gel, they move more slowly than the smaller fragments.

DNA fragments isolated from a gel in this way can be joined with DNA from another source, either of the same or a different species, into a new, recombinant DNA molecule by enzymes. Usually, such DNA fragments are joined with DNA from subcellular organisms—"parasites" that live inside another organism but have their own DNA. Plasmids and viruses are two such examples. Viruses consist only of nucleic acids encapsulated in a protein coat. Though they can exist outside the cell, they are inactive. Inside the cell, they take over its metabolic machinery to manufacture more

KEY TERMS

Codon— The base sequence of three consecutive nucleotides on DNA (or RNA) that codes for a particular amino acid or signals the beginning or end of a messenger RNA molecule.

Cytoplasm—The fluid inside a cell which surrounds the nucleus and other membrane-enclosed compartments.

Gene—The segment of a DNA molecule that stores the information needed to make a protein molecule.

Genome—The complete genetic content of an organism.

Genetic code—The relationship between the sequence of nucleotides in DNA to the corresponding sequence of amino acids in the protein molecule encoded by that DNA sequence.

Genetic engineering—The manipulation of the genetic content of an organism for the sake of genetic analysis or to produce or improve a product.

Nucleotide—The basic unit of DNA. It consists of deoxyribose, phosphate, and a ring-like nitrogen-containing base.

Nucleus—A compartment in the cell which is enclosed by a membrane and

which contains its genetic information.

Replication—The synthesis of a new DNA molecule from a pre-existing one.

Transcription—The synthesis of RNA using a strand of DNA as a template.

Translation—The process of protein synthesis.

---

microorganisms, such as bacteria or yeast, to produce large quantities of medically or commercially important proteins normally present only in scant amounts in the cell. For example, human insulin and interferon have been produced in this manner.

In recent years a technique has been developed which permits analysis of very small samples of DNA without repeated cloning, which is laborious. Known as the polymerase chain reaction, this technique involves "amplifying" a particular fragment of DNA by repeated synthesis using the enzyme DNA polymerase. This method can increase the amount of the desired DNA fragment by a million-fold or more.

See also Chromosome; Enzyme; Gene; Genetics; Meiosis; Mitosis; Mutation; Nucleic acid; Ribonucleic acid.

Further Reading:

Berg, Paul and Maxine Singer. *Dealing with Genes-The Language of Heredity*. Mill Valley, California: University Science Press, 1992.

Blueprint for Life. Journey Through the Mind and Body series. Alexandria, Virginia: Time-Life Books, 1993.

Lee, Thomas F. *Gene Future*. New York: Plenum Publishing Corporation, 1993.

Rosenfeld, Israel, Edward Ziff and Borin Van Loon. *DNA for Beginners*. New York: Writers and Readers Publishing Cooperative Limited, 1983.

Sofer, William H. *Introduction to Genetic Engineering*. Stoneham, Massachusetts: Butterwoth-Heineman, 1991.

Patricia V. Racenis

---

virus particles, eventually destroying their host. Plasmids are simpler than viruses in that they never exist outside the cell and have no protein coat. They consist only of circular double-stranded DNA. Plasmids replicate their DNA independently of their hosts. They are passed on to daughter cells in a controlled way as the host cell divides.

Cells that contain the same recombinant DNA fragment are clones. A clone harboring a recombinant DNA molecule that contains a specific gene can be isolated and identified by a number of techniques, depending upon the particular experiment. Thus, recombinant DNA molecules can be introduced into rapidly growing

Deposit

A deposit is an accumulation of Earth materials, usually loose sediment or minerals, that is laid down by a natural agent. Deposits are all around you—the sand on the beach, the soil in your backyard, the rocks in a mountain stream. All of these consist of earth materials transported and laid down (that is, deposited) by a natural agent. These natural agents may include flowing water, ice, or gusts of wind (all operating under the influence of gravity), as well as gravity acting alone. For example, gravity alone can cause a rock fall along a highway, and the rock fall will form a deposit at the base of the slope. The agents of transport and deposition mentioned above are mechanical in nature and all operate in the same way. Initially, some force causes a particle to begin to move. When the force decreases, the

This canyon in the Valley of 10,000 Smokes, Katmai National Park, Alaska, is made up of deposits of tuff (consolidated volcanic ash) from the 1912 eruption of the Novarupta and Mt. Katmai volcanoes.

rate of particle motion also decreases. Eventually particle motion ceases and mechanical deposition occurs.

Not all deposits form by mechanical deposition. Some deposits form instead by chemical deposition. As you may know, all naturally occurring water has some minerals dissolved in it. Deposition of these minerals may result from a variety of chemical processes; however, one of the most familiar is evaporation. When water evaporates, dissolved minerals remain behind as a solid residue. This residue is a chemical deposit of minerals.

Ocean water is very rich in dissolved minerals—that is why ocean water tastes salty. When ocean water evaporates, a deposit containing a variety of minerals accumulates. The mineral halite (that is, table salt) would make up the bulk of such a deposit. Large, chemically derived mineral deposits, which formed by the evaporation of ancient saline lakes, are currently being mined in several areas of the western United States. The Bonneville Salt Flats in Utah is a good example of an "evaporite" mineral deposit. Due to the arid climate, evaporite minerals are still being deposited today at Great Salt Lake in Utah.

The term "deposit" generally applies only to accumulations of earth materials that form at or near the earth's surface, that is, to particles, rocks, or minerals that are of sedimentary origin. However, ore deposits are an exception to this generality. The phrase "ore deposit" applies to any valuable accumulation of minerals, no matter how or where it accumulates. Some ore deposits do form by mechanical or chemical deposition (that is, they are of sedimentary origin).

For example, flowing streams deposit gold-bearing sand and gravel layers, known as placers. Placers, therefore, form by mechanical deposition. Some iron ores, on the other hand, form when subsurface waters chemically deposit iron in porous zones within sediments or rocks. However, many ore deposits do not form by either mechanical or chemical deposition, and so are not of sedimentary origin.

See also Minerals; Ore; Sediment and sedimentation.

Depositional environment see **Sediment and** sedimentation

Depression

Psychiatrists use the term "depression" in a confusing variety of ways: It can designate a short-lived mood, a long-lasting symptom, a syndrome (a group of symptoms commonly found together), a mental disorder, or a group of disorders. The general public may be particularly confused to discover that people with depressive syndromes or disorders do not necessarily have depressed moods.

"Depressed mood" refers to a pervasive sense of sadness—the "blues," or being "down in the dumps." Everyone experiences depressed mood from time to time. When the feeling persists for weeks without apparent reason, however, it may be a symptom of a psychiatric disorder.

The American Psychiatric Association's (APA's) definition of a major depressive episode illustrates the way in which symptoms are grouped together into a depressive syndrome. In a major depressive episode, either depressed mood or a marked lack of interest and pleasure in almost all activities persists for most of the day, nearly every day, for at least two weeks. In addition, many or all of the following symptoms occur: (1) changes in weight or sleeping habits; (2) fatigue; (3) visible agitation (or, alternatively, slow response to surrounding events); (4) feelings of guilt or worthlessness; (5) diminished ability to think or concentrate; (6) recurrent thoughts of death, often including suicidal thoughts or plans, or even a suicide attempt.

People with major depression are also very likely to experience headaches, stomach aches, or, indeed, pains or aches almost anywhere in the body. They often regard pain as their primary problem, believing that it causes their insomnia, poor appetite, and depressed, irritable mood. Furthermore, besides these pains of apparently psychological origin, depressed people may feel clearly physical pain with unusual intensity.

People experiencing a major depressive episode are also likely have intense feelings of hopelessness and worthlessness. They often feel so guilty they become convinced they do not deserve happiness. Nor, they think, is there any hope for improvement—even trying to make things better is an exercise in futility. Unfortunately, these feelings—these symptoms of the disorder—represent a major roadblock to effective treatment and recovery. Indeed, the overwhelming majority of depressed individuals do not even seek medical help unless friends or loved ones intervene.

PSYCHOLOGICAL

Loss of interest
Unexplained anxiety
Inappropriate feelings of guilt
Loss of self-esteem
Worthlessness
Hopelessness
Thoughts of death and suicide
Tearfulness
Irritability
Brooding

PHYSICAL

Headache, vague aches and pains
Changes in appetite
Changes in weight
Sleep disturbances
Loss of energy
Neuroendocrine disturbances
Loss of libido
Gastrointestinal disturbances

INTELLECTUAL

Slowed thinking
Indecisiveness
Poor concentration
Impaired memory

Signs and symptoms of depression.

Types of depressive disorder

The two most common types of depressive disorder are major depressive disorder and dysthymia. Major depressive disorder is characterized by recurring episodes of major depression. In dysthymia, the symptoms are never severe enough to meet the definition of a major depressive episode but persist for two years or more. Some individuals may also experience double depression—major depression and dysthymia superimposed on one another.

Less common is schizoaffective disorder, which the APA defines as combining episodes of major depression with hallucinations or delusions that may occur even when there are no mood symptoms. Some psychiatrists, however, question whether schizoaffective disorder is truly an illness in its own right. They suggest that it may be simply a variant of major depression or of schizophrenia—or, perhaps, that it is nothing more than the same patient suffering from both disorders.

An even more controversial diagnostic category is pre-menstrual dysphoric disorder. No one questions that some women become extremely depressed during the days immediately before their menstrual periods; the controversy concerns whether this is a distinct, identifiable depressive disorder. Some psychiatrists consider it a variant of major depressive disorder in which the hormonal changes associated with a woman's menstrual cycle affect the severity of her symptoms. Uncertainty about how these mood changes relate to the physical symptoms called pre-menstrual syndrome (PMS) only intensifies the controversy.

The case for regarding pre-menstrual dysphoric disorder as a hormone-influenced variant of major depression may be strengthened by analogy to post-partum depression. Most psychiatrists now believe that this is not a distinct disorder, but simply major depression triggered by the hormonal changes accompanying birth of a baby.

There may also be an analogy to seasonal affective disorder (SAD), a variant of major depressive disorder in which episodes recur every year during the darkest days of winter. (In a much rarer form, the episodes occur during summer.) Annual recurrence of SAD is no coincidence: Short, dark days appear to directly trigger the episodes, possibly by influencing secretion of certain hormones.

What is more, the episodes can be prevented or ended by sitting in front of bright lights (5-10 times the brightness of ordinary room lights) for 4-6 hours a day. Psychiatrists disagree, however, about whether this extra "daylight" must be in the morning before the sun is up: Some say it can equally well be in the evening after the sun has gone down. Some even suggest it could be split between the two—that only the length of the "day" is important.

When depressive syndrome is not depressive disorder

Two problems that are not actually depressive disorders—manic-depressive (bipolar) disorder and reactive depression—are nevertheless characterized by major depressive episodes.

Manic-depressive disorder often looks like depression at first: Several depressive episodes may occur before the first manic episode signals the correct diagnosis. This may be part of the reason traditional classification schemes (including that of the APA) group manic-depression with the depressive disorders. Today, however, the two types of disorder are treated with totally different medications: depressive disorders with antidepressants and manic-depression with lithium. Using antidepressants to treat manic-depressive individuals can sometimes make their conditions worse.

Reactive depression, which the APA describes as an adjustment disorder, is a direct response to some loss—for example, of a loved one, a job, or one's health. By definition, the degree of depression is proportionate to the extent of loss given the individual's psychological make-up and previous life experiences.

A divorce, for example, is traumatic for almost everyone. For someone who has been deeply hurt by previous rejections, however, it may be enough to plunge him or her into the depths of despair. All the characteristics of a major depressive episode, including the risk of suicide, may then follow. Yet the depression is still reactive, because it is proportionate to the psychological loss—even though that loss is greater than most people would experience in similar circumstances.

Although the theoretical distinction between major depressive disorder and reactive depression is clear, they are often difficult to tell apart in a given, concrete situation. The immediate symptoms are fundamentally the same. And although reactive depression results from an external loss, neither the existence of the loss nor the factors that account for the resulting degree of depression are necessarily obvious. Furthermore, recent research suggests that most initial episodes of major depression (and sometimes later ones as well) may also be triggered by external losses.

Sometimes previous events may suggest one diagnosis or the other. If the affected person has had previous depressive episodes, or if others in his or her family have suffered from depressive disorders, then major depression is more likely. Yet neither the absence nor the presence of previous episodes can be conclusive: There must always be an initial episode of major depression, while multiple losses may cause an individual to suffer from reactive depression on several different occasions.

Some psychiatrists believe they can tell the two conditions apart by the absence of "somatic" or "vegetative" symptoms—fatigue and changes in eating and sleeping habits—in reactive depression. Others question whether the difference in symptoms is sufficiently consistent to be helpful. Perhaps the most positive way to decide uncertain cases is with what physicians call a therapeutic trial: antidepressants will usually relieve major depression but have little or no effect on reactive depression.

Biological causes

No one knows the fundamental cause of depressive disorders. Scientists do know, however, that all the medications used to treat them raise the levels of certain chemicals known as neurotransmitters. These are chemicals released when a nerve impulse reaches the end of the cell carrying it; they then diffuse to the neighboring cell and create a new impulse there. In effect, they are a chemical means of transmitting an electrical impulse from one cell to another.

The effectiveness of antidepressant medications suggests that depression may result from an abnormally low level of one or more neurotransmitters. Confusingly, however, the older tricyclic antidepressants and monoamine oxidase inhibitors primarily raise the level of a transmitter known as norepinephrine; most of the newer atypical antidepressants, on the other hand, affect one known as serotonin. It thus seems that both norepinephrine and serotonin may play some role in causing depression. Perhaps, it has been suggested, both may act on a common target that is directly responsible for depression.

The effectiveness of antidepressant medications suggests that depression may be more a biological than a psychological disorder. This conclusion is supported by the way depression often runs in families—up to 25% of those with depression have a relative with a mood disorder of some kind. Furthermore, if one member of a pair of identical twins has major depression, the odds are about two in five that the other one will, too.

Social and demographic risk factors

The origin of depressive disorders is not entirely biological, of course. If it were, then identical twins would always experience depression at the same time. The observation that initial depressive episodes are often preceded by a loss also suggests that psychological factors are important: Even people biologically predisposed to the disorder, it seems, may escape if they lead generally happy lives with adequate sources of social support.

Several studies have confirmed the importance of social support—family, friends, and other relationships. According to these studies, depressed people who lack social support experience more severe and longer-lasting symptoms than those who have it. The sequence of cause and effect remains unclear, however. Someone suffering from fatigue and feelings of hopelessness and worthlessness is likely to have trouble making new friends or even maintaining contact with old ones. Perhaps, then, people with severe symptoms are less able to maintain their social support networks, rather than people who lack social support being more likely to develop severe symptoms.

The more interesting question is whether social support can help prevent depression. Although only a few studies have addressed this question, the answer appears to be that it can. Still unsettled is whether social support directly protects one from depressive disorders or, alternatively, acts by limiting the emotional impact of the losses everyone experiences from time to time.

In view of the protection social support offers, it may seem surprising that women are twice as likely as men to suffer from depressive disorders. Three potential explanations have been advanced: (1) Women are biologically more susceptible to depression, possibly because of their monthly hormonal changes; (2) In our society, women's lives are particularly likely to be frustrating and stressful; this can lead to feelings of powerlessness that may culminate in depression; (3) The rate of depression is actually the same for men and women, but men—trained to ignore their feelings and to regard seeking help as a sign of weakness—are less likely to admit that they experience depressive symptoms. No one presently knows which of these explanations is right. Perhaps all three are to varying degrees.

Depression can occur at any age. It is seen in children, and may occur in elderly people who have never experienced a depressive episode before; unfortunately, depression often goes unrecognized in both groups. The frequency of depressive disorders does vary with age, however. One study from Finland suggests that women's first episodes are most likely to occur when they are past age 40. Men, on the other hand, are most likely to experience their first episode around retirement age.

Most studies find that depression is much more common in cities than in rural areas. In reality, however, urban versus rural location may not be the critical factor. Finland has two major urbanized, industrialized areas—one with the highest rate of depression in the country, the other with the lowest. The most obvious difference between the two areas is that only in the one with high depression rates has there been extensive recent immigration from rural areas. Perhaps, then, the real risk factor is migration from a rural to an urban area. Or perhaps rapid urban growth produces social strains that increase the risk of depression for everyone who lives there.

In the United States, researchers find that African Americans are more likely to experience depressed mood than are whites. The difference between the races disappears, however, when the people being compared are similar in social and economic status. It also disappears when the measurement compares episodes of major depression—an actual psychiatric illness—rather than of the depressed mood that may result from a bad situation.

Hispanics are not truly a single group. Studies have found that Puerto Ricans living in the eastern United States experience high levels of depression; on the other hand, major depressive episodes among Mexican-Americans in the Los Angeles area are less common than among non-Hispanic whites.

Reported rates of depression among Asian-Americans are very low. This may reflect inaccurate reporting, however: Asian cultures generally view any type of psychological problem as extremely shameful, so even the most ill people will deny it if they can.

Depression and society

Depression is a relatively common condition. A survey of 18,000 Americans found that 270 (15 per 1,000) had major depression at that time, and that almost 800 (44 per 1,000) had it at some time in their lives. Another 31 per 1,000 had experienced dysthymia. Studies in other countries have largely confirmed these numbers.

Evidence from around the world suggests that the number of people with depression is rising steadily. Only 1% of Americans born before 1905 ever experienced a major depressive episode in their entire lives—yet 6% of those born after 1955 have had one by age 25. Nor is this trend unique to the United States: An international survey found depression becoming increasingly common in all three countries studied. Surprisingly, however, although Americans born in the late 1930s were the first to experience this phenomenon, it began 10 years earlier in Canada and 10 years later in Italy. As a further contrast, a different study found that the rate of depression in Finland actually fell among those born after 1945.

The impact of depression, on the individual and on society, cannot be overestimated. At the societal level, the U.S. Agency for Health Care Policy and Research estimates that the disorder cost the country $27 million in 1989 alone. This includes $17 million in lost work time and $10 million in healthcare and other costs.

At the individual level, depression is a truly crippling disorder. A recent study compared patients with nine chronic conditions. As expected, it was depression that created the greatest disruption in individuals' ability to function socially. Surprisingly, however, depression also interfered with their physical function more

than did arthritis, diabetes, high blood pressure, gastrointestinal disorders (such as ulcers), lung disorders (such as asthma or emphysema), or back problems. Only severe coronary artery (heart) disease and angina (heart pain, a milder form of heart disease) resulted in greater physical limitations.

Major depression can be life-threatening as well. As an episode worsens, suicide often comes more and more to occupy the depressed person's thoughts. This may then lead to suicidal plans and on to suicide attempts—which all too often succeed. The APA estimates that up to 15% of individuals with severe major depressive disorder will kill themselves; furthermore, research shows that between 30% and 70% of all suicides occur in depressed individuals.

Given the severity of the disorder, it is astonishing that so few depressed individuals are effectively treated for their condition. As previously mentioned, feelings of helplessness, hopelessness, and worthlessness prevent the overwhelming majority of depressed people from seeking medical help unless someone else intervenes. Beyond this, however, if they do see a physician—whether for depressive symptoms or for an unrelated condition—they are often not diagnosed correctly.

This is partially because depressed individuals frequently give misleading descriptions of their condition. They may focus on a single quasi-physical symptom such as insomnia, or may present a long and confusing list of symptoms ranging from headaches to fatigue. All too often they do not even mention their emotional state, mistakenly regarding this as a sign of character weakness—and, in any case, as unrelated to the physical symptoms that are a physician's proper domain.

Conversely, many family physicians remain unaware of how common depression is in all social groups. Further, many have not been trained to recognize the common thread beneath the varied symptoms this disorder may present. When lack of awareness and training are combined with the difficulties in patient presentation, inadequate diagnosis becomes at least partially understandable.

Once diagnosed, however, two-thirds of patients are not treated with anti-depressants. Although anti-depressants are not the only appropriate treatments for depression, they are regarded as the most generally effective. What is more, many of those not on anti-depressants also receive little or no psychotherapy—in effect, they are not being treated at all. While some lack of treatment may result from patients failing to understand their condition and its therapy, and thus not complying with the program their doctor has recommended, many physicians appear not to treat depression as the serious disorder it is.

Treatment

Medications known as antidepressants are considered standard therapy for depression. These medications offer relief to at least two-thirds of those treated, although it usually takes two or three weeks for improvement to become apparent.

Psychotherapy, used either alone or along with medication, is also an effective treatment for depression. The improvement often seen with psychotherapy highlights the extent to which depression feeds on itself: Patients typically feel guilty over being ill and are unable to function normally, mistakenly believing that a person of stronger character would be able to "snap out of it" on their own. This guilt, and the resulting depressed mood, reinforces and intensifies the symptoms of their illness. It thus further limits their ability to function and creates still more guilt. Psychotherapy allows the psychiatrist to point out that, since depression is no more subject to personal control than is cancer, there is no reason to feel guilty about having it.

People who have been depressed frequently or for long periods may also have trouble distinguishing between their true personalities and the symptoms of their disorder. Psychotherapy can help them draw this distinction, as well as assist them in dealing with the problems the disorder has created in their lives.

Both medication and psychotherapy typically take several weeks or months to become fully effective, and neither can help everyone. For those who are not helped, or whose symptoms are so severe that a faster start on the road to recovery is essential, an alternative is electroconvulsive therapy (ECT—sometimes informally called shock therapy). In this therapy, electrodes are applied to the head (or to one side of the head) and the patient receives an electric shock strong enough to cause muscle spasms and convulsions.

ECT acquired a bad name in the 1950s when the practice was abused by some professionals. Today, however, the main drawback to ECT is a sometimes distressing degree of temporary memory loss. Patients usually recover most of their missing memories within six to nine months, however; only the few days immediately preceding the therapy are permanently lost. Since ECT can be a literally life-saving treatment for severely depressed individuals, it is appropriate when nothing else can provide help fast enough.

Sleep deprivation, although still considered experimental, seems to hold promise. Several studies indicate

that depressed individuals get better if they remain awake for 40 hours in a row. Sleeping only part of the night for several nights in a row brings similar benefits. There are even indications that people can benefit from going to bed earlier and getting up earlier, with no change in the total amount of sleep they get.

Whatever the therapies available, however, treatment cannot be effective if it is not used. The greatest need continues to be getting help to those who need it, but who currently remain untreated.

See also Antidepressants; Manic depression; Neurotransmitter; Psychology; Psychoanalysis; Stress.

Further Reading:
Cronkite, Kathy. *On the Edge of Darkness: Conversations about Conquering Depression.* New York: Doubleday, 1994.

KEY TERMS

Electroconvulsive therapy (ECT—Therapy in which a strong electrical current is applied to the head; a rapid, effective treatment for depression, although it causes temporary memory loss. Also known as "shock therapy."

Dysthymia—A feeling of sadness or lack of pleasure in life that persists for at least two years.

Major depression—A persistent syndrome (or, in other contexts, a disorder) characterized by either sadness or lack of pleasure, accompanied by a certain number of other physical or emotional symptoms; major depression, also called endogenous depression, is by definition not an appropriate response to an external loss.

Premenstrual dysphoric disorder—A controversial diagnostic category describing a condition in which a woman becomes highly depressed during the days immediately before her menstrual period; possibly a hormone-influenced variant of major depression.

Reactive depression—A feeling of sadness or lack of pleasure in life that is an appropriate response to an external loss, given the individual's psychological makeup and previous life experiences.

Seasonal affective disorder—A variant of major depression that recurs regularly during the shortest, darkest days of winter (or, much more rarely, in summer).

Mondimore, Francis Mark. *Depression: The Mood Disease.* Baltimore: The Johns Hopkins University Press, 1990.

Robbins, Paul R. *Understanding Depression.* Jefferson, North Carolina: McFarland & Co., 1993.

Stokes, Peter E. "Current Issues in the Treatment of Major Depression." *Journal of Clinical Psychopharmacology* 13 (1993): 2S-9S.

W. A. Thomasson

Depth perception

Depth perception is the ability to see the environment in three dimensions and to estimate the spatial distances of objects from ourself and from each other. Depth perception is vital for our survival, being necessary to effectively navigate around and function in the world. Without it we would be unable to tell how far objects are from us, and thus how far we would need to move to reach or avoid them. Moreover, we would not be able to distinguish between, for instance, stepping down a stair from stepping off of a tall building.

Our ability to perceive depth encompasses space perception, or the ability to perceive the differential distances of objects in space. While researchers have discovered much about depth perception, numerous interesting questions remain. For instance, how are we able to perceive the world in three dimensions when the images projected onto the retina are basically two-dimensional and flat? And how much of a role does learning play in depth perception? While depth perception results primarily from our sense of vision, our sense of hearing also plays a role. Two broad classes of cues used to aid visual depth perception have been distinguished—the monocular (requiring only one eye), and the binocular (requiring both eyes working together.)

Monocular cues

The following cues require only one eye for their perception. They provide information that helps us estimate spatial distances and to perceive in three dimensions.

Interposition

Interposition refers to objects appearing to partially block or overlap one another. When an object appears partially blocked by another, the fully visible object is perceived as being nearer, and this generally corresponds to reality.

Shading and lighting

In general, the nearer an object is to a light source, the brighter its surface appears to be, so that with groups of objects, darker objects appear farther away than brighter objects. And in looking at single objects, the farther parts of an object's surface are from the source of light, the more shadowed and less bright they will appear. Varying shading and lighting then provide information about distances of objects from the source of light, and may serve as a cue to the distance of the object from the observer. In addition, some patterns of lighting and shading seem to provide cues about the shapes of objects.

Aerial perspective

Generally, objects having sharp and clear images appear nearer than objects with blurry or unclear images. This occurs because light is scattered or absorbed over long distances by particles in the atmosphere such as water vapor and dust which leads to a blurring of objects' lines. This is why on clear days, very large objects such as mountains or buildings appear closer than when viewed on hazy days.

Elevation

This cue, sometimes referred to as "height in the plane" or "relative height," describes how the horizon is seen as vertically higher than the foreground. Thus objects high in the visual field and closer to the horizon line are perceived as being farther away than objects lower in the visual field and farther away from the horizon line. Above the horizon line this relationship is reversed, so that above the horizon, objects that are lower and nearer to the horizon line appear farther away than those up higher and at a greater distance from the horizon line.

Texture gradients

Textures that vary in complexity and density are a characteristic of most object surfaces and they reflect light differentially. Generally, as distance increases, the size of elements making up surface texture appear smaller and the distance between the elements also appears to decrease with distance. Thus if one is looking at a field of grass, the blades of grass will appear smaller and arranged more closely together as their distance increases. Texture gradients also serve as depth and distance cues in groupings of different objects with different textures in the visual field, as when looking at a view of a city. Finally, abrupt changes in texture usually indicate an alteration in the direction of an object's surface and its distance from the observer.

Linear perspective

Linear perspective is a depth cue based on the fact that as objects increase in distance from the observer their images on the retina are transformed so that their size and the space separating them decrease until the farthest objects meet at what is called the vanishing point. It is called the vanishing point because it is the point where objects get so small that they are no longer visible. In addition, physically parallel lines such as those seen in railroad tracks are perceived as coming closer together until they meet or converge at the vanishing point.

Motion parallax

Whenever our eyes move (due to eye movement alone, or head, or body movement) in relation to the spatial environment, objects at varying distances move at different rates relative to their position and distance from us. In other words, objects at different distances relative to the observer are perceived as moving at different speeds. Motion parallax refers to these relatively perceived object motions which we use as cues for the perception of distance and motion as we move through the environment.

As a rule, when the eyes move, objects close to the observer seem to move faster than objects farther away. In addition, more distant objects seem to move smaller distances than do nearer objects. Objects that are very far away, such as a bright star or the moon, seem to move at the exact same rate as the observer and in the same direction.

The amount and direction of movement are relative to the observer's fixation point or where they are focussing. For instance, if you were travelling on a train and focussing on the middle of a large field you were passing, any objects closer to you than your fixation point would seem to be moving opposite to your direction of movement. In addition, those objects beyond your fixation point would appear to be moving in the same direction as you are moving. Motion parallax cues provide strong and precise distance and depth information to the observer.

Accommodation

Accommodation occurs when curvature of the eye lens changes differentially to form sharp retinal images of near and far objects. To focus on far objects the lens becomes relatively flat and to focus on nearer objects the lens becomes more curved. Changes in the lens shape are controlled by the ciliary muscles and it seems that feedback from alterations in ciliary muscle tension may furnish information about object distance.

Retinal size

As an object's distance from the viewer increases, the size of its image on the retina becomes smaller. And, generally, in the absence of additional visual cues, larger objects are perceived as being closer than are smaller objects.

Familiarity

While not exactly a visual cue for perceiving space or depth as are the previous ones discussed, our familiarity with spatial characteristics of an object such as its size or shape due to experience with the object may contribute to estimates of distance and thus spatial perception. For instance, we know that most cars are taller or higher than children below the age of five, and thus in the absence of other relevant visual cues, a young child seen in front of a car who is taller than the car would be perceived as being closer than the car.

Binocular cues

Monocular cues certainly provide a great deal of spatial information, but depth perception also requires binocular functioning of the eyes, that is, both eyes working together in a coordinated fashion. Convergence and retinal disparity are binocular cues to depth perception.

Convergence

Convergence refers to the eyes' disposition to rotate inward toward each other in a coordinated manner in order to focus effectively on nearby objects. With objects that are farther away, the eyes must move outward toward one's temples. For objects further than approximately 20 ft (6 m) away no more changes in convergence occur and the eyes are essentially parallel with each other. It seems that feedback from changes in muscular tension required to cause convergence eye movements may provide information about depth or distance.

Retinal disparity and stereopsis

Retinal disparity refers to the small difference between the images projected on the two retinas when looking at an object or scene. This slight difference or disparity in retinal images serves as a binocular cue for the perception of depth. Retinal disparity is produced in humans (and in most higher vertebrates with two frontally directed eyes) by the separation of the eyes which causes the eyes to have different angles of objects or scenes. It is the foundation of stereoscopic vision.

Stereoscopic vision refers to the unified three-dimensional view of objects produced when the two different images are fused into one (binocular fusion). We still do not fully understand the mechanisms behind stereopsis but there is evidence that certain cells in some areas of the brain responsible for vision are specifically responsive to the specific type of retinal disparity involving slight horizontal differences in the two retinal images. This indicates that there may be other functionally specific cells in the brain that aid depth perception. In sum, it seems that we use numerous visual depth cues, binocular vision, and functionally specific cells in the nervous system to make accurate depth judgements.

Auditory depth cues

Auditory depth cues are used by everyone but are especially important for the blind. These include the relative loudness of familiar sounds, the amount of reverberation of sounds as in echoes, and certain characteristics of sounds unique to their frequency. For instance, higher frequency sounds are more easily absorbed by the atmosphere.

Development of depth perception

A theme running throughout the study of perception in general since the time of the ancient Greeks has been whether perceptual processes are learned (based on past experience) or innate (existent or potential at birth). In terms of depth perception, research using the visual cliff with animals and human infants too young to have had experience with depth perception indicates that humans and various species of animals are born with some innate abilities to perceive depth.

The visual cliff is one the most commonly used methods of assessing depth perception. It is an apparatus made up of a large box with a clear or see-through panel on top. One side of the box has a patterned surface placed immediately under the clear surface, and the other side has the same patterned surface placed at some distance below the clear surface. This latter side gives the appearance of a sharp drop-off or cliff. The subject of the study will be placed on the glass and consistent movement toward the shallow side is seen as an indication of depth perception ability. Newborn infants who cannot crawl commonly show much distress when placed face down over the "cliff" side.

Research with animals raised without opportunities to see (for example if reared in the dark) sustain long-lasting deficits in their perceptual abilities. Indeed, such deprivation may even affect the weight and biochem-

KEY TERMS

Accommodation—Refers to changes in curvature of the eye lens to form sharp retinal images of near and far objects, it may function as a cue for depth.

Aerial-perspective—A monocular visual cue referring to how objects with sharp and clear images appear nearer than objects with blurry or unclear images.

Binocular cues—Visual cues that require the coordinated use of both eyes.

Convergence—The tendency of the eyes to rotate toward each other in a coordinated manner in order to focus effectively on nearby objects.

Elevation—A monocular visual cue referring to an object's placement in relation to the horizon.

Interposition—A monocular cue referring to how when objects appear to partially block or overlap with each other, the fully visible object is perceived as being nearer.

Linear perspective—A monocular depth cue involving the apparent convergence of parallel lines in the distance, as well as the perceived decrease in the size of objects and the space between them with increasing distance from the observer.

Monocular cues—Visual cues that one eye alone can perceive.

Motion parallax—The perception of objects moving at different speeds relative to their distance from the observer.

Retina—An extremely light-sensitive layer of cells at the back part of the eyeball. Images formed by the lens on the retina are carried to the brain by the optic nerve.

Stereoscopic vision—The unified three-dimensional view of objects produced when the two slightly different images of objects on the two retinas are fused into one.

Texture gradient—A monocular visual cue referring to how changes in an object's perceived surface texture indicate distance from the observer and changes in direction of the object.

istry of their brains. This research indicates that while humans and some animal species have innate mechanisms for depth perception, these innate abilities require visual experience in order to develop and become fully functioning. This research also suggests that animals and humans may have developmentally sensitive periods in which visual experience is necessary or permanent perceptual deficits may occur.

Current research/future developments

In sum, while environmental cues, binocular vision, and physiological aspects of the nervous system can account for many aspects of depth perception, numerous questions remain. Advances in understanding the physiological basis of vision have been great since the 1950s and this has greatly influenced research and theorizing in perception in general, and depth perception in particular. Researchers are eagerly looking at the structure of the nervous system to see if it might explain further aspects of depth perception. In particular, researchers continue to explore the possibility that additional fine tuned detector cells may exist that respond to specific visual stimuli. Finally, some psychologists have begun using certain basic principles of associative learning theory to explain a number of well-known yet poorly understood elements of perceptual learning. Both of these approaches show great potential for furthering our understanding of many processes in perception.

See also Vision.

Further Reading:

Coren, S., L.M. Ward, and J.T. Enns. *Sensation and perception*, 4th Ed. Fort Worth, TX: Harcourt Brace Jovanovich, 1994.

Masin, S.C., ed. *Foundations of perceptual theory*. New York: Elvesier Science, Inc., 1993.

Ono, T., et al., eds. *Brain mechanisms of perception and memory: From neuron to behavior*. New York: Oxford University Press, 1993.

Schiffman, H.R. *Sensation and perception: An integrated approach*, 3rd Ed. New York: John Wiley & Sons, 1990.

Marie Doorey

Derivative

In mathematics, the derivative is the exact rate at which one quantity changes with respect to another. Geometrically, the derivative is the slope of a curve at a point on the curve, defined as the slope of the tangent to the curve at the same point. The process of finding the derivative is called differentiation. This process is central to the branch of mathematics called differential calculus.

History and usefulness

Calculus was first invented by Sir Isaac Newton around 1665. Newton was a physicist as well as a mathematician. He found that the mathematics of his time was not sufficient to solve the problems he was interested in, so he invented new mathematics. About the same time another mathematician, Goltfried Leibnez, developed the same ideas as Newton. Newton was interested in calculating the velocity of an object at any instant. For example, if you sit under an apple tree, as legend has it Newton did, and an apple falls and hits you on the head, you might ask how fast the apple was traveling just before impact. More importantly, many of today's scientists are interested in calculating the rate at which a satellite's position changes with respect to time (its rate of speed). Most investors are interested in how a stock's value changes with time (its rate of growth). In fact, many of today's important problems in the fields of physics, chemistry, engineering, economics, and biology involve finding the rate at which one quantity changes with respect to another, that is, they involve finding the derivative.

The basic concept

The derivative is often called the "instantaneous" rate of change. A rate of change is simply a comparison of the change in one quantity to the simultaneous change in a second quantity. For instance, the amount of money your employer owes you compared to the length of time you worked for him determines your rate of pay. The comparison is made in the form of a ratio, dividing the change in the first quantity by the change in the second quantity. When both changes occur during an infinitely short period of time (in the same instant), the rate is said to be "instantaneous," and then the ratio is called the derivative.

To better understand what is meant by an instantaneous rate of change, consider the graph of a straight line (see figure 1).

The line's slope is defined to be the ratio of the rise (vertical change between any two points) to the run (simultaneous horizontal change between the same two points). This means that the slope of a straight line is a rate, specifically, the line's rate of rise with respect to the horizontal axis. It is the simplest type of rate because it is constant, the same between any two points, even two points that are arbitrarily close together. Roughly speaking, arbitrarily close together means you

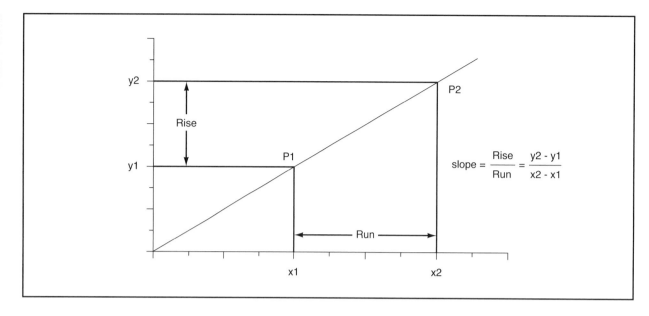

Figure 1.

can make them closer than any positive amount of separation. The derivative of a straight line, then, is the same for every point on the line and is equal to the slope of the line.

Determining the derivative of a curve is somewhat more difficult, because its instantaneous rate of rise changes from point to point (see figure 2).

We can estimate a curve's rate of rise at any particular point, though, by noticing that any section of a curve can be approximated by replacing it with a straight line. Since we know how to determine the slope of a straight line, we can approximate a curve's rate of rise at any point, by determining the slope of an approximating line segment. The shorter the approximating line segment becomes, the more accurate the estimate becomes. As the length of the approximating line segment becomes arbitrarily short, so does its rise and its run. Just as in the case of the straight line, an arbitrarily short rise and run can be shorter than any given positive pair of distances. Thus, their ratio is the instantaneous rate of rise of the curve at the point or the derivative. In this case the derivative is different at every point, and equal to the slope of the tangent at each point. (A tan-

gent is a straight line that intersects a curve at a single point.)

A concrete example

A fairly simple, and not altogether impractical example is that of the falling apple. Observation tells us that the apple's initial speed (the instant before letting go from the tree) is zero, and that it accelerates rapidly. Scientists have found, from repeated measurements with various falling objects (neglecting wind resistance), that the distance an object falls on the earth (call it S) in a specified time period (call it T) is given by the following equation (see figure 2):

(1) $S = 16 T^2$

Suppose you are interested in the apple's speed after it has dropped 4 ft (1.2 m). As a first approximation, connect the points where $Sl_1=0$ and $Sl_2=8$ (see figure 3 and line 1 of Table 1).

Using equation (1), find the corresponding times, and calculate the slope of the approximating line segment (use the formula in figure 1). Repeat this process numerous times, each time letting the two points get

	TABLE 1					
$_x1$	$_x2$	$_t1$	$_t2$	$_x2-_x1$	$_t2-_t1$	$(_x2-_x1)/(_t2-_t1)$
0	8	0	0.707106781	8	0.707106781	11.3137085
1	7	0.25	0.661437828	6	0.411437828	14.58300524
3	5	0.433012702	0.559016994	2	0.126004292	15.87247514

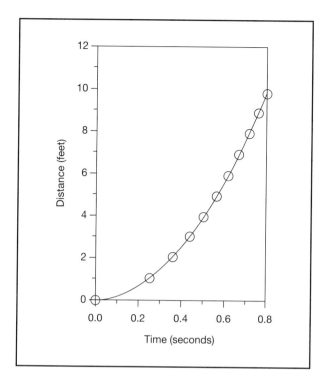

Figure 2.

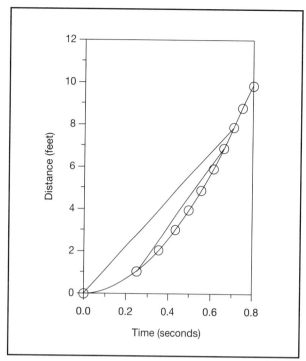

Figure 3.

closer together. If a calculator or computer spreadsheet is available this is rather simple. Table 1 shows the result for several approximating line segments. The line segments corresponding to the first two entries in the table are drawn in figure 3. Looking at figure 3, it is clear that as the approximating line gets shorter, its

slope approximates the rate of rise of the curve more accurately.

See also Calculus.

Further Reading:

Allen, G.D., C. Chui, and B. Perry. *Elements of Calculus*. 2nd ed. Pacific Grove, California: Brooks/Cole Publishing Co, 1989.

Boyer, Carl B. *A History of Mathematics*. 2nd ed. Revised by Uta C. Merzbach. New York: John Wiley and Sons, 1991.

Downing, Douglas. *Calculus the Easy Way*. 2nd ed. Hauppauge, New York: Barron's Educational Services, Inc., 1988.

McLaughlin, William I. "Resolving Zeno's Paradoxes." *Scientific American*. 271(1994): 84-89.

J. R. Maddocks

DES see **Diethylstilbestrol**

KEY TERMS

Infinitesimal—Approaching zero in length. When the separation between two points approaches zero but never quite gets there, the separation is said to be infinitesimal.

Instantaneous—Occurring in an instant or an infinitely short period of time.

Rate—A comparison of the change in one quantity to the simultaneous change in a second quantity. The comparison is made by forming a ratio.

Ratio—The fraction formed when two quantities are compared by division, that is, one quantity is divided by the other.

Slope—Slope is the ratio of the vertical distance separating any two points on a line, to the horizontal distance separating the same two points.

Desalination

Desalination, also called desalting, is the removal of salt from seawater. It provides essential water for drinking and industry in desert regions or wherever the local water supply is brackish. In 1991, about 3.5 billion gallons of desalinated water were produced in about 4,000 desalination plants world-wide. Most of this water was produced through distillation. However, other methods, including reverse osmosis and electrodialysis, are becoming increasingly important.

At its simplest, distillation consists of boiling the seawater to separate it from dissolved salt. The water vapor rises to a cooler region where it condenses as pure liquid water. Heat for distillation usually comes from burning fossil fuels. To reduce costs and pollution, desalination plants are designed to use as little fuel as possible. Many employ flash distillation, in which heated seawater is pumped into a low pressure chamber. The low pressure causes the water to vaporize, or "flash," even though it is below its boiling temperature. Therefore, less heat is required. Multi-stage flashing passes the seawater through a series of chambers at successively lower pressures. For even greater efficiency, desalination plants can be linked with electrical power plants. Heat from the hot gasses that turn the generators is recycled to warm the incoming seawater. Distillation is widely used in the Middle East, where fossil fuel is plentiful but fresh water is scarce.

Reverse osmosis uses high pressure to force pure water out of salt water. Normal osmosis occurs when pure water and salt water are separated by a semipermeable membrane, which permits only water to flow through. Under these conditions, the pure water will move into the salt water side, but if the salt water is squeezed under high enough pressure, fresh water moves out of it. Pressures on the order of 60 atmospheres (800-1,200 psi) are required to push pure water out of seawater. Reverse osmosis is widely used to desalinate brackish water, which is less salty than seawater and therefore requires pressures only about half as great.

Like reverse osmosis, electrodialysis is presently best suited for desalinating brackish water. Salts consist of ions, which are atoms that have acquired electrical charge by losing or gaining electrons. Because of their charge, ions are attracted to oppositely charged electrodes immersed in the salt water. They move toward the electrodes, leaving a region of pure water behind. Special membranes prevent the ions from drifting back into the purified water as it is pumped out.

Ongoing research seeks to improve existing desalination methods and develop new ones. The costs of distillation could be greatly reduced if clean, renewable energy were used to heat the water. Solar, geothermal,

and oceanic temperature differences are among the energy sources being studied. Reverse osmosis could be used on a larger scale, and with saltier water, through development of semipermeable membranes able to withstand higher pressures for longer times. All desalination methods leave extremely salty residues. New methods for disposing of these must be developed as the world's use of desalination grows.

See also Distillation; Salt; Saltwater.

Desert

A desert is an arid land area, one that loses more water through evaporation, than it gains through precipitation—rain, sleet, or snow. These areas generally receive fewer than 10 in (250 mm) of water annually. Average annual precipitation in the world's deserts ranges from about 0.4-1 in (10-25 mm) in the driest areas to 10 in (250 mm) in semiarid regions. The term desert can also be defined by comparing the solar energy an area receives with the its annual precipitation. In the eastern Sahara and the Peruvian desert, two of the driest places on earth, the sun can evaporate 200 times as much water as falls in an average year, giving these regions an aridity index of 200. Regions classified as semiarid, like those east of the U.S. Rocky Mountains have an aridity index of 1.5-4, and are able to support a diversity of life. Common characteristics of desert systems worldwide are sparse, erratic precipitation, frequently high winds, low humidity, and temperatures that can fluctuate dramatically between seasons and during each day. Days with maximum temperatures above 90°F (32.2°C) and minimums below 32°F (0°C) are not uncommon in desert areas.

Most of the world's desert ecosystems are located in two arid systems, governed by high-pressure weather systems, that almost completely encircle the earth to the north and south of the equator. These belts of aridity are shaped by intense sun at the equator, which heats that region's air, causing it to expand and become lighter. This light, hot air rises from the equator, drifts north and south into cooler latitudes, and descends. Equatorial air currents, which were initially quite humid, cool as they rise, and their moisture condenses into clouds and falls to the earth as rain. Having shed their moisture and cooled, these currents lose altitude as they move toward the Tropic of Cancer in the north and the Tropic of Capricorn in the south. As this

Cactus in the Sonoran Desert, Organ Pipe Cactus National Park, Arizona.

cool, dry air moves back toward the earth's surface, it is rewarmed, making it even drier. Finally, its low humidity draws moisture away from the land on its journey back toward the equator. So the air that reaches the tropics not only brings little or no precipitation, but it draws away whatever moisture is available from the land.

This recurring weather pattern has helped create the harsh conditions that define life in the arid lands along the edges of the tropics. Under the fierce, cloudless skies in the northern half of the globe lies north Africa's vast Sahara desert, an area 3,000 mi (4,800 km) wide and 1,000 mi (1,600 km) deep. Just 20% of the Sahara is sand, while the rest is plains of rock, pebble, and salt flats, punctuated by mountains. Because the Sahara is a low-lying desert, much of it below sea-level, and it can experience temperatures that rise and fall 100°F (38°C). in a single day, while a decades can go by without rain. By contrast, the deserts of Turkestan and central India, the frigid Gobi—a 500,000 square mile (129,500,000 ha) expanse—and Taklaman deserts, are found at higher altitudes where temperatures remain below freezing most of the year. The northern hemisphere is also home to the less arid deserts of the southwestern United States.

In the southern hemisphere lie Africa's Kalahari and Namib deserts, a coastal desert like the Atacama, along Chile's coast, as well as Australia's outback, a desert region that fills the interior of the continent. Antarctica, the land mass at the southern pole of the globe, is a polar desert, and is one of the driest places on earth, receiving only a dusting of snow each year, while experiencing warmest summer temperatures of 25°F (-4°C).

Some of these desert systems have developed under environmental stresses in addition to the high pressure weather systems described above. Continental deserts, such as the Gobi and Australia's great desert system, are so far from the oceans that they receive no moisture. Rain-shadow deserts, those that lie in the shadow of mountain ranges, receive little precipitation because as air ascends on the other side air of the mountains, it drops its rain, and is free of moisture as it descends down the eastern mountain slopes. Among rain shadow deserts are California's Death Valley, in the shadow of the Sierra Nevadas, Argentina's Patagonian and Monte deserts, in the shadow of Chile's great mountain range, and the Iranian desert, which lies under the Zagros Mountains. Coastal deserts, which lie along the western coastlines of three continents, are created as air passes over the frigid waters on these coasts. As it cools, this air loses its capacity to hold water. By the time the air has reached land, all the moisture has been turned to rain over the sea or dense fog over the coastline, leaving little or no water for the land.

Over the earth's lifespan, the intensity of desert conditions has fluctuated and deserts expanded and contracted, probably in response to global changes in atmospheric circulation. About 15 million years ago, toward the end of the Tertiary Period, the current configuration of desert lands started to develop. Three to 4 million years ago, at the onset of the Pleistocene Epoch, the deserts as we know them were in place. Today, almost 33% of the earth's land surface is desert, a proportion that is increasing by as much as 40 square miles (10,360 ha) each day. Of the total land surface area of the earth, 4% (5.4 million square km/2.2 million square mi) is extremely arid, 15% (20.3 million square km/7.8 square mi) is arid, and 14.6% (19.7 million square km/7.9 million square mi) is semiarid.

The hot, dry desert of sand dunes is the most easily evoked image of "desert," yet it accounts for only a small percentage of arid land areas. The world's deserts greatly diverse, and include semiarid deserts, composed of scattered trees, scrub, and grasses, the barren, freezing deserts of the Antarctic ice cap, paved deserts, flat lands covered with dense coats of large rock fragments, which give the land the look of a cobbled street, and the blinding white salt plains formed in the beds of extinct seas, such as Lake Assale in the Ethiopian highlands.

The deserts of the United States are located at higher latitudes and in higher altitudes than is typical of many other arid regions of the world. Death Valley represents the arid extreme of the North American continent; it is both extremely arid and extremely hot in the summer. And it is warmer than the neighboring Mojave Desert and drier than the Sonoran.

Life in the desert

The plants and animals that are able to survive the extremes of desert conditions have all evolved ways of compensating for the uncertain availability of water. For both plants and animals, the environmental stresses of the desert are extreme. Because plant growth in deserts is restricted by the lack of water, little organic matter is added to the soil. Desert soils typically contain

Windblown rock at Racetrack Playa, Death Valley, California. Some scientists believe that precipitation and low temperatures during a storm can create a micro-layer of ice between rocks and the muddy surface of the desert, a layer that reduces friction enough to allow the storm winds to move the rocks.

higher concentrations of salts that soils in regions that get more precipitation. Clear daytime skies allow most of the sun's heat and radiation to reach the earth. While water can be plentiful in some arid regions in some seasons, conditions in desert habitats can change quickly from favorable to unfavorable. Around the world, organisms have evolved similar mechanisms to deal with the deserts' dearth of water.

Plants that are able to thrive in the desert include lichens, which are actually two plants—algae and fungus growing together in symbiosis. Lichens have no roots and can absorb water and nutrients from rain, dew, and the dust on which they grow.

Annuals, plants such as many grasses, grow from seeds each year, and succeed in desert settings by responding quickly when conditions are favorable. In the southwestern United States, for example, precipitation is highly variable from year to year. With rainfall, seeds that may have lain dormant for as long as 50 years rapidly sprout and flower, and give the desert the appearance of a flower garden.

Succulents include the American cacti and agaves and the African euphorbias can quickly absorb rainwater when it comes, and store it in their stems and leaves, if they have them. Cacti, like the Southwest's giant Saguaro, are typically leafless, spiny, and covered with a thick, waxy cuticle—all means of conserving water. Other plants store nutrients in their roots and stems or develop specialized storage organs such as tubers.

KEY TERMS

· ·

Arid—Climate condition in which very little precipitation falls—average annual precipitation from about 10 to 25 mm.

Rain-shadow deserts—Areas that lie in the shadow of mountain ranges, and receive little precipitation rain has dropped from the air on the other side air of the mountains.

Precipitation—Water that falls to the ground in the form of rain, sleet, or snow.

Many desert shrubs have evolved into inverted cone shapes that collect larger amounts of rain on their surfaces, funneling it down to the base of the plant. And some desert plants have also evolved the ability to withdraw water from soils at very high pressures.

Desert animals

The many animals that have adapted to harsh desert life include insects, arachnids, reptiles, birds, and mammals. Unlike plants, these animals can seek shelter from the scorching sun, burning cold, and shipping winds by crawling into underground burrows. Reptiles, whose body temperature is controlled by the temperature of their environment, travel between sunlight and shade to stay cool. Birds, which show few adaptations except for the paler color of most desert animals, can soar to cool upper levels, and they may migrate during the harsher seasons.

Just as the seeds of desert annuals can stay dormant for decades, so can those of egg-laying desert animals. Amphibians and freshwater shrimp hatch, mature, mate, and lay their own eggs rapid succession in desert pools created by infrequent storms.

Some small mammals, such as rodents, excrete only concentrated urine and dry feces, and perspire little as a way of conserving body fluids. The camel's body temperature can soar to 105°F (40.5°C) before this mammal sweats, and it can lose up to a third of it body weight and replace it at a single drinking.

Desert insects protect themselves from hot dry conditions with a waxy coating, long legs that keep them elevated above the hot ground, and virtually moistureless excretions.

See also Biome.

Further Reading:

Polis, Gary A. *The Ecology of Desert Communities*. University of Arizona, 1991.

Beth Hanson

Desertification

Desertification denotes the gradual conversion of productive arid or semi-arid land to biologically unproductive land. The term desertification entered the popular vocabulary in 1949, when French botanist Aubreville used it to refer to the transformation of productive land into desert-like conditions.

However, the processes whereby arid lands are stripped of their productivity need not always result in desert; most desertified land does not look like Death Valley. In some cases desertification has been successfully reversed and desertified areas restored to productivity through careful land stewardship. In the worst case, even desert itself can become desertified, losing its sparse complement of plants and animals and becoming barren, gullied wasteland.

The processes of desertification are both natural and human-induced, and desertification in some form has probably been ongoing for eons in conjunction with long-cycle climatic changes. Until the twentieth century, however, humans could simply move away from land rendered unusable. The past century's global population increase and the lack of unsettled lands have jointly focused attention on the degradation of once-productive land.

Desertification claimed major international attention in the 1970s, following years of severe drought in the Sahel that affected six countries on the southern border of the Sahara Desert. Millions of livestock died during the drought, and the human toll was tremendous. Relief measures were instituted late, for the region had experienced drought before, and there was some uncertainty as to the severity of the 1968-1973 drought. One of the aftereffects of the drought was the United Nations Conference on Desertification, held in August and September, 1977, in Nairobi, Kenya. The conference brought together 700 officials from almost 100 countries. The delegates approved 26 recommendations for slowing or reversing desertification, with the intention of achieving zero increase in desertified lands by the year 2000. This goal is unlikely to be met. However, as the end of the twentieth century approaches, much more is known about desertification than was known during the UN conference, and ways of measuring the ecosystem effects of a single variable are being refined.

The arid lands of North America are among those most affected by desertification; almost 90% are moderately to severely desertified. The arid and semi-arid lands of the western and southwestern United States are highly vulnerable to aexploitation. The perennial grasses that dominate arid-land vegetation provide good forage for cattle, which, when confined in one spot, churn up the soil and destroy the roots of the grasses. Conversely, cattle may trample soil to a fine powder that cakes into a hard shell through wetting and drying, so that little water penetrates to the roots of arid-land vegetation. Water is drawn off aquifers to irrigate crops and supply large cities, exceeding the ability of the water table to replenish itself. Ore deposits, rich in the west, are mined for industrial uses; in fact, most of the U.S. energy resources—not only fossil fuels but wind and solar resources—are concentrated in the arid western region. The promotion of recreational pursuits on arid and desert lands has brought a new habitat threat in the form of land erosion by off-road vehicles.

Studies of pre-industrial, native people in the western and southwestern United States show that human contributions to desertification are not limited to modern society. Even a small band of people, if reliant on one resource, can introduce long-lasting changes. As an example, the Chihuahuan Desert, which extends from Arizona, New Mexico, and Texas in the United States deep into Mexico, has undergone changes in human history. Indians reliant on mesquite beans for food apparently transported them through the desert; stands of mesquite grew up around campsites and watering holes, replacing the desert grasses. The Pueblan group, which flourished in southwestern United States beginning around 800 A.D., used the meager supplies of trees for housing materials, and this practice was later followed by European missionaries and colonists. Thus, cultural practices of even a few people could, if continued over time, dramatically and unfavorably alter the ecosystem.

Processes of desertification

The decline in biological productivity of arid lands occurs gradually. Gradualism, incorporated into the definition, implies both potential reversibility and a continuum of change. Desertification, then, is best thought of as a process of degradation of a terrestrial ecosystem—including both plants and animals, as well as geophysical resources such as water and soil—that involves a continuum of undesirable changes. Desertification is ordinarily graded from slight to very severe, although these gradations are impossible to apply uniformly from area to area. Although desertification is sometimes thought to mean the advance of a desert ecology, that is not correct. Desertification takes hold in a focus of continued land abuse, which may occur in rain forests, tropical mountainous areas, or even within the desert itself. Because the role of climate in relation to desertification is highly marked in dry lands, desertification is usually discussed in the context of dry areas.

The physical characteristics of a land undergoing desertification include increasing loss of climax species (plants of a mature ecology) from the ecosystem; increasing loss of topsoil; increasing salinity (saltiness) of the soil, reducing crop yield and sometimes producing a salty crust to the soil, which hinders passage of water into the deeper soil layers; and an increasing number of deep gullies or sand dunes as the land is eroded, or through wind action.

The actions that produce these physical changes may be divided into natural, human/cultural, and administrative. Among the natural forces are wind and water erosion of soil, long-term changes in rainfall patterns, and other alterations in climate. The role of drought is variable and related in part to duration: a long drought accompanied by poor land management may be lethal when a shorter drought would not. Drought thus serves to stress an ecosystem without necessarily degrading it permanently. Rainfall similarly plays a variable role that depends on its duration and the pattern of its distribution.

The list of human or cultural processes is long but includes overgrazing, strip mining, the exhaustion of groundwater supplies, rechanneling of surface water, burning, removal of forests, the importation of non-native species, better veterinary services (more livestock live, increasing the pressure on water resources), and physical compaction of the soil (as may occur around camping sites as well as on rangeland). Human effects on the landscape have a long historical trail; there is evidence of human-caused desertification around the Tigris and Euphrates rivers in ancient Mesopotamia. Administrative forces contributing to desertification are those that tend to encourage cultivation of a single crop for export, the concentration of populations in arid lands, and various food policies and military policies. Governments desiring to halt desertification may lack the capital to assist farmers and ranchers in developing an alternative economic base that the land could support. Administrative policies may also encourage an asymmetrical transfer of resources: mining, for example, removes raw materials from a source area, but the government may have made no provision for investment to support development once the ore is exhausted.

When all these factors are put together, desertification emerges as a process of degradation that occurs over time and space and that interweaves natural, human, and economic forces. Ecosystem degradation must therefore be attacked on multiple fronts at once. Fortunately, scientists believe that severe desertification, rendering the land unreclaimable, is rare, and that most desertified areas can be reclaimed biologically, if socioeconomic and cultural factors allow it to be done.

Land management

Land management measures to combat desertification focus on improving sustainability and long-term productivity. It is not always possible or desirable to return a desertified area to its pre-desertified state, for an area that has been desertified once can be desertified again, and for the same reasons. Thus, reversing desertification means not restoring the ecosystem to its previous condition but converting it to a new state that can withstand local cultural and climatic pressures. Specific measures include developing a resilient vegetation cover of mixed trees, shrubs, and grasses that is suitable to local conditions. The soil must be protected against wind and water erosion, compaction, and salinization. Water diversions that critically lower the water table must be reversed, and new sources of water found for human and animal populations.

Principles of land management that would halt or reverse desertification have been known in North America since the end of the nineteenth century, but have only recently been put into practice. Even the ravages of the Dust Bowl, a phenomenon combining extended drought with severe wind erosion, did not suffice to move the public will toward instating broad anti-desertification measures. A focus on short-term profits and the autonomy of the private landowner or corporation has hindered significant progress. U.S. federal policies do support soil preservation in croplands and rangelands, but only about one third of such land is under federal protection. Elsewhere in the world, where political unrest is the norm and subsistence relies on exploiting local natural resources, there has been no progress toward reversing desertification. In areas of the world where subsistence means nomadic pastoralism—moving about with livestock from fertile spot to fertile spot—local governments' attempts either to limit the size of the herds or to deny access to traditional rangelands have been unsuccessful.

Managing land use requires the consent of many people, and often the best way to obtain that consent is

KEY TERMS

Arid land—Land receiving less than 10 inches (250 mm) of rainfall annually, with a high rate of evaporation and supporting a thin vegetation cover, chiefly grasses and shrubs.

Gradualism—A slow rate of change, implying that processes are spread out over time as well as space.

Sahel zone—A semi-arid region along the southern border of the Sahara in western Africa with a dry savanna type of vegetation; in recent years has been encroached on by the Sahara Desert, partly as a result of poor land management.

to provide people with viable alternatives. If rangeland is to be restricted while vegetation rejuvenates, the remaining rangeland must be populated with nutritious grasses capable of sustaining herds of livestock for years. The development of drought-resistant, highly nutritious grasses for this purpose is an ongoing research goal for botanists in the developed world. If trees are planted for use as fuel, it is better if they can also be used for fodder. A system of self-regulation, whereby a pastoral association assumes responsibility for maintaining a watering hole and surrounding rangeland, receiving in return free veterinary services, has been tried with good results in Niger, Mali, and Senegal. By these and similar means, economic concerns, cultural habitude, sustenance, and ecological preservation are addressed in a single program. Such comprehensive anti-desertification programs have usually been successful on a limited, regional scale, in part because cultural concerns must be addressed, in part because no accurate measure of desertification exists, so it is sometimes measured in the very pragmatic terms of how the land is intended to be used. Thus, any anti-desertification program must necessarily be adapted to local conditions, including climatic, cultural, and historical-use conditions.

Further Reading:

Sheridan, David. *Desertification of the United States.* Washington, DC: Council on Environmental Quality, U.S. Government Printing Office, 1981.

Marjorie Pannell

Desert rat see **Jerboas**

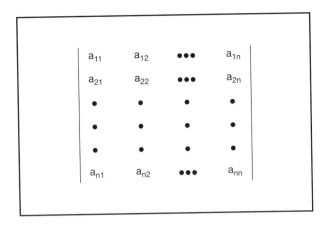

Figure 1.

Determinants

A determinant, signified by two straight lines ||, is a square array of numbers or symbols that has a specific value. For a square matrix, say, A, there exists an associated determinant, |A|, which has elements identical with the corresponding elements of the matrix. When matrices are not square, they do not possess corresponding determinants.

In general, determinants are expressed as shown in Figure 1, in which a_{ij}s are called elements of the determinant, and the horizontal and vertical lines of elements are called rows and columns, respectively. The sloping line consisting of a_{ii} elements is called the principal diagonal of the determinant. Sometimes, determinants can be written in a short form, $|a_{ij}|$. The n value, which reflects how many n^2 quantities are enclosed in ||, determines the order of a determinant.

For determinants of third order, that is, n = 3, or three rows of elements, we can evaluate them as illustrated in Figure 2.

By summing the products of terms as indicated by the arrows pointing towards the right-hand side and subtracting the products of terms as indicated by the arrows pointing towards the left-hand side, we can obtain the value of this determinant. The determinant can also be evaluated in terms of second-order determinants (two rows of elements), as in Figures 3(a) or 3(b).

Each of these second-order determinants, multiplied by an element a_{ij}, is obtained by deleting the *i*th row and the *j*th column of elements in the original third-order determinant, and it is called the "minor" of the element a_{ij}. The minor is further multiplied by $(-1)^{i+j}$, which is exactly the way we determine either the "+" or "-" sign for each determinant included in Figures 3 as shown, to become the "cofactor", C_{ij}, of the corresponding element.

Determinants have a variety of applications in engineering mathematics. Now, let's consider the sys-

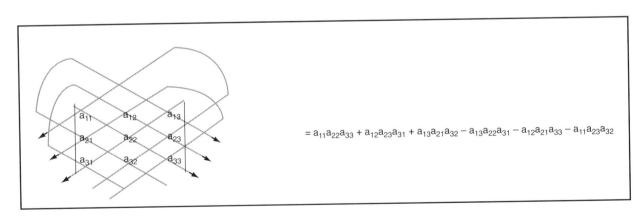

$$= a_{11}a_{22}a_{33} + a_{12}a_{23}a_{31} + a_{13}a_{21}a_{32} - a_{13}a_{22}a_{31} - a_{12}a_{21}a_{33} - a_{11}a_{23}a_{32}$$

Figure 2.

(a)

$$a_{11}\begin{vmatrix} a_{22} & a_{23} \\ a_{32} & a_{33} \end{vmatrix} - a_{21}\begin{vmatrix} a_{12} & a_{13} \\ a_{32} & a_{33} \end{vmatrix} + a_{31}\begin{vmatrix} a_{12} & a_{13} \\ a_{22} & a_{23} \end{vmatrix}$$

or

(b)

$$-a_{12}\begin{vmatrix} a_{21} & a_{23} \\ a_{31} & a_{33} \end{vmatrix} + a_{22}\begin{vmatrix} a_{11} & a_{13} \\ a_{31} & a_{33} \end{vmatrix} - a_{32}\begin{vmatrix} a_{11} & a_{13} \\ a_{21} & a_{23} \end{vmatrix}$$

Figure 3.

tem of two linear equations with two unknowns x_1 and x_2: $a_{11}x_1 + a_{12}x_2 = b_1$ and $a_{21}x_1 + a_{22}x_2 = b_2$.

We can multiply these two equations by a_{22} and $-a_{12}$, respectively, and add them together. This yields $(a_{11}a_{22} - a_{12}a_{21})x_1 = b_1a_{22} - b_2a_{12}$, i.e., $x_1 = (b_1a_{22} - b_2a_{12})/(a_{11}a_{22} - a_{12}a_{21})$. Similarly, $x_2 = (b_1a_{21} - b_2a_{11})/(a_{12}a_{21} - a_{11}a_{21})$ can be obtained by adding together the first equation multiplied by a_{21} and second equation multiplied by $-a_{11}$. These results can be written in determinant form as in Figure 4.

This is generally called Cramer's rule. Notice that in Figure 4, elements of the determinant in the denominator are the same as the coefficients of x_1 and x_2 in the two equations. To solve for x_1 (or x_2), we then replace the elements that correspond to the coefficients of x_1 (or x_2) of the determinant in the numerator with two constant terms, b_1 and b_2. When b_1 and b_2 both are equal to zero, the system defined by the two equations is said to be homogeneous. In this case, it will have either only

the trivial solution $x_1 = 0$ and $x_2 = 0$ or additional solutions if the determinant in the denominator in figure 5 is zero. When at least b_1 or b_2 is not zero (that is, a nonhomogeneous system) and the denominator has a value other than zero, the solution to the system is then obtained from figure 4. Cramer's rule is also applicable to systems of three linear equations. Therefore, determinants, along with matrices, have been used for solving simultaneous linear and differential equations involved in various systems, such as reactions in chemical reactors, stiffness of spring-connected masses, and currents in an electric network.

Pang-Jen Kung

Deuterium

Deuterium is an isotope of hydrogen with atomic mass of 2. It is represented by the symbols ^2H or D. Deuterium is also known as heavy hydrogen. The nucleus of the deuterium atom, consisting of a proton and a neutron, is known as a deuteron and is represented in nuclear equations by the symbol d.

Discovery

The possible existence of an isotope of hydrogen with atomic mass of two was suspected as early as the late 1910s after Frederick Soddy had developed the concept of isotopes. Such an isotope was of particular interest to chemists. Since the hydrogen atom is the

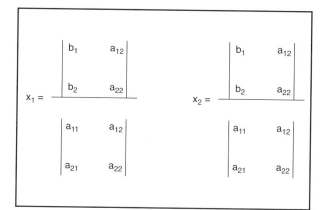

Figure 4.

simplest of all atoms—consisting of a single proton and a single electron—it is the model for most atomic theories. An atom just slightly more complex—one that contains a single neutron also—could potentially contribute valuable information to existing atomic theories.

Among those who sought for the heavy isotope of hydrogen was Harold Urey, at the time professor of chemistry at Columbia University. Urey began his work with the realization that any isotope of hydrogen other than hydrogen-1 (also known as protium) must exist in only minute quantities. The evidence for that fact is that the atomic weight of hydrogen is only slightly more than 1.000. The fraction of any isotopes with mass greater than that value must, therefore, be very small. Urey designed an experiment, therefore, that would allow him to detect the presence of heavy hydrogen in very small concentrations.

Urey's search for deuterium

Urey's approach was to collect a large volume of liquid hydrogen and then to allow that liquid to evaporate very slowly. His hypothesis was that the lighter and more abundant protium isotope would evaporate more quickly than the heavier hydrogen-2 isotope. The volume of liquid hydrogen remaining after evaporation was nearly complete, then, would be relatively rich in the heavier isotope.

In the actual experiment, Urey allowed 4.2 qt (4 l) of liquid hydrogen to evaporate until only .034 oz (1 ml) remained. He then submitted that sample to analysis by spectroscopy. In spectroscopic analysis, energy is added to a sample. Atoms in the sample are excited and their electrons are raised to higher energy levels. After a moment at these higher energy levels, the electrons return to their ground state, giving off their excess energy in the form of light. The bands of light emitted in this process are characteristics for each specific kind of atom.

By analyzing the spectral pattern obtained from his .034 oz (1 ml) sample of liquid hydrogen, Urey was able to identify a type of atom that had never before been detected, the heavy isotope of hydrogen. The new isotope was soon assigned the name deuterium. For his discovery of the isotope, Urey was awarded the 1934 Nobel Prize in chemistry.

Properties and preparation

Deuterium is a stable isotope of hydrogen with a relative atomic mass of 2.014102 compared to the atomic mass of protium, 1.007825. Deuterium occurs to the extent of about 0.0156% in a sample of naturally occurring hydrogen. Its melting point is 18.73 K (compared to 13.957 K for protium) and its boiling point is 23.67 K (compared to 20.39 K for protium). Its macroscopic properties of color, odor, taste, and the like are the same as those for protium.

Compounds containing deuterium have slightly different properties from those containing protium. For example, the melting and boiling points of heavy water are, respectively, 38.86°F (3.81°C) and 214.56°F (101.42°C). In addition, deuterium bonds tend to be somewhat stronger than protium bonds. Thus chemical reactions involving deuterium-containing compounds tend to go more slowly than do those with protium.

Deuterium is now prepared largely by the electrolysis of heavy water, that is, water made from deuterium and oxygen (D_2O). Once a great rarity, heavy water is now produced rather easily and inexpensively in very large volumes.

Uses

Deuterium has primarily two uses, as a tracer in research and in thermonuclear fusion reactions. A tracer is any atom or group of atoms whose participation in a physical, chemical, or biological reaction can be easily observed. Radioactive isotopes are perhaps the most familiar kind of tracer. They can be tracked in various types of changes because of the radiation they emit.

Deuterium is an effective tracer because of its mass. When it replaces protium in a compound, its presence can easily be detected because it weights twice as much as a protium atom. Also, as mentioned above, the bonds formed by deuterium with other atoms are slightly different from those formed by protium with other atoms. Thus, it is often possible to figure out what detailed changes take place at various stages of a chemical reaction using deuterium as a tracer.

Fusion reactions

Scientists now believe that energy produced in the sun and other stars is released as the result of a series of thermonuclear fusion reactions. The term fusion refers to the fact that two small nuclei, such as two hydrogen nuclei, fuse—or join together—to form a larger nucleus. The term thermonuclear means that such reactions normally occur only at very high temperatures, typically a few millions of degrees Celsius. Interest in fusion reactions arises not only because of their role in the manufacture of stellar energy, but also because of their potential value as sources of energy here on Earth.

Deuterium plays a critical role in most thermonuclear fusion reactions. In the solar process, for example, the fusion sequence appears to begin when two protium nuclei fuse to form a single deuteron. The deuteron is used up in later stages of the cycle by which four protium nuclei are converted to a single helium nucleus.

In the late 1940s and early 1950s scientists found a way of duplicating the process by which the sun's energy is produced in the form of thermonuclear fusion weapons, the so-called hydrogen bomb. The detonating device in this type of weapon was lithium deuteride, a compound of lithium metal and deuterium. The detonator was placed on the casing of an ordinary fission ("atomic") bomb. When the fission bomb detonated, it set off further nuclear reactions in the lithium deuteride which, in turn, set of fusion reactions in the larger hydrogen bomb.

For more than four decades, scientists have been trying to develop a method for bringing under control the awesome fusion power of a hydrogen bomb for use in commercial power plants. One of the most promising approaches appears to be a process in which two deuterons are fused to make a proton and a triton (the nucleus of a hydrogen-3 isotope). The triton and another deuteron then fuse to produce a helium nucleus, with the release of very large amounts of energy. So far, the technical details for making this process a commercially viable source of energy have not been completely worked out.

See also Hydrogen; Isotope; Nuclear fusion; Radioactive tracers.

Further Reading:

Asimov, Isaac. *Asimov's Biographical Encyclopedia of Science & Technology.* 2nd revised edition. Garden City, NY: Doubleday & Company, Inc., 1982, 739-40.

Greenwood, N. N., and A. Earnshaw. *Chemistry of the Elements.* Oxford: Pergamon Press, 1984, 1990, 40-7.

Joesten, Melvin D., David O. Johnston, John T. Netterville, and James L. Wood. *World of Chemistry.* Philadelphia: Saunders, 1991, 232-35.

Thomson, John F. *Biological Effects of Deuterium.* New York: Macmillan, 1963.

David E. Newton

Developmental processes

Developmental processes are the series of biological changes associated with information transfer, growth, and differentiation during the life cycle of organisms. Information transfer is the transmission of DNA and other biological signals from parent cells to daughter cells. Growth is the increase in size due to cell expansion and cell division. Differentiation is the change of unspecialized cells in a simple body pattern to specialized cells in single-celled bacteria, undergo development of some sort; the developmental process of complex multicellular organisms is emphasized here. In these organisms, development begins with the manufacture of male and female sex cells. It proceeds through fertilization and formation of an embryo. Development continues following birth, hatching, or germination of the embryo and culminates in aging and death.

History

Until the mid-1800s, many naturalists supported a theory of development called epigenesis, which held that the eggs of organisms were undifferentiated, but had a developmental potential which could be directed by certain external forces. Other naturalists supported a theory of development called preformationism, which held that the entire complex morphology of mature organism is present in miniature form in the egg, a developmental form called the homunculus.

These early theories of development relied on little experimental evidence. Thus, biologists often criticized the original theory of epigenesis because it seemed to propose that mystical forces somehow directed development, a view clearly outside the realm of science. Biologists also rejected preformationism, since studies of cytology and embryology clearly showed that development is much more than the simple growth of a preformed organism.

The modern view is that developmental processes have certain general features of both preformationism and epigenesis. Thus, we know that the simple cells of an egg are preformed in the sense that they contain a preformed instruction set for development which is encoded in their genes. Similarly, we know that the egg is relatively formless, but has the potential to develop into a complex organism as it grows. Thus modern developmental biology views development as the expression of a preformed genetic program which controls the epigenetic development of an undifferentiated egg into a morphologically complex adult.

Evolutionary aspects

People have long been interested in the connection between the development or an organism, its ontogeny, and the evolutionary ancestry of the species, its phylogeny. Anaximander, a philosopher of ancient Greece, noted that human embryos develop inside a fluid-filled wombs and proposed that human beings evolved from fish as creatures of the water.

This early idea was a progenitor to recapitulation theory, proposed in the 1800s by Ernst Haeckel, a German scientist. Recapitulation theory is summarized by the idea that the embryological development of an individual is a quick replay of its evolutionary history. As applied to humans, recapitulation theory was accepted by many evolutionary biologists in the 1800s. It also influenced the intellectual development of other disciplines outside of biology, including philosophy, politics, and psychology.

By the early 1900s, developmental biologists had disproven recapitulation theory and had shown that the relationship between ontogeny and phylogeny is more complex than proposed by Haeckel. However, like Haeckel, modern biologists hold that the similarities in the embryos of closely related species and the transient appearance of certain structures of mature organisms early in development of related organisms indicates a connection between ontogeny and phylogeny. One modern view is that new species may evolve when evolution alters the timing of development, so that certain features of ancestral species appear earlier or later in development.

Information transfer

Nearly all multicellular organisms pass through a life cycle stage where they exist as a single undifferentiated cell or as a small number of undifferentiated cells. This developmental stage contains molecular information which specifies the entire course of development encoded in its many thousands of genes. At the molecular level, genes are used to make proteins, many of which act as enzymes, biological catalysts which drive the thousands of different biochemical reactions inside cells.

Adult multicellular organisms can consist of one quadrillion (a one followed by fifteen zeros) or more cells, each of which has the same genetic information. (There are a few notable exceptions, such as the red blood cells of animals, which do not have DNA, and certain cells in the unfertilized eggs of amphibians, which undergo gene amplification and have multiple copes of some genes.) F.C. Steward first demonstrated the constancy of DNA in all the cells of multicellular organism in the 1950s. In a classical series of experiments, Steward separated a mature carrot plant into individual cells and showed that each cell, whether it came from the root, stem, or leaf, could be induced to develop into a mature carrot plant which was genetically identical to its parent. Although such experiments cannot typically be done with multicellular animals, animals, also have the same genetic information in all their cells.

Many developmental biologists emphasize that there are additional aspects of information transfer during development which do not involve DNA directly. In addition to DNA, a fertilized egg cell contains many proteins and other cellular constituents which are typically derived from the female. These cellular constituents are often asymmetrically distributed during cell division, so that the two daughter cells derived from the fertilized egg have significant biochemical and cytological differences. In many species, these differences act as biological signals which affect the course of development. There are additional spatial and temporal interactions within and among the cells of a developing organism which act as biological signals and provide a form of information to the developing organism.

Growth

Organisms generally increase in size during development. Growth is usually allometric, in that it occurs simultaneously with cellular differentiation and changes in overall body pattern. Allometry is a discipline of biology which specifically studies the relationships between the size and morphology of an organism as it develops and the size and morphology of different species.

A developing organism generally increases in complexity as it increases in size. Moreover, in an evolutionary line, larger species are generally more complex that the smaller species. The reason for this correlation is that the volume (or weight) of an organism varies with the cube of its length, whereas gas exchange and food assimilation, which generally occur on surfaces, vary with the square of its length. Thus, an increase in size requires an increase in cellular specialization and morphological complexity so that the larger organism can breathe and eat.

Depending on the circumstances, natural selection may favor an increase in size, a decrease in size, or no change in size. Large size is often favored because it generally make organisms faster, giving them better protection against predators, and makes them better at dispersal and food gathering. In addition, larger organisms have a higher ratio or volume to surface area, so they are less affected by environmental variations, such as temperature variation. Large organisms tend to have a prolonged development, presumably so they have more time to support their large size. Thus, evolutionary selection for large size leads to a prolongation of development as well as morphological complexity.

Sometimes the coordination between growth and differentiation goes awry, resulting in a developmental abnormality. One such abnormality is an undifferentiated mass of cells called a tumor. A tumor may be benign, in which case it does not invade adjacent cells; alternatively, it may be malignant, or cancerous, in which case the proliferating cells invade their neighbors. Cancers often send colonies of tumor cells throughout the body of an individual, a process called metastasis.

Cancers can be caused by damaging the DNA, the molecular information carrier, of a single cell. This damage may be elicited by a variety of factor such as carcinogenic chemicals, viral infection, or ultraviolet radiation. In addition, some cancers may arise from unprovoked and spontaneous damage to DNA. Basic studies of the different developmental processes may lead to a better understanding of cancer and how it might be prevented or cured.

Differentiation

Differentiation is the change of unspecialized cells in a simple body pattern to specialized cells in a more complex body pattern. It is highly coordinated with growth and includes morphogenesis, the development of the complex overall body pattern.

Below, we emphasize molecular changes in organisms which lead to development. However, this does not imply that external factors have no role in development. In fact, external factors such as changes in light, temperature, or nutrient availability often elicit chemical changes in developing organisms which lead to a profound influence on development.

The so-called "Central Dogma of Biology" says that spatial and temporal differences in gene expression cause cellular and morphological differentiation. Since DNA makes RNA, and RNA makes protein, there are basically three levels where a cell can modulate gene expression: 1) by altering the transcription of DNA into RNA; 2) by altering the translation of RNA into protein; and 3) by altering the activity of the protein, which is usually an enzyme. Since DNA and RNA are themselves synthesized by proteins, the gene expression pat-

---

KEY TERMS

. . . .

Differentiation—Developmental change of unspecialized cells in a simple body pattern to specialized cells in a more complex body pattern.

Gene expression—Molecular process in which a gene is transcribed into a specific RNA (ribonucleic acid), which is then translated into a specific protein.

Morphogenesis—Development of the complex overall body form of an organism.

Ontogeny—Entire developmental life history of an organism.

Phylogeny—Evolutionary history or lineage of an organism or group of related organisms.

---

terns of all cells are regulated by highly complex biochemical networks.

A few simple calculations provide a better appreciation of the complexity of the regulatory networks of gene expression which control differentiation. Starting with the simplifying assumption that a given point (gene product) can be either absent or present in a cell, there are at least ten centillion (a one followed by 6000 zeros) different patterns of gene expression in a single cell at any time. Given that a multicellular organism contains one quadrillion or more cells, and that gene expression patterns change over time, the number of possible gene expression patterns is enormous.

Perhaps the central question of developmental biology is how an organism can select the proper gene expression pattern among all these possibilities. This question has not yet been satisfactorily answered. However, in a 1952 paper, Alan Turing showed that simple chemical systems, in which the component chemicals diffuse and react with one another over time, can create complex spatial patterns which change over time. Thus, it seems possible that organisms may regulate differentiation by using a Turing-like reaction-diffusion mechanism, in which proteins and other molecules diffuse and interact with one another to modulate gene expression. Turing's original model, while relatively simple, has been a major impetus for research about pattern development in biology.

Lastly, aging must also be considered a phase of development. Many evolutionary biologists believe that all organisms have genes which have multiple effects, called pleiotropic genes, that increase reproductive success when expressed early in development, but cause the onset of old age when expressed later in development. In this view, natural selection has favored genes which cause aging and death because the early effects of these genes outweigh the later effects.

Further Reading:

Hall, B.K. *Evolutionary Developmental Biology.* Chapman and Hall, Inc., 1992.

Kugrens, P. *Developmental Biology.* Kendall-Hunt Publishing Co., 1993.

Peter Ensminger

Developmental toxicant see **Teratogen**

Devil's Hole pupfish see **Killifish**

Dextroamphetamine see **Amphetamines**

Diabetes mellitus

Diabetes mellitus is a serious disorder caused by an absence of or insufficient amount of insulin in the bloodstream. Insulin is a hormone produced by the pancreas in varying amounts depending on the concentration of glucose (sugar). When the pancreas is unable to secrete enough insulin to maintain a normal concentration of glucose in the blood, the blood-glucose concentration becomes elevated. Large amounts of glucose are then excreted in the urine. Insulin allows glucose to be absorbed by the liver and fat cells where it is stored as glycogen. In times of stress, exercise, or an emergency, the glycogen is reconverted back to glucose. It also sends glucose to the muscle cells where it is then converted to energy.

The history of the disease dates back to the ancient Greeks and Romans. Records from 2000-3000 B.C. show when it was given its name. The word diabetes means siphon, which stands for a major symptom of the condition: frequent urination. Mellitus means honey, and stands for one of the early signs of diabetes: sugar in the urine.

Incidence

More than 12 million Americans are affected by diabetes. There is a 5-6% increase in the number of those affected each year by the disease, primarily due to the population's increased rate of longevity. A rising rate of obesity, a prime cause for incidences of diabetes over the age of 40, also contributes to the increasing frequency of diabetes. It is estimated that for each reported new case of diabetes, there is an unreported one because symptoms of the early stages of adult diabetes tend to go unrecognized. Symptoms usually progress from mild to severe as the disease progresses.

Approximately 300,000 deaths each year are attributed to diabetes. Its prevalence increases with age, from about 0.2% in persons under 17 years of age to about 10% in persons aged 65 years and over. Females have a higher rate of incidence for the disease, while higher income groups in the United States show a lesser incidence than lower income groups. The incident rate is markedly different among ethnic groups; it is 20% higher in non-Caucasians than in Caucasians. However, for reasons as yet unknown, the rate of diabetes in ethnic groups such as Native Americans, Latin Americans, and Asian Americans is especially high and continues to rise.

Types

There are two forms of diabetes mellitus. Type I is called insulin-dependent and type II, non-insulin-dependent. Insofar as they are both caused by environmental and genetic factors, they are further classified as primary diabetes as opposed to secondary diabetes which is caused by either damage to or surgical removal of the pancreas.

Aside from the similarities of intense thirst and excessive urination, diabetes insipidus is a rare disease which has nothing else in common with diabetes mellitus. It is caused by inadequate production of vasopressin, also called antidiuretic hormone. Vasopressin is in the posterior portion of the pituitary gland and controls body water retention.

Type I

Insulin-dependent diabetes (type I) generally starts in childhood and is characterized by severe insulin deficiency. It is probably due to the destruction of the insulin-secreting cells of the pancreas, which is often caused by an autoimmune disorder. Without insulin, the person develops ketoacidosis, a condition where high levels of ketone bodies are present in the blood. When the body is deprived of glucose, which can occur as a result of insulin deprivation or fasting, the body begins to break down fat for fuel. Ketones are the result of this lipid metabolism. The resulting lowered blood pH value leads to the acidosis.

Ketoacidosis is a serious condition and can lead to confusion, unconsciousness, and death if it is not treated. It can be diagnosed by urine tests which detect ketones in the urine. Untreated or uncontrolled diabetes will lead to ketosis, but fasting or starvation also produces ketones. Other symptoms of ketoacidosis include vomiting, abdominal pain, loss of appetite, and nausea.

A very high blood glucose level in insulin-dependent diabetes can also lead to heart failure and coma.

Type II

Non-insulin dependent diabetes (type II) usually occurs in people over age 40. This group comprises about 80%-85% of the diabetic population. Even though they may have more than normal levels of insulin, they are resistant to its action. Unlike those with type I diabetes, people with type II diabetes rarely have ketoacidosis. Instead insulin action can be impaired by obesity. Therefore people who gain too much weight and ethnic groups that have changed to higher carbohydrate diets appear to be particularly prone to type II diabetes.

Pregnancy can also elevate a woman's glucose level. This condition is known as gestational diabetes. Although their glucose levels may return to normal after they give birth, these woman may be at risk of developing type II diabetes in the future.

Tests

For those people who are in a high risk group for getting diabetes (those who have had relatives with diabetes, adults over the age of 40 who are overweight, and women who have had babies weighing nine pounds or more at birth), there is a quick and simple screening test. The test requires a drop of blood from the finger and takes about one to two minutes to complete. The test shows if there is a high or low blood-sugar level in the blood. After the results of the screening test other tests can be done, if necessary.

If the screening test shows blood-sugar levels that are either too high or too low, a fasting plasma glucose test can be given. One or more samples of blood are taken after the individual fasts for 10-16 hours. Blood-glucose levels of less than 115 milligrams per decaliter (mg/dl) are normal. Fasting plasma glucose levels of more than 140 mg/dl indicates diabetes.

The oral glucose tolerance test also starts with a fast but adds a glucose drink taken after the fasting plasma glucose is tested. It is followed by several other tests to determine blood glucose levels.

There are other tests used to monitor the condition, including self-tests.

The presence of circulating islet antibodies is a good predictor of insulin-dependent diabetes. Research

KEY TERMS

Glucose—Simple sugar made from other carbohydrates that is circulated in the blood at a narrow limit of concentration. Also known as blood sugar.

Glycogen—Converted excess blood sugar (glucose) is created by glycogen, a complex carbohydrate stored in the liver and muscles for future use in exercise or emergencies. The conversion is done by insulin and other hormones. When the blood sugar is low, glycogen is converted back to glucose by a hormone called glucagon. As a sucrose, it then returns to the blood.

Insulin-dependent—A form of diabetes that requires the daily injection of insulin. It is the usual condition of juvenile diabetes. Also known as type I diabetes.

Ketoacidosis—Formation of ketones (acetones) in the blood from lipid (fat) metabolism and a high blood acid content. Usually the symptom of type I diabetes. Also known as diabetic coma.

Ketones—Acids indicating insufficient insulin that convert fat into glucose in the blood.

Non-insulin-dependent—A form of diabetes that is often caused by obesity and can be controlled by diet, exercise, and oral medication rather than daily injections of insulin. The type of diabetes that occurs after the age of 40. Also known as type II diabetes.

Pancreas—The organ responsible for secreting insulin.

is being done on genetic tests to predict the risk of developing diabetes.

Treatment

Deaths from ketoacidosis and diabetic coma decreased after the discovery of isolating insulin by Frederick G. Banting and Charles Best in 1921. However, long-term complications from diabetes began to increase as diabetics' life span increased. Some of these complications are kidney failure, heart disease, blindness, and nervous system disorders, all of which are believed to be the results of elevated blood-glucose levels.

Injections of an insulin that is absorbed slowly and given one or two times daily was the standard treatment for insulin-dependent diabetes. However, blood glucose is not controlled well with this procedure. Today glucose levels are controlled much more effectively by injecting a rapidly absorbed insulin just before each meal. Added to this dosage, the slowly absorbed insulin can then be injected or pumped in by a prosthetic implant device between meals to maintain low insulin concentrations. The amounts required are determined by frequent blood-glucose measurements.

For overweight, non-insulin-dependent diabetics, controlling diet, avoiding foods high in sugar and carbohydrates, and encouraging weight loss may be sufficient treatment. A regular program of physical exercise is also recommended as an important part of diabetes treatment. Exercise utilizes surplus blood glucose and helps to both lose and maintain weight. In addition non-insulin-dependent-type oral drugs may stimulate the pancreas to secrete additional insulin. It may be necessary to give injections of insulin.

A relatively new treatment for type II diabetes lies in the recently approved drug Glucophage (generic name: metformin). Glucophage affects how the body handles its own insulin, increasing its effectiveness. With only a few side effects (diarrhea, nausea, bloating) that fade after the body adjusts to the medication, Glucophage offers an alternative to those who don't respond to changes in diet and exercise.

See also Autoimmune disease; Insulin.

Further Reading:

Anstett, Patricia. "Newly approved drug controls most common type of diabetes." *Detroit Free Press* (5 May 1995): 1A-2A.

Davidson, Mayer B. *Diabetes Mellitus: Diagnosis and Treatment*. New York: Churchill Livingstone, 1991.

Gordon, Neil F. *Diabetes: Your Exercise Guide*. Dallas: Human Kinetics, 1993.

National Institute of Health. "Consensus Development Conference on Diet and Exercise in Non-Insulin-Dependent Diabetes Mellitus." *Diabetes Care* 10(1987): 639-44.

United States. "Diabetes Mellitus: An unrelenting threat to the health of minorities," (Report on hearing before the select committee on aging) House of Representatives, 102nd Congress, April 16, 1992.

Jordan P. Richman

Diagnosis

Diagnosis, from *gnosis*, the Greek word for knowledge, is the process of identifying a disease or disorder in a person by examining the person and studying the results of medical tests.

The diagnosis begins when the patient is presented to the doctor with a set of symptoms or perceived abnormalities such as pain, nausea, fever, or other untoward feeling. Often the diagnosis is relatively simple, and the physician can arrive at a clinical conclusion and prescribe the proper treatment. At other times, the symptoms may be subtle and seemingly unrelated, making the diagnosis difficult to finalize and requiring laboratory work.

The diagnosis is based on data the physician obtains from three sources, the first being the patient. This includes the patient's perception of his or her symptoms, medical history, family history, occupation, and other relevant facts. The physician then narrows the diagnosis with a second set of information obtained from the physical examination of the patient. The third source is the data obtained from medical tests, such as a blood test, x ray, or electrocardiogram.

Patient information

The physician begins the examination by asking about the patient's symptoms. The patient may be asked to describe the symptoms and how long he or she has been experiencing them. If the patient is in pain, information is collected about the location, type, and duration of the pain. Other symptoms that may be present but may not have been noticed by the patient must be explored.

The patient's occupation may have a bearing on his or her illness. Perhaps he or she works around chemicals that may cause illness. A job of repetitive bending and lifting may result in muscle strain or back pain. A police officer or fire fighter may have periods of boredom interrupted by periods of stress or fear.

The physician must learn when the symptoms first appeared and whether they have worsened over time or remained the same in intensity. If the patient has more than one symptom, the physician must know which appeared first and in what order the others appeared. The doctor will also ask if the symptoms are similar to ones the patient has experienced in the past or if they are entirely new.

The medical history of the patient's family also may be helpful. Some diseases are hereditary and some, though not hereditary, are more likely to occur if the patient's parent or other close relative has had such a disease. For example, the person whose father has had a heart attack is more likely to have a heart attack than is a person whose family has been free of heart disease.

Personal habits, such as smoking or drinking large amounts of alcohol, also contribute to disease. Lack of exercise, lack of sleep, and an unhealthy diet are all involved in bringing about symptoms of disease.

The physical examination

In addition to exploring the patient's clinical history, the physician will carry out a physical examination to further narrow his list of possible conditions. The patient's temperature, blood pressure, and rate of respiration will be measured. He or she will be weighed and his or her height measured. The physician will use an otoscope to examine the eardrums and to look into the throat for signs of inflammation, infection, or other abnormal conditions.

The heart and lungs can be examined superficially using a stethoscope. Abnormalities in the heartbeat or in the functioning of the heart valves can be heard in this way, and the presence of water or other fluid in the lungs can be heard as noises called rales. The physician also can study the sounds made by the intestines by listening to them through the stethoscope.

Using his fingers, a technique called palpation, the physician probes the abdomen for signs of pain or an abnormal lump or growth. He also feels the neck, the axillary area (armpit) and other locales to locate any enlarged lymph nodes, a sign of an infection. Such probing also may bring to light the presence of a tender area previously unknown to the patient.

If the patient is complaining of an injury, the physician can carefully palpate around the injury to determine its size. He can bend an leg or arm to assess the integrity of the joint. Using other maneuvers, he can determine whether a ligament has been torn and if it may need surgical correction.

The laboratory examination

Having learned the patient's clinical history and made his physical examination, the physician may then decide to submit specimens from the patient to a laboratory for testing. Fluids such as blood, urine, stomach fluid, or spinal fluid can be collected.

Basic laboratory tests of blood include a count of the number of white and red blood cells. An elevated number of white blood cells indicates an infection is present, but does not pinpoint the location of the infection. Blood also carries hormones and other components that are directly affected by disease or inflammation.

Far from the laboratory of the 1960s, the modern clinical laboratory is one of automation and high technology. Whereas before the laboratory technician was required to mix together the chemicals for each test,

newer technology requires only that a blood specimen be placed in one end of a machine. The blood is carried through the machine and minute amounts of the chemicals are added as needed and the results printed out. This technology also enables the measurement of blood or urine components in amounts much smaller than previous technology allowed—often at microgram levels. A microgram is one millionth of a gram. To measure such a minute amount, the chemistry involved is precise and the reading of the results is beyond the capability of the human eye.

Both blood and urine may contain evidence of alcohol, illicit drugs, or toxic substances that the patient has taken. Infectious organisms from the blood or urine can be grown in culture dishes and examined to determine what they are. Bacteria in blood or urine are often too sparsely distributed to be seen under the microscope, but bacteria in a blood specimen wiped across a plate of culture medium will grow when the plate is placed in an incubator at body temperature.

The physician also may want to obtain x rays of an injured area to rule out the possibility of a fractured bone. The presence of a heart condition can often be determined by taking an electrocardiogram (ECG), which measures the electrical activity of the heart. Changes in the ECG can indicate the presence of heart disease or give evidence of a past heart attack. CAT (computerized axial tomography) scans use x rays to produce images of one layer of hard or soft tissue, a procedure useful in detecting small tumors. Magnetic resonance imaging (MRI) uses radio waves in a magnetic field to generate images of a layer of the brain, heart, or other organ. Ultrasound waves are also sometimes used to detect tumors.

Physicians can collect other kinds of information by injecting substances into the patient. Injection of radiopaque liquids, which block the passage of x rays, allow x-ray examination of soft tissues, such as the spinal cord, that are normally undetectable on x-ray photographs. Metabolic disorders can sometimes be pinpointed using a procedure called scintigraphy, in which a radioactive isotope is circulated through the body. A gamma camera is then used to record the concentration of the isotope in various tissues and organs.

Other laboratory specimens can be obtained by invasive techniques. If the physician finds a suspicious lump or swelling and needs to know its nature, he can remove part of the lump and send it to the laboratory to be examined. The surgical removal of tissue for testing is called a biopsy. In the laboratory, the specimen is sliced very thinly, dyed to accentuate differences in tissues, and examined under the microscope. This enables the physician determine whether the lump is malignant (cancerous) or benign (noncancerous). If it is cancer, further tests can determine if it is the primary tumor or if it has grown (metastasis) as a result of being spread from the primary tumor. Other tests can determine what kind of cancer it is.

The method of actually looking into the body cavity used to mean a major surgical procedure called a laparotomy. In that procedure, an incision was made in the abdomen so the physician could look at each organ and other internal structure in order and determine the presence of disease or parasite. Now the laparotomy is carried out using a flexible scope called a laparoscope, which is inserted into the body through a small incision. The scope is attached to a television monitor that gives the physician an enlarged view of the inside of the body. The flexibility of the scope allows it to be guided around the organs, and a light attached to the scope helps the physician see each organ. Also, the laparoscope is equipped with the means to collect biopsy specimens or suction blood out of the abdomen. Minor surgery can also be carried out to stop a bleeding blood vessel or remove a small growth from an organ.

Once the above steps the physician deems necessary have been carried out, he or she will then study the evidence collectively and arrive at a diagnosis. Once having determined the diagnosis, he or she can prescribe the proper treatment.

Larry Blaser

Dialysis

Dialysis is a process by which small molecules in a solution are separated from large molecules. The principle behind the process was discovered by the Scottish chemist Thomas Graham in about 1861. Graham found that the rate at which some substances, such as inorganic salts, pass through a semipermeable membrane is up to 50 times as great as the rate at which other substances, such as proteins, do so. We now know that such rate differences depend on the fact that the openings in semipermeable membranes are very nearly the size of atoms, ions, and small molecules. That makes possible the passage of such small particles while greatly restricting the passage of large particles.

In a typical dialysis experiment, a bag made of a semipermeable membrane is filled with a solution to be dialyzed. The bag is then suspended in a stream of running water. Small particles in solution within the bag gradually diffuse across the semipermeable membrane and are carried away by the running water. Larger molecules are essentially retained within the bag. By this process, a highly efficient separation of substances can be achieved.

The kidney is a dialyzing organ. By the process described above, it filters waste products such as urea out of the blood and forces them into the urine, in which they are excreted from the body. Proteins and other important large molecules are retained in the blood.

A person whose kidneys have been damaged by disease or physical injury requires some artificial method for cleansing her or his blood. A device for carrying out this task—the artificial kidney machine—was developed in the early 1910s largely through the efforts of John J. Abel and his colleagues at the Johns Hopkins University. In the kidney machine, blood is removed from a person's arm, passed through a dialyzing system, and then returned to the patient. The machine functions much as does a natural kidney with one important exception. A natural kidney has a mechanism known as reverse dialysis for returning to the body certain small molecules (primarily glucose) that should not be excreted. The kidney machine is unable to do so, and glucose that it removes must be replaced by intravenous injection.

Electrodialysis is a form of dialysis in which the separation of ions from larger molecules is accelerated by the presence of an electrical field. In one arrangement, the solution to be dialyzed is placed between two other solutions, each of which contains an electrode. Cations within the middle solution are attracted to one electrode and anions to the other. Any large molecules in the middle solution remain where they are.

One possible application of electrodialysis is the desalination of water. In this procedure, sodium ions from seawater migrate to the cathode and chloride ions to the anode of an electrodialysis apparatus. Relatively pure water is left behind in the central compartment.

See also Osmosis.

Diamond see **Carbon**

Diaphragm, vaginal see **Contraception**

Dielectric materials

Dielectric materials are substances that have very low conductivity. That is, they are electrical insulators through which an electrical current flows only with the greatest of difficulty. Technically, a dielectric can be defined as a material with electrical conductivity of less than one millionth of a mho (a unit of electrical conductance) per centimeter.

In theory, dielectrics can include solids, liquids, and gases, although in practice only the first two of these three states of matter have any practical significance. Some of the most commonly used dielectrics are various kinds of rubber, glass, wood, and polymers among the solids; and hydrocarbon oils and silicone oils among the liquids.

The dielectric constant

A common measure of the dielectric properties of a material is the dielectric constant. The dielectric constant can be defined as the tendency of a material to resist the flow of an electrical current across the material. The lower the value of the dielectric constant, the greater its resistance to the flow of an electrical current.

The standard used in measuring dielectric constant is a vacuum, which is assigned the value of one. The dielectric constants of some other common materials are as follows: dry air (at one atmosphere of pressure): 1.0006; water: 80; glass: 4 - 7; wax: 2.25; amber: 2.65; mica: 2.5 - 7; benzene: 2.28; carbon tetrachloride: 2.24; and methyl alcohol: 33.1. Synthetic polymers are now widely used as dielectrics. The dielectric constants for these materials range from a low of about 1.3 for polyethylene and two for polytetrafluoroethylene (Teflon) to a high of about 7.2 - 8.4 for a melamine-formaldehyde resin.

Uses

Almost any type of electrical equipment employs dielectric materials in some form or another. Wires and cables that carry electrical current, for example, are always coated or wrapped with some type of insulating (dielectric) material. Sophisticated electronic equipment such as rectifiers, semiconductors, transducers, and amplifiers contain or are fabricated from dielectric materials. The insulating material sandwiched between two conducting plates in a capacitor is also made of some dielectric substance.

Liquid dielectrics are also employed as electrical insulators. For example, transformer oil is a natural or synthetic substance (mineral oil, silicone oil, or organic esters, for example) that has the ability to insulate the coils of a transformer both electrically and thermally.

Synthetic dielectrics

A number of traditional dielectric materials are still widely used in industry. For example, paper impregnated with oil is often still the insulator of choice for coating wires that carry high-voltage current. But synthetic materials have now become widely popular for many applications once filled by natural substances, such as glass and rubber. The advantage of synthetic materials is that they can be designed so as to produce very specific properties for specialized uses. These properties include not only low dielectric constant, but also strength, hardness, resistance to chemical attack, and other desirable qualities.

Among the polymers now used as dielectrics are the polyethylenes, polypropylenes, polystyrenes, polyvinyl chlorides, polyamides (Nylon), polymethyl methacrylates, and polycarbonates.

Breakdown

When a dielectric material is exposed to a large electrical field, it may undergo a process known as breakdown. In that process, the material suddenly becomes conducting, and a large current begins to flow across the material. The appearance of a spark may also accompany breakdown. The point at which breakdown occurs with any given material depends on a number of factors, including temperature, the geometric shape of the material, and the type of material surrounding the dielectric. The ability of a dielectric material to resist breakdown is called its intrinsic electric strength.

Breakdown is often associated with the degradation of a dielectric material. The material may oxidize, physically break apart, or degrade in some other way that will make conductance more likely. When breakdown does occur, then, it is often accompanied by further degradation of the material.

See also Electronics; Oxidation state; Transformer.

Further Reading:

Hawley, Gessner G., ed. *The Condensed Chemical Dictionary*, 9th edition. New York: Van Nostrand Reinhold, 1977, pp. 284 - 285.

Scaife, B. K. *Principles of Dielectrics*. New York: Oxford University Press, 1989.

David E. Newton

Diencephalon see **Brain**

Diesel engine

Diesel engines are a class of internal-combustion engine in which the fuel is burned internally and the combustion products are used as the working fluid. Unlike the spark-ignited (SI) engines found in the majority of today's automobiles in which the premixed fuel-air mixture is ignited by an electric spark, diesel engines are characterized by a spontaneously initiated combustion process where the ignition is brought about by very high temperature compressed air. A small amount of diesel fuel is injected at the end of the compression stroke into the cylinder where the fuel autoignites. Because of their higher actual operating efficiencies, as compared with SI engines that require pre-ignition, diesel engines are primarily used in heavy-duty vehicles such as trucks, ships, locomotives, etc.

Diesel engines were first developed by Rudolf Diesel (1858-1913) in the late nineteenth century. The original concept was to build a multifuel engine and to use coal as a primary fuel. However, for some reason, coal-fueled diesel engines so far have gained only occasional interest from the industry (e.g., when fuel-oil prices are high), most of the diesel engines currently being used rely on petroleum fuels. They are four-stroke cycle engines, and operate from several hundred up to around one thousand rpm. In addition to pistons, cylinders, crankshaft, and various valves, diesel engines are also equipped with controlled fuel injection systems, exhaust systems, cooling systems, and so on. Sufficient lubrication is required to prevent excessive wear of various parts in engines. Since pre-ignition is not required, the compression step can be continued to reach a higher pressure or a higher compression ratio than that in SI engines. This results in compressed air with a temperature exceeding the ignition point of the injected fuel for auto-ignition. To achieve high combustion efficiency, the fuel jets must draw in and mix well with air, ignite, and burn, all within less than one millisecond, when they impact on the cold combustion chamber walls. Engine performance is closely related to compression ratio, piston speed, supercharging, turbocharging, etc., and engine size is normally in terms of power rating (i.e., horsepower; for instance, 20,000 hp applicable for ship propulsion). In principle, the same engine frame can be designed for different output by varying the number of cylinders (10, 12, 16 cylinders, and so on).

In reality, because the fuel-air mixture is burned and the products of combustion are emitted, the process for work production via combustion in diesel engines is complex and not cyclical. However, in order to analyze it, the actual operation is frequently represented approximately by a cyclical process, called "Diesel cycle." From the point of view of thermodynamics, the working fluid is assumed to be air, the compression and expansion stages are assumed to be adiabatic (without the loss or gain of heat) and reversible, and the combustion and exhaust strokes are replaced by constant-pressure heat-absorption and constant-volume heat-rejection stages. As shown in Fig. 1 a typical pressure-volume (P-V) diagram for air-standard diesel engine operation, after the intake, air is compressed adiabatically along the path 1-2 and its temperature is increased substantially. At point 2 where the piston begins to reverse its motion, the fuel is injected and added slowly so that combustion is initiated and sustained at constant pressure following the path 2-3. After completion of the combustion, there is the work stroke, i.e., along the path 3-4 where the high-temperature and

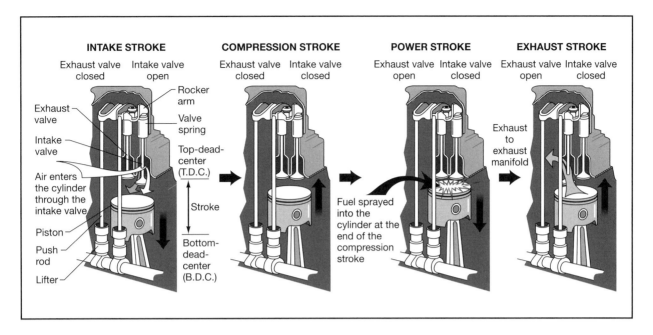

INTAKE STROKE
Exhaust valve   Intake valve
closed   open

COMPRESSION STROKE
Exhaust valve   Intake valve
closed   closed

POWER STROKE
Exhaust valve   Intake valve
open   closed

EXHAUST STROKE
Exhaust valve   Intake valve
open   closed

Exhaust
valve

Intake
valve

Air enters
the cylinder
through the
intake valve

Piston

Push
rod

Lifter

Rocker
arm

Valve
spring

Top-dead-
center
(T.D.C.)

Stroke

Bottom-
dead-
center
(B.D.C.)

Fuel sprayed
into the
cylinder at the
end of the
compression
stroke

Exhaust
to
exhaust
manifold

The combustion cycle of the Diesel engine.

high-pressure products of combustion are expanded to produce mechanical work. Then the exhaust valve is opened, the spent combustion products and waste heat are exhausted, and the pressure is rapidly reduced as the path 4-1. This, therefore, completes typical four strokes in each cycle of engine operation. The thermal efficiency of the cycle can be obtained from the net work produced divided by the heat absorbed during the entire cyclical process.

Overall, diesel engines can be viewed as a piston-and-cylinder assembly and the work-producing

machine. Their operation cycle is similar to that in SI engines which are based on the Otto (after the German inventor for the first internal-combustion engine produced in the mid 1860s) cycle; however, the latter require an external combustion initiator and have combustion occurring under an almost constant-volume condition, which is different from the path 2-3 as shown in

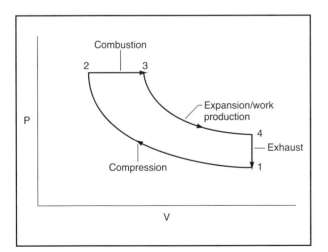

Combustion

2   3

Expansion/work
production

4
Exhaust

Compression   1

P

V

Figure 1. A typical pressure-volume (P-V) diagram for air-standard cycle of diesel engines.

KEY TERMS

Adiabatic—A process during which no heat is transferred between the system and surroundings is described as "adiabatic."

Heat engine—A device converts heat to mechanical work in a periodic process.

Reversible—A process occurs in such a way that both the system and its surroundings can be returned to their initial states.

Supercharging—Methods to increase the inlet manifold air pressure above ambient pressure so that power output in engines is increased.

Thermal efficiency—The ratio of net work to thermal energy input.

Turbocharging—An approach to utilizing high-temperature exhaust gas by expanding it through a turbine for driving the supercharging compressor.

Fig. 1. In these engines, the chemical (molecular) energy of the fuel (hydrocarbons) is released by a combustion process. Energy is evolved as heat and part of the heat is subsequently converted into useful work or mechanical energy. Because of the loss of heat during the process, research and development efforts have been made constantly in chamber design, new coatings for rings and liner, emission control, alternative fuels, and associated compressor and turbine technologies to improve the conversion efficiency. As can be expected, diesel engines will continue finding a variety of applications in the future, such as power generation as well as land, marine, and aircraft transport.

See also Internal combustion engine.

Further Reading:

S.D. Haddad, ed., *Advanced Diesel Engineering and Application*, New York: John Wiley & Sons, 1988.

T.W. Ryan III, "Coal-Fueled Diesel Development: A Technical Review," *Journal of Engineering for Gas Turbines and Power*, 1994.

Pang-Jen Kung

Diethylstilbestrol (DES)

The substance diethylstilbestrol (DES) is a synthetic, nonsteroidal estrogen, which was first made in 1938. Initially the substance was seen as a great scientific breakthrough, drawing on research which documented the importance of naturally-occurring estrogen in women. Widescale use of DES by pregnant women to prevent miscarriage beginning in the 1940s ended in 1971 when researchers discovered that some daughters of women who took DES had developed a rare cancer, called clear-cell adenocarcinoma of the vagina. Researchers have since found that daughters of women who took DES face a higher risk of certain cancers and of structural abnormalities in the genital area. The example of DES, used by 2-3 million American women, has been used to dramatize the risk of improperly tested medicine during pregnancy.

Medical breakthrough

The development of DES by British scientist Edward Dodds (1899-1973) was one in a long line of twentieth century medical advances which reflected new understanding of the female reproductive system. While doctors had observed pregnancy, childbirth, mis-

carriages, and infertility for centuries, they did not gain an understanding of the hormonal functions behind these processes until the twentieth century. Through a series of discoveries, researchers learned that the process of pregnancy required a complicated series of hormonal triggers to occur successfully. They also learned that hormones were critical for the development of sexual characteristics in both men and women.

An early breakthrough was the successful isolation in 1923 of estrogen, the female sex hormone produced in men and women. Initially, the natural form of estrogen was extracted from animal ovaries, a process that was time-consuming and expensive. By 1936, the first synthetic estrogen was manufactured from plant steroids. In 1942 DES was approved by the U.S. Food and Drug Administration for use by menopausal women and for several other purposes. The drug was not approved for use by pregnant women until 1947, following reports that the drug could reduce the incidence of miscarriage.

At the time DES was first used for pregnant women, the substance was seen as a new weapon against infertility, stillbirths, and prematurity, according to a 1991 account by Edith L. Potter, a pathologist who specialized in obstetrics and gynecology during the time DES was prescribed. George and Olive Smith, the Harvard Medical School researchers who promoted the use of DES during pregnancy, believed that stillbirths and premature births were caused by a failure of the placenta to produce sufficient quantities of progesterone, Potter observes. They thought DES would relieve this condition, so that the pregnancies could be carried to term.

In the observation of practicing physicians, the substance appeared to cause no harm. Potter examined more than 10,000 infants who died of unrelated causes during this time, and she writes of seeing no apparent abnormalities due to DES. Problems did not become apparent until the DES infants were no longer infants.

Contemporary critics have faulted studies promoting DES for pregnant women because they did not include control groups—individuals given a placebo to help gauge the true effectiveness of DES. Without control groups, there was no scientific way to tell if the use of DES made women less likely to miscarry.

Signs of trouble

The largest number of DES prescriptions were ordered in 1953. By the middle 1950s, a series of studies suggested that DES did not actually help prevent miscarriages. Yet the drug continued to be given to

1128

pregnant women throughout the 1960s. Then, in the late 1960s, doctors noticed a series of cases of vaginal cancer in teenaged girls and women in their twenties. This was troubling, because vaginal cancer had previously been seen primarily in much older women. By 1971, researchers had definitely linked DES to the vaginal cancer cases, and a report of the association appeared in the influential *New England Journal of Medicine*. That same year, the FDA prohibited the use of DES during pregnancy.

A total of about 600 cases of cancer of the cervix and vagina have been diagnosed in DES daughters. Daughters also are at higher risk of structural abnormalities of the reproductive tract and of poor pregnancy outcome. About one-half of all DES daughters experience an ectopic pregnancy, a premature birth, or a miscarriage. In addition, DES daughters are at a higher risk of infertility than women whose mothers did not take the drug.

The most common health problem reported by DES daughters is adenosis of the vagina. Adenosis is the abnormal development of glandular tissue. This occurs in 30% or more of DES daughters. About 25% of DES daughters have physical abnormalities of the cervix or vagina. Vaginal cancer occurs in less than 1 per 1,000 females whose mothers took DES.

Daughters of women who took DES are not the only ones at higher risk of health problems. Mothers who took DES face a slightly increased risk of breast cancer, and anecdotal evidence suggests that DES sons have a higher risk of testicular and semen abnormalities. Infertility and a higher risk of some types of cancer have also been reported among some DES sons.

Effects on the developing embryo

Various theories to account for the effects of DES have been presented. What is clear is that the diseases associated with DES derive from structural damage of the fetus caused by the drug. The drug is most damaging when taken early in pregnancy, when the reproductive organs are formed. (Researchers have found that daughters of mothers who took DES in their 18th week of pregnancy or later had fewer abnormalities.)

One explanation suggests that DES exposure causes abnormal development of the Mullerian ducts, paired structures present in the early embryo. During a normal pregnancy, the Mullerian ducts form the female reproductive tract, including the uterus, the fallopian tubes, the vagina, and the cervix. DES causes the persistence of a type of glandular, or secreting, epithelial cell in the vagina. During normal development, this

---

KEY TERMS

. . . .

Adenocarcinoma—Cancer of the glandular tissue.

Adenosis—Abnormal development or disease of the glands.

Cervix—The front portion, or neck, of the uterus.

Endometrium—The inner membrane of the uterus.

Epithelium—Layer of cells that covers external and internal surfaces of the body. The many types of epithelium range from flat cells to long cells to cubed cells.

Mullerian ducts—Paired structures present in the early embryo from which some of the reproductive organs develop.

---

type of cell is transformed to a squamous, or flattened, cell. The persistence of this type of cell, researchers speculate, could make affected women more susceptible to a cancer-promoting factor. They have also suggested that vaginal cancer does not develop until after menstruation begins because this susceptible tissue reacts to estrogens released naturally in women who menstruate.

To explain the higher rate of premature deliveries and infertility in DES daughters, scientists point to the abnormal development of the cervix or endometrium in the embryo. Another possible explanation is that DES somehow causes defects in the connective tissue of the fetal cervix and uterus, so that these organs cannot develop normally.

There is also a possibility that the abnormal cells in the vagina and cervix of DES daughters will become malignant later in life. While this is unusual, physicians are advised to examine DES daughters regularly to monitor their condition. Arthur L. Herbst reports that only 16 of the hundreds of thousands of DES daughters who have been examined have had tumors develop from vaginal adenosis or a related condition of the cervix, cervical ectropion.

Predictions that the number of DES daughters with cancer would continue to grow dramatically have fortunately proven false. But researchers warn that DES daughters, sons, and mothers may face other health complications as they get older. The legacy of DES has been long-lasting and troubling, a reminder of the power of medicine to hurt as well as help.

See also Hormones; Reproductive system.

Further Reading:

Colton, Theodore, et al. "Breast Cancer in Mothers Prescribed Diethylstilbestrol in Pregnancy: Further Follow-up." *Journal of the American Medical Association* 269 (April 28, 1993): 2096.

Henderson, Charles. "DES Registries in Need of Update." *Cancer Weekly* (June 22, 1992): 10.

Herbst, Arthur L. "Problems of Prenatal DES Exposure," in *Comprehensive Gynecology.* Edited by Arthur L. Herbst, Daniel R. Mishell, Jr., Morton A. Stenchever, and William Droegemueller. St. Louis: Mosby Year Book, 1992, 410-22.

Kushner, Susan. "In the Graveyard of Western Medicine." *East West Natural Health* (July-August 1992): 144.

Potter, Edith L. "A Historical View: Diethylstilbestrol Use During Pregnancy: A 30-Year Historical Perspective." *Pediatric Pathology* 11 (1991): 781-89.

Patricia Braus

Diffraction

Diffraction is the deviation from a straight path that occurs when a wave such as light or sound passes around an obstacle or through an opening. The importance of diffraction in any particular situation depends on the relative size of the obstacle or opening and the wavelength of the wave that strikes it. The diffraction grating is an important device that makes use of the diffraction of light to produce spectra. Diffraction is also fundamental in other applications such as x-ray diffraction studies of crystals and holography.

Fundamentals

All waves are subject to diffraction when they encounter an obstacle in their path. Consider the shadow of a flagpole cast by the Sun on the ground. From a distance the darkened zone of the shadow gives the impression that light traveling in a straight line from the Sun was blocked by the pole. But careful observation of the shadow's edge will reveal that the change from dark to light is not abrupt. Instead, there is a gray area along the edge that was created by light that was "bent" or diffracted at the side of the pole.

When a source of waves, such as a light bulb, sends a beam through an opening or aperture, a diffraction pattern will appear on a screen placed behind the aperture. The diffraction pattern will look something like the aperture (a slit, circle, square) but it will be surrounded by some diffracted waves that give it a "fuzzy" appearance.

If both the source and the screen are far from the aperture the amount of "fuzziness" is determined by the wavelength of the source and the size of the aperture. With a large aperture most of the beam will pass straight through, with only the edges of the aperture causing diffraction, and there will be less "fuzziness." But if the size of the aperture is comparable to the wavelength, the diffraction pattern will widen. For example, an open window can cause sound waves to be diffracted through large angles.

Fresnel diffraction refers to the case when either the source or the screen are close to the aperture. When both source and screen are far from the aperture, the term Fraunhofer diffraction is used. As an example of the latter, consider starlight entering a telescope. The diffraction pattern of the telescope's circular mirror or lens is known as Airy's disk, which is seen as a bright central disk in the middle of a number of fainter rings. This indicates that the image of a star will always be widened by diffraction. When optical instruments such as telescopes have no defects, the greatest detail they can observe is said to be diffraction limited.

Applications

Diffraction gratings

The diffraction of light has been cleverly taken advantage of to produce one of science's most important tools—the diffraction grating. Instead of just one aperture, a large number of thin slits or grooves—as many as 25,000 per inch—are etched into a material. In making these sensitive devices it is important that the grooves are parallel, equally spaced, and have equal widths.

The diffraction grating transforms an incident beam of light into a spectrum. This happens because each groove of the grating diffracts the beam, but because all the grooves are parallel, equally spaced and have the same width, the diffracted waves mix or interfere constructively so that the different components can be viewed separately. Spectra produced by diffraction gratings are extremely useful in applications from studying the structure of atoms and molecules to investigating the composition of stars.

X-ray diffraction

X-rays are light waves that have very short wavelengths. When they irradiate a solid, crystal material

KEY TERMS

· ·

Airy's disk—The diffraction pattern produced by a circular aperture such as a lens or a mirror.

Bragg's law—An equation that describes the diffraction of light from plane parallel surfaces.

Diffraction limited—The ultimate performance of an optical element such as a lens or mirror that depends only on the element's finite size.

Diffraction pattern—The wave pattern observed after a wave has passed through a diffracting aperture.

Diffractometer—A device used to produce diffraction patterns of materials.

Fresnel diffraction—Diffraction that occurs when the source and the observer are far from the diffraction aperture.

Interference pattern—Alternating bands of light and dark that result from the mixing of two waves.

Wavelength—The distance between consecutive crests of a wave.

X-ray diffraction—A method used for studying the structure of crystals.

they are diffracted by the atoms in the crystal. But since it is a characteristic of crystals to be made up of equally spaced atoms, it is possible to use the diffraction patterns that are produced to determine the locations and distances between atoms. Simple crystals made up of equally spaced planes of atoms diffract x-rays according to Bragg's Law. Current research using x-ray diffraction utilizes an instrument called a diffractometer to produce diffraction patterns that can be compared with those of known crystals to determine the structure of new materials.

Holography

When two laser beams mix at an angle on the surface of a photographic plate or other recording material, they produce an interference pattern of alternating dark and bright lines. Because the lines are perfectly parallel, equally spaced, and of equal width, this process is used to manufacture holographic diffraction gratings of high quality. In fact, any hologram (holos-whole:gram-message) can be thought of as a complicated diffraction grating. The recording of a hologram involves the mixing of a laser beam and the unfocused diffraction pattern of some object. In order to reconstruct an image of

the object (holography is also known as wavefront reconstruction) an illuminating beam is diffracted by plane surfaces within the hologram, following Bragg's Law, such that an observer can view the image with all of its three-dimensional detail.

See also Diffraction grating; Hologram and holography; Wave motion.

John Appel

Diffraction grating

A diffraction grating is an optical device consisting of many closely spaced parallel lines or grooves. In a transmission type of grating, light passes through the narrow transparent slits that lie between the dark lines on a glass or plastic plate. In a reflecting grating, light is reflected by the many parallel, narrow, smooth surfaces and absorbed or scattered by the lines cut in the reflecting surface of the grating.

During the 1870s, Henry Rowland, a physics professor at Johns Hopkins University, developed a machine that used a fine diamond point to rule glass gratings with nearly 15,000 parallel lines per inch. Today, there are carefully ruled gratings that have as many as 100,000 lines per inch. On the other hand, you can obtain inexpensive replica gratings reproduced on film with 13,400 lines per inch. To diffract very short electromagnetic waves, such as x rays, the distance between the lines in the grating must be comparable to the distance between atoms. Gratings with these small separations are obtained by using the regularly arranged rows of closely spaced ions found in the lattice structure of salt crystals.

Like a prism, a diffraction grating separates the colors in white light to produce a spectrum. The spectrum, however, arises not from refraction but from the diffraction of the light transmitted or reflected by the narrow lines in the grating. When light passes through a narrow opening, it is diffracted (spread out) like water waves passing through a narrow barrier as shown in the photograph. With a transmission type diffraction grating, light waves are diffracted as they pass through a series of equally spaced narrow openings. (A similar effect takes place if light is reflected from a reflecting grating.) The beam formed by the combination of diffracted waves from a number of openings in a transmission grating forms a wave front that travels in the same direction as the original light beam. This beam is often referred to as the central maximum.

If the light is not monochromatic, the direction of the diffracted beams will depend on the wavelength. The first order beam for light of longer wavelength, such as red light, will travel at a greater angle to the central maximum than the first order beam for light of a shorter wavelength, such as blue light. As a result, white light diffracted by the grating will form a spectrum along each ordered beam. If light from a glowing gas, such as mercury vapor, passes through a diffraction grating, the separate spectral lines characteristic of mercury will appear.

Knowing the distance between the slits in the grating and the geometry of the interference pattern produced by the diffracted light, it is possible to measure the wavelength of the light in different parts of the spectrum. For this reason, diffraction gratings are often used in spectroscopes to examine the spectral lines emitted by substances undergoing chemical analysis.

An ordinary LP record or CD when held at a sharp angle to a light source will produce a spectrum characteristic of a reflection grating. The narrow, closely spaced grooves in the disc diffract the reflected light and produce the interference pattern that separates light into colors. A simple transmission grating can be made by looking at the light from a showcase filament with your eyes nearly closed. Light passing through the narrow openings between your eyelashes will be diffracted and give rise to an interference pattern with its characteristic bright and dark bands.

See also Diffraction; Spectrum; Wave motion.

Diffusion

Diffusion is the movement of molecules along a concentration gradient, from an area of high concentration to one of low concentration. Diffusion proceeds until the two concentrations are equal. Diffusion occurs in both gases and liquids.

Concentration gradients

Molecules always diffuse from areas of high concentration to areas of low concentration. The difference between the concentration of a substance in one area compared to another area is the concentration gradient. For example, placing ink on surface of water establishes a concentration gradient, in which the surface of the water has a high concentration of ink, and the rest of the water has a low concentration. As the ink diffuses, it moves from the area of high concentration to the area of low concentration, eventually resulting in a solution with equal concentrations of ink.

The importance of diffusion

Diffusion takes place not only in liquid solutions, but in gases. The odor of bread wafting through a house is an example of the diffusion of bread-smell chemicals from a high concentration to a lower concentration.

Diffusion in cells

Cells are bounded by a double membrane composed of lipids. This membrane is punctured intermittently with tiny pores. The membrane of a cell is thus selectively permeable: it keeps out certain substances but lets others pass through. The substances that pass through move in either direction, either into or out of the cell, depending on the concentration gradient. For example, very small ions pass through the lipid membrane through tiny pores in the membrane. Ions move down the concentration gradient that exists between the cytoplasm of the cell and the environment outside the cell, called the extracellular fluid. The extracellular fluid usually contains less ions than the highly concentrated cytoplasm, so ions tend to move from the cytoplasm, down the concentration gradient, into the extracellular fluid. This process is called simple diffusion.

Substances such as glucose or urea can't pass easily into the cell because their molecules are too large, or because they are electrically charged. In these cases, the substances need assistance in getting across the membrane. Special molecules called carrier molecules, situated within the cell membrane, bind to glucose and other substances and bring about their passage into the cell. Because these substances are moving down a concentration gradient, but are assisted by carrier molecules, this type of diffusion is called carrier-facilitated diffusion.

Water diffusion: osmosis

The special case of diffusion of water into and out of cells is called osmosis. Because osmosis is the diffusion of water, it is the movement of water from an area with a high concentration of water molecules to an area with a low concentration of water molecules; that is, water diffuses from an area in which water is abundant to an area in which water is scarce. Osmosis in cells is usually defined in different terms, however. It is the movement of water from a low concentration of salts to

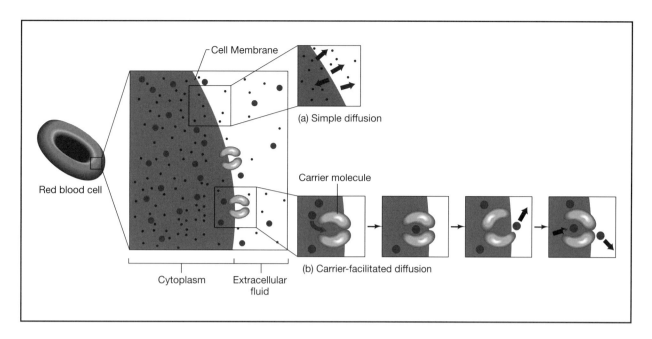

Simple diffusion (top) and carrier-facilitated diffusion (bottom) in a red blood cell.

an area with a high concentration of salts, across a semi-permeable membrane.

See also Membrane; Osmosis (cellular).

Further Reading:

Byrne, John H. *An Introduction to Membrane Transport and Bioelectricity: Foundations of General Physiology and Electrochemical Signaling,* 2nd ed. New York: Raven Press, 1994.

Denny, Mark. *Air and Water: The Biology and Physics of Life's Media.* Princeton, N.J.: Princeton University Press, 1993.

Yeagle , Philip. *The Membrane of Cells,* 2nd ed. San Diego: Academic Press, 1993.

Kathleen Scogna

KEY TERMS

Carrier-facilitated diffusion—The movement of substances down a concentration gradient assisted by carrier molecules.

Concentration gradient—The difference between the concentration of a substance in one area and that of another area.

Selectively permeable membrane—A membrane that allows some substances to pass through but blocks other substances.

Simple diffusion—Movement of substances down a concentration gradient across a selectively permeable membrane.

Digestive system

The digestive system is a group of organs responsible for the conversion of food into absorbable chemicals which are then used to provide energy for growth and repair. The digestive system is also known by a number of other names, including the gut, the digestive tube, the alimentary canal, the gastrointestinal (GI) tract, the intestinal tract, and the intestinal tube. The digestive system consists of the mouth, esophagus, stomach, and small and large intestines, along with several glands, such as the salivary glands, liver, gall bladder, and pancreas. These glands secrete digestive juices containing enzymes that break down the food chemically into smaller, more absorbable molecules. In addition to providing the body with the nutrients and energy it needs to function, the digestive system also separates and disposes of waste products ingested with the food.

Food is moved through the alimentary canal by a wavelike muscular motion known as peristalsis, which consists of the alternate contraction and relaxation of

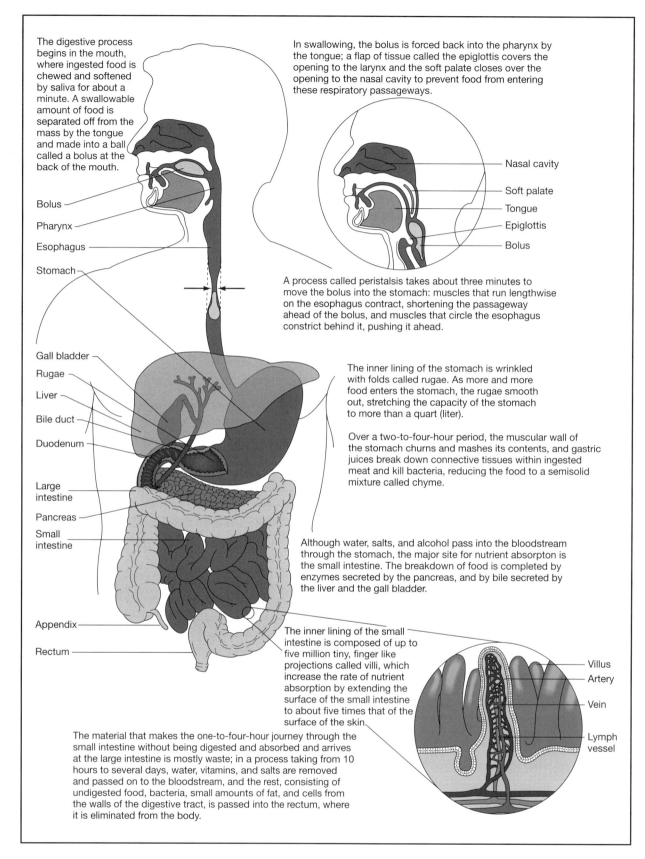

The digestive process begins in the mouth, where ingested food is chewed and softened by saliva for about a minute. A swallowable amount of food is separated off from the mass by the tongue and made into a ball called a bolus at the back of the mouth.

In swallowing, the bolus is forced back into the pharynx by the tongue; a flap of tissue called the epiglottis covers the opening to the larynx and the soft palate closes over the opening to the nasal cavity to prevent food from entering these respiratory passageways.

Bolus

Pharynx

Esophagus

Stomach

Nasal cavity

Soft palate

Tongue

Epiglottis

Bolus

A process called peristalsis takes about three minutes to move the bolus into the stomach: muscles that run lengthwise on the esophagus contract, shortening the passageway ahead of the bolus, and muscles that circle the esophagus constrict behind it, pushing it ahead.

Gall bladder

Rugae

Liver

Bile duct

Duodenum

Large intestine

Pancreas

Small intestine

Appendix

Rectum

The inner lining of the stomach is wrinkled with folds called rugae. As more and more food enters the stomach, the rugae smooth out, stretching the capacity of the stomach to more than a quart (liter).

Over a two-to-four-hour period, the muscular wall of the stomach churns and mashes its contents, and gastric juices break down connective tissues within ingested meat and kill bacteria, reducing the food to a semisolid mixture called chyme.

Although water, salts, and alcohol pass into the bloodstream through the stomach, the major site for nutrient absorpton is the small intestine. The breakdown of food is completed by enzymes secreted by the pancreas, and by bile secreted by the liver and the gall bladder.

The inner lining of the small intestine is composed of up to five million tiny, finger like projections called villi, which increase the rate of nutrient absorption by extending the surface of the small intestine to about five times that of the surface of the skin.

Villus

Artery

Vein

Lymph vessel

The material that makes the one-to-four-hour journey through the small intestine without being digested and absorbed and arrives at the large intestine is mostly waste; in a process taking from 10 hours to several days, water, vitamins, and salts are removed and passed on to the bloodstream, and the rest, consisting of undigested food, bacteria, small amounts of fat, and cells from the walls of the digestive tract, is passed into the rectum, where it is eliminated from the body.

The digestive process.

the smooth muscles lining the tract. In this way, food is passed through the gut in much the same manner as toothpaste is squeezed from a tube. *Churning* is another type of movement that takes place in the stomach and small intestine, which mixes the food so that the digestive enzymes can break down the food molecules.

Food in the human diet consists of carbohydrates, proteins, fats, vitamins, and minerals. The remainder of the food is fiber and water. The majority of minerals and vitamins pass through to the bloodstream without the need for further digestive changes, but other nutrient molecules must be broken down to simpler substances before they can be absorbed and used.

Ingestion

Food taken into the mouth is first prepared for digestion in a two step process known as mastication. In the first stage, the teeth tear break down the food into smaller pieces. In the second stage, the tongue rolls these pieces into balls (boluses). Sensory receptors on the tongue (taste buds) detect taste sensations of sweet, salt, bitter, and sour, or cause the rejection of bad-testing food. The olfactory nerves contribute to the sensation of taste by picking up the aroma of the food and passing the sensation of smell on to the brain.

The sight of the food also stimulates the salivary glands. Altogether, the sensations of sight, taste, and smell cause the salivary glands, located in the mouth, to produce saliva which then pours into the mouth to soften the food. An enzyme in the saliva called amylase begins the breakdown of carbohydrates (starch) into simple sugars, such as maltose. Ptyalin is one of the main amylase enzymes found in the mouth; ptyalin is also secreted by the pancreas.

The bolus of food, which is now a battered, moistened, and partially digested ball of food, is swallowed, moving to the throat at the back of the mouth (pharynx). In the throat, rings of muscles force the food into the esophagus, the first part of the upper digestive tube. The esophagus extends from the bottom part of the throat to the upper part of the stomach.

The esophagus does not take part in digestion. Its job is to get the bolus into the stomach. There is a powerful muscle (the esophageal sphincter), at the junction of the esophagus and stomach which acts as a valve to keep food, stomach acids, and bile from flowing back into the esophagus and mouth.

Digestion in the stomach

Chemical digestion begins in the stomach. The stomach, a large, hollow, pouched-shaped muscular organ, is shaped like a lima bean. When empty, the stomach becomes elongated; when filled, it balloons out.

Food in the stomach is broken down by the action of the gastric juice containing hydrochloric acid and a protein-digesting enzyme called *pepsin*. Gastric juice is secreted from the linings of the stomach walls, along with *mucus* which helps to protect the stomach lining from the action of the acid. The 3 layers of powerful stomach muscles churn the food into a fine semiliquid paste called *chyme*. From time to time, the chyme is passed through an opening (the pyloric sphircler), which controls the passage of chyme between the stomach and the beginning of the small intestine.

Gastric juice

There are several mechanisms responsible for the secretion of gastric juice in the stomach. The stomach begins its production of gastric juice while the food is still in the mouth. Nerves from the cheeks and tongue are stimulated and send messages to the brain. The brain in turn sends messages to nerves in the stomach wall, stimulating the secretion of gastric juice before the arrival of the food. The second signal for gastric juice production occurs when the food arrives in the stomach and touches the lining. This mechanism provides for only a moderate addition to the amount of gastric juice that was secreted when the food was in the mouth.

Gastric juice is needed mainly for the digestion of protein by pepsin. If a hamburger and bun reach the stomach, there is no need for extra gastric juice for the bun (carbohydrate), but the hamburger (protein) will require a much greater supply of gastric juice. The gastric juice already present will begin the breakdown of the large protein molecules of the hamburger into smaller molecules polypeptides and peptides. These smaller molecules in turn stimulate the cells of the stomach lining to release the hormone *gastrin* into the bloodstream.

Gastrin then circulates throughout the body, and eventually reaches the stomach, where it stimulates the cells of the stomach lining to produce more gastric juice. The more protein there is in the stomach, the more gastrin will be produced, and the greater the production of gastric juice. The secretion of more gastric juice by the increased amount of protein in the stomach represents the third mechanism of gastric juice secretion.

Alexis St. Martin's stomach

An understanding of the complex mechanisms of gastric juice secretion began with an American army doctor, William Beaumont (1785-1853). He was able to directly observe the process of digestion in the stomach from the wound of a soldier named Alexis St. Martin.

In 1822, Beaumont treated the soldier for an accidental gunshot wound. This wound left a large hole in the left side of St. Martin's body, tearing away parts of the ribs, muscles, and stomach wall. When the wound healed, the stomach wall had grown to the outer body wall, leaving a permanent hole from the outer body to the interior of the stomach. When St. Martin ate, bandages were needed to keep the food in place. For the first time in medical history, a physician was able to study the inner workings of the stomach. Beaumont's observations and experiments on St. Martin's stomach extended over eleven years.

In that time, he observed the secretion of gastric juice and placed the fluid from St. Martin's stomach on a piece of meat. There he could observe the digestion of protein. He was also able to observe the churning movements of the stomach when food entered it. Beaumont's investigation of St. Martin's stomach laid the groundwork for later investigations into the complexities of the digestive process.

Digestion and absorption in the small intestine

While digestion continues in the small intestine, it also becomes a major site for the process of absorption, that is, the passage of digested food into the bloodstream, and its transport to the rest of the body.

The small intestine is a long, narrow tube, about 20 ft (6 m) long, running from the stomach to the large intestine. The small intestine occupies the area of the abdomen between the diaphragm and hips, and is greatly coiled and twisted. The small intestine is lined with muscles which move the chyme toward the large intestine. The mucosa, which lines the entire small intestine, contains millions of glands that aid in the digestive and absorptive processes of the digestive system.

The small intestine, or small bowel, is sub-divided by anatomists into three sections, the duodenum, the jejunum, and the ileum. The duodenum is about 1 ft (0.3 m) long and connects with the lower portion of the stomach. When fluid food reaches the duodenum it undergoes further enzymatic digestion and is subjected to pancreatic juice, intestinal juice, and bile.

The pancreas is a large gland located below the stomach that secretes pancreatic juice into the duodenum via the pancreatic duct. There are three enzymes in pancreatic juice which digest carbohydrates, lipids, and proteins. Amylase, (the enzyme that is also found in saliva) breaks down starch into simpler sugars such as

maltose. The enzyme maltase in intestinal juice completes breaks maltose down into glucose.

Libases in pancreatic juice break down fats into fatty acids and glycerol, while proteinases continue the break down of proteins into amino acids. The gall bladder, located next to the liver secretes bile into the duodenum. While bile does not contain enzymes; it contains bile salts and other substances that help to emulsify (dissolve) fats which are otherwise insoluble in water. The fats so broken down into small globules allow the lipase enzymes a greater surface area for their action.

Chyme passing from the duodenum next reaches the jejunum of the small intestine, which is about 3 ft (0.91 m) long. Here, in the jejunum, the digested breakdown products of carbohydrates, fats, proteins, and most of the vitamins, minerals, and iron are absorbed. The inner lining of the small intestine is composed of up to five million tiny, finger-like projections called villi. The villi increase the rate of absorption of the nutrients into the bloodstream by extending the surface of the small intestine to about five times that of the surface area of the skin.

There are two transport systems that pick up the nutrients from the small intestine. Simple sugars, amino acids, glycerol, and some vitamins and salts are conveyed to the liver in the bloodstream. Fatty acids and vitamins are absorbed and then transported through the lymphatic system, the network of vessels which carry lymph and white blood cells throughout the body. Lymph eventually drains back into the bloodstream and so circulates throughout the body.

The last section of the small intestine is the ileum. It is smaller and thinner-walled than the jejunum, and it is the preferred site for vitamin B_{12} absorption and bile acids derived from the bile juice.

Absorption and elimination in the large intestine

The large intestine, or colon, is wider and heavier then the small intestine, but much shorter—only about 4 ft (1.2 m) long. It rises up on one side of the body (the ascending colon), crosses over to the other side (the transverse colon), descends (the descending colon), forms an s-shape (the sigmoid colon), reaches the rectum, and anus, from which the waste products of digestion (feces or stool), are passed out, along with gas. The muscular rectum, about 5 in (13 cm) long, expels the feces through the anus, which has a large muscular sphincter that controls the passage of waste matter.

The large intestine extracts water from the waste products of digestion and returns some of it to the bloodstream, along with some salts. Fecal matter contains undigested food, bacteria, and cells from the walls of the digestive tract. Certain types of bacteria of the large intestine help to synthesize the vitamins needed by the body. These vitamins find their way to the bloodstream along with the water absorbed from the colon, while excess fluids are passed out with the feces.

Liver

The liver is the largest organ in the body and plays a number of vital roles, including metabolizing the breakdown products of digestion, and detoxifying substances that are harmful to the body. The liver also provides a quick source of energy when the need arises and it produces new proteins. Along with the regulation of stored fats, the liver also stores vitamins, minerals, and sugars. The liver controls the excretion and production of cholesterol and metabolizes alcohol into a mild toxin. The liver also stores iron, maintains the hormone balance, produces immune factors to fight infections, regulates blood clotting, and produces bile.

The most common liver disorder in the United States and other developed countries is cirrhosis of the liver. The main cause for this disease is alcoholism. Cirrhosis is characterized by the replacement of healthy liver cells by fibrous tissue. The replacement process is gradual and extends over a period of 2-10 years to complete. There is no cure for the disease. Symptoms may not be noticed in its early development, but in its advanced stages there are a number of symptoms and the condition can lead to coma. Close medical attention is required to treat the disease.

Another common liver disorder is hepatitis. It is an inflammation of the liver caused by viruses. The most noticeable symptom of this disease is jaundice, that is, the skin, eyes, and urine turn yellow. There are three types of hepatitis, A virus, B virus, and a third type which as yet has not been identified.

Gallbladder

The gallbladder lies under the liver and is connected by various ducts to the liver and the duodenum. The gallbladder is a small hollow organ resembling a money pouch. Its main function is to store bile until it is concentrated enough to be used by the small intestine. The gall bladder can store about two ounces of bile. Bile consists of bile salts, bile acids, and bile pigments. In addition, bile contains cholesterol dissolved in the bile acids. If the amount of cholesterol in the bile acids increases or the amount of acid decreases, then some of the cholesterol will settle out of the acid to form gall-

stones that accumulate and block the ducts to the gallbladder.

Infection in the gallbladder can be another cause for gallstones. Gallstones may be in the gallbladder for years without giving any signs of the condition, but when they obstruct the bile duct they cause considerable pain and inflammation. Infection and blockage of the bile flow may follow. Surgical removal of the gallbladder may be necessary to treat this condition. Since the liver both produces and stores sufficient amounts of bile, the loss of the gallbladder does not interfere with the digestive process provided fat intake in the diet is regulated.

If the gallstones contain mainly cholesterol, drug treatment for gallstones may be possible. But if there is too much other material in the gallstones, surgery may still be necessary. Even after the condition has been treated successfully by drugs and diet, the condition can return. The drug treatment takes years to dissolve the gallstones.

Appendix

The appendix is a hollow finger-like projection that hangs from the occum at the junction between the small intestine and the large intestine. The appendix does not function in humans; however, in some animals, such as rabbits, the appendix is rather large and helps in the digestion of cellulose from bark and wood which rabbits eat. The appendix in humans is therefore a vestigial organ, which may have had uses for earlier types of ancestral human digestive processes before the evolution of *Homo sapiens*.

If food gets trapped in the appendix, an irritation of its membranes may occur leading to swelling and inflammation, a condition known as appendicitis. If the condition becomes serious, removal of the appendix is necessary to avoid a life-threatening condition if it were to rupture.

Pancreas

When food reaches the small intestine, the pancreas secretes pancreatic juices. When there is no food in the small intestine, the pancreas does not secrete its juices. The economy of this process puzzled researchers who wondered what the mechanism for this control might be. In 1902, William Bayliss and Ernest Starling, two British physiologists, conducted experiments to find the answer. They reasoned that the same mechanism that initiated gastric juices when food first enters the mouth might be the same mechanism for releasing the flow of pancreatic juices.

These researchers made an extract from the lining of small intestine and injected it into an experimental animal. The extract caused the animal to secrete large amounts of pancreatic juice. They concluded that the extract from the intestinal lining must have some substance responsible for the flow, which they named secretin. The experiment gave the first real proof for the existence of hormones, substances secreted by one group of cells that travel around the body which target other groups of cells.

Insulin is another important hormone secreted by a group of cells within the pancreas called the islets of Langerhans, which are part of the endocrine system rather than the digestive system. Insulin released into the bloodstream targets liver and muscle cells, and allows them to take excess sugar from the blood and store it in the form of glycogen. When the pancreas does not produce sufficient insulin to store dietary sugar, the blood and urine levels of sugar reach dangerous levels. Diabetes mellitus is the resultant disease. Mild cases can be controlled by a properly regulated diet, but severe cases require the regular injection of insulin.

Other disorders of the digestive system

Several disorders of the esophagus are esophagitis, esophageal spasm, and esophageal cancer. Esophagitis (heartburn) is an inflammation of the esophagus usually caused by the reflux of gastric acids into the esophagus and is treated with (alkalis) antacid. Esophageal spasm is also caused by acid reflux and is sometimes treated with nitroglycerine placed under the tongue. Esophageal cancer can be caused by smoking and is generally fatal.

Disorders of the stomach include hiatal hernia, ulcers, and gastric cancer. A hiatal hernia occurs when a portion of the stomach extends upwards into the thorax through a large opening in the diaphragm. It is a condition that commonly occurs to people over the age of 50. Stomach ulcers are sores that form in the lining of the stomach. They may vary in size from a small sore to a deep cavity, surrounded by an inflamed area, sometimes called ulcer craters. Stomach ulcers and ulcers that form in the esophagus and in the lining of the duodenum are called peptic ulcers because they need stomach acid and the enzyme pepsin to form. Duodenal ulcers are the most common type. They tend to be smaller than stomach ulcers and heal more quickly. Ulcers that form in the stomach lining are called gastric ulcers. About 4 million people have ulcers and 20% of those have gastric ulcers. Those people who are at most risk for ulcers are those who smoke, middle-age and older men, chronic users of alcohol, and those who take anti-inflammatory drugs, such as aspirin and ibuprofen.

Until 1993, the general belief in the medical community concerning the cause of stomach ulcers was that there were multiple factors responsible for their development. By 1993 there was mounting evidence that an S-shaped bacterium, *Helicobacter pylori*, could be one of the factors causing ulcers. *Helicobacter pylori* live in the mucous lining of the stomach near the surface cells and may go undetected for years. Researchers argued that irritation to the stomach caused by the bacteria weakened the lining, thus making it more susceptible to damage by acid and resulting in the formation of ulcers.

Barry Marshall, an Australian gastroenterologist, was the chief proponent of the theory that stomach ulcers are caused by *H. pylori* infections, rather than a multiple factor explanation, such as stress or poor diet. Although Marshall was discouraged by his colleagues from pursuing this line of research, he demonstrated his hypothesis by swallowing a mixture containing *H. pylori*. Marshall soon developed gastritis, which is the precursor condition to ulcers.

The treatment of ulcers has undergone a radical change with Marshall's discovery that stomach ulcers are caused by *H. pylori* infections. Ulcer patients today are being treated with antibiotics and antacids rather than special diets or expensive medicines. It is believed that about 80% of stomach ulcers may be caused by the bacterial infection, while about 20% may be from other causes, such as the use of antiinflammatory medicines.

Further Reading:

Maryon-Davis, Alan and Steven Parker. *Food and digestion*. London; New York: F. Watts, 1990.
Peikin, Steven R. *Gastrointestinal Health*. New York, NY : HarperCollins, 1991.

Jordan P. Richman

Digital audio tape see **Magnetic recording/audiocassette**

Digitalis

Digitalis is a drug that has been used for centuries to treat heart disease. The active ingredient in the drug is glycoside, a chemical compound that contains a sugar molecule linked to another molecule. The glycoside compound can be broken down into a sugar and nonsugar compound. Though current digitalis drugs are synthetic, that is, man-made, early forms of the drug were derived from a plant.

Digitalis is a derivative of the plant *Digitalis purpurea*, or purple foxglove. The plant's name, Digitalis (from the Latin *digit*, finger) describes the finger-shaped purple flowers it bears. The effects of the plant extract on the heart were first observed in the late eighteenth century by William Withering, who experimented with the extract in fowls and humans. Withering reported his results in a treatise entitled, "The Foxglove and an Account of its Medical Properties, with Practical Remarks on Dropsy." His explanations of the effects of foxglove on the heart have not stood up to the test of

time, but his prediction that it could be "converted to salutary ends" certainly has. Indeed, digitalis remains in use today, the oldest drug in use for the treatment of heart disease as well as the most widespread.

The digitalis drugs come in many forms, differing in their chemical structure. As a group they are classified as cardiac inotropes. Cardiac, of course, refers to the heart. An inotrope is a substance that has a direct effect on muscle contraction. Positive inotropism is an increase in the speed and strength of muscle contraction, while negative inotropism is the opposite. Digitalis has a positive inotropic effect on the heart muscle.

How digitalis is used

Digitalis is used to bolster the ailing heart in congestive heart failure. In this condition, the heart muscle has stretched while straining to pump blood against a back pressure. The back pressure may be caused by high blood pressure, or it may be the result of a leak caused by a faulty aortic valve or a hole in the wall (septum) dividing the right and left halves of the heart. When these conditions occur, the heart muscle, or myocardium, must exert greater and greater pressure to force blood through the body against the resistant force. Over time the strain will stretch the heart muscle, and the size of the heart increases. As the heart muscle changes in these ways, its pumping action becomes less and less effective. Congestive heart failure occurs when the myocardium has been stretched too far. At this juncture the patient must have a heart transplant, or he will die.

The administration of digitalis, however, can forestall the critical stage of the disease. Digitalis has a direct and immediate effect on the myocardium. By a mechanism not well understood, digitalis increases the levels of intracellular calcium, which plays an important role in the contraction of the muscles. Almost as soon as the drug has been administered, the heart muscle begins to contract faster and with greater force. As a result, its pumping efficiency increases and the supply of blood to the body is enhanced. Digitalis also tends to bring about a decrease in the size of the ventricles of the failing heart as well as a reduction in wall tension.

In addition to its immediate effect on the heart muscle, the drug affects the autonomic nervous system, slowing the electrical signal that drives the heartbeat. As heart contractions become more efficient, the heart rate slows. For this reason, the drug is said to have a negative chronotropic effect (the prefix *chrono-* refers to time).

As digitalis stabilizes the myocardium, appropriate steps can also be taken to correct the original cause of the disease, if possible. The patient's blood pressure can

KEY TERMS

· ·

Aortic valve—The one-way valve that allows blood to pass from the heart's main pumping chamber, the left ventricle, into the body's main artery, the aorta.

Cardiologist—A physician who specializes in the diagnosis and treatment of heart disease.

Myocardium—The heart muscle.

Oxygenation—The process, taking place in the lungs, by which oxygen enters the blood to be transported to body tissues.

Septum—The wall that divides the right side of the heart (which contains "used" blood that has been returned from the body) from the left side of the heart (which contains newly oxygenated blood to be pumped to the body).

Other drugs to treat heart disease have been developed over time, of course, but none has replaced digitalis as the standard therapy for heart failure. A drug of ancient lineage, digitalis remains one of the most reliable and most used medicines.

See also Heart diseases.

Further Reading:

Basic Health Care and Emergency Aid. Nashville: The Varsity Co., 1990.

The Complete Drug Reference: United States Pharmacopeia. Yonkers, N.Y.: Consumer Reports Books, 1992.

Larson, David E., ed. *Mayo Clinic Family Health Book.* New York: William Morrow and Company, Inc., 1990.

Larry Blaser

be lowered with medications, or heart surgery can be performed to replace a faulty valve or patch a hole in the septum. When it is not possible to improve cardiac function by other means, the patient can be maintained on digitalis for many years.

Risks and side effects

The effect of digitalis is dose related. The higher the dose, the more pronounced the cardiac reaction. It is this immediate and direct effect of the drug that dictates that the physician closely monitor his patient and adjust the digitalis dosage as needed to provide the corrective effect, while being careful not to institute a toxic reaction. Digitalis is a very potent and active drug and can quickly create an overdose situation if the patient is not closely watched. In the case of an overdose, the patient's heart will begin to beat out of rhythm (arrhythmia) and very rapidly (tachycardia). In addition, the drug may affect the nervous system and cause headaches, vision problems such as blurring and light sensitivity, and sometimes convulsions.

Withering already recognized the toxicity of digitalis and warned against the careless administration of the drug in too high a dose. Despite Withering's warnings, physicians in the early nineteenth century often overdosed their patients. As a consequence, the drug was considered too dangerous for the greater part of the nineteenth century and was used little. Later in the same century, however, the beneficial properties of digitalis were reassessed, and the drug became an essential element in the cardiologist's pharmacopeia.

Dik-diks

Dik-diks (genus *Madogna*) are small (dog-sized) African antelopes belonging to the family of Bovidae, which includes cattle, sheep, and goats, as well as deer, antelope, gazelles, and impalas. Like all bovids, dik-diks have even-toed hooves, horns, and a four-chambered stomach. There are five species of dik-dik—Kirk's (the largest), Günther's, Salt's, Red-bellied, and Swayne's (the smallest), as well as 21 subspecies.

Dik-diks belong to the tribe Neotragini, the dwarf antelopes. These small animals weigh only up to 12 lb (6 kg), stand a little over 1 ft (40 cm) in height at the shoulders, and are less than 2 ft (67 cm) in length. Dik-diks are found in the Horn of Africa, East Africa, and in some parts of southwest Africa. In spite of their small size, dik-diks are heavily hunted for their skin, which is used to make gloves. Dik-diks have big eyes, a pointed snout, and a crest of erect hair on their forehead. These antelopes can withstand prolonged high temperatures because of their ability to cool down by nasal panting.

Habitat and diet

Dik-diks live in arid bush country and eat a diet of fallen leaves, green leaves, and fruit. This diet is digested with the aid of microorganisms in the dik-dik's four-chambered stomach and by the regurgitation and rechewing of food (chewing the cud). Because of their small size, the dik-dik's rumination process is much faster than in larger hoofed animals. With the reduction of forest habitat in Africa over the past 12 million years,

A Kirk's dik-dik in Tsavo National Park, Kenya.

it is believed that the small size of animals like the dik-dik has been favorable to their survival.

The dik-dik, like all cud-chewing animals, has a specialized jaw and tooth structure that is adaptable to its diet. The front part of the dik-dik jaw is large compared to the brain area of its skull. The jaws come together elongated, and there are no teeth at the end of the upper jaw. The overall structure functions like a shovel that can tear off great quantities of food at a fast pace and then chop it up for the rumination process.

Social organization

A male and a female dik-dik form a permanent pair bond and together they occupy a territory 12-75 acres (5-30 ha) in size. The female is slightly larger than the male, which reflects her greater role in caring for her offspring. Dik-diks give birth twice a year (coinciding with the rainy seasons) to one offspring at a time. For the first few weeks after its birth, the young dik-dik lies hidden in the bush. Its mother makes contact by bleating sounds which are answered by the offspring.

Like other dwarf antelopes, dik-diks have efficient scent glands that are used to mark their territory. These glands are located in the front part of the eyes (suborbital glands) and on their hooves. Dik-diks are therefore able to mark both the ground and bushes of their territory with their scents.

Territorial behavior

Another distinctive aspect of dik-dik territorial behavior is a ritual that accompanies defecation and urination. The female urinates first, then defecates on a pile of dung that marks their territory. The male waits behind her while she squats during this activity. He then sniffs, scrapes, squats, and deposits his urine and feces over the female's. Some scent marking of neighboring plants is also part of this ritual. There can be between 6-13 such locations around a dik-dik pair's territory.

The male dik-dik defends the territory from both male and female intruders. Generally, conflicts over territory are infrequent. While rival males will engage in a rushing ritual, they rarely attack one another physically. The offspring of a dik-dik pair is allowed to remain in the territory until it reaches maturity, which is about six months for females and twelve months for male offspring. The male dik-dik usually intervenes when the mature male offspring tries to approach the mother. The adult male challenge leads to submissive behavior by the younger male. Eventually, the male or female offspring are driven from the territory but they quickly bond with another young dik-dik in an unclaimed territory.

Further Reading:

Estes, Richard D. *Behavior Guide to African Mammals.* Berkeley: University of California, 1991.
The Safari Companion. Post Mills, VT: Chelsea Green, 1993.

Vita Richman

Dill see **Carrot family**

Dingo see **Canines**

Dinoflagellates see **Red tide**

Dinosaur

Dinosaurs are a group of now-extinct, terrestrial reptiles in the order Dinosauria that lived from about

225 million years ago to 66 million years ago, during the Mesozoic Era. Species of dinosaurs ranged from chicken-sized creatures such as the 2 lb (1 kg) predator *Compsognathus*, to colossal, herbivorous animals known as sauropods, which were larger than any terrestrial animals that lived before or since. Some dinosaurs were enormous, awesomely fierce predators, while others were mild-mannered herbivores, or plant eaters, which reached an immense size. The word dinosaur is derived from two Greek words, meaning "terrible lizard," in reference to some of the huge and awesome predatory dinosaurs, which were the first of these extinct reptiles to be discovered, and were initially thought to be lizard-like in appearance and biology.

Dinosaurs were remarkable and impressive animals, but are rather difficult to define as a zoological group. They were terrestrial animals that had upright legs, rather than legs that sprawled outward from the body. Their skull had two temporal openings on each side (in addition to the opening for the eyes), as well as other common and distinctive features. Much of what distinguished the dinosaurs, however, includes distinctive aspects of their behavior, physiology, and ecological relationships. Unfortunately, relatively little is known about these traits, because we can only learn about dinosaurs using their fossil traces, which are rare and incomplete. Still, it is clear from the available evidence that some species of dinosaurs were large predators, others were immense herbivores, and yet others were smaller predators, herbivores, or scavengers. Sufficient information is available to allow paleontologists to assign scientific names to many of these dinosaurs, and to hypothesize about their evolutionary and ecological relationships.

Although they are now extinct, the dinosaurs were among the most successful large animals ever to live on Earth. The dinosaurs arose during the interval of geologic time known as the Mesozoic ("middle life") Era, often called the "golden age of reptiles" or "the age of dinosaurs." Radiometric dating of volcanic rocks associated with dinosaur fossils suggests they first evolved 225 million years ago, during the late Triassic Period and became extinct 66 million years ago, at the end of the Cretaceous Period. Dinosaurs lived for about 160 million years, and were the dominant terrestrial animals on Earth throughout the Jurassic and Cretaceous Periods—a span of over 100 million years.

Interestingly, mammal-like animals coexisted almost continuously with the dinosaurs, and obviously prospered after the last of the dinosaurs became extinct. However, although they co-existed in time with dinosaurs, mammals were clearly subordinate to these reptiles, in an ecological sense. It was not until the dis-

A dinosaur foot print in Tuba City, Arizona.

appearance of the last of the dinosaurs that an adaptive radiation of larger species of mammals occurred, and they could then become the dominant large animals on Earth.

It is not known exactly what caused the last of the dinosaurs to become extinct. It must be stressed, however, that the dinosaurs were remarkably successful animals. These creatures were dominant on Earth for an enormously longer length of time than the few tens of thousands of years that humans have been a commanding ecological force.

Biology of dinosaurs

The distinguishing characteristics of the dinosaurs include aspects of the structure of their skull and other bones. Dinosaurs typically had 25 vertebrae, plus three vertebrae that were fused to their pelvic bones. However, the dinosaurs displayed an enormous range of forms and functions, and they filled a wide array of ecological niches. Some of the dinosaurs were, in fact, quite bizarre in their shape and, undoubtedly, their behavior.

The smallest dinosaurs were chicken-like carnivores that were only about 1 ft (30 cm) long and weighed 5-6 lb (2-3 kg). The largest dinosaurs reached a length of over 100 ft (30 m), and weighed 80 tons or more—more than any other terrestrial animal has ever achieved. The largest blue whales can weigh more than this, about 110 tons, representing the largest animals ever to occur on Earth. However, the weight of these aquatic animals is partially buoyed by the water that they live in—whales do not have to fully support their immense weight against the forces of gravity. When compared with the largest living land animal, the African elephant, which weighs as much as 7.5 tons, the large species of dinosaurs were enormous creatures.

Most species of dinosaurs had a long tail and long neck, but this was not the case for all species. Most of the dinosaurs walked on their four legs, although some species were bipedal, using only their rear legs for locomotion, their forelegs being greatly reduced in size and probably used only for grasping. The species that were tetrapods, that is, walked on four legs, were all peaceful herbivores. In contrast, many of the bipedal dinosaurs were fast-running predators.

The teeth of dinosaur species were highly diverse. Many species were exclusively herbivorous, and their teeth were correspondingly adapted for cutting and grinding vegetation. Other dinosaurs were fierce predators, and their teeth were shaped like serrated knives, and were adaptive to seizing and stabbing their prey, and cutting it into smaller pieces that could be swallowed whole.

Until recently, it was widely believed that dinosaurs were rather stupid, slow-moving, cold-blooded (or poikilothermic) creatures. However, some scientists now believe that dinosaurs were intelligent, social, quick-moving, and probably warm-blooded (or homoiothermic) animals. This is a rather controversial topic, and scientific consensus has not been reached on the issue of whether at least some of the dinosaurs were able to regulate their body temperature by producing heat through metabolic reactions. However, it is absolutely undeniable that dinosaurs were extremely capable animals. This should not be a surprise to us, considering the remarkable evolutionary successes that these animals attained.

Fossils and other evidence of the dinosaurs

Humans have never co-existed with dinosaurs on Earth, yet a surprising amount is known about these remarkable reptiles. Evidence about the existence and nature of dinosaurs is entirely indirect, and has been gleaned from fossilized traces that these animals left in sediment deposits.

The first evidence suggesting the existence of the huge, extinct creatures that we now know as dinosaurs was the discovery of traces of their ancient footprints in sedimentary rocks. Dinosaurs left their footprints in soft mud as they moved along a marine shore or riverbank. That mud was subsequently covered over as a new layer of sediment accumulated, and later solidified into rock. Under very rare circumstances, this process preserved traces of the footprints of dinosaurs. Interestingly, the footprints were initially attributed to giant birds, because of their superficial resemblance to tracks made by the largest of the living birds, such as the ostrich and emu.

The first fossilized skeletal remains to be identified as those of giant, extinct reptiles were discovered by miners in western Europe. These first discoveries were initially presumed to be astonishingly gigantic, extinct lizards. However, several naturalists recognized substantial anatomical differences between the fossil bones and those of living reptiles, and so the dinosaurs were "discovered." The first of these finds were bones of a 35-50 ft (10-15 m) long carnivore named *Megalosaurus* (this was the first dinosaur to be named scientifically), and a large herbivore named *Iguanodon*, found in sedimentary rocks in mines in England, Belgium, and France.

Discoveries of fantastic, extinct mega-reptiles in Europe were soon followed by even more exciting finds of dinosaur fossils in North America and elsewhere. These events captured the fascination of both naturalists and the general public. Museums started to develop extraordinary displays of re-assembled dinosaur skeletons, and artists prepared equally extraordinary depictions of dinosaurs and their fabricated ecosystems.

This initial hey-day of dinosaur fossil discoveries occurred in the late nineteenth and early twentieth centuries. During this period many of the most important finds were made by North American paleontologists, who discovered and began to mine rich deposits of fossils in the prairies. There was intense scientific interest in these American discoveries of fossilized bones of gargantuan, seemingly preposterous animals, such as the awesome predator *Tyrannosaurus*, and the immense herbivore *Apatosaurus* (initially known as *Brontosaurus*.)

Unfortunately, the excitement and scientific frenzy led to a rather passionate competition among some of the paleontologists, who wanted to be known for discovering the biggest, or the fiercest, or the weirdest dinosaurs. The most famous rivals were two American scientists, Othniel C. Marsh and Edwin Drinker Cope.

Other famous discoveries of fossilized dinosaur bones have been made in the Gobi Desert of eastern Asia. Some of those finds include nests with eggs that contain fossilized embryos that are used to study dinosaur development. Some nests contain hatchlings, suggesting that dinosaur parents cared for their young. In addition, the clustering of the nests of some dinosaurs suggests aspects of the social structure of these animals, including communal nesting, possibly for mutual protection against marauding predatory dinosaurs.

By now, fossilized dinosaur bones have been discovered on all continents. Discoveries of fossils in the high Arctic and in Antarctica suggest that the climate was much warmer when dinosaurs roamed the Earth. It is also likely polar dinosaurs were migratory, probably traveling to high latitudes to feed and breed during the summer, and returning to lower latitudes during the winter. These migrations may have occurred mostly in response to the lack of sunlight during the long polar winters, rather than because of the cooler temperatures.

Although the most important fossil records of dinosaurs involve their bones, there are other sorts of evidence as well. In addition to footprints, eggs, and nests, there have also been finds of imprints of dinosaur skin, feces (known as coprolites), rounded gizzard stones (known as gastroliths), and even possible stomach contents. In addition, fossilized plant remains are sometimes associated with deposits of dinosaur fossils, and these can be used to infer something about the habitats of these animals. Inferences can also be based on the geological context of the locations of fossils, for example, their proximity to a marine shore, or geographical position, as is the case of polar dinosaurs. All of these types of information have been studied and used to infer the shape, physiology, behavior, and ecological relationships of extinct dinosaurs.

Major groups of dinosaurs

There is only incomplete knowledge of the evolutionary relationships of dinosaurs with each other, and with other major groups of reptiles. This results, of course, from the fact that dinosaurs, as well as any other extinct organism, can only be studied through their fossilized remains, which are often rare and fragmentary, especially those that are millions or hundreds of millions of years old. Nevertheless, some dinosaur species bear clear resemblances to each other, while also being obviously distinct from certain other dinosaurs.

The dinosaurs evolved from a group of early reptiles known as *thecodonts*, which arose during the Permian period (290-250 million years ago) and were dominant throughout the Triassic (250-208 million years ago). It appears that two major groups of dinosaurs evolved from the thecodonts, the ornithischian ("bird hips") dinosaurs, and the saurischian ("lizard hips") dinosaurs. These two groups are distinguished largely on the basis of the anatomical structure of their pelvic or hip bones.

Both of these dinosaur lineages originated at about the same time. Both evolved many species, were ecologically important, and persisted until about 66 million years ago. Both groups included quadrupeds that walked on all four legs, as well as bipeds, walking erect on their much-larger, hind legs. All of the ornithischians had a bird-like beak on their lower jaw, and all were herbivores. Most of the carnivorous, or predatory, dinosaurs were saurischians, as were some of the her-

bivorous species. Interestingly, despite some resemblance between ornithischian dinosaur and bird physiology, it appears that the first birds actually evolved from saurischians.

Carnivorous dinosaurs

The carnosaurs were a group of saurischian predators, or theropods, that grew large and had enormous hind limbs but tiny fore limbs. *Tyrannosaurus rex* was the largest carnivore that has ever stalked Earth's landscape; its scientific name is derived from Greek words for "tyrant reptile king." This fearsome, bipedal predator of the Late Cretaceous could grow to a length of 45 ft (14 meters), and may have weighed as much as 7-9 tons. *Tyrannosaurus rex* (T. rex) had a massive head, and a mouth full of about 60 dagger-shaped, 6 in (15 cm) long, very sharp, serrated teeth, which were renewed throughout the life of the animal. This predator likely ran in a lumbering fashion, using its powerful hind legs, which may also have been wielded as sharp-clawed, kicking weapons. It is thought that *T. rex* may have initially attacked its prey with powerful head-butts, and then torn the animal apart with its enormous, 3 ft (1 m) long jaws. Alternatively, *T. rex* may have largely been a scavenger of dead dinosaurs. The relatively tiny fore legs of *T. rex* probably only had minor uses. The long and heavy tail of *T. rex* was used as a counter-balance for the animal while it was running, and as a stabilizing prop while it was standing.

Albertosaurus was also a large theropod of the Late Cretaceous. *Albertosaurus* was similar to *Tyrannosaurus*, but it was a less massively built animal, and somewhat smaller at about 25 ft (8 m) long and two tons in weight. However, *Albertosaurus* was probably a considerably faster-moving predator than *Tyrannosaurus*.

Allosaurus was a gigantic, bipedal predator of the Late Jurassic. *Allosaurus* could grow to a length of 36 ft (12 m) and a weight of two tons. The jaws of *Allosaurus* were loosely hinged, and they could detach to swallow large chunks of prey.

Spinosaurus was a "fin-back" (or "sail-back") dinosaur of the Late Cretaceous period that was distantly related to *Allosaurus*. *Spinosaurus* had long, erect, skin-covered, bony projections from its vertebrae that may have been used in regulating body temperature or perhaps as behavioral displays to impress each other or attract a mate. *Spinosaurus* could achieve a length of 40 ft (13 m), and a weight of seven tons. These animals had small, sharp teeth, and were probably carnivores. *Dimetrodon* and *Edaphosaurus*, early Permian pelycosaurs (mammal-like reptiles, not dinosaurs), are

Dinosaur bones being excavated near Kauchanaburi, Thailand.

sometimes confused with *Spinosaurus* as they also had sail-like back spines.

Not all of the fearsome dinosaurian predators, or theropods, were enormous. *Deinonychus*, for example, was an Early Cretaceous dinosaur that grew to about 10 ft (3 m) and weighed around 220 lbs (100 kg). *Deinonychus* was one of the so-called "running lizards," which were fast, agile predators that likely hunted in packs. As a result, *Deinonychus* was probably a fearsome predator of animals much larger than itself. *Deinonychus* had one of its hind claws enlarged into a sharp, sickle-like, slashing weapon, which was wielded by jumping on its prey and then kicking, slashing, and disembowelling the victim. The scientific name of *Deinonychus* is derived from the Greek words for terrible claw.

The most infamous small theropod is *Velociraptor*, or swift plunderer, a 6 ft (2 m) long animal of the Late Cretaceous. Restorations of this fearsome, highly intelligent, pack-hunting, "killing machine" were used in the famous movie, *Jurassic Park*.

Oviraptosaurs (egg-stealing reptiles) were relatively small, probably highly intelligent theropod dinosaurs that were fast-running hunters of small animals, and some are believed to have also been specialized predators of the nests of other dinosaurs. The best known of these animals is Late Cretaceous *Oviraptor*. *Ingenia*, a somewhat smaller oviraptorsaur, was about 6 ft (2 m) long, weighed about 55 lb (25 kg), and also lived during the Late Cretaceous. *Microvenator* of the early Cretaceous was less than 3 ft (1 m) long, and weighed about 12 lb (6 kg).

Herbivorous dinosaurs

The sauropods were a group of large saurischian herbivores that included the world's largest-ever terrestrial animals. This group rumbled along on four, enormous, pillar-like, roughly equal-sized legs, with a long tail trailing behind. Sauropods also had a very long neck, and their head was relatively small, at least in comparison with the overall mass of these immense animals. The teeth were peg-like, and were mostly used for grazing, rather than for chewing their diet of plant matter. Digestion was probably aided by large stones in an enormous gizzard, in much the same way that modern, seed-eating birds grind their food. The sauropods were most abundant during the Late Jurassic. They declined afterwards, to be replaced as dominant herbivores by different types of dinosaurs, especially the hadrosaurs.

Apatosaurus (previously known as *Brontosaurus*, or the ground-shaking, "thunder lizard") was a large sauropod that lived during the late Jurassic, and could achieve a length of 65 ft (20 m) and a weight of 30 tons. *Diplodocus* was a related animal of the late Jurassic, but it was much longer in its overall body shape. A remarkably complete skeleton of *Diplodocus* has been found, which was 90 ft (27 m) long overall, with a 25 ft (8 m) neck and a 45 ft (14 m) tail, and an estimated body weight of 11 tons. In comparison, the stouter-bodied *Apatosaurus* was slightly shorter, but considerably heavier. *Brachiosaurus* also lived during the Late Jurassic and was an even bigger herbivore, with a length as great as 100 ft (30 m), and an astonishing weight that may have reached 80 tons, although conservative estimates are closer to 55 tons. *Supersaurus* and *Ultrasaurus* were similarly large. *Seismosaurus* may have been longer than 160 ft (50 m), and *Argentinosaurus*, recently discovered in Patagonia, South America, may set a new weight record of 100 tons.

Stegosaurus was a 30 ft (9 m) long, late Jurassic tetrapod, with a distinctive row of triangular, erect, bony plates running along its back. These may have been used to absorb or radiate heat, depending on the time of day. *Stegosaurus* had sharp-spiked projections at the end of its tail, which were lashed at predators as a means of defense. *Dacentrurus* was a 13 ft (4 m) long, Jurassic-age animal related to *Stegosaurus*, but it had a double row of large spikes along the entire top of its body, from the end of the tail to the back of the head.

The ceratopsians were various types of "horned" dinosaurs. *Triceratops* was a three-horned dinosaur, and could be as long as 33 ft (10 m), and weigh six tons. *Triceratops* lived in the late Cretaceous, and it had a large bony shield behind the head, and three horns projecting from the forehead and face, which were used as defensive weapons. *Anchiceratops* was a seven-ton animal that lived somewhat later, and was one of the last of the dinosaurs, becoming extinct 66-million years ago at the end of the Cretaceous period. There were also rhinoceros-like, single-horned dinosaurs, such as the 20 ft (6 m), two-ton *Centrosaurus* of the late Cretaceous. Fossilized skeletons of this animal have been found in groups, suggesting that it was a herding dinosaur. The horned dinosaurs were herbivores, and they had a parrot-like beak, useful for eating vegetation.

Ankylosaurus was a late Cretaceous animal that could be as long as 36 ft (11 m) and weigh five tons. *Ankylosaurus* was a stout, short-legged, lumbering herbivore. This animal had very heavy and spiky body armor, and a large bony club at the end of its tail that was used to defend itself against predators.

The duck-billed dinosaurs or hadrosaurs included many herbivorous species of the Cretaceous period. Hadrosaurs are sometimes divided into groups based on aspects of their head structure; they could have a flattish head, a solid crest on the top of their head, or an unusual, hollow crest. Hadrosaurs were the most successful of the late Cretaceous dinosaurs in terms of their relative abundance and wide distribution.

Hadrosaurs apparently were social animals, living at least part of the year in herds, and in some places undertaking seasonal migrations. Hadrosaurs appear to have nested communally, incubated their eggs, and brooded their young. Hadrosaurs had large hind legs and could walk on all four legs, or bipedally if more speed was required—these animals were probably very fast runners.

Hadrosaurus was a five-ton, late Cretaceous animal, and was the first dinosaur to be discovered and named in North America—in 1858 from fossils found in New Jersey. *Corythosaurus* was a 36 ft (11 m) long, four-ton, late Cretaceous herbivore that had a large, hollow, helmet-like crest on the top of its head. *Parasaurolophus* of the late Cretaceous was similar in size, but it had a curved, hollow crest that swept back as far as 6-10 ft (2-3 m) from the back of the head. It has been suggested that this exaggerated helmet may have assisted with breathing when this animal was feeding underwater on aquatic plants. However, a more likely use of the swept-back helmet was in species recognition, and for giving resonance to the loud sounds made by these hadrosaurs. *Edmontosaurus* was a large, non-helmeted hadrosaur that lived in the Great Plains during the late Cretaceous, and could be as long as 40 ft (13 m) and weigh three tons. *Anatosaurus* was a three-ton hadrosaur that lived as recently as 66 million years ago, and was among the last of the dinosaurs to become extinct. The hadrosaurs probably were a favorite prey for some of the large theropods, such as *Tyrannosaurus rex*.

Other extinct orders of Mesozoic-age reptiles

Several other orders of large reptiles lived at the same time as the dinosaurs, and are also now extinct.

The pterosaurs (order Pterosauria) were large, flying reptiles that lived from the late Triassic to the late Cretaceous. Some species of pterosaurs had wingspans as great as 40 ft (12 m), much wider than any other flying animal has ever managed to achieve. Functional biologists studying the superficially awkward designs of these animals have long wondered how the animals managed to fly. At least some species of pterosaurs are thought to have fed on fish, which were presumably scooped up as the pterosaur glided just above the water surface.

The ichthyosaurs (Ichthyosauria), plesiosaurs (Plesiosauria) and mosasaurs (Mososauria) were orders of carnivorous marine reptiles that became extinct in the Late Cretaceous. The ichthyosaurs were shark-like in form, except that their vertebral column extended into the lower part of their caudal (or tail) fin, rather than into the upper part as in the sharks. Of course, ichthyosaurs also had well-developed, bony skeletons, whereas sharks have a skeleton composed entirely of cartilage rather than bone. The plesiosaurs were large animals, reaching a length as great as 45 ft (14 m). These marine reptiles had paddle-shaped limbs, and some species had very long necks, while others had short necks. Mosasaurs were large lizards that had fin-shaped limbs and looked something like a cross between a crocodile and an eel, but grew to lengths of more than 30 ft (9 m).

What became of the dinosaurs?

There are many theories about what caused the extinction of the last of the dinosaurs, which occurred at the end of the Cretaceous period, about 66 million years ago. Some of the more interesting ideas include: the intolerance of these animals to rapid climate change, the emergence of new species of dominant plants that contained toxic chemicals that the herbivorous dinosaurs could not tolerate, an inability to compete successfully with the rapidly evolving mammals, insatiable destruction of dinosaur nests and eggs by mammalian predators, and some sort of widespread disease to which dinosaurs were not able to develop immunity. All of these hypotheses are interesting, but the supporting evidence for any of them is not enough to convince most paleontologists.

Interestingly, at the time of the extinction of the last of the dinosaurs, there were also apparently mass extinctions of other groups of organisms. These included the reptilian order Pterosauria, along with many groups of plants and invertebrates. In total, perhaps three quarters of all species and one half of all genera may have become extinct during the end-of-Cretaceous mass extinction. A popular hypothesis for the cause of this catastrophic, biological event involves an estimated 6 mi (10 km) wide meteorite hitting the Earth. This impact could have spewed an enormous quantity of fine dust into the atmosphere, which in turn could cause climate changes that most large animals and other organisms could not tolerate. As with the other theories about the end of the dinosaurs, this one is

KEY TERMS

Adaptive radiation—The relatively rapid, evolutionary diversification of a related group of organisms, usually in response to diverse ecological opportunities.

Homoiothermic—Refers to "warm-blooded" animals that regulate their body temperature independently of the ambient, environmental temperature.

Mass extinction—The extinction of an unusually large number of species in a geologically short period of time.

Poikilothermic—Refers to animals that do not have a physiological mechanism to control their internal body temperature, and so adopt the temperature of the ambient environment, as in "cold-blooded" animals.

controversial. Many scientists believe that the extinctions of the last of the dinosaurs were more gradual, and were not caused by the shorter-term effects of a rogue meteorite.

Another interesting concept concerns the fact that dinosaurs share many anatomical characteristics with Aves, the birds, a group that clearly evolved from a dinosaurian ancestor. In fact, there are excellent fossil remains of an evolutionary link between birds and dinosaurs. The 3 ft (1 m) long, Late Jurassic fossil organism *Archaeopteryx* looked remarkably like *Compsognathus*, but had a feathered body, and could fly, or at least glide. Moreover, some of the living, flightless birds such as emus and ostriches, and recently extinct birds such as elephant birds and moas, bear a remarkable resemblance to certain types of dinosaurs. Because of the apparent continuity of anatomical characters between dinosaurs and birds, a minority of paleontologists believes that the dinosaurs did not actually become extinct. In other words, the dinosaur lineage survives today in a substantially modified form, as the group Aves, the birds.

See also Evolution; Extinction; Fossil and fossilization; Geologic time; Paleontology.

Further Reading:

Carpenter, K. and P.J. Currie. *Dinosaur Systematics. Approaches and Perspectives.* Cambridge, UK: Cambridge University Press, 1990.
Cowen, R. *History of Life.* London: Blackwell Scientific Publishing, 1995.

Weishampel, D.B., ed. *The Dinosauria.* Berkeley, CA: University of California Press, 1990.

Bill Freedman

Diode

A diode is an electronic device that has two electrodes arranged in such a way that electrons can flow in only one direction. Because of this ability to control the flow of electrodes, a diode is commonly used as a rectifier, a device which connects alternating current into direct current. In general, two types of diodes exist. Older diodes were vacuum tubes containing two metal components, while newer diodes are solid state devices consisting of one n-type and one p-type semiconductor.

The working element in a vacuum tube diode is a metal wire or cylinder known as the cathode. Surrounding the cathode or placed at some distance from it is a metal plate. The cathode and plate are sealed inside a glass tube from which all air is removed. The cathode is also attached to a heater which, when turned on, causes the cathode to glow. As the cathode glows, it emits electrons.

If the metal plate is maintained at a positive potential difference compared to the cathode, electrons will flow from the cathode to the plate. If the plate is negative compared to the cathode, however, electrons are repelled and there is no electrical current from cathode to plate. Thus, the diode acts as a rectifier, allowing the flow of electrons in only one direction, from cathode to plate.

One use of such a device is to transform alternating current to direct current. Alternating current is current that flows first in one direction and then the other. But alternating current fed into a diode can move in one direction only, thereby converting the current to a one-way or direct current.

Newer types of diodes are made from n-type semiconductors and p-type semiconductors. N-type semiconductors contain small impurities that provide an excess of electrons with the capability of moving through a system. P-type semiconductors contain small impurities that provide an excess of positively charged "holes" that are capable of moving through the system.

A semiconductor diode is made by joining an n-type semiconductor with a p-type semiconductor through an external circuit containing a source of electrical current. The current is able to flow from the n-semiconductor to the p-semiconductor, but not in the other direction. In this sense, the n-semiconductor corresponds to the cathode and the p-semiconductor to the plate in the vacuum tube diode. The semiconductor diode has most of the same functions as the older vacuum diode, but it operates much more efficiently and takes up much less space than does a vacuum diode.

See also Cathode; Electrical conductivity; Electric current.

Dioxin

Chlorinated dioxins are a diverse group of organic chemicals. TCDD, or 2,3,7,8-tetrachlorodibenzo-*p*-dioxin, is a particular dioxin that is toxic to some species of animals in extremely small concentrations. As such, TCDD is the most environmentally controversial of the chlorinated dioxins, and the focus of this entry.

TCDD and other dioxins

Dioxins are a class of organic compounds, with a basic structure that includes two oxygen atoms joining a pair of benzene rings. Chlorinated dioxins have some amount of substitution with chlorine for hydrogen atoms in the benzene rings. A particular chemical, 2,3,7,8-tetrachlorodibenzo-*p*-dioxin (abbreviated as TCDD, or as 2,3,7,8-TCDD), is one of 75 chlorinated derivatives of dibenzo-*p*-dioxin. There is a very wide range of toxicity within the larger group of dioxins and chlorinated dioxins, but TCDD is acknowledged as being the most poisonous dioxin compound, at least to certain species of animals.

Dioxins have no particular uses. They are not manufactured intentionally, but are synthesized incidentally during some industrial processes. For example, under certain conditions relatively large concentrations of dioxins are inadvertently synthesized during industrial reactions involving 2,4,5-trichlorophenol. A well known case of this phenomenon is the manufacture of the phenoxy herbicide, 2,4,5-T (2,4,5-trichlorophenoxy acetic acid). This chemical (which is no longer used) was manufactured in large amounts, and much of the material was badly contaminated by TCDD. Concentrations in the range of 10-50 parts per million (ppm, or mg per liter) occurred in 2,4,5-T manufactured for use during the Vietnam War. However, there were much smaller contaminations (less than 0.1 ppm) in 2,4,5-T manufactured after 1972, in accordance with regulations enacted by the U.S. Environmental Protection Agency.

TCDD is also a trace contaminant of other products manufactured from trichlorophenol, including hexachlorophene, once commonly used as an antibacterial treatment. TCDD is also incidentally synthesized when wood pulps are bleached using chlorine-based oxidants. Low-temperature combustions of chlorine-containing organic materials (for example, in cigarettes, burning garbage dumps, and barbecues) also produce dioxins, including TCDD. The incineration of municipal wastes also synthesizes small quantities of TCDD, although the relatively high temperatures reduce the yield of dioxins compared with the smoldering combustions just mentioned. Dioxins are also synthesized naturally in trace quantities, mostly during forest fires.

TCDD is a persistent chemical in the environment, and because it is virtually insoluble in water, but highly soluble in fats and oils, it strongly biomagnifies and occurs in especially large concentrations in predators at the top of the food web. Moreover, TCDD is globally distributed, meaning that any chemical analysis of a biological tissue, especially of the fat of an animal, will detect residues of this dioxin (assuming that the analytical chemistry is sensitive enough).

Toxicity

TCDD is the most toxin of the chlorinated dioxins, while octachlorodioxin may be least so. However, there are large differences in the susceptibility of species to suffering toxicity from TCDD. The guinea pig, for example, is extremely sensitive to TCDD, thousands of time more so than the hamster.

Short-term or acute toxicity is often indicated by a laboratory assay known as LD or the dose of a chemical that is required to kill one-half of a test population of organisms over a period of several days. Guinea pigs have a LD for TCDD in food of only 0.0006 mg/kg (that is, 0.0006 mg of TCDD per kg body weight). In comparison, rats have a LD_{50} for TCDD in food of 0.022-0.045 mg/kg, while hamsters have a LD_{50} of 1 mg/kg. Clearly, TCDD is a highly toxic chemical, although species vary in sensitivity.

Depending on the dose and biological sensitivity, the symptoms of TCDD toxicity in mammals can include severe weight loss, liver damage, lesions in the vascular system, stomach ulcers, a persistent acne known as chloracne, birth defects, and ultimately, death.

Much of what is known about the toxicity of TCDD to humans has come from studies of: (1) industrial exposures of chemical workers, (2) people living near a toxic waste dump at Times Beach, Missouri, and (3) an accidental event at Seveso, Italy, in 1976. The latter case involved an explosion at a chlorophenol plant that released 2.2-11 lbs (1-5 kg) of TCDD to the surroundings, and caused residues as large as 51 ppm to occur in environmental samples. This accident caused the deaths of some livestock within 2-3 days, but remarkably it was not until 2.5 weeks had passed that about 700 people were evacuated from the severely contaminated residential area near the factory. The exposure of humans to TCDD at Seveso caused 187 diagnosed cases of chloracne, but there were apparently no statistically detectable increases in the rates of human diseases, or of deformities of children born to exposed women.

Overall, studies of humans suggest they are among the least-sensitive mammals to suffering toxicity from TCDD. Although a persistent, sometimes scarring chloracne is a common symptom of an acute human exposure to TCDD, the evidence showing increased rates of TCDD-related disease, mortality, cancer, or birth defects are equivocal, and controversial. Some scientists believe that there is no evidence that a human has ever died from an acute exposure to TCDD. However, there is unresolved scientific controversy about the possible effects of longer-term, chronic exposures of humans to TCDD, which might result in increased rates of developmental abnormalities or cancers. Unless large, these effects would be difficult to detect, because of the great environmental and genetic variations that must be overcome in epidemiological studies of humans.

TCDD in Vietnam

To deprive their enemy of food and cover during the Vietnam War, the U.S. military sprayed large quantities of herbicides. More than 56,000 square miles (1.4 million ha) of terrain were sprayed at least once. The most commonly used herbicide was a 50:50 mixture of 2,4,5-T and 2,4-D, known as Agent Orange. More than 46 million lb (21 million kg) of 2,4,5-T and 55 million lb (25 million kg) of 2,4-D were sprayed during this military program.

An important aspect of the military use of herbicides in Vietnam was contamination of the 2,4,5-T by TCDD. A concentration as large as 45 ppm was measured in Agent Orange, but the average concentration was about 2 ppm. In total, 243-375 lb (110-170 kg) of TCDD was sprayed with herbicides onto Vietnam.

Because TCDD is known to be extremely toxic to some laboratory animals, there has been tremendous controversy over the possible short and long-term effects of exposure of soldiers and civilians to TCDD in Vietnam. Although claims have been made of effects in exposed populations, the studies have not been convinc-

KEY TERMS

. . . .

Acute toxicity—Observable short-term damages caused by an intense exposure to some toxic agent, for example, tissue damage, behavioral change, or death.

Chronic toxicity—Long-term damages caused by a relatively small exposure to a toxic chemical, and manifest in decreases in growth or productivity, or possibly the development of reproductive abnormalities or cancer.

Epidemiology—The study of the incidence, control, and transmission of diseases in large populations.

ing to many scientists, and there is still controversy. The apparent, mainstream opinion from the most rigorous epidemiological studies suggests that large toxic effects have not occurred, which is encouraging. It is also likely that the specific effects of TCDD added little to the very substantial ecological effects caused by the use of military use of herbicides during the Vietnam War.

See also Biomagnification.

Further Reading:

Freedman, B. *Environmental Ecology,* 2nd ed. San Diego: Academic Press, 1994.

Harris, W.E. "Dioxins - an overview." *Tappi Journal,* (April 1990): 267-69.

Bill Freedman

Diphtheria

Diphtheria is a serious disease caused by the bacterium *Corynebacterium diptheriae.* Usually, the bacteria initially infect the throat and pharynx. During the course of the infection, a membrane-like growth appearing on the throat can obstruct breathing. Some strains of this bacterium release a toxin, a substance that acts as a poison in the body. This toxin, when released into the bloodstream, travels to other organs of the body and can cause severe damage.

Diphtheria was first formally described as a disease in 1826. In 1888, *Corynebacterium diptheriae* was identified as the cause of the disease. A few years later, researchers discovered the antitoxin, or antidote, to the diphtheria toxin. If the antitoxin is given to a person

with diphtheria in the early stages of the infection, the antitoxin neutralizes the toxin. This treatment, along with an aggressive vaccination program, has virtually eliminated the disease in the United States. Other countries that do not have an aggressive vaccination program, have numerous cases of diphtheria, many of which end in death.

Incidence of diphtheria

Since most children in the United States are vaccinated against diphtheria, the domestic incidence of the disease is very low. When diphtheria does occur, it tends to strike adults, because fewer adults than children have been immunized against the disease. In developing countries, where less than 10% of the children are vaccinated against diphtheria, about one million deaths are caused each year by this disease. Diphtheria is highly contagious. The disease is prevalent in densely-populated areas, especially during the winter months when more people crowd together indoors. Transmission of the bacteria occurs when an infected person sneezes or coughs and a susceptible person breathes in the saliva or mucus droplets form the air.

Diphtheria toxin

Interestingly, diphtheria toxin is produced by strains of *Corynebacterium diptheriae* that have themselves been infected with a special type of virus called a bacteriophage. The particular bacteriophage that infects *C. diptheriae* carries with it the gene that produces the diphtheria toxin. Strains of *C. diptheriae* without the bacteriophage do not produce the toxin.

The diphtheria toxin consists of two subunits, A and B. The B subunit binds to the plasma membrane of a cell. Once it is bound to the membrane, it pulls the A subunit into the cell. The A subunit is the active segment of the toxin, producing most of the effects. Once inside the cell, the A subunit disrupts protein synthesis; once this mechanism is disrupted, the cell cannot survive for long. Diphtheria toxin thus kills cells. Cells in the throat and respiratory tract are killed first; if the toxin spreads in the bloodstream to other organs—such as the heart, kidney, and brain—severe and even fatal damage can result.

Symptoms

The incubation period—the time from exposure to the bacteria to the first symptoms—is 1-7 days. The first symptoms of diphtheria are fatigue, a low-grade fever, and a sore throat. As the disease progresses, the throat swells, sometimes so much that the patient has noticeable neck swelling. The bacteria infect the throat first before spreading to the larynx (voice box) and trachea (windpipe). At the site of infection, the throat is red and sore. In reaction to the infection, the throat tissues release a discharge containing fibrous material and immune cells. This discharge covers the throat tissues and appears as a grayish, membrane-like material. The throat and trachea continue to swell; if not relieved, the swelling may obstruct the airway, leading to death by suffocation.

Sometimes the diphtheria bacteria infect the skin first. When this type of infection occurs, skin lesions appear. For reasons that are not clear, the diphtheria characterized by skin infection is more contagious than the disease characterized by respiratory infection. The skin-type of diphtheria is more common in tropical and sub-tropical countries.

Treatment

Diphtheria is treated with an antitoxin that can only neutralize the toxin that has not yet bound to a cell membranes; it cannot neutralize the toxin that has already bound to and penetrated a cell. For this reason, antitoxin must be administered early in infection. In fact, some experts recommend giving doses of antitoxin if diphtheria is even suspected, since the additional time spent waiting for confirming lab results allows for more of the toxin to spread and penetrate the cells.

Vaccine

The diphtheria vaccine consists of a small amount of the toxin that has been altered so as not to cause toxic effects. The vaccine works by prompting the body's immune system to make antitoxin against the altered vaccine toxin. The diphtheria toxin is combined with the tetanus toxin and the pertussis (whooping cough) toxin in one vaccine, abbreviated DPT. The DPT is given in four doses. In the United States, infants are given their first DPT dose at about 6-8 weeks of age. If all four doses are administered before age 4, the child should have a DPT "booster" before beginning kindergarten. This shot "boosts" the immunity to the disease.

A person can be tested for their immunity to diphtheria by the Schick test, which demonstrates the presence of antitoxin within the body. In this test, a small amount of diphtheria toxin is placed under the skin of the forearm. If the site develops a reaction—such as redness or swelling—the person has not developed the antitoxin from a previous infection or a vaccine, and is therefore susceptible to diphtheria. If no reaction is present, the person had already developed the antitoxin. The Schick test is useful for adults who cannot find their immunization records or cannot remember if they had diphtheria in childhood.

KEY TERMS

Antitoxin—A antidote to a toxin that neutralizes its poisonous effects.

Bacteriophage—A type of virus that infects bacteria. When a bacteriophage that carries the diphtheria toxin gene infects diphtheria bacteria, the bacteria produce diphtheria toxin.

Schick test—A test that checks for the presence of diphtheria antitoxin in the body.

Toxin—A substance produced by bacteria that acts as a poison in the body.

See also Childhood diseases; Vaccine.

Further Reading:

Kleinman, Lawrence C. "To End an Epidemic: Lessons From the History of Diphtheria." *New England Journal of Medicine* 326 (12 March 1992): 773.

"Misfiring Magic Bullets (Report on Adverse Effect from Diphtheria-Pertussis-Tetanus and Rubella Vaccines)." *Science News* 140 (20 July 1991): 45.

Peter, Georges. "Childhood Immunizations." *New England Journal of Medicine* 327 (7 December 1992): 25.

Kathleen Scogna

Diplopia see **Vision disorders**

Dipole

Dipole, literally, means "two poles," two electrical charges, one negative and one positive. Dipoles are common in atoms whenever electrons (-) are unevenly distributed around nuclei (+), and in molecules whenever electrons are unevenly shared between two atoms in a covalent bond.

When a dipole is present, the atom or covalent bond is said to be polarized, or divided into negative and positive regions. This is indicated by the use of partial negative (d-) and partial positive (d+) signs. The magnitude and direction of the electrical charge separation is indicated by using an arrow, drawn from the positive pole in a molecule to the negative pole.

In covalent bonds, permanent dipoles are caused when two different atoms share their electrons unevenly. The atom that is more electronegative—the one which holds electrons more tightly—pulls the electrons closer

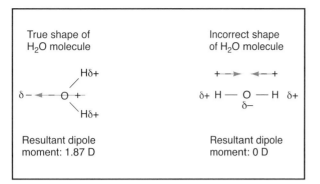

Figure 1.

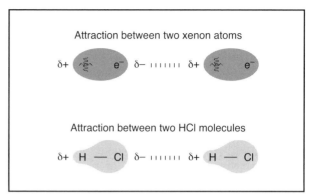

Figure 2.

to itself, creating a partial negative charge there. The less electronegative atom becomes partially positive as a result, because it has lost partial possession of the electrons. The electric strength of a dipole generally increases as the electronegativity difference between the atoms in the bond increases. This strength, called a dipole moment, can be measured experimentally. The size of a dipole moment is expressed in Debye units in honor of the Dutch chemist, Peter Debye (1884-1966).

The dipole moments of a series of molecules are listed below:

Molecule	Dipole Moment (in Debye units, D)
HF	1.91 D
HCl	1.03 D
HBr	0.78 D
HI	0.38 D

The measurement of dipole moments can help determine the shape of a molecule. The net dipole moment of a water molecule (H_2O) represents the overall electrical charge distribution in that molecule. (See Figure 1.)

The H_2O molecule is bent. Its dipole vectors do not cancel. The water molecule has a net resultant dipole moment of 1.87 D. If the molecule were linear, the measured dipole moment would be zero. Its individual dipoles in the two oxygen-hydrogen covalent bonds would have cancelled each other out.

Individual atoms (and ions) will be naturally polarized if their electrons happen to move irregularly about their nuclei creating, at least temporarily, lopsided looking atoms with d+ and d- portions. Natural collisions occurring between atoms can induce this temporary deformity from an atom's normal spherical, symmetric shape. Larger atoms are considered to be "softer" than smaller, "harder" atoms. Larger atoms are then more

likely to be polarized or to have stronger dipoles than smaller atoms.

The presence of dipoles helps to explain how atoms and molecules attract each other. Figure 2 shows how the electrically positive side of one xenon atom (Xe) lines up and pulls towards the negative side of another xenon atom. Likewise, the positive side of one H-Cl molecule is attracted to the negative side of another H-Cl molecule. When many atoms and molecules are present in matter, these effects continue on indefinitely from atom to atom and molecule to molecule.

Dipole forces tend to organize matter and pull it together. Atoms and molecules most strongly attracted to each other will tend to exist as solids. Weaker interactions tend to produce liquids. The gaseous state of matter will tend to exist when the atoms and molecules are non-polar, or when virtually no dipoles are present.

See also Atom; Molecule.

Direct current see **Electric current**

Directrix see **Conic sections**

Direct variation

If one quantity increases (or decreases) each time another quantity increases (or decreases), the two quantities are said to vary together. The most common form of this is direct variation in which the ratio of the two amounts is always the same. For example, speed and distance traveled vary directly for a given time. If you travel at 4 miles per hour for three hours, you go 12 miles, but at 6 mph you go 18 miles in three hours. The ratio of distance to speed is always 3 in this case.

The common ratio is often written as a constant in an equation. For example, if s is speed and d is distance, the relation between them is direct variation for d = ks, where k is the constant. In the example above, k = 3, so the equation becomes d = 3s. For a different time interval, a different k would be used.

Often, one quantity varies with respect to a power of the other. For example, of $y = kx^2$, then y varies directly with the square of x. More than two variables may be involved in a direct variation. Thus if z = kxy, we say that z is a joint (direct) variation of z with x and y. Similarly, if $z = kx^2/y$, we say that z varies directly with x^2 and inversely with y.

Dirigibles see **Airship**

Disaccharide see **Carbohydrate**

Disease

Disease can be defined as a change in the body processes that impairs its normal ability to function. Every day the physiology of the human body demands that oxygenation, acidity, salinity, and other functions be maintained within a very narrow spectrum. A deviation from the norm can be brought about by organ failure, toxins, heredity, radiation, or invading bacteria and viruses.

Normally the body has the ability to fight off or to neutralize many pathogenic organisms that may gain entrance through an opening in the skin or by other means. The immune system mobilizes quickly to rid the body of the offending alien and restore or preserve the necessary internal environment. Sometimes, however, the invasion is one that is beyond body's resistance, and the immune system is unable to overcome the invader. A disease may then develop. When the internal functions of the body are affected to the point that the individual can no longer maintain the required normal parameters, symptoms of disease will appear.

The infection brought about by a bacterium or virus usually generates specific symptoms, that is, a series of changes in the body that are characteristic of that invading organism. Such changes may include development of a fever (an internal body temperature higher than the norm), nausea, headache, copious sweating, and other readily discernable signs.

Much more important to the physician, though, are the internal, unseen changes that may be wrought by such an invasion. These abnormalities may appear only as changes from the norm in certain chemical elements of the blood or urine. That is the reason patients are asked to contribute specimens for analysis when they are ill, especially when their symptoms are not specific to a given disease. The function of organs such as the liver, kidneys, thyroid gland, pancreas, and others can be determined by the levels of various elements in the blood chemistry.

For a disease that is considered the result of a pathogenic invasion, the physician carries out a bacterial culture. Certain secretions such as saliva or mucus are collected and placed on a thin plate of culture material. The bacteria that grow there over the next day or so are then analyzed to determine which species are present and thus which antibiotic would be most effective in eradicating them.

Viruses present special challenges, since they cannot be seen under a microscope and are difficult to grow in cultures. Also, viruses readily adapt to changes in their environment and become resistant to efforts to treat the disease they cause. Some viral diseases are caused by any number of forms of the same virus. The common cold, for example, can be caused by any one of some 200 viruses. For that reason it is not expected that any vaccine will be developed against the cold virus. A vaccine effective against one or two of the viruses will be completely useless against the other 198 or 199 forms.

The agents that cause a disease, the virus or bacterium, are called the etiologic agents of the disease. The etiologic agent for strep throat, for example, is a bacterium within the *Streptococcus* genus. Similarly, the tubercle bacillus is the etiologic agent of tuberculosis.

Modern medicine has the means to prevent many diseases that plagued civilization in the recent past. Polio, a crippling disease brought about by the poliomyelitis virus, was neither preventable nor curable until the middle 1950s. Early in that decade an outbreak of polio affected an abnormally large number of young people. Research into the cause and prevention of polio immediately gained high priority, and by the middle of the decade Dr. Jonas Salk had developed a vaccine to prevent polio. Currently all young children in developed countries can be vaccinated against the disease.

Similar vaccines have been developed over the years to combat other diseases that previously were lethal. Whooping cough, tetanus, diphtheria, and other diseases that at one time meant certain death to victims, can be prevented. The plague, once a dreaded killer of thousands, no longer exists among the human population. An effective vaccine has eradicated it as a dread disease.

The resistance to disease is called immunity. A few people are naturally immune to some diseases, but most have need of vaccines. This type of immunity, attained by means of a vaccine, is called artificial immunity. Vaccines are made from dead bacteria and are injected into the body. The vaccine causes the formation of antibodies which alert the immune system in the event a live bacterium invades.

The body's immune system, responsible for guarding against invading pathogens, may itself be the cause of disease. Conditions such as rheumatoid arthritis and Lupus are considered to be the result of the immune system mistaking its own body for foreign tissue and organizing a reaction to it. This kind of disease is called an autoimmune disease—auto, meaning one's own, and immune referring to the immune system. Scientists have found that little can be done to combat this form of disease. The symptoms can be treated to ease the patient's discomfort or preserve his life, but the autoimmune reaction seldom can be shut down.

See also Epidemic; Epidemiology; Etiology; Syndrome.

Larry Blaser

Dissociation

Dissociation is the process by which a molecule separates into ions. It may also be called ionization, but because there are other ways to form ions, the term dissociation is preferred. Substances dissociate to different degrees, ranging from substances that dissociate very slightly, such as water, to those that dissociate almost completely, such as strong acids and bases. The extent to which a substance dissociates is directly related to its ability to conduct an electric current. A substance that dissociates only slightly (as in the case of a weak acid like vinegar) is a weak electrolyte, as it conducts electricity poorly. A substance that is almost completely dissociated (such as table salt, NaCl, or hydrochloric acid, HCl) conducts electricity very well. The ability to conduct electricity is based on the ionic makeup of a substance. The more ions a substance contains, the better it will conduct electricity.

Dissociation of water

Pure water dissociates only slightly. About one water molecule out of every 10 million is dissociated and the rest remain in non-dissociated (or molecular) form. This ionization of water (sometimes called self- or auto-ionization) can be summarized by the following formula. Pure water produces very few ions from its dissociation and so is a poor electrolyte, or conductor of electricity.

The following equation describes the process in which a water molecule ionizes (separates into ions) to form a hydrogen ion (proton) and a hydroxide ion.

$$H_2O \longleftrightarrow H^+ + OH^-$$

Another way to describe the dissociation of water is as follows:

$$H_2O + H_2O \longleftrightarrow H_3O^+ + OH^-$$

where two water molecules form a hydronium ion (essentially a water molecule with a proton attached) and a hydroxide ion.

Dissociation of acid and bases

Acids are molecules that can donate protons (hydrogen or H^+ ions) to other molecules. An alternate view is that an acid is a substance that will cause an increase in the concentration of hydrogen ions in a solution.

The dissociation of a strong acid (such as hydrochloric acid, HCl) is essentially 100%.

$$HCl \rightarrow H^+ + Cl^-$$

In this case, nearly every HCl molecule is dissociated (separated into ions). When any substance dissociates, both positive and negative ions will be formed. In this case, the positive ion (cation) is a proton, and the negative ion (anion) is the chloride ion. A strong acid is a strong electrolyte and a good conductor of an electric current. In the case of a strong base, nearly 100% of the molecules are dissociated as well, and strong bases (such as sodium hydroxide, NaOH) are also strong electrolytes.

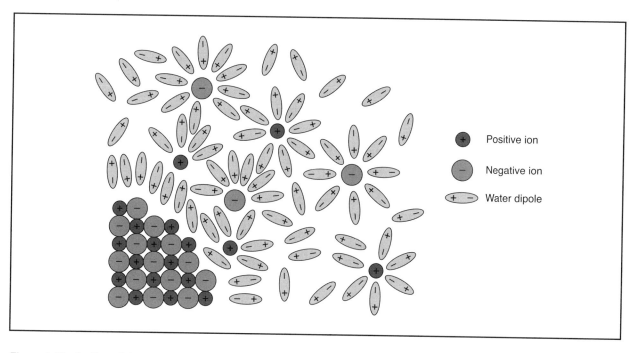

Figure 1. Illustration of the solvation process, in which the negative end of a water molecule faces the positive sodium ion and the positive end faces the negative ion.

Legend:
- + Positive ion
- − Negative ion
- +/− Water dipole

$$NaOH \rightarrow Na^+ + OH^-$$

A weak acid, such as hydrofluoric acid is only slightly dissociated. Many more of the molecules exist in the molecular (undissociated or unionized) form than in the ionized form. Since it forms fewer ions, a weak acid will be a weak electrolyte.

$$HF \longleftrightarrow H^+ + F^-$$

In the case of a weak base, such as aluminum hydroxide, $Al(OH)_3$, only a small percent of molecules ionize, producing few ions, and making weak bases weak electrolytes as well.

$$Al(OH)_3 \longleftrightarrow Al^{+3} + 3OH^-$$

In any dissociation reaction, the total charges will mathematically cancel each other out. The case above has a positive three charge on the aluminum ion and a negative one charge on each of the three hydroxide ions, for a total of zero.

Dissociation of salts

Salts are the product of the neutralization reaction between an acid and a base (the other product of this neutralization reaction being water). Salts that are soluble in water dissociate into their ions and are electrolytes. Salts that are insoluble or only slightly soluble in water form very few ions in solution and are nonelectrolytes or weak electrolytes. Sodium chloride, NaCl, is a water-soluble salt that dissociates totally in water.

$$NaCl \rightarrow Na^+ + Cl^-$$

The process by which this takes place involves the surrounding of each positive sodium ion and each negative chloride ion by water molecules. Water molecules are polar and have two distinct ends, each with a partial positive or negative charge. Since opposite charges attract, the negative end of the water molecule will face the positive sodium ion and the positive end will face the negative ion. This process, illustrated in Figure 1, is known as solvation.

See also Ionization.

Further Reading:

Carafoli, Ernest, and John Penniston. "The Calcium Signal," *Scientific American*, 253 (November, 1985).
Ezzell, Carol. "Salt's Technique for Tickling the Taste Buds," *Science News*, 140 (November 2, 1991).

Louis Gotlib

Distance

Distance has two different meanings. It is a number used to characterize the shortest length between two

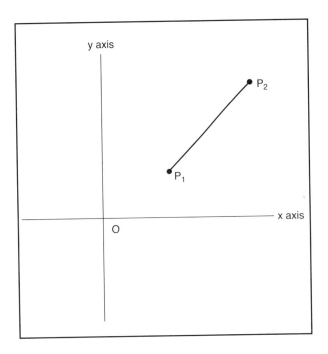

Figure 1. Two points are plotted in a perpendicular coordinate system.

geometric figures, and it is the total length of a path. In the first case, the distance between two points is the simplest instance.

Distance, the length between two points, can only be a positive number. It can never be a negative number, and can only be zero when the two points are identical. The two points P_1 and P_2 can only be connected with one straight line. The length of this line is the shortest distance between the two points P_1 and P_2.

For two lines that are parallel, the distance is the length of two points, each of which is on one of the lines, and both of which are on the perpendicular to the two lines. For figures such as line segments, triangles, circles, cubes, and so forth, if the figures do not intersect, then the distance between them is the shortest distance between any pair of points, each of which lies on a different figure.

The other meaning of distance is the length of a path. This is easily understood if the path consists entirely of line segments, such as around a pentagon. The distance is the sum of the lengths of the line segments. For curves that are not line segments, a continuous path can usually be approximated by a sequence of line segments. Using shorter line segments produces a better approximation. The limiting case, when the

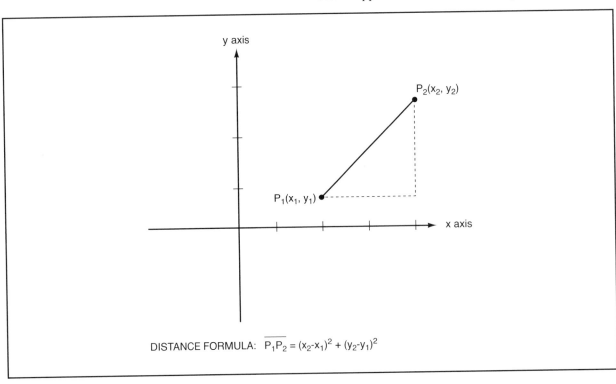

Figure 2. The shortest distance between the two points can be calculated using the distance formula based on the Pythagorean theorem.

TABLE 1

METRIC			ENGLISH		
picometer (pm)	=	10^{-12}m	12 inches	=	1 foot
Angstrom (A)	=	10^{-10}m	3 feet	=	1 yard
nanometer (nm)	=	10^{-9}m	1 mile	=	1758.84 yards
micrometer (μm)	=	10^{-6}m			
millimeter (mm)	=	10^{-3}m			
centimeter (cm)	=	10^{-2}m			
decimeter (dm)	=	10^{-1}m			
meter (m)	=	100m	CONVERSION		
hectometer (hm)	=	10^{2}m	1 inch	=	2.54 cm
kilometer (km)	=	10^{3}m	1 yard	=	0.9144 m
megameter (Mm)	=	10^{6}m	1 mile	=	1.609 km
1 light year	=	9.46×10^{12}km			

lengths of the line segments go to zero, is the distance. A common example would be the circumference of a circle, which is a distance.

For travel along a path, there is a distance formula, d = rt, or distance equals rate times time. Distance can be expressed in various units using the metric or English systems. Table 1 shows the units of both systems and the conversion from one to the other.

Distance formula

A different distance formula is used for points in a coordinate system. The coordinate system employs a horizontal axis (x) and vertical axis (y). Both axes are infinite for positive and negative values. The crossing point of the lines is the origin (O), at that point both x and y values are zero. (See Figure 1.)

The coordinates of point P_1 are denoted by (x_1, y_1), and for point P_2 by $(x_2$ and $y_2)$. The distance, the length of the connecting straight line $(P_1 P_2)$ which is the shortest distance between the two points, can be calculated by the distance formula based on the Pythagorean theorem. (See Figure 2.)

Further Reading:

Diagram group, *Comparison of distance, size, area, volume, mass, weight, density, energy, temperature, time, speed and number throughout the universe.* New York: St. Martin's Press, 1990.

Jeanette Vass

Distillation

Distillation is one of the most important processes for separating the components of a solution. The solution is heated to form a vapor of the more volatile components in the system, and the vapor is then cooled, condensed, and collected as drops of liquid. By repeat-

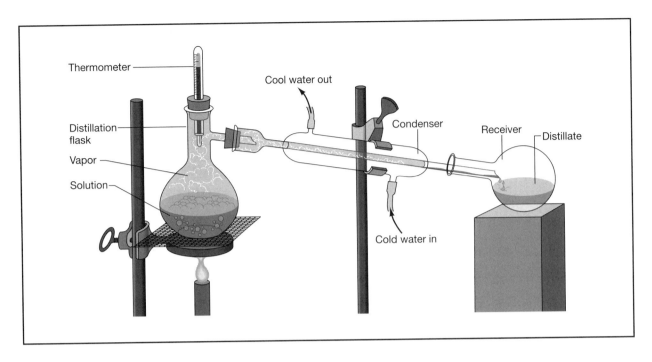

Thermometer

Cool water out

Condenser

Receiver

Distillate

Distillation flask

Vapor

Solution

Cold water in

A typical laboratory distillation setup.

ing vaporization and condensation, individual components in the solution can be recovered in a pure state. Whiskey, essences, and many pure products from the oil refinery industry are processed via distillation.

General principles

Distillation has been used widely to separate volatile components from non-volatile compounds. The underlying mechanism of distillation is the differences in volatility between individual components. With sufficient heat applied, a gas phase is formed from the liquid solution. The liquid product is subsequently condensed from the gas phase by removal of the heat. Therefore, heat is used as the separating agent during distillation. Feed material to the distillation apparatus can be liquid and/or vapor, and the final product may consist of liquid and vapor. A typical apparatus for simple distillation used in chemistry laboratories is one in which the still pot can be heated with a water, steam, or oil bath. When liquids tend to decompose or react with oxygen during the course of distillation, the working pressure can be reduced to lower the boiling points of the substances and hence the temperature of the distillation process.

In general, distillation can be carried out either with or without reflux involved. For the case of single-stage differential distillation, the liquid mixture is heated to form a vapor that is in equilibrium with the residual liquid. The vapor is then condensed and removed from the system without any liquid allowed to

return to the still pot. This vapor is richer in the more volatile component than the liquid that is removed as the bottom product at the end of the process. However, when products of much higher purity are desired, part of the condensate has to be brought into contact with the vapor on its way to the condenser and recycled to the still pot. This procedure can be repeated for many times to increase the degree of separation in the original mixture. Such a process is normally called "rectification."

Applications

Distillation has long been used as the separation process in the chemical and petroleum industries because of its reliability, simplicity, and low-capital cost. It is employed to separate benzene from toluene, methanol or ethanol from water, acetone from acetic acid, and many multicomponent mixtures. Fractionation of crude oil and the production of deuterium also rely on distillation.

Today, with 40,000 distillation towers in operation, distillation makes about 95% of all current industrial separation processes; however, distillation systems also have relatively high energy consumption. Significant effort, therefore, has been made to reduce the energy consumption and to improve the efficiency in distillation systems. This includes incorporating new analytical sensors and reliable hardware into the system to achieve advanced process control, using heat rejected

KEY TERMS

. . . .

Activity coefficient—The ratio of the partial pressure of a component in the gas phase to the product of its mole fraction in the liquid phase and its vapor pressure as a pure liquid which is an important factor encountered in many vapor-liquid separation processes.

Bubble point—For a saturated liquid, because any rise in temperature will form bubbles of vapor, the liquid is said at its bubble point.

Dew point—For a saturated vapor, because any drop in temperature will form drops of liquid, the vapor is said at its dew point.

Differential distillation—During distillation, only a very small portion of the liquid is flashed each time and the vapor formed on boiling the liquid is removed at once from the system.

Distillate—The product withdrawn continuously at the top of the distillation column.

Reflux—Part of the condensate from the condenser is returned to the top tray of the distillation column as reflux to provide liquid flow above the feed point for increasing separation efficiency.

from a condenser of one column to reboil other columns, and coupling other advanced process such as adsorption and crystallization with distillation to form energy-saving hybrid operation systems.

See also Volatility.

Pang-Jen Kung

Distributive property

The distributive property states that the multiplication "distributes" over addition. Thus $a \times (b + c) = a \times b + a \times c$ and $(b + c) \times a = b \times a + c \times a$ for all real or complex numbers a, b, and c.

The distributive property is behind the common multiplication algorithm. For example, 27×4 means $4 \times (2 \text{ tens} + 7 \text{ ones})$. To complete the multiplication,

you use the distributive property: $4 \times (20 + 7) = (4 \times 20) + (4 \times 7) = 80 + 28 = 108$.

We use the distributive property more than once in carrying out such computations as $(3x + 4)(x + 2)$. Thus $(3x + 4)(x + 2) = (3x + 4)x + (3x + 4)2$ where $3x + 4$ is "distributed over" $x + 2$ and then $(3x + 4)x + (3x + 4)2 = 3x^2 + 4x) + (6x + 8) = 3x^2 + 10x + 8$ where x and 2 are "distributed" over $3x + 4$.

Disturbance, ecological

In the ecological context, disturbance is regarded as an event of intense environmental stress occurring over a relatively short period of time and causing large changes in the affected ecosystem. Disturbance can result from natural causes or from the activities of humans.

Disturbance can be caused by physical stressors such as volcanic eruptions, hurricanes, tornadoes, earthquakes, and over geological time, glacial advance, and retreat. Humans can also cause physical disturbances, for example, through construction activities. Wildfire is a type of chemical disturbance caused by the rapid combustion of much of the biomass of an ecosystem and often causing mortality of the dominant species of the community such as trees in the case of a forest fire. Wildfires can ignite naturally usually through a lightning strike, or humans can start the blaze sometimes deliberately as a management activity in forestry or agriculture. Events of unusually severe pollution by toxic chemicals, nutrients, or heat may also be regarded as a type of disturbance if they are severe enough to result in substantial ecological damages. Disturbance can also be biological as when a severe infestation of defoliating insects causes substantial mortality of trees in a forest, or of crops in agriculture. The harvesting of forests and other ecosystems by humans is another type of biological disturbance.

Whenever an ecosystem is affected by a substantial disturbance event, species may suffer a great deal of mortality, and other ecological damages occur. However, once the actual disturbance event is finished, a process known as succession begins which may eventually restore a similar ecosystem to the one that existed prior to the disturbance.

Disturbance can occur over various spatial scales. The most extensive disturbances involve landscape-scale events such as glaciation which can affect entire continents. Wildfires can also affect very large areas,

A forest in Homestead, Florida, that was destroyed by Hurricane Hugo.

sometimes millions of acres in extent. Some disturbances, however, are much more local in their effects. For example, the primary disturbance regime in old-growth forests is associated with the death of individual, large trees caused by disease, insect attack, or a lightning strike. This sort of microdisturbance event results in a gap in the otherwise closed forest canopy and further ecological changes when the dead tree falls to the ground and slowly rots. Diverse processes of ecological recovery occur in response to the within-stand patch dynamics associated with the deaths of large trees in old-growth forests.

See also Ecosystem; Stress, ecological; Succession.

Division

Division is the mathematical operation which is the inverse of multiplication. If one multiplies 47 by 92 then divides by 92, the result is the original 47. In general, (ab)/b = a. Likewise, if one divides first then multiplies, the two operations nullify each other: (a/b)b = a. This lat-

ter relationship can be taken as the definition of division: a/b is a number which, when multiplied by b, yields a.

In the real world using ordinary arithmetic, division is used in two basic ways. The first is to partition a quantity of something into parts of a known size, in which case the quotient represents the number of parts, for example, finding how many 3-egg omlettes can be made from a dozen eggs. The second is to share a quantity among a known number of shares, as in finding how many eggs will be avaiable per omlette for each of five people. In the latter case the quotient represents the size of each share. For omlettes, if made individually you could use two eggs each for the five people and still have two left over, or you could put all the eggs in one bowl, so each person would get two and two-thirds eggs.

The three components of a division situation can represent three distinct categories of things. While it would not make sense to add dollars to earnings-per-share, one can divide dollars by earnings-per-share and have a meaningful result (in this case, shares). This is true, too, in the familiar distance-rate-time relationship R = D/T. Here the categories are even more distinct. Distance is measured with a tape; time by a clock; and rate by the wind in one's hair.

Another example would be in preparing a quarterly report for share holders, a company treasurer would divide the total earnings for the quarter by the number of shares in order to compute the earnings-per-share. On the other hand, if the company wanted to raise, say, $6,000,000 in new capital by issuing new shares, and if shares were currently selling for $18 1/8, the treasurer would use division to figure out how many new shares would be needed, i. e., about 330,000 shares.

Division is symbolized in two ways, with the symbol ÷ and with a bar, horizontal or slanted. In a/b or a ÷ b, a is called the dividend; b, the divisor; and the entire expression, the quotient.

Division is not commutative; 6/4 is not the same as 4/6. It is not associative; $(8 ÷ 4) ÷ 2$ is not the same as $8 ÷ (4 ÷ 2)$. For this reason care must be used when writing expressions involving division, or interpreting them. An expression such as

$$\frac{\frac{3}{4}}{7}$$

is meaningless. It can be given meaning by making one bar noticeably longer than the other

$$\frac{\frac{3}{4}}{7}$$

to indicate that 3/4 is to be divided by 7. The horizontal bar also acts as a grouping symbol. In the expressions

$$\frac{14 - 7}{8 + 2} \qquad \frac{3/4}{7} \qquad \frac{x^2 - 1}{x + 1}$$

The division indicated by the horizontal bar is the last operation to be performed.

In computing a quotient one uses an algorithm which finds an unknown multiplier digit by digit or term by term.

$$4\overline{)3.00} \quad \begin{array}{r} .75 \\ \underline{2\ 8} \\ 20 \\ \underline{20} \end{array} \qquad x + 1\overline{)x^2\quad -1} \quad \begin{array}{r} x - 1 \\ \underline{x^2 + x} \\ -x - 1 \\ \underline{-x - 1} \end{array}$$

In the algorithm on the left, one starts with the digit 7 (actually .7) because it is the biggest digit one can use so that $4 × 7$ is 30 or less. That is followed by 5 (actually .05) because it is the biggest digit whose product with the divisor equals what remains of the dividend, or less. Thus one has found (.7 + .05) which, multiplied by 4 equals 3. In the algorithm on the right, one does the same thing, but with polynomials. One finds the polynomial of biggest degree whose product with the divi-

sor is equal to the dividend or less. In the case of polynomials, "less" is measured by the degree of the polynomial remainder rather than its numerical value. Had the dividend been $x^2 - 4$, the quotient would still have been x - 1, with a remainder of -3, because any other quotient would have left a remainder whose degree was greater than or equal to that of the divisor.

These last two examples point up another way in which division is a less versatile operation than multiplication. If one is working with integers, one can always multiply two of them an have an integer for a result. That is not so with division. Although 3 and 4 are integers, their quotient is not. Likewise, the product of two polynomials is always a polynomial, but the quotient is not. Occasionally it is, as in the example above, but had one tried to divide $x^2 - 4$ by x + 1, the best one could have done would have been to find a quotient and remainder, in this case a quotient of x - 1 and a remainder of -3. Many sets that are closed with respect to multiplication (i. e. multiplication can always be completed without going outside the set) are not closed with respect to division.

One number that can never, ever be used as a divisor is zero. The definition of division says that (a/b)b = a, but the multiplicative property of zero says that (a/b)•0 = 0. Thus, when one tries to divide a number such as 5 by zero, one is seeking a number whose product with 0 is 5. No such number exists. Even if the dividend were zero as well, division by zero wouldn't work. In that case one would have (0/0)0 = 0, and 0/0 could be any number whatsoever.

Unfortunately division by zero is a trap one can fall into without realizing it. If one divides both sides of the equation $x^2 - 1 = 0$ by x - 1, the resulting equation, x + 1 = 0, has one root, namely -1. The original equation had two roots, however, -1 and 1. Dividing by x - 1 caused one of the roots to disappear, specifically the root that made x - 1 equal to zero.

The division algorithm shown above on the right converts the quotient of two numbers into a decimal, and if the division does not come out even, it does so only approximately. If one uses it to divide 2 by 3, for instance, the quotient is .33333... with the 3's repeating indefinitely. No matter where one stops, the quotient is a little too small. To arrive at an exact quotient, one must use fractions. Then the "answer," a/b, looks exactly like the "problem," a/b, but since we use the bar to represent both division and the separator in the ratio form of a rational number, that is the way it is.

The algorithm for dividing rational numbers and leaving the quotient in ratio form is actually much simpler. To divide a number by a number in ratio form, one simply multiplies by its reciprocal. That is, $(a/b) \div (c/d) = (a/b)(d/c)$.

See also Algorithm; Multiplication.

Further Reading:

Gardner, Martin. *Mathematical Puzzles and Diversions.* New York: Simon and Schuster, 1961.

Jourdain, Philip E. B. "The Nature of Mathematics" in *The World of Mathematics,* Newman, James R., Editor. New York: Simon and Schuster, 1956.

Olds, C. D. *Continued Fractions.* Washington, D. C.: Mathematical Association of America, 1963.

J. Paul Moulton

DNA see **Deoxyribonucleic acid**

Dobsonflies

Dobsonflies are species of medium- to large-sized insects in the order Neuroptera, family Corydalidae.

The life cycle of dobsonflies is characterized by a complete metamorphosis, with four developmental stages: egg, larva, pupa, and adult. Adult dobsonflies are usually found near freshwater, especially streams, either resting on vegetation or engaged in an awkward, fluttering flight. Sometimes adult dobsonflies can be abundant at night around lights, even far from water. The immature stages of dobsonflies are aquatic and are usually found beneath stones or other debris in swiftly flowing streams.

Dobsonflies have rather soft bodies. The adults of North American species generally have body lengths of 0.75-1.5 in (2-4 cm)and wing spans of 2 in (5 cm) or

greater. These insects have four wings with distinctive, many-veined membranes. The wings are held tent-like over the back when the animal is at rest. Dobsonflies have piercing mouthparts. Male dobsonflies have large mandibles about three times longer than the head and projecting forward. Female dobsonflies have much smaller mandibles. Adult dobsonflies are active at night and are not believed to feed, so the function of the exaggerated mandibles of the male insects are unknown. Dobsonflies lay their eggs on vegetation near water, and the larvae enter the water soon after hatching.

Larval dobsonflies are sometimes known as hellgrammites and are predators of other aquatic invertebrates. Larval dobsonflies are quite large, often longer than 3 in (8 cm) or more, with distinctive, tracheal gills projecting from the segments of their large abdomen. Larval dobsonflies are sometimes used as bait for trout fishing.

Various species of dobsonflies occur in North America. The species *Corydalus cornutus* is common but not abundant in eastern parts of the continent, while the genus *Dysmicohermes* is widespread in western regions.

Dog see **Canines**

Dogwood tree

Dogwood refers to certain species of trees and shrubs in the dogwood family (Cornaceae). The dogwoods are in the genus *Cornus*, which mostly occur in temperate and boreal forests of the Northern Hemisphere.

Species in the dogwood family have seasonally deciduous foliage. The leaves are simple, usually untoothed, and generally have an opposite arrangement on the twig. The flowers of dogwoods develop in the early springtime, often before the leaves. The flowers are small and greenish, and are arranged in clusters at the terminus of twigs. The flowers are sometimes surrounded by whitish leaves that are modified as petal-like, showy bracts, giving the overall impression of a single, large flower. The fruit is a drupe, that is, a hard-seeded structure surrounded by an edible pulp.

Several North American species of dogwood achieve the size of small trees. The flowering dogwood (*Cornus florida*) of the eastern United States can grow as tall as 43 ft (13 m), and is a species of rich hardwood forests. The flowering dogwood is an attractive species

A dogwood in bloom, Georgia.

that is often cultivated for its large and showy, white-bracted inflorescences, its clusters of scarlet fruits, and the purplish coloration of its autumn foliage. The Pacific dogwood (*C. nuttallii*) is a component of conifer-dominated rainforests of the Pacific coast, and is also a popular ornamental species, for reasons similar to the flowering dogwood. Other tree-sized dogwoods of the western United States include western dogwood (*C. occidentalis*) and black-fruited dogwood (*C. sessilis*), while stiffcornel dogwood (*C. stricta*) occurs in the east.

Many other species of dogwoods are shrub sized, including alternate-leaved dogwood (*C. alternifolia*) and roughleaf dogwood (*C. drummondii*) of eastern North America. The widespread red-osier dogwood (*C. stolonifera*) is sometimes cultivated for its attractive, red twigs, which contrast well with the snows of winter.

The bunchberry or dwarf cornel (*C. canadensis*) is a diminutive species of dogwood that grows in the ground vegetation of northern forests.

The wood of tree-sized dogwoods is very hard, and has had a few specialized uses, for example, in the manufacturing of shuttles for fabric mills, golf-club heads, and other uses where a very durable material is required. However, the major economic benefit of dogwoods is through their attractive appearance, which is often exploited in horticulture.

Dogwood stems are an important food for wild animals such as rabbits, hares, and deer that browse on woody plants during the winter. In addition, many species of birds and mammals feed on the fruits of various species of dogwoods.

Dollarbird see **Rollers**

Dolphins see **Cetaceans**

Domain

The domain of a relation is the set that contains all the first elements, x, from the ordered pairs (x,y) that make up the relation. In mathematics, a relation is defined as a set of ordered pairs (x,y) for which each y depends on x in a predetermined way. If x represents an element from the set X, and y represents an element from the set Y, the Cartesian product of X and Y is the set of all possible ordered pairs (x,y) that can be formed with an element of X being first. A relation between the sets X and Y is a subset of their Cartesian product, so the domain of the relation is a subset of the set X. For example, suppose that X is the set of all men and Y is the set of all women. The Cartesian product of X and Y is the set of all ordered pairs having a man first and women second. One of the many possible relations between these two sets is the set of all ordered pairs (x,y) such that x and y are married. The set of all married men is the domain of this relation, and is a subset of X. The set of all second elements from the ordered pairs of a relation is called the range of the relation, so the set of all married women is the range of this relation, and is a subset of Y. The variable associated with the domain of the relation is called the independent variable. The variable associated with the range of a relation is called the dependent variable.

Many important relations in science, engineering, business and economics can be expressed as functions of real numbers. A function is a special type of relation in which none of the ordered pairs share the same first element. A real-valued function is a function between two sets X and Y, both of which correspond to the set of real numbers. The Cartesian product of these two sets is the familiar Cartesian coordinate system, with the set X associated with the x-axis and the set Y associated with the y-axis. The graph of a real-valued function consists of the set of points in the plane that are contained in the function, and thus represents a subset of the Cartesian plane. The x-axis, or some portion of it, corresponds to the domain of the function. Since, by definition, every set is a subset of itself, the domain of a function may correspond to the entire x-axis. In other cases the domain is limited to a portion of the x-axis, either explicitly or implicitly.

Example 1. Let X and Y equal the set of real numbers. Let the function, f, be defined by the equation y= $3x^2 + 2$. Then the variable x may range over the entire set of real numbers. That is, the domain of f is given by the set D = {x| $-\infty \leq x \leq \infty$}, read "D equals the set of all x such that negative infinity is less than or equal to x and x is less than or equal to infinity."

Example 2. Let X and Y equal the set of real numbers. Let the function f represent the location of a falling body during the second 5 seconds of descent. Then, letting t represent time, the location of the body, at any time between 5 and 10 seconds after descent begins, is given by $f(t) = 1/2gt^2$. In this example, the domain is explicitly limited to values of t between 5 and 10, that is, D = {t | $5 \leq t \leq 10$}.

Example 3. Let X and Y equal the set of real numbers. Consider the function defined by $y = \pi x^2$, where y is the area of a circle and x is its radius. Since eht radius of a circle cannot be negative, the domain, D, of this function is the set of all real numbers greater than or equal to zero, D = x | ≥ 0}. In this example, the domain is limited implicitly by the physical circumstances.

Example 4. Let X and Y equal the set of real numbers. Consider the function given by y = 1/x. The variable x can take on any real number value but zero, because division by zero is undefined. Hence the domain of this function is the set D{x | x $\neq$ 0}. Variations of this function exist, in which values of x other than zero make the denominator zero. The function defined by y = 1/ 2-x is an example; x=2 makes the denominator zero. In these examples the domain is again limited implicitly.

See also Cartesian coordinate plane.

Further Reading:
Allen, G. D., C. Chui, and B. Perry. *Elements of Calculus.* 2nd ed. Pacific Grove, Cal.: Brooks/Cole Publishing Co., 1989.
McKeague, Charles P. *Elementary Algebra.* 5th ed. Fort Worth: Saunders College Publishing, 1995.
Swokowski, Earl W. *Pre Calculus, Functions, and Graphs,* 6th. ed. Boston: PWS-KENT Publishing Co., 1990.

J. R. Maddocks

Donkeys

Domestic donkeys, members of the order Perissodactyla, are large single-hoofed horse-like mammals with elongated heads. Donkeys usually stand between 9.5 and 11 hands high measured at the withers, that is, 38-44 inches (95-110 cm) tall. Because of the large amount of interbreeding among different donkey species, donkeys differ markedly in appearance. They can be brown, gray, black, roan (a mixture of white and usually brown hair), or broken colored (a combination of brown or black and white markings). Also known as asses, donkeys originated in Africa and are very well suited to hot dry climates, but are sensitive to the cold. Donkeys are intelligent, calm, and require little food in relation to the amount of work they are able to perform.

Members of the Order Perissodactyla, the odd-toed ungulates, are medium-sized to very large animals. The third digit of their limbs is the longest, and all four of their limbs are hoofed. These fast-running herbivores have a life expectancy of around 40 years. Today, there are only three families of odd-toed ungulates, the tapirs, the rhinoceros, and the horses.

Donkeys belong the horse family Equidae which has only one genus (Equus) and six species. The African wild ass (*Equus africanus*) is thought to be the ancestor of donkeys.

The domestic donkey can be traced back to three subspecies of African wild ass. The first subspecies, the Nubian wild ass, used to be found throughout Egypt and the Sudan. Today, these asses are very rare; in fact, only a few survive in zoos. The Nubian wild ass is a small yellow-gray animal with a dark strip across its shoulder and one long stripe down its back. The two stripes together are known as the cross, and can be found in many of its ancestors. The second subspecies, the North African wild ass, is now extinct. The third species, the Somali wild ass, is larger and taller than the Nubian wild ass. These asses are grayish with a pink hue and have stripes on their legs. Their manes are very dark and stand upright, and these asses have a nearly black tassel on their tails. Like their cousins, they are declining in numbers. Indeed, there are only a few hundred of these animals in Somalia and a few thousand in Ethiopia.

In around 4000 B.C., inhabitants of the Nile Valley of Egypt first domesticated descendants of the donkey, specifically, Nubian wild asses. Thus, donkeys were domesticated a long time before horses were. Later, Nubian wild asses were domesticated in Arabia and throughout Africa as well.

Eventually, the Somali wild asses were also domesticated, and the two subspecies of asses were mixed. Human use of donkeys as pack animals during wartime and for transporting tradable goods during times of peace accelerated the breeding of various subspecies of donkeys. Today's donkeys have characteristics of both Nubian and Somali wild asses.

It is thought that the Etruscans, traveling from Turkey to Italy, brought the first donkeys to Europe in around 2000 B.C., and that donkeys were brought to Greece by way of Turkey. In Greece, donkeys were commonly used for work in vineyards because of their sure-footedness. Soon, people throughout the Mediterranean used donkeys to help cultivate grapes. The Romans used donkeys throughout their empire, for pack animals and for grape cultivation, which they promoted as far north as France and Germany. The Romans also brought donkeys to Britain when they invaded.

Donkeys and horses existed in North America before the last ice age, over 10,000 years ago, but then became extinct. These did not reappear in North America until the Spanish brought them on their explorations in the 1600s. One hundred years later, the Spanish brought donkeys to South America.

Donkeys have a long work history. Aside from being used as pack animals and for grape cultivation, donkeys have been used to draw wagons, pull water from wells, and help grind grain. These animals were popular because of their efficiency and hardiness. In fact, few domestic animals require as little food as donkeys for the amount of work they can accomplish. Their diet is relatively simple; they survive very well on grass and hay. Furthermore, they can work into their old age, about 40 years. Contrary to popular myth, donkeys are cautious, brave, and very intelligent. Like their ancestors, donkeys can be aggressive if the need arises. When they are attacked, they form a circle and fend of predators by kicking and biting.

Interestingly, the name "donkey" is the word that most English speaking people have for asses. It is derived from the Old English word "dun," referring to the animals' gray-brown color, and the "ky," a suffix for small. Thus, the early English people used the word "dunky" to describe the pony-sized dun-colored animal.

Further Reading:

Svendsen, Elisabeth D., MBE. *The Professional Handbook of the Donkey.* Devon, England: The Sovereign Printing Group, 1989.

Kathryn Snavely

Doodlebugs see **Antlions**

Dopamine

Dopamine is a neurotransmitter (a chemical used to send signals between nerve cells) in the same family as epinephrine (adrenaline). A decrease in the amount of dopamine in specific sections of the brain has been implicated as a possible cause of Parkinson's Disease, while an excess of dopamine is some regions of the brain has been suggested as a possible cause of schizophrenia. Recently, dopamine has been used as a treatment for victims of heart attacks. Dopamine is also thought to play a role in depression.

Basic definitions and chemical information

Dopamine is one of a group of chemicals known as catecholamine neurotransmitters. Catecholamines are a group of chemicals that include epinephrine (adrenalin); histamine, which is responsible for many of the symptoms of allergies; and serotonin, a molecule that has been suggested as aiding in sleep. This group of compounds is sometimes collectively known as the biogenic amines. Neurotransmitters are chemicals used by the body to signal or send information between nerve cells or nerve and muscle cells. The chemical structure of dopamine is shown below. The NH_2 group on the molecule is the "amine" group in the term "biogenic amines." This entire group of chemicals has been implicated in depression and general moods.

Figure 1. The chemical structure of dopamine.

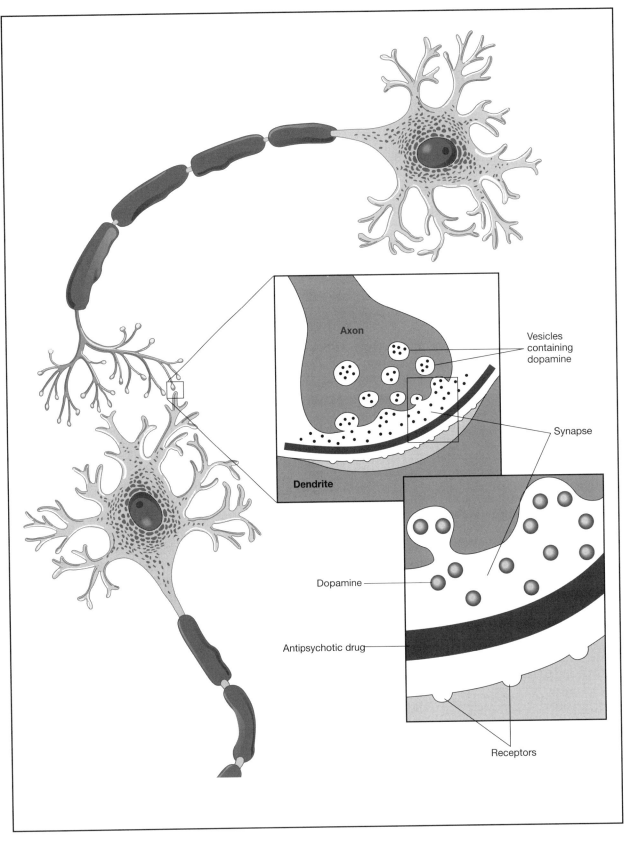

A representation of how an antipsychotic drug inhibits dopamine released by presynaptic neurons from reaching receptors on postsynaptic neurons.

Dopamine and Parkinson's disease

Parkinson's disease is a disorder of the nervous system that is characterized by slow movements and difficulty in initiating movements, a shuffle when walking, and increased muscular rigidity. It is estimated to affect as many as one million Americans and is far more prevalent in the elderly. The main cause of Parkinson's disease is thought to be a lack of dopamine in a region of the brain known as the substantia nigra. Whether the cells in that area do not produce enough dopamine or whether there are too few of the dopamine-producing cells is a matter of debate and active research. A chemical known as Levodopa or L-dopa, which our bodies rapidly metabolize to dopamine, is the main treatment. Levodopa reduces the symptoms of the disease, but does not stop the progression of the disease. A lack of dopamine in some areas of the brain has been implicated in depression.

Dopamine and schizophrenia

Schizophrenia is a form of psychosis or loss of contact with reality. It is estimated to affect about 1% of the population, or over 2.5 million Americans. A great deal of research is being done on the origins of schizophrenia and one widely accepted theory is that it is caused by an excess of dopamine or dopamine receptors. Receptors are proteins on the surfaces of cells that act as signal acceptors for the cells. They allow cells to send information, usually through neurotransmitter molecules. This hypersensitivity to dopamine (the prefix "hyper" means over or excessive) is treated by using chemicals that block (or inactivate) the receptors for the dopamine signals. Other approaches to the treatment of schizophrenia have focussed on decreasing the amounts of dopamine in the brain. In doing so, however, symptoms of Parkinson's disease often result, since less dopamine (or the ability to respond to dopamine) is present. The origins of schizophrenia are unclear; dopamine excess is probably not the sole cause of the disease as strong evidence for genetic and environmental factors exists as well. To date, treatments that focus of excess dopamine sensitivity have been the most successful.

Dopamine as heart medicine

Dopamine is used as a treatment for shock (low blood pressure throughout the body) which carries the risk of damage to major organs in patients who have suffered serious heart attacks. It helps to raise the blood pressure and causes small blood vessels to constrict, thus raising the blood pressure throughout the body.

KEY TERMS

Neurotransmitter—A chemical used to send information between nerve cells or nerve and muscle cells.

Receptors—Protein molecules on cells surfaces that act as "signal receivers" and allow communication between cells.

Psychosis—A loss of contact with reality. It may be caused by drugs, chemical imbalances, or even severe stress or depression.

Chemically related molecules such as adrenaline act similarly and both are often used to help patients.

See also Neurotransmitter; Parkinson's disease; Schizophrenia.

Further Reading:

Ackerman, S. *Discovering the Brain*. National Academy Press, 1992.

Bower, Bruce. "The Birth of Schizophrenia: A Debilitating Mental Illness May Take Root in the Fetal Brain." *Science News* (29 May 1993): 346.

Miller, Susan. "Picking up Parkinson's Pieces." *Discover* (May 1991): 22.

Restak, Richard M. *Receptors*. Bantam Press, 1994.

Zamula, Evelyn. "Drugs Help People with Parkinson's Disease." *FDA Consumer* (Jan-Feb 1992): 28.

Louis J. Gotlib

Doppler effect

The Doppler effect was named after Johann Christian Doppler (1803-1853). This Austrian physicist observed and explained the changes in pitch and frequency of sound and light waves, as well as all other types of waves, caused by the motion of moving bodies. The general rule of the Doppler effect is that the wave frequencies of moving bodies rise as they travel toward an observer and fall as they recede from the point of observation.

While Doppler, in 1842, demonstrated the phenomenon named after him in the area of sound waves, in the same year he also predicted that light waves could be

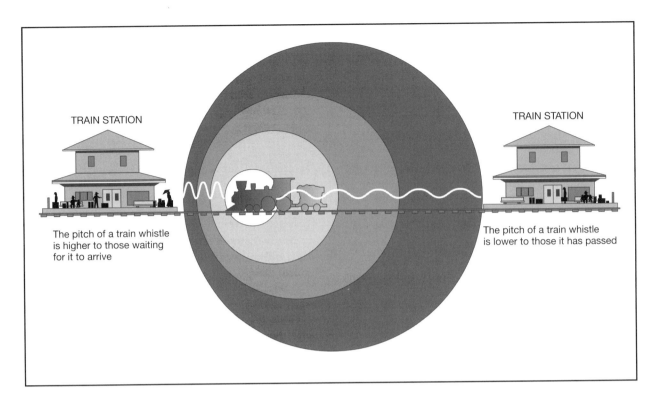

TRAIN STATION

TRAIN STATION

The pitch of a train whistle is higher to those waiting for it to arrive

The pitch of a train whistle is lower to those it has passed

The Doppler effect.

shown to exhibit the same response to the movement of bodies similar to those of sound waves.

Doppler effect in sound waves

The response of sound waves to moving bodies is illustrated in the example of the sounding of the locomotive whistle of a moving train. When the train blows its whistle while it is at rest in the station, stationary listeners who are either ahead of the engine or behind it will hear the same pitch made by the whistle, but as the train advances, those who are ahead will hear the sound of the whistle at a higher pitch. Listeners behind the train, as it pulls further away from them, hear the pitch of the whistle begin to fall.

The faster the train moves the greater will be the effect of the rising and falling of the pitch. Also, if the train remains at rest but the listeners either move toward the sounding train whistle or away from it, the effect will be the same. Those who move toward the train will hear a higher pitch, while those who travel away from the train will hear a lower pitch.

When the train is at rest it is the center of the sound waves it generates in circles around itself. As it moves forward, it ceases to be the center of the sound waves it produces. The sound waves move in the same direction of the train's motion. The train is chasing or crowding its waves up front, compressing them, so that the listener in front of the direction of its movement hears more waves per second, thus producing the effect of a higher frequency. The listener standing behind the train hears a lower pitch because the waves have spread out behind the forward motion of the train. Thus, there are fewer waves per second. The listener is now hearing a lower frequency than is actually being produced by the whistle.

In 1845, the Doppler effect received further confirmation in an elaborate experiment devised by a Dutch meteorologist, Christopher Heinrich Buys-Ballot. He placed a band of trumpet players on an open railroad flatcar and had it ride by listeners with perfect pitch who recorded their impressions of the notes produced by the whistle. Their written recordings of the pitches clearly demonstrated the Doppler wave effect.

Doppler effects in light waves

The Doppler effect in light waves can be observed by the spectral analysis of light emitted by luminous objects.

The light from a stationary distant object whose chemical composition is known is refracted at a specific band of light on a spectroscope. That band is known as its index of refraction. If the light, instead, appears at another frequency band in the spectroscope, it can be inferred from the Doppler effect that the body is in motion. When the light appears at a higher frequency band, then the body is no longer stationary but moving toward the observer. The Doppler effected light wave is displaced toward the higher frequency band, which is the blue end of the spectroscope. If the known body's light waves appear at a lower frequency band of the spectroscope, towards the red end, then the body is now in motion away from the observer.

With the use of the spectroscope, astronomers have been able to deduce the chemical composition of the stars. The Doppler effect enables them to determine their movements. In our own galaxy, all stars will be shifted either to the blue or red end because of a slight Doppler effect, indicating either a small movement toward or away from the earth. In 1923, however, Edwin Hubble, an American astronomer found that the light from all the galaxies outside our own were shifted so much toward the red as to suggest that they were all speeding away from our own at very great velocities. At the same time he saw that the recession of galaxies nearer to us was much less than those further away.

In 1929, Hubble and Milton Humason established a mathematical relationship that enables astronomers to determine the distance of galaxies by determining the amount of the galaxy's red shifts. This mathematical relationship is known as Hubble's law or Hubble's constant. Hubble's law shows that the greater the velocity of recession, the further away from the earth the galaxy is.

The concept of the expanding universe along with the corollary idea of the "Big Bang," that is, the instant creation of the universe from a compressed state of matter, owes much of its existence to Hubble's work which in turn is an important development of the Doppler effect in light waves. While some recent research challenges the red shift phenomenon for galaxies, most astronomers continue to accept Hubble's findings.

Other uses of the Doppler effect

In addition to its uses in science, the Doppler effect has many practical applications. In maritime navigation, radio waves are bounced off orbiting satellites to measure shifts which indicate changes in location. In highway traffic speeding detection, radar employs the Doppler effect to determine automobile speeds. There are also a number of medical applications of the Doppler effect found in ultrasonography, echocardiography, and radiology, all of which employ ultrasonic waves.

See also Wave motion.

Further Reading:

Bruning, David. "Seeing a Star's Surface." *Astronomy*, (October 1993): 34.

Powell, C. "The Redshift Blues." *Scientific American*, (January 1990).

Stroh, Michael. "Gust Work: Meteorologists Decipher the Winds with Radar." *Science News*, (July 11, 1992): 28-29.

Jordan P. Richman

Dories

Dories are bony fish in the family Zeidae. A dory has an oval body with a back that rises so that the main part of the body is higher than the head. The body itself is relatively thin and compressed and appears oval in side view.

Another distinguishing mark of the dories is a dark spot on each side of the body surrounded by a yellow ring. Dories typically are found in the middle depths of the seas where they live. Dories have extensible jaws, which can be extended outward as they capture their prey. This ability may explain why dories only have relatively small teeth for a carnivore. Dories move slowly toward their prey, then display a burst of speed while extending their jaws to finish the kill.

The best known of the dories is *Zeus faber*, the john dory, which is found in the Atlantic from Northern Europe to the tip of Africa, in the Mediterranean, and in the Pacific. The tasty john dory is a popular target for commercial fishermen. Specimens of *Zeus faber* can reach sizes of up to 3.3 ft (1 m). In Australia, the silver dory (*Cyttus australis*) is also a popular commercial fish. Despite the usual aversion that people have to the "fishy" taste and smell of seafood that is not freshly caught, the john dory is said to taste better when aged several days after being caught.

The American john dory, *Zeus ocellata*, can be found all along the Atlantic coast of North America reaching 2.3 ft (0.7 m). It is not a popular commercial species, unlike its European counterpart.

Fishermen often call the john dory "St. Peter's fish," a name that refers to the Apostle Peter who was at one time a fisherman. Two dark spots appear on the john dory as on other dories, one on each side of the body, which are said to be St. Peter's fingerprints.

Dormouse

Dormice are approximately ten species of rodents that make up the family Gliridae. Dormice typically live in trees, bushes, hedgerows, gardens, and rock piles. Dormice have a superficial resemblance to squirrels (family Sciuridae), but they are smaller and differ in many other anatomical and behavioral characters.

Dormice have soft fur, and a long, bushy tail. Their forefeet have four digits and the hindfeet have five, and all have claws that aid in climbing. If a predator grabs a dormouse by the tail, that appendage is shed, giving the dormouse a chance to escape. Dormice are nocturnal animals, mostly foraging on plant materials, but also opportunistically taking arthropods and the contents of bird nests. In fact, in some places predation by dormice is believed to cause significant reductions in the populations of breeding birds.

Dormice become quite fat by the end of the autumn, approximately doubling their normal summer weight. Dormice spend most of the winter sleeping in their nest, except for relatively warm and sunny days, when they awake and eat food that they have stored.

The fat dormouse (*Glis glis*) is a rather arboreal species that occurs widely from Spain and France to western Russia, and has been introduced to southern England. The usual natural habitat is angiosperm and mixedwood forests. However, the fat dormouse also occurs in proximity to rural and suburban humans, and often nests in buildings. The fat dormouse is sometimes considered to be an important agricultural pest, especially in orchards where they may eat large quantities of valuable crops such as walnuts, or take small bites out

of large numbers of softer fruits, making the produce unsalable. They are particularly regarded as a problem in Britain, where the populations of these animals are not well controlled by natural predators.

The fat dormouse is the largest of the dormice and it is sometimes eaten by people, some of whom consider the flesh of this animal to be a delicacy. In some respects, this epicurean taste for the fat dormouse is a leftover from the cuisine of the ancient Romans, who used to breed this dormouse in special pens for consumption when the animals were at their fattest.

The hazel mouse or common dormouse (*Muscardinus avellanarius*) is the smallest species in this family, and occurs through much of Europe, Asia Minor, and western Russia. The usual habitat of these arboreal animals is forests and hedgerows, especially if there is a dense canopy of shrubs.

The garden or orchard dormice (*Eliomys quercinus* and *E. melanurus*) occur in Europe, western Russia, Asia Minor, and northern Africa. These animals live in forests, swamps, and rocky habitats.

The tree or forest dormouse (*Dryomys nitedula*) occurs in forests and shrubby habitats of much of Europe and Asia Minor. The Japanese dormouse (*Glirulus japonicus*) only occurs in montane forests on the islands of Japan in eastern Asia. The mouse-like dormouse (*Myomimus personatus*) is a rare species that is only known from a few specimens collected in central Asia and Asia Minor. The African dormice (*Graphiurus* spp.) are three species that occur in a wide range of habitats in sub-Saharan Africa.

Double-blind study

New drugs undergo double-blind testing to determine whether they are effective. The test is called double-blind because neither the doctor who is administering the medication nor the patient who is taking it knows whether the patient is getting the experimental drug or a neutral substitute, called a placebo.

Getting a new drug approved is a long, complex process in order to ensure the drug is safe and effective and does what the manufacturer says it will do. The testing is done to satisfy the United States Food and Drug Administration (FDA), the government bureau that administers laws affecting the purity and safety of food and drugs.

A new medication first undergoes testing to insure that it is safe for humans to consume, that is, nontoxic. The drug then is tested to make certain it is effective against a specific disease in humans. Early testing must have shown it was effective against a bacterium or virus in the test tube (in vitro testing), but conditions are different in the human body. After passing toxicity and efficacy testing, the drug is placed in a double-blind study to compare it to other drugs used for similar purposes.

Thousands of patients in medical centers throughout the nation are assigned to the experimental group which receives the new drug, or the control group which receives the placebo or other older medication. Neither the patient nor his or her doctor know which group the patient is in.

The patient receives medication as stipulated by the doctor. The placebos are made to resemble the new drug's appearance and taste to make it difficult to tell the difference. These studies may take years to complete, so that a sufficient number of patients can be analyzed.

A safety committee oversees the study and determines which group each patient is in. If they notice that many patients become ill with the new drug, they can stop the test. If the new drug is proving exceptionally effective, they can stop the test to allow the drug to be given to all patients.

See also Placebo.

Double bond see **Chemical bond**

Dovekie see **Auks**

Doves see **Pigeons and doves**

Down's syndrome

Down's syndrome is a condition caused by a chromosomal abnormality and is characterized by a number of mental and physical defects. Named for Dr. John Langdon Down (an English physician who identified the characteristics of the condition among children in the late nineteenth century), Down's syndrome currently accounts for 33% of all forms of genetically based mental retardation. About 7000 children a year (1 in 800 births) are born with the chromosomal abnormality that causes Down's syndrome. The severity of the condition varies with each individual. Many of the physical defects that characterize Down's syndrome,

such as heart malformations, can be corrected surgically. Other defects, such as mental retardation and hypotonia (decreased muscle tone), can be helped with specialized education and physical therapy. Although no definitive treatment is available to people born with Down's syndrome, many individuals with the condition are able to work and live independently. The life expectancy of people with Down's syndrome has risen from 9 years in 1929 to 30 in 1980. Presently 25% of people with the condition live to the age of 50.

Chromosomal basis of Down's syndrome

Down's syndrome is caused by nondisjunction of chromosome 21 which results in a chromosomal abnormality called trisomy (three bodies) 21. Normally human cells contain 23 pairs of chromosomes. Researchers studying these chromosomes can induce the chromosomes in a cell to divide, photograph the chromosomes, and then match the pairs according to size and shape. The arrangement that results from this process called a karyotype. The chromosome pairs in a karyotype are numbered 1-23. In people with Down's syndrome an extra chromosome has been added to the chromosome 21 pair. Instead of the normal two, people with Down's syndrome have three chromosomes at position 21.

This abnormal number of chromosomes in people with Down's syndrome usually results from faulty cell division in the egg of the mother or the sperm of the father. When human eggs or sperm are formed cells must divide in such a way that each sex cell ends up with 23 chromosomes (in contrast to non-sex cells which divide in such a way that each cell ends up with 23 pairs of chromosomes). During conception the egg and sperm unite their genetic material forming a zygote (the cell that eventually becomes a fetus) that has 23 pairs of chromosomes. Sometimes a chromosome pair fails to separate during the cell division that forms an egg cell or sperm cell. This failure to separate is called nondisjunction. As a result of nondisjunction the sex cell receives 24 chromosomes not 23. When this sex cell unites with another during conception the zygote has an unequal number of chromosomes. If the nondisjunction occurs at chromosome 21 in the egg or sperm cell the zygote will develop into a child with Down's syndrome.

Nondisjunction is not the only abnormality that causes Down's syndrome. Another abnormality called translocation occurs in 4% of all people with Down's syndrome. In translocation a piece of chromosome 21 breaks off during sex cell formation in the mother or father and attaches to chromosome 13, 14, or 22. In mosaicism, which occurs in less than 1% of people with

Preschoolers with Down's syndrome at the Children's School for Early Development, Hawthorne, New York.

Down's syndrome, some cells of the zygote divide incompletely resulting in an abnormal number of chromosomes in only some of the zygote cells. Because the chromosomal abnormality occurs in only some of the cells the physical abnormalities in mosaicistic people vary according to how many cells have the abnormal number of chromosomes.

Risk factors

The risk of producing eggs with an abnormal number of chromosomes increases as a woman ages. From ages 15-30 the risk of having a child with Down's syndrome is 1 in 1000. At age 35 the risk jumps to 1 in 400, and at age 40 the risk is 1 in 105. Although the nondisjunction that results in Down's syndrome occurs 30% of the time in sperm, researchers still are not certain about what risk factors contribute to its occurrence.

Mental and physical defects of Down's syndrome

Researchers have found that chromosome 21 contains genes that encode a number of enzymes including superoxide dismutase-1 (SOD-1), cystathionine-*beta*-synthetase (CBS), and phosphofructokinase (PFKL). When chromosome 21 is triplicated as it is in people with Down's syndrome the levels of these enzymes increase in the body causing changes in metabolism. Researchers still are not certain about the exact mechanisms that link the abnormal levels of enzymes to the mental and physical disabilities of Down's syndrome.

The most common Down's syndrome characteristics are: a flat nasal bridge, slanting eyes with a fold at the corners, folded ears, and an inability to draw arms across the chest. Hypotonia (poor muscle tone) is common in people with Down's syndrome. Less common characteristics include an open mouth, protruding or furrowed tongue, upcurved fifth finger, and abnormal teeth.

Most people with Down's syndrome have some mental retardation although severity varies. Many people with Down's syndrome can be helped with special education and become productive members of the workforce. People with Down's syndrome can also live independently from their families in group homes or semi-independent living arrangements.

Down's syndrome also is characterized by a number of physical defects. The most common is malformation of the heart occurring in 40% of people with Down's syndrome. These defects can be corrected surgically. A more life-threatening problem is an increased risk of leukemia. Experts contend that people with Down's syndrome are 10-30 times more likely to develop leukemia during their lifetimes than people without Down's syndrome. The reason for this increased risk is unknown but some researchers believe that the leukemia may be linked to alterations in oncogenes (cancer-causing genes) on chromosome 21.

Another puzzling physical consequence of Down's syndrome is its link to Alzheimer's disease. This disease is marked by structural and biochemical changes in the brain resulting in changes in memory and behavior. Some people with Down's syndrome have the structural and biochemical changes but do not exhibit the symptoms of Alzheimer's; others do show the symptoms but usually after age 40.

Other physical abnormalities include skeletal defects such as a small skull, small facial bones, abnormal ribs, and abnormal pelvic structures. People with Down's syndrome also have a greater risk for atlantoaxial instability in which the first two vertebrae in the neck are unstable. This condition may lead to a spinal cord disability.

Prenatal detection of Down's syndrome

Many women, especially those over 35, opt for tests that detect Down's syndrome in a fetus. Until recently the only tests available involved looking within fetal cells by withdrawing some of the amniotic fluid that surrounds the fetus from the uterus or sampling tissue from the placenta. Both procedures carry an increased risk of miscarriage. Now researchers offer a test that probes for levels of certain hormones in the mother's blood. Researchers have found that an increased risk for Down's syndrome may be reflected in decreased levels of two fetal hormones alpha-fetoprotein and unconjugated estriol, and increased levels of a placental hormone, chorionic gonadotropin. If a preg-

---

KEY TERMS

. . . .

Atlantoaxial instability—Instability of the first two vertebrae of the neck which may lead to spinal cord disability.

Chromosome—The structures within the nuclei of cells that contain the cell's genetic material.

Karyotype—The arrangement of photographs of chromosomes by shape and size.

Nondisjunction—Failure of a chromosome pair to separate during cell division. If it occurs during formation of sex cells the resulting sex cell will have an abnormal number of chromosomes.

Translocation—Breakage of a chromosome during cell division; the broken piece may attach to another chromosome.

Trisomy 21—A condition in which an extra chromosome is added to chromosome pair 21 resulting in Down's syndrome.

Zygote—The cell that is formed from the uniting of egg and sperm and develops into a fetus.

---

nant woman is found to have these levels of hormones in her blood she is advised to have the more risky procedures that definitively test for trisomy 21 in fetal cells. Because these hormone tests can be performed on every pregnant woman they could detect an increased risk for Down's syndrome in many more fetuses than possible previously.

See also Birth defects; Congenital.

Further Reading:

"Down's Syndrome." *Pediatrics for Parents* 12 (January 1991): 4-6.

Fackelmann, Kathy. "New hope or false promise? Study shows futility of alternative Down's syndrome treatment." *Science News* 137 (17 March 1990): 168-70.

Hanson, Amy. "New math (triple blood test screen pregnant women for carrying baby with Down's syndrome)." *Harvard Health Letter* 16 (May 1991): 1-3.

"Maternal testing for Down's syndrome." *American Family Physician* 45 (April 1992): 1893-95.

Mathew, Prasad, et. al. "Long term follow-up of children with Down's syndrome with cardiac lesions." *Clinical Pediatrics* 29 (October 1990): 569-75.

Michaels, Evelyne. "Medical advances, positive attitudes brighten future of Down's syndrome children." *Canadian Medical Association Journal* 143 (15 September 1990): 546-49.

Kathleen Scogna

Dragonflies

Dragonflies are large flying insects in the order Odonata. Dragonflies can be as large as 3 in (7.5 cm) in length, with a wing span of up to 8 in (20 cm). The fossilized remains of a huge dragonfly-like insect which had a wingspread of more than 2 ft (70 cm) is known from the Carboniferous Period, some 300 million years ago.

Dragonflies are very distinctive insects, with large eyes that almost cover the entire head, a short thorax, a long slender abdomen, and glassy membranous wings. Dragonflies are classified in the Suborder Anisoptera since their hindwings are larger than their forewings, and the wings are habitually held straight out when at rest. They feed on other insects, which they catch in flight.

Dragonflies are usually found around streams and ponds, where they feed, mate, and lay their eggs. The mating habits of dragonflies are conspicuous and unusual. The male generally sets up a territory over a part of a stream or pond which he patrols for most of the day. When a newly emerged female flies in to the territory, the male flies above her and lands on her back, bends his abdomen far forward and deposits sperm on the underside of his second abdominal segment, which is the site of his penis. Then, grasping the female behind the head with a pair of forceps-like structures at the end of his abdomen, he flies off with her in tandem. When she is ready to mate, she curls her abdomen down and forward to place its end under the male's second abdominal segment, which has structures to hold it in place while the sperm are transferred to her reproductive tract. The pair may fly around in this unusual "wheel" configuration for several minutes. Egg-laying begins within a short time, with the male either continuing to hold the female while she dips her abdomen into the water to lay the eggs, or waiting above her and then regrasping her after each egg-laying session. The eggs hatch into aquatic larval form (naiad) after a few days.

Like the adults, the wingless naiads feed on insects and other small aquatic animals. The lower lip (labium)

A dragonfly.

of the larvae is retractable with jaws that can be thrust out in front of the head to catch and pull the prey back to the chewing mandibles. The naiads have gills in the last segments of the abdomen and ventilate the gills by pumping water in and out. The contraction of the pumping muscles also allows the larvae to "jet" forward rapidly out of harm's way. During the winter, the larvae live in the water, where they grow, shedding the external skeleton (molting) several times. In the spring, the larvae climb out of the water, molt again, and the newly-transformed adult dragonflies emerge and unfurl their wings.

Some 5,000 species of dragonflies are known, living in every continent except Antarctica, and on most islands as well. The principal families of dragonflies are the high-flying darners, the Aeshnidae, and the skimmers, the Libellulidae.

Further Reading:

Borror, D.J., D.M. Delong, & C.A. Triplehorn. *An Introduction to the Study of Insects*, 4th Ed. New York: Holt, Reinhart & Winston, 1976.

Borror, D.J. and R.E. White. *A Field Guide to the Insects of America North of Mexico*. Boston: Houghton Mifflin, 1980.

d'Aguilar, J., J.-L. Dommanget, & R. Prechac. *A Field Guide to the Dragonflies of Britain, Europe and North Africa*. London: Collins, 1986.

Needham, J.G., and M.J. Westfall. *A Manual of the Dragonflies of North America (Anisoptera)*. Berkeley: University California Press, 1954.

Herndon G. Dowling

KEY TERMS

Globe-skimmer—One of the most widely distributed of all dragonflies.

Naiad—The aquatic larval stage of dragonflies.

Thorax—The body region of insects which supports the legs and wings.

Dream see **Sleep**

Drift net

Drift nets are lengthy, free-floating, 26-49 ft (8-15 m) deep nets, each as long as 55 mi (90 km). Drift nets are used to snare fish by their gills in pelagic, open-water situations. Because drift nets are not selective of species, their use results in large by-catches of non-target fish, sharks, turtles, seabirds, and marine mammals, which are usually jettisoned, dead, back to the ocean. Drift nets are an extraordinarily destructive fishing technology.

Ecological damages caused by drift nets

Drift-net fisheries are mounted in all of the world's major fishing regions, and unwanted by-catch is always a serious problem. This has proven true for pelagic fisheries for swordfish, tuna, squid, salmon, and other species. One example is the drift-net fishery for swordfish in the Mediterranean, 90% of which is associated with Italian fishers. This industry kills excessive numbers of striped dolphin and sperm whale, and smaller numbers of fin whale, Cuvier's beaked whale, long-finned pilot whale, and Risso's, bottlenose, and common dolphins, along with other non-target marine wildlife. As a result of concerns about the excessive by-catch in this swordfish fishery during the early 1990s, the European Union banned the use of drift nets longer than 1.5 mi (2.5 km) (prior to this action, the average set was 26 mi (12 km) in length). However, some fishing nations have objected to this regulation and do not enforce it. It remains to be seen whether this length restriction will prove to be useful in preventing the non-target, drift-net mortality.

There are few monitoring data that actually demonstrate the non-target by-catch by drift nets. One measurement was made during a one-day monitoring of a typical drift-net set of 11 mile/day (19 km/day) in the Caroline Islands of the south Pacific. That single net, in one day, entangled 97 dolphins, along with 11 larger cetaceans, and 10 sea turtles. World-wide during the late 1980s, pelagic drift nets were estimated to have annually killed as many as one million dolphins, porpoises, and other cetaceans, along with millions of seabirds, tens of thousands of seals, thousands of sea turtles, and untold numbers of sharks and large, non-target species of fish.

Although there are no hard data to verify the phenomenon, there are anecdotal reports of substantial reductions in the abundance of some of these groups of animals in regions that have experienced a great deal of drift netting. Consequently, the drift-net by-catch is per-

ceived (by proponents of this type of fishing technology) to be less of a problem than formerly, because the unintended by-catches are apparently smaller. However, this really reflects the likelihood that this rapacious fishing practice has created marine deserts, that only support sparse populations of large animals.

In addition, great lengths of drift nets and other fishing nets are lost at sea every year, especially during severe storms. Because the nets are manufactured of synthetic materials that are highly resistant to degradation, they continue to snare fish, sharks, mammals, birds, turtles, and other creatures for many years, as so-called "ghost nets." Little is known about the magnitude of this problem, but it is undoubtedly an important source of mortality of marine animals and other creatures.

In response to mounting concerns about unsustainable by-catches of non-target species of marine animals, which in some cases are causing population declines, the United Nations in 1993 banned the use of drift nets longer than 1.5 mi (2.5 km). Although this regulation would not eliminate the by-catches associated with drift netting, it would reduce the amount of this unintended mortality, possibly by as much as 2/3. Unfortunately, there has been a great deal of resistance from the fishing industry and fishing nations to the implementation of even this minimal regulation, and many fisheries continue to use much longer nets.

Clearly, non-selective by-catches associated with drift nets cause an unacceptable mortality of non-target animals, some of which are threatened by this practice. A rapid improvement of this unsatisfactory state of environmental affairs could be achieved by using shorter drift nets, or by banning their use altogether. Unfortunately, because of economic self interest of the world's nations and the fishing industry, this obvious and simple betterment has not yet proved possible.

Further Reading:
Freedman, B. *Environmental Ecology,* 2nd ed. San Diego: Academic Press, 1994.

KEY TERMS

By-catch—A harvest of species of animals that are not the target of the fishery, caught during fishing directed towards some other, commercially desirable species.

Gill net—A net that catches fish by snaring their gill covering.

LaBudde, S. *Stripmining the Seas. A Global Perspective on Drift Net Fisheries.* Honolulu, Hawaii: Earthtrust, 1989.

Bill Freedman

Drill (animal) see **Baboons**

Dromedary see **Camels**

Drongos

Drongos are 20 species of handsome birds that make up the family of perching birds known as Dicruridae. Drongos occur in Africa, southern and southeastern Asia, and Australasia. Their usual habitats are open forests, savannas, and some types of cultivated areas with trees.

Drongos are typically black colored, though with a beautiful, greenish or purplish iridescence. The wings of these elegant, jay-sized birds are relatively long and pointed, and the tail is deeply forked. The tail of some species is very long, with the outer feathers developing extremely long filaments with a "racket" at the end. The beak is stout and somewhat hooked, and is surrounded by short, stiff feathers known as rictal bristles, a common feature on many fly-catching birds other than drongos. The sexes are identical in color and size.

Drongos are excellent and maneuverable fliers, though not over long distances. They commonly feed by catching insects in flight, having discovered their prey from an exposed, aerial perch. Some species follow large mammals or monkeys, feeding on insects that are disturbed as these heavier animals move about.

Drongos sing melodiously to proclaim their territory, often imitating the songs of other species. They are aggressive in the defense of their territory against other drongos as well as potential predators. Some other small birds deliberately nest close to drongos because of the relative protection that is afforded against crows, hawks, and other predators.

Drongos lay 3-4 eggs in a cup-shaped nest located in the fork of a branch. The eggs are mostly incubated by the female, but both sexes share in the feeding and caring of the young.

The greater racket-tailed drongo (*Dicrurus paradiseus*) of India, Malaya, and Borneo has a very long tail, which is about twice the length of the body of the bird. More than one-half of the length of the tail is made up of the extended, wire-like shafts of the outer-two tail feathers, which end in an expanded, barbed surface—the racket. These seemingly ungainly tail-feathers flutter gracefully as these birds fly, but do not seem to unduly interfere with their maneuverability when hunting flying insects. The greater racket-tailed drongo is also famous for its superb mimicry of the songs of other species of birds.

Another well-known species is the king-crow (*Dicrurus macrocercus*) of India, so-named because of its aggressive dominance of any crows that venture too closely, and of other potential predators as well. Like other drongos, however, the king-crow is not a bully—it only chases away birds that are potentially dangerous.

Drought

Drought is an extended period of time during which water supplies are inadequate to support the demands of plants, animals, and people. A drought condition is characterized by low precipitation, compared to the normal amount for the particular region in which it occurs, low humidity, high temperatures, and/or high wind velocities.

Drought is a temporary condition that occurs in moist climates. It differs from the conditions of arid regions which experience low average rainfall or available water. For example, deserts receive less than 10 in (25 cm) of rain per year. Under both drought and arid conditions, individual plants and animals may die, but the populations to which they belong survive. Both drought and aridity differ from situations of desiccation, in which entire populations become extinct due to a prolonged period of intensifying drought. An example of desiccation is the droughts lasting two to three decades in Africa and Australia. The loss of crops and cattle in these areas caused widespread suffering.

Unlike a storm or a flood, there is no specific time that constitutes the beginning or end of a drought. Its duration may differ according to who is monitoring it. Hydrologists measure the frequency and severity of droughts on river basins and other water bodies. Climatologists and meteorologists follow the effects of ocean winds and volcanoes on weather patterns that cause droughts. Agriculturalists measure a drought's effects on plant growth. They may notice the onset of a drought long before hydrologists record drops in underground water table levels. Meteorologists, observing weather cycles, may be able to predict the occurrence of future droughts.

Severe drought in Botswana, Africa was the result of an El Niño weather pattern that began in 1989.

drought by storing water in their tissues. Other plants, for example, mesquite trees, become dormant. Still others, such as the creosote bush, simply endure drought by adaptations such as reduced leaf size or a waxy coating that loses less moisture.

History

Studies of tree rings in the United States have identified prehistoric droughts occurring as early as 1220. The thickness of annual growth rings of some tree species, such as red cedar and yellow pine, indicates the wetness of each season. The longest drought identified by this method began in 1276 and lasted 38 years. The tree ring method identified 21 droughts lasting five or more years during the period from 1210 to 1958. The earliest recorded drought in the United States was in 1621.

In other countries, a drought in northern China in 1876 dried up crops in a 3 sq mi (7.77 sq km) region. Millions of people died from lack of food. Russia experienced severe droughts in 1890 and 1921. The latter drought, along the Volga River basin, caused the deaths of up to five million people—more than had died during World War I which had just ended.

India normally receives most of its rain during the monsoon season which lasts from June to September. Winds blowing in from the Indian Ocean bring most of the country's rainfall during this season. The monsoon winds did not come during two droughts in 1769 and 1865. An estimated ten million people died in each of those droughts, many from diseases like smallpox due to their weakened condition.

The best known American drought was during the Dust Bowl years on the Great Plains from 1931 to 1936. 1934 and 1936 were the two driest years in the recorded history of U.S. climate. The Dust Bowl encompassed an area approximately 399 mi (644 km) long and 298 mi (483 km wide) in parts of Colorado, New Mexico, Kansas, Texas, and Oklahoma. In more recent history, the United States experienced severe to extreme drought in over half of the country during 1987-89. This drought was emphasized by the extensive fires in Yellowstone National Park in 1988.

More recent severe droughts in other countries include England (1921, 1933-34, and 1976), Central Australia (1945-72), and the Canadian prairies (1983-85). One of the worst droughts occurred in the Sahel and Sudan in the early 1970s to late 1980s. The Sahel averages only (10-30 cm) of rainfall annually. An estimated 50,000-200,000 people died from the Sahel drought. Although these African areas received some rain in 1974, the drought returned and many areas were

In addition to its duration, the intensity of a drought is measured, to a large extent, by the ability of the living things in the affected vicinity to tolerate the dry conditions. Although a drought may end abruptly with the return of adequate rainfall, the effects of a drought on the landscape and its inhabitants may last for years.

Many factors affect the severity of a drought's impact on living beings. Plants are vulnerable to drought when water stored in the soil cannot keep up with the amount of soil moisture being lost to evaporation. Plants in impermeable soils with little water storage capacity and young plants that have not developed mature root systems are more vulnerable to drought.

Plants have several mechanisms that enable them to tolerate drought conditions. Many desert annuals escape drought altogether by having a short life span. Their life cycle lasts only a few weeks during the desert's brief, moist periods. The rest of the time they survive as seeds. Other plants, such as the cactus, evade

Drought: A Disaster! book. Brookfield, Connecticut: Milbrook Press, 1992.

Hamilton, Virginia. *Drylongso.* San Diego: Harcourt Brace Jovanovich, 1992.

Knapp, Brian. *Drought.* Austin, Texas: Steck-Vaughn Company, 1990.

Riebsame, William E., Stanley A. Changnon, Jr., and Thomas R. Karl. *Drought and Natural Resources Management in the United States: Impacts and Implications of the 1987-89 Drought.* Boulder, Colorado: Westview Press, Inc., 1991.

Karen Marshall

experiencing crisis conditions by 1985, especially in Ethiopia. This drought affected almost the entire continent of Africa.

Drought management

Crop and soil management practices can increase the amount of water stored within a plant's root zone. For example, contour plowing and terracing decreases the slope gradient of a hillside and thus the amount and velocity of water runoff. Vegetation, as both living plants and crop residues left by minimum tillage practices, reduces soil crusting from the impact of raindrops. Permeable soils absorb more rainfall than crusty soils.

Other farming practices that lessen the impact of drought on crop production include strip cropping, windbreaks, and irrigation. Windbreaks or shelterbelts are strips of land planted with shrubs and trees perpendicular to the prevailing winds. Windbreaks prevent soil and its moisture-retaining properties being blown away by wind. Plants can also be specifically bred to adapt to the effects of weather extremes. For example, shorter plants encounter less wind. Crinkled leaves create small pockets of still air, thus preserving water.

Drought severity, from a social standpoint, is also influenced by the vulnerability of an area or population to its effects. Vulnerability is a product, in part, of the demand for water, the age and health of the population affected by the drought, and the functionality of water supply and energy supply systems. Drought's effects are also more pronounced in areas that have lost wetlands that recharge aquifers, that are dependent on agriculture, that have low existing food stocks, or whose governments have not developed drought response mechanisms.

See also Desertification; Erosion; Hydrologic cycle; Water conservation.

Further Reading:

Defreitas, Stan. *The Water-Thrifty Garden.* Dallas, Texas: Taylor Publishing Company, 1993.

Ducks

Ducks are waterfowl in the order Anseriformes, in the family Anatidae, which also includes geese and swans. Ducks occur on all continents except Antarctica, and are widespread in many types of aquatic habitats. Almost all ducks breed in freshwater habitats, especially shallow lakes, marshes, and swamps. Most species of ducks also winter in these habitats, sometimes additionally using grainfields and other area developed by humans. Some species of sea ducks breed on marine coasts, wintering in near-shore habitats. Most species of ducks undertake substantial migrations between their breeding and wintering grounds, in some cases flying thousands of kilometers, twice each year.

Ducks are well adapted to aquatic environments, and are excellent swimmers with waterproof feathers, short legs, and webbed feet. The feathers are waterproofed by oil transferred from an oil gland at the base of the tail by the bill. Ducks eat a wide range of aquatic plants and animals, with the various species of ducks having long necks, wide bills and other attributes that are specialized for their particular diets. Most ducks obtain their food by either dabbling or diving. Dabbling ducks feed on the surface of the water, or they tip up to submerge their head and feed on reachable items in shallow water. Diving ducks swim underwater to reach deeper foods. Ducks have great economic importance as the targets of hunters and several species have been domesticated for agriculture. In general, duck populations have greatly declined world-wide, as a combined result of overhunting, habitat loss, and pollution.

Ducks are divided by systematists into a number of subfamilies, which are described below.

A lone mallard (*Anas platyrhynchos*) amid a group of black ducks in Castalia, Ohio.

Dabbling ducks

Dabbling ducks (subfamily Anatinae) are surface-feeding birds that eat vegetation and invertebrates found in shallow water that they can reach without diving. Their plant foods include colonial algae, small vascular plants such as duckweed (e.g., *Lemna minor*), roots and tubers of aquatic plants, and the seeds of pondweed (*Potamogeton* spp.), smartweed (*Polygonum* spp.), wild rice (*Zizania aquatica*), sedges (*Carex* spp.), and bulrushes (*Scirpus* spp.). Dabbling ducks also eat aquatic invertebrates, and in fact these are the most important foods of rapidly growing ducklings.

Two widespread species of dabbling duck are mallards (*Anas platyrhynchos*) and pintails (*A. acuta*). These ducks range throughout the Northern Hemisphere, occurring in both North America and Eurasia. Other North American species include black ducks (*A. rubripes*), American widgeons (*Mareca americana*), shovelers (*Spatula clypeata*), blue-winged teals (*A. discors*), and wood ducks (*Aix sponsa*).

Bay and sea ducks

Bay and sea ducks (Aythyinae) are diving ducks that swim beneath the surface of the water in search of aquatic animals. Some species also eat plants, but this is generally less important than in the herbivorous dabbling ducks. Some bay and sea ducks for example, common goldeneye (*Bucephala clangula*), ring-necked duck (*Aythya collaris*), and hooded merganser (*Lophodytes cucullatus*) eat mostly arthropods occurring in the water column. Other species including old-squaws (*Clangula hyemalis*), lesser scaups (*Aythya affinis*), surf scoters (*Melanitta perspicillata*), and common eiders (*Somateria mollissima*) specialize on bottom living invertebrates. Some of these species are remarkable divers, descending as deep as 246 ft (75 m) in the case of oldsquaw ducks.

Tree or whistling ducks

Tree ducks (Dendrocygninae) are long-legged birds, and are much less common than most dabbling or diving ducks. Tree ducks tend to be surface feeders in aquatic habitats, but they also forage for nuts and seeds on land. Tree ducks have a generally southern distribution in North America. The most common North American species is the fulvous tree duck (*Dendrocygna bicolor*).

Stiff-tailed ducks

Stiff-tailed ducks (Oxyurinae) are small diving ducks with distinctive, stiffly-erect tails. This group is represented in North America by the ruddy duck (*Oxyura jamaicensis*).

Mergansers

Mergansers (Merginae) are sleek, diving ducks that are specialized for feeding on small fish, and have serrated bills which apply a firm grip on their slippery prey. The most abundant species are the common merganser (*Mergus merganser*) and the red-breasted merganser (*M. serrator*).

Economic importance of ducks

Wild ducks have long been hunted for food, and more recently for sport. In recent decades, hunters kill about 10-20 million ducks each year in North America, shooting about 20% in Canada, and the rest in the United States. Duck hunting has a very large economic impact, because of the money that hunters spend on travel license fees, private hunting fees, and on firearms, ammunition, and other paraphernalia.

Prior to the regulation of the hunting of ducks and other game animals, especially before the 1920s, the killing of ducks was essentially uncontrolled. In areas where ducks were abundant, there were even commercial hunts to supply ducks to urban markets. The excessive hunting during these times caused tremendous decreases in the populations of ducks and other waterfowl, as well as in other species of edible birds and mammals. Consequently, governments in the United States and Canada began to control excessive hunting, to protect breeding habitat, and to provide a network of habitat refuges to provide for the needs of waterfowl during migration and wintering. These actions have allowed subsequent increases in the populations of most species of waterfowl, although the numbers of some species still remain much smaller than they used to be.

A relatively minor but interesting use of ducks concerns the harvesting of the down of wild common eiders. The female of this species plucks down from her breast for use in lining the nest, and this highly insulating material has long been collected in northern countries, and used to produce eiderdown quilts and clothing.

Several species of ducks have been domesticated, and in some areas they are an important agricultural commodity. The common domestic duck is derived from the mallard, which was domesticated about 2,000 years ago in China. Farm mallards are usually white, and are sometimes called Peking duck. The common domestic muscovy duck (*Cairina moschata*) was domesticated by aboriginal South Americans prior to the European colonization of the Americas.

Ducks are being increasingly used in a non-consumptive fashion. For example, bird watchers often go to great efforts to see ducks and other birds, trying to view as many species as possible, especially in natural habitats. Like hunters, birders spend a great deal of money while engaging in their sport, to travel, to purchase binoculars and books, and to belong to birding, natural-history, and conservation organizations.

Factors affecting the abundance of ducks

The best aquatic habitat for ducks and other waterfowl are those with relatively shallow water, with very productive vegetation and large populations invertebrates. Those habitats with a large ratio of shoreline to surface area, favors the availability of secluded nesting sites. These sorts of habitat occur to some degree in most regions, and are mostly associated with wetlands, especially marshes, swamps, and shallow, open water. In North America and elsewhere during the past century, extensive areas of these types of wetlands have been lost or degraded, mostly because they have been drained or infilled for agricultural, urban, or industrial use. Wetlands have also been degraded by eutrophication caused by excessive nutrient inputs, and by pollution by toxic chemicals and organic materials. These losses of habitat, in combination with overhunting, have caused large decreases in the populations of ducks throughout North America, and in most other places where these birds occur. Consequently, there are now substantial efforts to preserve or restore the wetlands required as habitat by ducks and other wildlife, and to regulate hunting of these animals.

The most important breeding habitats for ducks in North America occur in the fringing marshes and shallow open-water wetlands of small ponds in the prairies, known as "potholes." The marshy borders of potholes provide important breeding habitat for various species of dabbling ducks such as mallard, pintail, widgeon, and blue-winged teal, while deeper waters are important to lesser scaup, canvasbacks (*Aythya valisneria*), redheads (*Aythya americana*), and ruddy ducks. Unfortunately, most of the original prairie potholes have been filled in or drained to provide more land for agriculture. This extensive conversion of prairie wetlands has increased the importance of the remaining potholes as breeding habitat for North America's declining populations of ducks, and for other wildlife. As a result, further conversions of potholes are resisted by the conservation community, although agricultural interests still encourage the drainage of these important wetlands.

In years when the prairies are subject to severe drought, many of the smaller potholes are too dry to allow ducks to breed successfully, and ponds and wetlands farther to the north in Canada become relatively important for breeding ducks. Another important source of natural mortality of ducks and other waterfowl are infectious disease, such as avian cholera, which can sweep through dense staging or wintering populations, and kill tens of thousands of birds in a short period of time. When an epidemic of avian cholera occurs, wildlife managers attempt to manage the problem by collecting and burning or burying as many carcasses as possible, in order to decrease the exposure of living birds to the pathogen.

Lead shot is an important type of toxic pollution that kills large numbers of ducks and other birds each year. Lead shot from spent shotgun pellets on the surface mud and sediment of wetlands where ducks feed, may be ingested during feeding and retained in the duck's gizzard. There the shot is abraded, dissolved by acidic stomach fluids, absorbed into the blood, and then transported to sensitive organs, causing toxicity. An estimated 2-3% of the autumn and winter duck population of North America (some 2-3 million birds) dies each year from lead toxicity. As few as one or two pellets retained in the gizzard can be enough to kill a duck. Fortunately, steel shot is rapidly replacing lead shot, in order to reduce this unintended, toxic hazard to ducks and other wildlife.

Ducks and other aquatic birds may also be at some risk from acidification of surface waters as a result of acid rain. Although it is unlikely that acidification would have direct, toxic effects on aquatic birds, important changes could be caused to their habitat, which might indirectly affect the ducks. For example, fish are very sensitive to acidification, and losses of fish populations would be detrimental to fish-eating ducks such as mergansers. However, in the absence of the predation pressure exerted by fish in acidic lakes, aquatic invertebrates would become more abundant, possibly benefitting other species of ducks such as common goldeneye, ring-necked duck, and black duck. These scenarios are inevitably speculative, for not much is known about the effects of acid rain on ducks.

Ducks can also be affected by eutrophication in aquatic habitats, a condition that is characterized by large increases in productivity caused by large nutrient loads from sewage dumping or from the runoff of agricultural fertilizers. Moderate eutrophication often improves duck habitat, by stimulating plant growth and their invertebrate grazers. However, intense eutrophication kills fish and severely degrades the quality of aquatic habitats for ducks and other wildlife.

Some species of ducks nest in cavities in trees, a niche that has become increasingly uncommon because of forestry and losses of woodlands to agriculture and urbanization. Together with overhunting, the loss of natural cavities was an important cause of the decline of the wood duck and hooded merganser (*Lophodytes cucullatus*) in North America. Fortunately, these species will nest in artificial cavities provided by humans, and these ducks have recovered somewhat, thanks in part to widespread programs of nest box erection in wetland habitats.

Agencies and actions

Because the populations of ducks and other waterfowl have been badly depleted by overhunting and habitat loss, conservation has become a high priority for governments and some private agencies. In North America, the U.S. Fish and Wildlife Service and the Canadian Wildlife Service have responsibilities for waterfowl at the federal level, as do states and provinces at the regional level. Ducks Unlimited is a non-governmental organization whose central concern is the conservation of duck populations. The Ducks Unlimited mandate is mostly pursued by raising and spending money to increase duck productivity through habitat management, with an aim of providing more birds for hunters. Other organizations have a non-consumptive mandate that is partly relevant to ducks, for example, the World Wildlife Fund, The Nature Conservancy, and the Nature Conservancy of Canada. On the international stage, the *Convention on Wetlands of International Importance, Especially as Waterfowl Habitat* is a treaty among national governments that is intended to facilitate worldwide cooperation in the conservation of wetlands, thereby benefitting ducks and other wildlife.

All of these agencies are undertaking important activities on behalf of ducks, other animals, and natural ecosystems. However, duck populations are still much smaller than they used to be, and some species are endangered. Much more must be done to provide the ducks of North America and the world with the protection and habitat that they require.

See also Eutrophication; Geese; Swans; Wetlands.

Further Reading:
Bellrose, F. C. *Ducks, Geese, and Swans of North America.* Harrisburg, PA: Stackpole Books, 1976.
Freedman, B. *Environmental Ecology.* 2nd ed. San Diego: Academic Press, 1994.
Godfrey, W. E. *The Birds of Canada.* Toronto: University of Toronto Press, 1986.

Johnsgard, P. A. *Ducks in the Wild. Conserving Waterfowl and Their Habitats.* Swan Hill Press, 1992.
Owen, M., and J. M. Black. *Waterfowl Ecology.* London: Blackie Pub., 1990.

Bill Freedman

Duckweed

Duckweeds are small, floating to slightly submerged species of flowering plants in the genus *Lemna,* family . The simple body is leaf-like, generally flat on top and convex below, lacks stems or leaves, is oval to tear-dropped in shape, and has one unbranched root that lacks vascular (conducting) tissue. The upper surface of the plant is covered with waxy compounds so as to shed water.

Duckweeds are abundant throughout the world in freshwater ponds, lakes, and backwaters where the water is still, with the exception of the Arctic. Plants range in size from 0.05-0.8 in (1.5-20 mm) in length. One of the most widely distributed species, *Lemna minor,* typically grows to a length of 0.05-0.15 in (1.5-4 mm).

Reproduction in duckweeds is almost exclusively asexual, occurring as outgrowths from one end which break off, often resulting in the development of a dense, green mat on the surface of the water. Individual bodies are generally short-lived, five to six weeks for Lemna minor. Sexual reproduction is rare in duckweeds, and appears to occur mostly in warmer regions. Flowers are unisexual and extremely simple, consisting of only one stamen in male and one pistil in female flowers. Each flower arises from a pouch in the body and is covered by a small, highly modified leaf called a spathe.

The watermeal (*Wolffia,*) is a close relative of duckweed, and is the smallest flowering plant. Some species of watermeal consist of only a globular, rootless body, as small as 0.02 in (0.5 mm). Duckweeds and watermeals are an important food for waterfowl, which feed on these plants on the water surface.

Dugong see **Manatee**

Duikers

Duikers are small African antelopes in the large family of Bovidae. This family of hoofed animals includes deer, antelope, gazelles, as well as cattle, sheep, and goats. Like all bovids, duikers have even-toed hooves, horns, and a four-chambered stomach structure that allows them to digest a diet of plants. Duikers are found throughout sub-Saharan Africa. These small antelopes range in size from 22 in (55 cm) to as much as 57 in (1.45 m) in length, and weigh from as little as 3 lb (1.35 kg) to as much as 176 lb (80 kg).

There are 17 species of forest-dwelling duikers (*Cephalophus*). These are the blue, yellow-backed, bay, Maxwell's, Jentink's, black-fronted, red-flanked, Abbot's, banded or zebra, black, red, Ader's duiker, Peter's, Harvey's or Zanzibar duiker, bay or black-striped, Gabon or white-bellied, and Ogilby's duiker. There is only one species of savanna duiker, the grey (or Grimm's) duiker (*Sylvicapra grimmia*), which is found in thin forest and savanna woodlands. Duikers are heavily hunted for their meat, and many of the forest species are threatened or endangered.

Adaptation

Duikers have not been studied to any great extent in the wild because they live in dense rain forest habitats and are difficult to observe. They are, nonetheless, much sought after for their meat. The number of species of duikers increases with the size of the rain forests they inhabit.

The word duiker means divers or those that duck in Afrikaans. When duikers are alarmed they dive for cover into thickets. The front legs of duikers are shorter than the powerful hind legs. Duikers have a relatively big head, with a wide mouth, small ears, short backward-slanting horns, and a crest of erect hair on the forehead. Female duikers are on average a little larger than males and also possess horns.

Some species are active only during daylight hours (diurnal), some are active only at night (nocturnal), while and others are active during both times of day. Duikers are browsers, that is, animals that eat the tender shoots, twigs, and leaves of bushy plants, rather than grazing on grass. Some species of duikers also eat buds, seeds, bark, and fruit, and even small rodents and birds. The moisture content of leaves is usually sufficient to satisfy their water needs during the rainy season, when duikers do not drink. Duikers are preyed upon by leopards, large predatory birds, and even baboons.

Social life

Duikers are not social animals and are usually seen alone or in pairs. Like other small browsing antelope, duikers are territorial and monogamous (they mate for life). The size of the territory of a pair of duikers is between 5-10 acres (2-4 ha), and both sexes defend it from intrusion by other members of their species.

The care of the young is done mainly by the females. The first born offspring leaves its parents before a younger sibling is born. Within the territory, the male and female duikers rest and feed at different times, and often wander away from one another, which may be why they are seen alone so often.

The courtship ceremony of duikers includes close following of the female by the male, circling and turning by the female, hiding, moaning and snorting by both, mutual scenting, and then mating. Females give birth to one offspring at a time and may have from one to three young a year. Pregnancy usually lasts from between 4-5 months or longer. The newborn duiker lies concealed for the first few weeks of its life when it is nursed by its mother.

Male duikers have scent glands underneath their eyes and on their hooves. The glands under their eyes extend downward and secrete through a series of pores rather than through one opening, as in other antelopes. Duikers in captivity have been seen to mark their territory as frequently as six times within ten minutes. Male duikers also use their scent glands to mark their opponents in battle, as well as engaging in mutual marking with their mates and their offspring.

Further Reading:

Estes, Richard D. *Behavior Guide to African Mammals.* Berkeley: University of California, 1991.
The Safari Companion. Post Mills, VT: Chelsea Green, 1993.

Spinage, C. A. *The Natural History of Antelopes.* New York: Facts on File, 1986.

Vita Richman

Duilbers see **Antelopes and gazelles**

Dune

A dune is a wind-blown pile of sand. The sand is usually composed of the mineral quartz eroded from rocks, deposited along streams or oceans or lakes, picked up by the wind, and redeposited as dunes. Sand collects and dunes begin to form in places where the wind speed drops suddenly, behind an obstacle such as a rock or bush, for example, and can no longer transport its load of sand. The wind constantly shifts this sand into a myriad of shapes and heights, so one can visit the same dune field year after year and enjoy a new pattern each time. Wind sculpts sand piles into a wide variety of shapes. Among the more common are crescent, linear, and star.

Dunes move as wind bounces sand up the dune's gently-sloping windward side (facing the wind) to the peak of the slope where the wind's speed drops and sends sand cascading down the steeper lee side (downwind). As this process continues, the dune migrates in the direction the wind blows. The steeper lee side of the dune, called the slip face, maintains a 34° angle (called the angle of repose), much greater than the flatter (10° to 12°) windward side. The sand may temporarily build up to an angle greater than 34°, but eventually it avalanches back to the angle of repose. Given enough sand and time, dunes override dunes to thicknesses of thousands of feet, as in the Sahara desert, or as in the fossilized dunes preserved in the sandstone of Zion and Arches National Parks in Utah. In the famous Navajo Sandstone in Zion National Park, crossbeds, sloping bedding planes in the rock, represent the preserved slip faces of 180 million year old former dunes.

Three basic dune shapes—crescent, linear, and star—range in size up to 330 ft (100 m) high and up to a thousand feet long and wide. Barchan and parabolic dunes are crescent-shaped like the letter C. Barchans form where the sand supply is minimal. The two ends of the barchan's crescent point downwind toward the direction the dune moves. In contrast, the pointed ends of a parabolic dune stab into the wind, a mirror image of a barchan. Bushes or some other obstruction anchor the tips of a parabolic dune.

Massive moving dunes engulf a forest in Nags Head, North Carolina.

Transverse and longitudinal dunes form as long, straight, or snake-like ridges. Transverse ridges run perpendicular to a constant wind direction, form with an abundance of sand available, and are asymmetric in cross section (the windward side gently-sloped, the slip face steep). The ridges of longitudinal dunes, however, run parallel to a slightly varying wind direction and are symmetrical in cross section—have slip faces on either side of the ridge. Longitudinal dunes are also known as linear or seif (Arabic for sword) dunes.

Duplication of the cube

Along with squaring the circle and trisecting an angle, duplication of a cube is considered one of the three "unsolvable" problems of mathematical antiquity.

According to tradition, the problem of duplication of the cube arose when the Greeks of Athens sought the assistance of the oracle at Delos in order to gain relief from a devasting epidemic. The oracle told them that to do so they must double the size of the altar of Apollo which was in the shape of a cube.

Their first attempt at doing this was a misunderstanding of the problem: They doubled the length of the sides of the cube. This, however, gave them eight times the original volume since $(2x)^3 = 8\ x^3$.

In modern notation, in order to fulfill the instructions of the oracle, we must go from a cube of side x units to one of y units where $y^3 = 2x^3$, so that $y = \sqrt[3]{2}\ x$.

Thus, essentially, given a unit length, they needed to construct a line segment of length $\sqrt[3]{2}$ units. Now there are ways of doing this but not by using only a compass and an unmarked straight edge—which were the only tools allowed in classical Greek geometry.

Thus there is no solution to the Delian problem that the Greeks would accept and, presumably, the epidemic continued until it ran its accustomed course.

Further Reading:

Stillwell, John. *Mathematics: Its History.* Springer-Verlag, 1991.

Roy Dubisch

Dura mater see **Brain**

Dust devil

A dust devil is a relatively small, rapidly rotating wind that stirs up dust, sand, leaves, and other material as it moves across the ground. Dust devils are also known as whirlwinds or, especially in Australia, willy-willys. In most cases, dust devils are no more than 10 ft (3 m) in width and less than 300 ft (100 m) in height.

Dust devils form most commonly on hot dry days in arid regions such as a desert. They originate when a layer of air lying just above the ground is heated and begins to rise. Cooler air then rushes in to fill the space vacated by the rising column of warm air.

At some point, the rising column of air begins to spin. Unlike much larger storms such as hurricanes and tornadoes, dust devils may rotate either cyclonically or anticyclonically. Their size is such that the Earth's rotation appears to have no effect on their direction of spin, and each direction occurs with approximately equal frequency. The determining factor as to the direction any one dust devil takes appears to be the local topography in which the storm is generated. The presence of a small hill, for example, might direct the storm in a cyclonically direction.

Some large and powerful dust devils have been known to cause property damage. In the vast majority of cases, however, such storms are too small to pose a threat to buildings or to human life.

See also Wind.

Dwarf antelopes

These small antelopes belong to the ruminant family Bovidae, and are grouped with the gazelles in the sub-

A dust devil in Kenya.

family Antilopinae. The 13 species of dwarf antelopes are in the tribe Neotragini. Dwarf antelopes range from extremely small (3.3-4.4 lb or 1.5-2 kg) hare-sized royal antelopes and dik-diks to the medium-sized oribi and beira weighing from 30-50 lb (10-25 kg). Dwarf antelopes engage in territorial scent marking and possess highly developed scent glands. They are browsers, consuming a diet of young green leaves, fruit, and buds. Dwarf antelopes are also usually not dependent upon regular supplies of drinking water for their survival.

The food of the herbivorous dwarf antelope is digested by means of the four-chambered ruminant stomach. Dwarf antelopes browse or graze, consuming vegetation that is nutritionally rich. They lightly chew their food as they tear leaves from branches. After the food is swallowed, it enters the rumen of the stomach. Digestion is then aided by the process of bacteria breaking down nutrients. The food pulp is then regurgitated and chewed as cud to further break down the food before being swallowed and digested more completely.

Habitat

Dwarf antelopes are found in various terrains throughout the sub-Saharan regions of Africa. The klipspringer (*Oreotragus oreotragus*) is found in rocky areas in eastern and southern Africa. Four species of dik-diks are found in dry bush country in the horn of Africa, that is, Somalia and Ethiopia, as is the beira antelope (*Dorcatragus megalotis*). Oribis (*Ourebia ourebi*) are found in the savanna country, from West to East Africa and in parts of southern Africa.

Steenbok (*Raphicerus campestris*) inhabit bushy plains or lightly wooded areas in southern Africa, while the two species of grysbok (*R. melanotis* and *R. sharpei*) are found in stony, hilly areas and scrubby flat country in east-central Africa and the extreme south of the continent. The royal antelope (*Neotragus pygmaeus*) is found in dense forests in West Africa, and Bates' pygmy antelope (*N. batesi*) is found in the forests of the Zaire. Suni antelopes (*N. moschatus*) live in forests along the southeastern edge of Africa.

Characteristics

The horns of dwarf antelopes are short, straight spikes found only in the males, although klipspringer females sometimes have horns. Colorations are usually pale, varying from yellow to gray or brown with a white rump patch, while the steenbok is brick-colored. All dwarf antelopes have well-developed scent glands, particularly preorbital glands which can be easily seen on most species as dark slits beneath the eyes. Dwarf antelopes generally have narrow muzzles, prominent ears, and their nostrils are either hairy or bare.

Dwarf antelopes are territorial and many are in lifetime monogamous relationships. They tend to be solitary even though a mated pair shares the same territory. Territories can range in size from several hundred square feet to tens of acres depending upon the nature of the territory and the density of the group's population. Some monogamous pairs may have a second female, usually a female offspring, that has not left the parental territory. Some dwarf antelope males may have two or more females within a small territory.

Scenting behavior among dwarf antelopes maintains the mating bond and protects the territory from intruders. Males mark their territory with the scent glands found under their eyes (preorbital glands), and on their hooves (pedal glands). They can mark both the ground of their territory, as well as branches and bushes. Additionally, males will scent their mates, which strengthens the ties between them. Ceremonial behavior in dunging is also seen. A pair will follow one another and deposit urine and feces on the same pile.

KEY TERMS

Monogamy—Mating relationship where a male and female tend to become permanently paired.

Preorbital scent glands—Glands located below the eyes that are used to mark territory.

Scenting—Behavior whereby animals make deposits from their scent glands on trees and bushes to mark their territory and their mates.

Males can be aggressive in defending their territories. They have been known to use their sharp horns to wound intruders. Usually, however, male rivals for females will more often only display aggressive behavior to one another before one retreats. The display of aggressive behavior can include pawing the ground, horning, alarm calls, chasing, and pretending to attack.

Parenting

Dwarf antelope females give birth to one offspring at a time, coinciding with seasonal rains. The gestation period is around six months, depending on the species. Infants hide in the grass for several weeks and the mother returns to feed them twice a day. As the fawn grows, it begins to follow the mother. Young females mature by the age of 6-10 months, while males reach maturity around 14 months. Somewhere between 9-15 months, young dwarf antelopes leave the territory to establish themselves on their own.

In klipspringer families, the pair are found close together, on the average 4-15 yd (4-15 m) apart, and the male assumes the role of lookout while the female cares for the offspring. The male may even become involved with feeding the young klipspringer.

See also Antelopes and gazelles; Dik-diks; Gazelles.

Further Reading:

Estes, Richard D. *Behavior Guide to African Mammals.* Berkeley: University of California, 1991.

Estes, Richard D. *The Safari Companion.* Post Mills, Vermont: Chelsea Green, 1993.

Haltenorth, T., and H. Diller. *A Field Guide to the Mammals of Africa.* London: Collins, 1992.

Vita Richman

Dyes and pigments

Color scientists use the term "colorant" for the entire spectrum of coloring materials, including dyes and pigments. While both dyes and pigments are sources of color, they are different from one another. Pigments are particles of color that are insoluble in water, oils, and resins. They need a binder or to be suspended in a dispersing agent to impart or spread their color. Dyes are usually water soluble and depend on physical and/or chemical reactions to impart their color. Generally, soluble colorants are used for coloring textiles, paper, and other substances while pigments are used for coloring paints, inks, cosmetics and plastics. Dyes are also called dyestuffs. The source of all colorants is either organic or inorganic.

Colorants are classified according to their chemical structure or composition (organic or inorganic), method of application, hue, origin (natural or synthetic), dyeing properties, utilization, and, sometimes, the name of the manufacturer and place of origin. The Society of Dyers and Colourists and the American Association of Textile Chemists and Colorists have devised a classification system, called the Color Index, that consists of the common name for the color, and a five-digit identification number.

Organic and inorganic colorants

Organic colorants are made of carbon atoms and carbon-based molecules. Most organic colors are soluble dyes. If an organic soluble dye is to be used as a pigment, it must be made into particle form. Some dyes are insoluble and must be chemically treated to become soluble.

Vegetable-based organic colorants are produced by obtaining certain extracts from the plants. An example of a dye that is not water soluble is indigo. Indigo is derived from plants of the genus Indigofera. By an oxidation process where the plant is soaked and allowed to ferment, a blue-colored, insoluble solid is obtained. To get the indigo dye into solution, a reducing agent (usually an alkaline substance such as caustic soda) is used. The blue dye, after reduction, turns a pale yellow. Objects dyed with indigo react with the air, oxidize, and turn blue. The imparted color is not always that of the dye itself. Animals are another, rather interesting, source of organic colorants. Royal purple, once worn only by royalty as the name suggests, is obtained from the Murex snail. Sepia is obtained from cuttlefish, and Indian yellow is obtained from the urine of cows that have been force- fed mango leaves.

Organic sources of color often have bright, vivid hues, but are not particularly stable or durable. Dyes that are not affected by light exposure and washing are called colorfast, while those that are easily faded are called fugitive. Most organic natural dyes need a fixing agent (mordant) to impart their color.

Inorganic colorants are insoluble, so by definition, they are pigments. This group of colorants is of mineral origin— elements, oxides, gemstones, salts, and complex salts. The minerals are pulverized and mixed with a dispersing or spreading agent. Sometimes heating the minerals produces different hues.

Synthetic colorants

Organic and inorganic colorants can be produced synthetically. Synthetic organic and inorganic colorants are copies of vegetable, animal, and mineral-based colorants, and are made in a laboratory. Until the nineteenth century, all colorants were of natural origin. The first synthetically made commercial colorant, mauve, was developed from aniline, a coal tar derivative, by William Henry Perkins in 1856. Today, chemists arrange and manipulate complex organic compounds to make dyes of all colors. Synthetic dyes, made in a controlled atmosphere, are without impurities and the colors are more consistent from batch to batch. Natural dyes still have some commercial value to craftspeople, but synthetic colorants dominate the manufacturing industry.

Pigments

The color of a pigment is deposited when the spreading agent dries or hardens. The physical property of a pigment does not change when it is mixed with the agent. Some organic dyes can be converted into pigments. For example, dyes that have salt groups in their chemical structure can be made into an insoluble salt by replacing the sodium molecule with a calcium molecule. Dyes that depend on chemical treatment to become soluble such as indigo, can also be used as pigments. Pigments are also classified, in addition to classification mentioned above, by their color—white, transparent, or colored.

Pigments are also used for other purposes than just coloring a medium. Anticorrosive pigments, such as oxides of lead, are added to paint to prevent the rusting of objects made of iron. Metallic pigments such as aluminum, bronze, and nickel are added to paints and plastics for decorative, glittery effects. Pulverized mica produces a sparkle effect and bismuth oxychloride gives a pearlescent appearance to paints and cosmetics.

Luminous pigments have the ability to radiate visible light when exposed to various energy sources. The luminous pigments that emit light after exposure to a light source and placed in the dark are called phosphorescent or commonly, glow-in-the-dark. Phosphorescent pigments are made from zinc or calcium sulfides and other mineral additives that produce the effect. Another good example of how dyes are made into pigments are some of the fluorescent pigments. Fluorescent pigments are those that are so intense that they have a glowing effect in daylight. These pigments are added to various resins, ground up, and used as a pigment. Some fluorescent pigments are illuminated by an ultraviolet light source (black light).

Dyes

Dyes are dissolved in a solution and impart their color by staining or being absorbed. What makes one organic source a dye and another not depends on a particular groups of atoms called chromophores. Chromophores include the azo group, thio group, nitroso group, carbonyl group, nitro group, and azoxy group. Other groups of atoms called auxochromes donate or accept electrons and attach to the dye molecule, enhance the color and increase solubility. Auxochrome groups include amino, hydroxyl, sulfonic, and substituted amino groups.

Other than chemical structure, dyes are classified by their dyeing properties. There are a great number of dyes and a greater number of fibers and materials that incorporate colorants in their manufacture. Certain dyes are used for specific materials depending on the chemical properties of the dye and the physical properties of the material to be dyed, or dyeing properties. Dyeing properties are categorized as basic or cationic, acid and premetalized, chrome and mordant, direct, sulfur, disperse, vat, azoic, and reactive dyes.

Utilization

Every manufactured object is colored by a dye or pigment. There are about 7,000 dyes and pigments, and new ones are patented every year. Dyes are used extensively in the textile industry and paper industry. Leather and wood are colored with dyes. Food is often colored with natural dyes or with a synthetic dye approved by a federal agency. Petroleum-based products such as waxes, lubricating oils, polishes, and gasoline are colored with dyes. Plastics, resins, and rubbers are usually colored by pigments. Dyes are used to stain biological samples, fur, and hair. Special dyes are added to photographic emulsions for color photographs.

See also Paper; Textiles.

Further Reading:

Gottsegen, Mark D. *The Painter's Handbook.* New York: Watson-Guptill Publications, 1992.

Gutcho, M.H. (ed.). *Inorganic Pigments: Manufacturing Processes,* 1980.

Lyttle, Richard B. *Paints, Inks, and Dyes.* New York: Holiday House, 1974.

Christine Miner Minderovic

Dysentery

Dysentery is an infectious disease that has ravaged armies and prisoner-of-war camps throughout history. The disease still is a major problem in tropical countries with primitive sanitary facilities. Refugee camps in Africa resulting from many civil wars are major sinks of infestation for dysentery.

Shigellosis

The acute form of dysentery, called *shigellosis* or bacillary dysentery, is caused by the bacillus (bacterium) of the genus Shigella, which is divided into four subgroups and distributed worldwide. Type A, *Shigella dysenteriae,* is a particularly virulent species. Infection begins from the solid waste from someone infected with the bacterium. Contaminated soil or water that gets on the hands of an individual often is conveyed to the mouth, where the person contracts the infection. Flies help to spread the bacillus.

Young children living in primitive conditions of overcrowded populations are especially vulnerable to the disease. Adults, though susceptible, usually will have less severe disease because they have gained a limited resistance. Immunity as such is not gained by infection, however, since an infected person can become reinfected by the same species of Shigella.

Once the bacterium has gained entrance through the mouth it travels to the lower intestine (colon) where it penetrates the mucosa (lining) of the intestine. In severe cases the entire colon may be involved, but usually only the lower half of the colon is involved. The incubation period is from one to four days, that is the time from infection until symptoms appear.

Symptoms may be sudden and severe in children. They experience abdominal pain or distension, fever, loss of appetite, nausea, vomiting, and diarrhea. Blood and pus will appear in the stool, and the child may pass

20 or more bowel movements a day. Left untreated, he will become dehydrated from loss of water and will lose weight rapidly. Death can occur within 12 days of infection. If treated or if the infection is weathered, the symptoms will disappear within approximately two weeks.

Adults experience a less severe course of disease. They will initially feel a griping pain in the abdomen, develop diarrhea, though without any blood in the stool at first. Blood and pus will appear soon, however, as episodes of diarrhea recur with increasing frequency. Dysentery usually ends in the adult within four to eight days in mild cases and up to six weeks in severe infections.

Shigella dysenteriae brings about a particularly virulent infection that can be fatal within 12-24 hours. The patient has little or no diarrhea, but experiences delirium, convulsions, and lapses into a coma. Fortunately infection with this species is uncommon.

Treatment of the patient with dysentery usually is by fluid therapy to replace the liquid and electrolytes lost in sweating and diarrhea. Antibiotics may be used, but some Shigella species have developed resistance to them, so they may be relatively ineffective. Fluid therapy should be tendered with great care because patients often are very thirsty and will overindulge in fluids if given access to them. A hot water bottle may help to relieve abdominal cramps.

Some individuals can harbor the bacterium without having symptoms. Like those who are convalescent from the disease, the carriers without symptoms can spread the disease. This may occur by someone with improperly washed hands preparing food, which becomes infected with the organism.

Amebic dysentery

Another form of dysentery called amebic dysentery or intestinal amebiasis is spread by a protozoan, *Entamoeba histolytica*. The protozoan occurs in an active form, that which infects the bowel, and an encysted form, that which forms the source of infection. If the patient develops diarrhea the active form of amoeba will pass from the bowel and rapidly die. If no diarrhea is present the amoeba will form a hard cyst about itself and pass from the bowel to be picked up by another victim. Once ingested it will lose its shell and begin the infectious cycle. Amebic dysentery can be waterborne, so anyone drinking infested water that is not purified is susceptible to infection.

Amebic dysentery is common in the tropics and relatively rare in temperate climates. Infection may be so subtle as to be practically unnoticed. Intermittent bouts of diarrhea, abdominal pain, flatulence, and cramping mark the onset of infection. Spread of infection may occur with the organisms entering the liver, so abdominal tenderness may occur over the area of the liver. Because the amoeba invades the lining of the colon, some bleeding may occur, and in severe infections the patient may require blood transfusions to replace that which is lost.

Treatment again is aimed at replacement of lost fluids and the relief of symptoms. Microscopic examination of the stool will reveal the active protozoan or its cysts. Special medications aimed at eradicating the infectious organism may be needed.

An outbreak of amebic dysentery can occur seemingly mysteriously because the carrier of the amoeba may be without symptoms, especially in a temperate zone. This is the person with inadequate sanitation who can spread the disease through food that he has handled. Often the health officials can trace a disease outbreak back to a single kitchen and then test the cooks for evidence of amebic dysentery.

Before the idea of the spread of infectious agents was understood, dysentery often was responsible for more casualties among the ranks of armies than was actual combat. It also was a constant presence among prisoners who often died because little or no medical assistance was available to them. It is still a condition present throughout the world that requires vigilance. Prevention is the most effective means to maintain the health of populations living in close quarters. Hand washing, especially among food preparation personnel, and water purification are the most effective means of prevention. Adequate latrine facilities also help to contain any infectious human waste. A carefully administered packet of water and electrolytes to replace those lost can see a child through the infection.

See also Digestive system.

Larry Blaser

Dyslexia

Dyslexia is a disorder that falls under the broad category of learning disabilities. It is often described as a neurological syndrome in which otherwise normal people have difficulty reading and writing. Frequently, dyslexia is defined by what it is not—dyslexia is not mental retardation, a psychiatric or emotional disorder, or a vision problem. Dyslexia is not caused by poverty, psychological problems, lack of educational opportunities, or laziness; those who are identified as dyslectic have normal or above-normal intelligence, normal eyesight, and tend to come from average families.

There are dozens of symptoms associated with dyslexia. In reading and writing, those with dyslexia may skip words, reverse the order of letters in a word (for instance, writing or reading "was" for "saw"), or drop some letters from a word (for example, reading "run" instead of "running"). They may concoct strange spellings for common words, have difficulty remembering and following sequences (like reciting the alphabet in order), and have cramped, illegible handwriting. There is often a gap between what the person seems to be capable of doing and performance; it's not unusual for a student with dyslexia to earn straight As in science and fail English.

Reading and the brain

Sigmund Freud, the father of modern psychiatry, wrote in 1900 that painful childhood experiences or hatred of one or both parents caused dyslexia. He reasoned that children who could not openly rebel against a harsh mother or father defied their parents by refusing to learn to read. Freud recommended psychoanalysis to resolve such emotional problems.

Today, experts reject the psychoanalytic explanation of dyslexia. It is generally agreed that dyslexia results from a neurological problem in the areas of the brain involved in reading. Several regions of the brain—all located in the brain's left side—have been identified as key processing units for the complicated task of reading and writing. The angular gyrus, Wernicke's area, the frontal lobe's lower portion, and the occipital lobe all seem to play a part in reading. What part of the reading task is processed in each area is not yet clear; even more mysterious is how the brain translates abstract symbols like printed letters into ideas.

Current research supports the notion that specific areas of the brain control reading and writing. Investigators have studied those with brain lesions (abnormal growths such as tumors) in these areas of the brain. Although they had no reading difficulties before the lesion was large enough to detect, patients with brain lesions developed reading problems identical to those associated with dyslexia. Those with dyslexia also tend to have rapid, jerky, hard-to-control eye movements when they read—another indication of a misfire in the brain.

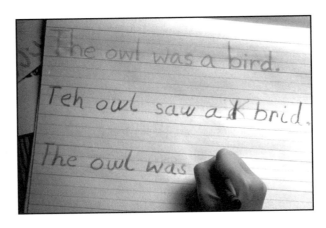

A student with dyslexia has difficulty copying words.

How we read

Reading is a complicated chain of events coordinated in the brain. Imagine a busy, computerized railroad yard: trains pull in on hundreds of tracks from all directions. The cargo of each train is documented in a central tower, then matched with a destination and assigned to one of dozens of tracks. Some trains may be sent to a holding area until their cargo is needed; others may be routed so they can make multiple stops. The computer system must analyze hundreds of pieces of information for each train pulling in, each train pulling out—so even a brief power failure can clog the railroad yard with thousands of trains, blocked from reaching their destination.

Scientists suspect a similar power failure in the brain is the cause of dyslexia. In normal reading, the eye sends pictures of abstract images—the printed word—to the brain. Each symbol is routed to various portions of the brain for processing or storage, symbols are interpreted and combined in combinations that make sense, then transferred to other portions of the brain that recognize the importance of the messages. Sometimes the messages are relayed to the lips, tongue, and jaw—reading aloud—or the fingers and hands—writing.

Investigators have identified three major "tracks" for sending written messages to the brain for interpretation. The phonic route recognizes individual letters and, over time, builds a list of groups of letters that generally appear together. The direct route is a "mental dictionary" of whole words recognized as a unit; the lexical route breaks strings of letters into a base word, prefixes, and suffixes. The lexical route might, for example, break the word "together" into "to-get-her."

The areas of the brain responsible for channeling words along these different routes, processing them, then moving them along as a message that makes sense, coordinate thousands of pieces of information in normal reading. These bits of information are moved through the brain over neurons, the roadways of the nervous system, on neurotransmitters, naturally occurring chemicals that make it possible for messages to travel from one nerve cell to the next. In dyslexia, something jams the signals brain and interferes with the interpretation of the written word.

Causes of dyslexia

Researchers generally agree that genetics play a role in dyslexia. Studies of twins show that if one twin is dyslexic, the other is far more likely to have the disorder. Other studies show that dyslexia, which affects about 8% of the population, tends to run in families. It's common for a child with dyslexia to have a parent or other close relative with the disorder.

Because dyslexia affects males far more often than females (the rate is about three to one), investigators are exploring the relationship of male hormones to dyslexia. Several studies indicate that an excess of the male hormone testosterone prior to birth may slow the development of the left side of the fetus's brain. Other researchers argue, however, that those with dyslexia rarely have problems with spoken language, which is also controlled by the left side of the brain and depends on some of the same areas that control reading and writing.

Treating dyslexia

Those with mild cases of dyslexia sometimes learn to compensate on their own, and many with dyslexia

reach remarkable levels of achievement. Leonardo Da Vinci, the famous Renaissance inventor and artist who painted the Mona Lisa, is thought to have been dyslexic; so was Albert Einstein.

The severity of the disorder, early diagnosis, and prompt treatment seem to be the keys to overcoming the challenges of dyslexia. Linguistic and reading specialists can help those with dyslexia learn how to break reading and writing into specific tasks, how to better remember and apply reading skills, and how to independently develop reading and writing skills. Studies with community college students indicate that intensive sessions with a specialist significantly increase a student's reading and writing skills, and experts believe earlier intervention is even more effective.

Although dyslexia occurs independently, it can spark social, behavioral, and emotional problems. Children with dyslexia may be frustrated by their inability to understand and embarrassed by their "failure" in the classroom. They may perceive themselves as "stupid" and develop problems with self-esteem and motivation.

Future developments

One key in helping those with dyslexia is to better understand exactly how the brain processes the writing, and positron emission tomography (PET) is a promising tool for mapping what the brain does and how it does it. A PET scan tracks the movement and concentrations of a radioactive substance through the brain; it creates images showing which portions of the brain are active and the biochemical reactions that occur when the brain is stimulated. These images may ultimately pinpoint what portions of the brain act when during the process of reading or writing.

Researchers are also exploring the use of various drugs known to affect chemical activity in the brain. Trials using the drug priacetam, for example, have shown some promise, but definite benefits have yet to be documented.

Further Reading:

Facts About Dyslexia. National Institutes of Health, National Institutes of Child Health and Human Development. Washington, DC: U.S. Government Printing Office, 1993 (U.S. Government Printing Office NIH Publication 93-0384-P).

Selikowitz, Mark. *Dyslexia and Other Learning Difficulties: The Facts*. New York: Oxford University Press, 1993.

Ziminsky, Paul C. *In a Rising Wind: A Personal Journey Through Dyslexia*. Lanham: University Press of America, 1993.

A. Mullig

Dysplasia

Dysplasia is a combination of two Greek words; dys- which means difficult or disordered; and plassein, to form. In other words, dysplasia is the abnormal or disordered formation of certain structures. In medicine, dysplasia refers to cells which have acquired an abnormality in their form, size, or orientation with respect to each other.

Dysplasia may occur as the result of any number of stimuli. Sunburned skin, for example, is dysplastic, but will correct itself as the sunburned skin heals itself. Any source of irritation causing inflammation of an area will result in temporary dysplasia. If the source of irritation is removed the dysplasia will rectify itself, and cell structure and organization will return to normal.

Unfortunately, dysplasia can become permanent. This can occur when a source of irritation to a given area cannot be identified and corrected, or for completely unknown reasons. The continually worsening area of dysplasia can develop into an area of malignancy (cancer). A tendency toward dysplasia can be genetic and/or can result from exposure to irritants or toxins, such as cigarette smoke, viruses, or chemicals.

The Pap smear, a medical procedure commonly performed on women, is a test for cervical dysplasia. The degree of dysplasia present in cervical cells can indicate progression to a cancerous condition.

Dysprosium see **Lanthanides**

Dziggetai see **Asses**

e (number)

The number e, like the number pi, is a useful mathematical constant that is the basis of the system of natural logarithms. Its value correct to nine places is 2.718281828... The number e is used in complex equations to describe a process of growth or decay. It is therefore utilized in the biology, business, demographics, physics, and engineering fields.

The number e is widely used as the base in the exponential function $y = Ce^{kx}$. There are extensive tables for e^x, and scientific calculators usually include an e^x key. In calculus one finds that the slope of the graph of e^x at any point is equal to e^x itself, and that the integral of e^x is also e^x plus a constant.

Exponential functions based on e are also closely related to sines, cosines, hyperbolic sines, and hyperbolic cosines: $e^{ix} = \cos x + i\sin x$; and $e^x = \cosh x + \sinh x$. Here I is the imaginary number $\sqrt{-1}$. From the first of these relationships one can obtain the curious equation $e^{i\pi} + 1 = 0$, which combines five of the most important constants in mathematics.

The constant e appears in many other formulae in statistics, science, and elsewhere. It is the base for natural (as opposed to common) logarithms. That is, if $e^x = y$, then $x = \ln y$. (ln x is the symbol for the natural logarithm of x.) ln x and e^x are therefore inverse functions.

The expression $(1 + 1/n)^n$ approaches the number e more and more closely as n is replaced with larger and larger values. For example, when n is replaced in turn with the values 1, 10, 100, and 1000, the expression takes on the values 2, 2.59..., 2.70..., and 2.717....

Calculating a decimal approximation for e by means of the this definition requires one to use very large values of n, and the equations can become quite complex. A much easier way is to use the Maclaurin series for e^x : $e^x = 1 + x/1! + x^2/2! + x^3/3! + x^4/4! + ...$ By letting x equal 1 in this series one gets $e = 1 + 1/1 + 1/2$ + 1/6 + 1/24 + 1/120 + ... The first seven terms will yield a three–place approximation; the first twelve will yield nine places.

See also Logarithms.

Eagles

Eagles are large, diurnal birds of prey in the subfamily Buteonidae, which also includes buzzards and other broad–winged hawks. The buteonids are in the order Falconiformes, along with falcons, osprey, goshawks, and vultures.

Like all of these birds, eagles have strong, raptorial (or grasping) talons, a large, strongly hooked beak, and extremely acute vision. Eagles are broadly distinguished by their great size, large, broad wings, wide tail, and their commonly soaring flight. Their feet are large and strong, armed with sharp claws, and well–adapted for grasping prey. Some species of eagles are uniformly dark–brown colored, while others have a bright, white tail or head. Male and female eagles are similarly colored, but juveniles are generally quite dark. Female eagles are somewhat larger than males.

Species of eagles occur on all of the continents, except for Antarctica. Some species primarily forage in terrestrial habitats, while others are fish–eating birds that occur around large lakes or ocean shores. Eagles are fierce predators, but they also scavenge carrion when it is available.

North American eagles

The most familiar and widespread species of eagle in North America is the bald eagle (*Haliaetus leucocephalus*). Mature bald eagles have a dark–brown body, and a white head and tail. Immature birds are browner, only gradually developing the rich adult plumage, which is complete when the birds are sexually mature at four to five years of age. The bald eagle mostly feeds on fish caught or scavenged in rivers, lakes, and ponds, or in brackish estuaries.

Bald eagles nest on huge platform nests built of sticks, commonly located in a large tree. Because the nests are used from year to year, and new sticks are added each breeding season, they can eventually weigh several tons. Northern populations of bald eagles commonly migrate to the south to spend their non–breeding season. However, these birds are tolerant of the cold, and will remain near their breeding sites as long as there is open water and a dependable source of fish to eat. Other birds may winter south of the breeding range of the species.

The golden eagle (*Aquila chrysaetos*) is an uncommon species in North America, breeding in the northern tundra, in mountainous regions, and in extensively forested areas. The golden eagle also breeds in northern Europe and Asia. This species has dark–brown plumage, and its wingspan is as great as 6.5 ft (2 m). These birds can predate on animals as large as young sheep and goats, but they more commonly take smaller mammals such as marmots and ground squirrels.

Golden eagles nest in a stick nest built onto a large tree, or on a steep cliff. As with the bald eagle, the nest may be used for many seasons, and they can eventually become massive structures. Usually, two to three white–downed eaglets are hatched, but it is uncommon for more than one to survive and fledge. It takes four to five years for a golden eagle to become sexually mature.

Eagles elsewhere

The largest species of eagle is the harpy eagle (*Harpia harpyja*) of tropical forests of South America. This species largely feeds on monkeys and large birds. The Philippine monkey–eating eagle (*Pithecophaga jefferyi*) and New Guinea harpy eagle (*Harpyopsis novaguineae*) are analogous species in Southeast Asia.

The sea eagle or white–tailed eagle (*Haliaetus albicilla*) is a widespread species, breeding in coastal habitats from Greenland and Iceland, through Europe, to Asia. This species has a dark–brown body and white tail. Another fishing eagle (*H. vocifer*) breeds in the vicinity of lakes and large rivers in Africa.

The imperial eagle (*Aquila heliaca*) and spotted eagle (*A. clanga*) are somewhat smaller versions of the golden eagle, breeding in plains, steppes, and other open habitats from central Asia to Spain and northwestern Africa. These birds tend to eat smaller–sized mammals than the golden eagle.

The harpy eagle (*Harpia harpyja*) dwells in the forests of southeastern Mexico, Central America, and South America (as far south as Paraguay and northern Argentina), where it hunts monkeys, sloths, porcupines, reptiles, and large birds. Since it prefers virgin forest, its numbers have decreased wherever there is regular human access to forest habitat.

The short–toed or snake eagle (*Circaetus gallicus*) breeds extensively in mountainous terrain in southern Europe and southwestern Asia. This species feeds on small mammals and snakes. Because it predates on large numbers of poisonous vipers, the short–toed eagle is highly regarded by many people living within its range.

The black eagle (*Ictinaetus malayensis*) is a species of tropical forests, ranging from India and southern China to the Islands of Java and Sumatra in Indonesia.

Eagles and humans

Because of their fierce demeanor and large size, eagles have long been highly regarded as a symbol of power and grace by diverse societies around the world.

Eagles have figured prominently in religion, mythology, art, literature, and other expressions of human culture.

In North America, for example, the bald eagle is an important symbol in many Native American cultures. Many tribes believe that the feathers of this bird have powerful qualities, and they use these to ornament clothing and hats, or will hold a single feather in the hand as a cultural symbol and source of strength. Various tribes of the Pacific coast knew the bald eagle as the "thunder bird," and they accorded it a prominent place on totem poles.

Today, most North Americans regard the bald eagle as a valued species—it is even a national symbol of the United States. However, some consider eagles to be pests. Perhaps believing the birds to be predators of domestic animals such as sheep, or of economically important fish, individuals have killed these birds using guns, traps, or poison. Fortunately, these misguided attitudes are now in an extreme minority—very few people still persecute these magnificent predators.

However, eagles and many other species of raptors are also damaged by other, less direct, human influences. These include the toxic effects of insecticides used in agriculture, some of which accumulate in wild animals and affect them or their reproduction. Eagles have also been poisoned by eating poisoned carcasses set out to kill other scavengers, such as coyotes or wolves. Eagles are also affected detrimentally by ecological changes in their necessary breeding, migrating, and wintering habitats, especially those changes associated with agriculture, urbanization, and forestry.

Because of these and other damaging effects of human activities, most of the world's species of eagles are much less abundant than they were a century or so ago. Many local populations of these magnificent birds are endangered or have actually been extirpated. In more extreme cases of endangerment, some species are at risk of total biological extinction. The monkey–hunting harpy eagle, for example, is an extremely rare bird that requires extensive tracts of tropical rainforest in South America and is believed to be significantly endangered because of its declining populations.

See also Birds of prey.

Further Reading:

Freedman, B. *Environmental Ecology,* 2nd ed. San Diego: Academic Press, 1994.

Gerrard, J. and G. Bortolotti. *The Bald Eagle.* Washington, D.C.: Smithsonian Press, 1988.

Johnsgard, P. A. *Hawks, Eagles, and Falcons of North America: Biology and Natural History.* Washington, D.C.: Smithsonian Press, 1990.

KEY TERMS

Diurnal—Refers to animals that are active during the day.

Extirpated—A situation in which a species formerly occurred in some area, but now only survives elsewhere.

Raptor—A bird of prey. Raptors have feet adaptive for seizing, and a beak designed for tearing.

Savage, C. *Eagles of North America.* New York: Douglas & McIntyre, 1988.

Scholz, F. *Birds of Prey.* Harrisburg, PA: Stackpole Books, 1993.

Bill Freedman

Ear

The human ear is the anatomical structure responsible for hearing and balance. The ear consists of three parts, the outer, middle and inner ears.

Outer ear

The outer ear collects sounds from the environment and funnels them through the auditory system. The outer ear is composed of three parts, the pinna (or auricle), the external auditory canal (or external auditory meatus), and the tympanic membrane (or eardrum).

Pinna

The two flap–like structures on either side of the head commonly called ears are actually the pinnas of the outer ear. Pinnas are skin–covered cartilage, not bone, and are therefore flexible. The lowest portion of the pinna is called the lobe or lobule and is the most likely site for earrings. The pinnas of most humans cannot move, but these structures are very mobile in other mammals, such as cats and dogs.

External auditory canal

The external auditory canal is a passageway in the temporal lobe of the skull which begins at the ear and extends inward and slightly upwards. In the adult

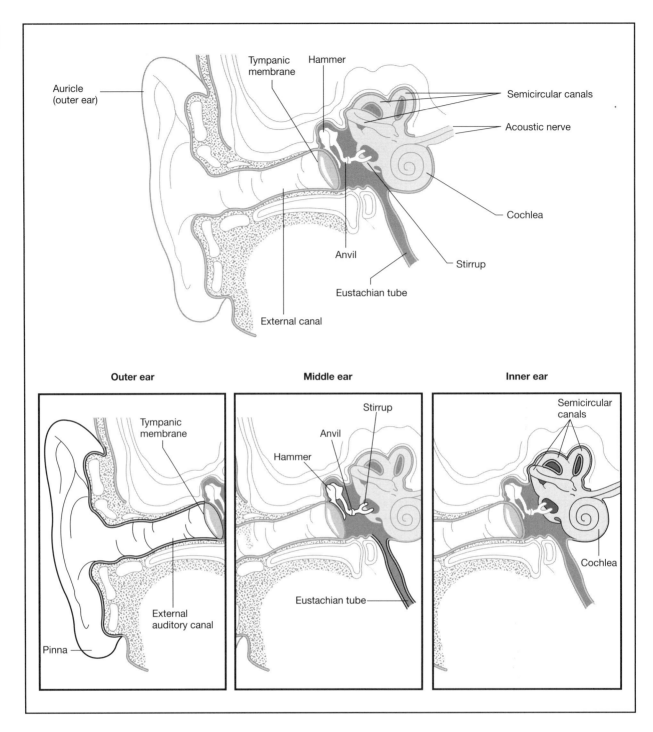

The anatomy of the human ear.

human it is lined with skin and hairs and is approximately one inch (2.5 cm) long.

The outer 1/3 portion of the canal is lined with a membrane containing ceruminous (ear wax producing) cells, and hair cells. The purpose of the cerumen and hairs is to protect the eardrum (which lies at the end of the canal) by trapping dirt and foreign bodies and keep-

ing the canal moist. In most individuals, cleaning of the external auditory canal (with Q–tips for example) is not needed. The inner 2/3rds of the external auditory canal contains no glands or hair cells.

Tympanic membrane/eardrum

The human tympanic membrane or eardrum is a

thin, concave membrane stretched across the inner end of the external auditory canal much like the skin covering the top of a drum. The eardrum marks the border between the outer ear and middle ear. The eardrum serves as a transmitter of sound by vibrating in response to sounds traveling down the external auditory canal, and beginning sound conduction in the middle ear.

In the adult human, the tympanic membrane has a total area of approximately 63 square mm, and consists of three layers which contribute to the membrane's ability to vibrate while maintaining a protective thickness. The middle point of the tympanic membrane (the umbo) is attached to the stirrup, the first of three bones contained within the middle ear.

Middle ear

The middle ear transmits sound from the outer ear to the inner ear. The middle ear consists of an oval, air–filled space approximately 2 cubic cm in volume. The middle ear can be thought of as a room, the outer wall of which contains the tympanic membrane. The back wall, separating the middle ear from the inner ear, has two windows, the oval window and the round window. There is a long hallway leading away from the side wall of the room, known as the eustachian tube. The brain lies above the room and the jugular vein lies below. The middle ear is lined entirely with mucous membrane (similar to the nose) and is surrounded by the bones of the skull.

Eustachian tube

The eustachian tube connects the middle ear to the nasopharynx. This tube is normally closed, opening only as a result of muscle movement during yawning, sneezing, or swallowing. The eustachian tube allows for air pressure equalization, permitting the air pressure in the middle ear to match the air pressure in the outer ear. The most noticeable example of eustachian tube function occurs when there is a quick change in altitude, such as when a plane takes off. Prior to takeoff, the pressure in the outer ear is equal to the pressure in the middle ear. When the plane gains altitude, the air pressure in the outer ear decreases, while the pressure in the middle ear remains the same, causing the ear to feel "plugged." In response to this the ear may "pop." The popping sensation is actually the quick opening and closing of the eustachian tube, and the equalization of pressure between the outer and middle ear.

Bones/ossicles and muscles

Three tiny bones (the ossicles) in the middle ear form a chain which conducts sound waves from the tympanic membrane (outer ear) to the oval window (inner ear). The three bones are the hammer (malleus), the anvil (incus) and the stirrup (stapes). These bones are connected and move as a link chain might, causing pressure at the oval window and the transmission of energy from the middle ear to the inner ear. Sound waves cause the tympanic membrane to vibrate, which sets up vibrations in the ossicles, which amplify the sounds and transmits them to the inner ear via the oval windows.

In addition to bones, the middle ear houses the two muscles, the stapedius and the tensor tympani, which respond reflexively, that is, without conscious control.

Inner ear

The inner ear is responsible for interpreting and transmitting sound (auditory) sensations and balance (vestibular) sensations to the brain. The inner ear is small (about the size of a pea) and complex in shape, where its series of winding interconnected chambers, has been compared to (and called) a labyrinth. The main components of the inner ear are the vestibule, semicircular canals and the cochlea.

Vestibule

The vestibule, a round open space which accesses various passageways, is the central structure within the inner ear. The outer wall of the vestibule contains the oval and round windows (which are the connection sites between the middle and inner ear). Internally, the vestibule contains two membranous sacs, the utricle and the saccule, which are lined with tiny hair cells and attached to nerve fibers, and which serve as the vestibular (balance/equilibrium) sense organs.

Semicircular canals

Attached to the utricle within the vestibular portion of the inner ear are three loop–shaped, fluid filled tubes called the semicircular canals. The semicircular canals are named according to their location ("lateral," "superior" and "posterior") and are arranged perpendicular to each other, like the floor and two corner walls of a box. The semicircular canals are a key part of the vestibular system and allow for maintenance of balance when the head or body rotates.

Cochlea

The cochlea is the site of the sense organs for hearing. The cochlea consists of a bony, snail–like shell which contains three separate fluid–filled ducts or canals. The upper canal, the scala vestibuli, begins at

KEY TERMS

· ·

Auricle—Also called pinna or external ear, is the flap–like organ on either side of the head.

Cerumen—Also known as ear wax, is an oily, fatty fluid secreted from glands within the external auditory canal.

Cochlea—Snail–like structure in the inner ear which contains the anatomical structures responsible for hearing.

Eustachian tube—A passageway leading from the middle ear to the nasopharynx or throat.

External auditory canal—Also called a meatus, is the tunnel or passageway which begins from the external ear and extends inward towards the eardrum.

Organ of Corti—A structure located in the scala media of the cochlea, contains hair cells responsible for hearing.

Ossicles—Three tiny, connected bones located in the middle ear.

Stapedius muscle—A muscle located in the middle ear which reflexively contracts in response to loud sounds.

Tympanic membrane—Also known as the eardrum, is a thin membrane located at the end of the external auditory canal, separates the outer ear from the middle ear.

Vestibular system—System within the body that is responsible for balance and equilibrium.

the oval window, while the lower canal, the scala tympani, begins at the round window. Between the two canals lies the third canal, the scala media. The scala media is separated from the scala vestibuli by Reissner's membrane and from the scala tympani by the basilar membrane. The scala media contains the organ of Corti, (named after the 19th century anatomist who first described it). The organ of Corti lies along the entire length of the basilar membrane. The organ contains hair cells and is the site of the conversion of sound waves into nerve impulses, which are sent to the brain, for auditory interpretation along Cranial Nerve VIII, also known as the Auditory Nerve.

Further Reading:

Mango, Karin. *Hearing Loss*. New York: Franklin Watts, 1991.

Martin, Frederick. *Introduction to Audiology, 4th Ed.* New Jersey: Prentice Hall, 1991.

Mestel, Rosie. "Pinna to the Fore." *Discover*, v.14 (June, 1993): 45–54.

Kate Glynn

Earth

The Earth is our home planet. Its surface is mostly water (about 70%), and it has a moderately dense nitrogen–and–oxygen atmosphere that supports life— the only known life in the Universe. Rich in iron and nickel, the Earth is a dense, rocky ball orbiting the Sun with its only natural satellite, the Moon. A complete revolution of the Earth around the Sun takes about one year, while a rotation on its axis takes one day. The surface of the Earth is constantly changing, as the continents slowly drift about on the turbulent foundation of partially molten rock beneath them. Collisions between landmasses build mountains; erosion wears them down. Slow changes in the climate cause equally slow changes in the vegetation and animals inhabiting a place.

Physical parameters of the earth

The Earth is the third of nine planets in our solar system. It orbits the Sun at a distance of about 93,000,000 miles (150,000,000 km), taking 365.25 days to complete one revolution. Earth is small by planetary standards; with a diameter of 7,921 miles (12,756 km), it is only one–tenth the size of Jupiter. Its mass is 2.108 x 10^{26} oz (about six trillion kg), and it must speed this huge bulk along at nearly 19 miles (30 km) per second to remain in a stable orbit. The mean density of our planet is 5.5 grams per cubic centimeter. Unlike the outer planets, which are composed mainly of light gases, Earth is made of heavy elements such as iron and nickel, and is therefore much denser. These characteristics—small and dense—are typical of the inner four planets, or terrestrial planets.

It was not until 1957, when the first manmade satellite was launched, that humans could see the Earth as a beautiful whole. It seemingly floats in empty space, a world distinguished first by its vast oceans and only secondarily by its landmasses, everywhere draped in white swirls of clouds. This is a planet in the most fragile ecological balance, yet resilient to repeated catastrophe. It is our home, and it bears close examination.

The coastlines of Africa, Antarctica and Arabia are visible in this photo of the Earth taken in December, 1972, by Apollo 17.

The formation of Earth

About 4.5 billion years ago, our Sun was born from a contracting cloud of interstellar gas. The cloud heated as it shrank, until its central part blazed forth as the mature, stable star that exists today. As the Sun formed, the surrounding gas cloud flattened into a disk. In this disk the first solid particles formed and then grew as they accreted additional matter from the surrounding gas. Soon sub–planetary bodies, called planetesimals, built up, and then they collided and merged, forming the planets. The high temperatures in the inner solar system ensured that only the heavy elements, those that form rock and metal, could survive in solid form.

Thus were formed the small, dense terrestrial planets. Hot at first due to the collisions that formed it, Earth began to cool. Its components began to differentiate, or separate themselves according to their density, much as the ingredients in a bottle of salad dressing will separate if allowed to sit undisturbed. To Earth's core went the heavy abundant elements, iron and nickel. Outside the core were numerous elements compressed into a dense but pliable substance called the mantle. Finally, a thin shell of cool, silicon–rich rock formed at Earth's surface: the crust, or lithosphere. Formation of the crust from the initial molten blob took half a billion years.

Earth's atmosphere formed as a result of outgassing of carbon dioxide from its interior, and accretion of gases from space, including elements brought to Earth by comets. The lightest elements, such as helium and most of the hydrogen, escaped to space, leaving behind an early atmosphere consisting of hydrogen compounds such as methane and ammonia as well as water vapor and nitrogen– and sulfur– bearing compounds released by volcanoes. Carbon dioxide was also plentiful, but was soon dissolved in ocean waters and deposited in carbonate rocks. As the gases cooled, they condensed, and rains inundated the planet. The lithosphere was uneven, containing highlands made of buoyant rock such as granite, and basins of heavy, denser basalt. Into these giant basins the rains flowed, forming the oceans. Eventually life forms appeared, and over the course of a billion years, plants enriched the atmosphere with oxygen, finally producing the nitrogen–oxygen atmosphere we have today.

Earth's surface

Land

The lands of our planet are in a constant, though slow, state of change. Landmasses move, collide, and break apart according to a process called plate tectonics. The lithosphere is not one huge shell of rock; it is composed of several large pieces called plates. These pieces are constantly in motion, because Earth's interior is dynamic, with its core still molten and with large–scale convective currents in the upper mantle. The giant furnace beneath all of us moves our land no more than a few centimeters a year, but this is enough to have profound consequences.

Consider North America. The center of the continent is the magnificent expanse of the Great Plains and the Canadian Prairies. Flat and wide is the land around Winnipeg, Topeka, and Amarillo. On the eastern edge, the rolling folds of the Appalachian Mountains grace western North Carolina, Virginia, and Pennsylvania. In the west, the jagged, crumpled Rockies thrust skyward, tall, stark, and snow–capped.

These two great ranges represent one of the two basic land–altering processes: mountain building. Two hundred million years ago, North America was moving east, driven by the restless engine beneath it. In a shattering, slow–motion collision, it rammed into what is now Europe and North Africa. The land crumpled, and the ancient Appalachians rose. At that time, they were the mightiest mountains on Earth. A hundred million years later, North America was driven back west. Now the western edge of the continent rumbled along over the Pacific plate, and about 80 million years ago, a massive spate of mountain building formed the Rockies.

During the time since the Appalachians rose, the other land–altering process, erosion, has been hard at work on them. Battered by wind and water, their once sheer flanks have been worn into the low, rolling hills of today. Eventually they will be gone—and sometime long after that, so will the Rockies.

Mountain building can be seen today in the Himalayas, which are still rising as India moves northward into the underbelly of Asia, crumpling parts of Nepal and Tibet nearly into the stratosphere. Erosion rules in Arizona's Grand Canyon, which gradually is deepening and widening as the Colorado river slices now into ancient granite two billion years old. In time, the Canyon too will be gone.

This unending cycle of mountain building (caused by movement of the crustal plates) and erosion (by wind and water) has formed every part of Earth's surface today. Where there are mountains, as in the long ranks of the Andes or the Urals, there is subterranean conflict. Where a crustal plate rides over another one, burying and melting it in the hot regions below the lithosphere, volcanoes rise, dramatically illustrated by Mt. St. Helens in Washington and the other sleeping giants that loom near Seattle and Portland. Where lands lie wide and arid, they are sculpted into long, scalloped cliffs, as one sees in the deserts of New Mexico, Arizona, and Utah. Without ever being aware of it, we humans spend our lives on the ultimate roller coaster.

Water

Earth is mostly covered with water. The mighty Pacific Ocean covers nearly half the Earth; from the proper vantage point in space one would see nothing but water, dotted here and there with tiny islands, with only Australia and the coasts of Asia and the Americas rimming the edge of the globe.

The existence of oceans implies that there are large areas of the lithosphere that are lower than others. This is because the entire lithosphere rides on a pliable layer of rock in the upper mantle called the asthenosphere. Parts of the lithosphere are made of relatively light rocks, while others are made of heavier, denser rocks. Just as corks float mostly above water while ice cubes float nearly submerged, the less dense parts of the lithosphere ride higher on the asthenosphere than the more dense ones. Earth therefore has huge basins, and early in the planet's history these basins filled with water condensing and raining out of the primordial atmosphere. Additional water was brought to Earth by the impacts of comets, whose nuclei are made of water ice.

The atmosphere has large circulation patterns, and so do the oceans. Massive streams of warm and cold water flow through them. One of the most familiar is the Gulf Stream, which brings warm water up the eastern coast of the United States.

Circulation patterns in the oceans and in the atmosphere are driven by temperature differences between adjacent areas and by the rotation of the Earth, which helps create circular, or rotary, flows. Oceans play a critical role in the overall energy balance and weather patterns of our planet. Storms are ultimately generated by moisture in the atmosphere, and evaporation from the oceans is the prime source of such moisture. Oceans respond less dramatically to changes in energy input than land does, so the temperature over a given patch of ocean is far more stable than one on land.

Earth's atmosphere and weather

Structure of the atmosphere

Earth's atmosphere is the gaseous region above its lithosphere, composed of nitrogen (78% by number), oxygen (21%), and other gases (1%). It is only about 50 miles (80 km) from the ground to space: on a typical, 12–inch (30 cm) globe the atmosphere would be less than two millimeters thick. The atmosphere has several layers. The densest and most significant of these is the troposphere; all weather occurs in this layer, and commercial jets cruise near its upper boundary, 6 miles (10 km) above Earth's surface. The stratosphere lies between 6 and 31 miles (10 and 50 km) above, and it is here that the ozone layer lies. In the mesosphere and the thermosphere one finds aurorae occurring after eruptions on the Sun; radio communications "bounce" off the ionosphere back to Earth, which is why you can sometimes pick up a Memphis AM radio station while you are driving through Montana.

The atmosphere is an insulator of almost miraculous stability. Only 50 miles (80 km) away is the cold of outer space, but the surface remains temperate. Heat is stored by the land and the atmosphere during the day, but the resulting heat radiation (infrared) from the surface is prevented from radiating away by gases in the atmosphere that trap infrared radiation. This is the well–known greenhouse effect, and it plays an important role in the atmospheric energy budget. It is well for us that Earth's climate is this stable. A global temperature decrease of two degrees could trigger the next advance of the current ice age, while an increase of three degrees could melt the polar ice caps, submerging every coastal city in the world.

Weather

Despite this overall stability, the troposphere is nevertheless a turbulent place. It is in a state of constant circulation, driven by Earth's rotation as well as the constant heating and cooling that occurs during each 24–hour period.

The largest circulation patterns in the troposphere are the Hadley cells. There are three of them in each hemisphere, with the middle, or Ferrel cell, lying over the latitudes spanned by the continental United States.

Northward–flowing surface air in the Ferrel cell is deflected toward the east by the Coriolis force, with the result that winds—and weather systems—move from west to east in the middle latitudes of the northern hemisphere.

Near the top of the troposphere are the jet streams, fast–flowing currents of air that circle the Earth in sinuous paths. If you've ever taken a commercial plane flight, you have experienced the jet stream: eastbound flights get where they are going much faster than westbound flights.

Circulation on a smaller scale appears in the cyclones and anticyclones, commonly called low and high pressure cells. Lows typically bring unsettled or stormy weather, while highs mean sunny skies. Weather in most areas follows a basic pattern of alternating pleasant weather and storms, as the endless progression of highs and lows, generated by Earth's rotation and temperature variation, passes by. This is a great simplification, however, and weather in any given place may be affected, or even dominated, by local features. The climate in Los Angeles is entirely different from that in Las Vegas, though the two cities are not too far apart. Here, local features—specifically, the mountains between them—are as important as the larger circulation patterns.

Beyond the atmosphere

Earth has a magnetic field that extends tens of thousands of kilometers into space and shields Earth from most of the solar wind, a stream of particles emitted by the Sun. Sudden enhancements in the solar wind, such as a surge of particles ejected by an eruption in the Sun's atmosphere, may disrupt the magnetic field, temporarily interrupting long–range radio communications and creating brilliant displays of aurorae near the poles, where the magnetic field lines bring the charged particles close to the Earth's surface.

Farther out, at a mean distance of about 248,400 miles (400,000 km), is the Earth's only natural satellite, the Moon. Some scientists feel that the Earth and the Moon should properly be considered a "double planet," since the Moon is larger relative to our planet than the satellites of most other planets.

Life

The presence of life on Earth is, as far as we know, unique. Men have walked on the Moon, and it seems certain there is no life on our barren, airless satellite. Unmanned spacecraft have landed on Venus and Mars and have flown close to every other planet in the solar

KEY TERMS

. . . .

Core—The innermost layer of Earth's interior. The core is composed of molten iron and nickel, and it is the source of Earth's magnetic field.

Erosion—One of the two main processes that alter Earth's surface. Erosion, caused by water and wind, tends to wear down surface features such as mountains.

Mantle—The thick layer of Earth's interior between the core and the crust.

Mountain–building—One of the two main processes that alter Earth's surface. Mountain–building occurs where two crustal plates collide and crumple, resulting in land forms thrust high above the surrounding terrain.

Lithosphere—The outermost layer of Earth's interior, commonly called the crust. The lithosphere is broken into several large plates that move slowly about. Collisions between the plates produce mountain ranges and volcanism.

Terrestrial planet—The term used to describe the four inner, earthlike planets of the solar system. Earth is the largest terrestrial planet.

Troposphere—The lowest layer of Earth's atmosphere, where all weather occurs. The troposphere is about 6 miles (10 km) thick.

system except Pluto. The most promising possibility, Mars, yielded nothing to the automated experiments performed by the Viking spacecraft that touched down there.

The origin of life on Earth is not understood, but a promising experiment was performed in 1952 that may hold the secret. Stanley Miller and Harold Urey simulated conditions in Earth's early oceans, reproducing the surface and atmospheric conditions thought to have existed more than three billion years ago. A critical element of this experiment was simulated lightning in the form of an electric arc. Miller and Urey found that under these conditions, amino acids, the essential building blocks of life, had formed in their primitive "sludge." Certainly this was a long way from humans—or even an amoeba—but the experiment proved that the early Earth may have been a place where organic compounds, the compounds found in living creatures, could form.

Life has existed on dry land only for the most recent 10% of Earth's history, since about 400 million years ago. Once life got a foothold beyond the oceans, however, it spread rapidly. Within 200 million years

forests spread across the continents and the first amphibians evolved into dinosaurs. Mammals became dominant after the demise of the dinosaurs 65 million years ago, and only in the last 2 million years—0.05% of Earth's history—have humans come on the scene.

See also Africa; Asia; Antarctica; Atmosphere, composition and structure of; Australia; Cartography; Continental drift; Earth science; Earth's interior; Earth's magnetic field; Earth's rotation; Earthquake; Europe; Geologic time; Geology; Hydrologic cycle; Lithosphere; Moon; North America; Ocean; Paleontology; Planet; Plate tectonics; South America; Solar system; Sun; Volcano.

Further Reading:

Ballard, R. D. *Exploring Our Living Planet.* Washington, D.C.: National Geographic Society, 1983.
Beatty, J., and A. Chaikin. *The New Solar System.* Cambridge: Cambridge, 1991.
"The Dynamic Earth," special issue. *Scientific American,* 249 (September 1983): 46-78+.

Jeffrey C. Hall

Earth hares see **Jerboas**

Earthquake

An earthquake is a geological event inside the Earth that generates strong vibrations. When the vibrations reach the surface, the Earth shakes, often causing damage to natural and manmade objects, and sometimes killing and injuring people and destroying their property. Earthquakes can occur for a variety of reasons, however, the most common source of earthquakes is movement along a fault.

Causes of earthquakes

Plate collisions

Some earthquakes happen when plates, large sections of the Earth's crust and upper mantle, move past each other like opposite lanes of traffic. Earthquakes along the San Andreas and Hayward faults in California occur because of this. Earthquakes also occur if one plate overruns another, as on the western coast of South America, the northwest coast of North America, and in Japan. If plates collide but neither is overrun, as they do from Spain to Vietnam across Eurasia, earthquakes

Earthquake damage in Alaska. The elongated area of downthrown land between the two parallel faults is called a graben.

result as the plates' rocks compress into high mountain ranges. In all three of these settings, the earthquakes result from movement along faults.

Gravity's effect on fault blocks

A fault block may also move due to gravity, sinking between other fault blocks that surround and support it. Sinking fault blocks and the mountains that surround them form a distinctive topography of basins and mountain ranges. This type of fault block topography is typified by the North American Basin and Range province. In such places, every foot of elevation lost by the valleys as they sink between the mountains is accompanied by some kind of tremor or earthquake. Another kind of mountain range born amid earthquakes rises because of an active thrust fault. Tectonic compression (*tectonic* = having to do with the forces that deform the rocks of planets) shoves the range up a natural ramp—the active thrust fault.

Igneous activity

Molten rock, called magma, moves beneath the Earth's surface in volcanically active regions. Earth-quakes sometimes accompany volcanic eruptions as huge masses of magma move underground.

Explosions

Nuclear bombs exploding underground cause small local earthquakes, which can be felt by people standing within a few miles of the test site. The earthquakes caused by nuclear bombs are tiny when compared with natural earthquakes, but have a distinctive "sound," and their location can be pinpointed. This is how nuclear bomb testing in one country can be monitored by other countries around the world.

Faults and fault mechanics

The Earth is covered by a crust of solid rock, which is broken into numerous plates that move around on the surface, bumping into each other, overrunning each other, and pulling away from each other. One kind of boundary between rocks within a plate, as well as at the edges of the plates, is a *fault*.

A crack in a rock lying loose on the surface is not a fault. Faults are breaks in the Earth's crust, in which the rock on one side of the fault has been moved parallel to the rock on the other side of the fault by tectonic forces. *Fault blocks* are large to giant pieces of crust that are separated from the rocks around them by faults.

When the forces pushing on the fault blocks cannot move one block past the other, *potential energy* is stored up in the fault zone. (This is the same potential energy that a giant boulder holds when it is poised, motionless, at the top of a steep slope. If something happens to overcome the friction holding the boulder in place, its potential energy will convert into *kinetic energy* as it thunders down the slope.) In the fault zone, the potential energy builds up until the friction that sticks the fault blocks together is overcome. Then, in seconds, all the potential energy built up over the years turns to kinetic energy as the rocks surge past each other.

The snapping and shattering vibrations of a fault block on the move can be detected by delicate instruments in rocks on the other side of the planet. Although this happens on a grand scale, it is remarkably like pushing on a stuck window or sliding door. Friction holds the window or door stuck in its tracks. Once enough force is applied to overcome the friction, the window or door jerks open.

Some fault blocks are stable, no longer experiencing the forces that moved them in the first place. The fault blocks that face each other across an *active fault*, however, are still influenced by tectonic forces in the ever–moving crust. They grind past each other parallel to the fault as they move in different directions.

Fault blocks can move in a variety of ways, which helps define the different types of faults. In a vertical fault, one block moves upwards compared to the other. For example, at the surface of the Earth, a vertical fault would form a cliff, known as a *fault scarp*. The sheer eastern face of the Sierra Nevada is a fault scarp. In most vertical faults, the fault scarp is not vertical, so that one of the fault blocks "hangs" over the other. This upper block is then called the hanging wall and the lower block, the foot wall.

In horizontal faults, the blocks slide past one another without either block being lifted upwards. In this case the objects on the two sides of the fault would simply slide past one another, for example, a road might be offset by tens of feet. Of course, some faults blocks display complex movements that involve both vertical and horizontal displacement, these are called complex faults.

Any one of the following fault types can generate an earthquake:

Normal fault—A vertical fault in which the hanging wall moves down compared to the foot wall.

Reverse fault—A vertical fault in which the hanging wall moves up compared to the foot wall.

Thrust fault—A low–angle (less than 30°) reverse fault, similar to an inclined floor or ramp. The lower fault block is the ramp itself, and the upper fault block is gradually shoved up the ramp. The "ramp" may be shallow or steep, or even curved, but the motion of the upper fault block is always in an "uphill" direction (the fault is underground and "uphill direction" has nothing to do with hills on the surface). A thrust fault caused the January 1994 earthquake in Los Angeles.

Strike–slip (or transform) fault—A fault along which one fault block moves horizontally (sideways), past another fault block——like opposing lanes of traffic. The San Andreas fault is one of the best known of this type.

The motion of earthquakes: seismic waves

When a falling rock splashes into a motionless pool of water, waves move out from the point of impact. These waves appear at the interface of water and air as circular ripples. But the waves occur below the surface, too, traveling down into the water in a spherical pattern. In rock, as in water, a wave–causing event makes not one wave, but a number of waves, moving out from their source one after another, like an expanding bubble.

Tectonic forces shove bodies of rock inside the earth, perhaps displacing a mountain range several feet in a few seconds, and generate tremendous vibrations called seismic waves. The earthquake's *focus* (also called the *hypocenter*) is the point (usually in the subsurface) where the sudden sliding of one rock mass parallel to a fault releases the stored potential energy of the fault zone. The first shock wave emerges at the surface at a point typically directly above the focus, called the *epicenter*. Seismometers detect seismic waves that reach the surface. Seismographs (devices which record seismic phenomena) record the times of arrival for each group of vibrations on a *seismogram* (a recording, either paper or digital).

Like surfaces in an echoing room that reflect or absorb sound, the boundaries of rock types within the earth change or block the direction of movement of seismic waves. Waves moving out from the earthquake's focus in an ever–expanding sphere become distorted, bent, and reflected. Seismologists (geologists who study seismic phenomena) analyze the distorted patterns made by seismic waves, searching through the data for clues about the Earth's internal structure.

Differing kinds of earthquake–generated waves, moving at different speeds, arrive at the surface in a particular order, one after another. The successive waves that arrive at a single site are called a *wave train*. Seismologists compare information about wave trains that are recorded passing through a number of data–collecting sites after an earthquake. By doing this, they can pinpoint the map location and depth, of the earthquake's focus.

These are the most important types of seismic waves:

P–waves—The fastest waves, these compress and stretch the rock in their path through the Earth, moving at about 4 miles (6.4 km) per second.

S–waves—As they move through the Earth, these waves move the rock in their path up and down and side to side, moving at about 2 miles (3.2 km) per second.

Rayleigh waves and Love waves—These two types of "surface waves" are named after seismologists. Moving at less than 2 miles (3.2 km) per second, they lag behind P–waves and S–waves—but cause the most damage. Rayleigh waves causes the ground surface in their path to ripple with little waves. Love waves move in a zigzag along the ground, and can wrench buildings from side to side.

The relative size of earthquakes is measured by the Richter Scale, which compares the energy an earthquake releases to the energy released by other earthquakes. Each whole number increase in value on the Richter scale indicates ten–fold increase in the energy released and a thirty–fold increase in ground motion. Therefore, an earthquake of 8 on the Richter scale is ten times more powerful than an earthquake with a value of 7, which is ten times more powerful than an earthquake with a value of 6. Another scale—the Modified Mercalli Scale—compares the surface effects of earthquakes to each other. It is called an intensity scale.

Hazards of earthquakes

Collapse of architectural structures

Earthquakes would not affect humans significantly if humans did not live in the heavy, flimsy structures we call buildings. To build a house or tower under normal conditions, the construction materials need only to be stacked up and balanced. Buildings are not designed to accelerate rapidly and change directions, like ships or trains. And because noticeable earthquakes do not happen every day, people do not commonly recognize that the objects and buildings around them represent potential mortal danger. Therefore, it is not movement of the ground surface alone that kills people. Instead, deaths from earthquakes result from the collapse of buildings and the things in them. The architectural style whose

collapse causes the most fatal injuries in earthquakes is traditional unreinforced brick, stone, or concrete-walled buildings.

Additional small earthquakes, called *aftershocks*, may cause even more injury and death. An aftershock may not exert enough force to knock down an undamaged building. But it can tumble down a building that the main shock left on the verge of collapse.

The most shock–resistant permanent building is a low wooden structure, anchored to a concrete foundation, and sheathed with thick plywood. Some of the traditional architecture of Japan approximates this shock–resistant design, including wooden buildings more than a thousand years old. Unfortunately, wood and paper houses are highly flammable. Even with many relatively shock–resistant structures, earthquakes have repeatedly killed tens of thousands of people in Japan. Both unreinforced masonry and shock–resistant wood houses are used by different cultures in areas of high earthquake risk. Apparently, the mere fact that a culture has lived in earthquake country for thousands of years does not make them any more prepared to deal with earthquakes than anyone else. In addition, no matter how well prepared a population is, there is no way to protect everyone in an earthquake.

Active faults lie under many parts of the world that do not commonly experience earthquakes. The crust under such places as Italy, California, and Central America moves often enough that an earthquake there, although still unpredictable, is not entirely unexpected. But other populated areas, such as the U.S. east coast and Mississippi valley, are periodically hit by earthquakes just as big as any "earthquake–prone" part of the world.

Landslide

Sometimes a mass of rock or soil perches precariously on a slope, the way you might sit unsteadily on a steep pile of loose gravel. If someone pushed you, you would start sliding downhill, unable to stop yourself. When an earthquake shock strikes an unsteady mass of rock or soil, the potential energy of the unsteady mass turns into unstoppable kinetic energy. An entire hill or mountainside can overrun the land below it within a few hundred seconds, spreading out into the valley or plain, sometimes behaving like a liquid. Large landslides move so much mass that no human agency can do anything to stop them. Besides, landslides happen so quickly and unexpectedly, that even if it were possible for humans to hold up a mountainside on the move, there would not be sufficient time to apply this technology before the event was over.

The only way to minimize the danger of landslides is for people not to live and work beneath hills or mountains where an unstable geologic setting has stored up potential energy. Local governments can make zoning regulations to prevent development on or under potentially unstable hillsides. Locating such dangerous places requires extensive, neighborhood–scale geological field work as part of an *active disaster policy*. But such costly measures find little support from geologically uninformed populations.

Landslides can reshape the landscape significantly. In 1959, an earthquake triggered a landslide that dammed the Madison river in Montana, creating Hebgen Lake. To prevent this accidental natural dam from washing out and causing catastrophic floods, the U.S. Army Corps of Engineers hastily installed a spillway through the landslide material. This enabled them to control the release of the water from the new lake. Prehistoric landslides have dammed the Columbia River, and could be the source of a legend of the Northwest Indians. In this legend, tribes walked across the Columbia River on a bridge of land to meet each other. Such an event today would greatly disrupt the economy of the U.S. Northwest.

Liquefaction of soil

Violent shaking changes sediments such as clay or sand into a liquid–like mass that will not support heavy loads, such as buildings. This phenomenon, called liquefaction, causes much of an earthquake's violence. Downtown Mexico City rests on the old lakebed of Lake Texcoco. In the Mexico City earthquake of 1985, the wet clay ground beneath tall buildings turned to slurry, as if the buildings stood on the surface of a huge bowl of vibrating gelatin. Most of the 10,000 people who died that day died in buildings that collapsed as their foundations sank into liquified clay.

Jets of sand or clay sometimes burst from the ground during an earthquake. These *sand geysers* or *mud volcanoes* happen when formations of soft, wet sediment, liquified by seismic vibration, get forcefully squeezed out of cracks in the ground. They have no relation to real geysers or volcanoes, and cause insignificant damage.

Subsidence

In the sudden rearrangement of fault blocks in the Earth's crust that cause an earthquake, the elevation of a land surface (the dropped–down side of the fault) can fall several feet. On a populated coastline, this can wipe out a city. Port Royal, on the south shore of Jamaica, subsided several feet in an earthquake in 1692, and suddenly disappeared as the sea rushed into the new depression. Eyewitnesses recount the seismic destruc-

tion of the infamous pirate anchorage: "…in the space of three minutes, Port–Royall, the fairest town of all the English plantations, exceeding of its riches,…was shaken and shattered to pieces, sunk into and covered, for the greater part by the sea….The earth heaved and swelled like the rolling billows, and in many places the earth crack'd, open'd and shut, with a motion quick and fast…in some of these people were swallowed up, in others they were caught by the middle, and pressed to death….The whole was attended with…the noise of falling mountains at a distance, while the sky…was turned dull and reddish, like an glowing oven."

Ships arriving later in the day found a small shattered remnant of the city still above the water. Charts of the Jamaican coast soon appeared printed with the words *Port Royall Sunk*.

In the New Madrid (Missouri) earthquake of 1811, a large area of land subsided around the bed of the Mississippi River in west Tennessee and Kentucky. The Mississippi was observed to flow backwards as it filled the new depression, to create what is now known as Reelfoot Lake.

The last great earthquake in the U.S. Pacific Northwest occurred two years before Port Royal sank, in 1690. In the three hundred years since then, no major earthquake has released the potential energy that has been building under the crust. Without major earthquakes to remind them of the danger, city leaders have been slow to adopt earthquake–hazard building codes. Geologists have found ancient low–lying environments that were periodically buried by catastrophic floods along the coast. Knowing this, a logical conclusion would be that such events will happen again. Some towns on the estuaries of northwest coast rivers are built entirely on previously annihilated landscapes. In addition, Seattle, Vancouver, Portland, and Tacoma could be severely damaged by sudden flooding following earthquake–related down-dropping. These cities contain many buildings built of unreinforced masonry (the kind of construction that turns into a low pile of rubble when shaken violently), or pier–and–beam towers, where metal bolts can shear, causing a tall building to collapse into a stack of concrete slabs (called *pancaking*). A regional flood, due to subsidence or a tsunami, might prevent the success of rescue operations for people trapped in the rubble.

Tsunami

An earthquake beneath the ocean may instantly change the volume of an ocean basin as part of the ocean floor rises or drops. This makes a giant wave, called a *tsunami* or *seismic sea wave*. The tsunami crosses the deep ocean, only detectable on the surface as a low swell (a wave with no crest). Where the ocean becomes shallow near the shore, however, the giant wave no longer fits in the sea—but it has to go somewhere. The fast–moving tsunami rises out of the sea and strikes the shore with unstoppable force. Just before it hits, the sea sometimes retreats from the shore. In a small, mountain–ringed bay, a tsunami can rush hundreds of feet up a sea–facing mountainside, scraping off all the trees and soil. A wall of water forms when a large tsunami enters straight into a shallow bay or estuary, and can move upriver for many miles. Sometimes tsunamis are mistakenly referred to as tidal waves, because they resemble a tide–related wave called a tidal bore.

The most destructive tsunamis in history, caused by earthquakes or volcanic eruptions, have killed tens of thousands of people. The coastal towns eradicated in these disasters had no topographic barriers between them and the energy source, and had no warning. For this reason, seacoast dwellers everywhere should learn about the risk of tsunamis in their area and know where to go to seek refuge in case one occurs. Building a breakwater to divert a tsunami and expend its energy is an option for otherwise unprotected coastal towns.

Secondary hazards: fire, disease, famine

Cities depend on networks to distribute water, power, food, and to remove sewage and waste. These networks, whether power lines, water mains, or roads, are easily damaged by earthquakes. Elevated freeways collapse readily, as demonstrated by the San Francisco Bay Bridge in 1989 and Kobe's National Highway Number 2 in 1995. The combination of several networks breaking down at once multiplies the damage done to lives and property. Live power lines fall into water from broken water mains, creating a deadly electric shock hazard. Fires may start at ruptured gas mains, or chemical storage tanks. Although emergency services are needed more than ever, many areas may not be accessible to fire trucks and other emergency vehicles. If the water mains are broken, there will be no pressure at the fire hydrants, and the firefighters' hoses are useless. The great fire that swept San Francisco in 1906 could not be stopped by regular firefighting methods. Only dynamiting entire blocks of buildings could halt the fire's progress. Both Tokyo and Yokohama burned after the Kwanto earthquake struck in 1923, and 143,000 people died, mostly in the fire.

Famine and epidemic disease quickly strike large displaced populations deprived of their usual food distribution system, sanitation services, and clean water. Furthermore, collapsed hospitals may be of no use to a stricken community that urgently needs medical services. After an earthquake, relief operations commonly include inoculation against infectious diseases. In countries that do not have sufficient organization or resources to handle the earthquake–generated refugee population, more people may die of secondary causes than those killed during the earthquake. Even in the most prepared countries, the disruption of networks may prevent relief operations from working as planned for a considerable time. In the aftermath of the January, 1995, earthquake in Kobe, Japan, plans for emergency relief made before the disaster did not work as well as planned. The population, wary of the danger of aftershocks, had to live outdoors in winter, without food, water, or power.

Incidence of earthquakes

Popular doomsayers excite uncomprehending fear by saying that earthquakes happen more frequently now than in former times, which can only result in the end of the world in the near future. It is true that more people than ever are at risk from earthquakes—but this is because the world's population grows larger every year, and so more people are living in earthquake prone areas—not because earthquakes are more frequent.

Today, sensitive seismometers "hear" every noteworthy earth–shaking event, recording it on a seismogram. These results become available on the worldwide information net within minutes of the earthquake. News agencies can report the event the same day. The reason that there seem to be so many earthquakes now is that people are now able to know of every earthquake that happens anywhere on Earth. And the Earth experiences a lot of earthquakes—the planet never ceases to vibrate with the motion of its tectonic forces. It has been resounding with the violence of earthquakes for more than four billion years. Earthquakes are a way of knowing that the planet beneath us is still experiencing normal operating conditions, full of heat and kinetic energy, and is nowhere near a stopping point.

Catastrophic earthquakes happened just as often in the past as they do today. Earthquakes shattered stone–walled cities in the ancient world, sometimes hastening the end of a civilization. Knossos, Chattusas, and Mycenae, capitals of countries located in tectonically active mountain ranges, fell to pieces and were eventually deserted. Scribes have documented earthquakes in the chronicles of ancient realms. An earthquake is recorded in the Bible's Book of Zechariah, and the apostle Paul wrote that he got out of jail when the building fell apart around him in an earthquake. Without international news services, only a few people from other regions ever heard the story of an earthquake. Only a few handwritten accounts have survived, giving

KEY TERMS

Active fault—A fault where movement has been known to occur.

Aftershock—A smaller earthquake that follows the most powerful earthquake, which originates from the same place.

Epicenter—The location where the seismic waves of an earthquake first appear on the surface, usually almost directly above the *focus*.

Fault—A crack running through rock that is the result of tectonic forces.

Fault block—A mass of rock whose boundaries are faults. Active, or moving fault blocks are one cause of earthquakes.

Fault scarp—A cliff that forms as one fault block moves up or down in relation to another.

Focus—The underground location of the seismic event that causes an earthquake. Also called the earthquake's *hypocenter*.

Foot wall—The fault block, in a vertical fault, which supports the overlying (hanging) block.

Foreshock—A small earthquake, or tremor, that precedes a larger earthquake shock.

Hanging wall—The fault block, in a vertical fault, which is supported by or rests on, the underlying block. This block "hangs" over the block below.

Horizontal fault—A fault in which fault blocks slide past one another without either block being lifted upwards.

Modified Mercalli scale—A scale used to compare earthquakes based on the effects they cause.

Normal fault—A vertical fault in which the hanging wall moves down compared to the foot wall.

Reverse fault—A vertical fault in which the hanging wall moves up compared to the foot wall.

Richter scale—A scale used to compare earthquakes based on the energy released by the earthquake.

Seismic gap—A fault zone where seismologists believe seismic activity should be occurring but it is not, that is, a fault zone where large amounts of seismic energy are being stored, rather than periodically released.

Seismic waves—P waves, S waves, and surface waves are vibrations in rock and soil that transfer the force of the earthquake from the focus into the surrounding area.

Strike–slip fault—A fault along which one fault block moves horizontally, (sideways) past another fault block—like opposing lanes of traffic, with the lane going one way stalled and the lane going the other way moving past it in the opposite direction.

Subsidence—The sinking of the land surface, due to the repositioning of fault blocks during an earthquake.

Thrust fault—A low–angle (less than 30°) reverse fault, similar to an inclined floor or ramp. The lower fault block is the ramp itself, and the upper fault block is gradually shoved up the ramp.

Vertical fault—fault in which one fault block moves upwards compared to the other.

---

us limited knowledge of earthquakes in antiquity. Thus, because of lost data, earthquakes seem to have been less common in ancient times than today. But in China, home of the first seismometer, the Imperial government has recorded earthquakes for over a thousand years. Their frequency has not changed through the ages.

Earthquakes were not remarkable phenomena to people in the ancient world—they knew all about them. Earthquakes happened, some cultures believed, when a god or spirit grew angry with the people who existed to mollify it. If they had not done enough to make the supernatural being happy, then the spirit would shake their houses down on top of them. In a dramatic discovery on the island of Crete, archaeologists found the bodies of priests and priestesses killed in an earthquake more than three thousand years ago. Their stone temple shook to pieces even as they offered a man as a human sacrifice—perhaps a rushed ceremony to calm spirits that had rumbled under the mountains only minutes before. In Japan, earthquakes occur so commonly that popular cartoons were printed about them. One cartoon shows a displaced population vengefully attacking the giant catfish that caused earthquakes by peevishly flopping around underground while the god who controlled it was distracted.

Predicting earthquakes

Whether shamans or geologists are performing the service, earthquakes have been predicted throughout human history. Geologists today implore governments to act to prevent needless deaths before the inevitable release of stresses within the Earth's crust causes the next earthquake.

Ultrasensitive instruments placed across faults at the surface can measure the slow, almost imperceptible movement of fault blocks, which tell of great potential energy stored at the fault boundary. In some areas, *foreshocks*, that is small earthquakes that precede a larger event, may help seismologists predict the larger event. In other areas, where seismologists believe seismic activity should be occurring but it is not, this *seismic gap* may be used instead to predict an inevitable large–scale earthquake.

Other instruments measure additional fault–zone phenomena which seem to be related to earthquakes. The rate at which radon gas issues from rocks near a fault has been observed to change before an earthquake. The properties of the rocks themselves have been observed to change, such as their ability to conduct electricity, as the tectonic force exerted upon them slowly alters the rocks of the fault zone between earthquakes. Peculiar animal behavior has been reported before many earthquakes, and research into this phenomenon is a legitimate area of scientific inquiry, even though no definite answers have been found.

Seismologists must make a hard choice when their data interpretations suggest an earthquake is about to happen. If they fail to warn a population of danger they strongly suspect is imminent, many people might die needlessly. But if a population is evacuated from potentially dangerous areas, and no earthquake happens, then people will lose confidence in the seismologists. The next time the seismologists felt an earthquake was coming, perhaps members of the public might not heed their warnings.

As more is discovered about how and why earthquakes occur in an area, that knowledge can be used to prevent the conditions that allow earthquakes to cause harm. The most effective way to minimize the hazards of earthquakes is to build buildings or refit old ones to withstand the short, high–speed acceleration of earthquake shocks. Inhabitants of areas potentially threatened by landslides or tsunamis can be bought out by an economically sound local government.

Geophysical events, however, do not usually excite voters to protect themselves until after the event is over. Sociologists have found that geologically–informed populations are much more likely to demand that their government act to prevent earthquake hazards.

See also Continental drift; Fault; Mass wasting; Plate tectonics; Seismograph; Subsidence.

Earth science

Earth science is the study of the physical components of the Earth—its water, land, and air—and the processes that influence them. As such, Earth science is concerned with not just the solid Earth, but also the atmosphere and the oceans. This distinguishes Earth science from geology. Earth science can also be thought of as the study of the five physical spheres of Earth: atmosphere (gases), lithosphere (rock), pedosphere (soil and sediment), hydrosphere (liquid water), and cryosphere (ice). As a result, Earth scientists must consider interactions between all three states of matter—solid, liquid, and gas—when performing investigations. The subdisciplines of Earth science are many, and include the geosciences, oceanography, and the atmospheric sciences.

The geosciences involve studies of the solid part of Earth and include geology, geochemistry, and geophysics. Geology is the study of Earth materials and processes. Geochemistry examines the composition and interaction of Earth's chemical components. Geophysicists study the dynamics of Earth and the nature of interactions between its physical components.

Oceanography involves the study of all aspects of the oceans: chemistry, water movements, depth, topography, etc. Considerable overlap exists between oceanography and the geosciences. However, due to the special tools and techniques required for studying the oceans, oceanography and the geosciences continue to be thought of as separate disciplines.

The atmospheric sciences, meteorology and climatology, involve the study of the atmosphere. Meteorology is the study of the physics and chemistry of the atmosphere. One of the primary goals of meteorology is the analysis and prediction of short–term weather patterns. Climatology is the study of long–term weather patterns, including their causes, variation, and distribution.

Due to the interactions between the different spheres of Earth, scientists from these different subdisciplines often must work together. Together, Earth scientists can better understand the highly involved and interrelated systems of Earth and find better answers to the difficult questions posed by many natural phenomena. In addition, due to the interwoven nature of the biotic (living) and abiotic (nonliving) parts of Earth's environment, Earth scientists sometimes work with life scientists (i.e., biologists, ecologists, agronomists, etc.) who study the Earth's biosphere.

Today, Earth science research focuses on solving the many problems posed by increasing human populations, decreasing natural resources, and inevitable natural hazards. Computer and satellite technologies are increasingly utilized in the search for and development of Earth's resources for present and future use.

See also Atmosphere observation; Earth; Ecology; Geology; Oceanography; Weather.

Earth's core see **Earth's interior**

Earth's crust see **Earth's interior**

Earth's interior

It is 3,950 miles (6,370 km) from the Earth's surface to its center. We understand the rock units and layers near the surface from direct observation, core samples, and drilling projects. However, the depth of our drill holes, and therefore, the direct observation of earth materials at depth, is severely limited. Even the deepest drill holes (7.5 mi, 12 km) penetrate less than 0.2% of the distance to the Earth's center. Thus, we know far more about the layers near the Earth's surface, and can only investigate the conditions within the Earth's interior (density, temperature, composition, solid versus liquid phase, etc.) through more indirect means.

Geologists collect information about the Earth's remote interior from several different sources. Some rocks found at the Earth's surface, known as kimberlite and ophiolite, originate deep in the Earth's crust and mantle. Some meteorites are also believed to be representative of the rocks of the Earth's mantle and core. These rocks provide geologists with some idea of the composition of the Earth's interior.

Another source of information, while more indirect, is perhaps more important. That source is earthquake, or seismic waves. When an earthquake occurs anywhere on Earth, seismic waves travel outward from the earthquake's center. The speed, motion, and direction of seismic waves changes dramatically at different levels within the Earth, known as *seismic transition zones*. Therefore, we can make various assumptions about the Earth's character above and below these transition zones through careful analysis of seismic data. This information reveals that the Earth is composed of three basic sections, the crust (the thin outer layer), the mantle, and the core.

The crust

The outermost layer of the Earth is the crust, or the thin "shell" of rock that covers the globe. There are two types of crust: the continental crust, which consists mostly of light–colored rock of granitic composition that underlies the Earth's continents; and the oceanic crust, which is a dark–colored rock of basaltic composition that underlies the Earth's oceans. One of the most important differences between continental and oceanic crust is their difference in density. The lighter–colored continental crust is also lighter in weight, with an average density of 2.6 g/cm³ (grams per cubic centimeter), compared to the darker and heavier basaltic oceanic crust, which has an average density of 3.0 g/cm³. It is this difference in density that causes the continents to have an average elevation of about 2000 feet (600 m) above sea level, while the average elevation (depth) of the ocean bottom is 10,000 feet (3,000 m) below sea level. The heavier oceanic crust sits lower on the Earth's surface, creating the topographic depressions for the ocean basins, while the lighter continental crust rests higher on the Earth's surface, causing the elevated and exposed continental land masses.

Another difference between the oceanic crust and continental crust is the difference in thickness. The heavier oceanic crust forms a relatively thin layer of 3–6 miles (5–10 km), while the continental crust is lighter, and the underlying material can support a thicker layer. The continental crust averages about 20 miles (35 km) thick, but can reach up to 40 miles (70 km) in certain sections, particularly those found under newly elevated and exposed mountain ranges such as the Himalayas.

The base of the crust (both the oceanic and continental varieties) is determined by a distinct seismic transition zone called the Mohorovičić discontinuity. The Mohorovičić discontinuity, commonly referred to as "the Moho" or the "M–discontinuity," is the transition or boundary zone between the bottom of the Earth's crust and the underlying unit, which is the uppermost section of the mantle called the lithospheric mantle. Like the crust, the lithospheric mantle is solid, but it is considerably denser. Since the thickness of the Earth's crust varies, the depth to the Moho also varies from 3–6 miles (5–10 km) under the oceans to 20–40 miles (35–70 km) under the continents.

This transition between the crust and the mantle was first discovered by the Croatian seismologist Andrija Mohorovičić in 1908. On October 8, 1908, Mohorovičić observed seismic waves (those generated through the earth by earthquake activity) that emitted from an earthquake in Croatia. He noticed that both the compressional, or primary (P), waves and the shear, or secondary (S), waves, at one point in their journey, picked up speed as they traveled farther from the earthquake. This suggested that the waves had been

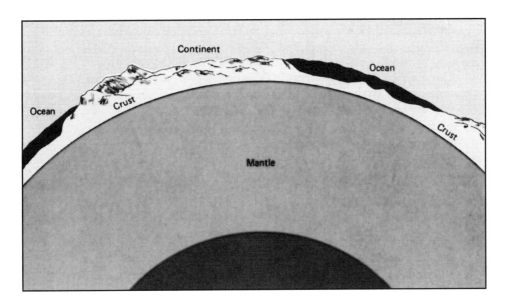

The structure of the Earth. The crust is not drawn to scale.

deflected, as if they had encountered something that had affected their energy. He noted that this increase in speed seemed to occur at a depth of about 30 miles (50 km). Since seismic waves travel faster through denser material, he reasoned that there was an abrupt transition from the rocky material in the Earth's crust, to denser rocks below. In honor of Mohorovičić's discovery, this transition zone marking the base of the Earth's crust was named after him.

The Moho is a relatively narrow transition zone estimated to be somewhere between 0.1–1.9 miles (0.2–3 km) thick. Currently, the Moho is defined by the level within the Earth where P wave velocity increases abruptly from an average speed of about 4.3 mi/second (6.9 km/second) to about 5.0 mi/second (8.1 km/second).

The mantle

Underlying the crust is the mantle. The uppermost section of the mantle, which is a rigid layer, is called the lithospheric mantle. This section extends to an average depth of about 40 miles (70 km), although it fluctuates between 30–60 miles (50–100 km). The density of this layer is greater than that of the crust, and averages 3.3 g/cm^3. But like the crust, this section is solid and brittle, and relatively cool compared to the material below. This rigid uppermost section of the mantle (the lithospheric mantle), combined with the overlying solid crust, is called the lithosphere, which is derived from the Greek word "lithos" which means "rock."

At the base of the lithosphere, a depth of about 40 miles (70 km), there is another distinct seismic transition called the Gutenberg low velocity zone. At this level, the velocity of S waves decreases dramatically, and all seismic waves appear to be absorbed more strongly than elsewhere within the Earth. Scientists interpret this to mean that the layer below the lithosphere is a "weak" or "soft" zone of partially melted material (with between 1–10% molten material). This "soft" zone is called the *asthenosphere*, from the Greek word "asthenes" meaning "weak."

This transition zone between the lithosphere and the asthenosphere is named after Beno Gutenberg, a mid–20th century geologist who made several important contributions to the study and understanding of the Earth's interior. It is at this level that some important Earth dynamics occur, affecting those of us here at the Earth's surface. At the Gutenberg low velocity zone, the lithosphere is carried "piggyback" on top of the weaker, less rigid asthenosphere which seems to be in continual motion. This motion creates stress in the rigid rock layers above it, and the slabs or plates of the lithosphere are forced to jostle against each other, much like ice cubes floating in a bowl of swirling water. This motion of the lithospheric plates is known as *plate tectonics*, and it is responsible for many of the Earth's activities that we experience at the surface today, including earthquakes, certain types of volcanic activity, and continental drift.

The asthenosphere extends to a depth of about 155 miles (250 km). Below that depth, seismic wave velocity increases, suggesting an underlying denser, but solid phase.

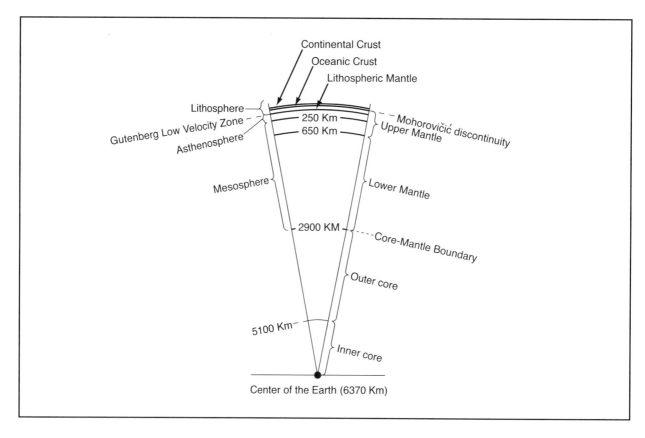

Figure 1. The interior of the earth.

The rest of the mantle, from the base of the asthenosphere at 155 miles (250) km to the core at 1,800 miles (2,900 km), is called the mesosphere (or "middle" sphere). There are mineralogical and compositional changes suggested by sharp velocity increases within the mesosphere. Notably, there is a thin zone at about the 250 miles (400 km) depth attributed to a possible mineralogical change (presumably from an abundance of the mineral olivine to the mineral spinel), and there is another sharp velocity increase at about the 400 mile (650 km) level, attributed to a possible increase in the ratio of iron to magnesium in mantle rocks. Except for these variations, down to the 560 mile (900 km) level the mesosphere seems to contain predominantly solid material that displays a relatively consistent pattern of gradually increasing density and seismic wave velocity with increasing depth and pressure. Below the 560 mile (900 km) depth, the P and S wave velocities continue to increase, but the rate of increase declines with depth.

The core

At a depth of 1,800 miles (2,900 km) there is another abrupt change in the seismic wave patterns, known as the Gutenberg discontinuity, or more often referred to as the core–mantle boundary (CMB). At this level, P waves decrease while S waves disappear completely. Since S waves can not be transmitted through liquids, it is believed that the CMB denotes a phase change from the solid mantle above, to a liquid outer core below. This phase change is believed to be accompanied by an abrupt temperature increase of 1300°F (700°C). This hot, liquid outer core material is denser than the cooler, solid mantle, probably due to a greater percentage of iron. It is believed that the outer core consists of a liquid of 80–92% iron, alloyed with a lighter element. The composition of the remaining 8–20% is not well understood, but it must be a compressible element that can mix with liquid iron at these immense pressures. Various candidates proposed for this element include silicon, sulphur, or oxygen.

The actual boundary between the mantle and the outer core is a narrow, uneven zone that contains undulations that may be 3–6 miles (5–8 km) high. These undulations are affected by heat–driven convection activity within the overlying mantle, which may be the driving force for plate tectonics. The interaction between the solid mantle and the liquid outer core is very important to Earth dynamics for another reason. It is the

KEY TERMS

· ·

Continental crust—The Earth's relatively thin layer or crust (about 35 km thick) of light colored, relatively light weight granitic rock that floors the Earth's continents.

Core—The section of the Earth below the 1,800 mi (2,900 km) level. Includes a liquid outer core and a solid inner core.

Gutenberg discontinuity—The seismic transition zone that occurs at the 1,800 mi (2,900 km) depth level separating the lower mantle (which is solid) and the underlying outer core (liquid). Also commonly referred to as the core–mantle boundary (CMB).

Gutenberg low velocity zone—The transition zone that occurs at the 30–60 mi (50–100 km) depth between the rigid lithosphere and the underlying "soft" or partially melted asthenosphere.

Lithospheric mantle—The rigid uppermost section of the mantle, less than 60 mi (100 km) thick. This section, combined with the crust, constitutes the Lithosphere, or the solid and rocky outer layer of the Earth.

Mantle—The thick middle section of the Earth that extends from the base of the crust to the outer core, a thickness of almost 1,800 mi (2,900 km). The mantle is predominantly solid, although it includes the partially melted asthenosphere.

Mesosphere—The solid section of the mantle directly beneath the asthenosphere. Extends from the 150 mi (250 km) depth level to 1,800 mi (2,900 km).

Mohorovičić discontinuity—The seismic transition zone indicated by an increase in primary seismic wave velocity that marks the transition from the crust to the uppermost section of the mantle.

Oceanic crust—The Earth's thin (3–6 mi/5–10 km thick) outer layer or crust that floors the Earth's ocean basins and is composed of basaltic rock, a dark colored, relatively heavy fine–grained material made from cooled lava.

P waves—Primary or compression waves that travel through the Earth, generated by seismic activity such as earthquakes, which can travel through solids or liquids.

S waves—Secondary or shear waves that travel through the Earth, generated by seismic activity such as earthquakes, which can not travel through liquids.

Seismic waves—Vibrations in the Earth's interior caused by earthquakes.

Seismic transition zone—An interval within the Earth's interior where seismic waves, or earthquake waves, display a change in speed and shape. These zones are layers where the character of the Earth materials differ from those above and below.

eddies and currents in the core's iron–rich fluids which are ultimately responsible for the Earth's magnetic field.

Although the core–mantle boundary is currently situated at a depth of about 1,800 miles (2,900 km), this depth has not been constant through geologic time. As the heat of the Earth's interior is constantly but slowly dissipated, the molten core within the Earth gradually solidifies and shrinks, causing the core–mantle boundary to slowly move deeper and deeper within the Earth's core.

There is one final, even deeper transition evident from seismic wave data. Within the Earth's core, at the 3,150 mile (5,100 km) level, P waves speed up and are reflected from yet another seismic transition zone. This indicates that the material in the inner core below 3150 miles (5100 km) is solid. The phase change from liquid

to solid is probably due to the immense pressures present at this depth.

In addition to this phase change in the inner core from liquid to solid, seismic wave velocities, as well as the Earth's total weight, suggest that the inner core has a different composition than the outer core. This could be accounted for by a relatively pure iron–nickel composition for the inner core. Although no direct terrestrial evidence for a solid iron–nickel inner core exists, comparative evidence from meteorites supports this theory. Numerous meteorites, fragments presumably from the interior of shattered extraterrestrial bodies within our solar system, often contain relatively pure iron or iron–nickel compositions. It is likely that the composition of the core of our own planet is very similar to the composition of these extraterrestrial travelers.

See also Earthquake; Magma; Lithosphere; Gutenberg discontinuity; Plate tectonics.

Further Reading:

Magill, Frank, N., ed. *Magill's Survey of Science, Earth Science Series.* 1990.

Mary D. Albanese

Earth's magnetic field

Our planet acts as though it were a huge dipole magnet with the positive and negative poles near the North and South Poles. This does not mean that the Earth is literally a dipole magnet—there are too many variations in the field—but that the best fit for a model of the field is two poles of a magnet, rather than a quadrupole or other shape. The magnetic field of the earth allows magnetic compasses to work, making navigation much easier. It also molds the configuration of van Allen belts, bands of high–energy charged particles around the Earth's atmosphere.

Most of the Earth's magnetic field (90%) occurs below the surface and possibly exists because the Earth's core doesn't move at the same rate as the Earth's mantle (the layer between the Earth's core and its crust). The external 10% of the field is generated by movement of ions in the upper atmosphere.

The Earth's magnetic field may help some animals navigate as they migrate. People have been using magnetic compasses for navigation since the fifteenth century. Because it is has been so important for navigation, the magnetic field has been mapped all over the surface of the Earth.

The magnetic field can also be used in other ways. For example, an instrument called a geomagnetic electrokinetograph determines the direction and speed of ocean currents while a ship is moving by measuring the voltage induced in the moving conductive sea water by the magnetic field of the Earth.

The Earth's magnetic field can change quickly and temporarily or slowly and permanently, depending on the cause of the change.

The magnetic field can change very quickly, within an hour, in magnetic storms. These occur when the magnetic field is disturbed by sunspots, which send clouds of charged particles into the Earth's atmosphere. (These same protons and electrons excite oxygen, nitrogen, and hydrogen atoms in the upper atmosphere,

causing the aurora borealis and aurora australis.) These disturbances can be measured all over the globe and can cause static on radio stations.

The orientation of the magnetic field also changes slowly over centuries. In the planet's lifetime, the magnetic field has changed and even reversed (north pole becomes south and vice–versa) several times. Evidence for this is seen in reversed paleomagnetism of some sedimentary and igneous rock. In the 1960s, Allan Cox and Richard Doell showed that the rocks formed at a particular interval in geologic time all indicate a magnetic field with the same orientation; older or younger rocks may show a reversed orientation. The cause of these paleomagnetic reversals is not yet known.

Today, the magnetic poles are not at the same place as the poles of the Earth's rotational axis. Therefore, "magnetic north" is not quite the direction of "true north." The difference is known as the magnetic declination. Accordingly, scientists have established a series of geomagnetic coordinates, including latitude and longitude. These are centered on the magnetic dipole of the earth and designed (like geographic latitude and longitude) as though the Earth were a perfect sphere.

See also Electromagnetic field; Magnetism; Van Allen belts.

Earth's mantle see **Earth's interior**

Earth's rotation

All objects in the universe and our solar system move in space. The Earth moves in two ways. It rotates like a top on its axis, an imaginary line through the north and south poles, and revolves in an orbit around the Sun. Centrifugal force results from the Earth's rotation which, without gravity, could cause objects to fly into space. Because the force of gravity is 289 times the centrifugal force, it prevents objects from leaving the surface. Centrifugal force causes the Earth to bulge at the equator, making it slightly ovoid in shape.

The Earth's counterclockwise rotation is in the opposite direction of the apparent movement of heavenly bodies. Because the Sun and stars appear to move from east to west, the Earth rotates from west to east.

Rotation is used to define time. Since man began to measure time, it's been done by the movement of Sun and stars. One rotation of the Earth makes up one 24 hour day. This is in contrast to the time of revolution around the Sun of 365 days or one year. Because the Earth's axis is not perpendicular to the equator, but leans at a 23 1/2 degree angle, the amount of daylight varies over the course of a year.

The rotation of the Earth can be proven in several ways. One is the Foucault experiment. This was first conducted in 1851, by the Frenchman Léon Foucault. He suspended a heavy iron ball from a 200 ft (61 m) wire, creating a pendulum, from the dome of the Pantheon in Paris. He put sand underneath the pendulum, and placed a pin on the bottom of the ball, so it would leave a mark on its swing from side to side. On each swing, over the course of twenty four hours, the mark in the sand would move to the right. The direction in the path showed movement of the Earth against the swing of the pendulum.

A more modern proof of the rotation is shown by the orbits of artificial satellites. A satellite is launched from the Kennedy Space Center at a 30 degree angle to an orbit 100 mi (161 km) above the Earth. Its orbit stays at approximately the same plane in space. If the Earth did not rotate, the satellite would pass over Cape Canaveral each time it completed an orbit, but it doesn't. As it completes the first orbit, it flies over Alabama and over Louisiana on the third. Each time the satellite passes over U. S. locations, it is 1,000 mi (1,609 km) to the west. Tracking stations have made this observation with hundreds of satellites.

Another way of proving rotation is through the prevailing winds. In the northern hemisphere, they move in a counter clockwise direction, while in the southern hemisphere, they blow clockwise.

Over time the speed of Earth's rotation has slowed. Knowing how fast it spins, at any given time, is important to navigators and pilots in finding locations.

See also Gravity and gravitation; Orbit; Solar system; Time.

Earthworms see **Segmented worms**

Earwigs

Earwigs are long–bodied insects with chewing mouthparts and many–jointed antennae in the order Dermaptera. Earwigs have small, vestigial forewings modified into a wing case, but their membranous hindwings are large, folded, and functional, although they are not often used for flying. Earwigs hatch into nymphs which closely resemble the adults, only they are much smaller. Metamorphosis in earwigs is simple, with no radical changes in shape during development from the nymphal stages to the adult form.

The most readily distinguishing characteristic of earwigs is the pair of unjointed, forceps–like structures that terminate their abdomen. These unusual organs are modified from common insect structures known as cerci, and they differ between the sexes, those of females having less curvature. The pincers are brandished when earwigs are disturbed, and can give a significant pinch to the finger, so they are clearly useful in defense. The pincers may also have other uses, possibly in folding the rather complicated wings after a flight.

Earwigs are nocturnal animals, and they hide during the day in dark, damp places. Most species of the more than 1,200 species of earwigs are scavengers of a wide range of organic debris, including carrion. Some species are herbivorous, some are opportunistic predators of other insects, and a few, specialized species are parasites of mammals.

The most common native earwig in Europe is *Forficula auricularia*, a species that is now also widespread in North America, New Zealand, and elsewhere due to accidental introductions by humans. The European earwig is omnivorous, eating a wide range of dead organic matter, and also preying on other insects. The female of this species broods her eggs and young hatchlings. During summers when the European earwig is particularly abundant, it may be considered to be a pest because of its ubiquitous presence in flower gardens, under all manner of moist things, in basements and kitchens, and in laundry hanging on clotheslines. These earwigs may damage vegetables and flowers during their feeding, but they are not really an important pest. In fact, the European earwig may be beneficial in some respects, by cleaning up organic debris, and perhaps by preying on other, more important insect pests.

A total of 18 species of earwigs occur in North America. The seaside earwig (*Anisolabis maritima*) is a native species that occurs on both the Atlantic and Pacific coasts of North America. The red–legged earwig (*Euborellia annulipes*), striped earwig (*Labidura bidens*), and handsome earwig (*Prolabia pulchella*) occur in the southern United States. The toothed earwig (*Spongovostox apicedentatus*) occurs in dry habitats in the southwestern states. The little earwig (*Labia minor*) is another species that was introduced from Europe.

Some species of earwigs have relatively unusual, specialized lifestyles. *Arixenia* is a small earwig that is a viviparous breeder, giving birth to live young. This species is an ectoparasite of the Indian bat (*Cheiromeles torquatus*). *Hemimerus* is also a small, viviparous earwig, and a blind ectoparasite of the giant rat (*Cricetomys gambianus*) of west Africa.

Earwigs received their common name from the folk belief that these insects would sometimes crawl into the ears of people as they slept, seeking refuge in those dark, moist cavities. This may, indeed, sometimes occur, and it would certainly be disconcerting to have an earwig, or any other insect in one's ear. However, there is no evidence that earwigs in the ear are a common problem, except as very rare accidents.

Bill Freedman

Eating disorders

Eating disorders are psychological conditions that involve either overeating, voluntary starvation, or both. No one is sure what causes eating disorders, but researchers think that family dynamics, biochemical abnormalities, and society's preoccupation with thinness all may contribute. Eating disorders are virtually unknown in parts of the world where food is scarce and within less affluent socioeconomic groups in developed countries. Although these disorders have been known throughout history, they have gained attention in recent years, in part because some celebrities have died as a result of their eating disorders.

Young people are more likely than older people to develop an eating disorder—the condition usually begins before age 20. Although both men and women can develop the problem, it is more common in women. Only about 5% of people with eating disorders are male. In either males or females, eating disorders are considered serious and potentially deadly. Many large hospitals and psychiatric clinics have programs especially designed to treat these conditions.

Anorexia nervosa, anorexic bulimia, and obesity are the most well known types of eating disorders. The word anorexia comes from the Greek for "lack of appetite." But the problem for people with anorexia is not that they aren't hungry. They starve themselves out of fear of gaining weight, even when they are severely underweight. The related condition, anorexic bulimia, literally means being "hungry as an ox." People with this problem go on eating binges, often gorging on junk food. Then they force their bodies to get rid of the food, either by making themselves vomit or by taking large amounts of laxatives. A third type of eating disorder is obesity caused by uncontrollable overeating. Being slightly overweight is not a serious health risk. But being 25% or more over one's recommended body weight can lead to many health problems.

Anorexia

People with anorexia starve themselves until they look almost like skeletons. But their self-images are so distorted that they see themselves as fat, even when they are emaciated. Some refuse to eat at all; others nibble only small portions of fruit and vegetables or live on diet drinks. In addition to fasting, they may exercise strenuously to keep their weight abnormally low. No matter how much weight they lose, they always worry about getting fat.

This self–imposed starvation takes a heavy toll on the body. Skin becomes dry and flaky. Muscles begin to waste away. Bones stop growing and may become brittle. The heart weakens. With no body fat for insulation, it's hard to keep warm. Downy hair starts to grow on the face, back and arms in response to lower body temperature. In women, menstruation stops and permanent infertility may result. Muscle cramps, dizziness, fatigue, even brain damage, kidney and heart failure are possible. An estimated 10–20% of people with anorexia die, either as a direct result of starvation or by suicide.

Researchers believe that anorexia is caused by a combination of biological, psychological and social factors. They're still trying to pinpoint the biological factors, but they have zeroed in on some psychological and social triggers of the disorder. Many people with anorexia come from families in which parents are overprotective and have unrealistically high expectations of their children. The condition seems to run in families, which leads researchers to believe it may have a genetic basis. Anorexia often seems to develop after a young person goes through some stressful experience, such as moving to a new town, changing schools, or going through puberty. Low self-esteem, fear of losing control and fear of growing up are common characteristics of anorectics (people with anorexia). The need for approval, combined with our culture's idealization of extreme thinness, also contributes.

The obvious cure for anorexia is eating, but that's the last thing a person with anorexia wants to do. It is unusual for the person himself or herself to seek treatment—usually a friend, family member or teacher initiates the process. Hospitalization, combined with psychotherapy and family counseling, often is needed to get the condition under control. Force feeding may be necessary if the person's life is in danger. Some 70% of anorexia patients who are treated for about six months return to normal body weight. About 15 to 20% can be expected to relapse, however.

Bulimia

Like anorexia, bulimia results in starvation. But there are behavioral, physical and psychological differences between the two conditions. Bulimia is much more difficult to detect because people who have it tend to be of normal weight or overweight, and they hide their habit of binge eating followed by purging by vomiting or using laxatives. In fact, bulimia was not widely recognized, even among medical and mental health professionals, until the 1980s. Unlike anorectics, bulimics (people with bulimia) are aware that their eating patterns are abnormal, and they often feel remorse after a binge. For them, overeating offers an irresistible escape from stress. Many suffer from depression, repressed anger, anxiety and low self esteem, combined with a tendency toward perfectionism. About 20% of bulimics also have problems with alcohol or drug addiction, and they are more likely than other people to commit suicide.

Many people occasionally overeat, but are not considered bulimic. According to the American Psychiatric Association's definition, a bulimic binges on enormous amounts of food at least twice a week for three months or more.

Bulimics plan their binges carefully, setting aside specific times and places to carry out their secret habit. They may go from restaurant to restaurant, to avoid being seen eating too much in any one place. Or they may pretend to be shopping for a large dinner party, when actually they intend to eat all the food themselves. Because of the expense of consuming so much food, some resort to shoplifting.

During a binge, bulimics favor high carbohydrate foods, such as doughnuts, candy, ice cream, soft drinks, cookies, cereal, cake, popcorn and bread, consuming many times the amount of calories they normally would consume in one day. No matter what their normal eating habits, they tend to eat quickly and messily during a binge, stuffing the food in their mouths and gulping it down, sometimes without even tasting it. Some say they get a feeling of euphoria during binges, similar to the "runner's high" that some people get from exercise.

The self–induced vomiting that often follows eating binges can cause all sorts of physical problems, such as damage to the stomach and esophagus, chronic heartburn, burst blood vessels in the eyes, throat irritation, and erosion of tooth enamel from the acid in vomit. Excessive use of laxatives can be hazardous, too. Muscle cramps, stomach pains, digestive problems, dehydration and even poisoning may result. Over time, bulimia causes vitamin deficiencies and imbalances of critical body fluids, which in turn can lead to seizures and kidney failure.

Some researchers believe that an imbalance in the brain chemical serotonin underlies bulimia, as well as other types of compulsive behavior. The production of serotonin, which influences mood, is affected by both antidepressant drugs and certain foods. But most research on bulimia focuses on its psychological roots.

Bulimia is not as likely as anorexia to reach life–threatening stages, so hospitalization usually is not necessary. Treatment generally involves psychotherapy and sometimes the use of antidepressant drugs. Unlike anorectics, bulimics usually admit they have a problem and want help overcoming it. Estimates of the rates of recovery from bulimia vary widely, with some studies showing low rates of improvement and others suggesting that treatment usually is effective. Even after apparently successful treatment, some bulimics relapse.

Obesity

Obesity is an excess of body fat. But the question of what constitutes an excess has no clear answer. Some doctors classify a person as obese whose weight is 20% or more over the recommended weight for his or her height. But other doctors say standard height and weight charts are misleading. They maintain that the proportion of fat to muscle, measured by the skinfold "pinch" test, is a better measure of obesity. A person who is overweight, they point out, is not necessarily obese. A very muscular athlete, for example, might have very little body fat, but still might weigh more than the recommended weight for his or her height.

The causes of obesity are complex and not fully understood. While compulsive overeating certainly can lead to obesity, it is not clear that all obesity results from overindulging. Recent research increasingly points to biological, as well as psychological and environmental factors that influence obesity.

In the United States, people with low incomes are more likely to be obese than are the wealthy. Women are almost twice as likely as men to have the problem, but both men and women tend to gain weight as they age.

In those people whose obesity stems from compulsive eating, psychological factors seem to play a large role. Some studies suggest that obese people are much more likely than others to eat in response to stress, loneliness, or depression. As they are growing up, some

KEY TERMS
. . . .

Morbid—From the Latin word for sick, pertaining to or inducing disease.

Risk factor—Any habit or condition that renders an individual more susceptible to disease. Cigarette smoking, for example, is a significant risk factor for lung cancer and heart disease.

people learn to associate food with love, acceptance and a feeling of belonging. If they feel rejected and unhappy later in life, they may use food to comfort themselves.

Just as emotional pain can lead to obesity, obesity can lead to psychological scars. From childhood on, obese people are taunted and shunned. They may even face discrimination in school and on the job. The low self-esteem and sense of isolation that result may contribute to the person's eating disorder, setting up an endless cycle of overeating, gaining more weight, feeling even more worthless and isolated, then gorging again to console oneself.

People whose obesity endangers their health are said to be morbidly obese. Obesity is a risk factor in diabetes, high blood pressure, arteriosclerosis, angina pectoralis (chest pains due to inadequate blood flow to the heart), varicose veins, cirrhosis of the liver and kidney disease. Obesity can cause complications during pregnancy and in surgical procedures. Obese people are about one and one half times more likely to have heart attacks than are other people. Overall, the death rate among people ages 20 to 64 is 50% higher for the obese than for people of normal weight.

Since compulsive eating patterns often have their beginnings in childhood, they are difficult to break. Some obese people get caught up in a cycle of binging and dieting — sometimes called yo–yo dieting — that never results in permanent weight loss. Research has shown that strict dieting itself may contribute to compulsive eating. Going without their favorite foods for long periods makes people feel deprived. They are more likely, then, to reward themselves by binging when they go off the diet. Other research shows that dieting slows the dieter's metabolism. When the person goes off the diet, he or she gains weight more easily.

The most successful programs for dealing with overeating teach people to eat more sensibly and to increase their physical activity to lose weight gradually without going on extreme diets. Support groups and therapy can help people deal with the psychological aspects of obesity.

Further Reading:

Epstein, Rachel. *Eating Habits and Disorders.* New York: Chelsea House Publishers, 1990.

Matthews, John R. *Eating Disorders.* New York: Facts On File, 1991.

Porterfield, Kay Marie. *Focus on Addictions.* Santa Barbara: ABC–CLIO, 1992.

Nancy Ross–Flanigan

Ebola virus

The Ebola virus is one of several recently identified and highly lethal viruses that cause severe hemorrhaging, or uncontrolled bleeding. In the electron microscope, the RNA–containing Ebola virus looks like a thread or filament, often with a loop at one end. It is a member of the filovirus family and kills 50–90% of its victims, often just days or weeks after infection. There is no vaccine or cure for the disease caused by Ebola virus. Because the virus is spread through direct contact with body secretions, it can be controlled by isolating victims and using strict safety precautions, including gloves, masks, and gowns when caring for patients.

Outbreaks of Ebola virus

In the last 25 years, many previously unknown, dangerous viruses have been discovered or identified. Most were probably in existence long before they came to the attention of Western medicine. These newly discovered or re–emerging viruses originated in tropical parts of the Africa, South America, and Asia. For example, HIV, the virus that causes AIDS, is believed to have originated in tropical Africa. Twenty years ago, AIDS was virtually unknown. Yet, it may infect 40 million people by the year 2000.

Some epidemiologists believe that as humans cultivate previously undeveloped lands and delve into more isolated parts of the world, such as African and Amazon forests, they may be exposed to more "emerging" viruses like Ebola and the only other known filovirus, Marburg. In 1967, Ugandan green monkeys carried the virus from Africa to Europe, where Marburg infected 30 people, bringing it to the attention of Western medicine. The virus killed seven people in West Germany and Yugoslavia.

There are three subtypes of Ebola virus, Ebola Zaire, Ebola Sudan, and Ebola Reston. These three subtypes, along with Marburg, make up the family of filoviruses. The Ebola virus is named after the Ebola River in Northern Zaire where it was discovered.

Outbreaks of filoviruses fortunately have been rare. The first Ebola outbreak occurred in Zaire and western Sudan in 1976. This outbreak took the lives of more than 400 persons, 90% of all those infected. Three years later, Ebola struck again, and 90% of those infected died. The third Ebola outbreak occurred in May 1995 in Kikwik, Zaire. By June 1995, more than 150 victims had did. Poor sanitation and hygiene in hospitals has contributed to some outbreaks. The disease may also have been spread, in at least one of the outbreaks, when corpses were cut open as dictated by certain African funeral rituals.

No one knows where the virus resides between outbreaks. It might exist in an animal that can carry the virus but does not get sick from it.

Effects of Ebola virus on humans

Like HIV, the virus that causes AIDS, Ebola can be spread from person to person in body secretions. Unlike HIV, which can take ten or more years to kill its victims, Ebola can kill within days of infection.

The illness starts 2-21 days after the virus enters the body. Its first symptoms include a fever and other flu–like symptoms, sudden tiredness, sore throat, muscle pain, and headache. Bloody diarrhea and vomiting follow. Blood cells die and clog capillaries, the narrowest blood vessels in the body. This causes damage to the skin which may slough off or dissolve after bruising and blistering. After a week or so, hemorrhaging causes blood to flow from the eyes, nose, and ears. Internal organs begin to liquefy and the victim's vomit is black with blood. The liver, spleen and kidney are most susceptible to damage by the disease but the heart, pancreas, brain, and spinal cord may also be damaged. Death usually occurs within nine or ten days from uncontrolled bleeding.

There are many reasons Ebola is less of a worldwide threat than the severity of its symptoms might suggest. First, Ebola kills humans so quickly it has a limited chance to spread to other victims. In close quarters, such as a primitive hospital where protective equipment like gloves are not used routinely and syringes are reused routinely, the virus may spread rapidly from patient to patient and from patient to health care worker. But outside of such close confines, most people, excluding family or caregivers, have less chance of coming into direct contact with virus–contaminated body fluids. The Ebola virus tends to kill its victim

KEY TERMS

Epidemiologist—A physician or scientist who studies the distribution, sources, and control of diseases in populations.

Filovirus—a family of lethal thread-shaped viruses that includes Ebola and Marburg.

before he or she has a chance to spread the virus to other persons unless someone comes into contact with the victim's blood, urine, saliva, or other body fluids. Also, the Ebola virus is destroyed by the ultraviolet light in sunlight.

New "emerging viruses"

Other viruses that concern health officials around the world include the arboviruses, Oropouche, identified in 1961, and Rift Valley Fever, identified in the 1950s. The arenaviruses, Junin (1953), Sabia (1990), Machupo (re–emerged in Bolivia in 1994) and Lassa, which has long been known to cause African hemorrhagic fever, also concern officials at the World Health Organization and the United States Centers for Disease Control. Lassa kills approximately 5,000 persons each year in West Africa and infects hundreds of thousands. New strains of Dengue, carried by mosquitoes in Latin America and Asia, and Hanta viruses, carried by mice in Asia and the United States, are other viruses that have created concern among epidemiologists and in the media.

See also Virus.

Further Reading:
Garrett, Laurie. *The Coming Plague: Newly Emerging Diseases in a World Out of Balance.* New York: Farrar, Straus and Giroux, 1994.
"Outbreak of Fear." *Newsweek* (22 May 1995): 48–55.
Preston, Richard. *The Hot Zone.* New York: Random House, 1994.

Dean Allen Haycock

Ebony

Ebony (*Diospyros* spp., family Ebenaceae) is a tropical hardwood favored for its hard and beautiful wood. Only the black or brown heartwood is used commercially. There are more than 300 species of ebony, ranging in size from shrubs to trees taller than 100 feet (30 m). The best commercial ebony comes from India, Madagascar, Nigeria, Zaire, and the Celebes Islands. Most species of ebony are found in the tropics but some can be found in warm temperate zones such as the American persimmon, (*Diospyrus virginiana*), whose heartwood is not a full black and does not have the extreme density that is so desirable. Aggressive harvesting of ebony has rendered these plants rare and, consequently, quite valuable.

The Ebenaceae family has simple alternate, coriaceous leaves that are oblong or lanceolate and vary in length according to species. The flowers are white or greenish white with at least four stamens. The globular fruits are sought by animals and humans alike because of their sweetness when ripe. Some native tribes use the fruit to make beer. The leaves and other parts of the tree are used to treat worms, wounds, dysentery, and fevers, but no laboratory tests have verified the success of this medicinal usage.

The wood of the ebony is so dense that it rapidly dulls tools used for working, sawing, or turning it. Even termites will bypass a fallen ebony log. This density contributes to ebony's commercial appeal as it results in a finish that will take a high polish, adding to its beauty. The properties, attributed to ebony through both fact and myth, have been recognized for many generations. It was a favorite material for carving in Africa. Some rulers in India had scepters made from it and also used it for their drinking vessels as it was believed to neutralize poisons. Today, ebony is used for many purposes, including tool and knife handles, furniture, inlay work, wall paneling, golf club heads, and musical instruments. For many years ebony was used for the black keys on the piano, but increasing costs have necessitated the use of substitutes. Today, only the most expensive concert pianos are still made with ebony. Ebony is also used in stringed instruments for tension pegs and fingerboards.

Although there are many species of ebony, only a few provide commercial–grade wood, and the demand far exceeds the supply. Africa is the source of the most desirable jet–black heartwood. It comes from the species *Diospyrus crassiflora*, commonly called African ebony. This ebony is prized for its intense black core. With a weight of 64 lb/cubic ft (1,030 kg/cubic m), it has a specific gravity of 1.03 and will not float in water. It is found in Ghana, Nigeria, Zaire, and Cameroon.

Diospyrus macassar, commonly called Macassar ebony, is not as plentiful as the African species, but its

KEY TERMS

Accrescent—Increasing in size with age, especially the calyx.

Calyx—All the sepals of a flower, collectively.

Coriaceous—Leathery in texture, thicker than normal.

Dioecious—Having male and female flowers on separate plants

Lanceolate—Lance shaped.

Sepals—Usually outermost division of the calyx.

greater density makes it even more useful in certain types of manufacture. With a weight of 68 lb/cubic ft (1,090 kg/cubic m), it is even more dense than African ebony. It has a specific gravity of 1.09, and does not float. Macassar ebony is found mostly in the Celebes Islands of Indonesia with some minor growth in India. The heartwood is frequently streaked with lighter bands, and this type is favored by piano makers. Because they are so difficult to dry, the trees are usually girdled to kill them and then left standing for two years to dry out. After they are felled and cut into lumber, they must dry for another six months.

Diospyros mespiliformis, also known as the Jakkalsbessie (Jackal's berry), Transvaal ebony, or Rhodesian ebony, is a straight tree, which grows 70 ft (21 m) tall with a trunk up to 4 ft (1.4 m) or more in diameter. It is more widespread and abundant than other ebonies but the heartwood is more brown than black, limiting its appeal. Among many native cultures, it serves a medicinal purpose and concoctions derived from the leaves and bark are used to treat wounds, fevers, and worms. Color aside, the density of Rhodesian ebony renders it desirable for furniture, knife handles, and flooring. The fruit is edible.

Diospyrus virginiana, the persimmon or American ebony, is a native of the southeast United States. It takes approximately 100 years to mature and grows to a height of at least 65 ft (20 m). Like the tropical ebonies, it has simple, alternate coriaceous leaves. The flowers are yellowish green and the fruit is yellow, globose, and somewhat larger than its tropical cousins—up to 2.5 in (6.4 cm) in diameter—filled with seeds and a sweet, custard–like interior. Due to its hardness, the wood is used for handles, furniture, and golf club heads. Since there are no vast groves of persimmon, it is not of great economic importance. Persimmon weighs 53–55 lbs/cubic ft (826–904 kg/cubic m).

The growing scarcity of all types of commercial ebony has steadily increased its value, causing users to search for suitable substitutes with little success.

Further Reading:

Dale, Ivan R. *Kenya Trees and Shrubs*. London: Hatchards, 1991.

Kaiser, Jo Ann. *Wood of the Month Annual*. Vol. I.

J. Gordon Miller

Echidna see **Anteaters; Monotremes; Spiny anteaters**

Echiuroid worms

Echiuroid worms, or echiurans, commonly called spoon worms, are soft–bodied, unsegmented, marine animals of worldwide distribution. The approximately 125 species in the phylum Echiura occur mostly in the shallow intertidal zone of oceans. Most burrow or form tubes in sand or mud. Some live in discarded shells of sea urchins and sand dollars. Others inhabit cracks and crevices in rocks or coral fragments. Body length varies from a fraction of an inch to 20 inches (50 cm) or more. There are two body divisions: the body proper, or trunk; and a proboscis, which is highly mobile and extensible, but not retractable into the trunk. The trunk may be smooth, or it may have rows of small papillae or tubercles, giving it a superficially segmented appearance. At its anterior end, close to the base of the proboscis, it bears a pair of curved or hooked chitinous processes called setae. (Presence of setae is a major characteristic of the phylum Annelida, in which the setae are more numerous.) In some species there are additional setae near the posterior end of the trunk. The body wall is muscular, and a spacious, fluid–filled cavity separates it from the gut. This cavity does not extend into the proboscis. The gut is much longer than the trunk, and parts of it are coiled. It begins at the mouth at the base of the proboscis, and terminates at the anus at the opposite end.

The proboscis may be short, broad, and spoon–shaped, as in the common genus *Echiurus*, or it may be much longer than the trunk, narrow, and divided into two branches at the tip as in *Bonellia*. Its edges are rolled over ventrally to form a trough which is lined by cilia and mucus–secreting cells. It is used in feeding to collect organic particles from the sandy or muddy substrate and to transport it to the mouth. Tube–dwelling echiurans, for example *Urechis*, collect their food by filter–feeding. This worm secretes a mucus funnel which strains out particles from water pumped into the tube. From time to time the mucus is transported to the mouth and ingested, and a new funnel is formed.

Respiratory gas exchange in echiuroid worms occurs between the body fluid and sea water, usually across the body wall. But at least in some species, water is pumped in and out of the lower part of the gut through the anus, and gas exchange takes place across the wall of the gut. Although a circulatory system of closed vessels is present, the blood is colorless and serves mainly to transport nutrients. Excretion is performed by tubular structures called nephridia whose number varies widely among the species. One end of each nephridium is funnel–shaped and ciliated, and opens into the body cavity. The other end is narrow and opens to the outside by means of a minute pore. The nervous system is simple, without a brain or specialized sense organs. Sexes are separate. Each individual has a single gonad, testis, or ovary, which develops from the lining of the body cavity. Immature gametes are shed into the body cavity. Upon maturation they are transported to the outside through the nephridial tubes. Fertilization is external, and a planktonic "trochophore" larva (found also in the segmented worms, phylum Annelida, and a few other groups) develops.

Although in most echiurans males and females of a particular species look alike, an interesting example of sexual dimorphism and sex differentiation is presented by the European form *Bonellia viridis*. In this species, the male, which is ciliated and lacks a proboscis, is about 1–2 mm long. In contrast, the female's trunk alone is 2.3–3.1 inches (6–8 cm), with a proboscis which is even longer. The male lives in the female's pharynx or occasionally in her body cavity. The trochophore larva in this species develops into a female if it settles (at metamorphosis) some distance away from an existing female. On the other hand, if it settles close to a female, it develops into a male. It has been suggested that females produce and release into the surrounding water a "hormone" which has a masculinizing effect on the developing trochophore.

Echo see **Acoustics**

Echolocation

In the animal kingdom, echolocation is an animal's determination of the position of an object by the interpretation of echoes of sounds produced by the animal.

Echolocation is an elegant evolutionary adaptation to a low–light niche. The only animals that have come to exploit this unique sense ability are mammals—bats, dolphins, porpoises, and toothed whales. It is now believed that these animals use sound to "see" objects in equal or greater detail than humans can see with reflected light.

Echolocation is an adaptation to night life or to life in dark, cloudy waters. Long ago, bats that ate insects during the day might have been defeated in the struggle for survival by birds, which are agile and extremely sharp–sighted insectivores. Similarly, toothed whales, porpoises, and dolphins might have been quickly driven to extinction by sharks, which have a very keen sense of smell. These marine mammals not only compete with sharks for food sources, but have themselves been preyed upon by sharks. Echolocation helps them find food and escape from predators.

Bats

Echolocation in bats was first clearly described in 1945 in a seminal paper by Griffin and Galambos entitled *Development of the Concept of Echolocation*. Bats that eat frogs, fish, and insects use echolocation to find their prey in total or near–total darkness. After emitting a sound, these bats can tell the distance, direction, size, surface texture, and material of an object from information in the returning echo. Although the sounds emitted by bats are at high frequencies, out of the range of human hearing, these sounds are very loud—as high as 100 decibels, which is as loud as a chainsaw or jackhammer. People may hear the calls as clicks or chirps. The fruit–eating and nectar–loving bats do not use echolocation. These daytime and dusk–active bats have strong eyes and noses for finding food.

Bats use echolocation to hunt for food and to avoid collisions. A group of insect–eating bats was trained to tell the difference between insect larvae with fuzzy bristles and larvae that had their bristles removed. Researchers injected the bristle–less larvae with a chemical that made them taste bitter, then offered both the normal and the nonfuzzy larvae to the bats; the bats could instantly distinguish between them. In another experiment, a group of bats was conditioned to detect very thin wires in total darkness.

One question that puzzled scientists is how a bat can hear the echo of one sound while it is emitting another sound; why is the bat not deafened or distracted by its own sounds? The answer is that the bat is deafened—but only for a moment. Every time a bat lets out a call, part of its middle ear moves, preventing sounds from being heard. Once the bat's call is made, this

structure moves back, allowing the bat to hear the echo from the previous call.

One family of bats, the Vespertilionidae, emits ultrasonic sound pulses from their mouths in a narrow directed beam and uses their large ears to detect the returning echoes. Each sound pulse lasts from 5 to 10 milliseconds and decreases in frequency from about 100,000 Hz at the beginning down to about 30,000 Hz. This change in frequency (or frequency modulation) is roughly equivalent to a human looking at an object under a range of different colors of light. When the bat is just "looking around" it puts out approximately 10 pulses per second. If it hears something interesting, it takes a closer look by increasing the number of pulses per second to approximately 200. This is roughly equivalent to a person shining a brighter light on an object under investigation.

Marine mammals

Echolocation may work better under water than it does on land because water is a more effective and efficient conveyer of sound waves. Echolocation may be more effective for detecting objects underwater than light–based vision is on land. Sound with a broad frequency range has a more complex interaction with the objects that reflect it than does light. For this reason, sound can convey more information than light.

Like bats, marine mammals such as whales, porpoises, and dolphins emit pulses of sounds and listen for the echo. Also like bats, these sea mammals use sounds of many frequencies and a highly direction–sensitive sense of hearing to navigate and feed. Echolocation provides all of these mammals with a highly detailed, three–dimensional image of their environment.

Whales, dolphins, and porpoises all have a weak sense of vision and of smell, and all use echolocation in a similar way. They first emit a frequency–modulated sound pulse. A large fatty deposit, sometimes called a melon, found in its head helps the mammal to focus the sound. The echoes are received at a part of the lower jaw sometimes called the acoustic window. The echo's vibration is then transmitted through a fatty organ in the middle ear where it is converted to neural impulses and delivered to the brain. The brains of these sea mammals are at least as large relative to their body size as is a human brain relative to the size of the human body.

Captive porpoises have shown that they can locate tiny objects and thin wires and distinguish between objects made of different metals and of different sizes. This is because an object's material, structure, and texture all affect the nature of the echo returning to the porpoise.

Like bats, the toothed whales have specially adapted structures in the head for using echolocation. Some species of toothed whales have a bony structure in the head that insulates the back of the skull where sounds are received from the front of the skull where sounds are produced. The middle ear cavity is divided into a complex sinus that may help to acoustically separate the right and the left ears. This would enable the whale to more easily glean information from the echoes it receives. Other structures help to reduce the confusion of transmitted and received sound throughout the skull.

See also Acoustics; Bats; Cetaceans; Radar; Sonar.

Further Reading:

Harrison, Richard, and M. M. Bryden, eds. *Whales, Dolphins, and Porpoises.* New York: Facts on File, 1988.

Starr, Cecie, and Ralph Taggart. *Biology: The Unity of Life.* 6th ed. Belmont, CA: Wadsworth, 1992.

John Henry Dreyfuss

Eclipses

It is a happy coincidence of nature that the apparent size of the sun and the moon in the sky are about the same. Thus on those rare occasions when the orbital motion of the earth and moon cause them to align with the sun, as seen from points on the earth the moon will just cover the surface of the sun and day will suddenly become night. Those who are located in the converging lunar shadow which just reaches the earth will see a *total eclipse* of the sun. We call the converging shadow cone,

within which the sun is completely hidden by the moon, the umbral shadow of the moon. One can imagine a diverging cone with the moon at its apex in which only part of the sun is covered by the moon. This shadow is called the penumbra, or partially dark shadow. Folks on the earth located in this shadow will see the sun partially obscured or covered by the moon. Such an eclipse is called a *partial solar eclipse.* Because the base of this shadow cone is far larger than the umbral shadow, far more people see partial solar eclipses than see total solar eclipses. However, the impact on the observer of a total solar eclipse is far greater. Even a nearly total solar eclipse permits a small fraction of the solar surface to be visible, but covering the bright photosphere completely drops the light–level to a millionth of its normal value. During totality one can safely look directly at the sun and its corona, but this should not be done outside of totality during any partial or annular phases. The photospheric surface of the sun is so bright that its focused image on the retina of the eye can do permanent damage to an individual's vision, including total blindness. Even viewing the sun through colored or smoked glass should be avoided, for the filter may pass infrared or ultraviolet light not obvious to the observer, but which can still do extensive damage. While specially designed "sun filters" may provide viewing safety, the safest approach to looking at the sun is projecting its image from a small telescope or monocular onto a screen. Direct viewing and photographs of the projected image can then be made in relative safety.

To the observer of a total solar eclipse many strange phenomena are visible at the same time. The progressive coverage of the solar photosphere by the moon reduces the solar heating of the earth, causing the local temperature to fall. The drop in temperature is accompanied by a rise in humidity and often a wind change. The covering of the central part of the sun's disk also brings about a subtle color shift toward the yellow. In the final seconds before totality the last bright regions of the sun's disk shine through the valleys at the limb of the moon, causing bright spots called "Baily's Beads." As the last of these disappear, the blood–red upper atmosphere of the sun called the *chromosphere* will briefly appear before it too is covered, revealing the winding–sheet–white corona which constitutes the outer atmosphere of the sun and is less bright than the full moon. This sequence takes just seconds and then it is night, complete with stars and planets. Birds fly to roost and animals behave as if night had truly arrived. All the senses are assaulted at once both by the changes in the local environment and the changes to the sun. A solar eclipse makes such an impression on people that it is said St. Patrick used one to convert the Celtic Irish to Christianity in the 5th century. The ancient historian Herodotus reported that a total solar eclipse which occurred during a battle between the Lydians and the Medes in 585 B.C. caused the soldiers to throw down their weapons and leave the field. Otherwise professional astronomers have been known to stand and stare at the phenomenon, forgetting to gather the data they have practiced for months and traveled thousands of miles to obtain.

Outside the narrow band traced across the earth by the tip of the moon's umbral shadow, part of the sun will be covered from those located in the expanding cone of the lunar penumbral shadow. An eclipse seen from such locations is said to be a partial solar eclipse. If the moon is near its farthest point from the earth, its dark umbral shadow doesn't quite reach the earth. Should this occur when the alignment for a solar eclipse is correct, the bright disk of the sun will only be partially covered. At the middle of the eclipse a bright annulus of the solar photosphere will completely surround the dark disk of the moon. Such eclipses are called *annular eclipses* and may be considered a special case of a partial solar eclipse. Since part of the photosphere is always visible, one never sees the chromosphere or corona and the sky never gets as dark as during a total solar eclipse. However, there is a definite change in the color of the sunlight. Since the visible photosphere at the limb of the annularly eclipsed sun is cooler and yellower than the center of the solar disk, the effect is for the daylight color to be shifted to the yellow. The effect is quite pronounced for eclipses occurring around local noon.

Because the area on the earth covered by the moon's umbra during a total eclipse is so small, it is quite rare for an individual to see one even though their frequency of occurrence is somewhat greater than lunar eclipses. Lunar eclipses occur when the moon passes into the shadow cast by the earth. During a lunar eclipse, the bright disk of the full moon will be progressively covered by the dark disk of the umbral shadow of the earth. If the eclipse is total, the moon will be completely covered by that shadow. Should the alignment between the sun, earth, and moon be such that the moon simply grazes the earth's umbra, the eclipse is called a partial. Lunar orbital paths that pass only through the penumbral shadow of the earth are called *penumbral lunar eclipses*. The dimming of the moon's light in these eclipses is so slight that it is rarely detected by the human eye so little notice of these eclipses is made.

Since the moon is covered by the shadow of the earth, any point on the earth from which the moon can be seen will be treated to a lunar eclipse. Thus they are far more widely observed than are total eclipses of the

A total solar eclipse in La Paz, Baja California, Mexico, on July 11, 1991.

sun. However, because the sun is so much brighter than the full moon, the impact of a total lunar eclipse is far less than for a total solar eclipse. Unlike a solar eclipse where the shadow cast by the moon is totally dark, some light may be refracted by the earth's atmosphere into the earth's umbra so that the disk of the moon does not totally disappear during a total lunar eclipse. Since most of the blue light from the sun is scattered in the atmosphere making the sky blue, only the red light makes it into the earth's umbral shadow. Therefore the totally eclipsed moon will appear various shades of red depending on the cloud cover in the atmosphere of the earth.

Lunar eclipses do not occur every time the moon is full, nor do solar eclipses happen each time the moon is new. Although the line–up between the sun, earth, and moon is close at these lunar phases, it is not perfect. The orbital plane of the moon is tipped about 5 degrees to the orbital plane of the earth. These two planes intersect in a line called the line of nodes. That line must be pointed at the sun in order for an eclipse to occur. Should the moon pass by the node between the earth and the sun while the line of nodes is aimed at the sun, the alignment between the sun, moon, and earth will be perfect and a solar eclipse will occur. If the moon passes through the node lying beyond the earth when the line of nodes is properly oriented, we see a lunar eclipse. Except for slow changes to the moon's orbit, the line of nodes maintains an approximately fixed orientation in space as it is carried about the sun by the earth's motion. Therefore, about twice a year the line of nodes is pointing straight at the sun and eclipses can occur. If the alignment is closely maintained during the two weeks between new moon and full moon, a solar eclipse will be followed by a lunar eclipse. A quick inspection of the table of pending eclipses shows that

20 of the 47 listed eclipses occur within two weeks of one another, indicating that these are times of close alignment of the line of nodes with the sun. A further inspection shows that these pairs occur about 20 days earlier each year indicating that the line of nodes is slowly moving westward across the sky opposite to the annual motion of the sun. At this rate it takes about 18.6 years for the nodes to complete a full circuit of the sky. Thus every 18 to 19 years eclipses will occur at about the same season of the year. After three of these seasonal cycles, or 56 years, the eclipses will occur on, or about, the same day. It is this long seasonal cycle that Gerald Hawkins associated with the 56 "Aubry Holes" at Stonehenge. He used this agreement to support his case that Stonehenge was used to predict eclipses and the Aubry Holes were used to keep track of the yearly passage of time between seasonal eclipses. There are other cycles of eclipses which have been known since antiquity. It is a reasonable question to ask how long it will be before an eclipse will re–occur at the same place on the earth. The requirements for this to happen are relatively easy to establish. First, the moon must be at the same phase (i.e. either new or full depending on whether the eclipse in question is a solar or lunar eclipse). Secondly, the moon must be at the same place in its orbit with respect to the orbital node. Thirdly, the sun and moon must have the same distance from the earth for both eclipses. Finally, if the solar eclipses are to have similar paths across the earth, they must happen at the same time of the year. The first two conditions are required for an eclipse to happen at all. Meeting the third condition assures that the umbral shadow of the moon will reach the earth to the same extent for both eclipses. This means that the two eclipses will be of the same type (i.e., total or annular in the case of the sun). The last condition will be required for solar eclipses to be visible from the same location on the earth.

The interval between successive phases of the moon is called the *synodic month* and is 29.5306 days long. Due to the slow motion of the line of nodes across the sky, successive passages of a give node, called the *nodal month*, occur every 27.2122 days. Finally, successive intervals of closest approach to the earth (i.e. perigee passage) are known as the *anomalistic* month which is 27.55455 days long. For the first three conditions to be met the moon must have traversed an integral number of synodic, nodical, and anomalistic months in a nearly integral number of days. One can write the these constraints as equations whose solutions are integers. However, such equations, called *Diophantine Equations*, are notably difficult to solve in general. So we look for a solution as the ancient Babylonians did, by trial and error. They found that 223 synodic

KEY TERMS

. . . .

Anomalistic month—The length of time required for the moon to travel around its orbit from its point of closest approach to the earth and back again.

Chromosphere—The bright red "color sphere" seen surrounding the sun as a narrow band when the photosphere is obscured.

Corona—A pearly white irregular shaped region surrounding the sun. It is visible only when the photosphere and chromosphere are obscured.

Node—The intersection of the lunar orbit with the plane of the earth's orbit about the sun.

Nodical month—The length of time required for the moon to travel around its orbit from a particular node and back again.

Penumbra—From the Greek meaning "partially dark." Within the penumbral shadow part of the light source contributing to the eclipse will still be visible.

Photosphere—From the Greek meaning "light–sphere." This is the bright surface which we associate with sunlight.

Saros—A cycle of eclipses spanning 18 years and 11 days first recorded by the Babylonians.

Synodic month—The length of time required for the moon to travel around its orbit from a specific phase and back again.

Umbra—From the Greek meaning dark. Within the umbral shadow no light will be visible except in the case of the earth's umbral shadow where some red sunlight may be refracted by the atmosphere of the earth.

months, 242 nodical months, and 239 anomalistic months all contained about 6585 and a third days which turns out to be just 11 days in excess of 18 years. They referred to the cycle as the Saros cycle for it accurately predicted repeats of lunar eclipses of the same type and duration. However, the cycle missed being an integral number of days by about eight hours. Thus, solar eclipses would occur eight hours later after each Saros, which would be more than enough to move the path of totality away from any given site. After three such cycles, sometimes referred to as the Triple Saros lasting 54 years and a month, even the same solar eclipses would repeat with fairly close paths of totality. Since the integral multiples of the various months do not

TABLE OF ECLIPSES 1995-2010

Date	Type of Eclipse	Time of Mid-Eclipse-EST*	Duration of Eclipse**	Total Length of Eclipse	Region of Visibility†
Apr. 15, 95	Lunar-Partial	7:19 AM	—	1h 12min	E. Hemisph.
Apr. 29, 95	Solar-Annular	1 AM	6min 38sec	—	Pacific S. America
Oct. 24, 95	Solar-Total	Midnight	2min 10sec	—	Asia, Borneo, Pacific Ocean
Apr. 3, 96	Lunar-Total	7:11 PM	86min	3h 36min	W. Hemisph.
Sep. 26, 96	Lunar-Total	9:55 PM	70min	3h 22min	W. Hemisph.
Mar. 8, 97	Solar-Total	8 PM	2min 50sec	—	Siberia
Mar. 23, 97	Lunar-Partial	11:41 PM	—	3h 22min	W. Hemisph.
Sep. 16, 97	Lunar-Total	1:47 PM	62min	3h 16min	E. Hemisph.
Feb. 26, 98	Solar-Total	Noon	4min 8sec	—	W. Pacific, S. Atlantic
Aug. 21, 98	Solar-Annular	9 PM	3min 14sec	—	Sumatra, Pacific Ocn.
Feb. 16, 99	Solar-Annular	2 AM	1min 19sec	—	Indian Ocn., Australia
Jul. 28, 99	Lunar-Partial	6:34 AM	—	2h 22min	Europe-Asia
Aug. 11, 99	Solar-Total	6 AM	2min 23sec	—	Atlantic Ocn., Europe-Asia
Jan. 20, 00	Lunar-Total	11:45 PM	76min	3h 22min	W. Hemisph.
Jul. 16, 00	Lunar-Total	8:57 AM	106min	3h 56min	E. Hemisph.
Jan. 9, 01	Lunar-Total	3:22 PM	60min	3h 16min	E. Hemisph.
Jun. 21, 01	Solar-Total	7 AM	4m 56sec	—	S. Atlantic, S. Africa
Jul. 5, 01	Lunar-Partial	9:57 AM	—	2h 38min	E. Hemisph.
Dec. 14, 01	Solar-Annular	4 PM	3min 54sec	—	Pacific Ocn., Cent. Amer.
Jun. 10, 02	Solar-Annular	7 PM	1min 13sec	—	Pacific Ocn.
Dec. 4, 02	Solar-Total	3 AM	2min 4sec	—	Indian Ocn., Australia
May 15, 03	Lunar-Total	10:41 PM	52min	3h 14min	W. Hemisph.
May 30, 03	Solar-Annular	11 PM	3min 37sec	—	Iceland &E. Arctic
Nov. 8, 03	Lunar-Total	8:20 PM	22min	3h 30min	W. Hemisph.
Nov. 23, 03	Solar-Total	6 PM	1min 57sec	—	Antarctica
May 4, 04	Lunar-Total	3:32 PM	76min	3h 22min	E. Hemisph.

TABLE OF ECLIPSES 1995-2010 (cont'd)

Date	Type of Eclipse	Time of Mid-Eclipse-EST*	Duration of Eclipse**	Total Length of Eclipse	Region of Visibility†
Oct. 27, 04	Lunar-Total	10:05 PM	80min	3h 38min	W. Hemisph.
Apr. 8, 05	Solar-Annular-Total	4 PM	42sec	—	N. Central, Pacific Ocn.
Oct. 3, 05	Solar-Annular	6 AM	4m 32sec	—	Atlantic Ocn., Spain, Africa
Oct. 17, 05	Lunar-Partial	7:04 AM	—	56min	E. Hemisph.
Mar. 29, 06	Solar-Total	5AM	4min 7sec	—	Atlantic Ocn., Africa, Turk.
Sep. 7, 06	Lunar-Partial	1:52 PM	—	1h 30min	E. Hemisph.
Sep. 22, 06	Solar-Annular	7 AM	7min 9sec	—	N.E. of S.Amer. Atlan.
Mar. 3, 07	Lunar-Total	6:22 PM	74min	3h 40min	W. Hemisph.
Aug. 28, 07	Lunar-Total	5:38 AM	90min	3h 32min	W. Hemisph.
Feb. 6, 08	Solar-Annular	11 PM	2min 14sec	—	S. Pacific, Antarctic
Feb. 20, 08	Lunar-Total	10:57 PM	50min	3h 24min	W. Hemisph.
Aug. 1, 08	Solar-Total	5 AM	2min 28sec	—	Arctic-Cand., Siberia
Aug. 16, 08	Lunar-Partial	4:11 PM	—	3h 8min	E. Hemisph.
Jan. 26, 09	Solar-Annular	3 AM	7min 56sec	—	S. Atlantic, Indian Ocn.
Jul. 21, 09	Solar-Total	10 PM	6min 40sec	—	East Asia, Pacific Ocn.
Dec. 31, 09	Lunar-Partial	2:24 PM	—	1h 00min	E. Hemisph.
Jan. 15, 10	Solar-Annular	2 AM	11min 10sec	—	Africa, Indian Ocn.
Jun. 26, 10	Lunar-Partial	6:40 AM	—	2h 42min	E. Hemisph.
Jul. 11, 10	Solar-Total	3 PM	5min 20sec	—	Pacific Ocn., S. America
Dec. 21, 10	Lunar-Total	3:18 AM	72min	3h 28min	W. Hemisph.

* Eastern Standard time is used for convience. Since the path of a Solar Eclipse spans a good part of the Earth, only an approximate time to the nearest hour is given the mid-point of that path.

** The time of the eclipse duration is for maximum extend of totality, except for annular eclipses where it marks the maximum duration of the annular phase.

† The visible location of lunar eclipses is approximately half the globe where the Moon is visible. For convience, the globe has been split into eastern and western hemispheres. Depending on the time of mid-eclipse, more or less of the entire eclipse may be visible from the specified hemisphere.

exactly result in an integral number of days, the repetitions of the eclipses are not exactly the same, but they are close enough to verify the predictability and establish the cycles. It is impressive that the Babylonians were able to establish the Saros with some certainty. Their ability to do so supports Hawkins' notion that the people who built Stonehenge were also capable of establishing the seasonal eclipse cycle.

It is tempting to look for cycles of even longer duration in search of a set of synodic, nodical, and anomalistic months that would yield a more close integral number of days, but such a search would be fruitless. There are other subtle forces perturbing the orbit of the moon so that longer series of eclipses fail to repeat. Indeed, any series of lunar eclipses fails to repeat after about 50 Saros or about 870 years. Similar problems exist for solar eclipses. While the present family of solar eclipses provides little opportunity for an observer in North America for the balance of the century, one should still consider making the effort to see a total eclipse in another land if the occasion presents itself. The phenomenon has awed people of the past, present, and will likely do so for the indefinite future.

See also Calendars; Moon; Sun.

Further Reading:

Arny, T.T., *Explorations: An Introduction to Astronomy*, 1994, Mosby, St. Louis, pp. 156–161 .

Hawkins, G.S. *Stonehenge Decoded*, 1965, Dell Publishing Co. Inc., New York, pp. 132–148.

Schaefer, B.E. "Solar Eclipses that Changed the World," Sky and Telescope, 87, 1984, pp. 36–39.

George W. Collins, II

Ecological climax see **Climax (ecological)**

Ecological community see **Biological community**

Ecological disturbance see **Disturbance, ecological**

Ecological economics

Conventional and ecological economics

Economics is conventionally considered to be a social science that examines the allocation of scarce resources among various potential uses that are in competition with each other. Economics attempts to predict and understand the patterns of consumption of goods and services by individuals and society. A core assumption of conventional economics is that individuals and corporations seek to maximize their profits within the marketplace.

In conventional economics, the worth of any goods or services is judged on the basis of their direct or indirect utilities to humans. In almost all cases, the goods and services are assigned value (that is, are valuated) in units of tradable currency, such as dollars. This is true of: (1) manufactured goods such as televisions, automobiles, and buildings, (2) the services provided by people like farmers, doctors, teachers, and baseball players, and (3) all natural resources that are harvested and processed for use by humans, including nonrenewable resources such as metals and hydrocarbons, and renewable resources such as agricultural products, fish, and wood.

Ecological economics differs from conventional economics by attempting to value goods and services in ways that are not only biased by their usefulness to humans, that is, in a nonanthropocentric fashion. This means that ecological economics attempts to take into account the many environmental and social costs that are associated with the depletion of natural resources as well as the degradation of ecological systems through pollution, extinction, and other environmental stressors. Many of these important damages are associated with the diverse economic activities of humans, but these degradations are often not accounted for by conventional economics. From the environmental perspective, the most important problem with conventional economics has been that the marketplace has not recognized the value of important ecological goods and services, and therefore their degradation has not been considered to be a cost of doing business. Ecological economics attempts to find ways to consider and account for the very real costs of environmental damages.

Ecological goods and services

Humans have an absolute dependence on a continuous flow of natural resources to sustain their economic systems. There are two basic types of natural resources, nonrenewable and renewable. Sustainable economic systems and sustainable human societies cannot, by definition, be based on the use of nonrenewable resources because these are always depleted by usage, a process that is referred to as "mining." Ultimately, sustainable systems can only be supported by the use of renewable resources which, if harvested and managed sensibly, can be available forever. Because most renewable resources are the goods and services of ecosystems, economic and ecological systems are highly interdependent.

Potentially, renewable natural resources can sustain harvesting indefinitely. However, to achieve a condition of sustainable usage, the rate of harvesting must be smaller than the rate of renewal of the resource. For example, flowing water can be sustainably used to produce hydroelectricity or for irrigation as long as the usage does not exceed the capacity of the landscape to yield water. Similarly, biological natural resources such as trees and hunted fish, waterfowl, and deer can be sustainably harvested to yield valuable products as long as the rate of cropping does not exceed the renewal of the resource. These are familiar examples of renewable resources partly because they all represent ecological goods and services that are directly important to human welfare, and that can be valuated in terms of dollars.

Unlike conventional economics, ecological economics also considers other types of ecological resources to be important even though they may not be of direct importance to humans, and they are not valuated in dollars. Because the marketplace does not assign value to these resources, they can be degraded without conventional economic cost even though this results in tremendous ecological damages and ultimately harms society. Some examples of ecological resources that markets consider to be "free" goods and services include: (1) nonexploited species of plants and animals that are not utilized as an economic resource but are nevertheless important because they may have undiscovered uses to humans perhaps as medicines or as food, as they are part of the aesthetic environment and have intrinsic value which exists even if they are not useful to humans; and (2) ecological services such as control over erosion, provision of water and nutrient cycling, and cleansing of pollutants emitted into the environment by humans as occurs when growing vegetation removes carbon dioxide from the atmosphere and when organisms detoxify chemicals such as pesticides.

Use of renewable resources by humans

As noted above, sustainable economic systems can only be based on the wise use of renewable resources. However, the most common way in which humans have used potentially renewable resources is by "overharvesting," that is, exploitation that exceeds the capacity for renewal so that the stock is degraded and sometimes made extinct. In other words, most use of potentially renewable resources has been by mining, or use as if it were a nonrenewable resource.

There are many cases of the mining and degradation of potentially renewable resources from all parts of the world and from all human societies. In a broad sense, this syndrome is represented by extensive deforestation, collapses of wild fisheries, declines of agricultural soil capability, and other resource degradations. The extinctions of the dodo, great auk, Steller's sea cow, and passenger pigeon all represent overhunting so extreme that it took potentially renewable resources beyond the brink of biological extinction. The overhunting of the American bison and various species of seals and whales all represent biological mining that took potentially renewable resources beyond the brink of economic extinction so that it was no longer profitable to exploit the resource.

These and many other cases of degradation of renewable resources occurred because conventional economics did not value resource degradation properly so that profit was only determined on the basis of costs directly associated with catching and processing the resource and not on the costs of renewal and depletion. Similarly, conventional economics considers nonvaluated goods and services such as biodiversity, soil conservation, erosion control, water and nutrient cycling, and cleansing air and water of pollutants to be free resources so that no costs are associated with their degradation.

Ecologically sustainable systems

The challenge of ecological economics is to design systems of resource harvesting and management that are sustainable so that human society can be supported forever into the future without degrading their essential, ecological base of support.

Ecologically sustainable systems must sustain two clusters of values: (1) the health of economically valuated, renewable resources, such as trees, fish, and agricultural soil capability, and well as (2) acceptable levels of ecological goods and services that are not conventionally valuated. Therefore, a truly sustainable system must be able to yield natural resources that humans need and to provide that sustenance forever. However, the system must also provide services related to clean air and water and nutrient cycling while also sustaining sufficient habitat for native species and their natural ecological communities.

To achieve this goal, ecologically sustainable systems will have to based on two ways of managing ecosystems: (1) as working ecosystems, and (2) as ecological reserves. The "working ecosystems" will be harvested and managed to yield sustainable flows of valuated resources such as forest products, hunted animals, fish, and agricultural commodities. However, some environmental costs will be associated with these uses of ecosystems. For example, although many species will find habitats available on working lands to be acceptable to their purposes, other native species and most natural communities will be at risk on working landscapes. To sustain the ecological values that cannot be accommodated by working ecosystems, a system of ecological reserves will have to be developed. These reserves must be designed to ensure that all native species are sustained at viable population levels, that there are viable areas of natural communities, and that ecosystems will be able to supply acceptable levels of important services such as control over erosion, nutrient cycling, and cleansing of pollution.

So far ecologically sustainable systems of the sort described above are no more than a concept. None exist today. In fact, humans mostly exploit the potentially renewable goods and services of ecosystems in an unsustainable fashion. Clearly this is a problem because humans rely on these resources to sustain their endeavors. Ecological economics provides a framework for the design of better, ecologically sustainable systems of resource use. However, it remains to be seen whether human societies will be wise enough to adopt these sustainable methods of organizing their economies and their interactions with ecosystems.

See also Alternative energy sources; Deforestation; Ecosystem; Sustainable development.

Further Reading:

Costanza, R. *Ecological Economics: The Science and Management of Sustainability*. New York: Columbia University Press, 1991.
Freedman, B. *Environmental Ecology*. 2nd ed. San Diego: Academic Press, 1994.
Jansson, A. M., M. Hammer, C. Folke, and R. Costanza, eds. *Investing in Natural Capital: The Ecological Economics Approach to Sustainability*. Washington, DC: Island Press, 1994.

Bill Freedman

Ecological integrity

Ecological integrity is a relatively new concept that is being actively discussed by ecologists. However, a consensus has not yet emerged as to the definition of ecological integrity. Clearly, human activities result in environmental changes that enhance some species, communities, and ecological processes, while at the same time causing important damages to others. The challenge for the concept of ecological integrity is to provide a means of distinguishing between responses that represent improvements or degradations of the quality of ecosystems.

Ecological integrity is analogous to health. A healthy individual is relatively vigorous in his or her physical and mental capacities, and is uninfluenced by disease. Health is indicated by diagnostic symptoms that are bounded by ranges considered to be normal, and by attributes that are regarded as desirable. Unhealthy conditions are indicated by the opposite, and may require treatment to prevent further deteriorations. However, the metaphor of human and ecosystem health is imperfect in some important respects, and has been criticized by ecologists. This is mostly because health refers to individual organisms, while ecological contexts are much more complex, involving many individuals of numerous species, and both living and nonliving attributes of ecosystems.

Environmental stress—challenge to ecological integrity

Environmental stress refers to physical, chemical, and biological constraints on the productivity of species and the development of ecosystems. When they increase or decrease in intensity, stressors elicit ecological responses. Stressors can be natural environmental factors, or they can be associated with the activities of humans. Some environmental stressors are relatively local in their influence, while others are regional or global in their scope. Stressors are challenges to ecological integrity.

Species and ecosystems have some capacity to tolerate changes in the intensity of environmental stressors, an attribute known as resistance. However, there are limits to resistance, which represent thresholds of tolerance. When these thresholds are exceeded, substantial ecological changes occur in response to further increases in the intensity of environmental stress.

Environmental stressors can be categorized as follows:

Physical stress

Physical stress refers to brief but intense events of kinetic energy. Because of its acute, episodic nature, this is a type of disturbance. Examples include volcanic eruptions, windstorms, and explosions.

Wildfire

Wildfire is another disturbance, during much of the biomass of an ecosystem combusts, and the dominant species may be killed.

Pollution

Pollution occurs when chemicals occur in concentrations that are large enough to affect organisms, and thereby cause ecological changes. Toxic pollution can be caused by gases such as sulfur dioxide and ozone, elements such as mercury and arsenic, and pesticides. Nutrients such as phosphate and nitrate can distort ecological processes such as productivity, causing a type of pollution known as eutrophication.

Thermal stress

Thermal stress occurs when releases of heat cause ecological responses, as occurs near natural, hot water vents in the ocean, or with industrial discharges of heated water.

Radiation stress

Radiation stress is associated with excessive loads of ionizing energy. This can be important on mountaintops, where there are intense exposures to ultraviolet radiation, and in places where there are uncontrolled exposures to radioactive wastes.

Climatic stress

Climatic stress is caused by excessive or insufficient regimes of temperature, moisture, solar radiation, or combinations of these. Tundra and deserts are climatically stressed ecosystems, while tropical rainforests occur in places where climate is relatively benign.

Biological stress

Biological stresses are associated with the complex interactions that occur among organisms of the same or different species. Biological stresses can result from competition, herbivory, predation, parasitism, and disease. The harvesting and management of species and ecosystems by humans is a type of biological stress.

Large changes in the intensity of environmental stress result in various types of ecological responses. For example, when an ecosystem is disrupted by an intense disturbance, there may be substantial mortality of its species and other damages, followed by recovery through succession. In contrast, a longer–term intensification of environmental stress, possibly associated with chronic pollution or climate change, causes more permanent ecological adjustments to occur. Relatively vulnerable species are reduced in abundance or eliminated from sites that are stressed over the longer term, and their modified niches are assumed by more tolerant species. Other common responses include a simplification of species richness, and decreased rates of productivity, decomposition, and nutrient cycling. These changes represent an ecological conversion, or a longer–term change in the character of the ecosystem.

Components of ecological integrity

Many studies have been made of the ecological responses to disturbance and to longer–term changes in the intensity of environmental stress. These studies have examined stressors associated with, for example, pollution, the harvesting of species of ecosystems, and the conversion of natural ecosystems into managed agroecosystems. The commonly observed patterns of change in these sorts of stressed ecosystems are considered to represent some of the key elements of ecological integrity. Such observations can be used to develop indicators of ecological integrity, which are useful in determining whether this condition is improving or being degraded over time. It has been suggested that greater ecological integrity is displayed by systems with the following characteristics:

Resiliency and resistance

Ecosystems with greater ecological integrity are, in a relative sense, resilient and resistant to changes in the intensity of environmental stress. In the ecological context, resistance refers to the capacity of organisms, populations, and communities to tolerate increases in stress without exhibiting significant responses. Resistance is manifest in thresholds of tolerance. Resilience refers to the ability to recover from disturbance.

Biodiversity

In its simplest interpretation, biodiversity refers to the number of species occurring in some ecological community or in a designated area, such as a park or a country. However, biodiversity is better defined as the total richness of biological variation, including genetic variation within populations and species, the numbers of species in communities, and the patterns and dynamics of these over large areas.

Complexity of structure and function

The structural and functional complexity of ecosystems is limited by natural environmental stresses associated with climate, soil, chemistry, and other factors, and by stressors associated with human activities. As the overall intensity of stress increases or decreases, structural and functional complexity responds accordingly. Under any particular environmental regime, older ecosystems will generally be more complex than younger ecosystems.

Presence of large species

The largest, naturally occurring species in any ecosystem generally appropriate relatively large amounts of resources, occupy a great deal of space, and require large areas to sustain their populations. In addition, large species are usually long–lived, and therefore integrate the effects of stressors over an extended time. Consequently, ecosystems that are subject to an intense regime of environmental stress cannot support relatively large species. In contrast, mature ecosystems of relatively benign environments are dominated by large, long–lived species.

Presence of higher–order predators

Because top predators are dependent on a broad base of ecological productivity, they can only be sustained by relatively extensive and/or productive ecosystems.

Controlled nutrient cycling

Recently disturbed ecosystems temporarily lose some of their capability to exert biological control over nutrient cycling, and they often export large quantities of nutrients dissolved or suspended in streamwater. Systems that are not "leaky" of their nutrient capital in this way are considered to have greater ecological integrity.

Efficient energy use and transfer

Large increases in environmental stress commonly cause community respiration to exceed productivity, so that the standing crop of biomass decreases. Ecosystems that are not degrading in their capital of biomass are considered to have greater integrity than those in which biomass is decreasing over time.

Ability to maintain natural ecological values

Ecosystems that can naturally maintain their species, communities, and other important characteristics, without interventions by humans through manage-

ment, have greater ecological integrity. For example, if a rare species of animal can only be sustained through intensive management of its habitat by humans, or by management of its demographics, possibly by a captive–breeding and release program, then its populations and ecosystem are lacking in ecological integrity.

Components of a "natural" community

Ecosystems that are dominated by non–native, introduced species are considered to have less ecological integrity than ecosystems that are composed of native species.

The last two indicators involve judgements about "naturalness" and the roles of humans in ecosystems, which are philosophically controversial topics. However, most ecologists would consider that self–organizing, unmanaged ecosystems have greater ecological integrity than those that are strongly influenced by human activities. Examples of the latter include agroecosystems, forestry plantations, and urban and suburban ecosystems. None of these systems can maintain themselves in the absence of large inputs of energy, nutrients, and physical management by humans.

Indicators of ecological integrity

Indicators of ecological integrity vary widely in their scale, complexity, and intent. For example, certain metabolic indicators can suggest the responses by individuals and populations to toxic stresses, as is the case of assays of detoxifying enzyme systems that respond vigorously to exposures to persistent chlorinated hydrocarbons, such as DDT and PCBs. Indicators related to populations of endangered species are relevant to the viability of those species, as well as the integrity of their natural communities. There are also indicators relevant to processes occurring at the level of landscape. There are even global indicators, for example, relevant to climate change, depletion of stratospheric ozone, and deforestation.

Sometimes, relatively simple indicators can be used to integrate the ecological integrity of a large and complex ecosystem. In the western United States, for instance, the viability of populations of spotted owls (*Strix occidentalis*) is considered to be an indicator of the integrity of the types of old–growth forests in which this endangered bird breeds. If plans to harvest and manage those forests are judged to pose a threat to the viability of a population of spotted owls or the species, this would indicate a significant challenge to the integrity of the entire old–growth forest ecosystem.

KEY TERMS

· ·

Stress—Environmental constraints that cause ecological disruptions (that is, disturbance), or that limit the potential productivity of species or development of ecosystems. Environmental stress is a challenge to ecological integrity.

Ecologists are also beginning to develop holistic indicators of ecological integrity. These are designed as composites of various indicators, analogous to certain economic indices such as the Dow–Jones Index of stock markets, the Consumer Price Index, and gross domestic product indices of economies. Composite economic indicators like these are relatively simple to design because all of the input data are measured in a common way, for example, in dollars. However, in ecology there is no common currency among the various indicators of ecological integrity, and it is therefore difficult to develop composite indicators that people will agree upon.

In spite of all of the difficulties, ecologists are making progress in their development of indicators of ecological integrity. This is a very important activity for ecologists, because individual people and their larger societies need objective information about changes in the integrity of species and ecosystems so that actions can be taken to prevent unacceptable degradations. It is being increasingly recognized that human economies can only be sustained over the longer term by ecosystems with integrity. These must be capable of supplying continuous flows of renewable resources, such as trees, fish, agricultural products, and clean air and water. There are also important concerns about the intrinsic values of native species and their natural ecosystems, all of which must be sustained along with humans. Truly sustainable economies can only be based on ecosystems with integrity.

See also Biodiversity; Ecosystem; Indicator species; Pollution; Stress, ecological; Wildfire.

Further Reading:

Freedman, B. *Environmental Ecology*. 2nd ed. San Diego: Academic Press, 1994.

Karr, J. "Defining and Assessing Ecological Integrity: Beyond Water Quality." *Environmental Toxicology and Chemistry* 12 (1993): 1521–1531.

Woodley, S., J. Kay, and G. Francis, eds. *Ecological Integrity and the Management of Ecosystems*. Boca Raton, FL: St. Lucie Press, 1993.

Bill Freedman

Ecological monitoring

Governments everywhere are increasingly recognizing the fact that human activities are causing serious environmental and ecological damages. To effectively deal with this environmental crisis, it is important to understand its dimensions and dynamics. What, specifically, are the damages, how are they changing over time, and what are the best means of prevention or mitigation? To develop answers to these important questions, longer–term programs of monitoring and research must be designed and implemented. These programs must be capable of detecting environmental and ecological changes over large areas, and of developing an understanding of the causes and consequences of those changes.

Humans and their societies have always been sustained by environmental resources. For almost all of human history the most important resources have been potentially renewable, ecological resources. Especially important have been fish and terrestrial animals that could be hunted, edible plants that could be gathered, and the productivity of managed, agricultural ecosystems. More recently, humans have increasingly relied on the use of nonrenewable mineral resources that are mined from the environment, especially fossil fuels and metals.

However, the ability of ecosystems to sustain humans is becoming increasingly stressed, largely because of the negative consequences of two, interacting factors: (1) the extraordinary increase in size of the human population, which numbered about 5.8 billion in 1995, and (2) the equally incredible increase in the quantities of resources used by individual humans, especially people living in developed countries with advanced economies, such as those of North America and Western Europe.

Environmental and ecological degradations are important for two reasons: (1) they represent decreases in the ability of Earth's ecosystems to sustain humans and their activities, and (2) they represent catastrophic damages to other species and to natural ecosystems, which have their own intrinsic values, irrespective of their importance to humans. The role of programs of environmental and ecological monitoring is to detect those degradations, to understand their causes and consequences, and to find ways to effectively deal with the problems.

Monitoring, research and indicators

In the sense used here, environmental monitoring is an activity that involves repeated measurements of inorganic, ecological, social, and/or economic variables. This is done with a view to detecting important changes over time, and to predicting future changes. Within this larger context, ecological monitoring deals with changes in the structure and functioning of ecosystems.

Monitoring investigates scientific questions that are rather uncomplicated, involving simple changes over time. However, the success of monitoring depends on: (1) astute choice of a few, appropriate indicators to measure over time, from a diverse array of potential indicators, and (2) successful data collection, which can be expensive and difficult, and requires longer–term commitments because important changes may not detectable by short–term studies.

It is important to understand that monitoring programs must be integrated with research, which examines relatively complex questions about the causes and consequences of important environmental and ecological changes that may be detected during monitoring. The ultimate goals of an integrated program of ecological monitoring and research are to: (1) detect or forecast changes, and (2) determine the causes and implications of those changes.

Monitoring involves the repeated measurement of indicators, which are relatively simple measurements related to more complex aspects of environmental quality. Changes in indicators are determined through comparison with their historical values, or with a reference or control situation. Often, monitoring may detect changes in indicators, but the causes of those changes may not be understood because the base of environmental and ecological knowledge is incomplete. To discover the causes of those changes, research has to be undertaken.

For example, monitoring of forests might detect a widespread decline of some species of tree, or of an entire forest community. In many cases the causes of obvious forest declines are not known, and but they are suspected to be somehow related to environmental stressors, such as air pollution, insect damage, climate change, or forestry. These possibilities must be investigated by carefully designed research programs. The ecological damages associated with forest declines are very complex, and are related, for example, to changes in productivity, amounts of living and dead biomass, age–class structure of trees and other species, nutrient cycling, soil erosion, and biodiversity values. However, in an ecological monitoring program designed to study forest health, only a few well–chosen indicators would be measured. A sensible indicator of changes in the forest as an economic resource might be the productivity of trees, while a species of mammal or bird with spe-

cific habitat needs could used as an indicator of the ecological integrity of mature or older–growth forests.

Indicators can be classified according to a simple model of stressor—exposure—response: (1) Stressors are the causes of environmental and ecological changes, and are associated with physical, chemical, and biological threats to environmental quality. Stressors and their indicators are often related to human activities, for example, emissions of sulfur dioxide and other air pollutants, concentrations of secondary pollutants such as ozone, the use of pesticides and other toxic substances, or occurrences of disturbances associated with construction, forestry, or agriculture. Natural stressors include wildfires, hurricanes, volcanic eruptions, and climate change.

(2) Exposure indicators are relevant to changes in the intensity of stressors, or in doses accumulated over time. Exposure indicators might only measure the presence of a stressor, or they might be quantitative and reflect the actual intensities or extent of stressors. For example, appropriate exposure indicators of ozone in air might be the concentration of that toxic gas, while disturbance could be indicated by the extent of habitat changes caused by forest fires, agriculture, clear–cutting, or urbanization.

(3) Response indicators reflect ecological changes that are caused by exposure to stressors. Response indicators can include changes in the health of organisms, populations, communities, or landscapes.

Indicators can also take the form of composite indices, which integrate complex information. Such indices are often used in finance and economics, for example, stock–market indices such as the Dow–Jones, and consumer price indices. For reporting to the public, it is very desirable to have composite indices of environmental quality, because complex changes would be presented in a simple manner. However, the design of composite indices of environmental quality or ecological integrity are controversial, because of difficulties in selecting component variables and weighing their relative importance. This is different from composite economic indicators, in which all variables are measured in a common currency, such as dollars.

Monitoring addresses important issues

Environmental monitoring programs commonly address issues related to changes in: (1) environmental stressors, for example, the chemical quality of water, air, and soil, and activities related to agriculture, forestry, and construction; (2) the abundance and productivity of economically important, ecological resources such as agricultural products, forests, and hunted fish, mammals, and birds; and (3) ecological values that are not economic resources but are nevertheless important, such as rare and endangered species and natural communities.

Monitoring programs must be capable of detecting changes in all of the above values, and of predicting future changes. In North America, this function is carried out fairly well for categories (1) and (2), because these deal with economically important activities or resources. However, there are some important deficiencies in the monitoring of noneconomic ecological values. As a result, significant environmental issues involving ecological changes cannot be effectively addressed by society, because there is insufficient monitoring, research, and understanding. A few examples are described below: (1) Is a widespread decline of populations of migratory songbirds occurring in North America? If so, is this damage being caused by stressors occurring in their wintering habitats in Central and South America? Or are changes in the breeding habitats in North America important? Or both? What are the causes of these changes, and how can society manage the stressors that are responsible? (2) What is the scope of the global biodiversity crisis that is now occurring? Which species are affected, where, and why? How are these species important to the integrity of the biosphere, and to the welfare of humans? Most of the extinctions are occurring because of losses of tropical forests, but how are people of richer countries connected to the biodiversity-depleting stressors in poorer countries? (3) What are the biological and ecological risks of increased exposures to ultraviolet radiation, possibly caused by depletions of stratospheric ozone resulting from emissions of chlorofluorocarbons by humans? (4) What constitutes an acceptable exposure to potentially toxic chemicals? Some toxins, such as metals, occur naturally in the environment. Are there thresholds of exposure beyond which human emissions should not increase the concentrations of these chemicals? Is any increase acceptable for non-natural toxins, such as synthetic pesticides, TCDD, PCBs, and radionuclides?

These are just a small sample of the important ecological problems that have to be addressed by ecological monitoring, research, and understanding. To provide the information and knowledge that is needed to deal with environmental problems, many countries are now designing programs for longer-term monitoring and research in ecology and environmental science.

In the United States, for example, the Environmental Monitoring and Assessment Program (EMAP) of the Environmental Protection Agency is intended to provide information on ecological changes across large areas, by monitoring indicators at a large number of sites spread across the entire country. Another program has been established by the National Science Foundation and involves a network of Long-Term Ecological Research (LTER) sites, although these are mostly for fundamental ecological research, and not necessarily relevant to environmental problems. These are important programs in ecological monitoring and research, but they are still in their infancy and it is too soon to determine how well they will contribute to resolution of the environmental crisis.

State-of-the-environment reporting and social action

The information from programs of environmental monitoring and research must be reported to government administrators, politicians, corporations, and individuals. This information can influence the attitudes of these groups, and thereby affect environmental quality. Decision makers in government and industry need to understand the causes and consequences of environmental damages, and the costs and benefits of alternative ways of dealing with those changes. Their decisions are based on the balance of the perceived costs associated with the environmental damages, and the shorter-term, usually economic benefits of the activity that is causing the degradation.

Information from environmental monitoring and research is interpreted and reported to the public by the media, educational institutions, state-of-the-environment reporting by governments, and by nongovernmental organizations. All of these sources of information help to achieve environmental literacy, which eventually influences public attitudes. Informed opinions about the environment will then influence individual choices of lifestyle, which has important, mostly indirect effects on environmental quality. Public opinion also influences politicians and government administrators to more effectively manage and protect the environment and ecosystems.

See also Biodiversity; Ecosystem; Indicator species; Population, human; Stress, ecological.

Further Reading:
Freedman, B. *Environmental Ecology*. 2nd ed. San Diego: Academic Press, 1994.
Goldsmith, F. B., ed. *Monitoring for Conservation and Ecology*. London: Chapman and Hall, 1991.
Spellerberg, I. F. *Monitoring Ecological Change*. Cambridge, U.K.: Cambridge University Press, 1991.

Bill Freedman

Ecological productivity

Ecological productivity refers to the primary fixation of solar energy by plants and the subsequent use of that fixed energy by plant–eating herbivores, animal–eating carnivores, and the detritivores that feed upon dead biomass. This complex of energy fixation and utilization is called a food web.

Ecologists refer to the productivity of green plants as primary productivity. Gross primary productivity is the total amount of energy that is fixed by plants, while net primary productivity is smaller because it is adjusted for energy losses required to support plant respiration. If the net primary productivity of green plants in an ecosystem is positive, then the biomass of vegetation is increasing over time.

Gross and net secondary productivities refer to herbivorous animals, while tertiary productivities refer to carnivores. Within food webs, a pyramid–shaped structure characterizes ecological productivity. Plants typically account for more than 90% of the total productivity of the food web, herbivores most of the rest, and carnivores less than 1%. Any dead plant or animal biomass is eventually consumed by decomposer organisms, unless ecological conditions do not allow this process to occur efficiently, in which case dead biomass will accumulate as peat or other types of nonliving organic matter.

Because of differences in the availabilities of solar radiation, water, and nutrients, the world's ecosystems differ greatly in the amount of productivity that they sustain. Deserts, tundra, and the deep ocean are the least productive ecosystems, typically having an energy fixation of less than 0.5×10^3 kilocalories per square meter per year (thousands of kcal/m^2/yr; it takes one calorie to raise the temperature of one gram of water by 1°C under standard conditions, and there are 1,000 calories in a kcal). Grasslands, montane and boreal forests, waters of the continental shelf, and rough agriculture typically have productivities of $0.5–3.0 \times 10^3$ kcal/m^2/yr. Moist forests, moist prairies, shallow lakes, and typical agricultural systems have productivities of $3–10 \times 10^3$ kcal/m^2/yr. The most productive ecosystems are fertile estuaries and marshes, coral reefs, terrestrial vegetation on moist alluvial deposits, and intensive agriculture, which can have productivities of $10–25 \times 10^3$ kcal/m^2/yr.

See also Carnivore; Ecological pyramids; Food chain/web; Herbivore.

Ecological pyramids

Ecological pyramids are graphical representations of the trophic structure of ecosystems. Ecological pyramids are organized with the productivity of plants on the bottom, that of herbivores above the plants, and carnivores above the herbivores. If the ecosystem sustains top carnivores, they are represented at the apex of the ecological pyramid of productivity.

A fact of ecological energetics is that whenever the fixed energy of biomass is passed along a food chain, substantial energy losses occur during each transfer. These energy losses are a necessary consequence of the so–called Second Law of Thermodynamics. This universal principle states that whenever energy is transformed from one state to another, the entropy of the universe must increase (entropy refers to the randomness of distributions of matter and energy). In the context of transfers of fixed biological energy along the trophic chains of ecosystems, increases in entropy are represented by losses of energy as heat (because energy is converted from a highly ordered state in biomass, to a much less–ordered condition as heat). The end result is that transfers of energy between organisms along food chains are inefficient, and this causes the structure of productivity in ecological food webs to always be pyramid shaped.

Ecological food webs

Ecological food webs are based on the productivity of green plants (or photoautotrophs), which are the only organisms capable of utilizing diffuse solar radiation to synthesize simple organic compounds from carbon dioxide and water. The fixed energy of the simple organic compounds, plus inorganic nutrients, are then used by plants in more complex metabolic reactions to synthesize a vast diversity of biochemicals. Plants utilize the fixed energy of their biochemicals to achieve growth and reproduction. On average, plant photosynthesis utilizes less than 1% of the solar radiation that is received at the surface of the Earth. Higher efficiencies are impossible for a number of reasons, including the Second Law of Thermodynamics, but also other constraining factors such as the availability of nutrients and moisture, appropriate temperatures for growth, and other environmental limitations. However, even relatively fertile plant communities can only achieve conversion efficiencies of 10% or so, and only for relatively short periods of time.

The solar energy fixed by green plants in photosynthesis is, of course, the energetic basis of the productivity of all heterotrophic organisms that can only feed upon living or dead biomass, such as animals and microorganisms. Some of the biomass of plants is consumed as food by animals in the next trophic level, that of herbivores. However, herbivores cannot convert all of the energy of the vegetation that they eat into their own biomass. Depending on the digestibility of the food being consumed, the efficiency of this process is about 1–20%. The rest of the fixed energy of the plant foods is not assimilated by herbivores, or is converted into heat. Similarly, when carnivores eat other animals, only some of the fixed energy of the prey is converted into biomass of the predator. The rest is ultimately excreted, or is converted into heat, in accordance with the requirement for entropy to increase during any energy transformation.

Ecological pyramids

It is important to recognize that the Second Law of Thermodynamics only applies to ecological productivity (and to the closely related variable of energy flow). Consequently, only the trophic structure of productivity is always pyramid shaped. In some ecosystems other variables may also have a trophic structure that is pyramid shaped, for example, the quantities of biomass (also known as standing crop) present at a particular time, or the sizes or densities of populations. However, these latter variables are not pyramid shaped for all ecosystems.

One example of plants having a similar, or even smaller total biomass as the herbivores that feed upon them occurs in the open ocean. In that planktonic ecosystem the phytoplankton (or single–celled algae) typically maintain a similar biomass as the small animals (called zooplankton) that feed upon these microscopic plants. However, the phytoplankton cells are relatively short–lived, and their biomass is regenerated quickly because of the high productivity of these microorganisms. In contrast, the herbivorous zooplankton are longer lived, and they are much less productive than the phytoplankton. Consequently, the productivity of the phytoplankton is much larger than that of the zooplankton, even though at any particular time their biomasses may be similar.

In some ecosystems, the pyramid of biomass may be inverted, that is, characterized by a larger biomass of herbivores than of plants. This can sometimes occur in grasslands, where the dominant plants are relatively small, herbaceous species that may be quite productive, but do not maintain much biomass at any time. In contrast, the herbivores that feed on the plants may be relatively large, long–lived animals, and they may maintain a larger total biomass than the vegetation. Inverted biomass pyramids of this sort occur in some temperate and tropical grasslands, especially during the dry seasons when there can be large populations, and biomasses, of long–lived herbivores such as deer, bison, antelopes, gazelles, hippopotamuses, rhinos, elephants, and other big animals. Still, the annual productivity of the plants in grasslands is much larger than that of the herbivores.

Similarly, the densities of animals are not necessarily less than those of the plants that they eat. For example, insects are the most important herbivores in most forests, where they can maintain very large population densities. In contrast, the densities of tree populations are much smaller, because each individual organism is large and occupies a great deal of space. In such a forest, there are many more small insects than large trees or other plants, so the pyramid of numbers is inverted in shape. However, the pyramid of productivity in the forest is still governed by the Second Law of Thermodynamics, and it is much wider at the bottom than at the top.

Sustaining top carnivores

Because of the serial inefficiencies of energy transfer along food chains, there are intrinsic, energetic limits to the numbers of top carnivores that ecosystems can sustain. If top predators such as lions or killer whales are to be sustained in some minimal viable productivity and population size, there must be a suitably large productivity of animal prey that these animals can exploit. Their prey must in turn be sustained by a suitably large productivity of appropriate plant foods. Because of these ecological constraints, only very productive or extensive ecosystems can sustain top predators.

African savannas and grasslands sustain more species of higher–order carnivores than any other existing terrestrial ecosystems. The most prominent of these top predators are lion, leopard, cheetah, hyena, and wild dog. Although these various species may kill each other during some aggressive interactions (lions and hyenas are well known for their mutual enmity), they do not eat each other, and each can therefore be considered to be a top predator. In this unusual case, a large number of top predators can be sustained because the ecosystem is very extensive, and also rather productive of vegetation in most years. Other, very extensive but unproductive ecosystems may only support a single species of top predator, as is the case of the wolf in the arctic tundra.

See also Autotroph; Carnivore; Ecological productivity; Food chain/web; Herbivore; Heterotroph; Trophic levels.

KEY TERMS

. . . .

Trophic—Pertaining to the means of nutrition.

Further Reading:

Odum, E. P. *Ecology and Our Endangered Life Support Systems.* New York: Sinauer, 1993.
Ricklefs, R. E. *Ecology.* New York: W. H. Freeman, 1990.

Bill Freedman

Ecological stress see **Stress, ecological**

Ecological succession see **Succession**

Ecology

Ecology can be defined as the study of the relationships of organisms with their living and nonliving environment. Most ecologists are interested in questions involving the natural environment. Increasingly, however, ecologists are concerned about degradations associated with the ecological effects of humans and their activities. Ultimately, ecological knowledge will prove to be fundamental to the design of systems of resource use and management that will be capable of sustaining humans over the longer term, while also sustaining other species and their natural communities.

The subject matter of ecology

The subject matter of ecology is the relationships of organisms with their biological and nonliving environment. These are complex, reciprocal interactions—organisms are influenced by their environment, but they also cause environmental change, and are components of the environment of other organisms.

Ecology can also be considered to be the study of the factors that influence the distribution and abundance of organisms. Ecology originally developed from natural history, which deals with the richness and environmental relationships of life, but in a nonquantitative manner.

Although mostly a biological subject, ecology also draws upon other sciences, including chemistry, physics, geology, mathematics, computer science, and others. Often, ecologists must also deal with socioeconomic issues, because of the rapidly increasing importance of human impacts on the environment. Because it draws upon knowledge and information from so many disciplines, ecology is a highly interdisciplinary field.

The biological focus of ecology is apparent from the fact that most ecologists spend much of their time engaged in studies of organisms. Example of common themes of ecological research include: (1) physical and physiological adaptations of organisms to their environment, (2) patterns of the distribution of organisms in space, and how these are influenced by environmental factors, and (3) changes in the abundance of organisms over time, and the environmental influences on these dynamics.

Levels of integration within ecology

The universe can be organized along a spectrum of levels according to spatial scale. Ordered from the extremely small to the extremely large, these levels of integration are: subatomic particles ... atoms ... molecules ... molecular mixtures ... tissues ... organs ... individual organisms ... populations of individuals ... communities of populations ... ecological landscapes ... the biosphere ... the solar system ... the galaxy ... the universe. Within this larger scheme, the usual realm of ecology involves the levels including individuals organisms through the biosphere. These elements of the ecological hierarchy are described below in more detail.

The individual

In the ecological and evolutionary contexts, an individual is a particular, distinct organism, with its unique complement of genetic information encoded in DNA. (Note that although some species reproduce by nonsexual means, they are not exceptions to the genetic uniqueness of evolutionary individuals.) The physical and physiological attributes of individuals are a function of (1) their genetically defined capabilities, known as the genotype, and (2) environmental influences, which affect the actual expression of those genetic capabilities, known as the phenotype. Individuals are the units that are "selected" for during evolution.

The population

A population is an aggregation of individuals of the same species, that are actively interbreeding, or exchanging genetic information. Evolution refers to changes over time in the aggregate genetic information of a population. Evolution can occur as a result of random "drift," as directional selection in favor of advantageous phenotypes, or as selection against less-well-adapted genotypes.

The community

An ecological community is an aggregation of populations, interacting physically, chemically, and behavioral in the same place. Strictly speaking, a community consists of all plant, animal, and microbial populations occurring together on a site. Often, however, ecologists study functional "communities" of similar organisms, for example, bird or plant communities.

The ecological landscape

This level of ecological organization refers to an aggregation of communities on a larger area of terrain. Sometimes, ecological units are classified on the basis of their structural similarity, even though their actual species may differ among widely displaced locations. The biome is such a unit, examples of which include alpine and arctic tundra, boreal forest, deciduous forest, prairie, desert, and tropical rainforest.

The biosphere

The biosphere is the integration of all life on Earth, and is spatially defined by the occurrence of living organisms. The biosphere is the only place in the universe known to support life.

Energy and productivity

Less than 1% of the solar energy that reaches Earth's surface is absorbed by green plants and used in photosynthesis. However, this fixed solar energy is the energetic basis of the structure and function of ecosystems. The total fixation of energy by plants is known as gross primary production (GPP). Some of that fixed energy is used by plants to support their own metabolic demands, or respiration (R). The quantity of energy that is left over (that is, GPP – R) is known as net primary production (NPP). If NPP has a positive value, then plant biomass accumulates over time, and is available to support the energy requirements of herbivorous animals, which are themselves available as food to support to carnivores. Any plant or animal biomass that is not directly consumed eventually dies, and is consumed by decomposers (or detritivores), the most important of which are microorganisms such as bacteria and fungi. The complex of ecological relationships among all of the plants, animals, and decomposers is known as a food web.

Environmental and influences and biological interactions

Compared with the potential biological "demand," the environment has a limited ability to "supply" the requirements of life. As a result, the rates of critical ecological processes, such as productivity, are constrained by so–called limiting factors, which are present in the least supply relative to the biological demand. A limiting environmental factor can be physical or chemical in nature, and the factors act singly, but sequentially. For example, if a typical unproductive lake is fertilized with nitrate, there would be no ecological response. However, if that same lake was fertilized with phosphate, there would be a tremendous increase in the productivity of single–celled algae. If the lake was then fertilized with nitrate, there would be a further increase of productivity, because the ecological requirement for phosphate, the primary limiting factor, had previously been satiated.

This example illustrates the strong influence that the environment has on rates of processes such as productivity, and on overall ecological development. The most complex, productive, and highly developed ecosystems occur in relatively benign environments, where climate and the supplies of nutrients and water are least limiting to organisms and their processes. Tropical forests and coral reefs are the best examples of well-developed, natural ecosystems of this sort. In contrast, environmentally stressed ecosystems are severely constrained by one or more of these factors. For example, deserts are limited by the availability of water, and tundra by a cold climate.

In a theoretically benign environment, with an unlimited availability of the requirements of life, organisms can maximize the growth of their individual biomass and of their populations. Conditions of unlimited resources might occur (at least temporarily), perhaps, in situations that are sunny and well supplied with water and nutrients. Population growth in an unlimited environment is exponential, meaning that the number of individuals doubles during a fixed time interval. For example, if a species was biologically capable of doubling the size of its population in one week under unlimited environmental conditions, then after one week of growth an initial population of N individuals would grow to $2N$, after two weeks $4N$, after three weeks $8N$, after four weeks $16N$, and after eight weeks it would be $256N$. A financial analogy will help to put this tremendous rate of increase into perspective—an initial $100 investment growing at that rate would be worth $25,600 after only 8 weeks.

Clearly this is an enormous rate of growth, and it would rarely be sustainable under real world ecological or economic conditions. Before long, environmental conditions would become limiting, and organisms would begin to interfere with each other through an ecological process known as competition. In general, the more similar the ecological requirements of individuals or species, the more intense is the competition that they experience. Therefore, competition among similar-sized individuals of the same species can be very intense, while individuals of different sized species (such as trees and mosses) will compete hardly at all.

Competition is an important ecological process, because it limits the growth rates of individuals and populations, and influences the sorts of species that can occur together in ecological communities. These ecological traits are also profoundly influenced by other interactions among organisms, such as herbivore, predation, and disease.

The goal of ecology

The larger objective of ecology is to understand the nature of environmental influences on individual organisms, their populations and communities, on landscapes and, ultimately, the biosphere. If ecologists can achieve an understanding of these relationships, they will be well placed to contribute to the development of systems by which humans will be able to sustainably use ecological resources, such as forests, agricultural soils, and hunted animals such as deer and fish. This is a very important goal because humans are, after all, completely reliant on ecologically goods and services as their only source of sustenance.

See also Biological community; Biome; Biosphere; Competition; Ecological productivity; Ecosystem; Limiting factor; Stress, ecological.

Further Reading:

Begon, M., Harper, J.L., and Townsend, C.R. *Ecology: Individuals, Populations and Communities. 2nd ed.* London: Blackwell Sci. Pub., 1990.

Freedman, B. *Environmental Ecology.* 2nd ed. San Diego: Academic Press, 1994.
Ricklefs, R. E. *Ecology.* New York: W.H. Freeman, 1990.

Bill Freedman

Ecology, human see **Human ecology**

Ecosystem

The notion of ecosystem (or ecological system) refers to indeterminate ecological assemblages, consisting of communities of organisms and their environment. Ecosystems can vary greatly in size. Small ecosystems can be considered to occur in tidal pools, in a back yard, or in the rumen of an individual cow. Larger ecosystems might encompass lakes or stands of forests. Landscape-scale ecosystems comprise larger regions, and may include diverse terrestrial and aquatic communities. Ultimately, all of Earth's life and its physical environment could be considered to represent an entire ecosystem, known as the biosphere.

Often, ecologists develop functional boundaries for ecosystems, depending on the particular needs of their work. Depending on the specific interests of an ecologist, an ecosystem might be delineated as the shoreline vegetation around a lake, or perhaps the entire waterbody, or maybe the lake plus its terrestrial watershed. Because all of these units consist of organisms and their environment, they can properly be considered to be ecosystems.

Through biological productivity and related processes, ecosystems take sources of diffuse energy and simple inorganic materials, and create relatively focused combinations of these, occurring as the biomass of plants, animals, and microorganisms. Solar electromagnetic energy, captured by the chlorophyll of green plants, is the source of diffuse energy most commonly utilized by ecosystems. The most important of the simple inorganic materials are carbon dioxide, water, and ions or small molecules containing nitrogen, phosphorus, potassium, calcium, magnesium, sulfur, and some other nutrients.

Because diffuse energy and simple materials are being ordered into much more highly structured forms such as biochemicals and biomass, ecosystems (and life more generally) represent rare islands in which negative entropy is accumulating within the universe. One of the fundamental characteristics of ecosystems is that they

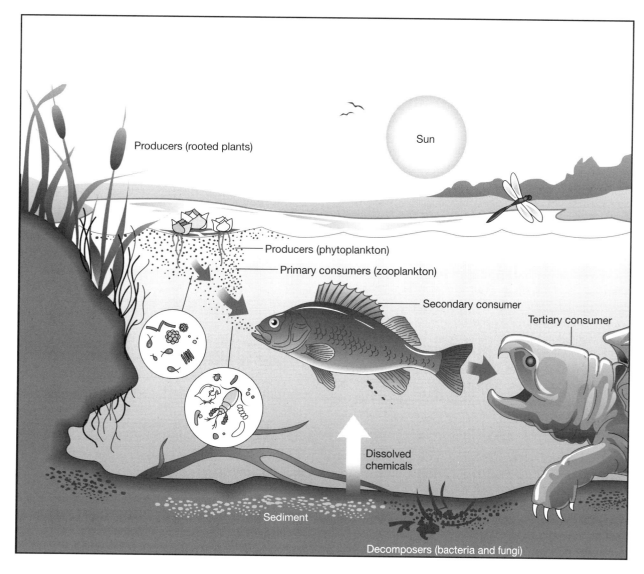

Producers (rooted plants)

Sun

Producers (phytoplankton)

Primary consumers (zooplankton)

Secondary consumer

Tertiary consumer

Dissolved chemicals

Sediment

Decomposers (bacteria and fungi)

A freshwater ecosystem.

must have access to an external source of energy to drive the biological and ecological processes that produce these localized accumulations of negative entropy. This is in accordance with the Second Law of Thermodynamics, which states that spontaneous transformations of energy can only occur if there is an increase in entropy of the universe; consequently, energy must be put into a system to create negative entropy. Virtually all ecosystems (and life itself) rely on inputs of solar energy to drive the physiological processes by which biomass is synthesized from simple molecules.

To carry out their various functions, ecosystems also need access to materials—the nutrients referred to above. Unlike energy, which can only flow through an ecosystem, nutrients can be utilized repeatedly. Through biogeochemical cycles, nutrients are recycled

from dead biomass, through inorganic forms, back into living organisms, and so on.

One of the greatest challenges facing humans and their civilization is to develop an understanding of the fundamentals of ecosystem organization—how they function and how they are structured. This knowledge is absolutely necessary if humans are to design systems that allow a sustainable utilization of the products and services of ecosystems. Humans are sustained by ecosystems, and there is no tangible alternative to this relationship.

See also Biological community; Biosphere; Ecological productivity.

Bill Freedman

Ecotone

An ecotone is a zone of transition between distinct ecological communities or habitats. Usually, the word is used to refer to relatively sharp, local transitions, also known as edges.

Because many physical and chemical changes in the environment tend to be continuous, ecological transitions are often similarly gradual. For example, climate and precipitation change steadily across continents and up the slopes of mountains. Because these environmental changes are gradual, communities of plants and animals often intergrade through wide, continuous transitions.

Frequently, however, there are relatively sharp environmental interfaces associated with rapid changes occurring naturally at the edges of major geological or soil discontinuities along the interface of aquatic and terrestrial habitats or associated with the boundaries of disturbances such as landslides and wildfires. These are the sorts of environmental contexts in which ecotones occur naturally. Human activities also favor the occurrence of many ecotones, for example, along the edges of clearcuts, agricultural fields, highways, and residential areas.

Disturbance–related ecotones exist in space, but often they eventually become indistinct as time passes because of the ecological process known as succession. For example, in the absence of an intervening disturbance, an ecotone between a forest and a field will eventually disappear if the field is abandoned and succession allows a mature forest to develop over the entire area.

The sharp ecological discontinuities at ecotones provide habitat for so–called "edge" species of plants and animals. These have a relatively broad ecological tolerance and within limits can utilize habitat on both sides of the ecotone. Examples of edge plants include many shrubs and vines that are abundant along the boundaries of forests in many parts of the world. Some animals are also relatively abundant in edges and in habitat mosaics with a large ratio of edge to area. Some North American examples of edge animals include white–tailed and mule deer, snowshoe hare, cottontail rabbit, blue jay, and robin.

Because human activities have created an unnatural proliferation of ecotonal habitats in many regions, many edge animals are much more abundant than they used to be. In some cases this has resulted in important ecological problems. For example, the extensive range expansion of the brown–headed cowbird, a prairie–forest edge species, has caused large reductions in the breeding success of many small species of native birds, contributing to large declines in some of their populations. This has happened because the cowbird is a very effective social parasite which lays its eggs in the nests of other species who then rear the cowbird chick to the severe detriment of their own young.

See also Biological community; Habitat.

Edema

Edema is the accumulation of fluid in any given location in the body. Edema can result from trauma, as in a sprained ankle, or from a chronic condition such as heart or kidney failure. The word edema is from the Greek and means "swelling."

The presence of edema can be an important diagnostic tool for the physician. A patient who is developing congestive heart failure often will develop edema in the ankles. Congestive heart failure means that the heart is laboring against very high blood pressure and the heart itself has enlarged to the point that it is not effectively circulating the blood. Excess fluid will leave the circulatory system and accumulate between the cells in the body. Gravity will pull the fluid to the area of the ankles and feet, which will swell. The physician can press on the swollen area and the depression left by his finger will remain after he lifts the pressure. The patient with congestive heart failure will develop edema in the lungs as well, and thus has a chronic cough.

Individuals who have liver failure, often because of excessive alcohol consumption over a period of years, will develop huge edematous abdomens. The collection of fluid in the abdomen is called ascites (ah–SITE–eez, from the Greek word for bag).

The presence of edema is not a diagnosis in itself. It signifies a more serious clinical condition that requires immediate attention. The failing heart reaches a point that it can no longer cope with the huge load of fluid and will become an ineffective pump. At that point the only cure for the patient is to undergo a heart transplant. If the underlying problem is kidney failure, the patient can be placed on a dialysis machine several times a week to filter the excess water from the system along with any accumulated toxins.

Medications are available to help rid the body of excess fluid. These drugs are called diuretics and stimulate the kidneys to filter greater volumes of fluid which is eliminated as urine. These are potent medications,

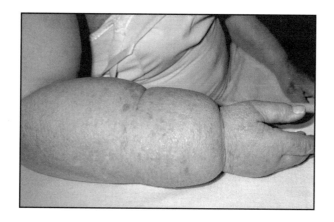

Gross lymphoedema in the arm of an elderly woman following radiotherapy treatment for breast cancer.

however, that require close monitoring by the physician.

EDTA see **Ethylenediaminetetraacetic acid**

Eel grass

Eel grasses are 18 species of herbaceous aquatic plants in the family Zosteraceae, 12 species of which are in the genus *Zostera*. However, some plant systematists have treated the eel grasses as a component of a much larger family, the pondweeds or Potamogetonaceae.

Eel grasses have long, strap–like leaves that emerge from a thin rhizome that grows in the surface sediment of the shallow–water, estuarine, or marine wetlands of the temperate zone where these plants grow. At the end of the growing season, the dead leaves and stems of eel grass break away from the perennating (living over from season to season) rhizomes of this plant and wash up on shores in large quantities.

The flowers of eel grasses are small, either male or female, and are aggregated into an inflorescence that may be unisexual or may contain flowers of both sexes. The fruit is a small seed.

Zostera marina is a common species of eel grass in North America. This species is widespread in estuaries and shallow, marine bays. It is eaten by many marine invertebrates, and by swans, geese, and ducks of estuaries and other marine wetlands.

In the past, the large quantities of eel grass debris that often accumulate along shores in the autumn were collected and used for packing delicate objects and instruments for shipping, and for packing into the walls of houses as insulation. Today, the major economic importance of eel grasses is through the habitat and food they provide for aquatic wild life.

Eels see **Spiny eels; Swamp eels; True eels**

Eggplant see **Nightshade**

Egret see **Herons**

Eiders see **Ducks**

Einsteinium see **Element, transuranium**

Eland

Eland (*Taurotragus oryx*) are the largest African antelopes, weighing up to a 2,205 lbs (1,000 kg) and standing 6.6 ft (2 m) at the shoulder. They belong to the family Bovidae in the order Artiodactyla, the even–toed hoofed mammals. Eland belong to the tribe Tragelaphini, a closely-related group of spiral-horned antelopes, whose members are not territorial. Both sexes posses long horns, and females are slightly smaller than males.

Characteristics

The horns of eland are about 2 ft (0.6 m) long, with one or two tight spirals. Eland have five or six white stripes on their bodies and white markings on their legs as well. The young are reddish brown, while older males are a bluish gray. Other distinctive markings include a crest running along their spines, a tuft of hair on the tail (like a cow tail), and a large loose flap of skin below the neck (the dewlap). This adds to the eland's bulky appearance.

Eland are not fast runners, but they can trot at a speed of 13 mph (21 kph) for long periods and can easily jump over a 6 ft (2 m) fence. They are gregarious, living in loosely structured herds where bonding is only evident between mothers and their calves. The size of herds can be as large as 500 with subgroups made up of eland of the same gender and age. Their home range areas can encompass more than 150 sq mi (389 sq km) and they travel over greater distances throughout the year.

Female eland reach maturity at three years, males at four or five years. Males continue to grow even after

A bull eland in eastern Africa.

maturity. Eland mate every other year. The gestation period lasts about nine months, resulting in a single calf. The newborn calf lies concealed in the grass or undergrowth for about a month and is visited for nursing by its mother twice a day. After this, the calf joins other young calves, forming a nursery group, watched over by female eland who protect the young from predators.

Adaptation

Eland can adapt to a wide range of conditions. They can be found in arid regions, savannas, woodland and grassland areas, and in mountain ranges as high as 15,000 ft (457 m). Eland, like all bovids, are ruminants (cud–chewing animals) living on a diet of leaves, fruits, seed pods, flowers, tubers, and bark. They sometimes break down higher branches with their horns to feed on leaves of trees. Eland are adept at picking out high qual-ity food from among poorer vegetation, a habit known as foliage gleaning. During rainy seasons eland graze on green grass.

Eland are found in East Africa (Kenya, Malawi, and Mozambique) and in southern Africa (from Zimbabwe to South Africa). In West Africa (from Senegal to Sudan) a second species, the giant eland (*T. derbianus*) is found from Senegal in West Africa to southern Sudan and northern Uganda. Like other antelopes, eland are somewhat independent of drinking, since they are able to meet most of their needs from the water contained in plants they eat. Some of the strategies eland use in water conservation are common to all antelopes. Seeking shade during the hottest part of the day and feeding during the coolest part is one strategy. Other water–conservation strategies include the ability to concentrate urine, heat storage, the ability to allow body temperature to rise, and exhaling dry air by recovering water that would otherwise be lost.

Domestication and conservation

Rock paintings indicate a domestic relationship between eland and bushmen. In Natal, South Africa, eland have been domesticated for use as both dairy and draft animals, and for their tough hides. On their own and in low–density areas, they are endangered by agricultural development, which diminishes their range, and by hunting. Their meat is considered delicious and is prized as a source of protein. Ranched eland are susceptible to ticks. These antelope also died in large numbers during the rinderpest epidemic of 1896. Conservationists support planned domestication since it preserves species otherwise threatened by the encroaching land use of humans. The populations of eland today are much reduced. These formerly abundant antelope are now found mainly in reserves in South Africa and Botswana.

See also Antelopes and gazelles.

Further Reading:
Estes, Richard D. *Behavior Guide to African Mammals.* Berkeley: University of California, 1991.

Estes, Richard D. *The Safari Companion.* Post Mills, Vermont: Chelsea Green, 1993.

Grzimek, Bernhard. *Encyclopedia of Mammals.* New York: McGraw –Hill, 1990.

Haltenorth, T., and H. Diller. *A Field Guide to the Mammals of Africa.* London: Collins, 1992.

Macdonald, David, ed. *The Encyclopedia of Mammals.* New York: Facts on File, 1987.

Nowak, Ronald M. *Walker's Encyclopedia of Mammals.* 5th ed. Baltimore, MD: Johns Hopkins University Press, 1991.

Vita Richman

Elapid snakes

Elapid snakes are extremely venomous snakes such as cobras, mambas, kraits, tiger snakes, and coral snakes in the family Elapidae. The elapids are about 120 species in the subfamily Elapinae. The sea snakes (subfamily Hydrophiinae) and subfamily Laticaudinae make up the other two subfamilies in the Elapidae. Elapid snakes have a wide distribution from warm temperate climates to tropical climates, and are found on all continents except Antarctica.

Biology of elapid snakes

Elapid snakes have teeth on the front part of the upper jaw that are modified as paired fangs to inject venom into their victims. The fangs deliver the venom in much the same way that a hypodermic syringe delivers a drug, i.e., as a subcutaneous injection under pressure through narrow tubes. The fangs of elapid snakes are permanently erect, and when the mouth is closed they are enclosed within a pocket in the outer lip, outside of the lower mandible. At any one time, only two fanged teeth are functionally capable of delivering venom. However, there are a series of smaller, developing fangs available as replacements, should the primary ones be damaged, lost during use, or shed. Elapid snakes bite to subdue their prey, and when attempting to protect themselves from their own predators.

Three species of elapid snakes have the ability to deliver their venom through the air, by "spitting" rather accurately towards the eyes of a predator, in some species to a distance of up to 9.8 ft (3 m). This is primarily a defensive behavior, rather than one used for hunting. The spitting cobra (*Hemachatus hemachatus*) of South Africa is especially accurate, and can propel its venom as far as 6.5 ft (about 2 m). Other spitting cobras are the African black–necked cobra (*Naja nigricollis*) and a subspecies of the Asian cobra (*Naja naja sputatrix*). If the venom of a spitting cobra is not quickly washed from the eyes, blindness could occur.

When cobras feel threatened, they will raise the front of their body above the ground, and face the danger. At the same time, cobras use extensible neck ribs to spread their so–called "hood," as a further warning to the potential predator. The erect stance and spread hood of cobras is a warning display, used to caution predators about meddling with a dangerous snake.

Most elapid snakes are oviparous, meaning they lay eggs, that after a period of incubation hatch into young that are small replicas of the adult animals. Some species of elapid snakes, most commonly cobras, guard

A siamese cobra.

their eggs until they hatch. Some species, including the spitting cobra, are ovoviviparous, meaning the eggs are retained within the body of the female until they hatch, so that live snakes are born. Australian snakes in the genus *Denisonia* are viviparous, meaning true eggs are never formed by the female, and live young are born.

The greatest recorded longevity of an elapid snake was for the forest cobra (*Naja melanoleuca*), which lived for 29 years in captivity.

Fish–eating sea snakes can reach a body length of 9.2 ft (2.8 m) and occur in tropical waters in eastern Africa and the Red Sea, Asia, Australia, and many Pacific islands. Sea snakes have very toxic venom, but most species are not aggressive, and they rarely bite humans. Sea snakes have a laterally compressed, pad-dle–shaped tail, well adaptive to swimming, and most species are ovoviviparous. Some species of sea snakes occasionally form mass aggregations, probably for

breeding, and such gatherings have been estimated to contain several million individuals.

One especially seafaring species, the pelagic sea snake (*Pelamis platurus*), ranges from the east coast of Africa, through the Indo–Pacific region, and has even crossed the Pacific Ocean, occuring in tropical waters of western South America. Sea snakes are probably the basis of folk legends about sea serpents, although the living sea snakes do not closely resemble the fantasti-cally large and aggressive serpents of folk lore.

Species of elapid snakes

Perhaps the world's most famous species of elapid snake is a subspecies of the Asian cobra (*Naja naja*) known as the Indian cobra (*N. n. naja*), which is the ser-pent that is most often used by snake charmers. Often, the cobra emerges from the urn or sack in which it is kept, and then assumes its warning stance of an erect fore–body and spread hood. In addition, the serpent "dances" sinuously in response to the movements of the flute, as it is waved about in front of the cobra. Actually, the cobra is deaf to most of the music played by the charmer's flute—it is only responding to the movement of the instrument.

The world's longest venomous snake is the king cobra (*Ophiophagus hannah*), which can attain a length of 18 ft (5.5 m). This impressive but uncommon snake occurs in India and southeast Asia, and it feeds primarily on other species of snakes.

The mambas are four species of African elapids, of which the black mamba (*Dendroapsis polylepis*) is most feared, because it is relatively common and many people are bitten each year. This snake can grow to a length of 13 ft (4 m), and is probably the most swiftly moving of all snakes.

Elapid snakes are relatively diverse and abundant in Australia, where species of venomous snakes actually outnumber nonvenomous snakes by four to one. The largest, most dangerous species is the taipan (*Oxyuranus scutellatus*), an uncommon, aggressive, tropical species that can reach a length of 11.5 ft (3.5 m). However, several species of tiger snakes (*Notechis scutatus* and *N. ater*) are more common and widespread, and have particularly deadly venom. The death adders (*Acanthophis antarcticus* and *A. pyrrhus*) are viper–like elapids that are relatively common and widespread.

American elapids are represented by about 40 species of coral snakes, in the genera *Micrurus* and *Micruroides*. These snakes have extremely potent venom. However, coral snakes are not very aggressive, possessing relatively short fangs and a small mouth, so they cannot easily bite most parts of the human body, with fingers and toes being notable exceptions. Coral snakes are brightly colored with rings of black, red, and yellow.

The most widespread species in North America is the eastern coral snake (*Micrurus fulvius fulvius*), occurring widely in the southeastern United States from southern North Carolina to eastern Louisiana. The eastern coral snake likes to burrow, and is not often seen unless it is specifically looked for. This snake feeds almost entirely on reptiles, with frogs and small mammals also occasional prey. The eastern coral snake has brightly colored rings of red, yellow, and black on its body. These are a warning or aposematic coloration, intended to alert predators to the dangers of messing with this potentially dangerous, venomous snake.

However, in the coral snake the red and yellow rings occur adjacent to each other, unlike similarly colored but nonpoisonous species such as the scarlet

KEY TERMS

Antivenin—An antitoxin that counteracts a specific venom, or a group of similar venoms. Antivenins are available for most types of snake venoms.

Aposematic—Refers to a bright coloration of an animal, intended to draw the notice of a potential predator, and to warn of the dangers of toxicity or foul taste.

kingsnake (*Lampropeltis triangulum*) and the scarlet snake (*Cemophora coccinea*). These latter snakes are mimics of the coral snake, which share aspects of its coloration to gain some measure of protection from predators. A folk saying was developed to help people remember the important differences in coloration between the coral snake and its harmless mimics: "Red touch yellow—dangerous fellow. Red touch black—venom lack." The Texas coral snake (*Micrurus fulvius tenere*) occurs in parts of the central and southwestern United States and Mexico.

Elapid snakes and humans

Species of elapid snakes are among the most feared of the serpents, and each year many people die after being bitten by these animals. This is especially true of certain tropical countries, particularly in India and tropical Asia, and in parts of Africa. For example, thousands of fatal snake bites occur each year in India alone. Wherever elapids and other poisonous snakes occur, there is a tangible risk of snake bite.

However, in many places the magnitude of the risks of being snake–bitten are grossly overestimated by people. Except in the case of unusually aggressive species of snakes, it is extremely unlikely that a careful person will be bitten by a venomous snake, even where these animals are abundant. In the greater scheme of things, snake bites may be deadly, but in terms of actual risk, snakes are not usually very dangerous. This is especially true in North America, but somewhat less so in some tropical countries.

However, any bite by a poisonous snake should be treated as a medical emergency. First–aid procedures in the field can involve the use of a constriction band to slow the absorption of the venom into the general circulation, and perhaps the use of incision and suction to remove some of the poison. Antivenins are also available for the venoms of many species of poisonous snakes. Antivenins are commercially prepared serums that serve as antidotes to snake venoms if they are administered in time.

It is regrettable that so many poisonous snakes—and harmless snakes—are killed each year by people with fears that are essentially misguided and overblown. Snakes are a valuable component of natural ecosystems. Moreover, many species of snakes provide humans with useful services, for example, by preying on rodents that can potentially cause great damage in agriculture, or serve as the vectors of human diseases.

See also Snakes.

Further Reading:
Goin, C. J., O. B. Goin, and G. R. Zug. *Introduction to Herpetology.* 3rd ed. San Francisco: Freeman & Co., 1978.

Halliday, T. R., and K. Adler. *The Encyclopedia of Reptiles and Amphibians.* New York: Facts on File, 1986.

Mattison, C. *Snakes of the World.* Poole U.K.: Blandford Press, 1986.

Bill Freedman

Elasticity

Elasticity is the ability of a material to return to its original shape and size after being stretched, compressed, twisted or bent. Elastic deformation (change of shape or size) lasts only as long as a deforming force is applied to the object, and disappears once the force is removed. Greater forces may cause permanent changes of shape or size, called plastic deformation.

In ordinary language, a substance is said to be "elastic" if it stretches easily. Therefore, rubber is considered a very elastic substance, and rubber bands are even called "elastics" by some people. Actually, however, most substances are somewhat elastic, including steel, glass, and other familiar materials.

Stress, strain and elastic modulus

The simplest description of elasticity is Hooke's Law, which states, "The stress is proportional to the strain." This relation was first expressed by the British scientist, Robert Hooke (1635–1702). He arrived at it through studies in which he placed weights on metal springs and measured how far the springs stretched in response. Hooke noted that the added length was always proportional to the weight; that is, doubling the weight doubled the added length.

In the modern statement of Hooke's law, the terms "stress" and "strain" have precise mathematical definitions. Stress is the applied force divided by the area the force acts on. Strain is the added length divided by the original length.

To understand why these special definitions are needed, first consider two bars of the same length, made of the same material. One bar is twice as thick as the other. Experiments have shown that both bars can be stretched to the same additional length only if twice as much weight is placed on the bar that is twice as thick. Thus, they both carry the same stress, as defined above.

The special definition of strain is required because, when an object is stretched, the stretch occurs along its entire length, not just at the end to which the weight is applied. The same stress applied to a long rod and a short rod will cause a greater extension of the long rod. The strain, however, will be the same on both rods.

The amount of stress required to produce a given amount of strain also depends on the material being stretched. Therefore, the ratio of stress to strain is a unique property of materials, different for each substance. It is called the elastic modulus (plural: moduli). It is also known as Young's modulus, after Thomas Young (1773–1829) who first described it. It has been measured for thousands of materials. The greater the elastic modulus, the stiffer the material is. For example, the elastic modulus of rubber is about six hundred psi (pounds per square inch). That of steel is about 30 million psi.

Other elastic deformations

All deformations, no matter how complicated, can be described as the result of combinations of three basic types of stress. One is tension, which stretches an object along one direction only. Thus far, our discussion of elasticity has been entirely in terms of tension. Compression is the same type of stress, but acting in the opposite direction.

The second basic type of stress is shear stress. This results when two forces push on opposite ends of an object in opposite directions. Shear stress changes the object's shape. The shear modulus is the amount of shear stress divided by the angle through which the shape is strained.

Hydrostatic stress, the third basic stress, squeezes an object with equal force from all directions. A familiar example is the pressure on objects under water due to the weight of the water above them. Pure hydrostatic stress changes the volume only, not the shape of the object. Its modulus is called the bulk modulus.

Elastic limit

The greatest stress a material can undergo and still return to its original dimensions is called the elastic limit. When stressed beyond the elastic limit, some materials fracture, or break. Others undergo plastic deformation, taking on a new permanent shape. An example is a nail bent by excessive shear stress of a hammer blow.

Elasticity on the atomic scale

The elastic modulus and elastic limit reveal much about the strength of the bonds between the smallest particles of a substance, the atoms or molecules it is composed of. However, to understand elastic behavior on the level of atoms requires first distinguishing between materials that are crystalline and those that are not.

Crystalline materials

Metals are examples of crystalline materials. Solid pieces of metal contain millions of microscopically small crystals stuck together, often in random orientations. Within a single crystal, atoms are arranged in orderly rows. They are held by attractive forces on all sides. Scientists model the attractive force as a sort of a spring. When a spring is stretched, a restoring force tries to return it to its original length. When a metal rod is stretched in tension, its atoms are pulled apart slightly. The attractive force between the atoms tries to restore the original distance. The stronger the attraction, the more force must be applied to pull the atoms apart. Thus, stronger atomic forces result in larger elastic modulus.

Stresses greater than the elastic limit overcome the forces holding atoms in place. The atoms move to new positions. If they can form new bonds there, the material deforms plastically; that is, it remains in one piece but assumes a new shape. If new bonds cannot form, the material fractures.

The ball and spring model also explains why metals and other crystalline materials soften at higher temperatures. Heat energy causes atoms to vibrate. Their vibrations move them back and forth, stretching and compressing the spring. The higher the temperature, the larger the vibrations, and the greater the average distance between atoms. Less applied force is needed to separate the atoms because some of the stretching energy has been provided by the heat. The result is that the elastic modulus of metals decreases as temperature increases.

Elastomers

To explain the elastic behavior of materials like rubber requires a different model. Rubber consists of molecules, which are clusters of atoms joined by chem-ical bonds. Rubber molecules are very long and thin. They are polymers, long chain–like molecules built up by repeating small units. Rubber polymers consist of hundreds or thousands of atoms joined in a line. Many of the bonds are flexible, and can rotate. The result is a fine structure of kinks along the length of the molecule. The molecule itself is so long that it tends to bend and coil randomly, like a rope dropped on the ground. A piece of rubber, such as a rubber band, is made of vast numbers of such kinked, twisting, rope–like molecules.

When rubber is pulled, the first thing that happens is that the loops and coils of the "ropes" straighten out. The rubber extends as its molecules are pulled out to their full length. Still more stress causes the kinks to straighten out. Releasing the stress allows the kinks, coils and loops to form again, and the rubber returns to its original dimensions. Materials made of long, tangled molecules stretch very easily. Their elastic modulus is very small. They are called elastomers because they are very "elastic" polymers.

The "kink" model explains a very unusual property of rubber. A stretched rubber band, when heated, will suddenly contract. It is thought that the added heat provides enough energy for the bonds to start rotating again. The kinks that had been stretched out of the material return to it, causing the length to contract.

Sound waves

Elasticity is involved whenever atoms vibrate. An example is the movement of sound waves. A sound wave consists of energy that pushes atoms closer together momentarily. The energy moves through the atoms, causing the region of compression to move forward. Behind it, the atoms spring further apart, as a result of the restoring force.

The speed with which sound travels through a substance depends in part on the strength of the forces between atoms of the substance. Strongly bound atoms readily affect one another, transferring the "push" due to the sound wave from each atom to its neighbor. Therefore, the stronger the bonding force, the faster sound travels through an object. This explains why it is possible to hear an approaching railroad train by putting one's ear to the track, long before it can be heard through the air. The sound wave travels more rapidly through the steel of the track than through the air, because the elastic modulus of steel is a million times greater than the bulk modulus of air.

Measuring the elastic modulus

The most direct way to determine the elastic modulus of a material is by placing a sample under increasing

KEY TERMS

. . . .

Elastic deformation—A temporary change of shape or size due to applied force, which disappears when the force is removed.

Elastic modulus—The ratio of stress to strain (stress divided by strain), a measure of the stiffness of a material.

Plastic deformation—A permanent change of shape or size due to applied force.

Strain—The change in dimensions of an object, due to applied force, divided by the original dimensions.

Stress—The magnitude of an applied force divided by the area it acts upon.

stresses, and measuring the resulting strains. The results are plotted as a graph, with strain along the horizontal axis and stress along the vertical axis. As long as the strain is small, the data form a straight line for most materials. This straight line is the "elastic region." The slope of the straight line equals the elastic modulus of the material. Alternatively, the elastic modulus can be calculated from measurements of the speed of sound through a sample of the material.

Further Reading:

Goodwin, Peter H. *Engineering Projects for Young Scientists.* New York: Franklin Watts, 1987.
Williams, Gurney, III. "Smart Materials." *Omni,* (15 April 1993): 42–44+.
"A Figure Less Than Greek," *Discover,* 13 (June 1992): 14.

Sara G. B. Fishman

Electrical conductivity

Conductivity is the term used to describe the ability of a material medium to permit the passage of particles or energy. Electrical conductivity refers to the movement of charged particles through matter. Thermal conductivity refers to the transmission of heat energy through matter. Together, these are the most significant examples of a broader classification of phenomena known as transport processes. In metals, electrical con-

ductivity and thermal conductivity are related since both involve aspects of electron motion.

History

The early studies of electrical conduction in metals were done in the 18th and early 19th centuries. Benjamin Franklin (1706–1790) in his experiments with lightning (leading to his invention of the lightning rod), reasoned that the charge would travel along the metallic rod. Alessandro Volta (1745–1827) derived the concept of electrical potential from his studies of static electricity, and then discovered the principle of the battery in his experiments with dissimilar metals in common contact with moisture. Once batteries were available for contact with metals, electric currents were produced and studied. Georg Simon Ohm (1787–1854) found the direct proportion relating current and potential difference, which became a measure of the ability of various metals to conduct electricity. Extensive theoretical studies of currents were carried out by André Marie Ampère (1775–1836).

To honor these scientists, the système internationale (S.I.) units use their names. The unit of potential difference is the volt, and potential difference is more commonly called voltage. The unit of electrical resistance is the ohm, and the unit of current is the ampere. The relation among these functions is known as Ohm's Law.

Franklin is remembered for an unlucky mistake. He postulated that there was only one type of electricity, not two as others thought, in the phenomena known in his day. He arbitrarily called one form of static electric charge positive and attributed the opposite charge to the absence of the positive. All subsequent studies continued the convention he established. Late in the 19th century, when advancements in both electrical and vacuum technology led to the discovery of cathode rays, streams of particles issuing from a negative electrode in an evacuated tube, Sir Joseph John Thomson (1856–1940) identified these particles as common to all metals used as cathodes and negatively charged. The historical concept of a positive current issuing from an anode is mathematically self–consistent and leads to no analytical errors, so the convention is maintained but understood to be a convenience.

Materials

Electrical conduction can take place in a variety of substances. The most familiar conducting substances are metals, in which the outermost electrons of the atoms can move easily in the interatomic spaces. Other conducting materials include semiconductors, electrolytes, and ionized gases, which are discussed later in this article.

Metals

Metals are now known to be primarily elements characterized by atoms in which the outermost orbital shell has very few electrons with corresponding values of energy. The highest conductivity occurs in metals with only one electron occupying a state in that shell. Silver, copper, and gold are examples of high–conductivity metals. Metals are found mainly toward the left side of the Periodic Table of the elements, and in the transition columns. The electrons contributing to their conductivity are also the electrons that determine their chemical valence in forming compounds. Some metallic conductors are alloys of two or more metal elements, such as steel, brass, bronze, and pewter.

A piece of metal is a block of metallic atoms. In individual atoms the valence electrons are loosely bound to their nuclei. In the block, at room temperature, these electrons have enough kinetic energy to enable them to wander away from their original locations. However, that energy is not sufficient to remove them from the block entirely because of the potential energy of the surface, the outermost layer of atoms. Thus, at their sites, the atoms are ionized—that is, left with a net positive charge—and are referred to as ion cores. Overall, the metal is electrically neutral, since the electrons' and ion cores' charges are equal and opposite. The conduction electrons are bound to the block as a whole rather than to the nuclei.

These electrons move about as a cloud through the spaces separating the ion cores. Their motion is random, bearing some similarities to gas molecules, especially scattering, but the nature of the scattering is different. Electrons do not obey classical gas laws; their motion in detail must be analyzed quantum–mechanically. However, much information about conductivity can be understood classically.

A particular specimen of a metal may have a convenient regular shape such as a cylinder (wire) or a prism (bar). When a battery is connected across the ends of a wire, the electrochemical energy of the battery imparts a potential difference, or voltage between the ends. This electrical potential difference is analogous to a hill in a gravitational system. Charged particles will then move in a direction analogous to downhill. In the metal, the available electrons will move toward the positive terminal, or anode, of the battery. As they reach the anode, the battery injects electrons into the wire in equal numbers, thereby keeping the wire electrically neutral. This circulation of charged particles is termed a current, and the closed path is termed a circuit. The battery acts as the electrical analog of a pump. Departing from the gravitational analogy, in which objects may fall and land, the transport of charged particles requires a closed circuit.

Current is defined in terms of charge transport:

$$I = q/t$$

where I is current, q is charge, and t is time. Thus q/t is the rate of charge transport through the wire. In a metal, as long as its temperature remains constant, the current is directly proportional to the voltage. This direct proportion in mathematical terms is referred to as linear, because it can be described in a simple linear algebraic equation:

$$I = GV$$

In this equation, V is voltage and G is a constant of proportionality known as conductance, which is independent of V and remains constant at constant temperature. This equation is one form of Ohm's Law, a principle applicable only to materials in which electrical conduction is linear. In turn, such materials are referred to as ohmics.

The more familiar form of Ohm's Law is:

$$I = V/R$$

where R is 1/G and is termed resistance.

Conceptually, the idea of resistance to the passage of current preceded the idea of charge transport in historical development.

The comparison of electrical potential difference to a hill in gravitational systems leads to the idea of a gradient, or slope. The rate at which the voltage varies along the length of the wire, measured relative to either end, is called the electric field:

$$E = -(V/L)$$

The field E is directly proportional to V and inversely proportional to L in a linear or ohmic conductor. This field is the same as the electrostatic field defined in the article on electrostatics. The minus sign is associated with the need for a negative gradient to represent "downhill." The electric field in this description is conceptually analogous to the gravitational field near the earth's surface.

Experimental measurements of current and voltage in metallic wires of different dimensions, with temperature constant, show that resistance increases in direct proportion to length and inverse proportion to cross–sectional area. These variations allow the metal itself to be considered apart from specimen dimensions.

Using a proportionality constant for the material property yields the relation:

$$R = \rho \, (L/A)$$

where ρ is called the resistivity of the metal. Inverting this equation places conduction rather than resistance uppermost:

$$G = \sigma \, (A/L)$$

where σ is the conductivity, the reciprocal $(1/\rho)$ of the resistivity.

This analysis may be extended by substitution of equivalent expressions:

$$G = I/V$$
$$\sigma(A/L) = I/EL$$
$$\sigma = I/AE$$

Introducing the concept of current density, or current flowing per unit cross–sectional area:

$$J = I/A$$

yields an expression free of all the external measurements required for its actual calculation:

$$\sigma = J/E$$

This equation is called the field form of Ohm's Law, and is the first of two physical definitions of conductivity, rather than mathematical.

The nature of conductivity in metals may be studied in greater depth by considering the electrons within the bulk metal. This approach is termed microscopic, in contrast to the macroscopic properties of a metal specimen. Under the influence of an internal electric field in the material, the electron cloud will undergo a net drift toward the battery anode. This drift is very slow in comparison with the random thermal motions of the individual electrons. The cloud may be characterized by the concentration of electrons, defined as total number per unit volume:

$$n = N/U$$

where n is the concentration, N the total number, and U the volume of metal (U is used here for volume instead of V, which as an algebraic symbol is reserved for voltage). The total drifting charge is then:

$$q = Ne = nUe$$

where e is the charge of each electron.

N is too large to enumerate; however, if as a first approximation each atom is regarded as contributing one valence electron to the cloud, the number of atoms can be estimated from the volume of a specimen, the density of the metal, and the atomic mass. The value of n calculated this way is not quite accurate even for a univalent metal, but agrees in order of magnitude. (The corrections are quantum–mechanical in nature; metals of higher valence and alloys require more complicated quantum–based corrections.)

The average drift velocity of the cloud is the ratio of wire length to the average time required for an electron to traverse that length. Algebraic substitutions similar to those previously shown will show that the current density is proportional to the drift velocity:

$$J = nev_d$$

The drift velocity is superimposed on the thermal motion of the electrons. That combination of motions, in which the electrons bounce their way through the metal, leads to the microscopic description of electrical resistance, which incorporates the idea of a limit to forward motion. The limit is expressed in the term mobility:

$$\mu = v_d / E$$

so that mobility, the ratio of drift velocity to electric field, is finite and characteristic of the particular metal.

Combining these last two equations produces the second physical definition of conductivity:

$$\sigma = J/E = nev_d/E = ne\mu$$

The motion of electrons among vibrating ion cores may be analyzed by means of Newton's Second Law, which states that a net force exerted on a mass produces an acceleration:

$$F = ma$$

Acceleration in turn produces an increasing velocity. If there were no opposition to the motion of an electron in the space between the ion cores, the connection of a battery across the ends of a wire would produce a current increasing with time, in proportion to such an increasing velocity. Experiment shows that the current is steady, so that there is no net acceleration.

Yet the battery produces an electric field in the wire, which in turn produces an electric force on each electron:

$$F = eE$$

Thus, there must be an equal and opposite force associated with the behavior of the ion cores. The analogy here is the action of air molecules against an object falling in the atmosphere, such as a raindrop. This fluid friction generates a force proportional to the velocity, which reaches a terminal value when the frictional force becomes equal to the weight. This steady state, for which the net force is zero, corresponds to the drift velocity of electrons in a conductor. Just as the raindrop quickly reaches a steady speed of fall, electrons in a metal far more quickly reach a steady drift velocity manifested in a constant current.

Thus far, this discussion has required that temperature be held constant. For metals, experimental measurements show that conductivity decreases as temperature increases. Examination suggests that, for a metal with n and e fixed, it is a decrease in mobility that accounts for that decrease in conductivity. For moderate increases in temperature, the experimental variation is found to fit a linear relation:

$$\rho = \rho_0[1 + \alpha(T - T_0)]$$

Here the subscript "0" refers to initial values and α is called the temperature coefficient of resistivity. This coefficient is found to vary over large temperature changes.

To study the relationship between temperature and electron mobility in a metal, the behavior of the ion cores must be considered. The ion cores are arranged in a three–dimensional crystal lattice. In most common metals the structure is cubic, and the transport functions are not strongly dependent on direction. The metal may then be treated as isotropic, that is, independent of direction, and all the foregoing equations apply as written. For anisotropic materials, the orientational dependence of transport in the crystals leads to families of equations with sets of directional coefficients replacing the simple constants used here.

Temperature is associated with the vibrational kinetic energy of the ion cores in motion about their equilibrium positions. They may be likened to masses interconnected by springs in three dimensions, with their bonds acting as the springs. Electrons attempting to move among them will be randomly deflected, or scattered, by these lattice vibrations, which are quantized. The vibrational quanta are termed phonons, in an analogy to photons. Advanced conductivity theory is based on analyses of the scattering of electrons by phonons.

With the increase in vibrational energy as temperature is increased, the scattering is increased so that the drift motion is subjected to more disruption. Maintenance of a given current would thus require a higher field at a higher temperature.

If the ion cores of a specific metal were identical and stationary in their exact equilibrium lattice sites, the electron cloud could drift among them without opposition, that is, without resistance. Thus, three factors in resistance can be identified: (a) lattice vibrations, (b) ion core displacement from lattice sites, and (c) chemical impurities, which are wrong ion cores. The factors (a) and (b) are temperature–dependent, and foreign atoms contribute their thermal motions as well as their wrongness. Additionally, sites where ions are missing, or vacancies, also are wrong and contribute to scatter-

ing. Displacements, vacancies, and impurities are classed as lattice defects.

A direct extension of thermal behavior downward toward the absolute zero of temperature suggests that resistance should fall to zero monotonically. This does not occur because lattice defects remain wrong and vibrational energy does not drop to zero—quantum mechanics accounts for the residual zero–point energy. However, in many metals and many other substances at temperatures approaching zero, a wholly new phenomenon is observed, the sudden drop of resistivity to zero. This is termed superconductivity.

Semiconductors

Semiconductors are materials in which the conductivity is much lower than for metals, and widely variable through control of their composition. These substances are now known to be poor insulators rather than poor conductors, in terms of their atomic structure. Though some semiconducting substances had been identified and studied by the latter half of the 19th century, their properties could not be explained on the basis of classical physics. It was not until the mid–20th century, when modern quantum–mechanical principles were applied to the analysis of both metals and semiconductors, that theoretical calculations of conductivity values agreed with the results of experimental measurements.

In a good insulator, electrons cannot move because nearly all allowed orbital states are occupied. Energy must then be supplied to remove an electron from an outermost bound position to a higher allowed state. This leaves a vacancy into which another bound electron can hop under the influence of an electric field. Thus, both the energized electron and its vacancy become mobile. The vacancy acts like a positive charge, called a hole, and drifts in the direction opposite to electrons. Electrons and holes are more generally termed charge carriers.

In good insulators the activation energy of charge carriers is high, and their availability requires a correspondingly high temperature. In poor insulators, that is, semiconductors, activation occurs at temperatures moderately above 27°C (300 K). Each substance has a characteristic value.

There are many more compounds than elements that can be classed as semiconductors. The elements are a few of those in column IV of the periodic table, which have covalent bonds: carbon (C), germanium (Ge), and silicon (Si). For carbon, only the graphite form is semiconducting; diamond is an excellent insulator. The next element down in this column, tin (Sn), undergoes a transition from semiconductor to metal at 59°F (15°C), below room temperature, indicative of an unusefully low activation energy. Other elements that exhibit semiconductor behavior are found in the lower portion of column VI, specifically selenium (Se) and tellurium (Te).

There are two principal groups of compounds with semiconducting properties, named for the periodic table columns of their constituents: III–V, including gallium arsenide (GaAs) and indium antimonide (InSb), among others; and II–VI, including zinc sulfide (ZnS), selenides, tellurides, and some oxides. In many respects these compounds mimic the behavior of column IV elements. Their chemical bonds are mixed covalent and ionic. There are also some organic semiconducting compounds, but their analysis is beyond the scope of this article.

A semiconductor is called intrinsic if its conductivity is the result of equal contributions from its own electrons and holes. The equation must then be expanded:

$$\sigma = n_e e\, \mu_e + n_h e\, \mu_h$$

In an intrinsic semiconductor, $n_e = n_h$, and e has the same numerical value for an electron (–) and the hole left behind (+). The mobilities are usually different. These terms add because the opposite charges move in opposite directions, resulting in a pair of like signs in each product.

For application in devices, semiconductors are rarely used in their pure or intrinsic composition. Under carefully controlled conditions, impurities are introduced which contribute either an excess or a deficit of electrons. Excess electrons neutralize holes so that only electrons are available for conduction. The resulting material is called n–type, n for negative carrier. An example of n–type material is Si with Sb, a column IV element with a column V impurity known as a donor. In n–type material, donor atoms remain fixed and positively ionized. When a column III impurity is infused into a column IV element, electrons are bound and holes made available. That material is called p–type, p for positive carrier. Column III impurities are known as acceptors; in the material acceptor atoms remain fixed and negatively ionized. An example of p–type material is Si with Ga. Both n–type and p–type semiconductors are referred to as extrinsic.

Thermal kinetic energy is not the only mechanism for the release of charge carriers in semiconductors. Photons with energy equal to the activation energy can be absorbed by a bound electron which, in an intrinsic semiconductor, adds both itself and a hole as mobile carriers. These photons may be in the visible range or in the near infrared, depending on E_G. In extrinsic semiconductors, photons of much lower energies can contribute to the pool of the prevailing carrier type, provided the material is cooled to cryogenic temperatures in order to reduce the population of thermally activated carriers. This behavior is known as photoconductivity.

Each separate variety of semiconductor is ohmic, with the conductivity constant at constant temperature. However, as the temperature is increased, the conductivity increases very rapidly. The concentration of available carriers varies in accordance with an exponential function:

$$n \propto \exp[-(E_G/kT)]$$

where E_G is the gap or activation energy, k is Boltzmann's constant (1.38×10^{23} joules/kelvin), T is absolute (Kelvin) temperature, and the product kT is the thermal energy corresponding to temperature T. The increase in available charge carriers overrides any decrease in mobility, and this leads to a negative value for α. Indeed, a decrease in resistance with increasing temperature is a reliable indication that a substance is a semiconductor, not a metal. Graphite is an example of a conductor that appears metallic in many ways except for a negative α. The converse, a positive α, is not as distinct a test for metallic conductivity.

The Fermi level, E_F, can be shown differently for intrinsic, n–type, and p–type semiconductors. However, for materials physically connected, E_F must be the same for thermal equilibrium. This is a consequence of the laws of thermodynamics and energy conservation. Thus, the behavior of various junctions, in which the interior energy levels shift to accommodate the alignment of the Fermi level, is extremely important for the semiconductor devices.

Non–ohmic conductors

Non–ohmic conduction is marked by nonlinear graphs of current vs. voltage. It occurs in semiconductor junctions, electrolytic solutions, some ionic solids not in solution, ionized gases, and vacuum tubes. Respective examples include semiconductor p–n diodes, battery acid or alkaline solutions, alkali halide crystals, the ionized mercury vapor in a fluorescent lamp, and cathode ray tubes.

Ionic conductivities are much lower than electronic, because the masses and diameters of ions make them much less mobile. While ions can drift slowly in a gas or liquid, their motions through the interstices of a solid lattice are much more restricted. Yet, with their thermal kinetic energy, ions will diffuse through a lattice, and in the presence of an electric field, will wander toward the appropriate electrode. In most instances, both ionic and electronic conduction will occur, depending on impurities. Thus, for studies of ionic conductivity, the material must be a very pure solid.

In gases, the gas atoms must be ionized by an electric field sufficient to supply the ionization energy of the gas in the tube. For stable currents, the ratio of field to gas pressure, E/P, is a major parameter. Electrons falling back into bound states produce the characteristic spectrum of the gas, qualitatively associated with color, e.g., red for neon, yellow–orange for sodium vapor, or blue–white for mercury vapor.

The basic definition of a plasma in physics includes all material conductors, ohmic and non–ohmic. A plasma is a medium in which approximately equal numbers of opposite charges are present, so that the medium is neutral or nearly so. In a metal the negative electrons are separated from an equal number of positive ion cores. In a semiconductor there may be holes and electrons (intrinsic), holes and ionized acceptors (p–type), or electrons and ionized donors (n–type). In an electrolytic solution and in an ionic solid there are positive and negative ions. An ionized gas contains electrons and positive ions. A small distinction among these may be made as to whether the medium has one or two mobile carriers.

In contemporary usage, the term plasma usually refers to extremely hot gases such as those used in the Tokamak for nuclear fusion experiments. High–energy plasmas are discussed in the article on fusion as a means of generating electric power.

The remaining non–ohmic conduction category is the vacuum tube, in which a beam of electrons is emitted from either a heated cathode (thermionic) or a suitably illuminated cathode (photoelectric), and moves through evacuated space to an anode. The beam in its passage is subjected to electrostatic or magnetic fields for control. The evacuated space cannot be classed either as a material with a definable conductivity or as a plasma, since only electrons are present. However, there are relations of current and voltage to be analyzed. These graphs are generally nonlinear or linear over a limited range. But vacuum tubes are not called ohmic even in their linear ranges because there is no material undergoing the lattice behavior previously described as the basis for ohmic resistance.

Electrical conduction in the human body and other animal organisms is primarily ionic, since body fluids contain vital electrolytes subject to electrochemical action in organs. Further information is available in other articles, particularly those on the heart, the brain, and neurons.

See also Chemical bond; Electrolyte; Metal; Non-metal; Periodic Table; Valence.

Further Reading:

Halliday, David, Resnick, Robert, and Krane, Kenneth. *Physics* 4th ed. New York: John Wiley and Sons, 1992.
Serway, Raymond A. *Physics for Scientists and Engineers* 3rd ed. Philadelphia: W. B. Saunders Co.

Frieda A. Stahl

Electric conductor

An electric conductor is any material that can efficiently conduct electricity, such as a metal, ionic solution, or ionized gas. Usually, this term refers to the current–carrier component of an electric circuit system.

Conduction of electricity

Conduction, the passage of charges in an electrical field, is done by the movement of charged particles in the conducting medium. Good *conductors* are materials that have available negative or positive charges, like electrons or ions. *Semiconductors* are less effective in conducting electricity, while most other materials are *insulators*.

In metals, the atomic nuclei form crystalline structures, where electrons from outer orbits are mobile, or "free." The *current* (the net transfer of electric charge per unit time) is carried by the free electrons. Yet the transfer of energy is done much faster than the actual movements of the electrons. Among metals at room temperature, silver is the best conductor, followed by copper. Iron is a relatively poor conductor.

In electrolytic solutions, the positive and negative ions of the dissolved salts can carry current. Pure water is a good insulator, and various salts are fair conductors; together, as sea water, they make a good conductor.

Gases are usually good insulators. Yet when they become ionized under the influence of strong electrical fields, they may conduct electricity. Some of the energy is emitted as light photons, with most spectacular effects are seen in lightning.

In semiconductors like germanium and silicon, a limited number of free electrons or holes (positive charges) are available to carry current. Unlike metals, the conductivity of semiconductors increases with temperature, as more electrons are becoming free.

Types of conductors

Electrical energy is transmitted by metal conductors. Wires are usually soft and flexible. They may be bare, or coated with flexible insulating material. In most cases, they have a circular cross–section. Cables have larger cross–sections than wires, and they are usually stranded, built up as an assembly of smaller solid conductors. Cords are small–diameter flexible cables that are usually insulated. Multi–conductor cable is an assembly of several insulated wires in a common jacket. Bus–bars are rigid and solid, made in shapes like rectangular, rods or tubes, and are used in switchboards.

Most conductors are made from copper or aluminum, which are both flexible materials. While copper is a better conductor, aluminum is cheaper and lighter. For overhead lines the conductors are made with a steel or aluminum–alloy core, surrounded by aluminum. The conductors are supported on insulators, which are usually ceramic or porcelain. They may be coated with rubber, polyethylene, asbestos, thermoplastic, and varnished cambric. The specific type of the insulating material depends on the voltage of the circuit, the temperature, and whether the circuit is exposed to water or chemicals.

Resistance to electrical energy

A perfect conductor is a material through which charges can move with no resistance, while in a perfect insulator it is impossible for charges to move at all. However, all conducting materials have some resistance to the electrical energy, with several major effects. One is the loss of electrical energy that converts to heat; the other is that the heating of the conductors causes them to age. In addition, the energy loss within the conductors causes a reduction in the voltage at the load. The voltage drop needs to be taken into consideration in the design and operation of the circuit, since most utility devices are operating within a narrow range of voltage, and lower than desired voltage may not be sufficient for their operation.

Superconductors

Superconductors carry electric current without any resistance, therefore without energy loss. In addition, under the extremely high currents they are able to carry, superconductors exhibit several characteristics that are unknown in common conductors. For instance, they may repel external magnetic fields; magnets placed over superconducting materials will remain suspended in the air. While there is a great potential in using superconductors as carriers of electrical energy, and for frictionless means of transportation, currently their use is limited. One of the reasons is their relatively low operating temperature; mostly close to the absolute zero, some higher, up to 130 K (–143°C).

See also Electricity; Electronics.

Electrical power supply

An electrical power supply is a device that provides the energy needed by electrical or electronic equipment to perform their functions. Often, that energy originates from a source with inappropriate electrical characteristics, and a power supply is needed to change the power to meet the equipment's requirements. Power supplies usually change alternating current into direct current, raise or lower the voltage as required, and deliver the electrical energy with a more constant voltage than the original source provides. Power supplies often provide protection against power source failures that might damage the equipment. They may also provide isolation from the electrical noise that is usually found on commercial power lines.

An electrical power supply can be a simple battery or may be more sophisticated than the equipment it supports. An appropriate power supply is an essential part of every working collection of electrical or electronic circuits.

The requirement for power supplies

Batteries could be used to supply the power for almost all electronic equipment if it were not for the high cost of the energy they provide compared to commercial power lines. Power supplies were once called battery eliminators, an apt name because they made it possible to use less expensive energy from a commercial power line where it is available. Batteries are still an appropriate and economical choice for portable equipment having modest energy requirements.

Batteries as power supplies

Two basic types of chemical cells are used in batteries that supply power to electronic equipment. Primary cells are normally not rechargeable. They are intended to be discarded after their energy reserve is depleted. Secondary cells, on the other hand are rechargeable. The lead–acid secondary cell used in an automobile's battery can be recharged many times before it fails. Nickel–Cadmium batteries are based on secondary cells.

Plug–in power supplies

The electrical energy supply for homes and businesses provided through the commercial power lines is delivered by an alternating current (AC). Electronic equipment, however, almost always requires direct–current power (DC). Power supplies usually change AC to DC by a process called rectification. Semiconductor diodes that pass current in only one direction are used to block the power line's current when its polarity reverses. Capacitors store energy for use when the diodes are not conducting, providing relatively constant voltage direct current as needed.

Power supply voltage regulation

Poor power line voltage regulation causes lights in a home to dim each time the refrigerator starts. Similarly, if a change in the current from a power supply causes the voltage to vary, the power supply has poor voltage regulation. Most electronic equipment will perform best when it is supplied from a nearly constant voltage source. An uncertain supply voltage can result in poor circuit performance.

Analysis of a typical power supply's performance is simplified by modeling it as a constant–voltage source in series with an internal resistance. The internal resistance is used to explain changes in the terminal voltage when the current in a circuit varies. The lower the internal resistance of a given power supply, the more current it can supply while maintaining a nearly–constant terminal voltage. An ideal supply for circuits requiring an unvarying voltage with changing load current, would have an internal resistance near zero. A power supply with a very–low internal resistance is sometimes called a "stiff" power supply.

An inadequate power source almost always compromises the performance of electronic equipment. Audio amplifiers, for example, may produce distorted sound if the supply voltage drops with each loud pulse of sound. There was a time when the pictures on television sets would shrink if the AC–line voltage fell below a minimum value. These problems are less significant now that voltage regulation has been included in most power supplies.

There are two approaches that may be used to improve the voltage regulation of a power supply. A simple power supply that is much larger than required

by the average equipment demand will help. A larger power supply should have a lower effective internal resistance, although this is not an absolute rule. With a lower internal resistance, changes in the current supplied are less significant and the voltage regulation is improved compared to a power supply operated near its maximum capacity.

Some power supply applications require a higher internal resistance. High–power radar transmitters require a power source with a high internal resistance so that the output can be shorted each time the radar transmits a signal pulse without damaging the circuitry. Television receivers artificially increase the resistance of the very high voltage power supply for the picture tube by adding resistance deliberately. This limits the current that will be delivered should a technician inadvertently contact the high voltage which might otherwise deliver a fatal electrical shock.

Voltage–regulation circuits

Voltage–regulated power supplies feature circuitry that monitors their output voltage. If this voltage changes because of external current changes or because of shifts in the power line voltage, the regulator circuitry makes an almost instantaneous compensating adjustment.

Two common approaches are used in the design of voltage–regulated power supplies. In the less–common scheme, a shunt regulator connects in parallel with the power supply's output terminals and maintains a constant voltage by wasting current the external circuit, called the load does not require. The current delivered by the unregulated part of the power supply is always constant. The shunt regulator diverts almost no current when the external load demands a heavy current. If the external load is reduced, the shunt regulator current increases. The disadvantage of shunt regulation is that it dissipates the full power the supply is designed to deliver, whether or not the external circuit requires energy.

The more–common series voltage regulator design depends upon the variable resistance created by a transistor in series with the external circuit current. The transistor's voltage drop adjusts automatically to maintain a constant output voltage. The power supply's output voltage is sampled continuously, compared with an accurate reference, and the transistor's characteristics are adjusted automatically to maintain a constant output.

A power supply with adequate voltage regulation will often improve the performance of the electronic device it powers, so much so that voltage regulation is a very common feature of all but the simplest designs. Packaged integrated circuits are commonly used, simple three–terminal devices that contain the series transistor and most of the regulator's supporting circuitry. These "off the shelf" chips have made it very easy to include voltage regulation capability in a power supply.

Power supplies and load interaction

When a single power supply serves several independent external circuits, changes in current demand imposed by one circuit may cause voltage changes that affect the operation of the other circuits. These interactions constitute unwanted signal coupling through the common power source, producing instability. Voltage-regulators can prevent this problem by reducing the internal resistance of the common power source.

Ripple reduction

When an alternating current is converted to direct current, small voltage variations at the supply frequency are difficult to smooth out, or filter, completely. In the case of power supplies operated from the 60–Hz power line, the result is a low–frequency variation in the power supply's output called ripple voltage. Ripple voltage on the power supply output will add with the signals processed by electronic circuitry, particularly in circuits where the signal voltage is low. Ripple can be minimized by using more elaborate filter circuitry but it can be reduced more effectively with active voltage regulation. A voltage regulator can respond fast enough to cancel unwanted changes in the voltage.

Minimizing the effects of line–voltage changes

Power–line voltages normally fluctuate randomly for a variety of reasons. A special voltage–regulating transformer can improve the voltage stability of the primary power. This transformer's action is based on a coil winding that includes a capacitor which tunes the transformer's inductance into resonance at the power line frequency. When the line voltage is too high, the circulating current in the transformer's resonant winding tends to saturate the magnetic core of the transformer, reducing its efficiency and causing the voltage to fall. When the line voltage is too low, as on a hot summer day when air conditioners are taxing the capabilities of the generators and power lines, the circulating current is reduced, raising the efficiency of the transformer. The voltage regulation achieved by these transformers can be helpful even though it is not perfect. An early TV brand included resonant transformers to prevent picture–size variations that accompanied normal line–voltage shifts.

Resonant power transformers waste energy, a serious drawback, and they do not work well unless heavily loaded. A regulating transformer will dissipate nearly its full rated power even without a load. They also tend to distort the alternating–current waveform, adding harmonics to their output, which may present a problem when powering sensitive equipment.

Laboratory power supplies

Voltage–regulated power supplies are necessary equipment in scientific and technical laboratories. They provide an adjustable, regulated source of electrical power to test circuits under development.

Laboratory power supplies usually feature two programmable modes, a constant–voltage output over a selected range of load current and a constant–current output over a wide range of voltage. The crossover point where the action switches from constant voltage to constant current action is selected by the user. As an example, it may be desirable to limit the current to a test circuit to avoid damage if a hidden circuit fault occurs. If the circuit demands less than a selected value of current, the regulating circuitry will hold the output voltage at the selected value. If, however, the circuit demands more than the selected maximum current, the regulator circuit will decrease the terminal voltage to whatever value will maintain the selected maximum current through the load. The powered circuit will never be allowed to carry more than the selected constant–current limit.

Simple transformer power supplies

Alternating current is required for most power lines because AC makes it possible to change the voltage to current ratio with transformers. Transformers are used in power supplies when it is necessary to increase or decrease voltage. The AC output of these transformers usually must be rectified into direct current. The resulting pulsating direct current is filtered to create nearly-pure direct current.

Switching power supplies

A relatively new development in power–supply technology, the switching power supply, is becoming popular. Switching power supplies are lightweight and very efficient. Almost all personal computers are powered by switching power supplies.

The switching power supply gets its name from the use of transistor switches which rapidly toggle in and out of conduction. Current travels first in one direction then in the other as it passes through the transformer. Pulsations from the rectified switching signal are much higher frequencies than the power line frequency, therefore the ripple content can be minimized easily with

KEY TERMS

. . . .

Alternating current—Current continually reversing direction, abbreviated AC.

Direct current—Current in one direction only, abbreviated DC.

Filter—Electrical circuitry designed to smooth voltage variations.

Harmonic—Whole–number multiple of a fundamental frequency.

Hz—SI abbreviation for Hertz, the unit of frequency.

Internal resistance—Fictitious resistance proposed to explain voltage variation.

Modeling—Analysis of a complicated device with a simpler analogy.

Ohms—Unit of electrical resistance, equal to 1 Volt per Ampere.

Parallel—Side–by–side electrical connection.

Rectification—Changing AC to DC by blocking reverse flow of charge.

Ripple—Repetitive voltage variation from inadequate filtering.

---

small filter capacitors. Voltage regulation can be accomplished by varying the switching frequency. Changes in the switching frequency alter the efficiency of the power supply transformer enough to stabilize the output voltage.

Switching power supplies are usually not damaged by sudden short circuits. The switching action stops almost immediately, protecting the supply and the circuit load. A switching power supply is said to have stalled when excessive current interrupts its action.

Switching power supplies are light in weight because the components are more efficient at higher frequencies. Transformers need much less iron in their cores at higher frequencies.

Switching power supplies have negligible ripple content at audible frequencies. Variations in the output of the switching power supply are inaudible compared to the hum that is common with power supplies that operate at the 60 Hz AC–power line frequency.

The importance of power supplies

Electrical power supplies are not the most glamorous part of contemporary technology, but without

them many electronic products that we take for granted would not be possible.

See also Electricity; Electronics.

Further Reading:

Cannon, Don L. *Understanding Solid–State Electronics*, 5th ed. SAMS division of Prentice Hall Publishing Company, 1991.

Giancoli, Douglas C. *Physics: Principles With Applications*, 3rd ed. Prentice Hall, 1991.

Donald Beaty

Electrical resistance

The electrical resistance of a wire or circuit is a way of measuring the resistance to the flow of an electrical current. A good electrical conductor, such as a copper wire, will have a very low resistance. Good insulators, such as rubber or glass insulators, have a very high resistance. The resistance is measured in Ohms, and is related to the current in the circuit and voltage across the circuit by Ohm's law. For a given voltage, a wire with a lower resistance will have a higher current.

The resistance of a given piece of wire depends of three factors: the length of the wire, the cross–sectional area of the wire, and the resistivity of the material composing the wire. To understand how this works, think of water flowing through a hose. The amount of water flowing through the hose is analogous to the current in the wire. Just as more water can pass through a fat fire hose than a skinny garden hose, a fat wire can carry more current than a skinny wire. For a wire, the larger the cross–sectional area, the lower the resistance; the smaller the cross–sectional area, the higher the resistance. Now consider the length. It is harder for water to flow through a very long hose simply because it has to travel farther. Analogously, it is harder for current to travel through a longer wire. A longer wire will have a greater resistance. The resistivity is a property of the material in the wire that depends on the chemical composition of the material but not on the amount of material or the shape (length, cross–sectional area) of the material. Copper has a low resistivity, but the resistance of a given copper wire depends on the length and area of that wire. Replacing a copper wire with a wire of the same length and area but a higher resistivity will produce a higher resistance. In the hose analogy, it is like filling the hose with sand. Less water will flow through the hose filled with sand than through an identical unobstructed hose. The sand in effect has a higher resistivity to water flow. The total resistance of a wire is then the resistivity of the material composing the wire times the length of the wire, divided by the cross–sectional area of the wire.

Electric arc

An electric arc is a high–current, low–voltage electrical discharge between electrodes in the presence of gases. In an electric arc, electrons are emitted from a heated cathode. Arcs can be formed in high, atmospheric, or low pressures, and in various gases. They have wide uses as highly luminous lamps, as furnaces for heating, cutting and welding, and as tools for spectrochemical analysis.

Electrical conduction in gases

Gases consist of neutral molecules, and are, therefore, good insulators. Yet under certain conditions, a breakdown of the insulating property occurs, and current can pass through the gas. Several phenomena are associated with the electric discharge in gases; among them are spark, dark (Townsend) discharge, glow, corona, and arc.

In order to conduct electricity, two conditions are required. First, the normally neutral gas must create charges or accept them from external sources, or both. Second, an electric field should exist to produce the directional motion of the charges. A charged atom or molecule, or ion, can be positive or negative; electrons are negative charges. In electrical devices, an electric field is produced between two electrodes, called anode and cathode, made of conducting materials. The process of changing a neutral atom or molecule into an ion is called ionization. Ionized gas is called plasma. Conduction in gases is distinguished from conduction in solids and liquids in that the gases play an active role in the process. The gas not only permits free charges to pass though, but itself may produce charges. Cumulative ionization occurs when the original electron and its offspring gain enough energy, so each can produce another electron. When the process is repeated over and over, the result is an avalanche.

For any gas at a given pressure and temperature there is a certain voltage value, called *breakdown potential*, that will produce ionization. Application of a voltage above the critical value would initially cause the current to increase due to cumulative ionization, and

the voltage is then decreased. If the pressure is not too low, conduction is concentrated into a narrow, illuminated, "spark" channel. By receiving energy from the current, the channel becomes hot and may produce shock–waves. Natural phenomena are the lightning and the associated thunder, that consist of high voltages and currents that cannot be artificially achieved.

An arc can be produced in high pressure following a spark. This occurs when steady conditions are achieved, and the voltage is low but sufficient to maintain the required current. In low pressures, the transient stage of the spark leads to the glow discharge, and an arc can later be formed when the current is further increased. In arcs, the *thermionic effect* is responsible for the production of free electrons that are emitted from the hot cathode. A strong electric field at the metallic surface lowers the barrier for electron emission, and provides a *field emission*. Because of the high temperature and the high current involved, however, some of the mechanisms of arcs cannot be easily studied.

Properties of the arc

The electric arc was first detected in 1808 by British chemist Humphry Davy. He saw a brilliant luminous flame when two carbon rods conducting a current were separated, and the convection current of hot gas deflected it in the shape of an arc. Typical characteristics of an arc include a relatively low potential gradient between the electrodes (less than a few tens of Volts), and a high current density (from 0.1 amperes to thousands amperes or higher). High gas temperatures (several thousands or tens of thousands degrees Kelvin) exist in the conducting channel, especially in high gas pressures. Vaporization of the electrodes is also common, and the gas contains molecules of the electrodes material. In some cases, a hissing sound may be heard, making the arc "sing."

The potential gradient between the electrodes is not uniform. In most cases, one can distinguish between three different regions: the area close to the positive electrode, termed *cathode fall*; the area close to the negative electrode, or *anode rise*; and the main arc body. Within the arc body there is a uniform voltage gradient. This region is electrically neutral, where the cumulative ionization results in the number of positive ions equals the number of electrons or negative ions. The ionization occurs mainly due to excitation of the molecules and the gain of high temperature.

The cathode fall region is about 0.01 millimeters with a potential difference of less than about ten Volts. Often thermionic emission would be achieved at the cathode. The electrodes in this case are made of refractive materials like tungsten and carbon, and the region contains an excess of positive ions and a large electric current. At the cathode, transition is made from a metallic conductor in which current is carried by electrons, to a gas in which conduction is done by both electrons or negative ions and positive ions. The gaseous positive ions may reach the cathode freely and form a potential barrier. Electrons emitted from the cathode must overcome this barrier in order to enter the gas.

At the anode, transition is made from a gas, in which both electrons and positive ions conduct current, to the metallic conductor, in which current is carried only by electrons. With a few exceptions, positive ions do not enter the gas from the metal. Electrons are accelerated towards the anode and provide, through ionization, a supply of ions for the column. The electron current may raise the anode to a high temperature, making it a thermionic emitter, but the emitted electrons are returned to the anode, contributing to the large negative space charge around it. The melting of the electrodes and the introduction of their vapor to the gas adds to the pressure in their vicinities.

Uses of electric arcs

There are many types of arc devices. Some operate at atmospheric pressure and may be open, and others operate at low pressure and are therefore closed in a container, like glass. The property of high current in the arc is used in the mercury arc rectifiers, like the thyratron. An alternate potential difference is applied, and the arc transfers the current in one direction only. The cathode is heated by a filament.

The high temperature created by an electric arc in the gas is used in furnaces. *Arc welders* are used for welding, where a metal is fused and added in a joint. The arc can supply the heat only, or one of its electrodes can serve as the consumable parent metal. *Plasma torches* are used for cutting, spraying, and gas heating. Cutting may be done by means of an arc formed between the metal and the electrode.

Arc lamps provide high luminous efficiency and great brightness. The light comes from the highly incandescence (about 7,000°F/4000°C) electrodes, as in *carbon arcs*, or from the heated, ionized gases surrounded the arc, as in *flame arcs*. The carbon arc, where two carbon rods serve as electrodes, was the first practical commercial electric lighting device, and it is still one of the brightest sources of light. It is used in theater motion–picture projectors, large searchlights, and lighthouses. Flame arcs are used in color photography and in photochemical processes because they closely approximate natural sunshine. The carbon is impregnated with

KEY TERMS

Artificial (hot) arc—An electric arc whose cathode is heated by an external source to provide thermionic emission, and not by the discharge itself.

Cold cathode arc—An electric arc that operates on low boiling–point materials.

Thermionic arc— An electric arc in which the electron current from the cathode is provided predominantly by thermionic emission.

volatile chemicals, which become luminous when evaporated and driven into the arc. The color of the arc depends on the material, that could be calcium, barium, titanium, or strontium. In some, the wavelength of the radiation is out of the visible spectrum. Mercury arcs produce ultraviolet radiation at high pressure. They can also produce visible light in a low pressure tube, if the internal walls are coated with fluorescence material such as phosphor; the phosphor emits light when illuminated by the ultraviolet radiation from the mercury.

Other uses of arcs include valves (used in the early days of the radio), and as a source of ions in nuclear accelerators and thermonuclear devices. The excitation of electrons in the arc, in particular the direct electron bombardment, leads to narrow spectral lines. The arc, therefore, can provide information on the composition of the electrodes. The spectra of metal alloys are widely studied using arcs; the metals are incorporated with the electrodes material, and when vaporized, they produce distinct spectra.

See also Electricity; Electronics

Ilana Steinhorn

Electric charge

Rub a balloon or styrofoam drinking cup against a wool sweater. It will then stick to a wall (at least on a dry day) or pick up small bits of paper. Why? The answer leads to the concept of electric charge.

Electromagnetic forces are one of the four fundamental forces in nature. The other three are gravitational, strong nuclear, and weak nuclear forces. The electromagnetic force unifies both electrical and magnetic forces. The magnetic forces occur whether the charges are moving or at rest. Electric charge is our way of measuring how much electric force an object can exert or feel.

Electric charge plays the same role in electric forces as mass plays in gravitational forces. The force between two electric charges is proportional to the product of the two charges divided by the distance between them squared, just as the force between two masses is proportional to the product of the two masses divided by the distance between them squared. These two force laws for electric and gravitational forces have exactly the same mathematical form.

There are however differences between the electric and gravitational forces. One difference is the electrical force is much stronger than the gravitational force. That is why the styrofoam cup mentioned above can stick to a wall. The electrical force pulling it to the wall is stronger than the gravitational force pulling it down.

The second major difference is that the gravitational force is always attractive. The electrical force can be either attractive or repulsive. There is only one type of mass, but there are two types of electric charge. Like charges will repel each other and unlike charges will attract. Most matter is made up of equal amounts of both types of charges, so electrical forces cancel out over long distances. The two types of charge are called positive and negative, the names given by Benjamin Franklin, the first American physicist. Contrary to what many people think, the terms positive and negative don't really describe properties of the charges. The names are completely arbitrary.

An important property of electric charges that was discovered by Benjamin Franklin is that charge is conserved. The total amount of both positive and negative charges must remain the same. Charge conservation is part of the reason the balloon and cup mentioned above stick to the wall. Rubbing causes electrons to be transferred from one object to another, so one has a positive charge and the other has exactly the same negative charge. No charges are created or destroyed; they are just transferred. The objects then have a net charge and electrical forces come into play.

Electric charge forms the basis of the electrical and magnetic forces that are so important in our modern electrical and electronic luxuries.

Electric circuit

An electric circuit is a system of conducting elements designed to control the path of electric current

for a particular purpose. Circuits consist of sources of electric energy, like generators and batteries; elements that transform, dissipate, or store this energy, such as resistors, capacitors and inductors; and connecting wires. Circuits often include a fuse or circuit breaker to prevent a power overload.

Devices that are connected to a circuit are connected to it in one of two ways: in series or in parallel. A series circuit forms a single pathway for the flow of current, while a parallel circuit forms separate paths or branches for the flow of current. Parallel circuits have an important advantage over series circuits. If a device connected to a series circuit malfunctions or is switched off, the circuit is broken, and other devices on the circuit cannot draw power. The separate pathways of a parallel circuit allows devices to operate independently of each other, maintaining the circuit even if one or more devices are switched off.

The first electric circuit was invented by Alessandro Volta in 1800. He discovered he could produce a steady flow of electricity using bowls of salt solution connected by metal strips. Later, he used alternating discs of copper, zinc, and cardboard that had been soaked in a salt solution to create his voltaic pile (an early battery). By attaching a wire running from the top to the bottom, he caused an electric current to flow through his circuit. The first practical use of the circuit was in electrolysis, which led to the discovery of several new chemical elements. Georg Ohm (1787–1854) discovered some conductors had more resistance than others, which affects their efficiency in a circuit. His famous law states that the voltage across a conductor divided by the current equals the resistance, measured in *ohms*. Resistance causes heat in an electrical circuit, which is often not wanted.

See also Electrical conductivity; Electrical power supply; Electrical resistance; Electric current; Electricity; Electronics; Integrated circuit.

Electric current

Electric current is the result of the relative motion of net electric charge. In metals, the charges in motion are electrons. The magnitude of an electric current depends upon the quantity of charge that passes a chosen reference point during a specified time interval. Electric current is measured in amperes, with one ampere equal to a charge–flow of one coulomb per second.

A current as small as a picoampere (one–trillionth of an ampere) can be significant. Likewise, artificial currents in the millions of amperes can be created for special purposes. Currents between a few milliamperes to a few amperes are common in radio and television circuits. An automobile starter motor may require several hundred amperes.

Current and the transfer of electric charge

The total charge transferred by an unvarying electrical current equals the product of current in amperes and the time in seconds that the current flows. If one ampere flows for one second, one coulomb will have moved in the conductor. If a changing current is graphed against time, the area between the graph's curve and the time axis will be proportional to the total charge transferred.

The speed of an electric current

Electrical currents move through wires at a speed only slightly less than the speed of light. The electrons, however, move from atom to atom more slowly. Their motion is more aptly described as a drift. Extra electrons added at one end of a wire will cause extra electrons to appear at the other end of the wire almost instantly. Individual electrons will not have moved along the length of the wire but the electric field that pushes the charge against charge along the conductor will be felt at the distant end almost immediately. To visualize this, imagine a cardboard mailing tube filled with ping–pong balls. When you insert an extra ball in one end of the tube, an identical ball will emerge from the distant end almost immediately. The original ball will not have traveled the length of the tube, but since all the balls are identical it will seem as if this has happened. This mechanical analogy suggests the way that charge seems to travel through a wire very quickly.

Electric current and energy

Heat results when current flows through an ordinary electrical conductor. Common materials exhibit an electrical property called resistance. Electrical resistance is analogous to friction in a mechanical system. Resistance results from imperfections in the conductor. When the moving electrons collide with these imperfections, they transfer kinetic energy, resulting in heat. The quantity of heat energy produced increases as the square of the current passing through the conductor.

Electric current and magnetism

A magnetic field is created in space whenever a current flows through a conductor. This magnetic field will exert a force on the magnetic field of other nearby current–carrying conductors. This is the principle behind the design of an electric motor.

An electrical generator operates on a principle similar to an electric motor. In a generator, mechanical energy forces a conductor to move through a magnetic field. The magnetic field forces the electrons in the conductor to move, which causes an electric current.

Direct current

A current in one direction only is called a direct current, or DC. A steady current is called pure DC. If DC varies with time it is called pulsating DC.

Alternating current

If a current changes direction repeatedly it is called an alternating current, or AC. Commercial electrical power is transported using alternating current because AC makes it possible to change the ratio of voltage to current with transformers. Using a higher voltage to transport electrical power across country means that the same power can be transferred using less current. For example, if transformers step up the voltage by a factor of 100, the current will be lower by a factor of 1/100. The higher voltage in this example would reduce the energy loss caused by the resistance of the wires to 0.01% of what it would be without the use of AC and transformers.

When alternating current flows in a circuit the charge drifts back and forth repeatedly. There is a transfer of energy with each current pulse. Simple electric motors deliver their mechanical energy in pulses related to the power line frequency.

Power lines in North America are based on AC having a frequency of 60 Hertz (Hz). In much of the rest of the world the power line frequency is 50 Hz. Alternating current generated aboard aircraft often has a frequency of 400 Hz because motors and generators can work efficiently with less iron, and therefore less weight, when this frequency is used.

Alternating current may also be the result of a combination of signals with many frequencies. The AC powering a loudspeaker playing music consists of a combination of many superimposed alternating currents with different frequencies and amplitudes.

Current flow vs. electron flow

We cannot directly observe the electrically-charged particles that produce current. It is usually not important to know whether the current results from the motion of positive or negative charges. Early scientists made an unfortunate choice when they assigned a positive polarity to the charge that moves through ordinary wires. It seemed logical that current was the result of positive charge in motion. Later it was confirmed that it is the negatively–charged electron that moves within wires.

The action of some devices can be explained more easily when the motion of electrons is assumed. When it is simpler to describe an action in terms of the motion of electrons, the charge motion is called electron flow. Current flow, conventional current, or Franklin convention current are terms used when the moving charge is assumed to be positive.

Conventional current flow is used in science almost exclusively. In electronics, either conventional current or electron flow is used, depending on which flow is most convenient to explain the operation of a particular electronic component. The need for competing conduction models could have been avoided had the original charge–polarity assignment been reversed.

See also Electricity; Electronics.

Further Reading:

Hewitt, Paul G. *Conceptual Physics*, 7th ed. Harper Collins, 1993.
Hobson, Art, *Physics: Concepts and Connections.* Prentice–Hall, Inc., 1995.
Ostdiek, Vern J., and Bord, Donald J. *Inquiry Into Physics.* West Publishing Company, 1995.

Donald Beaty

Electricity

Electricity is a natural phenomenon resulting from one of the most basic properties of matter, electrical

Electricity arcing over the surface of ceramic insulators.

charge. Our understanding of electrical principles has developed from a long history of experimentation. Electrical technology, essential to modern society for energy transmission and information processing, is the result of our knowledge about electrical charge at rest and electrical charge in motion.

Electrical charge

Electrical charge is a fundamental property possessed by a few types of particles that make up atoms. Electrical charge is found with either positive or negative polarity. Positive charge exactly neutralizes an equal quantity of negative charge. Charges with the same sign repel while unlike charges attract. The unit of electrical charge is the coulomb, named for Charles Coulomb, an early authority on electrical theory.

The most obvious sources of electric charge are the negatively–charged electrons from the outer parts of atoms and the positively–charged protons found in atomic nuclei. Electrical neutrality is the most probable condition of matter because most objects contain nearly equal numbers of electrons and protons. Physical activities that upset this balance will leave an object with a net electrical charge, often with important consequences.

Excess static electric charges can accumulate as a result of mechanical friction, as when someone walks across a carpet. Friction transfers charge between shoe soles and carpet, resulting in the familiar electrical shock when the excess charge sparks to a nearby person.

Many semiconductor devices used in electronics are so sensitive to static electricity that they can be destroyed if touched by a technician carrying a small excess of electric charge. Computer technicians often wear a grounded wrist strap to drain away an electrical charge that might otherwise destroy sensitive circuits they touch.

Electric fields

Charged particles alter their surrounding space to produce an effect called an electric field. An electric field is the concept we use to describe how one electric charge exerts force on another distant electric charge. Whether electric charges are at rest or moving, they are acted upon by a force whenever they are within an electric field. The ratio of this force to the amount of charge is the measure of the field's strength.

An electric field has vector properties in that it has both a unique magnitude and direction at every point in space. An electric field is the collection of all these values. When neighboring electrical charges push or pull each other, each interacts with the electric field produced by the other charge.

Electric fields are imagined as lines of force that begin on positive charges and end on negative charges. Unlike magnetic field lines, which form continuous loops, electric field lines have a beginning and an ending. This makes it possible to block the effects of an electric field. An electrically conducting surface surrounding a volume will stop an external electric field. Passengers in an automobile may be protected from lightning strikes because of this shielding effect. An electric shield enclosure is called a Faraday Cage, named for Michael Faraday.

Coulomb's Law and the forces between electrical charges

Force, quantity of charge, and distance of separation are related by a rule called Coulomb's Law. This law states that the force between electrical charges is proportional to the product of their charges and inversely proportional to the square of their separation.

The coulomb force binds atoms together to form chemical compounds. It is this same force that accelerates electrons in a TV picture tube, giving energy to the beam of electrons that creates the television picture. It is the electric force that causes charge to flow through wires.

The electric force binds electrons to the nuclei of atoms. In some kinds of materials, electrons stick tightly to their respective atoms. These materials are electrical insulators that cannot carry a significant current unless acted upon by an extremely strong electrical field. Insulators are almost always nonmetals. Metals are relatively good conductors of electricity because their outermost electrons are easily removed by an electric field. Some metals are better conductors than others, silver being the best.

Current

The basic unit of electric current is the ampere, named for the French physicist Andre Marie Ampere. One ampere equals 1 coulomb of charge drifting past a reference point each second.

Voltage

Voltage is the ratio of energy stored by a given a quantity of charge. Work must be performed to crowd same–polarity electric charges against their mutual repulsion. This work is stored as electrical potential energy, proportional to voltage. Voltage may also be thought of as electrical pressure.

The unit of voltage is the volt, named for Alessandro Volta. One volt equals one joule for every coulomb of electrical charge accumulated.

Resistance

Ordinary conductors oppose the flow of charge with an effect that resembles friction. This dissipative action is called resistance. Just as mechanical friction wastes energy as heat, current through resistance dissipates energy as heat. The unit of resistance is the ohm, named for Georg Simon Ohm. If 1 volt causes a current of 1 ampere, the circuit has 1 unit of resistance. It is useful to know that resistance is the ratio of voltage to current.

Mechanical friction can be desirable, as in automobile brakes, or undesirable, when friction creates unwanted energy loss. Resistance is always a factor in current electricity unless the circuit action involves an extraordinary low–temperature phenomenon called superconductivity. While superconducting materials exhibit absolutely no resistance, these effects are confined to temperatures so cold that it is not yet practical to use superconductivity in other than exotic applications.

Ohm's Law

Ohm's Law defines the relationship between the three variables affecting simple circuit action. According to Ohm's Law, current is directly proportional to the net voltage in a circuit and current is inversely proportional to resistance.

Electrical power

The product of voltage and current equals electrical power. The unit of electrical power is the watt, named for James Watt. One watt of electrical power equals 1 joule per second. If 1 volt forces a 1–ampere current through a 1–ohm resistance, 1 joule per second will be wasted as heat. That is, 1 watt of power will be dissipated. A 100–watt incandescent lamp requires 100 joules for each second it operates.

Electricity provides a convenient way to connect cities with distant electrical generating stations. Electricity is not the primary source of energy, rather it serves as the means to transport energy from the source to a load. Electrical energy usually begins as mechanical energy before its conversion to electrical energy. At the load end of the distribution system the electrical energy is changed to another form of energy, as needed.

Commercial electrical power is transported great distances through wires, which always have significant resistance. Some of the transported energy is unavoidably wasted as heat. These losses are minimized by using very high voltage at a lower current, with the product of voltage and current still equal to the power required. Since the energy loss increases as the square of the current, a reduction of current by a factor of 1/100 reduces the power loss by a factor of 1/10,000. Voltage as high as 1,000,000 volts is used to reduce losses. Higher voltage demands bigger insulators and taller transmission towers, but the added expense pays off in greatly–reduced energy loss.

Alternating current and direct current

Direct current, or DC, results from an electric charge that moves in only one direction. A car's battery, for example, provides a direct current when it forces electrical charge through the starter motor or through

---

KEY TERMS

Ampere—The basic unit of current flow.

Conductors—Materials that permit electrons to move freely.

Coulomb force—Another name for the electric force.

Electric field—The set of spatially–dependent vectors caused by electric charge.

Generator—A device used to change mechanical energy to electric energy.

Insulators—A material lacking the ability to conduct electricity easily.

Joule—The unit of energy in the mks system of measurements.

Ohm—The unit of electrical resistance.

Semiconductor devices—Electronic devices made from a material that is neither a good conductor or a good insulator.

Volt—The basic unit of electrical pressure.

Watt—The basic unit of electrical power equal to 1 joule per second.

---

the car's headlights. The direction of this current does not change.

Current that changes direction periodically is called alternating current, or AC. Our homes are supplied with alternating current rather than direct current because the use of AC makes it possible to step voltage up or down, using an electromagnetic device called a transformer. Without transformers to change voltage as needed, it would be necessary to distribute electrical power at a safer low voltage but at a much higher current. The higher current would increase the transmission loss in the powerlines. Without the ability to use high voltages, it would be necessary to locate generators near locations where electric power is needed.

Southern California receives much of its electrical power from hydroelectric generators in the state of Washington by a connection through an unusually long DC transmission line that operates at approximately one million volts. Electrical power is first generated as alternating current, transformed to a high voltage, then converted to direct current for the long journey south. The direct–current power is changed back into AC for final distribution at a lower voltage. The use of direct current more than compensates for the added complexity of the AC to DC and DC to AC conversions.

Further Reading:

Asimov, Isaac. *Understanding Physics: Light, Magnetism, and Electricity,* Volume II, Signet Books, The New American Library.

Giancoli, Douglas C., *Physics, Principles With Applications,* 3rd ed. Prentice Hall, 1991.

Hewitt, Paul G., *Conceptual Physics,* 7th ed. Harper Collins, 1993.

Donald Beaty

A cross section of a simple direct-current electric motor. At its center is the rotor, a coil wound around an iron armature, which spins within the poles of the magnet that can be seen on the inside of the casing.

Electric motor

An electric motor is a machine used to convert electrical energy to mechanical energy. Electric motors are extremely important to modern-day life, being used in many different places, e.g., vacuum cleaners, dishwashers, computer printers, fax machines, video cassette recorders, machine tools, printing presses, automobiles, subway systems, sewage treatment plants and water pumping stations.

The major physical principles behind the operation of an electric motor are known as Ampère's Law and Faraday's Law. The first states that an electrical conductor sitting in a magnetic field will experience a force if any current flowing through the conductor has a component at right angles to that field. Reversal of either the current or the magnetic field will produce a force acting in the opposite direction. The second principle states that if a conductor is moved through a magnetic field, then any component of motion perpendicular to that field will generate a potential difference between the ends of the conductor.

An electric motor consists of two essential elements. The first, a static component which consists of magnetic materials and electrical conductors to generate magnetic fields of a desired shape, is known as the *stator*. The second, which also is made from magnetic and electrical conductors to generate shaped magnetic fields which interact with the fields generated by the stator, is known as the *rotor*. The rotor comprises the moving component of the motor, having a rotating shaft to connect to the machine being driven and some means of maintaining an electrical contact between the rotor and the motor housing (typically, carbon brushes pushed against slip rings). In operation, the electrical current supplied to the motor is used to generate mag-

netic fields in both the rotor and the stator. These fields push against each other with the result that the rotor experiences a torque and consequently rotates.

Electrical motors fall into two broad categories, depending on the type of electrical power applied—direct current (DC) and alternating current (AC) motors.

The first DC electrical motor was demonstrated by Michael Faraday in England in 1821. Since the only available electrical sources were DC, the first commercially available motors were of the DC type, becoming popular in the 1880s. These motors were used for both low power applications and high power, such as electric street railways. It was not until the 1890s, with the availability of AC electrical power that the AC motor was developed, primarily by the Westinghouse and General Electric corporations. Throughout this decade, most of the problems concerned with single and multi-phase AC motors were solved. Consequently, the principal features of electric motors were all developed by 1900.

DC motor

The operation of a DC motor is dependent on the workings of the poles of the stator with a part of the rotor, or armature. The stator contains an even number of poles of alternating magnetic polarity, each pole consisting of an electromagnet formed from a pole winding wrapped around a pole core. When a DC current flows through the winding, a magnetic field is formed. The armature also contains a winding, in which the current flows in the direction illustrated. This armature current interacts with the magnetic field in accordance with Ampère's law, producing a torque which turns the armature.

KEY TERMS

. . . .

AC—Alternating current, where the current round a circuit varies regularly in a periodic fashion.

DC—Direct current, where the current round a circuit is approximately constant with time.

Rotor—That portion of an electric motor which is free to rotate, including the shaft, armature and linkage to a machine.

Stator—That portion of an electric motor which is not free to rotate, including the field coils.

Torque—A turning force.

If the armature windings were to rotate round to the next pole piece of opposite polarity, the torque would operate in the opposite direction, thus stopping the armature. In order to prevent this, the rotor contains a commutator which changes the direction of the armature current for each pole piece that the armature rotates past, thus ensuring that the windings passing, for example, a pole of north polarity will all have current flowing in the same direction, while the windings passing south poles will have oppositely flowing current to produce a torque in the same direction as that produced by the north poles. The commutator generally consists of a split contact ring against which the brushes applying the DC current ride.

The rotation of the armature windings through the stator field generates a voltage across the armature which is known as the counter EMF (electromotive force) since it opposes the applied voltage: this is the consequence of Faraday's Law. The magnitude of the counter EMF is dependent on the magnetic field strength and the speed of the rotation of the armature. When the DC motor is initially turned on, there is no counter EMF and the armature starts to rotate. The counter EMF increases with the rotation. The effective voltage across the armature windings is the applied voltage minus the counter EMF.

Types of DC motor

DC motors are more common than we may think. A car may have as many as 20 DC motors to drive fans, seats, and windows. They come in three different types, classified according to the electrical circuit used. In the shunt motor, the armature and field windings are connected in parallel, and so the currents through each are relatively independent. The current through the field winding can be controlled with a field rheostat (variable resistor), thus allowing a wide variation in the motor speed over a large range of load conditions. This type of motor is used for driving machine tools or fans, which require a wide range of speeds.

In the series motor, the field winding is connected in series with the armature winding, resulting in a very high starting torque since both the armature current and field strength run at their maximum. However, once the armature starts to rotate, the counter EMF reduces the current in the circuit, thus reducing the field strength. The series motor is used where a large starting torque is required, such as in automobile starter motors, cranes and hoists.

The compound motor is a combination of the series and shunt motors, having parallel and series field windings. This type of motor has a high starting torque and the ability to vary the speed and is used in situations requiring both these properties such as punch presses, conveyors and elevators.

AC motors

AC motors are much more common than the DC variety because almost all electrical supply systems run alternating current. There are three main different types of motor, namely polyphase induction, polyphase synchronous, and single phase motors. Since three phase supplies are the most common polyphase sources, most polyphase motors run on three phase. Three phase supplies are widely used in commercial and industrial settings, whereas single phase supplies are almost always the type found in the home.

Principles of three phase motor operation

The main difference between AC and DC motors is that the magnetic field generated by the stator rotates in the ac case. Three electrical phases are introduced through terminals, each phase energizing an individual field pole. When each phase reaches its maximum current, the magnetic field at that pole reaches a maximum value. As the current decreases, so does the magnetic field. Since each phase reaches its maximum at a different time within a cycle of the current, that field pole whose magnetic field is largest is constantly changing between the three poles, with the effect that the magnetic field seen by the rotor is rotating. The speed of rotation of the magnetic field, known as the synchronous speed, depends on the frequency of the power supply and the number of poles produced by the stator winding. For a standard 60 Hz supply, as used in the U.S., the maximum synchronous speed is 3600 rpm.

In the three phase induction motor, the windings on the rotor are not connected to a power supply, but are essentially short circuits. The most common type of rotor winding, the squirrel cage winding, bears a strong resemblance to the running wheel used in cages for pet gerbils. When the motor is initially switched on and the rotor is stationary, the rotor conductors experience a changing magnetic field sweeping by at the synchronous speed. From Faraday's Law, this situation results in the induction of currents round the rotor windings; the magnitude of this current depends on the impedance of the rotor windings. Since the conditions for motor action are now fulfilled, that is, current carrying conductors are found in a magnetic field, the rotor experiences a torque and starts to turn. The rotor can never rotate at the synchronous speed because there would be no relative motion between the magnetic field and the rotor windings and no current could be induced. The induction motor has a high starting torque.

In squirrel cage motors, the motor speed is determined by the load it drives and by the number of poles generating a magnetic field in the stator. If some poles are switched in or out, the motor speed can be controlled by incremental amounts. In wound–rotor motors, the impedance of the rotor windings can be altered externally, which changes the current in the windings and thus affords continuous speed control.

Three–phase synchronous motors are quite different from induction motors. In the synchronous motor, the rotor uses a DC energized coil to generate a constant magnetic field. After the rotor is brought close to the synchronous speed of the motor, the north (south) pole of the rotor magnet locks to the south (north) pole of the rotating stator field and the rotor rotates at the synchronous speed. The rotor of a synchronous motor will usually include a squirrel cage winding which is used to start the motor rotation before the DC coil is energized. The squirrel cage has no effect at synchronous speeds for the reason explained above.

Single phase induction and synchronous motors, used in most domestic situations, operate on principles similar to those explained for three phase motors. However, various modifications have to be made in order to generate starting torques, since the single phase will not generate a rotating magnetic field alone. Consequently, split phase, capacitor start, or shaded pole designs are used in induction motors. Synchronous single phase motors, used for timers, clocks, tape recorders etc., rely on the reluctance or hysteresis designs.

Further Reading:

Anderson, Edwin P. and Rex Miller, *Electric Motors*, New York: Macmillan, 1991.

Iain A. McIntyre

Electrocardiogram (ECG)

The electrocardiogram, or ECG, directly measures microvoltages in the heart muscle (myocardium) occurring over specific periods of time in a cardiac, i.e., a heartbeat, otherwise known as a cardiac impulse. With each heartbeat, electrical currents called action potentials, measured in millivolts (mV), travel at predictable velocities through a conducting system in the heart. The potentials originate in a sinoatrial (SA) node which lies in the entrance chamber of the heart, called the right atrium. These currents also diffuse through tissues surrounding the heart whereby they reach the skin. There they are picked up by external electrodes which are placed at specific positions on the skin. They are in turn sent through leads to an electrocardiograph. A pen records the transduced electrical events onto special paper. The paper is ruled into mV against time and it provides the reader with a so–called rhythm strip. This is a non–invasive method to used evaluate the electrical counterparts of the myocardial activity in any series of heart beats. Careful observation of the records for any deviations in the expected times, shapes, and voltages of the impulses in the cycles gives the observer information that is of significant diagnostic value, especially for human medicine. The normal rhythm is called a sinus rhythm if the potentials begin in the sinoatrial (SA) node.

A cardiac cycle has a phase of activity called systole followed by a resting phase called diastole. In systole, the muscle cell membranes, each called a sarcolemma, allow charged sodium particles to enter the cells while charged potassium particles exit. These processes of membrane transfer in systole are defined as polarization. Electrical signals are generated and this is the phase of excitability. The currents travel immediately to all cardiac cells through the mediation of end–to–end high–conduction connectors termed intercalated disks. The potentials last for 200 to 300 milliseconds. In the subsequent diastolic phase, repolarization occurs. This is a period of oxidative restoration of energy sources needed to drive the processes. Sodium is actively pumped out of the fiber while potassium diffuses in. Calcium, which is needed to energize the force of the heart, is transported back to canals called endoplasmic reticula in the cell cytoplasm.

The action potentials travel from the superior part of the heart called the base to the inferior part called the apex. In the human four–chambered heart, a pacemaker, the SA node, is the first cardiac area to be excited because sodium and potassium interchange and energize both right and left atria. The impulses then pass downward to an atrioventricular (AV) node in the lower

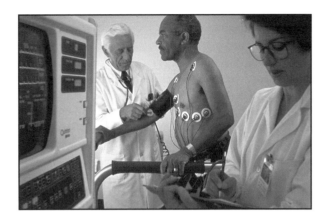

In electrocardiogram (ECG) testing, sensors attached to the patient relay information about cardiac activity to the computer display.

right atrium where their velocity is slowed, whereupon they are transmitted to a conducting system called the bundle of His. The bundle contains Purkinje fibers that transmit the impulses to the outer aspects of the right and left ventricular myocardium. In turn, they travel into the entire ventricular muscles by a slow process of diffusion. Repolarization of the myocardial cells takes place in a reverse direction to that of depolarization, but does not utilize the bundle of His.

The place where electrodes are positioned on the skin is important. In what are called standard leads, one

electrode is fastened to the right arm, a second on the left arm, and a third on the left leg. They are labeled Lead I (left arm to right arm), II (right arm to left leg) and III (left arm to left leg). These three leads from angles of an equilateral triangle called the Einthoven triangle. In a sense, the galvanometer is looking at the leads from three different points of view. The standard leads are in pairs called bipolar and the galvanometer measures them algebraically, not from zero to a finite value. The ECG record is called frontal, which is a record of events downward from base to apex.

The ECG displays a second set of leads called precordial. This means that they are positioned anterior to the heart at specific places on the skin of the chest. They measure electrical events, not in a frontal plane like the standard leads do, but tangentially, from anterior (ventral) to posterior (dorsal) or vice versa across the chest wall. They are numbered from their right to left positions as V1 through V6. This allows them to sense impulses directly beneath the particular electrode put into the circuit. Events in these horizontal planes add significantly to diagnosis.

The ECG also shows a third set of leads which are three in number. These are called vectorial and are essential in obtaining vectorcardiograms because the transmission of action potentials in the heart is a directional or vector process. The direction of travel of the action potentials is found by vectorial analysis as it is in

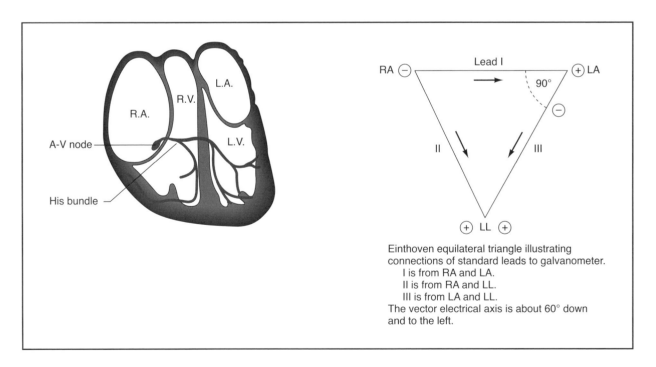

Einthoven equilateral triangle illustrating
connections of standard leads to galvanometer.
   I is from RA and LA.
   II is from RA and LL.
   III is from LA and LL.
The vector electrical axis is about 60° down
and to the left.

Figure 1.

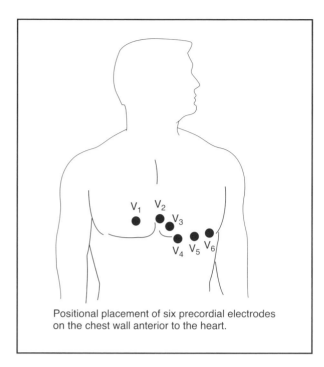

Figure 2.

Positional placement of six precordial electrodes on the chest wall anterior to the heart.

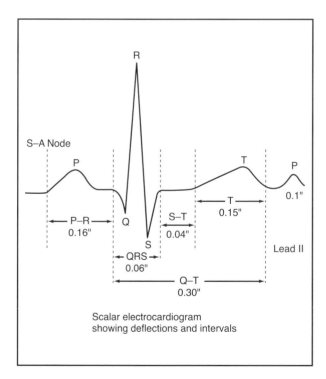

Figure 3.

Scalar electrocardiogram showing deflections and intervals

physics. The direction of travel of the action potentials is found by vectorial analysis as it is in physics. It takes two measurements of a completed record that are at right angles to one another to determine the resultant direction of all the potentials occurring at a given time. The resultant, computed as an arrow with a given length and direction, is considered to be the electrical axis of the heart. In the normal young adult it is predictably about minus 60

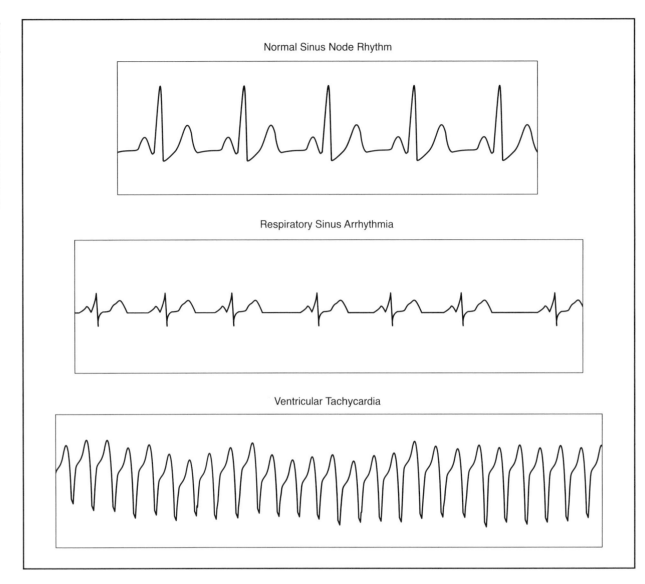

Normal Sinus Node Rhythm

Respiratory Sinus Arrhythmia

Ventricular Tachycardia

Figure 4.

degrees below the horizontal isoelectric base line. The three vectorial leads are each 30 degrees away from the standard leads, appearing like spokes on a wheel. They explain why twelve leads appear in an ECG strip. In the recordings they are designated a VR, a VL and a VF. The lower case "a" means augmented, V is voltage and R, L and F are for the right arm, left arm and left foot.

The normal sinus ECG

A few selected examples of ECGs are displayed herein. In the normal ECG, as taken from standard lead II, there are three upward or positive deflections, P, R, and T and two downward negative deflections, Q and S. The P wave indicates atrial depolarization. The QRS complex shows ventricular activity. The S–T segment as well as the T wave indicate ventricular repolarization. There are atrial repolarization waves but they are too low in voltage to be visible.

The time line on the X axis is real time. The recording paper is read on this line as 0.04 seconds for each small vertical subdivision if the paper is running at 0.98 in (25 mm) per second. At the end of each group of five of these, which corresponds to 0.2 seconds, the vertical line is darker on the ruled paper. If the pulse rate is found to be 75 per minute, the duration of a cardiac cycle is 60/75 or 0.8 seconds. Variations in expected normal times for any part of a cycle indicate specific cardiac abnormalities. This is used to diagnose arrhythmias which have a basis in time deviation.

On the Y axis, every 0.4 in (10 mm) corresponds to 1 mV of activity in the heart. Although time on the X axis is real, the mV on the Y axis cannot always be taken literally. Voltages may partly lose significance in that a fatty person can to some extent insulate cardiac currents from reaching the skin.

Respiratory sinus arrhythmia

The young adult male, while resting, breathes about 12 times per minute. Each cycle takes five seconds, two for inspiration, and three for expiration. The ECG shows these differences graphically in every respiratory cycle and they are easily measurable between successive P waves. This is the only arrhythmia that is considered to be normal.

Ventricular tachycardia

The effect of the form of the wave on the ECG, as distinguished from the effect of the direction and force is illustrated in this disorder. Prominent signs include an extraordinary height of the waves and also the rapidity of the heart beat. Both X and Y axes must be examined.

See also Heart.

Further Reading:

Eckert, Roger, Randall, David and Augustine, George. *Animal Physiology*. Third edition. New York: W.H. Freeman and Company, 1988.

Fox, Stuart I. *A Laboratory Guide to Human Physiology*. Fifth edition. Dubuque, Iowa: Wm. C. Brown Publisher, 1990.

Ganong, William F. *Review of Medical Physiology*. Sixteenth edition. East Norwalk, Connecticut: Appleton & Lange, 1993.

Guyton, Arthur C. *Human Physiology and Mechanisms of Disease*. Fourth edition. Philadelphia: W.B. Saunders Co., 1987.

Harold M. Kaplan and Kathleen A. Jones

Electrochemical cell see **Cell, electrochemical**

Electrode see **Battery**

Electroencephalogram (EEG)

An electroencephalogram, usually abbreviated EEG, is a medical test that records electrical activity in the brain. During the test, the brain's spontaneous electrical signals are traced onto paper. The *electroencephalograph* is the machine that amplifies and records the electrical signals from the brain. The *electroencephalogram* is the paper strip the machine produces. The EEG changes with disease or brain disorder, such as epilepsy, so it can be a useful diagnostic tool, but usually must be accompanied by other diagnostic tests to be definitive.

To perform an EEG, electrodes, which are wires designed to detect electrical signals, are placed on the cranium either by inserting a needle into the scalp or by attaching the wire with a special adhesive. The electrodes are placed in pairs so that the difference in electric potential between them can be measured. The wires are connected to the electroencephalograph, where the signal is amplified and directed into pens that record the waves on a moving paper chart. The tracing appears as a series of peaks and troughs drawn as lines by the recording pens.

Basic alpha waves, which originate in the cortex, can be recorded if the subject closes his eyes and puts his brain "at rest" as much as possible. Of course, the brain is never still, so some brain activity is going on and is recorded in waves of about 6–12 per second, with an average of about 10 per second. The voltage of these waves is from 5–100 microvolts. A microvolt is one-one millionth of a volt. Thus, a considerable amount of amplification is required to raise the voltage to a discernable level.

The rate of the waves, that is, the number that occur per second, appears to be a better diagnostic indicator than does the amplitude, or strength. Changes in the rate indicating a slowing or speeding up are significant, and unconsciousness occurs at either extreme. Sleep, stupor, and deep anesthesia are associated with slow waves and grand mal seizures cause an elevated rate of brain waves. The only time the EEG line is straight and without any wave indication is at death. A person who is brain dead has a straight, flat EEG line.

The rates of alpha waves are intermediate compared with other waves recorded on the EEG. Faster waves, 14–50 waves per second, that are lower in voltage than alpha waves are called beta waves. Very slow waves, averaging 0.5–5 per second, are delta waves. The slowest brain waves are associated with an area of localized brain damage such as may occur from a stroke or blow on the head.

The individual at rest and generating a fairly steady pattern of alpha waves can be distracted by a sound or touch. The alpha waves then flatten somewhat, that is their voltage is less and their pattern becomes more irregular when the individual's attention is focused. Any difficult mental effort such as multiplying two four–digit numbers will decrease the amplitude of the waves, and any pronounced emotional excitement will flatten the pattern. The brain wave pattern will change to one of very slow waves, about three per second, in deep sleep.

Though the basic EEG pattern remains a standard one from person to person, each individual has his own unique EEG pattern. The same individual given two separate EEG tests weeks or months apart will generate the same alpha wave pattern, assuming the conditions of the tests are the same. Identical twins will both have the same pattern. One twin will virtually match the second twin to the extent that the two tracings appear to be from the same individual on two separate occasions.

Though the EEG is a useful diagnostic tool, its use in brain research is limited. The electrodes detect the activity of only a few neurons in the cortex out of the billions that are present. Electrode placement is standardized so the EEG can be interpreted by any trained neurologist. Also, the electrical activity being measured is from the surface of the cortex and not from the deeper areas of the brain.

The brain

The brain is the center of all human thought, feeling, emotion, movement, and touch, among other facilities. It consists of the prominent cerebrum, the cerebellum, and the medulla oblongata. The cerebral cortex, or outer layer, has specialized areas for sight, hearing, touch, smell, taste, and so on.

The basic cell of the brain is the neuron, which monitors information coming in to it and directs an appropriate response to a muscle or to another neuron. Each neuron is connected to other neurons through axons, which carry information away from a neuron, and dendrites, which carry information to the neuron. Thus, an axon from one neuron will end at a dendrite of another. The very tiny space between the two nerve endings is a synapse. The message is passed across the synapse by the release of certain chemical "messengers," from the axon which cross the space and occupy receptor areas in the dendrite. These chemicals are called neurotransmitters. Thus neurons are in constant electrical contact with other neurons, receiving and passing on information at the rate of billions of reactions a second.

Neuronal connections are established early in life and remain intact throughout one's lifetime. An interruption of those connections because of a stroke or acci-

dent results in their permanent loss. Sometimes, with great effort, alternative pathways or connections can be established to restore function to that area, but the original connection will remain lost.

Uses of the EEG

The electroencephalogram is a means to assess the degree of damage to the brain in cases of trauma, or to measure the potential for seizure activity. It is used also in sleep studies to determine whether an individual has a sleep disorder and to study brain wave patterns during dreaming or upon sudden awakening.

The EEG is also a useful second–level diagnostic tool to follow–up a computerized tomogram (CT) scan to assist in finding the exact location of a damaged area in the brain. The EEG is one of a battery of brain tests available and is seldom used alone to make a diagnosis. The EEG tracing can detect an abnormality but cannot distinguish between, for example, a tumor and a thrombosis (site of deposit of a blood clot in an artery).

Although persons with frequent seizures are more likely to have an abnormal EEG than are those who have infrequent seizures, EEGs cannot be solely used to diagnose epilepsy. Approximately 10% of epilepsy patients will have a normal EEG. A normal EEG, therefore, does not eliminate brain damage or seizure potential, nor does an abnormal tracing indicate that a person has epilepsy. Something as simple as visual stimulation or rapid breathing (hyperventilation) may initiate abnormal electrical patterns in some patients.

If the EEG is taken at the time the patient has a seizure, the pattern will change. A grand mal seizure will result in sharp spikes of higher voltage and greater frequency (25–30 per second). A petit mal seizure also is accompanied by sharp spikes, but at a rate of only 3 waves per second.

Also, the EEG is not diagnostic of mental illness. The individual who is diagnosed with schizophrenia or paranoia may have an EEG tracing interpreted as normal. Most mental illness is considered to be a chemical imbalance of some sort, which does not create abnormal electrical activity. However, an EEG may be taken of an individual who exhibits bizarre, abnormal behavior to rule out an organic source such as thrombosis as the cause.

Patients being diagnosed for a brain disorder can be monitored on a 24–hour basis by a portable EEG unit. A special cap with electrodes is fitted onto the head where it will remain during the time the test is being run. The electroencephalograph is worn on the belt. A special attachment on the machine enables the patient to telephone the physician and transmit the data the machine has accumulated.

See also Brain.

Further Reading:

Rosman, Isadore, ed. *Basic Health Care and Emergency Aid*, New York: Thomas Nelson, Inc. 1990.

Larry Blaser

Electrolysis

Electrolysis is the process of causing a chemical reaction to occur by passing an electric current through a substance or mixture of substances, most often in liquid form. Electrolysis frequently results in the decomposition of a compound into its elements. To carry out an electrolysis, two electrodes, a positive electrode (anode) and a negative electrode (cathode), are immersed into the material to be electrolyzed and connected to a source of direct (DC) electric current.

The apparatus in which electrolysis is carried out is called an *electrolytic cell*. The roots *–lys* and *–lyt* come from the Greek *lysis* and *lytos*, meaning to cut or decompose; electrolysis in an electrolytic cell is a process that can decompose a substance.

The substance being electrolyzed must be an electrolyte, a liquid that contains positive and negative ions and therefore is able to conduct electricity. There are two kinds of electrolytes. One kind is a solution of any compound that produces ions when it dissolves in water, such as an inorganic acid, base, or salt. The other kind is a liquefied ionic compound such as a molten salt.

In either kind of electrolyte, the liquid conducts electricity because its positive and negative ions are free to move toward the electrodes of opposite charge—

the positive ions toward the cathode and the negative ions toward the anode. This transfer of positive charge in one direction and negative charge in the opposite direction constitutes an electric current, because an electric current is, after all, only a flow of charge, and it doesn't matter whether the carriers of the charge are ions or electrons. In an ionic solid such as sodium chloride, for example, the normally fixed–in–place ions become free to move as soon as the solid is dissolved in water or as soon as it is melted.

During electrolysis, the ions move toward the electrodes of opposite charge. When they reach their respective electrodes, they undergo chemical oxidation–reduction reactions. At the cathode, which is pumping electrons into the electrolyte, chemical reduction takes place—a taking–on of electrons by the positive ions. At the anode, which is sucking electrons out of the electrolyte, chemical oxidation takes place—a loss of electrons by the negative ions.

In electrolysis, there is a direct relationship between the amount of electricity that flows through the cell and the amount of chemical reaction that takes place. The more electrons are pumped through the electrolyte by the battery, the more ions will be forced to give up or take on electrons, thereby being oxidized or reduced. To produce one mole's worth of chemical reaction, one mole of electrons must pass through the cell. A mole of electrons, that is, 6.02×10^{23} of them, is called a *faraday*. The unit is named after Michael Faraday (1791–1867), the English chemist and physicist who discovered this relationship between electricity and chemical change. He is also credited with inventing the words *anode*, *cathode*, *electrode*, *electrolyte* and *electrolysis*.

Various kinds of electrolytic cells can be devised to accomplish specific chemical objectives.

Electrolysis of water

Perhaps the best known example of electrolysis is the electrolytic decomposition of water to produce hydrogen and oxygen:

$$2H_2O \quad + \quad energy \quad \rightarrow \quad 2H_2 \quad + \quad O_2$$

| water | | | hydrogen gas | oxygen gas |

Because water is such a stable compound, we can only make this reaction go by pumping energy into it—in this case, in the form of an electric current. Pure water, which doesn't conduct electricity very well, must first be made into an electrolyte by dissolving an acid, base, or salt in it. Then an anode and a cathode, usually made of graphite or some non–reacting metal such as

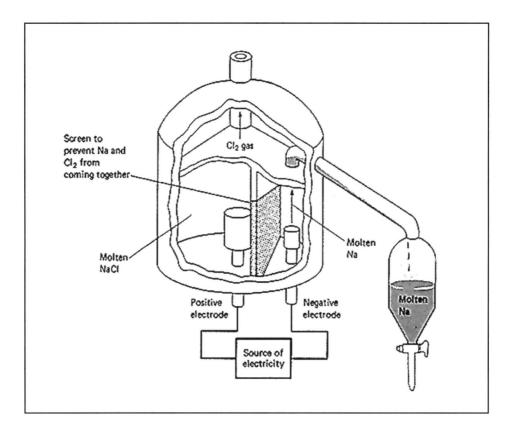

The Downs cell.

platinum, can be inserted and connected to a battery or other source of direct current.

At the cathode, where electrons are being pumped into the water by the battery, they are taken up by water molecules to form hydrogen gas:

$$4H_2O \quad + \quad 4e^- \quad \rightarrow \quad 2H_2 \quad + \quad 4OH^-$$

water   electrons   hydrogen   hydroxide
                   gas   ions

At the anode, electrons are being removed from water molecules:

$$2H_2O \quad - \quad 4e^- \quad \rightarrow \quad O_2 \quad + \quad 4H^+$$

water   electrons   oxygen   hydrogen
                   gas   ions

The net result of these two electrode reactions added together is

$$2H_2O \rightarrow 2H_2 + O_2.$$

(Note that when these two equations are added together, the four H^+ ions and four OH^- ions on the right–hand side are combined to form four H_2O molecules, which then cancel four of the H_2O molecules on the left–hand side.) Thus, every two molecules of water have been decomposed into two molecules of hydrogen and one molecule of oxygen.

The acid, base, or salt that made the water into an electrolyte was chosen so that its particular ions cannot be oxidized or reduced (at least at the voltage of the battery), so they don't react chemically and serve only to conduct the current through the water. Sulfuric acid, H_2SO_4, is commonly used.

Production of sodium and chlorine

By electrolysis, common salt, sodium chloride, NaCl, can be broken down into its elements, sodium and chlorine. This is an important method for the production of sodium; it is used also for producing other alkali metals and alkaline earth metals from their salts.

To obtain sodium by electrolysis, we'll first melt some sodium chloride by heating it above its melting point of 801°C. Then we'll insert two inert (non–reacting) electrodes into the melted salt. The sodium chloride must be molten in order to permit the Na^+ and Cl^- ions to move freely between the electrodes; in solid sodium chloride, the ions are frozen in place. Finally, we'll pass a direct electric current (DC) through the molten salt.

The negative electrode (the cathode) will attract Na^+ ions and the positive electrode (the anode) will attract Cl⁻ ions, whereupon the following chemical reactions take place.

At the cathode, where electrons are being pumped in, they are being grabbed by the positive sodium ions:

$$Na^+ \quad + \quad e^- \quad \rightarrow \quad Na$$

| sodium | electron | sodium |
| ion | | atom |

At the anode, where electrons are being pumped out, they are being ripped off the chloride ions:

$$Cl^- \quad - \quad e^- \quad \rightarrow \quad Cl$$

| chloride | electron | chlorine |
| ion | | atom |

(The chlorine atoms immediately combine into diatomic molecules, Cl_2.) The result is that common salt has been broken down into its elements by electricity.

Production of magnesium

Another important use of electrolysis is in the production of magnesium from sea water. Sea water is a major source of that metal, since it contains more ions of magnesium than of any other metal except sodium. First, magnesium chloride, $MgCl_2$, is obtained by precipitating magnesium hydroxide from seawater and dissolving it in hydrochloric acid. The magnesium chloride is then melted and electrolyzed. Similar to the production of sodium from molten sodium chloride, above, the molten magnesium is deposited at the cathode, while the chlorine gas is released at the anode. The overall reaction is $MgCl_2 \rightarrow Mg + Cl_2$.

Production of sodium hydroxide, chlorine and hydrogen

Sodium hydroxide, NaOH, also known as lye and caustic soda, is one of the most important of all industrial chemicals. It is produced at the rate of 25 billion pounds a year in the U.S. alone. The major method for producing it is the electrolysis of brine or "salt water," a solution of common salt, sodium chloride in water. Chlorine and hydrogen gases are produced as valuable byproducts.

When an electric current is passed through salt water, the negative chloride ions, Cl⁻, migrate to the positive anode and lose their electrons to become chlorine gas.

$$Cl^- \quad + \quad e^- \quad \rightarrow \quad Cl$$

| chloride | electron | chlorine |
| ion | | atom |

(The chlorine atoms then pair up to form Cl_2 molecules.) Meanwhile, sodium ions, Na⁺, are drawn to the

negative cathode. But they don't pick up electrons to become sodium metal atoms as they do in molten salt, because in a water solution the water molecules themselves pick up electrons more easily than sodium ions do. What happens at the cathode, then, is

$$2H_2O \quad + \quad 2e^- \quad \rightarrow \quad H_2 \quad + \quad OH^-$$

| water | electrons | hydrogen | hydroxide |
| | | gas | ions |

The hydroxide ions, together with the sodium ions that are already in the solution, constitute sodium hydroxide, which can be recovered by evaporation.

This so–called *chloralkali* process is the basis of an industry that has existed for well over a hundred years. By electricity, it converts cheap salt into valuable chlorine, hydrogen and sodium hydroxide. Among other uses, the chlorine is used in the purification of water, the hydrogen is used in the hydrogenation of oils, and the lye is used in making soap and paper.

Production of aluminum

The production of aluminum by the Hall process was one of the earliest applications of electrolysis on a large scale, and is still the major method for obtaining that very useful metal. The process was discovered in 1886 by Charles M. Hall, a 21–year–old student at Oberlin College in Ohio, who had been searching for a way to reduce aluminum oxide to the metal. Aluminum was a rare and expensive luxury at that time, because the metal is very reactive and therefore difficult to reduce from its compounds by chemical means. On the other hand, electrolysis of a molten aluminum salt or oxide is difficult because the salts are hard to obtain in anhydrous (dry) form and the oxide, Al_2O_3, doesn't melt until 2072°C.

Hall discovered that Al_2O_3, in the form of the mineral bauxite, dissolves in another aluminum mineral called cryolite, Na_3AlF_6, and that the resulting mixture could be melted fairly easily. When an electric current is passed through this molten mixture, the aluminum ions migrate to the cathode, where they are reduced to metal:

$$Al^{3+} \quad + \quad 3e^- \quad \rightarrow \quad Al$$

| aluminum | electrons | molten |
| ion | | aluminum metal |

At the anode, oxide ions are oxidized to oxygen gas:

$$2O^{2-} \quad - \quad 2e^- \quad \rightarrow \quad O_2$$

| oxide | electrons | oxygen |
| ion | | gas |

The molten aluminum metal sinks to the bottom of the cell and can be drawn off.

Notice that three moles of electrons (three faradays of electricity) are needed to produce each mole of aluminum, because there are three positive charges on each aluminum ion that must be neutralized by electrons. The production of aluminum by the Hall process therefore consumes huge amounts of electrical energy. The recycling of beverage cans and other aluminum objects has become an important energy conservation measure.

Refining of copper

Unlike aluminum, copper metal is fairly easy to obtain chemically from its ores. But by electrolysis, it can be refined and made very pure—up to 99.999%. Pure copper is important in making electrical wire, because copper's electrical conductivity is reduced by impurities. These impurities include such valuable metals as silver, gold and platinum; when they are removed by electrolysis and recovered, they go a long way toward paying the electricity bill.

In the electrolytic refining of copper, the impure copper is made from the anode in an electrolyte bath of copper sulfate, $CuSO_4$, and sulfuric acid H_2SO_4. The cathode is a sheet of very pure copper. As current is passed through the solution, positive copper ions, Cu^{2+}, in the solution are attracted to the negative cathode, where they take on electrons and deposit themselves as neutral copper atoms, thereby building up more and more pure copper on the cathode. Meanwhile, copper atoms in the positive anode give up electrons and dissolve into the electrolyte solution as copper ions. But the impurities in the anode do not go into solution because silver, gold and platinum atoms are not as easily oxidized (converted into positive ions) as copper is. So the silver, gold and platinum simply fall from the anode to the bottom of the tank, where they can be scraped up.

Electroplating

Another important use of electrolytic cells is in the electroplating of silver, gold, chromium and nickel. Electroplating produces a very thin coating of these expensive metals on the surfaces of cheaper metals, to give them the appearance and the chemical resistance of the expensive ones.

In silver plating, the object to be plated (let's say a spoon) is made from the cathode of an electrolytic cell. The anode is a bar of silver metal, and the electrolyte (the liquid in between the electrodes) is a solution of silver cyanide, AgCN, in water. When a direct current is passed through the cell, positive silver ions (Ag^+) from

the silver cyanide migrate to the negative anode (the spoon), where they are neutralized by electrons and stick to the spoon as silver metal:

$$2H_2O \ + \ \text{energy} \ \rightarrow \ 2H_2 \ + \ O_2$$
$$\text{water} \qquad\qquad\qquad \text{hydrogen} \quad \text{oxygen}$$
$$\text{gas} \qquad\quad \text{gas}$$

Meanwhile, the silver anode bar gives up electrons to become silver ions:

$$Ag \ - \ e^- \ \rightarrow \ Ag^+$$
$$\text{silver} \qquad \text{electron} \qquad \text{silver}$$
$$\text{atom} \qquad\qquad\qquad \text{ion}$$

Thus, the anode bar gradually dissolves to replenish the silver ions in the solution. The net result is that silver metal has been transferred from the anode to the cathode, in this case the spoon. This process continues until the desired coating thickness is built up on the spoon—usually only a few thousandths of an inch—or until the silver bar has completely dissolved.

In electroplating with silver, silver cyanide is used in the electrolyte rather than other compounds of silver such as silver nitrate, $AgNO_3$, because the cyanide ion, CN^-, reacts with silver ion, Ag^+, to form the complex ion $Ag(CN)_2^-$. This limits the supply of free Ag^+ ions in the solution, so they can deposit themselves only very gradually onto the cathode. This produces a shinier and more adherent silver plating. Gold plating is done in much the same way, using a gold anode and an electrolyte containing gold cyanide, AuCN.

Further Reading:

Chang, Raymond. *Chemistry*. New York: McGraw–Hill, 1991.

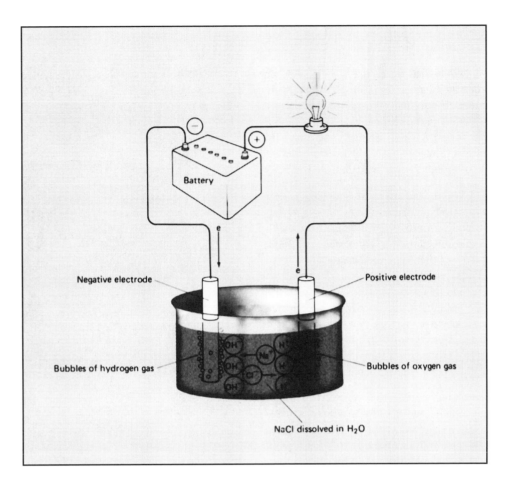

Conduction of electricity by a salt solution.

Sherwood, Martin and Sutton, Christine, ed. *The Physical World*. New York: Oxford, 1991.

Robert L. Wolke

Electrolyte

An electrolyte is a substance that will allow current to flow through the solution when dissolved in water. Electrolytes promote this current flow because they produce positive and negative ions when dissolved. The current flows through the solution in the form of positive ions (cations) moving toward the negative electrode and negative ion (anions) moving the positive electrode.

Electrolytes can be classified as strong electrolytes and weak electrolytes. Strong electrolytes are substances that completely break apart into ions when dissolved.

The most familiar example of a strong electrolyte is table salt, sodium chloride. Most salts are strong electrolytes, as are strong acids such as hydrochloric acid, nitric acid, perchloric acid, and sulfuric acid. Strong bases such as sodium hydroxide and calcium hydroxide are also strong electrolytes. Although calcium hydroxide is only slightly soluble, all of the compound which dissolves in completely ionized.

Weak electrolytes are substances which only partially dissociate into ions when dissolved in water. Weak acids such as acetic acid, found in vinegar, and weak bases such as ammonia, found in cleaning products, are examples of weak electrolytes. Very slightly soluble salts such as mercury chloride are also sometimes classified as weak electrolytes. Ligands and their associated metal ions can be weak electrolytes.

Not all substances that dissolve in water are electrolytes. Sugar, for example, dissolves readily in water, but remains in the water as molecules, not as ions. Sugar is classified as a non–electrolyte. Water itself ionizes slightly and is a very, very weak electrolyte.

Electromagnetic field

An electromagnetic field is an area in which electric and magnetic forces are interacting. It arises from electric charges in motion. Electromagnetic fields are directly related to the strength and direction of the force that a charged particle, called the "test" charge, would be subject to under the electromagnetic force caused by another charged particle or group of particles, called the source.

An electromagnetic field is best understood as a mathematical function or property of spacetime, but may be represented as a group of vectors, arrows with specific length and direction. For a static electric field, meaning there is no motion of source charges, the force $\vec{F}$ on a test charge is $\vec{F} = q\vec{E}$, where q is the value of the test charge and $\vec{E}$ is the vector electric field. For a static magnetic field (caused by moving charge inside an overall neutral group of charges, or a bar magnet, for example) the force is given by $\vec{F} = q\vec{v} \times \vec{B}$, where $\vec{v}$ is the charge velocity, $\vec{B}$ is the vector magnetic field, and the x indicates a cross–product of vectors.

A stationary charge produces an electric field, while a moving charge additionally produces a magnetic field. Since velocity is a relative concept dependent on one's choice of reference frame, magnetism and electricity are not independent, but linked together, hence the term electromagnetism.

Superposition of fields

Since all charges, moving or not, have fields associated with them, we must have a way to describe the total field due to all randomly distributed charges that would be felt by a positive charge, such as proton or positron, at any position and time. The total field is the sum of the fields produced by the individual particles. This idea is called the principle of superposition.

Let us look at arrow or vector representations of the fields from some particular charge distributions. There is an infinite number of possibilities, but we will consider only a few simple cases.

Electric fields

The field of a static point charge

According to Coulomb's law, the strength of the electric field from a nonmoving point charge depends directly on the charge value q and is inversely proportional to the distance from the charge. That is, farther from the source charge will be subject to the same strength of force regardless of whether it is above,

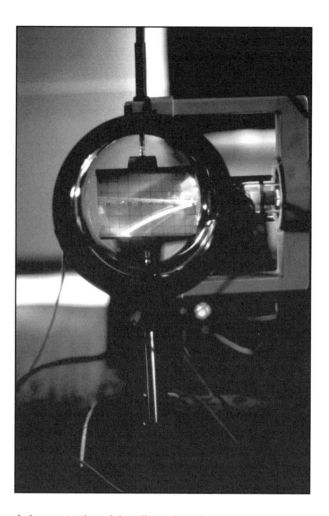

A demonstration of the effect of an electromagnetic field on an electron beam. The dark circles are the coils of wire of an electromagnet. Current flowing in the wire produces a magnetic field along the axis of the coils which deflects the electron beam in a direction perpendicular it.

below, or to the side of the source, as long as the distance is the same. A surface of the same radius all around the source will have the same field strength. This is called a surface of equipotential. For a point source charge, the surface of equipotential is a sphere, and the force F will push a positive charge radially outward. A test charge of mass m and positive charge q will feel a push away from the positive source charge with an acceleration a directly proportional to ($\propto$) the field strength and inversely proportional to the mass of the test charge. The equation is written: $F = ma \propto q/d^2$, so that $a \propto q/(md^2)$ where $F = ma$ is given by Newton's second law, which tells us that force causes acceleration. The letter d represents the distance from the source charge to the test charge.

If a charge does not move because it is acted upon

by the electromagnetic force equally from all directions, it is in a position of stable equilibrium.

The dipole field

Now let us consider the field from two charges, one positive and one negative, a distance d apart. We call this combination of charges a dipole. Remember, opposite charges attract, so this is not an unusual situation. A hydrogen atom, for example, consisting of an electron (negative charge) and a proton (positive charge) is a very small dipole, as these particles do not sit right on top of each other. According to the superposition principle mentioned above, we can just add the fields from each individual charge and get a rather complicated field. If we only consider the field at a position very far from the dipole, we can simplify the field equation so that the field is proportional to the product of the charge value and the separation of the two charges. There is also dependence on the distance along the dipole axis as well as radial distance from the axis.

The field of a line of charge

Next, we consider the field due to a group of positive charges evenly distributed along an infinite straight line, defined to be infinite because we want to neglect the effect of the endpoints as an unnecessary complication here. Just as the field of a point charge is directed radially outward in a sphere, the field of a line of charge is directed radially outward, but at any specific radius the surface of equipotential will be a cylinder.

Magnetic fields

Recall that the force of a stationary charge is $\vec{F} = q\vec{E}$, but if the charge is moving the force is $\vec{F} = q\vec{E} + q\vec{v} \times \vec{B}$. A steady (unchanging in time) current in a wire, generates a magnetic field. Electric current is essentially charges in motion. In an electrical conductor like copper wire, electrons move, while positive charges remain steady. The positive charge cancels the electric charge so the overall charge looks like zero when viewed from outside the wire, so no electric field will exist outside the wire, but the moving charges create a magnetic field from $\vec{F} = q\vec{v} \times \vec{B}$ where $\vec{B}$ is the magnetic field vector. The cross product results in magnetic field lines circling the wire. Because of this effect, solenoids (a current–carrying coil of wire that acts as a magnet) can be made by wrapping wire in a tight spiral around a metallic tube, so that the magnetic field inside the tube is linear in direction.

Relating this idea to Newton's first law of motion, which states that for every action there is an equal and opposite reaction, we see that an external magnetic field (from a bar magnet, for example) can exert a force on a current–carrying wire, which will be the sum of the forces on all the individual moving charges in the wire.

Electromagnetic fields

A simple example of a combination of electric and magnetic fields is the field from a single point charge, say a proton, traveling through space at a constant speed in a straight line. In this case, the field vectors pointing radially outward would have to be added to the spiral magnetic field lines (circles extend into spirals because an individual charge is moving) to get the total field caused by the charge.

Maxwell's equations

A description of the field from a current which changes in time is much more complicated, but is calculable owing to James Clerk Maxwell (1831–1879). His equations, which have unified the laws of electricity and magnetism, are called Maxwell's equations. They are differential equations which completely describe the combined effects of electricity and magnetism, and are considered to be one of the crowning achievements of the nineteenth century. Maxwell's formulation of the theory of electromagnetic radiation allows us to understand the entire electromagnetic spectrum, from radio waves through visible light to gamma rays.

See also Electromagnetic spectrum; Electromagnetism; Magnetism.

Electromagnetic induction

Electromagnetic induction is the generation of an electromotive force in a closed electrical circuit. It results from a changing magnetic field as it passes through the circuit. Some of the most basic components of electrical power systems—such as generators and transformers—make use of electromagnetic induction.

Fundamentals

The phenomenon of electromagnetic induction was discovered by the British physicist Michael Faraday in 1831 and independently observed soon thereafter by the American physicist Joseph Henry. Prior to that time, it was known that the presence of an electric charge would cause other charges on nearby conductors to redistribute themselves. Furthermore, in 1820 the Danish physicist Hans Christian Oersted demonstrated that

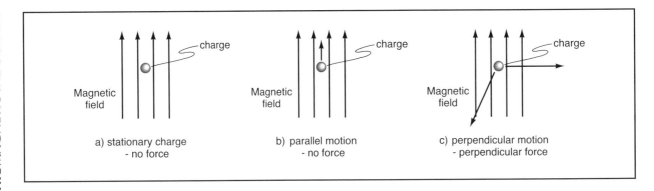

Figure 1.

an electric current produces a magnetic field. It seemed reasonable, then, to ask whether or not a magnetic field might cause some kind of electrical effect, such as a current.

An electric charge that is stationary in a magnetic field will not interact with the field in any way. Nor will a moving charge interact with the field if it travels parallel to the field's direction. However, a moving charge that crosses the field will experience a force that is perpendicular both to the field and to the direction of motion of the charge (see Figure 1). Now, instead of a single charge, consider a rectangular loop of wire moving through the field (see Figure 2). Two sides of the loop will be subjected to forces that are perpendicular to the wire itself so that no charges will be moved. Along the other two sides charge will flow, but because the forces are equal the charges will simply bunch up on the same side, building up an internal electric field to counteract the imposed force, and there will be no net current.

How can a magnetic field cause current to flow through the loop? Faraday discovered that it was not simply the presence of a magnetic field that was required. In order to generate current the magnetic flux through the loop must change with time. The term flux refers to the flow of the magnetic field lines through the area enclosed by the loop. The flux of the magnetic field lines is like the flow of water through a pipe and may increase or decrease with time.

To understand how the change in flux generates a current, consider a circuit made of many rectangular loops connected to a light bulb (see Figure 3). Under what conditions will current flow and the light bulb shine? If the circuit is pulled through a uniform magnetic field there will be no current because the flux will be constant. But, if the field is non–uniform, the charges on one side of the loop will continually experience a force greater than that on the other side. This difference in forces will cause the charges to circulate around the loop in a current that lights the bulb. The work done in moving each charge through the circuit is called the electromotive force or EMF. The units of electromotive force are volts just like the voltage of a battery which also causes current to flow through a circuit. It makes no difference to the circuit whether the changing flux is caused by the loop's own motion or that of the magnetic field, so the case of a stationary circuit and a moving non–uniform field is equivalent to the previous situation and again the bulb will light.

Yet a current can be induced in the circuit without moving either the loop or the field. While a stationary loop in a constant magnetic field will not cause the bulb to light, that same stationary loop in a field that is changing in time (such as when the field is being turned on or off) will experience an electromotive force. This comes about because a changing magnetic field generates an electric field whose direction is given by the right–hand rule—with the thumb of your right hand pointing in the direction of the change of the magnetic flux, your fingers can be wrapped around in the direction of the induced electric field. With an EMF directed around the circuit, current will flow and the bulb will light.

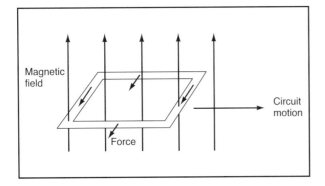

Figure 2.

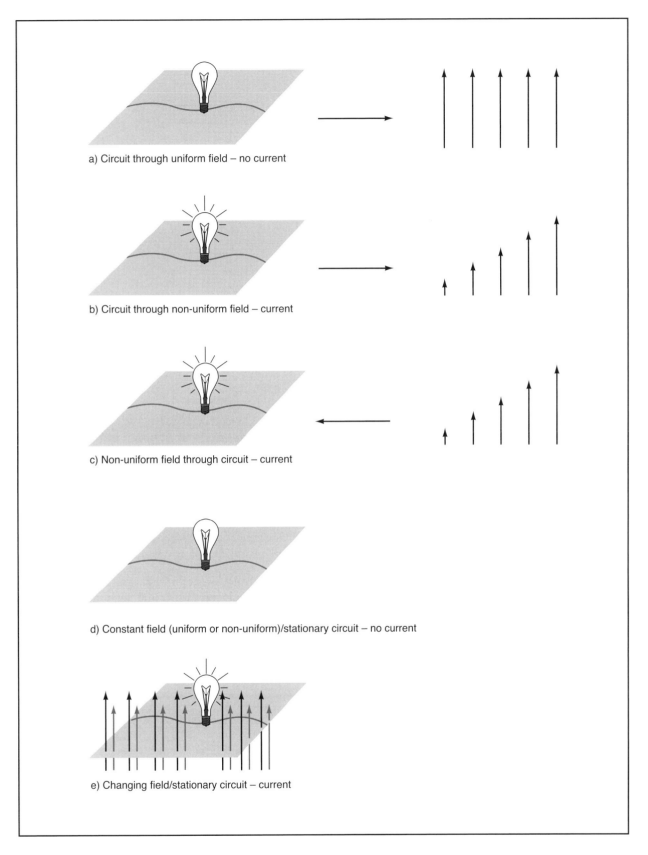

a) Circuit through uniform field – no current

b) Circuit through non-uniform field – current

c) Non-uniform field through circuit – current

d) Constant field (uniform or non-uniform)/stationary circuit – no current

e) Changing field/stationary circuit – current

Figure 3.

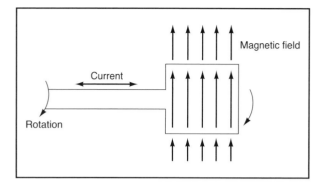

Figure 4.

The different conditions by which a magnetic field can cause current to flow through a circuit are summarized by Faraday's Law of Induction. The variation in time of the flux of a magnetic field through a surface bounded by an electrical circuit generates an electromotive force in that circuit.

What is the direction of the induced current? A magnetic field will be generated by the induced current. If the flux of that field were to add to the initial magnetic flux through the circuit, then there would be more current, which would create more flux, which would create more current, and so on without limit. Such a situation would violate the conservation of energy and the tendency of physical systems to resist change. So the induced current will be generated in the direction that will create magnetic flux which opposes the variation of the inducing flux. This fact is known as Lenz's Law.

The relation between the change in the current through a circuit and the electromotive force it induces in itself is called the self–inductance of the circuit. If the current is given in amperes and the EMF is given in volts, the unit of self–inductance is the henry. A changing current in one circuit can also induce an electromotive force in a nearby circuit. The ratio of the induced electromotive force to the rate of change of current in the inducing circuit is called the mutual inductance and is also measured in henrys.

Applications

An electrical generator is an apparatus that converts mechanical energy into electrical energy. Consider the diagram in Figure 4. In this case the magnetic field is stationary and does not vary with time. It is the circuit that is made to rotate through the magnetic field. Since the area which admits the passage of magnetic field lines changes while the circuit rotates, the flux through

KEY TERMS

Ampere—A standard unit for measuring electric current.

Faraday's Law of Induction—The variation in time of the flux of a magnetic field through a surface bounded by an electrical circuit generates an electromotive force in that circuit.

Flux—The flow of a quantity through a given area.

Generator—An apparatus designed to convert mechanical energy into electrical energy.

Henry—A standard unit for measuring inductance.

Lenz's law—The direction of a current induced in a circuit will be such as to create a magnetic field which opposes the inducing flux change.

Mutual inductance—The ratio of the induced electromotive force in one circuit to the rate of change of current in the inducing circuit.

Right–hand rule (for electric fields generated by changing magnetic fields)—With the thumb of the right hand along the direction of change of magnetic flux, the fingers curl to indicate the direction of the induced electric field.

Self–inductance—The electromotive force induced in a circuit that results from the variation with time in the current of that same circuit.

Volt—A standard unit of electric potential and electromotive force.

the circuit will change, thus inducing a current. Generally, a turbine is used to provide the circuit's rotation. The energy required to move the turbine may come from steam generated by nuclear or fossil fuels, or from the flow of water through a dam. As a result, the mechanical energy of rotation is changed into electric current.

Transformers are devices used to transfer electric energy between circuits. They are used in power lines to convert high voltage electricity into household current. Common consumer electronics such as radios and televisions also use transformers. By making use of mutual inductance, the transformer's primary circuit induces current in its secondary circuit. By varying the physical characteristics of each circuit, the output of the transformer can be designed to meet specific needs.

John Appel

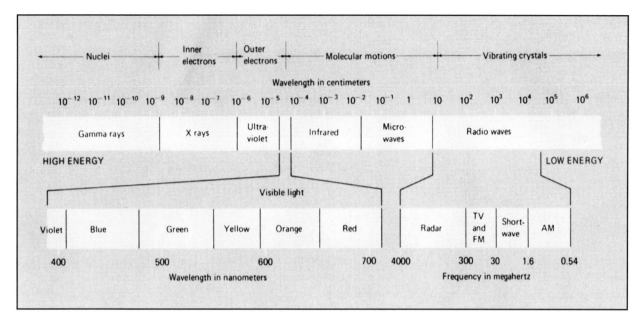

The electromagnetic spectrum.

Electromagnetic radiation see **Radiation**

Electromagnetic spectrum

The light which we see is just a small part of a continuum of electromagnetic radiation, which extends from radio waves to gamma rays. Phenomena as diverse as radio waves, which we use to transmit information; microwaves, which we use to cook our food; and x–rays, which we use for medical purposes are all part of the electromagnetic spectrum. Although each type of radiation has distinct properties, they can all be described in the same simple terms.

Wavelength, frequency, and energy

The characteristic of electromagnetic radiation which causes its properties to vary is its wavelength. The wave–like properties of electromagnetic radiation are similar to the waves created when an object is dropped into water. The wavelength of the wave is the distance between two successive peaks. The wavelength of radiation is sometimes given in units with which we are familiar, such as inches or centimeters, but for very small wavelengths, they are often given in angstroms (abbreviated Å). There are 10,000,000,000 angstroms in one meter.

An alternative way of describing a wave is by its frequency, or the number of peaks which pass a particular point in one second. Frequencies are normally given in cycles per second, or hertz (abbreviation Hz), after Heinrich Hertz, who was the first to artificially generate radio waves. Other common units are kilohertz (kHz, or thousands of cycles per second), megahertz (MHz, millions of cycles per second), and gigahertz (GHz, billions of cycles per second). The frequency and wavelength, when multiplied together, give the speed of the wave. For electromagnetic waves in empty space, that speed is the speed of light, which is approximately 186,000 miles per second (300,000 km per sec).

In addition to the wave–like properties of electromagnetic radiation, it also can behave as a particle. The energy of a particle of light, or photon, can be calculated from its frequency by multiplying by Planck's constant. Thus, higher frequencies (and lower wavelengths) have higher energy. A common unit used to describe the energy of a photon is the electron volt (eV). Multiples of this unit, such as keV (1000 electron volts) and MeV (1,000,000 eV), are also used.

Properties of waves in different regions of the spectrum are commonly described by different notation. Visible radiation is usually described by its wavelength, for example, while x–rays are described by their energy. All of these schemes are equivalent, however; they are just different ways of describing the same properties.

Wavelength regions

The electromagnetic spectrum is typically divided into wavelength or energy regions, based on the characteristics of the waves in each region. Because the prop-

TABLE 1

Region	Frequency (Hz)	Wavelength (m)	Energy (eV)	Size Scale
Radio waves	$< 10^9$	> 0.3	$< 7 \times 10^{-7}$	Mountains, building, humans
Microwaves	$10^9 - 3 \times 10^{11}$	$0.001 - 0.3$	$7 \times 10^{-7} - 2 \times 10^{-4}$	
Infrared	$3 \times 10^{11} - 3.9 \times 10^{14}$	$7.6 \times 10^{-7} - 0.001$	$2 \times 10^{-4} - 0.3$	
Visible	$3.9 \times 10^{14} - 7.9 \times 10^{14}$	$3.8 \times 10^{-7} - 7.6 \times 10^{-7}$	$0.3 - 0.5$	Bacteria
Ultraviolet	$7.9 \times 10^{14} - 3.4 \times 10^{16}$	$8 \times 10^{-9} - 3.8 \times 10^{-7}$	$0.5 - 20$	Viruses
X-rays	$3.4 \times 10^{16} - 5 \times 10^{19}$	$6 \times 10^{-12} - 8 \times 10^{-9}$	$20 - 3 \times 10^4$	Atoms
Gamma Rays	$> 5 \times 10^{19}$	$< 6 \times 10^{-12}$	$> 3 \times 10^4$	Nuclei

erties vary on a continuum, the boundaries are not sharp, but rather loosely defined.

Radio waves are familiar to us due to their use in communications. The standard AM radio band is at 540–1650 kHz, and the FM band is 88–108 MHz. This region also includes shortwave radio transmissions and television broadcasts.

We are most familiar with microwaves because of microwave ovens, which heat food by causing water molecules to rotate at a frequency of 2.45 GHz. In astronomy, emission of radiation at a wavelength of 8.2 inches (21 cm) has been used to map neutral hydrogen throughout the galaxy. Radar is also included in this region.

The infrared region of the spectrum lies just beyond the visible wavelengths. It was discovered by William Herschel in 1800 by measuring the dispersing sunlight with a prism, and measuring the temperature increase just beyond the red end of the spectrum.

The visible wavelength range is the range of frequencies with which we are most familiar. These are the wavelengths to which the human eye is sensitive, and which most easily pass through the Earth's atmosphere. This region is further broken down into the familiar colors of the rainbow, which fall into the wavelength intervals listed in Table 2.

A common way to remember the order of colors is through the name of the fictitious person ROY G. BIV (the I stands for indigo).

The ultraviolet range lies at wavelengths just shortward of the visible. Although we do not use UV to see, it has many other important effects on Earth. The ozone

TABLE 2

Red	6300 - 7600 Å
Orange	5900 - 6300 Å
Yellow	5600 - 5900 Å
Green	4900 - 5600 Å
Blue	4500 - 4900 Å

layer high in the Earth's atmosphere absorbs much of the UV radiation from the sun, but that which reaches the surface can cause suntans and sunburns.

We are most familiar with X rays due to their uses in medicine. X radiation can pass through the body, allowing doctors to examine bones and teeth. Surprisingly, X rays do not penetrate the Earth's atmosphere, so astronomers must place X ray telescopes in space.

Gamma rays are the most energetic of all electromagnetic radiation, and we have little experience with them in everyday life. They are produced by nuclear processes, for example, during radioactive decay or in nuclear reactions in stars or in space.

See also Electromagnetism; Frequency; Light; Radio waves; X rays.

David Sahnow

Electromagnetic waves see
Electromagnetism

Electromagnetism

Electromagnetism is a branch of physical science that involves all the phenomena in which electricity and magnetism interact. This field is especially important to electronics because a magnetic field is created by an electric current. The rules of electromagnetism are responsible for the way charged particles of atoms interact.

Some of the rules of *electrostatics*, the study of electric charges at rest, were first noted by the ancient Romans, who observed the way a brushed comb would attract particles. It is now known that electric charges occur in two different types, called positive and negative. Like types repel each other, and differing types attract.

The force that attract positive charges to negative charges weakens with distance, but is intrinsically very strong. The fact that unlike types attract means that most of this force is normally neutralized and not seen in full strength. The negative charge is generally carried

by the atom's electrons, while the positive resides with the protons inside the atomic nucleus. There are other less well known particles that can also carry charge. When the electrons of a material are not tightly bound to the atom's nucleus, they can move from atom to atom and the substance, called a conductor, can conduct electricity. On the contrary, when the electron binding is strong, the material is called an insulator.

When electrons are weakly bound to the atomic nucleus, the result is a semiconductor, often used in the electronics industry. It was not initially known if the electric current carriers were positive or negative, and this initial ignorance gave rise to the convention that current flows from the positive terminal to the negative. In reality we now know that the electrons actually run from the negative to the positive.

Electromagnetism is the theory of a unified expression of an underlying force, the so–called electromagnetic force. This is seen in the movement of electric charge, which gives rise to magnetism (the electric current in a wire being found to deflect a compass needle), and it was a Scotsman, James Clerk Maxwell, who in 1865 published the theory unifying electricity and magnetism. The theory arose from former specialized work by Gauss, Coulomb, Ampère, Faraday, Franklin, Coulomb, and Ohm. However, one factor that did not contradict the experiments was added to the equations by Maxwell so as to ensure the conservation of charge. This was done on the theoretical grounds that charge should be a conserved quantity, and this addition led to the prediction of a wave phenomena with a certain anticipated velocity. Light, which has the expected velocity, was found to be an example of this electromagnetic radiation.

Light had formerly been thought of as consisting of particles (photons) by Newton, but the theory of light as particles was unable to explain the wave nature of light (diffraction and the alike). In reality, light displays both wave *and* particle properties. The resolution to this duality lies in quantum theory, where light is neither particles or wave, but both. It propagates as a wave without the need of a media and interacts in the manner of a particle. This is the basic nature of quantum theory.

Classical electromagnetism, useful as it is, contains contradictions (acausality) that make it incomplete and drive one to consider its extension to the area of quantum physics, where electromagnetism, of all the fundamental forces of nature, it is perhaps the best understood.

There is much symmetry between electricity and magnetism. It is possible for electricity to give rise to magnetism, and symmetrically for magnetism to give rise to electricity (as in the exchanges within an electric transformer). It is an exchange of just this kind that constitutes electromagnetic waves. These waves, although they don't need a medium of propagation, are slowed when traveling through a transparent substance.

Electromagnetic waves differ from each other only in amplitude, frequency and orientation (polarization). Laser beams are particular in being very coherent, that is, the radiation is of one frequency, and the waves coordinated in motion and direction. This permits a highly concentrated beam that is used not only for its cutting abilities, but also in electronic data storage, such as in CD-ROMs.

The differing frequency forms are given a variety of names, from radio waves at very low frequencies through light itself, to the high frequency X and gamma rays.

Many a miracle depends upon the broad span of the electromagnetic spectrum. The ability to communicate across long distances despite intervening obstacles, such as the walls of buildings, is possible using the radio and television frequencies. X rays can see into the human body without opening it. These things, which would once have been labeled magic, are now ordinary ways we use the electromagnetic spectrum.

The unification of electricity and magnetism has led to a deeper understanding of physical science, and much effort has been put into further unifying the four forces of nature. The remaining known forces are the so called weak, strong, and gravitational forces. The weak force has now been unified with electromagnetism, called the electroweak force. There are proposals to include the strong force in a grand unified theory, but the inclusion of gravity remains an open problem.

The fundamental role of special relativity in electromagnetism

Maxwell's theory is in fact in contradiction with Newtonian mechanics, and in trying to find the resolution to this conflict, Einstein was lead to his theory of special relativity. Maxwell's equations withstood the conflict, but it was Newtonian mechanics that were corrected by relativistic mechanics. These corrections are most necessary at velocities, close to the speed of light. The many strange predictions about space and time that follow from special relativity are found to be a part of the real world.

Paradoxically, magnetism is a counter example to the frequent claims that relativistic effects are not noticeable for low velocities. The moving charges that compose an electric current in a wire might typically only be traveling at several feet per second (walking speed), and the resulting Lorentz contraction of special relativity is indeed minute. However, the electrostatic forces at balance in the wire are of such great magnitude, that this small contraction of the moving (negative) charges exposes a residue force of real world magnitude, namely the magnetic force. It is in exactly this way that the magnetic force derives from the electric. Special relativity is indeed hidden in Maxwell's equations, which were known before special relativity was understood or separately formulated by Einstein.

Technological uses of electromagnetism

Before the advent of technology, electromagnetism was perhaps most strongly experienced in the form of lightning, and electromagnetic radiation in the form of light. Ancient man kindled fires which he thought were kept alive in trees struck by lightning.

Much of the magic of nature has been put to work by man, but not always for his betterment or that of his surroundings. Electricity at high voltages can carry energy across extended distances with little loss. Magnetism derived from that electricity can then power vast motors. But electromagnetism can also be employed in a more delicate fashion as a means of communication, either with wires (as in the telephone), or without them (as in radio communication). It also drives our electronics devices (as in computers).

Magnetism has long been employed for navigation in the compass. This works because the Earth is itself a huge magnet, thought to have arisen from the great heat driven convection currents of molten iron in its center. In fact, it is known that the Earth's magnetic poles have exchanged positions in the past.

Electromotive force

In an electric circuit, electromotive force is the work done by a source on an electrical charge. Because it is not really a force, the term is actually a misnomer; it is more commonly referred to by the initials EMF. EMF is another term for electrical potential, or the difference in charge across a battery or voltage source. For a circuit with no current flowing, the potential difference is called EMF.

Electrical sources that convert energy from another form are called seats of EMF. In the case of a complete circuit, such a source performs work on electrical charges, pushing them around the circuit. At the seat of

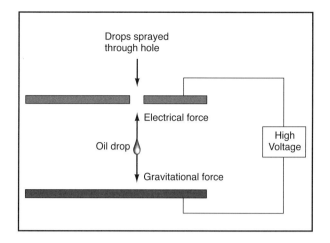

Drops sprayed through hole

Electrical force

Oil drop

Gravitational force

High Voltage

Figure 1.

EMF, charges are moved from low electrical potential to higher electrical potential.

Water flowing downhill in a flume is a good analogy for charges in an electric circuit. The water starts at the top of the hill with a certain amount of potential energy, just as charges in a circuit start with high electrical potential at the battery. As the water begins to flow downhill, its potential energy drops, just as the electrical potential of charges drops as they travels through the circuit. At the bottom of the hill, the potential energy is minimum, and work must be performed to pump it to the top of the hill to travel through the flume again. Similarly, in an electrical circuit, the seat of EMF performs work on the charges to bring them to a higher potential after their trip through the circuit.

Electron

The electron is a negatively charged subatomic particle which is an important component of the atoms which make up ordinary matter. The electron is fundamental, in that it is not believed to be made up of smaller constituents. The size of the charge on the electron has for many years been considered the fundamental unit of charge found in nature. All electrical charges were believed to be integral multiples of this charge. Recently, however, considerable evidence has been found to indicate that particles classified as mesons and baryons are made up of objects called quarks, which have charges of either 2/3 or 1/3 the charge on the electron. For example, the neutrons and protons, which make up the nuclei of atoms, are baryons. However, sci-

entists have never been able to observe an isolated quark, so for all practical purposes the charge on the electron can still be considered the fundamental unit of charge found in nature. The magnitude of this charge, usually designated by e, has been measured very precisely and is 1.602177×10^{-19} coulombs. The mass of the electron is small even by atomic standards and has the value 9.109389×10^{-31} kg, being only about 1/1836 the mass of the proton.

All atoms found in nature have a positively charged nucleus about which the negatively charged electrons move. The atom is electrically neutral and thus the positive electrical charge on the nucleus has the same magnitude as the negative charge due to all the electrons. The electrons are held in the atom by the attractive force exerted on them by the positively charged nucleus. They move very rapidly about the nucleus in orbits which have very definite energies, forming a sort of electron cloud around it. Some of the electrons in a typical atom can be quite close to the nucleus, while others can be at distances which are many thousands of times larger than the diameter of the nucleus. Thus, the electron cloud determines the size of the atom. It is the outermost electrons that determine the chemical behavior of the various elements. The size and shape of the electron clouds around atoms can only be explained utilizing a field of physics called quantum mechanics.

In metals, some of the electrons are not tightly bound to atoms and are free to move through the metal under the influence of an electric field. It is this situation that accounts for the fact that most metals are good conductors of electricity and heat.

Quantum theory also explains several other rather strange properties of electrons. Electrons behave as if they were spinning, and the value of the angular momentum associated with this spin is fixed; thus it is not surprising that electrons also behave like little magnets. The way electrons are arranged in some materials, such as iron, causes these materials to be magnetic. The existence of the positron, the antiparticle of the electron, was predicted by French physicist Paul Dirac in 1930. To predict this antiparticle, he used a version of quantum mechanics which included the effects of the theory of relativity. The positron's charge has the same magnitude as the electron's charge but is positive. Dirac's prediction was verified two years later when the positron was observed experimentally by Carl Anderson in a cloud chamber used for research on cosmic rays. The positron does not exist for very long in the presence of ordinary matter because it soon comes in contact with an ordinary electron and the two particles annihilate, producing a gamma ray with an energy equal to the energy equivalent of the two electron masses, according to Einstein's famous equation $E = mc^2$.

History

As has been the case with many developments in science, the discovery of the electron and the recognition of its important role in the structure of matter evolved over a period of almost 100 years. As early as 1838, English physicist Michael Faraday found that when a charge of several thousand volts was applied between metal electrodes in an evacuated glass tube, an electric current flowed between the electrodes. It was found that this current was made up of negatively charged particles by observing their deflection in an electric field. Credit for the discovery of the electron is usually given to the English physicist J. J. Thomson. He was able to make quantitative measurements of the deflection of these particles in electric and magnetic fields and measure e/m, the ratio of their charge to mass.

Later, similar measurements were made on the negatively charged particles emitted by different cathode materials and the same value of e/m was obtained. When the same value of e/m was also obtained for "electrons" emitted by hot filaments (called thermionic emission) and for photoelectrons emitted when light hits certain surfaces, it became clear that these were all the same type of particle, and the fundamental nature of the electron began to emerge. From these and other measurements it soon became known that the charge on the electron was roughly 1.6×10^{-19} coulombs. But the definitive experiment, which indicated that the charge on the electron was the fundamental unit of charge in nature, was carried out by Robert A. Millikan at the University of Chicago between 1907 and 1913. A schematic diagram of this famous "oil drop" experiment is shown in Figure 1. Charged oil drops, produced by an atomizer, were sprayed into the electric field maintained between two parallel metal plates. By measuring the terminal velocity of individual drops as they fell under gravity and again as they rose under an applied electric field, Millikan was able to measure the charge on the drops. He measured the charge on thousands of drops and was able to follow some drops for long periods of time and to observe changes in the charge on these drops produced by ionizing x rays. He observed many drops with only a single electronic charge and never observed a charge that was not an integral multiple of this fundamental unit. Millikan's original measurements gave a value of 1.591×10^{-19} coulombs. These results do not prove that nonintegral charges do not exist, but because many other different experiments later confirmed Millikan's result, he is generally credited with discovering the fundamental nature of the charge on the electron, a discovery for which he received the Nobel Prize in physics in 1923.

See also Electron cloud; Neutron; Nucleus, atomic; Proton; Quantum mechanics; Subatomic particles.

Robert L. Stearns

Electron cloud

The term electron cloud is used to describe the area around an atomic nucleus where an electron will probably be. It is also described as the "fuzzy" orbit of an atomic electron.

An electron bound to the nucleus of an atom is often thought of as orbiting the nucleus in much the same manner that a planet orbits a sun, but this is not a valid visualization. An electron is not bound by gravity, but by the Coulomb force, whose direction depends on the sign of the particles' charge. (Remember, opposites attract, so the negative electron is attracted to the positive proton in the nucleus.) Although both the Coulomb force and the gravitational force depend inversely on the square of the distance between the objects of interest, and both are central forces, there are important differences. In the classical picture, an accelerating charged particle, like the electron (a circling body changes direction, so it is always accelerating) should radiate and lose energy, and therefore spiral in towards the nucleus of an atom . . . but it does not.

Since we are discussing a very small (microscopic) system, an electron must be described using quantum mechanical rules rather than the classical rules which govern planetary motion. According to quantum mechanics, an electron can be a wave or a particle, depending on what kind of measurement one makes. Because of its wave nature, one can never predict where in its orbit around the nucleus an electron will be found. One can only calculate whether there is a high probability that it will be located at certain points when a measurement is made.

The electron is therefore described in terms of its probability distribution or probability density. This probability distribution doesn't have definite cutoff points; its edges are somewhat fuzzy. Hence the term "electron cloud."

This cloudy probability distribution takes on different shapes, depending on the state of the atom. At room temperature, most atoms exist in their lowest energy state or "ground" state. If energy is added—by shooting a laser at it, for example—the outer electrons can "jump" to a higher state (think larger orbit, if it helps). According to quantum mechanical rules, there are only certain specific states to which an electron can jump. These discrete states are labeled by *quantum numbers*. The letters designating the basic quantum numbers are n, l, and m, where n is the principal or energy quantum number, l relates to the orbital angular momentum of the electron, and m is a magnetic quantum number. The principal quantum number n can take integer values from 1 to infinity. For the same electron, l can be any integer from 0 to $(n-1)$, and m can have any integer value from $-l$ to l. For example, if $n = 3$, we can have states with $l = 2$, 1, or 0. For the state with $n = 3$ and $l = 2$, we could have $m = -2, -1, 0, 1$, or 2.

Each set of n, l, m quantum numbers describes a different probability distribution for the electron. A larger n means the electron is most likely to be found farther from the nucleus. For $n = 1$, l and m must be 0, and the electron cloud is spherical about the nucleus. For $n = 2$, $l = 0$, there are two concentric spherical shells of probability about the nucleus. For $n = 2$, $l = 1$, the cloud is more barbell-shaped. We can even have a daisy shape when $l = 3$. The distributions can become quite complicated.

Experiment has verified these distributions for one-electron atoms, but the wave function computations can be very difficult for atoms with more than one electron in their outer shell. In fact, when the motion of more than one electron is taken into account, it can take

days for the largest computer to output probability distributions for even a low–lying state, and simplifying approximations must often be made.

Overall, however, the quantum mechanical wave equation, as developed by Schrödinger in 1926, gives an excellent description of how the microscopic world is observed to behave, and we must admit that while quantum mechanics may not be precise, it is accurate.

Electronegativity see **Chemical bond**

Electronics

Electronics is the branch of physics that deals with the flow of electrons and other carriers of electric charge. This flow of electric charge is known as *electric current*, and a closed path through which current travels is called an *electric circuit*.

The modern era of electronics originated in the early 20th century with the invention of the electron tube, a device which stores electric charges and amplifies electronic signals. In 1947 the industry took a giant leap forward when John Bardeen, Walter Brattain, and William Shockley of Bell Telephone Laboratories developed the smaller, more efficient transistor which lead to a new generation of miniature electronics. In the late 1950s Robert Noyce and Gordon Moore, of Fairchild Semiconductor Company, invented the silicon integrated circuit, a still more efficient way to process electronic impulses which has carried the electronics industry into the computer age. Most recently, the 1980s saw the development of achievement of circuits employing very–large–scale integration (VLSI), which involves placement of 100,000 or more transistors on a single silicon chip. VLSI greatly expands the computational speed and ability of computers, and researchers believe that eventually it may be possible to fit a billion or more transistors on a single chip. Today, electronics has a vast array of applications, including television, computers, microwave ovens, radar, radio, sound recording and reproduction equipment, video technology, and x–ray tubes. The term electronics is also used broadly to describe devices which employ electricity for many purposes.

Electron microscope see **Microscopy**

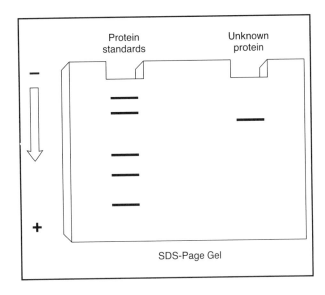

Figure 1.

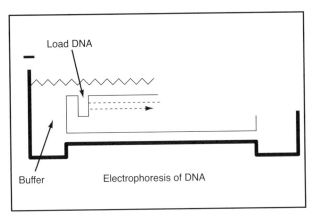

Figure 2.

tional coefficient. The frictional coefficient relates to the size and the shape of the particle. From equation (2) it can be seen that electrophoretic mobility decreases for larger particles and increases with higher charge.

Electrophoresis

Electrophoresis is a technique used for the separation of biological molecules based on their movement due to the influence of a direct electric current. The technique was pioneered in 1937 by the Swedish chemist Arne Tiselius for the separation of proteins. It has now been extended to the separation of many other different classes of biomolecules including nucleic acids, carbohydrates and amino acids.

Electrophoresis has become increasingly important in the laboratory for basic research, biomedical research and in clinical settings for the diagnosis of disease. Electrophoresis is not commonly used to purify proteins in large quantities because other methods exist which are simpler, faster, and more efficient. However, it is valuable as an analytical technique for detecting and quantifying minute traces of many biomolecules in a mixture. It is also useful for determining certain physical properties such as molecular weight, isoelectric point, and biological activity.

Electrophoretic theory

Electrophoretic separations are based upon the fact that the electrical force (F) on a charged particle (ion) in an electrical field (E) is proportional to the charge of the particle (q), or $F = qE$ (Eq 1).

The migration of the charged particle in the electric field, called the electrophoretic mobility (μ), is defined as $\mu = v/E = q/f$ (Eq 2), where v is the velocity of the charged particle and f is a complex term called the fric-

Methodology and applications

The electrophoresis equipment can have several designs. The simplest approach is the *moving boundary technique*. As diagramed in Figure 3, the charged molecules (I.E. proteins) to be separated are electrophoresed upward through a buffer solution toward electrodes immersed on either side of a U–shaped tube. The individual proteins are resolved because they have different mobilities as described above. This technique separates the biomolecules on the basis of their charges. Positively charged molecules migrate toward the negative electrode (cathode) and negatively charged particles move to the positive electrode (anode). The migration of the particles to the electrodes can be followed by instruments which measure the refractive index or absorption of light by the solution.

The most important class of electrophoresis is *zone electrophoresis*. In zone electrophoresis, the sample to be separated is applied to a solid matrix through which it migrates under the force of an applied electric potential. Two major classes of zone electrophoresis will be discussed below.

Gel electrophoresis

The sample is loaded into a gel matrix support. This has many important advantages:

1. The density and porosity of gels can be easily controlled and adjusted for different biomolecules or different experimental conditions. Since the gel pore size is on the order of the dimensions of the macromolecules, the separations are based on *molecular sieving* as

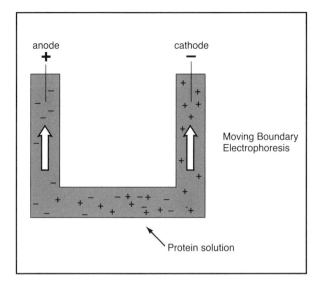

anode
+

cathode
−

Moving Boundary
Electrophoresis

Protein solution

Figure 3.

well as electrophoretic mobility of the molecules. Large molecules are retarded relative to smaller molecules as they can not pass as easily through the gel during electrophoresis.

2. Gels are easy to chemically modify, for related techniques such as affinity electrophoresis which separates biomolecules on the basis of biomolecular affinity or recognition.

3. Excellent separation power.

Gel electrophoresis of DNA

Highly purified agarose, a major component of sea weed, is used as the solid gel matrix into which the DNA samples are loaded for electrophoresis. By varying the agarose concentration in the gel, DNA fragments in different size ranges can be separated.

The agarose is dissolved in water, heated and cast as a gel slab approximately 0.2 inch (0.5 cm) in thickness. Wells are formed at one end of the gel for the loading of the DNA sample. The slab is then placed horizontally into the electrophoresis buffer chamber.

The DNA migrates in bands toward the positive electrode. The smaller molecules pass through the matrix more rapidly than the larger ones which are restricted. The DNA bands are then stained using a fluorescent dye such as ethidium bromide. The stained gel is then viewed directly under ultraviolet light and photographed. A diagram of a submarine DNA electrophoresis is illustrated in Figure 2.

Gel electrophoresis of proteins

Because proteins are typically much smaller than DNA, they are run in gels containing polymers of much smaller pore size. The most common technique for protein separation is known as SDS–Polyacrylamide Gel Electrophoresis (SDS–PAGE). In this approach the proteins are treated with a detergent (sodium dodecyl sulfate) which unfolds them and gives them similar shape and ratio of charge to mass. Thus, proteins, treated with SDS separate on the basis of mass, with the smaller proteins migrating more rapidly through the gel. The gel matrix is polyacrylamide, a synthetic copolymer which has excellent molecular sieving properties. Polyacrylamide gels are cast between glass plates to form what is called a "sandwich."

Protein gels are generally run in a vertical fashion. The electrophoresis apparatus has an upper and lower buffer tank. The top and bottom of the sandwich is in contact with either buffer. Protein is loaded into the wells in the upper buffer tank and current is applied. The proteins thus migrate down through the gel in bands, according to their sizes. After electrophoresis, the polyacrylamide gel is removed from between the glass plates and chemically stained to show protein bands which can then be studied. The SDS–PAGE technique allows researchers to study parts of proteins and protein–protein interactions. If a protein has different subunits they will be separated by SDS treatment and will form separate bands (see Figure 1).

Paper electrophoresis

This technique is useful for the separation of small charged molecules such as amino acids and small proteins. A strip of filter paper is moistened with buffer and the ends of the strip are immersed into buffer reservoirs containing the electrodes. The samples are spotted in the center of the paper, high voltage is applied, and the spots migrate according to their charges. After electrophoresis, the separated components can be detected by a variety of staining techniques, depending upon their chemical identity.

Electrophoretic techniques been also been adapted to other applications such as the determination of protein isoelectric points. Affinity gels with biospecific properties are used to study binding sites and surface features of proteins. Continuous flow electrophoresis is applied to separations in free solution and has found very useful application in blood cell separation. Recently, High Performance Capillary Electrophoresis (HPCE) has been developed for the separation of many classes of biological molecules.

Further Reading:

Lehninger, A.L., D.L. Nelson & M.M. Cox. *Principles of Biochemistry,* 2nd ed, New York: Worth Publishers, 1993.

Robyt, J.F. & B.J. White. *Biochemical Techniques, Theory and Practice,* Prospect Heights, IL: Waveland Press, Inc., 1990.

Scopes, R.K. *Protein Purification, Principles and Practice*, 3rd ed, New York: Springer–Verlag, 1994.

Wilson, K. & J. Walker. *Principles and Techniques of Practical Biochemistry*, 4th ed. New York: Cambridge University Press, 1994.

Leonard D. Holmes

Electrostatic devices

Electrostatics is the study of the behavior of electric charges that are at rest. The phenomenon of static electricity has been known for well over 2,000 years, and a variety of electrostatic devices have been created over the centuries.

The ancient Greek philosopher Thales (624–546 B.C.) discovered that when a piece of amber was rubbed, it could pick up light objects, a process known as triboelectrification. The Greek name for amber, *elektron*, gave rise to many of the words we use in connection with electricity. It was also noted that lodestone

A Van de Graaff generator is a device that is capable of building up a very high electrostatic potential. In this photo, the charge that has accumulated in the dome is leaking into the hair of a wig that has been placed on top of the generator. Because the charge is of one polarity, the hairs repel each other.

had the natural ability to pick up iron objects, although the early Greeks did not know that electricity and magnetism were linked.

In the late 16th century, William Gilbert (1544–1603) began experimenting with static electricity, pointing out the difference between static electric attraction and magnetic attraction. Later, in the mid–1600s, Otto von Guericke built the first electrostatic machine. His device consisted of a sulfur globe that was rotated by a crank and stroked by hand. It released a considerable static electric charge with a large spark.

A similar device was invented by Francis Hawkesbee in 1706. In his design, an iron chain contacted a spinning globe and conducted the electric charge to a suspended gun barrel; at the other end of the barrel another chain conducted the charge.

In 1745, the first electrostatic storage device was invented nearly simultaneously by two scientists working independently. Peter von Muschenbrock, a professor at the University of Leyden, and Ewald von Kleist of the Cathedral of Camin, Germany, devised a water–filled glass jar with two electrodes. A Leyden student who had been using a Hawkesbee machine to electrify the water touched the chain to remove it and nearly died from the electric shock. This device, known as the Leyden jar, could accumulate a considerable electric charge, and audiences willingly received electric shocks in public displays. One of these displays aroused the curiosity of Benjamin Franklin, who obtained a Leyden jar for study. He determined that it was not the water that held the electric charge but the glass insulator. This is the principle behind the electri-

The Vivitron electrostatic particle accelerator under construction at the Centre des Recherches Nucleaires, Strasbourg, Germany. Vivitron, the largest Van de Graaff generator in the world, can generate a potential of up to 35 million volts. The accelerator will be used to fire ions of elements such as carbon at other nuclei. Under the right conditions this creates superdeformation, a relatively stable state in which the rotating nuclei have an elliptical form. Gamma rays given off by these nuclei reveal much about the internal structure of the nucleus.

cal condenser (capacitor), one of the most important electrical components in use today.

Charles F. DuFay (1698–1739) discovered that suspended bits of cork, electrified with a statically charged glass rod, repelled each other. DuFay concluded that any two objects which had the same charge repelled each other, while unlike charges attracted. The science of electrostatics, so named by André Ampère (1775-1836), is based on this fact.

French physicist Charles Coulomb (1736–1806) became interested in the work of Joseph Priestly (1733–1804), who had built an electrostatic generator in 1769, and studied electrical repulsion. Coulomb used his torsion balance to make precise measurements of the force of attraction between two electrically charged spheres and found they obeyed an inverse square law. The mathematical relationship between the forces is known as Coulomb's law, and the unit of electric charge is named the coulomb in his honor.

Alessandro Volta invented a device in 1775 that could create and store an electrostatic charge. Called an electrophorus, it used two plates to accumulate a strong positive charge. The device replaced the Leyden jar, and the two–plate principle is behind the electrical condensers in use today.

Several other electrostatic machines have been devised. In 1765 John Reid, an instrument maker in London, built a portable static electric generating machine to treat medical problems. In 1783, John Cuthbertson built a huge device that could produce electrical discharges 2 ft (61 cm) in length. The gold leaf electroscope, invented in 1787, consists of two leaves which repel each other when they receive an electric charge. In 1881, British engineer James Wimshurst invented his Wimshurst machine, two glass discs with metal segments spinning opposite each other. Brushes touching the metal segments removed the charge created and conducted it to a pair of Leyden jars where it was stored for later use.

The most famous of all the electrostatic devices is the Van de Graff generator. Invented in 1929 by Robert

J. Van de Graff, it uses a conveyor belt to carry an electric charge from a high–voltage supply to a hollow ball. It had various applications. For his experiments on properties of atoms, Van de Graff needed to accelerate subatomic particles to very high velocity, and he knew that storing an electrostatic charge could result in a high potential. Another generator was modified to produce x rays for use in the treatment of internal tumors. It was installed in a hospital in Boston in 1937. Van de Graff's first generator operated at 80,000 volts, but was eventually improved to five million volts. It remains one of the most widely used experimental exhibits in schools and museums today.

See also Capacitor; Electric charge.

Element, chemical

A chemical element is a pure substance that is made up of only one single kind of atom. A chemical compound, on the other hand, is made up of two or more different kinds of atoms combined together in certain proportions.

By "kind of atom," we mean atoms having the same atomic number—the number of protons in the atomic nucleus, which is equal to the number of electrons outside the nucleus. Because the chemical properties of an atom are determined purely by its number of electrons, every element has its own unique set of chemical properties.

Some elements, such as the rare gases, exist as collections of single atoms; they are *monatomic*. Others exist as molecules that consist of two or more atoms of the element bonded together. For example, oxygen (O) can exists as either *diatomic* (two–atom) molecules (O_2) or *triatomic* (three–atom) molecules (O_3); the latter form is called *ozone*. Phosphorus (P) exists as four–atom molecules (P_4), while sulfur (S) exists as eight–atom molecules (S_8).

Even though they have the same number of protons, atoms of the same element may differ in the numbers of neutrons in their nuclei. Atoms with different numbers of neutrons are called isotopes. Some elements have only one stable (non–radioactive) isotope, while others have two or more. Tin (Sn) has ten stable isotopes, and all of these atoms have the same chemical properties. Some elements have no stable isotopes; they're all radioactive. An element's total number of isotopes, stable plus radioactive, which many reference books quote, is meaningless because a new radioactive isotope that lasts for only a tiny fraction of a second may some day be made. (If it lasts for a billionth of a second, do you count it, or not?)

Ninety–two different elements occur naturally on Earth; others have been made synthetically (artificially). Since 1937, when technetium (Tc), the first synthetic element, was made, the number of known elements has grown as nuclear chemists made new atoms with higher and higher atomic numbers: synthetic elements with atomic numbers higher than 92, which is the atomic number of uranium (U). At last count (November 1994), there were 110 known elements, ranging from hydrogen (H), whose atoms have only one electron, to the as–yet unnamed element whose atoms contain 110 electrons. Because the highest–atomic–number atoms are very radioactive and can exist for only tiny fractions of a second, it is not worth arguing over exactly how many elements there are, unless you are a nuclear chemist. New elements are so hard to produce today—only a few atoms can be made at a time—that the scientists usually squabble for several years before everybody agrees on who discovered what and when.

Figure 1 lists all the currently known elements, with their symbols and atomic numbers.

A survey of the elements

Of the 110 currently known elements, 97 are solids at ordinary room temperature, only two are liquids, and 11 are gases. (We have to guess that a few of the more recently discovered ones are solids, because not enough atoms have been produced to actually see samples of them.) Many elements, such as iron (Fe), copper (Cu), and aluminum (Al), are familiar everyday substances, but many more may sound strange and unfamiliar, either because they are not very abundant on Earth or because they are not used very much by human beings. Elements you may never have heard of have names such as dysprosium (Dy), thulium (Tm) and protactinium (Pa).

As you can see, every element has been assigned a name and a one– or two–letter symbol for convenience in writing formulas and chemical equations; the symbols are shown above in parentheses. For example, to distinguish the four elements that begin with the letter *c*, calcium has been given the symbol Ca, cadmium is Cd, californium is Cf, and carbon is just plain C because it "got there first"—it was known, named and given a symbol long before the others.

Many of the symbols for chemical elements don't seem to make sense in terms of their English names.

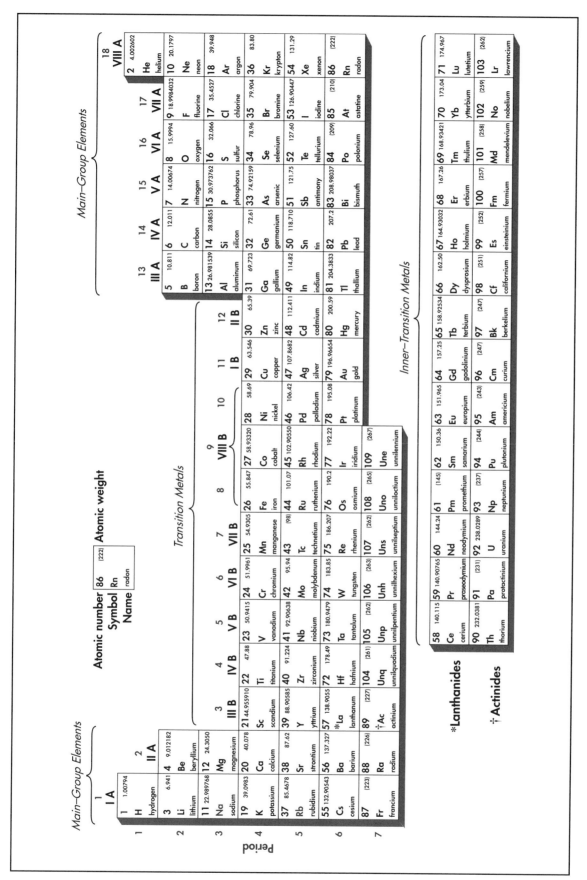

Figure 1.

TABLE 1. TWO DOZEN OF THE MOST COMMON AND/OR IMPORTANT CHEMICAL ELEMENTS.

| Element | Symbol | Percent of all atoms[a] | | | | Characteristics under ordinary room conditions |
		In the universe	In the earth's crust	In sea water	In the human body	
Aluminum	Al	—	6.3	—	—	A lightweight, silvery metal
Calcium	Ca	—	2.1	—	0.2	Common in minerals, seashells, and bones
Carbon	C	—	—	—	10.7	Basic in all living things
Chlorine	Cl	—	—	0.3	—	A toxic gas
Copper	Cu	—	—	—	—	The only red metal
Gold	Au	—	—	—	—	The only yellow metal
Helium	He	7.1	—	—	—	A very light gas
Hydrogen	H	92.8	2.9	66.2	60.6	The lightest of all elements; a gas
Iodine	I	—	—	—	—	A nonmetal; used as antiseptic
Iron	Fe	—	2.1	—	—	A magnetic metal; used in steel
Lead	Pb	—	—	—	—	A soft, heavy metal
Magnesium	Mg	—	2.0	—	—	A very light metal
Mercury	Hg	—	—	—	—	A liquid metal; one of the two liquid elements
Nickel	Ni	—	—	—	—	A noncorroding metal; used in coins
Nitrogen	N	—	—	—	2.4	A gas; the major component of air
Oxygen	O	—	60.1	33.1	25.7	A gas; the second major component of air
Phosphorus	P	—	—	—	0.1	A nonmetal; essential to plants
Potassium	K	—	1.1	—	—	A metal; essential to plants; commonly called "potash"
Silicon	Si	—	20.8	—	—	A semiconductor; used in electronics
Silver	Ag	—	—	—	—	A very shiny, valuable metal
Sodium	Na	—	2.2	0.3	—	A soft metal; reacts readily with water, air
Sulfur	S	—	—	—	0.1	A yellow nonmetal; flammable
Titanium	Ti	—	0.3	—	—	A light, strong, noncorroding metal used in space vehicles
Uranium	U	—	—	—	—	A very heavy metal; fuel for nuclear power

[a] If no number is entered, the element constitutes less than 0.1 percent.

TABLE 2. A WHO'S WHO OF THE ELEMENTS.		
Element	**Distinction**	**Comment**
Astatine (At)	The *rarest*	Rarest of the naturally occurring elements
Boron (B)	The *strongest*	Highest stretch resistance
Californium (Cf)	The *most expensive*	Sold at one time for about $1 billion a gram
Carbon (C)	The *hardest*	As diamond, one of its three solid forms
Germanium (Ge)	The *purest*	Has been purified to 99.99999999 percent purity
Helium (He)	The *lowest melting point*	-271.72° C at a pressure of 26 times atmospheric pressure
Hydrogen (H)	The *lowest density*	Density 0.0000899 g/cc at atmospheric pressure and 0°C
Lithium (Li)	The *lowest-density metal*	Density 0.534g/cc
Osmium (Os)	The *highest density*	Density 22.57 g/cc
Radon (Rn)	The *highest-density gas*	Density 0.00973 g/cc at atmospheric pressure and 0°C
Tungsten (W)	The *highest melting point*	3420°C

Those are mostly elements that have been known for thousands of years and that already had Latin names before chemists began handing out the symbols. Iron, for example, is Fe for its Latin name, *ferrum*. Gold is Au for *aurum*, sodium is Na for *natrium*, copper is Cu for *cuprum*, and mercury is Hg for *hydrargyrum*, meaning liquid silver, which is exactly what it looks like, but isn't.

Table 1 lists some of the most common and important chemical elements. Note that many of these are referred to in the last column as metals. In fact, fully 89 out of the 110 elements are metals; the other 21 are nonmetals.

Notice that only two elements taken together—hydrogen and helium—make up 99.9 percent of the atoms in the entire universe. That's because virtually all the mass in the universe is in the form of stars, and stars are made mostly of H and He. Here on Earth, however, only three elements, oxygen, silicon and aluminum,

make up more than 87 percent of our planet's crust—that 17–or–so–kilometer–thick, hard surface beneath our feet. Adding only half a dozen more—hydrogen, sodium, calcium iron, magnesium and potassium—we account for more than 99 percent of the Earth's crust.

The *abundance* of an element can be quite different from its *importance* to us as human beings. Nutritionists believe that no fewer than 24 elements are essential to life, even though many of them are fairly rare and are needed in only the tiniest amounts.

History of the elements

Many substances that we now know are elements that have been known since ancient times, but without any understanding of their true nature. Gold (Au) was found and made into ornaments during the late stone age, some ten thousand years ago. More than 5,000 years ago in Egypt, the metals iron (Fe), copper (Cu), silver (Ag), tin each time (Sn), and lead (Pb) were also used for various purposes. Arsenic (As) was discovered around 1250 A.D., and phosphorus (P) was discovered around 1674. By 1700, about 12 elements were known, but they were not yet recognized for what they are.

The concept of elements—that there are a limited number of fundamental pure substances out of which all other substances are made—goes back to the ancient Greeks. Empedocles (c.495–c.435 B.C.) proposed that there are four basic "roots" of all materials: earth, air, fire and water. Plato (427?–347 B.C.) referred to them as *stoicheia*, or elements. Aristotle (384–322 B.C.), a student of Plato's, proposed that an element is "one of those simple bodies into which other bodies can be decomposed and which itself is not capable of being divided into others." Except for nuclear fission and other nuclear reactions that were discovered more than two thousand years later, this definition is still good today.

Of course, there were many wrong ideas along the way; that is how all science proceeds. For example, the Swiss physician and alchemist Theophrastus Bombastus von Hohenheim (1493?–1541), known as Paracelsus, proposed that everything was made of three "principles": salt, mercury and sulfur, while an alchemist named van Helmont (1577?–1644?) tried to boil everything down (figuratively) to just two elements: air and water.

Eventually, Robert Boyle (1627–91) revived Aristotle's definition and ran with it. By 1789, Antoine Lavoisier (1743–94) was able to publish a list of chemical elements that met Boyle's definition. Even though some of them later turned out to be compounds (that is, they could be broken down into real elements), that set the stage for the adoption of standard names and symbols for the various elements.

The Swedish chemist J. J. Berzelius (1779–1848) was the first person to employ the modern method of classification: a one– or two–letter symbol for each element. These symbols could then be put together to show how the elements combine into compounds. For example, writing two Hs and one O together as H_2O would mean that the particles (molecules) of water consist of two hydrogen atoms and one oxygen atom, tied together. Berzelius published a table of 24 elements, including their atomic weights, most of which are very close to the values used today.

In the year 1800, only about 25 true elements were known, but progress was relatively rapid throughout the nineteenth century. By the time Dmitri Ivanovich Mendeleev (1834–1907) organized his periodic table in 1869, he had about 60 elements to reckon with. By 1900 there were more than 80. The list quickly expanded to 92, ending at uranium (atomic number 92), where it stayed until 1940, when synthesis of the transuranium elements began.

Organization of the elements

The task of organizing more than a hundred elements into some sensible arrangement would seem to be very difficult. Mendeleev's periodic table, however, is the answer. It even accommodates the modern synthetic transuranium elements without any strain. In this encyclopedia, each individual chemical element is discussed under one of three headings: (1) Fourteen particularly important elements are discussed under their own headings. They are Aluminum, Calcium, Carbon, Chlorine, Copper, Hydrogen, Iron, Lead, Nitrogen, Oxygen, Silicon, Sodium, Sulfur and Uranium.

(2) Elements that belong to any of seven families of elements—groups of elements that have very similar chemical properties—are discussed under their family–name headings. They are Actinides, Alkali metals, Alkaline earth metals, Halogens, Lanthanides, Rare gases and Transuranium elements.

(3) Elements that are not discussed either under their own name or in a family ("orphan elements") are discussed briefly below. Any element that is not discussed below can be found in the headings described above.

"Orphan" elements

Actinium. The metallic chemical element of atomic number 89. Symbol Ac, specific gravity 10.07, melting point 1832°F (1051°C), boiling point 5702.4±482.4°F (3200±300°C). All isotopes of this element are radioactive; the half–life of its most stable isotope, actinium–227 is 21.8 years. It's name is from the Greek *aktinos*, meaning ray.

Antimony. The metallic chemical element of atomic number 51. Symbol Sb, atomic weight 121.8, specific gravity 6.69, melting point 1077.73°F (630.74°C), boiling point 3092.4°F (1750°C). One of its main uses is as an alloy with lead in automobile batteries; it makes the lead harder.

Arsenic. The metallic chemical element of atomic number 33. Symbol As, atomic weight 74.92, specific gravity 5.73 in gray metallic form, melting point 1413°F (817°C), sublimes (solid turns to gas) at 1045.8° (613°C). Arsenic compounds are poisonous.

Bismuth. The metallic chemical element of atomic number 83. Symbol Bi, atomic weight 209.0, specific gravity 9.75, melting point 431°F (271.1°C), boiling point 2757.6±48.6°F (1564±5°C). Bismuth oxychloride is used in "pearlized" cosmetics. Bismuth subsalicylate, an insoluble compound, is the major ingredient in Pepto–Bismol. The soluble compounds of bismuth, however, are poisonous.

Boron. The non–metallic chemical element of atomic number 5. Symbol B, atomic weight 10.81, specific gravity (amorphous form) 2.37, melting point 4082.4° (2300°C), boiling point 4532.4°F (2550°C). Common compounds are borax, $Na_2B_4O_{10}$. $10H_2$, used as a cleansing agent and water softener, and boric acid, H_3BO_3, a mild antiseptic and an effective cockroach poison.

Cadmium. The metallic chemical element of atomic number 48. Symbol Cd, atomic weight 112.4, specific gravity 8.65, melting point 520°F (320.9°C), boiling point 1319.4°F (765°C). A soft, highly toxic metal used in silver solder, in many other alloys, and in nickel–cadmium rechargeable batteries. Because it is an extraordinary absorber of neutrons, it is used in control rods for nuclear reactors.

Chromium. The metallic chemical element of atomic number 24. Symbol Cr, atomic weight 52.00, specific gravity 7.19, melting point 3295.8±21.6°F (1863±20°C), boiling point 4752°F (2672°C). A hard, shiny metal that takes a beautiful, high polish. Used to electroplate steel for protection against corrosion and as the major ingredient (next to iron) in stainless steel. Alloyed with nickel, it makes Nichrome, a high–electrical–resistance metal that gets red hot when electric current passes through it; electric toaster and heater coils are made of Nichrome wire. Chromium was named from the Greek *chroma* meaning color, because most of its compounds are highly colored. Chromium is responsible for the green color of emeralds.

Cobalt. The metallic chemical element of atomic number 27. Symbol Co, atomic weight 58.93. Cobalt is a grayish, hard, brittle metal closely resembling iron and nickel. These three metals are the only naturally occurring magnetic elements on Earth.

Gallium. The metallic chemical element of atomic number 31. Symbol Ga, atomic weight 69.72, melting point 3.996°F (29.78°C), boiling point 4268°F (2403°C). Gallium is frequently used in the electronics industry and thermometers which measure a wide range of temperatures.

Germanium. The metallic chemical element of atomic number 32. Symbol Ge, atomic weight 72.61. In pure form, germanium is a brittle crystal. It was used to make the world's first transistor, and is now used as a semiconductor in electronics devices.

Gold. The metallic chemical element of atomic number 79. Symbol Au, atomic weight 196.97. This most malleable of metals was probably the first element known to humans. It is usually alloyed with harder metals for use in jewelry, coins, or decorative pieces.

Hafnium. The metallic chemical element of atomic number 72. Symbol Hf, atomic weight 178.49, melting point 3951±21.6°F (2227±20°C), boiling point 4572°F (4602°C). Hafnium is very strong and resistant to corrosion. It also absorbs neutrons well, making it useful in control rods of nuclear reactors.

Indium. The metallic chemical element of atomic number 49. Symbol In, atomic weight 114.82, melting point 224.2°F (156.61°C), boiling point 3686°F (2080°C). Indium is lustrous, silvery metal that bends easily. It is often alloyed with other metals in solid–state electronics devices.

Iridium. The metallic chemical element of atomic number 77. Symbol Ir, atomic weight 192.22. Iridium is an extremely dense metal that resists corrosion better than most others. In its pure state, it is often used in special aircraft spark plugs.

Manganese. The metallic chemical element of atomic number 25. Symbol Mn, atomic weight 54.94. The biggest use of manganese is in steelmaking, where it is alloyed with iron. The element is required by all plants and animals, so it is sometimes added as magnesium oxide to animal feed.

Mercury. The metallic chemical element of atomic number 80. Symbol Hg, atomic weight 200.59, melting point −12.36°F (−38.87°C). Mercury is highly poisonous and causes irreversible damage to the nervous and excretory systems. The element is useful in thermometers because it expands and contracts at a nearly constant rate.

Molybdenum. The metallic chemical element of atomic number 42. Symbol Mo, atomic weight 95.94, melting point 4653°F (2617°C). Molybdenum is used to make superalloyed metals designed for high–temperature processes. It is also found as a trace elements in plant and animal tissues.

Nickel. The metallic chemical element of atomic number 28. Symbol Ni, atomic weight 58.71. Nickel is often mixed with other metals, such as copper and iron, to increase the alloy's resistance to heat and moisture.

Niobium. The metallic chemical element of atomic number 41. Symbol Nb, atomic weight 92.91, melting point 4379.4±39.6°F (2468±10°C), boiling point 8460° (4742°C). Niobium is used to strengthen alloys used to make lightweight aircraft frames.

Osmium. The metallic chemical element of atomic number 76. Symbol Os, atomic weight 190.2. Osmium is very hard and dense, weighing twice as much as lead. The metal is used to make fountain pen tips and electrical devices.

Palladium. The metallic chemical element of atomic number 46. Symbol Pd, atomic weight 106.42. Palladium is very soft. It also readily absorbs hydrogen, and is used to purify the gas.

Phosphorus. The nonmetallic chemical element of atomic number 15. Symbol P, atomic weight 30.97. Phosphorus is required by all plant and animal cells. In humans, most phosphorus exists in the bones and teeth. Phosphorus is heavily used in agricultural fertilizers.

Platinum. The metallic chemical element of atomic number 78. Symbol Pt, atomic weight 195.08, melting point 3132°F (1772°C), boiling point 6831°F (3827±100°C). Platinum withstands high temperatures well and is used in rocket and jet engine parts. It is also used as a catalyst in chemical reactions because it is relatively unreactive itself.

Polonium. The metallic chemical element of atomic number 84. Symbol Po, atomic weight 209. Polonium is a product of uranium decay and is 100 times as radioactive as uranium in its pure form.

Rhenium. The metallic chemical element of atomic number 75. Symbol Re, atomic weight 186.21, specific gravity 21.0, melting point 5666.4°F (3180°C), boiling point 10,071°F (5627°C, estimated). Rhenium is used in chemical and medical instruments, as a catalyst for the chemical and petroleum industries, and in photoflash lamps.

Rhodium. The metallic chemical element of atomic number 45. Symbol Rh, atomic weight 102.91. This element is similar to palladium. Electroplated rhodium, which is very hard and highly reflective, is used as material for optical instruments.

Ruthenium. The metallic chemical element of atomic number 44. Symbol Ru, atomic weight 101.07, specific gravity 12.5, melting point 4100.4°F (2310°C), boiling point 6962.4°F (3900°C). This element is alloyed with platinum and palladium to form very hard, resistant contacts for electrical equipment that must withstand a great deal of wear.

Scandium. The metallic chemical element of atomic number 21. Symbol Sc, atomic weight 44.96, melting point 2716.2°F (1541°C). Scandium is a silvery–white metal that develops a yellowish or pinkish cast when exposed to air. It has relatively few commercial applications.

Selenium. The nonmetallic chemical element of atomic number 34. Symbol Se, atomic weight 78.96. Selenium is able to convert light directly into electricity, and its resistance to electrical current decreases when it is exposed to light. Both properties make the element useful in photocells, exposure meters, and solar cells.

Silver. The metallic chemical element of atomic number 47. Symbol Ag, atomic weight 107.87. Silver has long been used in the manufacture of coins. It is also an unparalleled conductor of heat and electricity, which makes it useful in the chemical and photographic industries.

Tantalum. The metallic chemical element of atomic number 73. Symbol Ta, atomic weight 180.95, melting point 5335.2°F (2996°C). Tantalum is a heavy, gray, very hard metal that is used in alloys to pen points, analytical weights, and laboratory equipment.

Technetium. The metallic chemical element of atomic number 43. Symbol Tc, atomic weight 98. Technetium was the first element to be produced synthetically; scientists have never detected the natural presence of the element on Earth.

Tellurium. The nonmetallic chemical element of atomic number 52. Symbol To, atomic weight 127.60, melting point 751.5°F (449.5±0.3°C), boiling point 1724°F (989.8±3.8°C). It is a grayish–white, lustrous, brittle metal. Tellurium is a semiconductor that is used in the electronics industry.

Thallium. The metallic chemical element of atomic number 81. Symbol Tl, atomic weight 204.38. Thallium is a bluish–gray metal that is soft enough to be cut with a knife. Thallium sulfate is used as a rodenticide and ant poison.

Tin. The metallic chemical element of atomic number 50. Symbol Sn, atomic weight 118.71. Tin is alloyed with copper and antimony to make pewter. It is also used as a soft solder and as coating to prevent other metals from corrosion.

Titanium. The metallic chemical element of atomic number 22. Symbol Ti, atomic weight 47.88, melting point 2930±39.6°F (1660±10°C), boiling point 5859°F (3287°C). This element occurs as a bright, lustrous brittle metal or dark gray powder. Titanium alloys are very strong for their weight and can withstand large changes in temperature.

Tungsten. The metallic chemical element of atomic number 74. Symbol W, atomic weight 183.85, melting point 6080.4±21.6°F (3410±20°C). The melting point of tungsten is higher than that of any other metal. Its chief use is as a filament in electric light bulbs.

Vanadium. The metallic chemical element of atomic number 23. Symbol V, atomic weight 50.94. Pure vanadium is bright white. This metal finds its biggest use in strengthening steel.

Yttrium. The metallic chemical element of atomic number 39. Symbol Y, atomic weight 88.91, melting point 2682±43.2°F (1522±8°C), boiling point 5950.8°F (3338°C). Yttrium is a relatively active metal that decomposes in cold water slowly and in boiling water rapidly. Compounds containing yttrium have been shown to become superconducting at relatively high temperatures.

Zinc. The metallic chemical element of atomic number 30. Symbol Zn, atomic weight 65.37. Zinc, a brittle metal at room temperature, forms highly versatile alloys in industry. One zinc alloy is nearly as strong as steel, but has the malleability of plastic.

Zirconium. The metallic chemical element of atomic number 40. Symbol Zr, atomic weight 91.22, melting point 3276°F (1852±2°C), boiling point 7821°F (4377°C). Neutrons which are exposed to zirconium pass through the metal without being absorbed. This makes it highly desirable as a construction material in nuclear power plants.

See also Actinides; Alkali metals; Alkaline earth metals; Aluminum; Ammonia; Atom; Atomic number; Atomic weight; Calcium; Carbon; Chlorine; Compound, chemical; Copper; Deuterium; Elements, families of; Element, transuranium; Hydrogen; Iron; Lanthanides; Lead; Mercury; Nitrogen; Oxygen; Periodic table; Rare gases; Sodium; Sulfur; Tritium; Uranium; Valence.

Further Reading:

CRC Handbook of Chemistry and Physics, 73rd ed., CRC Press, 1992.

Emsley, J., *The Elements,* Clarendon, 1991.

Greenwood, N.N. and A. Earnshaw, *Chemistry of the Elements,* Pergamon Press, 1986.

Robert L. Wolke

Element, families of

A family of chemical elements usually consists of elements that are in the same group (the same column) of the Periodic Table, although the term is also applied to certain closely related elements within the same period (row). Just as the individual members in a human family are all different but may have certain characteristics in common, for example, the color of their hair, so the elements in a chemical family have certain properties in common, although each element also has properties that make it unique.

The search for patterns among the elements

Johann Döbereiner (1780–1849) made one of the earliest attempts to organize the elements into families in 1829, when he observed that for certain groups of three elements, called triads, the properties of one element were approximately mid–way between those of the other two. However, because the number of elements known to Döbereiner was far less than it is today, the number of triads that he was able to find was very limited.

In 1864, John Newlands (1837-1898) noticed that when the known elements were arranged in order of increasing atomic weight, every eighth element showed similar properties. This observation, which was at first dismissed by the chemical community as being purely coincidental, is readily explicable using the modern periodic table and the concept of families of elements.

After organizing the elements known in 1869 so that those with similar properties were grouped together, Dmitri Mendeléev (1834–1907) predicted the existence and properties of several new elements. The subsequent discovery of these elements, and the accuracy of many of Mendeléev's predictions, fully justified the notion that the elements could be organized into families. Today, we recognize that the basis for this classification is the similarity in the electronic configurations of the atoms concerned.

The main–group families

For those families of elements found among the main–group elements, that is, elements in groups 1, 2 and 13 through 18 of the periodic table, each member of a given family has the same number of valence electrons. A detailed examination of the electron configurations of the elements in these families reveals that each family has its own characteristic arrangement of electrons. For example, each element in group 1, the alkali metals, has its valence electron in an s sublevel. As a result, all the elements in this family have an electron configuration which, when written in linear form, terminates with ns^1, where n is an integer representing the principal quantum number of the valence shell. Thus, the electron configuration of lithium is $1s^2\, 2s^1$, that of sodium is $1s^2\, 2s^2\, 2p^6\, 3s^1$, potassium is $1s^2\, 2s^2\, 2p^6\, 3s^2\, 3p^6\, 4s^1$, and so on. In a similar way, the elements in group 2, the alkaline earth metals, each have two valence electrons and electron configurations that terminate in ns^2.

For example, beryllium is $1s^2 2s^2$, magnesium is $1s^2 2s^2 2p^6 3s^2$, calcium is $1s^2 2s^2 2p^6 3s^2 3p^6 4s^2$. Because the s sub–level can only accommodate a maximum of 2 electrons, the members of group 13, which have 3 valence electrons, all have electron configurations terminating in $ns^2 np^1$; for example, aluminum is $1s^2 2s^2 2p^6 3s^2 3p^1$. The remaining main–group families, group 14 (the carbon family), group 15 (the pnicogens), group 16 (the chalcogens), group 17 (the halogens) and group 18 (the rare gases) have 4, 5, 6, 7 and 8 valence electrons, respectively. Of these valence electrons, two occupy an s sublevel and the remainder occupy the p sub–level having the same principal quantum number.

The similarity in electron configurations within a given main–group family results in the members of the family having similar properties. For example, the alkali metals are all soft, highly reactive elements with a silvery appearance. None of these elements is found uncombined in nature, and they are all willing to give up their single valence electron in order to form an ion with a charge of 1+. Each alkali metal will react with water to give hydrogen gas and a solution of the metal hydroxide.

Characteristic patterns of behavior can also be identified for other main–group families; for example, the members of the carbon family all form chlorides of the type ECl_4 and hydrides of the type EH_4, and have a tendency towards *catenation*, that is, for identical atoms to join together to form long chains or rings. Similarly, although little is known about the heaviest, radioactive halogen, astatine, its congeners all normally exist as diatomic molecules, X_2, and show a remarkable similarity and predictability in their properties. All the members of this family are quite reactive—fluorine, the most reactive, combines directly with all the known elements except helium, neon and argon—and they all readily form ions having a charge of 1–.

The family of elements at the far right of the periodic table, the rare gases, consists of a group of colorless, odorless gases that are noted for their lack of reactivity. The first compounds of these elements were not prepared until 1962. Even today there are only a limited number of krypton compounds known and still no known compounds of helium, neon, or argon.

Hydrogen: The elemental orphan

When the elements are organized into families, hydrogen presents a problem. In some of its properties, hydrogen resembles the alkali metals, but it also shows some similarities to the halogens. Many periodic tables include hydrogen in group 1; others show it in groups 1 and 17. An alternative approach is to recognize hydrogen as being unique and not to assign it to a family.

Other families of elements

In addition to the main–group families, other families of elements can be identified among the remaining elements of the periodic table.

The transition metals

The elements in groups 3 through 12, the transition metals or d–block elements, could be considered as one large family. Their characteristic feature, with some exceptions, is the presence of an incomplete d sublevel in their electron configurations. As with any large family, transition metals show considerable diversity in their behavior, although there are some unifying features, such as their ability to form ions with a charge of 2+. Another similarity between these elements is that most of their compounds are colored.

The coinage metals and the platinum metals

At least two small family units can be identified within the larger transition–metal family. One of these small families, the coinage metals, consists of copper, silver and gold, the three elements in group 11. The other family, the platinum metals, includes elements from three groups: ruthenium and osmium from group 8; rhodium and iridium from group 9; and palladium and platinum from group 10.

The coinage metals are resistant to oxidation, hence their traditional use in making coins. Unlike the majority of the transition metals, the coinage metals each have a full d sublevel and one electron in an s sublevel, that is, an electron configuration that terminates in $(n-1)d^{10} ns^1$. One result of this electron configuration is that each of these metals will form an ion of the type M^+, although it is only for silver that this ion is relatively stable.

The platinum metals occur together in the same ores, are difficult to separate from one another, and are relatively unreactive.

The lanthanides and actinides

The lanthanides (or rare–earth elements) and actinides are two families that are related because they both result from electrons being added into an f sub–level. Both families have fourteen members, the lanthanides consisting of the elements with atomic numbers 58 through 71, and the actinides including the elements with atomic numbers 90 through 103. However, it is sometimes convenient to consider lanthanum (atomic number 57) as an honorary member of the lanthanide family and to treat actinium (atomic number 89) in a similar manner with respect to the actinides.

The lanthanides are usually found together in the same ores and despite their alternative name of the rare–earth elements, they are not particularly rare. In contrast, only two of the actinides, thorium and uranium, occur in nature, the remainder having been synthesized by nuclear scientists. Members of both families form ions with a charge of 3+, although other ions are also formed, particularly by the actinides.

See also Actinides; Alkaline metals; Alkali earth metals; Atomic number; Atomic weight; Element, chemical; Element, transuranium; Lanthanides; Periodic table; Valence.

Further Reading:

Emsley, John. *The Elements*. 2nd ed. Oxford: Oxford University Press, 1991.

Norman, Nicholas C. *Periodicity and the p–Block Elements*. Oxford: Oxford University Press, 1994.

Silberberg, Martin. *Chemistry: The Molecular Nature of Matter and Change*. St. Louis: Mosby, 1996.

Arthur M. Last

Element (mathematics) see **Locus; Set theory**

Element, rare earth see **Lanthanides**

Elementary particles see **Subatomic particles**

Elements, formation of

Elements are identified by the nuclei of the atoms of which they are made. For example, an atom having six protons in its nucleus is carbon, and one having 26 protons is iron. There are over 80 naturally occurring elements, with uranium (92 protons) being the heaviest (heavier nuclei have been produced in reactors on Earth). Nuclei also contain certain neutrons, usually in numbers greater than the number of protons.

Heavy elements can be formed from light ones by nuclear fusion reactions; these are nuclear reactions in which atomic nuclei merge together. The simplest reactions involve hydrogen, whose nucleus consists only of a single proton, but other fusion reactions, involving mergers of heavier nuclei, are also possible. When the universe formed in an initial state of very high temperature and density called the big bang, the first elements to exist were the simplest ones: hydrogen, helium (two

protons), and little else. But we and the Earth are made of much heavier elements, so a major question for scientists is how these heavier elements were created.

When the universe was created in the big bang only the lightest elements formed: hydrogen, helium, and tiny quantities of lithium and beryllium. Hydrogen and helium dominated; the lithium and beryllium were only made in trace quantities. The other 88 elements found in nature were created in nuclear reactions in the stars and in huge stellar explosions known as supernovas. Stars like the Sun and planets like the Earth containing elements other than hydrogen and helium could only form after the first generation of massive stars exploded as supernovas, and scattered the atoms of heavy elements throughout the galaxy to be recycled.

History

The first indications that stars manufacture elements by nuclear reactions came in the late 1930s when Hans Bethe and C. F. von Weizsäcker independently deduced the energy source for the Sun and stars. Stars burn hydrogen into helium in fusion in their cores. They received the Nobel prize in physics for this work.

George Gamow championed the big bang theory in the 1940s. Working with Ralph Alpher, he suggested all the elements formed during the big bang. With Robert

Herman in the early 1950s they used early computers to try to work out in detail how all the elements could be formed during the big bang. This attempt was unsuccessful, but was one of the first large scientific problems to be tackled with early computers. Astronomers now realize that heavier elements cannot form this way. The problem was that the universe cooled too rapidly as it expanded, and the extremely high temperatures required for nuclear reactions to occur did not last long enough for the creation of elements heavier than lithium or beryllium. By the time the universe had the raw materials to form the heavier elements, it was too cool.

In 1957, Margaret Burbidge, Geoffery Burbidge, William Fowler, and Fred Hoyle (referred to as B^2FH) published a monumental paper in which they outlined the specific nuclear reactions that occur in stars and supernovas to form the heavy elements. Fowler received the 1983 Nobel Prize in physics for his role in understanding nuclear processes in stars.

Formation of elements

During most of their lives, stars fuse hydrogen into helium in their cores, but little helium is produced this way. Most of the helium in the universe was made during the initial big bang. However, when the star's core runs out of hydrogen, the star begins to die out and in the process make heavier elements. The star expands, into a red giant star. A typical red giant at the Sun's location would extend to roughly the Earth's orbit. The star now begins to manufacture carbon atoms by fusing three helium atoms. Occasionally a fourth helium atom combines to manufacture oxygen. Stars of about the Sun's mass stop with this helium burning stage and collapse into white dwarfs about the size of the Earth expelling their outer layers in the process. Only the more massive stars play a significant role in manufacturing heavy elements.

Massive stars become much hotter internally than stars like the Sun, and additional reactions can occur after all the hydrogen in the core has been converted to helium. The massive stars then begin a series of nuclear burning, or reaction, stages: carbon burning, neon burning, oxygen burning, and silicon burning. In the carbon burning stage, carbon undergoes fusion reactions to produce oxygen, neon, sodium, and magnesium. During the neon burning stage, neon fuses into oxygen and magnesium. During the oxygen burning stage, oxygen forms silicon and other elements between magnesium and sulfur on the periodic table. These elements then produce elements near iron on the periodic table, during the silicon burning stage. Massive stars produce iron and the lighter elements by these fusion reactions and

Hans Bethe.

subsequent radioactive decay of unstable isotopes. Elements heavier than iron are more difficult to make. Fusion reactions of elements lighter than iron release energy, but elements heavier than iron require energy to fuse, so the reactions in a star's core stop once iron has been created.

How then are elements heavier than iron made? There are two processes, both triggered by the addition of neutrons to atomic nuclei: the s (slow) process and the r (rapid) process. In both processes, a nucleus captures a neutron, which emits an electron and decays into a proton, a reaction called a beta decay. One proton at a time, these processes build up elements heavier than iron. Some elements can be made by either process, but the s process can only make elements up to bismuth (83 protons) on the periodic table. Elements heavier than bismuth require the r process.

The slower s process occurs the star is still in the red giant stage. This is possible because the reactions create excess energy, which keeps the star stable. But once iron has formed in the star's core, further reactions suck heat energy from the core, leading to catastrophic collapse, followed by rebound and explosion. The r process occurs rapidly when the star explodes. During a supernova, the star releases as much energy as the Sun does in 10 billion years and also releases the large number of neutrons needed for the r process, creating new elements during the outburst. The elements that were made during the red giant stage, and those that are made during the supernova explosion, are spewed out into space. The atoms are then available as raw materials for the next generation of stars, which can contain elements that were not made during the big bang. These elements are the basic materials for life as we know it. During their death throes, massive stars sow the seeds for life in the universe.

KEY TERMS

. . . .

Beta decay—The splitting of a neutron into a proton and electron.

Fusion—Nuclear reactions in which two atoms join to make a heavier atom.

Red giant—An extremely large star that is red because of its relatively cool surface.

r process—Rapid process, the process by which some elements heavier than iron are made in a supernova.

s process—Slow process, the process by which some elements heavier than iron are made in a red giant.

See also Big bang theory; Cosmology; Nuclear fission; Nuclear fusion; Star; Stellar evolution; Supernova.

Further Reading:
Bartusiak, Marcia. *Through a Universe Darkly.* New York: HarperCollins, 1993.

Kirshner, Robert. "The Earth's Elements." *Scientific American* (October 1994): 59.

Riordan, Michael and David N. Schramm. *The Shadows of Creation.* New York: Freeman, 1991.

Zeilik, Michael. *Astronomy: The Evolving Universe.* 7th ed. New York: Wiley, 1994.

Paul A. Heckert

Element, transuranium

A transuranium (beyond uranium) element is any of the chemical elements with atomic numbers higher than 92, which is the atomic number of uranium.

Ever since the eighteenth century when chemists began to recognize certain substances as chemical elements, uranium had been the element with the highest atomic weight; it had the heaviest atoms of all the elements that could be found on Earth. The general assumption was that no heavier elements could exist on this planet. The reasoning went like this: Heavy atoms are heavy because of their heavy nuclei, and heavy nuclei are unstable, or radioactive; they spontaneously transform themselves into other elements. Uranium and several even lighter elements—all those with atomic numbers higher than 83 (bismuth)—were already radioactive. Therefore, still heavier ones would probably be so unstable that they could not have lasted for the billions of years that the Earth has existed, even if they were present when the Earth was formed. In fact, uranium itself has a half–life that is just about equal to the age of the Earth (4.5 billion years), so only one–half of all the uranium that was present when the Earth was formed is still here.

If we could create atoms of elements beyond uranium, however, perhaps they would be stable enough to hang around long enough for us to study them. A few years, or even hours, would do. But in order to make an atom of an element with an atomic number higher than uranium which has 92 protons in its nucleus, we would have to add protons to its nucleus; one added proton would make an atom of element number 93, two added protons would make element 94, and so on. There was no way to add protons to nuclei, though, until the invention of the cyclotron in the early 1930s by Ernest Lawrence at the University of California at Berkeley. The cyclotron could speed up protons or ions (charged atoms) of other elements to high energies and fire them at atoms of uranium (or any other element) like machine–gun bullets at a target. In the resulting nuclear smashup, maybe some protons from the bullet nuclei would stick in some of the "hit" target nuclei, thereby transforming them into nuclei of higher atomic numbers. And that is exactly what happened. Shooting light atoms at heavy atoms has turned out to be the main method for producing even heavier atoms far beyond uranium.

Such processes are called *nuclear reactions*. Using nuclear reactions in cyclotrons and other "atom smashing machines," nuclear chemists and physicists over the years have learned a great deal about the atomic nucleus and the fundamental particles that make up the universe. Making new transuranium elements has been only a small part of it.

The road beyond uranium

Like any series of elements, the transuranium elements have similarities and differences in their chemical properties. Also like any other series of elements, they must fit into the periodic table in positions that match their atomic numbers and electronic structures. The transuranium elements are often treated as a "family," not because their properties are closely related (although some of them are), but only because they represent the latest, post–1940 extension of the periodic table. Uniting them is their history of discovery and their radioactivity, more than their chemical properties.

Inner–Transition Metals

*Lanthanides	58 140.115 Ce cerium	59 140.90765 Pr praseodymium	60 144.24 Nd neodymium	61 (145) Pm promethium	62 150.36 Sm samarium	63 151.965 Eu europium	64 157.25 Gd gadolinium	65 158.92534 Tb terbium	66 162.50 Dy dysprosium	67 164.93032 Ho holmium	68 167.26 Er erbium	69 168.93421 Tm thulium	70 173.04 Yb ytterbium	71 174.967 Lu lutetium
†Actinides	90 232.0381 Th thorium	91 (231) Pa protactinium	92 238.0289 U uranium	93 (237) Np neptunium	94 (244) Pu plutonium	95 (243) Am americium	96 (247) Cm curium	97 (247) Bk berkelium	98 (251) Cf californium	99 (252) Es einsteinium	100 (257) Fm fermium	101 (258) Md mendelevium	102 (259) No nobelium	103 (262) Lr lawrencium

Figure 1.

Transuranium elements and the periodic table

We can think of the atomic numbers of the transuranium elements as mileposts along a Transuranium Highway that begins at uranium (milepost 92) and runs onward into transuranium country as far as milepost 110. As we begin our trip at 92, however, we realize that we are already three mileposts into another series of elements that began back at milepost 89: the *actinides*. Actinide Road runs from milepost 89 to 103, so it overlaps the middle of our 92–110 transuranium trip. (The road signs between 92 and 103 read both "Actinide Road" and "Transuranium Highway.")

Figure 1 is the bottom row of the periodic table, showing where the actinides and all of the transuranium elements fit in. The names that go along with the symbols of the elements from 93 to 109 are: Np = neptunium, Pu = plutonium, Am = americium, Cm = curium, Bk = berkelium, Cf = californium, Es = einsteinium, Fm = fermium, Md = mendelevium, No = nobelium, Lr = lawrencium, Ru = rutherfordium, Ha = hahnium, Sg = seaborgium, Ns = nielsbohrium, Hs = hassium, and Mt = meitnerium. Element 110 has not yet been named.

The names of some of the transuranium elements and who discovered them have been the subjects of a raging battle among the world's chemists. In one corner of the name–game ring is the International Union of Pure and Applied Chemistry (IUPAC), a more–or–less official organization that among other things "makes the rules" about how new chemicals should be named. In another corner is the American Chemical Society (ACS) and most of the American and German scientists who discovered transuranium elements. The names listed above and in Fig. 1 are the ACS recommendations.

History of the transuranium elements

In 1940, the first element with an atomic number higher than 92 was found, element number 93, now known as neptunium. This set off a search for even heavier elements. In the 15 years between 1940 and 1955 eight more were found, going up to atomic number 101 (mendelevium). Most of this work was done at the University of California laboratories in Berkeley, led by nuclear chemists Albert Ghiorso and Glenn Seaborg. Since 1955, the effort to find new transuranium elements has continued, although with rapidly diminishing returns. As of 1995 a total of 18 transuranium elements had been made, ranging up to atomic number 110. While the first nine transuranium elements were discovered within a 15 year period, discovering the last nine took almost 40 years. It wasn't that the experiments took that long; they had to await the development of more powerful cyclotrons and other ion–accelerating machines. This is because these transuranium elements do not exist on Earth; they have to be synthesized—made artificially in the laboratory.

The transuranium story began when nuclear fission was discovered by Otto Hahn and Fritz Strassman in Germany in 1938. Chemists were soon investigating the hundreds of new radioactive isotopes that were formed in fission, which spews its nuclear products over half the periodic table. In 1940, E. M. McMillan and P. Abelson at the University of California in Berkeley found that one of those isotopes could not be explained as a product of nuclear fission. Instead, it appeared to have been formed by the radioactive transformation—rather than the fission— of uranium atoms, and that it had the atomic number 93.

When uranium was bombarded with neutrons, some uranium nuclei apparently had become radioactive and had increased their atomic number from 92 to 93 by emitting a (negative) beta particle. (It was already known that radioactive beta decay could increase the atomic number of an atom.) Because uranium had been named after Uranus, the seventh planet from the sun in our solar system, the discoverers named their "next" element *neptunium*, after the next (eighth) planet. When McMillan and other chemists at Berkeley, including G. Seaborg, E. Segrè, A. Wahl and J. W. Kennedy, found that neptunium further decayed into the next higher element with atomic number 94, they named it plutonium, after the next (ninth) planet, Pluto. From there on, new transuranium elements were synthesized by using nuclear reactions in cyclotrons and other accelerators.

These experiments become more and more difficult as atomic numbers increase. For one thing, if you want to make the next higher transuranium element, you have to have some of the preceding one to use as a target, and the world's supply of that one may be only a few micrograms—a very tiny target indeed. It's worse than trying to hit a mosquito at 50 yards with a BB gun. While the probability of hitting one of these target nuclei with a "bullet" atom is incredibly small, the probability is even smaller that you will transform some of the nuclei you *do* hit into a particular higher atomic number nucleus, because once a "bullet" atom crashes into a target atom many different nuclear reactions can happen. To make matters even worse, the target element is likely to be very unstable, with a half–life of only a few minutes. So it's not only an incredibly tiny target, it's a rapidly disappearing one. The mosquitoes are vanishing before your eyes while you're trying to shoot them.

The heaviest transuranium elements have therefore been made literally one atom at a time. Claims of discovery of new transuranium elements have often been based on the production of only half a dozen atoms. It is no wonder that the three major groups of discoverers, Americans, Russians and Germans, have had "professional disagreements" about who discovered which element first. When organizations such as IUPAC and the ACS get into the act, trying to choose a fair name that honors the true discoverers of each element, the disagreements can get rather heated.

Cruising the transuranium highway

Following is a brief sketch of each of the transuranium elements. The chemical properties of these elements have in most cases been determined by nuclear chemists using incredibly ingenious experiments, often working with one atom at a time, and with radioisotopes that last only a few minutes. We will omit the chemical properties of these elements, however, because they are not available in sufficient quantities to be used in any practical chemical way; only their *nuclear* properties are important.

Neptunium (93)—Named after the planet Neptune, the next planet "in line" after Uranus, for which uranium (92) was named. Discovered in 1940 by McMillan and Abelson at the Radiation Laboratory of University of California, Berkeley (now called the Lawrence Radi-

ation Laboratory), as a product of the radioactive decay of uranium after it was bombarded with neutrons. The neutrons produced uranium–239 from the "ordinary" uranium–238. The resulting uranium–239 has a half–life of 23.5 minutes, changing itself into to neptunium–239, which has a half–life of 2.35 days. Trace amounts of neptunium actually occur on Earth, because it is continually being formed in uranium ores by the small numbers of ever–present neutrons.

Plutonium (94)—First found in 1940 by Seaborg, McMillan, Kennedy, and Wahl at Berkeley as a secondary product of the radioactive decay of neutron-bombarded uranium. The most important isotope of plutonium is plutonium–239, which has a half–life of 24,390 years. It is produced in large quantities from the neutron bombardment of uranium–238 while ordinary nuclear power reactors are operating. When the reactor fuel is reprocessed, the plutonium can be recovered. This fact is of critical strategic importance because plutonium–239 is the major ingredient in nuclear weapons.

Americium (95)—Named after the Americas because europium, its just–above neighbor in the periodic table, had been named after Europe. Found by Seaborg, James, Morgan, and Ghiorso in 1944 in neutron–irradiated plutonium during the Manhattan Project (the atomic bomb project) in Chicago in 1944.

Curium (96)—Named after Marie Curie, the discoverer of the elements radium and polonium and the world's first nuclear chemist, and her husband, physicist Pierre Curie. First identified by Seaborg, James, and Ghiorso in 1944 after bombarding plutonium–239 with helium nuclei in a cyclotron.

Berkelium (97)—Named after Berkeley, California. Discovered in 1949 by Thompson, Ghiorso, and Seaborg by bombarding a few milligrams of americium–241 with helium ions. By 1962 the first visible quantity of berkelium had been produced. It weighed three billionths of a gram.

Einsteinium (99)—Named after Albert Einstein. Discovered by Ghiorso and his coworkers at Berkeley in the debris from the world's first large thermonuclear (hydrogen bomb) explosion, in the Pacific Ocean in 1952. About a hundredth of a microgram of einsteinium was separated out of the bomb products.

Fermium (100)—Named after physicist Enrico Fermi. Isolated in 1952 from the debris of a thermonuclear explosion in the Pacific by Ghiorso, working with scientists from Berkeley, the Argonne National Laboratory, and the Oak Ridge National Laboratory. Also produced by a group at the Nobel Institute in Stockholm by bombarding uranium with oxygen ions in a *heavy ion accelerator*, a kind of cyclotron.

Mendelevium (101)—Named after Dmitri Mendeleev, originator of the periodic table. Made by Ghiorso, Harvey, Choppin, Thompson, and Seaborg at Berkeley in 1955 by bombarding einsteinium–253 with helium ions. The discovery was based on the detection of only 17 atoms.

Nobelium (102)—Named after Alfred Nobel, Swedish discoverer of dynamite and founder of the Nobel Prizes. Produced and positively identified in 1958 by Ghiorso, Sikkeland, Walton, and Seaborg at Berkeley, by bombarding curium with carbon ions. It was also produced, but not clearly identified as element 102, by a group of U.S., British, and Swedish scientists in 1957 at the Nobel Institute of Physics in Stockholm. IUPAC hastily named the element for the Swedish workers. The Berkeley chemists eventually agreed to the Swedish name, but not to the Swedes' credit for discovery. Ironically, in 1992 the International Unions of Pure and Applied Chemistry and of Pure and Applied Physics (IUPAC and IUPAP) credited the discovery of nobelium to a group of Russian scientists at the Joint Institute for Nuclear Research at Dubna, near Moscow.

Lawrencium (103)—Named for Ernest O. Lawrence, inventor of the cyclotron. Produced in 1961 by Ghiorso, Sikkeland, Larsh and Latimer at Berkeley by bombarding californium with boron ions.

Elements 104 to 110—The identities of the true discoverers of these elements are tangled in an assortment of very difficult experiments performed by different groups of scientists at the American Lawrence Radiation Laboratory in Berkeley, the German Gesellschaft für Schwerionenforschung (Institute for Heavy–Ion Research) in Darmstadt, the Russian Joint Institute for Nuclear Research in Dubna, and the Swedish Nobel Institute of Physics in Stockholm.

The end of the road?

The Transuranium Highway would appear to be coming to a dead end for two reasons. Chemists don't have large enough samples of the heaviest transuranium elements to use as targets in their cyclotrons, and the materials are so radioactive anyway that they only last for seconds or at most a few minutes.

Element 110 has been made by a slightly different trick—shooting medium–weight atoms at each other. The nuclei of these atoms can fuse together and hopefully stick, to make a nucleus of a transuranium element. In November of 1994, a group of nuclear chemists at the Heavy Ion Research Center at Darmstadt, Germany reported that by shooting nickel atoms (atomic number 28) at lead atoms (atomic number 82),

they had made three atoms of element 110 (=28+82), which lasted for about a ten–thousandth of a second.

In spite of this gloomy picture, nuclear chemists are trying very hard to make *much* heavier—"super-heavy"—elements. There are theoretical reasons for believing that they would be more stable and would stick around much longer.

The Transuranium Highway may be still under construction.

See also Elements, families of; Periodic table; Radioactivity.

Further Reading:
Harvey, Bernard G., "Criteria for the Discovery of Chemical Elements," *Science*, Vol. 193, 1976, pp. 1271–2.
Hoffman, Darleane C., "The Heaviest Elements," *Chemical & Engineering News*, May 2, 1994, pp. 14–34.
Seaborg, Glenn T. and Loveland, Walter D., *The Elements Beyond Uranium*, New York: John Wiley & Sons, Inc., 1990.

Robert L. Wolke

Elephant

Elephants are large four–legged, herbivorous mammals, with a tough, almost hairless hide a long, flexible trunk, and usually two ivory tusks growing from the upper jaw. Only two species of elephant exist today, the African elephant (*Loxodonta africana*) and the Asian (or Indian) elephant (*Elephas maximus*), both of which are threatened or endangered. The two species differ in appearance but are similar in structure and behavior. African elephants are the largest land animals, weighing up to 5 tons. There are two subspecies, the African bush elephant (*Loxodonta africana africana*) and the African forest elephant (*Loxodonta africana cyclotis*). Bush elephants inhabit grasslands, while forest elephants live in equatorial rain forests. Asian elephants are widely domesticated, with the few surviving wild elephants living mainly in forests and woodlands. Field workers have differing opinions of the elephant's life span, some estimating between 60 and 80 years while others estimate over 100 years.

Evolution

The order Proboscidea includes three suborders, including the Elephantoidea. The ancestors of today's elephants lived between 50 and 70 million years ago, and were small beasts, standing about two feet (0.75 m) high. The suborder Elephantoidea once included three families, several genera, and hundreds of species, originating in North Africa long before it became desert. From there, elephants spread to every continent except Australia and Antarctica. The family Elephantidae includes only two species today: the Asian or Indian elephant and the African elephant. Mammoths and mastodons also belong to the suborder Elephantoidea, becoming extinct only about 10,000 years ago.

About 400,000 years ago Asian elephants inhabited a wider range, including Africa. This species now survives only in Asia, from India to Sumatra and Borneo. The single species of Asian elephant has three subspecies, *Elephas maximus maximus* of Sri Lanka, *E. m. indicus* of India, Indochina, and Borneo, and *E. m. sumatranus* of Sumatra. African elephants only ever existed in Africa, appearing about four million years ago. As recently as a hundred years ago, some 10 million African elephants inhabited that continent. By 1990 their numbers were reduced to just 600,000.

Body

Asian and African elephants can be distinguished by the shape of their backs, the Asian having a convex, gently sloping back and the African a concave or saddle–shaped back. Male elephants (bulls) are larger than females (cows), being 20%–40% taller and up to 70% heavier. The average African adult bull weighs about five tons and measures about eight ft (2.4 m) to the shoulder. The largest elephant on record is a magnificent bull, now mounted in the Smithsonian Museum in Washington, D.C., standing a massive 13 ft 2 in (4 m) at the shoulder.

Skin texture varies from the tough, thick, wrinkled, folds of the back and forehead, to the soft, thin, pliable skin of the breast, ears, belly, and the underside of the trunk. The tough skin bears a few, scattered, bristly hairs, while the thin skin on the trunk, chin, ear openings, eyelids, knees, wrists, and tip of the tail has thicker hair. Daily skin care includes showers, dusting with sand, and full–bodied mud–packs which are later rubbed off against a tree or boulder, removing dead skin as well. This keeps the skin moist, supple, protected from the sun and insects, and also helps keep the animal cool.

Limbs

Supporting the elephant's massive body are four sturdy, pillar–like legs. Although the back legs are slightly longer than the front legs, the shoulder makes the forelimbs look longer. The back legs have knees with knee–caps, while the front leg joints are more like wrists. Elephants kneel on their "wrists," stand upright on their back legs, sit on their haunches, and have even been trained to balance on their front feet. The feet have thick, sponge–like pads with ridged soles which act as shock–absorbers and climbing boots, helping these sure–footed animals climb steep embankments and negotiate narrow pathways with amazing dexterity. The African species has four toenails on its round front feet, and three on its oval–shaped back feet; the Asian species has five toes on the front feet and four toes on the back feet. In spite of their size, elephants can move quickly, but cannot make sustained runs, as all four feet are never off the ground at one time. Elephants often doze on their feet, but sleep lying down for about one to three hours at night.

Head

Elephants have a large skull which supports the massive weight of their tusks. The size and shape of the skull helps distinguish between African and Asian elephants and between female and male of the same species. Asian elephants have a high, dome–shaped forehead while African elephants display a lower, more gently angled forehead. Heads of the males are larger in both species. Also in both species, the neck is short, making the head relatively immobile. To see behind, elephants must move their entire body; they display excited, restless behavior and turn quickly when detecting unfamiliar sounds or smells from the rear.

Mouth and Trunk

Elephants have a small mouth and a large, mobile tongue which will not extend past the short lower lip. Contributing to the elephant's unique appearance is its long, strong, flexible trunk, which is a fusion and elongation of the nose and upper lip. The trunk, with no bones and more than 100,000 muscles, is so strong and flexible it can coil like a snake around a tree and uproot it. At the end of this mighty "limb," which trails on the ground unless curled up at the end, are two nostrils and flexible finger–like projections, making the tip so sensitive it can wipe a grain of sand from the elephant's eye and detect delicate scents blowing in the breeze. With this fascinating appendage, the elephant feeds by plucking grass from the ground or foliage from a tree and placing them in its mouth. Water drawn up the trunk may either be squirted into the mouth for drinking or sprayed over the body for bathing. Loud trumpeting sounds and soft, affectionate murmurs echo through the trunk, which tenderly disciplines, caresses and guides young offspring; strokes its mate; fights off

Wild asiatic elephants (*Elephas maximus*) in Yala National Park, Tissamaharama, Sri Lanka.

predators; and pushes over trees. The trunk is an essential and vulnerable organ, the object of attack by an enemy and to which damage causes extreme pain and can even lead to the animal's death.

Teeth

The tusks of elephants begin as two front teeth which drop out after about a year. In their place grow ivory tusks which eventually protrude from beneath the upper lip. The tusks of female Asian elephants, however, remain very short and are barely visible. Male African elephants grow the largest tusks, the longest recorded measuring approximately 137 in (348 cm) and weighing over 220 lbs (100 kg) each. Today, however, tusks are generally much smaller in wild elephants because many of the older animals have been slaughtered for their ivory. Although there are some variations, the long, cylindrical tusks grow in a gradual upward curve, somewhat resembling the sliver of a new moon. Elephants use their tusks as weapons in combat, to dig up roots, strip bark off trees, lift objects, and—for females—to establish feeding dominance. Tusks continue to grow throughout the animal's life at an average of about 5 in (12.7 cm) a year; however, their length is

not an accurate measure of the animals age, as the tips wear and break with daily use and during combat use.

Elephants have large grinding, molar teeth which masticate (grind) their plant diet with a backward–forward jaw action. These teeth fall out when worn down, and are replaced by new, larger teeth. During its lifetime, an elephant will grow 24 of these large molar teeth, each weighing up to nine pounds (four kg) in older animals. Only four teeth, two on each side of the jaw, are in use at any one time. As the teeth wear down, they move forward; the new teeth grow from behind and the worn teeth drop out. This pattern repeats six times over the elephant's lifetime and the most common method of determining an elephant's age is by tooth and jaw examination. Once all of its teeth have fallen out, an elephant can no longer eat, and will soon die.

Ears

One astute elephant observer noted that "the ears of Asian elephants are shaped like India, and African elephants like Africa!" The ears of African elephants are much larger than those of Asian elephants, and the ears of the African bush elephants are larger than those of the African forest elephants. African elephants cool off

An African elephant (*Loxodonta africana*) in Amboseli National Park, Kenya.

by fanning themselves with their ears and, conversely, in extreme cold elephants must increase their activity levels to produce enough body heat to prevent their ears being severely frostbitten. Elephants have a keen sense of hearing, and spread their ears wide to pick up distant sounds; the spread out ears also intimidate enemies by making the elephants appear larger.

Eyes

The eyes of elephants are about the same size as a human's. The eyes are usually dark brown, with upper and lower lids, and long eyelashes on the upper lid. With one eye on either side of their head elephants have a wide visual field, although their eyesight is relatively poor, particularly in bright sunlight.

Social Behavior

Few animals other than humans have a more complex social network than elephants, which fieldworkers are just beginning to decipher. These outgoing, emotionally demonstrative animals rarely fight among themselves and peacefully coexist with other animals. Elephants give and receive love, care intensely for their young, grieve deeply for their dead, get angry, show fear, and are more intelligent than all other animals except the higher primates.

Group Structure

Each elephant troop has its own home range, but territorial fights are rare even though ranges often overlap. While several hundred elephants may roam a similar range, small "kin groups" form between female relatives. The leader of each group is a respected old female with years of accumulated knowledge. This matriarch is the mother and grandmother of other members but sometimes allows her sisters and their offspring to join the group. Once a male reaches maturity, he is forced to leave. The entire group looks to the matriarch for guidance, particularly in the face of danger. Her actions, based on her superior knowledge, will determine whether the group flees or stands its ground. Young members learn from their elders how to find water and food during drought, when to begin travel, and many other survival skills. This knowledge is passed on from generation to generation.

Once a male elephant reaches sexual maturity at 12 years or older, the matriarch no longer tolerates him in the group. He will live basically alone or perhaps join a small, loosely–knit group of other males. Bull elephants seldom form long–term relationships with other males, but often one or two young males accompany an old

bull, perhaps to protect, but more importantly, to learn from him. Bulls often spar with each other to establish a dominance hierarchy. Elephants have excellent memories: once this social hierarchy is established, the same two elephants not only recognize each other, perhaps after many years, but know which one is dominant. This way, they avoid fighting again to reestablish dominance. After about 25 years of age, male elephants experience annual periods of heightened sexuality called "musth," which lasts about a week in the younger animals and perhaps three or four months as they near their 50s. During this time they aggressively search out females, challenge other bulls, and even more dominant males will back down. Different bulls come into musth at different times of the year; however, two bulls in musth will often fight to the death.

Mating

Female elephants come into estrus (heat), marking ovulation and the ability to get pregnant, for only a few days each year. Because the mating season is short, female elephants are never far from adult males. The scent of female elephants in estrus attracts male bulls, and a receptive female will hold her head high, producing a low, rumbling invitation as she leaves her group and runs quickly across the plains chased by the bulls. It appears she actually chooses her mate, for she seldom stops for a young bull but slows down for a larger, dominant male who, once she allows him to catch her, gently rests his trunk across her back in a caress. They may mate several times, and he may stay with her until the end of her estrus, warding off other bulls and fighting if necessary. She may, however, mate with others. Because males play no part in raising the young and are not needed to protect the mother or baby, their role appears to be purely reproductive.

At the end of estrus, the cow returns to her group and the male goes off in search of another mate. The gestation period of female elephants lasts for 22 months, longer than any other animal; pregnancies are spaced from three to nine years apart. There is usually only one offspring, but twin births do occur and both calves may survive under favorable conditions. There is much excitement in the group during a birth, and another female almost always tends to the birthing mother. An adult female and her sexually immature offspring are a "family unit" within the group. However, females assist each other in raising the young, with one mother even sometimes nursing the calf of another. In general, females reach sexual maturity between the age of 12 to 15 years and, over the course of 60 years, will bear anywhere from five to 15 offspring.

Communication

Elephants teach and learn by behavioral examples and "talk" with vocalized sounds which can be described as screams, trumpets, growls, and rumbles. Originating from the throat or head, these calls can signal danger and express anger, joy, sadness and sexual invitation. An animal separated from its family will make "contact rumbles," low, vibrating sounds which can be heard at great distances. Once reunited, the family engages in a "greeting ceremony," reserved strictly for close relatives, in which excited rumbling, trumpeting, touching of trunks, urinating and defecating occurs. Vocal sounds range from high–pitched squeaks to extremely powerful infrasonic sounds of a frequency much lower than can be heard by the human ear.

Death

Elephants mourn deeply for their dead and often cover them with leaves, dirt, and grass. An animal will stand over the body of a dead loved one, gently rocking back and forth as other animals caress the mourner with their trunks. One field–worker watching such a display wrote: "This isn't just a dead elephant; it is a living elephant's dead relative or friend."

Habitat and Food

Because of their high intelligence level, elephants can adapt to and modify habitat, while their wide range of food products permit habitation of a diverse range of environments, including forests, woodlands, grassy plains, swampy areas, and sparsely vegetated desert lands. Unfortunately, because of massive poaching for ivory and the destruction of much of the elephant's natural habitat, most African elephants are now restricted to the protection of national parks. Not so long ago, however, they freely followed age–old seasonal migration routes from one habitat to another.

Elephants need massive quantities of food, perhaps 300–350 lbs (136–159 kg) a day, although when body mass is divided by bodyweight elephants eat less than mice. The diet of elephants includes roots, bark, grass, leaves, berries, and seedpods. Elephants will uproot trees to obtain tasty treats from the top, or delicately pluck a single berry from a branch. Elephants never roam far from water, and will travel great distances in search of it. They may drink up to 50 gallons of water a day, and after drinking their fill, will splash themselves with water and mud, wash their young, and sometimes just frolic, tossing and squirting water about while their young splash, play, and roll in the mud. Surprisingly, populations of these water–loving creatures inhabit desert areas, using their tusks and trunk to dig for water

KEY TERMS

Estrus—Time during which a female elephant can conceive.

Musth—Period of heightened sexuality and aggressiveness in the male elephant.

under dry river beds. Knowing where to dig is handed down from one generation to another.

The Future

Only a few surviving elephant herds remain in the wild. In Asia, elephants are venerated; however they are highly valued as domestic animals for work and for transport and each tamed animal must be captured from the wild. One–third of the remaining 35,000 Asian elephants are now domesticated, threatening the survival of wild herds.

The combination of habitat loss and ivory poaching have brought the African elephants close to extinction. Ivory has been traded for thousands of years, but this trade escalated dramatically after the middle of this century. During the 1980s, 100,000 elephants were being slaughtered each year, their tusks ending up as billiard balls, piano keys, jewelry and ornaments. The oldest males, bearing the biggest tusks, were killed first, but as their populations diminished, younger males and females were also slaughtered, leaving young calves to grieve inconsolably and possibly die of starvation.

The "elephant holocaust" was brought to public attention in the 1970s and long and bitter battles ensued between government authorities, ivory traders, and conservationists. Not until 1989 was a ban imposed on commercial ivory trade. In the early 1990s, elephant kills in Kenya and other African countries dropped to almost zero but by then the total surviving population of elephants had been reduced to very low levels. Today, elephants are worth more alive than dead, for ivory prices have crashed from $30 a kilogram to $3, and tourists coming to see the elephants bring hard currency to African governments, totaling more than $200 million a year.

Further Reading:

Douglas–Hamilton, Iain and Oria. *Battle For the Elephant.* New York: Viking Penguin, 1992.

Hayes, Gary. *Mammoths, Mastodons, and Elephants—Biology, Behavior and the Fossil Record.* Cambridge: Cambridge University Press, 1991.

Redmond, Ian. *The Elephant Book.* Woodstock: The Over-
    look Press, 1991.
Moss, Cynthia. *Elephant Memories: Thirteen Years of Life in
    an Elephant Family.* New York: William Morrow and
    Company, Inc, 1988.
Scullard, H. H. *The Elephant in the Greek and Roman World.*
    Ithaca: Cornell University Press, 1974.

Marie L. Thompson

Elephant fish see **Chimaeras**

Elephantiasis

Elephantiasis is an extreme symptom of human infection by a type of roundworm or nematode. It involves massive swelling of a limb or of the scrotum. The leg of an individual suffering from elephantiasis can become enlarged to two or three times normal diameter.

The actual name of the disease or infection which causes elephantiasis is lymphatic filariasis. Lymphatic filariasis is an important parasitic infection (a parasite is any organism which survives by living within another organism) in Africa, Latin America, the Pacific Islands, and Asia, and causes infection in about 250 million individuals (more than the number suffering from malaria). At one time, there was a small focus of infection which occurred in South Carolina, but this ended in the 1920s.

How lymphatic filariasis is spread

Lymphatic filariasis is caused by infestation by one of three nematodes (*Wucheria bancrofti, Brugia malayi,* or *Brugia timori*). These nematodes are spread to humans through the bite of mosquitoes. The mosquitoes are considered vectors, meaning that they spread the nematode, and therefore the disease. Humans are considered hosts, meaning that actual reproduction of the nematode occurs within the human body.

The nematode has a rather complicated lifecycle. The larval form lives within the mosquito, and it is this form which is transmitted to humans through the bite of an infected mosquito. The larvae pass into the human lymphatic system, where they mature into the adult worm. Adult worms living within the human body produce live offspring, known as microfilariae, which find their way into the bloodstream.

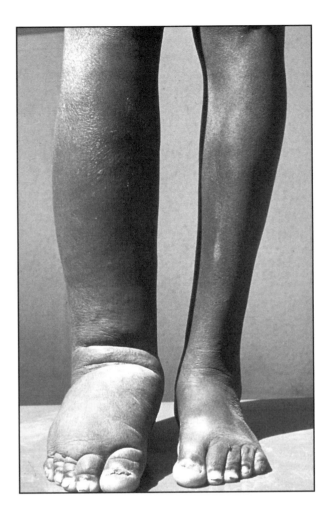

Elephantiasis.

Microfilariae have interesting properties which cause them to be released into the bloodstream primarily during the night; this property is called nocturnal periodicity. Therefore, the vectors (carriers) of filariasis, which deliver the infective worm larvae to the human host, tend to be the more nocturnal (active at night) species of mosquito.

Symptoms and progression of filarial disease

The majority of the suffering caused by filarial nematodes occurs because of blockage of the lymphatic system. The lymphatic system is made up of a network of vessels which serve to drain tissue fluid from all the major organs of the body, including the skin, and from all four limbs. These vessels pass through lymph nodes on their way to empty into major veins at the base of the neck and within the abdomen. While it was originally thought that blockage of lymph flow occurred due to the live adult worms coiling within the lymphatic vessels, it is now thought that the worst obstructions occur after the adult worms die.

While the worm is alive, the human immune system attempts to rid itself of the foreign invader by sending a variety of cells to the area, causing the symptoms of inflammation (redness, heat, swelling) in the infected node and lymph channels. The skin over these areas may become thickened and rough. In some cases, the host will experience systemic symptoms as well, including fever, headache, and fatigue. This complex of symptoms lasts seven to ten days, and may reappear as often as ten times in a year.

After the worm's death, the inflammatory process is accelerated, and includes the formation of tough, fibrous tissue which ultimately blocks the lymphatic vessel. Lymph fluid cannot pass through the blocked vessel, and the back up of fluid results in swelling (also called edema) below the area of blockage. Common areas to experience edema are arms, legs, and the genital area (especially the scrotum). These areas of edema are also prone to infection with bacterial agents. When extreme, lymphatic obstruction to vessels within the abdomen and chest can lead to rupture of those vessels, with spillage of lymph fluid into the abdominal and chest cavities.

An individual who picks up filarial disease while traveling does not tend to experience the more extreme symptoms of elephantiasis which occur in people who live for longer periods of time in areas where the disease is common. It is thought that people who live in these areas receive multiple bites by infected mosquitoes over a longer period of time, and are therefore host to many, many more nematodes than a traveler who is just passing through. The larger worm load, as the quantity of nematodes present within a single individual is called, contributes to the severity of the disease symptoms suffered by that individual.

Diagnosis

An absolutely sure diagnosis (called a definitive diagnosis) of filarial disease requires that the actual nematode be identified within body tissue or fluid from an individual experiencing symptoms of infection. This is not actually easy to accomplish, as the lymph nodes and vessels in which the nematodes dwell are not easy to access. Sometimes, blood samples can be examined to reveal the presence of the microfilariae. Interestingly enough, because of the nocturnal periodicity of these microfilariae, the patient's blood must be drawn at night to increase the likelihood of the sample actually containing the parasite.

KEY TERMS

Host—An animal or plant within which a parasite lives.

Microfilariae—Live offspring produced by adult nematodes within the host's body.

Nocturnal—Occurring at night.

Periodicity—The regularity with which an event occurs.

Vector—Latin for "one who carries." An organism which delivers an agent of infection to its host.

Many times, however, diagnosis is less sure, and relies on the patient's history of having been in an area where exposure to the nematode could have occurred, along with the appropriate symptoms, and the presence in the patient's blood of certain immune cells which could support the diagnosis of filarial disease.

Treatment

A drug called diethylcarbamazine (DEC) is quite effective at killing the microfilariae as they circulate in the blood, and injuring or killing some of the adult worms within the lymphatic vessels. An individual may require several treatment with DEC, as any adult worms surviving the original DEC treatment will go on to produce more microfilariae offspring.

As the nematodes die, they release certain chemicals which can cause an allergic–type reaction in the host, so many individuals treated with DEC will also need treatment with potent anti–allergy medications such as steroids and antihistamines. The tissue damage caused by elephantiasis is permanent, but the extreme swelling can be somewhat reduced by surgery or the application of elastic bandages or stockings.

Prevention

Prevention of lymphatic filariasis is very difficult, if not impossible, for people living in the areas where the causative nematodes are commonly found. Travelers to such areas can minimize exposure to the mosquito vectors through use of insect repellant and mosquito netting. Work is being done to determine whether DEC has any use as a preventive measure against the establishment of lymphatic filariasis.

See also Roundworms.

Further Reading:

Andreoli, Thomas E., et al. *Cecil Essentials of Medicine.* Philadelphia: W. B. Saunders Company, 1993.

Berkow, Robert, and Andrew J. Fletcher. *The Merck Manual of Diagnosis and Therapy.* Rahway, NJ: Merck Research Laboratories, 1992.

Isselbacher, Kurt J., et al. *Harrison's Principles of Internal Medicine.* New York: McGraw Hill, 1994.

Mandell, Douglas, et al. *Principles and Practice of Infectious Diseases.* New York: Churchill Livingstone, 1995.

Sherris, John C., et al. *Medical Microbiology.* Norwalk, CT: Appleton & Lange, 1994.

Rosalyn Carson–DeWitt

Elephant's ear see **Arum family**

Elephant shrews

Elephant shrews are relatively small mammals in the family Macroscelididae, order Insectivora. Elephant shrews have a characteristic long, narrow snout that is broad at the base, and very sensitive and flexible but not retractile. This snout is movable in circular manner at the base, and has nostrils at the end. There are five genera with some 185 species of elephant shrews, living in continental Africa and on the island of Zanzibar. Elephant shrews live in thorn bush country, grassy plains, thickets, the undergrowth of forests, and on rocky outcrops.

The head and body length is 3.7–12.3 in (95–315 mm) and the tail 3.1–10.3 in (80–265 mm). The tail is usually slender and covered with bristles, which may be rough at the underside and terminating in knobs. There is a naked black musk gland under the tail which secretes a highly scented substance, especially in females. The body is covered with soft fur which is lacking on the rump. The two bones of the hind legs are joined. The feet have four or five toes, and the hands have five fingers. The females have two or three pairs of mammae.

The elephant shrews are active mainly in daytime, but in hot weather they may they may be nocturnal. These animals may hide during the day when harassed by diurnal predators, but are often seen sun bathing. They reside singly or in pairs in burrows, ground depressions, rock crevices, and in the crevices of termite mounds. Burrows of rodents are occasionally used. When running elephant shrews leave runways with a broken appearance because of their jumping locomo-

An elephant shrew (*Elephantulus rozeti*).

tion which is like a bouncing ball, running on their hind legs, with the tail extended upward.

The smaller species of elephant shrews feed on ants, termites, and slender shoots, roots, and berries, while some larger species prefer beetles. The members of the genus *Elephantulus* and *Rhynchocyon* produce squeaks, while *Petrodromus* make cricket–like calls. *Elephantulus* and *Petrodromus* rap their hind feet when nervous or to give an alarm. Species of *Petrodromus* and *Rhynchocyon* are known to beat their tails on the ground.

Gestation takes about two months and one or two young are born relatively large and well developed, fully covered with fur and with eyes open at birth or soon after. There is a short nursing period and elephant shrews become sexually mature at five to six weeks of age. The life span in the wild is probably 18 months or less, but captive North African elephant shrews lived 40 months. Larger elephant shrews of the genus *Petrodromus* of East Africa are snared and eaten by natives.

See also Shrews.

Elephant snout fish

Elephant snout fish belong to a diverse group of fishes that comprise the Family Mormyridae. All are freshwater species that are confined to tropical parts of the African continent. Some 150 species have been described so far. The group takes its common or English name from the animals' extended snout. This adaptation is taken to the extreme in the genus *Gnathonemus* which has a pendulous, trumpet–shaped snout. This species, like many other in the genus, feeds almost exclusively on small crustaceans. In some species, the snout is so modified that it possesses only a tiny mouth equipped with just a few, but relatively large, teeth. In some species the "trunk" is pendulous, while in others it may be held straight out from the head. Although this adaptation may, at first sight appear at odds to a predatory fish, because these animals often frequent muddy waters, this slender, highly tactile snout is ideally suited for detecting and grasping small prey that hide in vegetation or amongst rubble or mud on the base of streams and lakes.

All mormyroid fish possess specialized electric organs, a feature that is not unusual in species living in either deep or gloomy waters. In the elephant snout fish, this feature is probably related to helping the fish to move around and avoid obstacles, as well as assisting with the location of prey. By emitting a series of short, pulsed electrical signals, the fish is able to detect and avoid obstacles. In the same way, it can detect and pinpoint living animals that also give off a small electric field. In this way they are able to identify potential food items and avoid conflict with other electric–producing snout fish. Members of the family Mormyridae probably constitute the most diverse group of electric fishes; most swim by synchronous movements of the opposite dorsal and anal fins, thereby keeping the electric organs arranged along the sides of the body in perfect alignment with the body.

Elevator

An elevator is an enclosed car that moves in a vertical shaft between the multi–story floors of a building carrying passengers or freight. All elevators are based on the principle of the counterweight, and modern elevators also use geared, electric motors and a system of cables and pulleys to propel them. The world's most often used means of mechanical transportation, it is also the safest. The elevator has played a crucial role in the development of the high–rise or skyscraper and is largely responsible for how our cities look today. It has become an indispensable factor of modern urban life.

History

Lifting loads by mechanical means goes back at least to the Romans who used primitive hoists operated by human, animal, or water power during their ambitious building projects. An elevator employing a counterweight is said to have been built in the 17th century by a Frenchman named Velayer, and it was also in that country that a passenger elevator was built in 1743 at the Versailles Palace for King Louis XV. By 1800, steam power was used to power such lift devices, and in 1830, several European factories were operating with hydraulic elevators that were pushed up and down by a plunger that worked in and out of a cylinder.

All of these lifting systems were based on the principle of the counterweight, by which the weight of one object is used to balance the weight of another object. For example, while it may be very difficult to pull up a heavy object using only a rope tied to it, this job can be made very easy if a weight is attached to the other end of the rope and hung over a pulley. This other weight, or counterweight, balances the first and makes it easy to pull up. Thus an elevator, which uses the counterweight system, never has to pull up the total weight of its load, but only the difference between the load–weight and that of the counterweight. Counterweights are also found inside the sash of old–style windows, in grandfather clocks, and in dumbwaiters.

Until mid–19th century, the prevailing elevator systems had two problems. The plunger system was very safe but also extremely slow, and it had obvious height limitations. If the plunger system was scrapped and the elevator car was hung from a rope to achieve higher speeds, the risk of the rope or cable breaking was an ever–present and very real danger. Safety was the main technical problem that the American inventor, Elisha Graves Otis (1811–1861) solved when he invented the first modern, fail–safe passenger elevator in 1853. In that year, Otis demonstrated his fail–safe mechanism at the Crystal Palace Exposition in London. In front of an astonished audience, he rode his invention high above the crowd and ordered that the cable holding the car be severed. When it was, instead of crashing to the ground, his fail–safe mechanism worked automatically and stopped the car dead.

The secret of Otis's success was a bow–shaped wagon spring device that would flex and jam its ends into the guide rails if tension on the rope or cable was released. What he had invented was a type of speed governor that translated an elevator's downward motion into a sideways, braking action. On March 23, 1857, Otis installed the first commercial passenger elevator in the Haughwout Department Store in New York, and the age of the skyscraper was begun. Until then, large city buildings were limited to five or six stories which was the maximum number of stairs people were willing to climb. When the iron–frame building was developed by architects in the 1880s, the elevator was ready to service them. By then, electric power had replaced the old

KEY TERMS
. . . .

Centrifugal force—The inertial reaction which causes a body to move away from a center about which it revolves.

Counterweight—The principle in which the weight of one object is used to balance the weight of another object; for an elevator, it is a weight which counterbalances the weight of the elevator car plus approximately 40% of its capacity load.

Hydraulic elevator—A power elevator where the energy is applied, by means of a liquid under pressure, in a cylinder equipped with a plunger or a piston; a direct-plunge elevator had the elevator car attached directly to the plunger or piston which went up and down a sunken shaft.

Microprocessor—The central processing unit of a microcomputer that contains the silicon chip which decodes instructions and controls operations.

Sheave—A wheel mounted in bearings and having one or more grooves over which a rope or ropes may pass.

Speed governor—A device that mechanically regulates the speed of a machine, preventing it from going any faster than a preset velocity.

steam-driven elevator, and the first commercial passenger elevator to be powered by electricity was installed in 1889 in the Desmarest Building in New York. In 1904, a "gearless" feature was added to the electric motor, making elevator speed virtually limitless. By 1915, automatic leveling had been introduced and cars would now stop precisely where they should.

Modern elevators

Today's passenger elevators are not fundamentally different from the Otis original. Practically all are electrically propelled and are lifted between two guide rails by steel cables that loop over a pulley device called a *sheave* at the top of the elevator shaft. They still employ the counterweight principle. The safety mechanism, called the overspeed governor, is an improved version of the Otis original. It uses centrifugal force that causes a system of weights to swing outward toward the rails should the car's speed exceed a certain limit. Although the travel system has changed little, its control system has been revolutionized. Speed and automation now characterize elevators, with microprocessors gradually replacing older electromechanical control systems. Speeds ranging up to 1,800 ft (550 m) per minute can be attained. Separate outer and inner doors are another essential safety feature, and most now have electrical sensors that pull the doors open if they sense something between them. Most also have telephones, alarm buttons, and emergency lighting. Escape hatches in their roofs serve both for maintenance and for emergency use.

Modern elevators can also be programmed to provide the fastest possible service with a minimum number of cars. They can further be set to sense the weight of a car and to bypass all landing calls when fully loaded. The 110-story twin towers of the World Trade Center in New York divide each building into three layers to minimize the space required for elevator service. In addition to regular passenger or freight elevators, today's specialized lifts are used in ships, dams, and even on rocket launch pads. Today's elevators are safe, efficient, and an essential part of our daily lives.

See also Building design/architecture.

Further Reading:

Jackson, Donald Dale. "Elevating Thoughts from Elisha Otis and Fellow Uplifters," *Smithsonian*. (November 1989): 211+.
Strakosch, George R. *Vertical Transportation: Elevators and Escalators*. New York: John Wiley & Sons, 1983.
The First One Hundred Years. New York: The Otis Elevator Company, 1953.

Leonard C. Bruno

Elk see **Moose**

Ellipse

An ellipse is a kind of oval. It is the oval formed by the intersection of a plane and a right circular cone—one of the four types of conic sections. The other three are the circle, the hyperbola, and the parabola. The ellipse is symmetrical along two lines, called *axes*. The *major axis* runs through the longest part of the ellipse and its center, and the *minor axis* is perpendicular to the major axis through the ellipse's center.

Other definitions of an ellipse

Ellipses are described in several ways, each way having its own advantages and limitations:

1. The set of points, the sum of whose distances from two fixed points (the foci, which lie on the major axis) is constant. That is, P: $PF_1 + PF_2$ = constant.

2. The set of points whose distances from a fixed point (the focus) and fixed line (the directrix) are in a constant ratio less than 1. That is, P: PF/PD = e, where 0 |less than| e |less than| 1. The constant, e, is the eccentricity of the ellipse.

3. The set of points (x,y) in a Cartesian plane satisfying an equation of the form $x^2/25 + y^2/16 = 1$. The equation of an ellipse can have other forms, but this one, with the center at the origin and the major axis coinciding with one of the coordinate axes, is the simplest.

4. The set of points (x,y) in a Cartesian plane satisfying the parametric equations x = a cos t and y = b sin t, where a and b are constants and t is a variable. Other parametric equations are possible, but these are the simplest.

Features

In working with ellipses it is useful to identify several special points, chords, measurements, and properties:

The major axis: The longest chord in an ellipse that passes through the foci. It is equal in length to the constant sum in Definition 1 above. In Definitions 3 and 4 the larger of the constants a or b is equal to the semimajor axis.

The center: The midpoint, C, of the major axis.

The vertices: The end points of the major axis.

The minor axis: The chord which is perpendicular to the major axis at the center. It is the shortest chord which passes through the center. In Definitions 3 and 4 the smaller of a or b is the semiminor axis.

The foci: The fixes points in Definitions 1 and 2. In any ellipse, these points lie on the major axis and are at a distance c on either side of the center. If a and b are the semimajor and semiminor axes respectively, then $a^2 = b^2 + c^2$. In the examples in Definitions 3 and 4, the foci are 3 units from the center.

The eccentricity: A measure of the relative elongation of an ellipse. It is the ratio e in Definition 2, or the ratio FC/VC (center–to–focus divided by center-to-vertex). These two definitions are mathematically equivalent. When the eccentricity is close to zero, the ellipse is almost circular; when it is close to 1, the ellipse is almost a parabola. All ellipses having the same eccentricity are geometrically similar figures.

The angle measure of eccentricity: Another measure of eccentricity. It is the acute angle formed by the major axis and a line passing through one focus and an end point of the minor axis. This angle is the arc cosine of the eccentricity.

The area: The area of an ellipse is given by the simple formula πab, where a and b are the semimajor and semiminor axes.

The perimeter: There is no simple formula for the perimeter of an ellipse. The formula is an elliptic integral which can be evaluated only by approximation.

The reflective property of an ellipse: If an ellipse is thought of as a mirror, any ray which passes through one focus and strikes the ellipse will be reflected through the other focus. This is the principle behind rooms designed so that a small sound made at one location can be easily heard at another, but not elsewhere in the room. The two locations are the foci of an ellipse.

Drawing ellipses

There are mechanical devices, called ellipsographs, based on Definition 4 for drawing ellipses precisely, but lacking such a device, one can use simple equipment and the definitions above to draw ellipses which are accurate enough for most practical purposes.

To draw large ellipses one can use the pin-and-string method based on Definition 1: Stick pins into the drawing board at the two foci and at one end of the minor axis. Tie a loop of string snugly around the three pins. Replace the pin at the end of the minor axis with a pencil and, keeping the loop taut, draw the ellipse. If string which does not stretch is used, the resulting ellipse will be quite accurate.

To draw small and medium sized ellipses a technique based on Definition 4 can be used: Draw two concentric circles whose radii are equal to the semimajor axis and the semiminor axis respectively. Draw a ray from the center, intersecting the inner circle at y and outer circle at x. From y draw a short horizontal line and from x a short vertical line. Where these lines intersect is a point on the ellipse. Continue this procedure with many different rays until points all around the ellipse have been located. Connect these points with a smooth curve. If this is done carefully, using ordinary drafting equipment, the resulting ellipse will be quite accurate.

Uses

Ellipses are found in both natural and artificial objects. The paths of the planets and some comets around the Sun are approximately elliptical, with the sun at one of the foci. The seam where two cylindrical pipes are joined is an ellipse. Artists drawing circular objects such as the tops of vases use ellipses to render them in proper perspective. In Salt Lake City the roof of the Mormon Tabernacle has the shape of an ellipse rotated around its major axis, and its reflective properties give the auditorium its unusual acoustical properties. (A pin dropped at one focus can be heard clearly by a person standing at the other focus.) An ellipsoidal reflector in a lamp such as those dentists use will, if the light source is placed at its focus, concentrate the light at the other focus.

Because the ellipse is a particularly graceful sort of oval, it is widely used for esthetic purposes, in the design of formal gardens, in table tops, in mirrors, in picture frames, and in other decorative uses.

Further Reading:

Finney, Thomas, Demana, and Waits. *Calculus: Graphical, Numerical, Algebraic*. Reading, Mass; Addison Wesley Publishing Co., 1994.

J. Paul Moulton

Elm

Elms are trees (occasionally shrubs) of flowering plants in the genus *Ulmus*. Elm leaves possess stipules, and often have a nonsymmetrical leaf, that is, one half is larger than the other so that the bottom ends do not meet where they are attached to the mid–rib. Elms flower in the spring. Their flowers lack petals, form reddish brown clusters in the tops of the trees, appear

American elm trees in Washington, D.C.

before the leaves have fully expanded, and are pollinated by the wind. The fruits are samaras that are technically equivalent to the keys (fruits) of maple, although in elm the seed is surrounded entirely by a greenish, papery wing so that the oval or circular fruit (seed plus wing) resembles a fried egg.

There are about 30 species of elms in the world. Most occur in north temperate regions of North America, Europe, and Asia, and on mountains of tropical Asia. Elms rarely occur in large tracts in forests. Instead they are usually found interspersed among other deciduous trees.

Elm has, until recently, been an important ornamental and shade tree. In eastern North America there is hardly a single town without an Elm Street, named after the stately white or American elm (*Ulmus americana*), which is a tall tree reaching heights of 130 ft (40 m). American elm has elegant upswept limbs that arch down at the ends. Unfortunately, these beautiful trees are becoming rare because of a devastating disease called Dutch elm disease that was accidentally imported from Europe, probably on infected timber.

Dutch elm disease derives its name from the fact that it was first discovered on elm trees in Holland in 1921. There is no tree known as Dutch elm, and the disease originated in Asia. The disease appeared in the United States in 1930 and spread rapidly throughout the range of elm in eastern North America.

Dutch elm disease is caused by an ascomycete fungus (*Ophiostoma ulmi*) in partnership with an insect. Although the fungus causes the disease, an insect is generally necessary as an agent in spreading fungal spores from infected trees to healthy trees. The bark beetles *Scolytus multistriatus*, *S. scolytus*, and *Hylurgopinus rufipes* are the common agents of spread, although birds and, to a limited extent, water and wind can also spread the disease. The fungus can also spread from diseased trees to healthy trees by natural root grafts. Once a tree has been infected, the fungus initially grows within the water–conducting cells called vessels, where spores (different from those produced on coremia) are produced and released. Carried in the water of the vessels, these spores spread the infection to other parts of the tree. The symptoms shown by infected trees include: yellowing of the leaves, followed by wilting and their premature fall, death of branches causing the crown to appear sparse, and browning of the sap-wood. If the infection spreads throughout the vascular system, death of the tree can occur within weeks of the infection, although many trees survive for several years before succumbing to the disease. In the later stages of the disease, the fungus moves out of the water–conducting cells into other tissues. There is no satisfactory method for managing Dutch elm disease. Not all species of elm have been affected by Dutch elm disease. Asiatic species, such as Siberian and Chinese elms, are generally resistant.

Elm wood is economically valuable. Most species produce fine timber with a distinctive pattern. The timber resists decay when waterlogged, thus making it quite useful in certain specialized uses, such as serving as underwater pilings. Before metalworking, elm was used in Europe in water pipes and water pumps; 200–year–old pipes are often dug up in London, England. The grain of elm wood is strongly interlocked so that it is very difficult to split. For this reason, elm wood is often used for certain kinds of furniture, such as the seats of chairs, since the driving in of legs and backs tends to split most other woods, and also for wheel–hubs and mallet heads. Elm wood has also been extensively used for coffin boards and shipping cases for heavy machinery.

KEY TERMS

Samara—A simple, dry, fruit that is unopen at maturity, usually contains 1 seed, and has one or more wings.

Stipule—An appendage found at the base of a leaf where it joins a branch or stem.

The inner bark of elm, especially of roots, is fibrous and can be made into rope, and string for fishing–line, nets, or snares. The fruits are eaten by many birds and squirrels. Twigs and leaves are eaten by deer and rabbits. The leaves are quite nutritious and in ancient times in Europe, branches were cut off so that livestock could feed on the foliage. Elms have little value as food for people, although in times of famine, the ground bark, leaves, and fruits have been eaten by the Chinese, and bark ground into a meal and mixed with flour for bread has similarly been used in times of scarcity in Norway. The inner bark of slippery elm reputedly has some medicinal properties.

Les C. Cwynar

El Niño and La Niña

El Niño and La Niña are the names given to changes in the winds, atmospheric pressure, and sea water that occur in the Pacific Ocean near the equator. El Niño and La Niña are like winter and summer—they are opposite phases of a back and forth cycle in the Pacific Ocean and the atmosphere above it. Unlike winter and summer, however, El Niño and La Niña do not change with the regularity of the seasons; they repeat on average about every three or four years. This vast repeating cycle is called the Southern Oscillation.

Although El Niño and La Niña take place in a small portion of the Pacific, the changes caused by Southern Oscillation can affect the weather in large parts of Asia, Africa, Indonesia and North and South America. Scientists have only recently become aware of the far reaching effects of the Southern Oscillation on the world's weather. A recent El Niño, during 1982–83, was associated with record snowfall in parts of the Rocky Mountains, flooding in the southern United States, and heavy rain storms in southern California, which brought about floods and mud slides.

Early signs of El Niño and the Southern Oscillation

The name El Niño comes from Peruvian fishermen, who noticed that near the end of each year, the sea water off the South American coast became warmer, which made fishing much poorer. Since the change appeared each year close to Christmas, the fishermen dubbed it El Niño, Spanish for "the boy child" referring to the Christ child. Every few years, the changes brought with El Niño were particularly strong or long lasting. During these strong El Niños, the warmer sea waters nearly wiped out fishing and brought significant changes in weather. For example, normally dry areas on shore could receive abundant rain, turning deserts into lush grasslands while these strong El Niños lasted. In the 1950s and 60s it was found that strong El Niños were associated with increased sea surface temperatures throughout the eastern tropical Pacific. In recent years, these strong El Niños have been recognized as not just a local change in the sea, but as one half of a vast atmospheric–oceanic cycle.

The other half of the repeating cycle has been named La Niña, or the girl child. This phase of the Southern Oscillation is also sometimes called El Viejo, or the old man.

The Southern Oscillation was discovered in the early 1920s by Sir Gilbert Walker. He was trying to understand the variations in the summer monsoons (rainy seasons) of India by studying the way atmospheric pressure changed over the Pacific Ocean. Based on meteorologists' previous pressure observations from many stations in the southern Pacific and Indian oceans, Walker established that over the years, atmospheric pressure seesawed back and forth across the ocean. In some years, pressure was highest over northern Australia and lowest over the southeastern Pacific, near the island of Tahiti. In other years, the pattern was reversed. The two pressure patterns had specific weather patterns associated with each, and the change from one phase to the other could mean the shift from rainfall to drought or from good harvests to famine. In the late 1960s, Jacob Bjerknes, a professor at the University of California, first proposed that the Southern Oscillation and the strong El Niño sea warming were two aspects of the same vast atmosphere–ocean cycle.

The two phases of the Southern Oscillation

El Niño and the Southern Oscillation (often referred to as ENSO) take place in the tropics, a part of the world dominated by prevailing winds called the trade winds. Near the equator in the tropical Pacific, these easterly (east to west) winds blow day in and day out and tend to pull the surface water of the ocean along with them. This pulls the warm surface water westward, where it collects on the western edge of the ocean basin, the area that includes Indonesia, eastern Australia and many Pacific Islands. The warm waters literally pile up in these areas, where the sea level is about 16 inches (40 cm) higher than in the eastern Pacific. Meanwhile, along the coast of South America, colder water from the ocean depths rises to the top since the warmer water has been blown westward. The result is called upwelling, and it occurs along much of the coasts of South and North America. Upwelling has two important consequences. The cold deep waters tend to have more nutrients than surface water; these nutrient are essential to phytoplankton, the tiny plants of the sea which provide food for many other types of sea life. Thus upwelling zones are very productive for fish and the animals (and people) who depend on fish for food. The second result of upwelling cold water is that it cools the air above it. Cool air is denser than warm air, and cool air in the atmosphere can not begin rising to form clouds and thunderstorms. As a result, the areas near upwelling zones tend to be arid (desert–like) because rain clouds rarely form.

The warmer water that builds up in the western Pacific warms the air above it. This warm moist air frequently rises to form clouds which eventually produce rainfall. When the trade winds are blowing the warm water their way, the lands along the western Pacific enjoy abundant rainfall. Many rain forests are found in these areas, such as those of Borneo and New Guinea.

The pattern of winds described above is the La Niña phase of the Southern Oscillation. It sets up the areas of high and low atmospheric pressure observed by Walker and others; in the west, warm air rising produces low pressure, while farther east the cooler, denser air leads to areas of high pressure.

The atmosphere and the ocean form a system that is coupled, that is, they respond to each other. Changes in the ocean will cause a response in the winds above it, and vice versa. For reasons not yet fully understood, the coupled atmosphere–ocean of the La Niña phase begins to change during the beginning of an El Niño. The trade winds weaken somewhat, so that they pull less warm water to the western edge of the Pacific. This causes far reaching changes. Fewer rain clouds form over the lands along the western Pacific. The lush rain forests dry out and become fuel for forest fires. The area of heavy rain shifts to the mid–southern Pacific, where formerly desert island are soaked day after day. In the eastern Pacific, the surface water becomes warmer, since it is no longer being driven westward. Ocean upwelling is weakened, so the water near the surface soon runs low on nutrients which support the ocean food chain. Many species of fish are driven elsewhere to find food; in severe El Niño years fish populations may be almost completely wiped out. Bird species that depend on fish must look elsewhere, and the human fishing population faces economic hardship. At the same time the warmer waters offshore encourage the development of clouds and thunderstorms. Normally dry areas in western South America, such as Peru and Ecuador, may experience torrential rains and flooding during the El Niño phase.

Global effects of El Niño

While its effects have long been noted in the tropical Pacific, El Niño is now being studied for its impact on weather around the world. The altered pattern of winds and ocean temperatures during an El Niño is believed to change the high level winds, called the jet streams, that steer storms over North and South America. El Niños have been linked with milder winters in western Canada and the northern United States, as most severe storms are steered northward to Alaska. As Californians saw in 1982–83, El Niño can cause extremely wet winters along the west coast, bringing torrential rains to the low lands and heavy snow packs to the mountains. The jet streams altered by El Niño can also contribute to storm development over the Gulf of Mexico, which bring heavy rains to the southeastern United States. Similar changes occur in countries of South America, such as Chile and Argentina, while droughts may affect Bolivia and parts of Central America.

El Niño also appears to affect monsoons, which are annual shifts in the prevailing winds that bring on rainy seasons. The rains of the monsoon are critical for agriculture in India, southeast Asia and portions of Africa; when the monsoon fails, millions of people are at risk of starvation. At present it appears that while El Niños do not always determine monsoons, they are associated with weakened monsoons in India and southeastern Africa, while tending to strengthen those in eastern Africa. These changes are reversed during La Niña years.

Predicting El Niño and La Niña

The widespread weather impacts of the two phases of the Southern Oscillation make their understanding and prediction a high priority for atmospheric scientists. Researchers have developed computer models of the Southern Oscillation which mimic the behavior of the real atmosphere–ocean system. These computer simulations require the input of mountains of data about sea

---

KEY TERMS
· ·

Coupled system—A system with parts that are linked in such a way that they respond to changes in each other. The atmosphere and the ocean form a coupled system, so that changes in one will cause a response in the other, which will in turn cause another change in the first, etc.

El Niño—The phase of the Southern Oscillation characterized by increased sea water temperatures and rainfall in the eastern Pacific, with weakening trade winds and decreased rain along the western Pacific.

ENSO—Abbreviation for El Niño/Southern Oscillation.

Jet streams—High velocity winds that blow at upper levels in the atmosphere and help to steer major storm systems.

La Niña—The phase of the Southern Oscillation characterized by strong trade winds, colder sea water temperatures and dry weather in the eastern Pacific, with increased rainfall along the western Pacific.

Monsoon—An annual shift in the direction of the prevailing wind that brings on a rainy season and affects large parts of Asia and Africa.

Southern Oscillation—A large scale variation in the winds, ocean temperatures and atmospheric pressure of the tropical Pacific Ocean which repeats about every three to four years.

---

and wind conditions in the equatorial Pacific. The measurements are provided by a large and growing network of instruments. Ocean buoys, permanently moored in place across the Pacific, constantly relay information on water temperature, wind, and air pressure to weather prediction stations around the world. The buoys are augmented by surface ships, island weather stations, and Earth observing satellites.

Even with mounting data and improving computer models, El Niño, La Niña and the Southern Oscillation remain difficult to predict. However, the Southern Oscillation models are now being used in several countries to help prepare for the next El Niño. Countries most affected by the variations in El Niño, such as Peru, Australia and India, have begun to use El Niño prediction to improve agricultural planning.

See also Atmospheric pressure; Ocean; Weather; Wind.

Further Reading:

"El Niño and Climate Prediction," UCAR Reports to the Nation On Our Changing Planet #3, University Corporation for Atmospheric Research, Spring 1994.

Kerr, R.A., "A Successful Forecast of an El Niño Winter," *Science*, (January 24, 1992): 402.

Monastersky, R.A., "Exploiting El Niño to Avert African Famine," *Science News*, (July 23, 1994): 52.

Williams, Jack. *The Weather Book*, New York: Vintage Books, 1992.

James Marti

Embiids

Embiids are small, cylindrical, soft–bodied insects in the order Embioptera that spin tubular galleries of silk, an ability that gives them the common name web–spinners. They have chewing mouthparts, and undergo paurometabolism, or gradual metamorphosis, exhibiting a definite egg, nymph, and adult stage. In the phylogeny, or evolutionary history of the class Insecta, embiids are thought to be most closely related to the orders Dermaptera (the earwigs) and Plecoptera (the stone flies).

A distinguishing morphological feature of the web–spinners is that the silk glands are in the tarsal segments of the front legs. Another unique characteristic of these insects is that the wings of the males are flexible when the insect is not in flight. Their wing veins are hollow, and fill with blood in order to stiffen the wing for flight.

Embiids are gregarious, or group–living, insects in which the wingless females live in silken galleries where they care for their young. The males of this order are often, but not always winged, and do not feed as adults. Rather they die soon after finding and mating with a female. Individuals in all developmental stages have the ability to spin silk. They spin galleries in the soil, under bark, in dead plant matter, in rock crevices, and other such inconspicuous substrates. The females and nymphs living in the galleries are flightless but they are adapted to run backwards through the tunnel to flee potential predators that may discover the opening of the chamber.

These secretive insects are rare, with only 200 species known to exist, most of which are tropical. In the United States, there are ten species, all of which have a southern distribution. The main food source of Embioptera is dead plant matter, and this fact, as well as their relative rarity, make embiids of little known economic significance to humans.

Embolism

An embolism is the sudden blockage of a blood vessel by a blood clot that has been brought to that location by the bloodstream. The clot, called an embolus, from the Greek word meaning plug, is a blood clot that has formed inside the circulatory system and is floating in the bloodstream. It will remain on the move until it encounters a blood vessel too small for it to fit through, where it will plug the vessel and prevent any further circulation of blood through it.

A blood clot that forms in a given location and remains there is called a thrombus, from the Greek word for clot.

An embolism is named by the location in which the clot lodges. A pulmonary embolism is an embolus that has plugged a blood vessel, usually an artery, in one of the lungs. A coronary embolism is obscuring the channel in one of the coronary arteries, which feed the heart muscle. A cerebral embolism lodges in a blood vessel in the brain and perhaps precipitates a stroke.

When an embolus plugs a blood vessel, the tissues that are bathed by the blood in the vessel will die when the blood supply is cut off. Death of tissue resulting from the lack of blood is called an infarct. If the embolism is in a coronary artery and the infarct is in the heart muscle it is a heart attack. The seriousness of the attack is determined by which vessel the clot blocks and how much of the heart muscle is infarcted.

The same situation applies to other organs. A cerebral embolism can cause brain damage and bring about a stroke. A pulmonary embolism causes damage to the lung tissue that can be serious. Any of these embolisms can be fatal and must be treated quickly.

Drugs can be given to dissolve the clot and other drugs can be taken to prevent the formation of any more clots.

What causes most emboli to form is not known. Some may form after surgery if air gets into the bloodstream.

See also Circulatory system.